HANDBOOK OF BUSINESS-TO-BUSINESS MARKETING

About the ISBM

Founded in 1983, Penn State's Institute for the Study of Business Markets (ISBM) is a Center of Excellence in the Smeal College of Business at Penn State. As a global network of leading-edge researchers and practitioners, it has two main missions:

- To expand research and teaching in business-to-business marketing and sales in academia, and
- To improve the practice of business-to-business marketing and sales for member firms in industry.

This *Handbook* is dedicated to help fulfill both those missions.

**Institute for
the Study of
Business Markets**

Handbook of Business-to-Business Marketing

Edited by

Gary L. Lilien

Distinguished Research Professor of Management Science, The Pennsylvania State University, USA

Rajdeep Grewal

Irving & Irene Bard Professor of Marketing, The Pennsylvania State University, USA

Edward Elgar
Cheltenham, UK • Northampton, MA, USA

Published by
Edward Elgar Publishing Limited
The Lypiatts
15 Lansdown Road
Cheltenham
Glos GL50 2JA
UK

Edward Elgar Publishing, Inc.
William Pratt House
9 Dewey Court
Northampton
Massachusetts 01060
USA

A catalogue record for this book
is available from the British Library

Library of Congress Control Number: 2011934813

ISBN 978 1 78100 536 1 (paperback)
ISBN 978 1 84980 142 3 (cased)

Typeset by Servis Filmsetting Ltd, Stockport, Cheshire

For Alanna and Calina, who make me smile . . .
– Gary
For Rima, Rana, Ranjit, and Randeep, who made it possible and for Angad and
Kabir, who make it worth it . . .
– Raj

Contents

About the editors

Gary L. Lilien is Distinguished Research Professor of Management Science at the Smeal College of Business at Pennsylvania State University, University Park, PA. He is also co-founder and Research Director of the Institute for the Study of Business Markets (ISBM). Previously, Professor Lilien was a member of the faculty at the Sloan School at MIT. He received his bachelor's, master's and doctoral degrees from Columbia University. His research interests include B2B marketing, marketing engineering, market segmentation, new product modeling, marketing mix issues for business products, bargaining and negotiations, modeling the industrial buying process, the implementation of marketing science and innovation diffusion modeling.

He is the author or co-author of 12 books (including *Marketing Models* with Philip Kotler, *Marketing Engineering* and *Principles of Marketing Engineering*), as well as more than 100 professional articles. He was Departmental Editor, Marketing for *Management Science*; is on the editorial board of *International Journal for Research in Marketing*; is functional Editor for Marketing for *Interfaces*, and is Area Editor at *Marketing Science*. He was Editor-in-Chief of *Interfaces* for six years. He is the former President and Vice President/Publications for The Institute of Management Sciences. He is an Inaugural INFORMS Fellow, was honored as Morse Lecturer for INFORMS and received the Kimball Medal for distinguished contributions to the field of operations research. He is an Inaugural Fellow of the European Marketing Academy, VP External Relations for the INFORMS Society for Marketing Science (ISMS) and an Inaugural ISMS Fellow. He sits on the Board of Directors of the American Marketing Association.

Professor Lilien has received honorary doctorates from the University of Liege, University of Ghent and Aston University and received the 2008 AMA/Irwin/McGraw-Hill Educator of the Year Award. In 2010 the ISMS–MSI Practice Prize for the best applied work in marketing science globally was renamed the Gary Lilien ISMS–MSI Practice Prize in his honor.

Rajdeep Grewal is Irving & Irene Bard Professor of Marketing at the Smeal College of Business at the Pennsylvania State University, University Park, PA. He is also the Associate Research Director of the Institute for the Study of Business Markets at the Smeal College of Business at the Pennsylvania State University at University Park, PA. His research focuses on empirically modeling strategic marketing issues with a focus on issues related to business-to-business markets.

His research has appeared in prestigious journals such as the *Journal of Marketing*, *Journal of Marketing Research*, *Marketing Science*, *Management Science*, *Journal of Consumer Psychology*, *MIS Quarterly* and *Strategic Management Journal*, among others. Currently he serves as an Associate Editor for the *Journal of Marketing*. He is serving or has served on the Editorial Boards for the *Journal of Marketing*, *Marketing Science*, *International Journal of Research in Marketing*, *Journal of the Academy of Marketing Science* and *Decision Sciences*. He has received several awards for his research including a doctoral dissertation award from the Procter & Gamble Market Innovation

Research Fund. His research also received the Honorable Mention Award at the prestigious MSI/JM competition on 'Linking Marketing to Financial Performance and Firm Value', the 2003 Young Contributor Award from the Society of Consumer Psychology for his 2003 article in the *Journal of Consumer Psychology*, and his article on incentive-aligned conjoint analysis was the finalist for the 2006 Paul E. Green Award and 2010 O'Dell Award for best article published in the *Journal of Marketing Research* in 2005. His article on governance in electronic markets was also a finalist for the 2010 Maynard Award at the *Journal of Marketing* for the best theory-based article. In 2003 he was named in the Marketing Science Institute's Young Scholars (individuals with PhD after 1995 selected on the basis of research productivity in top tier marketing journals). He also received the AMA Marketing Strategy SIG Early Career Award in 2007 and was cited among the most productive scholars in marketing from 1982–2006 in terms of publication rate (ranked 15 globally) in a study by Seggie and Griffin published in the *Journal of Marketing* (2009).

Contributors

Michael Ahearne is the C.T. Bauer Chaired Professor in Marketing and Executive Director of the Sales Excellence Institute at the Bauer College of Business, University of Houston. His research focuses primarily on two areas: the performance of sales organizations and building brand identity and corporate image.

Sönke Albers is Professor of Marketing and Innovation and Dean of Research at Kühne Logistics University in Hamburg, Germany. His research interests are in the fields of sales management, marketing mix planning, electronic business and the diffusion of innovations. He works primarily with quantitative models but also does empirical research testing hypotheses.

Kersi D. Antia is Assistant Professor of Marketing, School of Business, University of Wisconsin–Madison. His research deals with the governance of inter-firm relationships (vertical channel relationships, franchising, strategic alliances) and the impact of technology, particularly the Internet and its information-sharing capabilities, on these relationships. Though trained as a survey researcher, Kersi has developed a significant interest in longitudinal analysis.

Ranjan Banerjee is the Director and Group COO of Insta Worldwide. His research interests center on distribution channel design and management and customer relationship management, including how to use analytical and empirical approaches to explain the existence of multiple channels of distribution, as well as the performance implications of channel governance choices.

Roger Baxter is a Senior Lecturer at AUT University, Auckland, New Zealand. He researches value creation and resource flows in relationships. He has published in *Industrial Marketing Management* and the *Journal of Business Research*. Before entering academia, he worked in senior sales and marketing positions in multinational corporations.

Joshua T. Beck is a marketing PhD student at the University of Washington in Seattle. His research interests in the relationship marketing domain center on trying to understand how relational assets are created and implemented along with other strategic assets to enhance a firm's competitive advantage in various market environments. His research has appeared in the *Journal of Consumer Psychology*.

Mark Bergen is the James D. Watkins Chair in Marketing at the Carlson School of Management. Bergen's research focuses on pricing and channels of distribution, where he has studied issues such as pricing as a strategic capability, price wars, price pass-throughs, branded variants, dual distribution, gray markets, co-op advertising and quick response.

Torsten Bornemann is Assistant Professor of Marketing at the University of Mannheim, Germany. His research interests include innovation management, marketing strategy and business-to-business marketing.

Douglas Bowman is Professor of Marketing, Area Coordinator for Marketing, and Senior Associate Dean for External Relations at Emory University's Goizueta Business School. His research interests include marketing strategy, marketing mix analysis and customer relationship management.

Kevin Bradford is Associate Professor, Mendoza College of Business, University of Notre Dame. Kevin conducts research on developing an understanding of significant issues within the marketing system and its relationship to society. His work has centered on the marketing domain (e.g. salespeople, sales management, development of relationships), the customer domain (e.g. buyer–seller relationships) and public policy domain (e.g. firearm diversion, distribution channel capability, responsibility).

Steven P. Brown is Bauer Professor of Marketing at the C.T. Bauer College of Business, University of Houston. His research interests focus on identifying ways of building and sustaining competitive advantage through effective sales and service organizations.

Frank Cespedes is a Senior Lecturer at Harvard Business School where he has taught Marketing, Strategy and Entrepreneurial Management in the MBA and various executive education programs. For 12 years he was Managing Partner at the Center for Executive Development (CED), a firm that worked with firms in the United States, Asia and Europe on strategy implementation issues. He is the author of six books, and articles in *Harvard Business Review*, *Journal of Personal Selling & Sales Management*, *Organization Science*, *Wall Street Journal*, and other publications.

Jennifer D. Chandler is Assistant Professor of Management at California State University Fullerton, Mihalyo College of Business and Economics. She holds a BA from UCLA, an MBA from the University of Hawaii at Manoa and a PhD from the University of California, Irvine. Dr Chandler focuses on strategy, the resource-based view of the firm and social network analysis. She is interested in innovation, learning and knowledge management.

Rajesh K. Chandy is Professor of Marketing and Academic Director of the Institute for Innovation and Entrepreneurship at London Business School, where he also holds the Tony and Maureen Wheeler Chair in Entrepreneurship. Dr Chandy's areas of expertise include innovation, technology management, emerging markets and marketing strategy. His research and publications have received several awards, including the *Journal of Marketing* Harold Maynard Award for contributions to marketing theory and thought. His papers have also been named as finalists for the *Journal of Marketing Research* William O'Dell Award for the most significant long-term contribution to marketing, the INFORMS Society for Marketing Science Practice Prize, and the *Journal of Marketing Research* Paul Green award for contributions to the practice of marketing research.

Robert G. Cooper is President of the Product Development Institute Inc.; Professor Emeritus, DeGroote School of Business, McMaster University, Hamilton, Ontario, Canada; and ISBM Distinguished Research Fellow at Penn State University's Smeal College of Business Administration. His research interests focus on the management of service and product innovation.

Anne T. Coughlan is J.L. & Helen Kellogg Professor of Marketing, Kellogg School of Management, Northwestern University. Coughlan's main research interests are in the areas of distribution channels, sales force management and compensation, and pricing. Current research projects include modeling optimal restocking fees in returns management and how they affect consumer behavior and optimal pricing; optimal sales force diversification and group incentive payments; and an international study of how taxation policies and job challenge interact in the setting of sales compensation in several European countries.

George E. Cressman Jr is founder and president of World Class Pricing, a consultancy specializing in helping clients build world-class pricing managers. George has over 28 years of experience in the chemicals industry, having worked in positions of pricing, marketing and business management, finance, research and manufacturing.

Shantanu Dutta works in the Marshall School of Business at the University of Southern California. He is an expert on strategic marketing, especially in high-technology markets. He also studies how firms use distribution, partnerships and value pricing to build competitive advantages. His research has been published in leading marketing, economics and management journals, including the *Journal of Marketing*; *Journal of Marketing Research*; *Marketing Science*; *Quarterly Journal of Economics*; *Journal of Law and Economics*; *Journal of Law, Economics and Organization*; *Management Science* and *Strategic Management Journal*. He serves on the editorial boards of the *Journal of Marketing Research* and *Marketing Science* and is Secretary of the Informs Society for Marketing Science.

Liam Fahey is co-founder and executive director of Leadership Forum, Inc. He serves as Professor of Management Practice at Babson College. His academic research, organization consulting and executive teaching focus on the creation and use of 'marketplace intelligence': developing superior understanding of the competitive present and future to shape and inspire more informed and incisive decision-making.

Shankar Ganesan is the Karl Eller Professor of Marketing in the Department of Marketing at the Eller College of Management, University of Arizona. Professor Ganesan's research interests focus on the areas of inter-organizational relationships, buyer–seller negotiations, service failure and recovery, and new product innovation.

Mrinal Ghosh is the W.H. and Callie Clark Associate Professor of Marketing at the Eller College of Management, University of Arizona. His primary research interests lie in using the lens of organizational economics to study marketing problems in the domain of business-to-business marketing, marketing strategy, entrepreneurship and innovation, marketing channels and sales force compensation and design.

Srinath Gopalakrishna's research focuses on quantitative modeling approaches to problems in B2B marketing and sales. His research examines the effectiveness of B2B communications such as advertising, direct mail and trade shows and how they can be integrated with personal selling. He has received the Distinguished Research Fellowship Award, the O'Brien Award and the Kemper Award for Teaching Excellence at the University of Missouri.

Abbie Griffin holds the Royal L. Garff Presidential Chair in Marketing and is Chair of the Marketing Department at the University of Utah's David Eccles School of Business.

Professor Griffin's research investigates how to measure and improve the process of new product development. She is an avid environmentalist, skier, hiker and quilter.

Ernan Haruvy is Associate Professor of Marketing, School of Management, University of Texas at Dallas.

Hillbun (Dixon) Ho is an assistant professor in the Division of Marketing and International Business and a fellow of the Institute on Asian Consumer Insight at Nanyang Technological University, Singapore. His research areas include business-to-business marketing, distribution channels, retailer strategies and consumer search behavior. Before joining NTU, he taught at Monash University in Australia.

Christian Homburg is Professor of Marketing, Chair of the Marketing Department, and Director of the Institute for Market-Oriented Management at the University of Mannheim, Germany. He is also Professorial Fellow at the Department of Management and Marketing at the University of Melbourne, Australia. His research interests include business-to-business marketing, sales management, and marketing strategy.

Sandy Jap is the Dean's Term Chair Professor of Marketing at the Goizueta Business School, Emory University. Sandy is a leading expert in the field on the development and management of inter-organizational relationships, multichannel issues, online procurement and B2B e-commerce. Her PhD is from the University of Florida (Go Gators!).

George John holds the General Mills and Paul S. Gerot Chair in Marketing at the Carlson School of Management, University of Minnesota, Twin Cities. His research interests are in extending and applying transaction cost economics and new empirical industrial organization approaches to marketing problems in business-to-business marketing, marketing channels, sales force compensation and marketing strategy.

Wesley J. Johnston is CBIM Roundtable Professor of Marketing, Georgia State University. Johnston's research interests include the application of behavioral sciences to marketing in the areas of customer relationship management and strategic account programs. He is an expert in network dynamics and relationship strategies, especially in sales force management.

Kissan Joseph is Associate Professor and Stockton Research Fellow at the University of Kansas. His research interests include sales force compensation, pricing, advertising budgeting and topics residing at the marketing–finance interface. His research has appeared in the *Journal of Marketing*, *Marketing Science*, *Marketing Letters*, *Journal of Interactive Marketing* and other outlets.

Kevin Lane Keller is the E.B. Osborn Professor of Marketing at the Tuck School of Business at Dartmouth College. Professor Keller's general area of expertise lies in marketing strategy and planning and branding. Professor Keller is currently conducting a variety of studies that address strategies to build, measure and manage brand equity.

Philip Kotler is the S.C. Johnson & Son Distinguished Professor of International Marketing at Northwestern University's Kellogg School of Management, and one of the world's leading authorities on marketing. His writing had defined marketing around the world for the past 40 years. The recipient of numerous awards and honorary degrees from schools all over the world, he holds an MA from the University of Chicago and a PhD from MIT, both in economics. Kotler has an incredible international presence – his books have been translated into approximately 25 languages, and he regularly speaks on the international circuit.

V. Kumar (VK) is the Lenny Distinguished Chair Professor of Marketing and Executive Director, Center for Excellence in Brand & Customer Management, J. Mack Robinson College of Business, Georgia State University. He has been recognized with seven lifetime achievement awards in Marketing Strategy, Inter-Organizational Issues, Retailing and Marketing Research from the AMA and other professional organizations.

Son K. Lam is Assistant Professor of Marketing at Terry College of Business, University of Georgia. His research focuses on sales management, internal marketing and customer–brand relationships. Son's research has appeared in the *Journal of Marketing Research*, *Journal of Marketing* and *Journal of Retailing*.

Sally E. Lorimer is a consultant and business writer. She was previously a principal at ZS Associates, where she consulted with numerous companies on sales force effectiveness. She holds a Master of Management degree from the Kellogg School of Management at Northwestern University. She is the co-author of three books on sales force management.

Robert F. Lusch is Professor of Marketing and holder of the James and Pamela Muzzy Chair in Entrepreneurship and Innovation. His research interests are in strategic marketing, marketing channels and the service-dominant logic.

Murali K. Mantrala is Sam M. Walton Distinguished Professor of Marketing at the University of Missouri, Columbia. His research interests fall in the areas of B2B market segmentation, sales management and resource allocation; two-sided markets and media marketing mix modeling; retail assortment and pricing strategies.

Detelina Marinova is an Assistant Professor of Marketing at the University of Missouri-Columbia. Detelina's research interests lie at the intersection of marketing strategy and econometric modeling. Her current research focuses on market learning and innovation, marketing strategy mechanisms in service organizations and judgment dynamics in managerial and customer decision-making.

Jakki J. Mohr is the Jeff & Martha Hamilton, Regents Professor of Marketing at the University of Montana. Dr Mohr's primary research is on the marketing strategies of high-technology companies and has been published in the *Journal of Marketing*, *Strategic Management Journal* and *Journal of the Academy of Marketing Science*, among others. An award-winning teacher, Dr Mohr also conducts executive education classes with mid-level and senior executives at universities and companies worldwide.

Neil A. Morgan is an Associate Professor and the PetSmart, Inc. Distinguished Professor of Marketing Chair in the Kelley School of Business, Indiana University. His research interests include marketing strategy implementation and linking marketing-related resources and capabilities with firms' product market, accounting and stock market performance.

Ralph Oliva is the Executive Director of the Institute for the Study of Business Markets (ISBM), and Professor of Marketing in the Smeal College of Business Administration at Pennsylvania State University. He is driving the growth of ISBM as the leading academic center devoted to advancing knowledge and practice in B2B marketing worldwide. The ISBM is supported by over 70 major firms and a network of more than 100 researchers, all focused on B2B.

Robert W. Palmatier holds the John C. Narver Chair of Business Administration at the University of Washington's Foster School of Business. His research interests are focused on relationship marketing and business strategy. His research has appeared in the *Journal of Marketing, Journal of Marketing Research, Marketing Science, Journal of Retailing* and *Journal of Consumer Psychology.*

Jaideep C. Prabhu is Jawaharlal Nehru Professor of Indian Business and Enterprise and Director of the Centre for India & Global Business at Judge Business School, University of Cambridge. His current research is mainly on the globalization of innovation and the role of emerging economies in this process.

Sourav Ray is Associate Professor of Marketing in the DeGroote School of Business at McMaster University. Dr Ray's research interest is in industrial and retail marketing strategies, focusing on strategic pricing and distribution channel issues. Recent topics of his research include asymmetric and dynamic pricing in the grocery retail sector and systems marketing practices in high-tech markets. He explores both profit and policy implications of such marketing strategies using theoretical and empirical quantitative methodologies.

Werner Reinartz is a Professor of Marketing at the University of Cologne, Germany. His research interest and expertise focus on the subjects of customer management, services, retailing and distribution channel management. His research work in these domains has been published in leading marketing journals, and his work on customer lifetime value is widely cited.

Aric Rindfleisch is Department Chair and McManus-Bascom Professor in Marketing at the University of Wisconsin–Madison and Research Professor at Korea University. He has also served as a faculty member at the University of Arizona and Tilburg University and worked for J. Walter Thompson-Japan, Millward Brown and the US Army. Aric's research, which focuses on understanding inter-organizational relationships, consumption values and new product development, has been published in the *Journal of Marketing, Journal of Marketing Research* and numerous other journals.

Lisa K. Scheer is the Emma S. Hibbs Distinguished Professor and Professor of Marketing at the University of Missouri's Trulaske College of Business. Her research interests include interpersonal and B2B marketing relationships and the implementation of marketing strategy, with emphases on trust, fairness, interdependence, conflict and relationship-building processes and strategies.

Don E. Schultz is Professor (Emeritus-in-Service) Integrated Marketing Communications at Northwestern University, Evanston, IL. He holds a BBA from the University of Oklahoma and an MA and PhD from Michigan State University. He is President of Agora, Inc., a global marketing, communication and branding consulting firm.

Sanjit Sengupta is Professor of Marketing at San Francisco State University. His research interests include new product development and technological innovation, strategic alliances, sales management and international marketing. His research has appeared in many journals including the *Academy of Management Journal, Journal of Marketing* and *Journal of Product Innovation Management*. He has taught in many executive development programs in India, Finland, Poland, South Korea and the United States.

Venkatesh Shankar is Professor of Marketing and Coleman Chair in Marketing at the Mays Business School, Texas A&M University. Dr Shankar's areas of specialization include marketing strategy, innovation, international marketing, digital business, pricing and retailing. He has corporate experience in marketing and international business development. He has made over 150 presentations in diverse countries.

Jagdip Singh currently holds the H. Clark Ford Chair in Marketing at the Weatherhead School of Management, Case Western Reserve University. Jagdip's research involves issues related to building and sustaining effective and enduring connections between organizations and their customers, especially in service industries, and understanding how firms organize, implement and support change and knowledge management to balance the competing goals of productivity and quality in the frontlines.

Prabhakant Sinha is Founder and Co-chairman of ZS Associates, the leading sales management consultancy in the world. A former faculty member in the Marketing department at the Kellogg School of Management at Northwestern University, he has also taught in executive education programs at London Business School and the Indian School of Business. He has consulted with hundreds of firms around the world and has co-authored several books on sales force effectiveness.

Stanley Slater is the Lillis Professor of Business Administration at Colorado State University. Professor Slater won the 2011 Mahajan Award for Lifetime Contributions to Marketing Strategy Research, given by the Marketing Strategy Special Interest Group of the American Marketing Association. His research interests include the performance implications of a market orientation, marketing's role in business strategy success and processes for innovation management.

Rebecca J. Slotegraaf is Associate Professor of Marketing and Whirlpool Faculty Fellow at the Kelley School of Business, Indiana University. Dr Slotegraaf's research interests focus on the role of marketing resources, capabilities and new products as sources of competitive advantage.

Robert E. Spekman is the Tayloe Murphy Professor of Business Administration at the University of Virginia's Darden Graduate School of Business. He is a recognized authority on business-to-business marketing strategy, channels of distribution design and the implementation of go-to-market strategies. Robert is also well known for his research and corporate consultancy work in strategic alliances, partnerships and supply chain management. The author of more than 100 articles and papers, Robert has also written/edited eight books and monographs.

Raji Srinivasan is Associate Professor of Marketing at the University of Texas at Austin, McCombs School of Business. She has published in the *Journal of Marketing*,

Management Science, Journal of the Academy of Marketing Science and *International Journal for Research in Marketing*. She is the recipient of the Marketing Strategy SIG of the American Marketing Association's Varadarajan Award for Early Career Contributions to Marketing Strategy Research (2010) and the Inaugural Recipient of the American Marketing Association's Erin Anderson Award for an Emerging Female Marketing Scholar and Mentor (2009).

Gerard J. Tellis is Professor, Neely Chair of American Enterprise, and Director of the Center for Global Innovation, at the USC Marshall School of Business. He is an expert in innovation, advertising, global market entry, new product growth, quality and pricing. He has published four books and more than 100 papers, which have won over 20 awards.

Robert J. Thomas is Professor of Marketing in the McDonough School of Business at Georgetown University, where he has also been Senior Associate Dean, Director of Executive Programs and Associate Dean for Graduate Business Programs. He conducts research in the areas of market segmentation, new product development and organizational buying behavior.

Christophe Van den Bulte is an Associate Professor of Marketing at the Wharton School of the University of Pennsylvania. His research focuses on new product diffusion and social networks. Several of his projects involve business-to-business settings in which network structure is particularly important.

Rajan Varadarajan is Distinguished Professor of Marketing and Ford Chair in Marketing and E-Commerce at Texas A&M University. His primary teaching and research interests are in the areas of marketing strategy, innovation, international marketing and e-commerce. His research has been published in the *Journal of Marketing, Journal of the Academy of Marketing Science, Academy of Management Journal, Strategic Management Journal, Management Science* and other journals. Rajan served as editor of the *Journal of Marketing* from 1993 to 1996 and as editor of the *Journal of the Academy of Marketing Science* from 2000 to 2003.

Stephen L. Vargo is a Shidler Distinguished Professor and Professor of Marketing at the University of Hawai'i at Manoa. His primary research areas are marketing theory and thought and consumers' evaluative reference scales. Professor Vargo has been awarded the Harold H. Maynard Award by the American Marketing Association for his significant contributions to marketing theory and thought and the Sheth Foundation Award for his long-term contributions to the field of marketing.

Rajkumar Venkatesan is the Bank of America Research Associate Professor of Business Administration at the Darden Graduate School of Business, University of Virginia. Raj's research focuses on identifying profitable customer-centric marketing strategies. He has published articles in the *Journal of Marketing, Journal of Marketing Research, Marketing Science* and *Harvard Business Review*.

Barton A. Weitz is the JC Penney Eminent Scholar Professor of Marketing at the University of Florida. He is the recipient of the American Marketing Association/Irwin Distinguished Marketing Educator Award and was the co-author of *Selling: Building*

Partnerships; three of his articles were selected as the articles making the greatest impact on personal selling and sales management in the twentieth century.

Arch G. Woodside is Professor of Marketing, Boston College. He is a Fellow of the American Psychological Association, APS, Royal Society of Canada, Society for Marketing Advances and the International Academy for the Study of Tourism. He is a past president of the Society of Consumer Psychology. He is the Editor-in-Chief of the *Journal of Business Research*. He is the founder of the International Academy of Culture, Tourism, and Hospitality Research. He is the Editor of the Emerald Publishing book series, *Advances in Business Marketing and Purchasing*.

Stefan Wuyts is Associate Professor of Marketing, Koç University, and Tilburg University. Professor Wuyts teaches marketing strategy, business-to-business marketing, innovation and new product development and marketing channel management. His recent research focuses on the areas of marketing channels and other forms of inter-firm relationships (alliances, outsourcing relationships), innovation, technology-intensive industries and social networks.

Andris A. Zoltners, Founder and Co-Chairman of ZS Associates, is a Frederic Esser Nemmers Distinguished Professor Emeritus of Marketing at the Kellogg School of Management at Northwestern University, where he had been a faculty member for more than 30 years. Professor Zoltners' areas of expertise are sales force strategy; sales force size, structure and deployment; sales force compensation; and sales force effectiveness. He has personally consulted for over 100 companies in more than 20 countries. In addition to his consulting, he has spoken at numerous conferences and has taught sales force topics to several thousand Executive, MBA and PhD students.

Acknowledgments

Penn State's Institute for the Study of Business Markets (ISBM) was founded in 1983 with a dual mission: to expand research and teaching in B2B marketing in academia and to improve the practice of B2B marketing in industry. We viewed the former as the route to the latter, and the ISBM is dedicated to providing the platform for future best practices in B2B marketing.

When Alan Sturmer of Edward Elgar Publishing contacted us about putting together a B2B Marketing Handbook, the timing could not have been better: the ISBM had just celebrated its 25th anniversary. We have supported a great deal of research over the years, and many of the ideas the ISBM had championed had turned into (profitable) mainstream practices. But we could not point to any single work that consolidated our key learnings. What better vehicle than a handbook, co-published by Edward Elgar and the ISBM! Hence, we must first thank Alan Sturmer and Edward Elgar Publishing for inviting us to undertake this activity, as well as the ISBM sponsoring companies and staff, particularly the ISBM's Executive Director Ralph Oliva, for their enthusiastic support of this venture.

We view a book as a sort of iceberg. The visible book, the above-water bit, is one-seventh of the total, and there would be no book (or iceberg) without the six-sevenths that is out of sight. Hence the acknowledgements that follow here.

Each of the chapters received critical and constructive comments from at least two reviewers. Most of those reviewers were other authors, whom we will not name personally but rather thank as a group (their names are prominently displayed in the table of contents and elsewhere). In addition to the authors, we received excellent and helpful reviews from Anindita Chakravarty, Sharmila Chatterjee, Hubert Gatignon, Alok Kumar, Girish Mallapragada, Vithala Rao, Gaurav Sabnis, Gerrit van Bruggen, Qiong Wang, Fred Wiersema and Chen Zhou

Managing the period between the point an author or group of authors agree to contribute a chapter until that chapter is complete requires both administrative and editorial skills. Lori Nicolini provided the former. She kept close tabs on, cajoled and sometimes badgered authors to provide what they promised in a timely manner, coordinated the interaction with the editors and publisher and did whatever else was needed to produce this handbook. This work is as much hers as ours.

Elisabeth Nevins Caswell and Francesca Van Gorp Cooley, in conjunction with the staff at Edward Elgar, produced our editorial guidelines and mercilessly implemented and enforced them. Every chapter reflects their dedication and attention to detail, and every chapter is far better for having been subjected to their craft. We thank them profusely.

We are grateful for significant research support from several Penn State PhD students: Aditya Gupta, Mahima Hada and Alok Saboo.

All of those above put up with our unrealistic demands and unreasonable deadlines with unfailing good humor, and we thank them all.

Finally, we would like to thank our families – wives, children (and, in Lilien's case, grandchild) for providing the love and support and relinquishing the time that a project like this demands.

Gary L. Lilien, State College, PA
Rajdeep Grewal, State College, PA
November 2011

PART I

INTRODUCTION AND OVERVIEW

1 Business-to-business marketing: looking back, looking forward
Rajdeep Grewal and Gary L. Lilien

What we now call business-to-business (B2B) marketing used to be called industrial marketing (Webster 1978a), when it primarily focused on transactions of products produced for consumption by other businesses (machine tools, office supplies and the like) as well as the items that went into the production process of those other organizations (for example, raw materials like petroleum, timber or parts; other ingredients like valves, bearings, resins and polymers). In the past several decades, the term 'industrial marketing' has given way to the broader term 'B2B marketing', and its meaning has grown to encompass the activity of building mutually value-generating relationships (including both products and services) between organizations (which include businesses but also government agencies, not-for-profit organizations and the like) and the many individuals within them. In this latter sense, specific examples of marketing issues – such as a manufacturer–retailer relationship in consumer product markets (for example Walmart as the key account for Procter & Gamble), pharmaceutical firms marketing to doctors (who prescribe to patients) or agribusiness firms selling seeds, fertilizer and equipment to farmers – all fall within the purview of B2B marketing. In contrast business-to-consumer (B2C) marketing is mainly focused on the final transaction between the firm (and/or retailer) and the customer.

Table 1.1 sketches some key differences between B2B and B2C marketing. B2B marketers typically focus on far fewer and more varied customers, using more complex and more technically oriented sales processes than appear in consumer marketers. The complexity (multiple stakeholders – financial analysts, purchasing agents, engineers, manufacturing managers, lawyers and others – all of whom proceed through an intricate, multi-stage decision-making process) has led to a field of study specific to B2B marketing called 'organizational buying behavior'. The presence of a few powerful customers, which often account for a heavily skewed percentage of sales (for example, a telecom firm may count ExxonMobil and General Electric among its business customers but also serve hundreds of thousands of small to medium-sized enterprises), means that many common and powerful statistical tools, data mining methods and other research tools popular in the B2C domain are either inappropriate or must be adapted to the B2B domain. In addition, many B2C transactions still occur through common channels (for example, consumer packaged goods in retail stores, so retailers can host and capture data about the competitive consumer marketing landscape), but transactions in the B2B realm, especially larger ones, tend to be private, direct sales that often involve extensive negotiations or that occur through downstream distribution channels. Thus, data about the nature of the customer and the terms of the transaction are far from transparent.

Both the relative simplicity of the B2C marketing domain (compared with B2B) and the much larger number of public transactions historically has made that domain far

Table 1.1   Some key differences between B2B and B2C marketing

Business-to-Consumer	Business-to-Business
Marketing culture	Manufacturing/Tech culture
Market to end of chain	Market to value chain
Perceptual proposition	Technical proposition
Value in brand relationship	Value in use, quantifiable
Large customer segments	Small number of customers
Smaller-unit transactions	Large-unit transactions
Transaction linkage	Process linkage
More direct purchase	Complex buying sequence
Consumer decides	Web of decision participants

more attractive for researchers than the B2B domain, as a scan of the topics published in top journals will readily attest. A special issue of *Marketing Science* focusing on the impact of the Internet (Hoffman 2000) contained no articles and barely a mention of B2B e-commerce. Yet according to the most recent US Department of Commerce Statistics (see http://www.census.gov/econ/estats/2009), B2B e-commerce accounts for more than 91 per cent of the dollar volume of such transactions, versus less than 9 per cent for B2C e-commerce. In Chapter 33 of this book, Shankar notes that these numbers nearly flip when we consider the volume of academic e-commerce research.

And there is virtually no academic work on sales to the military or to federal, state and local governments in the US or elsewhere, according to a recent keyword search of top journals. Yet such sales are of enormous financial importance and represent virtually the sole business for many firms, both large and small. For example, the top five US government contractors in 2010 (Lockheed Martin, Northrop Grumman, Boeing, Raytheon and General Dynamics) accounted for nearly $50 billion in sales (see http://washington-technology.com/toplists/top-100-lists/2011.aspx).

Reid and Plank (2000) trace the modern history of B2B marketing from the 1930s (e.g., Frederick 1939; Lester 1936) and show that it was not until the late 1960s (e.g. Webster 1965) and 1970s (e.g. Sheth 1973; Webster and Wind 1972) that the area began to attract focused attention. In his review of the literature, Webster (1978b) noted that although B2B marketing comprised approximately half the economy, most research in top marketing journals focused on B2C marketing. The same seems to be true today: Department of Commerce statistics show that B2B transactions account for the same dollar value as B2C transactions, yet, especially in top-tier marketing journals, research on B2C marketing far outstrips research on B2B marketing. If we include research on B2B sales (which according to Lilien (1979) account for approximately 7 per cent of revenue for the average B2B firm; Belz and Bussman (2001) put the number at 13 per cent, according to a survey of 346 executives from 13 countries), the contrast is even more striking.

Over a decade has passed since Reid and Plank's (2000) comprehensive review of B2B literature (a journal article of 185 pages), and both the real world and the world of academia have evolved substantially. Rather than attempt another journal article, we have chosen this handbook format as a way to provide a broad perspective on the domain. Our objective is to provide as many diverse perspectives on B2B as possible and to engage prominent B2B scholars to guide future research in the domain. For every chapter we asked the contributors to focus on where we need to go as opposed to just providing a comprehensive review of where we have been. We also asked each contributor (especially those from practice fields) to provide clear takeaways for B2B practitioners. The careful reader will still find gaps; handbooks by their very nature are incomplete (for example this book contains little information on services, and nothing about marketing to the government) and are more supply than demand driven (i.e. the need for authors willing to contribute). But we are delighted with the contributions that we include here, because we believe each chapter contributes an insightful perspective on an important B2B domain, with clear research avenues for researchers and important takeaways for practitioners.

The goal of this introductory chapter is to provide a brief overview and perspective on the handbook and on the field. In the next section, we outline our view on why the field has attracted so (relatively) little academic attention and what we can do to address the challenges of performing research in the B2B domain. We then provide an overview of the handbook. Next we sketch a few ideas about where further research needs lie in the B2B domain. Each chapter suggests research directions on the particular topic it covers; we supplement those recommendations by focusing on areas not covered within them.

LOOKING BACK: ACCOMPLISHMENTS AND CHALLENGES

As Reid and Plank (2000) note, focusing on the period from 1978 to 1997, research in B2B marketing has come a long way and has produced much useful knowledge. Their review of 2194 articles and book chapters covers (1) planning; (2) organizational buying behavior and purchasing; (3) marketing sciences (including market research, segmentation and forecasting); (4) product (including new product and service development and management); (5) pricing; (6) channels; and (7) promotion (including advertising, sales promotion and sales force management and compensation). They show that B2B publications in top marketing journals are rare, appearing in the *Journal of Marketing* (*JM*) at a rate of about five a year, *Journal of Marketing Research* (*JMR*) at a rate of about two a year and *Marketing Science* (*MS*) at a rate of less than one a year; the *Journal of Consumer Research* (*JCR*) is completely focused on B2C issues. The bulk of B2B research appears in more specialized journals such as *Industrial Marketing Management* (37 per cent), *Journal of Business and Industrial Marketing* (8 per cent), *Journal of Business-to-Business Marketing* (2 per cent, though the journal only began in 1991, so the number would be higher today), *International Journal of Purchasing and Materials Management* (9 per cent) and *Journal of Personal Selling and Sales Management* (6 per cent). LaPlaca and Katrichis (2009) provide a recent update and find that not much has changed: since each journal's founding, B2B publications have represented 6.8 per cent of the articles in *JM*, 2.5 per cent in *JMR*, 1.3 per cent in *MS* and 0 per cent in *JCR*. It is clear that if B2B marketing has just as much economic import as B2C marketing, then the volume of top quality B2B research should be greater. We believe there are structural reasons, which we call hurdles, that explain this disparity.

Hurdle 1: Complexity and Heterogeneity

The most complex consumer behavior involves households of several individuals, normally spanning a generation or two. Rarely are more than two or three individuals involved in any purchase decision. In the B2B world, an organization may involve dozens of individuals with vastly different backgrounds in the purchasing decision-making process. And as we noted, a firm's prospect list may include firms of vastly different sizes and whose use of the focal firm's offering may differ widely. Consider a simple case. Titanium dioxide is an opacifying ingredient used in the manufacture of paper, plastic piping, paint and other materials. It has varying customer value and competes with different alternative ingredients in these and other applications. Conceptualizing and analyzing such market situations requires qualitatively different research approaches to deal with issues of purchasing complexity and customer/prospect heterogeneity than the approaches needed in the consumer marketplace. These difficulties are compounded by the small number of customers in many markets (for example, suppliers of parts for commercial airline engines may have only Boeing and Airbus as potential customers). Research methods that sacrifice breadth for depth (as discussed by Griffin in Chapter 35 and Woodside and Baxter in Chapter 36) or that make use of extensive survey and secondary source data thus are more appropriate to this domain than methods more commonly used in the B2C domain.

Hurdle 2: Lack of Domain Knowledge

We are all consumers: we understand the choice process for consumables and durables and even experience the challenges of family decision-making. We also understand (mostly) what products and services are supposed to do for us. In the B2B domain, some work experience within an organization, whether in sales, production or engineering, provides a similar background and thus is almost essential for a B2B researcher. In addition a background in science, technology or engineering is extremely helpful to understand the domain of study.[1] The solution seems clear: PhD students with work experience and a technology background have clear advantages over their peers in their ability to understand the B2B domain and the related research issues. For those with a technical background but no business experience, some company experience or internship would be most useful and should be considered part of the professional career development process.

Hurdle 3: Lack of Data Availability

A corollary to Hurdle 1 is that data for B2B research are rarer and more difficult and time consuming to collect than are data from consumer sources, be they experimental data used to study consumer behavior and psychology or secondary data used to develop consumer behavior models. This lack of data availability was one of the drivers of the development of the ISBM, whose mission includes connecting B2B researchers with organizations that share an interest in their research problem and thus facilitating the collection of primary source data. The ISBM hosts a data resources program (http://isbm.smeal.psu.edu/drp) to identify and document the location of and means of access to useful secondary source data. We believe that the use of software for customer relationship management (CRM) may increase the availability of secondary data from CRM suites to study B2B issues. Although this trend of greater data availability is a welcome sign, more needs to be done. The ISBM thus will be reaching out to B2B researchers, urging them to document and share their data. We believe such sharing will lead to differing approaches to the same data, as well as facilitating meta-analytic studies.

Hurdle 4: Diffuse Focus

Perhaps most important, the domain of B2B research encompasses many problems and relies on a variety of research foundations. The study of B2B markets is a substantive domain that builds on theories from a diverse set of parent disciplines, including economics, sociology, social psychology and psychology. Research on sales force management, the primary promotion mechanism in B2B markets, studies the same phenomena using behavioral (Bradford et al. 2010) and analytic (Mantrala et al. 2010) perspectives. The commonality of the substantive domain is helpful, but, in our opinion, insufficient; for example, scholars from each perspective on sales force management normally attend different academic conferences. The ISBM has developed a biennial academic conference to help encourage cross-perspective communication. B2B research also faces considerable heterogeneity in the unit of analyses – whether an individual sales manager in sales research, a buying unit in buying behavior research, a firm for B2B strategy and segmentation issues, an inter-firm relationship for distribution channels research or an inter-firm network for product development research. And research on these differing units of analysis relies on differing theoretical perspectives. Psychological theories might be most appropriate for sales managers, whereas the resource-based view informs firm-level studies, transaction cost economics clarifies inter-firm issues and sociological network perspectives are beneficial for studying inter-firm networks. We hope this handbook and related follow-up work will help facilitate cross-problem connections and scholarly links.

These hurdles are mere illustrations; the reader can surely add his or her own. Yet they are real, so the onus is on seasoned scholars in our field to build a community, share data, share expertise and recruit and nurture the young talent the field needs to address the many important and challenging problems the field presents.

OVERVIEW OF THE HANDBOOK

In structuring this handbook, we took a hybrid approach: Reid and Plank (2000) provide a useful, top-down (topic-driven) structure that we integrated with our understanding of where top B2B researchers might be willing and capable to make contributions. We received many acceptances (and a few declines, for the usual reasons). With our view toward engaging the practice community, we invited and received acceptances from several thoughtful practitioners.

Beyond this overview chapter (which constitutes Part I), the handbook comprises 37 chapters that we have divided into six parts:

II.   Perspectives in B2B research
III. B2B marketing mix and strategy

IV.   Inter-firm relationships in B2B markets
V.   Personal selling and sales management
VI.   Technology and B2B marketing
VII. Methodological issues

Part II contains eight chapters that provide a variety of lenses to view diverse B2B marketing issues. In Chapter 2, Oliva takes a high-level, value-based perspective on B2B markets and, based on his experience as a practitioner and his nearly 20 years as executive director of the ISBM, suggests why and how marketing organizations in B2B firms should view themselves as value-creating operations for the focal organization and that organization's customers. Banerjee, Bergen, Dutta and Ray apply an agency theory lens to the study of B2B markets in Chapter 3, and focus on the role of independent agents, including how B2B firms should structure their relationships with independent agents. They also discuss recent developments in agency theory that incorporate multitasking, non-linear compensation and structural econometric methods. In Chapter 4, Ghosh and John focus on governance value analysis, which integrates governance and strategy perspectives. They develop the notion of a 'value frame' to develop and assess the foundational architecture of strategic choice in value chains. Next, in Chapter 5, Wyuts and Van den Bulte investigate and apply a network governance approach, recognizing that firms in B2B markets operate in a social network of firms, and then theorize how firms might use their network position to govern their interactions with other firms. In Chapter 6, Morgan and Slotegraaf develop a marketing capabilities framework for B2B firms, in which they categorize a firm's marketing capabilities according to their lower-to-higher order (essentially, complexity and sophistication) and the organizational level at which those capabilities exist. Their chapter provides both a rich new set of research opportunities and a useful skills and capabilities inventory for B2B firms. Chapter 7 contains Lusch and Vargo's discussion of the ideas behind the service-dominant logic that B2B firms can use to gain competitive advantage; this logic views all B2B offerings as services and provides the rationale for firms to focus on customer experience and solutions to develop a sustainable and profitable service orientation. Cespedes then tackles the thorny issues related to managing the marketing–sales interface in B2B firms in Chapter 8; these issues are minor for most B2C firms but are of pervasive importance and understudied in the B2B domain. Finally, Chapter 9 provides Fahey's discussion of the critical importance of competitive intelligence in B2B markets, which consists of three interrelated activities: description, interpretation and assessment.

The 'B2B marketing mix and strategy' part contains five chapters. In Chapter 10, Schultz examines issues related to marketing communication in B2B markets and focuses on the marketing communication challenges that arise from the recent, dramatic advances in communications technology and the emergence of a global, networked world. In Chapter 11, Thomas discusses segmentation issues. Because of the small number of customers, their extensive heterogeneity and their diverse needs, segmentation approaches that have seen great success in the B2C world fall short in the B2B domain. He thus outlines some approaches that work and identifies important areas in need of research and methodological development. In Chapter 12, Keller and Kotler discuss the central role that brands and branding play in the B2B marketplace and provide guidelines for managing the branding function in B2B firms, which they predict will permeate the entire organization. In Chapter 13 Gopalakrishna and Lilien focus on the central role that trade shows play in the communication mix for B2B firms and examine trade shows from the perspective of the three main organizational actors: exhibitors, attendees and show organizers. The final chapter of this section (Chapter 14) contains Cressman's discussion of the concepts and components of value pricing in B2B markets; he provides a systematic approach to implement value pricing in B2B firms.

Inter-firm relationships are central to B2B marketing; Part IV, 'Inter-firm relationships in B2B markets', comprises eight chapters focused on this critical issue. In Chapter 15, Bowman notes that buyer–seller relationships evolve over time and require a longitudinal perspective in order to understand their evolution and manage those relationships properly. Beck and Palmatier advocate a multilevel, relationship marketing approach to understand and manage inter-firm relationships in Chapter 16. Then in Chapter 17, Venkatesan, Kumar and Reinartz discuss how to apply customer relationship marketing concepts to B2B firms, with a focus on how to adapt the tools of customer lifetime value measurement and management to this domain. Chapter 18 finds Scheer's investigation of trust, the most frequently studied construct in B2B inter-firm relationships. She also stresses the need to research the still poorly understood negative consequences of trust, in addition to the much more frequently studied positive consequences. In Chapter 19, Spekman discusses the complexities inherent in developing strategic alliances in B2B markets, which can undermine the strategic use of such alliances to gain access to B2B markets. Next, in Chapter 20, Ho and Ganesan discuss the importance of learning in coopetative relationships, that is, relationships that involve cooperative ventures with competitors. In Chapter 21, Johnston and Chandler elaborate on the history of the study of organizational buying and the emerging challenges in the domain, where buying centers must do much more than buy; they also must focus on innovation, knowledge management and brands. Finally, in Chapter 22 Varadarajan stresses the importance of outsourcing inter-firm relationships in global B2B markets and provides a fresh, insightful view of this increasingly important form of inter-firm relationship.

The seven chapters in Part V, 'Personal selling and sales management', focus on the most important promotional element for B2B firms. In Chapter 23, Bradford and Weitz discuss the two main roles of B2B salespeople, the traditional influencer role and the emerging value-creator/relationship-manager role, and suggest what those roles mean for researchers and practitioners. Singh, Marinova and Brown view salespeople as critical to establish and maintain connectivity with customers and thus, in Chapter 24, theorize that salespeople provide a significant, sustainable competitive advantage. In Chapter 25, Homburg and Bornemann focus on the importance of and research issues related to key account management that can help develop and sustain strategic inter-firm relationships. Then in Chapter 26, Coughlan and Joseph organize and summarize empirical and analytic research on sales force compensation, identify best practices and lay out research challenges. Ahearne and Lam develop a two-dimensional typology for sales force performance in Chapter 27, featuring valence (positive versus negative) and measurement (behavioral versus outcome). Zoltners, Sinha and Lorimer take a managerial perspective in Chapter 28 to outline a sales force systems framework that they have helped implement successfully to build winning sales forces in many B2B firms. In Chapter 29, the final chapter of this section, Mantrala and Albers discuss the effects of Internet-enabled technologies on the appropriate size and structure of the B2B sales force.

Reflecting the importance of technology in the B2B domain, Part VI comprises five chapters. In Chapter 30, Mohr, Sengupta and Slater propose a theory for marketing high-tech B2B products and employ a contingency approach to address differences in marketing strategy for different types of innovations. In Chapter 31, Tellis, Chandy and Prabhu present a three-stage conceptualization of the B2B innovation process – development, commercialization and fruits of innovation – and propose key research questions associated with each stage. Then Cooper expands on his Stage-Gate system for product innovation in Chapter 32 and discusses recent developments in practice related to idea development, project selection and new product development process improvements. In Chapter 33, Shankar provides an overview of B2B e-commerce, discussing electronic data interchange, extranets, B2B exchanges and international B2B e-commerce. In the final chapter in this section (Chapter 34), Haruvy and Jap discuss challenges underlying the design and execution of dynamic pricing mechanisms (particularly auctions) for B2B commerce.

The last part, 'Methodological issues', contains four chapters. The first two are devoted to the qualitative research methods that have seen widespread use in B2B academic work published to date. In Chapter 35, Griffin discusses when to use qualitative research and how to pursue such research with scientific rigor, and then in Chapter 36, Woodside and Baxter complement her discussion with a focus on the role and execution of case-based research – a specific type of qualitative B2B research. In Chapter 37, Rindfleisch and Antia discuss the challenges that survey researchers in B2B markets face and provide guidelines for producing more rigorous academic research that employs this methodology. Chapter 38 represents both the final chapter in this section and the closing chapter of the book; there Srinivasan discusses the challenges for developing marketing metrics in B2B markets, specifically when these metrics pertain to measures of performance.

As we acknowledged, it is possible to find many omissions here; in particular, many more methodological issues are relevant for B2B research than those discussed in Part VII. However we choose a 'glass half-full' perspective: what these expert authors have covered here, though far from exhaustive, is important, provocative and likely to provide intriguing research directions for academics along with useful guidance for practitioners.

RESEARCH OPPORTUNITIES

In each of the 37 chapters in this handbook, the authors lay out important research directions. Reid and Plank (2000), other authors cited in these chapters and other sources can add to these inventories. Thus we will not attempt a synthesis of research directions but instead urge readers to check the original sources – they are compelling and excellent.

We add two areas of research to those discussed in these sources though, because we believe they are vital to the B2B domain but remain dreadfully understudied: (1) the derived nature of demand in B2B markets; and (2) business-to-government (B2G) marketing.

Demand for B2B products is derived; it depends on final consumer demand. For example the demand for paint additives depends on demand for paint in consumer and industrial markets. In turn the demand for paint in industrial markets depends on the demand for consumer products produced by industrial firms that buy industrial paints. Thus B2B firms face the unique challenges of marketing not only to their immediate customers but also to customers of their customers – and so on down the value chain. The nature of this derived demand creates phenomena such as ingredient branding (e.g. Intel Inside) and corporate advertising in an attempt to build equity with customers' customers (e.g. BASF's tagline: 'We don't make the products you buy. We make the products you buy better'). The nature and coordination of value capture throughout the value chain (from raw materials to manufactured materials to component parts to finished goods, all flowing through multiple channels of distribution) present a host of issues for research and also suggest a domain in need of an integrated conceptual framework. Yet research on derived demand has not surfaced in top marketing journals.

As of this writing, the 2012 US Department of Defense budget is more than $670 billion (http://www.defense.gov/releases/release.aspx?releaseid=14263). And that is only one of a myriad of state, federal and local government agencies that procure products, technologies and services from B2B firms. Many well-known firms (for example Boeing, Lockheed Martin, Raytheon) obtain the vast majority of their sales by selling to governments. Selling to the government poses unique challenges, including the importance of instruments such as tenders and a marketing timeline that starts months or years before the tenders arrive. Governments at different levels and in different countries have varying and often unique institutional and legal arrangements. But they buy – and in very large quantities. Government accounts might be seen as key accounts (see Chapter 25), but they pose many challenges that differ from those in the private sector, including unique budget cycles, complex buying processes that involve many actors from divergent governmental bodies and the need for an influence and presence in the political arena. This area of enormous financial importance has seen little rigorous academic research.

Finally, the ISBM conducts a biennial marketing trends study (http://www.isbmtrends.com), in which we highlight the key issues that leading B2B academics and practitioners believe are the main issues that academics and practitioners should be addressing to be prepared for tomorrow's B2B marketplace. We urge readers, academics and practitioners alike, to investigate the most recent version of that study to complement the issues and directions raised here.

NOTE

1. A recruiter from a major chemical company visiting our university recently hired no business graduates, only chemical engineers, explaining to us, 'We can teach chemical engineers to sell, but we can't teach business grads enough chemistry to be credible in our market.'

REFERENCES

Belz, Christian and Wolfgang Bussman (2001), *Performance Selling*, St. Gallen, Switzerland: Thexis and Mercuri.
Bradford, Kevin, Steven Brown, Shankar Ganesan, Gary Hunter, Vincent Onyemah, Robert Palmatier, Dominique Rouziès, Rosann Spiro, Harish Sujan and Barton Weitz (2010), 'The embedded sales force: connecting buying and selling organizations', *Marketing Letters*, **21** (3), 239–53.

Frederick, John H. (1939), 'The place of industrial marketing in distribution', *Journal of Marketing*, **4** (1), 31–5.

Hoffman, Donna L. (2000), 'The revolution will not be televised: introduction to special issue on marketing science and the Internet', *Marketing Science*, **19** (1), 1–3.

LaPlaca, Peter and Jerome M. Katrichis (2009), 'Relative presence of business-to-business research in the marketing literature', *Journal of Business-to-Business Marketing*, **16** (1), 1–22.

Lester, Bernard (1936), 'Changing methods in the marketing of industrial equipment', *Journal of Marketing*, **1** (1), 46–52.

Lilien, Gary L. (1979), 'Advisor 2: modeling the marketing mix decision for industrial products', *Management Science*, **25** (2), 191–204.

Mantrala, Murali K., Sönke Albers, Fabio Caldieraro, Ove Jensen, Kissan Joseph, Manfred Krafft, Chakravarthi Narasimhan, Srinath Gopalakrishna, Andris Zoltners, Rajiv Lal and Leonard Lodish (2010), 'Sales force modeling: state of the field and research agenda', *Marketing Letters*, **21** (3), 255–72.

Reid, David A. and Richard E. Plank (2000), 'Business marketing comes of age: a comprehensive review of the literature', *Journal of Business-to-Business Marketing*, **7** (2), 9–186.

Sheth, Jagdish N. (1973), 'A model of industrial buyer behavior', *Journal of Marketing*, **37** (October), 50–56.

Webster, Frederick E. (1965), 'Modeling the industrial buying process', *Journal of Marketing Research*, **2** (4), 370–76.

Webster, Frederick E. (1978a), 'Is industrial marketing coming of age?' in G. Zaltman and T. Bonoma (eds), *Review of Marketing*, Chicago: American Marketing Association, pp. 138–59.

Webster, Frederick F. (1978b), 'Management science in industrial marketing', *Journal of Marketing*, **42** (1), 21–7.

Webster, Frederick E. and Yoram Wind (1972), 'A general model for understanding organizational buying behavior', *Journal of Marketing*, **36** (April), 12–19.

PART II

PERSPECTIVES IN B2B RESEARCH

2   A high-level overview: a value perspective on the practice of business-to-business marketing
Ralph Oliva

The goal of this chapter is to provide an overview of the practice of B2B marketing for practitioners and outline the research issues for academics researching the field. After setting the stage and some foundation principles behind the practice, the chapter is organized following a framework developed in the Institute for the Study of Business Markets (ISBM), headquartered in the Smeal College of Business at Penn State, and illustrated in Figure 2.1.

In the common parlance and practice of marketing, the term 'marketing' itself is often misunderstood and is subject to a wide variety of interpretations, depending on the context of the discussion (for relevant online resources and a glossary of important B2B terms used in practice, please see the online Web Appendix for this chapter at http://handbook.isbm.org). In general parlance, the term is often used as a synonym for 'advertising' or other parts of the process and is generally associated with marketing B2C products and services.

The American Marketing Association provides a broad definition of the term 'marketing': 'Marketing is the activity, set of institutions, and processes for creating, communicating, delivering, and exchanging offerings that have value for customers, clients, partners, and society at large.'

In my view, in B2B markets it is important to recognize the value of marketing to the Chief Financial Officer as well. I would thus propose another definition of B2B marketing: 'The set of processes and activities that optimize the value of a firm's assets – and free cash flow – by connecting those assets to the exact right demand.'

B2B marketing can extend across the entire value chain and can be applied to transactions that occur in marketing basic raw materials, manufactured components, and services of all sorts, from first purchase consideration all the way through to the point where the product or service is used or recycled.

Transactions between businesses make up the largest share of total commerce in the United States. Of the $22.4 trillion in 'shipments sales and revenue' cited by the US Census in 2008, $11.6 trillion was cited as B2B and $10.8 trillion as B2C. B2B activity is larger than the total of consumer transactions, because before a consumer buys anything, many B2B transactions typically have to happen first.

The realm of B2B marketing traverses diverse offerings, from 'foundation goods' (big-ticket products such as machine tools), 'entering goods' ('direct material' or 'ingredients' used in another firm's manufacturing process) and end products sold from B2B to a broad array of B2B services and maintenance repair and operating (MRO) supplies.

In these diverse realms, while purchasing new products B2B buyers start their processes when they have a problem or need they cannot fulfill on their own. Their purchase is driven by the need to support the profitability of their firm. Buying can also happen cyclically following a schedule, or episodically following some change in process or direction for their firm (the notion of modified and straight rebuy). 'Impulse buys' are rare but do happen in B2B. The B2B buying process is usually one of careful consideration, by multiple people with different roles and functions, and can take quite a long period of time.

Keeping in mind the complexity of the B2B buying process, and the multiple actors involved in different departments and at various levels, it is essential to unravel and understand the different needs and motives of the multiple stakeholders involved. Over the last 15 years the study of organization buying behavior has evolved considerably. It includes levels of analysis such as organizational, situational, group and individual levels. It has become essential to consider questions like: what are the best practices for integrating the organizational buying process with product design, development and innovation? How can technology, media and automation be leveraged in the buying process (Johnston and Chandler 2012)?

Another element of B2B is the forecasting and management of 'derived demand'. The B2B marketer needs a view down the value chain, as to how demand will be created. It's difficult for the B2B marketer to stimulate 'primary demand' through the value chain on its own. (For example, the demand for truck axles derives from the primary demand for trucks. If people aren't buying trucks, the axle manufacturer will also have no business.) This need has given rise to use of electronic data interchange (EDI) and extranets for the coordination and optimization of the supply chain (Shankar 2012).

The foundation of the B2B marketing discipline is an understanding of the concept of value – in tangible, numeric terms – and implementing a systemic process for creating, managing and harvesting a fair share of value. In fact management of that 'fair share' in pricing strategy is an important element of B2B practice (Anderson et al. 2010).

The ISBM 'Value Delivery Framework' in Figure 2.1 lists the categories of processes that define B2B marketing management. Understanding a total process such as this is crucial for B2B marketers. The ISBM Value Delivery Framework has formed the core of the central processes of B2B marketing for firms such as DuPont, General Electric (GE), Kennametal and Parker Hannifin. Through the remainder of this chapter, I will be using the Value Delivery Framework to organize my coverage of the practice. It is important to note that though the Value Delivery Framework implies that parts of the process happen in a 'linear' fashion, in practice these processes form a 'web', with many elements overlapping and happening simultaneously.

How a firm defines, develops and delivers value to its customer is a function of the firm's marketing capabilities. These capabilities determine how the firm meets market needs by combining, transforming and deploying its resources. Marketing capabilities need to be aligned with the firm's core offering, target customers' needs and address the competitive landscape, keeping in mind the dynamic market environment (Morgan and Slotegraaf 2012).

Further on in the chapter, I look at how B2B marketers can better understand value; how firms can use their marketing capabilities to design, communicate and deliver value to their customers; and finally how firms can manage the life cycle of B2B customers. Throughout the chapter there are suggested research pathways as the discussion progresses. The chapter closes by gazing into the future of B2B.

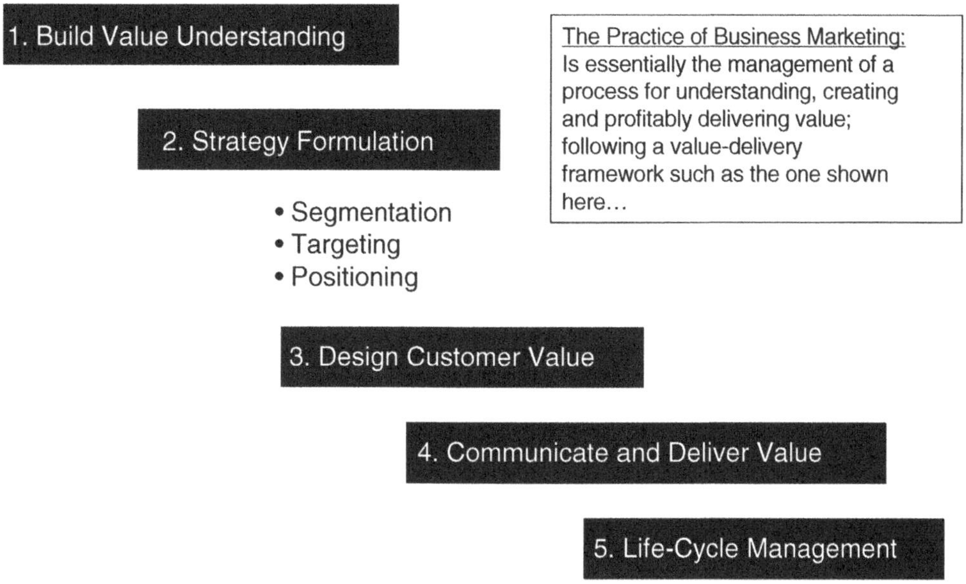

1. Build Value Understanding

The Practice of Business Marketing:
Is essentially the management of a process for understanding, creating and profitably delivering value; following a value-delivery framework such as the one shown here…

2. Strategy Formulation

• Segmentation
• Targeting
• Positioning

3. Design Customer Value

4. Communicate and Deliver Value

5. Life-Cycle Management

Source: ©1999, ISBM – Penn State.

Figure 2.1   ISBM Value Delivery Framework

BUILDING VALUE UNDERSTANDING IN BUSINESS MARKETS

Value understanding and management is the heart of all marketing practice, especially so in B2B marketing. Across many of the member firms of the ISBM, it is observed that marketers generally have a firm understanding of the concept of price (though tools and techniques used in pricing are often surprisingly primitive). The same holds for the concept of cost (even though actual costs are often known with far less precision than most managers realize). But when businesspeople are asked, 'What is value?' the answers are often much less clear.

Mixed definitions of the term 'value' can lead to real communication problems within a firm and, more so, across firms. Is value a tangible construct, or is it 'perceived' in the eye of the customer? Is it some view of 'quality for the price charged' (whatever 'quality' means)? Or is value whatever the customer is willing to pay to acquire a given set of product and service benefits?

Because understanding value is critical, ISBM has recommended a definition based on a calculation of the impact of an offering for a customer firm as the offering is put into use:

The value of an offering to a particular customer for a particular application is the hypothetical price for that offering which leaves the customer at overall economic break-even with respect to the next best alternative for performing that same application.

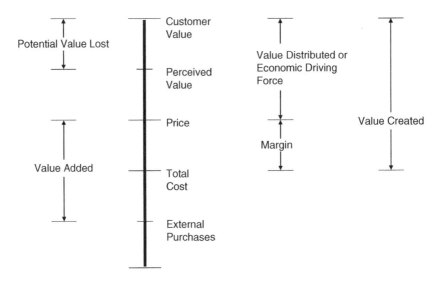

Source: Irwin Gross.

Figure 2.2   Taxonomy for conceptualizing value, costs, prices

This definition has formed the core of a value taxonomy that has been widely deployed across ISBM member firms, as depicted in Figure 2.2. When suppliers and customers work together to solve problems and build solutions better than any previous alternative, they create new value together. That 'customer value' is depicted at the top of the line chart. Often a customer's 'perceived value' is lower. The gap between the real customer value and customer's perceived value is identified as 'potential value lost' in subsequent discussions on price. Price is the 'knife' that divides the customer value into the margin for the supplier firm and the value delivered to the customer: the customer's 'economic driving force' for doing business with the supplier.

The total value of an offering to a business customer can have several components:

- Functional value-in-use, as described. Computing this value requires understanding the tangible impact of an offering on the customer's business in hard currency terms. In B2B, it is usually the largest and most crucial element of the offering. (These might be termed 'tangible, financial benefits'.) In B2B markets, the tangible value in use of an offering can usually be discerned by analysing the product's use downstream in the marketplace and comparing that offering to the next best alternative – or the 'design around' – for the downstream customer.
- Supplier reputation, relationship and brand value are part of the offering as well. These 'intangibles' can have a powerful influence in B2B markets. The supplier's know-how, understanding of a customer's business and ability to build confidence all add value to the offering. Furthermore the supplier's reputation, trust and brand relationships fill in the uncertainties of a transaction. These components

of value are also translatable to economic impact but involve more research and forensics with the customer in order to quantify them.

Value-based Pricing

Understanding customer needs, and the creation of offerings of real value to satisfy those needs, is at the core of a firm's function. Accurate quantification of the value of those offerings is critical to setting prices. As B2B marketers learn better ways to understand the total value they actually deliver to customers, they often find they have underpriced products or services, particularly if they follow the discredited but still widely used practice of pricing based on 'cost plus a target' margin. It sometimes comes as a surprise when practitioners realize that price and cost are fundamentally unrelated.

Pricing based on cost can create significant pricing mistakes and missed profit opportunities. With value-based pricing, companies learn that when their marketing and sales programs enable customers to understand the value they receive in crisp, currency-based terms, those customers are frequently willing to pay more. For more on the management of a value-based approach to B2B marketing, readers might refer to the excellent book *Value Merchants: Demonstrating and Documenting Superior Value in Business Markets* (Anderson et al. 2007).

Value-based pricing is an essential tool in the B2B marketer's toolkit. Cressman (2012) expands on this point, looking at successful pricing strategies, managing this value exchange with customers, structuring the offering, communicating value and value-based negotiating.

Discerning Value-based Market Opportunities

B2B marketers are faced with the challenge of developing new approaches and methods to better understand what their customers really need, beyond what they can say or articulate. The discernment of customer needs is a key enabler of the creation of real, new value.

A process framework for systemically understanding customer needs and customer value is in Figure 2.3. As customers navigate between their present state and the desired new state, B2B marketers have to tune in to their functional and economic needs – those that can be objectively measured and calculated, using hard-edged analytical techniques. But beyond that, B2B marketers need to dig into the perceived and psychological needs of the customer and bring them into the equation as well.

B2B market transactions can be quite sizable and often carry with them great amounts of risk. For many customer firms, fear, uncertainty about how an offering will work in their process, questions about whether a supplier will stand behind them if something goes wrong and bonds of friendship between individuals in the buying and selling firm are very real parts of the buying equation. Measures of perceptual value need to be developed and employed to bring these 'softer' parts of the offering into the selling process. The role of relationship marketing can be important for the B2B marketer. Beck and Palmatier (2012) provide a framework for understanding relationship marketing, look at various drivers of inter-firm relationships and connect these drivers to performance-related outcomes.

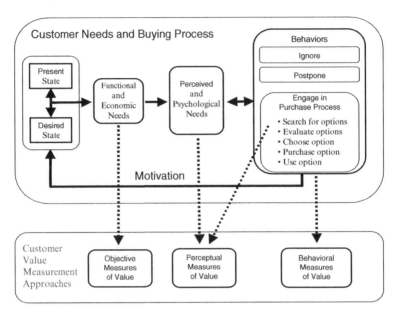

Source: Robert J. Georgetown.

Figure 2.3   Customer needs and customer value measurement

A variety of tools can help identify value creation opportunities.

- A family of powerful techniques available to B2B marketers is clustered around the *Voice of the Customer* analysis (Griffin and Hauser 1993, 1996). A practical guide to value discernment incorporating Voice of the Customer techniques is the field manual *Customer Visits* by McQuarrie (1998).
- *Quality Function Deployment* (or QFD), a technique that is often used as part of the Six-Sigma quality improvement process, takes a systemic approach to outlining customers' specific need points, their worth in numerical terms and approaches to serving those needs profitably.
- *Conjoint Analysis* enables marketers to identify which features/benefits are most important – and worth more – to specific groups of customers in a complex offering environment.
- The ISBM *Marketing Engineering Toolkit* brings powerful tools such as conjoint analysis and others to the desktop of the B2B marketer (Lilien et al. 2007; Parry 2002).
- *Revealed Choice Models* can be another important approach. Carefully documenting past customer buying behavior, and modeling what they may do in the future can help in understanding and discerning needs – and their likely buying patterns in the future.
- *Ethnography* is an observational approach that develops a detailed qualitative description of how people are actually behaving in a variety of different situations, based on direct observation in the field (McFarland 2001). The ethnographer

attempts to get a detailed understanding of needs and the context surrounding them through direct observation of relatively few subjects. Ethnographic accounts are explanatory and interpretive. The ethnographer must determine the signifi- cance of what he or she observes without gathering broad, statistical information.

- More recently, techniques normally used in consumer marketing, such as the *Zaltman Metaphor Elicitation Technique* (ZMET) are being used to better deter- mine how intangible elements of an offering factor into the B2B value equation. In this technique carefully selected respondents are asked to find and bring pictures describing their feelings and relationship to a problem, proposition, brand or other feature to a specially structured interview session. Through the interview process, deep feelings and metaphors can be revealed, which enable marketers to get to the feelings underneath the purchase (Zaltman 1998).

While B2B marketers focus all their energy on understanding and meeting the needs of the customer, they also need to keep one eye on what the competition has to offer. Understanding competition is an essential part of how value proposition is structured and communicated to customers.

Competition: The 'Next Best Alternative'

The value of new offerings as viewed by the customer almost always involves a compari- son to the current alternative the customer is using for performing a set of functions or filling a need. Value is defined with respect to the 'next best alternative'.

An excellent reference on competitor analysis and market intelligence is *Competitors: Outwitting Outmaneuvering Outperforming* (Fahey 1997). Additional insight on plotting competitive scenarios can be found in *Learning from the Future* (Fahey and Randall 1998). Fahey (2012) looks at this interesting and essential topic of competitive intel- ligence and how competitor intelligence and B2B marketing strategy can be better connected.

Another challenge that B2B marketers face in the current environment is the pace of change. Increased globalization, quick product obsolescence, ever-changing customer demands and the fast pace of technological innovation have forced B2B marketers to look beyond traditional strategies and to look at cooperative strategies with downstream and upstream partners. The competitive ground has changed from firms competing against each other to one ecosystem against another ecosystem of partners. The coopera- tive environment has opened a whole new way of looking at how firms conceptualize and deliver value as members of the ecosystem (Ho and Ganesan 2012).

Suggested Research Pathways: Value Understanding in Business Markets

Understanding, discovering, discerning and quantifying value is at the very core of B2B marketing practice. B2B marketers would be well served by new knowledge and research outcomes that shed additional light on how to better uncover stated and unstated cus- tomer needs and how to better overcome barriers to building dialogue through the value chain to foster the development of new value, as well as new models for building effective value propositions in B2B markets.

STRATEGY FORMULATION IN BUSINESS MARKETS

Building on a true understanding of what value is in the marketplace, the needs that customers have and the current competitive alternatives they are using set the stage for B2B marketing strategy. At the core of modern B2B marketing strategy are three concepts: segmentation, targeting and positioning (STP).

Segmentation

Segmentation is an analytic discovery process for dividing a large group of customers or prospects into smaller groups (or aggregating individual customers into groups) that will react similarly to some marketing action. Discerning how similar customers can be grouped together and approached with tailored offerings is crucial to effective deployments of resources. Segmentation techniques are used for a variety of reasons: to target communications, focus the sales force, create new and tailored offerings, allocate resources and optimize marketing investment (Wind and Cardozo 1974).

In consumer markets, segmentation typically entails statistically grouping large numbers of customers with similar needs who can be reached with similar marketing and advertising appeals. Because consumer marketers can often amass huge amounts of data on consumer behavior, demographics, psychographics, buying patterns and so on, advanced statistical and data mining techniques are often used to group customers into clusters who might respond similarly to the marketing of an offering.

In B2B markets the process of segmentation can be very different. Consumer marketers may have literally millions of customers but only know a few of them by name. They focus on clusters of customers in segments of interest. Business marketers often know all of their customers and the universe of prospects – by name. B2B market segmentation usually must deal with much smaller customer populations resistant to large group statistical analysis such as data mining. A segment might be as small as an individual customer or firm.

Targeting

Once appropriate segments have been identified, the selection of the best segment to focus on, targeting, is the next step. This step involves systemic decision-making to allocate finite marketing resources to produce optimal business results. Segmentation and targeting working together look 'from the market back' and tie a firm's resources to customers with needs that the supplier firm is especially prepared to serve. Segmentation and targeting also look from the 'inside out' to optimize the value of the firm's capital assets and consider the question: do we have the right customers for our capacity to enable us to deliver optimal value to customers, at an optimal profit to our firm? B2B marketers help set priorities for assigning sales resources and developing distribution channels.

It's important when selecting target segments to ensure that the mix of customers, and the size of the segments that a firm addresses, represent a good and well-founded business opportunity. Segments that are too small to address can absorb resources without enough return. Relying on one or two big customers can be very dangerous.

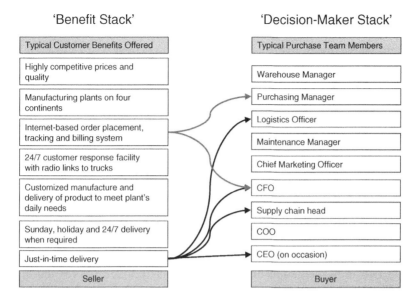

'Benefit Stack'   'Decision-Maker Stack'

Typical Customer Benefits Offered		Typical Purchase Team Members

Seller / Buyer

Figure 2.4   Value–message alignment in business markets

B2B markets can be very dynamic, and targeting segments with only one or two customers might enable a focused short-term profit but in the long term can lead to volatility in demand that can significantly hurt a firm that needs to keep its factory running at high utilization to maintain profitability.

Positioning

Once a B2B firm has developed a segmentation approach and selected the segments that are most profitable, the firm addresses the positioning of its offerings (and brand) in that segment.

As defined by Al Ries and Jack Trout in *Positioning: The Battle for your Mind* (2001), positioning involves creating a real difference in the mind of the buyer for the supplier's offering (and brand) from those alternatives also being considered at the time of purchase. In B2B however, this differentiating must often be accomplished across many minds – the minds of the people who make up the buying center inside the customer firm. As illustrated in Figure 2.4, each element of the customer buying center may have its own picture of the competitive landscape, making this process more complex than the challenges faced by consumer marketers.

Positioning involves demonstrating superior, differentiated value before the sale, based on unique points of difference with real economic impact for the customer, and clearly creating a separation for those offerings from those of the competitive set. A simple scheme might be to position offerings as:

- Unique: 'The only product/service offering with XYZ'.
- Different: 'More than twice the (feature) vs. (competitor)'.
- Similar: 'Same functionality as (competitor), lower price'.

Positioning often relates to the brand of the offering being delivered, but ties closely to the 'unique value proposition' for specific offerings for specific customers. In any B2B offering there are 'points of parity' (POP), which are usually required to even be a viable alternative in the category. Key to positioning are compelling, relevant and unique 'points of difference' (POD), which will be the key influence in the buy decision.

The implementation of effective and successful segmentation in B2B market situations has been difficult. It can involve sales force realignment and changes in compensation, breaking some customer relationships, nurturing others or selling to a different part of the buying center inside a customer firm. All of these things can be quite difficult to implement in practice. Some of the possible reasons for the variation in outcomes of segmentation in B2B are organization differences, market situational differences, segmentation methodology differences, targeting difference, positioning and marketing strategy formulation and implementation differences. Thomas (2012) explores the interaction between B2B market segmentation processes and practices. He outlines the challenges facing B2B segmentation scholars and practitioners and looks at ways to overcome such challenges. The ISBM research director Gary Lilien recommends carefully understanding the implementation implications of any segmentation study before beginning. Segmentation, targeting and positioning are powerful elements of the B2B marketing arsenal – but only if they are done with an eye to the realities of implementation.

Suggested Research Pathways: Strategy Formulation

Marketers would benefit from a better understanding of how the concept of 'segment' is changing with the advent of social media and other mechanisms by which customers and markets are constantly connecting to one another. Is the whole concept of a 'segment' changing in some way? How? What actions can marketers take to better focus their resources? What segmentation approaches and tools work best in different cultural and organizational situations? Are there new analytic methodologies, geared for B2B, that would enable us to better discern segments from the data sets B2B marketers encounter and to better enable us to target them? Finally, any research on overcoming barriers to implementation of STP would be quite valuable. Across ISBM member firms, for example, many B2B segmentations simply do not work.

DESIGNING CUSTOMER VALUE

Technically sophisticated customers, working with their best suppliers, can create exciting new solutions with greatly increased value from the current next best alternative. In the face of market downturns and stress, however, low price often becomes the highest priority. When that happens, value chains tend to focus their innovative capability on efficiency, lowering costs and streamlining, rather than on innovation and the creation of fundamental new value. Firms need to constantly innovate or face the danger of perishing. Innovation is the critical driver that can help firms meet customer needs in a better way, improve firm performance and contribute to firms' growth and success. Tellis et al. (2012) identify 10 major topics in innovation, summarize the major contributions in the topic of innovation and outline key research questions for the future.

It is important to note that innovation goes beyond the core product to include all elements of the total 'offering' for the customer in a particular situation. B2B services are big business, and for many B2B markets, the service wrapped around the core 'product' offers the opportunity for greater value added and real differentiation. Deep understanding of the target segment and customer needs is crucial to designing new offerings in the business marketing arena. Marketers pay particular attention, and deploy specialized tools and approaches, at different points in the new offering realization process:

- *The 'Front End': Market Understanding and Ideation.* This part of the new offering realization process is often euphemistically referred to as the 'fuzzy front end'. This is the place where innovation, creativity and discipline all come together in the ideation of product and service offerings of significant new value. The process begins with good answers to the questions: do we really understand what our markets, especially downstream markets, need from us? Have we put enough front-end and market intelligence work into our research and development and innovation processes? Do we have an ongoing and repeatable process for generating fresh new insights and ideas that feed the new offering process? Do we understand likely new offerings by the competition?

    Firms employ a wide variety of approaches to generate new offering ideas: from traditional 'brainstorming' techniques, to basic ideas emerging from R&D, to nurturing the firm's 'serial innovators' (Griffin et al. 2007; Sim et al. 2007), to buying new ideas (from early concept to full product specification) from online sources (Nambisan and Sawhney 2008).
- *From Idea to Offering: Stages/Gates.* Once a product concept is selected for development, the ongoing investment and importance of key decisions along the way warrant a disciplined and systematic approach (Cooper 1993). Cooper (2012) details the stage and gate approach. He highlights how firms can adopt Stage-Gate® to improve their innovation process and implement a robust idea to launch system.
- *New Offering Portfolio Management.* As the new offering realization process continues, a portfolio approach to managing initiatives to achieve the right mix of risk and reward is key. Is the firm pushing the envelope sufficiently with investments in true innovations, which can be risky? Are those initiatives balanced with relatively low-risk offerings, such as product extensions? Is the firm effectively 'killing' new offering initiatives that will not work early in the process, freeing resources for redeployment on more profitable investments?
- *Launch.* Finally, there is the suite of processes around new product launch. Product debuts require special attention in B2B markets. Are all elements of the selling force, channel partners and the customer buying center addressed with elements of an integrated market communications program? Are results being tracked in ways that allow for mid-course adjustments to support product success? Schultz (2012) highlights how the forces of competition, pace of technology, rise of brands

and today's global and networked organizations are changing how B2B marketing is planned, developed and executed. The age-old linear, primarily outbound persuasive personal sales and selling system is being challenged. This change calls for re-evaluating current practices of B2B marketing and communication and giving them new direction.

B2B Services

The new offering process for many B2B firms involves a harder-edge product offering, with services 'wrapped around it'. As B2B markets continue to emerge, however, a wide variety of 'pure B2B service' innovations offerings are coming into play, with businesses finding ways to move entire processes of their operations to outside firms and agencies that might be better able to accomplish the entire function (Bitner et al. 2008).

An often-cited example is General Electric (GE) in the servicing of jet engines. As airlines worked to keep their jet engines in good working order, many of which are manufactured by GE, they often bought service packages or training for their mechanics to do a better job. GE recognized that what airlines really needed was not so much better tools and techniques for maintaining engines, or even services to maintain engines better, but reliable 'power by the hour'. This GE service offering allows it to re-engineer the value chain to the benefit of all of the players involved – a move toward the service-dominant logic (Vargo and Lusch 2004). Lusch and Vargo (2012) look at the advantages of the service-centric view, including how firms are now part of a service ecosystem and strive for better resource integration to attain higher order competences.

Suggested Research Pathways: Designing Customer Value

Research that would enable firms to better understand and systematize the innovation process, and importantly mobilize the powerful new global resources afforded by the web and social media, would be very important, looking forward. Which innovation processes work best in which circumstances? Can we recognize and build a model of the new offering innovation space in today's connected environment? Which development processes are right for which sorts of offering? The Stage-Gate® process has been around for a while; can research build on the best of that process to enable 'tailoring' for specific sorts of new offering development opportunities?

COMMUNICATE AND DELIVER VALUE

As the value delivery framework and process unfolds, effectively communicating the value of offerings to the marketplace is the next important step. It is especially important at product launch, when B2B marketers are often bringing significant new alternatives to their customers that in turn enable them to create new, differentiated products for their customers downstream.

Schultz and colleagues (e.g. Schultz and Schultz 2004; Schultz et al. 1993) provide processes, tools and techniques for focused and carefully time-phased communications in B2B markets. For example, marketers can adopt a Behavioral Timeline® approach for mapping communications timed to the actions that customers take in the buying process (Lauterborn 1998 [2001]). In B2B marketing the whole 'demand decision chain' has to be taken into consideration as communications plans are developed and as value is communicated. The Behavioral Timeline® is a tool expressly designed to assist marketers in detailed mapping of actions for all elements of the chain.

The challenge and opportunity of B2B market communications is illustrated in the 'benefit stack' and the 'decision-maker stack' in Figure 2.4 (Narayandas 2005). Different organizational elements in the decision-maker stack have different views as to the most important benefits of a supplier's offering in a given situation, depending on these individuals' position and point of view. Johnston and Chandler (2012) review the fundamental constructs discussed in organizational buying literature; evaluate the emergent role of partnerships, alliances and outsourcing; and propose a framework that links the three emergent topics of Innovation and solutions, Knowledge management and technology, and Brands and relationship processes.

B2B Market Communications

Because of the complexity of the buying process and the nature of the decision-maker stack, B2B market communications need to be effectively delivered to elements of the buying center at 'just the right place' and 'just the right time'. B2B market communications involve some of the more conventional suite of communications tools such as marketing media relations, print advertising, direct mail, email, and special websites, but it is leading the way in aggressively exploring social media and the impact of networking across customers, influentials and market geographies.

A good B2B website can be an especially important component of market communications between businesses. Because the buying process and the offerings involved can be complex, custom websites that allow various elements of the customer decision-maker stack to tune into the information they need, just when they need it, can be especially valuable. For this reason many B2B websites look like 'an ocean of links' on their main landing page. In practice, however, customers often access the websites of their suppliers through custom interfaces that have been especially designed for them.

In B2B market communications it is often said that 'content is king'. Various elements of the decision-maker stack inside customer firms are very busy, and market communications is often very much a 'value-based contract' with the receiver, involving the delivery of important information at the right place at the right time. Careful targeting and a valuable message are essential.

Trade shows are often a very important part of the B2B market communications mix. Although under fire in recent years for their high expense and lack of trackable results, trade shows continue as a place where customers, suppliers and other influentials gather, and they afford an opportunity for a great deal of communication and connection to happen at one time. Gopalkrishna and Lilien (2011) look from the perspective of three stakeholders – exhibitors, attendees and show organizers – and provide guidelines for practitioners and possible research agendas for researchers.

The emergence of 'social media' is adding a spectrum of new channels and interesting new dimensions of direct dialog across and between many players in the buying process. Emerging channels such as blogs, Twitter, Facebook, LinkedIn, YouTube and others are making new sorts of dialog, discussion and co-creation possible between corporations. With this comes a whole array of issues with regard to 'official policies' on how and when to deploy these resources, protection of proprietary information, the investment involved in resourcing these new channels and others. As of this writing, experiments are underway across B2B practice, and B2B marketers are just beginning to develop principles by which to mobilize these new tools.

Value Propositions in Business Markets

Building strong value propositions in B2B markets requires investments of time and effort to understand customers' business, their value chains and their unique requirements and preferences. Supplier claims on value delivered, cost savings and so on need to be backed up in accessible, persuasive language with a focus on the differences between a supplier's offerings and rivals' offerings, which matter most to customers.

Anderson et al. (2006) outline an approach for creating what they term 'resonating focus' value propositions. They suggest that focusing on the one or two most important points of difference in the supplier firm's offering (and perhaps a Point of Parity that a customer may not recognize you have) can be key to much better results. A resonating focus value proposition answers the customer question: 'What is *most* worthwhile for my firm to keep in mind about your offering?'

Building strong value propositions requires deep knowledge of how a supplier's firm offering differs and delivers superior value to customers, compared with the next best alternative that the customer is considering in the specific buying situation. Savvy B2B marketers 'demonstrate' value before the sale, in hard-hitting economic terms, and then continue to 'document' value after the sale, with value forensics they conduct together with customers. Documentation of value furthers the learning of how a supplier can better serve a customer and brings the customer on board in documenting and verifying that the value promised was actually delivered.

Brands in B2B Markets

An important additional component of value in B2B markets is the brand and reputation of the supplier. The whole business of brands and brand equity is often not that well understood by B2B marketers and often does not receive the importance or investment it deserves. In our work at ISBM, we define a brand as 'A relationship with a market or market segment that has an economic impact in the marketing of an offering'. That economic impact can include higher prices, lower cost of sales, faster uptake, more willingness to try new offerings, ability to forestall competitive encroachment – a variety of factors. These factors in the aggregate, the economic impact of a brand, are termed 'brand equity'. Brand equity comes into play when customers encounter things such as trademarks, logos or people they recognize as coming from a firm they know and trust.

Brands themselves reside in the minds of customers. Firms can own trademarks, and the economic effects of brands (brand equity), but they are dealing with a powerful and valuable asset that they actually do not own themselves. Brands are built over time through an accumulation of experiences a customer has with a supplier firm. From the performance of offerings (products and services) to the relationships developed between employees, to the market communications messages sent and received; all of these act to add up to the 'brand' in the mind of the customer. (In consumer markets, many of the 'core offerings' in a category are close to identical. Real functional differentiation may be very difficult to see or discern. The real differentiating feature is in the brand and brand experience.)

B2B transactions are often quite complex, involve very high stakes and incorporate a great deal of risk or fear, uncertainty and doubt. The risks involved when a consumer purchases a tube of toothpaste on a trial basis are relatively minor. If a toothpaste manufacturing firm is considering the purchase of several hundred thousand pounds of a chemical for use in its product, the risks and complications can be quite a bit higher. Despite all of the 'left brain' quantitative analysis that goes on in a B2B buy, customers like working with suppliers they trust. Strong B2B brands 'fill in the gaps' of uncertainty that reside in every B2B buying situation. A strong brand that assures customers that the supplier will stand behind the product it sells and work to ensure that any problems will be handled can be a very important part of any value proposition in B2B markets (Kotler and Pfoertsch 2006).

Many B2B firms fail to understand and utilize the importance of branding. Keller and Kotler (2011) provide some answers on branding for B2B firms. They look at issues such as why B2B firms fail to use B2B branding, what differentiates major B2B firms that make good use of B2B branding, what B2B firms need to know about branding as a starting point and what steps a B2B firm should take to build a strong brand.

In some situations, the supplier's 'ingredient' in a customer's product creates *the* differentiating feature sold to the next step (or to a player farther down) in the value chain. A supplier often provides an essential, and sometimes invisible, element of value or a key, compelling, differentiating benefit that the customer then uses in its selling situations. Pioneered by DuPont (with Stainmaster, Teflon, Nomex and others), an ingredient branding strategy spans a wide variety of business models. These business models vary greatly across cases such as NutraSweet, Dolby, Intel Inside, DLP and others. Ingredient brands enable a supplier firm to reach 'down the value chain' and create downstream market 'pull' for their products, as well as enabling different sorts of negotiation in the direct sale to the next step in the value chain (Kotler and Pfoertsch 2010; Oliva et al. 2006).

Channel Strategies

Channel strategies and channel management come into play at this phase of the process, as offerings move downstream toward the eventual user. In B2B markets, the right channel partners are often the keys to value-added marketing. The nature of the channel partner relationship spans a broad range of business designs. Some channel partners are 'pure resellers': they find buyers and 'make the market', break bulk and handle basic transactions. Other channel partners – 'value added resellers' (VARs) – start with the supplier's offering and add significant additional value. VARs frequently provide application know-how, access to customers, inventory management, product integration and other contributions to the basic product or service offering coming from a supplier, on its way downstream to the next customer in the value chain.

Identifying, selecting and working with the dealers, distributors, resellers, retailers and other intermediaries operating between a company and users of its products and services is a special mix of art and science (Friedman and Furey 1999). Critical issues include how a given channel adds value, what portions of that value it captures through pricing and how the suppliers' offering enables the channel partner to make money. B2B marketers are learning that channel strategy becomes fluid and challenging as disruptive technologies such as the Internet create opportunities for new channel experiments. Customers develop new performance expectations, and new channels disrupt old and familiar relationships. In most B2B situations, multiple channels to market, including electronic channels, often exist side by side, enabling better coverage and more custom service to different customer segments, but they also present challenges to channel managers (Rangan 2006).

B2B 'eBusiness'

Although the Internet has occupied mass consciousness for nearly two decades, we're still in the early days of seeing its potential for marketers. The tools and techniques of electronic communication and networked marketing are enabling firms to understand, create, deliver and profitably harvest value with even greater efficiency and effectiveness. New channels for communication, supply chain integration, demand forecasting and transaction management are being constantly tested. Innovative market experiments are underway as suppliers use digital/networked tools to customize offerings, focus communications, create new sorts of dialog and manage prices.

Although consumer-oriented online commerce often captures more headlines, 2008 census data reports that B2B e-commerce, at $3.4 trillion, dwarfs consumer e-business at $288 billion. The size and frequency of individual transactions and the large dollar value of supplier–buyer relationships make B2B fertile ground for digital/networked experiments. Digital technologies enable B2B companies to tap storehouses of technical knowledge and move them into complex offerings. Custom 'extranets' (websites created by one firm for private access by another firm) enable virtual integration of a firm's competencies up and down its value chain and provide new dimensions in sales support. Using extranets and EDI, firms across a value chain can link with one another and share real-time information. This information exchange is critical for better demand prediction and supply chain optimization (Shankar 2012).

The Sales Force

The most critical element of the marketing value-delivery framework often boils down to where the rubber meets the road: the sales force and the capabilities of individual salespeople.

The sales force is the face of the firm for the customer. The firm's performance and profitability is directly related to the performance and effectiveness of the sales force. The success of the sales force directly leads to the success of the firm in terms of better results and profit. Zoltners et al. (2012) look at what defines sales force success and identify five key drivers for sales force effectiveness.

The salesperson is also a crucial link in the brand relationship with the customer. Salespeople are the organization's front line and are crucial in establishing and maintaining effective connectivity, communication and relationships with business customers.

Singh et al. (2012) review boundary role theory in marketing and present myths associated with boundary roles.

The salesperson also plays multiple roles in the firm's marketing program as (1) informer; (2) persuader; (3) problem solver; and (4) value creator (Wotruba 1991). The salesperson's effectiveness in these roles is essential for the salesperson's success. Bradford and Weitz (2012) focus on behaviors of salespeople, their knowledge, skills and abilities (KSAs) and management practices that can be used to develop these KSAs and support the transition of a salesperson from a traditional influencer role to a value creation role.

In B2B marketing, I often find that the terms 'sales' and 'marketing' are merged and frequently confused. Sometimes the terms are used interchangeably, even though they are distinct, albeit tightly symbiotic and complementary, functions. B2B marketing manages the understanding, creation and delivery of value. The selling force interprets that value for individual customers, ensures that customers receive the value they purchase and translates customer needs in ways that allow the firm to improve the value of its offerings.

In theory, marketing provides direct support for the selling process, such as competitive intelligence, pricing information, sales aids, channel programs, training and technical support. Marketing sets the stage so that salespeople can build profitable relationships, overcome obstacles and close transactions.

In practice, I often find a separation or conflict between B2B marketers and salespeople. When these functions are poorly aligned, the marketing function is usually marginalized, and focused more on market communications that the sales force does not recognize as valuable. The bigger issue for the salespeople in such situations, however, is that they may be focused on the wrong segments, greatly reducing their productivity.

Where the connection works, and both functions are integrated into a well-defined demand-generation process, the combined effects are quite powerful. Salespeople are focused on the right segments, with superior offerings, a keen understanding of competition and the tools needed to be 'value merchants'. Cespedes (2012) investigates the reasons for differences and conflicts between marketing and sales. Further practices and methodologies are presented to improve marketing–sales coordination.

In ongoing discussions on this topic at several ISBM members' meetings, we have seen that building three key 'linkages' across these functions is key (Oliva 2006):

- Linkages in language: the common language of value.
- Linkages in process: following the value-delivery framework outlined in Figure 2.1.
- Linkages in organization: enabling sales and marketing to work together, aligned toward common goals.

Although ideally only a last resort, profitably harvesting value often boils down to tough negotiation. Marketers must work with the sales force to help build the skills and strategies that enable successful negotiation. Creating distinctive, unique value in offerings (and building strong brands) assists salespeople in negotiating profitable prices (Anderson et al. 2007).

Suggested Research Pathways: Communicating and Delivering Value

As of this writing, a broad variety of experiments are underway, exploring social media in new sorts of market communications between firms. Research-based insights into these new tools would be very valuable through the coming decade. An important research pathway revolves around the question: 'What is the model of the communications "receiver" in today's markets?' Members of the decision-maker stack are now connected across countries, cultures, firms, suppliers and competition. Messages are no longer delivered in isolation, and marketers would greatly benefit from insights into how to more effectively, and efficiently, create communications between customers and suppliers (Schultz 2012).

The emergence of new channels, often mediated by the Internet, affords another whole pathway for research. When do multiple channels make sense? How can 'e-channels' and more conventional channels accent and help each other?

Finally, the whole business of how to motivate, compensate and equip the sales force to navigate the turbulent and changing markets of the coming decade is fertile ground for research (Zoltners et al. 2009). The subject of sales force compensation has always been a challenge to both academicians and practitioners. While in theory compensation can be used as a strategic tool to align salesperson goals and activities with the firm's own profit-maximizing goals, in reality there is often divergence between the objectives of the firm and the salesperson. Coughlan and Joseph (2012) review literature on sales force compensation and suggest an amalgamated framework to arrive at an optimal compensation structure.

MANAGING THE LIFE CYCLE OF THE B2B CUSTOMER

The B2B customer is an ever-changing and complex entity whose behavior follows cycles driven by business designs and the various value-creating processes inside the customer firm (Narayandas 2003). There are times when a B2B customer needs many value-added services from its suppliers and relies heavily on supplier help in the co-creation of new value for its downstream customers. At other times the same customer may be only focused on taking cost out of its process and move toward the behavior of a commodity buyer, even to the extent of deploying reverse auction techniques to squeeze every ounce of cost out of the buy.

B2B marketers must have understanding of where their customers are in the life cycle of their connection – for each offering over time. This is another distinctive characteristic of B2B compared with B2C marketing practice. Although there are a wide variety of B2B customer 'life cycle phenomena', I focus on the buying process cycles I find most common in B2B marketing practice: the design-in, straight rebuy, modified rebuy and MRO buying patterns.

The Design-in

In a design-in situation, the customer is usually designing a new offering for downstream customers and is looking to build in as much innovation and new value as possible so

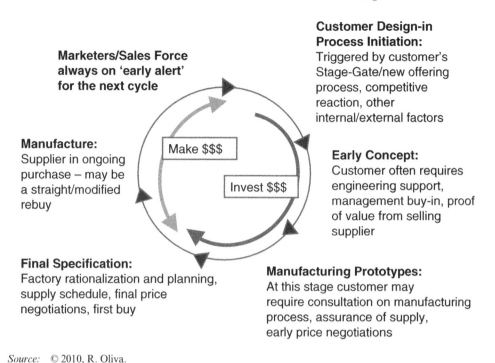

Marketers/Sales Force always on 'early alert' for the next cycle

Customer Design-in Process Initiation: Triggered by customer's Stage-Gate/new offering process, competitive reaction, other internal/external factors

Manufacture: Supplier in ongoing purchase – may be a straight/modified rebuy

Make $$$

Invest $$$

Early Concept: Customer often requires engineering support, management buy-in, proof of value from selling supplier

Final Specification: Factory rationalization and planning, supply schedule, final price negotiations, first buy

Manufacturing Prototypes: At this stage customer may require consultation on manufacturing process, assurance of supply, early price negotiations

Source: © 2010, R. Oliva.

Figure 2.5   The 'design-in' cycle in B2B marketing and sales

that it can be competitive in its market. Consider the designer of a complex new consumer electronic product, a new chemical formulation, a new sort of paper or an entirely new service; something where the B2B customer is innovating to create new value and looking to suppliers to help with 'value-added ingredients'.

In this situation the supplier firm is often selling important and new offerings of its own – 'direct material' – that will become part of the customer's offering. B2B marketers managing a design-in phase are involved in a risky, difficult and complex cycle, as shown conceptually in Figure 2.5. For customers for which design-in is a key factor, it is important for the B2B marketer to understand the cycle and to intercept it at just the right times. (If a B2B marketer 'misses' the design cycle in a customer firm, it may not have another chance to participate in another buy until the next cycle comes along.)

At this stage of the process, B2B marketers work with the customer to provide the best alternative possible as they develop the early concept of their new offering. Marketers are often investing heavily in engineering support, making connections with the management of the customer firm, building understanding of the value that the customer is trying to create downstream and providing prototypes or simulation software to prove the value of their offering in the final product.

In the next phase of this process the customer might be working on building manufacturing prototypes to understand how the design works, assessing its manufacturability and beginning to put the supply chain together to build the product. Often a B2B customer will be leery of buying from a single source for any critical element of its manufacturing process. The B2B marketer needs to understand which other sources will be available and needs to be there at the right place, at the right time, with the right offering and the right final price to win the first buy.

This first buy is all-important, because it will constitute the lot of products the customer uses to assemble its first build. The customer will gain experience with the supplier's offering in the manufacturing process. At this point, switching to another supplier gets difficult – a 'switching cost' is developed – as the customer learns more and more about how to use the supplier's ingredients.

The Straight Rebuy

Over time, this same customer will be likely to need more of the supplier's product as its manufacturing processes continue. As successful downstream sales continue, the B2B marketer moves into a different role with the customer – and the customer takes on a different role to the supplier. Savvy B2B marketers understand that this changing relationship is a natural part of the B2B marketing cycle. Once a supplier's product has been designed in as 'direct material' into a customer's product, and the customer needs to buy more, it often happens through what is called a 'straight rebuy' process. Here the B2B marketer often negotiates long-term contracts, building a supply chain to enable the customer to rely on a stable, high quality, low variability supply of the ingredients it is purchasing. At this point in the cycle the supplier has the opportunity to reap significant profits and pay back some of the investment that it made early on to win the design-in phase.

Modified Rebuy

Over time the customer will typically drive to reduce the cost of its offerings and begin asking the supplier for changes in its offerings, regarding how they are delivered or their price. This is a natural part of the B2B marketing life cycle, and at this point competitive alternatives may emerge; market conditions downstream for the customer may dictate that cost reduction is essential.

The savvy B2B marketer works to understand the customer's changing needs and the fact that all of the value it added in the design-in phase is now being harvested by the customer as it passes its products downstream. As this phase continues, the customer will tend to move more and more to commodity-like buying behavior. It has developed knowledge on the use of the supplier's ingredient in its product situation and is focused more and more on taking cost and complexity out of the manufacturing process to improve its profitability. In this phase of the process B2B marketers work to drive their costs down and provide pricing that enables their customers to harvest profit as they in turn face what usually are their own more challenging market conditions downstream in the value chain.

Beyond that, B2B marketers are always working to create 'the next innovation', the next round of technology, the next best alternative ingredient so that they can win the next design-in. Strategic B2B marketing involves linking the supplier firm's business design to the business design of customer firms in ways that enable the ongoing discernment, creation, delivery, computation and profitable harvest of value.

Maintenance, Repair, Operating Supplies (MRO)

Some B2B marketing operations involve the sale of MRO supplies. These are the things businesses need to get on with business and keep things going day-to-day. They are often items such as shop supplies, office supplies, wipers, goggles, gloves, non-specialty fasteners and so on.

In this situation, the basic offerings themselves can be viewed as commodities, and without careful marketing, price might be the only differentiating factor. As has been proven by W.W. Grainger, however (Anderson et al. 2007), innovation in offering design can be the key to profitable success even in this sort of market. Taking cost out of providing the total solution, streamlining the link between the supplier and the customer at the lowest possible overhead, anticipating need and keeping inventories low can spell better profits and more satisfied customers even in this highly competitive B2B marketplace.

Customer Relationship Management in Business Markets

Keeping track of complex buying cycles, and how one cycle will fold into another, as well as the complex nature of the transactions between businesses, is the realm of customer relationship management. Doing this well requires an active, dynamic and accessible database enabling B2B marketers and salespeople to understand the changing nature of the customer relationship, as well as to anticipate customer needs over the life cycle of their relationship.

From simply tracking transactions with customers, to keeping tabs on key personnel in the decision-maker stack and how they migrate through a customer firm over time, to understanding seasonalities and product development cycles inside a customer firm, a comprehensive database can be a valuable tool. A great customer database comprehends the dimensionality of the relationship between the supplier and the customer and tracks changes in these dimensions over time to enable more focused, effective and profitable marketing decisions (Venkatesan et al. 2012).

Ongoing Support After the Sale: Customer Satisfaction in Business Markets

B2B marketing is often a very personal business. Working with a customer through various elements of the buying cycle until the sale is made and a supplier's product is installed in the customer's process can take a long time. A B2B buy may take many months, and ongoing purchase of the product after that can go on for years. Once a sale is made, an ongoing focus on 'service after the sale' is critical to ensure satisfaction, foster the customer relationship and build very important market-based assets for the supplying firm: customer advocates.

A variety of techniques are in use to measure 'customer satisfaction and loyalty' in B2B markets. As of this writing, the various tools and techniques that are being used are often quite controversial and the subject of significant debate.

A popular metric for measuring customer satisfaction and loyalty is the 'net promoter score' popularized by Fred Reichheld and described in his book *The Ultimate Question* (Reichheld 2006).

A firm's net promoter score in a segment boils down to asking customers how strongly they agree to this focal statement: 'I would recommend this firm (product/brand/solution) in confidence to a peer or friend'. Respondents are asked to score their response on a 1–10 scale, with 10 being 'strongly agree' and 1 being 'totally disagree'. The 9s and 10s are added together, and the 1–6s are subtracted to get to a firm's net promoter score. The net promoter score is cited as having more correlation with true customer loyalty and advocacy behavior than a broad variety of other survey techniques and metrics.

To come up with metrics that more strongly correlate with customer behavior usually involves a more in-depth approach, such as Gallup's Customer Engagement 11 (or CE11), which explores and quantifies both 'rational advocacy' (tied to the basic performance of a product or service) and 'emotional advocacy' (reflective of the total relationship between the customer and the supplier) (Fleming 2007).

'Customer loyalty', whether in B2B or B2C markets, is a matter of some controversy. It is clear that retaining the right customers and managing the total relationship with them is more affordable than the ongoing acquisition of new customers – especially the wrong customers. Segmentation, targeting and positioning done well leads to coupling the right customers with firms' total capacity, which optimizes the value of their capital and other assets, improves profits, reduces waste and drives increased free cash flow.

Firms have always paid particular attention to their most important customers. Key account management (KAM) is a focused and intensive form of customer relationship management. If KAM is applied ineffectively it may not yield any benefits to the firm, and the customer may become unprofitable. Homburg and Bornemann (2012) address the conceptualization and theoretical underpinning of KAM, along with determinants, design elements and prototypical approaches of KAM and their respective performance outcomes.

Suggested Research Pathways: Managing the Life Cycle of the B2B Customer

The ongoing application of advanced information technology to a broad array of business processes is changing the behavior of industrial firms and their various business cycles. Processes that once worked in isolation are now connected together through enterprise resource planning (ERP) systems such as those provided by SAP. Research on how marketers can better identify cycles and processes inside customers, and better attach to them, navigate them and work through them profitably, would be extremely helpful.

Insights on what sort of investments in customer relationship management, and which approaches are antecedents to better business results, would be especially helpful as the nature of the relationship between customers and suppliers, and between customers and other customers, undergoes rapid change driven by social media.

A WORD ON THE FUTURE OF B2B . . .

Through the years that ISBM has been tracking B2B markets and the practice of B2B marketing, we've seen the evolution of the practice moving through distinct cycles. For B2B firms that do not fully understand the impact of marketing, investments in marketing – and hiring of marketing professionals – accelerated during an upturn, and it was considered 'an expense we can afford'.

In those same firms with little understanding of marketing practice, where marketing is primarily viewed as downstream marketing, sales support and market communications, things get brutal for marketers during a downturn. Marketing is considered pure 'SG&A' (sales, general and administrative), and severe cuts marginalize the practice, sending even talented B2B marketers off looking for work. Through many years of these cycles, we've seen the practice of marketing marginalized for many B2B firms (Webster et al. 2005).

There is evidence, however, driven by several leading firms, that the practice is coming into maturity. These firms are recognizing that – upturn or downturn – without better connectivity to their customers and markets, careful STP, ongoing innovation, better pricing and a better understanding of 'upstream' and 'downstream' marketing, they will not be able to compete in the challenging marketplaces of the coming decade.

These firms, including several well-known and notable firms such as GE, DuPont and Cisco, as well as smaller firms such as New Pig, Kennametal and Sabert, are working to turn B2B marketing into a formidable competitive advantage (Comstock et al. 2010).

They usually begin by creating a common language of value-based marketing, defining stronger marketing processes, assembling leading-edge tools and making them available and fostering a community of learning and practice among their marketing team. This effort is often accompanied by significant investments in training, professional development and rotational assignments, which enable marketers to develop the connections across the firm required for them to be effective.

For these firms, the maturity level of the B2B marketing practice itself is being tracked. Marketing, and B2B marketers, are seen as essential ingredients in driving organic growth, optimizing the value of capital and other assets and ensuring healthy, free cash flows. As these leading firms gain traction, they set the stage for the practice of B2B marketing itself to emerge as an essential component of the enterprise, with a seat at the table with the C-level officers, guiding the future of the firm.

At ISBM, we see firms working to identify the sort of talent and human resources that are required to lead the charge, and then creating exciting careers with great impact for those with the right mix of left-brain analytic skills to mobilize data for insight, and right-brain creative skills to innovate new solutions, business designs and pathways to profitability through challenging markets.

Over the next few years, certain key elements of B2B marketing practice will surface as of 'perennial importance':

- B2B marketers must develop tools, techniques and competencies for understanding, quantifying and communicating value.
- B2B marketers must bring to their firms new tools and techniques for discerning the opportunity to add new value – getting down to the real 'voice of the customer'.
- And . . . B2B marketers will need to step up to be the drivers of organic growth for their firms. Organic growth will come from the opportunities presented by new emerging markets, such as the BRIC countries, as well as going deeper with current customers and helping them transform their own businesses as we move through the decade.

In coming years, B2B marketers will be called upon for ever more important contributions and will become an even more critical element in driving business success throughout their companies. The decade of the 2010s may very well be seen as 'the decade of business marketing'.

REFERENCES

Anderson, J.C., Nirmalya Kumar and James Narus (2007), *Value Merchants: Demonstrating and Documenting Superior Value in Business Markets*, Boston: Harvard Business School Press.
Anderson, J., James Narus and W. van Rossum (2006), 'Customer value propositions and business markets', *Harvard Business Review*, **84** (3), 90–99.
Anderson, J.C., M. Wouters and W. van Rossum (2010), 'Why the highest price isn't the best price', *MIT Sloan Management Review*, **51** (2), 69–76.
Beck, Joshua and Rob Palmatier (2012), 'Relationship marketing', chapter 16 in Gary Lilien and Rajdeep Grewal (eds), *Handbook of Business-to-Business Marketing*, Cheltenham, UK and Northampton, MA, USA: Edward Elgar.
Bitner, Mary J., Amy Ostrom and F. Morgan (2008), 'Services blueprinting: a practical technique for service innovation', *California Management Review*, **50** (3), 66–94.
Bradford, Kevin and Bart Weitz (2012), 'Salesperson effectiveness: a behavioral perspective', chapter 23 in Gary Lilien and Rajdeep Grewal (eds), *Handbook of Business-to-Business Marketing*, Cheltenham, UK and Northampton, MA, USA: Edward Elgar.
Cespedes, Frank (2012), 'Coordinating marketing and sales in B2B organizations', chapter 8 in Gary Lilien and Rajdeep Grewal (eds), *Handbook of Business-to-Business Marketing*, Cheltenham, UK and Northampton, MA, USA: Edward Elgar.
Comstock, B., R. Gulati and S. Ligouri (2010), 'Unleashing the power of marketing', *Harvard Business Review*, **88** (October), 90–98.
Cooper, Robert G. (1993), *Winning at New Products*, 2nd edn, Boston: Perseus.
Cooper, Robert G. (2012), 'The Stage-Gate® system for product innovation in B2B firms', chapter 32 in Gary Lilien and Rajdeep Grewal (eds), *Handbook of Business-to-Business Marketing*, Cheltenham, UK and Northampton, MA, USA: Edward Elgar.
Coughlan, Anne T. and Kissan Joseph (2012), 'Sales force compensations: research insights and research potential', chapter 26 in Gary Lilien and Rajdeep Grewal (eds), *Handbook of Business-to-Business Marketing*, Cheltenham, UK and Northampton, MA, USA: Edward Elgar.
Cressman, George (2012), 'Value based pricing: a state-of-the-art review', chapter 14 in Gary Lilien and Rajdeep Grewal (eds), *Handbook of Business-to-Business Marketing*, Cheltenham, UK and Northampton, MA, USA: Edward Elgar.
Fahey, Liam (1997), *Competitors: Outwitting Outmaneuvering Outperforming*, New York: John Wiley & Sons.
Fahey, Liam (2012), 'Competitor intelligence: enabling B2B marketing strategy', chapter 9 in Gary Lilien and Rajdeep Grewal (eds), *Handbook of Business-to-Business Marketing*, Cheltenham: Edward Elgar.
Fahey, Liam and Robert M. Randall (1998), *Learning from the Future*, New York: John Wiley & Sons.
Fleming, John (2007), *Human Sigma*, New York: Gallup Press.
Friedman, L. and T. Furey (1999), *The Channel Advantage*, Brazil: BH Press.
Gopalkrishna, Srinath and Gary Lilien (2012), 'Trade shows in the business marketing communications mix', chapter 13 in Gary Lilien and Rajdeep Grewal (eds), *Handbook of Business-to-Business Marketing*, Cheltenham, UK and Northampton, MA, USA: Edward Elgar.
Griffin, Abbie and John Hauser (1993), 'The voice of the customer', *Marketing Science*, **12** (1), 1–27.
Griffin, Abbie and John Hauser (1996), 'Integrating R&D and marketing: a review and analysis of the literature', *Journal of Product Innovation Management*, **13**, 191–215.
Griffin, Abbie, N. Hoffman, R. Price and B. Vojak (2007), 'How serial innovators navigate the fuzzy front end of new product development', *ISBM Working Series Paper 03*.
Ho, Hillbun and Shankar Ganesan (2012), 'Learning in coopetitive relationships', chapter 20 in Gary Lilien and Rajdeep Grewal (eds), *Handbook of Business-to-Business Marketing*, Cheltenham, UK and Northampton, MA, USA: Edward Elgar.
Homburg, Christian and Torsten Bornemann (2012), 'Key account management', chapter 25 in Gary Lilien and Rajdeep Grewal (eds), *Handbook of Business-to-Business Marketing*, Cheltenham, UK and Northampton, MA, USA: Edward Elgar.
Johnston, Wesley J. and Jennifer Chandler (2012), 'The organizational buying center: innovation, knowledge

management and brand', chapter 21 in Gary Lilien and Rajdeep Grewal (eds), *Handbook of Business-to-Business Marketing*, Cheltenham, UK and Northampton, MA, USA: Edward Elgar.

Keller, Kevin L. and Philip Kotler (2012), 'Branding in B2B firms', chapter 12 in Gary Lilien and Rajdeep Grewal (eds), *Handbook of Business-to-Business Marketing*, Cheltenham, UK and Northampton, MA, USA: Edward Elgar.

Kotler, Philip and Waldemar Pfoertsch (2006), *BtoB Brand Management*, New York: Springer.

Kotler, Philip and Waldemar Pfoertsch (2010), *Ingredient Branding: Making the Invisible Visible*, New York: Springer.

Lauterborn, R. (1998 [2001]), 'The behavioral timeline®', *ISBM Note*.

Lilien, Gary, Arvind Rangaswamy and Arnaud DeBruyn (2007), *Principles of Marketing Engineering*, Victoria, Canada: Trafford Publishing.

Lusch, Robert F. and Stephen L. Vargo (2012), 'Gaining competitive advantage with service-dominant logic', chapter 7 in Gary Lilien and Rajdeep Grewal (eds), *Handbook of Business-to-Business Marketing*, Cheltenham, UK and Northampton, MA, USA: Edward Elgar.

McFarland, J. (2001), 'Margaret Mead meets consumer fieldwork', *Harvard Management Update*, Reprint U0108C.

McQuarrie, Edward (1998), *Customer Visits*, 2nd edn, Thousand Oaks, CA: Sage Publications.

Morgan, Neil and Rebecca Slotegraaf (2012), 'Marketing capabilities for B2B firms', chapter 6 in Gary Lilien and Rajdeep Grewal (eds), *Handbook of Business-to-Business Marketing*, Cheltenham, UK and Northampton, MA, USA: Edward Elgar.

Nambisan, Satish and Mohanbir Sawhney (2008), *The Global Brain*, Philadelphia, PA: Wharton School Publishing.

Narayandas, N. (2003), 'Customer management strategy in business markets', *Harvard Business School Note 9-503-060*, 9 May.

Narayandas, N. (2005), 'Building loyalty in business markets', *Harvard Business Review*, **83** (9), 131–9.

Oliva, Ralph (2006), 'The three linkages: important connections between marketing and sales', *ISBM Note*, June.

Oliva, Ralph, R. Srivastava, W. Pfoertsch and J. Chandler (2006), 'Insights on ingredient branding', *ISBM Note*, 15 November.

Parry, M. (2002), 'Conjoint analysis', Background Note, Darden Business Publishing, Harvard Business School, product number UV2940-pdf-eng.

Rangan, V.K. (2006), *Transforming Your Go to Market Strategy: The Three Disciplines of Channel Management*, Boston, MA: Harvard Business School Publishing.

Reichheld, Fred (2006), *The Ultimate Question*, Boston, MA: Harvard Business School Publishing.

Ries, Al and Jack Trout (2001), *Positioning: The Battle for Your Mind*, 20th edn, New York: McGraw-Hill.

Schultz, Don E. (2012), 'B2B Marketing Communication in a Transformational Marketplace', chapter 10 in Gary Lilien and Rajdeep Grewal (eds), *Handbook of Business-to-Business Marketing*, Cheltenham, UK and Northampton, MA, USA: Edward Elgar.

Schultz, Don and Heidi Schultz (2004), *IMC: The Next Generation*, New York: McGraw-Hill.

Schultz, Don, Stanley Tannenbaum and Robert Lauterborn (1993), *Integrated Marketing Communications*, Lincolnwood, IL: NTC Business Books.

Shankar, Venkatesh (2012), 'B2B e-commerce', chapter 33 in Gary Lilien and Rajdeep Grewal (eds), *Handbook of Business-to-Business Marketing*, Cheltenham, UK and Northampton, MA, USA: Edward Elgar.

Sim, E., Abbie Griffin, R. Price and B. Vojak (2007), 'Exploring differences between inventors, champions, implementers, and serial innovators in developing new products in large, mature firms', *ISBM Working Series Paper 04-2007*.

Singh, Jagdip, Detelina Marinova and Steven Brown (2012), 'Boundary work and customer connectivity in B2B front lines', chapter 24 in Gary Lilien and Rajdeep Grewal (eds), *Handbook of Business-to-Business Marketing*, Cheltenham, UK and Northampton, MA, USA: Edward Elgar.

Tellis, Gerard, Rajesh Chandy and Jaideep Prabhu (2012), 'Key Questions on innovation in the B2B context', chapter 31 in Gary Lilien and Raj Grewal (eds), *Handbook of Business-to-Business Marketing*, Cheltenham, UK and Northampton, MA, USA: Edward Elgar.

Thomas, Robert J. (2012), 'Business-to-business market segmentation', chapter 11 in Gary Lilien and Rajdeep Grewal (eds), *Handbook of Business-to-Business Marketing*, Cheltenham, UK and Northampton, MA, USA: Edward Elgar.

Vargo, Stephen L. and Robert F. Lusch (2004), 'Evolving to a new dominant logic for marketing', *Journal of Marketing*, **68** (January), 1–17.

Venkatesan, Rajkuma, Werner Reinartz and V. Kumar (2012), 'Customer relationship management in business markets', chapter 17 in Gary Lilien and Rajdeep Grewal (eds), *Handbook of Business-to-Business Marketing*, Cheltenham, UK and Northampton, MA, USA: Edward Elgar.

Webster, F., A. Malter and S. Ganesan (2005), 'The decline and dispersion of marketing competence', *Sloan Management Review*, **46** (4), 35–43.

Wind, Y. and R. Cardozo (1974), 'Industrial market segmentation', *Industrial Marketing Management*, **3**, 153–66.

Wotruba, T.R. (1991), 'The evolution of personal selling', *Journal of Personal Selling and Sales Management*, **11** (3), 1–12.

Zaltman, G. (1998), 'The ZMET Research Process', *Harvard Business School Note* #9-599-056, September.

Zoltners, Adris, Prabhakant Sinha and Sally Lorimer (2009), *Building a Winning Salesforce*, New York: Amacom.

Zoltners, Andris A., Prabhakant Sinha and Sally E. Lorimer (2012), 'Building a winning sales force in B2B markets: a managerial perspective', chapter 28 in Gary Lilien and Rajdeep Grewal (eds), *Handbook of Business-to-Business Marketing*, Cheltenham, UK and Northampton, MA, USA: Edward Elgar.

3 Applications of agency theory in B2B marketing: review and future directions

Ranjan Banerjee, Mark Bergen, Shantanu Dutta and Sourav Ray

The important role of independent 'facilitating agents' in B2B markets cannot be overstated, because 'Most goods and services are distributed through intermediaries – such as wholesalers, retailers, or franchisees – who act as agents . . . of the manufacturer' (Bergen et al. 1992, p. 2). From distribution channels to sales forces, these intermediaries perform essential business functions such as bringing a product to market, enhancing awareness of a firm's product or service, educating customers on specific functionalities or performing warehousing and logistic functions. Unfortunately these relationships also involve substantial challenges for motivating, contracting, coordinating and controlling the independent agents. This scenario creates a fundamental dilemma for B2B marketers, academics and practitioners: how should firms structure their relationship with their facilitating agent most effectively to provide agents with proper incentives?

Agency theory has emerged as one of the foundational theories for tackling such questions. Such theory pertains to situations in which one party (the principal) depends on another party (the agent) to undertake some action on its behalf. Both channel and sales force relationships are classic agency problems, because 'A distribution channel constitutes a set of agency relationships' (Bergen et al. 1992, p. 13) and 'The relationship between sales manager and sales person is an agency relationship' (Bergen et al. 1992, p. 8). The key challenge in these situations arises when some information is relevant and known to one party but unknown to the other. For example, facilitating agents often have private information about the levels of effort they undertake on the principal's behalf, local market characteristics, or their individual characteristics. These issues, broadly characterized as *information asymmetry* problems, are prevalent in business markets, which makes agency theory a useful tool for exploring such issues. Facilitating agents can use their private information opportunistically to shirk and free-ride on the actions of other marketers. Agency theory focuses on how firms should structure relationships to provide agents with appropriate incentives (Hurwicz 1972). In particular, because the efforts undertaken by agents are unobservable but often related to measurable outputs (e.g. sales, customer service), managers must determine how to condition contracts on measurable outputs and their dependence on agent and task characteristics.

Despite the relevance of agency theory to business markets, no comprehensive review addresses the current and potential applications of agency theory in business markets (for more general reviews see Bergen et al. 1992; Lafontaine and Slade 1996). This chapter covers that gap by explaining the major constructs embedded in agency theory, as well as what we have learned about agency according to agent and task characteristics. We explore recent developments in multitasking, non-linear compensation and structural econometric methods, which might expand the reach of agency models. We also offer a discussion of opportunities in business markets for both academics and managers.

FUNDAMENTALS OF AGENCY THEORY: AGENT AND TASK CHARACTERISTICS

Agency theory focuses on situations in which one party delegates work to another. The instrument used by the delegating party (principal) to achieve its objectives is the contract. The focus of agency theory is determining the nature of the most efficient contract from the principal's point of view. The party to whom the work is delegated (agent) should behave optimally in response to the offered contract. Typically some information is known to the agent but not to the principal, and the design of efficient contracts in the face of such information asymmetry is the heart of the agency problem. Because efficiency reflects the principal's point of view, an efficient contract typically induces the best possible outcome for the principal, given the constraints imposed by the agent's anticipated behavior. The nature of the contracting problem depends crucially on the nature of the information asymmetry, which may reflect pre- or post-contractual problems. The former involves the hidden information of the agent, whereas the latter are hidden actions by that agent. With our interest in applications of agency theory to B2B settings, for which problems of hidden action are of particular relevance, we offer a detailed review of this latter class; we refer readers to Bergen et al. (1992) for a discussion of pre-contractual asymmetric information problems.

Problems of hidden action arise when the principal cannot observe the effort of the agent – a common feature in channels and sales force settings, when the manufacturer cannot gauge the efforts undertaken by outside parties to satisfy customers directly. Agency models also note situations in which the principal cannot observe effort directly but can attain a noisy measure of effort. This measure is often an output measure, such as sales volume or customer satisfaction. These outcomes are related to effort, but they reflect it only imperfectly, and their noisiness refers to the degree of imprecision. Problems arise in these relationships not only because output measures are noisy but also because the principal and the agent have different attitudes toward risk. Agency models capture this attitude by the degree of risk aversion for a given party, which captures a preference for certain outcomes (that is risk-averse parties prefer certain outcomes, whereas risk-neutral parties are only concerned with expected outcomes). The principal's problem is to design contracts that balance returns (i.e. stronger incentives) with insurance (i.e. less variability in income, a prerequisite for getting risk-averse agents to accept contracts). Agency models assume that the principal is risk neutral and agents are risk averse, with an underlying assumption that principals are large firms that can diversify their earnings and spread risk, whereas agents depend far more or exclusively on the principal for employment.

This central tension is primary in the classic sales force compensation problem of salary versus commission. Salespeople often have private information about their sales efforts that remains hidden from the firm but also relates to sales volume. Making their sales compensation more heavily weighted on commissions gives them stronger incentives to provide effort but puts more of the burden of risk and uncertainty on their shoulders. Making sales compensation more heavily salary oriented reduces the burden of risk and uncertainty but also reduces incentives for effort. In a channel context, the classic decision problem involves when to use an independent channel agent or salesperson as opposed to bringing the intermediary in house. In agency theoretic models, bringing the intermediary in house is equivalent to paying a flat wage and relying on monitoring mechanisms to ensure effort. In contrast, an independent contract uses a combination of flat wages and incentives to motivate agents. A similar trade-off applies between incentives and the burden of uncertainty and risk, in this case for the independent channel member. Prior literature refers to them as high- and low-powered incentives; contracts characterized by high incentive intensity are designated high-powered contracts, whereas flat wage contracts or those with low incentive intensity are designated low-powered contracts.

Broadly speaking, the extant literature studies two dimensions of agency relationships: agent characteristics, such as risk aversion and agent ability, and task characteristics, such as imprecise mapping of effort onto outputs and the nature of the interdependence between tasks and their impact on the optimal contract.

Agent Characteristics

Agent characteristics highlight the effect of agents' concerns about the risk burden imposed by incentive contracts, which suggests managers may need to temper the use and degree of incentives for business partners. They also refer to agent ability, in the sense that the use and degree of incentives should be applied where they are most effective. We summarize some key findings related to specific agent characteristics in channels and sales force management and their impact on contract design.

The effect of risk
Traditional agency models suggest that an increase in the risk borne by the agent leads to the greater use of low-powered incentives or a greater propensity to integrate vertically. Building on Holmström (1979), Basu et al.'s (1985) agency models propose an optimal mix of salary and commission in various alternative conditions, such that as the risk aversion of agents increases, contracts should become less high powered. Various empirical studies seek to test these propositions. With survey data from the compensation plans used by 161 manufacturing firms, John and Weitz (1989) find support for many of Basu et al.'s (1985) predictions. In a cross-sectional study of 367 salespeople from more than 100 firms, Oliver and Weitz (1991) find that agents who are more risk averse tend to select lower powered contracts. Mishra et al. (1998) extend these results to show that price premiums can be incentives to ameliorate moral hazard problems. With data from 287 managers involved in automotive services, they find support for their hypotheses regarding when to use an independent agent or salesperson rather than bringing the intermediary in house.

Channel models in this tradition (e.g. Norton 1988; Stiglitz 1974) assume that franchisors cannot observe the behavior of franchisees in providing local inputs. Because there is stochasticity in the relationship between franchisee effort and observed sales, efforts cannot be inferred directly from sales. With the assumption that franchisees are risk averse and franchisors risk neutral, a share of revenue (or franchise) contract therefore offers a compromise between the need to provide risk-averse franchisees with insurance and the need for incentives to motivate higher levels of effort. However, empirical studies that test this prediction have tended to support the opposite result; both Norton (1988) and Lafontaine (1992) find that increased risk leads to greater use of high-powered contracts. One possible reason suggested for this result counters the fundamental premises of agency theory (Lafontaine and Slade 1996) by citing the difficulty associated with operationalizing outlet or agent risk levels. Empirical studies also use imperfect proxies, such as the variance of detrended sales and the fraction of outlets discontinued.

The importance of agent effort
The greater the importance of the agent's effort, the greater the responsiveness of outputs to changes in effort. This measure is presented as a characteristic of the agent, but it could be affected by the nature of the task. Agency models predict that incentive intensity increases with the importance of the agent's effort. Models that consider agent ability typically consider the notion that outputs are more responsive to efforts by agents with greater ability. In this sense the responsiveness of outputs to efforts, or the importance of agent effort, is an ability parameter. The importance of agent effort has been operationalized with measures of labor intensity (e.g. employee/sales, capital/labor) or measures of employee value added. Lafontaine (1992), using measures of franchisee value added and franchisee business experience as proxies for the importance of franchisee input, finds that more important franchisee input leads to the use of higher powered contracts, consistent with theory. In another study, Scott (1995) surveys business format franchising across sectors and finds that a higher capital/labor ratio (that is more important outlet level input) leads to the greater use of high-powered incentives.

Task Characteristics

Task characteristics focus on the effects of the tasks that managers require their business partners to undertake. We focus on environmental uncertainty, monitoring costs and task interdependence in multitask settings. The use and degree of incentives applied must vary not only across agents but also across the degree of uncertainty and ability to monitor outcomes. However, incentives are less useful when uncertainty and the costs of monitoring outcomes increase. When multiple tasks are required, agency theory suggests modifying the use and degree of incentives to make them more effective. We turn our attention to the impact of task characteristics on the optimal contract.

Environmental uncertainty
Analytical models (Basu et al. 1985; Holmström 1979) typically suggest that greater stochasticity in the mapping of effort onto outputs increases the use of vertical integration (flat wage contracts), because incentive contracts are less effective in these noisy settings. Anderson (1985) and John and Weitz (1989) offer empirical support for these propositions. Environmental uncertainty plays a similar role in channel design and management, such as in the choice to vertically integrate channel activities or use independent channel agents.

Monitoring costs

Agency models predict that higher costs of monitoring should lead to less vertical integration and higher powered contracts, consistent with the notion that monitoring is best achieved within firm boundaries. An increase in monitoring costs, which increases the relative cost of behavioral monitoring compared with outcome monitoring (Oliver and Anderson 1994), should result in greater use of incentive contracts. Empirical evidence tends to support this prediction. For example Baker and Hubbard (2003) note the introduction of onboard computers in trucking and find that it lowered the cost of monitoring and resulted in the use of lower powered contracts. Other measures of monitoring costs include geographic distance or the distance of agents from the monitors located in the principal company's headquarters.

ADDITIONAL DEVELOPMENTS IN AGENCY THEORY RESEARCH

Research in agency theory has developed in many interesting directions in the past 20 years, from purely analytical to purely empirical to emerging work that takes a hybrid approach and develops structural models of optimizing behavior. We explore three particularly interesting areas: managing multitask situations, extending the range of incentive options to explore nonlinear contracts, and using structural models.

Multitasking

Members of marketing channels frequently must perform multiple interrelated tasks. Agency theoretic models suggest that when multiple tasks are required of the same channel member, the optimal contract depends on the interdependence of the tasks, the extent to which the tasks can be mapped onto contractible outputs, and the relative importance of the tasks in the principal's benefit function. Holmström and Milgrom (1991) show that when firms require channel members to perform multiple tasks, the optimal contract is always a flat wage if the following conditions hold: (1) one of the tasks has a contractible output measure, while the other does not; (2) the unmeasurable task is necessary; and (3) the two tasks are substitutable in the agent's cost function. When tasks are substitutes in the agent's cost function, the incentives for one task should affect not only effort on that task but also the relative allocation of effort between tasks. Thus when an unmeasurable task is necessary, the only way to ensure sufficient effort is to withhold incentives for an alternative task.

Zhang and Mahajan (1995) explore such multitasking issues for the design of an optimal sales force compensation plan for multiple products. They extend agency theory to include multidimensional sales effort response distributions. For two independent products, their optimal sales force compensation plan is a base salary plus commissions, whose rates vary for every product. For two substitutable products, optimal compensation features a base salary plus a commission for total sales. For two complementary products, optimal compensation is a base salary plus a commission for the product with greater sales effort effectiveness.

Slade (1996) looks at the contracts employed by gasoline stations in Vancouver,

Canada, and uses a multitask model to derive and test predictions about the impact of interdependence between an external second task and incentives for the internal sales task. When all profits from the external task go to the channel member and the tasks are complementary, the incentives for the internal task should be lower powered. When the incentives on the external task are high powered and the tasks are complementary (each raises the output of the other task), there is less need for incentives for the internal task. Conversely, if the tasks are substitutes (independent of each other), incentives for the internal task will be high powered. The empirical application to 96 gasoline stores supports these model predictions.

Baker and Hubbard (2003) look at multitasking in the for-hire trucking industry, for which the tasks in question are shipping and cargo handling. Onboard computers in trucking make coordination easier and lower the cost of multitasking; their adoption prompted lower powered contracts. Empirical tests support this prediction, particularly in contexts in which multitasking is important.

In a similar light, salespeople may be asked to undertake a mix of selling and non-selling activities or to sell multiple products that differ in the responsiveness of outputs to their effort. Some recent work builds on work by Holmström and Milgrom (1991) by applying multitask models. For example Lal and Srinivasan (1993) consider a multiproduct salesperson. In some conditions, such as a linear sales response function and equal effectiveness in selling different products, equal commission rates across products are optimal. If sales efforts are complementary across products, as Bharadwaj (1998) shows, commission rates on the second product are always lower than commission rates on the first. Joseph and Thevaranjan (1998) also consider a salesperson engaged in two tasks, of which one task can be monitored directly. A firm that elects to monitor and pay directly for this effort offers a lower powered incentive contract than a firm that eschews monitoring.

The problem of short- and long-run effects of multiple tasks is taken up by Hauser and colleagues (1994). In their setting, the salesperson's efforts have both short-term, ephemeral components, which yield observed sales, and long-term, enduring components, which yield future sales by influencing customer satisfaction. Thus current-period sales are the observed output of ephemeral effort, but customer satisfaction survey data provide the output of enduring effort. Optimal contracts combine the two output measures in direct proportion to their precision: if customer satisfaction measures are more precise, the relative weight given to customer satisfaction should increase. Despite considerable analytical work on contract design in multitask settings, little empirical work in sales force settings explicitly considers multitasking. In our view, it is a profitable area for future exploration.

Non-linear Incentive Contracts

Other work extends the range of incentive options used to create more effective incentive plans. Literature in the sales force management field considers the use of non-linear contracts in greater detail, as well as a variety of alternative contract forms observed in practice in business markets. A more detailed review appears in Chapter 26 of this volume on sales force compensation by Coughlan and Joseph (2012).

Linear and non-linear contracts

Analytical work in marketing literature regarding sales force compensation largely focuses on linear contracts, with a fixed wage and a linear incentive based on output measures. In addition to the analytical convenience offered by linear contracts, a commonly offered justification for their use comes from Holmström and Milgrom (1987), who show that for a risk-averse agent with an exponential utility function and normally distributed errors, linear contracts are optimal. Yet though linear contracts are often observed in practice, a variety of alternative contract forms also are commonly observed. Research has employed agency theoretic models to study these alternative contract structures. In a survey of *Fortune* 500 firms, Joseph and Kalwani (1998) report that 95 per cent of compensation schemes use some combination of quotas and commissions. Economics and marketing literature also draw on agency theoretic models to explore possible explanations for the widespread use of non-linear compensation schemes. Raju and Srinivasan (1996) analyze optimal compensation under various alternative assumptions and suggest that one reason for the widespread deployment of quotas is that in certain conditions, quota-based incentives offer a good approximation of the concave optimal compensation profile predicted by theory. The use of quotas stems from the competing desires to design a contract that is both close to the ideal and simple in form. To this end, Oyer (2000) demonstrates that when a salesperson enjoys rents from current employment and is risk neutral, the optimal contract entails paying a bonus when sales reach a quota. Lazear and Rosen (1981) find that a rank-order tournament, with pay-offs based on relative performance, can achieve a first-best outcome; Park (1995) and Kim (1997) show that a bonus for meeting quotas also may lead to first-best agent effort.

Empirical evidence about non-linear compensation schemes

Two inefficiencies arise from the use of quota-based contracts. First, when an incentive spans multiple periods, salespeople may periodically review their performance relative to the quota and readjust their effort levels, depending on their proximity to the quota. Such readjustments might result in accelerated effort if they are close to the quota, but they could mean less effort than the salespeople would otherwise exert if they are far from the quota. Second, when a firm increases next-period quotas for high performing salespeople, those salespeople pull back their effort after they reach their initial quota to minimize their losses due to ratcheting.

Empirical evidence on the desirability of non-linear compensation schemes thus has been mixed. Steenburgh (2008) and Sudhir, Chung, and Steenburgh (2009) use agency-based models to study the impact of quotas in durable goods sales. Their studies suggest limited inefficiencies of non-linear compensation schemes, such that quota-based schemes accelerate output. Conversely Misra and Nair (2010) find that limits caused by ratcheting and withheld effort make quota-based schemes inefficient, so a straight linear incentive would outperform quota-based schemes. To reconcile these findings, we might consider that the quota scheme that Misra and Nair study has a ceiling beyond which no incentives are paid, so the firm has a tendency to increase quotas for high-performing salespeople.

Recent laboratory and field experiments also study alternative forms of sales compensation. Lim et al. (2009) use a combination of laboratory and field experiments to empirically test the predictions of Kalra and Shi (2001). They find that though having multiple prizes in a sales tournament is optimal, sales effort and revenues are not affected by rank-ordered prizes.

Use of Structural Econometric Models

These extant studies are concerned with reduced form tests that can validate the predictions of agency models in real-world settings. The emphasis is on testing whether contracts observed in practice correspond with contracts predicted by theory. However, such studies are subject to certain limitations. As pointed out by Salanie (2005), reduced form tests cannot estimate unobservable features, such as effort, cost of effort or risk aversion. Furthermore it is difficult to evaluate the consequences of alternative contract structures, because such contracts are not observed. This problem has particular relevance because contracts frequently depend on agent characteristics and environmental characteristics, and contract choices are rarely exogenous. Salanie thus suggests structural models to resolve some of these difficulties. A structural model uses an optimizing model of agent behavior and applies it to data. The structure provided by the model allows for an estimation of unobservable features. Because such models enable us to estimate unobservable variables and underlying deep parameters, we can counterfactually compute the performance implications of alternative contract structures.

Paarsch and Shearer (2000) consider contracts used in tree planting in British Columbia, Canada, which includes two activity dimensions: the number of trees planted (quantity dimension) and the number of bad trees planted (quality dimension). A structural model can account for the dependence of the optimal contract on the environmental conditions. Therefore with their structural model, they estimate an incentive effect of 22.6 per cent, defined as the increase in productivity per unit change in incentive. However, some of this productivity gain comes at the expense of quality, with more bad trees planted with higher powered contracts.

Banerjee (2010) considers a channel structure in which a firm employs a mix of contracts in its retail channel. The channel performs two tasks: acquisition, which affects the number of customers who sign up, and matching, which involves understanding customer needs and recommending an appropriate offering, such that it affects the revenues per acquired customer. They use a multitask model of how contracts depend on location, then estimate it using data about customer acquisitions and observed contracts. Their counterfactual estimation suggests that the observed channel structure (with multiple contracts) outperforms any single channel (with a single contract) by more than 10 per cent. They also find support for Holmström and Milgrom's (1991) prediction that incentives are dampened in the presence of an unmeasured second task.

Recent work in sales force settings also uses structural econometric models to estimate efforts in response to quota-based incentives and to account for intertemporal effort allocation by salespeople. Non-linearities make the computation of an optimal contract difficult, but the use of structural models supports the design of alternative contracts that outperform the contract currently in practice. Sudhir et al. (2009) find that quota-based incentives with shorter time horizons reduce inefficiencies. Misra and Nair (2010) find that a simple linear incentive can outperform quarterly quota-based incentive schemes in practice (see also Holmström and Milgrom 1987). Using a unique data set with survey-based measures of effort, Jiang and Palmatier (2009) find that contracts used in practice deviate from optimal versions; they also derive the level of the optimal incentive.

CONCLUSIONS AND FURTHER DIRECTIONS

Agency theory has come a long way in 20 years. It has substantially increased understanding of the role of incentives for independent facilitating agents, as well as how to manage these issues more effectively in terms of the kinds of contracts that work better in which conditions. We have come to understand how information asymmetry problems can be solved in a way that is incentive compatible for the agent, as well as how the optimal use of high- and low-powered incentives depends on variables such as environmental uncertainty, costs of monitoring output, risk aversion and the importance of agent effort. Emerging research has also enabled us to understand how to manage multiple tasks, select from a wider range of incentive schemes and apply these models in new ways to generate more effective policy prescriptions.

This summary is not to suggest that agency theory is a panacea. Not everything has worked as agency theory has predicted. The findings on risk aversion have been mixed. The tenuous importance of risk aversion has been raised eloquently by authors such as Prendergast (2002). The imperfect fit of agency models to sales force compensation has been documented by Albers (1996, 2002). Some findings regarding non-linear compensation contracts have also been mixed, though this confusion may be due to some industry-specific factors, such as the use of ratcheting by the firm (that is the firm hikes the quota targets for high-achieving salespeople so salespeople adjust, leading to lower effort). Studies that observe ratcheting find inefficiencies. Another factor that matters but is difficult to account for is the ability of the firm to set targets or quotas appropriately. The use of structural models continues to develop; only time and further studies that provide additional validation and generalizability can reveal what these promising new studies will ultimately bring to our understanding of these issues. Nor is agency theory the only lens to use to study the management of independent intermediaries in B2B contexts. Looking at the big picture, work in transaction cost economics, behavioral economics and organizational behavior and strategy promises to inform understanding of the management of B2B markets. Work exploring the boundaries of these literature streams is also very interesting, albeit very difficult, and well worth pursuing (for an example of how transaction cost analysis and agency theory might fit structural and contractual decisions, see Albers et al. 2004). For any specific issue there can be a variety of explanations that might inform our understanding. For example the use of quotas might be driven by elements other than agency considerations, such as heterogeneity across territories or issues of fairness and equity (Albers 2002).

Our recommendations regarding the applicability of agency theory to business markets, for both managers and academics, are the same as we suggested 20 years ago:

> Agency theory is likely to prove most useful for examining situations characterized by factors unique to the theory – factors that make contracting with and controlling the performance of

agents particularly difficult. Hence, the theory might be used most productively to examine situations involving (1) substantial goal conflict between a principal and its agents, (2) sufficient environmental uncertainty to trigger the risk sharing implications of the theory, (3) substantial information asymmetries, and/or (4) difficulty in evaluating performance (e.g. creative, team oriented or long-term marketing activities) (Bergen et al. 1992, p. 19).

For managers, agency theory can provide a more comprehensive approach to handling independent facilitating agents and a wider range of actions for creating more effective incentives for the partners. Agency theory can support better channel and sales force design and restructuring, which are often done on the basis of 'gut feelings' or past performance. The concern about using past performance is that performance itself is contingent on the contract and the incentives created for these independent agents. This problem is one that agency theoretic models can help solve. Recent research suggests that structural models, drawing on agency theoretic frameworks, can be applied to archival firm data to estimate the parameters of interest (e.g. effort, agent and task characteristics). We are optimistic about the potential of this work to provide estimates that can be used to compute counterfactually the agent's response to alternative contracts. Estimates of performance enhancements achieved from alternative contracts range from 5 to 10 per cent, suggesting significant managerial benefits from these methods. Real-world validity has received support from two recent studies (Banerjee 2010, Misra and Nair 2010) that implemented their proposed incentive schemes and demonstrated some favorable enhancements. These improvements even appear in settings with non-linear contracts and when optimal contracts are difficult to compute. That is, improvements can be achieved when the firm's interest is in finding a 'better contract' that outperforms the current contract, even if contract complexity is high.

For academics there are many promising areas for B2B research, ranging from issues that remain open 20 years later, to the use of new methodologies to study the more complex challenges that managers face, to more complex questions being raised by academics.

- *Multichannel structures.* Firms frequently use multiple channels to reach customers, which increases the complexity of agency problems. Limited theoretical and empirical research explores the antecedents and consequences of multiple channel structures. For this profitable area of exploration, recent developments in econometric methods indicate the potential of applying structural models that adopt agency-based models of optimizing behavior as their underlying theoretical framework.
- *Power-dependence structure.* Agency models typically assume a situation in which principals are large and have greater power than the agent. Such a structure may not appear in some B2B situations, such as when modern firms engage in transactions with giant retailers (e.g. Procter & Gamble dealing with Walmart). To recognize this characteristic of modern business relations, researchers should incorporate aspects of bargaining in agency models and consider situations in which principals may be risk averse. In other situations the manufacturer–retailer interactions involve an ongoing relationship, and agency models should be modified to incorporate forward-looking behavior.
- *Applying econometric tools to study unobserved variables.* A common constraint for sales forces is that effort is unobserved. Recent studies show that a structural model might help estimate efforts and counterfactually determine the likely con-

sequences of alternative incentive schemes. Such empirical studies not only shed light on alternative compensation forms in practice but also provide managerial guidance regarding the appropriate compensation form to adopt. Misra and Nair (2010) and Jiang and Palmatier (2009) provide a useful beginning, but there is tremendous scope for further work along these lines, particularly considering the vast variety of alternative contract structures (e.g. tournaments, team-based incentives) that remain underexplored. Recent advances in the econometric tools available to estimate such models (Arcidiacono and Miller 2010; Bajari et al. 2007) also reduce the inherent computational burden involved in estimating models for these applications and make the methods easier to apply.

- *Laboratory and field experiments.* Another area of potentially great value is the use of laboratory and field experiments to study responses to incentive structures. An issue with empirical studies based on agency models is the difficulty associated with operationalizing agency theory constructs such as risk aversion. However, as shown by Ghosh and John (2000) and Lim et al. (2009), laboratory experiments based on agency models can be used profitably to ameliorate such difficulties.

- *Multimethod studies.* Finally, when multiple methods are used in tandem, they can enhance the applicability of agency models and illuminate sales force management issues. To highlight two primary examples, Lim et al. (2009) combine laboratory experiments with a field experiment, and Jiang and Palmatier (2009) use survey and archival data in combination with a structural model. Researchers working in this domain therefore can explore emerging issues in sales force management by expanding their toolkit to include multiple methods. To that end, there is room for profitable partnerships among researchers from different schools of methodological persuasion, designed to achieve comprehensive tests of agency theory models.

ACKNOWLEDGMENTS

We thank Professors Gary Lilien and Rajdeep Grewal for this opportunity and their patient and helpful support throughout this process. We also thank Professors Chen Zhou and Sönke Albers for their thoughtful comments on this chapter; we hope our final product does justice to their suggestions. We thank Professors George John and Mrinal Ghosh and all the faculty who attended the authors' meeting in August for their helpful feedback and sage advice. Many thanks to Madhu Viswanathan from the University of Minnesota and Jeffrey Boichuk and Zach Hall from the University of Houston for their thoughtful suggestions and detailed feedback. The future is bright in the marketing profession with PhD students like them.

REFERENCES

Albers, Sönke (1996), 'Optimization models for sales force compensation', *European Journal of Operational Research*, **89**, 1–17.
Albers, Sönke (2002), 'Salesforce management – compensation, motivation, selection and training', in Barton Weitz and Robin Wensley (eds), *Handbook of Marketing*, London: Sage, pp. 248–66.

Albers, Sönke, Manfred Krafft and Rajiv Lal (2004), 'Relative explanatory power of agency theory and transaction cost analysis in German salesforces', *International Journal of Research in Marketing*, **21**, 265–83.

Anderson, Erin (1985), 'The salesperson as outside agent or employee: a transaction cost analysis', *Marketing Science*, **4** (3), 234–53.

Arcidiacono, P. and R. Miller (2010), 'CCP estimation of dynamic discrete choice models with unobserved heterogeneity', working paper, Department of Economics, Duke University.

Bajari, P., C.L. Benkard and J. Levin (2007), 'Estimating dynamic models of imperfect competition', *Econometrica*, **75** (5), 1331–70.

Baker, G.P. and T.N. Hubbard (2003), 'Make versus buy in trucking: asset ownership, job design, and information', *American Economic Review*, **93** (3), 551–72.

Banerjee, Ranjan (2010), 'Essays on the application of multitasking in marketing channels', Dissertation, University of Minnesota.

Basu, A.K., R. Lal, V. Srinivasan and R. Staelin (1985), 'Salesforce compensation plans: an agency theoretic perspective', *Marketing Science*, **4** (4), 267–91.

Bergen, Mark, Shantanu Dutta and Orville C. Walker Jr (1992), 'Agency relationships in marketing: a review of the implications and applications of agency and related theories', *Journal of Marketing*, **56** (July), 1–24.

Bharadwaj, P. (1998), 'Essays on issues in sales force management', Dissertation, University of Toronto.

Coughlan, Anne and Kissan Joseph (2012), 'Sales force compensation: research insights and research potential', Chapter 26 in Gary Lilien and Raj Grewal (eds), *Handbook of Business-to-Business Marketing*, Cheltenham, UK and Northampton, MA, USA: Edward Elgar.

Ghosh, Mrinal and George John (2000), 'Experimental evidence for agency models of sales force compensation', *Marketing Science*, **19** (4), 348–65.

Hauser, John R., Duncan I. Simester and Berger Wernerfelt (1994), 'Customer satisfaction incentives', *Marketing Science*, **13** (4), 327–50.

Holmström, B. (1979), 'Moral hazard and observability', *Bell Journal of Economics*, **10** (1), 74–91.

Holmström, B. and P. Milgrom (1987), 'Aggregation and linearity in the provision of intertemporal incentives', *Econometrica*, **55** (2), 303–28.

Holmström, B. and P. Milgrom (1991), 'Multitask principal–agent analyses: incentive contracts, asset ownership, and job design', *Journal of Law, Economics, & Organization*, **7** (Special Issue: Papers from the Conference on the New Science of Organization, January), 24–52.

Hurwicz, L. (1972), 'On informationally decentralized systems', in Roy Radner and C.B. McGuire (eds), *Decision and Organization: A Volume in Honor of Jacob Marschak*, Amsterdam: North Holland Publishing Company, pp. 297–336.

Jiang, R. and Robert Palmatier (2009), 'Structural estimation of a moral hazard model: an application to business selling', working paper, U.C. Davis School of Management.

John, George and Barton Weitz (1989), 'Salesforce compensation: an empirical investigation of factors related to use of salary versus incentive compensation', *Journal of Marketing Research*, **26** (February), 1–14.

Joseph, Kissan and M.U. Kalwani (1998), 'The role of bonus pay in sales force compensation plans', *Industrial Marketing Management*, **27** (2), 147–59.

Joseph, Kissan and A. Thevaranjan (1998), 'Monitoring and incentives in sales organizations: an agency-theoretic perspective', *Marketing Science*, **17** (2), 107–23.

Kalra, Ajay and M. Shi (2001), 'Designing optimal sales contests: a theoretical perspective', *Marketing Science*, **20** (2), 170–93.

Kim, S.K. (1997), 'Limited liability and bonus contracts', *Journal of Economics Management Strategy*, **6** (4), 899–913.

Lafontaine, F. (1992), 'Agency theory and franchising: some empirical results', *RAND Journal of Economics*, **23** (2), 263–83.

Lafontaine, F. and M.E. Slade (1996), 'Retail contracting and costly monitoring: theory and evidence', *European Economic Review*, **40** (3–5), 923–32.

Lal, R. and V. Srinivasan (1993), 'Compensation plans for single- and multi-product sales forces: an application of the Holmstrom–Milgröm model', *Management Science*, **39** (7), 777–893.

Lazear, E.P. and S. Rosen (1981), 'Rank-order tournaments as optimum labor contracts', *Journal of Political Economy*, **89** (5), 841–64.

Lim, N., M.J. Ahearne and S.H. Ham (2009), 'Designing sales contests: does the prize structure matter?', *Journal of Marketing Research*, **46** (3), 356–71.

Mishra, D.P., Jan B. Heide and S.G. Cort (1998), 'Information asymmetry and levels of agency relationships', *Journal of Marketing Research*, **33** (August), 277–95.

Misra, S. and H. Nair (2010), 'A structural model of sales-force compensation dynamics: estimation and field implementation', *Quantitative Marketing and Economics*, **8** (March), 1–47.

Norton, S.W. (1988), 'An empirical look at franchising as an organizational form', *Journal of Business*, **61** (2), 197–218.

Oliver, Richard L. and Erin Anderson (1994), 'An empirical test of the consequences of behavior- and outcome-based sales control systems', *Journal of Marketing*, **58** (October), 53–67.

Oliver, Richard L. and Barton Weitz (1991), *The Effects of Risk Preference, Uncertainty, and Incentive Compensation on Salesperson Motivation*, Cambridge, MA: Marketing Science Institute.

Oyer, P. (2000), 'A theory of sales quotas with limited liability and rent sharing', *Journal of Labor Economics*, **18** (3), 405–26.

Paarsch, H.J. and B. Shearer (2000), 'Piece rates, fixed wages, and incentive effects: statistical evidence from payroll records', *International Economic Review*, **41** (1), 59–92.

Park, E.S. (1995), 'Incentive contracting under limited liability', *Journal of Economics Management Strategy*, **4** (3), 477–90.

Prendergast, C. (2002), 'The tenuous trade-off between risk and incentives', *Journal of Political Economy*, **110** (October), 1071–102.

Raju, J.S. and V. Srinivasan (1996), 'Quota-based compensation plans for multiterritory heterogenous sales-forces', *Management Science*, **42** (10), 1454–62.

Salanie, Bernard (2005), *The Economics of Contracts: A Primer*, 2nd edn, Cambridge, MA: MIT Press.

Scott, F.A. (1995), 'Franchising vs. company ownership as a decision variable of the firm', *Review of Industrial Organization*, **10** (1), 69–81.

Slade, M.E. (1996), 'Multitask agency and contract choice: an empirical exploration', *International Economic Review*, **37** (2), 465–86.

Steenburgh, T.J. (2008), 'Effort or timing: the effect of lump-sum bonuses', *Quantitative Marketing and Economics*, **6** (3), 235–56.

Stiglitz, J.E. (1974), 'Incentives and risk sharing in sharecropping', *Review of Economic Studies*, **41** (2), 219–55.

Sudhir, K., D. Chung and T. Steenburgh (2009), 'Do bonuses enhance sales productivity? A dynamic structural analysis of bonus based compensation plans', Harvard Business School Working Paper No. 1491283.

Zhang, C. and V. Mahajan (1995), 'Development of optimal salesforce compensation plans for independent, complementary and substitutable products', *International Journal of Research in Marketing*, **12** (November), 355–62.

4 Progress and prospects for governance value analysis in marketing: when Porter meets Williamson

Mrinal Ghosh and George John

Firms rarely create value in isolation, and cooperation between firms has become so pervasive that it has fundamentally reshaped the field of marketing strategy (Webster 1992, p. 1). Indeed, such cooperation and coordination between firms has been fundamental to the successes of many prominent companies in a variety of channels contexts, including business-format franchising (e.g. McDonald's, Coca-Cola), original equipment manufacturers (OEMs) and supplier relationships (e.g. Toyota and its Keiretsu system), industrial distribution (e.g. Caterpillar's dealer network) and the PC industry (e.g. the Wintel systems of Microsoft and Intel), to name a few. In accordance with this shift, increasing attention has been paid by academicians to understand the design and management of relationships between B2B companies in a variety of marketing contexts, including industrial purchasing, channel relationships, international market entry and so on.

During the past 25 years, transaction cost analysis (TCA) has been the most dominant framework used to analyze these and related issues. Since the pioneering work of the Nobel Prize-winning economists Ronald Coase and Oliver Williamson, the focus of TCA has been to understand how firms structure their formal as well as informal relationships with other value-chain partners (e.g. suppliers, distributors, customers) and their rationale for these choices. TCA argues that the central role of governance in an exchange is to provide *safeguards* and foster *adaptation* with the purpose of curbing potential conflict between parties to an exchange that could undermine opportunities to realize mutually beneficial gains. This core principle has generated refutable predictions that can be succinctly summarized as follows: transactions that vary in their attributes (e.g. level of specific investments, uncertainty and measurement difficulties) will be aligned with governance forms (e.g. vertical integration, level of contractual completeness, informal relational norms) in a *discriminating* fashion. These predictions have found broad support in empirical studies across a variety of substantive contexts, including make-versus-buy decisions in both domestic and international markets, formal (contractual) and informal (normative) aspects of buyer–seller and manufacturer–distributor relationships, R&D contracts, joint ventures, component branding, exclusive distribution and dealing, and so on.

Despite its success, TCA has been criticized on a variety of fronts, with the key criticisms emerging from the strategy-oriented research. One key criticism is that TCA is inconsequential to business strategy because of its inability to account for how organizational heterogeneity and *firm-specific* motivations and resources matter in the design and structuring of organizational arrangements, such as inter-firm ties (e.g. Ghoshal and Moran 1996; Madhok 2002; Zajac and Olsen 1993). Specifically, scholars have argued that if firms possess unique capabilities and skills, these endowments should influence their motives in organizing their exchanges (e.g. Madhok 2002; Williamson 1999). The offshoot of this neglect is that TCA cannot provide a satisfactory explanation for why firms within the same industry, presumably facing the same competitive and environmental pressures, opt for demonstrably different approaches to bring their product to market. Likewise, it is not clear how or why firms with different positioning profiles in their customer markets design their upstream and downstream value chains in a differential fashion. A related criticism of TCA is that it focuses exclusively on the cost minimization calculus at the expense of explicating value-enhancing options (e.g. Zajac and Olsen 1993). This debate has led scholars to call for a *strategic* theory of the firm to be generated (e.g. Foss 2005) which provides a better understanding of value-generating organizational forms.

Ghosh and John (1999) put forth the Governance Value Analysis (GVA) framework to address these issues by explicitly incorporating firm-specific motivations and resources in the design of inter-organizational exchanges. The GVA model extends the *economizing calculus* approach of TCA into a *strategizing calculus* to show how four core constructs – namely, the unique *resources* and capabilities of the firm; its *positioning* in customer markets; the *transactional attributes*; and *governance structures* – interact to enable a firm to create and claim value in its exchange relationships. In essence, governance decisions are affected not only by the *efficiency* concerns arising from economizing on transaction costs but also from *strategic* concerns about leveraging or protecting valuable resources and capabilities.

The model sheds light on the specific trade-offs that firms must make between these four factors and asks (and provides an approach to answer) questions such as the following: why do firms in the same industry demonstrate starkly different approaches to bringing their products to market? How does the possession of unique assets (e.g. product development resources) differentially affect their ability to structure value-enhancing ties with channel partners and customers? How do positioning differences between firms and how do customer brand equity, technology and channel resource differences influence the design of their supply chain and end-customer governance forms? The intent was to shed light on how firms with unique assets *design* and *manage* their relationships to leverage these assets into sources of strategic advantage.

In this chapter, we provide a brief sketch of the principal components of GVA but, more important, through evidence provided by systematic empirical studies in a variety of B2B contexts, we show how the GVA logic sheds light on the interlinks between the design and management of the exchanges (with suppliers, channel partners and customers) and the unique, idiosyncratic resource base and/or motivation of these firms. We then suggest some key directions for future research and offer useful prescriptions to a practitioner-manager. The discussion and analysis here pertains to other works published in this handbook, especially those on strategic alliances (Spekman), technology marketing (Mohr, Sengupta and Slater), cooperation and competition in B2B markets (Ho and Ganesan) and survey research (Rindfleisch and Antia).

GVA

Figure 4.1 shows the core components of the GVA model. We begin with a description of each component.

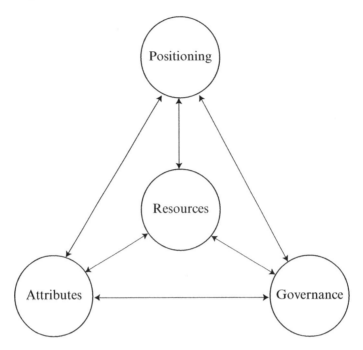

Figure 4.1   The GVA model

Positioning

Positioning refers to the particular set of attributes/benefits the firm generates and offers to its end customers. Positioning is the most central part of a firm's marketing strategy, and firms generally have a variety of options in deciding on what positioning strategy to choose. These positioning strategies can be broadly classified according to Porter's (1985) generic categorization: cost leadership, differentiation and niche; however, even within a particular category, firms have a multiplicity of positioning spaces. For example, in the automotive market, Toyota differentiates itself on fit-and-finish and quality/reliability dimensions, whereas Porsche and BMW generally differentiate themselves on the performance dimension. The GVA maintains that securing the desired positioning is a key motive in the organization of a firm's inter-firm relationships.

Resources

Resources refer to the imperfectly mobile and scarce skills or assets that are owned by the focal parties to the exchanges. These resources exist because of the development of enterprise-specific routines and processes to accomplish various activities within the firm, and such resources can be leveraged to generate competitive advantage, either through activities within the firm or through activities between a variety of value-chain partners (e.g. suppliers, channel members, customers). Resources can be of many types, including technological (engineering design, manufacturing, product development), customer-side (brand equity, customer orientation) and marketing (channel relationships, sales force skills, market coverage). The GVA maintains that firms design inter-organizational relationships to both leverage and protect their non-imitable resources.

Attributes

John and Reve (2010) offer a succinct set of motives (S-A-M) that implicate governance structures in TCA, namely, to create Safeguards that prevent the underinvestment in at-risk assets, to promote Adaptation to changing circumstances and to mitigate the undersupply of activities that lack verifiable output Measures. Operationally, these motives have been distilled into three sets of transactional attributes: specialized investments (e.g. human asset specificity), uncertainty (e.g. technological or market demand uncertainty) and measurement difficulty (e.g. performance ambiguity). These are the attributes that have been crucially implicated in governance design in accordance with TCA.

Governance

Governance refers to the institutional form the firm chooses to manage a particular transaction in accordance with TCA. Again, in general, governance structures can be effectively classified into market, hierarchical or relational governance.

The essence of the GVA model is this: the 'best' strategic choice is the one in which the positioning option is aligned with the resource profile, the levels of the exchange attributes and the deployed governance form. The bidirectional arrows in Figure 4.1 indicate this alignment. Furthermore, although the model appears static, it is not necessarily so. In particular, it also suggests that any change along one dimension (e.g. the firm changes its positioning) is likely to throw the current alignment into disarray and thus would require an adjustment in the other dimensions to regain the best strategic choice status (for the new level of positioning). The precise adjustments depend on the trade-offs that firms with specific characteristics face and thus are context dependent. Next, we illustrate some of these links. TCA-based research has extensively studied the links between attributes and governance; therefore, we focus here on the links between positioning and resources (i.e. the firm-specific factors) and the other dimensions.

Positioning effects
A firm's positioning choice needs to be aligned with resources, the transactional attributes and governance forms. Consider, for example, a firm in the automotive industry (e.g. Toyota) that is positioned as a brand offering highly reliable vehicles with superior fit and finish. Because reliability and fit and finish depend primarily on the quality of assembly, firms positioned along these attributes in their customer markets need to make specialized investments in their manufacturing and assembly-line processes. This argument is supported in data obtained by Whitney (1992) that show dramatic differences between Toyota and General Motors. Specifically, consistent with our argument, Toyota has focused on making specialized investments in machine tools, computer-aided design and computer-aided manufacturing, assembly-line robots and so forth, which enhance the quality of its manufacturing processes; in turn, these developments have been governed by vertical integration into these manufacturing processes. In contrast, General

Motors has lower levels of investments in assembly processes and consequently is not vertically integrated into the same.

Positioning also needs to be aligned with the resource base of the firm. Consider, for example, the case of ICI Explosives, which wanted to position itself away from its traditional commodity business (selling dynamite) to a customer-centric solutions business model (generating rock of certain size and quality). To generate this shift in positioning effectively, ICI needed to generate two specific sets of resource skills: (1) a deep, human expertise in understanding particular customer needs; and (2) engineering models that optimized the layout and sequencing of the explosives to match customer requirements (size and quality of rocks) and the type of material (density and hardness of rocks). Equally importantly, note that this shift in positioning also creates a shift in the transactional attributes. For example, the difficulty of measuring output is significantly higher for 'generating rock of certain size and quality' than for 'selling dynamite'. This increased difficulty in accurately assessing performance then necessitates a concurrent reorganization of the governance form. In particular, under the old positioning, in which ICI sold a commodity product (dynamite), the usual pricing structure would be to pay a price per 'tonnage of explosives'. This governance rule would be completely inadequate as the positioning shifts to the more ambiguous 'quality of rock'. In turn, ICI has had to shift the governance form to a fundamentally different pricing/contract structure that 'pays for broken rock' with associated penalties for not achieving targets.

It is equally important to note the reverse causality from these dimensions to positioning. Again to wit, the specific positioning desired by ICI cannot be achieved unless the firm possesses the appropriate resource expertise. Similarly, if General Motors wants to achieve a positioning similar to Toyota's, it would be less successful in achieving it without realigning its supply chain investments and infrastructure to support the appropriate manufacturing and assembly-line processes. The four-way alignment per the GVA thus is effectuated.

Resource effects
A firm's resource base – technological, brand or supply-chain based – should also be aligned with the transactional attributes and governance form. Consider, for example, technology-intensive capital goods markets in which superior technology is the key resource for long-term profitability. Firms that position themselves as the most advanced and state-of-the-art in these markets need to incorporate frequent engineering changes and upgrades to their equipment. This is because, given the relatively long life of this capital equipment, existing customers would be disadvantaged compared with new customers if the technological developments are only available to the latter (through latter generation machines). This problem can be resolved by leasing, rather than selling, the said equipment to the customers. Leasing aligns better with the more severe adaptation problem because, under leasing (more precisely, operating leases), the ownership of the equipment lies with the vendor and gives it the hierarchical authority to implement those needed changes. Similar impacts can be drawn for other types of resources, such as brand equity and supply chain intensity.

In essence, the GVA model enhances the governance-design perspective of TCA in three key directions.

1. It explicitly clarifies that the essential goal in the design of governance mechanisms is 'joint value maximization', with both value creation and value claiming being the central elements of this motive. Unlike TCA, however, these motives are not independent of the specific resource profiles of the firm or the positioning they seek in the customer marketplace. In other words, depending on their desired positioning as well as their ability to leverage their own resource profiles, firms choose attribute levels (e.g. specialized investments in human and technical assets) and governance forms to curb potential conflicts that undermine opportunities to realize mutually beneficial gains.
2. By incorporating the dual role of positioning and resource profile of the parties, GVA makes firm strategy a key component of relationship and governance design. As the ICI example illustrates, changes in positioning can be successfully achieved only after a concomitant realignment of the resource profile and the governance choices. Both value creation and value claiming are central to this realignment.
3. The GVA model also provides guidance on how to test comprehensive models that incorporate both value creation and value claiming. Classic TCA-based empirical studies have focused on reduced-form analysis, in which the value-creating transactional attributes (e.g. investments) are taken as given (exogenous), and then have investigated their impact on governance forms. As such, the value-creating motive (e.g. why make investments in specialized assets) is effectively curbed and creates a false impression that governance models are only cost minimization devices. GVA would argue that testing both the value creation and the value-claiming aspects necessarily means that research models should endogenize both the investment and governance decisions.

EMPIRICAL EVIDENCE

To date, the core principle of GVA has been subject to a few empirical tests. We classify these tests into two categories: *main evidence*, which directly investigates some of the core issues in GVA, and *additional evidence*, which reviews empirical approaches and studies that are consistent with the GVA model. To make evident the broad scope of this analysis for strategic marketing questions, we organize the studies into substantive areas of interest to marketing and strategy scholars.

Main Evidence

International distribution
Nickerson et al. (2001) use GVA to link Porter's (1985) strategic positioning framework to Williamson's (1985) TCE, and study the relationship of market position, resources and governance structure in the context of international courier and small package services in Japan. Building on the GVA logic, they argue that an organization's competitive strategy (i.e. the target market position it operates in) is supported by a resource profile (i.e. the necessary investments) and that this resource profile must be paired with an appropriate governance structure to generate the product/service attributes that are consistent with the intended target market position. Operationally, this is a non-trivial

task because a test of this framework requires specifying (1) the resource activities/profiles that serve different target market positions; (2) the desired organizational choice to support that resource profile; and (3) the implication of this resource/governance pairing on performance (product attributes).

Firms in the international courier and small package services market in Japan are primarily positioned as 'package specialists', 'document specialists' or 'full-line services'. The crucial product attributes for differentiation in this industry are delivery reliability and speed, with document specialists positioned at the high end (faster and more reliable delivery), package specialists positioned at the low end and full-line service providers positioned between the two. Nickerson et al. (2001) argue that the time- and reliability-sensitive nature of document specialists requires these firms to customize the IT tracking systems in their transportation segments to store, sort and use large amounts of information; thus, the idiosyncratic investments made by document specialists are higher than those made by full-line service providers, which in turn are higher than those required by package specialists. As a consequence, compared with full-line service providers, the likelihood of integration into the transportation segment would be higher for document specialists and lower for package specialists. Using a three-stage, endogenous, self-selection model, the research finds strong evidence that firms positioned at the high end of the spectrum (document specialists) (1) make more idiosyncratic IT investments than firms positioned at the medium (full-line service providers) and low (package specialists) end; (2) are more vertically integrated into the transportation segment; and (3) have faster delivery time. In essence, firms must properly align their investment–governance relationship to generate the desired market positioning.

Organization of production
In their study of the liquefied natural gas (LNG) industry, Ruester and Neumann (2009) use Porter's (1985) strategic positioning framework approach to identify three strategic target market positions from which LNG producers can choose: chain optimization, flexibility strategy and nationalized companies. Then, depending on the institutional context of the natural gas industry, they argue that these market positions need to be supported by varying levels of specialized investments. In particular, LNG producers choosing chain optimizer strategy should make more idiosyncratic investments than producers choosing a flexibility strategy, which in turn should make more idiosyncratic investments than producers that are nationalized oil companies. As a consequence, the likelihood of vertical integration along the LNG value chain should be the highest for chain optimizers, followed by firms using a flexibility strategy and then by nationalized oil companies. The evidence is consistent with their theoretical prediction. It is again crucial to note the central link between value creation (through the choice of a firm's positioning strategy) and the governance of its value chain.

OEM–supplier relationships
Ghosh and John (2005) study the link between a firm's overall positioning strategy and governance choices in the context of alliance-type relationships between industrial OEMs and their component suppliers. Building on the strategizing calculus of GVA, they hypothesize that (1) the correct fit between governance (measured as flexibility in price and design terms of formal contracts) and specific investments depends on the

value-added outcome (cost reduction vs. quality enhancement) desired in the relationship; and (2) firms seeking such cooperative alliances are not atomistic, faceless entities but bring firm-specific endowments (the market strength of the OEM in its customer market) and, thus, particularistic motivations that moderate the efficient alignment relationships drawn from the first point. Using primary, contract-level data and simultaneous equation modeling, they find evidence of a discriminating fit among firm resources, specific investments, governance forms and outcomes. Specifically, they find that cost reduction benefits are improved when specific investments align with more complete contracts and that quality-enhancing benefits are improved when specific investments align with more incomplete (or flexible) price and design terms in the contracts. Furthermore, they find that OEMs with stronger presence in their downstream customer markets use more complete contracts to protect this resource from being potentially appropriated by an opportunistic supplier; however, because more complete contracts are not conducive to fostering adaptation and cooperation that is essential for quality-enhancing benefits, these OEMs end up sacrificing some gains in quality enhancement (but not cost reduction). In effect, the OEMs' unique downstream resources limit their flexibility and force them to sacrifice these gains from efficient alignment.

Taken together, these results provide the first demonstration of the efficiency–strategy considerations at the heart of GVA.

Additional Evidence

Other studies have investigated this strategy–governance link that is consistent with the spirit of the GVA model. We provide a review of this research next.

The scope of the firm

Wernerfelt (2005) melds insights from the resource-based view (RBV) with his adjustment cost theory (1997) to show how the product development resources a firm possesses can affect its *vertical scope* (whether the firm makes versus buys its inputs) and *horizontal scope* (whether the firm sells more versus fewer lines of output). Specifically, he argues that the possession of high levels of product development resources/processes requires frequent adjustments in the firm's supply chain, which then can be more efficiently managed by internalizing the supplier (broadening the vertical scope) than by contracting for the input. This governance choice is driven by the desire to manage the trade-off between forgoing the design adjustments and clamping down on the costs of adjustments. Likewise, because product development skills are generally tacit to the firm and non-codifiable, firms possessing such skills cannot effectively demonstrate the value of these resources to an independent buyer through a contract; such firms are likely to broaden their horizontal scope and enter into new product markets themselves. The results are consistent with predictions. Note that it is the comparative advantage of one governance form over another (vertical integration versus contracting) that enables Wernerfelt to make this link between the resource profile and the scope of the firm.

Supply-chain link

In two related articles, Heide and colleagues show how the strategy–governance link influences the interface between successive links in a vendor's value chain, be they inter-firm or intra-firm. First, Mishra, Heide and Cort (1998) argue that both adverse selection (did the customer choose the right vendor) and moral hazard (would the vendor take the right action) problems concurrently arise in many buyer–seller contexts, such as the automotive service sector. Building on the classic signaling argument, they contend that customer-side adverse selection problems can be mitigated by charging a price premium and posting customer bonds; in effect, higher ambiguity in performance should be related to higher price premiums for the vendor's product and higher levels of customer bonds being posted by the vendor. However, vendors getting such price premiums should, in turn, take actions to ensure the supply of high-quality service *ex post*. One way to ensure this action (i.e. reduce moral hazard) is to prequalify their service employees, compensate them on customer inputs and provide a more team-oriented rather than individual-oriented culture. The results are again consistent with their hypotheses. The article clearly shows that when quality is unobservable, firms positioned at the high end of the quality spectrums (and which secure high price premiums in return) need to organize their internal governance structures that ensure the supply of the desired level of quality.

Second, Wathne and Heide (2004) use a similar argument, in principle, in their study on the interrelationship between successive links in a supply chain. In the context of the apparel industry, they examine how a firm's strategy in its downstream customer relationship is affected by how its upstream supplier-side relationship is organized. They argue that in uncertain downstream market conditions, the focal firm can show high levels of flexibility in its downstream customer relationships if, on its upstream supplier side, (1) it undertakes a high level of supplier qualification effort and (2) supplier-side hostages are matched by the focal firm's hostages. The data provide support to this highly nuanced prediction.

Note the similarities and differences between this article and Ghosh and John's (2005) work. Both articles examine the interlinks between a firm's customer-side positioning and supplier-side activities. The contrast is that whereas Ghosh and John (2005) evaluate the impact of the downstream customer-side resources (downstream market strength) on upstream supplier-side governance, Wathne and Heide (2004) examine the impact of upstream supplier-side governance on downstream customer-side positioning. In that sense, the articles complement each other and provide a robust assessment of the GVA model.

Product customization in industrial markets

Do customers or vendors control the customization decision in industrial markets? Ghosh et al. (2006) find that firms with greater knowledge mobilization resources (i.e. greater ability to absorb customer information to generate customized solutions) are better positioned to lower the coordination costs, and vice versa. For example, the higher the customer's knowledge/expertise, the more likely the customer is to take charge of the product customization decision. However, the authors find that the vendor's knowledge mobilization resource moderates this relationship. Vendors with high levels of this resource have the absorptive capacity (Cohen and Levinthal 1990) to understand the language and precise needs of expert customers better than poorly resourced vendors; as such, these aspects enhance the ease with which these vendors can design customized solutions and lower the knowledgeable buyer's need to control the customization decision. In essence, the authors generate an integrated RBV/TCA model that shows how firms with different resource profiles make different governance decisions.

Branded components

Branded component contracts are arrangements in which the systems manufacturer (OEM) explicitly contracts with a component brand vendor to use the vendor's brand name in the marketing and promotional activities of the OEM's end product in its downstream market. Given that these contracts are attempts to leverage a unique resource base of the constituent brands to generate downstream differentiation, they offer a unique context to study the interaction among positioning, RBV and governance theories. In two related articles, Ghosh and colleagues study these effects in more detail.

Ghosh and John (2009) propose that leveraging the vendor's brand reputation and safeguarding the vendor's customization investments (which increase the differentiation of the OEM's end product in its customer markets) are the key motives for choosing branded component contracts. Using contract data from OEMs in three engineering-intensive industry sectors, they find support for both the leveraging and the safeguarding arguments. The safeguarding motivation is relevant even to suppliers with modest brand reputation. The authors also find that OEMs that selectively chose these contracts in accordance with their framework were able to lower supplier-side opportunism. The article strongly suggests that governance structures (branded vs. non-branded component contracts) not only enable firms to leverage the existing resource profiles of their supplier partners but, through the supplier investment in customized investments, also create unique points of differentiation for the OEM's product in their customer markets.

In a related article, Lo et al. (2011) study the rigidity of the price format for branded components. Integrating RBV with TCA, they argue that these transacting parties create value not only through partner-specific investment and coordination of their activities but also through matching of the heterogeneous and firm-specific resource profiles of the parties. In turn, the governance structures – price format for branded components in this case – reflect a discriminating alignment with these two distinct forms of value-creating activities and resources.

Lo et al. also investigate the conditions under which the price formats for branded components are agreed on (more fixed) *ex ante* versus negotiated (more flexible) *ex post* and find that the chosen governance form reflects a trade-off between safeguarding and adaptation motives. They find a significant contrast in the price arrangements for the differentiation-generating pre-existing resources that are *independent* of the relationship, with the price arrangement for differentiation-generating investments and coordination efforts that are *relationship specific*. Specifically, both parties prefer fixed price formats when the pre-existing differentiating capability of the component brand or the OEM market strength is high, suggesting their desire to safeguard their own firm-specific but not relationship-specific resource from being appropriated. In contrast, parties prefer more flexible price formats when technical complexity or technological uncertainty is high, suggesting their desire to encourage within-relationship, value-enhancing adjustments. Furthermore, they find evidence that the pre-existing resources that both parties bring to the table can serve as mutual safeguards in the spirit of Williamson's (1983) hostage model. Price formats are more flexible when both the pre-existing differentiation capability of the vendor and the brand strength of the OEM are high. The results clearly suggest that even valuable, firm-specific resources that pre-exist outside the exchange relationship are at stake in these cooperative but contractually incomplete relationships and that, together with relationship-specific investments and activities, they have a significant impact on governance design.

One important implication is that firms earning rents from their pre-existing resources might willingly forgo more efficient adaptive governance that could have generated incremental rents because such adaptive governance structures create appropriation hazards that expose their pre-existing resources. In essence, firms with pre-existing resources seem to be constrained in their ability to use *ex post* adaptation mechanisms to generate *ex post* value-add. This strategy–efficiency trade-off seems to be the most salient consequence of a combined RBV/TCA lens, which is the core of the GVA model.

Dual sourcing: securing customer commitments
Consider the case in which customers must make vendor-specific investments to generate the productive value from the vendor's products. An illustrative example is the early years of the PC industry in which customers needed to purchase both proprietary hardware and operating systems/applications software from the same vendor (e.g. Digital Electronics Corporation, Bull, Wang Labs, IBM). In each of these cases, the proprietary nature of the hardware/software combination meant that customers could not easily switch between vendors and were open to opportunistic price gauging *ex post*. These lock-in hazards were problematic because, at the margins, customers were likely to forgo these investments. In a masterful strategic move, IBM secured these customer-side investments by *inviting* its own competition. Specifically, IBM licensed its proprietary technology, free of cost, to any vendor that would use the IBM architecture to offer similar 'cloned' products to the customers. This reduced a customer's lock-in hazards because any attempt by IBM to substantially raise prices *ex post* could be neutralized by switching to a clone supplier.

Dutta and John (1995) investigate this phenomenon using a multimethod approach (a game-theoretic model and experiments). They show that inviting one's own competition by licensing one's own proprietary technology at a nominal licensing fee reduces customer-side lock-in hazards and generates a primary growth in the market. But they go one step further and show how competitive strategy implications are intertwined with governance issues by contending that focal vendors with greater differentiation ability will find this strategy of 'invited competition' more valuable. To wit, if the licensor has little differentiation ability, the availability of compatible products would lead to end users claiming most of the value from the technology at the expense of the competing vendors. Given this, a far-sighted licensor might forgo the additional value created by second sourcing and be content with claiming the value generated from a single-sourcing/proprietary arrangement. In contrast, a licensor with an ability to differentiate its products *ex post* can gain from expanding the market size (by inviting its competition) and by differentiating its product from the compatible product offered by the licensee vendor. This differentiation ability of the vendor, through its marketing-based brand equity or technical equity, clearly influences the chosen governance form.

Managing retail relationships
Two recent articles have used the GVA framework to show the contingent strategy–governance alignment in retail management. Kim et al. (2011) examine the fashion-apparel

retail market in South Korea in which they find the prominent use of a partially integrated channel; that is, employees of the brand manufacturer work on a full-time basis on the premises of the retailer and perform many of the activities traditionally undertaken by the retailer. Using the GVA framework, they show how the brand resource profile of the manufacturer and transactional attributes, such as market uncertainty and salesperson performance ambiguity, jointly affect the control the manufacturer seeks over the sales operations and the flexibility the manufacturer demonstrates in its relationship with the retailer. In particular, they argue and find that manufacturers with high brand reputation are more likely to be flexible in their dealings with the retailer and more likely to seek control over their salespeople's activities as the downstream uncertainty and salesperson ambiguity increase, respectively.

Gooner et al. (2011) use the theoretical lens of the GVA to study category management in the grocery retail sector and find that two key aspects of category management (the intensity of category management effort and the lead supplier influence) are affected by both the marketing capabilities of the retailer and the unique resources the retailer brings to the relationship. These, in turn, are hypothesized to affect the opportunistic behaviors of the lead supplier.

In summary, in a wide variety of marketing contexts, we find empirical support for the basic tenet of the GVA model – that governance and strategy/positioning issues are critical in the design of exchange relationships. The key, however, is to accentuate the links that are particularized to a context. For example, certain resource profiles can constrain a focal party's use of specific governance structures, as we explained with the Ghosh and John (2005) and Lo et al. (2011) articles, but other resource profiles (e.g. Ghosh et al. 2006) enable an enhancement of the activity set that is possible through these governance structures.

DIRECTIONS FOR FUTURE RESEARCH

Value Frame

Many observers of strategy insist that one of the most critical marketing strategy questions is, where should a firm participate in the value chain? Or equivalently, what product form should the firm use to sell its innovation in the marketplace (Jacobides and Billinger 2006)? Broadly speaking, three principal strategic alternatives exist with respect to this framing question: transact in *intellectual know-how* (by licensing one's intellectual property (IP) as a *licensor*), transact in *intermediate products* (by marketing components/subsystems as a *vendor*), or transact in *end products* (by marketing complete systems/solutions/services as an *OEM*). We use this licensor–vendor–OEM frame as shorthand notation hereinafter.

This frame is fundamental because it occurs before classical marketing strategy notions of product positioning or differentiation. In other words, questions such as 'Should we position our product/service as a high-quality, premium brand?' are in general preceded by resolving 'What product form should we sell?' In addition, this frame has implications for core marketing issues such as 'Who is our direct customer' and/or 'Who is our direct competitor?' Finally, this frame is of substantive importance because it encapsulates the behavior of a broad range of firms in a variety of business sectors. For example, many pharmaceutical and cosmetics/personal goods OEMs (e.g. Procter & Gamble) are also the most prominent licensors of their technologies. Likewise, during the past decade, IBM has transformed itself from a vertically integrated OEM-only frame eschewing IP transactions or intermediate components to a licensor–vendor–OEM frame. It has consciously worked to increase its revenues from licensing its IP as well as marketing components and technology to other OEMs.[1]

Despite its strategic value on subsequent marketing decisions, no systematic decision framework or evidence about the value frame yet exists. However, we believe that GVA provides a way forward with this issue for several reasons. First, note that the boundaries among the licensor, vendor and OEM categories are inherently institutional in nature. Thus, GVA, which is rooted in TCA, is able to order these categories readily. Second, the pioneering work of Frias (2010) on this issue indicates that the relevant constructs are embedded within GVA.

Frias (2010) investigates early-stage development projects undertaken in venture capital-supported start-up enterprises in the high-technology and biomedical sectors, and her results provide clues to this link between GVA and the value frame decision. This is a valuable setting to study the value frame because (1) the core technology/idea/ innovation that motivates the start-up is readily identifiable and described; (2) venture capitalists' use of structured, deliberative processes and criteria to evaluate start-up feasibility traces out the value frame decisions; and (3) the venture capitalists' heterogeneous resource profiles (financial support plus managerial resources and product–market development skills on occasion) provide variation on important drivers.

Frias's (2010) 'emergent-theory' approach consisting of in-depth interviews with venture capitalists on individual start-up projects surfaces their mental model for making their value frame choice for each innovation. The key insight that emerged was that concern about leakage of the core technology (appropriability concerns) and ability to garner resources to develop and commercialize the technology (coordination concerns) drive the choices, which the venture capitalists articulate as (1) license IP; (2) commercialize an intermediary component; and (3) commercialize an end product. Note that with our value frame terminology, these can be restated as (1) licensor; (2) vendor; and (3) OEM frames, respectively. Frias concludes that the appropriability and resource availability drivers manifest through a variety of technological characteristics (e.g. tacitness), industry characteristics (e.g. legal regime) and market characteristics (e.g. breadth of potential applications).

Note that the two key motives she unearthed, safeguarding and coordination, are indeed the fundamental motives underlying the TCA/GVA framework. We can readily interpret her insights into the desire to secure one's innovation and the ability to garner complementary resources as a driver of value frame choices as another instantiation of the resource profile–governance links posited in GVA. Thus, GVA seems a very promising framework that would enable us to tackle one of the central questions in marketing strategy and issues related to it. For example, a firm's value frame choice would be intertwined with the quality and type of relationships the firm is able to develop with its supplier and channel partners. What would these relationships look like? Likewise, selling in international markets brings with it associated hazards because of variation in the legal and enforceability norms in those countries. The GVA would propose that firms are likely to modify their product frames to account for the variation in these hazards.

Dyadic Analysis of Divergent Relational Norms

Marketing scholars have focused a lot of attention on how relational norms support inter-firm exchanges (e.g. Dwyer et al. 1987; Heide 1994). In general, these dyadic norms are defined and measured as common expectations of behavior in a bilateral exchange.

Empirical work on relational contracting/norms based on TCE generally work under the assumption of convergent expectations of these dyadic norms. Methodologically, this means that 'convergent validity' (or, for some, random measurement error) is the key criterion for assessing the psychometric scales of these norms, obtained from both sides of the dyad. Data, however, have persistently shown that such dyadic measures of social norms fit these models (common expectations plus random measurement error) quite poorly (e.g. John and Reve 1982) and lead to questions about the value of psychometric measures and, by association, the survey-based methods primarily used to collect these data.

However, the GVA model would argue that this focus on achieving high convergent validity is conceptually inappropriate because each party to a dyadic exchange brings its own individual resources and endowments as well as motivations that should systematically influence its own perceptions of the norm. This suggests that we should focus on models that do not rely on invariant adherence to a cooperative or relational norm. This view is consistent with the observations made by sociologists (e.g. Pondy and Boje 1980) that adherence to any given norm could vary across the relevant actors either because parties have different perceptions of the norms or because they believe that violation of a norm has a differential impact on one party over the other. We sketch two recent streams of research along these lines.

Collective action

Consider, for example, the problem of collective action, or contributing to a common good. Public goods can be successfully provided even when there are marked differences between people with respect to a norm of cooperation. Fehr and Gächter (2000) show that a supply of public goods can be maintained in one-shot stranger–stranger interactions absent any contract enforcement or market reputation mechanism, *as long as an investor can punish free-riders after the fact.*

Why? A few but sufficient number of people are inclined to be 'altruistic punishers',[2] which is a social motive rooted in the evolutionary pressures fostering collective action in hunter–gatherer societies. Altruistic punishment maintains cooperation because it induces a credible belief among potential free-riders that their behavior will be punished. We observe that this example would be relevant to vertically administered contractual arrangements, such as franchising. Franchisors and franchisees are quite likely to hold different interpretations about the same contractual clause.[3] The GVA model can help construct testable models of such divergent norms for rigorous testing that might shed a better light on the management of collective actions.

Two-sided alliances

Another argument against the adherence to the notion of common expectations is that parties to an exchange might have different expectations about what they seek from a relationship. Madhok (2002) concludes that General Motors and Toyota had very different expectations from their NUMMI (New United Motor Manufacturing Inc.) alliance. Thus, their adherence to relational norms was by no means invariant to their particularistic motives. Nevertheless, these parties were able to sustain this alliance for quite some time and to meet their particularistic goals.

Consistent with these examples, we believe that instead of adhering to the notion of a common expectation, a more realistic view is that parties to an exchange do share some normative expectations but that they also have their own systematic perceptions of the norms in addition to random errors. On the theoretical side, the GVA model can provide a compelling rationale on why and when these systematic variations might occur in the interpretation of these norms. On the methods side, these models can then be tested with hierarchical linear models or similar types of random coefficient models using nested data.

This should provide two key benefits and directions to future research. First, models that account for common/shared and systematic differences between the parties will not only provide a richer and more complex understanding on the use and value of social norms on design and management of dyadic ties but also provide a better fit to the data. Second, and probably more important, the efficacy of these models should enhance the value of perceptual measures and, therefore, survey methods, in our understanding of complex and nuanced issues in inter- and intra-organizational studies. If parties to a contract have systematically different interpretations on how they should act in the relationship, the analysis of formal contracts, as preferred by economics and strategy researchers, is likely to provide an incomplete, and quite possibly misguided, understanding of these complex phenomena, and researchers will need to rely on survey-based primary data collection methods to tackle these issues.

INSIGHT FOR BUSINESS PRACTITIONERS

The GVA model attempts to integrate strategic motives with governance decisions and, as various empirical studies have shown, has been applied in a wide variety of marketing contexts. Consider a few specific insights based on existing empirical evidence.

Implementing Different Positioning Profiles

The GVA model offers a link among the positioning a firm seeks for its products/services, the activity set (i.e. transaction attributes such as investments) that needs to be implemented for generating that positioning and the rules of engagement (i.e. governance) that need to be put in place to ensure the alignment between the positioning and the activity set. The ICI illustration shows how positioning shifts need to have a commensurate shift in the customer-side activity set and the pricing rules. Nickerson et al.'s (2001) research suggests a similar set of links in which more valuable (time-sensitive and speedy) positioning profiles needed more proprietary investments in IT, which could be accomplished only if the firm sought a more hierarchical form of governance.

Managing the Value Chain Through Strategic Contract and Relationship Design

Contract design does not come naturally to marketing managers; however, we suggest that managers should think of themselves as 'governance value engineers' (Gilson 1984) who add value by engineering appropriate contracts. For example, Ghosh and John's (2005) research suggests that component supply relationships geared toward cost reduction need to be supported by fixed price and design contracts (with potential gain sharing) whereas supply relationships geared toward quality and performance enhancement need to be supported by more flexible price and design formats; however, while accomplishing the latter, the OEM needs to be cognizant that such contracts do not expose the margins they earn in their customer markets to risk. Likewise, Mishra et al.'s (1998) research suggests that automotive maintenance service shops that seek higher premiums from their customers need to undertake extra effort to qualify their service employees and compensate them more on customer inputs. Similar conclusions on strategically organizing governance structures are obtained from Wathne and Heide's (2004) study on supply chains, Kim et al.'s (2011) study on partially integrated channels and Gooner et al.'s (2011) study on category management.

Choosing Between Open and Proprietary Product Designs

Compared with open systems, proprietary systems lock in buyers to the vendor technology (but also offer higher value/performance through more integrated design than can be obtained under an open system), making reasonably far-sighted buyers more hesitant to buy these proprietary systems from the start. Dutta and John (1995) show how vendors can break this logjam by inviting their own competition to license their technology for free (or at nominal licensing fee) and, in the process, generate primary market growth that can be beneficial to both the licensor and the licensee. However, consistent with the GVA, they also suggest that the focal vendor would be enticed to do so only if it possesses the resources to differentiate its offering (e.g. through brand, channel or technology equity) from that of the licensee's clone. The domination of the IBM-compatible PC and the current tussle between the Google–Android open architecture and the Apple iPhone closed architecture reflect these conflicting strategic motives. Frias's (2010) work also suggests how a firm's value frame choice (e.g. to sell intermediate components or final end systems) is affected by whether the firm expects to profit from selling open versus proprietary designs. In short, the GVA framework would contend that managers/firms need to be cognizant of the technology features and their own resource profiles and capabilities when choosing the governance format.

Creating and Enhancing Brand Value

OEMs frequently use their association with highly reputed component vendors to generate a differentiated position in their customer marketplace. However, managers are far less aware of the use of branded component contracts to support the development of unique components that are developed exclusively for the OEM's end product and that provide a unique point of differentiation for that end product. Such creation and enhancement of brand value through co-branding arrangements is valuable even in B2B service markets. For example, during the early years of the Internet, the renowned consulting firm Andersen Consulting touted the ability of the far less reputable Fasturn e-business solutions and their joint ability to create a web-enabled marketplace for retailers that would combine Fasturn's e-business solutions with Andersen's industry experience and knowledge to deliver high-value results. Although Fasturn was the less reputable firm, Andersen might have realized the potential value that could be added by Fasturn's innovative product. However, that would require Fasturn to undertake a significant level of non-verifiable development effort to ensure a successful integration and co-implementation with Andersen's consulting business. To incentivize Fasturn, Andersen used its own reputation (brand equity) to create potential future value (and possibly a positive revenue stream) for the Fasturn brand; in essence, the OEM created rather than leveraged the supplier brand to secure the supplier's commitment to create a significant quality/performance enhancement of the OEM's solution. Again, the relationship between strategic positioning and governance design becomes apparent here.

CONCLUSIONS

The GVA framework was an attempt by Ghosh and John (1999) to show how the efficiency-based governance lens of TCA could be intertwined with the calculus inherent in strategic decisions. In this chapter, we provide an up-to-date review of the literature based on GVA. The review not only shows how researchers have generated nuanced predictions on the strategy–governance links but also reveals the wide range of substantive areas in the B2B marketing domain in which such strategy–governance links have been studied. This review demonstrates the inherent value of the GVA framework and suggests several key directions for future research.

NOTES

1. However, note that its de-emphasis on hardware sales versus business services does not move it away from its OEM frame.
2. This is labeled altruistic because the punisher's behavior cannot be rationalized from a self-interest viewpoint or even from an extended self-interest viewpoint that incorporates future gains from reputation effects. Counterintuitively, punishment represents a gain to the non-punishing investors as well as the target because it induces a credible belief that sustains higher cooperation at no additional personal cost.
3. Private conversations with Professors Patrick Kaufmann at Boston University and Francine Lafontaine at University of Michigan.

REFERENCES

Cohen, Wesley M. and Daniel A. Levinthal (1990), 'Absorptive capacity: a new perspective on learning and innovation', *Administrative Science Quarterly*, **35** (1), 128–52.
Dutta, Shantanu and George John (1995), 'Combining lab experiments and industry data in transaction cost analysis: the case of competition as a safeguard', *Journal of Law, Economics, and Organization*, **11** (1), 87–111.

Dwyer, Robert F., Paul H. Schurr and Sejo Oh (1987), 'Developing buyer–seller relationships', *Journal of Marketing*, **51** (2), 11–27.

Fehr, Ernst and Simon Gächter (2000), 'Cooperation and punishment in public goods experiments', *American Economic Review*, **90** (4), 980–94.

Foss, Nicolai J. (2005), *Strategy, Economic Organization, and the Knowledge Economy: The Coordination of Firms and Resources*, New York: Oxford University Press.

Frias, Kellilynn M. (2010), 'Product form choice in high-technology entrepreneurial ventures', working paper, University of Arizona.

Ghosh, Mrinal and George John (1999), 'Governance value analysis and marketing strategy', *Journal of Marketing*, **63** (Special Issue), 131–45.

Ghosh, Mrinal and George John (2005), 'Strategic fit in industrial alliances: an empirical test of governance value analysis', *Journal of Marketing Research*, **42** (3), 346–57.

Ghosh, Mrinal and George John (2009), 'When should original equipment manufacturers use branded component contracts with suppliers?', *Journal of Marketing Research*, **41** (5), 597–611.

Ghosh, Mrinal, Shantanu Dutta and Stefan Stremersch (2006), 'Customizing complex products: when should the vendor take control?', *Journal of Marketing Research*, **43** (4), 664–79.

Ghoshal, Sumantra and Peter Moran (1996), 'Bad for practice: a critique of the transaction cost framework', *Academy of Management Journal*, **21** (1), 13–47.

Gilson, Ronald (1984), 'Value creation by business lawyers: legal skills and asset pricing', *Yale Law Journal*, **94** (December), 239–313.

Gooner, Richard A., Neil A. Morgan and William D. Perreault Jr. (2011), 'Is retail category management worth the effort (and does a category captain help or hinder)?', *Journal of Marketing*, **75**, forthcoming.

Heide, Jan B. (1994), 'Interorganizational governance in marketing channels', *Journal of Marketing*, **58** (1), 71–85.

Jacobides, Michael G. and Stephan Billinger (2006), 'Designing the boundaries of the firm: from "make, buy, or ally" to the dynamic benefits of vertical architecture', *Organization Science*, **17** (2), 249–61.

John, George and Torger Reve (1982), 'The reliability and validity of key informant data from dyadic relationships in marketing channels', *Journal of Marketing Research*, **19** (4), 517–24.

John, George and Torger Reve (2010), 'Transaction cost analysis in marketing: looking back, moving forward', *Journal of Retailing*, **86** (3), 248–56.

Kim, Stephen K., Richard G. McFarland, Soongi Kwan, Sanggi Son and David A. Griffith (2011), 'Understanding governance decisions in a partially integrated channel: a contingent alignment framework', *Journal of Marketing Research*, **48** (3), 603–16.

Lo, Desmond, Kellilynn M. Frias and Mrinal Ghosh (2011), 'Price formats for branded components in industrial markets: an integration of transaction cost economics and the resource-based view', *Organization Science*, forthcoming.

Madhok, Anoop (2002), 'Reassessing the fundamentals and beyond: Ronald Coase, the transaction cost and resource-based theories of the firm and the institutional structure of production', *Strategic Management Journal*, **23** (6), 535–50.

Mishra, Debi Prasad, Jan B. Heide and Stanton G. Cort (1998), 'Information asymmetry and levels of agency relationships', *Journal of Marketing Research*, **35** (3), 277–95.

Nickerson, Jack A., Barton H. Hamilton and Tetsuo Wada (2001), 'Market position, resource profile, and governance: linking Porter and Williamson in the context of international courier and small package services in Japan', *Strategic Management Journal*, **22** (3), 251–73.

Pondy, Louis R. and David M. Boje (1980), 'Bringing mind back in', in William M. Evan (ed.), *Frontiers in Organization and Management*, New York: Praeger Publishers, pp. 83–101.

Porter, Michael E. (1985), *The Competitive Advantage: Creating and Sustaining Performance*, New York: The Free Press.

Ruester, Sophia and Anne Neumann (2009), 'Linking alternative theories of the firm: a first empirical application to the liquefied natural gas industry', *Journal of Institutional Economics*, **5** (1), 47–64.

Wathne, Kenneth H. and Jan B. Heide (2004), 'Relationship governance in a supply chain network', *Journal of Marketing*, **68** (1), 73–89.

Webster, Frederick E. (1992), 'The changing role of marketing in a corporation', *Journal of Marketing*, **56** (4), 1–17.

Wernerfelt, Birger (1997), 'On the nature and scope of the firm: an adjustment-cost theory', *Journal of Business*, **70** (October), 489–504.

Wernerfelt, Birger (2005), 'Product development resources and the scope of the firm', *Journal of Marketing*, **69** (2), 15–23.

Whitney, Daniel E. (1992), 'State of the art in Japanese CAD methodologies for mechanical products: industry practice and university research', *Office of the Naval Research Scientific Information Bulletin*, **17** (1), 89–111.

Williamson, Oliver E. (1983), 'Credible commitments: using hostages to support exchanges', *American Economic Review*, **73** (September), 519–40.
Williamson, Oliver E. (1985), *The Economic Institutions of Capitalism*, New York: The Free Press.
Williamson, Oliver E. (1999), 'Strategy research: governance and competence perspective', *Strategic Management Journal*, **20**, 1087–108.
Zajac, Edward J. and Cyrus P. Olsen (1993), 'From transaction cost to transactional value analysis: implications for the study of interorganizational strategies', *Journal of Management Studies*, **30** (1), 131–45.

5   Network governance
Stefan Wuyts and Christophe Van den Bulte

Social networks pervade industries and have an important bearing on individual firms' actions and outcomes. European retailers, for example, join forces as buyer groups to increase their bargaining position with manufacturers (IGD 2006). Many manufacturers use small-scale networks of exchange relationships with multiple competing suppliers both to protect themselves against opportunistic suppliers and to maintain their flexibility (Wuyts 2007). Firms in high-technology industries build alliance networks both to gain access to technologies and to market new products (Wuyts et al. 2004a). Even traditional distribution channels connecting suppliers to vendors to customers are networks (Wuyts et al. 2004b).

The notion that 'no business is an island' has long been accepted outside marketing (e.g. Braudel 1985; Granovetter 1985; Macaulay 1963). Yet the current marketing literature does not provide much systematic guidance on the processes and mechanisms through which network structure beyond the focal buyer–seller or manufacturer–distributor dyad affects firm behavior. Particularly for B2B networks, in which the 'actors' or 'nodes' in the network are intrinsically driven by self-serving motives such as bottom-line performance, it is important to understand how networks can improve inter-organizational governance. When does a network help curb exchange partners' opportunistic tendencies and generate 'control benefits'? When does a network help align different actors to achieve synergy and other 'coordination benefits'? What are the possible disadvantages of being embedded in a network?

This chapter provides an overview of various network governance mechanisms in business markets. We do so by discussing the control and coordination benefits as well as the constraints that result from firms and dyads being embedded in social networks. First, we identify network control mechanisms that help firms monitor and steer the behaviors of their exchange partners. We also discuss the conditions that need to be fulfilled for these mechanisms to be effective. These conditions involve both the structure of the network and the strategic motivations of the organizations. Second, we discuss how social networks can stimulate positive behavior and help align different parties for the sake of mutual gain. Third, we acknowledge that social networks can have a dark side. Firms may influence the behavior of other firms in the network by changing the logic of exchange from instrumental and self-centered to normative and collectivist. This shift in logic can inhibit economic effectiveness.

THE CURRENT LITERATURE ON NETWORK GOVERNANCE

Prior Marketing Literature on Governance and Control

Dyadic exchange is central to the marketing channels literature. The power and conflict theory that flourished in the 1970s and 1980s (e.g. Gaski 1984) was grounded in sociological interpretations of dyadic interaction (e.g. Deutsch 1969; Emerson 1962) and social exchange theory (Thibaut and Kelley 1959). The political economy paradigm that emerged in the late 1980s and emphasized control, conflict and institutional change similarly focused on dyadic interaction (Stern and Reve 1980), albeit with some acknowledgment of the importance of the broader channel environment (Achrol et al. 1983). The relationship marketing school of thought that followed did not elaborate on the channel environment but shifted the focus back to dyadic relationships, a development that is perhaps most strongly conveyed by the popular marriage analogy for channel relationships (Anderson and Weitz 1989; Dwyer et al. 1987). The rise of transaction cost analysis reinforced the focus on the dyad (e.g. Heide and John 1990).

Although marketing scholars recognize that 'individual relationships are embedded in a context of other relationships that could have governance implications' (Heide 1994, p. 81), network governance effects have not received much attention. Taking much of its conceptual foundations from social psychology and economics, marketing theory kept its focus on dyadic exchange and did not keep up with sociology in which social exchange theory was gradually replaced by network exchange theory (Cook and Whitmeyer 1992; Markovsky et al. 1988). This theory views exchange networks as sets of two or more connected exchange relationships, with exchange relationships being connected when one relationship is contingent on exchange (or non-exchange) in the other relationships (Cook and Emerson 1978). One exception to this pattern of disconnect was a research community often referred to as the Industrial Marketing and Purchasing (IMP) Group (e.g. Ford 1990). Its early programmatic statements on business-markets-as-networks explicitly incorporated notions from network exchange theory. However, later IMP research became conceptually disconnected from mainstream sociology and marketing, a theoretical disconnect further amplified by the IMP community's methodological preference for qualitative case studies. Today, IMP research is characterized by soliloquy and mutual disregard for mainstream marketing thought (Van den Bulte 2009).

In short, little progress has been made in understanding network governance and control consequences for exchange in marketing. This is due in part to the dyadic focus of early power/conflict theory, the political economy paradigm, relationship marketing theory and transaction cost theory, respectively, and in part to the failure of a marketing research tradition committed to network issues to connect with mainstream marketing research and theory. As a result, the marketing literature offers little guidance for managers on the specifics of network governance mechanisms, the conditions under which these mechanisms are likely to be activated, or the effectiveness and potential drawbacks of networks (Van den Bulte 2010; Van den Bulte and Wuyts 2007).

A few recent marketing studies, however, do provide empirical evidence that the broader network has governance implications. Franchisors refrain from punishing contract infringements by well-connected franchisees out of fear of retaliation (Antia and Frazier 2001). Buyers of IT systems prefer to work closely with vendors that have close ties to upstream component suppliers (Wuyts et al. 2004b). Detailed contracts curb a supplier's opportunistic behavior more effectively when the buyer and supplier share close ties to mutual others (Wuyts and Geyskens 2005). The amount of word of mouth among customers of different distributors limits the appeal of providing product exclusivity to any of the distributors (Peres and Van den Bulte 2010). Rigorous evidence is mounting for the relevance of network governance in B2B marketing. A thorough discussion of the actual network governance mechanisms that may explain these findings, however, is lacking.

Limitations of Network Governance Literature

The marketing literature has not systematically discussed network governance, and the literature in related fields is rather limited as well. It is restricted in three fundamental ways. First, much of the work focuses on goal-directed networks as purposely designed organizational forms (e.g. Coleman 1990; Koza and Lewin 1999) rather than on network structures that emerge more serendipitously from the actions of the network members (Kilduff and Tsai 2003). The network theory of organization has focused mainly on enabling coordinated interaction to achieve collective/individual interests (Salancik 1995) or on alternative approaches to actively govern organizational networks (e.g. Provan and Kenis 2008). The emphasis on purposive design is also evident in empirical research, as illustrated by the work of Grewal et al. (2010) on electronic market community building and the active role of market makers in the creation of trust and integrity. What all this work has in common is that the network structure is the result of particular network goals; that is, the involved actors deliberately strive toward particular network structures. This is not what we observe in many B2B settings, where the strategic goals of firms are often formulated at the dyadic level and the network structure results from large numbers of dyadic decisions. Let us illustrate the difference. A buyer group in the European retail market is a goal-directed network because the strategic goals are formulated at the buyer group level and the group's structure is deliberately chosen to attain that goal (for example, to reach a certain level of critical mass to counter the powerful grocery manufacturers). In contrast, the complex network of collaborative agreements in the information and communications technology market for Internet solutions results from large numbers of strategic decisions to ally at the dyad level (that is, between pairs of industry participants). In the former case, network formation is driven by network goals; in the latter case, network formation emerges from an accumulation of strategic goals at the dyad level.

A second limitation of the current body of thought is in many ways the opposite of the first. Just as much work emphasizes purposive design, another sizable body of work focuses on providing network explanations of behavior with little to no attention to the possibility of agency or purposive behavior in these networks (Emirbayer and Goodwin 1994). In layman's terms, firms have no free will, and their actions are determined by the structure of the network of which they are a part. This is problematic because a firm's position in the broader network mostly affects its opportunities and constraints and, as such, only affects its potential for action. To fully understand action, we need also to consider actors' motivations. Yet, as Stevenson and Greenberg (2000, p. 653) note, 'network theorists have often emphasized the macro-social properties of network position and downplayed the more micro-behavioral aspects of action'. This overly deterministic approach to explain behavior solely by the social context in which it takes place leads to an oversocialized conception of action (Wrong 1961) that is not very helpful in guiding managers.

The third limitation in the current work on network governance is that considerable attention has been devoted to the question of whether network control is a hybrid of market and hierarchy (e.g. Park 1996) or a new form of control (e.g. Powell 1990). Although this discussion is worthwhile from an abstract-theoretical point of view, it provides little insight relevant to marketers into how network control mechanisms actually work.

CONTROL BENEFITS OF SOCIAL NETWORK STRUCTURES[1]

This section provides some insight into how different network control mechanisms work and when they are likely to be activated and operate effectively. We pay attention to both network structure and individual motivation. We discuss four mechanisms: two-step leverage, negative gossip, group norms and *tertius gaudens*. The first two are directed at one specific individual actor, whereas the last two are not. Negative gossip, for example, is directed toward one specific actor being bad-mouthed. In contrast, group norms, such as generalized trust conventions, affect firms across the entire network. This distinction is important because if actors perceive the use of a control mechanism as coercive or punitive, they can instigate a vicious cycle of retaliation (John 1984; Lusch 1976). In an interpersonal setting, we can distinguish between personal and impersonal mechanisms (Wuyts 2010); in a B2B context, we prefer the labels 'direct' versus 'indirect'. Another dimension along which to organize the four mechanisms pertains to the objective that is being pursued. Negative gossip and *tertius gaudens* weaken the position of counterparties, whereas two-step leverage and group norms align the interests of the parties involved. Table 5.1 summarizes these differences. The categorization is somewhat loose because the categories are not completely mutually exclusive and definitely not collectively exhaustive. Nevertheless, keeping in mind these distinctions among the mechanisms is useful because particular network positions and motivations may be more amenable to one particular network control mechanism than to another.

One can also distinguish among network control mechanisms according to whether they operate locally or globally. Local refers to the ego-network comprised of the focal actor, the adjacent actors, and the ties among them, whereas global refers to the overall network (Scott 1992). Although this distinction has practical consequences that we discuss subsequently, it is not fundamental for our purpose. First, most global network control mechanisms can in principle occur in a triad as well (e.g. group norms). Second, the fundamental step in network theory is the step from dyad to triad, enabling the researcher to examine situations of brokerage, structural balance, and structural imbalance. Subsequent steps to larger networks (e.g. four or five or more nodes) are not typically considered fundamental in the network literature (Simmel [1908] 1950). Still, our

Table 5.1   Network control mechanisms

		Nature of influence	
		Direct	Indirect
Objective of influence	Alignment of interests	Two-step leverage	Group norms
	Competitive threat	Negative gossip	*Tertius gaudens*

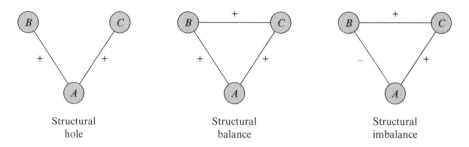

Figure 5.1   Three triadic structures of special importance

discussion of the different network control mechanisms does consider the consequences for each mechanism when moving from the triad to larger networks.

Next, we discuss the network-structural and motivational conditions that determine the effectiveness of alternative network control mechanisms. We limit the discussion of network-structural conditions primarily to three fundamental triadic structures: structural hole, structural balance, and structural imbalance (see Figure 5.1).

When an actor links two unconnected actors, he or she is said to serve as a broker. An example is a systems integrator that connects component suppliers with end customers. Prior research has shown that such a network position conveys advantages through arbitrage of business opportunities and knowledge (Burt 1992).

When three actors are fully connected and all ties are positive in valence, the triad does not engender discomfort among the actors and is said to display structural balance (Heider 1958). Such all-positive structural balance is found in many business cooperatives, a centuries-old organizational form that unites small business owners for the sake of economic protection and increased negotiation power. Note that a triad with two negative ties and one positive tie is also balanced – a situation in which 'the enemies of my enemies are my friends' does not create attitudinal conflict – but we focus on all-positive balance.

When three actors are fully connected but two of the three ties are positive in valence and the third one is negative in valence, the triad is said to display structural imbalance (Heider 1958). An example is a situation in which a consultancy firm provides advice to two competing firms.

Two-step Leverage

Two-step leverage works as follows: Firm A calls on firm B to exert influence on firm C, such that firm C behaves in alignment with firm A's interests (Gargiulo 1993). Thus, as noted in Table 5.1, the influence in two-step leverage is directed toward one particular firm (C) and the objective is alignment. An example, taken from a colleague's experience, is a car owner calling on the car manufacturer to exert influence on a negligent car dealer. Two-step leverage may explain Wuyts et al.'s (2004b) finding that a buyer's preference for system integrators with intensive ties to component suppliers is increased if the buyer has direct ties to component suppliers. In the event that the system integrator underperforms, the buyer firm, which may not have sufficient leverage to influence the system integrator directly, may call on the component suppliers to exert influence on the system integrator.

Triadic conditions

We expect two-step leverage to be especially effective when the triad is characterized by structural imbalance. Say customer A believes that his car dealer, B, does not handle the repairs to his car quickly enough, creating a negatively valenced tie between A and B. The customer may decide to contact the car manufacturer C directly to exert influence on B. For manufacturer, C, to be willing and able to exert such influence, it must obviously care enough about customer A and must also have a good relationship with dealer B. Thus, we advance, two-step leverage is a mechanism to control or redirect a specific actor's behavior in situations of structural imbalance.

From triads to larger networks

Two-step leverage can also be used at the global network level. Boycotts are an example, such as the episode when the environmental organization EII (Environmental Impact Initiative) called on US consumers to boycott StarKist products so that the latter would refrain from purchasing tuna from foreign firms using netting methods banned by the United States (Frooman 1999). Note that the ultimate objective was not to have StarKist change its behavior but rather to achieve behavioral change in the fishing industry at large. The same is true of the efforts of many non-governmental organizations targeting major retailers, such as Tiffany & Co. in jewelry or Home Depot in construction materials, to change the behavior of raw materials producers.

Motivational conditions

Although two-step leverage is typically used in imbalanced triadic structures, its effectiveness is also a function of the willingness of the called-on firm to actually exert influence. This firm must foresee either social or economic benefits from exerting influence. For a car manufacturer, the potential loss of a high-value customer may hinge on the dealer's behavior toward this customer, providing the car manufacturer with economic benefits to redirect the dealer's misbehavior toward the customer.

Negative Gossip

Negative gossip can also be a powerful control mechanism. Spreading negative information about an actor can damage its reputation (Dollinger et al. 1997), which in turn can result in a loss of future business (Greif 1993; Houston and Johnson 2000). Negative gossip thus is directed toward a specific firm with the objective to weaken that firm's position.

Triadic conditions

Negative gossip is likely to be used effectively in triadic structures characterized by brokerage or structural imbalance. A disgruntled customer, A, may pass on negative information about firm B to either a potential or an existing customer, C, of this firm. The former would be an instance of brokerage, and the latter would be one of imbalance. Either way, the threat of losing a (potential) customer may induce the firm to redirect its behavior toward A.

From triad to larger networks

Previous research has shown that network closure (that is, the presence of a dense pattern of connections among one's own network neighbors) facilitates reputation building, which is crucial for the negative gossip mechanism (Buskens 1998; Jones et al. 1997; Raub and Weesie 1990). Real-life social networks are seldom characterized by perfect closure, but the latter is not required for gossip to be effective. All that is needed is a fast-spreading and convincing message among the contacts of the party one wants to bad-mouth. Having many connections to other firms that, in turn, are linked to many other firms (that is, they have high 'eigenvector centrality'; Bonacich 1987) also boosts one's ability to devalue the reputations of counterparties because information disseminated by these firms travels more extensively through the network. In turn, this puts the firm in a better position to effectively bad-mouth transgressors (Robinson and Stuart 2007; Yang et al. 2010).

Motivational conditions

Next to triadic conditions, the motivations of the firms that receive the negative message influence the effectiveness of negative gossip as well. If firms are not motivated to reconsider their (potential) relationships with the firm that is the subject of negative gossip, the mechanism will have little effect. When the firm being bad-mouthed is a monopolist, for example, firms that receive the negative messages may not have any alternative available to them. The negative gossip mechanism is also less effective when receivers of the negative message see no benefit in passing on the negative information to other firms. Motivational problems can be quite important in preventing word-of-mouth information from reaching the intended targets (Dodds et al. 2003).

Group Norms

Group norms can influence behavior in business networks through trust and moral obligation (Larson 1992). Although norms are not an actual network mechanism, their effectiveness may be greatly enhanced or dampened by the structure of the network. Framing the workings of group norms in line with Table 5.1, group norms are indirect (that is, not directed toward one specific firm) and are intended to align the interests of involved firms.

Triadic conditions

Group norms curtailing opportunistic behavior arise in close-knit networks of positive valence. Positive structural balance facilitates the emergence and sustainability of cooperative group norms. For example, when a manufacturer shares a close relationship with an intermediary and both invest in the development of a close tie with a business customer, the firms involved may develop an implicit understanding of what constitutes appropriate behavior and forgo the need to monitor each other closely.

From triad to larger networks

More generally, the presence of a dense pattern of positive relationships tends to favor group norms. Provan and Sebastian (1998) find that group norms develop more easily among firms if they are connected by multiple and overlapping links. Such high levels of closure lead to feelings of identification and commonality and thus facilitate the emergence of group norms. Macy and Skvoretz (1998) indeed find that the coordination of effective trust conventions is facilitated in tightly knit networks.

Group norms are less likely to be effective in networks consisting of clusters that are internally densely interconnected but have only a moderate number of ties running across them. The feeling of identification with the group, a precondition for an actor to be susceptible to group norms, is likely to be lower among members that belong to different local clusters. The real problem is that actors bridging multiple clusters may be exposed to conflicting modes of behavior, each dominant in one of the clusters to which they belong. So, whichever mode of behavior they engage in, they end up being oddballs violating one or the other local norm. As a consequence, the network may be stuck in inferior behaviors. For example, Watts and Strogatz (1998) find that it is difficult for the tit-for-tat strategy to establish itself as the dominant strategy when an iterated prisoner's-dilemma game is being played in such a network structure rather than within disconnected dyads. Tilly (1978) similarly notes that collective resource mobilization, which is facilitated by a group norm of solidarity, is more readily achieved in networks that are dense and in which actors lack strong ties to outsiders.

Motivational conditions
Low levels of identification with the rest of the network can undermine the effectiveness of group norms. First, there may be a free-rider problem in the inculcation and enforcement of social norms. To the extent that popularizing and enforcing norms impose costs, some firms will want others to bear the burden of educating newcomers and punishing transgressors. Unless a sufficiently large number of firms care enough about the norm, it may never get established, or may erode quickly. Second, firms that identify less with the social network may interpret group norms as overly restrictive normative pressure, which in turn can cause reactance and willful resistance. These adverse consequences of group norms have been documented in consumer networks (Algesheimer et al. 2005) and are likely to apply to B2B settings as well.

Tertius Gaudens

Tertius gaudens is a network control mechanism that aims to reduce dependency on exchange partners by exploiting competition, or at least the lack of contact, among the exchange partners (Simmel [1908] 1950). This network control mechanism is not directed toward one specific firm and is intended to weaken the other firms' competitive positions. In its strong version, the *tertius gaudens* principle is also referred to as '*divide et impera*' (divide and rule), in which competing firms are set up against one another. However, it is not necessary to actively increase tension and division among competitors. The very fact that, for example, company A is connected to several firms competing with one another can be sufficient to curb these firms' opportunistic tendencies toward A and may even stimulate them to display positive behaviors that will benefit company A. When a buyer firm follows a multisourcing strategy, the very presence of competing suppliers may stimulate each supplier to do more than what is formally required in order to outperform the competition and ensure a favorable share of business (Wuyts 2007).

Triadic conditions

The conditions under which the *tertius gaudens* mechanism is effective pertain to both the local network structure and the motivations of the adjacent actors. Both structural imbalance and brokerage may provide the opportunity to use the *tertius gaudens* mechanism. In the case of brokerage, firms B and C in Figure 5.1 are not in contact with each other, which provides firm A with brokerage benefits in the form of unique information or arbitrage opportunities. In the case of structural imbalance, B and C share a negatively valenced tie with each other, which ensures that A can play B and C against each other.

From triad to larger networks

The *tertius gaudens* mechanism can be effective beyond the confines of a triad. Multisourcing, for example, is not restricted to triads. Many firms build large portfolios of relationships with alternative suppliers and offer the status of preferred supplier only to those that outperform competing suppliers. Similarly, franchisors build networks with franchisee-operated outlets but often also operate several outlets themselves to benchmark one type of outlet against the other (e.g. Bradach 1997). More generally, the *tertius gaudens* principle applied to larger networks is equivalent to Burt's (1992) notion of brokerage through structural holes. As long as the relationships between the counterparties are negatively valenced (for example, they are competitors such as in multisourcing), collusion against the broker is unlikely to occur and the brokerage advantage is sustainable.

Motivational conditions

For the *tertius gaudens* mechanism to be effective, actors B and C should not have an incentive to collude against A. Collusion would undermine the mechanism, whether in brokerage or in structural imbalance scenarios. Collusion is more of a concern when the *tertius gaudens* mechanism is based on brokerage in the triad than when it is based on structural imbalance in which the negative tie between B and C is more likely to stand in the way of effective collusion.

COORDINATION BENEFITS OF SOCIAL NETWORK STRUCTURES

Social network structures not only provide protection against negative behaviors, like opportunistic exploitation, but also convey synergistic benefits. The marketing literature on inter-firm exchange devotes most of its attention to protection against negative behaviors, and mostly ignores positive behaviors. To provide a more complete understanding of the consequences of networks for exchange, we now discuss mechanisms that facilitate coordination and so may translate into synergistic benefits. In particular, we discuss structural embeddedness, generalized reciprocity, and *tertius iungens*.

Embedded Ties

Granovetter (1985) introduced the concept of structural embeddedness as a response to the oversocialized sociological perspective that network structure determines the behavior of individual actors (the industry network structure determines why firms behave the way they do) and the undersocialized economic perspective that ignores network embeddedness (firms are driven by their own economic rationalizations in isolation of the network in which they are embedded). Granovetter's argument was that all economic action is socially embedded and that elements from the economics and sociological perspectives should be integrated to fully grasp behavior. When Uzzi (1997) examined this phenomenon in the apparel industry, he found that long-standing and trusting relationships improved coordination and pooling of resources and so helped overcome challenges such as shifts in customer preferences and business slowdowns. These improvements were Pareto-efficient in that they benefited at least one firm without generating any losses to other firms. Joint problem solving, trust and fine-grained information transfer were the key elements of what Uzzi labeled 'embedded ties'. Because of their consequences for adaptation and resource reallocation, embedded ties are important in B2B settings. Note, however, that Uzzi's findings were really about dyadic ties rather than network structure.

Generalized Reciprocity

Generalized reciprocity refers to a 'group-based exchange relationship in which members expect quid pro quo exchanges within the group but not necessarily with any specific member' (Das and Teng 2002, p. 449). So, it is a particular kind of group norm, but the expectation on how to behave applies to all members diffusely rather than to each member separately. By stimulating network members to display goodwill and help out others, which in turn fosters trust and solidarity, generalized reciprocity is a group norm that is beneficial to individual member firms (Das and Teng 2002; Gouldner 1960).

Generalized reciprocity is more likely to take hold and flourish in closed and positively balanced triads. The presence of 'cycles' of ties in the network also helps. Being kind in observance of the norm may induce the counterparty to observe the norm as well and be kind to others, and so on. To the extent that there are cycles of ties in the network (for example from A to B to C to D back to A), the chain of benevolent acts is likely to cycle back to the originator (Ho and Weigelt 2005).

Tertius Iungens

Tertius iungens (Obstfeld 2005) is a counterpart to Burt's (1992) conceptualization of the *tertius gaudens* principle in brokerage situations. The idea is that while serving as a bridge between otherwise disconnected actors can provide a party with unique information and control benefits, the completion of value-generating projects sometimes requires direct contact ties between the parties on opposite sides of the bridge. In such situations, brokerage is ineffective. What the actor in the middle needs to do instead is act as a matchmaker, introducing both parties to each other and, if necessary, educating them on the benefits of working together. The *tertius iungens* principle thus captures the activity of joining actors to produce coordinated action. It has been related to successful innovation (Obstfeld 2005). Following a similar line of logic, Hargadon (2003) discusses 3M's creation of the Optical Technology Center (OTC), the purpose of which was to find alternative applications across all 3M's divisions for a technology called 'microreplication'. Thus, the OTC joined people and created bridges that resulted in new innovative product opportunities. *Tertius iungens* differs fundamentally from *tertius gaudens* in that its objective is collective synergy rather than individual gain. It differs from negative gossip and two-step leverage in that it is not primarily aimed at reducing conflict and avoiding negative behaviors but rather at coordinating often in the absence of competing claims or tensions.

A Comment on Competition

Coordination among firms affects the nature and extent of competition. The popular phrase that 'no firm can go it alone' in uncertain and complex industries conveys the need to network with others to be successful. Network coordination may also affect price levels. Uzzi and Lancaster (2004) find that in the corporate law market, the reduced transaction and production costs that result from embedded ties with customers allow for lower prices without loss of margins. Still more intriguing is Ingram and Roberts's (2000) examination of the hotel industry in Sydney. They find that hotel yields substantially increase when managers of competing hotels belong to cohesive friendship networks. What sets this study apart from the stream of research on collusion (for example, through price-fixing arrangements; see Baker and Faulkner 1993) is that the increased collaboration among competitors leads to improved information exchange and better awareness of strategic positions, which in turn stimulate a legal form of tacit collusion associated with improved economic performance. Clearly, the debate about the consequences of embedded ties and coordination among competitors is ongoing.

CONSTRAINT AND SOCIAL NETWORK STRUCTURES

The same network forces that curb opportunistic behavior and engender positive behavior for one actor can be experienced by another as restrictive or even coercive. In a context of exchange in which individual actors try to attain economic benefits, social network structures and the behaviors they facilitate can stand in the way of economically optimal behavior. A higher density of ties in the network often facilitates cooperation (Van den Bulte and Wuyts 2007). However, when internal ties come at the detriment of external ties, the pool of information that can be accessed and shared is more homogenized and less novel (Uzzi and Spiro 2005). The resulting myopia may not only harm innovation but also make the network members more vulnerable to changes in the broader environment. In addition, group norms can effectively curb behaviors that go against group interests, but there is a risk of the group interest becoming too restrictive for achieving economic optimality individually. In other words, social networks can demotivate individual actors from pursuing their interests and so can stifle effective economic action (Uzzi 1997). Similarly, two-step leverage and other mechanisms geared toward sharing resources can divert resources from their best use or can demotivate actors who feel that they cannot sufficiently enjoy the fruits of their efforts (Stevenson and Greenberg 2000).

   When network control mechanisms are direct in nature, their use can trigger retaliation and relationship deterioration. The reason is that influence attempts directed toward a specific other may be experienced as coercion and so paradoxically increase rather than decrease conflict and opportunism (John 1984; Lusch 1976).

The constraining nature of network control mechanisms also becomes apparent when considering the use of different network control mechanisms simultaneously, or in combination with dyadic control mechanisms. Different control mechanisms may rely on different and incompatible logics. Group norms, for example, rely on a logic of cooperation and alignment, and so do some dyadic control mechanisms. Negative gossip and the *tertius gaudens* principle rely on a logic of threat and competition, often leading to a more competitive rather than cooperative atmosphere, which is again similar to some dyadic control mechanisms. Similar to the incompatibility of contract enforcement and relational norms (Jap and Ganesan 2000; Macaulay 1963; Nooteboom et al. 1997), the *tertius gaudens* principle may cause adverse reactions if deployed in a close-knit network in which interaction is guided by group norms. Incompatibility problems can also occur when network governance mechanisms are combined with dyadic governance mechanisms. While a competition-based multisourcing strategy and a collaborative atmosphere within each dyad both stimulate supplier extra-role behavior, multisourcing *undermines* the effectiveness of a collaborative atmosphere when both governance mechanisms are deployed simultaneously (Wuyts 2010).

CONCLUSION

This chapter examined different mechanisms behind network control and network coordination. Network control may result from shared group norms, the threat of bad-mouthing, triadic influence strategies like two-step leverage, and deliberate attempts to divide and rule. The effectiveness of each of these mechanisms hinges on both the network structure and the motivations of the actors involved. Regarding coordination, we have discussed embedded ties, generalized reciprocity, and *tertius iungens* as three coordination mechanisms that have been associated with economic benefits in prior research. But here again contingencies matter. In close-knit cohesive networks, embedded ties and generalized reciprocity may be activated. In situations of brokerage, however, *tertius iungens* is a constructive and potentially beneficial alternative to its control counterpart, *tertius gaudens*. In what follows, we discuss the implications of these insights for researchers and managers, respectively.

Implications for Researchers

Given (1) the importance of channel governance for marketing; (2) the dyadic tradition in the marketing channel literature; and (3) the insights from social exchange theory and network embeddedness studies in sociology, we call for more research on network governance in marketing channels. A parallel with developments in research on word-of-mouth dynamics and social contagion in general may be informative. Much of this research benefits from new data opportunities, but the very best is guided by sound theory rather than mere data opportunism (Van den Bulte 2010). We expect that the importance of theory will be even greater for network governance research because the data are more difficult to obtain. In addition, we believe that the conceptual foundations for a theoretically informed research program on network governance are likely to be found in sociology rather than marketing, where work on network governance is in its infancy (Van den Bulte and Wuyts 2007).

Another, and complementary rather than competing, approach to advance this field is to empirically assess the effectiveness of network control mechanisms in inter-organizational settings of interest to B2B marketers. We hope that research will move beyond case studies and cross-sectional survey designs toward methods with higher internal validity, both experiments and panel data structures, to investigate the effectiveness of various network mechanisms (Van den Bulte 2009).

Little empirical evidence is available to guide firms in making trade-offs between the benefits and constraints associated with social networks. Studying these trade-offs has the potential to generate novel insights that are both theoretically significant and practically useful. Until researchers and consultants offer more empirically validated advice, we hope that our discussion of various mechanisms and the conditions under which they are most likely to be effective will provide guidance to managers on how and when to use network governance to their advantage.

Implications for Managers

We still know little about network governance mechanisms and their effectiveness in B2B markets. Although several findings in the marketing literature suggest that network governance is highly relevant, the managerial implications of these empirical findings are often little more than glorified guesswork. The reason is the inability to distinguish among possible explanations of observed effects. Disentangling different network control mechanisms and identifying those at work in a particular setting are essential to managers.

Let us illustrate with two examples. A firm suspects that one of its suppliers is opportunistically distorting information about its available production capacity and its efforts to meet delivery times. To better control this supplier's behavior, the client firm sees little value in confronting the supplier directly and decides to use multisourcing or bad-mouthing. Although both mechanisms seem like alternative means to the same end, which of them is more effective depends on the specifics of the situation. In the case of multisourcing, the client firm selects a competing supplier to perform similar tasks; the success of this strategy hinges on the two suppliers being unwilling or unable to collude against the client. In the case of bad-mouthing, the client firm instigates the spread of negative gossip in the client network; the success of this alternative strategy hinges on whether other clients are motivated to pass on the message and willing to reduce their own business interactions with the client firm. In other words, before deciding between the two actions, the client firm needs to understand both the supply network in the industry (for example, the competitive nature of ties between suppliers) and the demand side network in the industry (for example, the network structure among client firms, the value of the negative gossip to other client firms, their willingness to punish the opportunistic supplier).

As a second example, a supplier experiences delayed payments by one of its customers, a franchisee of a retail chain. The supplier cannot easily solve this problem with dyadic forms of governance because enforcing contracts through courts is costly and difficult.

Instead, the supplier considers using two-step leverage or negative gossip. Which is likely to be best? Here again, it depends. The franchisee may be so large and dominant that other suppliers are unlikely to reduce their business with this client after hearing about the payment delays, in which case negative gossip is unlikely to be effective. Moreover, if the franchisee's suppliers are competitors, they are unlikely to share a dense communication network through which the negative gossip can spread quickly. Two-step leverage may seem like a more effective solution. The supplier may ask the franchisor to exert influence on its franchisee. The effectiveness of two-step leverage hinges on the franchisor's ability and motivation to exert such influence. Thus, the supplier's choice between negative gossip and two-step leverage should be guided by insight into network structures as well as the motivations of individual actors.

Networks offer opportunities not only for control but also for coordination. For example, entrepreneurs should attempt not only to exert control over other players but also to create new business opportunities. Networks can help in this regard. Open source systems are excellent examples of generalized reciprocity, in which contributors freely share knowledge with others. Although sharing valuable knowledge for free seems non-economical, the system thrives on generalized reciprocity: the contributor knows he or she will benefit from others' achievements later. In the B2B domain, *tertius iungens* is also quite common: firms such as IDEO are classic examples of innovators that create value for client firms by uniquely bridging industries and using recombination and integration to solve new problems. Being aware of various governance mechanisms and of how they work helps marketers leverage their business networks to their advantage.

NOTE

1.   This section is based in part on Wuyts (2010).

REFERENCES

Achrol, Ravi S., Torger Reve and Louis W. Stern (1983), 'The environment of marketing channel dyads: a framework for comparative analysis', *Journal of Marketing*, **47** (Fall), 55–67.
Algesheimer, René, Uptal M. Dholakia and Andreas Herrmann (2005), 'The social influence of brand community: evidence from European car clubs', *Journal of Marketing*, **69** (July), 19–34.
Anderson, Erin and Barton Weitz (1989), 'Determinants of continuity in conventional industrial channel dyads', *Marketing Science*, **8** (4), 310–23.
Antia, Kersi and Gary L. Frazier (2001), 'The severity of contract enforcement in interfirm channel relationships', *Journal of Marketing*, **65** (October), 67–81.
Baker, Wayne E. and Robert R. Faulkner (1993), 'The social organization of conspiracy: illegal networks in the heavy electrical equipment industry', *American Sociological Review*, **58**, 837–60.
Bonacich, P. (1987), 'Power and centrality: a family of measures', *American Journal of Sociology*, **92**, 1170–82.
Bradach, Jeffrey L. (1997), 'Using the plural form in the management of restaurant chains', *Administrative Science Quarterly*, **42** (2), 276–303.
Braudel, Fernand (1985), *Civilization and Capitalism, 15th–18th Century: The Wheels of Commerce*, Vol. 2, London: Fontana Press.
Burt, Ronald S. (1992), *Structural Holes: The Social Structure of Competition*, Cambridge, MA: Harvard University Press.
Buskens, Vincent (1998), 'The social structure of trust', *Social Networks*, **20** (3), 265–89.

Coleman, James S. (1990), *Foundations of Social Theory*, Cambridge, MA: Harvard University Press.

Cook, Karen S. and Richard M. Emerson (1978), 'Power, equity, and commitment in exchange networks', *American Sociological Review*, **43** (October), 721–39.

Cook, Karen S. and J.M. Whitmeyer (1992), 'Two approaches to social structure: exchange theory and network analysis', *Annual Review of Sociology*, **18**, 109–27.

Das, T.K. and Bing-Sheng Teng (2002), 'Alliance constellations: a social exchange perspective', *Academy of Management Review*, **27** (3), 445–56.

Deutsch, M. (1969), 'Conflict: productive and destructive', *Journal of Social Issues*, **25** (January), 7–42.

Dodds, Peter Sheridan, Roby Muhamad and Duncan J. Watts (2003), 'An experimental study of search in global social networks', *Science*, **301**, 827–9.

Dollinger, Marc J., Peggy A. Golden and Todd Saxton (1997), 'The effect of reputation on the decision to joint venture', *Strategic Management Journal*, **18** (2), 127–40.

Dwyer, F. Robert, Paul H. Schurr and Sejo Oh (1987), 'Developing buyer–seller relationships', *Journal of Marketing*, **51** (April), 11–27.

Emerson, Richard M. (1962), 'Power-dependence relations', *American Sociological Review*, **27** (February), 31–41.

Emirbayer, Mustafa and Jeff Goodwin (1994), 'Network analysis culture and the problem of agency', *American Journal of Sociology*, **99** (6), 1411–54.

Ford, David (ed.) (1990), *Understanding Business Markets: Interaction, Relationships, Networks*, London: Academic Press.

Frooman, Jeff (1999), 'Stakeholder influence strategies', *Academy of Management Review*, **24** (2), 191–205.

Gargiulo, Martin (1993), 'Two-step leverage: managing constraint in organizational politics', *Administrative Science Quarterly*, **38** (1), 1–19.

Gaski, John F. (1984), 'The theory of power and conflict in channels of distribution', *Journal of Marketing*, **48** (Summer), 9–29.

Gouldner, Alvin (1960), 'The norm of reciprocity: a preliminary statement', *American Sociological Review*, **25** (2), 161–78.

Granovetter, Mark (1985), 'Economic action and social structure: the problem of embeddedness', *American Journal of Sociology*, **91** (3), 481–510.

Greif, Avner (1993), 'Contract enforceability and economic institutions in early trade: the maghribi traders' coalition', *American Economic Review*, **83** (3), 525–48.

Grewal, Rajdeep, Anindita Chakravarty and Amit Saini (2010), 'Governance mechanisms in business-to-business electronic markets', *Journal of Marketing*, **74** (July), 45–62.

Hargadon, Andrew (2003), *How Breakthroughs Happen: The Surprising Truth about how Companies Innovate*, Boston, MA: Harvard Business School Press.

Heide, Jan B. (1994), 'Interorganizational governance in marketing channels', *Journal of Marketing*, **58** (January), 71–85.

Heide, Jan B. and George John (1990), 'Alliances in industrial purchasing: the determinants of joint action in buyer–supplier relationships', *Journal of Marketing Research*, **27** (February), 24–36.

Heider, Fritz (1958), *The Psychology of Interpersonal Relations*, New York: John Wiley & Sons.

Ho, T.H. and K. Weigelt (2005), 'Trust building among strangers', *Management Science*, **51** (4), 519–30.

Houston, Mark B. and Shane A. Johnson (2000), 'Buyer–supplier contracts versus joint ventures: determinants and consequences of transaction structure', *Journal of Marketing Research*, **37** (February), 1–15.

IGD (2006), 'European grocery buying groups', IGD MyReports, available at http://www.igd.com/Analysis/Hub.aspx?id=60&tid=9&mr=1&mtab=6&cid=37, accessed 31 January 2011.

Ingram, Paul and Peter W. Roberts (2000), 'Friendships among competitors in the Sydney hotel industry', *American Journal of Sociology*, **106** (2), 387–423.

Jap, Sandy D. and Shankar Ganesan (2000), 'Control mechanisms and the relationship life cycle: implications for safeguarding specific investments and developing commitment', *Journal of Marketing Research*, **37** (May), 227–45.

John, George (1984), 'An empirical investigation of some antecedents of opportunism in a marketing channel', *Journal of Marketing Research*, **21** (August), 278–89.

Jones, Candace, William S. Hesterly and Stephen P. Borgatti (1997), 'A general theory of network governance: exchange conditions and social mechanisms', *Academy of Management Review*, **22** (4), 911–45.

Kilduff, Martin and Wenpin Tsai (2003), *Social Networks and Organizations*, London: Sage Publications.

Koza, Mitchell P. and Arie Y. Lewin (1999), 'The coevolution of network alliances: a longitudinal analysis of an international professional service network', *Organization Science*, **10** (5), 638–53.

Larson, Andrea (1992), 'Network dyads in entrepreneurial settings: a study of the governance of exchange relationships', *Administrative Science Quarterly*, **37**, 76–104.

Lusch, Robert F. (1976), 'Sources of power: their impact on intrachannel conflict', *Journal of Marketing Research*, **13** (November), 382–90.

Macaulay, Stewart (1963), 'Non-contractual relations in business: a preliminary study', *American Sociological Review*, **28** (1), 55–67.
Macy, Michael W. and John Skvoretz (1998), 'The evolution of trust and cooperation between strangers: a computational model', *American Sociological Review*, **63** (October), 638–60.
Markovsky, Barry, David Willer and Travis Patton (1988), 'Power relations in exchange networks', *American Sociological Review*, **53** (2), 220–36.
Nooteboom, Bart, Hans Berger and Niels G. Noorderhaven (1997), 'Effects of trust and governance on relational risk', *Academy of Management Journal*, **40** (2), 308–38.
Obstfeld, David (2005), 'Social networks, the *tertius iungens* orientation, and involvement in innovation', *Administrative Science Quarterly*, **50** (1), 100–130.
Park, Seung H. (1996), 'Managing an interorganizational network: a framework of the institutional mechanism for network control', *Organization Studies*, **17** (5), 795–824.
Peres, Renana and Christophe Van den Bulte (2010), 'How customer word of mouth affects the benefits of new product exclusivity to distributors', working paper, University of Pennsylvania.
Powell, Walter W. (1990), 'Neither market nor hierarchy: network forms of organization', in Barry M. Staw and L.L. Cummings (eds), *Research in Organizational Behavior*, Vol. 12, Greenwich, CT: JAI Press, pp. 295–336.
Provan, Keith G. and Patrick Kenis (2008), 'Modes of network governance structure, management, and effectiveness', *Journal of Public Administration Research and Theory*, **18** (2), 229–52.
Provan, Keith G. and Juliann G. Sebastian (1998), 'Networks within networks: service link overlap, organizational cliques, and network effectiveness', *Academy of Management Journal*, **41** (4), 453–63.
Raub, Werner and Jeroen Weesie (1990), 'Reputation and efficiency in social interactions: an example of network effects', *American Journal of Sociology*, **96** (3), 626–54.
Robinson, David T. and Toby E. Stuart (2007), 'Network effects in the governance of strategic alliances', *Journal of Law, Economics, and Organization*, **23** (1), 242–73.
Salancik, G.R. (1995), 'Wanted: a good network theory of organization', *Administrative Science Quarterly*, **40** (2), 345–9.
Scott, J. (1992), *Social Network Analysis*, Newbury Park, CA: Sage Publications.
Simmel, Georg ([1908] 1950), 'Quantitative aspects of the group', in Kurt H. Wolff (ed.), *The Sociology of Georg Simmel*, New York: The Free Press, pp. 87–177.
Stern, Louis W. and Torger Reve (1980), 'Distribution channels as political economies: a framework for comparative analysis', *Journal of Marketing*, **44** (Summer), 52–64.
Stevenson, William B. and Danna Greenberg (2000), 'Agency and social networks: strategies of action in a social structure of position, opposition, and opportunity', *Administrative Science Quarterly*, **45**, 651–78.
Thibaut, John W. and Harold Kelley (1959), *The Social Psychology of Groups*, New York: John Wiley & Sons.
Tilly, C. (1978), *From Mobilization to Revolution*, Reading, MA: Addison-Wesley.
Uzzi, Brian (1997), 'Social structure and competition in interfirm networks: the paradox of embeddedness', *Administrative Science Quarterly*, **42** (1), 35–67.
Uzzi, Brian and Ryon Lancaster (2004), 'Embeddedness and price formation in the corporate law market', *American Sociological Review*, **69** (3), 319–44.
Uzzi, Brian and Jarrett Spiro (2005), 'Collaboration and creativity: the small world problem', *American Journal of Sociology*, **111** (2), 447–504.
Van den Bulte, Christophe (2009), 'Some suggestions for doing social network research in B-to-B marketing', *ISBM Research Quarterly*, **2** (1), 2–3.
Van den Bulte, Christophe (2010), 'Opportunities and challenges in studying customer networks', in Stefan Wuyts, Marnik G. Dekimpe, Els Gijsbrechts and Rik Pieters (eds), *The Connected Customer: The Changing Nature of Consumer and Business Markets*, London: Routledge, pp. 7–35.
Van den Bulte, Christophe and Stefan Wuyts (2007), *Social Networks and Marketing*, Cambridge, MA: Marketing Science Institute.
Watts, Duncan J. and Steven H. Strogatz (1998), 'Collective dynamics of "small-world" networks', *Nature*, **393**, 440–42.
Wrong, Dennis (1961), 'The oversocialized conception of man in modern sociology', *American Sociological Review*, **26** (2), 183–93.
Wuyts, Stefan (2007), 'Extra-role behavior in buyer–supplier relationships', *International Journal of Research in Marketing*, **24** (4), 301–11.
Wuyts, Stefan (2010), 'Connectivity, control, and constraint in business markets', in Stefan Wuyts, Marnik G. Dekimpe, Els Gijsbrechts and Rik Pieters (eds), *The Connected Customer: The Changing Nature of Consumer and Business Markets*, London: Routledge, pp. 77–103.
Wuyts, Stefan and Inge Geyskens (2005), 'The formation of buyer–supplier relationships: detailed contract drafting and close partner selection', *Journal of Marketing*, **69** (October), 103–17.

Wuyts, Stefan, Shantanu Dutta and Stefan Stremersch (2004a), 'Portfolios of interfirm agreements in technology-intensive markets: consequences for innovation and profitability', *Journal of Marketing*, **68** (April), 88–100.

Wuyts, Stefan, Stefan Stremersch, Christophe Van den Bulte and Philip Hans Franses (2004b), 'Vertical marketing systems for complex products: a triadic perspective', *Journal of Marketing Research*, **41** (November), 479–87.

Yang, Haibin, Zhiang Lin and Ya Lin (2010), 'A multilevel framework of firm boundaries: firm characteristics, dyadic differences, and network attributes', *Strategic Management Journal*, **31**, 237–61.

6 Marketing capabilities for B2B firms
Neil A. Morgan and Rebecca J. Slotegraaf

Broadly defined, marketing capabilities are the processes by which organizations define, develop and deliver value to their customers by combining, transforming and deploying their resources in ways that meet market needs (e.g. Day 1994; Vorhies and Morgan 2005). Although the literature on marketing capabilities is relatively new, growing evidence suggests that firm-level marketing capabilities are associated with superior product-market (e.g. Dutta et al. 1999; Morgan et al. 2003) and financial (e.g. Krasnikov and Jayachandran 2008; Morgan et al. 2009b) performance outcomes. To enhance understanding of the nature and value of marketing capabilities for B2B firms, we expand the conceptualization of capabilities to encompass the levels of organizational analysis (ranging from the individual employee level to the inter-organizational level) and the hierarchal level of capabilities (ranging from specialized single-task capabilities to higher-order learning capabilities).

Consider, for example, customer relationship management (CRM) capabilities. At the firm level, this marketing capability may be an important driver of a B2B firm's ability to develop and sustain a competitive advantage (e.g. Krasnikov et al. 2010). Yet managers tasked with building an organization's CRM capabilities require greater direction and insight. In particular, what are the contributing skills and processes underlying this capability, and how can they be enhanced and better orchestrated? The theoretical literature suggests that CRM capabilities are ultimately based on individual-level knowledge and skills that are applied to a range of activities, from specific single-task activities (e.g. call handling) to more complex processes that draw together the various resources and skills required to execute and coordinate different activities (e.g. a salesperson providing a customized solution to a particular customer). In turn, to create an organization-level CRM capability, these individual-level capabilities must be combined with other resources and capabilities. For example, individuals' call-handling skills and knowledge must be organized with technology and management systems to allow the systematic collection of customer-related data that provide an important input to other CRM subprocesses, such as customer analysis. All the contributing CRM subprocesses (e.g. customer data acquisition, customer analysis, pricing, product management, customer service delivery) then must be orchestrated so that the organization can use its overall CRM capability to efficiently transform its available knowledge, technology, financial, production, human and other resources into strong relationships with customers.

For an organization's CRM capability to contribute to superior performance, it must also be combined with architectural marketing capabilities, such as market planning, to ensure that the organization focuses on the markets and customer segments to which it is best able to efficiently provide superior value offerings. If the value of an organization's CRM capabilities is to be sustained in the face of dynamic marketplaces, the organization also needs to be able to complement its current CRM capabilities with higher-order learning capabilities, such as market sensing, benchmarking and continuous process improvement. Such complementary learning capabilities enable the organization to guide its investments in new CRM resources and CRM capability enhancement in ways that ensure they match changing marketplace needs.

The CRM capability example suggests that B2B managers and researchers can benefit by adopting a more comprehensive conceptualization of marketing capabilities. Here, we aim to provide such a conceptualization. We begin by describing the nature of marketing capabilities and the characteristics that determine their underlying value to an organization. We then outline a new taxonomy that we developed to shed light on the characteristics of different types of marketing capabilities within B2B firms, and we subsequently review the extant B2B marketing literature using the taxonomy as a theoretical lens. Finally, we discuss the findings of our review and highlight new areas for B2B research in this important area.

THE NATURE OF MARKETING CAPABILITIES

A large body of capability literature in management, economics and marketing focuses on the firm level of analysis. At this level, capabilities are broadly viewed as the processes and routines by which a firm transforms its resources into valuable outputs (e.g. Reed and DeFillippi 1990; Teece et al. 1997). Grounded in the resource-based view, a firm's resources are the tangible or intangible assets controlled by the firm (Constantin and Lusch 1994), and they offer the greatest sources of competitive advantage when they are valuable, rare, inimitable and non-substitutable (Barney 1991). Brand equity, customer relationships and supplier relationships have been identified as three key marketing-based resources that a firm may deploy and leverage through its marketing capabilities (Srivastava et al. 1998). However, marketing capabilities also often deploy many different types of other resources. For example, a pricing capability draws on and deploys knowledge of customers, competitors and suppliers, along with its human, reputational, financial, relational and legal resources (Dutta et al. 2003). Indeed, capabilities connecting multiple related resources may play a particularly important role in attaining a sustained competitive advantage by making it more difficult for competitors to discern and imitate the process by which the various resources are combined and deployed to form the capability (Dierickx and Cool 1989; Milgrom and Roberts 1995).

Both the resource-based view and strategic marketing theory posit that capabilities are inherently hierarchical in nature as a result of the way they evolve and are developed within a firm (e.g. Dickson 1992; Grant 1996). From an evolutionary perspective, as similar problems facing the firm are addressed repeatedly over time, tacit response routines emerge (Nelson and Winter 1982). Over time, these routines become codified, integrated and coordinated at different organizational levels, and a hierarchy of capabilities develops (Grant 1996; Teece et al. 1997). At the lowest level, individuals working in a marketing role apply their unique knowledge and skills to solving marketing-related problems. An individual's marketing knowledge and skills may also be combined with those of other individuals, both within the marketing function (e.g. in subunits and work groups) and across other functions (e.g. through cross-functional teams). At higher levels, the integration of resources, specialized knowledge and lower-level capabilities becomes more expansive and complex (Grant 1996). Broader integration across multiple levels enhances the difficulty involved in successfully mastering the capability but also establishes a greater contribution toward sustainable advantage (Porter 1996).

As capabilities develop over time, they become embedded in the firm as a result of the complex, interconnected nature of resources and coordinated patterns of skills, activities and knowledge that occur across different functions and at different levels of the organizational hierarchy (Day 1994; Grant 1991, 1996). The nested hierarchies and reliance on processes that are ingrained in shared understandings within the organization create an additional barrier to imitation and enhance the value of such embedded capabilities (Dacin et al. 1999; Dickson 1992; Grewal and Slotegraaf 2007).

To sustain a competitive advantage in dynamic market environments, a firm's resources and capabilities must be continually changed, developed and enhanced (e.g. Eisenhardt and Martin 2000; Morgan et al. 2009a). The extent to which a firm is able to encourage and tap individual, group and organizational learning about the market environment determines its ability to discover why and how its resources and capabilities should be changed and upgraded (Morgan et al. 2009b; Slater and Narver 1995). Given the dynamic nature of markets, capabilities that fail to evolve to fit the changing demands of the firm and its environment create organizational rigidities (Leonard-Barton 1992) that lead to suboptimal outcomes (e.g. Hunt and Morgan 1995). Thus, the dynamic nature of capabilities is critical in enabling a firm to sustain a competitive advantage over time.

In summary, the theoretical literature indicates that (1) marketing capabilities are inherently hierarchical in nature; (2) the extent to which they become embedded in the firm can elevate their value to the firm; and (3) the dynamic nature of marketing capabilities is essential to understanding firm performance over time in the face of changing market environments. To help identify and understand the various types of marketing capabilities that may be critical for B2B organizations, we propose a new taxonomy.

A TAXONOMY FOR UNDERSTANDING MARKETING CAPABILITIES

The marketing literature reveals several different approaches to classifying capabilities. Vorhies and Morgan (2003, 2005) offer a classification of marketing capabilities as either *specialized* capabilities (i.e. specific marketing program-related processes) or *architectural* capabilities (i.e. processes that orchestrate multiple specialized capabilities and their associated resource inputs). Our taxonomy for understanding B2B marketing capabilities captures two dimensions that subsume this prior approach by recognizing (1) the hierarchical nature of capabilities; and (2) the different units of analysis at which the underlying processes and routines occur and have been observed. First, within the hierarchical dimension of the taxonomy, we extend Vorhies and Morgan's (2003, 2005) classification by incorporating an additional, higher-order learning level. This highest level of capability reinforces the importance of generating new market-based insights in reconfiguring resources and upgrading existing capabilities to respond to changes in the environment. Consequently, this dimension of our

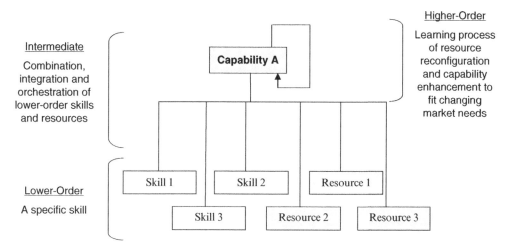

Figure 6.1   Exemplar of the hierarchy of B2B marketing capabilities

taxonomy captures the underlying hierarchical nature of marketing capabilities by recognizing capabilities that occur at a lower level (i.e. deployment of specific skills), at an intermediate or architectural level (i.e. orchestration of multiple activities) and at the highest level (i.e. learning capabilities that reflect an evolution of all skills, activities and routines to fit changing environmental conditions). Figure 6.1 illustrates this hierarchical perspective.

The second dimension of our taxonomy considers the organizational unit in which the underlying processes and routines that underpin the capability occur. We recognize firms as interrelated subsystems, in which individuals operate independently but also work within and across groups, departments and subunits that collectively represent the firm. In addition, acknowledging the importance to B2B firms of managing both upstream and downstream channels, we include an inter-organizational level. This level recognizes the importance of deploying resources that lie outside a firm's boundaries; for example, pooling other firms' resources to enhance new product development (Rindfleisch and Moorman 2001) and sharing strategic information with suppliers and distributors to improve planning and implementation efforts (Frazier et al. 2009). Thus, this dimension of our taxonomy acknowledges that capabilities can occur at the individual, group, organizational or inter-organizational level.

Within our taxonomy of B2B marketing capabilities, lower-order capabilities reflect activities and processes that are based on specific marketing tasks, and these can occur at the individual, group, organizational or inter-organizational level. These specialized marketing capabilities involve the specific individual marketing mix-based routines that transform available resources into valuable specialized outputs (e.g. Day 1994; Grant 1996; Vorhies and Morgan 2005), including specific activities pertaining to product management, pricing, marketing communications and distribution (Hunt and Morgan 1995), as well as selling and service delivery, in particular, within a B2B context.

Intermediate-order B2B marketing capabilities reflect processes that integrate multiple specialized capabilities and can occur at the individual, group, organizational or

Table 6.1   Taxonomy of B2B marketing capabilities: exemplar capabilities

	Individual	Group (e.g. Team or Function)	Organization (Firm)	Inter-organizational
Higher-Order [learning processes that involve resource reconfiguration and capability enhancement]	*Learning orientation* *Adaptive selling* *Process thinking*	*Channel transformation*	*Market sensing* *Organization learning* *Strategic flexibility* *Market orientation*	*Inter-organizational learning* *Benchmarking*
Intermediate [orchestrating, coordinating and organizing processes]	*Customization of customer value proposition* *Resolving customer complaints*	*Pricing* *Marketing communication* *Team selling*	*Product development* *Market planning* *Marketing strategy implementation* *CRM* *Customer service delivery*	*Channel management* *Supply chain management* *NPD alliances*
Lower-Order [specialized skills and activities]	*Call handling* *Relationship forging*	*Key account management*	*Marketing personnel recruitment and retention*	*Reverse logistics*

inter-organizational level. These capabilities are architectural in that they orchestrate multiple lower-order specialized capabilities and their associated resource inputs, and integrate them into a coherent whole (e.g. Galunic and Rodan 1998; Vorhies and Morgan 2005).

Higher-order B2B marketing capabilities reflect learning-based processes that span various lower-order and intermediate-order capabilities, involve changing and reconfiguring resources and capabilities to address dynamic environments, and can occur at the individual, group, organizational or inter-organizational level. These marketing capabilities reflect the processes by which firms learn about their market environment, integrate resource deployment activities to create new resources and use the knowledge and experience gained to acquire and upgrade their existing resources and capabilities (Eisenhardt and Martin 2000; Mengüc and Auh 2006). These capabilities therefore require an understanding of both the firm's lower- and intermediate-order routines and the shifting marketplace to eliminate resources and routines that have become unnecessary or inferior and to acquire, enhance or upgrade marketing capabilities and their associated resource inputs (Morgan et al. 2009b).

Table 6.1 reveals the two-dimensional, three-by-four categorization of our taxonomy of B2B marketing capabilities. In the next section, we use this taxonomy as a lens to review archetypical B2B marketing capabilities that have been identified and examined in the extant literature.

APPLYING THE TAXONOMY AS A LENS INTO B2B MARKETING CAPABILITIES

The literature on B2B marketing is extensive and has a long history. Conversely, the extant marketing capabilities literature has a much shorter history and is less rich. Therefore, it should come as no surprise that there has been little consideration of whether and how marketing capabilities differ between B2B and B2C firms. The widely cited distinctions between B2B and B2C firms and contexts suggest the potential for some differences. For example, the disparities between buying centers and consumers in terms of the number of people involved in purchase decisions and the level of expertise of decision-makers suggest that product management and selling may be relatively more important, and marketing communications less important, in B2B contexts. However, although the labels applied may sometimes differ (e.g. consumer insight vs. market research, product management vs. brand management), each of the marketing capabilities we identify is (or can be) valuable to both B2B and B2C firms. There is certainly no evidence to date to support the idea that B2B marketing capabilities fundamentally differ in some way from those of B2C companies. To the contrary, several studies in the general marketing literature have found that the same marketing capabilities are valuable in samples containing both B2B and B2C companies (e.g. Morgan et al. 2009a; Vorhies and Morgan 2005). Consequently, our focus on B2B marketing capabilities does not preclude the possibility of parity in their nature or value to B2C firms. To offer greater insight into the nature of specific B2B marketing capabilities we review some key exemplar skills,[1] activities and capabilities explored in the B2B marketing literature using the taxonomy as a lens, as Table 6.1 illustrates.

Lower-order, Individual-level Skills

This category within the taxonomy refers to the individual skills by which employees connect relevant resources with their own abilities to perform specific marketing tasks, such as a salesperson's ability to engage in *prospecting* or a customer service employee's *call-handling skills*. Relationships with customers are also facilitated by salespeople's *relationship-forging skills* through which they deploy specific resources, such as customer and market knowledge, with information technology to perform key sales tasks (e.g. Hunter and Perreault 2007). The nature of these individual-level skills makes it difficult to link them with higher-level organizational outcomes to calibrate their value. Most empirical studies examining such individual-level marketing skills link them with more causally adjacent outcomes, such as role performance, in the context of salespeople (e.g. Churchill et al. 1985).

Lower-order, Group-level Capabilities

Lower-order, group-level capabilities draw together individual-level skills and allied resources to perform specific marketing tasks by groups or departments that pertain to their organizational goals and responsibilities. For example, in selling to B2B customers, firms often use teams of salespeople. Research in B2B contexts indicates that the ability of such sales teams to perform specific selling tasks, such as prospecting and trust building with prospects, can have a positive impact on customer-level and, ultimately, firm performance (e.g. Jones et al. 2005; Workman et al. 2003).

Lower-order, Organizational-level Capabilities

Lower-order, organizational-level capabilities reflect the organization's ability to perform specific marketing tasks related to its goals. This typically involves integrating knowledge and skills across different functional subunits, such as marketing, sales and human resources, making them cross-functional in nature. Two examples of such single-task capabilities that have been examined in the B2B marketing literature are the firm's ability to retain salespeople as an important source of both cost saving and revenue generation (e.g. Chandrashekaran et al. 2000; Darmon 1990) and the firm's ability to design and operate effective sales force compensation systems (e.g. John and Weitz 1989; Joseph and Kalwani 1998).

Lower-order, Inter-organizational-level Capabilities

Lower-order, inter-organizational-level capabilities reflect the ability to integrate knowledge and skills across organizational boundaries to perform specific marketing tasks related to the organization's goals. One exemplar of such single-task marketing capabilities that span organizations within the firm's value chain and speaks directly to B2B firms is Autry's (2005) depiction of a reverse-logistics capability. Reverse logistics refers to a firm's ability to design and organize the specific mechanisms by which channel members can collect and return products to the manufacturer.

Intermediate, Individual-level Skills

Intermediate, individual-level skills reflect the ability of individual employees to effectively engage in more complex integrative marketing activities that involve the orchestration of multiple lower-level tasks and their associated resource inputs. One example is the ability of an individual service employee to resolve a customer complaint or create a customized value offering for a particular customer by coordinating his or her own customer-relating behavior and service-delivery skills with the resources available in the organization (e.g. Gwinner et al. 2005).

Intermediate, Group-level Capabilities

Carried out by specific groups or departments, intermediate, group-level capabilities draw together individual-level skills and available resources to perform more complex integrative marketing activities. We focus here on the sales and marketing functions as key groups within the firm and identify three intermediate marketing capabilities that have received particular attention within the B2B literature.

Pricing capability reflects the ability to set and realize prices to maximize both short- and long-term goals (e.g. Dutta et al. 2003). The ability to manage pricing effectively is a critical marketing capability (e.g. Dolan and Simon 1996). A strong pricing capability requires knowledge about the impact of price on customer value perceptions (e.g.

Davey et al. 1998) and competitors' current and planned pricing strategies (Blattberg and Wisniewski 1989). This knowledge is then shared across individuals within the marketing function and used to develop appropriate pricing strategies and effectively execute and communicate pricing changes when required (Marn and Rosiello 1992).

Marketing communications capability refers to the effectiveness and efficiency with which the marketing group creates desired message reception among target customers, suppliers and prospects (Vorhies and Morgan 2005). This is an essential marketing capability associated with customer value delivery (e.g. Akdeniz et al. 2010; McKee et al. 1992) and superior customer loyalty (Scheer et al. 2010) in B2B markets. Such communications capabilities are typically built on fundamental lower-level marketing capabilities, such as advertising and public relations (e.g. Vorhies and Morgan 2005).

Selling capability reflects the sales function's ability to acquire and fulfill customer orders (e.g. McKee et al. 1992). It involves the integration of individual-level selling skills and knowledge, such as prospecting and customer-specific insight (Szymanski 1988), with structural and processing procedures, such as a sales management system to recruit and retain skilled sales personnel (e.g. Vorhies and Morgan 2005), into a coherent whole. Strong selling capabilities in B2B markets may enhance not only supplier performance but also the channel partner's sales revenue performance (Akdeniz et al. 2010).

Intermediate, Organizational-level Capabilities

Prior literature has identified several intermediate, organizational-level capabilities that reflect an organization's ability to perform more complex, integrative marketing activities. Integration and coordination across functions is critical for these capabilities because the orchestration of multiple lower-level tasks and their resource inputs necessarily occurs across functions. Several capabilities of this type have been linked with stronger performance. We highlight five specific marketing capabilities.

A *product development and management capability* refers to the process of designing, developing and managing product or service offerings to satisfy customer needs (e.g. Greenley and Oktemgil 1997). This involves the integration of various lower-level skills and functional capabilities to create and manage revenue-producing products and services (e.g. Helfat and Raubitschek 2000). For example, producing valuable and appealing product offerings requires effective routines across the organization for designing product concepts (Adler et al. 1996), manufacturing the product or service offerings to closely fit customer needs, and launching and subsequently managing the product with the appropriate marketing mix. This capability therefore requires cross-functional teams that integrate skills and resources across levels of the organizational hierarchy (Salvato 2009). A product development and management capability generates positional advantages in general (e.g. Moorman and Slotegraaf 1999; Salvato 2009) as well as specifically in B2B contexts (Morgan et al. 2004).

A *marketing planning capability* reflects a firm's ability to generate and select among alternative courses of appropriate marketing actions (e.g. Slotegraaf and Dickson 2004). This involves integrating lower-order capabilities, such as customer need identification and competitive intelligence, along with their needed resource inputs. A marketing planning capability also includes the ability to segment markets (e.g. Vorhies and Morgan 2003) and to identify attractive market targets and appealing value propositions that will enable the organization to achieve its strategic objectives (e.g. Narver and Slater 1990). Because many of these planning activities require interfunctional interaction and resource inputs from other parts of the organization, marketing planning is an organizational- rather than group-level capability (Piercy and Morgan 1994). Research shows that firms with strong marketing planning capabilities can attain higher firm performance than the competition (Vorhies and Morgan 2005); yet very strong marketing planning capabilities can also form organizational rigidities that hinder performance (Slotegraaf and Dickson 2004).

Marketing strategy implementation capability reflects a firm's ability to enact its marketing strategy decisions (e.g. Day and Wensley 1988; Vorhies and Morgan 2005). This capability includes the ability to develop appropriate organizational designs (e.g. Vorhies and Morgan 2003; Walker and Ruekert 1987), acquire and allocate required resources from multiple sources inside the organization (e.g. Bonoma and Crittenden 1988) and monitor internal and marketplace progress (e.g. Jaworski 1988) to enable intended marketing strategies to be quickly and efficiently translated into consistent goal-directed action outcomes (e.g. Bonoma 1985). Needed resources (e.g. budgets, people, technology) and lower-level capabilities (e.g. compensation system design, hiring and training needed personnel, product and service delivery, accounting returns) for a marketing implementation capability are frequently cross-functional (Morgan et al. 2003).

A *CRM capability* reflects a firm's ability to establish and maintain beneficial relationships with target customers (e.g. Morgan et al. 2009a; Srivastava et al. 1999). Managing and nurturing relationships with customers and sales prospects is broadly recognized as an important capability in determining and sustaining firm performance (e.g. Day 2000; Verhoef 2003). For example, B2B firms with strong customer relationships can attain specific positional advantages (e.g. Bolton et al. 2008) and greater service responsiveness and innovativeness (e.g. Theoharakis et al. 2009).

A *customer service delivery capability* reflects a firm's ability to ensure that customers are satisfied with the delivery of services offered by the firm (Kordupleski et al. 1993). It involves integration of resources and lower-order capabilities related to the design and delivery of goods and services to the customer (Moorman and Rust 1999). From a marketing perspective, the connection between the customer and the firm is generally a frontline employee, whether a salesperson or customer service representative. However, to develop a strong customer service delivery capability, firms must integrate capabilities across marketing, operations and human resources functions or departments (Moorman and Rust 1999).

Intermediate, Inter-organizational-level Capabilities

Intermediate, inter-organizational-level capabilities reflect the ability to perform more complex integrative marketing activities that span organizations within the value chain and involve the orchestration of multiple lower-level tasks and their associated resource inputs. In general, a firm's inter-organizational cooperative capabilities refer to the processes by which the firm identifies, selects, initiates, maintains and leverages relationships with other organizations (e.g. Dyer and Singh 1998; Wucherer 2006) and have been linked with firm value. For example, Swaminathan and Moorman (2009) find that a firm's marketing alliance capability elevates value creation when the firm announces a new marketing alliance. Likewise, Theoharakis et al. (2009) report a strong relationship between B2B firms' strategic partnering capability and their innovativeness.

From a marketing perspective, intermediate, inter-organizational capabilities have most often been viewed within a channel context. For example, a firm's *channel management capability* reflects the ability to identify appropriate channels and to establish, maintain and leverage relationships with attractive channel partners (e.g. Vorhies and Morgan 2005). This involves activities that cross organizational boundaries, such as supporting channel member efforts and developing and maintaining mutually beneficial relationships (e.g. Anderson and Narus 1990; Buchanan 1992). Theoretically, the integration of resources, specific investments and governance mechanisms across organizational boundaries may elevate the firms' positional advantages (Ghosh and John 1999). Because channel members perform significant value-added activities in B2B markets (e.g. Bucklin et al. 1996), the ability to manage channel relationships has long been viewed as an important capability (e.g. Weitz and Jap 1995).

Another key intermediate, inter-organizational capability is a firm's *supply chain management capability*. This reflects the ability to build and maintain relationships with suppliers for necessary resource inputs and to coordinate and integrate these inputs to enable the design and delivery of the firm's value offering to target customers (e.g. Moller and Torronen 2003; Tracey et al. 2005). It involves integrating multiple specific capabilities and their associated resource inputs spanning different organizations in the firm's value chain, across procurement, purchasing, inbound transportation of components, materials warehousing, inventory control and outbound delivery scheduling (e.g. Tan 2001). Although this is a relatively new capability conceptualization in the literature, some evidence suggests that this capability can be linked with firm performance outcomes in B2B firms (e.g. Tracey et al. 2005).

More recently, the B2B marketing literature has also begun exploring how other capabilities associated with marketing that were typically viewed as within-firm capabilities may be affected when firms undertake them across different organizations in the value chain. For example, a *dispersed product development capability* refers to the cooperative development of new products, technologies or services and involves the ability to coordinate and manage activities and inputs in the development processes that span two or more firms. Perks (2005) describes how firms' inter-organizational abilities to collectively specify and synchronize development activities drive collaborative cross-firm new product development efforts.

Higher-order, Individual-level Skills

The capacity for individual employees to learn distinguishes the dynamic nature of these higher-order, individual-level skills. Such learning involves changing the individual-level resources available for deployment (for example, an employee gaining new knowledge) and enhancing the individual's lower- and intermediate-level skills through which these new resources can be deployed. One example of this type of skill is an individual salesperson's *learning orientation* (e.g. Kohli et al. 1998). A salesperson's learning orientation involves the development of knowledge and skills needed to experiment with new sales approaches and the willingness to change sales strategies to improve selling skills (Sujan et al. 1994). A similar example is *adaptive selling* skills, which reflect a salesperson's ability to alter his or her sales behavior during or across customer interactions according to perceived information about the nature of the situation (Weitz 1981; Weitz et al. 1986). Such adaptive selling skills can enhance individual salespeople's long-term selling effectiveness (Spiro and Weitz 1990).

Outside the sales context, such individual-level learning capabilities have generally not been given a great amount of attention in either the B2B or the general marketing literature. However, this does not necessarily suggest that such individual-level marketing skills are not important. Indeed, Dickson and colleagues (2009) identify an individual employee's *process thinking skills* as a capability that is critical for a firm to be able to develop other capabilities and is fundamental to understanding firm performance over time. At a broad level, these higher-order process thinking skills involve the ability to produce, reproduce and select the specific processes necessary for the situation (Dickson 2003). More specifically, this capability involves the integration of lower-level skills, such as those related to creative thinking, improvisation and the deployment of people and technology (Dickson et al. 2009).

Higher-order, Group-level Capabilities

Higher-order, group-level capabilities reflect the abilities of groups to learn and therefore change the processes, resources and lower- and intermediate-level routines and capabilities necessary to perform required tasks. This type of capability has received little attention in either the general or the B2B marketing literature; however, there has been some recent attention to one such capability – namely a firm's *channel transformation capability*. This pertains to the channel subunit's ability to learn about and resolve the sources of conflict with channel partners (Chang and Gotcher 2010) and to evolve its channel design and management systems to reflect changes in technology and customer needs (Wilson and Daniel 2007). This capability has been linked with performance in B2B contexts. For example, Chang and Gotcher (2010) report a strong relationship between channel conflict learning and the quality of joint firm–channel partner marketing strategies, which in turn affect the joint profit performance of the supplier firm and its channel partner.

Higher-order, Organizational-level Capabilities

Higher-order, organizational-level capabilities reflect the firm's ability to learn about its environment, reconfigure its resources and enhance its lower- and intermediate-level capabilities to meet marketplace needs. Any type of marketing capability may be more or less dynamic regarding the degree to which it is responsive to changes in the environment. However, the higher-order capabilities on which we focus are a distinct separable category of higher-order learning capabilities. In marketing, much of the *market orientation* research stream can be viewed as one form of such a higher-order learning capability.[2] Other specific higher-order, organizational-level capabilities have also been identified in the general and B2B marketing literature.

Market sensing capability reflects an organization's ability to acquire, interpret and use information regarding customers, competitors, channel members and the broader market environment (e.g. Day 1994; Sinkula 1994; Slater and Narver 1995). Moorman (1995) demonstrates that firms vary in the degree to which such market information is acquired and used, and that product outcomes vary depending on the information-processing and cultural factors present in the organization. Similarly, Johnson et al. (2004) find that a sensing capability affects B2B firms' ability to engage in successful relationships with customers. A market sensing capability also increases marketing strategy creativity and timeliness, leading to higher customer-based performance in B2B firms (Neill et al. 2007).

Organizational learning reflects an organization's ability to acquire, process, retrieve and store new knowledge (Fiol and Lyles 1985; Slater and Narver 1995). This is a more generalized capability than market sensing, in which sensing focuses on the market environment and learning reflects a firm's ability to learn in any domain. Furthermore, Grewal and Tansuhaj (2001) show that *strategic flexibility*, or a firm's ability to learn about and respond to economic and political risks, can help firm performance following an economic crisis. Day (1994) and March (1991) suggest that such learning is remembered through changes in the firm's organizational routines and procedures. This suggests that firms use the new knowledge generated by an organizational learning capability in ways that are consistent with our definition of dynamic capabilities.

Higher-order, Inter-organizational-level Capabilities

Higher-order, inter-organizational-level capabilities reflect an organization's ability to learn, modify and reconfigure firm-specific and inter-firm resources (e.g. knowledge), routines and lower-order capabilities. In general, the literature has tended to focus on cross-organization relationship-based capabilities (e.g. Anderson and Narus 1990; Wucherer 2006) rather than the higher-order ability to learn from such relationships. An exception is research examining *inter-organizational learning*. For example, Selnes and Sallis (2003) show that relational learning (i.e. organizational learning within a buyer–supplier relationship context) positively affects relationship performance. Emerging work from a supply chain perspective has also begun to adopt such a cross-organizational learning perspective. For example, organizational learning within supply chains can have a positive impact on both supply chain capabilities and business unit performance within a supply chain (e.g. Hult et al. 2007; Hult et al. 2003).

A ROADMAP FOR MANAGERS

Examining the literature through the lens of our typology reveals many capabilities that are crucial for B2B firms. Because evidence connecting firm-level marketing capabilities with superior firm performance is relatively sparse, it remains difficult to answer managerial questions regarding the return on investments made in different marketing capabilities. However, our typology and brief literature review provide B2B managers with a new way to organize their thinking about B2B marketing capabilities. In particular, managers are frequently asked to enhance their firms' marketing capabilities or develop 'world-class' marketing processes. However, few managers have a clear idea of what marketing capabilities actually are or how to begin developing them. We provide a clear framework for identifying marketing capabilities and show how the development of different capabilities requires the coordination of various resources, skills and routines. Moreover, developing specific firm-level marketing capabilities that are often touted (e.g. CRM capabilities, product development capabilities) is complicated, requiring the coordination of multiple group-level capabilities (subprocesses) that in turn draw on individual-level skills and activities.

As a result, managers can use our framework as a tool to map out their firms' marketing capabilities. For example, the typology can be used in focus-group discussions with managers and employees (in marketing and other functions) to identify specific resources, skills and capabilities that specific individuals, groups or teams possess. Managers can then develop detailed maps of how best to deploy these resources and capabilities to enhance or even develop specific firm-level or inter-organizational capabilities, by tracing its component group-level subprocesses, and the individual-level skills, activities and routines that contribute to each of these subprocesses. After each of the firm's marketing capabilities have been mapped, managers can develop a self-assessment audit tool, tapping managers and employees from marketing and other functions to gauge the firm's existing proficiency in each marketing capability. Such audit tools commonly use internal surveys or focus-group discussions, asking questions on perceived strengths and weaknesses in each specific lower-level activity and intermediate- and higher-level marketing process.

Marketing capability audits are an essential precursor to enhancing a firm's marketing capabilities. They provide a clear identification of areas of capability weakness, offering a starting point toward creating a marketing capability improvement plan. Such marketing capability improvement plans may include individual-level education and training, group-level process redesign and training, experimentation with new marketing activity coordination and management systems, and even the formation of benchmarking consortia with other firms to identify world-class benchmark sites from which to learn.

FUTURE RESEARCH

Our typology reinforces certain marketing capabilities that have been most extensively studied in the B2B literature and draws attention to the capabilities that have garnered less consideration but are crucial for B2B performance. In this regard, our typology-focused literature review offers the following four directions for future empirical research:

1. Examination of individual-level marketing capabilities in the extant B2B literature focuses almost exclusively on salespeople, with some emerging consideration of customer service personnel. Although the focus on salespeople may be appropriate given the relative importance of selling in B2B markets, evidence shows that salespeople may not share the same characteristics as other types of marketing employees (e.g. Homburg and Jensen 2007). As a result, there are few insights into the types, nature and performance consequences of the individual-level, task-related skills of other marketing employees, such as product managers, channel managers, CMOs and marketing planners.

2. With respect to group-level capabilities, most of the attention in the B2B literature focuses on either selling or new product development teams. This leaves much to be discovered about the nature and importance of many other group-level B2B marketing capabilities. For example, little or no insight exists regarding group-level marketing capabilities that are important in determining the effectiveness and efficiency of marketing planning teams or customer service teams.

3. Most of the existing work on higher-order marketing capabilities is purely conceptual in nature and involves identifying the need for resource reconfiguration and capability enhancement (for example, determining the need for stronger market sensing or organizational learning). Although firms may seek competitive benchmarking as a path for these processes, little research has focused on the nature and consequences of different approaches to resource reconfiguration and capability enhancement.

4. The inter-organizational level of analysis has been an area of growing interest. Much of the extant work in this area has adopted either a dyadic focus in terms of specific individual partners or a general 'cross-organization' framing covering all potential external partners. Yet, despite a long history of the study of networks in B2B markets and the many claims that B2B competition is increasingly taking place between supply networks, there have been few network-level studies and thus little evidence of such network-level processes regarding inter-organizational marketing capabilities.

In addition to these four domains, our typology reveals a need for further conceptual research. First, surprisingly little attention has been given to the question of whether, how and why marketing capabilities may be different for B2B versus B2C firms. While much attention has been paid to the distinctive nature of B2B markets, the marketing capabilities research stream has not been grounded in such differences. In addition, answers to these questions from a marketing capabilities perspective may not necessarily be intuitive. For example, classic distinctions between B2C and B2B customers emphasize the more rational nature of B2B buying behavior. This suggests that brand management capabilities, for example, should not be important drivers of B2B firm performance. Yet some evidence suggests that B2B customers are influenced by supplier brand image, and four of the world's five most valuable brands (IBM, Microsoft, General Electric and Nokia) are primarily B2B (e.g. Kotler and Pfoertsch 2007; Van Riel et al. 2005). Thus, brand management capabilities (reflecting an intermediate, organization-level capability) may also be valuable in B2B contexts.

Second, the extant literature offers surprisingly little insight into the relative value of different marketing capabilities. Vorhies and Morgan (2005) find evidence that each of the specialized and architectural marketing capabilities they examine positively covaries and that this covariance is valuable in enhancing firm performance. Other research also reinforces the importance of interconnectedness or complementarities in resources and capabilities (Dierickx and Cool 1989; Grewal and Slotegraaf 2007; Moorman and Slotegraaf 1999), illustrating the value that strength in multiple related capabilities can have on firm performance. Thus research generally suggests that in their capability development and enhancement efforts, firms should not try to achieve a particularly strong capability in one area and neglect others. Yet caution is needed regarding the focal capabilities selected. For example, Morgan et al. (2009a) find that different cross-functional marketing capabilities can have directionally different effects on the underlying components of profit growth. Thus further research is clearly needed to establish the relative value of different individual and combinations of marketing capabilities on different dimensions of firm performance in B2B firms.

Third, dynamic capabilities theory posits that the primary source of sustainable competitive advantage of any B2B firm should lie in its higher-order, organizational-level capabilities.[3] Thus, B2B firms need to develop both *capability-broadening* processes to acquire or develop new capabilities, and *capability-deepening* processes that enhance capabilities already possessed (Argyres 1996). Thus a firm's ability to 'learn how to learn' is likely to be the ultimate source of long-term superior performance in dynamic market environments (Dickson 1992). Although organizational learning approaches to marketing capability improvement through benchmarking offer some direction (Day 1994; Vorhies and Morgan 2005), extant conceptual developments are limited, and there is little empirical understanding of such learning-to-learn marketing capabilities. Given the importance of these capabilities in enabling B2B firms to uncover and respond to changes in their environment, it is likely that marketing capabilities will have a key role in B2B firms' ability to learn how to learn. Future research in this area therefore offers a rich opportunity to link marketing capabilities with the ultimate source of competitive advantage and to potentially elevate the role of marketing in B2B firms.

CONCLUSION

Marketing capabilities are clearly an area of growing interest among B2B marketing managers and scholars, but they remain relatively undeveloped. By revealing that various fundamental building blocks exist for different marketing capabilities, we offer a new typology for understanding and road mapping the processes that build different B2B marketing capabilities. Applying this taxonomy as a theoretical lens to the extant B2B marketing literature suggests several areas for theoretically interesting and managerially relevant future research. Overall, studying the effects of various marketing capabilities on performance outcomes, especially the outcomes that are of the utmost importance to upper management, provides a promising arena for calibrating and verifying the value of marketing in B2B firms.

NOTES

1. In keeping with the extant theoretical literature, we use the term 'skills' to denote individual-level capabilities.
2. Both information-processing and cultural market orientation approaches theoretically view understanding and using the firm's resources to respond to the market environment as the core of market orientation.
3. Although inter-organizational resource sharing approaches can increase the resources available to a firm, the associated capabilities may be less embedded in the firm, limiting their value.

REFERENCES

Adler, Paul S., Avi Mandelbaum, Vien Nguyen and Elizabeth Schwerer (1996), 'Getting the most out of your product development process', *Harvard Business Review*, (March–April), 134–52.

Akdeniz, M. Billur, Tracy Gonzalez-Padron and Roger J. Calantone (2010), 'An integrated marketing capability benchmarking approach to dealer performance through parametric and nonparametric analyses', *Industrial Marketing Management*, **39** (1), 150–60.

Anderson, James C. and James A. Narus (1990), 'A model of distributor firm and manufacturer firm working partnerships', *Journal of Marketing*, **54** (1), 42–58.

Argyres, Nicholas (1996), 'Evidence on the role of firm capabilities in vertical integration decisions', *Strategic Management Journal*, **17** (2), 129–50.

Autry, Chad W. (2005), 'Formalization of reverse logistics programs: a strategy for managing liberalized returns', *Industrial Marketing Management*, **34** (7), 749–57.

Barney, Jay (1991), 'Firm resources and sustained competitive advantage', *Journal of Management*, **17** (1), 99–120.

Blattberg, Robert C. and Kenneth J. Wisniewski (1989), 'Price-induced patterns of competition', *Marketing Science*, **8** (Fall), 291–309.

Bolton, Ruth N., Katherine Lemon and Peter C. Verhoef (2008), 'Expanding business-to-business customer relationships: modeling the customer's upgrade decision', *Journal of Marketing*, **72** (1), 46–64.

Bonoma, Thomas V. (1985), *The Marketing Edge: Making Strategies Work*, New York: The Free Press.

Bonoma, Thomas V. and Victoria L. Crittenden (1988), 'Managing marketing implementation', *Sloan Management Review*, **29** (Winter), 7–14.

Buchanan, Lauranne (1992), 'Vertical trade relationships: the role of dependence and symmetry in attaining organizational goals', *Journal of Marketing Research*, **29** (1), 65–75.

Bucklin, Christine B., Stephen P. DeFalco, John R. DeVincentis and John P. Levis (1996), 'Are you tough enough to manage your channels?', *McKinsey Quarterly*, **1**, 104–14.

Chandrashekaran, Murali, Kevin McNeilly, Frederick A. Russ and Detelina Marinova (2000), 'From uncertain intentions to actual behaviors: a threshold model of whether and when salespeople quit', *Journal of Marketing Research*, **37** (4), 463–79.

Chang, Kuo-Hsiung and Donald F. Gotcher (2010), 'Conflict-coordination learning in marketing channel relationships: the distributor view', *Industrial Marketing Management*, **39** (2), 287–97.

Churchill, Gilbert A., Neil M. Ford, Steven W. Hartley and Orville C. Walker (1985), 'The determinants of salesperson performance: a meta-analysis', *Journal of Marketing Research*, **22** (2), 103–18.

Constantin, James A. and Robert F. Lusch (1994), *Understanding Resource Management*, Oxford, OH: The Planning Forum.

Dacin, M. Tina, Marc J. Ventresca and Brent D. Beal (1999), 'The embeddedness of organizations: dialogue and directions', *Journal of Management*, **25** (3), 317–56.

Darmon, René Y. (1990), 'Identifying sources of turnover costs: a segmental approach', *Journal of Marketing*, **54** (2), 46–56.

Davey, K.K.S., Andy Childs and Stephen J. Carlotti (1998), 'Why your price band is wider than it should be', *McKinsey Quarterly*, **3**, 116–27.

Day, George S. (1994), 'The capabilities of market-driven organizations', *Journal of Marketing*, **58** (4), 37–52.

Day, George S. (2000), 'Managing market relationships', *Journal of the Academy of Marketing Science*, **28** (1), 24–30.

Day, George S. and Robin Wensley (1988), 'Assessing advantage: a framework for diagnosing competitive superiority', *Journal of Marketing*, **52** (2), 1–20.

Dickson, Peter R. (1992), 'Toward a general theory of competitive rationality', *Journal of Marketing*, **56** (1), 69–83.

Dickson, Peter R. (2003), 'The pigeon breeders' cup: a selection on selection theory of economic evolution', *Journal of Evolutionary Economics*, **13** (3), 259–80.

Dickson, Peter R., Walfried M. Lassar, Gary Hunter and Samit Chakravorti (2009), 'The pursuit of excellence in process thinking and customer relationship management', *Journal of Personal Selling & Sales Management*, **46** (2), 653–68.

Dierickx, Ingemar and Karel Cool (1989), 'Asset stock accumulation and sustainability of competitive advantage', *Management Science*, **35** (12), 1504–15.

Dolan, Robert J. and Hermann Simon (1996), *Power Pricing: How Managing Price Transforms the Bottom Line*, New York: The Free Press.

Dutta, Shantanu, Om Narasimhan and Surendra Rajiv (1999), 'Success in high-technology markets: is marketing capability critical?', *Marketing Science*, **18** (4), 547–68.

Dutta, Shantanu, Mark J. Zbaracki and Mark Bergen (2003), 'Pricing process as a capability: a resource-based perspective', *Strategic Management Journal*, **24** (7), 615–30.

Dyer, Jeffrey H. and Harbir Singh (1998), 'The relational view: cooperative strategy and sources of interorganizational competitive advantage', *Academy of Management Review*, **23** (4), 660–79.

Eisenhardt, Kathleen M. and Jeffrey A. Martin (2000), 'Dynamic capabilities: what are they?' *Strategic Management Journal*, **21**, 1105–21.

Fiol, C. Marlene and Marjorie A. Lyles (1985), 'Organizational Learning', *Academy of Management Review*, **10** (4), 803–13.

Frazier, Gary L., Elliot Maltz, Kersi D. Antia and Aric Rindfleisch (2009), 'Distributor sharing of strategic information with suppliers', *Journal of Marketing*, **73** (4), 31–43.

Galunic, D. Charles and Simon Rodan (1998), 'Resource recombination in the firm: knowledge structures and the potential for Schumpeterian innovation', *Strategic Management Journal*, **19** (12), 1193–201.

Ghosh, Mrinal and George John (1999), 'Governance value analysis and marketing strategy', *Journal of Marketing*, **63** (Special Issue), 131–45.

Grant, Robert M. (1991), 'The resource-based theory of competitive advantage: implications for strategy formulation', *California Management Review*, **33** (Spring), 114–35.

Grant, Robert M. (1996), 'Prospering in dynamically-competitive environments: organizational capability as knowledge integration', *Organizational Science*, **7** (July–August), 375–87.

Greenley, Gordon and Mehmet Oktemgil (1997), 'An investigation of modulator effects on alignment skill', *Journal of Business Research*, **39** (2), 93–105.

Grewal, Rajdeep and Rebecca J. Slotegraaf (2007), 'Embeddedness of organizational capabilities', *Decision Sciences*, **38** (3), 451–88.

Grewal, Rajdeep and Patriya Tansuhaj (2001), 'Building organizational capabilities for managing economic crisis: the role of market orientation and strategic flexibility', *Journal of Marketing*, **65** (2), 67–80.

Gwinner, Kevin P., Mary Jo Bittner, Stephen W. Brown and Ajith Kumar (2005), 'Service customization through employee adaptiveness', *Journal of Services Research*, **8** (2), 131–48.

Helfat, Constance E. and Ruth S. Raubitschek (2000), 'Product sequencing: co-evolution of knowledge, capabilities and products', *Strategic Management Journal*, **21** (10–11), 961–79.

Homburg, Christian and Ove Jensen (2007), 'The thought worlds of marketing and sales: which differences make a difference?', *Journal of Marketing*, **71** (July), 124–42.

Hult, G. Tomas M., David J. Ketchen and Mathias Arrfelt (2007), 'Strategic supply chain management: improving performance through a culture of competitiveness and knowledge development', *Strategic Management Journal*, **28** (10), 1035–52.

Hult, G. Tomas M., David J. Ketchen and Ernest L. Nichols (2003), 'Organizational learning as a strategic resource in supply management', *Journal of Operations Management*, **21** (5), 541–56.

Hunt, Shelby and Robert M. Morgan (1995), 'The comparative advantage theory of competition', *Journal of Marketing*, **59** (2), 1–15.

Hunter, Gary and William D. Perreault (2007), 'Making sales technology effective', *Journal of Marketing*, **71** (1), 16–34.

Jaworski, Bernard J. (1988), 'Toward a theory of marketing control: environmental context, control types, and consequences', *Journal of Marketing*, **52** (3), 23–9.

John, George and Barton Weitz (1989), 'Salesforce compensation: an empirical investigation of factors related to use of salary versus incentive compensation', *Journal of Marketing Research*, **26** (1), 1–14.

Johnson, Jean L., Ravipreet S. Sohi and Rajdeep Grewal (2004), 'The role of relational knowledge stores in interfirm partnering', *Journal of Marketing*, **68** (July), 21–36.

Jones, Eli, Andrea L. Dickson, Lawrence B. Chonko and Joseph P. Cannon (2005), 'Key accounts and team selling: a review, framework, and research agenda', *Journal of Personal Selling & Sales Management*, **25** (2), 182–98.

Joseph, Kissan and Manohar U. Kalwani (1998), 'The role of bonus pay in salesforce compensation plans', *Industrial Marketing Management*, **27** (2), 147–59.

Kohli, Ajay K., Tasadduq A. Shervani and Goutam N. Challagalla (1998), 'Learning and performance orientation of salespeople: the role of supervisors', *Journal of Marketing Research*, **35** (May), 263–74.

Kordupleski, Raymond, Roland T. Rust and Anthony J. Zahorik (1993), 'Why improving quality doesn't improve quality', *California Management Review*, **35** (Spring), 82–95.

Kotler, Philip and Waldemar Pfoertsch (2007), 'Being known or being one of many: the need for brand management for business-to-business (B2B) companies', *Journal of Business & Industrial Marketing*, **22** (6), 357–62.

Krasnikov, Alexander and Satish Jayachandran (2008), 'The relative impact of marketing, research-and-development, and operations capabilities on firm performance', *Journal of Marketing*, **72** (4), 1–11.

Krasnikov, Alexander, Satish Jayachandran and V. Kumar (2010), 'The impact of customer relationship management implementation on cost and profit efficiencies: evidence from the US commercial banking industry', *Journal of Marketing*, **73** (6), 61–76.

Leonard-Barton, Dorothy (1992), 'Core capabilities and core rigidities: a paradox in managing new product development', *Strategic Management Journal*, **13** (Summer), 111–25.

March, James G. (1991), 'Exploration and exploitation in organizational learning', *Organization Science*, **2** (1), 71–87.

Marn, Michael and Robert Rosiello (1992), 'Managing price, gaining profit', *Harvard Business Review*, (September–October), 84–94.

McKee, Daryl O., Jeffery S. Conant, P. Rajan Varadarajan and Michael P. Mokwa (1992), 'Success-producer and failure-preventer marketing skills: a social learning theory interpretation', *Journal of the Academy of Marketing Science*, **20** (1), 17–26.

Mengüç, Bülent and Seigyoung Auh (2006), 'Creating a firm-level dynamic capability through capitalizing on market orientation and innovativeness', *Journal of the Academy of Marketing Science*, **34** (1), 63–73.

Milgrom, Paul and John Roberts (1995), 'Complementarities and fit: strategy, structure, and organizational change in manufacturing', *Journal of Accounting and Economics*, **19** (2–3), 179–208.

Moller, K.E. Kristian and Pekka Torronen (2003), 'Business suppliers' value creation potential: a capability-based analysis', *Industrial Marketing Management*, **32** (2), 109–18.

Moorman, Christine (1995), 'Organizational market information processes: cultural antecedents and new product outcomes', *Journal of Marketing Research*, **32** (3), 318–35.

Moorman, Christine and Roland T. Rust (1999), 'The role of marketing', *Journal of Marketing*, **63** (Special Issue), 180–97.

Moorman, Christine and Rebecca J. Slotegraaf (1999), 'The contingency value of complementary capabilities in product development', *Journal of Marketing Research*, **36** (May), 239–57.

Morgan, Neil A., Anna Kaleka and Constantine S. Katsikeas (2004), 'Antecedents of export venture performance: a theoretical model and empirical assessment', *Journal of Marketing*, **68** (1), 90–108.

Morgan, Neil A., Rebecca J. Slotegraaf and Douglas W. Vorhies (2009a), 'Linking marketing capabilities with profit growth', *International Journal of Research in Marketing*, **26** (4), 284–93.

Morgan, Neil A., Douglas W. Vorhies and Charlotte H. Mason (2009b), 'Market orientation, marketing capabilities, and firm performance', *Strategic Management Journal*, **30** (8), 909–20.

Morgan, Neil A., Shaoming Zou, Douglas W. Vorhies and Constantine S. Katsikeas (2003), 'Experiential and informational knowledge, architectural marketing capabilities, and the adaptive performance of export ventures', *Decision Sciences*, **34** (2), 287–321.

Narver, John C. and Stanley F. Slater (1990), 'The effect of a market orientation on business profitability', *Journal of Marketing*, **54** (4), 20–35.

Neill, Stern, Daryl McKee and Gregory M. Rose (2007), 'Developing the organization's sensemaking capability: precursor to an adaptive strategic marketing response', *Industrial Marketing Management*, **36** (6), 731–44.

Nelson, Richard R. and Sidney G. Winter (1982), *An Evolutionary Theory of Economic Change*, Cambridge, MA: Harvard University Press.

Perks, Helen (2005), 'Specifying and synchronizing partner activities in the dispersed product development process', *Industrial Marketing Management*, **34** (1), 85–95.

Piercy, Nigel F. and Neil A. Morgan (1994), 'The marketing planning process: behavioral problems compared to analytical techniques in predicting plan credibility', *Journal of Business Research*, **29** (3), 167–79.

Porter, Michael E. (1996), 'What is strategy?', *Harvard Business Review*, (November–December), 2–19.

Reed, Richard and Robert J. DeFillippi (1990), 'Causal ambiguity, barriers to imitation, and sustainable competitive advantage', *Academy of Management Review*, **15** (1), 88–102.

Rindfleisch, Aric and Christine Moorman (2001), 'The acquisition and utilization of information in new product alliances: a strength-of-ties perspective', *Journal of Marketing*, **65** (2), 1–18.

Salvato, Carlo (2009), 'Capabilities unveiled: the role of ordinary activities in the evolution of product development processes', *Organization Science*, **20** (2), 384–409.

Scheer, Lisa K., C. Fred Miao and Jason Garrett (2010), 'The effects of supplier capabilities on industrial customers' loyalty: the role of dependence', *Journal of the Academy of Marketing Science*, **38** (1), 90–104.

Selnes, Fred and James Sallis (2003), 'Promoting relationship learning', *Journal of Marketing*, **67** (3), 80–95.

Sinkula, James M. (1994), 'Market information processing and organizational learning', *Journal of Marketing*, **58** (1), 35–45.

Slater, Stanley F. and James C. Narver (1995), 'Market orientation and the learning organization', *Journal of Marketing*, **59** (3), 63–74.

Slotegraaf, Rebecca J. and Peter R. Dickson (2004), 'The paradox of a marketing planning capability', *Journal of the Academy of Marketing Science*, **32** (4), 371–85.

Spiro, Rosann L. and Barton A. Weitz (1990), 'Adaptive selling: conceptualization, measurement, and nomological validity', *Journal of Marketing Research*, **27** (1), 61–9.

Srivastava, Rajendra K., Tasadduq A. Shervani and Liam Fahey (1998), 'Market-based assets and shareholder value: a framework for analysis', *Journal of Marketing*, **62** (1), 2–18.

Srivastava, Rajendra K., Tasadduq A. Shervani and Liam Fahey (1999), 'Marketing, business processes, and shareholder value: an organizationally embedded view of marketing activities and the discipline of marketing', *Journal of Marketing*, **63** (Special Issue), 168–79.

Sujan, Harish, Barton A. Weitz and Nirmalya Kumar (1994), 'Learning orientation, working smart, and effective selling', *Journal of Marketing*, **58** (3), 39–52.

Swaminathan, Vanitha and Christine Moorman (2009), 'Marketing alliances, firm networks, and firm value creation', *Journal of Marketing*, **73** (1), 52–69.

Szymanski, David M. (1988), 'Determinants of selling effectiveness: the importance of declarative knowledge to the personal selling concept', *Journal of Marketing*, **52** (1), 64–77.

Tan, Keah Choon (2001), 'A framework of supply chain management literature', *European Journal of Purchasing and Supply Chain Management*, **7** (1), 39–48.

Teece, D.J., G. Pisano and A. Shuen (1997), 'Dynamic capabilities and strategic management', *Strategic Management Journal*, **18** (7), 509–35.

Theoharakis, Vasilis, Laszlo Sajtos and Graham Hooley (2009), 'The strategic role of relational capabilities in the business-to-business service profit chain', *Industrial Marketing Management*, **38** (8), 914–24.

Tracey, Michael, Jeen-Su Lim and Mark A. Vonderembse (2005), 'The impact of supply-chain management capabilities on business performance', *Supply-Chain Management*, **10** (3), 179–91.

van Riel, Allard C.R., Charles Pahud de Mortanges and Sandra Streukens (2005), 'Marketing antecedents of industrial brand equity: an empirical investigation in specialty chemicals', *Industrial Marketing Management*, **34** (8), 841–7.

Verhoef, Peter C. (2003), 'Understanding the effect of customer relationship management efforts on customer retention and customer share development', *Journal of Marketing*, **67** (4), 30–45.

Vorhies, Douglas W. and Neil A. Morgan (2003), 'A configuration theory assessment of marketing organization fit with business strategy and its relationship with marketing performance', *Journal of Marketing*, **67** (1), 100–115.

Vorhies, Douglas W. and Neil A. Morgan (2005), 'Benchmarking marketing capabilities for sustained competitive advantage', *Journal of Marketing*, **69** (1), 80–94.

Walker, Orville C. and Robert W. Ruekert (1987), 'Marketing's role in the implementation of business strategies: a critical review and conceptual framework', *Journal of Marketing*, **51** (July), 15–33.

Weitz, Barton A. (1981), 'Effectiveness in sales interactions: a contingency framework', *Journal of Marketing*, **45** (1), 85–103.

Weitz, Barton A. and Sandy Jap (1995), 'Relationship marketing and distribution channels', *Journal of the Academy of Marketing Science*, **23** (4), 305–20.

Weitz, Barton A., Harish Sujan and Mita Sujan (1986), 'Knowledge, motivation, and adaptive behavior: a framework for improving selling effectiveness', *Journal of Marketing*, **50** (4), 174–91.

Wilson, Hugh and Elizabeth Daniel (2007), 'The multi-channel challenge: a dynamic capability approach', *Industrial Marketing Management*, **36** (1), 10–20.

Workman, John P., Christian Homburg and Ove Jensen (2003), 'Intraorganizational determinants of key account management effectiveness', *Journal of the Academy of Marketing Science*, **31** (1), 3–21.

Wucherer, Klaus (2006), 'Business partnering: a driving force for innovation', *Industrial Marketing Management*, **35** (1), 91–102.

7 Gaining competitive advantage with service-dominant logic

Robert F. Lusch and Stephen L. Vargo

Competitive advantage never comes easy. However, it is more difficult to achieve when operating with an outdated or inappropriate logic of the market and marketing. We argue that a goods-dominant (G-D) logic guided most of marketing and competitive practice during the past two centuries and largely continues today. Unfortunately, much of the educational foundations of current managers are also grounded in G-D logic. As we show later in the chapter, G-D logic is deeply entrenched in the division of labor and specialization in society. This logic of separation and division puts firms, their customers and suppliers, and other stakeholders at odds. Slowly replacing the G-D logic is the service-dominant (S-D) logic (Vargo and Lusch 2004, 2008). S-D logic is grounded in the service-providing nature of all economic actors who use their skills, capabilities and resources in general to provide benefits to other actors. S-D logic is grounded in togetherness, or the integration of resources, and focuses on how actors collaborate for the common purpose of value co-creation; in brief all B2B enterprises are co-creators of value.

More and more enterprises are beginning to recognize that to compete effectively they must view themselves and the strategies they develop as centered not on goods but on service provision. Though not yet fully recognized, compelling evidence shows that competing through service is becoming the central competitive reality in high-performance organizations in every industry and in every country throughout the world. Importantly, when firms compete through service the good or tangible product seldom disappears but is viewed as providing a flow of service(s). For example the Rolls Royce or General Electric jet propulsion engine is a distribution mechanism for providing thrust or propulsion service.

S-D logic is not about separateness of either buyers and sellers or goods or services but rather the interwoven fabric of individuals and organizations, brought together into networks and societies, specializing in and exchanging the application of their competences to provide service for the applied competences in the form they need for their own well-being (Lusch et al. 2007). Philosophically S-D logic is grounded in a commitment to collaborative processes with customers, partners, employees and all stakeholders of the enterprise. Enterprises that understand, internalize and act on this logic better than the competition (Lusch et al. 2007) will have increasing competitive advantage. In other words it is no longer useful to view B2B marketing as bringing stuff *to market* or *marketing to* distinct customers; rather the increasingly preferred and managerially useful perspective is about *marketing with* customers and suppliers to co-create value.

FOUNDATIONS OF G-D LOGIC

To understand S-D logic, it is necessary to compare it with G-D logic. G-D logic has paradigmatic status and has guided much of economic thinking and thus competitive B2B strategy. Sometimes G-D logic refers to manufacturing logic (Normann 2001), neo-classical economics tradition (Hunt 2000) or old enterprise logic (Zuboff and Maxmin 2002). Implied by the G-D name, the focus is on the production of goods or more generally 'products', which can include both tangible (goods) and intangible (services) units of output that firms exchange with the market. G-D logic can be summarized as follows (Vargo and Lusch 2004, 2008):

1. Economic exchange is fundamentally concerned with units of output (products).
2. These products are embedded with value during the manufacturing (or agricultural or extraction) process.
3. For efficiency, this production ideally (a) is standardized; (b) takes place in isolation from the customer; and (c) can be inventoried to even out production cycles in the face of irregular demand.
4. These products can be sold in the market by capturing and stimulating demand to maximize profits.

Each of these four foundational premises of G-D logic, however, is increasingly on shaky ground. First, what firms produce, distribute and sell is not products but solutions. And solutions increasingly involve a network of tangible goods and intangible offerings and a network of other firms and actors, with information technology increasingly central to the systems solution. Second, a product is never embedded with value because value is only something that can be realized in the use of a market offering. In other words value is not produced in the factory or through distribution and marketing but rather through the end use of a market offering. Third, production that is standardized and takes place in isolation from the customers may provide homogeneous quality and efficiency from a supplier's perspective or from an engineering perspective but not from the perspective of customers who want their needs and problems uniquely addressed. In brief, customers want heterogeneous and customized offerings and not homogeneous and standardized offerings, even if this is economically efficient.

G-D logic is primarily centered on outputs. Outputs are exchanged with customers, and customers receiving these outputs exchange money. Firms attempt to increase the positive spread between what the customer pays for this output and what they pay for the resources needed to produce and sell the output offered. The greater the spread, the more added value the firm has produced and the more it contributes not only to share-holder wealth but also to national wealth. Because of the central perceived importance to the firm's success, there is considerable pressure on management to (1) produce and sell a large quantity of output; (2) have a high share of industry or market output; and (3) increase the spread between the cost of resources and the prices obtained from customers and thus to put pressure on suppliers to lower their prices while developing marketing programs to convince customers to pay higher prices. The focus on maximizing outputs at low cost may serve the organization well in terms of efficiency, but increasingly it is not viewed as highly effective as we suggest a service-centric orientation is.

A SERVICE-CENTRIC VIEW

In contrast with G-D logic with its product- or output-centric focus, S-D logic has a process-centric focus. In S-D logic service is defined as the application of competences (knowledge and skills) for the benefit of another party. Of note is the strategically significant distinction between the plural 'services' and the singular 'service'. Services is a G-D logic that focuses on firms producing intangibles as units of output. For example the airline industry produces seat miles, the hotel industry produces filled beds, the banking industry produces deposits and loans, and the higher education industry produces credit hours and degrees. From an S-D perspective, however, service is the process of doing something for and with another party, and thus it is inherently a collaborative process. Importantly, it shifts thinking from value creation derived from the product and the exchange of tangible and static resources to the exchange of intangible and dynamic resources that result in the co-creation of value. Undoubtedly, goods can be part of a service exchange, but they are appliances for service provision; they are conveyors of competences. Thus service can be provided directly or through a good, but in either case it is the knowledge and skills (competences) of the providers and beneficiaries that represent the essential source of value creation, not the goods, which are only sometimes used to convey them. From this perspective a firm always provides service even if it sells what appears to be a strictly tangible good. Take for instance an office chair. An office chair is used and integrated with other office furniture and equipment to enable and assist workers to perform their work tasks and activities more efficiently and effectively. Thus the chair is an appliance used to provide a service. If the firm providing the chairs to another firm is able to observe how people use the chairs in work practices, with proper design principles it can offer a chair of enhanced capabilities and perhaps integrate it with other office furniture and information appliances that in turn render more service. In brief this constitutes the service-centric view of a tangible good.

Closely aligned with S-D logic is a fundamental distinction between resources as 'operand' and 'operant'. Operand resources are usually static and often tangible and reflect material that is acted on by another entity or actor. Examples include natural resources (e.g. timber, ore, land, water) and human artifacts (e.g. roadways, buildings, the office chairs discussed previously). G-D logic focuses on the exchange of operand resources. Conversely, operant resources are dynamic and often intangible. An operant resource acts on other resources to produce effects. Humans and, more specifically, their knowledge and skills (competences) are an example of operant resources. Not only does the firm making the offering treat humans in the form of employees as operant resources, but customers who use a firm's offerings are also viewed as an operant resource. The service-centric view implies that marketing is a continuous series of social and economic processes that largely focus on operant resources. The S-D logic can be summarized as follows:

1. Identify or develop core competences, or the fundamental knowledge and skills that can represent potential competitive advantage.
2. Identify other entities (potential customers) that could benefit from these competences.

3. Cultivate relationships that involve the customers in developing customized, competitively compelling value propositions to meet specific needs.
4. Gauge marketplace feedback by analyzing financial performance from exchange to learn how to improve the firm's offering to customers and firm performance.

FOUNDATIONS OF S-D LOGIC

S-D logic employs many concepts that reflect a gradual transition over the latter part of the twentieth century. Table 7.1 summarizes 12 of these conceptual transitions. The transition moves from a G-D mental model to transitional concepts to an emerging consensus S-D mental model. Understanding this shifting mental model requires fathoming the transition from a focus on goods (G-D logic) to services (transitional logic) to service (S-D logic), or from products (G-D logic) to offerings (transitional logic) to experiences (S-D logic), or from feature/attribute (G-D logic) to benefit (transitional logic) to solution (S-D logic). Take for instance the office chair we discussed previously; it could be viewed as a bundle of features and attributes, such as its weight, height, adjustability, synthetic or natural material, and color, or as conveying benefits, such as comfortable seating or affordable seating; under S-D logic it could be viewed as part of a solution, and thus the focus is on how the chair is part of a work system and provides a solution platform for many of the challenges faced in fostering efficient and effective work.

Overall, the S-D logic lexicon in Table 7.1 reflects the language needed to advance a service-centered logic. Nonetheless, in most industries the G-D lexicon still remains the foundation of conversation and practice when dealing with marketing, exchange and business. A clearer picture emerges when firms ask their executives or management team to indicate which column in the exhibit characterizes their organization for each of the 12 concepts.[1]

Table 7.1   Conceptual transitions in marketing practice and thought

G-D logic concepts	Transitional concepts	S-D logic concepts
Goods	Services	Service
Products	Offerings	Experiences
Feature/attribute	Benefit	Solution
Value-added	Co-production	Co-creation of value
Value-in-exchange	Value-in-use	Value-in-context
Profit maximization	Financial engineering	Financial feedback/learning
Price	Value delivery	Value proposition
Equilibrium systems	Dynamic systems	Complex adaptive systems
Supply chain	Value chain	Service ecosystem
Promotion	Integrated marketing communication	Dialog
To market	Marketing to	Marketing with
Product orientation	Market orientation	Service orientation

Evolution of Marketing

Table 7.1 captures an important conceptual transition that reflects the evolution of marketing practice and thought overall. This transition is from 'to market' (G-D logic), to 'marketing to' (transitional logic), to 'marketing with' (S-D logic). A further explanation helps expand this idea.

Formal marketing thought and practice emerged in the beginning of the twentieth century and was largely grounded in neoclassical economics; thus it embraced G-D logic. Marketing in the first half of the twentieth century was perceived as transferring ownership of goods and their physical distribution (Savitt 1990). For example, Shaw (1912, p. 764) viewed marketing as the 'application of motion to matter'. Marketing's role was to take products to market, and much of the enterprise's efforts to accomplish this were on physical distribution, distribution intermediaries and the sales process. Embracing this philosophy, in the mid-1930s the American Marketing Association defined marketing as the set of business activities that direct the flow of goods and services from producer to consumer.

By the mid-1900s the marketing discipline had purportedly shifted from a 'product orientation' to a 'consumer orientation', first through the marketing concept (Barksdale and Darden 1971; McNamara 1972) and then by investigating firms' practice as a customer or market orientation (Kohli and Jaworski 1990; Narver and Slater 1990; Webster 1988). Marketing was moving from a 'to-market' focus to a 'marketing-to' focus. However, the tie to manufacturing or old enterprise logic strongly continued. Even the leading marketing management textbook in the 1970s (Kotler 1972, p. 42, emphasis in original) stated that 'marketing management seeks to determine the settings of the company's *marketing decision variables* that will maximize the company's objective(s) in the light of the expected behavior of noncontrollable *demand variables*'. In short, competitive advantage was considered a function of utility maximization by embedding value in products through superior manipulation of the 4Ps, with an assumed passive consumer in mind. Essentially the consumer was treated as an operand resource – or something to be acted on. A G-D logic kept raising its head, as reflected in the focus on segmenting the customer and then targeting the customer, promoting to the customer, distributing to the customer, and hopefully capturing the customer by enticing him or her to purchase using heavy promotional programs in which transparency was the exception (Lusch et al. 2007).

Although some enterprises entered an era of 'marketing with' guided by S-D logic in the late twentieth century, most firms and especially B2C firms are now just beginning to learn about and adopt this logic. With a more enlightened logic of how markets and actors actually work, firms are realizing that 'marketing to' customers must be replaced by 'marketing with' customers. The S-D mental model treats customers as operant resources who are capable of acting with other resources and collaborating to co-create value. Customers are dynamic, knowledge-generating, and value-creating resources. In contrast with B2C firms, B2B firms have led the way in a 'marketing with' and S-D logic perspective. For example many B2B firms focus heavily on relationships and networks of relationships, interactivity, service and co-production activities (Vargo and Lusch 2008).[2]

With the G-D logic mind-set, just as customers were treated as operand resources so were employees and other network partners. Firms treated all these groups as static resources to be controlled and managed to help firms maximize output and profit. In contrast, S-D logic views all exchange partners as operant resources that firms should collaborate with to co-create value. Thus the primary sources of a firm's innovation, competence and value are employees, customers and other network partners. Therefore competitive advantage actually arises from collaborative advantage.

Foundational Premises

S-D logic has a rich heritage that draws on services and relationship marketing literature (Gronroos 1994; Gummesson 1995), resource theory (Hunt 2000; Penrose 1959), core competency theory (Day 1994; Prahalad and Hamel 1990) and network theory (Achrol and Kotler 1999; Hakansson and Snehota 1995; Normann and Ramirez 1993). Vargo and Lusch (2004, 2008) developed ten foundational premises for S-D logic based in part on this heritage but also on the work of Bastiat (1848 [1964], 1860) and Smith (1776 [1904]). Table 7.2 presents these foundational premises.

A Note on Learning

Considering the ten foundational premises as a whole, S-D logic with its focus on processes is fundamentally about the process of learning. Firms must learn to provide better service to potential beneficiaries and to serve them better. Competing through service is inherently a learning process. G-D logic focuses on knowledge, which is a stock and static resource, whereas S-D logic focuses on learning, which is a flow or dynamic resource.

S-D logic argues that in an attempt to improve their existing conditions, actors enter into exchange by improving the conditions of others by improving their service offering (Lusch et al. 2007). That is, S-D logic hypothesizes that if actors take certain actions (and changes), they will be better off. Nonetheless, this hypothesis is tested by the perceptions of service rendered by beneficiaries and the value derived through exchange and subsequent use. Actors enter into exchange and experience the consequences first hand. They learn that their hypotheses can be falsified, particularly when the service rendered does not contribute to the desired experience. All actors have an ongoing desire to improve their condition and thus, through exchange, learn what works and what does not. Actors then respond by returning to the market to integrate more resources, developing competences that enable them to better adapt the original service rendered in exchange or finding options to the market, such as more self-service and communal sharing, or through other institutions to enhance well-being.

Under S-D logic, the organization is adaptive, learning and changing. The more the enterprise treats all exchange partners as entities to learn from, the more it can innovate and better serve these partners. Finally, the firm that learns and responds the fastest is in a better position to compete for customers effectively (Dickson 1992). However, as we indicate next, the firm is set within a system of other actors and is not viewed as an industry, a market, a marketing channel or a supply chain, as was the case with the old manufacturing logic, but rather as a service ecosystem.

Table 7.2 Foundational premises of S-D logic

Foundational premise	Comment/explanation
FP1. Service is the fundamental basis of exchange.	The application of operant resources for the benefit of another, 'service' is the basis for all exchange.
FP2. Indirect exchange masks the fundamental basis of exchange.	Complex combinations of goods, money and institutions make the exchange of service not always apparent.
FP3. Goods are a distribution mechanism for service provision.	Goods (both durable and nondurable) derive their value from use – the service they provide.
FP4. Operant resources are the fundamental source of competitive advantage.	The comparative ability to cause desired change drives competition.
FP5. All economies are service economies.	Service is only now becoming more apparent with increased specialization and outsourcing.
FP6. The customer is always a co-creator of value.	Value creation is interactional.
FP7. The enterprise cannot deliver value but only offer value propositions.	Enterprises can offer their applied resources for value creation and can collaboratively (interactively) create value but cannot create and/or deliver value independently.
FP8. A service-centric view is inherently customer oriented and relational.	Because service is defined in terms of customer-determined benefit and co-created, it is *inherently* customer oriented and *relational*.
FP9. All social and economic actors are resource integrators.	Implies the context of value creation is networks of networks (resource integration).
FP10. Value is always uniquely and phenomenologically determined by the beneficiary.	Value is idiosyncratic, experiential, contextual and meaning laden.

SERVICE ECOSYSTEM

From the 1960s through the 1980s, the view of an 'extended firm' as an interlinked behavioral and economic system comprising suppliers, distributors, facilitating agencies and customers, was referred to as the marketing channel (Mallen 1967; Stern 1969; Stern and El-Ansary 1977). However, the term 'marketing channel' fell out of favor in the 1990s, during which the term 'supply chain management' was born to indicate the flow of materials and information both within and across firms (Mentzer 2001; Tayur et al. 1999). During this same time frame both marketing channels and supply chains began to be viewed as 'value networks' and 'constellations' (Bovet and Martha 2000; Normann and Ramirez 1993). Overlapping this work, the B2B subdiscipline took on a broader, more holistic approach, particularly through the interactive network orientation of the Industrial Marketing and Purchasing Group (e.g. Hakansson and Snehota 1995).

S-D logic finds that the value constellation and network perspective more closely capture how economic actors function and benefit in an economy. However, S-D logic adopts the service ecosystem concept (Lusch et al. 2010) because it is more explanatory and strategically insightful. A service ecosystem is a spontaneously sensing and responding spatial and temporal structure of largely loosely coupled value-proposing social and economic actors that interact through institutions, technology and language to (1) co-produce service offerings; (2) engage in mutual service provision; and (3) co-create value. The explanatory and strategic richness of the service ecosystem concept can be recognized by expanding on the eight key components of the definition.

1. *Spontaneously sensing and responding.* Actors interface with other actors and use their senses to determine how and when to respond or act. With the ascendance of information technology the sensing and responding is more and more spontaneous.
2. *Spatial and temporal structure.* Actors and resources are arrayed over geographic space and temporal dimensions.
3. *Largely loosely coupled.* Actors connect to others both within and outside organizations mostly through 'soft' contracts (versus 'hard' contracts).
4. *Value proposing actors.* Actors cannot create value for other actors but can make offers that have potential value. This occurs through value propositions.
5. *Use of language, institutions and technology.* To interface successfully, actors need a common language. They also rely on other social institutions (e.g. monetary systems, laws) to regulate interfacing and exchange. Finally, technology and especially innovation drive system evolution and performance.
6. *Co-producing service offerings.* Actors invite other actors to assist in the production of service offerings.
7. *Engaging in mutual service provision.* Actors do not get a free ride but must help other actors, through service exchange, either directly or indirectly (e.g. monetarily, generalized reciprocity).
8. *Co-creating value.* Actors, in the integration of service offerings with other resources (including other service offerings), create value that is unique to their situation and use of resources.

STRIVING FOR BETTER RESOURCE INTEGRATION[3]

Just as firms are constantly learning, evolving and adapting to changing requirements, so are service ecosystems. A central way this occurs is through increased resource integration (Normann 2001) by reconfiguring processes around form, time, place and possession (Normann 2001). In the end improved resource integration is fundamentally about helping the firm make more competitively compelling value propositions. These concepts require further explanation.

Central to S-D logic is the resource concept. Actors draw on resources to benefit another actor or to provide service. However, resources are seldom at a time and place when needed and also are seldom integrated or combined in an optimal manner. The density of resources reflects the extent to which optimality occurs when, at a given time, all the resources are brought together for a solution. Thus maximum density is the ideal combination of resources at the right time and place to provide a solution. Part of the challenge in improving resource integration is the physical movement of resources. However, more and more resources are information resources that can be digitized or liquefied and transmitted through the Internet and electromagnetic spectrum. Not only do liquefied resources benefit from low transport cost, but they can also move rapidly from place to place. Essentially the movement is toward time and space collapsing on a single dimension in which information can be provided at any time and at any place simultaneously and at minimal cost. Therefore, organizations in a global network economy can better adapt and serve by liquefying information resources (Lusch et al. 2007; Normann 2001).

To illustrate the concept of liquefied resources, consider a B2B salesperson in 1970, who needed to carry a multitude of product brochures, technical specification sheets, order forms and related tangible sales material. Compare this with a B2B salesperson today, who can walk into a client's office, open up his or her computer and have all the related information available. This salesperson can even use the customer's computer and Internet connection to go to a website with all the relevant information on a real-time basis. Other possibilities exist, such as an engineer being able to diagnose a problem with a robot in a factory without traveling to the factory for observation or to replace a part on a device (for example, a door handle on a truck) by sending the digitized engineering design through the Internet to the customer's place of business in which a three-dimensional fabricator makes the part on demand. In these illustrations information replaces physical movement of tangible matter. When this occurs, resource density increases.

Bases of Resource Integration

The fundamental structure of a service ecosystem can be conceptualized in terms of the form of resources, the time they are available, the place they are available, and their possession or use. Marketing has long focused on various utilities of products, such as form, time, place and possession utility. Indeed marketing has long attempted to improve total utility by adjusting the dimensions of form, time, place and possession. For example Alderson (1957) describes the postponement of product availability as a tool that helps determine the most efficient way to serve end customers (also see Garcia-Dastugue and Lambert 2007). In the supply chain and operations literature, Alderson's concept of postponement has been renamed manufacturing postponement, in which the form or identity of the product is delayed; geographic postponement serves to delay and therefore optimize the place of final location (Garcia-Dastugue and Lambert 2007). Neither manufacturing (form) postponement nor geographic (place) postponement can be separated from time postponement simply because delaying form and place consumes time.

Organizations can gain key insights into developing more competitively compelling value propositions by focusing on fundamental reconfigurations of form, time, place and possession. Often this causes organizations to closely examine the basic structure and flow of the underlying processes of the business that occur not only in a firm but also across firms in the service ecosystem. In a B2B context the market offer is a more compelling value proposition if the firm can identify possible substantive changes in the bundling of resources to improve density.

Reconfiguring form

Forms, or structures, have purpose or function and can be thought of as artifacts. Over time, dominant forms or artifacts emerge. Tangible examples are transportation vehicles, hospitals, packaging, office furniture, apparel or computers. Intangible artifacts include contracts, policies and procedures, and business processes. Although dominant forms emerge, it is important to question these forms with the intent of discovering whether they can be altered or reframed to better perform a function to become a more useful tool or appliance.

One aspect of reconfiguring with form, which is often discussed in the context of S-D logic, pertains to customization and outsourcing. By creating standardized components, especially through the use of modular architecture (Baldwin and Clark 1997), such as in componentized software and Web services, it is possible to outsource activities that are not core to organization competence. Ironically, by standardizing component processes, customization can rise (Baldwin and Clark 1997) because the customer is buying a unique service solution that involves the integration of many distinct components into a customized market offering with a compelling value proposition. It is similar to writers using a standardized language of thousands of words that they can then combine into an almost infinite number of narratives. Thus the offering can be customized even though it is made up of an integrated set of standardized components (McCarthy 2007).

One source of innovation in the late 1990s occurred with process re-engineering, in which a process was decomposed, standardized, mapped into a best practice and evaluated against the firm's core competency. Often the result of such re-engineering and redesign was an alteration of the form a business process takes within the firm and the way the associated information is manipulated by the people and technology (Marchand and Stanford 1995). For example an order fulfillment process, on decomposition, may lead to order configuration by the customer using the Internet, order validation by an intelligent software system within the firm, order filling to the factory floor or to a supplier (if the product is warehoused at a supplier), order shipment and tracking to an external partner (UPS or FedEx), and invoicing to an external application service provider. The same occurs with other processes that largely involve supply chain management and marketing, such as compliance, security, collaborative planning and integration.

Reconfiguring time

Another reconfiguration opportunity pertains to the time at which activities are performed. Mapping a set of activities that are involved in the sourcing of inputs for production, the production of the product, the distribution and sale of the product, and the customer's use of the product determines how these activities are arranged along a time continuum. Certain activities precede others, either by custom or by necessity. For example in building a distribution center the building process follows a PERT chart: stake the lot, dig footings, do the rough plumbing, pour the foundation, do the rough carpentry and rough electrical wiring, and so forth. However, again, this does not need to be the process. Why? Because it assumes that the distribution center is site built. However, walls can be assembled with rough electric at a factory as the foundation is being poured and then delivered and installed in a few hours. This illustrates the multiple new configurations that are possible when determining whether time truly is by custom or norm or by necessity.

Concurrent engineering (Zirger and Hartley 1996) has been successfully used both in product design and manufacturing and in software development with the goal of speeding up the time to market (Boehm and Turner 2003). Greater modularization and componentization of the development process itself has been critical to this increased speed (McCarthy 2007). For example start and smart parts in product life-cycle management are dramatically changing the time it takes to build a part. Because engineers can start with a default specification for a standard part ('start part') and revise it to meet customer requirements, intelligence embedded in the part ('smart part') ensures that the redesigned part is valid, when viewed in the context of where it is to be used. Similarly, in today's on-demand software configuration environment, reusable software components made available as Web services are altering dramatically the time it takes for software development.

Reconfiguring place
Another reconfiguring process deals with the place where activities occur. Digitization and networks have altered the concept of place, where a task is performed, and where resources are delivered. In today's world, in which firms are networked across the globe with their customers and suppliers/partners, an order may originate in the United States, the parts ordered from manufacturing sites in Taiwan and Europe, and the product assembled in Mexico. Similarly, a call center service request can be placed anywhere in the world, processed initially at some location in India, escalated up to someone in New York, and responded to within a few minutes. Personalized Web portals (e.g. myDell) can make the 'place' where a 'product' is ordered and delivered right on a consumer's desktop, from which the customer can track the order throughout the entire value network, from initial placement to final delivery.

Increasingly, collaborations throughout the ecosystem are occurring through virtual collaboration, in which the participants meet through the Internet to work on projects. Documents can be shared not only throughout the organization but also with any other relevant parties in the value network. Parties can work on these documents at their place of business or elsewhere and become part of a virtual organization, in which place is independent of work. This is being done not only with simple, repetitive and explicit tasks but also in collaborations involving more complex projects, such as new product development (Ganesan et al. 2005). Supporting this trend is the movement to a 7-day, 24-hour knowledge factory in which people continually pass work around the globe so the sun never sets on the project (Gupta et al. 2009).

Reconfiguring possession
According to conventional marketing and economic thought, value can be partially provided through ownership and possession of material things. However S-D logic argues that it is the service, including the flow of service from appliances (good), that matters rather than possession per se. This idea can be used to reconfigure ecosystems because it suggests that firms can lease assets or pay for use of service flows, rather than purchasing goods.

Reframing of possession can also occur with hardware. For example Rolls-Royce has moved away from selling engines to selling power by the hour, and Intel in its fabrication plants for microprocessors no longer buys expensive laser machines but acquires laser pulses on a service contract. No longer does a firm need to worry about owning a jet engine or an expensive laser beam machine, having it on its balance sheet, financing the capital equipment, and paying for constant repair and maintenance and operating supplies; rather it can focus on the value it obtains in the use of the capital equipment and pay an appropriate fee for this value-in-use. There are many other examples beyond high-technology and highly expensive products. Consider Chep, a container company that is deeply rooted in a commodity business, in which product differentiation is very difficult. One of the biggest product lines Chep produces is wood pallets. Traditionally, manufacturers or distributors must purchase a pallet, place goods on it, and absorb the cost, or transfer it as a shipping and handling fee. For large shippers or manufacturers the cost of these pallets can add up. Chep recognized that value was obtained not in the ownership and possession of the pallets but in their use. Instead of selling pallets Chep leases pallets to manufacturers, distributors and others within the value network and then picks up the empty pallets. Chep's value proposition therefore becomes the following: at the same cost of purchase, Chep provides the service provisioning the pallets offer, which is integrated into the customers' storage systems and requirements, without pallets piling up in the loading dock.

As a firm moves away from selling a product to selling a service flow, payment for the service can be based on customer outcomes. In the case of software as a service, it may be for use of an application; for Chep it is time usage of the pallet. Thus the offering of service flows and the structuring of outcome-based contracts are areas of strategic opportunity (Ng et al. 2009).

Higher-order Competences

Competitive advantage arises from the application of operant resources, as S-D logic's fourth foundational premise suggests. Although a firm can acquire many resources both more efficiently and effectively from other firms, we argue that there are four higher-order competences that are essential for all firms that want to compete effectively to be among the best. These competences address two fundamental realities that all firms confront. First, humans and organizations have been on a specialization trajectory for hundreds, if not thousands, of years. This trend is unlikely to subside. Second, as more and more actors connect through communication and transport networks, the service ecosystem within which they operate and in part create becomes more dynamic.

In this dynamic environment, firms cannot remain static in their value propositions or service offering; therefore service *innovations* are instrumental. These innovations are dependent on the collection of competences, which the firm can continually renew, create, integrate and transform. Accomplishing this feat requires the firm to develop absorptive competence, which is the firm's ability to comprehend important trends and know-how from the external environment. Absorptive competence helps transform the external environments into important resources that the firm can draw on for support. At the same time the firm must develop adaptive competence, which is the firm's ability to adjust to changing circumstances.

As we have discussed and illustrated, S-D logic focuses on togetherness through co-production, co-creation, dialog and conversation. Firms can do a better job at developing their absorptive and adaptive competences if they can work effectively with their suppliers, customers and other stakeholders. To accomplish this, firms need to develop relational competence, which goes hand in hand with S-D logic. Relational competence is enhanced through open two-way communication, trustworthiness and solidarity. It is also enhanced through development of collaborative competence or the ability to work well with others. Importantly by developing collaborative competence the firm can use its partner firms (suppliers and customers) as mechanisms for adapting to change brought about by complex and dynamic environments.

Organizations can use better collaborative and relational competency, coupled with improved absorptive competence and adaptive competence, to lower their relative resource cost and enhance their relative value proposition (Hunt 2000). Essentially, lower relative resource cost focuses on efficiency, and enhanced relative value focuses on effectiveness. As Hunt (2000) implies, the nirvana position is to offer more efficient and effective solutions to the marketplace. The only possible way to realize and maintain this nirvana position is to have superior collaborative and relational competency because it leverages firms' ability to absorb information and knowledge from the environment, customers and their value networks and thus enables them to adapt to dynamic and complex environments.

CONCLUDING COMMENT: A PRACTICE AND RESEARCH AGENDA

In many instances B2B marketing has led B2C marketing in both theoretical and practical development. Many concepts from B2B marketing, including 'relationship', 'value network' and 'use-value' have contributed directly to or are highly consistent with the emerging S-D logic of marketing. At the same time S-D logic provides an overarching and enriching framework that offers B2B firms a guiding philosophy not only for marketing as a functional area but, more generally, for the entire firm as well. Nonetheless, for S-D logic to be fully operational and applied, further academic research is required perhaps around mid-range theory. However, even at its current level of development firms can use the S-D logic to become more innovative, in both the development of market offerings and the organizational management of cross-functional and interenterprise (e.g. customers, suppliers) activities and processes. Several research opportunities thus include the following:

1. How can firms more effectively view and treat customers and employees as *operant resources*? Can the pay-off from treating customers and employees as operant resources be modeled and/or measured?
2. What are the fundamental determinants of collaborative competency? Is *collaborative competency* a stronger driver of the firm's financial performance than competitive strength?
3. How do firms develop and implement *competitively compelling value propositions*? Can or should customer and supplier communities help shape a firm's value propositions?
4. How can *design science* be coupled with S-D logic to develop offerings that represent competitively compelling value propositions?
5. How can firms establish *payment mechanisms and economic incentives* that encourage offering of service flows that lower systemwide waste and inefficiency but maintain or increase effectiveness?

Some firms may hesitate to adopt S-D logic until its normative implications are more fully developed and empirically validated. However, it should be stressed that S-D logic emerged from efforts to capture evolving company, industry and disciplinary perspectives and thus is a formalization of emerging marketing practices, especially among forward-thinking B2B firms. Even at its current stage of development, S-D logic points B2B firms toward the following practices:

1. Study the users of the market offerings provided to other firms. Observe them in a natural setting, and think about how your firm can provide a better solution that will often be a combination of tangible and intangible offerings.
2. Step back from your customer and look within your organization at all the business processes in which employees are providing service to each other and examine whether these processes can be improved.
3. Develop a graphic model of your enterprise's service ecosystem. Ask yourself the following: (a) Are the value propositions that connect actors mutually satisfying and compelling? (b) Is the language the actors use helping or hindering service? (c) Do you have the ability to sense and respond to rapid change in the ecosystem? and (d) Can your firm create more loosely coupled modules that can be part of new innovative offerings?
4. Determine what your opportunities are for reconfiguring resources around form, time, place and possession for improved resource utilization.
5. Assess your firm's collaborative, relational, absorptive and adaptive competences. Identify strengths and weaknesses, and develop an action plan for improvement.

From the outset S-D logic has been a collaborative and open effort among a community of scholars and increasingly practitioners, who found traditional manufacturing logic, neoclassical economics, and much of marketing management increasingly unable to explain and guide successful managerial action. We invite others to join this effort and share effective practices and research results.

NOTES

1. For this exercise labeling the columns with the terms in Table 7.1 may cause biased answers. Thus labeling them as I, II and III might be more beneficial.
2. We do not use the B2C designation because of its connotation that the firm produces value and the customer consumes value. Thus we view all exchange either as B2B or more preferably as actor to actor (see Vargo and Lusch 2011).
3. This section draws on Lusch et al. (2010).

REFERENCES

Achrol, Ravi and Philip Kotler (1999), 'Marketing in a network economy', *Journal of Marketing*, **63** (Special Issue), 146–63.
Alderson, Wroe (1957), *Marketing Behavior and Executive Action: A Functionalist Approach to Marketing Theory*, Homewood, IL: Richard D. Irwin.
Baldwin, Carliss and Kim Clark (1997), 'Managing in an age of modularity', *Harvard Business Review*, **75** (5), 84–93.

Barksdale, Hiram C. and Bill Darden (1971), 'Marketers' attitudes toward the marketing concept', *Journal of Marketing*, **35** (October), 29–36.

Bastiat, F. (1848 [1964]), *Selected Essays on Political Economy*, trans. Seymour Cain, George B. de Huszar (ed.), Princeton, NJ: D. Van Nordstrand.

Bastiat, F. (1860), *Harmonies of Political Economy*, trans. Patrick S. Sterling, London: J. Murray.

Boehm, Barry and Richard Turner (2003), *Balancing Agility and Discipline*, Boston: Addison-Wesley.

Bovet, David and Joseph Martha (2000), *Value Nets: Breaking the Supply Chain to Unlock Hidden Profits*, New York: John Wiley & Sons.

Day, George (1994), 'The capabilities of market-driven organization', *Journal of Marketing*, **58** (October), 37–52.

Dickson, Peter R. (1992), 'Toward a general theory of competitive rationality', *Journal of Marketing*, **56** (January), 69–83.

Ganesan, Shankar, Alan J. Malter and Aric Rindfleisch (2005), 'Does distance still matter? Geographic proximity and new product development', *Journal of Marketing*, **69** (October), 44–60.

Garcia-Dastugue, S.J. and D. Lambert (2007), 'Interorganizational time-based postponement in the supply chain', *Journal of Business Logistics*, **28** (1), 57–81.

Gronroos, Christian (1994), 'From marketing mix to relationship marketing: towards a paradigm shift in marketing', *Asia-Australia Marketing Journal*, **32** (2), 4–20.

Gummesson, Evert (1995), 'Relationship marketing: its role in the service economy', in William J. Glynn and James G. Barnes (eds), *Understanding Services Management*, New York: John Wiley & Sons, pp. 244–68.

Gupta, Amar, Elisa Mattarelli, Satwik Seshasai and Joseph Broschak (2009), 'Use of collaborative technologies and knowledge sharing in co-located and distributed teams: towards the 24-h knowledge factory', *Journal of Strategic Information Systems*, **18** (3), 147–61.

Hakansson, H. and I. Snehota (1995), *Developing Relationships in Business Networks*, London: Routledge.

Hunt, Shelby D. (2000), *A General Theory of Competition: Resources, Competences, Productivity, and Economic Growth*, Thousand Oaks, CA: Sage Publications.

Kohli, Ajay J. and Bernard Jaworski (1990), 'Market orientation: the construct, research propositions, and managerial implications', *Journal of Marketing*, **54** (April), 1–18.

Kotler, Philip (1972), *Marketing Management*, 2nd edn, Englewood Cliffs, NJ: Prentice Hall.

Lusch, Robert F., Stephen L. Vargo and Matthew O'Brien (2007), 'Competing through service: insights from service-dominant logic', *Journal of Retailing*, **83** (1), 5–18.

Lusch, Robert F., Stephen L. Vargo and Mohan Tanniru (2010), 'Service, value networks and learning', *Journal of the Academy of Marketing Science*, **38** (1), 19–31.

Mallen, Bruce (1967), *The Marketing Channel*, New York: John Wiley & Sons.

Marchand, D.A. and M.J. Stanford (1995), 'Business process redesign: a framework for harmonizing people, information and technology', in V. Grover and W. Kettinger (eds), *Business Process Change*, Hershey, PA: Idea Group, pp. 34–56.

McCarthy, R.M. (2007), 'Cost-effective supply chains: optimizing product development through integrated design and sourcing', in K. Butner, T. Gilliam, H. Goldstein, J. Kalina, C. Taylor and M. Witterding (eds), *Reshaping Supply Chain Management: Vision and Reality*, Boston, MA: Pearson Custom, pp. 102–35.

McNamara, Carlton P. (1972), 'The present status of the marketing concept', *Journal of Marketing*, **36** (January), 50–57.

Mentzer, John T. (2001), *Supply Chain Management*, Thousand Oaks, CA: Sage Publications.

Narver, John and Stanley Slater (1990), 'The effect of a market orientation on business profitability', *Journal of Marketing*, **54** (October), 20–35.

Ng, Irene, Roger Maull and Nick Yip (2009), 'Outcome-based contracts as a driver of systems thinking and service-dominant logic in service science: evidence from the defence industry', *European Management Journal*, **27** (6), 377–87.

Normann, R. (2001), *Reframing Business: When the Map Changes the Landscape*, Chichester: John Wiley & Sons.

Normann, Richard and Rafael Ramirez (1993), 'From value chain to value constellation: designing interactive strategy', *Harvard Business Review*, **71** (4), 65–77.

Penrose, E. (1959), *The Theory of the Growth of the Firm*, London: Basil Blackwell and Mott.

Prahalad, C.K. and G. Hamel (1990), 'The core competence of the corporation', *Harvard Business Review*, **68** (3), 79–91.

Savitt, Ronald (1990), 'Pre-Aldersonian antecedents to macromarketing: insights from the textual literature', *Journal of the Academy of Marketing Science*, **18** (4), 293–301.

Shaw, Arch (1912), 'Some problems in market distribution', *Quarterly Journal of Economics*, **12** (August), 703–65.

Smith, A. (1776 [1904]), *An Inquiry into the Nature and Causes of the Wealth of Nations*, London: Strahan and T. Cadell.

Stern, L.W. (1969), *Distribution Channels: Behavioral Dimensions*, Boston, MA: Houghton Mifflin.

Stern, Louis W. and Adel El-Ansary (1977), *Marketing Channels*, Englewood Cliffs, NJ: Prentice Hall.

Tayur, Sridhar, Ram Ganeshan and Michael Magazine (1999), *Quantitative Models for Supply Chain Management*, Boston, MA: Kluwer Academic Press.

Vargo, Stephen L. and Robert F. Lusch (2004), 'Evolving to a new dominant logic for marketing', *Journal of Marketing*, **68** (January), 1–17.

Vargo, Stephen L. and Robert F. Lusch (2008), 'From goods to service(s): divergences and convergences of logics', *Industrial Marketing Management*, **37** (3), 254–9.

Vargo, Stephen L. and Robert F. Lusch (2011), 'It's all B2B . . . and beyond: toward a systems perspective of the market', *Industrial Marketing Management*, **40**, 181–7.

Webster, Frederick E. (1988), 'The rediscovery of the marketing concept', *Business Horizons*, **31** (3), 29–39.

Zirger, B.J. and J.L. Hartley (1996), 'The effects of acceleration techniques on product development time', *IEEE Transactions on Engineering Management*, **43** (2), 143–52.

Zuboff, Shoshana and James Maxmin (2002), *The Support Economy*, New York: Penguin.

8 Coordinating marketing and sales in B2B organizations
Frank Cespedes

An executive I once interviewed described a common situation (Cespedes 1996a, p. 4): 'Our Marketing managers operate at a national level and with specific product orientations. They're not as familiar with regional or account differences. Meanwhile, Sales is driven by specific accounts, volume shipments, and trade deals.' A senior sales manager at this company described marketing managers as 'headquarters theorists, unaware of field realities', while a marketing manager responded that salespeople were 'primarily interested in the deepest deal that moves the most product in the current quarter – regardless of the impact on profitability' (Cespedes 1996a, p. 4). Meanwhile, service personnel complained that their activities were constantly being 'disrupted by the ad hoc arrangements that characterize Marketing–Sales interactions in a marketplace where customers are more powerful and demanding' (Cespedes 1996a, p. 4). Why do such conflicts arise between groups that, as the general manager of this division (along with most academics and consultants) repeatedly emphasized, 'should all be team players because they all work for the same company'? Why does a recent study (Miller Heiman 2008 Sales Best Practices Study, as cited in Levy 2008) indicate that only 37 per cent of respondents agreed that their marketing and sales organizations are aligned with what their customers want and need?

This chapter focuses on the topic of the coordination of marketing and sales activities in B2B organizations. I first provide a brief historical overview of the topic, including the recurring prescriptive advice that has been offered to practitioners and why this advice seems to have limited usefulness. This chapter then reviews some common delineations of marketing and sales activities in companies and their implications: both groups have inherent interdependencies and necessary differences. I conclude this chapter with a discussion of what some B2B companies have done to improve coordination between their marketing and sales functions, as well as some suggestions for further research.

HISTORICAL PERSPECTIVE AND SOME COMMON ADVICE

Coordinating marketing and sales is not a new issue. Consider several comments from a century ago. The first is from Truman De Weese, a marketing manager quoted in *Printers' Ink* (a trade publication) in July 1910: 'If the marketing department is what it should be, sales will be merely distributors. It is their job to keep in touch with the trade. They don't need to sell goods. The goods are already sold'. The second comes from Herbert Mildrum, a sales manager quoted in *Advertising & Selling* in February 1913: '99% of our marketing managers have never carried a sample case. Such a trip will knock a lot of foolishness out of them. No ad ever should be published without the approval of the sales department'. By the mid-twentieth century, textbooks and professors routinely distinguished between 'sales' and 'marketing'. Theodore Levitt (from a marketing point of view) summarized a common distinction: 'Selling is preoccupied with the seller's need to convert his product into cash; marketing with the idea of satisfying the needs of the customer by means of the product and the whole cluster of things associated with creating, delivering, and finally consuming it' (Levitt 1960, p. 26).

It is also important to emphasize that the issue of coordinating marketing and sales functions is not a phenomenon engendered primarily by particular selling 'biases' or sheer 'bigness' in terms of organizational size and scope. One view sketches an allegedly typical organizational evolution in which 'most small businesses' see no need to differentiate marketing and selling activities, but as they grow, 'successful small businesses add a marketing person (or persons) to help relieve the sales force of some chores' such that 'as companies become larger and more successful . . . Marketing becomes an independent player [and] starts to compete with Sales for funding' (Kotler et al. 2006, pp. 70–71). But decades of research on cross-functional coordination have demonstrated that the issue is endemic to organizational specialization in multiple forms (see literature dating back at least as far as Lawrence and Lorsch 1967; Pondy 1967; Robbins 1974), occurs between marketing/sales and other functions (Carroad and Carroad 1982; Griffin and Hauser 1996; Maltz and Kohli 2000; Menon et al. 1996; Ruekert and Walker 1987; Shapiro 1977; Shaw and Shaw 1988), was present when business firms were on average much smaller and less diversified in their product or geographical scope (Powers et al. 1987) and indeed is present in start-ups and small businesses as well as large corporations. Trade journals aimed at small businesses regularly carry stories about the need and difficulty of coordinating sales and marketing activities, as do books and blogs aimed at start-up firms and entrepreneurs (Moore 2002; see also the links compiled by Eisenmann 2009).

It should not be surprising therefore that the business trade press frequently highlights this issue in articles with titles such as 'The gap between marketing and sales' or 'Ending the war between sales & marketing'. Such articles tend to offer three types of advice to managers: (1) encourage 'more communication' between these groups through regular meetings, joint assignments and/or account reviews; (2) align incentives and metrics for marketing and sales, perhaps through shared revenues or profit targets or one common sales goal to which both sales and marketing commit; and (3) attempt a structural solution by having both marketing and sales report to the same person or office in the company (e.g. Chief Customer Officer) and/or through job rotation across marketing and sales positions. Kotler et al. (2006) offer a recent example and compendium of such advice: They recommend 'disciplined communication' through 'regular meetings . . . joint assignments [and] account reviews', 'common metrics' for the two groups and the appointment of 'a chief revenue (or customer) officer', and they encourage job rotation between marketing and sales.

But there are many complications that arise when companies attempt to follow such advice, other important factors that affect these groups and useful alternative approaches available to firms.

Coordination Costs and Goals

Terms like 'teamwork' and 'coordination' are value-laden words with positive connotations. Especially before confronting necessary trade-offs and resource constraints, few managers are *against* initiatives aimed at promoting better coordination. But coordination comes at a cost, and different approaches are implicitly choices about the kinds of ongoing issues a firm must monitor and manage. As even its proponents note, 'More communication is expensive. It eats up time, and it prolongs decision making' (Kotler et al. 2006, p. 70). These are especially significant costs in markets characterized by shorter product life cycles and more customer access to easily available sources of online information, including product and pricing comparisons. Thus Rouzies et al. (2005, p. 115) usefully distinguish sales–marketing integration from related concepts, such as involvement and communication, and emphasize that coordination

> is a dynamic process in which the two functional areas create more value for their firms by working together than they would create by working in isolation . . . the timing of the activities must be coordinated (i.e., concurrent or thoughtfully sequenced) . . . consistent in that they have the same goal, and they support each other in that each activity makes the other activity more effective.

Coordination and Specialization

To be effective in organizations, communication and coordination need content: managers presumably communicate about relevant analyses and decisions and attempt to coordinate actions and resources in accord with those analyses and decisions. As I outline subsequently, the delineation of marketing and sales activities often reflects necessary specialization, making advice such as 'encourage communication' or 'align incentives' difficult to implement and, often, sloganeering rather than an action plan. There are also major unexamined assumptions in such advice: that senior executives are not aware of differing incentive systems between marketing and sales groups, have not in fact tried various reward systems, and that effective coordination *requires* common metrics between groups. The topic of metrics and coordination by now constitutes a vast and varied literature, with no clear agreement about whether common rewards are a necessary ingredient for cooperative behaviors at multiple levels of organizational analysis, such as within teams, across functions or between companies. Ashforth and Lee (1990) and De Dreu and Weingart (2003) provide reviews, and Cespedes (1990, 1992) discusses compensation and coordination in the sales context in particular.

Structure versus Organization

Within and beyond the areas of marketing and sales, structure and organization are not synonymous. Firms of all sizes are networks of people and processes. At some point in the hierarchy of most firms, marketing and sales report to a common person (COO, CEO or LOB head, depending on the company). Does a change in an organization chart or renaming a current VP of sales or marketing as the 'Chief Customer Officer' really change the routines embedded in the network of people and processes responsible for marketing and sales activities? Many companies have experimented with job rotation between their marketing and sales groups; many find that in the end, they have damaged important human resource capabilities in their attempts to transform excellent salespeople into mediocre marketing managers, and vice versa. In the process necessary expertise often gets sacrificed.

More generally, terms like 'marketing manager' or 'salesperson' encompass a range of activities and possible organizational roles, depending on business strategy, the structure of the functions, the individuals who work within each function and the technical or go-to-market requirements of the product or service offering and its associated applications. It is important to understand these activities and thus the kinds of issues and tasks around which the coordination of marketing and sales does or does not occur in organizations.

A CONTINUUM OF ACTIVITIES

Figure 8.1 outlines tasks usually associated with marketing and sales groups.[1] On organization charts, such tasks are often grouped into designations labeled 'product management' or 'distribution'. But as Figure 8.1 suggests, these tasks can be viewed as a continuum of activities, such that one group has primary responsibility for tasks, whose achievement is affected by the plans and actions of another group. In B2B organizations, for example, marketing managers' market research should be informed by selling activities for customer accounts; pricing plans must be implemented by sales;

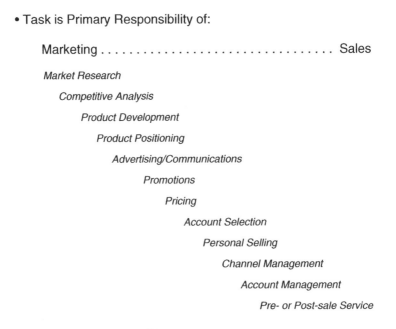

- Task is Primary Responsibility of:

Marketing . . . . Sales

Market Research

Competitive Analysis

Product Development

Product Positioning

Advertising/Communications

Promotions

Pricing

Account Selection

Personal Selling

Channel Management

Account Management

Pre- or Post-sale Service

Source: Adapted from Cespedes (1995, p. 32).

Figure 8.1   Responsibilities along a continuum of activities

and profit margins are affected by pre- or post-sales activities provided during the selling cycle.

This continuum means that market planning without sales input, or sales actions without market plans, will be incomplete or contradictory. But in most firms some differentiation of these activities occurs so that specialized expertise in (and, equally important, accountability for) a subset of this continuum can be developed and maintained. What follows is a representative delineation of the roles and responsibilities in each group that can help specify the nature of their inherent interdependencies (and thus why coordination between marketing and sales is important), as well as issues that separate the groups (and thus why coordination between marketing and sales is a perennial challenge in organizations).

Marketing Roles and Responsibilities

A characteristic of marketing management is its focus on making plans and monitoring the budgets and programs for one or more products or services sold by the company. An important motive for establishing such positions is the desire to put one person or group in charge of making a business plan work for an assigned portion of what the company offers in its market. Accountability and overall responsibility for managing the many tasks required to take a product or service to market are important in most B2B companies. But these qualities are often diffused throughout an organization, and as a result, many senior executives appreciate an organization in which they know whom to call with a question or problem about the marketing of a product or service.

As a response to external conditions, these positions often provide a means to handle the differing go-to-market requirements generated when a company has multiple products – many in different stages of their life cycles or with different technical or usage conditions – flowing through the same distribution channel to various customer groups.[2] In these situations somebody must manage ongoing trade-offs among maintaining efficient production, satisfying fluctuating demand across different segments and motivating the sales force to devote a 'fair share' of its time to each product or service sold through a common channel. A basic concern of many marketing managers in B2B firms then is to maximize the return on investments in production assets allocated to their assigned products or services, as well as to maintain a competitive brand in the face of changing demand and substitutes at the intermediary and/or end-user level of the marketplace.

In terms of actual responsibilities, marketing management positions differ widely – from staff coordinator to line manager with profit and loss (P&L) responsibility. But the paradigmatic form of the role in B2B organizations is probably the product manager. As one representative job description notes: 'The product manager assumes broad strategic responsibilities and serves as the company expert in all matters pertaining to the brand. The product manager is responsible for initiating and leading business development programs, executing and controlling the marketing plan, coordinating all department/staff resources, [and] developing strong working relationships' with other relevant functional groups' (Cespedes 1996a, p. 7). Compared with consumer firm brand managers, B2B marketing managers tend to spend more time on and have more responsibility for actual product design and development, but less for advertising and promotions (Cespedes 1993a; Cummings et al. 1984; Dawes and Patterson 1988). This outcome should not be surprising, given the generally greater reliance on media advertising and trade promotions in the marketing budgets of consumer versus B2B companies.

B2B marketing managers also often have a more prominent role than consumer marketing managers in activities such as assessing market size, conducting reseller and competitive analyses, developing applications and forecasting sales. These differences reflect two other characteristics of B2B versus consumer marketing. One is the derived nature of demand in most B2B markets and thus the greater need to track differing forms of product/service usage throughout the go-to-market chain. The other is the historical availability of information in these markets. Many consumer goods markets have long had syndicated research services and other information sources that over the years have provided consumer marketing managers with readily available data about market size, consumer behavior and competitive shares in their product categories. Until relatively recently by contrast, such data were not easily available in many B2B markets, and so these marketing managers often have had to conduct the research themselves. This situation may be changing as a result of e-commerce, online selling, digital marketing and other sources of direct customer feedback in B2B markets.

Sales Roles and Responsibilities

In its modern form, sales became a distinct function in the nineteenth century, in response to expanded mass production capabilities. Periodic gluts of unsold goods in businesses with high fixed costs made high rates of throughput crucial and increased the importance of forecasting sales volume accurately. This shift in turn prompted manufacturers in many industries to limit their reliance on tiers of wholesalers, concentrate on market share and instead develop in-house sales forces (Friedman 2004). By the turn of the twentieth century, as Chandler (1977) documents, modern sales organizations, with offices run by professional sales managers, were in place, integrating mass production together with mass distribution.

Today selling jobs vary greatly, depending on the kind of product or service sold, the number of customers a salesperson is responsible for and ancillary requirements (e.g. amount of travel, technical knowledge required, number and types of people contacted during the selling cycle). But in B2B organizations in which personal selling is an important part of the marketing mix, the salesperson is at the heart of the company's encounters with customers and plays a key *boundary role* in the organization (see Figure 8.2).

Salespeople represent the buying organization to groups in the seller's organization; they also represent their company and its capabilities to the customer. They must respond to the often conflicting rules, procedures and requirements of both organizations. Internally at their own companies, they often interact with sales, marketing, production or engineering managers; credit personnel in finance; and perhaps other service groups. Externally with clients they must often deal with purchasing and, depending on the product or buying process, a host of other purchase decision-makers and purchase influencers. Each of these groups has its own operating procedures that it considers especially important. Yet the essence of most selling jobs is to manage and, in practice, actively negotiate this boundary between the B2B selling organization and potential customer accounts. Moreover if a company indeed has a marketing strategy (as opposed to a merely abstract set of goals), it should have policies, procedures and programs in

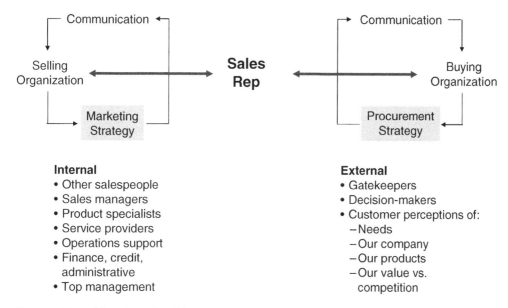

Internal
- Other salespeople
- Sales managers
- Product specialists
- Service providers
- Operations support
- Finance, credit,
  administrative
- Top management

External
- Gatekeepers
- Decision-makers
- Customer perceptions of:
  – Needs
  – Our company
  – Our products
  – Our value vs.
    competition

Source: Adapted from Cespedes (1995, p. 39).

Figure 8.2   Sales' boundary role in an organization

place that are intended to help execute that strategy consistently. But this means that salespeople, most of whom are usually responsible for multiple accounts, must deal with a variety of buying policies through the lens of the selling company's particular policies and procedures. For all these reasons the salesperson is likely to feel a certain psychological as well as physical distance from the firm. Studies of boundary-role personnel in various occupations have demonstrated the internal organizational conflicts inherent to these positions (Adams 1976; Singh 1993).

In terms of responsibilities a key sales objective is demand generation – calling on current and prospective customers to stimulate interest in the product or service, even if the ultimate sale occurs through resellers and/or another entity in the selling organization. For B2B firms a useful taxonomy outlines five basic types of selling activities (Moncrief 1986):

- obtaining direct customer contact through lead generation, call planning and making sales presentations;
- working with orders by expediting shipments or modifying standard terms and conditions for particular accounts;
- servicing the product and/or account through installation, repair, maintenance, training of customer personnel or other pre- or post-sale activities;
- working with resellers or other intermediaries; and
- undertaking information management by soliciting feedback and data from accounts and providing data to others in sales and marketing through call reports, account plans or competitive analyses.

Some B2B companies divide these activities across different components of the sales force or between sales and service personnel. For example, a key account manager might be responsible for direct customer contact, information management and some elements of account service at the headquarters level of a customer, whereas sales and service people in individual geographic territories are responsible for these and other activities with buyers and users at individual customer locations (Cespedes et al. 1989).

INTERDEPENDENCIES AND INHERENT DIFFERENCES

Delineating typical sets of responsibilities indicates why coordinating marketing and sales is so important in B2B firms: inherent to these roles are interdependencies that must be managed to achieve marketing effectiveness. Each unit is responsible for different aspects of the continuum of activities that affect customers. The need to understand evolving product plans and their place in the firm's strategy, for example, makes sales' effectiveness dependent on marketing management's expertise. Conversely the experience gained by salespeople during their interactions with current and prospective customers is a valuable source of market knowledge for marketing activities. Especially in B2B firms, moreover, service requirements often are generated as an output of sales activities, which affects product plans, and sales success in industrial markets is often tied to the provision of customized service activities.

One way to visualize these connections is as in Figure 8.3. To do its job effectively, marketing needs certain kinds of input from sales. At a minimum, this input usually

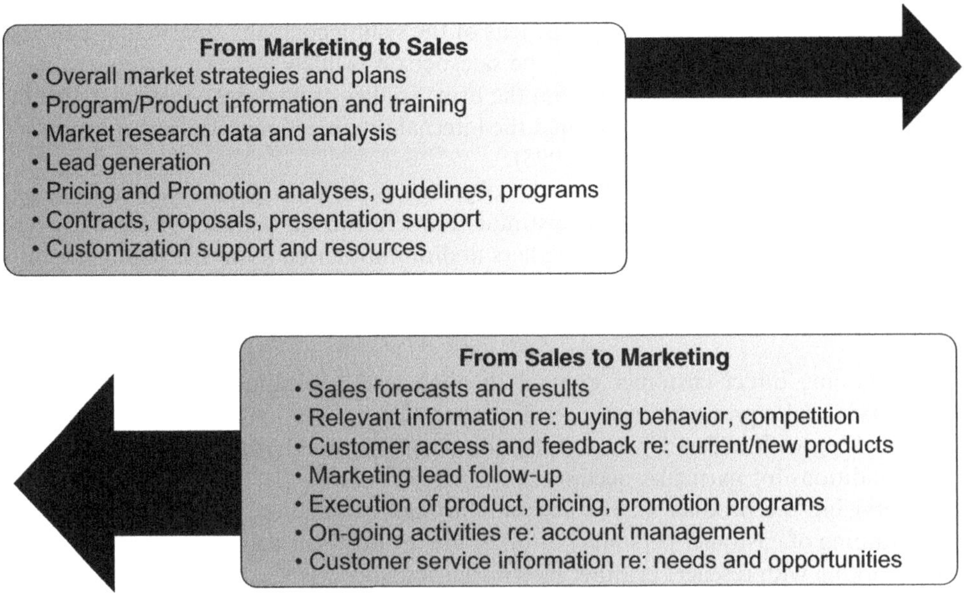

From Marketing to Sales
- Overall market strategies and plans
- Program/Product information and training
- Market research data and analysis
- Lead generation
- Pricing and Promotion analyses, guidelines, programs
- Contracts, proposals, presentation support
- Customization support and resources

From Sales to Marketing
- Sales forecasts and results
- Relevant information re: buying behavior, competition
- Customer access and feedback re: current/new products
- Marketing lead follow-up
- Execution of product, pricing, promotion programs
- On-going activities re: account management
- Customer service information re: needs and opportunities

Figure 8.3   Typical interdependencies: what each group needs from the other to achieve its tasks efficiently

includes sales forecasts, customer feedback about product performance and product/ service needs, and ongoing market information about buying behavior and competitive activities. Sales requires from marketing, on an ongoing basis, marketing strategies and plans, available research data, relevant literature or documentation about the product/ service offering and (in most firms) pricing parameters. The interlinked nature of their activities generates inherent task interdependencies.

But delineating roles and responsibilities also helps indicate issues that separate the groups and make coordination of marketing and sales a challenge. The groups differ in their orientation to the marketplace and time horizons, performance criteria and metrics, and required information priorities. The differences in themselves are neither good nor bad; they can provide valuable perspectives and information on multidimensional customer realities. In addition there is much evidence that specialization requirements are increasing in marketing and sales activities due to the information revolution, digital marketing opportunities, data available to buyers and sellers and other factors. The common allocation of responsibilities reflects these expertise requirements. But coordination problems often arise because of conflicting priorities: what each group considers as fundamental to 'good marketing' and what it takes for granted as part of its daily work versus what it considers discretionary in allocating its limited attention, resources and efforts.

Orientation and Time Horizons

In most B2B organizations, marketing managers' responsibilities mean that they operate across geographical territories but with specific product and/or market responsibilities. Their orientation is also strongly influenced by where in the value chain they concentrate: as I noted previously, marketing responsibilities are closely tied in B2B firms, with product development and ongoing product/service management issues. As a result their time horizons tend to be driven by product development and introduction cycles (which can stretch over multiple quarters or even years, depending on the market), as well as by the internal planning and budgeting processes of their firms (typically an annual process). By contrast, sales managers and sales reps tend to operate within geographical territories but with specific customer or individual account assignments. Their orientation and time horizons naturally tend to be driven by selling cycles at multiple accounts and external buying processes, rather than internal planning or budgeting processes. This orientation also means that sales often finds differences in product/service requirements among customers salient and vital to 'closing the sale'. Even as marketing managers often have an incentive to amortize development costs and stretch a product's applicability *across* customer groups, sales managers have an incentive to customize product/service applications and specify these requirements more narrowly *within* a particular segment or account.

The following comment from a B2B marketing manager (Cespedes 1995, p. 64) illustrates this tension:

> In our business, crucial product decisions must be made years before introduction, and consequences of those decisions linger for years afterward. But customers rarely look beyond a one-to-two year time horizon in assessing their needs. So, customer surveys and sales force feedback are limited means for making key decisions about product requirements.

In her firm, however, short-term and account-specific requirements drove field sales behavior. This difference was the source of sales complaints that 'marketing management is unresponsive . . . not customer-oriented' and parallel complaints by marketing managers that salespeople 'want us to be everything to everybody and so destroy the coherence of our marketing strategy'.

Performance Criteria and Metrics

What gets measured gets attention, particularly when performance metrics are tied to compensation and promotion. Differences in time horizons and orientation also reflect reward systems that in turn reflect a need in B2B firms to focus on and maintain accountability – a scarce resource in any complex organization characterized by inherent interdependencies. In the setting of quotas, performance appraisals and bonuses, the focus of sales metrics in most firms is primarily on sales volume rather than profit contribution or activities/tasks performed, occasionally complemented by 'customer satisfaction' indices based on surveys and/or customer retention measures. Marketing measures are more varied, but profit responsibility (or forms of return on assets measures) is usually more prominent.

These differing performance criteria can generate conflicts in the implementation of joint tasks, and as noted previously advocating 'common metrics' is probably the most frequent advice proffered to managers interested in improving cross-functional coordination. But companies encounter many constraints and unintended consequences when they try to follow this advice (see later in this chapter). Therefore a practical need in most B2B organizations is to manage interactions between marketing and sales in the context of different measurement systems.

Information Flows

The groups also differ in (1) their information priorities and type of data tracked by each and (2) the role and use of data that are tracked. Marketing managers naturally tend to view data about assigned products and markets as a priority. Sales people instead view timely information about specific accounts, their sales territory and the activities of resellers or others as priority data. An executive at a market research firm described the information differences in this way (Cespedes 1995, p. 76):

> Marketing managers tend to synthesize the information they receive; they're looking for commonalities across the data because they naturally think in terms of segments, or what seems common to aggregate groups of customers. Sales managers tend to disaggregate the information they receive, and look for exceptions – why account X differs from account Y – because they sell to specific customers, not 'segments'.

The organizational role and use of data also differ. Marketing managers in B2B firms typically need data relevant to product development, costing and pricing decisions. More than sales managers, marketing managers often work through formal presentations as part of their firms' market planning processes. Hence compatibility with the *selling* firm's budgeting vocabulary is a key criterion for useful data for marketing. Sales managers typically need data relevant to specific accounts, so compatibility with multiple *buying*

Table 8.1   Marketing dialects

Marketing	Sales
Span of Surveillance: Orientation	
• Across geographies, with specific product/ market responsibilities	• Within territories, with specific account responsibilities
Time Horizon Drivers	
• Program/product cycles	• Selling cycles
• Internal budgeting process	• External buying processes
• Career paths that emphasize frequent rotation among assignments	• Career paths that emphasize account continuity in a sales territory
Performance Criteria and Information Flows	
• Profit and/or ROA criteria	• Sales volume
• Product/Market information	• Geographical/Account information
• Synthesize for development, costing, pricing activities	• Disaggregate for selling and specific account management activities

vocabularies and purchase criteria is naturally more important to them. Similarly the groups' informational needs reflect fundamentally different usage cycles. With their responsibilities closer to R&D and product development activities in B2B firms, marketing managers must gather and present data to and from a variety of functional areas. Furthermore these data are often assembled for the firm's capital budgeting process, which in many companies adheres to a set annual schedule. In contrast, the timing of sales' information use is more irregular and less capable of being scheduled, because it is more influenced by external customers rather than internal processes.

Table 8.1 outlines these differences in roles, orientation, time horizons, performance metrics and information flows. I have previously used the term 'marketing dialects' (Cespedes 1993b) to refer to these differences between marketing and sales and the implications: individual managers in an organization may recognize that products *and* accounts *and* markets are all important and mutually interdependent, but the aggregate impact of these differences on their behavior still generates different priorities and coordination challenges. Furthermore, according to this analysis, the differences are necessary because they reflect core task requirements in each unit: the need to develop and maintain discrete types of expertise along a continuum of value creation and value delivery activities. Over time as each group focuses on its subset of activities, their separate operating procedures become part of the way things are done around here. The result for the organization as a whole, however, is what I call a 'competency trap': each unit's accumulated experience with established procedures provides efficiencies *within* its own domain but also inhibits coordinated interactions *between* the units.

This point is analogous to what others have called organizational 'routines' (Nelson and Winter 1982) or 'thought worlds' (Homburg and Jensen 2007): the pattern of activity that characterizes different subgroups in a firm, shapes the assumptions and marketplace interpretations of each group and over time shapes repertoires of capabilities and constraints. Any attempt to rechannel and manage these processes productively must understand its roots and therefore the challenge in coordinating marketing and sales:

how to link efficiently and effectively the knowledge, capabilities and operations necessarily located in different areas and marketing dialects in most firms (Table 8.1).

DEVELOPMENTS IN PRACTICE

What have B2B companies done to deal with the challenge of balancing demands for specialized expertise *and* cross-functional collaboration between marketing and sales? Documented initiatives include (1) structural linkages; (2) changes or investments in market research and information systems; and (3) changes in management processes, including account management and human resource (HR) processes such as career paths and training programs.

Structural Linkages

Different configurations of marketing and sales have been tried across industries to improve the coordination of these functions (Homburg et al. 2008). As part of their structural approaches, some firms have created or expanded positions to coordinate marketing and sales. Liaison units are most common when product development requires coordination far in advance of introduction (e.g. technology firms) or when go-to-market initiatives involve multiple marketing programs that share common distribution channels (e.g. many service businesses and multiproduct firms). Liaison units are intended to act as the 'voice of the field' for marketing managers and as product/service experts and customizers for salespeople, ensuring two-way information flows about interdependent tasks; this role is especially important in markets in which companies must launch more products faster to increasingly diverse segments.

As Microsoft grew and its product line and distribution channels expanded, for example, it established a 'Sales Operation Group' intended to play this role. Similarly IBM embedded this liaison activity within the responsibilities of its 'Assistant General Manager of Marketing' position. Another common structural device involves deploying 'Field Marketing Specialists': product, geography or dedicated vertical marketing specialists. These positions are intended to increase the field's ability to sell and service a new product or segment or to facilitate the coherent adaption of headquarters-based marketing programs to different regions, channels and selling requirements across a company's product line. Companies as varied as General Electric, MCI and Texas Instruments have adopted this device in different business units.

These structural linkages can legitimize marketing–sales collaboration in companies in which these activities have long resided in separate areas, each steeped in its own standard operating procedures. They offer a visible process for specifying required two-way information flows and capturing learning about joint activities. Without a formal structure, informal methods of managing marketing–sales coordination are often too time consuming, treated as a distant 'secondary priority' by each group or simply ineffective because attempts by managers to get involved in another group's plans are viewed as infringements, not collaboration. At the same time, liaison units represent another management layer with attendant costs in salaries, support systems, overhead and changes in decision-making processes. Research (e.g. Cespedes 1995) also indicates that these units depend heavily on the personal stature of their members, but attracting managers with visible track records of accomplishment to a liaison position (versus staff members regarded as 'expendable' by the core marketing or sales units) is a challenge.

Market Research and Information Systems

'More communication' is a frequent prescription for cross-functional coordination. But it requires a mutually relevant information infrastructure that serves groups that must collaborate around activities such as customer analysis, lead generation and lead follow-up (Carroll 2006; Chatterjee 1996; Rouzies et al. 2005). In the alignment of market research responsibilities established by most B2B firms, research usually reports to (and is funded by) marketing, and its key responsibility is to expedite research requests from marketing managers, not sales. Some companies have realigned their market research function to foster better coordination, placing research in closer contact with the firm's IT function (because more research data are driven by IT developments among research suppliers and the company) and positioning it as a cross-functional facilitator of joint marketing–sales information needs (rather than primarily a support or analytical resource for product management groups). In this type of alignment, the research budget may come from marketing, sales and IT. The goal, as one executive explained (Cespedes 1993b, p. 32), is to 'involve research more directly with decisions that increasingly require translation among relevant units. Making marketing programs congruent with distribution economies, for example, requires more data from more functions. Research should help to provide a common understanding of the impact of each unit's decisions on the other units involved'.

Moreover, market research in many B2B firms has been complemented by significant investments in customer relationship management (CRM) systems and other software initiatives intended to create a common information base and improve coordination between marketing and sales groups. IBM created a new function called 'Channel Enablement' intended, in part, to use CRM data to bridge marketing–sales gaps in areas such as new product announcements and linking advertising dollars spent to actual sales.

A realignment of research activities, in conjunction with new IT capabilities, often complements the role of formal liaison units. But the costs of realigning activities in this manner are considerable: hardware and software costs are significant, and incorporating shipment and account order information into these systems, data with high interest for sales, typically involves developing protocols that are compatible with various other processes throughout the company. Other costs involve technology upgrades, ongoing maintenance of the data, and time and costs involved in end-user training, especially because the customized and often account-specific data relevant to sales activities typically are more expensive to obtain and keep up-to-date than are the broader market and product surveys traditionally associated with marketing research at B2B firms. Finally a key thrust of these changes is to make local field data more prominent in marketing decision-making. But for various reasons, the quality of the inputs can be suspect. In B2B firms the input of the field salesperson is typically crucial to these information systems. But sales managers are often reluctant to involve the sales force because it takes time away from selling. Conversely there are questions about the ability and motivation of salespeople to provide accurate information. Sales personnel, trained and compensated to 'get the sale', tend to have well-documented biases (see research dating back to Albaum 1964; Lambert et al. 1990; Robertson 1974) regarding the relative importance of price, product attributes and the product performance levels desired by customers.

Management Processes

Some firms have altered management processes, including changes in career paths, training programs and core account management processes. Individual managers usually join specific areas in organizations, promotions typically mean acquiring successive levels of expertise along a given area's career path and career paths tend to reinforce the differing 'dialects' outlined in Table 8.1. In B2B firms, marketing managers are more likely than sales personnel to have MBAs; because account relationships are important, salespeople are more likely to remain with assigned accounts and in a given territory far longer than marketing managers stay with their assigned product or service. Yet people with different training and experience must nonetheless work on joint activities. To address this situation some firms have established explicit cross-functional career tracks in sales and marketing. Others have expanded the length and type of sales experience required for marketing managers. Still others have initiated joint performance evaluation processes for marketing and sales personnel who must coordinate various activities. At one firm, marketing and sales managers evaluate each other's contributions with a questionnaire that considers 'attitude, professionalism, quick response, and contribution to customer satisfaction'. These questionnaires are also completed by customers and reviewed by the managers to whom the relevant sales and marketing personnel report. It is unclear what the overall impact is, but as one executive at this firm notes, 'This procedure generates a discussion between Sales and Marketing of specific accounts – a considerable benefit in a business where, for good reasons, the sales rep has a select group of accounts but those accounts are among dozens or hundreds considered in Marketing analyses'.

Training programs have also been revised, which often involves joint training or 'action-learning' programs in which marketing and sales managers work together on a combination of activities. An influential model has been the Work-Out programs begun at General Electric (GE). Company-specific in focus, cross-functional in terms of participants and project-driven in agenda, these sessions deal with various issues within GE's business units (Jick 1990). Many involve the need for better integration of marketing and sales initiatives in the context of global competition, lower priced alternatives and a consequent emphasis on product/service solutions of various kinds. In initiating Work-Out, then-Chairman Jack Welch was explicit about the organizational challenge: 'Even in a horizontal structure you'll still have product managers, still need accountability. But the lines [between product marketing and other units] will blur' (Stewart 1991, p. 61).

Another approach is to establish multifunctional teams that bring together marketing and sales managers (and often other functions) for specific key accounts. This approach has been most prominently adopted by firms that sell consumer goods through a B2B relationship with major retail accounts or other institutional customers. Procter & Gamble staffs teams with salespeople from different divisions and marketing people assigned to a large account. Team members spend one to two years at customer sites and, as a marketing manager noted, 'You come away with an appreciation for what's involved in executing brand programs through the distribution channel' (Cespedes 1996b, p. 33). Hewlett-Packard and Oracle have created similar account teams. These assignments allow firms to move managers, information and capabilities to and from headquarters and local levels, where key customization tasks are located.

These changes in management processes are each intended to develop managers with experience on 'both sides' of the marketing–sales interface, as well as more awareness of the other unit's operating conditions and contributions. The goal is to build cross-functional knowledge and relations that are more likely to result in coordinated programs. But cross-functional career initiatives are time consuming and expensive and for this reason are usually limited to relatively few managers in each area. This limitation raises implementation obstacles precisely because most careers develop according to a different paradigm: people must assume the career risks in a situation in which most managers are evaluated and promoted by acquiring within-function (not cross-functional) expertise. Joint training programs thus usually entail *additional* training and expenses, beyond still-required functional knowledge in product management or selling skills. Similarly multifunctional account teams generate many transaction-specific investments that often 'duplicate' existing systems in established marketing and sales units, and rotations in and out of selling assignments are not simple, as the team seeks to build continuity and long-term relationships with customers, even as team members change.

SUGGESTIONS FOR FURTHER RESEARCH

If fruitful research areas are characterized by issues important to practitioners, relevant literature from multiple disciplines and specific topics for examination, then marketing–sales coordination is likely to be a prime research opportunity for some time. In the previous section I outlined several areas of interest to practitioners: the impact of different structural linkages on firms' abilities to coordinate marketing and sales activities; the benefits and vulnerabilities of HR initiatives such as career paths and training on these groups; and different methods of account management that might help or inhibit the alignment of marketing and sales deliverables. I conclude this chapter with additional suggestions, grouped into four categories: people, processes, reward systems and the impact of online technology and digital marketing on buying behavior and marketing–sales coordination tasks.

People

Ultimately coordination occurs between people. Practitioners attest to what can or cannot be accomplished in organizations, depending on the presence or absence of constructive relationships among people in different functions. One area of research focuses on individual-level factors that affect coordination. For example Massey and Dawes (2007) draw on exchange theory to build a model of how factors such as interpersonal trust influence effectiveness in marketing–sales relationships, and Dewsnap and Jobber (2002) employ social psychology to develop a model of trust in marketing–sales relations. This focus would seem to be a promising area of research: substantial academic marketing literature exists regarding trust in channel (Andaleeb 1995; Anderson and Narus 1990) and market research (Moorman et al. 1993) relationships, and practitioner sales literature is replete with references to 'trust-based' relationships (e.g. Green 2006). But surprisingly few studies draw on either literature stream to examine marketing–sales coordination.

An allied area pertains to the impact of globalization. As companies compete across markets in an increasingly wired world, their marketing–sales tasks involve people from more countries. This situation adds the differences in national culture to the 'marketing dialects' I detailed in Table 8.1. Further research thus might extend extant literature on cultural differences (Deshpande and Farley 2004; Quelch and Deshpande 2004) to marketing–sales coordination.

Processes

Another level of analysis looks at the connections between activities and outcomes that affect coordination between groups. This research recognizes the continuum of interdependent activities between marketing and sales groups (among others in a firm) and considers how activities and outcomes at one organizational level connect to activities and outcomes at a different level. Goodman (2000) provides a delineation of the concept, specific tools for organizational linkage analysis and case studies. Although his focus is much broader than marketing–sales interactions, his four types of linkage analytics (outcome coupling, use of negative and positive feedback systems, identification of limiting conditions and compensatory process mechanisms) seem well-suited to research in this area.

Similarly, if marketing–sales coordination in most firms means linking knowledge and action from different areas, research should examine perspectives on coordination beyond those typically assumed in current business literature. In his popular book on collective decision-making processes, Surowiecki (2004, pp. xix–xx) presents many examples that support a contrary view about coordination, information and decision-making:

> Diversity and independence are important because the best collective decisions are the product of disagreement and contest, not consensus or compromise. An intelligent group . . . does not ask its members to modify their positions in order to let the group reach a decision everyone can be happy with. Instead, it figures out how to use mechanisms – like market prices or intelligent voting systems – to aggregate and produce collective judgments that represent not what any one person thinks but rather, in some sense, what they all think. Paradoxically, the best way for a group to be smart is for each person in it to think and act as independently as possible.

A decade earlier, I had reached a similar conclusion (Cespedes 1995, p. 271), based on field research focusing on marketing and sales interactions in particular:

> Contrary to currently fashionable pronouncements about future organizations as boundaryless, a division of labor that develops and maintains appropriate product, sales, and service expertise is even *more* important as more work becomes knowledge work. . . .. To dismantle or diffuse this necessary expertise in the name of undifferentiated notions of teamwork is to short-circuit the continual organizational learning required [and] to unwittingly encourage lowest common-denominator approaches to the marketplace.

These views stress that absence of conflict may not be optimal for business performance (Homburg et al. 2008), which clearly runs counter to many commonly held assumptions about the role and purpose of 'teamwork' and 'coordination' between groups. It may or may not reflect the task realities of marketing and sales in B2B organizations. But it is an area worthy of research, especially because IT now makes easily accessible, for dispersed marketing and sales personnel, the kinds of independent interactions that Surowiecki (2004) documents in other contexts.

Reward Systems

Changes in reward systems represent a common response to coordination problems. In a field study (Cespedes 1995), I found that managers tend to adopt two theories-in-use about metrics for marketing and sales groups: a checks-and-balance versus common-metrics approach. Oscillation between these approaches over time and within the same firm was not uncommon. The first approach suggests that differing metrics between marketing and sales foster 'constructive conflict' or a check on each group's tendency to insulate itself from other valid enterprise concerns. In theory, profit-/margin-measured marketing management has an incentive to monitor sales' execution of marketing programs. In turn, volume-oriented sales managers will challenge and modify marketing plans with timely information from the field about requirements at specific sources of demand. In practice, however, these differing metrics often lead to internal competition between marketing units for field sales attention and resources, as well as coordination issues at major accounts that buy across the selling company's product line.

Faced with these conflicts, managers often attempt a common-metrics approach, typically by making profit or margin responsibility – instead of, or in addition to, volume metrics – a key component of sales as well as marketing metrics. But again my field research revealed obstacles and unintended consequences in implementation of common metrics for marketing and sales: a lack of information systems needed to generate the measurement data and unintended negative impacts on the sale and cost structures of many lower margin items that still required high volumes to maintain purchasing economies and manufacturing throughput for cost/price competitiveness (for example, many B2B firms sell commodity and specialty items that differ significantly in their profit margins but that also have important interrelationships in the firm in terms of purchasing, R&D and manufacturing economies).

But constraints in aligning reward systems clearly do not mean that performance metrics are irrelevant. Rather the complexities indicate a practice and research opportunity, namely, the need to find useful complementary relationships in the metrics for marketing and sales units.

Impact of Online Technologies

During the past decade, in both consumer and B2B markets, customers have become better equipped with information and technology in their buying processes. Sophisticated tools are readily available to conduct product searches, online price bids and specific comparisons (e.g. average maintenance costs or energy efficiency ratings for many B2B products). Meanwhile selling channels have proliferated. A B2B firm that once sold solely through a wholesale channel or its own direct sales force now also has a website, online catalog, mobile telephone connections with customers and new digital marketing techniques within its marketing mix. The net effect is to alter the dimensions of buying and selling and, as a result, the nature of the marketing–sales interfaces in many B2B organizations.

One article describing these developments outlines various impacts along the stages of a purchasing process and suggests concomitant impacts on the selling organization (Nunes and Cespedes 2003), including a de facto need for multichannel capabilities, new information requirements and cross-channel performance metrics. These factors necessarily affect the continuum of activities between marketing and sales. But while 'digital marketing' and 'social networks' have increasingly been the focus of research, the impact of new technologies on organizational requirements in general, and marketing–sales coordination issues in particular, has not.

This state of affairs leads to my concluding observation about this topic. Because of their central role in customer acquisition and retention, changes in marketing requirements always have wider organizational implications. Today those changes are at the heart of many challenges facing B2B firms worldwide: how to harness new technologies that alter buying behavior? How to develop talent capable of responding flexibly but coherently to market changes? How to establish processes and reward managers for increasingly complex tasks across national and organizational boundaries? How to encourage cross-functional efforts without diluting necessary expertise and accountability? The topic of coordinating marketing and sales is thus both a reflection of and a productive gateway into these important managerial and research issues.

NOTES

1. This section draws on the delineation of marketing and sales activities discussed in Cespedes (1995, chapter 2). Rouzies et al. (2005) and Kotler et al. (2006) provide similar analyses of these activities.
2. For useful historical perspectives on marketing management roles, see Buell (1975), Fulmer (1975) and Tull et al. (1991).

REFERENCES

Adams, J.S. (1976), 'The structure and dynamics of behavior in organizational boundary roles', in M. Dunnette (ed.), *Handbook of Industrial and Organizational Psychology*, New York: Rand McNally, pp. 317–51.

Albaum, G. (1964), 'Horizontal information flow: an exploratory study', *Journal of the Academy of Management*, **7** (March), 21–33.

Andaleeb, S.S. (1995), 'Dependence relations and the moderating role of trust: implications for behavioral intentions in marketing channels', *International Journal of Research in Marketing*, **12**, 157–72.

Anderson, J.C. and James A. Narus (1990), 'A model of distributor firm and manufacturer firm working partnerships', *Journal of Marketing*, **54** (January), 42–58.

Ashforth, B.E. and R.T. Lee (1990), 'Defensive behavior in organizations: a preliminary model', *Human Relations*, **43**, 621–48.

Buell, V.P. (1975), 'The changing role of the product manager', *Journal of Marketing*, **39**, 3–11.

Carroad, P.A. and C.A. Carroad (1982), 'Strategic interfacing of R&D and marketing', *Research Management*, **25** (January), 28–33.

Carroll, B.J. (2006), *Lead Generation for the Complex Sale*, New York: McGraw-Hill.

Cespedes, Frank V. (1990), 'A preface to payment: designing a sales compensation plan', *Sloan Management Review*, **32** (Fall), 59–69.

Cespedes, Frank V. (1992), 'Sales coordination: an exploratory study', *Journal of Personal Selling & Sales Management*, **12** (Summer), 13–29.

Cespedes, Frank V. (1993a), 'Coordinating sales and marketing in consumer goods firms', *Journal of Consumer Marketing*, **10** (Summer), 37–55.

Cespedes, Frank V. (1993b), 'Market research and marketing dialects', *Marketing Research*, **10** (Winter), 26–34.

Cespedes, Frank V. (1995), *Concurrent Marketing: Integrating Product, Sales, and Service*, Boston, MA: Harvard Business School Press.

Cespedes, Frank V. (1996a), 'The marketing gearbox', *Strategy and Business*, **3** (Spring), 4–21.

Cespedes, Frank V. (1996b), 'Beyond teamwork: how the wise can synchronize', *Marketing Management*, **5** (Spring), 25–37.

Cespedes, Frank V., S.X. Doyle and R.J. Freedman (1989), 'Teamwork for today's selling', *Harvard Business Review*, **67** (March–April), 44–58.

Chandler, A.D. (1977), *The Visible Hand: The Managerial Revolution in American Business*, Cambridge, MA: Harvard University Press.

Chatterjee, S.C. (1996), 'Management generated leads: panacea for enhancing salesforce productivity?', *Working Paper 22-1996*, Institute for the Study of Business Markets.

Cummings, W.T., D.W. Jackson and L. Ostrom (1984), 'Differences between industrial and consumer product managers', *Industrial Marketing Management*, **13** (3), 171–80.

Dawes, P.I. and P.G. Patterson (1988), 'The performance of industrial and consumer product managers', *Industrial Marketing Management*, **17** (2), 73–84.

De Dreu, C. and L.R. Weingart (2003), 'Task versus relationship conflict, team performance, and team member satisfaction: a meta analysis', *Journal of Applied Psychology*, **88** (4), 741–49.

Deshpande, Rohit and John U. Farley (2004), 'Organizational culture, market orientation, innovativeness and firm performance: an international research odyssey', *International Journal of Research in Marketing*, **14** (January), 3–22.

Dewsnap, B. and D. Jobber (2002), 'A social psychological model of relations between marketing and sales', *European Journal of Marketing*, **36** (4), 878–94.

Eisenmann, T. (2009), 'A compilation of the web's best advice for entrepreneurs', available at http://platform-sandnetworks.blogspot.com, accessed 15 July 2010.

Friedman, W.A. (2004), *Birth of a Salesman: The Transformation of Selling in America*, Cambridge, MA: Harvard University Press.

Fulmer, R.D. (1975), 'Product management: panacea or Pandora's box', *California Management Review*, **7** (Spring), 63–74.

Goodman, P.S. (2000), *Missing Organizational Linkages: Tools for Cross-Level Research*, Thousand Oaks, CA: Sage Publications.

Green, C.H. (2006), *Trust-Based Selling*, New York: McGraw-Hill.

Griffin, Abbie and John R. Hauser (1996), 'Integrating R&D and marketing: a review and analysis of the literature', *Journal of Product Innovation Management*, **13** (4), 191–215.

Homburg, Christian and Ove Jensen (2007), 'The thought worlds of marketing and sales: which differences make a difference?', *Journal of Marketing*, **71** (July), 124–42.

Homburg, Christian, Ove Jensen and H. Krohmer (2008), 'Configurations of marketing and sales: a taxonomy', *Journal of Marketing*, **72** (April), 133–54.

Jick, T.D. (1990), 'Customer–supplier partnerships: human resources as bridge builders', *Human Resource Management*, **29** (Winter), 435–54.

Kotler, Philip, N. Rackham and S. Krishnaswamy (2006), 'Ending the war between sales & marketing', *Harvard Business Review*, **84** (July–August), 68–78.

Lambert, D., H. Marmorstein and A. Sharma (1990), 'Industrial salespeople as a source of market information', *Industrial Marketing Management*, **19** (Spring), 141–8.

Lawrence, P. and J.W. Lorsch (1967), *Organization and Environment: Managing Differentiation and Integration*, Boston, MA: Graduate School of Business Administration, Harvard University.

Levitt, Theodore (1960), 'Marketing myopia', *Harvard Business Review*, **38** (July–August), 22–32.

Levy, J. (2008), 'Gaining value from the sales and marketing conversation', LeveragePoint Value Management Blog, available at http://blog.leveragepoint.com, accessed 28 March 2010.

Maltz, E. and A.J. Kohli (2000), 'Reducing marketing's conflicts with other functions: the differential aspect of integrating mechanisms', *Journal of the Academy of Marketing Science*, **28** (4), 479–92.

Massey, G. and P. Dawes (2007), 'Personal characteristics, trust, conflict, and effectiveness in marketing/sales working relationships', *European Journal of Marketing*, **41** (4), 1117–45.

Menon, A., S.G. Bharadwaj, and R. Howell (1996), 'The quality and effectiveness of marketing strategy: effects of functional and dysfunctional conflict in intraorganizational relationships', *Journal of the Academy of Marketing Science*, **24** (4), 299–313.

Moncrief, W.C. (1986), 'Selling activities and sales position taxonomies for industrial sales forces', *Journal of Marketing Research*, **23** (3), 261–70.

Moore, G. (2002), *Crossing the Chasm*, New York: HarperCollins.

Moorman, Christine, Rohit Deshpande and Gerald Zaltman (1993), 'Factors affecting trust in market research relationships', *Journal of Marketing*, **57** (January), 81–101.

Nelson, R. and S.G. Winter (1982), *An Evolutionary Theory of Economic Change*, Cambridge, MA: Harvard University Press.

Nunes, P. and Frank V. Cespedes (2003), 'The customer has escaped', *Harvard Business Review*, **81** (November), 106–15.

Pondy, L.R. (1967), 'Organizational conflict: concepts and models', *Administrative Science Quarterly*, **12** (2), 296–320.

Powers, T.L., W.S. Martin, H. Rushing and S. Daniels (1987), 'Selling before 1900: an historical perspective', *Journal of Personal Selling & Sales Management*, **7** (November), 1–7.

Quelch, J.A. and Rohit Deshpande (2004), *The Global Market: Developing a Strategy to Manage Across Borders*, San Francisco, CA: Jossey-Bass.

Robbins, S.P. (1974), *Managing Organizational Conflict*, Englewood Cliffs, NJ: Prentice-Hall.

Robertson, D. (1974), 'Communications and sales force feedback', *Journal of Business Communication*, **11** (1), 3–9.

Rouzies, D., Erin Anderson, A.J. Kohli, R.E. Michaels, Barton A. Weitz and A.A. Zoltners (2005), 'Sales and marketing integration: a proposed framework', *Journal of Personal Selling & Sales Management*, **25** (Spring), 113–22.

Ruekert, R.W. and O.C. Walker (1987), 'Marketing's interaction with other functional units: a conceptual framework and empirical evidence', *Journal of Marketing*, **51** (January), 1–19.

Shapiro, B.P. (1977), 'Can marketing and manufacturing coexist?', *Harvard Business Review*, **55** (September–October), 121–32.

Shaw, V. and C.T. Shaw (1988), 'Conflict between engineers and marketers', *Industrial Marketing Management*, **27** (3), 279–91.

Singh, J. (1993), 'Boundary role ambiguity: facets, determinants, and impacts', *Journal of Marketing*, **57** (January), 11–31.

Stewart, T.A. (1991), 'GE keeps those ideas coming', *Fortune*, **58** (August 12), 58–64.

Surowiecki, J. (2004), *The Wisdom of Crowds*, New York: Doubleday.

Tull, D.S., B.E. Cooley, M.R. Phillips and H.S. Watkins (1991), 'The organization of marketing activities of American manufacturers', Marketing Science Institute, Report No. 91-126.

9 Competitor intelligence: enabling B2B marketing strategy
Liam Fahey

Every B2B marketing strategy, no matter how brilliantly conceived or exquisitely executed, sooner or later faces the ultimate marketplace reality: can it withstand (and survive) the direct assault of rivals? Given the pace of change in and around B2B market spaces, it is increasingly sooner rather than later that rivals take aim at a winning strategy. The depressing irony in competitive strategy is that the more successful a strategy, the more it becomes a target for rivals. They see the marketplace opportunity inherent in the strategy; they conjure marketplace approaches (strategies) to garner a portion of that opportunity, often extending the scope and scale of the base opportunity. Thus, in any B2B market space, strategy is not just about attracting, winning and retaining customers; it must also be about outwitting, outmaneuvering and outperforming current and potential rivals. The latter requires competitor intelligence, that is, insight into competitors' current and potential strategies; not just what their strategies are or may be but why they pursue (or do not pursue) specific strategy options. In short, competitor intelligence is nothing short of critical to determining B2B marketing strategy content and preferred execution modes.

The goals of this chapter are fourfold: first, to define and describe the domain, scope and intent of competitor intelligence – what it is and what it is not; second, to illustrate how and why intelligence, as an understanding of competitors' current and potential strategies, is fundamental to designing and executing strategies that generate superior marketplace and financial returns; third, to describe the state of the practice of competitor analysis – how leading firms conduct competitor intelligence; and fourth, to offer a research agenda to advance how competitor intelligence and B2B marketing strategy can be better connected.

The four goals shape the structure of the chapter. I begin by briefly describing what competitor intelligence entails, with specific emphasis on its purpose in the context of B2B marketing strategy. I then connect competitor intelligence and B2B marketing strategy. The bulk of the chapter delineates the three core analysis activities at the heart of competitor intelligence: description, interpretation and assessment. Finally, I offer some ideas for a research program.

UNDERSTANDING THE COMPETITOR INTELLIGENCE DOMAIN

Domain Definition

Because competitor intelligence has been defined in so many ways (Brody 2008), it is essential to be clear on the content domain it encompasses: what it is, and what it is not.

Thus the two words 'competitor' and 'intelligence' need to be carefully delineated so that the confusion and ambiguity sometimes reflected in articles, books and speeches about competitor intelligence are avoided.

For the purposes of this chapter, competitor as an entity is defined very broadly. It includes both a time and a breadth dimension. It addresses current, emerging and potential competitors, not just those we are competing against today but also those we might compete against in the future. Who we compete against is viewed broadly. It is not just look-alike competitors but functional substitute rivals (organizations offering a product or solution that can substitute for our offering). It is, of course, the functional substitute rivals that often radically disrupt the long-lived stability in so many market spaces.

Intelligence as a concept is far more elusive. It is best viewed from a variety of related perspectives. Each contributes to understanding the scope, power and value of intelligence. First, intelligence can be viewed as an *output*: insight into competitors' current and potential strategies. Second, intelligence can be viewed as an *analysis process*: the analytical steps required to transform data about one or more competitors into insight. Third, intelligence can be viewed as a *value-enabling* activity: how insight is leveraged in marketing strategy-making and execution or, more broadly, in marketing decision-making (Fahey 2009). In summary, competitor intelligence addresses both the creation and the leveraging of superior understanding of rivals' current and future strategies.

Intent: Marketing Strategy Implications

Both literature and practice frequently misconstrue the purposes of competitor intelligence. It is not to develop and document detailed descriptions of rivals' strategies – that is not the end. It is not to understand everything possible about competitors, nor even to eliminate all possible surprise moves by competitors. Rather, the intent resides in how the analysis of such strategy descriptions can be leveraged to inform marketing decision-makers and influence strategy deliberations. A magnificently documented projection of how a rival might reconfigure its strategy to create a new, distinctive value proposition for an emerging customer segment results in little decision-making value until we derive its implications for our firm. In short, the intelligence intent must be to identify and assess marketing strategy implications for our firm: do we try to pre-empt this rival by developing a new breakthrough product? Do we quickly amend our current strategy to gain a temporary advantage with specific customer segments? Do we just wait to see how customers might react?

Scope: Breadth of Analysis

The scope of competitor intelligence work with respect to rivals' marketing strategies is almost boundless. Some broad categories of analysis include:

- detecting the emergence of new competitors;
- describing the current strategies of rivals;
- capturing change in rivals' strategies;
- projecting rivals' potential or likely strategic moves;

- evaluating the consequences of rivals' strategies for change in and around the industry or competitive space or specific market segments;
- interpreting the consequences of competitors' strategies (and, more specifically, strategic moves) for specific inputs to our strategy deliberations. For example, what does the evolution of a competitor's product offering indicate about emerging and future marketplace opportunities? Does a competitor's announcement about where it wants to take its R&D program indicate a significant threat to the dominant products in this market space?
- assessing the implications of competitors' strategies (and, more specifically, strategic moves) for our strategies.

Focus: Which Competitors?

Competitor intelligence as practiced in many B2B firms unfortunately leads to extensive wasted resources – time, attention, energy and cash – because one of its most basic questions is not critically addressed: which competitors should be the primary focus of analysis, and which should receive only secondary attention? As a consequence, firms commit the grievous error of not paying attention to rivals other than the current large market share rivals. Analysis thus forgoes the opportunity to learn from others and often to realize what cannot be learned from large market share rivals, no matter how systematic, detailed and creative the analysis.

Theoretically the answer to the question is clear: address the rivals that generate the insights most valuable for marketing strategy and decision-making purposes. But what criteria are appropriate in determining which rivals to address? Unfortunately, the intelligence and strategy literature is largely silent on this question.

In my experience, three guidelines have proved useful in screening potential competitors for attention and thus avoiding the errors noted previously. First, adopt a broad scope in identifying the relevant strategy and decision domain. For example, include related product and customer segments you may not currently compete in; do not confine the analysis only to current rivals, that is, largely look-alike rivals considered by your current customers. Incumbents in related segments might conceivably enter your current market space. The output is likely to be a long laundry list of rivals. Second, in the initial screening of 'relevant' rivals, adopt a broad definition of competitors. For example, a small market share rival may be developing a customer value proposition that will outperform rivals over time. The initial laundry list of rivals will be extended even further. Third, use the following types of questions to prune the list to a manageable few. These questions include:

1. *Winning rivals:* Which competitors have (sustained) a winning value proposition either in segments in which we compete or in segments we may enter?
2. *Leapfrog rivals:* Which competitors seem to be shaping a strategy that might leapfrog current (and even emerging) rivals?
3. *Local rivals:* Which competitors have had 'local' wins (or losses) that might indicate future strategy directions?
4. *Emergent rivals:* Which competitors could enter our current market space and win even though their product or offering does not look like ours?

With these criteria, it will rarely be necessary to conduct a 'full' or 'deep-dive' analysis on more than four or five competitors. Each chosen competitor, in effect, becomes representative of a class of rivals.

Some Glaring Misconceptions

A small set of misconceptions about competitor intelligence, some evident in the literature and all manifest in the practice, serve to inhibit realization of its full value. Each misconception negatively affects how competitor intelligence is understood and how it is practiced (Fahey 2009).

- Intelligence is something you gather. No. You gather data and then you create intelligence, that is, something of value to decision-makers.
- Intelligence should only be about facts. No. Facts address the present and the past. Intelligence is much more about the future, what competitors will do. There are not many facts about the future!
- Intelligence should not be about judgments. No. It is all about judgments. Every inference that is derived, without which intelligence is impossible, requires the judgment of the people involved.
- Intelligence should not identify implications for the business. No. Intelligence professionals can provide decision-makers with strategy or decision 'options'; they can point out possible types of actions that could be considered.

Adherence to these and many related false prescriptions renders competitor intelligence as nothing more than simple descriptions of what is happening and so circumscribes the thinking of those doing the work that genuine insights are most unlikely to ensue.

COMPETITOR INTELLIGENCE AND B2B MARKETING STRATEGY: A PERSPECTIVE AND RATIONALE

B2B marketing strategy can never be immune to attack by rivals. Thus the B2B marketing strategist must address fundamental challenges: how to outwit, outmaneuver and outperform individual and/or multiple rivals (Fahey 1999). Each contributes to superior market and economic performance. Intelligence plays a fundamental role in meeting each challenge.

Outwitting rivals involves, for example, capturing customer needs faster and better than rivals, anticipating rivals' moves and countermoves, and learning from rivals' assumptions about likely marketplace change. Intelligence enables each of these aspects of outwitting rivals.

Outmaneuvering rivals involves, for example, getting the right products to the market before rivals, creating and delivering *winning* value propositions to targeted customer segments, and developing alliances that inhibit rivals from partnering with key third parties. Again, intelligence contributes to each of these choices.

Outperforming rivals involves both marketplace and financial dimensions. Marketplace performance ranges from being the first to establish a new product–customer space, to launching new breakthrough products, to gaining market share or share of individual customers. Financial performance runs the gamut from getting cash faster and getting more of it to reducing cash flow volatility and vulnerability, all of which contribute to enhancing return on investment and shareholder value (Srivastava et al. 1998).

Attention to outwitting, outmaneuvering and outperforming rivals exemplifies the *intelligence* perspective advocated in this chapter (and what it is not). Competitor intelligence intent is not simply to emulate rivals, though in some cases that may lead to acceptable short-term returns. Rather, it is about how best to get ahead of rivals (outwitting), how best to execute more smartly than rivals (outmaneuvering) and what the appropriate measures of performance should be (outperforming). Although the immediate analysis focus is obviously current and potential competitors, competitor intelligence never takes its eyes off the ultimate prize: that is, attracting, winning and retaining customers.

The advocated *intelligence* perspective serves three crucial B2B marketing strategy-specific purposes, each of which contributes to winning in the marketplace. First, rivals' strategies and potential marketplace moves provide an external reference frame to counter the internal focus that seems to predominate especially in B2B firms. A rival's strategy that could be reasonable only if it is based on assumptions radically different from ours about, for example, overall market growth, customer switching tendencies and the emergence of substitute rivals immediately challenges the content of our assumptions, the bases for them and, most important, their acceptability as inputs to shaping (future) strategy. Simply put, we do not want to be outwitted by a rival that understands the emerging and potential future better than we do.

Second, it is only through comparison with rivals' current and potential strategies that any B2B firm can assess whether it possesses, can create and could sustain customer-based and competitor-based advantages (Christensen 2010). As discussed subsequently, understanding of competitors' modes of competing to deliver customer value enables critical assessment of whether a firm possesses distinctive customer-based advantage and whether it can sustain such advantage.

Third, rivals' strategies provide a necessary and unavoidable set of criteria in performance assessment. They shift the criteria from market share alone to market leadership: comparison with several rivals may indicate that we are winning a market share battle against some rivals but losing the war when the comparison is with the competitor that is about to launch breakthrough products and/or create a whole new market space.

COMPETITOR INTELLIGENCE PRACTICE: THREE CORE ACTIVITIES

Competitor intelligence as output, analysis process and value enabling is executed many different ways in practice. Some organizations focus on a narrow range of outputs, such as alerts and early warnings (for example, when and how a competitor might launch a new product). Others create myriad outputs, including projections of rivals' likely strategies, key insights, emerging marketplace opportunities and potential risks. Most organizations over time develop their preferred analytical tools and techniques. How organizations connect analysis outputs to marketing decision-making varies greatly

Table 9.1   Three core analysis activities: some key elements

	Description	Interpretation	Assessment
Broad purpose	Describe current, past and expected 'worlds' in and around competitors.	Transform description into inputs useful for strategy development and execution.	Derive and deploy implications for thinking and action (decision-making).
Sample foci of each activity	Which competitors should be addressed? What strategy change is evident or may occur?	What are the consequences of competitors' actions for the broader competitive space? What opportunities, threats and risks are present or emerging?	What change might be required in our current strategy? What new strategy alternatives should we consider?
Typical kinds of outputs	A competitor's current strategy. A competitor's likely strategic moves.	Change in customers' needs. Potential evolution of solutions. Emerging marketplace opportunities and risks. Assumptions about key marketplace change.	Specific change to the current strategy. Modifications to strategy execution. Further exploration of specific opportunities.
Core analysis challenges	Identifying patterns across discordant competitor data. Projecting alternative potential change in strategy.	Discerning specific potential marketplace consequences of rivals' strategy change. Delineating opportunities and risks with sufficient detail to be meaningful.	Determining implications that will maximize potential for winning strategy.
Common errors	Paying too much attention to the wrong competitors. Going overboard on details of competitors' strategies, behaviors, actions and intent.	Paying too little attention to interpretation as a process. Not developing and challenging key inferences about potential competitive consequences.	Running with the first implications that are noted. Not seriously considering implications beyond the current strategy (short-term focus).

across organizations. Yet at the heart of all this variety of competitor intelligence approaches lies three core or fundamental analysis activities: description, interpretation and assessment (see Table 9.1).

Description

Any B2B competitor cannot hide its marketplace strategy from its rivals. Its actions in the marketplace leave sufficient 'footprints in the sand' for any savvy analyst to construct the essential elements of the strategy. These footprints include the products or solutions it places in the marketplace; the customers it pursues; the functionality, features and related attributes of its products; the types of services it provides; its desired image and reputation; how it conducts selling; the channels it uses; and, of course, the prices it charges. It is important to emphasize that what is captured is the marketing strategy as *actually executed*, not the strategy that may be intended (in the minds of the rival's executive team) or the strategy as planned (the strategy delineated in the rival's strategic planning documents).

Description details and documents the competitor's current and potential strategy. It emphasizes change in the competitor's strategy over time: it delineates how the strategy is evolving and what its alternative future paths might be. In short, description endeavors to answer the following related set of questions:

- What is the competitor's current strategy?
- How has it evolved in the last few years?
- How is it changing and what is the likely future direction of the strategy?
- What forces within and outside the competitor are driving or are likely to drive (change in) the strategy?

Identifying the competitor's current strategy: Describing any rival's current marketplace strategy requires three key items: (1) a *framework* that details each of three key components that constitute any firm's marketplace strategy; (2) determination of the *relevant indicators and related data sources*; and (3) an *experienced analyst* who can observe and document patterns in the data – the patterns that enable the executed strategy to be deciphered and detailed. Although space prohibits a detailed description of the methodology that allows a competitor's strategy to be determined with sufficient clarity and certainty, I briefly discuss each one.

The required *framework* involves three key components (Fahey 1999): (1) marketplace scope: what product-market segments does the competitor serve? (2) competitive posture: how does the competitor compete to attract, win and retain customers within these segments? and (3) marketplace goals: what goals is the competitor trying to achieve? Marketplace scope addresses where the competitor is playing in the marketplace. Competitive posture addresses how the competitor is attempting to create customer-based advantage, that is, give the customer reasons to buy from it rather than from its rivals. Marketplace goals address what the competitor is trying to achieve in the marketplace.

Data gathering, if it is not to be ad hoc and haphazard, requires the determination of the *indicators* relevant to each of the three components. Typically, a small group in a two-hour session can identify the indicators specific to each component. The session often identifies indicators historically overlooked or downplayed.

Indicators determine what data need to be collected. They also help identify relevant data sources. For example, service may involve several indicators, including a toll-free number, online emergency support, on-site technical support, spare parts provision and access to third-party technical experts. Each indicator involves its own data sources.

Description generates understanding of the competitor's strategy only when an *experienced analyst* detects and develops patterns across the competitor data. No single component or indicator by itself provides the breadth of perspective that is required to detect and develop a description of a rival's strategy. However, connections across the components enable the discernment of a strategy: how the rival's actions cumulate to suggest the presence of a marketplace strategy.

The analyst can search for patterns within each component and then across the components. For example, one B2B firm discovered the following pattern in a competitor's competitive posture: high-level functionality performance (speed) tailored to meet customers' specifications, a breadth of services unique to the market and high price (compared with rivals). The analyst concluded the competitor was trying to put in place a distinct form of differentiation best described as high performance, high price and customization. This pattern, in conjunction with statements by the executive team and investments in the brand and the sales force, allowed a strong inference about the competitor's goals: the intent seemed to be to dominate the 'high end' of the market.

Projecting change in the competitor's strategy: Description cannot stop with the competitor's current strategy. Substantially different competitor insights emerge when the current strategy is projected over some reasonable period; in most cases, at least two or three years. For example, identifying strategic moves that may not be available to a competitor, because of resource limitations or agility constraints, may generate insights into its option set that would not be evident merely by analyzing its current strategy.

Change within each of the marketplace strategy components, scope, posture and goals, provides indicators of the competitor's potential strategy direction. Trends along product change and customer focus provide strong indicators as to how the strategy will evolve. For many years, for example, Japanese firms continued to add product lines to go up the product ladder. Many B2B competitors continue to extend their product reach, thus allowing projections on how they will target customers over the next two or three years.

Competitive posture tends to be more difficult to project than marketplace scope. Rivals possess more options with regard to posture change. They can execute change in each of the key posture dimensions: product line breath, functionality, features, service, image and reputation, availability, selling and relationships, and price (Fahey 1999). Indeed, continual posture change is necessary: if a firm is not continually adapting and augmenting its value proposition, it is allowing itself to become a 'sitting duck' for rivals.

However, sharp discontinuities in posture are relatively rare: B2B firms infrequently consummate a switch from a price-driven to a solution customization thrust or from a product-centric to a service-focused thrust. Importantly, from a future strategy perspective, such complete shifts in posture thrusts take time; they simply cannot be executed in a short number of months. Thus not only can they be tracked over time but also projected well in advance. Many B2B firms have found that surprisingly accurate projections are possible as to how a competitor will manage its competitive posture by carefully detecting the thrusts of change in posture over time and seeking key indicators of potential posture shifts.

Competitor insights often do not require that the strategy be projected in exquisite detail. For example, a set of indicators, such as product announcements, statements by the competitor's executives and sale force members, may enable a firm to infer how a competitor plans to move into adjacent customer segments.

Interpretation

Describing a competitor's strategy, by itself, generates little strategy-relevant insight. Description evolves into interpretation when current and projected strategy change is evaluated for signals of change in and around the *competitive context*. In this way, what a competitor is doing or plans to do no longer serves as the principal focus; rather, it enables 'context insight' that transcends competitors per se. Unfortunately, in my experience, too many B2B firms devote far too much time to description and far too little time to interpretation and assessment.

Interpretation is critical for at least three reasons. First, because a competitor's strategy (change) may significantly influence the competitive context in which all strategies will play out, it serves as a critical source of context insight. The competitor's strategy and, in particular, change in the strategy may portend key shifts in, for example, product evolution, value propositions, emergence and decline of market segments and, of course, competitive dynamics. Second, insight into the competitive context in turn helps shed light on key necessary *strategy inputs*, including emerging and potential marketplace opportunities, competitive threats, competitive risks and vulnerabilities specific to different types of strategies. Third, when interpretation is not fully developed or, worse, largely ignored, assessment is severely hampered and may lead to less-than-appropriate action guidance. The temptation is to move quickly from an understanding of what a competitor could do to isolating strategy implications without fully understanding how the competitive context might be altered by the competitor's potential actions.

Context insight

Competitor strategy change affords indicators of change in many dimensions of the competitive context. As noted previously, context insight is heavily influenced by which competitors serve as the focus of attention. Because of its importance to intelligence, five frequent types of context insight are addressed:

1. Customer needs: frequently, competitors' actions provide early indicators of emerging customer needs. Unfortunately, all too many B2B firms concentrate so emphatically on discovering more and more granular detail on what competitors are doing to attract, win and retain customers, that they ignore the signaling capacity of these actions to capture emerging and potential customer needs. Thus marketers must focus on deriving inferences about customers' needs, even when the competitor data may be somewhat discordant, incomplete and limited.
2. Solution evolution: competitors' product and related initiatives often portend where customer solutions are headed. A competitor that is winning customers by customizing its provision of technical support, after-sales support and application deployment may be the source of a strong signal that at least some customer segments no longer want just a product but rather a solution to a set of technical issues that pervade application and deployment of the product. A small rival's commitment to delivering a 'full' solution to selected customers in its local geographic region reveals to the market's dominant competitor that many of its customers might also prefer a full solution instead of product components. The shift toward solution provision enables the dominant firm to 'lock in' early several key accounts and thus inhibit migration to other rivals that follow suit. Patterns across competitors also often indicate the broad trajectory that products or solutions are likely to take. More specifically, attention to emerging or potential substitute rivals may indicate dramatic disruptions in product or solution evolution. A large provider of surgery

instruments discovered that the emergence of laser technology could quickly lead to two of its leading product lines becoming obsolete.

3. Value proposition: implicit in the discussion of customer needs and solution evolution is that successful competitor strategy change almost always reveals shifts in winning value propositions. The emphasis here is on winning: the value propositions that are successfully attracting, winning and retaining customers. Again, the unfortunate truth is that all too often B2B firms do not push their analysis of a competitor's competitive posture to determine what the underlying value proposition is and how and why it is winning or losing.

4. Customer migration: sometimes detecting patterns in rivals' competitive posture moves and early market share gains alerts analysts to the potential for dramatic customer migration, often before a full understanding of the underlying customer needs is derived. A midsized industrial components provider recognized that its customers would probably migrate to a recent foreign entrant from the experience of three of its customers in one sales area. The commitment of the foreign rival to partner with these customers in diagnosing their 'engineering challenges' and collaborating to solve them enabled the firm to infer that if other rivals also moved their value proposition in this direction, a mass migration of customers might transpire if corrective action were not taken.

5. Competitive dynamics: a projected change in one competitor's strategy can lead to an inference that suggests a potential dramatic shift in the competitive dynamics among a set of rivals. For example, a regional competitor projected to enter adjacent regions rapidly with a superior value proposition could cause rivalry to shift from a live-and-let-live complacency to a dynamic powered by intense rivalry on multiple dimensions, including services, support, functionality and price.

Strategy inputs

Understanding of change in and around competitors and the competitive context must be transformed into 'inputs' that directly enable strategy development and execution. If these strategy-relevant inputs are not created, interpretation is likely to degenerate, diving deeper into, for example, the nuances and details of change in customer needs or solution evolution or the transformation of value propositions or interesting speculations of future value chain configurations.

Interpretation outputs that constitute critical and proven inputs to the strategy development process include new marketplace opportunities, competitor threats, competitive risks, strategy vulnerabilities and assumptions. Each of these potential strategy inputs requires analysis across the types of context insight areas just discussed. These inputs are developed without respect to any individual competitor. For illustration purposes, I address two inputs.

1. New marketplace opportunities: marketing strategy is always about the pursuit of presumed marketplace opportunity. Thus, an indisputable truth: the analysis of competitors that does not bring new marketplace opportunities to the surface is of little marketing value. Change in competitors' strategies frequently indicates opportunities that heretofore may not have been detected or that may have been noted but then received little, if any, attention. Here are two common examples. Change in

product features often represents a response to a customer's application needs; thus a new use or application opportunity becomes manifest that may be relevant to a broad swath of customers. A competitor that announces a revenue goal or a goal of achieving a specific level of product sales may have inadvertently signaled to rivals that the product opportunity is far greater than it had realized. In these cases, inferences about potential latent opportunities are then tested through research.

2. Competitor threats and competitive risks: competitor threats and competitive risks constitute the flip side of opportunities. Competitor threats represent possible ways that rivals could negatively affect a firm's current strategies. Given the dominant traditional internal focus in many B2B firms, marketing strategy often was conceived and modified without full recognition of potential marketplace risks. Thus competitors' strategic moves and, in some cases, non-moves may draw attention to both current and potential risks. In one instance, a competitor's decision not to carry through on a research program as a launching pad for a new product indicated a regulatory risk (due to Environmental Protection Agency concerns) that had not been previously noted.

Assessment

Interpretation provides the inputs to determine the implications for the firm's current and potential marketplace strategy. The analysis focus now shifts from the competitor and competitive context to *our* business. Assessment aims to identify whether and how we might adapt, or even radically shift our strategy, according to the judgments at the heart of inputs stemming from interpretation. A substantial portion of assessment involves comparing our (current and anticipated) marketplace strategy and its performance with that of the chosen competitors.

Marketplace performance

A competitor's current and potential marketplace performance provides a reference point for assessing our firm's present and projected marketplace performance that is distinctly different from the typical internally focused criteria so dominant in many firms: past performance, stated (including stretch) goals and industry averages. One outcome is that the firm may see its own marketplace results in an entirely new light, one that can run the gamut from reassuringly positive to worryingly negative. Either way, significant implications may accrue for the firm's marketing strategy choices. Consider these two examples. A US firm reviewing its market performance in China concluded that even though it was hugely successful in terms of market share and positive cash flow, its local competitors were gaining so fast that it could not defend its current market position or financial returns. Its market and financial projections for the China market constructed a mere 12 months earlier had to be markedly turned downward. Another industrial products firm discovered that its projected 6–8 per cent industry growth over the next five years was considerably lower than a major rival's public projection of 12–14 per cent. If the firm achieved its planned sales forecast, it would have lost significant market share if the rival's industry projection proved correct. It concluded that there was significant evidence to move closer to the rival's projection and then adjusted its marketing strategy (and product output) accordingly.

Current marketplace strategy

It is never sufficient merely to determine that marketplace opportunities and competitive risks exist; it is necessary to determine their relevance to the firm's current marketplace strategy. Addressing the following questions provides one way to ensure that broad sets of potential implications are not overlooked:

1. Are marketplace opportunities being missed? The current marketing strategy was crafted in a previous period. The outputs of interpretation often identify opportunities that should be pursued, in part, because they are an extension of the current strategy. Typical examples include adding product lines (which a competitor has already introduced or plans to introduce), extending the intended customer reach (sometimes one or more competitors reveal customer segments that previously we had not addressed) and adapting distribution channels or even adopting new channels. Indeed, pursuing opportunities identified through competitor intelligence frequently enables a firm to leapfrog rivals or outmaneuver them because it moves faster.

2. Are key competitor threats addressed? Description and interpretation almost always identify competitor threats, that is, how one or more competitors could inhibit the success of our current strategy. Each such threat needs to be assessed to determine whether the strategy should be modified. Consider this example: one B2B firm recognized that a large look-alike rival was preparing to launch a full-scale frontal 'attack' on its key accounts in each geographic region. In effect, the rival proposed to 'buy' share in each key account by dramatically reducing price, adding to its service menu and providing some forms of technical expertise to ensure rapid product installation. The firm decided to modify some key elements in its long-term contract with these key accounts and to step up its sales force calls on these accounts to put the contracts in place much sooner than initially planned.

3. Are key competitive risks addressed? Every B2B strategy can be stress-tested to assess whether it can handle (competitive) risks beyond competitors' actions. For example, technology risks often emerge through consideration of competitors' strategy change. The surgical instrument provider briefly noted previously found that its current strategy's dependence on the traditional product lines could not offset the value added to be delivered to customers through the projected introduction of laser-based products.

4. To what is our strategy most vulnerable? Competitor and context insights can always be used to push beyond threats and risks to specifically identify how the current strategy could be most vulnerable. Rarely will key vulnerabilities not cause change to the strategy or how it should be executed. One firm discovered that its new product line was most vulnerable to a rival attacking it in the regulatory arena: it attempted to show that the Occupational Safety and Health Administration implications of the technology were unacceptable. Were it to succeed, the product would have to be dramatically reconfigured.

5. Do the key underlying assumptions hold? Assumptions about the marketplace emanating from interpretation offer a frame to assess the assumptions underpinning the current strategy; assumptions, it should be noted, that are often left implicit. Two classic cases illustrate the value of testing key assumptions. First, assumptions

about the direction of the marketplace may directly conflict with the strategy's assumptions. One firm discovered that the assumption about where the market was heading – more customized solutions across all segments – was in direct conflict with the assumption underpinning the current strategy that a substantial segment of customers would still want the firm's largely stand-alone and undifferentiated product. Second, assumptions about rivals' future strategy direction, and the intensity of it, may starkly contrast with the long-accepted assumption in a firm that rivals will predominantly stay the course with their established product and customer thrusts.

Customer-based advantage

Assessment of customer-based advantage involves directly comparing one or more rivals' value propositions and their acceptance by customers. The results can lead to major marketing strategy change. One firm discovered that its most direct competitor was experiencing powerful 'pull-through' in the leading channels because of its efforts to reposition its brand and to strengthen its relationship with individual channel members. These customer-based advantages overwhelmed the firm's generally accepted superior technology and product performance – the superior functionality simply did not matter much to many end users.

Potential strategy alternatives

Finally, as indicated previously, competitor intelligence often generates key insights into potential (new) marketplace opportunities, thus identifying potential new strategy alternatives. The strategy benefits do not apply only to enhancing the current marketing strategy.

ANALYSIS METHODS

The corporate intelligence literature is rife with methodologies that are deployed in varying levels of breadth and depth to facilitate and guide description, interpretation and assessment (Fleisher and Bensoussan 2003). These methodologies enable groups of individuals in a business to systematically address core analysis issues within these three core competitor intelligence activities. Space does not allow a detailed enumeration or discussion of these methods, but they include scenarios, simulations, response profiling, competitive gaming and invented competitors. Each of these methodologies involves distinct modes of data collection and creation, transformation of data into insights and connections to strategy and decision-making.

The creativity and value now common in deploying these methodologies is well exemplified in the case of invented competitors, that is, the strategy a competitor might pursue that is not currently in the marketplace (Fahey 2002). The methodology has been deployed by many B2B firms. Invented competitor analysis requires establishing how the competitor comes to be, perhaps through alliances between existing entities or as an outgrowth of a technology breakthrough. The strategy the invented competitor might pursue is then delineated in detail: marketplace scope, competitive posture and goals. How the strategy would be executed is then detailed, and the potential customer-based advantages are specified. One B2B firm in the financial services domain used the invented competitor method to identify a major new marketplace opportunity, devoted three years to realize the opportunity and became the dominant rival in this broad market space.

A RESEARCH AGENDA

Researchers active in competitor intelligence recognize the importance of moving the field forward by setting a research agenda (Ganesh et al. 2003). A small group of academics has evolved a concentrated research program dedicated to issues, topics and questions within competitor intelligence. Many of their outputs have appeared in the *Journal of Competitive Intelligence and Management.*

Competitor intelligence, however, is not yet an established and well-recognized academic field or discipline with accepted theory, burgeoning streams of research, noted researchers and visibility in recognized academic (peer-reviewed) outlets. The diversity of analysis questions noted previously and the breadth of germane topic areas (from intelligence topic identification, to data determination and collection, to analysis and insight creation, to business implications specification) render impossible the development of individual theories and research streams that encompass all these questions and areas. Research thus must focus on issues and questions that are likely to enhance both the practice and the understanding (theory) of intelligence. All facets of the work involved in description, interpretation and assessment cry out for well-designed and carefully executed academic research. With an eye toward B2B marketing, Table 9.2 identifies ten potential research areas, some key questions that should be addressed and the intelligence practice relevance of advancing understanding and insight in these research areas.

The choice criteria employed to determine this set of potentially valuable research areas were threefold. First, identify research pockets central to the practice of successful competitor intelligence. Thus, for example, outwitting rivals is critical to marketing strategy that wins in the marketplace, and deriving inferences is a crucial analytical task across all three core analysis activities. Second, pinpoint some research areas in which little, if any, systematic research has been conducted in the context of competitor intelligence. For example, communities of practice and the role of technology offer research opportunities that potentially could transform how many facets of intelligence work get done. Third, identify some research areas that address the organizational context within which competitor intelligence must not only exist but prosper as well. Thus organizational culture and the role and influence of bias represent two domains that offer many questions for productive research studies.

Much of the academic research relevant to B2B competitor intelligence research domains identified in Table 9.2 takes place in academic fields and disciplines as diverse as strategic management, marketing, information technology, accounting, systems thinking, knowledge management, futures research and even epistemology. The B2B competitor intelligence research agenda must leverage the theorizing and empirical work in these fields to address fundamental intelligence-related issues, questions and prescriptions across the three core intelligence activities: description, interpretation and assessment.

A fundamental research stream central to competitor intelligence needs to address 'who we actually compete against'. Given the variety of rivals noted in this chapter, the

Table 9.2   A research agenda for B2B competitor intelligence (CI)

Research Domain	Sample Key Questions	Potential Practice Insights
How to evaluate the presence or potential of outwitting rivals	What kinds of analysis best contribute to outwitting rivals? What criteria could be used to determine that outwitting has taken place or was likely to occur? What organizational conditions positively or negatively influence outwitting?	How to focus CI on outwitting; How to move faster toward outwitting.
How to evaluate the presence or potential of outmaneuvering rivals	What are the indicators of outmaneuvering rivals? How does CI enable outmaneuvering? What kinds of analysis methodologies best contribute to identifying outmaneuvering possibilities?	How to make outmaneuvering a primary focal point in CI work; How to achieve outmaneuvering better and faster than otherwise might occur.
How to evaluate outperforming rivals	What is the range of marketplace indicators of outperforming rivals? What insights into marketing strategy does each indicator provide? How can financial performance measures be linked to the marketplace indicators as a basis for assessing the return on investment of CI?	How to assess the value of CI projects and CI as a practice.
Setting the CI agenda	What criteria can be established to identify potential intelligence needs? What criteria are appropriate to determine the most critical intelligence needs? What organizational procedures can be established to apply these criteria?	How to establish the most productive CI focus and practice.
Data sources and data collection	How can key external human sources be identified? How can the potential value of individual external sources be assessed? How can relationships with human sources be developed and sustained over time? What are the relative merits of different data collection protocols? What are the most efficient methods to develop external human source networks? How should external human source networks best be managed when established?	How to best organize data gathering; How to build and sustain a network of data sources.
Communities of practice	What types of leaders are required to initiate and sustain an intelligence community of practice? How can a community of practice best contribute to distinct phases in data collection and pruning? What facets of a community of practice can be managed virtually? How can decision-makers become integral members of a community of practice?	How to best initiate and organize self-managing groups to generate data and conduct analysis.
The role of technology in CI	How can the social media be used in data gathering? How can information technologies contribute to 'mining' structured and unstructured data? How can technology enable virtual CI teams (across sites, geographies, business units)?	How to manage technologies in many phases of CI work.

Table 9.2   (continued)

Research Domain	Sample Key Questions	Potential Practice Insights
Deriving inferences	How do 'mental models' and implicit theories influence the derivation of inferences? How does the use of specific analysis frameworks shape and influence the types of inferences derived?	How to draw critical inferences consistently; How to test inferences in the context of ongoing change.
Role and influence of bias in CI	How does dependence on specific data sources and preferences for data types bias analysis and insights? What biases come into play in the choice of analysis frameworks, and how is analysis conducted?	How to identify prevailing biases and their implications; How to manage biases.
Organization culture	What is the ideal CI-supportive organization culture? What aspects of organization culture tend to support or inhibit development and deployment of basic CI practices?	How to develop a productive culture within the CI community; How to detect the prevailing organization culture and manage CI within it.

answer to this question often is not obvious and sometimes is badly misconstrued when the focus is on products and not the customer perspective (DeSarbo et al. 2006). How customers categorize and compare rivals' offerings would provide a frame of reference to compare with more conventional rivalry structures and inform firms' reference points for value proposition development.

Data are the lifeblood of description. Conceptual developments and empirical work in the domain of knowledge management (Nonaka and Takeuchi 1995) should buttress research efforts to address the profound issues and challenges characterizing all phases of data collection and analysis. A substantive research program is required to address the following questions: how should firms leverage their existing data on and about competitors as a means to determine more precisely what externally sourced data they should pursue? How should firms develop external networks of human sources as a means to obtain (legally and ethically) non-publicly available data and do so efficiently and effectively? How should firms determine the critical data gaps with respect to competitors' strategies, value chains and technology as a guide to determine what data to collect? And how should firms identify key indicators and track data on these indicators over time?

Description ultimately addresses the future: the strategic direction competitors may adopt, how they might redeploy marketing tactics and the value proposition they could create and deliver. Theories that develop explicit and different approaches to understanding and depicting B2B firms' approaches to marketing strategy change should inform research investigating the range and discontinuity characterizing competitors' strategy shifts. For example, the metaphors of 'invention' (the future can and should be designed; Ackoff 1970) and navigation (multiple forms of muddling through or logical incrementalism; Quinn 1980) provide two distinct alternatives to categorizing and analyzing competitors' potential strategy choices, well before such shifts might become evident in the marketplace.

Yet intelligence-focused research cannot stop at the borders of the prevailing competitor configuration in any specific market segment or even the broader marketplace. Intelligence must grapple with the ever-present prospect that one or more rivals at some future time may bear little resemblance to the profile and strategy of current rivals. Thus a fascinating and productive research challenge involves the development and deployment of one or more methodologies that aim to 'invent' potential rivals, that is, rivals with strategies that do not exist today. Such invented competitors (Fahey 2002) enable a marketing management team to challenge both the content of and the assumptions underpinning its current and projected strategy in ways that cannot be attained when the frame of reference is provided only by current rivals.

Intelligence requires the transformation of data into sharply scripted insights, often requiring the analyst to see beyond the 'raw' data, no matter how rich and comprehensive the data set. Thus intelligence offers a natural home for epistemological principles and practices. Narayanan and Zane (2011) demonstrate how attention to basic epistemological concerns can help theorists (and practitioners) draw inferences from disparate data and develop explanations for what they observe (patterns in data), both critical issues in competitor intelligence. Of perhaps especial research importance is the need to investigate the structure and quality of reasoning that generates insight: that is, understanding of rivals that did not previously exist.

An inviolable principle of good intelligence work, especially with respect to interpretation, is that analysis and thinking should never be allowed to fall within a single dominant 'frame' (a point of view, perspective or analytical tool). The complexity, turbulence and discontinuities so evident in the broader competitive context that faces all competitors demand multiple frames. Snowden and Stanbridge (2004) illustrate how a variety of conceptual frameworks can be used to structure thinking and analysis in the context of social and economic complexity – frameworks applicable to unraveling the often-hidden complexity surrounding rivals' strategies. Two research questions suggest themselves: which analysis frames (e.g. models of the industry or competitive space) enable marketers in the B2B world to best anticipate potential marketplace change and thus initiate significant game-changing strategy shifts? And which futures frames (e.g. scenario structures, competitive gaming, simulations) enable marketers to 'see the future before it unfolds' and thus be better positioned than rivals to configure marketing strategy?

Intelligence insights emerge from the interactions of individuals with different perspectives and often representing different functions both within and outside marketing. Communities of practice (Wenger et al. 2002) offer perhaps the most imaginative but realistic approach to studying how a collection of individuals can support one another in the pursuit of genuine intelligence – insights that make a difference in marketing decision-making. Communities of practice also present the opportunity to study how individuals outside the enterprise can be appropriately and productively involved in the process of intelligence work.

In summary, the importance of a systematic research approach to competitor intelligence cannot be overstated. The practice has mostly evolved with an emphasis on *how*:

how to gather data, how to conduct analysis, how to connect with decision-makers and so forth. Theory that addresses the underlying *why* questions – explanations for what works and what does not work – has received comparatively little attention.

REFERENCES

Ackoff, Russell (1970), *A Concept of Corporate Planning*, New York: Wiley-Interscience.
Brody, Roberta (2008), 'Issues in defining competitive intelligence: an exploration', *Journal of Competitive Intelligence and Management*, **4** (3), 3–16.
Christensen, H. Kurt (2010), 'Defining customer value as the driver of competitive advantage', *Strategy and Leadership*, **38** (5), 20–25.
DeSarbo, Wayne S., Rajdeep Grewel and Jerry Wind (2006), 'Who competes with whom? A demand-based perspective for identifying and representing asymmetric competition', *Strategic Management Journal*, **27** (2), 101–29.
Fahey, Liam (1999), *Outwitting, Outmaneuvering and Outperforming*, New York: John Wiley & Sons.
Fahey, Liam (2002), 'Invented competitors', *Strategy and Leadership*, **30** (6), 5–12.
Fahey, Liam (2009), 'The future direction of competitive intelligence: some reflections', *Competitive Intelligence Magazine*, **12** (1), 17–22.
Fleisher, Craig S. and Babette E. Bensoussan (2003), *Strategic and Competitive Analysis*, Upper Saddle River, NJ: Pearson Education.
Ganesh, Usha, Cynthia E. Miree and John Prescott (2003), 'Competitive intelligence field research: moving the field forward by setting a research agenda', *Journal of Competitive Intelligence and Management*, **1** (1), 1–12.
Narayanan, V.K. and Lee J. Zane (2011), 'Current theoretical debates in strategic management: epistemological analysis in strategic management', in C. Cassell and B. Lee (eds), *Challenges and Controversies in Management Research*, New York: Routledge, pp. 195–211.
Nonaka, Ikujiro and Hirotaka Takeuchi (1995), *The Knowledge-Creating Company: How Japanese Companies Create the Dynamics of Innovation*, New York: Oxford University Press.
Quinn, J.B. (1980), *Strategies for Change*, Homewood, IL: Richard D. Irwin.
Snowden, David and Peter Stanbridge (2004), 'The landscape of management: creating the context for understanding social complexity', *E:Co*, **6** (1–2), 140–48.
Srivastava, Rajendra, Tasadduq Shervani and Liam Fahey (1998), 'Market-based assets and shareholder value: a framework for analysis', *Journal of Marketing*, **62** (1), 2–18.
Wenger, Etienne, Richard A. McDermott and William Snyder (2002), *Cultivating Communities of Practice: A Guide to Managing Knowledge*, Cambridge, MA: Harvard Business School Press.

PART III

B2B MARKETING MIX AND STRATEGY

10 B2B marketing communication in a transformational marketplace
Don E. Schultz

B2B MARKETING AND COMMUNICATION IN A LINEAR, SUPPLY CHAIN SELLING SYSTEM

Almost all sales and marketing activities, particularly those in B2B markets, are the children of the industrial revolution of some 200 years ago. The producing firm created or developed products for sale, commonly inventoried them, pushed them out into the marketplace and then tried to create sales and selling situations in which customers could or would buy (Morris et al. 2001). The approach commonly was based on a supply chain structure, where economies of scale generally provided the returns and profit margins to the seller. Thus efficient volume has been the major determinant of either the success or failure of the firm. A typical supply chain model is illustrated in Figure 10.1.

As it shows, the manufacturing firm sources raw materials from suppliers, processes those raw materials in various ways and embeds what are perceived to be forms and levels of value into the products, which upon purchase by the buyer can be extracted and enjoyed. Often the purchaser creates additional value by combining several benefits into products and offers that can be developed and delivered further downstream. The primary focus of the B2B firm therefore has always been to build various types of value propositions (Gronroos 2007) that would benefit buyers immediately or could be combined to serve downstream markets.

Because many B2B 'value propositions' involve complex offers, multiple buying decision points and long-cycle selling situations, B2B organizations have relied on field-based sales forces to identify prospects, make sales calls, deliver the value propositions and even conduct some level of after-sales support.

Looking back, we can see how the linear, always outbound sales and marketing system developed. Personal selling was a key step in the process (Morris et al. 2001). Therefore leads for the field sales force or other distribution system members were the most critical elements in the process. Marketing and communication were clearly support systems, designed either to generate sales force leads or to provide selling and value proposition support materials that the field sales force could use in their sales calls. Because few B2B products or offers were purchased directly or without personal contact, marketing and communication were viewed as 'ingredients' in the sales mix and budgeted and evaluated that way (Best 2000).

Furthermore because B2B marketing and communication were support elements, they were budgeted, allocated and evaluated separately from the sales force costs (Morris et al. 2001). They were often considered 'expenses' or a cost of doing business. When sales were down, marketing and communication were reduced. When sales were up, the budget might be increased. And since the marketing and communication returns were

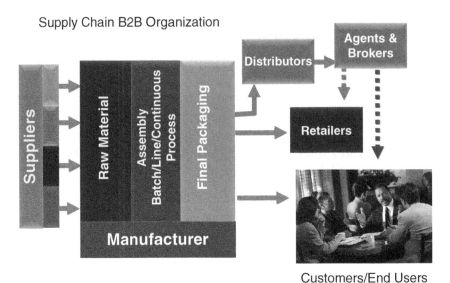

Figure 10.1   Supply chain graphic

often entwined with the sales force efforts, it has always been tremendously difficult to determine the return on investment (ROI) of B2B marketing and communication activities (Coe 2003).

Because marketing, communication and sales were quite different activities, commonly budgeted and managed separately, functional groups developed to manage each. This development often created internal competition for scarce organizational resources, resulting in each group trying to demonstrate that its functional activity was critical to the success of the firm.

Although this description does not fit every B2B organization, the idea of the firm embedding value or value propositions into its product offerings, which can then be extracted by the buyer and either used or passed along downstream, is common enough to set the stage for this chapter. What is most critical to our discussion is that the primary tools used by B2B organizations are outbound, linear sales systems that rely heavily on a field sales force that depends on the development of an ongoing supply of sales leads. With such a supply, it can present the product benefits and value propositions that the seller has developed and sell them through persuasive activities to a group of customers and prospects. It is this linear, primarily outbound, persuasive personal sales and selling system that is being challenged today. Thus it is the focus of this chapter.

THE ROLE OF MARKETING AND COMMUNICATION IN A SUPPLY CHAIN SYSTEM

The sales and marketing activities in most B2B organizations are fairly clearly defined. Whether the following activities are developed by an internal staff or external suppliers, such as agencies and other consultants, the primary 'sales force support tasks' are to (1) identify customers and prospects who might benefit from the value proposition that has been created; (2) encourage potential customers and prospects for those value propositions to identify themselves in some way; (3) from those who identify themselves, the field sales force can then make personal contacts; and (4) based on persuasive sales arguments developed in advance that could be delivered either personally by them or through the distribution system or through various marketing communication techniques, all of which have been designed to move prospective buyers through the 'sales funnel' (Coe 2003). Given this linear, outbound system, conflict between sales and marketing often occurs, depending on the quality of the leads developed or the appropriateness of the support materials created by the marketing and communication group. Those conflict issues are fairly common to most B2B organizations.

Despite the challenges, though, the system works. B2B selling organizations continue to develop products with embedded value propositions, buyers continue to purchase and extract those values for use in their own businesses, and sales and marketing continue to find ways to create persuasive materials that help sellers sell and buyers buy. Although the system is not perfect, it has been in place for more than a century and is well known and recognized by all parties.

THE LOOMING TECTONIC TRANSFORMATIONAL SHIFT

Today in spite of its success, almost all B2B sellers, marketers and communicators agree that the current system has flaws. Yet they have been loath to radically change it. The changes that have occurred therefore have generally been incremental, such as optimization of the sales force's time with customers (Siguaw et al. 2003), switches to more efficient communication delivery systems (Weigand et al. 2003), more focus on better customer segmentation and identification (Dibb and Simkin 2008), data analytics to better manage prospects through the sales cycle and the like (Siguaw et al. 2003). As a result, the system is essentially the same as it was in the middle of the twentieth century. It is (1) linear, that is, seller → sales program → buyers; (2) generally outbound, such that the B2B organization embeds value that the buyer extracts; (3) based on value propositions the seller creates and uses to 'persuade' buyers to accept; (4) focused on short-term returns, including sales force quotas and reward systems; and (5) organized and managed as groups of functional silos, such as sales, marketing/communication, operations, finance and so on. Everyone knows the system, and every organization tends to adopt the same rules.

Yet a major shift is occurring in the marketplace that will dramatically affect this traditional system, forcing it to evolve and change over the next few years. That shift will be created by the shift of control of information technology. This shift of knowledge, and therefore the shift in marketplace power from the manufacturer/marketer to the customer/consumer (Schultz et al. 2009), will radically change how sales, marketing and communication must be conducted by most B2B organizations in the next few years, as illustrated in Figure 10.2.

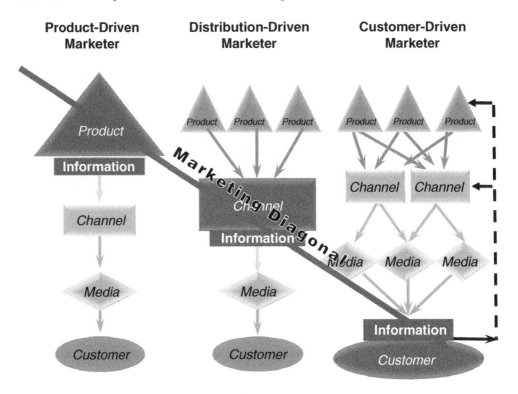

Figure 10.2   The shift of information technology

Power in the Manufacturer System

Historically most information about B2B products, services, systems, channels, technologies, value propositions, marketplace changes and the like has resided with the manufacturer/marketer, as shown in the left-hand column of Figure 10.2, labeled 'Product-driven Marketer'. Because the manufacturer had the facilities and capabilities to develop and produce products that downstream customers needed, wanted or could use to improve their business operations, it controlled the system. The primary advantages the manufacturer had were control of the research and development process, patents, access to raw materials and ownership of manufacturing facilities to produce products that would improve or make possible business success for its customers. Thus, the marketer controlled the system.

Because of that system control, the manufacturer also controlled the information buyers could acquire. B2B marketers doled out needed marketplace information through their sales forces and other communication channels, such as advertising expenditures in trade publications and industry trade shows (Moriarty and Spekman 1984). An outstanding example of this information control was the marketing campaign mounted by Intel in the 1980s to convince the entire laptop computer industry that 'Intel Inside' was the primary value proposition that drove the category (Norris 1993).

Because most B2B product and ingredient knowledge and applications resided in the manufacturer's sales force, that's where the control resided too. The sales force focused on how the manufacturer's/supplier's products could or would improve, enhance, simplify or reduce the costs of the customer's business operations. For example in the 1950s and 1960s, IBM maintained a huge field sales force, whose primary purpose was to visit customers and prospects, explain the value of the computers the organization made and detail how those products could improve the prospect's business operations. IBM had all the information about computers and their value. It allocated that information to customers and prospects through individual sales calls, which were supported by marketing communication materials that the organization either developed or had developed for it (Pine and Gilmore 1998). This persuasive selling of the highest order was emulated over time by other organizations seeking the same business success.

A Shift to Channel Control

The shift of information technology began when the manufacturer began to employ various types of distributors or middlemen organizations to help expand the range and extent of its field sales force. The B2B organization authorized distributors, dealers, value-added retailers and the like and either supplied them with product knowledge and sales support or worked directly with them to initiate sales calls (Brennan et al. 2007). Thus information technology slid down the marketing diagonal, from the manufacturer to the distribution channel partners.

It then became the responsibility of the various channel members to gather and allocate product knowledge and information to customers and prospects they selected (Dwyer and Tanner 2008). Manufacturers were generally willing to give up some of their marketplace control to the channels, because doing so expanded their sales opportunities at much lower costs than increasing their own sales organizations.

This new, distributed information technology system was, however, still focused on the same concepts and approaches, most of which were based on person-to-person persuasive selling. The only difference was who was doing that persuasive selling and who had direct contact with the customer. Thus we see a shift of marketplace power from the manufacturer to shared responsibility with various channel partners.

Customers Gain Information Control

In the third stage of this ongoing informational transitional shift, an increasing amount of the marketplace and product knowledge that customers need resides with them, as a result of technology changes such as the Internet, World Wide Web and mobile technologies, or else it can be easily and quickly accessed from third parties. As shown in the right-hand column in Figure 10.2, the customer has access to media systems, channel information and even product information, which the manufacturer makes available as a web page service to customers and prospects. Increasingly customers can access needed product and market information from various media sources, distribution channels, bloggers, consortiums and a host of other information sources (Block and Schultz 2009).

In this new marketplace, many B2B customers truly control the marketing system because they determine how, where, in what way and in what form they want to acquire information through various forms of technology. With this capability to acquire almost unlimited amounts of product and marketplace information, much of it specifically related to their needs and requirements, the power of the traditional B2B organization's persuasive selling system is sorely challenged.

It is this transition of information technology and product and marketplace knowledge from the seller to the buyer that radically changes the role, needs for, capabilities of and requirements for B2B sales, marketing and marketing communications. My hypothesis is that in the next decade, this transition from traditional marketer-controlled persuasive selling to shared buyer–seller knowledge, along with the development of networked and negotiated systems and the development of reciprocal information models, will radically change B2B sales, marketing and marketing communication (Schultz and Malthouse 2010).

This transformation of customer power through information technology will have major implications for all areas of B2B operations. The more knowledge the customer has, the less power the B2B manufacturer/marketer and its sales force have. To illustrate that change, it is useful to look back to see how our current B2B sales and marketing systems developed and thus predict where they are probably going.

TRADITIONAL OUTBOUND B2B MARKETING COMMUNICATION SYSTEMS

The marketing communication system now employed by B2B marketers followed the development of traditional outbound communication systems in the United States and Western Europe. Figure 10.3 illustrates that process (Schultz and Schultz 2010).

The B2B marketer, with the assistance of information distribution groups such as media firms, direct mail companies, trade show organizers, advertising agencies and the like, distributed outbound, generally persuasive communication materials about its products and services to customers and prospects that it believed might benefit from the value propositions it had developed. Messages and incentives were developed and delivered through a wide range of communication methodologies, commonly with a focus on vertical industries with known buying influences (Schultz and Schultz 2010).

B2B marketing communication groups devised what were perceived as persuasive messages and then sent them to customers and prospects, often through specialized media forms. These communications were viewed as either substitutes for a personal sales call or devices to encourage prospective customers to self-identify so that a sales-

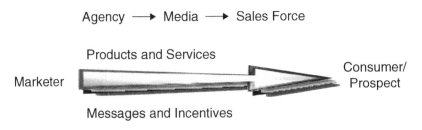

Figure 10.3   Outbound communication system

person could make the initial contact. Marketing communication was therefore often viewed as a precursor to an actual persuasive sales call or a supplement to such activities through various types of leave-behinds, follow-up devices and information request appeals (Morris et al. 2001).

Many B2B communication systems followed this marketing diagonal (Schultz and Schultz 1998). Therefore many B2B communication programs were outbound, linear and managed by the marketer or an external communication agency. The goal was to distribute product and market information in such a way that customers and prospects would be encouraged to contact the organization and/or members of the sales group so that a personal contact could be made (Schultz and Schultz 1998).

All these outbound systems assumed customers and prospects went through some type of identifiable purchasing process, often called the 'sales funnel' (Kotler et al. 2006). Marketing communication efforts aimed to move customers or prospects through the various stages of the purchasing process to the point at which the sales force could or would complete the sale with a personal contact (Morris et al. 2001).

In this persuasive B2B sales model, in place for the past 50 or so years, the focus of marketing communication has always been on supporting the efforts of the personal sales force, or the left-hand column in Figure 10.2. Sellers talked, customers listened.

Marketer-controlled Technologies

In the 1980s and 1990s, the B2B marketing communication model shifted to accommodate the development of new technologies that enabled the organization to electronically capture, store and manipulate substantial amounts of customer and prospect information. Operating under the general rubric of 'customer relationship management', or CRM, these computer-assisted models were designed primarily to help the organization better allocate its sales efforts. For example, through various customer analytic tools, B2B marketers could identify their best or most profitable customers, as well as those most likely prospects for upsales, cross-sales and add-ons, all of which helped move prospects through the 'purchase funnel' (Blattberg et al. 2001).

The entire outbound, persuasive B2B selling system changed radically, however, in the middle 1990s. The commercialization of the Internet and World Wide Web created those changes (Schultz and Schultz 2003). It is only now that the full impact of this systemic change is being felt in most B2B organizations. Yet many B2B sellers have continued to use the traditional sales force persuasive selling system.

The change is clear, however. Most B2B organizations are on the cusp of that change today, with some further along the developmental path than others.

NEW PUSH AND PULL MARKETING COMMUNICATION SYSTEMS

The development and introduction of new customer-activated and -controlled digital communication systems have resulted in a 'pull marketing communication' system. It has pushed information technology down the marketing diagonal, into the waiting hands of customers and prospects. Figure 10.4 contains an overlay of the new pull

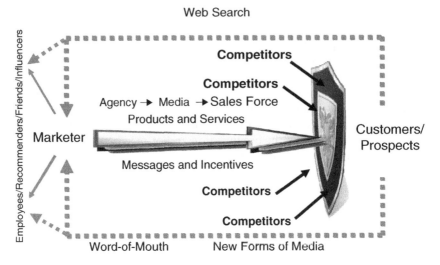

Figure 10.4   Push and pull communication in a B2B market

system on the traditional outbound push communication system to illustrate today's marketplace (Schultz et al. 2009).

Figure 10.4 identifies three major 'pull' communication systems that B2B customers and prospects can use to gather information about the market, products and services they need, require or would like to investigate. These customer-driven pull systems are (1) websites and Internet search engines; (2) new forms of communication, such as mobile and wireless devices and (3) expanded and enhanced electronic word-of-mouth methodologies, including new technologies such as LinkedIn, salesforce.com, Facebook, Twitter, industry-specific blogs and the like. These new technologies increase the information access capabilities of the buyer and diminish the impact and influence of the persuasive message-focused capabilities of the seller (Schultz et al. 2009).

With the additional knowledge that customers and prospects now have about alternatives to those offered by the B2B firm, the role of the sales force changes substantially. Rather than always being in a persuasive selling mode, the sales force is often put on the defensive, that is, in the role of a product purchase negotiator. With the buyers in control of information, which the sales force may not have acquired or know how to use, customers have more control of the sales discussion system and the traditional selling process (Schultz and Malthouse 2010).

Furthermore the concept of a sales funnel, a fundamental B2B sales and marketing tool, is sorely challenged. B2B customers now gather information on their own, through consortia, associations, affiliations and the like, to which the selling organization may or may not have access. Therefore it is difficult for the manufacturer's sales force to identify the stage of the purchase cycle in which the customer is operating, how fast they are moving through the system or what is driving that change. Often the customer introduces alternatives into the selling situation that the sales force may not realize even exist or that were being considered.

As Figure 10.5 shows, the B2B organization can and will continue to develop and

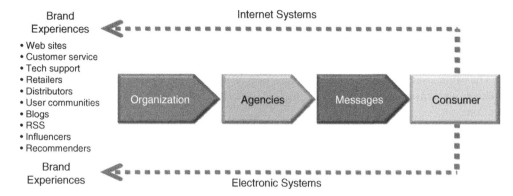

Figure 10.5   Where responses occur in B2B systems

implement outbound, persuasive communication programs (Schultz and Schultz 2010). After all, the entire organization is generally built around this model; management knows how to implement these types of programs and totally abandoning the present system is simply not feasible, no matter how clear future directions may appear. In addition many B2B customers prefer the existing system, have built their purchasing decisions around it and consider it perfectly adequate for their needs today and into the future. So while the direction of the change is clear, the speed at which it will appear in various markets and marketplaces and among various B2B categories is not quite so obvious.

The challenge that this shift of information technologies creates is not just the additional amount of information the customer has or is able to acquire. This shift of information technology, through new communication systems, challenges the basic communication capabilities of all B2B organizations. Enhanced information acquisition processes, now easily and quickly available to the B2B firm's customers and prospects, do not end with a changed impact on the sales force. The greater challenge is that the contact points customers now have with the B2B organization have multiplied exponentially. Whereas once the firm and the customer relied on interactions between the sales force and purchasing decision-makers, today those activities are more and more widely distributed. In the new pull systems the contact points and knowledge generation alternatives available to the customer/buyer seem to expand almost geometrically.

Figure 10.5 shows only a few of the new information resources available to buyers, such as customer service, technical support, distributors, bloggers, RSS, influencers and even the firm's own website, which are relevant and easily accessible resources (Schultz and Schultz 2010). Unfortunately, in too many cases these new buyer contact points have not been brought into the B2B sales and selling systems.

The silo structures of many B2B organizations keep the sales, support and, now, new information conduits in the selling organization separate and isolated (Schultz and Schultz 2003). Therefore the contact points of the B2B organization are often disjointed. The contact points B2B customers have with the firm's support units are often inadequately trained or simply not prepared to serve as surrogates for the sales force. Thus the information that B2B customers and prospects may receive may not support or even agree with what the sales force has developed as its primary persuasive selling message.

When these new channels join the communication mix, the challenge to the traditional controlled and coordinated sales message systems that the B2B marketers have developed is seriously challenged. And in many cases those disconnects are not even known to the organization's senior managers.

The other issue this change in customer-controlled contact and communication creates is the movement from persuasion selling to negotiated purchasing, as covered in the next section.

MOVING FROM PERSUASION TO NEGOTIATION

In the traditional outbound B2B selling system, persuasive communication was a critical ingredient. The sales force was trained in persuasive communication, and that concept dominated most of the firm's ongoing activities. Find the customer benefit. Sell that benefit. Answer any objections. Close the sale. That list has been the B2B selling mantra since the beginning of the modern industrial era (Haas 1992). Thus the marketing and communication efforts of the firm were focused on finding or developing benefits and value propositions for the sales force to sell, or else on taking the sales force's persuasive communication ideas and converting them into media-delivered persuasive selling approaches.

When the maker or seller controlled all or most of the information, these benefits were easily identified and communicated, which made B2B communication a fairly simple task. Simply enumerate the benefits, persuade the buyer they were important and either encourage a comparison with alternatives or rely on the persuasive nature of the sales force to carry the day.

Today, however, the marketplace is filled with a multitude of alternatives and competitors. And those competitors have quickly evolved from local or national to global in scope. Alternative suppliers that have developed do not always play by the same rules or on the same field that B2B organizations have staked out (Ewing et al. 2011). Thus the argument underlying the persuasive sales approach to B2B relationships is severely challenged.

With customers in control, the selling situation changes from persuasive selling to customer-controlled negotiation. When all the benefits are known to both parties, when comparisons between sellers are easy to make, when costs and pricing are known to both parties and when the buyer has as much (or more) information as the seller, then negotiation generally occurs. That is the case in many industries today, and that system is likely to grow in the future (Weigand et al. 2003).

In traditional negotiation, which has always existed in B2B situations, there were major advantages for the seller. Today, the buyer is often in control of the process, generally because its knowledge of its needs is better understood than the seller's. Therefore the previous advantages the manufacturer had in terms of product, solution and even persuasive selling arguments have become less relevant.

Some will respond with the argument that negotiation has always been part of B2B marketing, and to a certain extent, it is true. The buyer has one point of view; often the seller has another. The process of finding common ground between the two results in a successful conclusion of the sales process.

In the new push and pull marketplace, the rules change substantially. Historically the focus of the B2B marketing organization has been to optimize the returns from customer negotiations, that is, 'not to leave any money on the table'. Thus the focus of the seller has been on trying to extract the largest amount of money from the buyer as possible. The seller's goal and the sales force's task was to consummate the sale at maximum value and move on (Siguaw et al. 2003).

Some efforts have been made to develop long-term relationships with customers, yet the traditional incentive-based compensation systems employed by B2B organizations, which value short-term sales quotas over long-term relationships, still force the sales force to be 'immediate sale focused' (Coughlan and Narasimhan 1992).

In the negotiated marketplace, however, the focus of the B2B marketer's selling system is likely to be compromised, in favor of a solution that favors both parties. Therefore the emphasis by the B2B selling organization must move from persuasion and profit optimization to reciprocity, where each party's costs and benefits are equalized to the satisfaction of both. This outcome is dramatically different from that in the traditional persuasive selling model (Iacobucci 1996; Schultz and Bailey 2000).

Looking at both sides of the selling and buying equation and both parties' perspectives dramatically changes how marketing programs and marketing communication alternatives should be developed and delivered and how success can be measured.

MOVING FROM COMMUNICATION DISTRIBUTION TO COMMUNICATION CONSUMPTION

Historically, B2B marketing communication has focused on the efficient delivery of sales messages and incentives. That efficiency was determined by the manufacturer or seller. Thus a multitude of measures have been developed, all focused on communication optimization. Less emphasis has centered on how effective the distribution of those messages could have been in the marketplace (Block and Schultz 2009).

Over the years B2B marketers have been aided in the message distribution system by media owners and external measurement organizations. They have developed various methods to determine how many messages have been distributed, including measures of the number of copies of a trade publication printed and distributed, number of people visiting a trade show, number of direct mail letters posted and so on. All these measures were relevant in a marketplace in which information delivery by the manufacturer or seller was the most important criterion. If the marketer controlled the product and persuasive benefit information and was allocating it to relevant buyers and prospects, then determining the most efficient method of distributing messages and incentives made sense (Schultz and Pilotta 2004).

Over the past few years, though, new message and distribution systems, particularly electronic ones, have exploded. The B2B customer or prospect has a multitude of choices from which to select relevant messages, gather information, make comparisons and so on. With the customer in control, the question of distribution moves to customer message consumption. Therefore knowing how many messages or incentives were sent out is not as important as knowing how many messages or incentives were received, accepted or acquired by the intended customers or prospects. That shift means measuring marketing communication from the view of the customer rather than from the view of the marketer (Schultz et al. 2005, 2006).

The relevant issue in message distribution has become effectiveness, that is, how many relevant customers actually acquired the B2B marketer's messages and incentives. This radically different view of marketing communication becomes critical when the customer can acquire messages, incentives, comparisons and other alternatives at the click of a computer key rather than by scheduling a sales appointment or making a trip to a trade show.

Whether relevant customers or prospects acquire the information to be used in the sales negotiation also becomes a much more relevant measure of marketing communication success than simply how many messages were distributed. If the customer does not acquire the messages or incentives, the value of the marketer's expenditure is zero, no matter how many messages were distributed. In the new pull marketplace, traditional B2B marketing communication activities are generally not as effective or as reliable as in the past. Trade publications are sorely challenged as communication moves to electronic forms. Trade show attendance is generally down. Direct mail is being intercepted in the mail room. At the same time the new electronic systems, such as email, social media, pop-ups and banners, have become prevalent. Thus B2B marketing communication has expanded in some ways and contracted in others, making the job of the B2B marketing communications manager that much more difficult. This change in the focus of B2B marketing communication, from marketer distribution to customer/prospect acquisition, and the resulting negotiated marketplace signifies another dramatic shift in the required skills and capabilities of the B2B marketing communication manager. All these changes culminate, however, in the measure of B2B marketing communication value.

MEASURING THE IMPACT AND EFFECT OF B2B MARKETING COMMUNICATIONS

Historically, the impact and effect of B2B marketing communication programs relied heavily on the sales force's evaluation. That group commonly determined whether marketing communication activities helped improve their selling process or were a waste of resources. Persuasive selling ('feet on the street') has commonly dominated the allocation of finite corporate resources in B2B management systems. Simply put, persuasive personal selling has always been touted as a more powerful selling method than difficult-to-measure communication activities. These traditional B2B communication measurement approaches will probably continue in the near future. But as persuasive selling becomes less and less important to the organization and is replaced by negotiated buying, that too will change.

In a customer-controlled, dynamic, multifunctional marketplace, where negotiating power is increasingly in the hands of the buyer, the issue becomes not one of measuring the distribution or even the acceptance of the marketing communication messages; instead it is creating a mutually profitable, ongoing relationship between the seller and the buyer. In marketplaces historically limited both geographically and competitively, the B2B sales force could maintain contact with known customers and prospects. Getting in the car or on an airplane to visit the customer was a feasible method of keeping in contact. As the global marketplace has expanded and communications networks have

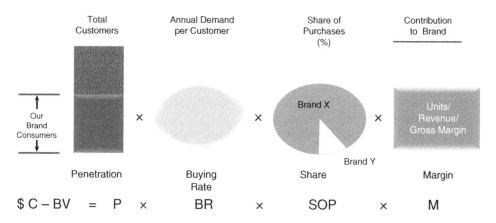

Figure 10.6   Determining B2B customer financial value

blossomed, several changes have occurred that demand a new view. Buyers are scattered around the globe, and transportation and language have become hindrances, not advantages. Competitors can keep up a constant barrage of communication to and with customers and prospects, and negotiations continue both before and after the sale, because both the buyer and the seller are able to identify and build shared value. B2B communication thus will become increasingly important for the selling organization, which means dramatic changes in the type, capabilities and responsibilities of the B2B marketing communications team.

Clearly new technologies will require much more focus on analytical and management skills than on traditional communication and design capabilities, because B2B communication will focus more on getting the consumer to access and acquire what the marketer has to say, rather than on trying to convince the buyer of the value of the seller's product through persuasive messaging.

In addition and historically, selling, and therefore marketing and communication, were conducted in spurts, generally driven by the selling organization. Communication was activated when the seller wanted or needed to sell rather than when the customer wanted or needed to buy (Schultz and Schultz 2003). With the customer in control, the selling and communication process for the B2B marketer never stops. Therefore new types of communication measurement will be needed. One example is shown as Figure 10.6.

One measurement approach that solves many traditional issues is based on identifying the B2B organization's short- and long-term returns on marketing communication. An example helps make the point. Most B2B organizations have customer records, and the sales force has lists of prospects. Knowing who buys in the category and who might be a good prospect for the firm's products enables the organization to develop a system, such as that shown in Figure 10.6 (Schultz et al. 2009).

The concept is simple: the customer creates a flow of income for the B2B firm. Thus customer income flows can be considered firm assets and managed accordingly. The task of the entire B2B organization is focused on acquiring, maintaining and/or growing customer income flows. The emphasis of the organization moves from selling products and services or even value propositions to generating ongoing customer income flows.

The methodology has four parts:

1. Penetration, or the number of total customers in the category compared with the number of customers the firm presently serves. Most of the information needed by the organization to develop this approach is already available to it. The selling organization generally knows the approximate number of buyers that exist in the categories in which they produce products.
2. Total category value, or how many units, pieces or parts the identified customers in the category use, buy or require during a certain time period, usually one year.
3. Unit sales by the B2B organization. In comparison with total category value, this element easily reveals market share.
4. Converting the number of customers and their demands into organizational income flows by multiplying the number of units demanded by the gross margin of the products sold. This product provides a measure of the financial value of the total customer base and the total category. If desired, this approach can be developed for each individual customer.

Using these simple calculations, an actual profit-and-loss calculation could be computed for each customer. (Profitability could be determined by the total income flow generated, less the cost to acquire and serve the customer.)

When customer income flow is known, various systems can be devised to determine how much the organization should invest in any customer or in aggregated customers to acquire, retain or grow those income flows to the firm. (This analysis might use the firm's internal rate of return [IRR] as a benchmark. Theoretically, it would be possible for the firm to invest up to the limit of the required IRR and use it as a budgeting process going forward.)

Using this type of measurement approach, it is a relatively simple task for the B2B marketer to measure the impact of its marketing communication activities. So much money was spent on new customer acquisition. So many new customers were identified or became active. So many customers had a certain level of income flow with the firm. So many units and dollars were retained by the firm – and so on. There are often difficulties in separating out or unraveling the exact level of contribution the marketing communications generated. Having this system in place helps the B2B firm immeasurably in terms of identifying how much to invest in each customer, as well as understanding the total returns generated. The determination of the value of marketing communication in the equation can rely on various methodologies, such as regression equations, econometric modeling or the like.

Although the description of this budgeting and measurement system is necessarily sketchy, it helps close the loop on how the value of B2B marketing and marketing communication might develop going forward. This point will be critical in the developing networked and negotiated marketplace.

A FINAL NOTE

This chapter provides a forward-looking view of the importance and value of marketing and marketing communication in a B2B setting in a radically changing marketplace. The view taken is that traditional B2B approaches, in which a sales force is dedicated to the process of persuasive selling, is rapidly being challenged by the diffusion of information technology. Whereas once the B2B organization controlled most of the information in the product category, then distributed it downstream to buyers through the sales force, the shift of information technology changes the value of that system. Today buyers in many B2B categories have as much knowledge, or perhaps more, than the selling organization. The buyer is often in control. That means the B2B organization is facing dramatic changes.

Some of the most evident changes are the need for the B2B organization to move to a reciprocal model of customer relationships, such that marketplace value is co-created by the seller and buyer (Gronroos 2007) and the resulting returns evenly distributed. Another element is the need for the B2B organization to start focusing on measures of customer acquisition and use of the firm's messages and incentives, rather than a message distribution model. Finally, the B2B firm must find more effective ways to measure the importance and value of its marketing communication efforts. This new approach can be tied to a new customer-focused measurement methodology that makes investments in customers through various communication approaches and then measures the resulting changes in customer income flows (Schultz and Schultz 2010).

How relevant are these concepts and approaches? Some may argue they are simply not appropriate for the existing B2B marketplace. Alternatively the argument could be made that the changes proposed in this chapter are only an interim step and must be continuously adapted and adjusted to meet the needs of both the buyer and seller in this transformational marketplace.

A brief illustration of the possible future of B2B marketing and marketing communication follows. If this description is the future of B2B marketing and communication, even the changes described in this chapter may not be radical enough to meet marketplace demands.

At the 2010 La Londe Services Marketing Conference hosted by Institut d'Administration des Enterprises, Université Paul Cezanne, France, Lei Guo and Irene Ng, both of the University of Exeter in the United Kingdom, presented a paper. They described a research project conducted in the area of performance-based logistics (PBL) (Guo and Ng 2010). In the United Kingdom, prime contractors have agreed to provide fastjet and missile services to the British Ministry of Defence (MoD) on a continuing basis. Rather than selling the airplanes and missiles to the government, the two B2B firms involved have agreed to provide a certain number of operating hours for the planes and a certain level of missile delivery capability over a period of time. Called availability contracting, these types of agreements, in which the firm does not sell B2B products but instead guarantees certain outcomes, challenge the traditional B2B persuasive selling system. The questions that these types of new agreements between buyers and sellers – or in this case, suppliers and users – create are mind boggling. The scenario I described in this chapter therefore may be only the tip of the iceberg in terms of how B2B marketing communications will develop in the months and years ahead. It is clear, however, that the B2B firm must move from a traditional persuasive mode into a more negotiated model. I hope this chapter has helped in that transformation.

Finally, this chapter raises some important new research issues for scholars and practitioners. Some that become immediately apparent are as follows:

1. The shift of information technology is clearly evident from marketplace observations. Can these technological shifts be forecast going forward, and if so, how? B2B marketers are always more interested in future results than past accomplishments. What types of new forecasting tools will be needed?
2. The decline in value of the traditional outbound communication approach demands new planning models and approaches. If the future is non-linear and networked, how and in what way can those approaches best be developed?
3. There must be better measures of customer communication consumption. This chapter has speculated on possible measures, but are there other methods and approaches that would be more relevant and effective?
4. This chapter has argued for customer income flows as relevant measures of marketing communication effectiveness. What other alternatives might also be developed?

REFERENCES

Best, Roger J. (2000), *Market-Based Management*, Upper Saddle River, NJ: Prentice-Hall.
Blattberg, R.C., G. Getz and J.S. Thomas (2001), *Customer Equity: Building and Managing Relationships as Valuable Assets*, Cambridge, MA: Harvard Business School Press.
Block, M.P. and Don E. Schultz (2009), *Media Generations: Media Allocation in a Consumer-Controlled Marketplace*, Worthington, OH: Prosper Publishing.
Brennan, R., L.E. Canning and R. McDowell (2007), *Business-to-Business Marketing*, Thousand Oaks, CA: Sage.
Coe, J. (2003), *The Fundamentals of Business to Business Sales and Marketing*, New York: McGraw-Hill.
Coughlan, Anne T. and C. Narasimhan (1992), 'An empirical analysis of sales-force compensation plans', *Journal of Business*, **64** (1), 93–121.
Dibb, Sally and Lyndon Simkin (2008), *Marketing Segmentation Success: Making It Happen!* New York: Haworth Press.
Dwyer, Robert F. and John F. Tanner (2008), *Business Marketing: Connecting Strategy, Relationships and Learning*, New York: McGraw-Hill.
Ewing, M.T., L. Windisch and Fiona J. Newton (2011), 'Corporate reputation in the People's Republic of China', *Industrial Marketing Management* (forthcoming).
Gronroos, C. (2007), *In Search of a New Logic for Marketing*, Hoboken, NJ: John Wiley & Sons.
Guo, Lei and Irene Ng (2010), 'Relational governance on interpersonal cooperation in equipment-based services', *Proceedings of the 11th International Research Seminar in Service Management*, LaLonde, France, May.
Haas, Robert W. (1992), *Business Marketing Management: An Organizational Approach*, 5th edn, Boston, MA: PWS-Kent Publishing.
Iacobucci, Dawn (1996), *Networks in Marketing*, Thousand Oaks, CA: Sage.
Kotler, Philip, N. Rackham and S. Krishnaswamy (2006), 'Ending the war between sales and marketing', *Harvard Business Review*, (July–August), 1–14.
Moriarty, R.T. and R.E. Spekman (1984), 'An empirical investigation of the sources of information used during the industrial buying process', *Journal of Marketing Research*, **21** (May), 137–47.
Morris, M.H., L.F. Pitt and E.D. Honneycutt Jr (2001), *Business-to-Business Marketing*, 3rd edn, Thousand Oaks, CA: Sage.
Norris, Donald G. (1993), '"Intel Inside": branding a component in a business market', *Journal of Business & Industrial Marketing*, **8** (1), 14–24.
Pine, J., II and J.H. Gilmore (1998), 'Welcome to the experience economy', *Harvard Business Review*, **76** (July–August), 97–105.
Schultz, Don E. and S. Bailey (2000), 'Customer/brand loyalty in an interactive marketplace', *Journal of Advertising Research*, **40** (3), 41–53.
Schultz, Don E. and E. Malthouse (2010), 'Understanding the new negotiated phase of relationship marketing: a proposed research agenda', Working Paper.
Schultz, Don E. and J.J. Pilotta (2004), 'Developing the foundation for a new approach to understanding how media advertising works', *Proceedings of the 3rd ESOMAR/ARF World Audience Measurement Conference*, 12–18 June, Geneva.

Schultz, Don E. and H.F. Schultz (1998), 'Transitioning marketing communication into the twenty-first century', *Journal of Marketing Communications*, **4** (1), 9–26.

Schultz, Don E. and H.F. Schultz (2003), *IMC: The Next Generation*, New York: McGraw-Hill.

Schultz, Don E. and H.F. Schultz (2010), 'IMC in today's "Push–Pull" Marketplace', *Proceedings from the ISBM-WESCO Training*, 13–14 January, Pittsburgh.

Schultz, Don E., J.J. Pilotta and M.P. Block (2005), 'Populating and implementing a media consumption model', *Proceedings of the 4th ESOMAR/ARF World Audience Measurement Conference*, 19–24 June, Montreal.

Schultz, Don E., J.J. Pilotta and M.P. Block (2006), 'Media consumption and consumer purchasing: connecting the dots . . . finally', *Proceedings of the ESOMAR Worldwide Multi Media Measurement*, 4–7 June, Shanghai.

Schultz, Don E., B.E. Barnes, H.F. Schultz and M. Azzaro (2009), *Building Customer–Brand Relationships*, Armonk, NY: M.E. Sharpe.

Siguaw, James A., S.E. Kimes and Jule B. Gassenheimer (2003), 'B2B sales force productivity: applications of revenue management strategy sales management', *Industrial Marketing Management*, **32** (7), 539–51.

Weigand, H., Aldo De Moor, Marieke Schoop and Frank Dignum (2003), 'B2B negotiation support: the need for a communication perspective', *Group Decision and Negotiation*, **12** (7), 3–29.

11 Business-to-business market segmentation
Robert J. Thomas

Market segmentation is a dynamic business decision process driven by a theory about how markets function. The theory is based primarily on economics literature pertaining to price discrimination developed during the 1920s and 1930s (Chamberlin 1965; Pigou 1920; Robinson 1954) but also has been well received in marketing literature (DeSarbo and DeSarbo 2007; Dickson and Ginter 1987; Frank et al. 1972; Moorthy 1984; Smith 1956). The theory suggests that customer heterogeneity supports the existence of demand-based segments from which firms can generate greater responses by shaping different offerings for those various segments, rather than by providing the same offering to the whole market. As a dynamic decision process, it resides in the domain of managerial decision-making and thus can be improved by concepts, methods and tools developed and tested by academics and practitioners.

As a decision process, market segmentation holds the promise of being used in practice by managers of a single firm facing competition to pursue business objectives through a more efficient and effective allocation of resources. This promise appears to have progressed in B2C marketing, where it has become an imperative to know target consumers well and build highly focused marketing programs to meet their needs (Yankelovich and Meer 2006). However, managers in B2B markets have been slower to adopt market segmentation, beyond just traditional industry or application segments.

Consider the case of Thomson Corporation, as reported by Harrington and Tjan (2008). A provider of information services to organizational customers, Thomson traditionally marketed to its direct customers (corporate information services managers) with little consideration for end users who might also influence the purchase of their services. The authors contrasted the benefits of going from an industry-based segmentation involving direct customers to a more comprehensive one based on the needs and problems of end users. They also studied the work flow of end users, measured their trade-offs for product features using conjoint analysis and clustered the resultant utilities to obtain need-based user segments. This information then enabled them to develop innovative products and marketing plans for target segments, thereby revitalizing Thomson's strategy.

What is notable about the Thomson approach is that it is almost identical to the methodology recommended by Wind et al. (1978) for scientific and technical information services – albeit some 30 years earlier! Although there is almost always a lag in the adoption of academic approaches among practitioners, it appears that B2B managers have been lax in taking advantage of this process. There may be several reasons, not the least of which may be difficulties in implementation, as reported by Robertson and Barich (1992), Dibb and Simkin (1994) and Berg et al. (2009). In this chapter, I review B2B market segmentation from both academic and business perspectives to clarify its potential effectiveness. In the next section, I consider major challenges of using B2B market segmentation, followed by a consideration of several activities required to complete a successful segmentation process. This analysis sets the stage for a discussion of directions for research that should be considered to improve the process and practice of B2B market segmentation.

CHALLENGES TO B2B MARKET SEGMENTATION

As derived from economic theory and marketing conceptualizations, B2B market segmentation can be summarized as the following belief typically held by marketing academics and practitioners:

> A market can be segmented into groups of business customers whose needs (or other bases of market response)[1] are similar within-group and different between-groups, and all firms competing in this market can extract more profit with offerings that meet the needs of the different groups than the same offering to meet total market needs.

This belief is generally supported by observations that multiple brands compete and profit in the same market application. Despite the apparent conviction that B2B market segmentation works, there are as of yet no broad-based empirical studies that support this belief. A review of prior literature reveals at least three major challenges to its potential effectiveness: (1) mixed reports on B2B segmentation success in practice; (2) B2B market structure complexities; and (3) variation in defining B2B segmentation processes.

Mixed Reports on B2B Segmentation Success in Practice

Few published comprehensive studies document the effectiveness of business market segmentation in practice.[2] These studies tend to support the notion that segmentation can work in practice, but not without deeper consideration of how it might work best in a given situation (Doyle and Saunders 1985). In a classic case study reporting a chance field experiment for ABB Electric, Gensch et al. (1990) provide compelling evidence of the effectiveness of B2B market segmentation. In a one-year test, they use a segmentation approach based on choice modeling applied to two of three geographic districts and attained sales increases of 18 per cent and 12 per cent, even as sales declined by 15 per cent for the industry overall and 10 per cent in the district without segmentation. The sales manager in the third district, who declined to participate in the segmentation approach, thus created an opportunity to demonstrate the value of segmentation while simultaneously revealing a key challenge: the importance of cooperation.

Waaser et al. (2004) report a segmentation of hospitals by Hill-Rom, a health care equipment manufacturer and service provider. They segment the market and identify two target segments. Following a redesign of the organization to better meet the needs of each segment, they reallocated the sales force to the two target segments. The results over a two-year period, attributable to the new segmentation scheme as implemented by management, included an 11 per cent increase in sales per employee, a customer satisfaction increase of 6 per cent and a gross margin increase of 6.7 per cent, yielding more than $70 million. Apparently the firm also anticipated and coped with sales force implementation problems, which indicates that such issues are not insurmountable.

An even more dramatic segmentation success story is Dow Corning's segmentation of its silicone market (Gary 2004). As a perennial market leader, it admittedly had become complacent. However, the threat of aggressive competitors and increasing costs for innovation and service compelled Dow Corning to consider segmentation as an option. In its segmentation, it learned that one segment no longer needed the added value of service, innovation or a broad product assortment of the silicone products; instead these customers just wanted the best price. Rather than lose them to aggressive price competitors, Dow Corning chose to launch a new brand, Xiameter©, with an Internet-based business model that could meet the segment's needs. The needs-based segmentation approach was so successful that it reportedly paid for itself in three months. The reasons given for the success are notable, including the role of the team responsible for implementing the Xiameter© business model and the way the entire organization prepared for and managed the new segmentation approach (Gary 2004).

Despite these successes, there also have been reports of problems with B2B market segmentation (Abratt 1993; Berg et al. 2009; Plank 1985). In an ISBM Segmentation Consortium, Jan Ekonomy (2000) of Sprint described a case study about how segmentation can fail to deliver promised benefits. She reported that some segmentation efforts were effective but not sufficiently actionable; others were actionable but not effective. After analyzing Sprint's past approaches and segmentation literature, she concluded that (1) none of the segmentation approaches used adequately modeled the complexity of the decision-making process within large business customers; (2) none of them provided a holistic view of the business market; and (3) the resources, time and leadership required for success were significantly underestimated.

Robertson and Barich (1992) lend credibility to this Sprint example, noting that the results of well-designed segmentations often include resounding rejections by the sales force. Dibb and Simkin (1994) express similar concerns about implementation and note that it is possible to develop a segmentation that managers and salespeople cannot implement. As a case in point, they describe a seven-segment solution based on factor analysis and clustering of 40 supplier requirements in the car parts after-market. Because no descriptor variables in the study could sufficiently discriminate across the segments, the segmentation was eventually abandoned in favor of a more traditional one, based on customer types.

What emerges from these examples is that B2B segmentation has worked better in some cases than in others, perhaps for a variety of reasons. A partial explanation may be the way managers and salespeople become involved in and understand the segmentation process. For example, Dolnicar and Leisch (2010) study 198 Australian marketing managers and find some 65 per cent had difficulties interpreting segmentation solutions, while many others lacked an understanding of how the data collected could result in the identification of segments. These difficulties may be due in part to the inherent complexities of business markets.

B2B Market Structure Complexities

The allure of using segmentation in business markets is promulgated by its apparent successes in consumer markets. The siren sounded by Robertson and Barich (1992, p. 5) is clear: 'Surprisingly, the sophisticated market segmentation methods that power decision making for the consumer products businesses are often strikingly ineffectual in the industrial arena'. It is not just that the sales force has difficulty implementing a segmentation approach; it is that business markets are inherently different and far more complex in structure than consumer markets, which makes them more difficult to understand and research.[3]

Business firms are part of commercial networks, value chains and inter-organizational and interpersonal relationships that complicate transactions. For example in a value chain, business firms as 'customers' participate in transactions upstream and downstream, whereas consumers as customers are the end of a value chain. Business firms often exist to serve other customers that have their own business model to generate profit or maintain a budget, whereas consumers seldom resell their purchases for a profit. Consumer markets are typically characterized by large numbers of individuals who can make numerous purchase decisions in a week or a day and who pay with cash or a credit card. Business markets typically contain fewer customers that make less frequent but often larger purchase decisions. They tend to include organizations with complex buying centers, several decision-makers, influencers inside and outside the buying organization and a professional purchasing agent trained to obtain the best price or value for the organization.

For example a manufacturer of automotive paint has some 50 potential customers in the world, of which the top 15 customers make more than 80 per cent of the 60 million automobiles sold globally (International Organization of Motor Vehicle Manufacturers 2009). The challenge for the paint supplier – segmenting large, complex automotive manufacturers with multiple product lines offered to millions of potential consumers globally – will be very different from that for an automobile manufacturer that must segment several million consumers who might purchase vehicles. The paint supplier has a compound task: to consider the needs and problems of not only its direct customers but also of its customers' customers (Tang and Mantrala 2010). For the paint manufacturer to be competitive, it must understand the segmented structure of both the automotive manufacturer market and the consumer market; thus, clearly, the multilevel B2B segmentation challenge is a complicated one.

Brown et al. (2007) provide a compelling set of differences between business and consumer markets on a continuum of ten dimensions. They propose that B2B markets, more than B2C markets, exhibit several general tendencies. Although the focus of their study is on branding, the differences are relevant for B2B segmentation too. Specifically B2B, compared with B2C, tends to be

1. higher in buying situation risk;
2. focused more on technological and utilitarian product drivers;
3. more likely to engage in group rather than individual purchase decision processes;
4. focused on economic and performance risk rather than social risk;
5. more rational than impulsive in purchasing;
6. more responsive to different types of reference groups;
7. focused more on a corporate brand than a product brand;
8. focused more on services that support the product;
9. more responsive to personal and interactive selling rather than mass communication;
10. more responsive to technical message content than to image-based content.

A final key difference is the accessibility of large amounts of scanning and other data in B2C markets relative to B2B markets; transaction data can be critical for segmentation research.

In addition to such differences, there are also complications in business markets with respect to the networks of firms within and adjacent to the value chain. These larger constellations of organizational purchasing reflect networks of activity that increasingly influence how organizations behave in general and in their purchases (Henneberg et al. 2009). The emergence of the Internet, telecommunication and other powerful drivers has created a much more interdependent world that affects organizational buying behavior in ways that are not yet fully understood (Wind and Thomas 2010). These kinds of differences have an impact on the activities involved in the process of segmentation and point to areas that academic research should pursue to better understand the theoretical and conceptual underpinnings of segmentation in B2B markets.

Variation in Defining B2B Segmentation Processes

Faced with business markets that are complex and highly situational, it is helpful for managers to have processes that provide some guidelines so they can capitalize on any opportunities from the use of market segmentation. A review of published segmentation processes over the past 50 years reveals many different formulations. Table 11.1 summarizes eight selected segmentation processes defined in prior literature. Each is briefly reviewed here, but interested readers should consult the original references for more comprehensive explanations.

Hummel (1960) proposes what might be labeled an 'industry-focused' segmentation process using standard industrial classification (SIC) codes[4] to classify markets by industry, then estimating size and value using company sales data, judgment and market surveys. Customer prospects can be identified and targeted using one or more of four suggested information sources: (1) industrial directories; (2) surveys; (3) trade show attendance lists; and (4) advertising and promotional inquiries.

Wind and Cardozo's (1974) survey of 25 industrial firms reveals that the most used approaches to industrial segmentation at that time were similar to Hummel's (1960). They propose a more formal, two-step, macro- and micro-segmentation approach that begins by identifying macro-segments of organizations with similar characteristics such as size, SIC code and geographic location. Each macro-segment then can be evaluated with regard to the extent to which it provides an 'attractive' opportunity (e.g. sales potential). The most attractive macro-segments become the focus of micro-segments, or small groups of firms defined by similarities and differences among their decision-making units (DMUs). A variety of bases and descriptor variables and methods can be used to develop a more refined understanding of micro-segments, which can be evaluated and selected according to their profitability and distinct responses to the firm's marketing program. Choffray and Lilien (1978) extend the macro- and micro-segmentation process with a 'decision matrix' approach applied to the heating and air conditioning equipment market. After identifying macro-segments, their decision matrix structures stages in the buying decision process according to the people in the DMU involved in the various stages.

As Table 11.1 shows, Thomas and Wind (1982) introduced a more comprehensive

Table 11.1 Eight B2B market segmentation processes

Industry-Focused Process Hummel (1960)	Macro- and Micro-Segmentation Process Wind and Cardozo (1974)	Macro-Micro Decision-Matrix Process Choffray and Lilien (1978)	Managerial Decision Process Thomas and Wind (1982)	Nesting Process Bonoma and Shapiro (1983)	Conjoint-Based Process Green and Krieger (1991)	Phased Process McDonald and Dunbar (2004)	Implementation Process Clarke (2009)
Use SIC code to classify industrial market	Macro-Segmentation: Identify macro-segments based on organizational characteristics	Phase 1: Macro-Segmentation	Segmentation decision (Should I segment this market?)	Demographics nest	Define initial researcher focus (customer or product)	Stage 1: Your Market and How it Works	1. Identification of purpose
Generate high probability prospects through:	Select set of macro-segments consistent with corporate objectives and resources	Phase 2: Micro-Segmentation	Segment identification decision (If so, how?)	Operating variables nest	Segmentation approach (a priori, post hoc, stepwise)	Step 1: Defining the 'market' (scope of the project)	2. Identification of market to segment

Table 11.1 (continued)

Industry-Focused Process Hummel (1960)	Macro- and Micro-Segmentation Process Wind and Cardozo (1974)	Macro-Micro Decision-Matrix Process Choffray and Lilien (1978)	Managerial Decision Process Thomas and Wind (1982)	Nesting Process Bonoma and Shapiro (1983)	Conjoint-Based Process Green and Krieger (1991)	Phased Process McDonald and Dunbar (2004)	Implementation Process Clarke (2009)
1. Industry directories	Evaluate each macro-segment according to response to marketing stimuli; if yes, select target and stop	Step 1: Measure the pattern of involvement in the purchasing process	Marketing resource allocation decision (What resources should be allocated to each segment?)	Purchasing approach nest	Optimal product design model finds best product for each of k segments (or best k products for stepwise segments)	Step 2: Market mapping (structure and decision-makers)	3. Identification of variables and model
2. Surveys of prospects in SIC code	Micro-Segmentation: Identify within each acceptable macro-segment, micro-segments based on DMU characteristics	Step 2: Define an index of inter-organizational similarity	Segment selection decision (Which segments should be selected?)	Situational factors nest	Total contribution to overhead profits is computed	Stage 2: Decision-Makers and Transactions	4. Segmenting and analysis

3. Trade show attendance lists	Select target micro-segment based on costs/benefits of reaching it	Step 3: Use cluster analysis to identify groups of organizations homogeneous in buying center composition	Segment implementation decision (Can this segmentation strategy be implemented?)	Personal variables rest	Background profile is found for selectors of each competitive product	Step 3: Who specifies what? (decision-makers and their purchases)	5. Verification, evaluation and selection of segments
4. Advertising and promotional inquiries	Identify complete profile of target segment	Step 4: Identification of the pattern of involvement in the purchasing process within each micro-segment				Stage 3: Segmenting the Market; Step 4: Why? (needs of decision-makers); Step 5: Forming segments (combining like-minded decision makers); Stage 4: Identifying Your Target Segments; Step 6: Segment attractiveness (segment potential); Step 7: Company competitive strengths by segment	6. Communication and implementation; 7. Monitoring and updating

189

'managerial decision process' to segment business markets, in which the first decision recognizes that managers should embrace the possibility that segmentation may or may not have a pay-off for them. The segment identification decision then might include a macro- and micro-segmentation process. The third decision involves determining the extent to which the firm can offer the necessary marketing resources (e.g. products, price, advertising, sales force) to the identified segments to obtain a desirable response. Notably, this stage precedes the segment selection or targeting decision, which requires managerial criteria to pick an optimal target segment. Finally, the segment implementation decision anticipates concerns mentioned more recently. In effect this segmentation process takes a wide-ranging decision perspective but still remains sequential.

The decision and staged approaches thus tend to be sequential, but Bonoma and Shapiro (1983) instead propose five sets of 'nested' variables, such that managers can begin at any nest and work their way through the others. The outermost nest begins with demographics, within which are nested operating variables, purchasing approach variables, situational factors and the micro-level personal characteristics of buyers. The authors note that as the nests go from the outer to the inner ones, the variables change in terms of visibility, permanence and intimacy; the outermost variables are higher on visibility and permanence and the innermost ones are higher on intimacy. Although they provide no specific decision rules to move from one nest to the next, the authors suggest managers should stop the process when they discover segments that appear economical and useful. The process differs from previous approaches in its nesting and the flexibility for managers to begin at any nest.

The conjoint-based segmentation process defined by Green and Krieger (1991) also affords considerable flexibility in identifying market segments because it uses conjoint analysis for data collection. The approach allows the manager/researcher to choose between defining segments by customers or by product attribute partworth utilities. Customers can be put into segments a priori, according to predetermined partworth utility values, or their utilities can be clustered *post hoc* to identify segments for which customers can be described. The process also includes a product optimizer model, which sets the stage for estimating segment profitability and the background characteristics of customers for targeting. The value of such an approach is that it links customer response to product design and other marketing variables through a conjoint task to identify a segment with the most profitable outcomes. The process differs from the others in that it illustrates the centrality of a specific methodology that involves various assumptions, which may be more appropriate for some situations than others.

McDonald and Dunbar (2004) propose a process with two major phases: (1) developing segments; and (2) prioritizing and selecting segments. The first phase involves five steps, including understanding the overall market structure, identifying key decision-makers and forming segments based on customer needs and other 'why' variables. The second phase involves estimating segment attractiveness to prioritize segments and selecting segments with respect to company strengths: in effect, a portfolio approach. The process is noteworthy because it recognizes market structures ('mapping') and the role of different decision-makers, and it is couched in a book that calls segmentation an important part of the marketing process.

The last process in Table 11.1 has a clear emphasis on implementation. Clarke (2009, p. 344) sets out to construct 'a market segmentation process and methodology that is practical in nature, easily approachable for companies, operational within the company, and that considers the eventual implementation ramifications throughout the segmentation process'. Working with a Danish company, she employs action research methodology involving an aggregative rather than disaggregative process to identify segments. It begins with understanding the company's purpose for the segmentation and clearly defining the market. Next, the approach identifies variables to use in the segmentation analysis and a verification, evaluation and selection of segments. How the segmentation is communicated throughout the organization to facilitate its implementation then sets the stage for its ongoing monitoring and updating.

What these eight selected segmentation processes make clear is that there are a variety of conceptualizations, variables, methods and targeting approaches to segmentation. Coupled with the complexity of business markets and the mixed results from using segmentation in practice, the variations in process suggest the need for a different approach. As Goller et al. (2002) note, it is difficult to generalize around segmentation variables and methods. Instead a focus on the activities involved in a process of segmentation may be of greater value.

CRITICAL ACTIVITIES FOR B2B MARKET SEGMENTATION

Given the challenges of developing effective B2B market segmentations and the variability in market situations encountered, the approach I recommend here is for managers to design their own segmentation process rather than adopt one that presumably works for every situation. On the basis of the processes in Table 11.1, I identify and present six *core segmentation activities* in Figure 11.1. Although each of these six activities is consistent with extant recommendations, not all have to be used to design a segmentation process, nor is the order meant to imply a step-by-step approach. For example, a marketing manager in the local subsidiary of a chemical firm may receive a well-defined positioning and marketing strategy from the global organization and only need to find the best target segment. This segmentation process would place 'positioning and marketing strategy' closer to the beginning than the end of the task. Consequently managers who use or who are asked to use market segmentation must be prepared to design and implement a process that best conforms to the situations they face. I consider each of the six core segmentation activities briefly in the following sections.

Decide on the Use of Segmentation

The decision to use B2B market segmentation has three critical components: (1) the *market uncertainties* faced from the outcome of a situation analysis; (2) the *importance of the marketing decisions* contemplated; and (3) the organization's *readiness to embrace segmentation*. The three aspects work together to provide a basis for defining the objectives of segmentation and ascertaining its value in terms of its benefits versus the investment of time and resources required to carry out a segmentation process. Generally the greater the uncertainties faced in a market situation (e.g. problems or opportunities), the more important the marketing decisions, and the greater the organization's readiness to embrace segmentation, the more likely a decision to use segmentation will produce

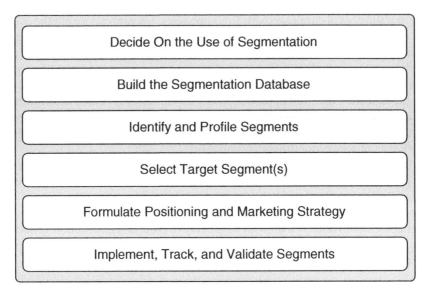

Figure 11.1   Core activities for B2B market segmentation

valuable results. Any other mixture of outcomes from these three possibilities requires a more careful analysis of the decision to use segmentation.

A market situation analysis is quite standard yet critical to all marketing activities, including the decision to segment (Rao and Steckel 1998). It involves the careful definition of the market or category and the trends that influence it. Analyses of customers, competitors, the value chain and the companies' own strengths and weaknesses within and across cultures in a global economy should lead to a clearly stated set of insights and challenges that help define the central marketing uncertainties facing managers. Using a marketing situation analysis, managers then can consider the marketing decisions that will ameliorate and/or capitalize on market uncertainties and decide whether segmenting the market will improve the quality of these decisions. The decisions may involve new markets that are sources of business development and growth, new product development, pricing, distribution, communication, customer relationship management or other critical marketing decisions. The issue is whether implementing a market segmentation process will reduce the market uncertainties linked to marketing decisions.

Although the market situation analysis and marketing decision problems are important, if the organization is not ready to embrace segmentation, the entire effort will be of little value. Organization structure, operations, size, leadership, communication styles, decision-making processes, teamwork and other factors may lead to differences in how segmentation is viewed and how it is implemented (Dibb and Simkin 2001). For example larger versus smaller organizations may have different resources that can influence how the segmentation process is staffed and funded. Furthermore the personnel involved in segmentation may not agree on the objectives or the resources required, or they may not have adequate analytical capabilities. As Jan Ekonomy (2000) noted, Sprint initially underestimated the resources, time and leadership necessary to commit to a segmentation process that would be effective for the organization.

Firms using segmentation for the first time occasionally or routinely also need to assess their organization's response. For example firms using it for the first time may confront what is essentially an organizational innovation, which often requires leadership and support from top management, including the CEO. Leadership must ensure that the rationale for segmentation links to the corporate vision, strategy and objectives. In addition to providing necessary resources, leaders can appoint a segmentation team with the responsibility for developing and implementing the segmentation process for organizations. Simkin (2008) proposes cross-functional teams, including some with a detailed appreciation of customers' purchasing behavior and needs. Clarke (2009) offers several characteristics of the people to include on the segmentation team, including expertise with segmentation, implementation power, a vested interest in the segmentation results and participation in involved departments, especially the sales force or those who might *resist* a new segmentation approach.

Such guidelines are useful, but little empirical research addresses questions about the leadership and teamwork responsibilities required for different kinds of segmentation processes or the extent to which these responsibilities vary over time while carrying out segmentation. As Clarke and Freytag (2008) propose, the extent and process of segmentation may differ according to the purpose of segmentation and the intended marketing offering. Their idea of developing a matrix that suggests different segmentation approaches for different situations is indicative of the kind of thinking required to better understand the decision to use segmentation.

Build the Segmentation Database

The emphasis in segmentation literature is typically on methods of analysis (Dibb and Stern 1995; Wright 1996), with less consideration given to the quality of segmentation data, such as the variables, measurement and data collection (Wind 1978; Wind and Bell 2008). All too often standard sets of questions are asked of single respondents from organizations in business markets, with little thought given to truly understanding customer needs or other relevant variables. Building a quality database for segmentation requires a consideration of (1) the unit of analysis; (2) the variables and measures used; (3) the research approach; and (4) the integration of multiple databases.

Unit of analysis data
With few exceptions the bulk of published research on B2B market segmentation relies on data from a single 'customer'. However, in practice, business customers mainly consist of buying centers (Robinson et al. 1967), with multiple participants who may have different needs and problems. A segmentation based on the needs of a purchasing manager may differ considerably from that based on responses from marketing or R&D managers. Despite numerous studies of buying centers (Johnston and Lewin 1996), few have considered the implications for market segmentation (Choffray and Lilien 1978; Thomas 1989; Narayandas 2005). Consider a buying center with three key participants, A, B and C. If their needs or responses to marketing stimuli are similar, there appears to be high agreement within that organization, which then can be treated as a unified customer voice. However, if their needs are different or if two have similar needs and one does not, there are different implications in terms of segmentation. In addition, buying centers can

Table 11.2   Illustrative segmentation variables

Bases Variables Used to Define Market Segments	Descriptor Variables Used to Describe and Target Segments	Response Variables Used to Develop Segment Positioning	Marketing Variables Used to Formulate Marketing Strategy
Needs (core reasons why customers are motivated to purchase)	Organizational characteristics (size, age, industry, etc.)	Awareness of major brands (top-of-mind, unaided, aided, etc.)	Product design, development, assortment, etc.
Value (benefits to meet needs in relation to price)	Buying center characteristics (e.g., size, influence, location)	Perceptions of major brands on needs and benefits, comprehension of brand meaning	Perceived value for pricing
Attitudes, interests, beliefs, and related psychological variables	Individual factors (age, income, occupation, gender, family, education)	Preference/likeability for major suppliers and brands	Channels of distribution, direct vs. indirect purchasing options
Intention-to-buy brands or new product concepts	Social and cultural factors	Intention to buy brands or new product concepts	Media usage and preferences, touch points, etc.
Purchasing processes (new task, modified, straight rebuy), product usage rates (heavy, medium, light), etc.	Time based and other variables such as customer life cycle, purchase frequency, etc.	Brand loyalty, usage rates, etc.	Sales force sensitivity, technical support, customer service, etc.

be extended to value chains and other market networks through interactive media that help form special interest communities, consortia or buying groups (Clarke and Freytag 2008; Henneberg et al. 2009; Wind and Thomas 2010). This situation makes it important to consider a more expanded definition of whom to sample in data collection.

Variables and measures

The second major concern in building a database for segmentation is the need to establish creative and insightful variables. Thomas and Wind (1982) and Wind and Thomas (1994) suggest three sets of variables to consider: marketing resource variables (e.g. product, price, sales force), market segmentation variables and market response variables at the organizational, buying center and individual levels. An alternative but similar view with four variables sets in Table 11.2 includes bases variables traditionally used to identify segments, descriptor variables to describe and target segments, response variables for positioning and targeting, and marketing variables to formulate marketing strategy.

With respect to the bases variables, the entire focus of the field of marketing has been to identify customer needs and develop offerings to meet them (Kotler and Keller 2009). Thus any effort to segment a business market should focus on customer need variables. In some ways managers intuitively select variables such as organizational size, usage or geographic location as surrogate indicators of customer need. Such variables are useful for identifying macro-segments, but competitors often adopt the same approach. To gain a competitive edge through segmentation, firms thus increasingly turn to customer needs and value (Lilien et al. 2010) and customer behavior (Rangan et al. 1992) to identify micro-segments.

Consequently the purpose of Table 11.2 is to encourage the development of a comprehensive set of variables, beginning with exploratory in-depth customer research as input to the segmentation research process. In addition, alternative measurement approaches beyond the ubiquitous importance rating scale should be considered. Along with conjoint analysis (Green and Krieger 1991), the development of the maximum differences (maxdiff) or best–worst scaling approaches (Louviere and Woodworth 1990) hold considerable promise for B2B segmentation. From a list of relevant customer needs or benefits, several sets of needs are provided to a respondent, who then indicates the most and least important ones. The resulting data, similar to paired comparisons, can be analyzed with a multinomial choice or hierarchical Bayes model to produce a ranking of needs, from most to least important. Unlike traditional rating scales, the maxdiff approach facilitates comparisons between respondents, which is essential for more discriminatory segmentations. When compared with five other approaches, maxdiff scaling offered the best accuracy, though it took longer to administer (Chrzan and Golovashkina 2006). Thus though the maxdiff approach holds promise, it requires both conceptual and practical development (Marley 2009), as well as specific consideration of its applicability in B2B segmentation, especially in the context of multiperson buying centers.

The emergence of the Internet, mobile communication and online marketing have been seen as commercial and research opportunities for business marketing. When customers visit a website's landing page, clickstream data can be captured on several variables: customer duration on a specific page, topic or the entire site; the number of clicks through to other pages or specific products; the number of times they return and when; and purchase outcomes. As Naik et al. (2008) note, such data are high-dimensional; imagine large databases of Variables×Alternatives×Subjects×Time (VAST matrix arrays), where any one or more dimensions might be very large. The data can be derived from social networks and are numeric or text-based, including blogs, customer comments and so on. Such data require new thinking about their collection and analysis for the purposes of segmentation. The value of such data is that they represent B2B customer *behaviors*, not just responses to survey questions. Unfortunately, few published studies use such data in B2B segmentation.

Research approach
Beyond its traditional marketing research decisions (e.g. sample, research instrument, data collection method), the overall segmentation research approach can take two forms: aggregative and disaggregative. In an aggregative approach, data collection begins one customer at a time, to build an understanding of market needs and how they are segmented (Clarke 2009). With deeper customer intimacy, a database can be developed that enables the grouping of even a few customers into meaningful segments. In larger markets, firms might collect data on individual customer organizations, one at a time, and then proceed to place those customers together that are most similar on the critical variables of interest. This process can be continued until adding new customers no longer leads to new segments.

The disaggregative research approach borrows heavily from consumer market segmentation techniques. Representative samples are drawn from large populations, and databases are assembled from questionnaires completed by various data collection procedures (e.g. online, in-person, mail, telephone). There is no evidence to indicate that one approach is better than another (Rao and Wang 1995); though case studies and research on the costs and benefits of each would be of value to both academics and practitioners.

Integrating multiple databases
All too often companies develop and maintain separate databases with the same customers, albeit for different purposes. Yet integrating relevant aspects of these databases into a single-source database provides greater opportunities to identify and profile segments. At issue is locating the data available that also are relevant to customer segmentation across different databases. For example, how should a database from a customer survey, a sales call database (e.g. from sales force software reports), clickstream data and/or an enterprise database (e.g. SAP, Oracle) be integrated into a single segmentation database for analysis? How should the segmentation database be cleaned, maintained and updated? Without a high quality database, the important tasks of identifying and profiling segments are at risk.

Identify and Profile Segments

The identification and profiling of target segments may be the most difficult challenge in market segmentation, as well as the reason published literature on this segmentation activity is so extensive relative to other topics (Wedel and Kamakura 2000). The challenge requires several decisions that both analysts and managers should consider, including (1) which method(s) should be used to identify groups of customers who are similar within groups and different between groups on selected variables; (2) how many segments should define the feasible set; and (3) how the segments should be profiled. Each is considered briefly.

Segment identification method
Many methods can be used to identify market segments and various classification schemes to organize these methods. Here my emphasis is on four segment identification methods that appear in prior literature and have also been used in B2B practice: (1) classifying customers on preselected categorical variables; (2) grouping customers on multiple variables with cluster analysis; (3) classifying customers with latent class analysis; or (4) optimizing segments using predefined criteria.

Method 1 involves selecting one or a few bases variables with defined categories and creating a priori classifications of organizational customers. For example, consider two variables and their categories: customer sensitivity to price (low or high) and similarity of needs within the buying center (similar or dissimilar). They produce four segments into which a sample of customers can be grouped for profiling and additional comparative analysis.

Method 2 involves the consideration of multiple bases variables that are typically constructed from rating scales, such as customer importance ratings of needs or benefits or customer agreement ratings on various attitude statements. Cluster analyses on these variables are conducted to identify segments. Whereas Method 1 started with predetermined segments (a priori), this multivariate approach enables the identification of numerous segments from *post hoc* analyses of the data (Green 1977). Due to the likelihood that these bases variables may be correlated, they are typically factor analyzed to identify a reduced set of variables that capture the underlying need, benefit or attitudinal 'factor' structure of the market. Individual-level 'factor' scores or selected variables from the factors are then submitted to a cluster analysis to identify potential segments.

While Method 2 is a popular approach practiced by many firms and research suppliers, it also is problematic. Selecting the best set of bases variables and rating scale measures to include in a questionnaire, assuming respondents answer them properly and summarizing them into underlying factors (that may explain only 50–60 per cent of the variation in the responses) introduces the potential for error in the data analyzed. This issue is compounded by concerns for selecting the best cluster analysis procedure (Arabie and Hubert 1994). There are decisions about which clustering procedure to use: overlapping (customers may be assigned to more than one cluster), non-overlapping (customers can be assigned to only one cluster) or fuzzy (customers can be assigned partially to different clusters). With non-overlapping clustering (the most common approach), a decision must be made to use either a hierarchical or non-hierarchical approach. With a hierarchical approach, the analyst needs to choose a similarity measure (typically a Euclidian distance measure) and a linkage method (e.g. Ward's method of minimum variance). Everitt et al. (2011) provide a comprehensive review of cluster analysis, including the various methods and decisions to consider.

Method 3, latent class analysis (LCA), has an objective similar to that of cluster analysis but identifies customer segments with a different set of assumptions, variables and models. Essentially LCA, often associated with finite mixture models, uses statistical procedures to identify a set of unobservable classes or clusters from observed variables. For example, we cannot directly observe if an organization's purchasing behavior is risk averse, but we can measure selected variables (e.g. how long it takes to make a decision, how many people get involved in the purchase) that, when analyzed, uncover the extent to which an organization can be classified as risk averse. The covariation in these observed variables should explain each observed variable's relationship to the unobserved one. The data for the observed variables in LCA can be based on a variety of measurement scales; they are not based on distance scores (as required for cluster analysis) but can be raw responses from customers. Despite these advantages, there are issues to be considered in using LCA (Dillon et al. 1994).

Whereas Methods 1–3 can be used to identify segments, they are unconstrained. That is, there are few limiting resources and criteria applied until the targeting phase of the segmentation process. Method 4 seeks to find a more 'optimized' set of segments by simultaneously including variables such as reachability, profitability and feasibility, in addition to customer needs and descriptors. DeSarbo and Grisaffe (1998) and DeSarbo and DeSarbo (2007) describe this more flexible approach using a methodology called NORMCLUS, which contains combinatorial optimization algorithms. The methodology is more flexible, in that it accommodates user-specified objective functions, single or multi-criterion objective functions, a variety of user-specified constraints, different forms or types of segments, multiple sets of data collected from the same customers and alternative models of market segmentation. Comparing this approach to more traditional ones in an application to the electric utility industry, DeSarbo and Grisaffe (1998) demonstrate its value by identifying managerially relevant segments.

Although there are other methods and procedures for identifying and profiling segments, the numerous possibilities suggest the need for research into guidelines to determine situations in which some methods are more relevant and valuable than others. If one method is better than others, will it yield marginally different results than others, and at what cost in terms of data collection and analysis? With few exceptions, these methods were also derived from B2C literature with the assumption of individual buyers, not buying centers.

Number of segments to define a feasible set

In a database of N customers it is theoretically possible to have $1-N$ segments. One segment implies that all customers are quite similar in terms of relevant variables, and the best marketing approach is to prepare one offering for the entire market. The case of N segments indicates that every customer is different, and the marketing offer should be customized to each. One of the challenges in B2B marketing practice is that the sales force often treats each customer as a separate segment, sensing each one's needs, recognizing the complexity of the customer's buying situation and coordinating the offering accordingly. The value of two or more segments in such cases is to make the sales call more efficient, that is, to provide the sales force with information that can enable salespeople to allocate their limited resources better to obtain greater customer response.

Consequently one of the key problems in segmentation is determining the appropriate number of segments, between 1 and N, to avoid under- or over-segmenting. There are basically two approaches: statistical analysis and managerial involvement. The core idea of segmentation is to identify segments that are similar within themselves and different from others on critical variables, so the use of segment variance calculations can help determine the number of segments. Milligan and Cooper (1985) test 30 such measures and find that the index by Calinski and Harabasz (1974) is the best indicator of the number of segments. Boone and Roehm (2002) suggest another approach using artificial neural networks to select the appropriate number of segments. Although these methods should prove useful in practice, they are often based on artificial data sets with a known segment structure or consumer applications. A second approach to determine the number of segments generally follows managerial rules of thumb. For example, some firms set the rule that no segment should be smaller than 10 per cent of the market; others indicate that the number of segments should be between 3 and 10. Until the statistical methods are applied and tested in B2B markets, it is strongly recommended that managers review the profiles of alternative segment structures and use their judgment and experience to decide on the appropriate number for the feasible set.

Profiling segments

The primary objectives of profiling segments are to define who the customers in each segment are and to assess the reachability of the customers in each segment. Given a feasible set of segments, there are three approaches to profiling: bivariate, multivariate, and model-based. The classical bivariate approach is often used with Methods 1 and 2: data are presented to managers in cross-tabulations, often with segments as the column variables and categorical descriptors of the segments (e.g. geographical location) as row variables. The column percentages then can be compared across the segments for each row variable to identify similarities and differences. Similarly, the mean or other statistical measures of interval and ratio-scaled variables (e.g. importance of a benefit on a five-point scale) can be compared across segments.

The typical multivariate approach employs a statistical model to identify the set of independent variables that best separates the segments. Multiple discriminant analysis, CART (classification and regression trees) and similar methods are useful to identify those variables that best define each segment. For example, discriminant analysis seeks to find the linear combinations of segment descriptor variables (e.g. organizational size, location, product application) that maximize between-segment variance relative to within-segment variance. If a discriminant analysis is effective, the variables that describe the segments can predict membership in a segment, which is useful for both validating the segments derived from a database and for predicting segment membership from customers not in the database, which in turns helps determine the reachability of segment.

The model-based approach is linked more closely with Methods 3 and 4. In this case, multiple variables appear in the model (e.g. LCA), such that segments are simultaneously identified and profiled (Kamakura et al. 1994). There is no need for a subsequent discriminant analysis to profile the segments. With the exception of case study applications, such as those by DeSarbo and Grisaffe (1998) and DeSarbo and DeSarbo (2007), there have been few published applications of these approaches for B2B market segmentation, let alone of their validity and comparison with other procedures.

Select Target Segments

A primary challenge of selecting a target segment is that the eventual response of any one segment can be influenced by the marketing offering to that segment. Even the definition of a segment can change depending on the resources the firm can offer to it. Typical approaches to segment selection tend to avoid this challenge by assuming that a segment is based on customer needs and that firm resources are unlimited in being able to provide the appropriate offering. This assumption can lead to segment selection decisions that meet customer needs but do not generate profit, due to the costs of serving the segment.

Early marketing theorists and managers tended to approach the targeting decision by first defining a set of criteria that would characterize ideal segments, such as measurability, substantiality, accessibility and actionability (Frank et al. 1972). Each can be defined by more specific metrics, and other criteria can be added. Callaghan and Morley (2002) conducted a survey among 124 Australian marketing managers to rank 40 potential segmentation criteria. Notably, the top 10 criteria in the list include characteristics of both the segment (e.g. size, growth, profitability) and the firm (e.g. fit with strategy, ability to add value to segment, ability to deliver the offer).

Using the selected criteria, managers can establish a rating scheme, weight the criteria if desired and evaluate each segment according to how well it meets the criteria.

A portfolio-based approach can provide even more structure to the targeting process (Wind and Thomas 1994). In this approach managers identify and weight criteria that define a dimension of *market attractiveness* (e.g. size, growth, profitability, reachability) and a dimension of *business competency* to serve the segment (e.g. brand strength, ability to develop an offer, financial resources). Each segment then can be rated and plotted on these two dimensions. The segments that are most attractive and for which the organization has the greatest competency are more likely to be chosen as targets. Sarabia (1996) extends this model by including multiple detailed variables, especially those involving the organization.

Target segment selection should be approached as a management decision process with multiple alternatives evaluated on selected criteria, preferably incorporated into a decision model, yet it is not easy to integrate all these elements while considering differences among individual managers involved in the process. Montoya-Weiss and Calantone (1999) tackle this problem in a B2B setting by modeling the trade-offs among evaluation criteria and organizational resource constraints. Essentially they employ a process that starts with structuring the problem and setting managerial criteria to evaluate the segments. Segments then form with a variety of well-known marketing research procedures. A two-year *post hoc* review of an application of the model for an automotive supplier enables the authors to conclude that the model enhances management's decision-making and business performance.

Hartmann (2010) proposes a targeting model based on game theoretic concepts and Bayesian estimates to incorporate the social interaction of group members. He shows that targeting an entire group generates a 1 per cent increase in profit, whereas targeting within the group increases profit by 20 per cent. Although his application involves golfers, it may be extended to buying centers and other B2B communities. Both Montoya-Weiss and Calantone's (1999) and Hartmann's (2010) applications of targeting are ambitious and apparently effective. However, it is unclear if these models would have been superior to a more traditional segment selection approach. That is, what remains missing is research on which targeting approaches work in which conditions or measures of managerial receptivity to more comprehensive versus simpler models. Montoya-Weiss and Calantone (1999) suggest that simpler is better as a reminder of the importance of managerial involvement.

Formulate Positioning and Marketing Strategy

Once a target segment is selected, the next recommended step usually is to develop a positioning statement and formulate a marketing strategy to achieve that positioning. Whereas data are important to inform positioning and marketing strategy statements (Berrigan and Finkbeiner 1992), all too often creativity and biases take over at this point. The frequent result is that the positioning diverges from the needs of customers in the target segment and reflects instead managerial beliefs about how customers should perceive the offering. This scenario is further complicated by the challenge of reaching the target segment with an effective communication approach. In many B2B marketing situations, the marketing plan and its implementation are handed off to the sales force. Different approaches to sales force training and who is targeted in the buying center can lead to different outcomes for segmentation.

Ideally, the potential positioning and marketing strategy gets incorporated as part of the segment identification and selection process. Among the segmentation models discussed in the previous sections, those that involve latent class structures and optimization algorithms hold the most promise. These models can incorporate various marketing decisions through conjoint analysis and other procedures, but they do not include customer brand perceptions. DeSarbo et al. (1991) creatively integrate cluster analysis and multidimensional scaling in a model to include customer perceptions and preferences and other segmentation-related variables simultaneously. Wedel and Kamakura (2000) define this class of models as STUNMIX (for STochastic UNfolding MIXture modeling). Clearly a variety of data, distribution and other modeling assumptions are required to make such models operational, but with further development, they hold the promise of creating a single modeling approach that can select an optimal segment using targeted criteria relevant for successful implementation. Unfortunately such models in B2B market segmentation have received little attention and application, let alone validation to prove their value in use.

Implement, Track and Validate Segments

In marketing literature segmentation processes usually end with the selection of a positioning and marketing strategy for the targeted segments, along with recommendations for implementation. Various implementation problems and approaches arise in the first set of segmentation activities, as discussed previously, and Maier and Saunders (1990) provide relevant advice for working with the sales force to enhance implementation. However, there has been very little concern for the recommended process of tracking and validating segments (Wind 1978). As Blocker and Flint (2007) discuss, markets and market segments can be unstable over time, and there must be at least a conceptual understanding of this concern, if not methodological rigor in tracking the existence of a segment structure of the market.

In effect, managers face a simple but critical question: *did the marketing program reach the identified target segment?* For some managers, if sales increased after the segmentation was implemented, it worked! However, sales could increase due to other factors or because the firm reached customers that had not been targeted. Tracking and validation are important challenges, yet there are few guidelines. In smaller markets tracking can be accomplished by the sales force, who can report results by customer, which can then be correlated with targeted segments. Sales force software can be designed to accommodate this effort.

In larger markets, one approach might be to identify early customers, obtain their characteristics from the sales force or a questionnaire and determine their segment membership. A more comprehensive follow-up segmentation study might be conducted, say one year after implementation, with the results compared with the original segmentation. Reported purchase data from the follow-up study could be correlated with segment membership. The possibility of B2B customer online panels and various commercial sources can also track and validate customer responses by segment, assuming such data are available in the relevant categories. Although there are possible tracking and validation methods, few have been reported or tested for their value in use.

CONCLUSIONS AND DIRECTIONS FOR FURTHER RESEARCH

B2B marketing managers strive to support the continuously profitable growth of organizations through the efficient and effective allocation of resources. Market segmentation promises to be a dynamic business decision process to support this objective, because it can identify one or more segments of target customers on which to focus a marketing strategy for long-run competitive advantage. The purpose of this chapter has been to consider the current state of B2B market segmentation, identify some major challenges to its effectiveness, and note the major activities involved in developing a segmentation process in prior literature.

The literature reviewed reveals success stories for B2B segmentation, as well as reports of it not working as well as expected. A comprehensive baseline survey of current segmentation practices and methods used by B2B organizations is missing and must be conducted. Relying solely on occasional case studies of segmentation effectiveness is insufficient to shed light on its true value to B2B firms. Several case studies bring to the surface the problems of implementing B2B segmentation; however, many methodological problems remain as well:

- The continued emphasis on single-respondent studies – when buying centers are almost always involved in purchase decisions – can lead to murky segmentation results.
- The types of variables, measures and data used in B2B segmentation research have not been adequately addressed, whether by traditional market research and surveys or newly emerging sources of data from the Internet and telecommunications applications.
- The approaches to identify and profile segments have moved well beyond cross-tabulations and cluster analysis, yet few published B2B segmentation applications involve latent class or optimization models that validate their utility for different situations.
- The implementation problems noted in recent literature need to be addressed in the form of guidelines for managers that enable them to get the most value from segmentation.

Table 11.3 summarizes a list of questions to stimulate research on these topics, as well as some guidelines for managers involved in segmenting B2B markets. To overcome these challenges, both academics and practicing managers must rethink the process that firms use to conduct B2B segmentation. The variety of B2B segmentation processes that have been proposed in the past 50 years provide the basis for identifying at least six major activities that managers can use to develop a more integrated segmentation process that fits their organization and markets (Figure 11.1). The six activities can be taken as a process, as presented, but a different logical order also may be more relevant for some situations than others. The challenges inherent in these six activities provide many opportunities for academic researchers and managers to improve B2B market segmentation.

Table 11.3   Directions for future B2B segmentation research and practice

Questions for Future B2B Segmentation Research	B2B Segmentation Guidelines for Managers
• What is the track record and effectiveness of B2B market segmentation across a variety of industries, cultures, organizational types and other factors? • What are the best ways to manage the organization for market segmentation to improve its internal acceptance, minimize barriers and enhance its implementation? • What is the best composition of segmentation 'teams' for different kinds of applications, and how effective are such teams in managing and accelerating the process? • What are the determinants of the value of conducting segmentation to make the proper allocation of resources to a segmentation process (e.g., does the greater importance of a marketing decision lead to a greater potential value from segmentation)? • How should data be collected and analyzed to account for similarities and differences of responses among participants in the buying center of a customer organization? How are buying centers defined within multinational organizations that span a variety of cultures? • What are the validity, reliability, costs and benefits of using importance ratings, constant sum scales, maxdiff or other scaling procedures to measure customer needs or other variables? Which measures are best for different cultures? • How can multiple data bases be linked to improve the segmentation process (e.g. how to integrate data from customer surveys, sales call reports, enterprise data bases, Internet activity)? • What are the conditions and circumstances under which aggregative versus disaggregative segmentation research approaches to collect data should be used? • What are the problems and prospects of organizing massive data bases using clickstream and other forms of electronic data for purposes of B2B segmentation?	• Learn as much as possible about market segmentation concepts and language to communicate effectively about it within your organization and with potential market research suppliers. • Do your marketing situation analysis homework up front to be very clear about the potential value of segmentation prior to starting such a process. Write down specific decisions and objectives you hope to achieve with the segmentation. • Make sure you understand your organization's propensity to embrace segmentation and recognize its potential value. Leadership 'buy-in' is critical for success. Set realistic expectations for the outcome of the segmentation. • Whatever the size and global extent of your market, focus on an expanded view of the buying center beyond a single individual. Explore the entire value chain and related interdependencies, especially your customer's customers, to develop new insights about the market to be segmented. • Be creative in developing new variables and measures that can be used for segmentation. Consider using conjoint analysis or the maxdiff scaling approaches rather than traditional rating scales of importance. Include positioning and marketing strategy variables to better link these decisions to the segments. • Use more than one analytical approach to identify segments and compare the findings of the approaches (e.g. cluster analysis and latent class analysis). Managers should review more than one segmentation solution to pick the best feasible set of segments from which to choose a target. • Profitability is a time-tested way to select a target segment; other strategic criteria can impact profitability and should be considered as well, such as reachability or consistency with strategic positioning.

Table 11.3   (continued)

Questions for Future B2B Segmentation Research	B2B Segmentation Guidelines for Managers
• Are there new variables and measures to identify and profile segments that can be used to expand the unit of analysis from individuals to buying centers, networks and business systems or to consider new forms of multilevel segmentation analysis? • Can guidelines be developed, situational or otherwise, that will provide insight into which variables are best to use for bases of segmentation? • Can a classification of segmentation decisions, data and methods be developed for various B2B marketing situations? What are the conditions for which latent class analysis should be preferred over traditional cluster analysis, for example? • What are the best data, methods and tools to track and validate a segmentation that has been implemented?	• Once a marketing approach has been identified for target segments, prepare an internal marketing communication plan for the sales force and other relevant players inside and outside the organization who may have an impact on the implementation of your segmentation approach. • Track and validate the response of your marketing approach for your segment(s). Use tracking tools to recognize the potential instability and dynamics in important target segments and make corrections accordingly. • Recognize that because of potential error in the variables selected, the data and the segmentation methods, there will most likely *not* be a single best segmentation or target market. Use your managerial experience and open-mindedness to let the segmentation findings improve your resource allocations, then learn from the outcomes.

NOTES

1. The term 'needs' as used here refers to a summary class of variables that provide a basis for dividing customers into groups. It can include a variety of operationalizations, such as customer value, attitudes, preference or usage.
2. Unfortunately studies from business practice about B2B segmentation effectiveness may be rare due to the constraints of confidentiality and because segmentation is often done for competitive reasons. In many published academic case studies, the firms are disguised and actual outcomes seldom known.
3. Wind (2006) cogently argues that B2B and B2C markets are converging due to the Internet, increasingly outsourced value chains, consumer co-creation with business, a blurred marketing function in firms due to widely available customer data and the move from an industrial to a knowledge-based society. Undeniably, these market drivers are at work, yet their impact on B2B segmentation serves to make the challenge even more difficult.
4. In 1997, the US government launched a six-digit North American Industry Classification System (NAICS) code to replace the four-digit SIC code, though some firms and government agencies continue to use SIC codes.

REFERENCES

Abratt, Russell (1993), 'Market segmentation practices of industrial marketers', *Industrial Marketing Management*, 22, 79–84.

Arabie, Phipps and Lawrence J. Hubert (1994), 'Cluster analysis in marketing research', in Richard Bagozzi (ed.), *Advanced Methods of Marketing Research*, London: Blackwell Publishers, pp. 160–89.

Berg, Brian, John Berrigan and Gary L. Lilien (2009), 'Why most B2B segmentations fail and what to do about it', presentation at M-Planet, Chicago: American Marketing Association.

Berrigan, John and Carl Finkbeiner (1992), *Segmentation Marketing*, New York: Harper Business.

Blocker, Christopher P. and Daniel J. Flint (2007), 'Customer segments as moving targets: integrating customer value dynamism into segment instability logic', *Industrial Marketing Management*, 36, 810–22.

Bonoma, Thomas V. and Benson P. Shapiro (1983), *Segmenting the Industrial Market*, Lexington, MA: Lexington Books.

Boone, Derrick S. and Michelle Roehm (2002), 'Evaluating the appropriateness of market segmentation solutions using artificial neural networks and the membership clustering criterion', *Marketing Letters*, 13 (4), 317–33.

Brown, Brian P., Daniel N. Bellenger and Wesley J. Johnston (2007), 'The implications of business-to-business and consumer market differences for B2B branding strategy', *Journal of Business Marketing*, 1 (3), 209–29.

Calinski, Tadeusz and J. Harabasz (1974), 'A dendrite method for cluster analysis', *Communications in Statistics*, 3, 1–27.

Callaghan, Bill and Clive Morley (2002), 'The hierarchy of target market selection criteria', *ANZMAC 2002 Conference Proceedings*, pp. 761–7.

Chamberlin, Edward H. (1965), *The Theory of Monopolistic Competition*, Cambridge, MA: Harvard University Press.

Choffray, Jean-Marie and Gary L. Lilien (1978), 'A new approach to industrial market segmentation', *Sloan Management Review*, (Spring), 17–29.

Chrzan, Keith and Natalia Golovashkina (2006), 'An empirical test of six stated importance measures', *International Journal of Market Research*, 48, 717–40.

Clarke, Ann H. (2009), 'Bridging industrial segmentation theory and practice', *Journal of Business-to-Business Marketing*, 16, 343–73.

Clarke, Ann H. and Per V. Freytag (2008), 'An intra- and inter-organisational perspective on industrial segmentation: a segmentation classification framework', *European Journal of Marketing*, 42, 1023–38.

DeSarbo, Wayne S. and Christian F. DeSarbo (2007), 'A generalized normative segmentation methodology employing conjoint analysis', in A. Gustafsson, A. Herrmann, F. Huber (eds), *Conjoint Measurement: Methods and Applications*, 4th edn, Berlin: Springer, pp. 321–45.

DeSarbo, Wayne S. and Douglas Grisaffe (1998), 'Combinatorial optimization approaches to constrained market segmentation: an application to industrial market segmentation', *Marketing Letters*, 9, 115–34.

DeSarbo, Wayne S., Daniel J. Howard and Kamel Jedidi (1991), 'Multiclus: a new method for simultaneously performing multidimensional scaling and cluster analysis', *Psychometrika*, 56, 121–36.

Dibb, Sally and Lyndon Simkin (1994), 'Implementation problems in market segmentation', *Industrial Marketing Management*, 23, 55–63.

Dibb, Sally and Lyndon Simkin (2001), 'Market segmentation: diagnosing and treating the barriers', *Industrial Marketing Management*, 30, 609–25.

Dibb, Sally and Philip Stern (1995), 'Questioning the reliability of market segmentation techniques', *Omega*, 23, 625–36.

Dickson, Peter R. and James L. Ginter (1987), 'Market segmentation, product differentiation, and marketing strategy', *Journal of Marketing*, 51, 1–10.

Dillon, William R., Ulf Böckenholt, Melinda Smith De Borrero, Ham Bozdogan, Wayne DeSarbo, Sunil Gupta, Wagner Kamakura, Ajith Kumar, Benkatraman Ramaswamy, and Michael Zenor (1994), 'Issues in the estimation and application of latent structure models of choice', *Marketing Letters*, 5, 323–34.

Dolnicar, Sara and Freidrich Leisch (2010), 'Evaluation of structure and reproducibility of cluster solutions using the bootstrap', *Market Letters*, 21, 83–101.

Doyle, Peter and John Saunders (1985), 'Market segmentation and positioning in specialized markets', *Journal of Marketing*, 49, 24–32.

Ekonomy, Jan (2000), 'Leveraging past failures into future opportunities', ISBM Segmentation Consortium (October).

Everitt, Brian S., Sabine Landau, Morven Leese and Daniel Stahl (2011), *Cluster Analysis*, Chichester: John Wiley & Sons.

Frank, Ronald E., William F. Massy and Yoram Wind (1972), *Market Segmentation*, Englewood Cliffs, NJ: Prentice Hall.

Gary, Loren (2004), 'Dow corning's push for organic growth', *Strategy and Innovation*, 2, 3–5.

Gensch, Dennis H., Nicola Aversa and Steven P. Moore (1990), 'A choice modeling market information system that enabled ABB Electric to expand its market share', *Interfaces*, 20, 6–25.

Goller, Susanne, Annik Hogg and Stavros P. Kalafatis (2002), 'A new research agenda for business segmentation', *European Journal of Marketing*, 36, 252–71.

Green, Paul E. (1977), 'A new approach to market segmentation', *Business Horizons*, 20, 61–73.

Green, Paul E. and Abba Krieger (1991), 'Segmenting markets with conjoint analysis', *Journal of Marketing*, 55 (4), 20–31.

Harrington, Richard J. and Anthony K. Tjan (2008), 'Transforming strategy one customer at a time', *Harvard Business Review*, (March), 62–72.

Hartmann, Wesley R. (2010), 'Demand estimation with social interactions and the implications for targeted marketing', *Marketing Science*, **29**, 584–601.

Henneberg, Stephan C., Stefano Mouzas and Peter Naudé (2009), 'Going beyond customers – A business segmentation approach using network pictures to identify network segments', *Journal of Business Marketing*, **3**, 91–113.

Hummel, Francis E. (1960), 'Pinpointing prospects for industrial sales', *Journal of Marketing*, **25**, 26–31.

International Organization of Motor Vehicle Manufacturers (2009), website available at http://oica.net/wp-content/uploads/ranking-2009.pdf.

Johnston, Wesley J. and Jeffrey E. Lewin (1996), 'Organizational buying behavior: toward an integrative framework', *Journal of Business Research*, **35**, 1–15.

Kamakura, Wagner A., Michel Wedel and Jagadish Agrawal (1994), 'Concomitant variable latent class models for conjoint analysis', *International Journal of Research in Marketing*, **11** (5), 451–64.

Kotler, Philip and Kevin Keller (2009), *Marketing Management*, Upper Saddle River, NJ: Pearson.

Lilien, Gary L., Rajdeep Grewal, Douglas Bowman, Min Ding, Abbie Griffin, V. Kumar, Das Narayandas, Renana Peres, Raji Srinivasan and Qiong Wang (2010), 'Calculating, creating, and claiming value in business markets: status and research agenda', *Marketing Letters*, **21**, 287–99.

Louviere, Jordan and George G. Woodworth (1990), 'Best–worst scaling: a model for largest difference judgments', Working Paper, Faculty of Business, University of Alberta.

Maier, Jens and John Saunders (1990), 'The implementation process of segmentation in sales management', *Journal of Personal Selling and Sales Management*, **10**, 39–48.

Marley, Anthony A.J. (2009), 'The best–worst method for the study of preferences: theory and application', Working Paper, Faculty of Business, University of Alberta.

McDonald, Malcolm and Ian Dunbar (2004), *Market Segmentation*, Oxford: Elsevier.

Milligan, Glenn W. and Martha C. Cooper (1985), 'An examination of procedures for determining the number of clusters in a data set', *Psychometrika*, **50**, 159–79.

Montoya-Weiss, Mitzi and Roger J. Calantone (1999), 'Development and implementation of a segment selection procedure for industrial product markets', *Marketing Science*, **18**, 373–95.

Moorthy, K. Sridhar (1984), 'Market segmentation, self-selection, and product line design', *Marketing Science*, **4**, 288–307.

Naik, Prasad, Michel Wedel, Lynd Bacon, Anand Bodapati, Eric Bradlow, Wagner Kamakura, Jeffrey Kreulen, Peter Lenk, David M. Madigan and Alan Montgomery (2008), 'Challenges and opportunities in high-dimensional choice data analyses', *Marketing Letters*, **19**, 201–13.

Narayandas, Das (2005), 'Building loyalty in business markets', *Harvard Business Review*, **83**, 131–9.

Pigou, Arthur C. (1920), *The Economics of Welfare*, London: Macmillan.

Plank, Richard (1985), 'A critical review of industrial market segmentation', *Industrial Marketing Management*, **14**, 79–81.

Rangan, V. Kasturi, Rowland T. Moriarty and Gordon S. Swartz (1992), 'Segmenting customers in mature industrial markets', *Journal of Marketing*, **56**, 72–82.

Rao, Chatrathi P. and Zhengyuan Wang (1995), 'Evaluating alternative segmentation strategies in standard industrial markets', *European Journal of Marketing*, **29**, 58–75.

Rao, Vithala and Joel Steckel (1998), *Analysis for Strategic Marketing*, Reading, MA: Addison Wesley.

Robertson, Thomas S. and Howard Barich (1992), 'A successful approach to segmenting industrial markets', *Planning Review*, **48**, 4–11.

Robinson, Joan (1954), *The Economics of Imperfect Competition*, London: Macmillan.

Robinson, Patrick J., Charles W. Faris and Yoram Wind (1967), *Industrial Buying and Creative Marketing*, Boston, MA: Allyn & Bacon.

Sarabia, Francisco J. (1996), 'Model for market segments evaluation and selection', *European Journal of Marketing*, **30**, 58–74.

Simkin, Lyndon (2008), 'Achieving market segmentation from B2B sectorisation', *Journal of Business and Industrial Marketing*, **23**, 464–74.

Smith, Wendell (1956), 'Product differentiation and market segmentation as alternative marketing strategies', *Journal of Marketing*, **21**, 3–8.

Tang, Yihui and Murali Mantrala (2010), 'A three-dimensional approach to B-to-B market segmentation: incorporating customers' customers', Paper presented at 32nd INFORMS Marketing Science Conference, Cologne.

Thomas, Robert J. (1989), 'Industrial market segmentation on buying center purchase responsibilities', *Journal of the Academy of Marketing Science*, **17**, 243–52.

Thomas, Robert J. and Yoram Wind (1982), 'Toward empirical generalizations on industrial market segmentation', in R. Spekman and D. Wilson (eds), *Issues in Industrial Marketing: A View to the Future*, Chicago: American Marketing Association, pp. 1–18.

Waaser, Ernest, Marshall Dahneke, Michael Pekkarinen and Michael Weissel (2004), 'How you slice it: smarter segmentation for your sales force', *Harvard Business Review*, **82**, 105–111.

Wedel, Michel and Wagner Kamakura (2000), *Market Segmentation: Conceptual and Methodological Foundations*, 2nd edn, Norwell, MA: Kluwer.

Wind, Yoram (1978), 'Issues and advances in segmentation research', *Journal of Marketing Research*, **15**, 317–37.

Wind, Yoram (2006), 'Blurring the lines: is there a need to rethink industrial marketing?', *Journal of Business & Industrial Marketing*, **21**, 474–81.

Wind, Yoram and David R. Bell (2008), 'Market segmentation', in M.J. Baker and S.J. Hart (eds), *The Marketing Book*, 6th edn, Oxford: Butterworth Heinemann.

Wind, Yoram and Richard Cardozo (1974), 'Industrial market segmentation', *Industrial Marketing Management*, **3**, 153–66.

Wind, Yoram and Robert J. Thomas (1994), 'Segmenting industrial markets', *Advances in Business Marketing and Purchasing*, **6**, 59–82.

Wind, Yoram and Robert J. Thomas (2010), 'Organizational buying behavior in an interdependent world', *Journal of Global Academy of Marketing Science*, **20**, 110–22.

Wind, Yoram, John F. Grashof and Joel D. Goldhar (1978), 'Market-based guidelines for design of industrial products', *Journal of Marketing*, **42**, 27–37.

Wright, Malcolm (1996), 'The dubious assumptions of segmentation and targeting', *Management Decision*, **34**, 18–24.

Yankelovich, Daniel and David Meer (2006), 'Rediscovering market segmentation', *Harvard Business Review*, **84**, 122–31.

12 Branding in B2B firms
Kevin Lane Keller and Philip Kotler

Brands are a powerful force in our everyday lives, whether we are thinking of buying a car, a pair of sneakers, a refrigerator or hotel lodging. We pay attention to brands and often have favorites. We choose a brand that we have heard about, others have talked about or with which we have had a good experience. In buying a new television set, we confront many different brands but probably focus on a smaller 'consideration set' of those few brands that we know and trust (Urban 2005). Because we know that Sony or Samsung will work well, we may feel we do not have to consider all the other brands. Branding simplifies our decision-making and reduces our felt risk.

Although we know the importance of branding in navigating our consumer purchases, we can ask whether branding plays the same important role in B2B purchasing (Bendixen et al. 2004; Mudambi et al. 1997). Suppose a car manufacturer must decide what brand of tires to purchase and mount on its cars. The car manufacturer can choose from such tire manufacturers as Michelin, Goodyear, Continental, Bridgestone and Pirelli. Does the brand matter? Certainly it does. All these brands carry meanings and associations about quality, price, experience, innovation and other dimensions.

We believe that B2B branding is just as important to business buyers as B2C branding is to consumers. Yet we also believe that many B2B businesses do a poor job of developing and managing their corporate brands, sub-brands and other brands. Our goal is to answer the following questions to help B2B firms do a better job of branding:

- Why do B2B firms often fail to make good use of branding?
- Which major B2B firms make very good use of branding?
- What does a B2B firm need to know about branding as a starting point?
- What steps should a B2B firm take if it wants to build a strong brand?

BARRIERS TO B2B FIRMS MAKING GOOD USE OF BRANDING

B2B firms tend to assume that purchasers of their products are so well-informed and professional that brands don't matter. Professional purchasing agents can find plenty of information from manufacturer catalogues as well as the unlimited resources of the Internet and the expertise of a network of experts. These agents know the qualities that they want in a product and know how to shop for the best price. They are not likely to be fooled by lavish, expensive ads or slick, fast-talking salespeople. The manufacturer's brand name is only enough to let the salesperson in, but it does not play much of a role in influencing the purchasing agent's decision.

As a result when B2B firms think about investing in a deep branding or rebranding effort, many will say that they do not need to do it. The winning formula is simply good products backed by good services and effective communications and a fair value price. Here are some major objections, as well as some straightforward counterarguments. In the following sections, we offer more detail into why and how B2B firms should build and manage their brands.

1. *Branding is only about choosing a name, logo and slogan. We already have these in our firm.* B2B branding depends on all aspects of the customer experience. The brand itself is only one part. Every encounter a corporate customer has with a product or service and how it is sold, distributed, serviced and so forth will affect its brand image and equity.

2. *Branding costs too much. You have to pay expensive consultants to shape your brand. Then you have to spend a fortune in costly advertising to establish your brand.* At the heart of a great brand is a great product or service. Successful B2B firms always focus on delivering a great customer experience. This delivery is the first step to building a great brand. And when it happens, corporate customers talk about the brand and the media write about it, and thus inexpensive word-of-mouth and public relations (PR) follow.

3. *The benefits of branding will not appear for a long time.* The benefits to B2B branding are immediate and affect every interaction and encounter that existing or potential corporate customers have with the brand. Sales calls, product or service experiences and price discounts can be interpreted very differently, depending on the brand involved. A strong brand makes B2B marketing more effective and efficient.

4. *It is very hard to measure the ultimate payback on the 'brand investment'.* Much of the investment in a B2B brand is already made anyway – in R&D, employee training, service centers – to enhance the corporate customer experience. Communication expenses to build a stronger brand image can be tracked in the marketplace. Movements in attitudes and perceptions can be related to different outcome measures of interest.

5. *We cannot spare people to spend time on a branding effort. Brand building is a complex and difficult process.* All B2B firms have brands, even if just the corporate brand. The question is whether the firm chooses to manage it properly and ensure that everyone in the organization understands the brand promise and acts accordingly. If not, the brand will still have an image and reputation but an unmanaged one that is completely a function of how the marketplace chooses to shape and influence it.

6. *Branding does not really figure very much in the final decision of the customer, especially in B2B marketing, where the purchasing agents are professional and well-informed.* In B2B purchase situations, corporate decision-makers take everything into consideration. Intrinsic and extrinsic brand factors all come into play and affect how corporate decision-makers interpret the brand's ability to satisfy the firm's needs, as well as their own personal needs.

B2B FIRMS THAT MAKE GOOD USE OF BRANDING

Recognizing the fallacy of these concerns, several B2B firms have made exceptionally good use of branding (Kotler and Pfoertsch 2006). Some notable B2B firms that have learned to use branding as a major tool include Siemens, Bosch, General Electric (GE), Saint-Gobain, UPS, FedEx, Tetra Pak, Caterpillar, Michelin, Tata Steel and Morgan Stanley.

Consider DuPont. DuPont does not sell directly to consumers, only to business buyers. Its task is to develop a new material or ingredient, brand it and get the brand to convey the image of superior performance that can justify a 10–15 per cent premium price over the competition. Business buyers are willing to pay this premium because their superiors can never complain that they did not buy the 'right' brand if something goes wrong. DuPont owns such names as Nylon, Dacron, Kevlar, Corian, Tyvek, Teflon and many others. Each commands a premium in its market.

Consider also IBM. IBM manages to earn premium prices for its services on the same basis, namely, selling strong products backed by powerful branding. Purchasing agents know that they will not be fired for choosing IBM. IBM advertising and salespeople work on the principle that choosing to buy a competitor's product would lead to 'FUD', or feelings of fear, uncertainty and doubt.

WHAT DOES A B2B FIRM NEED TO KNOW ABOUT BRANDING?

Savvy business marketers recognize the importance of their brand and how they must execute in a number of areas to gain marketplace success. Boeing, which makes everything from commercial airplanes to satellites, implemented its 'One Firm' brand strategy to unify all its different operations with a one-brand culture (Sullivan 2009). The strategy was based in part on a triple helix representation: (1) enterprising spirit (why Boeing does what it does); (2) precision performance (how Boeing gets things done); and (3) defining the future (what Boeing achieves as a firm).

NetApp is another good example of the increased importance placed on branding in B2B marketing (Dionne 2009; Levy 2009a). NetApp provides data management and storage solutions for medium- and large-sized clients. Despite some marketplace success, the firm found its branding efforts in disarray by 2007. Several variations of its name were in use, leading to a formal name change to NetApp in 2008. The branding consultant Landor also created a new identity, architecture, nomenclature, tone of voice and tagline ('Go further, faster') for the brand and its new name. Messages emphasized NetApp's superior technology, innovation and customer-centric, 'get things done' culture. NetApp also tapped into a number of social media outlets, including communities and forums, bloggers, Facebook, Twitter and YouTube.

Before a firm undertakes branding efforts, it must assess where it stands with its branding and what it needs to know about brand-building (Keller 2008). Regardless of the particular businesses and markets involved, management must answer the questions in Box 12.1. By answering these questions, the firm gains a better position from which to decide how to proceed in investing in brand-building.

Brand-building in a B2B setting requires some more specific advice, though. The next section therefore reviews and illustrates six key guidelines to build and manage a winning B2B brand.

BOX 12.1   BRAND MANAGEMENT SCORECARD

1. **Managers understand what the brand means to customers**.
   - Have you created detailed, research-driven mental maps of your target customers?
   - Have you attempted to define a brand mantra?
   - Have you outlined customer-driven boundaries for brand extensions and guidelines for marketing programs?
2. **The brand is properly positioned**.
   - Have you established necessary and competitive points of parity?
   - Have you established desirable and deliverable points of difference?
3. **Customers receive superior delivery of the benefits they value most**.
   - Have you attempted to uncover unmet customer needs and wants?
   - Do you relentlessly focus on maximizing your customers' product and service experiences?
4. **The brand takes advantage of the full repertoire of branding and marketing activities available to build brand equity**.
   - Have you strategically chosen and designed your brand name, logo, symbol, slogan packaging, signage and so forth to build brand awareness and image?
   - Have you implemented integrated push and pull strategies that target intermediaries and end customers, respectively?
5. **Marketing and communications efforts are seamlessly integrated (or as close as humanly possible). The brand communicates with one voice**.
   - Have you considered all the alternative ways to create brand awareness and link brand associations?
   - Have you ensured that common meaning is contained throughout your marketing communication program?
   - Have you capitalized on the unique capabilities of each communication option?
   - Have you been careful to preserve important brand values in your communications over time?
6. **The brand's pricing strategy is based on customer perceptions of value**.
   - Have you estimated the added value perceived by customers?
   - Have you optimized price, cost and quality to meet or exceed customer expectations?
7. **The brand uses appropriate imagery to support its personality.**
   - Have you established credibility by ensuring that the brand and the people behind the brand are seen as expert, trustworthy and likable?
   - Have you established appropriate user and usage imagery?
   - Have you crafted the right brand personality?

8. **The brand is innovative and relevant.**
   - Have you invested in product improvements that provide improved benefits and better solutions for your customers?
   - Have you stayed up-to-date and in touch with your customers?
9. **For a multiproduct, multibrand firm, the brand hierarchy and brand portfolio are strategically sound.**
   - For the brand hierarchy, are associations at the highest levels relevant to as many products as possible at the next lower levels, and are brands well differentiated at any one level?
   - For the brand portfolio, do the brands maximize market coverage while minimizing their overlap at the same time?
10. **The firm has in place a system to monitor brand equity and performance.**
    - Have you created a brand charter that defines the meaning and equity of the brand and how that character should be treated?
    - Do you conduct periodic brand audits to assess the health of your brands and to set your strategic direction?
    - Do you conduct routine tracking studies to evaluate current marketing performance?
    - Do you regularly distribute brand equity reports that summarize all brand-relevant research and information to assist marketing decision-making?
    - Have you assigned people within the organization the responsibility of monitoring and preserving brand equity?

WHAT STEPS ARE NECESSARY TO BUILD AND MANAGE A STRONG B2B BRAND?

Ensure the Organization Understands and Supports Branding and Brand Management

Fully recognizing and embracing the potential of branding throughout the organization is the first and most critical step in building a strong B2B brand. Unfortunately many B2B organizations are burdened with skeptics who do not really understand branding and, as a consequence, do not believe in the value of branding. They may mistakenly equate branding with naming or identity standards or view branding as only the responsibility of marketers in consumer product firms.

To counteract these forces, internal branding activities need to be designed so that all members of the organization are properly aligned with the brand. Employees must have a complete, up-to-date understanding of the vision for the brand and how they can help achieve that vision. Internal branding involves a host of different programs and activities, such as training, communications, monitoring, performance appraisal and so on (Davis 2005; Davis and Dunn 2002; Gad 2000; Ind 2004; Pringle and Gordon 2001).

Here we consider two internal branding issues particularly relevant to B2B marketers: (1) horizontal and vertical alignment; and (2) the role of a brand essence (also known as a brand mantra).

Horizontal and vertical alignment

To ensure that the entire firm enthusiastically supports branding efforts, it is useful to think of the firm in terms of vertical and horizontal dimensions. Vertically all levels of management, and horizontally all areas and departments of the firm, should be the recipients of internal branding efforts.

Top executives in B2B firms in particular must be believers in the importance of managing the brand properly. A top-down approach to internal branding involves senior management, reinforcing principles to the entire organization regarding how and why brands matter in B2B settings, how exactly the brand should be positioned, what makes the brand unique and what expectations of employees relate to delivering the brand promise. They must ensure that sufficient resources are available and that proper procedures, processes and guidance are put into place.

A CEO in a B2B firm can be the ultimate brand ambassador, signaling and communicating the importance and value of the brand both internally and externally. A CEO, managing director or other prominent senior executive can have a profound effect on public perceptions of a brand. These executives at least implicitly, if not explicitly, help convey the brand promise and set customer expectations.

Horizontally areas outside marketing must understand, appreciate and support branding. A particularly crucial area within the B2B organization is the sales force. Personal selling is often the profit driver of a B2B organization. The sales force must be properly aligned so that the department can more effectively leverage and reinforce the brand promise. If done right the sales force can ensure that target customers recognize the worth of the range of benefits of the brand's offerings, such that they would be willing to pay a price commensurate with the brand's potential value.

The sales force serves as the firm's personal link to corporate customers. Fred Hassan, CEO of the global pharmaceutical firm Schering-Plough, calls salespeople 'active representatives of the firm [who] can influence people's perception of it through their ability to interact, to customize, and to build relationships with customers' (Stewart and Champion 2006).

Brand mantras

As part of the internal branding effort for a firm, an internal brand slogan – a brand mantra – is useful as a rallying cry for employees (Keller 1999). A brand mantra is an articulation of the 'heart and soul' of the brand. Specifically, *brand mantras* are short, three- to five-word phrases that capture the irrefutable essence or spirit of the brand positioning. The purpose of a brand mantra is to ensure that all employees within the organization and all external marketing partners understand what the brand fundamentally should represent with customers so that they can adjust their actions accordingly. Some consumer marketing examples of a brand mantra are Disney's 'fun family entertainment' and Nike's 'authentic athletic performance'.

A brand mantra is a powerful device that provides guidance as to what products to introduce under the brand, what communications to issue, where and how the brand should be sold and so on. The influence of brand mantras, however, can extend beyond these tactical concerns. A brand mantra may even guide the most seemingly unrelated or mundane decisions, such as the look of a reception area, the way phones are answered and so on. In effect brand mantras create a mental filter to screen out brand-inappropriate marketing activities or actions of any type that may have a negative bearing on customers' impressions of the brand.

Brand mantras are important for several reasons. Any time a customer encounters a brand – in any way, shape or form – his or her knowledge about that brand may change, and as a result, the equity of the brand is affected. Because vast numbers of employees come into contact, either directly or indirectly, with customers in ways that may affect customer knowledge about the brand, the words and actions of employees must consistently reinforce and support the brand meaning.

Many employees or even marketing partners who could help or hurt brand equity may be far removed from the marketing strategy formulation and may not even recognize their role in influencing brand equity – especially in B2B firms. The existence and communication of a brand mantra signals the importance of the brand to the organization and an understanding of its meaning, as well as the crucial role of employees and marketing partners in its management. A brand mantra also provides memorable shorthand notes as to the crucial considerations of the brand that should be kept most salient and top-of-mind. A good brand mantra is simple, descriptive and inspiring.

A GE application

A brand mantra is designed for internal purposes for the firm; a brand slogan is designed to be used externally for communications and other purposes. Nike's mantra was distinct from its well-known external brand slogan, 'Just Do It'. In some cases however, they may be one and the same, as with Betty Crocker's 'Homemade Made Easy' or BMW's 'Ultimate Driving Machine'.

In a B2B setting, GE has developed brand slogans that it also uses internally as brand mantras to capture its brand positioning and improve its marketing. Although GE operates in areas as diverse as home appliances, jet engines, security systems, wind turbines and financial services, the firm has been a pioneer in B2B corporate branding. For GE, its long-running 'We Bring Good Things to Life' line was more than a corporate image ad slogan. It worked hard to make sure the entire organization, and even marketing partners, understood this brand promise.

To facilitate understanding and compliance with its brand positioning, GE created a written brand charter or 'brand bible', whose contents provided a short history of branding and the importance of brands; summarized research into the value of the GE brand; identified the brand's core promise ('better living'), personality and values; and offered guidelines for how the brand should be managed. These guidelines stressed consistency and discipline, summarized in a checklist of questions that forced GE marketing decision-makers to specify key product features and sales propositions and how they related to the core benefit promise of 'better living'.

Its subsequent campaign, called 'Imagination at Work', highlighted a renewed focus on innovation and new technology, again both internally and externally. The goal of GE's corporate advertising was to unify its divisions under the GE corporate brand while giving each of them a voice. 'When you're a firm like ours, with 11 different businesses, brand is really important in pulling the identity of the firm together', said Chief Marketing Officer Beth Comstock. 'Integration was important in communicating the brand across the organization and to all of our constituents . . . The GE brand is what connects us all and makes us so much better than the parts' (Maddox 2004; see also Colvin 2006; Fisher 2005; Kranhold 2006; Stewart 2006).

Adopt a Corporate Brand Strategy if Possible and Create a Well-defined Brand Hierarchy

Because firms selling in B2B markets are often characterized by many and complex product or service lines and variations, a logical and well-organized brand architecture needs to be devised. A *brand architecture* reflects the number and nature of common and distinctive brand elements applied to the different products sold by the firm. Brand architecture involves defining both brand boundaries and brand complexity. Which different products should share the same brand name? How many variations of that brand name should be employed?

Because of the breadth and complexity of the product or service mix, B2B firms are more likely to emphasize corporate brands (e.g. GE, Hewlett-Packard, IBM, ABB, BASF, John Deere). An increasing number of firms recognize the value of a strong corporate brand for dealing with other firms. At one time, Emerson Electric, global provider of power tools, compressors, electrical equipment and engineering solutions, was a conglomerate of 60 autonomous, and sometimes anonymous, firms. A new chief marketing officer (CMO) aligned the previously independent brands under a new global brand architecture and identity, allowing Emerson to achieve a broader presence so that the firm could sell locally while leveraging its global brand name. Record sales and stock price highs soon followed (Krauss 2006).

Corporate credibility

Various corporate image dimensions for a B2B corporate brand are possible. Making sure that corporate brands convey credibility is especially important in a business setting (Erdem and Swait 2004; Goldberg and Hartwick 1990). Corporate credibility is often a primary risk reduction heuristic adopted by B2B buyers. Corporate credibility refers to the extent to which customers believe that a firm can design and deliver products and services that satisfy customer needs and wants (Keller and Aaker 1998). Thus corporate credibility relates to the reputation that the firm has achieved in the marketplace; it depends on three factors:

- *Corporate expertise.* The extent to which a firm is seen as able to make and sell its products or conduct its services competently.
- *Corporate trustworthiness.* The extent to which a firm is seen as motivated to be honest, dependable and sensitive to customer needs.
- *Corporate likability.* The extent to which a firm is seen as likable, attractive, prestigious, dynamic and so forth.

In other words, a credible firm is good at delivering quality products and services, keeps customers' best interests in mind and is enjoyable to work with. Other characteristics can be related to these three credibility dimensions as consequences, such as success and leadership.

Creating a firm with a strong and credible reputation may offer benefits beyond the customer's response in the marketplace. A highly credible firm may be treated more favorably by other external constituencies, such as government or legal officials, and also increase its opportunity to attract better qualified employees. A highly credible firm may help motivate existing employees to be more productive and loyal.

A strong corporate reputation can help a firm survive a brand crisis and avert public outrage that could depress sales, encourage unionism or block expansion plans. As Harvard's Steve Greyser (1999) notes, 'Corporate reputation . . . can serve as a capital account of favorable attitudes to help buffer corporate trouble'.

Brand hierarchy
In completing the brand hierarchy for B2B firms using their corporate brand, individual brands and modifiers often take on descriptive product meaning for clarity and differentiation. Thus a particularly effective branding strategy for B2B marketers is to create sub-brands by combining a well-known and respected corporate brand name with descriptive product modifiers.

Yet if a firm has a distinctive line of business, a more clearly differentiated sub-brand may need to be developed, as with Praxair's Medipure brand of medical oxygen, GE's Lexan plastic, DuPont's Teflon coating or Intel's Centrino mobile technology. Given the effort and investment needed to establish a meaningful sub-brand, though, B2B marketers must employ them selectively.

Frame Value Perceptions

The biggest enemy to B2B marketers is commoditization (Low and Blois 2002). Commoditization eats away margins and weakens customer loyalty. Commoditization can only be overcome if target customers are convinced that meaningful differences exist in the marketplace and that paying more for the unique benefits supplied by the firm's offerings is worth the added expense. Thus a critical step in B2B marketing is to create and communicate relevant differentiation from competitors.

Differentiation can arise in several ways. The highly competitive nature of B2B markets implies that marketers must ensure that customers fully appreciate how the offerings by the firm differ. Framing occurs when customers employ a given perspective or point of view that allows the brand to 'put its best foot forward', so to speak. Framing can be as simple as making sure that customers realize all the benefits or cost savings offered by the brand, or by becoming more involved in the thought process behind how customers view the economics of purchasing, owning, using and disposing of a brand in a different way. Framing requires understanding how customers currently think of brands and choose among products and services, then determining how they ideally *should* think and choose.

Framing is often necessary when customers apply pressure for the firm to cut prices, a common occurrence with B2B purchases. B2B marketers can counter these requests in multiple ways. They may be able to show evidence that the 'total cost of ownership', that is, the 'life-cycle cost' of using their product, is lower than that of competitors' products. They can cite the value of the services the buyer now receives, especially if they are superior to those offered by competitors. For example, research has shown that service support and personal interactions, as well as a supplier's know-how and ability to improve customers' time to market, can be useful differentiators in achieving key supplier status (Ulaga and Eggert 2006).

Marketing communications can play a key role in framing. A different marketing communication mix exists for industrial products than with consumer products. Because of the well-defined target market and complex nature of product decisions, marketing communications tend to convey more detailed product information in a more direct or face-to-face manner. Thus personal selling plays an important role, and the sales force must be skilled at framing the buying decision in the right way.

Regardless of the means, at some point marketers must ensure that customers value product and service differences sufficiently to pay some type of price premium. When Timken, which manufacturers bearings and rotaries for firms in a variety of industries, saw its net income and shareholder returns dip compared with competitors, the firm became concerned that it was not investing in the most profitable areas. To identify businesses that operated in financially attractive sectors and that would be most likely to value its offerings, the firm conducted an extensive market study. It revealed that some customers generated a lot of business but had little profit potential, while for others, the opposite was true. As a result Timken shifted its attention away from the auto industry and into the heavy processing, aerospace and defense industries, and it also addressed customers that were financially unattractive or minimally attractive. By adjusting its products, prices and communications to appeal to the right types of firms, Timken earned record revenues of $5.7 billion in 2008 (Baker 2009; Levy 2009b).

Link Non-product-related Imagery Associations

Developing supportive marketing programs to build brand equity can differ for B2B firms compared with consumer goods firms because of the nature of the organizational buying process. With B2B marketing, product-related performance associations may play a relatively more important role than non-product-related imagery associations. As a consequence many B2B brand marketers emphasize functionality and cost/benefit considerations.

Nevertheless non-product-related associations can be useful in terms of other perceptions of the firm. In a B2B setting, imagery might relate to the size or type of firm. For example Microsoft or Oracle might be seen as 'aggressive' firms, whereas 3M or Apple might be seen as 'innovative'. Imagery may also be a function of the other organizations to which the firm sells. For example customers may believe that a firm with many customers is well established and a market leader.

In B2B markets one commonly adopted means of communicating credibility is to identify other leading or well-respected firms that are customers for the firm's products or services. Such endorsements may serve as a signal or cue of quality. The challenge in communicating this endorsement through advertising at least is ensuring that the other firms used as endorsers do not distract from the message about the advertised firm and its brands.

Non-product-related imagery in a B2B setting can relate to intangible aspects of a product or service offering or various other considerations. With sales of more than $1.1 billion and a huge fan club of IT customers, SAS, the business intelligence software firm, seemed in an enviable position in 1999. Yet its image was what one industry observer called 'a geek brand'. To extend its reach beyond IT managers with PhDs in mathematics or statistical analysis, the firm needed to connect with C-level executives in the largest firms – the kind of people who either did not have a clue what SAS's software was and what to do with the technology, or else did not think business intelligence was a strategic issue. Working with its first outside ad agency, SAS emerged with a new logo, a new slogan ('The Power to Know') and a series of television spots and print ads in business publications such as *BusinessWeek*, *Forbes* and *The Wall Street Journal*. Subsequent research showed that SAS had made the transition to a mainstream business decision-making support brand, both user-friendly and necessary (Lamons 2005).

Customer service

Many B2B firms distinguish themselves on the basis of the customer service they provide, in addition to the quality of their products. For example, Premier Industrial Corporation charges up to 50 per cent more than competitors for every one of the 250 000 industrial parts the firm stocks and distributes, because of its strong commitment to customer service (Phillips and Dunkin 1990).

As a further illustration, creative changes in customer service have similarly built brand equity and allowed Armstrong World Industries to charge higher prices for its floor tiles and Weyerhaeuser's wood-products division to command premiums for its commodity-like two-by-fours. Following IBM's lead, Lucent began to shift into more differentiated value-added services after losing ground in selling its telecommunications hardware to offer current customers more complete packages and to create new opportunities (Lyons 2004).

Uncover Relevant Emotional Associations for the Brand

Perhaps one of the biggest myths in B2B branding is that the nature of the decision process is so rational that emotions do not really play a significant role (Lynch and de Chernatony 2004). Undoubtedly consumer brands can more effectively tap into many different types of emotions than B2B brands can. But at least three emotions can be identified that play a key role in many different customer decisions in a B2B setting.

- *Security.* The brand gives customers a feeling of safety, comfort and self-assurance. As a result of the brand, customers do not experience worry or concerns that they might have otherwise felt.
- *Social approval.* The brand grants customers positive feelings or satisfaction about the reactions of others to themselves.
- *Self-respect.* The brand makes customers feel better about themselves; customers feel a sense of pride, accomplishment or fulfillment.

The rationale and mechanisms for each of these three types of emotions is straightforward and compelling.

As noted previously, B2B decisions are often characterized by a certain degree of risk because they affect the financial performance of a firm and the career prospects of the decision-makers involved. Reducing risk to improve customers' sense of security can be a powerful emotion that can drive many decisions and thus be an important source of brand equity.

A business decision-maker may also be concerned with his or her own reputation. Being seen as someone who works with other top firms may offer peer approval and personal recognition within the organization. Some may even believe that more intrinsic rewards, such as learning or skill development, can be gained from professional interactions with a top firm.

Finally and beyond respect and admiration from others, a business decision-maker may just feel more satisfied by virtue of working with top organizations and brands. A business decision-maker may feel more kinship and connection, whether real or aspirational, when dealing with a firm that has a strong brand reputation.

Emotions and decision-making
B2B marketers who do not explore the role of emotions in decision-making are missing a potentially big opportunity. For example research conducted by one industrial component manufacturer found that though top executives at small- and medium-sized firms stated they were comfortable in general with buying from other firms, they appeared to harbor subconscious insecurities about buying the manufacturer's product. Constant changes in technology had left them concerned about the internal effects within the manufacturer. Recognizing this unease, the manufacturer retooled its selling approach to emphasize more emotional appeals and how its product line actually enabled the customer's employees to improve their performance, relieving management of the complications and stress of component use (Donath 2006).

Ultimately individuals, not organizations, make purchasing decisions (Webster and Keller 2004). Individuals are motivated by their own needs and perceptions to maximize the rewards (pay, advancement, recognition, feelings of achievement) offered by the organization. Personal needs motivate the behavior of individuals, but organizational needs legitimate the buying decision process and its outcomes. People are not buying 'products'. They are buying solutions to two problems: the organization's economic and strategic problem and their own personal need for individual achievement and reward. In this sense B2B buying decisions are both 'rational' and 'emotional', because they serve both the organization's and the individual's needs (Ward and Webster 1991). Keeping both of these perspectives in mind in developing a B2B brand is critical.

Segment Customers Carefully and Develop Tailored Branding and Marketing Programs

As with any brand, it is important to understand how different customer segments view products and brands. In a B2B setting, however, different customer segments may exist both within and across organizations. Brand building must take these different segmentation perspectives in mind in building a brand.

Segmentation within organizations
Within an organization, many different segments may exist. Webster and Wind (1972a, 1972b) call the decision-making unit of a buying organization the buying center. The

buying center consists of 'all those individuals and groups who participate in the purchasing decision-making process, who share some common goals and the risks arising from the decisions' (Webster and Wind 1972a, p. 6). The buying center includes all members of the organization who play any of the following seven roles in the purchase decision process:

1. *Initiators:* users or others in the organization who request that something be purchased.
2. *Users:* those who will use the product or service. In many cases, the users initiate the buying proposal and help define the product requirements.
3. *Influencers:* people who influence the buying decision, often by helping define specifications and providing information for evaluating alternatives.
4. *Deciders:* people who decide on product requirements or suppliers.
5. *Approvers:* people who authorize the proposed actions of deciders or buyers.
6. *Buyers:* people who have formal authority to select the supplier and arrange the purchase terms. Buyers may help shape product specifications, but they play their major role in selecting vendors and negotiating.
7. *Gatekeepers:* people who have the power to prevent sellers or information from reaching members of the buying center (e.g. purchasing agents, receptionists, telephone operators who may help or prevent salespersons from contacting users or deciders).

Several people can occupy a given role, such as user or influencer, and one person may occupy multiple roles (Anderson and Narus 2004; Enright 2006; Webster and Wind 1972b). A purchasing manager, for example, often occupies the roles of buyer, influencer and gatekeeper simultaneously: she or he can determine which sales reps can call on other people in the organization; what budget and other constraints to place on the purchase; and which firm will actually get the business, even if others (e.g. deciders) select which two or more potential vendors meet the firm's requirements.

Clearly individuals in these different roles will have different needs and potentially different views of the brand too. Accordingly, and depending on the perceptions and preferences of the organizational segments involved, such as engineers, brand or marketing managers, accountants or purchasing managers and so forth, the particular associations that serve as sources of brand equity may differ, as might even the role of the brand itself (de Chernatony and McDonald 1998; Mudambi 2002; Rozin 2004).

Marketing programs must reflect the role of individuals in the buying center or process: initiator, influencer, purchaser, user and so on. Some individuals may be more concerned with developing a deep relationship with the firm and therefore place greater value on the trustworthiness dimension and corporate credibility; others may seek merely to make transactions and therefore place greater value on product performance and expertise.

Different types of communications will need to come into play that emphasize different types of information, but it is important to keep in mind that the essential aspects of the brand promise come across in all marketing activities and programs directed at different members of the buying center. The brand mantra can be helpful in providing this high-level guidance. At the same time, more customized marketing must come into play to connect effectively with these various parts of the organization. Having a varied communication mix that allows for different means of contacting and persuading different participants in the buying center can be crucial.

Segmentation across organizations

Firms in B2B markets can be segmented on the same basis as some of the variables used in consumer markets, such as geography, benefits sought and usage rate. Business marketers also use other variables, though. Industry and firm size are often important considerations for defining product needs. Business users also vary in terms of the technologies they use and other capabilities, how they organize purchasing and the purchasing policies they use, and even personal characteristics in terms of their risk and loyalty profiles.

These various factors can lead to different brand strategies and marketing programs. B2B marketers must arrive at the most compelling brand-building and sales-generating segmentation scheme. For example a rubber tire firm can sell tires to manufacturers of automobiles, trucks, farm tractors, forklift trucks or aircraft. Within a chosen target industry, a firm can further segment by firm size. The firm might set up separate operations for selling to large and small customers. Within a given target industry and customer size, a firm can segment further by purchase criteria. For example government laboratories need low prices and service contracts for scientific equipment; university laboratories need equipment that requires little service; industrial laboratories need equipment that is highly reliable and accurate.

Careful customer analysis is a prerequisite for the development of successful market segmentation. Just before it acquired Reuters, the global information services giant Thomson Corporation embarked on an extensive research study to understand its ultimate customers better. Thomson sold to businesses and professionals in the financial, legal, tax, accounting, scientific and health care sectors, but it felt it knew much more about how a financial services manager made purchases for an entire department, for example, than about how individual brokers or investment bankers used Thomson data, research and other resources to make day-to-day investment decisions for clients. Segmenting the market by these end users, rather than by purchasers, and studying how they viewed Thomson versus competitors allowed the firm to identify market segments that offered growth opportunities.

Then to understand these segments better, Thomson conducted surveys and 'day in the life' ethnographic research on how end users did their jobs. Using an approach called 'three minutes', researchers combined observation with detailed interviews to understand what end users were doing three minutes before and after they used one of Thomson's products. Insights from the research helped the firm develop new products and make acquisitions that led to significantly higher revenue and profits (Harrington and Tjan 2008; Reed 2007, 2008).

DISCUSSION

Careful branding is practiced by virtually all major B2C firms but is less applied by many B2B firms, which often see it as costly, with a hard-to-measure return that takes a long time to be realized and does not seem to make a fundamental difference in influencing

Table 12.1   B2B branding guidelines and corresponding research priorities

Branding Guidelines	Corresponding Research Priorities
1) Ensure the entire organization understands and supports branding and brand management.	1) What is the appropriate role of a corporate branding department in a B2B firm?
2) Adopt a corporate branding strategy if possible and create a well-defined brand hierarchy.	2) Is there any halo from a B2C division to a B2B division?
3) Frame value perceptions.	3) What decision processes and rules do B2B customers use in practice to assess value?
4) Link relevant non-product-related brand associations.	4) How do dimensions of corporate credibility interact to affect the decisions of a B2B customer?
5) Find relevant emotional associations for the brand.	5) How do perceptions of risk and other feelings color the perceptions of a B2B customer?
6) Segment customers carefully and develop tailored marketing programs.	6) How uniform must the image of a B2B brand be within and across firms?

the buyer's purchasing decision. Yet we have cited a number of B2B firms that have used branding especially well. They help establish the power of effective branding.

Before a firm decides whether to make a substantial investment in brand-building, management should answer the questions in Box 12.1 to assess its brand standing and its opportunities for moving forward.

If the firm decides to invest in stronger branding, it should employ the following branding guidelines:

1. Ensure the entire organization understands and supports branding and brand management;
2. Adopt a corporate branding strategy if possible and create a well-defined brand hierarchy;
3. Frame value perceptions;
4. Link relevant non-product-related brand associations;
5. Find relevant emotional associations for the brand;
6. Segment customers carefully and develop tailored marketing programs.

Each of these guidelines in turn suggests some future research priorities, as summarized in Table 12.1 and which also follow here:

1. Additional research should determine organizational structures, processes and responsibilities that facilitate good brand management by B2B firms. This work may be interdisciplinary in nature, involving collaborations with theorists and practitioners skilled in human resources, management and other business disciplines. Some basic questions include: should there be a centralized corporate branding department? If so, how should it be run? What actions should it take? Another set of questions might address the inherent value of branding for different types of B2B

firms. In particular, when does it make sense for a B2B firm to develop an ingredient branding strategy? Many factors, such as the importance of the B2B ingredient and the relative strength of the host versus ingredient brand, may be relevant here (Kotler and Pfoertsch 2010).

2. Many B2B firms also sell consumer products. How does brand equity flow across B2B and B2C divisions? Does the brand equity built in consumer markets affect business customers? How much value does Caterpillar create with its toys, boots and other licensed products? Kodak once ran a carefully conducted research study that demonstrated that business customers' perceptions of the Kodak brand as a consumer affected their professional decisions. One explanation of such a finding is that it is virtually impossible to compartmentalize reactions to a brand and that a halo exists in the marketplace, across the consumer and business settings. Understanding if, when and how this halo in brand image occurs is important for guiding both brand investments and tactical planning.

3. Understanding how to frame value calculations for B2B customers successfully is critically important. Many recent research advances in behavioral decision theory and behavioral economics may be relevant, such as applications of prospect theory, decision biases, mental accounting and so on. How do B2B decision-makers combine information? In what ways do their decisions *not* follow a classic linear compensatory decision rule? Are certain kinds of information typically ignored or undervalued? If this information would help the B2B brand, how can it be made more salient and prominent?

4. A particularly interesting research issue concerns the 'softer side' of a B2B brand's image and how its extrinsic, non-product-related associations enter into the value calculations of B2B customers. How are the different components of credibility factored into customer decision-making? Are there any multiplicative effects associated with being seen as expert, trustworthy and likable? Other corporate image dimensions of a B2B are important too. How important is it to seem 'innovative'? How about being seen as a good corporate citizen?

5. One interesting question for B2B brands is how best to create and activate emotional associations. Given the fundamental role of risk perceptions in branding, in what circumstances should fear appeals be employed to evoke feelings of risk? Should fear appeals in a B2B setting be thought of differently than in a B2C setting, where for example they are often used for public service campaigns? When are more outer-directed feelings of social approval versus more inner-directed feelings of self-respect most likely to emerge? How do they manifest themselves, and what are their implications for marketing to a B2B customer? If social approval is important, should marketing emphasize visible symbols of collaboration? Even if a firm is able to create these feelings, how can it ensure that the feelings influence a B2B customer's decision-making in the right way?

6. The complexity of segmentation in a B2B market, across and within firms, raises the interesting question of how uniform the brand positioning should be across segments. How much flexibility is appropriate in crafting relevant messages to different market segments? The ability to personalize communications through the Internet offers a means to reach more segments within a firm cost effectively, for example, but how coordinated do those messages need to be?

REFERENCES

Anderson, James C. and James A. Narus (2004), *Business Market Management: Understanding, Creating, and Delivering Value*, 2nd edn, Upper Saddle River, NJ: Prentice Hall.
Baker, Stephen (2009), 'Timken plots a rust belt resurgence', *BusinessWeek Online*, 15 October.
Bendixen, Mike, Kalala A. Bukasa and Russell Abratt (2004), 'Brand equity in the B2B market', *Industrial Marketing Management*, **33** (5), 371–80.
Colvin, Geoffrey (2006), 'What makes GE great?', *Fortune*, 6 March, 90–104.
Davis, Scott M. (2005), 'Building a brand-driven organization', in Alice M. Tybout and Tim Calkins (eds), *Kellogg on Branding*, Hoboken, NJ: John Wiley & Sons, pp. 226–43.
Davis, Scott M. and Kenneth Dunn (2002), *Building the Brand-Driven Business: Operationalize Your Brand to Drive Profitable Growth*, San Francisco, CA: Jossey-Bass.
de Chernatony, Leslie and Malcolm H.B. McDonald (1998), *Creating Powerful Brands*, 2nd edn, Oxford: Butterworth-Heinemann.
Dionne, Britt (2009), 'Behind the scenes with NetApp', *The Hub Online*, July/August.
Donath, Bob (2006), 'Emotions play key role in Biz brand appeal', *Marketing News*, 1 June , p. 7.
Enright, Allison (2006), 'It takes a committee to buy into B-to-B', *Marketing News*, 15 February, p. 12.
Erdem, Tulin and Joffre Swait (2004), 'Brand credibility, brand consideration and choice', *Journal of Consumer Research*, **31** (June), 191–8.
Fisher, Daniel (2005), 'GE turns green', *Forbes*, 15 August, pp. 80–85.
Gad, Thomas (2000), *4-D Branding: Cracking the Corporate Code of the Network Economy*, London: Financial Times Prentice-Hall.
Goldberg, Marvin E. and Jon Hartwick (1990), 'The effects of advertiser reputation and extremity of advertising claim on advertising effectiveness', *Journal of Consumer Research*, **17** (September), 172–9.
Greyser, Stephen A. (1999), 'Advancing and enhancing corporate reputation', *Corporate Communications*, **4** (4), 177–81.
Harrington, Richard J. and Anthony K. Tjan (2008), 'Transforming strategy one customer at a time', *Harvard Business Review*, (March), 62–72.
Ind, Nicholas (2004), *Living the Brand: How to Transform Every Member of Your Organization into a Brand Champion*, 2nd edn, London: Kogan Page.
Keller, Kevin Lane (1999), 'Brand mantras: rationale, criteria, and examples', *Journal of Marketing Management*, **15**, 43–51.
Keller, Kevin Lane (2008), *Strategic Brand Management*, 3rd edn, Upper Saddle River, NJ: Pearson Prentice-Hall.
Keller, Kevin Lane and David A. Aaker (1998), 'Corporate-level marketing: the impact of credibility on a firm's brand extensions', *Corporate Reputation Review*, **1** (August), 356–78.
Kotler, Philip and Waldemar Pfoertsch (2006), *B2B Brand Management*, Berlin: Springer.
Kotler, Philip and Waldemar Pfoertsch (2010), *Ingredient Branding: Making the Visible Invisible*, Berlin: Springer-Verlag.
Kranhold, Kathryn (2006), 'The immelt era, five years old, transforms GE', *The Wall Street Journal Online*, 11 September.
Krauss, Michael (2006), 'Warriors of the heart', *Marketing News*, 1 February, p. 7.
Lamons, Bob (2005), 'Branding, B-to-B style', *Sales and Marketing Management*, **157** (September), 46–50.
Levy, Piet (2009a), 'It's alive! Alive!', *Marketing News*, 30 April, p. 8.
Levy, Piet (2009b), 'Reeling in the hungry fish', *Marketing News*, 30 May, p. 6.
Low, John and Keith Blois (2002), 'The evolution of generic brands in industrial markets: the challenges to owners of brand equity', *Industrial Marketing Management*, **31** (5), 385–92.
Lynch, Joanne and Leslie de Chernatony (2004), 'The power of emotion: brand communication in B2B markets', *Journal of Brand Management*, **11** (5), 403–19.
Lyons, Daniel (2004), 'You want fries with that?', *Forbes Online*, 24 May.
Maddox, Kate (2004), 'GE's Comstock leads campaign to strengthen brand worldwide', *BtoB Online*, 25 October.
Mudambi, Susan M. (2002), 'Branding importance in B2B markets: three buyer clusters', *Industrial Marketing Management*, **31** (6), 525–33.
Mudambi, Susan M., Peter Doyle and Veronica Wong (1997), 'An exploration of branding in industrial markets', *Industrial Marketing Management*, **26** (5), 433–46.
Phillips, Stephen and Amy Dunkin (1990), 'King Customer', *BusinessWeek*, 12 March, pp. 88–92.
Pringle, Hamish and William Gordon (2001), *Brand Manners: How to Create the Self Confident Organization to Live the Brand*, New York: John Wiley & Sons.
Reed, Stanley (2007), 'The rise of a financial data powerhouse', *BusinessWeek Online*, 15 May.

Reed, Stanley (2008), 'Media giant or media muddle?', *BusinessWeek Online*, 1 May.

Rozin, Randall S. (2004), 'Buyers in B2B branding', *Journal of Brand Management*, **11** (5), 344–5.

Stewart, Thomas A. (2006), 'Growth as a process', *Harvard Business Review*, (June), 60–70.

Stewart, Thomas A. and David Champion (2006), 'Leading change from the top line: an interview with Fred Hassan', *Harvard Business Review*, **84** (July–August), 96–7.

Sullivan, Elisabeth (2009), 'Building a better brand', *Marketing News*, 15 September, 14–17.

Ulaga, Wolfgang and Andreas Eggert (2006), 'Value-based differentiation in business relationships: gaining and sustaining key supplier status', *Journal of Marketing*, **70** (January), 119–36.

Urban, Glen (2005), 'Where are you positioned on the trust dimensions?', in *Don't Just Relate – Advocate: A Blueprint for Profit in the Era of Customer Power*, Pennsylvania, PA: Wharton School Publishers.

Ward, Scott and Frederick E. Webster Jr (1991), 'Organizational buying behavior', in Tom Robertson and Hal Kassarjian (eds), *Handbook of Consumer Behavior*, Upper Saddle River, NJ: Prentice Hall, pp. 419–58.

Webster, Frederick E., Jr and Kevin Lane Keller (2004), 'A roadmap for branding in industrial markets', *Journal of Brand Management*, **11** (May), 388–402.

Webster, Frederick E., Jr and Yoram Wind (1972a), *Organizational Buying Behavior*, Upper Saddle River, NJ: Prentice Hall.

Webster, Frederick E., Jr and Yoram Wind (1972b), 'A general model for understanding organizational buying behavior', *Journal of Marketing*, **36** (April), 12–19.

13 Trade shows in the business marketing communications mix

Srinath Gopalakrishna and Gary L. Lilien

Trade shows have long been used as a forum for promoting sales of a variety of products, dating back to medieval times when artisans and village folk exhibited their wares at local fairs. Those fairs were a relatively inexpensive, yet convenient, way for local producers to gain access to large numbers of potential buyers who came to attend the events from neighboring towns and villages. That flavor has essentially remained unchanged as trade shows continue to occupy a prominent position within the B2B communications mix.

Trade shows also have a characteristic that differentiates them from personal selling, the dominant element in the B2B marketing mix: they bring current and prospective customers to the seller rather than vice versa. Industry surveys during the past decade repeatedly show that over 80 per cent of the attendees at a typical show have some influence on the eventual purchase decision and more than 50 per cent of show visitors have specific plans to buy one or more products exhibited at a show within the next 12 months (www.exhibitsurveys.com/trends). Such a high concentration of interested buyers and sellers in a setting that lasts several days, combined with the opportunity for meaningful face-to-face contact, creates a powerful forum for marketing communications.

Trade shows are big business. In 2009 the trade show industry in North America attracted over 60 million attendees and 1.5 million exhibitors, generating an estimated revenue of nearly $11.2 billion (CEIR 2010a). In the United States, Canada and Mexico more than 14 000 trade shows were held in 2010, totaling over 700 million square feet of exhibit space. The statistics covering 20 European countries reported by UFI, the Global Association of the Exhibition Industry (based in Paris), are just as impressive, with an estimated 112 million visitors and 1.3 million exhibitors attending over 4400 trade fairs spanning nearly 588 million square feet in 2008 (Euro Fair Statistics 2008). Expenditures on trade shows make up the largest share of the typical B2B communications budget (nearly 18.6 per cent), ahead of print advertising (13.8 per cent) and direct mail (10 per cent) (Stevens 2005). And the US exhibition industry grew substantially over the eight-year period from 2000 to 2008, with net square feet of exhibit space growing by 21 per cent and the number of attendees increasing by 10 per cent (CEIR 2010a). While the 2008–09 recession led to a downturn in exhibitions, industry experts have expressed cautious optimism in their outlook for the future (*Exhibitor Magazine* 2010), reinforced by strong third-quarter statistics for 2010 based on positive growth in net square feet, number of exhibitors and attendance (*Trade Show Executive* 2010).

Firms consistently report that lead generation is their most important objective for exhibiting at a show, followed by the desire to introduce new products and services (CEIR 2006). Other reasons they cite as important include building awareness, recruiting dealers/ distributors, maintaining company image and exposure, discovering new applications for existing products, monitoring competition and showing support for the sponsoring association. Wu et al. (2008) confirm work by Kerin and Cron (1987) and Hansen (1999) that suggests many firms have both short-term selling objectives (more amenable to measurement and value assessment) and longer-term, non-selling objectives (less amenable to value assessment). However, exhibitor decisions about which shows to attend and the economic justification for such decisions continue to challenge practitioners and academics alike.

For example there is much folk wisdom but little hard data associated with valuing the interaction that comes with trade show participation. The nature of the B2B context, which often involves complex, large dollar transactions involving multiple decision-makers, seems to suggest a need for face-to-face contact with prospective customers (Hutt and Speh 2010). Trade shows offer a cost-effective way of making at least the initial face-to-face contact. (Appendix 13.1 provides an illustrative cost-effectiveness analysis of trade show exhibiting.) Qualitative support for these observations also comes from surveys of attendees and exhibitors, more than 75 per cent of whom consider face-to-face interactions with potential suppliers/customers extremely important (CEIR 2003).

Assessing the non-sales value of trade shows has proven challenging, though. As Bonoma (1983) and others have noted, non-sales objectives are often imprecise and thus hard to measure and value. For example what does it mean when a company says it wants to 'maintain corporate image' by exhibiting? The relevant metrics for non-sales objectives are generally either poorly defined or non-existent, and their relationships to tangible outcomes are rarely established in a clear manner.

For a trade show to come about and be successful, three sets of actors must be involved: attendees (mostly prospective short- or long-term buyers), exhibitors (mostly prospective short- or long-term sellers) and show managers who organize and manage the event. Show management transacts with exhibitors for the sale of floor space and to provide other fee-based show services. They want exhibitors to have a successful experience, such that they will return to exhibit again at a future show. Exhibitors will return to a show only if the attendees they were able to attract to their booth were of good quality and the interactions led eventually to successful outcomes. Similarly, attendees will want to return only if they felt that they had a cost-effective experience that enabled them to find products/solutions from alternative suppliers.

In the rest of this chapter we first provide an overview of the impact of the technological revolution on traditional trade show strategies. We then review relevant knowledge on trade shows along three perspectives, starting with the exhibitor perspective where we cover issues related to the planning and execution of trade show strategy, followed by the viewpoints of trade show attendees and show management. We conclude with an overview of implications and opportunities for academic research in this domain, as well as lessons for managers.

TRADE SHOWS AND THE TECHNOLOGICAL REVOLUTION

The advent of the Internet and social media has had a dramatic impact on how B2B customers use and exchange information. A recent study (CEIR 2009a) reports that more than 75 per cent of show attendees rely on websites as their top source of industry information, over 50 per cent prefer to receive information about a trade show via email and nearly 90 per cent report being active on a social media website.

These statistics point to the increasingly important role that information technology (IT) is playing before, during and after the trade show. It is evident that IT has become an essential tool for effective management: both trade show organizers (show management) and exhibitors must develop comprehensive social media strategies to reach and engage the audiences of today's marketplace.

Building Communities Through Social Media

A CEIR survey of social media usage shows the increasing use of such media by younger managers; overall, 88 per cent use a social media website, and younger respondents are significantly more likely to use online sites than older respondents (CEIR 2009a). Facebook is the most frequently used social media site overall. It should come as no surprise that such tools are becoming increasingly important as complements to the face-to-face experience that trade shows provide. Hence event organizers and exhibitors are beginning to integrate Internet and social media strategies into their overall event planning processes. Two examples are instructive (*Exhibitor Magazine* 2009):

- Hewlett-Packard added a Twitter-based tactic to its exhibit marketing program to promote its Procurve business (a line of networking products) at the May 2009 Interop show in Las Vegas. The goal was to capture 400 leads at the show (13 per cent more than the 2008 show). But with expected show attendance down by more than 20 per cent from the previous year, this was clearly a challenging goal. The firm set up a Twitter account and recruited 150 initial followers through its website. Sales reps sent out a tweet once every other day, alerting recipients about the new Procurve technology to be showcased, the ten partner companies to be featured and the prizes to be given away. Tweeting increased in frequency to once or twice daily as the show approached; during the three-day event, the firm ratcheted its efforts up to five or six tweets a day, urging followers to come to the booth, locate one of eight products, find a specific staff member and mention a special password to win an iPod or a digital picture frame. Hewlett-Packard eventually garnered 600 leads, an increase the company attributes largely to its Twitter campaign.
- The consulting firm Rick Grant and Associates Inc. contacted 75 current and prospective clients who were not registered to attend the 2009 Technology in Mortgage Banking Conference & Expo and asked them to sign up for a micro-blogging medium. During the show, the firm updated Twitter followers about happenings, such as conference sessions, new offerings on the show floor, gossip overheard, the show facility, amenities and so on. The firm reported 'significantly enhanced' post-show relationships with clients who followed it on Twitter compared with those who did not, though the higher response from followers may be somewhat attributable to self-selection based on interest.

Event Websites

Websites are the most frequently used sources of industry information; it is imperative that they permit prospective attendees to

1. register online quickly and with ease;
2. create personalized schedules and download them to a smartphone;
3. access speaker presentations and the program handbook;
4. access all elements of the event.

A recent study examining the quality of trade show websites (Lee et al. 2008) may signal the start of more systematic empirical research in this area.

Improving Exhibition Marketing Performance Through Better Digital Integration

The exhibition industry is finding digital media, in their many forms, to be excellent means of increasing reach and improving efficiency. Marketers in this space attempt to enhance the attendee experience and deepen engagement. But there are very few reports of how to measure the effectiveness of online advertising, the emails sent prior to the event, the short/multimedia messaging services (SMS/MMS) used during the event, audio downloads after the event or really simple syndication (RSS). Although such digital media account for at least 10 per cent of the overall exhibit budget for most marketers, few of them actually measure the impact of these activities (CEIR 2010b).

Virtual Trade Shows

The potential to reduce travel and event management costs significantly makes virtual trade shows a potentially valuable complement to, or substitute for, live events (see Figure 13.1). However, personal engagement, a prime benefit of trade shows, is missing in this domain; a challenge for the industry and for researchers therefore is to assess the relative benefits and costs of online versus offline exhibitions.

Improved Attendee Tracking Technologies

Show attendees may believe their behavior at trade shows is anonymous. But new attendee tracking technologies are making that belief far from accurate. Barcode and radio frequency identification (RFID) devices (e.g. http://www.trakkers.com/) and video-based tracking methods (see http://videomining.com/, as currently applied in retail environments) capture the minute-by-minute movements of attendees, in much the same way that clickstream data follow online activities. These data are only beginning to be mined to help understand trade show dynamics and to assess effectiveness.

Implications for Research

These technological trends suggest that there are significant research opportunities to (1) use the new type of data being generated through new tracking technologies and those accompanying virtual shows to assess what works and why; and (2) determine the cost-effectiveness and synergies that new media may contribute to trade show performance. New conceptual and operational models are needed to perform these assessments, and several experiments conducted by firms and show organizers seem conducive to fruitful industry–academic research collaborations.

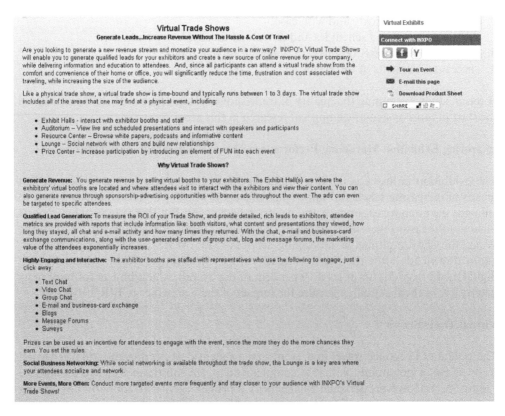

Source: Inexpo.com; see http://presentations.inxpo.com/InXpo/Tours/InXpo_Tours/VirtualTradeShows/
player.html for an example of how such shows work

Figure 13.1   Virtual trade shows

TRADE SHOWS: THE EXHIBITOR PERSPECTIVE

We review two elements of an exhibitor's perspective: planning (role, show selection and budgeting) and execution (pre-, during and post-show feedback and control).

Planning

Role of trade shows

The role of a trade show in the buying and selling process has engaged the attention of academic researchers (Banting and Blenkhorn 1974; Herbig et al. 1998). Trade shows can uncover previously unknown or inaccessible buying influences, project a favorable corporate image, provide product information, generate qualified leads for salespeople, handle customer complaints and so on (Hutt and Speh 2010). They also can satisfy competitive objectives (e.g. intelligence gathering), enhance employee morale and help support personal selling activities.

Customer Buying Process Stage	Marketer Communication Objective	Marketer Communication Task	Relative Communication Effectiveness
			Low High
Identify need	Arouse interest	Prospecting	
Research solutions	Be known to research team	Opening relationship, qualifying prospect	
Develop short list	Be selected for short list	Presenting sales message	
Request proposals	Submit winning proposal	Presenting sales message	
Review proposals	Create preference	Presenting sales message	
Negotiate	Preserve margins	Presenting sales message	
Select vendor	Win	Closing sale	
Install and use	Satisfy and support usage	Account service	Advertising Trade show Personal selling
Upgrade	Upsell, cross-sell	Build and enhance relationship	?

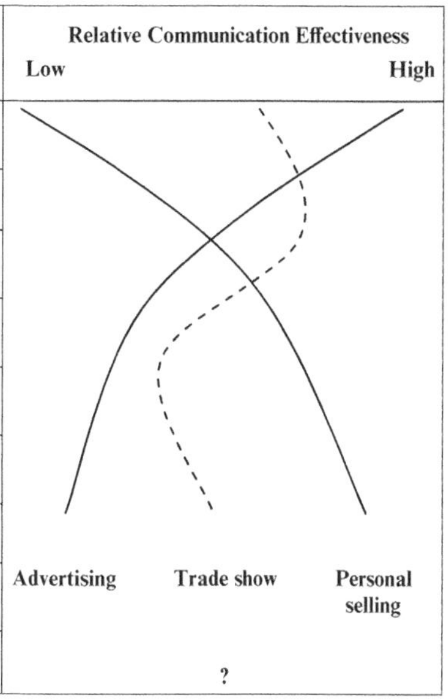

Source: Adapted from Gopalakrishna and Lilien (1995) and Stevens (2005).

Figure 13.2   The buying and selling process and the communications mix

The role of trade shows in the B2B communications mix can be best understood by investigating their potential role in buying and selling processes. The buying process in a B2B transaction has been characterized as a series of stages (Wind and Thomas 1994). Column 1 in Figure 13.2 highlights those stages. Buyers in each stage may have different information needs. Similarly, the marketer faces a multi-stage sales process involving different communication objectives (Column 2) that imply different sales tasks (Column 3). Some objectives (e.g. awareness generation) are handled more cost-effectively by impersonal communication channels, while others (e.g. customization) demand personal contact; thus most firms employ a mix of both.

Trade shows combine aspects of direct selling (there are almost always some sales-people at the booth) and advertising (the booth can generate awareness and answer some questions even without the involvement of salespeople). They may play a cost-effective role in the communications mix, especially in the early stages of the process; their effectiveness diminishes as the buying process progresses toward evaluation and selection, though they may be a bit more cost-effective in providing feedback on product/service performance after the sale (Gopalakrishna and Lilien 1995). Similarly, from the seller's perspective trade shows can be effective for prospecting, opening a relationship, qualifying prospects and even presenting the sales message (Churchill et al. 1993).

Objectives for participation
Research on trade show objectives has often been confined to noting their importance (Cavanaugh 1976) and documenting differing objectives across firms or industries (Barczyk et al. 1989) and exhibitors or visitors (Hansen 1996; Siskind 2006; Tanner and

Chonko 1995). Although large expenditures are involved in exhibiting, CEIR reports that more than 70 per cent of exhibitors go to a trade show without clearly stated objectives (Stevens 2005). Management may emphasize the importance of defining objectives and measuring performance for all marketing programs, yet the trade show literature offers only general suggestions to exhibitors, such as 'have objectives that are realistic yet challenging' or 'make sure your objectives are measurable' (Stevens 2005, p. 51).

Kerin and Cron (1987) study the specific articulation and measurement of performance on eight different exhibitor objectives using a survey of exhibit managers in different firms. They measure performance on a seven-point Likert scale and find that firms with successful trade show programs tend to exhibit more products, have more customers, have written objectives for show participation and focus less on horizontal shows. Their study represents the only reported academic research that formally documents performance according to objectives, though the measurements employed are subjective ratings by exhibit managers.

Stevens (2005) suggests linking the objectives with metrics that will allow for the measurement of results. She also suggests a variety of metrics for different exhibitor objectives, adding that metrics must reflect business reality if the objectives are to be realistic (for an illustration, see Table 13.1).

Although trade show return on investment (ROI) is a popular discussion topic, a clear demonstration of those returns in a given setting remains a challenge. The long and complex buying cycles for most B2B products and the presence of multiple channels for sales and customer contact create much confusion in sorting out the effects of different media over an extended period. Thus the ROI question often gets transformed into a discussion of return on objectives (ROO), such that managers set clear (non-financial) objectives for a trade show, specify the associated metrics and report how they delivered against those objectives. By doing so they are able to provide some form of reasonable justification of the value derived by exhibiting at the show, but they leave the ROI question largely unanswered (cf. Gopalakrishna et al. 1995).

Show selection and budgeting

An important element of any trade show strategy is the choice of the specific shows in which a firm decides to participate. Although literature on trade show practices in this domain provides various guidelines and rules of thumb, academic research is scant. Most firms seem to rely on inertia, competitive pressure or some ad hoc process that involves listing potential shows, then ranking them on the basis of the audience profile for each show, its net attendance in past years, projected attendance, number of likely exhibitors, cost of exhibiting and so on (CEIR 1993, 1995; Stevens 2005).

Academic research has addressed the show selection issue at a more general level. For example, Lilien (1983) shows that a firm is most likely to use trade shows as a communication medium if the product to be displayed is complex, is carried in inventory, has high sales levels, has high purchase frequency and involves many people in the purchase decision. Other research discusses show selection at a conceptual level (Shoham 1992), and the research by Kijewski et al. (1993) offers a model of the trade show decision process that involves setting exhibit objectives, developing a show consideration set, ranking show options, budget evaluation, show selection (Go/No Go), implementation and post-show audit.

Table 13.1   Setting specific metrics around objectives

Primary Objective	Examples of Associated Metrics	Ease of Measurement
Introduce new product	Number of demos given	Easy
	Number of samples ordered	Easy
	Number of press mentions	Moderately easy
	Number of booth visitors	Easy
Generate sales leads	Number of qualified leads	Easy
	Cost per qualified lead	Easy
Enter new market	Number of prospects by industry	Difficult
	Number of requests for proposals received	Easy
Generate company/brand awareness	Number of booth visitors	Easy
	Number of flyers distributed	Easy
	Visibility opportunities	Moderately easy
	Pre-/post-show awareness levels	Moderately easy
Recruit channel partners	Number of partners recruited	Easy
	Geographic penetration	Easy
Competitive research	Number of competitors at the show	Easy
	Competitive analyses done	Difficult
Retain current customers	Customer appointments scheduled and held	Easy
	New product demos to current customers	Easy
Support industry	Association events attended	Easy
	Investment in association sponsorship	Easy

Note: The appropriate metrics and their measurements may be known, but it is far more challenging to link them to bottom-line metrics such as return on investment.

Source: Adapted from Stevens (2005, pp. 54–5).

There is also limited research in the trade show budgeting domain. Lilien (1983) finds that the level of spending on trade shows is greater for products that have aggressive plans, high levels of sales and low customer concentration and are early in their life cycle. Such analyses can be used as norms or guidelines for show budgeting. In practice, setting trade show budgets is largely based on rules of thumb. For example, an approximate breakdown of exhibit spending on different expense categories appears in Table 13.2. Another rule of thumb noted by a trade show consulting firm is that the trade show budget must be at least four times the cost of booth space, plus a 10 per cent add-on for miscellaneous expenses (Stevens 2005).

Execution

Pre-show

The objective of pre-show promotions is to target the highest quality prospects and invite them to visit the firm's booth, make an appointment for a conversation or otherwise establish contact at the trade show (Stevens 2005). An effective pre-show strategy

Table 13.2   How an exhibit dollar is spent

Expense Category	Percentage Spent	Amount Spent ($Billion)
Exhibit space	31.1%	$7.5
Exhibit design	11.2%	$2.7
Show services	20.3%	$4.9
Shipping	10.8%	$2.6
Travel & entertainment	15.3%	$3.7
Promotion	7.5%	$1.8
Other	3.8%	$0.9
Total	100.0%	$24.1

Source: CEIR(2007).

typically has two aspects: *qualification* (determining which prospective show attendees represent good opportunities for the exhibitor and are therefore worthy of establishing contact) and *invitation* (promoting a visit to the booth for qualified attendees).

Pre-show tactics should align with the exhibiting objectives. For example, if the goal is to generate sales leads, the pre-show promotion strategy should be to attract qualified prospects to the booth. Similarly if the goal is to retain current customers, the strategy would be to maximize customer appointments and convey appreciation for the customers' business and their relationships. A 2000 CEIR study identifies direct mail, past show attendance, trade publication ads and word of mouth as the four top communication channels through which prospects can be reached effectively prior to the show (Stevens 2005). Attracting attendees to the booth also involves promotion activity at the show, and exhibitors report the use of email, giveaways, premiums, samples, print and online advertising and direct mail to great extents to achieve that objective (CEIR 2009c).

Exhibitors spend about 6 per cent of their entire trade show budget on promotion (Stevens 2005). Factors such as size of the trade show, type of show (vertical/horizontal) or the value of sales also influence the level of pre-show investment, but these issues have not been explored in a systematic way.

During the show
An exhibiting firm must deal with multiple tactical issues to ensure an effective presence at the show, including booth location, size, design, staffing and at-show promotion.

Booth location
There are several opinions about the 'ideal' location of a booth on the show floor. The common view holds that because of the sheer advantage of heavy traffic volume, locating near the entrance or exit is preferable to being in the middle of the show floor. Another view suggests that locating near a competitor or close to a big booth or a well-known brand name can be an advantage, as opposed to staying far away from competitors. These conjectures have not been subjected to rigorous empirical analysis and therefore appear to have little scientific basis. Exhibit Surveys Inc. has examined several trade shows held at McCormick Place in Chicago and the Houston Astrodome to investigate

the issue of booth location. They report no statistical correlation between booth location and booth traffic or memorability (Trade Show Bureau 1983).

Booth size
The space rented by a firm on the show floor is the largest single item in the overall exhibit budget, making up 31 per cent (see Table 13.2). Industry wisdom suggests that the booth size decision must be based on the firm's objectives for exhibiting (Stevens 2005). One heuristic considers the size of the target audience to be reached, the exhibit hall hours and number of possible demos per hour (Appendix 13.2, Part B, describes the details of one such approach).

Booth type, layout and design
The decision about the type of booth involves options such as standard (within a row, facing the aisle), island (aisles on four sides, which offer more dimensionality), peninsula (end of row, with aisles on three sides) and corner (end of row, bordered by two aisles) booths. Booth layout involves several dimensions, including the attraction strategy, the nature of the product and the activities planned for the booth (Stevens 2005). The attraction strategy refers to aspects such as whether the booth should have an open/inviting look or a closed/internally focused design, or else a combination. These choices are driven by the firm's objectives and the nature of the audience. (For an example of how effective booth design produced better results for Mattel, see *Exhibitor Magazine* 2003.) The activities planned for the booth, such as product demos, video monitors, computer stations, theaters, space for private meetings or refreshments also have an impact on booth layout. Booth design and graphics involve decisions about signage, lighting, carpets, color and images. Research on the impact of all these elements on booth traffic is scarce and difficult to conduct, because data on these variables are not collected or assembled systematically.

Booth staffing
Staffing involves decisions about the number of salespeople who need to be working the booth at any given time and adequate training for the booth staff in the set of skills needed for effective booth results. The business press offers plenty of ad hoc, judicious guidelines about staff selection, training and booth management. For example, there are suggestions about selecting booth personnel with characteristics similar to the audience, choosing neither seasoned salespeople nor rookies, striving for a mix of specialized product knowledge and technical skills and so on (Stevens 2005).

Giveaways and attention-getting techniques
These tactics are commonly used to draw audiences to the booth and can involve demos (which attract better quality visitors) or gimmicks, such as offering free pens and key chains, hosting a magic show or bringing in a celebrity to sign autographs (which typically draw lower quality visitors). Again these decisions are rarely subject to rigorous analysis or measurement.

Post-show
The focus in the post-show phase is collecting relevant data about performance metrics that correspond to appropriate exhibitor objectives. Much of these data are drawn from

post-show surveys of audiences and from visitors who stop at the booth during the show. The biggest hurdle is tracking sales leads generated at the show to see how many and which converted into a sale. The long purchase cycles and many intervening influences in most B2B sales situations create a measurement and analysis challenge, but such tracking is essential to assess the true effectiveness of trade shows.

Evaluation and Control

As noted previously, various ad hoc approaches to trade show planning and strategy execution have appeared in the trade journals. This aspect is true in the area of performance evaluation and control as well (Stevens 2005). There is limited documentation in the business press of the proven value of activities such as comparing post-show measurements with pre-show behaviors or tracking leads to eventual sales. Most practical managerial suggestions appear based on limited empirical work.

On the academic side, the issue of evaluating trade show effectiveness received only cursory interest (Bellizzi and Lipps 1984; Carman 1968) before researchers began to highlight the need for a systematic measurement of outcomes (Herbig et al. 1994). Some empirical research involving metrics, such as lead efficiency (Gopalakrishna and Williams 1992), has since led to the development of appropriate scales and the validation of performance metrics (Hansen 2004). Other academic studies, as briefly noted next, offer promise for more advanced empirical research in this domain.

We have developed a three-stage model of trade show performance that relies on different indices of performance at each stage: attraction, contact and conversion efficiency (Gopalakrishna and Lilien 1995). We view the process as a funnel, such that the target audience for a firm at a trade show is only a subset of total show attendance. A fraction of the target audience ends up visiting the firm's booth (attraction efficiency), a subset of those visiting the booth actually make contact with a salesperson (contact efficiency) and only a fraction of those contacted turn into a sales lead (conversion efficiency). We model the impacts of pre-show promotion, booth space, use of attention-getting techniques, competition, and the number and training of booth staff on these three indices, which we treat as performance outcomes (dependent variables). Our empirical results show significant and different impacts of the various managerial actions on the three dependent variables; this work provides a template for rigorously assessing the trade-offs and impact of tactical variables on a firm's trade show performance.

The value derived by exhibiting at a trade show and its impact on the bottom line is a subject of intense discussion among managers (Sashi and Perretty 1992). In a study to assess the ROI of a firm's participation in a trade show, Gopalakrishna et al. (1995) track a group of matched show attendees and non-attendees for one exhibiting firm and report significant positive economic returns to the firm. Their empirical results are not generalizable, but their approach can be used as a template to determine both the direct (sales) effects of show participation and other outcomes, such as greater product awareness and interest (indirect effects).

Smith et al. (2004) investigate the complementary effect of trade shows on personal selling from an integrated marketing communications perspective. With a field study involving a group of industrial distributors, they demonstrate that follow-up sales efforts can be reduced by about 50 per cent but generate the same level of sales if prospective customers have previously seen the product at a trade show. They also demonstrate how knowledge of a prospect's exposure to the firm's product at the trade show can help allocate post-show sales effort across prospective customers more effectively. Other researchers have acknowledged the leverage offered by trade shows for managing key accounts (Blythe 2002) and, more generally, enhancing the selling aspects (O'Hara 1993; Tanner 1994).

Implications for Research

All of the potentially relevant objectives for show participation are rarely equal in importance; they may vary across exhibitor firms, and for the same firms, they may vary across shows. Systematic measurement of these objectives and their antecedents should provide a foundation for a better understanding of show effectiveness and the role that managerial actions play in enhancing that effectiveness. For example, given a specific objective for trade show participation, which pre-show activities are most or least effective in achieving that objective? Can we determine, in a more scientific way, how investment in pre-show activity should be allocated across elements of the pre-show mix to optimize objectives for a specific show? Similar questions might be addressed for at-show and post-show marketing investments. In particular small firms may find the show environment rather challenging as they try to compete against bigger rivals. They face greater resource constraints and may benefit more from a different resource deployment strategy (Tanner 2002; Williams et al. 1993). Similarly, show selection decisions tend to draw heavily on managerial judgment and experience. Although attempts to reflect the entire trade show process from pre-show invitation to post-show sale have begun to appear (Lee and Kim 2008; Sridhar et al. 2011), more comprehensive studies are needed to model and trace the trade show process from end-to-end for different customer types, different products and different industry settings.

THE ATTENDEE PERSPECTIVE

Attendees represent a vital link in the value chain. Show management and exhibitors understand that a satisfying, enriching and fun experience for the attendee has a high likelihood of ensuring repeat visits and building show attendance in the future (Smith et al. 2003). Thus, gaining deeper insights into attendees' behavior and activities as they experience the show is an important and valuable element of organizing a successful trade show.

Efforts to understand why attendees visit trade shows appear in prior literature (Godar and O'Connor 2001). Bello (1992) examines buyer behavior at trade shows with an adaptive approach and finds that three elements of declarative knowledge, decisions made, information sought and sources used, vary with the attendee's role. In a follow-up study, Bello and Lohtia (1993) demonstrate that show attendees fit into two broad roles: administrative and production. To obtain high quality leads, they suggest that salespeople should actively try to contact all key members of the attendee firm's buying team. For highly qualified booth visitors, salespeople should base their show selling plans on an analysis of the size and composition of the attendee's buying center, with larger (customer) firms sending larger and more diverse teams than smaller firms. Production people appear more interested in technical information, but administrative people are more interested in transactional information.

Rosson and Seringhaus (1995) report that visitors from smaller firms have direct influence over purchasing, but attendees from larger firms are more likely to be middle managers collecting information that will merely be inputs for purchasing. They also report that

- multi-person attendance signals an immediate purchase or technology implementation;
- an invitation from a vendor is the most influential factor in an attendee's decision to attend;
- intensive and special-purpose users carefully map out their visits, using (online) exhibition directories, exhibitor invitations and discussions with colleagues;
- booths are best remembered if they are large and well-designed, with an effective staff and a live display.

Berne and Garcia-Uceda (2008) report that attendees consider the same show features as do potential exhibitors when deciding which shows to visit: the experience of the show organizer, the breadth and depth of the set of exhibitors, the show's capacity to attract visitors, the presence of competitors at the show, sponsorship or endorsement of the event by public and private associations and the cost/convenience of the place or timing.

Rinallo et al. (2010) use ethnographic methods to study ten shows in the textile industry and find that an attendee's typical visit starts with market leaders, continues with regular suppliers, and features residual time devoted to other suppliers. Attendees indicate that a valuable trade show experience provides cognitive stimulation, resulting in learning and new knowledge and an opportunity to relate to exhibitors and other visitors, which forges a sense of community.

Although most attendee research reported thus far has been survey based, new advances in technology now permit a finer level of data access and capture. Using data on booth visits captured with badge swipes across a large number of booths at a specific show, it is possible to track attendees in terms of the exact booths they visited and the sequence in which those visits happened. Gopalakrishna et al. (2010) study attendee behavior on the trade show floor and identify five distinct shoppers: a basic shopper, enthusiasts, the niche shopper, brand shoppers and apathetic shoppers. For example, brand shoppers seek out popular booths but also visit all the booths in which they are interested; they know what they want to accomplish and are efficient about doing so. In contrast, apathetic shoppers tend to be newcomers or attendees who have difficulty navigating the trade show floor or are unfamiliar with the trade show environment; their visits follow no discernible pattern.

Implications for Research

The advent of RFID devices affords opportunities not hitherto seen in this research domain. RFID enables more accurate tracking of attendee movements on the show floor or within the confines of a specific booth. It also provides information about how long a visitor looked at an exhibit. Hui et al. (2009a) propose a framework to analyze path data and provide some interesting insights on customer behavior in the context of grocery shopping (Hui et al. 2009b, 2009c). Similarly new video tracking systems that digitize video signals (movements) and monitor the trade show floor (videomining. com) provide a source of customer tracking data that can be used in a similar way to RFID data. It is exciting to consider the research implications of marrying these forms of data.

THE SHOW MANAGEMENT PERSPECTIVE

Academic research from the exhibitor and attendee perspectives may be scarce, but research from the trade show management perspective is almost non-existent. Show organizers are interested in developing (profitable) shows that provide high levels of satisfaction for both exhibitors and attendees. A recent study of exhibition organizers (CEIR 2009b) showed that more than 80 per cent believe that partnerships with exhibitors are critical to the success of their show. They also believe that using more than one advertising or promotional vehicle is critical to building a good base of attendees. According to the study, show organizers are of two types: those who favor online marketing (nearly 40 per cent) and those who favor traditional marketing methods (particularly direct mail). They believe that online marketing is less expensive but also less effective than direct mail.

Organizers also assert that traditional methods, such as direct mail, produce more success with older attendees, whereas new methods like email or social networking tools (LinkedIn, Facebook, Twitter) are effective with younger attendees. Some other findings from that study reveal that (1) direct mail and email comprise two-thirds of the organizers' marketing budgets; (2) the average expenditure on attendee marketing for the most recent exhibition was $247 000; and (3) 72 per cent of corporate event organizers believe traditional methods are becoming less reliable and plan to promote entirely online within three years (CEIR 2009b).

Acquiring new attendees remains an ongoing concern for trade show organizers. Allowing access to pre- and post-show attendee lists and working with exhibitors to institute new and innovative promotion activities through social networking or virtual booths represent avenues that potentially generate new revenue stream opportunities.

Many organizers use virtual events (e.g. webcasts/webinars, two- or three-dimensional simulated trade show environments) to complement live events (see Figure 13.1). And though social media seem to provide significant ROI with regard to the promotion of a trade show, few organizers have the means to measure that impact. Developing an effective strategy to promote the show to attract prospective exhibitors has become an important challenge for show management. For example, the National Association of Broadcasters show (a top digital media industry event) recently hired a vice president of strategic accounts to help retain and grow its exhibitor base.

Online channels provide greater insight into customers' preferences, offering audiences a platform to engage with the brands and their peers on their own terms. This movement toward a more customer-centric approach aligns closely with the increasingly experiential nature of the exhibition engagement model and marketers' efforts to build and nurture communities of interest around their events.

Implications for Research

One of the few research articles in this domain, by Wu et al. (2008), models the trade show formation process. Vertical shows that display a narrow range of products (such as the Association of Operating Room Nurses show) are more likely to attract participants with a high degree of interest in purchase transactions (by both buyers and sellers). Horizontal shows (such as National Manufacturing Week) that feature a broad range of products are more likely to attract attendees with less immediate interest in buying but who have a high breadth of product interests, and are likely to be especially prevalent in highly innovative industries. However, their research is descriptive in nature and says little about what show organizers should be doing. The link between marketing resources and exhibitor performance continues to engage and intrigue researchers (Li 2007, 2008). In particular, the globalization of B2B markets has focused attention on topics such as exporting products through trade shows (Bello and Barksdale 1986), cross-national comparisons of trade show performance (Dekimpe et al. 1997; Palumbo et al. 1998), exploring the value of non-selling activities and interactions at trade shows (Rice 1992; Sharland and Balogh 1996) and developing a broad research agenda for trade shows in the global arena (Seringhaus and Rosson 1994). There is a large amount of uncharted research territory here: what type of shows organizers should develop in different types of markets, how those shows should be marketed to exhibitors and attendees, what is the best mix of online and offline shows and how show organizers can manage their shows for the long term by applying customer lifetime value concepts to the equity they have created by investing in the shows they have organized.

DISCUSSION

The changing nature of the B2B environment, from both supplier and buyer perspectives, as driven largely by the technological revolution, is also changing the nature of the traditional trade show environment. That change, combined with increasing insistence on accountability, will provide incentives for exciting and relevant academic research in the years to come.

Managerial Implications

Our review has identified several templates for firms trying to determine which shows to attend; how much to spend on pre-show, at-show and post-show activities; and which promotional and measurement methods are appropriate. Our review also indicates that though some useful templates exist, their application is limited largely because managers do not understand or lack the discipline to develop the associated measurements or track the relevant metrics. The perfect may be the enemy of the good here. Even a simple, disciplined approach to setting and weighting specific objectives; determining appropriate metrics for those objectives; determining which shows to attend and what to do in terms of pre-, at-, and post-show activity; measuring the impact of those actions using the appropriate metrics; and updating show evaluation and effectiveness models can turn the trade show decision process into a business investment, rather than a business expense.

CONCLUSION

The technological revolution has forced retailers and shopping malls to evolve rapidly when sales functions that previously could only take place there moved online. And consumers now communicate with retailers and with one another in new ways. But shopping malls do not appear to be in any danger of disappearing; customers still want to touch products, talk to other buyers face-to-face and talk to real salespeople. So it is with trade shows: the technological revolution is changing the landscape drastically, but trade shows are in no danger of going away. However, they are evolving rapidly. The need for better measurement and accountability is converging with more cost-effective and unobtrusive attendee measurement methods, providing many of the exciting research opportunities we have noted. Trade shows will be around and thrive, both off- and online, in the years to come. And if these new data sources are used appropriately, show exhibitors should be able to justify show attendance as an investment rather than as an expense. Attendees will have better tools and information sources to plan their trade show visits and maximize their personal ROI. Trade show organizers will be able to provide a broader, deeper and more profitable range of offerings, on- and offline, for attendees and exhibitors alike.

ACKNOWLEDGMENTS

The authors thank Skip Cox, CEO and President, Exhibit Surveys, Inc., and Christophe Van den Bulte for their valuable suggestions. They also thank Stephen Hampton and Vamsi Kanuri, doctoral students in Marketing at University of Missouri, for their help in organizing the literature.

REFERENCES

Banting, Peter M. and David L. Blenkhorn (1974), 'The role of industrial trade shows', *Industrial Marketing Management*, 3, 285–95.
Barczyk, Casimir C., George B. Glisan and William C. Lesch (1989), 'Trade show participation: inter-industry and organizational motives', *Journal of Professional Services Marketing*, 4, 131–48.
Bellizzi, Joseph and Delilah Lipps (1984), 'Managerial guidelines for trade show effectiveness', *Industrial Marketing Management*, 13, 49–52.
Bello, Daniel C. (1992), 'Industrial buyer behavior at trade shows: implications for selling effectiveness', *Journal of Business Research*, 25, 59–80.
Bello, Daniel C. and Hiram C. Barksdale (1986), 'Exporting at industrial trade shows', *Industrial Marketing Management*, 15, 197–206.
Bello, Daniel C. and Ritu Lohtia (1993), 'Improving trade show effectiveness by analyzing attendees', *Industrial Marketing Management*, 22, 311–18.
Berne, Carmen and M.E. Garcia-Uceda (2008), 'Criteria involved in evaluation of trade shows to visit', *Industrial Marketing Management*, 37, 565–79.
Blythe, Jim (2002), 'Using trade fairs in key account management', *Industrial Marketing Management*, 31, 627–35.
Bonoma, Thomas V. (1983), 'Get more out of your trade shows', *Harvard Business Review*, (January–February), 61, 75–83.
Carman, James (1968), 'Evaluation of trade show exhibitions', *California Management Review*, 11, 35–44.
Cavanaugh, Suzette (1976), 'Setting objectives and evaluating the effectiveness of trade show exhibits', *Journal of Marketing*, 40, 100–103.
CEIR (1993), Center for Exhibition Industry Research Report MC 28, available at www.ceir.org.

CEIR (1995), Center for Exhibition Industry Research Report MC 25, available at www.ceir.org.

CEIR (2003), Center for Exhibition Industry Research Report F 01-03, available at www.ceir.org.

CEIR (2006), 'Exhibitor objectives', Center for Exhibition Industry Research, available at www.ceir.org.

CEIR (2007), Center for Exhibition Industry Research Report SM 22.07, October, available at www.ceir.org.

CEIR (2009a), 'Power of exhibitions in the 21st century', Center for Exhibition Industry Research Report, Section 4, available at www.ceir.org.

CEIR (2009b), 'Effective methods for visitor promotion, part I: exhibition organizers', Center for Exhibition Industry Research Report, MC 41, available at www.ceir.org.

CEIR (2009c), 'Effective methods for visitor promotion, part II: exhibitors', Center for Exhibition Industry Research Report, MC 42, available at www.ceir.org.

CEIR (2009d), 'Cost effectiveness of trade show exhibiting', Center for Exhibition Industry Research Report, SM 37 and SM 38, available at www.ceir.org.

CEIR (2010a), 'CEIR Index – an analysis of the 2009 exhibition industry and future outlook', Center for Exhibition Industry Research, available at www.ceir.org.

CEIR (2010b), 'Digital + exhibiting marketing insights 2010', Center for Exhibition Industry Research Report MC45, available at www.ceir.org.

Churchill, Gilbert A. Jr, Neil M. Ford and Orville C. Walker (1993), *Sales Force Management*, 4th edn, Homewood, IL: Irwin.

Dekimpe, Marnik G., Pierre François, Srinath Gopalakrishna, Gary L. Lilien and Christophe van den Bulte (1997), 'Generalizing about trade show effectiveness: a cross-national comparison', *Journal of Marketing*, **61**, 55–64.

Euro Fair Statistics (2008), 'UFI – the global association of the exhibition industry', available at www.ufi.org.

Exhibitor Magazine (2003), 'Best practices in trade shows and events', (December).

Exhibitor Magazine (2009), 'Best practices in trade shows and events', (August), pp. 21–6.

Exhibitor Magazine (2010), 'Best practices in trade shows and events', (June), pp. 34–7.

Godar, Susan H. and Patricia J. O'Connor (2001), 'Same time next year – buyer trade show motives', *Industrial Marketing Management*, **30**, 77–86.

Gopalakrishna, Srinath and Gary L. Lilien (1995), 'A three-stage model of industrial trade show performance', *Marketing Science*, **14**, 22–42.

Gopalakrishna, Srinath and Jerome D. Williams (1992), 'Planning and performance assessment of industrial trade shows: an exploratory study', *International Journal of Research in Marketing*, **9**, 207–24.

Gopalakrishna, Srinath, Catherine Roster and Shrihari Sridhar (2010), 'An exploratory study of attendee activities at a business trade show', *Journal of Business & Industrial Marketing*, **25** (4), 241–8.

Gopalakrishna, Srinath, Gary L. Lilien, Jerome D. Williams and Ian K. Sequeira (1995), 'Do trade shows pay off?', *Journal of Marketing*, **59**, 75–83.

Hansen, Kåre (1996), 'The dual motives of participants at international trade shows: an empirical investigation of exhibitors and visitors with selling motives', *International Marketing Review*, **13**, 39–53.

Hansen, Kåre (1999), 'Trade show performance: a conceptual framework and its implications for future research', *Academy of Marketing Science Review*, **8**, 1–12.

Hansen, Kåre (2004), 'Measuring performance at trade shows: scale development and validation', *Journal of Business Research*, **57**, 1–13.

Herbig, Paul, Bradley O'Hara and Frederick A. Palumbo (1994), 'Measuring trade show effectiveness: an effective exercise?', *Industrial Marketing Management*, **23**, 165–70.

Herbig, Paul, Bradley O'Hara and Frederick A. Palumbo (1998), 'Trade show: who, what, why', *Marketing Intelligence & Planning*, **16**, 425–35.

Hui, Sam K., Peter S. Fader and Eric T. Bradlow (2009a), 'Path data in marketing: an integrative framework and prospectus for model building', *Marketing Science*, **28** (2), 320–35.

Hui, Sam K., Peter S. Fader and Eric T. Bradlow (2009b), 'The traveling salesman goes shopping: the systematic deviations of grocery paths from TSP optimality', *Marketing Science*, **28** (3), 566–72.

Hui, Sam K., Peter S. Fader and Eric T. Bradlow (2009c), 'Testing behavioral hypotheses using an integrated model of grocery store shopping path and purchase behavior', *Journal of Consumer Research*, **36**, 478–93.

Hutt, Michael D. and Thomas W. Speh (2010), *Business Marketing Management*, 10th edn, Mason, OH: South-Western Cengage Learning Publishing.

Kerin, Roger A. and William L. Cron (1987), 'Assessing trade show functions and performance: an exploratory study', *Journal of Marketing*, **51**, 87–94.

Kijewski, Valerie, Eunsang Yoon and Gary Young (1993), 'How exhibitors select trade shows', *Industrial Marketing Management*, **22**, 287–98.

Lee, Chang Hyun and Sang Yong Kim (2008), 'Differential effects of determinants on multi-dimensions of trade show performance: by three stages of pre-show, at-show, and post-show activities', *Industrial Marketing Management*, **37**, 784–96.

Lee, Jumyong, Curtis Love and Taedong Han (2008), 'Trade show websites: an examination of critical websites' quality factors and content items', *Journal of Convention & Event Tourism*, **9** (1), 35–59.

Li, Ling-Yee (2007), 'Marketing resources and performance of exhibitor firms in trade shows: a contingent resource perspective', *Industrial Marketing Management*, **36**, 360–70.

Li, Ling-Yee (2008), 'The effects of firm resources on trade show performance: how do trade show marketing processes matter?', *Journal of Business & Industrial Marketing*, **23**, 35–47.

Lilien, Gary (1983), 'A descriptive model of the trade-show budgeting decision process', *Industrial Marketing Management*, **12**, 25–9.

O'Hara, Bradley S. (1993), 'Evaluating the effectiveness of trade shows: a personal selling perspective', *Journal of Personal Selling & Sales Management*, **13**, 67–77.

Palumbo, Frederick A., Brad O'Hara and Paul Herbig (1998), 'Differences between international and domestic trade show exhibitors', *Academy of Marketing Studies Journal*, **2** (2), 1–14.

Rice, Gillian (1992), 'Using the interaction approach to understand international trade shows', *International Marketing Review*, **9** (4), 32–45.

Rinallo, Diego, Stefania Borghini and Francesca Golfetto (2010), 'Exploring visitor experiences at trade shows', *Journal of Business & Industrial Marketing*, **25** (4), 249–58.

Rosson, Philip J. and F.H. Rolf Seringhaus (1995), 'Visitor and exhibitor interaction at industrial trade fairs', *Journal of Business Research*, **32**, 81–90.

Sashi, C. and Jim Perretty (1992), 'Do trade shows provide value?', *Industrial Marketing Management*, **21**, 249–55.

Seringhaus, F.H. Rolf and Philip J. Rosson (1994), 'International trade fairs and foreign market involvement: review and research directions', *International Business Review*, **3**, 311–29.

Sharland, Alex and Peter Balogh (1996), 'The value of non-selling activities at international trade shows', *Industrial Marketing Management*, **25**, 59–66.

Shoham, Aviv (1992), 'Selecting and evaluating trade shows', *Industrial Marketing Management*, **21**, 335–41.

Siskind, Barry (2006), 'Management by objectives: benchmarks for exhibit growth', Center for Exhibition Industry Research (CEIR), Guru Report G 11.06, available at www.ceir.org.

Smith, Timothy M., Srinath Gopalakrishna and Paul M. Smith (2004), 'The complementary effect of trade shows on personal selling', *International Journal of Research in Marketing*, **21**, 61–76.

Smith, Timothy M., Kazuyo Hama and Paul M. Smith (2003), 'The effect of successful trade show attendance on future show interest: exploring Japanese attendee perspectives of domestic and offshore international events', *Journal of Business & Industrial Marketing*, **18**, 403–18.

Sridhar, Shrihari, Clay Voorhees and Srinath Gopalakrishna (2011), 'Assessing the drivers of short- and long-term outcomes of business trade shows', Marketing Science Institute, Working Paper.

Stevens, Ruth P. (2005), *Trade Show and Event Marketing*, Mason, OH: Thomson/South-Western.

Tanner, John F. (1994), 'Adaptive selling at trade shows', *Journal of Personal Selling & Sales Management*, **14**, 15–23.

Tanner, John F. Jr (2002), 'Leveling the playing field: factors influencing trade show success for small companies', *Industrial Marketing Management*, **31**, 229–39.

Tanner, John F. and Lawrence B. Chonko (1995), 'Trade show objectives, management staffing practices', *Industrial Marketing Management*, **24**, 257–64.

Trade Show Bureau (1983), 'The effect of booth location on exhibit performance and impact', Research Report No. 20, Trade Show Bureau, East Orleans, MA.

Trade Show Executive (2010), 'Great Expectations', December, p. 19.

Williams, Jerome D., Srinath Gopalakrishna and Jonathan Cox (1993), 'Trade show guidelines for smaller firms', *Industrial Marketing Management*, **22**, 265–75.

Wind, Yoram and Robert Thomas (1994), 'Segmenting industrial markets', in Arch Woodside (ed.), *Advances in Business Marketing*, Vol. 6, Greenwich, CT: JAI Press, pp. 59–82.

Wu, Jianan, Gary L. Lilien and Aniruddha Dasgupta (2008), 'An exploratory study of trade show formation and diversity', *Journal of Business-to-Business Marketing*, **15**, 397–424.

APPENDIX 13.1   COST-EFFECTIVENESS OF TRADE SHOWS

In 2009, the Center for Exhibition Industry Research (CEIR) conducted a telephone survey among sales and marketing managers across various industry sectors. Annual sales for the firms in the study were greater than $50 million. Respondents answered several questions pertaining to sales effort, costs and so on, such as: 'Prior to a sales call, what is the average cost of identifying a prospect through means other than a trade show?' A summary of the findings from the survey reveals the following:

Cost of identifying a prospect at a trade show	$96
Cost of identifying a prospect through means other than a trade show	$443
Cost of making a face-to-face contact with a prospect in the field (sales call)	$596
Number of calls to close a sale starting with a trade show lead	3.5
Number of calls to close a sale without a trade show lead	4.5
Total cost to close the sale with a trade show lead	$2188
Total cost to close the sale without a trade show lead	$3102*

Notes:
Sample size was 214. The average annual cost of exhibiting reported by respondents, based on an average of 6.8 shows a year, was $153763.
*   Computed as follows: $596 × 4.5 + 443 = $3125. Numbers differ slightly due to rounding.

Source: CEIR 2009d.

Therefore, closing a sale with a potential customer from a trade show, versus one found in the field, saves an organization nearly $914 per new customer.

APPENDIX 13.2   LINKING METRICS TO REALISTIC GOALS

Part A

This example highlights the idea that the metrics employed for assessment must reflect the marketplace realities. Say a firm that manufactures pneumatic seals wants to introduce its product to a new industry segment (plastics) at a forthcoming show. It is important to research the trade show attendance, read the exhibitor guide and talk to show management. Say last year's attendance at the same show was 5000, of which 15 per cent represented the plastics industry. Of the 750 potential targets, show management suggests that approximately 50 per cent are likely to pass by the firm's booth during the exhibit hall hours. So, the metric may be:

Give a demo to as many of 375 prospects as possible.

Next, the firm must ensure that is a realistic goal, given the resources at its disposal. If a one-to-one demo takes 15 minutes and the plan is to have three salespeople at demo stations, it is possible to perform 12 demos per hour. With 375 likely prospects, the firm needs 31.25 hours of demos. But what if the exhibit hall is open for only 25 hours? The firm will need either to add more salespeople or reduce the number of possible demos it can realistically hope to make at the show.

Such analysis can help assess the viability of the metrics being used. The idea is to employ metrics that are aggressive yet attainable, given the realities of the trade show, the audience and the resources available at the firm's disposal.

Part B

If the target is 375 demos during the 25 exhibit hall hours and one rep can accomplish 4 demos per hour, the number of salespeople needed is as follows:

Number of salespeople $= 375/(25 \times 4) = 3.75$ (rounded to 4).

Typically, about 50 square feet of space is needed for one demo station. Thus, the firm will need at least 200 square feet of booth space (possibly a 10×20 foot booth). This illustration is adapted from Stevens (2005, pp. 55–6).

14 Value-based pricing: a state-of-the-art review
George E. Cressman Jr

Pricing in business markets is a neglected discipline. Hinterhuber (2004) notes that:

1. Pricing has been largely neglected by managers. McKinsey & Co. indicates that fewer than 15 per cent of companies do any systematic research on pricing.
2. Relatively little academic research focuses on pricing practices. Other areas of marketing effort receive far more attention.
3. Pricing changes have substantial impacts on profitability, usually far more than any other element of the marketing mix.

Hinterhuber further suggests that neglect of pricing strategy is a result of two factors. First, managers see business pricing as a zero sum game; what a seller gains the customer loses. This attitude leads to significant conflict in customer relationships. Second, managers seem to believe they cannot affect pricing in their industry; price points and competitive behavior are driven by the 'market'.

Unlike pricing in consumer markets, pricing in business markets is underresearched. This chapter therefore reviews business market pricing literature, proposes a model for the strategic management of the pricing function and poses fundamental research questions. Because much of the development of pricing work is currently being done by practicing managers and consultants, this chapter takes a practice perspective. Furthermore my review focuses on the development and implementation of a value-based pricing strategy. In this chapter I define pricing strategy and value pricing; I also provide an overview of the elements of a pricing strategy using the perspective of value-based pricing practices.

PRICING STRATEGY AND VALUE PRICING DEFINED

In their overview of pricing strategies employed by managers, Rao and Kartono (2009) find that the most commonly employed strategy is cost-plus pricing, followed by perceived value pricing. Both of these approaches are more appropriately described as methods to determine price points rather than a pricing strategy. A *pricing strategy* provides a systematic delineation of the elements that must be managed to achieve profitable performance in a business. Pricing strategy elements include customer targeting decisions, identification of the appropriate offerings for each target customer, communication to convince customers to buy, a sales negotiation process and a price setting methodology. In most business markets, sellers reach their ultimate customers through distribution channels, so a pricing strategy must also consider distributor selection and management. Pricing strategy then integrates many elements of what has classically been considered the marketing function: customer targeting, offering design, communication and selling.

Pricing tactics are the means by which the pricing strategy is implemented, including pricing processes, an organizational structure to carry out the pricing processes and the development of data systems to provide information for managing the pricing strategy implementation. *Value pricing* then is a cultural orientation that focuses a seller's business on designing and developing offerings with significant impact on the buyer's business, then pricing to capture a portion of that impact. Specifically, value pricing can be defined as the practice of pricing to capture a portion of a seller's economic impact on a target customer's business. As a cultural orientation, value pricing derives from a routinized set of organizational philosophies and practices that the seller uses to focus on affecting the customer's business success, and then insists on being rewarded profitably for that impact.

A seller can impact a customer's business in two ways:

● helping the customer achieve higher revenue flows;
● helping the customer achieve lower cost of operations.

Sellers who employ value pricing practices have a deep understanding of how their target customers pursue their business goals and develop insights into the offerings that enhance the target customers' business performance. The measure of success for firms implementing a value pricing culture thus is always how profitable the seller is in its efforts to impact the target customer's business. The profitable implementation of a value pricing culture results from a focus on two elements:

● achieving price points that reflect the economic impact the seller has on the customer's business by increasing the customer's revenue flow and/or decreasing the customer's cost of operations;
● deploying resources productively in the seller's business to develop and deliver the appropriate value-creating offerings to the target customer.

In their overview, Rao and Kartono (2009) list 19 'pricing strategies', but all of them actually are methods to set price; none of the described methods considers the integrative nature of a pricing strategy. The concept of value pricing – a cultural orientation focused on impacting target customers' businesses – is not included. In contrast, managerial literature contains many descriptions of a value pricing orientation (e.g. Holden and Burton 2008; Nagle and Cressman 2002; Nagle and Hogan 2006).

A basic tenet of the value pricing cultural orientation is that customer knowledge of a seller's economic impact on the customer's business can be changed. In contrast the perceived value concept measures a customer's view at a single point in time, so that view may be incomplete or purposely devalued for negotiation purposes. A profitable pricing strategy thus depends on ensuring the customer has a complete understanding of the seller's value impact and cannot play games to achieve lower prices.

SUCCESSFUL PRICING STRATEGY

What constitutes a successful pricing strategy remains hotly debated among marketing professionals and academics. Some argue that pricing success is the ability to establish

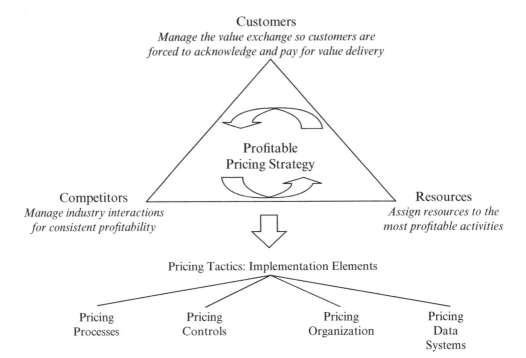

Figure 14.1   Elements of pricing strategy and tactics

price points that customers agree to pay. Others argue that success is the ability to price goods in a way that increases market share or customer preferences. Nagle and Cressman (2002) propose that a successful pricing strategy drives increasing firm profitability, which requires the active management of all elements of the pricing strategy. Tellis (1986, p. 147) takes a similar approach when he states, 'A pricing strategy is a reasoned choice from a set of alternative prices (or price schedules) that aim at profit maximization within a planning period in response to a given scenario'. This perspective uses profitability as the measure of a successful pricing strategy.

But why is managing pricing so important? Pricing has significant impacts on firm profitability; studies show small price changes can move firm profit by 8 to 11 per cent. Hansen and Solgaard (2004) argue that a significantly greater level of managerial attention is needed to manage the pricing function successfully, and Ohmae (1982) proposes that all strategy should consider three interrelated factors: customers, competitors and the company. For pricing strategy, this framework takes the form of Figure 14.1. The key elements of a pricing strategy are

- *Managing the value exchange with customers.* The objective is to create profit potential by forcing customers to recognize and pay for value delivery.
- *Managing competitive interactions.* The objective is to manage competitive dynamics so the value potential created by managing the exchange with customers is not given up due to competitive intensity.

- *Resource management.* The objective is to allocate all organizational resources to the most profitable activities.

In contrast with Hinterhuber's (2004) finding that managers perceive pricing as an area they cannot influence, value-based pricing provides a means to manage pricing actively in the market. The means to accomplish it is through the management of the three elements. I therefore outline all three elements before moving on to a tactical implementation.

MANAGING THE VALUE EXCHANGE WITH CUSTOMERS

This section introduces a process that enables the active management of the value exchange with customers. The value exchange provides customers with offerings that increase the monetary success of their business (whether through higher revenue flows or lower operating costs) while providing a reward for the seller in the form of a price proportional to the value delivery. The objective of managing the value exchange with customers is to have each customer recognize the value delivery and pay for it. The underlying premise is that customers will not pay for delivered value unless they recognize the delivered value and are forced to pay for it.

In business markets, firms must actively manage the value exchange. Price realization is the culmination of management of a series of marketing activities that provide the foundation for successful capture, with the pricing strategy, of a portion of the value delivered to customers. The marketing activity elements that lead to a successful pricing strategy are in Figure 14.2. Each step in this value pyramid must be implemented to achieve a value pricing strategy. Firms must work their way up through the value hierarchy in sequence, as described next.

Customer Segmentation

Segmentation literature is extensive, well developed and overviewed in a series of excellent papers (e.g. Beane and Enis 1993; Bennion 1987; Bonoma and Shapiro 1983; de Kluyver and Whitlark 1986; Dickson and Ginter 1987; Wind and Cardozo 1971). Yankelovich and Meer (2006) assert that recent segmentation work is not helpful, in that it does not identify where customer behavior can be changed, as is very evident in the pricing effort. For developing pricing strategies, and especially to manage the value exchange with customers, a useful segmentation scheme identifies underlying customer business practices in a way that allows the supplier to develop offerings that deliver unique value. Selecting some identified customers (i.e. targeting) should be based on the supplier's ability to deliver unique value to them at a competitive advantage. Smith (2002, p. 38) thus proposes segmentation by value delivery, with the assertion, 'A simple, but powerful, premise should govern value-driven market segmentation in B2B marketing: Own valuable market segments and focus on the segments you own'.

From a pricing perspective, segmentation and targeting may be the foundations for profitable pricing, but many segmentation schemes currently in use do not help marketing professionals develop value delivery or enable them to capture a portion of delivered value with their pricing strategy. The reason is that many segmentation schemes (e.g.

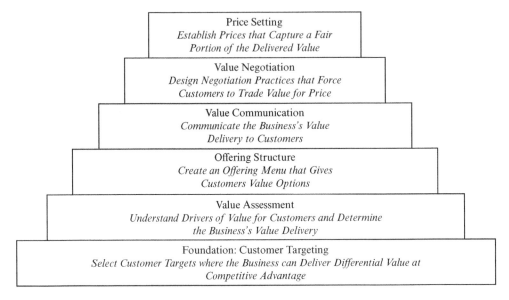

Figure 14.2   Elements of managing the value exchange

demographic, customer size) mix customers into broad groups, obscuring their underlying needs. In contrast, for a value-based pricing strategy, a useful segmentation scheme must (1) provide insights into the customer's business model in a way that (2) allows identification of valuable offering designs, so that (3) the seller can determine how to deliver valuable offerings at a competitive advantage.

Critical questions for further research are as follows:

- What segmentation methodology would allow for segmentation schemes directly related to value delivery? Consumer marketing techniques, considering the typically larger customer group sizes, often use indirect methods as a basis for inferring underlying customer needs. With smaller customer group sizes, business markets may be segmented using more direct methods. Nagle and Hogan (2006) state that the best direct method for identifying segments is customer interviews.
- What targeting methods would enable business marketers to select profitable customer targets? It is probable such methods must incorporate customer value, competitor intent and cost perspectives.

Value Assessment

Marketing professionals have repeatedly been urged to base their pricing strategy on value delivery. This of course raises the question: 'How can value delivery be determined?' Several overviews of value assessment practices offer some answers. Anderson et al. (1993) propose value measurement, arguing that customer willingness to pay (WTP) is an important measure of value delivery and the 'cornerstone' of marketing strategy. These authors explore the use of nine techniques (internal engineering assessment, field value-in-use assessment, indirect survey questions, focus group value assessment, direct survey questions, conjoint or trade-off analysis, benchmarks, compositional approaches and importance ratings). Respondents appeared least familiar with compositional approaches (e.g. asking for direct assessments of the monetary value of an offering feature) and most familiar with focus group assessments. Focus group assessments were also the most widely used assessment procedure. Both Hinterhuber (2008) and Jedidi and Jagpal (2009) overview various approaches to measuring WTP, including comparisons of purchase data and survey techniques. These authors conclude that the measurement of WTP using surveys is likely to involve considerable error.

Is willingness to pay even an accurate measure of value delivery, though? It is not if customers do not understand the total value (economic impact) of a seller's offering and/ or purposely understate value delivery to gain negotiating power. Managers should be especially wary of WTP estimates when they have not communicated their offering's value impact or have a long history of negotiating prices with customers. And as noted previously, a customer's understanding of value delivery can be managed and changed through the use of communication tools and effective negotiating tools (both described subsequently).

Other research has proposed a variety of alternative measurement techniques (Anderson et al. 2000; Flint et al. 2002; Homburg et al. 2001; Lindgreen and Wynstra 2007; Ulaga 2003; Ulaga and Eggert 2006; Wind 1990). Value is poorly defined (with many competing definitions), and the underlying drivers of value and how to manage value creation and delivery remain poorly researched. Lepak et al. (2007, p. 180) thus recognize that:

> while one would be hard pressed to find a management scholar who would disagree that value creation is important, one also would find it equally difficult to find agreement among such scholars regarding (1) what value creation is, (2) the process by which value is created, and (3) the mechanisms that allow the creator of value to capture the value.

Smith and Nagle (2005a, 2005b) instead describe the evolution of two general approaches to answering the value question. During the 1980s, two very different approaches to value assessment emerged, based on differing assumptions about customer behavior and with different implications for setting prices. Although both versions are cited often in marketing literature, they are not interchangeable. The first, customer value mapping (CVM), assumes that customers buy on the basis of delivered value and choose suppliers on the basis of their perceptions of delivered value. Customer value is quality relative to price (Gale 1994; see also Marn et al. 2004), and quality depends on a series of customer judgments about all non-price attributes of the offering. Respondents judge the relative (versus a competing offering) superiority of the offering's elements and their relative importance. They then must assess the relative price positions of competing offerings. However, there are several difficulties involved in completing a CVM assessment (see also Smith and Nagle 2002):

1. Respondents typically provide feedback on the offering elements they are asked to judge, which may not include the offering elements that drive their purchase choice. Careful construction of the judgment criteria thus is required.
2. CVM assumes the customer translates from the offering elements to delivered value, but customers may not be able to make this translation.

3. The process may ask respondents to evaluate offering elements that are not delivering any value, which would make the value translation moot.
4. The underlying assumption of CVM is that price is constrained by the customer's perception of the offering elements. Marketing effort can often change the customer's perceptions, but CVM does not recognize this effort.
5. CVM measures the response to queried offering elements but not value delivery. For example, suppose a CVM assessment finds that customers perceive firm A has twice as much of an offering element as firm B. But that offering element may deliver much more than twice the value; CVM thus may conclude firm A can double its price, whereas actual value delivery would indicate prices could be raised much more.

The second approach is economic value modeling (EVM), which Nagle and Hogan (2006) call economic value estimation (EVE). EVM attempts to measure objectively the economic worth of the benefits that customers receive from an offering, distinguishing between what they might receive from a competitor (commodity value) and what they obtain uniquely from a specific supplier (differentiation value). Forbis and Mehta (1981) are widely credited with developing the foundation for EVM practices. It builds a quantified model of value delivery by asking how a firm influences its customers by increasing their revenue and/or decreasing their cost of operations, always relative to a competing alternative. Nagle and Hogan (2006) provide a description of the process and numerous examples of quantified value delivery. Other examples appear in Anderson et al. (2007); Cressman (2001a) provides details of the quantification process.

Value assessment is clearly an embryonic field, still searching for generally accepted definitions of terms and methodologies. Developing agreement about what value delivery is and how to quantify it is a critical element for attaining better pricing processes. Important open questions include:

*   What definition of 'value' contributes most to the development of pricing strategy?
*   What is a robust, valid method for determining value delivery?

Structuring Offerings

To manage the value exchange with customers effectively, three issues are important in structuring offerings for customers:

*   creating offering options for customers;
*   bundling products and services;
*   pricing new products.

Fundamental to the development of a value-based pricing strategy is the concept of creating offering options. Offering options are critical because they force customers to trade value for price, which reduces customers' bargaining power and increases their value sensitivity while also decreasing their price sensitivity. In addition options can be structured to take advantage of the supplier's cost economies. Yet structuring offering options into a menu of choices is not described in prior academic literature, though Ottley (2002) provides a managerial perspective.

A specific tool for structuring offerings is bundling products and services, as described by Schmalensee (1982, 1984). However, prior literature seems more focused on the legal and cost issues of bundling than on its impact in delivering value and/or creating customer preferences. Yet bundling can be used as an active means for creating offering options for customers. As an important contribution to bundling literature, Stremersch and Tellis (2002) provide a consistent set of bundling definitions and a useful typology of practices. However, the concept of offering option development remains unconnected to bundling practices. Venkatesh and Mahajan (2009) also note that the use of bundling is increasing and provide an overview of its options, which demonstrates there is no universally 'correct' methodology for bundling.

Another critical question in offering creation involves pricing for new products. Marn et al. (2003) propose that companies regularly underprice new offerings. New products are becoming much more important to many firms as a hedge against competitive imitation and the commoditization of their offerings. This increased emphasis on new product development places more stress on managers to make profitable pricing decisions. Dean (1955) was the first to detail the process for pricing new products, arguing that novel products require a different pricing process from old products, while also recognizing the difficulties innovators face. Dean also introduces pricing options (skimming and penetration pricing) for new products. But the new product pricing issue seems to have lingered at this point for quite some time. Ingenbleek et al. (2003) acknowledge the complexity of pricing new products (and indeed of setting prices for all products) and thus propose a customer value–competitor–cost perspective. Bernstein and Macias (2002) also offer an interesting case study of new product pricing at Emerson Electric. Cressman (2004), though not focused on the pricing question explicitly, discusses issues related to pricing and managing a new product's early life cycle stage. More recently, Chatterjee (2009) provides a very useful organization of the new product pricing literature and notes the need for better tools to manage the longer-term issues of new product pricing. Important questions regarding the offering structuring include:

- How does offering structuring shape customer demand?
- How can managers use product and/or service bundling to create offering options for customers?
- What new product pricing processes should be used to facilitate product entry and profitability?
- What are the appropriate methodologies for building a longer-term, strategic new product pricing practice?

Value-based Communication

As noted, perceived value pricing can lead to incorrectly set price levels if customers do not fully understand the value of the seller's offerings. Value-based pricing strategies demand that managers actively communicate their value delivery. For a value-based pricing strategy, there are four main communication issues:

1. communicating the value delivery of the offering;
2. communicating to manage price sensitivity factors;

3.   communicating price points;
4.   communicating price changes.

Literature related to value and price communication is dominated by studies in consumer markets (for an excellent overview of how consumers perceive fairness, see Maxwell 2008). It is not clear to what extent findings developed in consumer markets can be applied to business markets. Monroe (2003), Baker (2006) and Holden and Burton (2008) briefly discuss value-based market communication. Nagle and Hogan (2006) also devote a chapter to communication.

Price sensitivity seems driven by emotive or psychological factors. It is not clear how, or even if, the factors that drive price sensitivity in business markets differ from those in consumer markets. Do managers leave their cognitive biases behind when they enter the business environment? While most texts in the pricing arena acknowledge the need for communication and the criticality of communication to the pricing effort, few provide details of how to undertake the communication effort. Critical questions include:

- What is the most effective way to communicate value delivery to target customers?
- How can price changes be framed? (Monroe (2003) and Chen et al. (1998) offer some discussion of this issue.)
- What drives customer price sensitivity in business markets, and how does it differ from consumer markets?
- How can customer communication be used to reduce customer price sensitivity?

Value-based Sales Negotiations

Many sales professionals have been trained in negotiation techniques. Unfortunately this training has successfully taught the sales team how to negotiate price points. There are several problems with negotiating price:

- Customers are trained that price aggression is worthwhile; the more they insist on lower prices, the lower their price.
- When price is negotiated, customers become more price-sensitive. Customers are trained that what they receive is less important than what they pay.
- It is very difficult to stop price negotiating once customers learn price aggression can be leveraged to lower prices.

Managing the value exchange with customers mandates replacing price negotiations with value negotiation. When negotiating value delivery, customers insist prices must be lower, so the seller responds by providing options that reduce the value delivery in exchange for a lower price. This process forces the customer to make a decision and trade value for price. The options customers consider come from the offering menu (see 'Structuring offerings' section above).

To implement value-based negotiation, the seller must first diagnose customer buying behavior and the customer's buying center. Buyer behavior literature is rich (Choffray and Lilien 1977; Hutt and Speh 1998; Johnston 1981; Johnston and

Spekman 1982, 1987, 1996; Lilien et al. 1992; Robinson et al. 1967; Sheth 1973; Soderlund et al. 2001; Webster and Wind 1972a, 1972b). Nagle and Holden (1995) offer a useful framework for determining buying behavior that diagnoses the behavior as price, relationship, value or convenience. The selling and negotiating strategy is then adapted to match the diagnosed buying behavior. For example, selling to loyal buyers requires a focus on security; selling to price-oriented buyers requires matching a competitive offer and price. Therefore, significant planning is required for the negotiation effort.

Next the seller must assess the buying center, including all those who influence and/ or make the purchase decision. Buying center literature is equally well developed (see Anderson et al. 1987; Bellizzi and McVey 1983; Bonoma 1982; Bristol 1992; Bunn 1993; Doyle et al. 1979; Ghingold and Wilson 1998; Jackson et al. 1984; Johnston and Bonoma 1981; Kohli 1989; Lilien and Wong 1984; McCabe 1987; Moriarty and Spekman 1984; Patton et al. 1986; Pettigrew 1993; Ronchetto et al. 1989; Silk and Kalwani 1982; Spekman and Stern 1979; Wilson 1971). Unfortunately, despite this extensive documentation of both buying behavior and buying center concepts, my experience suggests that neither concept is used widely by marketing and sales professionals. Rather they seem focused more on developing negotiating tactics, without regard to the customer personnel involved in the purchase decision or their behavior.

In contrast, purchasing professionals appear more aggressive and the purchasing tactics they deploy more sophisticated. Yama (2004) describes a wide variety of games that purchasing personnel use, from pre- to post-purchase. A particularly troubling game is the better deal price game, in which the buyer asserts that it has a lower (but confidential, of course) price offer. In many cases the seller cannot confirm the presence of a lower price offer and must decide whether to respond. Using a signal detection framework, Cressman (2007) offers some guidelines for making this decision, including those for assessing the credibility of a customer's assertion. Keiser (1988) also provides guidelines for negotiating with highly important customers.

Sales negotiations increasingly take place in a global arena. My experience suggests that though individual sales personnel may be well suited to an individual country, senior sales and marketing management – who must manage pricing strategies globally – often lack the skills to operate across many countries with unique cultures. Academic literature has begun to deal with this issue (e.g. Campbell et al. 1988; Simintiras and Thomas 1998), but little of this effort seems to have translated into marketing and sales professionals' actions. Thus important questions remain:

- How can managers implement buying process and buying center concepts in negotiating practice?
- What tools would help marketing and sales professionals diagnose buying behavior and tailor their selling strategies?
- How can managers manage negotiations in a global context?

Setting Price Points

Price points determine how much of the value delivery the supplier captures. Making this decision demands a trade-off between two incentives: to supply and to buy (see

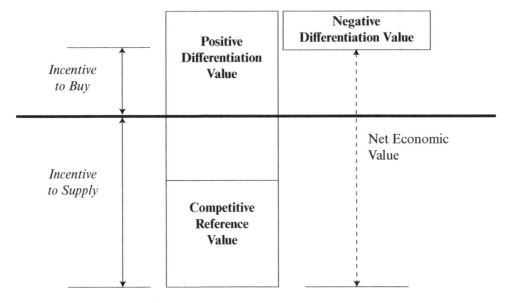

Figure 14.3   Price point determination

Figure 14.3). Setting the price fixes the level of these incentives. As early as the 1960s, Oxenfeldt (1960) called for managers to make sounder pricing decisions, noting that formulas provide little guidance. Morgenroth (1964) also attempted to integrate market and organizational factors in a model to determine price points in perhaps the first recognition that price setting was an organizational, and therefore political, decision (for a more recent view of the political nature of pricing, see Lancioni et al. 2005). Wentz (1966) then called for more realism in pricing decisions, because managers often used inappropriate decision models when establishing pricing policy. Oxenfeldt (1973) also noted a significant gap between academic understanding of the pricing decision and managerial application and thus provided a still useful list of pricing problems that required more managerial attention. Monroe and Della Bitta (1978) provided another early attempt to describe pricing models and inputs to the pricing decision. From these starting points, Shapiro and Jackson (1978), Ross (1984), Monroe (2003), Indounas (2006) and Nagle and Hogan (2006) have provided extended coverage of a managerial perspective on the price setting process. There is also significant, and often conflicting, academic research in this area (Avlontia and Indounas 2005; Hinterhuber 2004, 2008; Jain and Laric 1979; Mizik and Jacobson 2003; Monroe and Zoltners 1979; Morris and Calantone 1990; Morris and Fuller 1989; Morris and Joyce 1988; Noble and Gruca 1999; Samiee 1987; Shipley and Jobber 2001; Skinner 1970; Tellis 1986). The determination of how much of the firm's delivered value a firm can capture depends on:

- how thoroughly the target customer understands the delivered value – a communication issue;
- factors that drive customer price sensitivity;
- the firm's general pricing strategy.

Nagle and Hogan (2006) also describe a series of factors that drive customer price sensitivity. They suggest that as price sensitivity factors increase, firms must reduce the amount of delivered value captured with price.

Classic pricing strategy options include skimming, penetration and neutral (see Nagle and Hogan 2006). The choice of a pricing strategy also depends on the characteristics of target customers and the firm's underlying cost structure. Holden and Nagle (1998) discuss challenges of penetration strategies and caution about their use, though, particularly for new products. In addition, a price point implementation can lead to significant market difficulties. Cressman (2006) argues that confidential price offers actually increase customer price aggression and competitive intensity, because customers can reveal the confidential price proposal to a supplier's competitors, who must respond because they have no way to confirm the details of the offer. In that article, I therefore suggest firms should be more price transparent with price and offering details in the public domain, which helps reduce the 'fog' around competitive prices, as well as the purchasing agent's ability to play the better deal game. Another particular challenge for many companies is their apparent inability to achieve desired price points. McClearn (2004) argues that firms that have lost the power to set price often have not done an adequate job in designing offerings for target customers, have failed to thoroughly communicate their value delivery or have done a poor job of negotiating with customers. Another important and continuing question involves managing pricing activities globally.

The primary question is how to manage pricing practices across borders. The drivers of globalization/levers of strategy framework suggested by Yip (1992) offers some promise, but it has not been fully developed for the pricing domain. Emerging literature for global pricing practices focuses on the following topics:

- The conceptual basis for managing pricing globally (Cavusgil 1996; Cavusgil et al. 2003; Cavusgil et al. 2004; Diller and Bukhari 1994; Forman and Hunt 2005; Gaul and Lutz 1994; Lancioni 1989; Marsh 2000; Myers et al. 2002; Ozsomer and Prussia 2000; Shi et al. 2004; Weekly 1992). Zou and Cavusgil (2002) offer an excellent proposal on developing a global marketing strategy.
- The degree of standardization of strategy components as a strong strategy lever (Yip 1992). Literature on global pricing offers some coverage (Chung 2006; Jain 1989; Ozsomer and Simonin 2004; Schuh 2000; Sousa and Bradley 2008, 2009; Theodosiou and Katsikeas 2001).
- The currency selected for setting price points and the management of exchange rates in the pricing decision (Clark et al. 1999; Samiee and Anckar 1998).

What stand out in this research field are the multiple perspectives and varying conclusions reached in empirical work. There is still much work needed to formalize global pricing management. In particular, important questions include:

- How do price sensitivity factors influence value capture with price, and how can managers offset price sensitivity factors?
- How can managers systematize the price-setting process?
- What is a suitable process for managing pricing practices globally?

Conclusion: Managing the Value Exchange with Customers

In the framework in Figure 14.2 for managing the value exchange with customers, value assessment has received the most attention from researchers and marketing professionals. Other elements of this framework are much less developed. Significant work is required to understand and manage offering structuring, value communication, value-based negotiation and price point determinations.

MANAGING COMPETITIVE INTERACTIONS

Although managing the value exchange with customers is critical to driving profitable performance, it alone cannot ensure profitability. Udell (1964) argues that competitive strategy is critical to pricing practice and proposes that traditional approaches to pricing overlook real market environments. Practices that intensify competitive battles can significantly reduce the profit potential created by effectively managing the value exchange with customers. Firms that successfully manage the value exchange create the potential for superior profitability; to realize that potential, firms must also manage competitive interactions, which requires a carefully constructed strategy that considers pricing practices. This section therefore develops a process for incorporating the competitive strategy in pricing strategy development. As in the section above on managing the value exchange, my focus here is on how firms can actively manage competitive interactions rather than just responding to competitive developments.

An effective competitive strategy is tied directly to the decisions that firms make while managing the value exchange. Customer target selection and the offering design determine which competitors the firm will confront. Given customer targets and the firm's offerings, the starting point for a competitive pricing strategy is identifying the firm's competitors. Depending on their competitors' strategies, the evolution of the seller's offering structure and the sources of competitive advantage must also be planned. The framework provided by Chen (1996) can be adapted to identifying direct and potential competitors (see Figure 14.4). Using this framework, managers can identify which competitors require a competitive strategy, which require a contingency strategy and which can be safely ignored. However, many managers underestimate competition (Clark and Montgomery 1999), which causes them to fail to recognize competitors until they have established a significant position, when it is too late to respond (see Hodgkinson 1997). Clark and Montgomery (1999) propose that because managers typically fail to see all competitors, they should focus on competitors as customers see them. I have used the value analysis method described previously and the competitor identification grid (Figure 14.4) to help managers expand their views of competitors. Early detection of potential competitors and their evolution to direct competitors requires managerial vigilance. Geroski (1999) provides a framework to aid this vigilance, and the competitor identification grid in Figure 14.4 can provide assistance. The evaluation should address the following questions:

- What could this potential competitor do to enter the market of direct competitors?
- What can be done to discourage this entry?

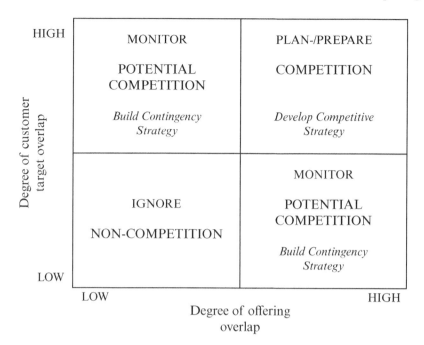

Source: Adapted from Chen (1996).

Figure 14.4 Identifying competitors

- If the entry cannot be discouraged, how will the competitor most likely enter?
- What actions should be undertaken if entry occurs?

Another essential input to competitive price strategy development is procuring source(s) of competitive advantage. The framework developed by Day and Wensley (1988) is especially useful in getting managers to address advantage sources. A critical component of the active management of competitive interactions is the evolution of the sources of advantage, which might erode due to competitor duplication. For direct competitors, the use of a SWOT (strength–weakness–opportunities–threats) analysis is traditionally recommended. However, it is not always helpful in developing a competitive pricing strategy because:

- SWOT does not deal explicitly with competitor intent and capabilities. A competitor with a threatening intent and the capabilities to execute its strategy is a powerful competitor but may be overlooked.
- Strengths and weaknesses may be evaluated without considering value delivery. A strength that cannot be converted into value delivery is an investment that may never generate a return. A weakness that does not impact value delivery may be irrelevant.
- Opportunities are only important if the firm has the capability to capitalize on them; without capability, an opportunity may be important only for a competitor.

- A threat is critical only if it affects the firm's ability to deliver value to target customers or the firm's capabilities.

These criticisms are sometimes managed in the development of SWOT analysis, but in my experience, they generally get overlooked altogether.

An alternative evaluation approach uses the following sequence for direct and potential competitors:

1. What is this competitor's strategic intent? Consider marketing, technology, operations, finance and general management functions.
2. What capabilities does this competitor have to support its intent? What barriers will the competitor encounter in pursuing its intent?
3. Comparing intent with barriers and capabilities, what will happen?
   a. Will the competitor succeed? If so, how will it behave?
   b. Will the competitor fail? If so, how will it behave?
4. What is the impact of this success/failure on the firm's strategic intent?
5. What actions should the firm take?

Hamilton et al. (1998) propose a similar approach; I provide the details of the methodology in Cressman (2001b).

How should competitive interactions be managed? I have previously argued (Cressman 2003) that the problem is not always the competitor's actions. Competitive problems may also be the result of actions the firm takes and to which the competitor responds. Cressman and Nagle (2002) propose competitors' moves should not always be countered; managers instead must weigh the long-range cost of responding. In that article we provide a framework for transforming insights into profitable responses. Smith and Cressman (2008) propose another framework for evaluating competitive responses in mature markets, for which the measure of success is profitable performance, not share growth.

Assuming competitive attacks evolve, how should they be managed? Fahey (1999) provides a comprehensive process for managing competitor attacks, and Clark (1998) offers a useful managerial perspective. Rao et al. (2000) also pose an interesting perspective on fighting price wars (avoid them, if possible!). Chen and Miller (1994) take the opposite tack, asking: when attacking, what forms of attack are likely to reduce the potential of retaliation? These authors propose that attacks that are less visible, difficult for competitors to respond to and distant from the central focus of the competitor's strategy are less likely to precipitate response. However, most research in the competitive arena has been developed outside of pricing concerns. From a value pricing perspective, important questions are:

- How can managers improve their capability to detect competitors and diagnose their strategies?
- What are effective strategies for preventing competitive entry into a marketplace?
- What is the impact of price wars on firm profits?
- Once in a price war, what are the most effective strategies for ending the war?

MANAGING RESOURCE ALLOCATIONS

In this section I examine the final component of pricing strategy: assigning resources to the firm's most profitable activities. It requires understanding how managerial decisions drive changes in profitability. The critical managerial issue is the level of resources to apply to managing the value exchange with customers and managing competitive inter- actions, as well as the impact this resourcing will have on business unit profitability. To some extent resourcing issues have been addressed in marketing modeling and market- ing engineering literature (for overviews see Lilien et al. 1992; Lilien and Rangaswamy 1998). However, the framework I propose creates significant resource assignment and optimality issues that have not been addressed.

For example, the financial impact of pricing decisions has been described. The key issue in assessing this financial impact is how a change in price alters volume and cost, and thus profits. Smith and Nagle (1994) provide an excellent overview of the analysis process involved in evaluating the profit impacts of pricing decisions. Nagle and Hogan (2006) also discuss price optimization and techniques for evaluating multiple price points, and Smith (2006) details profit leverage moves in low margin industries.

Another issue requiring more attention is the impact of scarce resources on pricing decisions. Firms typically have a scarce resource, such as an asset that creates high value for customers and is in limited supply. The management issue is to align this scarce resource with the firm's most profitable opportunities. Management teams might choose to reserve some scarce resource capacity to serve more profitable customers if demand is highly variable and uncertain. To do this, the firm must

- identify the firm's scare resource(s);
- determine what the demand pattern is for the scarce resource(s);
- prioritize opportunities for assigning the scarce resource(s);
- determine an inventory policy for reserves of the scarce resource(s) and/or how resource allocations can be changed readily.

The concept of revenue management in the airline sector attempts to deal with these questions. In the airline sector, the scarce resource is a seat on a specific flight, and air- lines have developed sophisticated tools for tracking demand for all flights. Thus airline operators can shift the availability of low-cost seats to optimize aircraft utilization and revenue flow on each flight. Revenue management has also been widely researched in the operations management sector. However, it has not been widely adopted in other busi- ness markets, perhaps because managers find it difficult to forecast demand or identify scarce resources. Whatever the cause, I believe business marketing professionals have ignored a significant opportunity to improve their profitability. Thus important ques- tions include:

- How can managers optimally assign resources to managing the value exchange with customers and managing competitive interactions?
- How can management teams operationalize revenue management concepts for their scarce resource(s)?
- How can firms assess their scarce resource(s)?

- How can firms determine adequate reserve capacity levels for their scarce resource(s)?

VALUE-BASED PRICING STRATEGY LINKAGES

The three strategy elements in Figure 14.1 (managing the value exchange with customers, managing competitive interactions and managing resources) are tightly integrated and interact in a value-based pricing strategy (see Figure 14.5):

- As customer targeting and offering design decisions are made, competitors can be identified who are or might target the same customers with similar offering structures.
- Competitor identification and examination of competitor strategies provides insights into how the seller must change its offering structure and renew its sources of competitive advantage.
- With customer targeting and offering design decisions, the seller can determine what resource skills are required and how to prioritize the investment of these resources. Decisions on the evolution of the offering structure and renewing sources of competitive advantage also drive resource skill levels and priorities.
- Resourcing decisions become part of profitability analyses and managerial decision-making.
- Finally, decisions on competitive strategy and managing competitor interactions form the basis for thinking through the profit impact of various competitive moves.

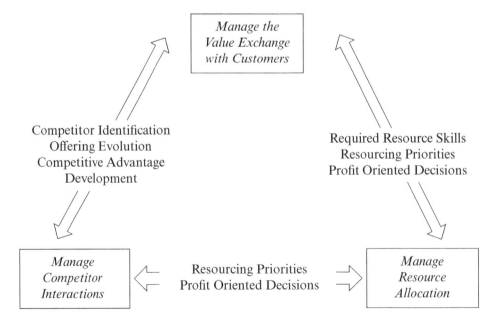

Figure 14.5   Pricing strategy element linkages

PRICING TACTICS: THE IMPLEMENTATION INFRASTRUCTURE CONNECTION

As for other types of organizational strategy, the development of a pricing strategy does not guarantee its implementation. Eugster et al. (2000) argue that a surprising number of firms lack the discipline to implement their price strategies. I have recently noted (Cressman 2009, 2010) that pricing strategies often fail because the firm does not adequately prepare its implementation elements and fails to communicate the strategy to the organization. There are four tactical implementation elements relevant to pricing strategy implementation:

1. pricing processes;
2. pricing organization;
3. pricing controls;
4. pricing data systems.

Pricing Process

The pricing process is the means for establishing price points and price discounts. It includes both the data inputs to the price/price discount setting effort and the way the data inputs are manipulated to determine price points and price discounts. The pricing process used in many companies seems more situational than planned. There is often little documentation of how pricing decisions were made, what data were considered or how the data had been manipulated. This situation frequently creates wide price variance, with no clear explanation for the different price points.

Literature regarding pricing processes is relatively underdeveloped. Rao et al. (2000) suggest this gap may be because practitioners assume the pricing process incurs low costs and is relatively simple, which makes it undeserving of strategic management. Rao (1984) cites pricing as the only element of the marketing mix that does not require resource expenditures; implying the pricing effort does not require strategic oversight. Yet Dutta et al. (2002, 2003) also propose that the processes for setting prices and determining price discounts is an organizational capability that can provide a basis for competitive advantage. Even though a firm delivers value to customers, it may not capture this value with pricing; rather it must develop pricing processes to set and manage pricing. Moreover, a firm cannot purchase pricing systems and skills but instead must develop processes that meet both its internal needs and customers' requirements. Therefore according to these authors, a pricing process consists of three components:

1. assessing competitive prices (input issue);
2. setting pricing strategy (data manipulation issue);
3. performing analyses of proposed prices and gaining commitment to new prices (data manipulation issue).

It is interesting to note, though, that the analysis of delivered value is not identified as an input factor. Dutta et al. (2003) propose that the objective of the pricing process is to set price points: if the only input item is competitive prices, then they are implicitly arguing that prices should be set relative to competitive prices. But clearly these authors also want to propose that a portion of the delivered value should be captured through price-setting. Somewhere value delivery must be determined as a critical input to the pricing process. Thus there is great need for more understanding of the elements of optimal pricing processes. Questions that need to be addressed include:

- What is a strategic process for managing pricing strategy development?
- How can the pricing process be connected to value analysis and value creation?
- What types of input data lead to pricing decisions that create profit improvements?
- How can firms validate customer and competitor information used in pricing decisions?

Organizing for Pricing Strategy Implementation: Delegating Pricing Decisions

Discussions of the advisability of delegating pricing decisions differ dramatically, as do pricing practices. Some firms grant wide authority to sales teams to determine price points; others strictly limit this authority (Dolan and Simon 1996). In a survey of 108 medical supply firms, Stephenson et al. (1979) find that 30 per cent of the firms allow no price delegation, while 70 per cent allow medium to high levels of delegation. The fundamental question, though, is whether delegating pricing authority helps or hinders profitability. These authors suggest delegation appears in certain conditions, such as when:

1. demand is highly elastic, because presumably price discounts drive the significant growth of sales volume;
2. firms are aggressive price negotiators, which may indicate an underlying culture that thrives in price negotiations;
3. product or service offerings are complex, which raises the question of whether negotiations are price driven or content driven (see the 'Structuring offerings' section above);
4. Wide variance marks customer types and sizes, which raises the question of whether the firm is designing offerings for unique customer segments or trying to force uniform offerings onto a diverse marketplace.
5. sales forces are relatively autonomous and demand pricing authority;
6. planned price points are difficult because of the size and structure of the offering, as is typical for many distributors;
7. the product line is perishable.

Weinberg (1975) instead proposes that profitable sales can be achieved by allowing the sales force to determine price levels and using achieved gross margin as the sales force incentive. This argument assumes a salesperson will seek to maximize personal income. However, many studies indicate that the sales team operates in a highly complex motivational environment (e.g. Walker et al. 1977; Winer 1983). To deal with this criticism Weinberg (1978) built a model in which a gross margin compensation system is optimal when salespeople are income maximizers, seek to minimize the work required to achieve a target sales level and/or trade off time for money. Lal (1986) suggests that if the incentives are appropriately structured, the sales team's knowledge of customers and evaluations of the firm's offerings make the delegation of pricing authority a reasonable decision. Delegating pricing authority to the sales team can be as profitable as centralized pricing when the salesperson and sales manager are equally knowledgeable about the market; it becomes more profitable when the salesperson's market knowledge is superior to that of the sales manager. Bhardwaj (2001) similarly finds that delegating pricing authority can increase profits. Using agency theory Mishra and Prasad (2005) study delegated pricing authority in competitive markets in symmetric and asymmetric information conditions. Their models suggest favorable profitability, regardless of the degree of delegated pricing authority.

Such studies provide a theoretical basis for delegating pricing authority to the sales force, but empirical support is lacking. Stephenson et al. (1979) thus provide empirical validation but find that as delegated pricing authority increases, profitability declines. Firms that grant the least pricing authority generate the highest gross margins; firms granting the highest levels of pricing authority generate the lowest gross margins. Furthermore, sales representative contributions (i.e. gross margin minus selling costs as a percentage of net sales) tend to decrease as sales forces receive higher levels of pricing authority, which implies that sales personnel might be using price discounts to achieve sales volume while ignoring the impact on their commissions. Thus incentives based on gross margins may not be powerful enough to overcome the desirability of a sale.

Perhaps the most interesting of Stephenson et al.'s (1979) findings is that firms that grant the lowest level of pricing authority achieve the highest rate of sales growth. However, firms granting medium levels of pricing authority achieve the highest level of sales per sales representative. The authors recognize the potential inconsistency of these results but do not offer an explanation. They then conclude that the delegation of pricing authority to sales personnel is likely to drive aggressive price discounting and harm profits and that sales growth and sales per sales representative are negatively affected by high levels of pricing authority. If pricing flexibility is desirable in the market situation, firms should allow the sales force to recommend discounts, but sales management needs to retain authority for granting discounts. Finally, Stephenson et al. (1979) identify five factors that should be considered when determining the desirability of delegating pricing authority:

1. Resulting sales behavior: Do sales behaviors increase profits and sales growth?
2. Market knowledge: Do salespeople have better knowledge of customer evaluations of offerings and WTP?
3. Competitive behavior: Does delegated pricing authority increase price competition?
4. Buying environment: Does delegated pricing authority increase customer price negotiations and customer price sensitivity?
5. Reward structures: Do gross margin incentive schemes encourage sales behavior that drives greater profitability?

Joseph's (2001) model recognizes that the sales team may have superior market knowledge but also may substitute price discounts for selling effort. Kissan's model thus revealed that though in some market environments, delegating pricing authority is optimal, it is not true in all market environments. The key factor is the effort cost of pursuing high value sales prospects; at very low and very high effort cost levels, the delegation of pricing authority is optimal.

Yuksel and Sutton-Brady (2006) instead explore the price authority delegation issue from the sales force's perspective. Granting pricing authority to the sales force enhances the sales team's motivation, performance and respect from customers. Perhaps these outcomes arise because the customer sees the salesperson as in charge of the selling effort. But Yuksel and Sutton-Brady find contradictions in the sales team's understanding of the impact of delegated pricing authority too: half the respondents believed delegated authority would increase sales volume and profit, whereas the other half predicted a directly opposite result. Some respondents saw delegated pricing authority as a burden. Therefore, these authors conclude that delegating pricing authority is dysfunctional unless it increases the sales force's motivation; they also note that motivation can be driven by factors other than delegated pricing authority.

Hansen et al. (2008) extend empirical testing of pricing authority delegation by proposing and testing two factors that might reduce the desirability of delegating authority:

1. Sales personnel may see the selling effort as too costly and then use price discounts to obtain a sale. In this case, delegating pricing authority may reduce profitability.
2. Incentive systems may limit the firm's ability to manage the delegation of pricing authority. For example, rewarding the sales force on gross margins might reveal the firm's cost structure to the sales team, who in turn might share it with customers. This sharing raises the potential for leaks to competitors, making centralized control of pricing a desirable preventative measure.

Although these researchers find that delegated pricing authority may be favorable for some firms, they highlight the real potential that sales personnel will use price discounts to reduce selling effort. Firms are less likely to delegate pricing authority when the revenue/profit impact of discounting is substantial. They also find that firms that closely monitor their sales forces can minimize the excessive use of price discounting for selling effort and thus might benefit from increased price authority delegation.

Frenzen et al. (2010) test the delegation decision issue further and find:

1. pricing delegation increases when there are more substantive differences in customer/market knowledge between the salesperson and the sales manager;
2. pricing delegation increases when it is difficult to monitor salesperson performance;
3. firm performance is enhanced by delegated pricing authority when salespeople have better market/customer knowledge and market-related uncertainty is high.

They thus conclude that rigid 'one-size-fits-all' pricing centralization is inappropriate for some markets and suggest consideration of pricing authority delegation. It is clear that the issue of delegated pricing authority is still not sufficiently understood. Significant questions remain:

- If the sales team uses pricing authority for price discounting, does delegating pricing authority increase customer price sensitivity by focusing customers on price points instead of value delivery?
- Does the increased use of price discounts increase competitive intensity through the actions of customers positioning to shift an order to a lower priced competitor?

Pricing Controls

For many companies, gathering data to monitor pricing performance systematically is a difficult process. Although a firm may have invested in a sophisticated accounting system, translating accounting data to pricing metrics is problematic for many reasons. Two types of pricing control plots can be helpful, though:

- Price dispersion. A plot of realized price by sales volume (by customer, salesperson, sales territory, region) helps identify adherence to pricing and discounting rules and can help identify customers who abuse their bargaining power to drive prices lower.
- Price waterfalls. A waterfall aims to identify the path between list price and the price the firm ultimately realizes (pocket price) by documenting all discounts and allowances.

Marn and Rosiello (1992) provide a good overview of the use of waterfalls. Another challenge many companies face is that instead of routine scrutiny, management teams frequently conduct pricing performance reviews only on a situational basis. These situational reviews are precipitated by some crisis (competitor gaining share, customer learning about significantly lower prices at another firm), and by the time the management review is underway, long-term systemic pricing processes may have already developed. These pricing processes may have significant negative impacts on prices and profitability but are very difficult to change. Routine monitoring of pricing performance is critical to detect and prevent the growth of bad pricing habits. Useful pricing controls are needed by many firms. Remaining questions include:

- What pricing performance indicators would motivate management teams to actively monitor and correct pricing problems?
- What tools would facilitate the move from occasional pricing performance reviews to routine reviews? That is, how can control systems be used to motivate behavior in the marketing function?
- What pricing performance indicators can provide an early indication of pricing problems? Price dispersion and price waterfalls are end-of-process measures; early indicators of problems are critical to prevent the development of more serious pricing problems.

Pricing Data Systems

Many firms have invested in sophisticated cost data systems that provide much-needed information on system costs. However, costs are frequently reported at an aggregate business unit level. Most fixed costs are distributed in allocation or absorption systems, disguising real product and customer costs. What is needed is a costing system that provides costs by

- individual customer;
- individual product;

- individual sales territory;
- individual geographic region.

The solution lies in the development of activity-based costing systems. Yet such systems are quite expensive, and construction times are often measured in years. My experience shows that effective activity costing systems for pricing purposes can also be constructed in spreadsheet form, with reasonable estimates of activity consumption by customer, product territory and region. Yet whereas cost data are often readily available for marketing professionals (even if the allocation process hides the real costs), the availability of customer and competitor data is much rarer in most firms. Most customer and competitor information required for making profitable pricing decisions is not routinely collected and validated. In many cases, marketing managers have not thought through the information they really need to make good customer decisions (see Indounas 2006). Thus an effective method to begin collecting good information is a marketing log book. Managers can use logs to track customer and competitor actions as product and price moves appear in the market, made by various firms. Many firms also do not task their sales and customer service teams with the routine collection of customer or competitor information. One way to collect customer information is to assign the sales and service teams to routinely report changes in customer priorities or competitor reports. Collecting competitor information can be facilitated by asking what competitors might do to thwart the firm's strategy and what must be known to detect those moves. The routine collection, analysis and reporting of this information is a necessary step in assembling valid customer and competitor information.

What information should be collected? For competitors, Fahey (1999) and Fuld (1994) provide good guidelines. Hutt et al. (1995) provide a useful process for analyzing competitor strategic intent, and Fahey (2003) discusses developing competitive scenarios. The framework provided by Campbell and Cunningham (2006) is useful in assessing customers. Although data collection may be regarded as a more pedestrian issue, value-based pricing strategy is deeply dependent on valid basic data; management teams seem to rely more on anecdotal, untested data rather than confirmed data. Important questions thus include:

- How can managers systematize the collection of competitor and customer information?
- How can managers validate collected customer and competitor information?
- How can managers improve the use of customer and competitor information in the pricing process?

SUMMARY

Despite the power of pricing management to affect firm profits, we know surprisingly little about profitable pricing practices. Pricing in practice is dominated by (sometimes) poorly founded managerial judgment and biases, and an amazingly small amount of effort gets spent on pricing by marketing professionals. Clearly the pricing management area calls for intensive research and development, as well as improved understanding of how both to develop and implement pricing strategies.

REFERENCES

Anderson, Erin, W. Chu and Barton Weitz (1987), 'Industrial purchasing: an empirical exploration of the buyclass framework', *Journal of Marketing*, **51** (July), 71–86.

Anderson, James C., D.C. Jain and P.K. Chintagunta (1993), 'Customer value assessment in business markets: a state-of-practice study', *Journal of Business-to-Business Marketing*, **1** (1), 3–29.

Anderson, James C., Nirmalya Kumar and James A. Narus (2007), *Value Merchants: Demonstrating and Documenting Superior Value in Business Markets*, Boston, MA: Harvard University Press.

Anderson, James C., J. Thomson and F. Wynstra (2000), 'Combining value and price to make purchase decisions in business markets', *Internal Journal of Research in Marketing*, **17**, 307–29.

Avlontia, G.J. and K.A. Indounas (2005), 'Pricing objectives and pricing methods in the services sector', *Journal of Services Marketing*, **19** (1), 47–57.

Baker, R.J. (2006), *Pricing On Purpose: Creating and Capturing Value*, Hoboken, NJ: John Wiley & Sons.

Beane, T.P. and D.M. Enis (1993), 'Market segmentation: a review', *European Journal of Marketing*, **21** (5), 20–42.

Bellizzi, J.A. and P. McVey (1983), 'How valid is the buy-grid model?', *Industrial Marketing Management*, **12** (February), 57–62.

Bennion, M.L., Jr (1987), 'Segmenting and positioning in a basic industry', *Industrial Marketing Management*, **16** (February), 9–18.

Bernstein, J. and D. Macias (2002), 'Engineering new-product success: the new product pricing process at Emerson', *Industrial Marketing Management*, **31**, 51–64.

Bhardwaj, P. (2001), 'Delegating pricing decisions', *Marketing Science*, **20** (Spring), 143–69.

Bonoma, Thomas V. (1982), 'Major sales: who really does the buying?', *Harvard Business Review*, (May–June), 111–19.

Bonoma, Thomas V. and B.P. Shapiro (1983), *Segmenting the Industrial Market*, Lexington, MA: Lexington Books.

Bristol, J.M. (1992), 'Influence strategies in organizational buying: the importance of connections to the right people in the right places', *Journal of Business-to-Business Marketing*, **1** (June), 63–98.

Bunn, M.D. (1993), 'Taxonomy of buying decision approaches', *Journal of Marketing*, **57** (January), 38–56.

Campbell, N.C.G. and M.T. Cunningham (2006), 'Customer analysis for strategy development in industrial markets', *Strategic Management Journal*, **4** (4), 369–80.

Campbell, N.C.G., J. Graham, L.A. Jolbert and H.G. Meissner (1988), 'Marketing negotiations in France, Germany, the United Kingdom, and the United States', *Journal of Marketing*, **52** (April), 49–62.

Cavusgil, S. Tamir (1996), 'Pricing for global markets', *Columbia Journal of World Business*, **31** (Winter), 66–78.

Cavusgil, S. Tamir, K. Chan and C. Zhang (2003), 'Strategic orientations in export pricing: a clustering approach to create firm taxonomies', *Journal of International Marketing*, **11** (Spring), 47–72.

Cavusgil, S. Tamir, S. Yeniyurt and J.D. Townsend (2004), 'The framework of a global company: a conceptualization and preliminary validation', *International Marketing Management*, **33** (November), 711–16.

Chatterjee, R. (2009), 'Strategic pricing of new products and services', in V. Rao (ed), *Handbook of Pricing Research in Marketing*, Cheltenham, UK and Northampton, MA, USA: Edward Elgar.

Chen, M. (1996), 'Competitive analysis and interfirm rivalry: toward a theoretical integration', *Academy of Management Review*, **21** (1), 100–134.

Chen, M. and D. Miller (1994), 'Competitive attack, retaliation and performance: an expectancy-valence framework', *Strategic Management Journal*, **15**, 85–102.

Chen, S.S., Kent B. Monroe and Y. Lou (1998), 'The effects of framing price promotion messages on consumers' perceptions and purchase intentions', *Journal of Retailing*, **74** (3), 353–72.

Choffray, J.M. and Gary L. Lilien (1977), 'Assessing response to industrial marketing strategy', *Journal of Marketing*, **41** (July), 20–31.

Chung, H.F.L. (2006), 'An investigation of crossmarket standardization strategies', *European Journal of Marketing*, **29** (11/12), 1345–71.

Clark, B.H. (1998), 'Managing competitor interactions', *Marketing Management*, (Fall/Winter), 9–20.

Clark, B.H. and D.B. Montgomery (1999), 'Managerial identification of competitors', *Journal of Marketing*, **63** (July), 67–83.

Clark, T., M. Kotabe and D. Rajaratnam (1999), 'Exchange rate pass-through and international pricing strategy: a conceptual framework and research propositions', *Journal of International Business Studies*, **30** (2), 249–68.

Cressman, George E. (2001a), 'Building business profitability: the value connection', *Chimica Oggi*, (June), 65–8.

Cressman, George E., Jr (2001b), 'Building business profitability: the value connection, part three', *Chimica Oggi*, (December).

Cressman, George E., Jr (2003), 'Dealing with "dumb competitors"', *The Pricing Advisor*, (April), pp. 1–2.

Cressman, George E. (2004), 'Reaping what you sow', *Marketing Management*, (March/April), pp. 34–40.

Cressman, George E. (2006), 'Fixing prices', *Marketing Management*, (September/October), pp. 32–7.

Cressman, George E., Jr (2007), 'Seeing through the fog: managing price demands', *Journal of the Professional Pricing Society*, no. 4, 22–27.

Cressman, George E., Jr (2009), 'Why pricing strategies fail', *The Journal of the Professional Pricing Society*, no. 2, 18–22.

Cressman, George E., Jr (2010), 'Selling value based pricing strategies: making pricing strategy work', *The Journal of the Professional Pricing Society*, no. 1, 16–19.

Cressman, George E., Jr, and T.T. Nagle (2002), 'How to manage an aggressive competitor', *Business Horizons*, (March–April), pp. 23–30.

Day, George S. and R. Wensley (1988), 'Assessing advantage: a framework for diagnosing competitive superiority', *Journal of Marketing*, **52** (April), 1–20.

Dean, J. (1955), 'Pricing a new product', *The Controller*, **23** (April), 163–5.

De Kluyver, C.A. and D.B. Whitlark (1986), 'Benefit segmentation for industrial products', *Industrial Marketing Management*, **15** (November), 273–86.

Dickson, P.R. and J.L. Ginter (1987), 'Market segmentation, product differentiation, and marketing strategy', *Journal of Marketing*, **51** (April), 1–10.

Diller, H. and I. Bukhari (1994), 'Pricing conditions in the European common market', *European Management Journal*, **12** (June), 163–70.

Dolan, R. and H. Simon (1996), *Power Pricing*, New York: The Free Press.

Doyle, P., Arch G. Woodside and P. Michell (1979), 'Organizations buying in new task and rebuy situations', *Industrial Marketing Management*, **8** (January), 7–11.

Dutta, Shantanu, M.J. Zbaracki and Mark Bergen (2003), 'Pricing process as a capability: a resource-based perspective', *Strategic Management Journal*, **24**, 615–30.

Dutta, Shantanu, Mark Bergen, D. Levy, M. Ritson and M. Zbaracki (2002), 'Pricing as a strategic capability', *Sloan Management Review*, (Spring), pp. 61–6.

Eugster, C.C., J.N. Kakkar and E.V. Roegner (2000), 'Bringing discipline to pricing', *The McKinsey Quarterly*, pp. 132–9.

Fahey, L. (1999), *Outwitting, Outmaneuvering, and Outperforming Competitors*, New York: John Wiley & Sons.

Fahey, L. (2003), 'Competitor scenarios', *Strategy and Leadership*, **31** (1), 32–44.

Flint, D., R. Woodruff and S. Gardial (2002), 'Exploring the phenomenon of customers' desired value change in a business-to-business context', *Journal of Marketing*, **66** (October), 102–17.

Forbis, J.L. and N.T. Mehta (1981), 'Value-based strategies for industrial products', *Business Horizons*, **24** (May–June), 32–42.

Forman, H. and J.M. Hunt (2005), 'Managing the influence of internal and external determinants on international industrial pricing strategies', *International Marketing Management*, **34** (February), 133–49.

Frenzen, H., A. Hansen, M. Krafft, M.K. Mantrala and S. Schmidt (2010), 'Delegation of pricing authority to the sales force: an agency-theoretic perspective of its determinants and impact on performance', *International Journal of Research in Marketing*, **27** (March), 58–68.

Fuld, L. (1994), *The New Competitive Intelligence: The Complete Resource for Finding, Analyzing, and Using Information About Your Competitors*, New York: John Wiley & Sons.

Gale, B.T. (1994), *Managing Customer Value*, New York: The Free Press.

Gaul, W. and U. Lutz (1994), 'Pricing in international marketing and Western European economic integration', *Management International Review*, **34** (2), 101–24.

Geroski, P.A. (1999), 'Early warning of new rivals', *Sloan Management Review*, (Spring), pp. 107–16.

Ghingold, M. and D.T. Wilson (1998), 'Buying center research and business marketing research: meeting the challenge of dynamic marketing', *Journal of Business and Industrial Marketing*, **13** (2), 96–108.

Hamilton, R.D., III, E.D. Eskin and M.P. Michaels (1998), 'Assessing competitors: the gap between strategic intent and core capability', *Long Range Planning*, **31** (3), 406–17.

Hansen, A., K. Joseph, and M. Krafft (2008), 'Price delegation in sales organizations: an empirical investigation', *Official Open Access Journal of VHB*, **1** (May), 94–104.

Hansen, T. and H.S. Solgaard (2004), 'Strategic pricing: fundamental considerations and future perspectives', *Marketing Review*, **4** (February), 99–111.

Hinterhuber, Andreas (2004), 'Towards value-based pricing – an integrative framework for decision making', *Industrial Marketing Management*, **33**, 765–78.

Hinterhuber, Andreas (2008), 'Creating and managing superior customer value', *Advances in Business Marketing and Purchasing*, **14**, 381–448.

Hodgkinson, G.P. (1997), 'Cognitive inertia in a turbulent market: the case of UK residential estate agents', *Journal of Management Studies*, **34** (November), 921–45.

Holden, R.K. and M. Burton (2008), *Pricing With Confidence: 10 Ways to Stop Leaving Money on the Table*, Hoboken, NJ: John Wiley & Sons.

Holden, R.K. and T.T. Nagle (1998), 'Kamikaze pricing', *Marketing Management*, (Summer), pp. 31–40.

Homburg, C., S. Kuster, N. Beutin and A. Menon (2001), 'Determinants of benefits in business-to-business markets – a cross cultural comparison', *Journal of International Marketing*, **13** (3), 1–31.

Hutt, M.D. and T.W. Speh (1998), *Business Marketing Management*, 6th edn, Hinsdale, IL: Dryden Press.

Hutt, M., B.B. Tyler, C. Hardee and D. Park (1995), 'Understanding strategic intent in the global marketplace', *The Academy of Management Executive*, **9** (May), 12.

Indounas, K. (2006), 'Making effective pricing decisions', *Business Horizons*, **49** (September–October), 415–24.

Ingenbleek, Paul, M. Debruyne, R.T. Frambach and T.M.M. Verhallen (2003), 'Successful new product pricing practices: a contingency approach', *Marketing Letters*, **14** (4), 289–305.

Jackson, D.W., Jr, J.E. Keith and Richard K. Burdick (1984), 'Purchasing agents' perceptions of industrial buying center influence: a situational approach', *Journal of Marketing*, **48** (Fall), 75–83.

Jain, S.C. (1989), 'Standardization of international marketing strategy: some research hypotheses', *Journal of Marketing*, **53** (1), 70–79.

Jain, S.C. and M.V. Laric (1979), 'A framework for strategic industrial pricing', *Industrial Marketing Management*, **6** (January), 75–80.

Jedidi, Kamil and S. Jagpal (2009), 'Willingness to pay: measurement and managerial implications', in V. Rao (ed.), *Handbook of Pricing Research*, Cheltenham, UK and Northampton, MA, USA: Edward Elgar.

Johnston, Wesley J. (1981), 'Industrial buying behavior: a state of the art review', in K. Roering (ed.), *Annual Review of Marketing*, Chicago: American Marketing Association, pp. 75–85.

Johnston, Wesley J. and Thomas V. Bonoma (1981), 'The buying center: structure and interactions patterns', *Journal of Marketing*, **45** (Summer), 143–56.

Johnston, Wesley J. and R.E. Spekman (1982), 'Special section on industrial buying behavior: introduction', *Journal of Business Research*, **10** (February), 133–4.

Johnston, Wesley J. and R.E. Spekman (1987), 'Industrial buyer behavior: where we are and where we need to go', in Jagdeth N. Sheth (ed.), *Research in Consumer Behavior*, Stamford, CT: JAI Press, pp. 83–111.

Johnston, Wesley J. and R.E. Spekman (1996), 'Organizational buying behavior: toward an integrative framework', *Journal of Business Research*, **35** (January), 1–15.

Joseph, K. (2001), 'On the optimality of delegating pricing authority to the sales force', *Journal of Marketing*, **65** (January), 62–70.

Keiser, T.C. (1988), 'Negotiating with a customer you can't afford to lose', *Harvard Business Review*, **66** (June), 30–33.

Kohli, Ajay (1989), 'Determinants of influence in organizational buying: a contingency approach', *Journal of Marketing*, **53** (July), 50–65.

Lal, R. (1986), 'Delegating pricing responsibility to the salesforce', *Marketing Science*, **5** (2), 159–68.

Lancioni, R.A. (1989), 'The importance of price in international business development', *European Journal of Marketing*, **23** (11), 45–50.

Lancioni, R.A., Hope J. Schau and M.P. Smith (2005), 'Intraorganizational influences on business-to-business pricing strategies: a political economy perspective', *Industrial Marketing Management*, **34** (February), 123–31.

Lepak, D., K. Smith and M. Taylor (2007), 'Value creation and value capture – a multilevel perspective', *Academy of Management Review*, **32** (1), 180–94.

Lilien, Gary L. and A. Wong (1984), 'An exploratory investigation of the structure of the buying center in the metalworking industry', *Journal of Marketing Research*, **21** (February), 1–11.

Lilien, Gary L. and G. Rangaswamy (1998), *Marketing Engineering: Computer-Assisted Marketing Analysis and Planning*, Reading, MA: Addison-Wesley.

Lilien, Gary L., Philip Kotler and K.S. Moorthy (1992), *Marketing Models*, Englewood Cliffs, NJ: Prentice Hall.

Lindgreen, Adam and F. Wynstra (2007), 'Value in business markets: what do we know? Where are we going?', *Industrial Marketing Management*, **35**, 180–94.

Marn, M.V. and R.L. Rosiello (1992), 'Managing price, gaining profit', *Harvard Business Review*, (September–October), 84–94.

Marn, M.V., Eric V. Roegner and C.C. Zawada (2003), 'Pricing new products', *McKinsey Quarterly*, (August).

Marn, M.V., Eric V. Roegner and C.C. Zawada (2004), *The Price Advantage*, Hoboken, NJ: John Wiley & Sons.

Marsh, G. (2000), 'International pricing – a market perspective', *Marketing Intelligence & Planning*, **18** (4), 200–205.

Maxwell, S. (2008), *The Price is Wrong: Understanding What Makes a Price seem Fair and the True Cost of Unfair Pricing*, Hoboken, NJ: John Wiley & Sons.

McCabe, D.L. (1987), 'Buying group structure: constriction at the top', *Journal of Marketing*, **51** (October), 89–98.

McClearn, Cameron C. (2004), 'When you've lost the power to set prices', *Across the Board*, (May/June), 37–42.

Mishra, B.K. and A. Prasad (2005), 'Delegating pricing decisions in competitive markets with symmetric and asymmetric information', *Marketing Science*, **24** (Summer), 490–97.

Mizik, N. and R. Jacobson (2003), 'Trading off between value creation and value appropriation: the financial implications of shifts in strategic emphasis', *Journal of Marketing*, **67** (January), 63–76.

Monroe, Kent B. (2003), *Pricing: Making Profitable Decisions*, 3rd edn, Boston: McGraw Hill-Irwin.

Monroe, Kent B. and A.J. Della Bitta (1978), 'Models for pricing decisions', *Journal of Marketing Research*, **15** (August), 413–28.

Monroe, Kent B. and Andris Z. Zoltners (1979), 'Pricing the product line during periods of scarcity', *Journal of Marketing*, **43** (Summer), 49–59.

Morgenroth, W.M. (1964), 'A method for understanding price determinants', *Journal of Marketing Research*, **1** (August), 17–26.

Moriarty, Robert T. and Robert E. Spekman (1984), 'An empirical investigation of the information sources used during the industrial buying process', *Journal of Marketing Research*, **21** (May), 137–47.

Morris, M.H. and R.G. Calantone (1990), 'Four components of effective pricing', *Industrial Marketing Management*, **19** (November), 321–9.

Morris, M.H. and D. Fuller (1989), 'Pricing an industrial service', *Industrial Marketing Management*, **18** (May), 139–46.

Morris, M.H. and M.L. Joyce (1988), 'How marketers evaluate price sensitivity', *Industrial Marketing Management*, **17**, 169–76.

Myers, M.B., S. Tamir Cavusgil and A. Diamantopoulos (2002), 'Antecedents of export pricing strategy: a conceptual framework and research propositions', *European Journal of Marketing*, **36** (1/2), 159–88.

Nagle, T.T. and George E. Cressman (2002), 'Don't just set prices, manage them', *Marketing Management*, (November/December), 29–33.

Nagle, T.T. and J.E. Hogan (2006), *The Strategy and Tactics of Pricing: A Guide to Growing More Profitably*, 4th edn, Upper Saddle River, NJ: Prentice Hall.

Nagle, T.T. and R.K. Holden (1995), *The Strategy and Tactics of Pricing: A Guide to Profitable Decision Making*, 2nd edn, Englewood Cliffs, NJ: Prentice Hall.

Noble, P.M. and T.S. Gruca (1999), 'Industrial pricing: theory and managerial practice', *Marketing Science*, **18** (3), 435–54.

Ohmae, K. (1982), *The Mind of the Strategist – The Art of Japanese Business*, New York: McGraw-Hill.

Ottley, G. (2002), 'Value-based pricing strategy in practice: the price menu – bringing structure to the uncertain world of pricing', *Journal of the Professional Pricing Society*, (Spring).

Oxenfeldt, A.R. (1960), 'Multi-stage approach to pricing', *Harvard Business Review*, (July/August), 125–33.

Oxenfeldt, A.R. (1973), 'A decision-making structure for price decisions', *Journal of Marketing*, **37** (January), 48–53.

Ozsomer, A. and G.E. Prussia (2000), 'Competing perspectives in international strategy: contingency and process models', *Journal of International Marketing*, **8** (1), 27–50.

Ozsomer, A. and B.L. Simonin (2004), 'Marketing program standardization: a cross-country exploration', *International Journal of Research in Marketing*, **21** (December), 397–419.

Patton, W.E., III, C.P. Puto and R.H. King (1986), 'Which buying decisions are made by individuals and not by groups?', *Industrial Marketing Management*, **15** (May), 129–38.

Pettigrew, A.M. (1993), 'The industrial purchasing decision as a political process', *European Journal of Marketing*, **9** (1), 4–19.

Rao, A., Mark Bergen and S. Davis (2000), 'How to fight a price war', *Harvard Business Review*, **78** (2), 107–16.

Rao, V. (1984), 'Pricing research in marketing: the state of the art', *Journal of Business*, **57** (1), S39–S60.

Rao, V.R. and B. Kartono (2009), 'Pricing objectives and strategies: a cross-country survey', in V. Rao (ed.), *Handbook of Pricing Research in Marketing*, Cheltenham, UK and Northampton, MA, USA: Edward Elgar.

Robinson, P.J., C.W. Faris and Y. Wind (1967), *Industrial Buying and Creative Marketing*, Boston, MA: Allyn and Bacon.

Ronchetto, J.R., Jr, Michael D. Hutt and P.H. Reingen (1989), 'Embedded influence patterns in organizational buying systems', *Journal of Marketing*, **53** (October), 51–62.

Ross, E.B. (1984), 'Making money with proactive pricing', *Harvard Business Review*, (November/December), 145–55.

Samiee, S. (1987), 'Pricing in marketing strategies of US- and foreign-based companies', *Journal of Business Research*, **15** (February), 17–30.

Samiee, S. and P. Anckar (1998), 'Currency choice in industrial pricing: a cross-national evaluation', *Journal of Marketing*, **62** (July), 112–27.

Schmalensee, R. (1982), 'Commodity bundling by single-product monopolies', *Journal of Law and Economics*, **25** (April), 67–71.

Schmalensee, R. (1984), 'Gaussian demand and commodity bundling', *Journal of Business*, **57** (1), S211–S230.

Schuh, A. (2000), 'Global standardization as a success formula for marketing in Central Eastern Europe?', *Journal of World Business*, **35** (2), 133–48.

Shapiro, B.P. and B.B. Jackson (1978), 'Industrial pricing to meet customer needs', *Harvard Business Review*, (November–December), 119–27.

Sheth, J.N. (1973), 'A model of industrial buying behavior', *Journal of Marketing*, **37** (October), 50–56.

Shi, L.H., S. Zou and S.T. Cavusgil (2004), 'A conceptual framework of global account management capabilities and firm performance', *International Business Review*, **13**, 539–53.

Shipley, D. and D. Jobber (2001), 'Integrative pricing via the pricing wheel', *Industrial Marketing Management*, **30**, 301–14.

Silk, A.J. and M.U. Kalwani (1982), 'Measuring influence in organizational purchase decisions', *Journal of Marketing Research*, **19** (May), 165–81.

Simintiras, A.C. and A.H. Thomas (1998), 'Cross-cultural sales negotiations', *International Marketing Review*, **11** (1), 10–28.

Skinner, R.C. (1970), 'The determination of selling prices', *Journal of Industrial Economics*, **18** (July), 201–17.

Smith, G.E. (2002), 'Segmenting B2B markets with economic value analysis', *Marketing Management*, (March/April), 35–9.

Smith, G.E. (2006), 'Leveraging profitability in low-margin markets', *Journal of Product & Brand Management*, **15** (6), 358–66.

Smith, G.E. and T.T. Nagle (1994), 'Financial analysis for profit-driven pricing', *Sloan Management Review*, **35** (Spring), 71–84.

Smith, G.E. and T.T. Nagle (2002), 'How much are customers willing to pay?', *Marketing Management*, (Winter), 20–25.

Smith, G.E. and T.T. Nagle (2005a), 'Pricing the differential', *Marketing Management*, (May/June), 28–32.

Smith, G.E. and T.T. Nagle (2005b), 'A question of value', *Marketing Management*, (July/August), 38–43.

Smith, R.D. and George E. Cressman Jr (2008), 'Share wars: finding new life in mature markets', *Journal of the Professional Pricing Society*, no. 3, 10–14.

Soderlund, M., M. Vilgon and J. Gunnarsson (2001), 'Predicting purchasing behavior on business-to-business markets', *European Journal of Marketing*, **33** (1/2), 168–81.

Sousa, C.M.P. and F. Bradley (2008), 'Antecedents of international pricing adaptation and export performance', *Journal of World Business*, **43** (July), 307–20.

Sousa, C.M.P. and F. Bradley (2009), 'Price adaptation in export markets', *European Journal of Marketing*, **43** (3/4), 438–58.

Spekman, Robert E. and L.W. Stern (1979), 'Environmental uncertainty and buying group structure: an empirical investigation', *Journal of Marketing*, **43** (Spring), 54–64.

Stephenson, P.R., W.L. Cron and Gary L. Frazier (1979), 'Delegating pricing authority to the sales force: the effects on sales and profit performance', *Journal of Marketing*, **43** (Spring), 21–8.

Stremersch, Stefan and Gerard J. Tellis (2002), 'Strategic bundling of products and prices: a new synthesis for marketing', *Journal of Marketing*, **66** (January), 55–72.

Tellis, Gerard J. (1986), 'Beyond the many faces of price: an integration of pricing strategies', *Journal of Marketing*, **50** (October), 146–60.

Theodosiou, M. and C. Katsikeas (2001), 'Factors influencing the degree of international pricing strategy standardization of multinational corporations', *Journal of International Marketing*, **9** (3), 1–18.

Udell, J.G. (1964), 'How important is pricing in competitive strategy?', *Journal of Marketing*, **28** (January), 44–8.

Ulaga, Wolfgang (2003), 'Capturing value creation in business relationships – a customer perspective', *Industrial Marketing Management*, **32**, 677–93.

Ulaga, Wolfgang and Andres Eggert (2006), 'Value-based differentiation in business markets – gaining and sustaining key supplier status', *Journal of Marketing*, **70** (January), 119–36.

Venkatesh, R. and V. Mahajan (2009), 'The design and pricing of bundles: a review of normative guidelines and practical approaches', in V. Rao (ed.), *Handbook of Pricing Research in Marketing*, Cheltenham, UK and Northampton, MA, USA: Edward Elgar.

Walker, Orville C., Jr, Gilbert A. Churchill Jr and N.M. Ford (1977), 'Motivation and performance in industrial selling: present knowledge and needed research', *Journal of Marketing Research*, **14** (May), 156–68.

Webster, F.E. and Y. Wind (1972a), 'A general model for understanding organizational buying behavior', *Journal of Marketing*, **36** (April), 12–19.

Webster, F.E. and Y. Wind (1972b), *Organizational Buying Behavior*, Chicago, IL: American Marketing Association.

Weekly, J.K. (1992), 'Pricing in foreign markets: pitfalls and opportunities', *Industrial Marketing Management*, **21** (May), 175–9.

Weinberg, C.B. (1975), 'An optimal commission plan for salesman's control over price', *Management Science*, **21** (April), 937–43.

Weinberg, C.B. (1978), 'Jointly optimal sales commissions for nonincome maximizing sales forces', *Management Science*, **24** (August), 1252–8.

Wentz, T.E. (1966), 'Realism in pricing analyses', *Journal of Marketing*, **30** (April), 19–26.

Wilson, D.T. (1971), 'Industrial buyers' decision making styles', *Journal of Marketing Research*, **13** (November), 433–6.

Wind, Y. (1990), 'Getting a read on market-defined value', *Journal of Pricing Management*, **1** (Winter), 41–9.

Wind, Y. and R. Cardozo (1971), 'Industrial market segmentation', *Industrial Marketing Management*, **3**, 53.

Winer, L. (1983), 'The effect of product sales quota on sales force productivity', *Journal of Marketing Research*, **10** (May), 180–83.

Yama, E. (2004), 'Purchasing hardball: playing price', *Business Horizons*, (September/October).

Yankelovich, D. and D. Meer (2006), 'Rediscovering market segmentation', *Harvard Business Review*, (February).

Yip, George S. (1992), *Total Global Strategy: Managing for Worldwide Competitive Advantage*, Englewood Cliffs, NJ: Prentice Hall.

Yuksel, U. and C. Sutton-Brady (2006), 'To delegate or not to delegate? That is the question of pricing authority', *Journal of Business & Economics Research*, **4** (2), 35–44.

Zou, S. and S. Tamir Cavusgil (2002), 'The GMS: a broad conceptualization of global marketing strategy and its effect on firm performance', *Journal of Marketing*, **66** (October), 40–56.

PART IV

INTER-FIRM RELATIONSHIPS IN B2B MARKETS

15 Evolution of buyer–seller relationships
Douglas Bowman

The importance of understanding how interorganizational buyer–seller relationships are created, persist, sometimes destroyed and occasionally re-established has been raised in multiple contexts. For many reasons, continuity is a focal construct of interest in business marketing contexts (Dwyer et al. 1987).

From the seller's perspective the relative cost of generating a new customer versus retaining a current customer (Fornell and Wernerfelt 1988) suggests that actions that promote continuity can be more profitable. As evidence, consider Kalwani and Narayandas's (1995) matched-pair analysis of manufacturing firms, which shows that compared with firms viewed as taking a transactional approach, those in long-term relationships achieve high profitability through means such as lower discretionary expenses. Kumar's (1999) matched-pair study of business services suppliers also reveals that compared with those focused on customer acquisition (i.e. transaction-oriented), firms involved in long-term client relationships typically achieve superior returns on their investment (ROI).

Customer retention is a key driver of customer lifetime value (Gupta and Zeithaml 2006), and the profit impact of underspending on retention can greatly exceed the profit impact of a comparable underspend on customer acquisition (Reinartz et al. 2005). In advertising agency–client relationships, the discontinuity in promotional strategy resulting from a change in agencies can weaken the brand image (Buchanan and Michell 1991). Relationships in distribution channels have been viewed as dyadic in nature (e.g. Anderson and Weitz 1989), and their continuity plays an important role in channel effectiveness. With an expectation of continuity, independent sales representatives in an industrial channel, for example, are more likely to assist the manufacturer in new product development, engage in activities such as customer education that have a longer-term pay-off and provide more informal market research (Anderson and Weitz 1989). Continuity may also influence elements of the marketing mix. Carlton (1986), in a study of purchases by *Fortune* 500 companies, reports a negative correlation between price rigidity and the length of the buyer–seller association; a shorter association means more rigid prices.

Continuity in buyer–supplier relationships is important in other ways too. Having long-term relationships with customers seems associated with a greater likelihood of survival for B2B firms, especially when products require high customization and relationship-specific knowledge (Hoetker et al. 2007). In business services, firms in long-term relationships are not as exposed to excessive price pressures over time as they maintain their gross margins (Kumar 1999). In computing support services, the length of the relationship also affects upgrade decisions (Bolton et al. 2008). Continuity may also influence the effectiveness of relational constructs, such as trust and commitment (Grayson and Ambler 1999).

Measuring the value of a business marketing relationship and developing strategies to maximize its value has been a topic of great research importance (e.g. Berger et al. 2002). Venkatesan and Kumar (2004) suggest methods to measure the customer lifetime value; Ramani and Kumar (2008) show how the relationship between buyers and sellers can be strengthened using an interaction orientation.

To date empirical research on buyer–seller relationships in business markets has largely concentrated on studying the status of an existing relationship, though, typically through cross-sectional investigations. Compared with longitudinal investigations, cross-sectional approaches have advantages, such as more cost effective data collection efforts. Many aspects of buyer–seller relationships in business markets evolve only slowly over time, in which cases cross-sectional studies are an acceptable approach. Considerably less attention has been devoted to the longitudinal aspects of relationships, though, so the objective of this chapter is to synthesize existing empirical research that examines the longitudinal aspects of buyer–seller relationships, with an eye to understanding how they form, evolve over time and sometimes break down.

CONTRACTUAL VERSUS NON-CONTRACTUAL RELATIONSHIPS

Although there are many ways to classify a business, according to how buyers and sellers interact, a commonly applied topology considers the type of relationship, contractual versus non-contractual, and transactions that are largely continuous or discrete (e.g. Schmittlein et al. 1987; Schmittlein and Peterson 1994). The distinction between contractual and non-contractual relationships is important when studying relationship continuity.

In a contractual relationship, the time when a customer becomes inactive or leaves a purchase relationship can be observed; in a non-contractual relationship, that time is not observable. In a contractual purchasing relationship, a formal contract might expire or, in the case of a continuous service such as a utility, the customer might explicitly discontinue one provider to switch to another. This distinction is important in explaining the behavior of sellers and their competitors over time as a function of when an account is up for review. It is also important in determining customer lifetime value (CLV) (Lilien et al. 2010). Figure 15.1 lists some example processes, in line with these two general conditions.

The challenges for studying longitudinal aspects of purchasing relationships differ when the opportunities for transactions are largely observable as distinct or periodic purchases versus continuous ones (i.e. when opportunities for transactions are largely unobservable to the researcher). In non-contractual situations, the strength and likely continuation of the relationship must be inferred. Much research in the business domain has focused on marketing activities and customer contacts that lead to enduring, collaborative relationships (Cardozo et al. 1987; McDonald et al. 1997; Weitz and Bradford 1999). Such relationships are typically costly (due to investments in customization) and entail risks (customer and/or supplier power or dependence) that present challenges to suppliers that hope to capture value (Ryals and Humphries 2007).

Type of Relationship with Customers

		Non-contractual	Contractual
Opportunities for Transactions	Continuous (or Unobserved)	• Supply purchases • Travel and lodging stays	• Corporate banking • Consulting services • Utilities
	Discrete (or Observed)	• Capital spending • Spot media buying	• Renewable service contracts • Auditing • Raw materials purchasing

Source: Adapted from Schmittlein et al. (1987, p. 16).

Figure 15.1   Relationships and transactions in business markets

APPROACHES TO STUDYING CONTINUITY IN A BUYER–SELLER RELATIONSHIP

To date the dominant approach for studying buyer–seller relationships is cross-sectional investigations; considerably less attention has been devoted to longitudinal aspects of relationships. A primary reason for this trend is certainly the challenge of obtaining longitudinal data. Thus though researchers have investigated aspects of the continuity of buyer–seller relationships in business markets, the nature of the data examined has influenced the insights and conclusions obtained to date.

It is useful to classify prior research into the continuity of buyer–seller relationships according to the nature of the data examined. Variables describing the underlying process can be broadly characterized as either unobservable attitudes, such as trust and commitment that are important antecedents of behavior, or observable characteristics typically associated with demographics (e.g. firm size) or the structure of the market (e.g. number of competitors). In contractual situations continuity can be measured with variables that describe future intentions or actual observed behavior, such as the renewal or non-renewal of a purchasing agreement. In non-contractual situations, continuity can be measured with the future intentions variables, but actual breakdown can be inferred only from patterns gleaned from the history of transactions.

Figure 15.2 provides a representative sample of prior research that examines the continuity of buyer–seller relationships in business markets, distinguished by the nature of the data examined. The rows reveal three broad classifications of the dependent variable used to describe continuity: (1) an attitude or behavioral intention from a cross-sectional investigation, (2) an observed binary continue–drop (switch–no-switch) behavior from a single-period (or two-period) investigation and (3) an observed continue–drop (switch–no-switch) behavior from a multiperiod study. No multiperiod studies use an attitude or behavioral intention as the terminal variable. The columns represent two broad characterizations of the focal explanatory variables: observable demographics, structural

Unobservable (attitude or intention)		Anderson and Weitz (1989); Gensch (1984); Jap and Anderson (2003); Morgan and Hunt (1994)
Switch–No Switch (binary event)	Bolton et al. (2006); Buchanan and Michell (1991); Seabright et al. (1992)	Doyle et al. (1980); Heide and Weiss (1995); Henke (1995)
Switch–No Switch (duration process)	Baker et al. (1998); Davies and Prince (1999); Levinthal and Fichman (1988)	

Dependent Variable

Observable (structural; service operations)　　　Subjective (perceptions; satisfaction or assessments of performance)

Focal Explanatory Variables

Figure 15.2   Characterizing studies of customer retention in business markets

descriptors of the marketplace or service operations versus subjective perceptions or assessments of relationship performance.

The top right cell of Figure 15.2 is by far the dominant approach to studying relationship continuity in business marketing contexts. Many studies have examined assumed correlates of future behavior, such as the effectiveness or expected continuity (behavioral intentions) of a B2B relationship. Examples include the supplier preference studied by Gensch (1984), likelihood of termination investigated by Anderson and Weitz (1989), expectations of continuity considered by Jap and Anderson (2003) and propensity to leave as studied by Morgan and Hunt (1994). Hypothesis testing relies on (cross-sectional) survey data, and the focal explanatory variables of interest are typically customer perceptions or assessments of vendor performance.

Longitudinal aspects can be investigated to some extent by classifying relationships a priori into different relationship stages (e.g. early, growth, mature), then comparing across these predefined groupings, as Fam and Waller (2008), Jap and Anderson (2007), Jap and Ganesan (2000) and Grayson and Ambler (1999) do. Each article cleverly studies the evolution of a relationship using cross-sectional data and comparing relationships at various stages of the relationship life cycle. A key finding by Jap and Ganesan shows that as many as 30 per cent of relationships do not follow a typical sequence; many relationships lapse back to earlier stages or rebuild and restart from a later phase over a multiyear period.

Research examining observed supplier dropping or switching behavior has studied either binary, switch–no-switch events in a pre-established relationship (e.g. Bolton et al. 2006;

Buchanan and Michell 1991; Heide and Weiss 1995; Henke 1995; Seabright et al. 1992) or the entire duration of a relationship (e.g. Baker et al. 1998; Davies and Prince 1999; Levinthal and Fichman 1988). The former are cross-sectional analyses, which can include explanatory variables that describe prior periods. For example Henke (1995) surveys clients using criteria for evaluating advertising agencies and satisfaction with the current agency; using data from a second survey one year later, Henke compares those who switched agencies with those who had not. Jap (1999) relates measures of the processes and actions taken to 'expand the pie' over a year to measures of outcomes in the next year.

Because business customer–supplier relationships often last years, retrospectively collecting data on variables that describe the process that leads to an observable switch–no-switch decision is challenging. The bottom left cell of Figure 15.2 contains a representative sample of studies that address the entire duration of a buyer–seller relationship. To date, such studies in business contexts have relied primarily on archival data sources, and thus explanatory variables describing past periods are limited to structural metrics such as firm size (e.g. Baker et al. 1998) or a vendor's service operations records (e.g. Bolton et al. 2006). Variables that describe a customer's perceptions or assessments of vendor performance over time have not been considered, because doing so would require either an extensive primary data collection over a period of years or access to firms' past records in situations in which they collected longitudinal data on the same measures.

Finally, some studies focus on a business marketing setting in which the seller, using transaction data, can effectively target the right buyer with the right product/service at the right time (e.g. Kumar et al. 2006, 2008).

CONTINUITY AND RELATIONSHIP ASSETS

Various plausible theoretical mechanisms that relate to the continuity (or breakdown) of a customer–supplier relationship in business markets have been advanced. When primary data are available, variables describing the mechanisms can be developed and measures collected. When data are collected retrospectively, usually in studies of the full duration of a relationship, a surrogate such as age is typically employed. For mechanisms that evolve over time, three general effects have been discussed.

First, research considers factors such as the accumulation of knowledge, 'internal friction' to change and the quality of external ties, whose ability to shield a relationship from negative outcomes increases monotonically with age. Assets specific to a relationship accrue over time, so longer-lasting relationships tend to persist. Increased switching costs are often cited as examples. Over time suppliers may come to better understand a buyer's needs or become better at proactively anticipating changes in a buyer's needs or understanding the intricacies of its decision-making processes. Interpersonal relationships involving boundary-spanning personnel may also develop.

Second, initial 'endowments', such as favorable prior beliefs, goodwill, benefit of the doubt and the need to justify a recent decision, can shield a relationship from breakdown in its early stages and attenuate over time (Levinthal and Fichman 1988). An initial stock of relationship assets, together with a relatively limited time in which to gather the information needed to make a rational decision, means that an initial 'honeymoon' period exists during which the relationship is shielded from negative outcomes. New buyer–seller relationships may begin with more forgiveness for destabilizing issues than they would at other times. A customer's internal organization can also make it difficult to dissolve a relationship with a buyer shortly after its initiation, especially if the decision-making unit went through an elaborate process to justify its initiation internally.

Third, some factors over time serve to destabilize and ultimately destroy a relationship from within. Collectively termed the 'dark side' (Grayson and Ambler 1999) of business relationships, these factors include opportunism by sellers, loss of objectivity and rising customer expectations (Moorman et al. 1992). Over time liabilities that can destabilize a buyer–seller relationship accrue. Buyers may come to demand increasing levels of service without accompanying pricing flexibility (Narayandas 2002). Sellers may use guile in their efforts to achieve a greater share of the relationship's benefits than previously agreed.

Reinartz and Kumar (2003) offer a set of many drivers that affect relationship length. Readers should refer to that source for a full list.

FACTORS AFFECTING CONTINUITY: EMPIRICALLY TESTED

Table 15.1 presents a sample of published research that has empirically investigated the continuity of a buyer–seller relationship in business markets, classified according to the (1) dependent process studied; (2) underlying theoretical process to explain continuity, if any; (3) methodology and data; and (4) sample findings. A striking aspect of this sampling is the narrowness of the set of contexts examined to date. Most studies are set in one of three contexts: auditing services, advertising services or distribution channels. This focus is probably driven by data availability. In auditing and advertising service industries, supplier changes are in the public domain, as part of publicly traded firms' annual reports (auditing) or industry trade publications (advertising). Trade associations of distributors in industries such as electronics components and chemicals, as well as firms with large distributor bases, have a long track record of cooperating with scholarly researchers on issues of mutual interest.

FACTORS PROPOSED TO AFFECT CONTINUITY, WITH LITTLE EMPIRICAL TESTING

Various factors might affect the continuity of buyer–seller relationship in business marketing contexts, but they have yet to be examined empirically and in a systematic way. For example Anderson et al. (2009) cite three factors that lead to unstable inter-organizational relationships in a buyer–reseller context. First, drawing on consulting work, they argue that legitimate cross-purposes contribute to relationship instability. Legitimate cross-purposes indicate that the supplier and reseller firms rely on different profit models that sometimes are at odds. Suppliers profit through economies of scale by producing and selling large quantities of a limited number of products. They prefer resellers to do the same. Resellers instead profit from economies of scope and from providing unique bundles or solutions that combine relatively small quantities of input from a variety of sources.

Table 15.1 Sample of empirical studies of continuity of buyer–seller relationships in business markets

Study	Dependent Process	Theoretical Perspective	Method/Data	Sample Finding
Doyle et al. (1980); advertising services	Observed switching	—	Means; match firm that switched agency with agency's perceptions	Breakdown is a process of creeping disenchantment, preceded by clear signals of vulnerability.
Gensch (1984); electrical generators	Switchable versus non-switchable, derived from preference rankings and intentions	—	Logit (cross-sectional)	Allocating resources from non-switchable to switchable customers increases sales.
Levinthal and Fichman (1988); auditing services	Observed switching	Social exchange; transaction cost	Hazard rate (parametric); 883 dyads over 13-year period	Age dependence is non-monotonic. Likelihood of failure declines with task complexity (buyer's size).
Anderson and Weitz (1989); channels (electronics)	Behavioral intentions: manufacturer expectation of continuity	Social exchange; negotiation	3SLS (cross-sectional); survey of 95 manufacturers from 690 dyads	Stability is enhanced by avoiding a reputation for switching, raising the stakes, and cultivating trust.
Buchanan and Michell (1991); advertising services	Observed switching	—	Logistic regression; 1222 UK accounts	Structural factors (e.g. size) explain stability.
Seabright et al. (1992); auditing services	Observed switching/non-switching	Social exchange; transaction cost	Logit (cross-sectional); 170 switchers matched with 170 non-switchers	Likelihood of dissolution increases with change in resource fit but decreases with presence of individual attachment.
Weiss and Anderson (1992); channels (electronics)	Behavioral intentions: manufacturer intention to integrate selling function	Organization ecology; transaction cost	3SLS (cross-sectional); survey of 258 manufacturers	Intention to integrate is impeded by perceptions of high switching costs, even when incentives to change are significant.
Moorman et al. (1992); marketing research services	Use of market research	Relationship marketing	OLS (cross-sectional); 84–779 dyads	Trust and perceived quality are most important in determining use.

Table 15.1 (continued)

Study	Dependent Process	Theoretical Perspective	Method/Data	Sample Finding
Heide and Weiss (1995); computer hardware	Consideration; new or existing vendor	Uncertainty; switching costs; buying process	Nested logit (workstation purchase); survey of 215 buyers	Probability of switching, given consideration, is higher for less experienced firms and more centralized firms and lower with rapid change and high switching costs.
Henke (1995); advertising services	Observed switching	—	Compare means (survey) for firms switching one year after survey	Initial focus on creative potential shifts to a focus on performance and service skills.
Baker et al. (1998); advertising services	Observed switching	Sociology network ties	H=hazard rate (parametric); 313 dyads over 10-year period	Competition, power, and institutional forces undermine relationships.
Keep et al. (1998); four industries	Relationship development	—	Qualitative; four case studies	Economic growth, information asymmetry, entry barriers, dependence asymmetry, and economies of scale affect relationship development.
Davies and Prince (1999); advertising services	Observed switching	—	Hazard rate (parametric); 313 dyads over 10-year period	Greater account stability is associated with larger agency size in both the US and UK.
Grayson and Ambler (1999); advertising services	Perceived commitment	Relationship marketing	SEM (cross-sectional); short-term versus with long-term dyads	Long-term relationships have a negative effect on service use, which dampens the impact of trust.
Skarmeas et al. (2002); channels	Perceived commitment	Transaction cost	SEM (survey); 216 distributors	Transaction-specific investments and opportunism affect commitment.
Farley et al. (2004); financial services	Choosing and upgrading	—	Two-stage process: selection and being among the top three	Marketing variables (price, product, promotion) have a greater impact in the US than the UK.

Source	Focal construct	Theoretical perspective	Methodology	Key findings
Narayandas and Rangan (2004); frequently purchased components, mature markets	Relationship development	—	Qualitative; three field case studies	Weak initial power in a relationship can be countered over time through interpersonal trust.
Bolton et al. (2006); technology services	Upgrade	Relationship marketing	Over 2000 service contracts	Satisfaction, service quality and price influence the decision to upgrade.
Jap and Anderson (2007); channels (chemicals)	Relationship stage (four categories)	Life cycle theory	Compare means (survey); cross-sectional; 4033 resellers	Relationship properties supporting expansion are highest in the build-up stage.
Palmatier et al. (2007); channels	Growth; financial performance; cooperation	Compares four theoretical perspectives	SEM (survey); 4 years 396 customers of a distributor	Trust and commitment are important; also need to account for relationship-specific investments.
Fam and Waller (2008); advertising services	Relationship stage (four categories)	—	Compare means (survey); cross-sectional; 82 advertisers	Lack of closeness, bonding and client dependence drive relationship failure.
Gedeon et al. (2009); various industries	Observed dissolution	—	Case studies; 11	Personal relationships between individuals shield a relationship from dissolution.
Hansen (2009); suppliers of Walmart	Cooperation	Service-dominant logic	Qualitative	As relationships get more cooperative, outcomes include co-managed inventory.
Sánchez et al. (2010); channels	Commitment	Relationship marketing	SEQ (survey); 181 manufacturers	Commitment is an antecedent of value creation.

Secondly, change is in many ways perpetual, so evolution in a marketplace may dramatically and unexpectedly alter the goals and resources of business marketing partners. Anderson et al. (2009) argue that as mutual self-interests and complementary resources diverge more and more, they prompt counterproductive actions that threaten the continued prosperity of a partnership. For example the Internet may affect long-standing relationships by providing a viable alternative way for producers to sell directly to customers or commoditize many offerings, which might prompt resellers to develop private-label products.

Thirdly, opportunism, defined as self-interest seeking with guile, may destabilize a relationship. One party may resort to misleading or otherwise devious behavior to claim a greater share of benefits than is warranted by the existing agreements.

IMPLICATIONS FOR PRACTICE

Unlike research by practitioners, which seeks knowledge and understanding that is unique to its context, provides an advantage over competition and is proprietary, scholarly research seeks generalizable findings. Despite many studies of behavioral intentions, the number of published studies of an observed breakdown of a buyer–seller relationship is modest. If findings from consumer contexts hold in business markets, then the link between intentions and behaviors is not clear (Mittal and Kamakura 2001).

The generalizable findings to date from research investigating the continuity of a buyer–seller relationship in business markets tend to be directional. The limited number of studies examining observed continuity and breakdown, and the limited set of industry contexts, makes it difficult to quantify the size of an effect. That said, there is reasonable evidence to support some generalizations. Firm size and trust are associated with continuity; competition, power and reduced usage contribute to increased likelihood of breakdown. Table 15.2 summarizes factors associated with continuity versus breakdown in prior empirical studies.

RESEARCH OPPORTUNITIES

Research seeking to understand the evolution of consumer preferences has benefited from the development of panel data sets (static panels) by researchers and panel data collected for commercial purposes that is made available to researchers. Data collected through transaction processing systems have the advantage of being relatively less intrusive and ensure that all transactions in the system are captured. Diary panels (e.g. Heilman et al. 2000) capture transactions through all channels and can include both behavioral and attitudinal measures. To date panel data studies of consumers have almost exclusively occurred in the domain of frequently purchased consumer goods. Advantages of this focus include the abilities to observe many purchase occasions within a relatively short observation window, to collapse the choice set into a manageable number of alternatives and to include acceptable measures of the important elements of the marketing mix.

As panel data sets in business markets develop and become available from commercial

Table 15.2 Determinants of continuity and switching in prior literature

	Determinants of Continuity			Determinants of Switching		
Relevant Literature	Decreases with age	Constant with age	Increasing with age	Decreases with age	Constant with age	Increasing with age
Perceptual/Decision Processes	• Initial relationship assets (i.e. favorable prior beliefs, benefit of doubt) • Initial sunk costs in hiring a new supplier loom large • Individual decision-maker's reluctance to admit a bad decision	• Perceptions of switching costs	• Perceptions of switching costs		• Power imbalance • Buyer prone to risk taking • Change in buyer's resource requirements	• Less uncertainty about any lack of fit between organizations
Industrial Organization/Structural/Institutional	• Time to implement a new strategy	• Size of buyer organization • Size of seller organization • Effort/resources to implement new strategy • Organizational bureaucracy	• Investments in relationship-specific assets • Difficulty of task		• Industry	

Table 15.2 (continued)

	Determinants of Continuity	Determinants of Switching
Social Exchange/ Relational	• Initial relationship assets (i.e. initial trust)	• Trust • Relationship-specific knowledge • Individual attachment, continuity of buyer–seller interface personnel	• Early 'shakeout' period of conflict and influence attempts
Strategic	• Desire not to establish a reputation for switching • Time to gather information to make a rational decision	• Different decision processes for hiring a new supplier versus straight rebuy	• Reputation for switching • Experience with substitution • Buyer competes using low cost versus differentiation strategy • Buyer under intense competitive pressure

288

research firms, researchers should pursue answers to several important questions regarding relationship continuity, such as:

- Longitudinal investigations that link the evolution of buyer perceptions, attitudes and assessments of supplier performance to observed purchasing behavior and relationship continuity.
- The relative effect of relationship 'assets' that shield relations from negative outcomes, increase the likelihood of a breakdown (i.e. the 'dark side') or start high and attenuate over time.
- The effects of the industry context. In business services, for example, longitudinal investigations should address continuity in business services contexts outside financial auditing and advertising services.
- Longitudinal studies of continuity that account for the development of the relationship prior to the initially observed transaction or contract, including, for example, whether the supplier entered using a foot-in-the-door product (Narayandas 2002) or a fuller portfolio of product and service offerings.
- The extent to which age dependence is really due to researchers' neglect of important variables that affect continuity.
- Longitudinal studies at the transaction level. Large-scale online marketplaces may provide a way around significant data collection challenges. Of course the need for comparable units of analysis across transactions still exists.
- Longitudinal studies of the value of references, following from its origin through to any resulting behavioral changes.

The importance of gathering results from longitudinal investigations should not be overlooked. Research has often traded off the richness of measures describing an underlying process that might be demanded of a cross-sectional investigation for a narrower set of explanatory variables in a longitudinal study. For example in the pharmaceutical industry, studies of the longitudinal prescribing behavior of physicians to date have studied physician data without accounting for important patient characteristics, such as the characteristics of the patient's pharmaceutical benefit plan.

CONCLUSION

Srivastava et al. (1999) argue that customer relationship management, along with product development management and supply chain management, is a core business process. They describe customer relationship management as the process that 'addresses all aspects of customers, creating customer knowledge, building customer relationships, and shaping customer perceptions of the organization and its products' (Srivastava et al. 1999, p. 169). This chapter has synthesized prior research that empirically examines the longitudinal aspects of a customer–supplier relationship in business marketing.

The efforts to study the dynamics of buyer–seller relationships through longitudinal investigations have been relatively modest. Empirical research on buyer–seller relationships has largely concentrated on studying the status of an existing relationship, typically through cross-sectional analyses. Considerably less attention has been devoted to longitudinal aspects.

The objective of this chapter has been to synthesize existing empirical research that examines longitudinal aspects of buyer–seller relationships, with an eye to understanding how they evolve over time and thereby result in continuity versus dissolution.

REFERENCES

Anderson, Erin and Barton Weitz (1989), 'Determinants of continuity in conventional industrial channel dyads', *Marketing Science*, **8** (4), 310–23.

Anderson, James C., James A. Narus and Das Narayandas (2009), *Business Market Management: Understanding, Creating, and Delivering Value*, 3rd edn, Englewood Cliffs, NJ: Prentice Hall.

Baker, Wayne E., Robert R. Faulkner and Gene A. Fisher (1998), 'Hazards of the market: the continuity and dissolution of interorganizational market relationships', *American Sociological Review*, **63** (2), 147–77.

Berger, Paul D., Ruth N. Bolton, Douglas Bowman, Elten Briggs, V. Kumar, A. Parasuraman and Creed Terry (2002), 'Marketing actions and the value of customer assets: a framework for customer asset management', *Journal of Service Research*, **5**, 39–54.

Bolton, Ruth N., Katherine N. Lemon and Michael D. Bramlett (2006), 'The effect of service experiences over time on a supplier's retention of business customers', *Management Science*, **52** (12), 1811–23.

Bolton, Ruth N., Katherine N. Lemon and Peter C. Verhoef (2008), 'Expanding business-to-business customer relationships: modeling the customer's upgrade decision', *Journal of Marketing*, **72** (1), 46–64.

Buchanan, Bruce and Paul C. Michell (1991), 'Using structural factors to assess the risk of failure in agency–client relations', *Journal of Advertising Research*, **31** (4), 688–75.

Cardozo, Richard N., Shannon H. Shipp and Kenneth J. Roering (1987), 'Implementing new business-to-business selling methods', *Journal of Personal Selling & Sales Management*, **7** (2), 17–26.

Carlton, Dennis W. (1986), 'The rigidity of prices', *American Economic Review*, **76** (4), 637–58.

Davies, Mark and Mel Prince (1999), 'Examining the longevity of new agency accounts: a comparative study of US and UK advertising experiences', *Journal of Advertising*, **28** (4), 75–89.

Doyle, Peter, Marcel Corstjens and Paul C. Michell (1980), 'Signals of vulnerability in agency–client relationships', *Journal of Marketing*, **44** (4), 18–23.

Dwyer, F. Robert, Paul H. Schurr and Sejo Oh (1987), 'Developing buyer–seller relationships', *Journal of Marketing*, **51** (1), 11–27.

Fam, Kim-Shyan and David S. Waller (2008), 'Agency–client relationship factors across life-cycle stages', *Journal of Relationship Marketing*, **7** (2), 217–36.

Farley, John U., Andrew F. Hayes and Praveen K. Kopalle (2004), 'Choosing and upgrading financial services dealers in the US and UK', *International Journal of Research in Marketing*, **21** (4), 359–75.

Fornell, Claes and Berger Wernerfelt (1988), 'A model for customer complaint management', *Marketing Science*, **7** (3), 287–98.

Gedeon, Joanna-Maria, Andrew Fearne and Nigel Poole (2009), 'The role of inter-personal relationships in the dissolution of business relationships', *Journal of Business & Industrial Marketing*, **24** (3/4), 218–26.

Gensch, Dennis H. (1984), 'Targeting the switchable industrial customer', *Marketing Science*, **3** (1), 41–54.

Grayson, Kent and Tim Ambler (1999), 'The dark side of long-term relationships in marketing services', *Journal of Marketing Research*, **36** (1), 132–41.

Gupta, Sunil and Valarie Zeithaml (2006), 'Customer metrics and their impact on financial performance', *Marketing Science*, **25** (6), 718–41.

Hansen, Jared M. (2009), 'The evolution of buyer–supplier relationships: an historical industry approach', *Journal of Business & Industrial Marketing*, **24** (3/4), 227–36.

Heide, Jan B. and Alan M. Weiss (1995), 'Vendor consideration and switching behavior for buyers in high-technology markets', *Journal of Marketing*, **59** (3), 30–43.

Heilman, Carrie M., Douglas Bowman and Gordon P. Wright (2000), 'The evolution of brand preferences and choice behaviors of consumers in a new market', *Journal of Marketing Research*, **37** (2), 139–55.

Henke, Lucy L. (1995), 'A longitudinal analysis of the ad agency–client relationship', *Journal of Advertising Research*, **35** (2), 24–30.

Hoetker, Glenn, Anand Swaminathan and Will Mitchell (2007), 'Modularity and the impact of buyer–supplier relationships on the survival of suppliers', *Management Science*, **53** (2), 178–91.

Jap, Sandy D. (1999), '"Pie-expansion" efforts: collaboration processes in buyer–supplier relationships', *Journal of Marketing Research*, **36** (4), 461–75.

Jap, Sandy D. and Erin Anderson (2003), 'Safeguarding interorganizational performance and continuity under ex post opportunism', *Management Science*, **49** (12), 1684–701.

Jap, Sandy D. and Erin Anderson (2007), 'Testing a life-cycle theory of cooperative interorganizational relationships: movement across stages and performance', *Management Science*, **53** (2), 260–75.

Jap, Sandy D. and Shankar Ganesan (2000), 'Control mechanisms and the relationship life cycle: implications for safeguarding specific investments and developing commitment', *Journal of Marketing Research*, **37** (2), 227–45.

Kalwani, Manohar U. and Narakesari Narayandas (1995), 'Long-term manufacturing–supplier relationships: do they pay off for supplier firms?', *Journal of Marketing*, **59** (1), 1–16.

Keep, William W., Stanley C. Hollander and Roger Dickinson (1998), 'Forces impinging on long-term business-to-business relationships in the United States: an historical perspective', *Journal of Marketing*, **62** (2), 31–45.

Kumar, Piyush (1999), 'The impact of long-term client relationships on the performance of business service firms', *Journal of Service Research*, **2** (1), 4–18.

Kumar, V., Rajkumar Venkatesan and Werner Reinartz (2006), 'Knowing what to sell, when to whom', *Harvard Business Review*, (March), 131–7.

Kumar, V., Rajkumar Venkatesan and Werner Reinartz (2008), 'Performance implications of adopting a customer-focused sales campaign', *Journal of Marketing*, **72** (5), 50–68.

Levinthal, Daniel A. and Mark Fichman (1988), 'Dynamics of interorganizational attachments: auditor–client relationships', *Administrative Science Quarterly*, **33** (3), 345–69.

Lilien, Gary L., Rajdeep Grewal, Douglas Bowman, M. Ding, Abbie Griffin, V. Kumar, Das Narayandas, Renana Peres, Raji Srinivasan and Qiong Wang (2010), 'Calculating, creating, and claiming value in business markets: status and research agenda', *Marketing Letters*, **21** (3), 287–99.

Mittal, Vikas and Wagner A. Kamakura (2001), 'Satisfaction, repurchase intent, and repurchase behavior: investigating the moderating effect of customer characteristics', *Journal of Marketing Research*, **38** (1), 131–42.

McDonald, Malcolm, Tony Millman and Beth Rogers (1997), 'Key account management: theory, practice and challenges', *Journal of Marketing Management*, **13** (8), 737–57.

Moorman, Christine, Gerald Zaltman and Rohit Deshpandé (1992), 'Relationships between providers and users of market research: the dynamics of trust within and between organizations', *Journal of Marketing Research*, **29** (3), 314–28.

Morgan, Robert M. and Shelby D. Hunt (1994), 'The commitment-trust theory of relationship marketing', *Journal of Marketing*, **58** (3), 20–38.

Narayandas, Das (2002), 'Note on customer management', Harvard Business School Publishing, no.502073.

Narayandas, Das and V. Kasturi Rangan (2004), 'Building and sustaining buyer–seller relationships in mature industrial markets', *Journal of Marketing*, **68** (3), 63–77.

Palmatier, Robert W., Rajiv P. Dant and Dhruv Grewal (2007), 'A comparative longitudinal analysis of theoretical perspectives of interorganizational relationship performance', *Journal of Marketing*, **71** (4), 172–94.

Ramani, Girish and V. Kumar (2008), 'Interaction orientation and firm performance', *Journal of Marketing*, **72** (1), 27–45.

Reinartz, Werner and V. Kumar (2003), 'The impact of customer relationship characteristics on profitable lifetime duration', *Journal of Marketing*, **67** (1), 77–99.

Reinartz, Werner, Jacquelyn S. Thomas and V. Kumar (2005), 'Balancing acquisition and retention resources to maximize customer profitability', *Journal of Marketing*, **69** (1), 63–79.

Ryals, Lynette J. and Andrew S. Humphries (2007), 'Managing key business-to-business relationships: what marketing can learn from supply chain management', *Journal of Service Research*, **9** (4), 312–26.

Sánchez, José Angel López, Maria Leticia Santos Vijande and Juan Antonio Trespalacios Gutiérrez (2010), 'The impact of relational variables on value creation in buyer–seller business relationships', *Journal of Business-to-Business Marketing*, **17** (1), 62–94.

Schmittlein, David C. and Robert A. Peterson (1994), 'Customer base analysis: an industrial purchase process application', *Marketing Science*, **13** (1), 41–67.

Schmittlein, David C., Donald G. Morrison and Richard Colombo (1987), 'Counting your customers: who they are and what will they do next?', *Management Science*, **33** (1), 1–24.

Seabright, Mark A., Danial A. Levinthal and Mark Fichman (1992), 'Role of individual attachments in the dissolution of interorganizational relationships', *Academy of Management Journal*, **35** (1), 122–60.

Skarmeas, Dionisis, Constantine S. Katsikeas and Bodo B. Schlegelmilch (2002), 'Drivers of commitment and its impact on performance in cross-cultural buyer–seller relationships: the importer's perspective', *Journal of International Business Studies*, **33** (4), 757–83.

Srivastava, Rajendra K., Tasadduq A. Shervani and Liam Fahey (1999), 'Marketing, business processes, and shareholder value: an organizationally embedded view of marketing activities and the discipline of marketing', *Journal of Marketing*, **63** (Special Issue), 168–79.

Venkatesan, Rajkumar and V. Kumar (2004), 'A customer lifetime value framework for customer selection and resource allocation strategy', *Journal of Marketing*, **68** (4), 106–25.

Weiss, Alan M. and Erin Anderson (1992), 'Converting from independent to employee salesforces: the role of perceived switching costs', *Journal of Marketing Research*, **29** (1), 101–15.

Weitz, Barton A. and Kevin D. Bradford (1999), 'Personal selling and sales management: a relationship marketing perspective', *Journal of the Academy of Marketing Science*, **27** (2), 241–54.

16 Relationship marketing
Joshua T. Beck and Robert W. Palmatier

Relationship marketing (RM), in both business practice and academic research, has received ever increasing attention, in line with the belief that strong buyer–seller relationships enhance exchange performance (Palmatier et al. 2006b). Although relationships exist in both B2B and B2C exchanges, the interdependent nature of B2B trade makes RM in this sphere most critical. As the number of exchange partners increases, as the transactions become faster paced and as the situation grows more uncertain, relationships become increasingly important as means to secure business partners and protect against business risk.

In support of this notion most developed countries have undergone dramatic shifts toward service economies; services now account for more than 80 per cent of US gross domestic product (Libai et al. 2009). Compared with products, services are less tangible, less consistent, more perishable and harder to evaluate, and they often require co-production (Zeithaml et al. 1985). Despite the difficulties associated with delivering and assessing services, B2B firms increasingly incorporate them into their value proposition to stabilize their cash flows (Lohr 2010). Xerox, Hewlett-Packard, IBM and Cisco all have recently announced the acquisition or expansion of their service offerings (Lohr 2010). Because of the complexities associated with services, strong relationships that maximize trust and knowledge transfer are integral to the success of this type of offering.

At the same time, advances in technology have pushed the use of relationship marketing. Many technology-supported initiatives, such as total quality management, demand close relationships with suppliers and rapid product development; therefore firms exhibit increasing desire to build persistent bonds with both suppliers and various other business partners (Sheth and Parvatiyar 2000). Similarly improvements in communication and logistics technologies enable producers and customers to interact directly, even at great distances. Customers demand trust and confidence, as can be developed in a relational-based exchange, before they will transact in such a global bazaar (Sheth and Parvatiyar 2000).

A final, critical trend that reinforces the role of relationships in exchange is the increase in both global competition and customer churn rates, largely as a result of the visibility of prices for commodity products and services worldwide. Firms that provide such products often initiate customer retention and loyalty programs to compete effectively, whereas traditional promotional expenditures, such as advertising, may prove less useful. A recent meta-analysis reveals that investments in salespeople provide greater returns than advertising expenditures, especially in the early stages of an offering's life cycle (Albers et al. 2008; 2010), which reflects the crucial role of relationships in exchange.

This chapter provides a framework for understanding relationship marketing. To help managers and researchers understand the nature of business relationships, we provide a review of the mechanisms that underlie the relationship process. We also highlight the importance of analyzing the multiple dyadic ties between firms at an aggregate level to appreciate the complementary nature of various types of relationships and their impact on performance. Next we offer insights into the various drivers of inter-firm relationships and connect these relationships to previously measured performance-related outcomes. We also provide a brief discussion of the moderators that leverage the effectiveness of relationships. As a conclusion this chapter suggests directions for additional research; to begin, though, we issue a formal definition of relationship marketing.

DEFINITION

When the American Marketing Association revised its definition of marketing in 2004 (Palmatier 2008b), it highlighted that 'marketing is an organizational function and a set of processes for creating, communicating, and delivering value to customers and for *managing customer relationships* in ways that benefit the organization and its stakeholders' (emphasis added). Other prominent marketing definitions delineate three predominant aspects of relationship marketing (Gronroos 1997; Sheth and Parvatiyar 2000):

1. Engagement activities across stages of the relationship life cycle. Marketing activities and exchange characteristics systematically vary in a dynamic process over time (Dwyer et al. 1987).
2. Target or scope of relationship marketing activities. Some definitions focus on customer relationships; others include links to any constituent (e.g. internal departments, competitors, customers, suppliers).
3. Locus of benefits derived from relationship marketing activities. To be successful, they must offer value to both the seller and the buyer in a dyad.

We rely on and extend these perspectives to propose the following definition:

> Relationship marketing (RM) is the process of identifying, developing, maintaining and terminating relational exchanges with the purpose of enhancing performance (see also Palmatier 2008b).

THEORETICAL UNDERPINNINGS OF RELATIONSHIP MARKETING

To fully appreciate how partners can build, manage and leverage relationships to effect desirable outcomes, we must understand the mechanisms underlying the relational process. Thus we provide a foundation, as illustrated in Figure 16.1, regarding how relationships operate in dyadic exchanges and how ties between firms reflect an aggregation of those dyadic bonds.

Dyadic Relational Constructs

As any long-married couple might assert, the hallmark of a successful relationship is the level of commitment and trust that exists between partners. In their seminal piece on RM, Morgan and Hunt (1994) show that commitment and trust, separate from

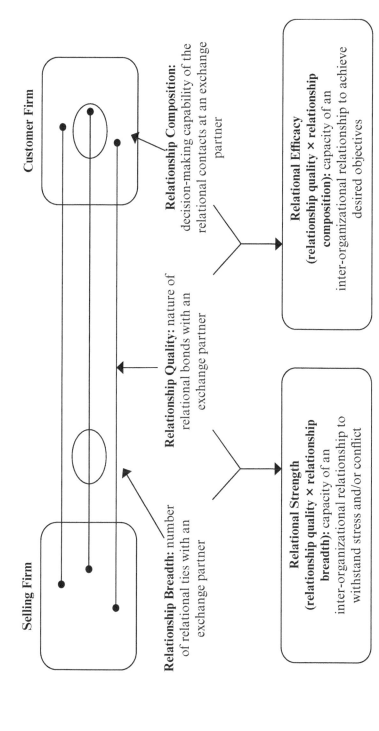

Customer Firm

Selling Firm

Relationship Composition: decision-making capability of the relational contacts at an exchange partner

Relationship Quality: nature of relational bonds with an exchange partner

Relationship Breadth: number of relational ties with an exchange partner

Relational Efficacy (relationship quality × relationship composition): capacity of an inter-organizational relationship to achieve desired objectives

Relational Strength (relationship quality × relationship breadth): capacity of an inter-organizational relationship to withstand stress and/or conflict

Figure 16.1   Five drivers of inter-firm relationship performance

power and dependence, are central to successful relationships. Their 'Commitment–trust theory of relationship marketing' integrates research from social exchange theory, marriage and organizational behavior to demonstrate that *commitment*, 'an enduring desire to maintain a valued relationship' (Moorman et al. 1992, p. 316), and *trust*, the 'confidence in an exchange partner's reliability and integrity' (Morgan and Hunt 1994, p. 23), are necessary concepts for any understanding of how relationships influence performance.

Relationships built on commitment and trust provide shelter from opportunistic threats (Gregoire et al. 2009) and facilitate cooperation, enhancing financial performance and other positive outcomes such as market penetration (Kumar et al. 1994; Morgan and Hunt 1994). Trust enhances performance directly; it also enhances commitment, which in turn drives performance (Hibbard et al. 2001; Mohr and Spekman 1994). This process has provided a theoretical foundation of more than a decade of research (Morgan and Hunt 1994; Palmatier et al. 2006b), though recent work also notes the important role of gratitude in translating RM efforts into desirable outcomes (Palmatier et al. 2009).

Gratitude refers to an emotional appreciation for benefits received and accompanies *reciprocity*, or the willful desire to return such favors (Moyer 1970; Palmatier et al. 2009). Customers experience gratitude when they receive favors (Goei and Boster 2005), such as extra efforts by firms, which they reward by complying with subsequent requests from that firm (Goei and Boster 2005; Morales 2005), sustaining the relationship (Young 2006), promoting trust and establishing long-term reciprocity norms (Palmatier et al. 2007b, 2009). However, if they perceive that sellers are acting only in their own self-interest, such feelings of gratitude and the corresponding desire to reciprocate are inhibited.

Commitment, trust, gratitude and reciprocity thus constitute four interceding tenets of dyadic relationship success. There are of course many dyadic ties that exist between firms. When two firms engage in business exchanges over time, the success of their exchanges depends on the relationships formed across these sets of individuals. The collection of such individual dyads constitutes the inter-firm relationship.

Multidimensional Perspective of Inter-firm Relationships

The relationship of one firm with another reflects an aggregation of dyadic relationships between boundary-spanning agents of both firms. Because the relational sum might be greater than its parts, it is important to describe these relationships broadly; in this section we provide some tools to do so. Specifically in the context of inter-firm relationships, five elements capture their nature and the way they assemble or interact to provide value for the firm. As we illustrate in Table 16.1, these elements are relationship quality, relationship breadth and relationship composition, and the higher-order elements are relationship strength and relationship efficacy.

Relationship quality, similar to the network theory concept of tie strength (i.e. relational bonds among actors), reflects the caliber of the relational bonds with an exchange partner. With this notion we can capture relational embeddedness, closeness and degree of reciprocity from social bond theory (Rindfleisch and Moorman 2001). We also align our work with prior research (Crosby et al. 1990; Kumar et al. 1995) that suggests relationship quality can capture unique aspects of relational bonds, such as commitment,

Table 16.1   *Theoretical underpinnings of relationship marketing*

Mechanism	Description	Marketing References
Dyadic Relational Constructs		
Commitment	Enduring desire to maintain a valued relationship.	Crosby et al. 1990; Moorman et al. 1992; Morgan and Hunt 1994
Trust	Confidence in an exchange partner's reliability and integrity.	Doney and Cannon 1997; Hibbard et al. 2001
Gratitude	Emotional acknowledgment of benefits received and subsequent desire to respond in kind.	Goei and Boster 2005; Morales 2005; Palmatier et al. 2009
Reciprocity	Returned efforts for benefits received in a relationship exchange.	Moyer 1970; Dahl et al. 2005
Multidimensional Perspective of Inter-firm Relationships		
Relationship quality	Caliber of relational bonds with an exchange partner.	Crosby et al. 1990; Kumar et al. 1995; Palmatier 2008b; Gregoire et al. 2009
Relationship breadth	Number of relational bonds with an exchange partner.	Rowley 1997; Tsai 2001; Bendapudi and Leone 2002; Palmatier 2008b
Relationship composition	Decision-making capability of relational contacts.	Palmatier 2008a
Relationship strength	Inter-organizational relationship's ability to withstand stress and conflict, related to the interaction between relationship quality and breadth.	Hess et al. 2003; Palmatier et al. 2007b
Relationship efficacy	Inter-organizational relationship's ability to achieve desired objectives, related to the interaction between relationship quality and composition.	Crosby et al. 1990; Anderson and Narus 1990; Morgan and Hunt 1994; Palmatier et al. 2007b

trust, reciprocity norms and exchange efficiency, even though the best understanding of these concepts requires them to appear in concert to summarize the close bonds and influence on exchange outcomes. The quality of inter-firm relationships is important, but it does not speak to the quantity of ties.

Instead we need the concept of *relationship breadth* to address the number of relational bonds with an exchange partner; when inter-firm relationships often include many inter-personal ties, they tend to uncover more key information, find added profit-enhancing opportunities and better withstand threats to individual bonds (e.g. turnover). Even when confronted with the loss of a key contact, for example, broad inter-firm relationships can recover and thus suffer less from this turnover (Bendapudi and Leone 2002). A wealth of interconnections also contribute to customer value (Palmatier 2008a), in that they enhance cooperation, knowledge transfer, communication efficiency and product development performance (Rowley 1997; Tsai 2001). We thus note the quality and number of relationships; it is also useful to understand the types of individual relationship participants.

For that understanding we rely on *relationship composition*, which is similar to the network concepts of diversity (Wasserman and Faust 1994) and attractiveness (Anderson et al. 1994) and entails the decision-making capability of relational contacts. When a seller possesses a diverse and authoritative contact portfolio, it can better effect change in buyer organizations, because it knows that different customer firm departments make key decisions, not just 'key' decision-makers with the most official authority. Relational composition, if adequate, can enhance the value of a customer (Palmatier 2008a). When this element combines with the preceding two unique aspects of inter-firm relationships, the results benefit the firm.

In particular they may lead to *relationship strength*, which is the inter-organizational relationship's ability to withstand stress and conflict. Many high-quality relational bonds result in strong, resilient relationships; this claim relates to the interaction between relationship quality and breadth. Prior service literature similarly implies that relationship duration and breadth enhance service recovery (Hess et al. 2003). Therefore we assert that relationship strength positively influences seller outcomes by increasing the ability of an inter-firm relationship to function well, even when it must withstand problems and conflict.

Finally *relationship efficacy* refers to the ability of an inter-firm relationship to achieve the desired objectives, largely due to the interaction between relationship quality and composition. When sellers have high-quality bonds in well-structured contact portfolios, they can execute effective selling strategies, whereas gaps in particular areas hinder such effectiveness. If the portfolio offers only poor quality (i.e. weak interpersonal bonds), even if it contains key decision-makers (high composition), these contacts will not disclose sufficient information (Crosby et al. 1990) or care much about the seller's needs. That is, only high-quality relationships can solidify a contact portfolio's potential ability to institute change, induce reciprocity and enable the seller to achieve its objectives (Morgan and Hunt 1994). On the other side, a portfolio with high-quality, broad relationships still fails overall if the contacts represent only one functional area with little decision-making ability (low composition), because in this case, the seller cannot access non-redundant information or promote customer change.

In short, five factors provide an expanded view of inter-firm relationships and extend understanding of the mechanisms that underlie dyadic exchange to reveal three unique inter-firm relational elements (quality, breadth, composition) and two interactive elements (strength, efficacy). Building ties among firms requires focused attention on the factors that drive and sustain lasting relationships.

ANTECEDENTS OF CUSTOMER RELATIONSHIPS

Establishing beneficial relationships between boundary-spanning agents can be a complex task. Therefore in this section we outline elements that drive favorable relationships, as listed in Table 16.2, and provide an overview of the critical components of strong relationships, a discussion of the efforts a firm can undertake to support relationships and a review of deleterious factors that must be avoided to protect relationships. In many instances the causal flows we describe are autocatalytic. For instance, communication may strengthen a relationship, and a strong relationship may result in greater communication. Although potentially part of a recursive process, we present these drivers as

Table 16.2   Antecedents of customer relationships

Driver	Impact	Description	Marketing References
Relationship-Enhancing Antecedents			
Similarity	High	The individual-level commonalities in appearance, lifestyle and status and organizational-level parallels in cultures, values and goals.	Doney and Cannon 1997; Nicholson et al. 2001; Homburg et al. 2009
Communication	Moderate	The amount, frequency and quality of information shared between exchange partners.	Anderson and Narus 1990; Morgan and Hunt 1994
Seller expertise	High	Perceived credibility of salesperson, increasing perceptions of reliability, value and persuasiveness of information shared.	Dholakia and Sternthal 1977; Lagace et al. 1991; Vargo and Lusch 2004
Dependence	Low	Control in the exchange relationship that results from a lack of alternatives and its subsequent effect on the weaker party.	Morgan and Hunt 1994; Hibbard et al. 2001; Palmatier et al. 2006b
Relationship marketing programs	High	Social, structural and financial efforts or incentives intended to establish or enhance customer relationships, with social-focused programs having the strongest impact.	Berry 1995; Corsten and Kumar 2005; Palmatier et al. 2006a
Organizational programs	High	Internal, company-focused initiatives aimed at promoting customer relationships through organizational strategy, leadership, culture, structure and controls.	Tushman and Nadler 1978; Narver and Slater 1990; Day 1994; Verhoef and Leeflang 2009
Relationship-Damaging Antecedents			
Conflict	Moderate	The overall level of disagreement between exchange partners.	Gaski 1984; Anderson and Weitz 1992; Samaha et al. 2010
Opportunism	Moderate	Sly or cunning self-interested behavior on the part of an exhange partner.	Williamson 1975; Swaminathan and Moorman 2009; Samaha et al. 2010
Unfairness	High	A distributive, procedural or interactional inequity or mistreatment in an exchange.	Scheer et al. 2003; Samaha et al. 2010

antecedents, in keeping with prior literature. The dynamic nature of these elements, and of relationships in general, remains a rich subject for inquiry.

Relationship-enhancing Antecedents

Certain elements of an interaction contribute to beneficial relationships and aid relationship construction. In particular, commonalities in individual appearance, lifestyle and status, as well as coordinating organizational cultures, values and goals, positively affect trust, commitment and relationship quality in the form of *similarity* (Doney and Cannon 1997; Nicholson et al. 2001). Such similarity, including common perspectives, also diminishes uncertainty about a partner's actions, and a shared identity drives willingness to pay and loyalty (Homburg et al. 2009). To realize the benefits of similarity, firms must engage in open and explorative dialogue.

That is, they need *communication*, a concept that summarizes the amount, frequency and quality of information shared between exchange partners (Mohr et al. 1996). Whereas unilateral information exchange involves disclosure or openness, bilateral communication can resolve disputes, align goals and expectations and reveal value-creating opportunities (Mohr and Nevin 1990; Morgan and Hunt 1994). The resulting guidance and clarified exchanges improve relationship trust, because both parties have confidence in the other's promises, and enhance relationship commitment, because they identify value-creating opportunities.

As another means to enhance trust, *seller expertise* exists when a buyer perceives a seller possesses knowledge and credibility, such that any information it provides seems persuasive, reliable and valuable (Dholakia and Sternthal 1977). Such information in turn makes the interaction with this competent seller more valuable, so the buyer considers this exchange relationship particularly important and worthy of greater effort to strengthen and maintain it (Lagace et al. 1991). As Vargo and Lusch's (2004) argument that skills and knowledge are fundamental to exchanges would suggest, seller expertise offers the greatest benefits, compared with the other antecedents, across all forms of relationship quality (Palmatier et al. 2006b). That is, well-trained employees are key.

Our discussion thus far has centered on the positive elements (similarity, communication, seller expertise) needed to build strong relationships. In contrast, prior views in marketing also emphasize *power*, or one firm's control over another, and *dependence*, which is the resulting reliance of one firm on the other due to its lack of alternatives in inter-firm ties (Morgan and Hunt 1994). Yet Morgan and Hunt (1994) do not consider power as central to RM, and empirical evidence suggests that it plays a relatively small role in relationships, increasing commitment but not trust (Palmatier et al. 2006b). The relational benefits of increasing dependence are slight, but there are some specific, dedicated initiatives a firm can pursue to build and enhance its customer relationships.

Relationship Marketing Programs

Companies that dedicate resources to building and sustaining their relationships with customers implement RM programs, which can be evaluated according to three categories that reveal their impact on objective performance: social, structural and financial. When RM programs focus on social engagements and customized communication to personalize the relationship or convey a customer's special status, they produce bonds that are difficult to duplicate. Furthermore these special customers should reciprocate, in the form of repeat sales and recommendations or by ignoring competitive offers (De Wulf et al. 2001). Therefore social RM programs produce the highest return on investment (ROI; Palmatier et al. 2006a).

The next best ROI derives from structural RM programs, which provide investments for tools that facilitate customer exchange, such as electronic order processing systems or customized packaging. These tools increase the customer's productivity, which means they offer hard-to-quantify but still significant customer benefits. In addition, if the relationship enjoys high customer trust, the perceptions of economic benefits from these investments increase (Corsten and Kumar 2005), in a virtuous cycle between investments and relationship development. Structural bonds also create competitive advantages; customers do more business with the seller to take advantage of these value-enhancing linkages (Berry 1995).

As their name clearly indicates, financial RM programs provide economic benefits such as extended payment terms, giveaways or discounts and free shipping. Although attractive, these advantages tend to be unsustainable because competitors can easily match them (Day and Wensley 1988), unless the programs reflect some unique source (e.g. low-cost structure). Furthermore customers attracted by financial incentives tend to search for deals and provide less profit to the seller (Cao and Gruca 2005). Even with these concerns Bolton et al. (2000) find sufficient returns on many financial programs, particularly among large firms (Liu and Yang 2009). Such efforts can be complemented by internal efforts aimed at creating an atmosphere that recognizes the importance of RM.

Organizational Programs

Organizational design theory (Tushman and Nadler 1978) cites the impact of five organizational dimensions on customer relationships: strategy, leadership, culture, structure and control. The organization's *strategy* refers to managerial vision and initiatives and sets the stage for buyer–seller engagements. A strategy focused on customers, or a market orientation (Narver and Slater 1990), supports relationship success. Its *leadership* drives this strategy through the managers' beliefs and expertise (Weinszimmer et al. 2003), which should inspire employees (Wieseke et al. 2009).

Leaders also help create the organizational *culture* – the values, norms and artifacts prevalent in an organization – which may focus on customers, prompt relational behaviors, and ultimately enhance financial performance (Homburg and Pflesser 2000). Related to the culture, the organizational *structure* captures the organization of employees and the arrangement of customer interface activities to support new and existing customer relationships. Three structural elements that bridge the front and back ends of the organization affect customer relationships: outside-in (e.g. market sensing, technology monitoring), inside-out (e.g. costs, logistics) and spanning processes (e.g. order fulfillment, customer service) (Day 1994).

Finally, the marketing department is essential for a successful market-oriented strategy, and accountability is a paramount factor (Verhoef and Leeflang 2009). Similarly the final element in organizational design theory is *control*, which pertains to the system designed to monitor, incentivize or punish employees according to their customer interface activities (Oliver and Anderson 1994). Organizational standards, metrics and feedback loops help optimize performance and learning to implement RM tactics (Payne and Frow 2005). In summary, proper attention and dedication to organizational elements enhance customer relationships, which ultimately drive performance outcomes.

When relationships exist and receive support, it next becomes important to protect these valuable bonds.

Relationship-damaging Antecedents

Building relationships demands financial and temporal investments that should not go to waste. Sustaining a relationship requires avoiding incidents that might undermine the relational bonds, and recent work highlights three prominent relational stressors: conflict, opportunism and unfairness (Samaha et al. 2010).

Conflict is the overall level of disagreement between exchange partners (Gaski 1984); it can destroy relationship quality and corrode customer confidence in the long-term intentions of the seller, as well as customer willingness to invest in relationship building or maintenance (Anderson and Weitz 1992). Not all conflict impairs relationships, and a healthy level of functional conflict may enhance trust if the disagreements can be amicably resolved (Morgan and Hunt 1994). However, unresolved disagreements fester and can undermine the relationship. Because people tend to pay more attention to negatives than to positives (Shiv et al. 1997), it is critical to resolve conflict, lest it permanently impair the relationship.

Opportunism instead refers to 'self-interest seeking with guile' (Williamson 1975, p. 26). It can be either active or passive; active opportunism characterizes partners who seek out opportunistic behaviors, such as intentionally violating contracts, whereas passive opportunism describes those who simply respond or react to circumstances opportunistically, such as ignoring partner requests (Wathne and Heide 2000). Interconnections among trade partners can decrease opportunism, though only to a point, because an abundance of connections inhibits managers' ability to share information selectively, which a partner could use to its own advantage (Swaminathan and Moorman 2009). Trust in relationships requires a common belief that partners will not act opportunistically (Srivastava and Chakravarti 2009), whereas manifest opportunistic behavior is likely to degrade trust and thus harms relationship quality.

Conceptually distinct from opportunism, *unfairness* results from a distributive imbalance in the perceived inputs or efforts and the corresponding outcomes or benefits in a relational exchange (Adams 1965). It also might reflect a procedural bias that partially and systematically favors some members or firms over others (Thibaut and Walker 1978), or it could imply an interpersonal, interactional mistreatment experienced during the exchange (Bies and Shapiro 1987). Perceptions of unfairness are particularly damaging to strong relationships, and customers in high-quality relationships are more prone to seek revenge for mistreatment than are low-quality relationship customers (Gregoire et al. 2009). In some cultures positive inequity, which describes a form of unfairness that benefits the customer, also has negative impacts on trust (Scheer et al. 2003). In summary, to manage relationships effectively, firms must grasp these relationship-destroying elements and safeguard against them.

In a relational exchange, conflict, opportunism and unfairness may separately or interactively undermine the quality of the relationship over time. Relationship managers therefore must attend quickly to resolve issues as they arise, rather than blindly allowing the relationship to erode or leave benefits unrealized.

OUTCOMES OF CUSTOMER RELATIONSHIPS

As should any business investment, customer relationships and the related efforts must be assessed continually to ensure the resource allocations are appropriate and merited. Because of the varied tangibility of different derived relational benefits, metrics must be adjusted accordingly. In particular the metrics differ for four outcomes, identified as particularly important for relationship marketing (see Table 16.3): cooperation, word of mouth, loyalty and objective performance (Palmatier et al. 2006b).

Referring to coordinated, complementary actions between partners to achieve a mutual goal, *cooperation* derives from strong relationships and increases customers' flexibility and adaptability to a seller's requests for changes, for information or for reciprocation of its efforts in the long term. Through cooperation both firms can attain value creation beyond that which each might achieve alone. However, one party usually receives its value enhancement first, which means trust in the relationship, as the other party waits for reciprocation, is critical (Anderson and Narus 1990). In addition, because committed customers are defined by their desire to maintain their valued relationships, they cooperate with sellers, even without *quid pro quo* benefits (Morgan and Hunt 1994). Therefore trust, commitment and relationship quality are critical for cooperation (Palmatier et al. 2006b).

When they enjoy such benefits, customers may comment positively about the seller to other potential customers (whether inside or outside the firm). That is, word of mouth (WOM) depends heavily on the relational bonds that drive customers to provide referrals and testimonials (Barksdale et al. 1997; Verhoef et al. 2002). Because WOM behaviors, especially Internet referrals, exclude potential contaminants such as switching costs or insufficient time and motivation, they provide effective customer loyalty indicators (Dick and Basu 1994): only strong and trusting relationship customers risk their reputations by recommending their seller (Reichheld 2003).

These customers also tend to be loyal; in this context *loyalty* is the likelihood that the customer provides the seller with an advantage or benefits in the exchange process, such

Table 16.3   Outcomes of customer relationships

Outcome	Impact	Description	Marketing Reference
Cooperation	High	The coordinated, complementary actions between partners to achieve a mutual goal.	Morgan and Hunt 1994; Palmatier et al. 2006b
Word of mouth	High	The likelihood that a customer comments positively about a seller to another potential customer.	Dick and Basu 1994; Barksdale et al. 1997
Customer loyalty	Moderate	The likelihood that the customer provides the seller with an advantage or benefits in the exchange process.	Dick and Basu 1994; Gabarino and Johnson 1999
Firm performance	Moderate	Objective performance measured using metrics consisting of four categories: sales-based, profitability-based, aggregate and knowledge-based.	Palmatier et al. 2006b

as automatic rebuys, a narrower search for competing bids, competitor quote disclosure and 'last looks'. Of the many ways to describe loyalty (Oliver 1999), most focus on behavioral intentions (e.g. repurchase, continuity) but also therefore suffer from situational influences (Dick and Basu 1994). If a customer expects the relationship to continue because switching would be too expensive, there is no guarantee that this customer does not also exhibit weak relational bonds and little 'ultimate loyalty' (Oliver 1999). Another perspective describes loyalty according to relationship-induced or favored status and thus focuses on behaviors that reflect relational bonds. When committed, trusting, high relationship quality customers perceive little risk in dealing with their partners, act on their sense of belonging and minimize their acquisition costs by buying from partners, they also develop greater loyalty toward the seller (Garbarino and Johnson 1999), which ultimately drives firm performance.

And thus we arrive at the ultimate relational outcome; *firm performance* can be measured using various seller-focused metrics that reflect the customer's relational behaviors. These metrics generally fall into four categories: sales-based, profitability-based, aggregate and knowledge-based. *Sales-based* outcome measures focus on the increase or reduced drops in sales or revenues due to relational behaviors (e.g. reciprocation, last look), such as annual sales growth, sales diversity, sales volatility or share of wallet. *Profitability-based* outcome measures include price premiums and reduced selling costs, focusing on the bottom line. Because the impact of RM programs is complex, *aggregate measures* of performance capture the broad impact of RM programs and thus are best. Metrics in this category include customer lifetime value and return on investment (ROI). Finally *knowledge-based outcomes* capture the less tangible benefits of relationship marketing that result from buyer insights, often related to innovation. For example, the number of patents, time to market and new product success rate are all indicators of relational benefits that financial measures cannot capture.

LEVERAGING RELATIONSHIP MARKETING EFFECTIVENESS

The benefits generated from relationship marketing often vary across different conditions. In this section we detail the situations in which the effectiveness of relationship marketing has been shown to differ.

Individual versus Organizational Relationship Targets

Relationships comprise various levels: person-to-person or interpersonal; person-to-firm or firm-to-person; and firm-to-firm or inter-firm. In turn relationships and associated decision-making vary across levels (Doney and Cannon 1997; Palmatier et al. 2007a). Yet relationships also can span multiple targets simultaneously, operate according to varying rules (Iacobucci and Ostrom 1996) and have unique or divergent effects on performance (Palmatier et al. 2007a). For example, trust depends strongly on the type of interaction or bond (Doney and Cannon 1997), and customer loyalty might be focused on the salesperson, the company or both. If a customer trusts a particular salesperson and therefore is loyal to him or her, and not to the company, this buyer would switch suppliers in the event of salesperson turnover (Reichheld and Teal 1996). Together with the intention to maintain the relationship, these unique and diverging elements drive performance differently, depending on the level (Palmatier et al. 2007a).

Why do customers judge individual salespeople separately from the collective firm (Lickel et al. 2000)? Most research suggests these variances reflect perceived differences in *entitativity*, that is, the degree to which the target exhibits coherence, unity or consistency (Hilton and von Hippel 1990). Firms with higher perceived entitativity generally have policies and procedures that emphasize employee uniformity, which make it easier for customers to form strong firm-level relationships (Palmatier et al. 2007a; 2007b). These relationships then determine the configuration of the distribution used by the relationship partners.

Channel Distribution Versus Direct Exchange

As a basic element of RM, exchanges between partners cannot be simple, direct buyer–seller transactions but instead demand interdependence, coordinated action and safeguards against opportunistic behavior (Anderson and Weitz 1989; Kumar et al. 1995). Accordingly channel partners often develop strong relationships to be successful. Strong relationships logically have a much greater impact on exchange performance than do simple, direct exchanges. In this sense relationship importance offers a distinction between consumer and business markets (Anderson and Narus 2004).

Product Versus Service Offering

As we noted previously, services are less tangible, less consistent and more perishable than products. Therefore customers and boundary spanners must cooperate in their production and consumption (Zeithaml et al. 1985), such that stronger relationships should be more critical for services than they are for products. These characteristics of services also make them relatively more difficult or ambiguous to evaluate, so trust may be more critical in service-oriented relationships.

Overall, to leverage RM, firms should pursue relationships with consistent partners (individuals or uniform entities) that are proximate and provide less standardized offerings. The drivers, roles and lasting effects of relationships in these settings are especially important.

CONCLUSION AND FURTHER RESEARCH DIRECTIONS

Research into RM is necessarily varied and complex. This chapter provides a framework for understanding relationships in a business context and thus should serve as a foundation for practitioners and academics interested in the field. Although the types of research questions and approaches vary, common themes have emerged in the domain that lend themselves to important further research topics, as we discuss in this section.

Experimental Analysis of Dynamic Effects

Relationships occur over time, but the methodology used to assess them at different stages generally involves cross-sectional surveys. Using dynamic experiments, additional approaches should consider causal models that test how relationships change over time, investigate moderating factors that enhance or diminish this process and note the mediating mechanisms responsible for this change. Attention should also focus on other mediators, such as gratitude, that may play varying roles over time (e.g. gratitude may be especially beneficial in the relationship growth stage).

Multilevel Methods

In addition to incorporating experimental methods, analyses should expand to encompass effects at varying levels within and between firms. As we have presented, relationships occur at multiple levels, ranging from individual to firm interactions. To understand the role of relationships in a business context, further analysis should capture customer-, salesperson- and firm-level effects, as well as their cross-level interactions.

Groups and Networks as Units of Analysis

In addition to multilevel analyses, researchers should conceptualize relationships as bundled, such that the whole is distinct from the sum of their parts. In this sense relationships might involve a focal firm and a group of exchange partners or a focal firm and a network of exchange partners. Each approach demands distinct methods and constructs that cannot be captured by a dyadic perspective. This effort may become increasingly critical as the importance and adoption of social media continues to grow.

Social Media and Relational Webs

Technological platforms that connect exchange partners increasingly influence and even dictate how business gets conducted. Research investigating how the relationships in this space can be built and then transition over time would provide innovative insights into ways to implement and exploit these technologies to drive performance outcomes, which remains an important business question.

Relationships, Risk and Uncertainty

In another important application for firms, relationships can buffer against uncertainty in business exchanges. Yet the way in which relationships might be used to manage risk in a dynamic environment is not fully understood. Researchers therefore should consider the role of RM as a means to help firms hedge against catastrophic events, such as the loss of a substantial customer or sudden, rapid advance in competing technologies.

Pitfalls of Relationship Marketing Programs

Finally, in distinct contrast to the preceding positive directions for further research, we note that RM programs can be very costly, and not just in terms of the resources demanded. Implementing poorly designed programs inevitably alters customer composition (e.g. by attracting price-sensitive customers) and may have other damaging effects on aspects of the business exchange. Exploring the negative or harmful effects of RM programs therefore is an important area for additional research.

REFERENCES

Adams, John S. (1965), 'Inequity in social exchange', in L. Berkowitz (ed.), *Advances in Experimental Social Psychology*, Vol. 2, New York: Academic Press.

Albers, Sönke, Murali Mantrala and Shrihari Sridhar (2008), 'A meta-analysis of personal selling elasticities', MSI Reports (08-100).

Albers, Sonke, Murali K. Mantrala and Shrihari Sridhar (2010), 'Personal selling elasticities: a meta-analysis', *Journal of Marketing Research*, **47** (5), 840–53.

American Marketing Association (2004), 'Marketing', available at http://www.marketingpower.com/_layouts/Dictionary.aspx?dLetter=M, accessed 7 June 2010.

Anderson, Erin and Barton A. Weitz (1989), 'Determinants of continuity in conventional industrial channel dyads', *Marketing Science*, **8** (4), 310–23.

Anderson, Erin and Barton A. Weitz (1992), 'The use of pledges to build and sustain commitment in distribution channels', *Journal of Marketing Research*, **29**, 18–34.

Anderson, James C. and James A. Narus (1990), 'A model of distributor firm and manufacturer firm working partnerships', *Journal of Marketing*, **54**, 42–58.

Anderson, James C. and James A. Narus (2004), *Business Market Management: Understanding, Creating, and Delivering Value*, Upper Saddle River, NJ: Prentice Hall.

Anderson, James C., Hakan Hakansson and Jan Johanson (1994), 'Dyadic business relationships within a business network context', *Journal of Marketing*, **58**, 1–15.

Barksdale, Hiram C., Jr, Julie T. Johnson and Munshik Suh (1997), 'A relationship maintenance model: a comparison between managed health care and traditional fee-for-service', *Journal of Business Research*, **40**, 237–47.

Bendapudi, Neeli and Robert P. Leone (2002), 'Managing business-to-business customer relationships following key contact employee turnover in a vendor firm', *Journal of Marketing*, **66** (1), 83–101.

Berry, Leonard L. (1995), 'Relationship marketing of services-growing interest, emerging perspectives', *Journal of the Academy of Marketing Science*, **23** (4), 236–45.

Bies, Robert J. and Debra L. Shapiro (1987), 'Interactional fairness judgements: the influence of causal accounts', *Social Justice Research*, **1**, 199–218.

Bolton, Ruth N., P. K. Kannan and Matthew D. Bramlett (2000), 'Implications of loyalty programs membership and service experiences for customer retention and value', *Journal of the Academy of Marketing Sciences*, **28** (1), 95–108.

Cao, Yong and Thomas S. Gruca (2005), 'Reducing adverse selection through customer relationship management', *Journal of Marketing*, **69**, 219–29.

Corsten, Daniel and Nirmalya Kumar (2005), 'Do suppliers benefit from collaborative relationships with large retailers? An empirical investigation of efficient consumer response adoption', *Journal of Marketing*, **69** (3), 80–94.

Crosby, Lawrence A., Kenneth R. Evans and Deborah Cowles (1990), 'Relationship quality in services selling: an interpersonal influence perspective', *Journal of Marketing*, **54** (3), 68–81.

Dahl, Darren W., Heather Honea and Rajesh V. Manchanda (2005), 'Three Rs of interpersonal consumer guilt: relationship, reciprocity, reparation', *Journal of Consumer Psychology*, **15** (4), 307–15.

Day, George S. (1994), 'The capabilities of market-driven organizations', *Journal of Marketing*, **58**, 37–52.

Day, George S. and Robin Wensley (1988), 'Assessing advantage: a framework for diagnosing competitive superiority', *Journal of Marketing*, **52** (2), 1–20.

De Wulf, Kristof, Gaby Odekerken-Schröder and Dawn Iacobucci (2001), 'Investments in consumer relationships: a cross-country and cross-industry exploration', *Journal of Marketing*, **65** (4), 33–50.

Dholakia, Ruby Roy and Brian Sternthal (1977), 'Highly credible source: persuasive facilitator of persuasive liabilities?', *Journal of Consumer Research*, **3**, 223–32.

Dick, Alan S. and Kunal Basu (1994), 'Customer loyalty: toward an integrated conceptual framework', *Journal of the Academy of Marketing Science*, **22** (2), 99–113.

Doney, Patricia M. and Joseph P. Cannon (1997), 'An examination of the nature of trust in buyer-seller relationships', *Journal of Marketing*, **61** (2), 35–51.

Dwyer, Robert F., Paul H. Schurr and Sejo Oh (1987), 'Developing buyer–seller relationships', *Journal of Marketing*, **51** (2), 11–27.

Garbarino, Ellen and Mark S. Johnson (1999), 'The different roles of satisfaction, trust, and commitment in customer relationships', *Journal of Marketing*, **63** (2), 70–87.

Gaski, John F. (1984), 'The theory of power and conflict in channels of distribution', *Journal of Marketing*, **48** (3), 9–29.

Goei, Ryan and Franklin J. Boster (2005), 'The roles of obligation and gratitude in explaining the effect of favors on compliance', *Communication Monographs*, **72** (3), 284.

Gregoire, Y., T. Tripp and R. Legoux (2009), 'When customer love turns into lasting hate: the effects of relationship strength and time on customer revenge and avoidance', *Journal of Marketing*, **73** (November), 18–32.

Gronroos, Christian (1997), 'Value-driven relational marketing: from products to resources and competencies', *Journal of Marketing Management*, **13** (4), 407–19.

Hess, Ron L., Shankar Ganesan and Noreen M. Klein (2003), 'Service failure and recovery: the impact of relationship factors on customer satisfaction', *Journal of the Academy Marketing Science*, **31** (2), 127–45.

Hibbard, Jonathan D., Nirmalya Kumar and Louis W. Stern (2001), 'Examining the impact of destructive acts in marketing channel relationships', *Journal of Marketing Research*, **38**, 25–61.

Hilton, John L. and William von Hippel (1990), 'The role of consistency in judgment of stereotype-relevant behaviors', *Personality and Social Psychology Bulletin*, **16** (1), 430–48.

Homburg, Christian and Christian Pflesser (2000), 'A multiple-layer model of market-oriented organizational culture: measurement issues and performance outcomes', *Journal of Marketing Research*, **37**, 449–62.

Homburg, Chrisian, Jan Wieseke and Wayne D. Hoyer (2009), 'Social identity and the service-profit chain', *Journal of Marketing*, **73** (March), 38–54.

Iacobucci, Dawn and Amy Ostrom (1996), 'Commercial and interpersonal relationships; using the structure of interpersonal relationships to understand individual-to-individual, individual-to-firm, and firm-to-firm relationships in commerce', *International Journal of Research in Marketing*, **13** (1), 53–72.

Kumar, Nirmalya, Jonathan D. Hibbard and Leonard D. Stern (1994), *The Nature and Consequences of Marketing Channel Intermediary Commitment*, Cambridge, MA: Marketing Science Institute.

Kumar, Nirmalya, Lisa K. Scheer and Jan-Benedict E.M. Steenkamp (1995), 'The effects of supplier fairness on vulnerable resellers', *Journal of Marketing Research*, **32** (1), 54–65.

Lagace, Rosemary R., Robert Dahlstrom and Jule B. Gassenheimer (1991), 'The relevance of ethical salesperson behavior on relationship quality: the pharmaceutical industry', *Journal of Personal Selling and Sales Management*, **11** (4), 39–47.

Libai, Barak, Eitan Muller and Renana Peres (2009), 'The diffusion of services', *Journal of Marketing Research*, **46** (2), 163–75.

Lickel, Brian, David L. Hamilton, Amy Lewis, Steven J. Sherman, Grazyna Wieczorkowska and A. Neville Uhles (2000), 'Varieties of group and the perception of group entitativity', *Journal of Personality and Social Psychology*, **78** (2), 223–46.

Liu, Yuping and Rong Yang (2009), 'Competing loyalty programs: impact of market saturation, market share, and category expandability', *Journal of Marketing*, **73** (1), 93–108.

Lohr, Steve (2010), 'Huge payoff for IBM after a shift', *The New York Times*, 20 May, B6.

Mohr, Jakki J. and John R. Nevin (1990), 'Communication strategies in marketing channels: a theoretical perspective', *Journal of Marketing*, **54**, 36–51.

Mohr, Jakki J. and Robert Spekman (1994), 'Characteristics of partnership success: partnership attributes, communication behavior, and conflict resolution techniques', *Strategic Management Journal*, **15** (2), 135–52.

Mohr, Jakki J., Robert J. Fisher and John R. Nevin (1996), 'Collaborative communication in interfirm relationships: moderating effects of integration and control', *Journal of Marketing*, **60**, 103–15.

Moorman, Christine, Gerald Zaltman and Rohit Deshpandé (1992), 'Relationships between providers and users of market research: the dynamics of trust within and between organizations', *Journal of Marketing Research*, **29** (3), 314–29.

Morales, Andrea C. (2005), 'Giving firms an "E" for effort: consumer responses to high-effort firms', *Journal of Consumer Research*, **31** (4), 806.

Morgan, Robert M. and Shelby D. Hunt (1994), 'The commitment–trust theory of relationship marketing', *Journal of Marketing*, **58** (3), 20–38.

Moyer, Reed (1970), 'Reciprocity: retrospect and prospect', *Journal of Marketing*, **34**, 47–54.

Narver, John C. and Stanley F. Slater (1990), 'The effect of a market orientation on business profitability', *Journal of Marketing*, **54** (4), 20–35.

Nicholson, Carolyn Y., Larry D. Compeau and Rajesh Sethi (2001), 'The role of interpersonal liking in building trust in long-term channel relationships', *Journal of the Academy of Marketing Science*, **29** (1), 3–15.

Oliver, Richard L. (1999), 'Whence consumer loyalty?', *Journal of Marketing*, **63** (Special Issue), 33–44.

Oliver, Richard L. and Erin Anderson (1994), 'An empirical test of the consequences of behavior and outcome-based sales control systems', *Journal of Marketing*, **58**, 53–67.

Palmatier, Robert W. (2008a), 'Interfirm relational drivers of customer value', *Journal of Marketing*, **72** (July), 76–89.

Palmatier, Robert W. (2008b), *Relationship Marketing*, Cambridge, MA: Marketing Science Institute.

Palmatier, Robert W., Lisa K. Scheer and J.B. Steenkamp (2007a), 'Customer loyalty to whom? Managing the benefits and risks of salesperson-owned loyalty', *Journal of Marketing Research*, **44** (2), 185–99.

Palmatier, Robert W., Srinath Gopalakrishna and Mark B. Houston (2006a), 'Returns on business-to-business relationship marketing investments: strategies for leveraging profits', *Marketing Science*, **25** (5), 477–93.

Palmatier, Robert W., Rajiv Dant, Dhruv Grewal and Kenneth Evans (2006b), 'Factors influencing the effectiveness of relationship marketing: a meta-analysis', *Journal of Marketing*, **70** (3), 136–53.

Palmatier, Robert W., C. Jarvis, J. Bechkoff and Frank Kardes (2009), 'The role of customer gratitude in relationship marketing', *Journal of Marketing*, **73**, 1–18.

Palmatier, Robert W., Lisa K. Scheer, Mark B. Houston, Kenneth R. Evans and Srinath Gopalakrishna (2007b), 'Use of relationship marketing programs in building customer–salesperson and customer–firm relationships: differential influences on financial outcomes', *International Journal of Research in Marketing*, **24** (September), 210–23.

Payne, Adrian and Pennie Frow (2005), 'A strategic framework for customer relationship management', *Journal of Marketing*, **69**, 167–76.

Reichheld, Fredrick F. (2003), 'The one number you need', *Harvard Business Review*, **81** (12), 46–54.

Reichheld, Fredrick F. and Thomas Teal (1996), *The Loyalty Effect*, Boston, MA: Harvard Business School Press.

Rindfleisch, Aric and Christine Moorman (2001), 'The acquisition and utilization of information in new product alliances: a strength-of-ties perspective', *Journal of Marketing*, **65** (2), 1–18.

Rowley, Timothy J. (1997), 'Moving Beyond Dyadic Ties: A network theory of stakeholder influences', *Academy of Management Review*, **22** (4), 887–910.

Samaha, Stephen A., Robert W. Palmatier and Rajiv P. Dant (2010), 'Perceived unfairness – relationship poison', University of Washington, Working Paper.

Scheer, Lisa K., Nirmalya Kumar and Jan-Benedict E.M. Steenkamp (2003), 'Reactions to perceived inequity in US and Dutch interorganizational relationships', *Academy of Management Journal*, **46** (3), 303–16.

Sheth, Jagdish N. and Atul Parvatiyar (2000), *Handbook of Relationship Marketing*, Thousand Oaks, CA: Sage Publications.

Shiv, Baba, Julie A. Edell and John W. Payne (1997), 'Factors affecting the impact of negatively and positively framed ad messages', *Journal of Consumer Research*, **24**, 285–94.

Srivastava, Joydeep and Dipankar Chakravarti (2009), 'Channel negotiations with information asymmetries: contingent influences of communication and trustworthiness reputations', *Journal of Marketing Research*, **46** (4), 557–72.

Swaminathan, Vanitha and Christine Moorman (2009), 'Marketing alliances, firm networks, and firm value creation', *Journal of Marketing*, **73** (5), 52–69.

Thibaut, John W. and Lauren S. Walker (1978), *Procedural Justice: A Psychological Analysis*, Hillsdale, NJ: Lawrence Erlbaum Associates.

Tsai, Wenpin (2001), 'Knowledge transfer in interorganizational networks: effects of network position and absorptive capacity on business unit innovation and performance', *Academy of Management Journal*, **44** (5), 996–1001.

Tushman, Michael L. and David A. Nadler (1978), 'Information processing as an integrating concept in organizational design', *Academy of Management Review*, **3**, 613–24.

Vargo, Stephen L. and Robert F. Lusch (2004), 'Evolving to a new dominant logic for marketing', *Journal of Marketing*, **68** (1), 1–17.

Verhoef, Peter C. and Peter S.H. Leeflang (2009), 'Understanding the marketing department's influence within the firm', *Journal of Marketing*, **73** (2), 14–37.

Verhoef, Peter C., Philip Hans Franses and Janny C. Hoekstra (2002), 'The effect of relational constructs on customer referrals and number of services purchased from a multiservice provider: does age of relationship matter?', *Journal of the Academy Marketing Science*, **30** (3), 202–16.

Wasserman, Stanley and Katherine Faust (1994), *Social Network Analysis*, Cambridge: Cambridge University Press.

Wathne, Kenneth H. and Jan B. Heide (2000), 'Opportunism in interfirm relationships: forms, outcomes, and solutions', *Journal of Marketing*, **64**, 36–51.

Weinszimmer, Laurence G., Edward U. Bond, Mark B. Houston and Paul C. Nystrom (2003), 'Relating marketing expertise on the top management team and strategic market aggressiveness to financial performance and shareholder value', *Journal of Strategic Marketing*, **11**, 133–59.

Wieseke, Jan, Michael Ahearne, Son K. Lam and Rolf Van Dick (2009), 'The role of leaders in internal marketing', *Journal of Marketing*, **73** (2), 123–45.

Williamson, Oliver E. (1975), *Markets and Hierarchies: Analysis and Antitrust Implications*, New York: The Free Press.
Young, Louise (2006), 'Trust: looking forward and back', *Journal of Business & Industrial Marketing*, **21** (7), 439–45.
Zeithaml, Valarie A., A. Parasuraman and Leonard L. Berry (1985), 'Problems and strategies in services marketing', *Journal of Marketing*, **49** (2), 33–46.

17 Customer relationship management in business markets

Rajkumar Venkatesan, V. Kumar and Werner Reinartz

Customer relationship management (CRM) has its origins in business markets. Business markets have long adopted key account management (Shapiro and Moriarty 1984) as a way to recognize individual customers who are valuable to a firm and to allocate resources to ensure satisfaction and retention of key accounts. Business markets have always faced the challenge of managing individual customers and customizing marketing, products, prices and sometimes channels to each customer's preferences (Narayandas 2005). Somewhat parallel to the trends in business markets, general marketing strategists recognized the value of customer relationships (Sheth and Parvatiyar 1995), the need to be market oriented and customer centric (Day 2006; Jaworski and Kohli 1993) and the potential of measuring and managing individual customer profitability (Reinartz and Kumar 2003; Rust et al. 2004; Venkatesan and Kumar 2004).

In this chapter we track the evolution of the strategic CRM literature from customer loyalty to the current state of the art for customer-centric organizations (Gulati 2010) and interaction orientation (Ramani and Kumar 2008). We define 'CRM' as the practice of analyzing and employing marketing databases and leveraging communication technologies to determine corporate practices and methods that maximize the lifetime value of each individual customer to the firm. We draw parallels between B2B and CRM research. We also discuss the implications of CRM findings for business markets and recognize the challenges in applying CRM to business markets. Our objective in this chapter is to spur interest among CRM researchers to recognize the unique aspects of business markets in their strategic frameworks and empirical models.

The domain of business markets includes a broad range of transactions and relationships. Firms in business markets differ depending on their emphasis on products or services, a transactional or relationship orientation, differentiated or commodity product portfolio and an enterprise-wide or unit-level value proposition. As we map research in CRM to business markets we specify the business market contexts that are most appropriate for application of the specific CRM concept. Figure 17.1 illustrates the conceptual link between research in CRM and relationship marketing, the aspect of B2B research most relevant to CRM. Both CRM and relationship marketing research adopt the premise that firms perform better if they are relationship rather than transaction oriented with their customers. The CRM research stream so far has primarily focused on quantifying the lifetime value of a customer, identifying the customers to select and proposing the optimal level of resources to allocate to selected customers. Conversely, the relationship marketing stream has focused on effective ways to spend the resources allocated to the selected customers and processes and organizational structures for better managing a firm's value chain that includes both the firm's suppliers and its customers.

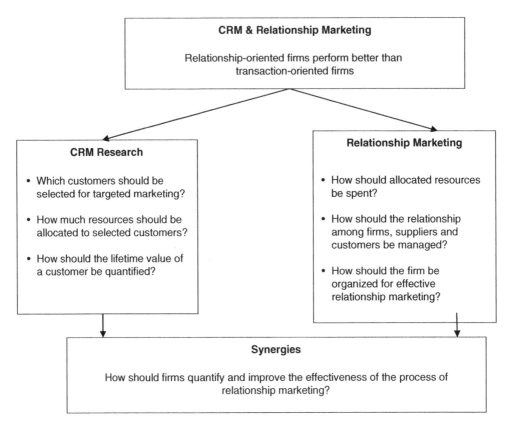

Figure 17.1   Links between CRM and B2B relationship marketing research

CUSTOMER LOYALTY FOR BUSINESS MARKETS

The meaning and development of customer loyalty can differ in business markets compared with consumer markets. In consumer markets, the loyalty construct refers to the affective and behavioral disposition of consumers toward a firm or a brand. Although a (limited) number of well-known firms (e.g. General Electric, Siemens) can generate sizable and positive brand attitudes because of their reputation around reliability and risk reduction, a common norm in business markets is that the role of the affective component is much more subdued (though not absent). For example, the more commoditized a product, the greater is the likelihood that buyers perceive little value and benefits from intangible brand assets. Many business markets are at risk of commoditization because of product parity, strong utilitarian features or lack of social identification with the brand. Moreover, because the decision-making process in business markets is much more driven by a group decision-making process with several domain experts, the objective utilitarian aspects of an offer can surface more readily (Dholakia et al. 1993). Overall, the construct of loyalty in business markets is more focused on the behavioral aspect of loyalty. Thus, knowing the importance of the behavioral element lends direction to the understanding, measurement and management of the loyalty aspect in business markets.

That organizations in B2B contexts build up ongoing relationships or at least show behavioral loyalty can be traced back to the notion of perceived customer value. At the core, loyalty in B2B markets is a consequence of perceived customer value created by suppliers (Morgan and Hunt 1994). Scholars and practitioners have widely recognized that creating superior customer value is paramount for a company's long-term survival and success (Woodruff 1997). In B2B markets in particular, customer value is the cornerstone of marketing management. Anderson et al. (2008, p. 4, italics in original) define business market management as 'the process of *understanding*, *creating*, and *delivering value* to targeted business markets and customers'.

Thus, from a customer's point of view, the creation of value to the customer is a necessary condition to build loyalty. That being said, customers still differ in the degree to which they *want* to engage in an ongoing relationship. It is well established in marketing literature (e.g. Day 2000) that customers locate on different points along the relationship continuum. At one extreme, customers may prefer individual arm's-length transactions without any commitment. On the other extreme, customers might engage in long-lasting, trustful collaborative exchanges. The preference for a location on the continuum is due to a host of factors, including individual intra-firm preferences and product and industry characteristics (Anderson and Narus 1991). And behavioral loyalty can result in both cases! In the case of a collaborative exchange, loyalty is the result of a clear commitment to the relationship in which both parties agree to invest in and harvest from the relationship. They are likely to share information, jointly define relationship objectives and manage conflict systematically. The outcome is not only a clear behavioral commitment of the customer to the focal supplier but also certain identification with the culture and values of the partner (Lambert and Knemeyer 2004). That is, two firms learn and build common routines and norms that help fortify the relationship and build positive attitudes. Even in the case of transactional exchange, de facto behavioral loyalty can result. That is, when an offer provides high utility to a customer even in the absence of any commitment, frequent repurchasing might readily occur.

However, many business customers put safeguards in place not to become overexposed to potential deleterious effects of loyalty. For example, many firms have mechanisms in place that govern the maximum share a single supplier can garner. This procedure relates to managing the risk of individual suppliers going out of business or abusing their privilege of securing a high customer share (a classic hold-up problem).

So far, the discussion has focused on the perspective of the customer. However, regardless of the customer's perception of value creation in an exchange and the customer's desire for a relational versus transactional mode, the focal supplier must monitor value capture as well. That is, from a supplier's perspective it is also important to link customer loyalty to the value customers generate for the focal organization (i.e. customer profitability). Especially in a B2B context it is crucial to create an understanding of a systems perspective on value creation – that is, value created for the customer and value created for the focal organization. Although loyalty is firms' ultimate goal (Reichheld 1996), it is tempered in the view of a systems perspective. The most prototypical systems perspective in this domain is the satisfaction–profit chain, which has been popular since the early 1990s, when companies realized the importance of measuring and managing customer

	Butterflies	Percentage of Customers	**True Friends**	Percentage of Customers
High Profitability	**B2B** Corporate service provider	20%	**B2B** Corporate service provider	30%
	B2C Grocery retail	15%	**B2C** Grocery retail	36%
	Mail-order	19%	Mail-order	31%
	Direct brokerage	18%	Direct brokerage	32%
	Strangers	Percentage of Customers	**Barnacles**	Percentage of Customers
Low Profitability	**B2B** Corporate service provider	29%	**B2B** Corporate service provider	21%
	B2C Grocery retail	34%	**B2C** Grocery retail	15%
	Mail-order	29%	Mail-order	21%
	Direct brokerage	33%	Direct brokerage	17%

Short-Term Customers   Long-Term Customers

Source: Reinartz and Kumar (2002).

Figure 17.2   Customer profitability–loyalty grid

satisfaction (Heskett et al. 1994). The key underlying idea is that improving product and service attributes will lead to an improvement in customer satisfaction. In turn, increased customer satisfaction should lead to greater customer retention, which is often used as a proxy for customer loyalty, which then should lead to greater profitability. Despite the almost self-evident nature of these positive links, empirical evidence shows only mixed support (Zeithaml 2000). Likewise, translating the conceptual framework into practical reality has been problematic for many firms. For example, a firm may have improved its performance on a key attribute only to discover that the overall satisfaction score did not noticeably increase. At other times, changes in overall satisfaction scores have failed to show a demonstrable impact on customer retention (Ittner and Larcker 1998). Consequently, firms must have a complete understanding of the entire satisfaction–profit chain to manage customers efficiently.

Reinartz and Kumar (2002) highlight the implications of firms having a thorough understanding of the satisfaction–profit chain. They investigate the profitability of a sample of more than 16000 individual customers across four different industries – both B2B and B2C. They find that the relationship between customer retention and customer profits is not as strong and straightforward as anticipated. As Figure 17.2 shows, they demonstrate across the different firms the existence of loyal but not very profitable segments of customers (due to excessive resource allocation) and segments that generate very high profits but only for a short time. Because these short-term customers can be very profitable, it is clear that loyalty is not the only path to profitability.

The key implication of their finding is that caution must be exercised when equating customer retention or loyalty with customer profitability. Therefore, firms ultimately must make an effort to obtain information on individual or segment profitability. Although the satisfaction–profit chain concept is conceptually sound, measuring and managing customer satisfaction is not enough. By not understanding the exact nature (e.g. strength, symmetry, non-linearity) of the various links, many companies seriously misallocate resources from an incorrect understanding of the underlying mechanics. Furthermore, customer profits are ultimately required to make good marketing decisions, especially in a B2B context in which the contribution of customers is significantly influenced by the firm resources those customers 'consume'. Likewise, understanding these effects across different segments is mandatory marketing practice.

CUSTOMER LIFETIME VALUE

Customer lifetime value (CLV) is a metric that captures the potential value or profits a customer provides to the firm. Interest in CLV among practitioners and academics is driven by several reasons. First, given the weak relationship between loyalty and customer profitability (Reinartz and Kumar 2002), CLV directly focuses managers' attention on the profits the customer provides rather than a proxy for profits. Second, CLV is an important metric in guiding an organization's transition from product to customer centricity (Gupta and Lehmann 2008). Third, CLV is a forward-looking metric that enables firms to select and target the customers they expect to be profitable in the future rather than focusing attention solely on customers who provided profits in the past (Venkatesan and Kumar 2004). Finally, CLV provides managers with a venue for connecting marketing actions to financial returns, both cash and stock market valuation (Kumar and Shah 2009; Rust et al. 2004).

Customer lifetime value refers to the net present value of future profits a customer provides over his or her life of business with the firm. In its basic form, the CLV of a customer is as follows (Gupta et al. 2004):

$$CLV = m* \frac{r}{1 + d - r} \tag{17.1}$$

where
m = margin provided by a customer,
r = retention rate and
d = risk-free discount rate for the firm.

The formulation assumes that margins and retention rates are constant over a customer's lifetime and provides an infinite time horizon for calculating CLV. Variants are obtained by relaxing these assumptions. For example, some industries and companies typically calculate four- to five-year customer values instead of using the infinite horizon. Over a short time horizon, however, changes in the technological or competitive landscape do not affect the CLV calculation. Thus, this consideration recommends that managers use an infinite horizon in mature industries with more stable consumer preferences, less competitive intensity and slower technological advances. In other words, an infinite time horizon is more appropriate for industries or companies with a smaller discount rate, and alternatively a shorter time horizon is more appropriate for calculating CLV when the discount rate is higher (Farris et al. 2010). Some researchers have recommended calculating CLV as the value of future cash flows assuming no changes in the current macro environment and including a prescient value (CLV-*p*) to accommodate major changes in the external environment (Berger et al. 2006). The formulation in equation (17.1) does not include acquisition costs when calculating CLV. In this form CLV provides the upper limit for a customer's acquisition cost. Other formulations have been proposed in which the acquisition cost is subtracted from equation (17.1) to calculate CLV (e.g. Gupta and Lehmann 2008). A more comprehensive formulation that incorporates the extensions discussed here may be represented as follows (Reinartz and Venkatesan 2008):

$$CLV_i = \sum_{t=1}^{T} \frac{\sum_{p=1}^{P} M_{tp}*Q_{itp} - \sum_{j=1}^{J} CS_{itj}}{(1 + r)^t} - \sum_{i=1}^{n} AC_i \qquad (17.2)$$

where

M_{tp} = gross margin (i.e. net of cost of goods sold) for product p in period t,
Q_{itp} = quantity purchased of product p by customer i in period t,
CS_{itj} = cost to serve customer i in period t through channel J,
AC_i = acquisition cost for customer i,
r = discount rate and
n = number of customers of the firm in time $t = 0$.

The major challenge in CLV measurement as represented in equation (17.2) for business settings is the recognition of multiple points of contact between a customer and the firm and the value created at each stage of the supply chain. Measuring CLV forms the basis for the major strategic decisions in CRM, including (1) which customers to select and (2) how to allocate resources to selected customers.[1] In this chapter we discuss empirical models that predict the major components of a CLV-based customer management strategy – namely, acquisition cost, retention rate and margins – and highlight the necessary modifications and challenges in a B2B setting.

Acquisition Cost

Strategic acquisition emphasizes acquiring more of the *right* customers rather than simply acquiring as many customers as possible (Reinartz et al. 2005). The objective of CRM acquisition campaigns is to acquire prospects that resemble current best customers. The two major objectives of acquisition models are to (1) review historical acquisition campaigns to understand those that were effective and also predict the expected acquisition probability (and cost) for a customer and (2) identify the right customers to acquire from a pool of prospects.

For the first category, logit or probit models are used to predict the acquisition probability of individual customers (Thomas 2001). Vector autoregressive models are appropriate for identifying interactions among different marketing instruments and estimating the long-term profitability of customers acquired through each marketing channel. However, vector autoregressive models are appropriate for modeling acquisition rates of a group of customers at each period rather than studying individual differences in acquisition probability and costs. Because a firm does not have access to a prospect's transaction history with the competition and, by definition, a prospect does not have any interaction with the firm, the firm's current customers and prospects are typically matched according to profile variables provided by secondary data services, such as Dun & Bradstreet. Prospect scoring (Bodapati and Gupta 2004) and clone marketing (Steenburgh et al. 2003) have been proposed under this context.

Several nuances of B2B markets necessitate modifications to current models for predicting acquisition probability. First, business sales cycles are typically longer and involve sophisticated sequencing and coordination of several activities. For example, selling solutions or services to firms involves first identifying and predicting customers' business challenges through business intelligence, establishing contact with the customer, understanding specific customer concerns, developing customer-specific solutions, executing pilots and demonstrating benefits of the vendor's solutions, and finally implementing the solution. These steps can extend over multiple years, which presents a challenge of modeling the interaction or synergy among these various activities for accurately predicting acquisition costs. Different types of businesses have different decision-making units with different decision-making processes. An effective CRM strategy should be able to identify these differences to harness firm resources effectively in order to reduce acquisition costs. In this regard, CRM models would need to integrate microsegmentation strategies (Rangan et al. 1992) into their acquisition models. Another challenge is that though sales costs can be directly attributable to a single customer, other activities, such as corporate advertising, trade shows and business intelligence functions, cannot be. Thus, the CLV approach provides an opportunity for firms to treat the sales function as a profit center by attributing all the acquisition costs (sometimes over multiple years) to the same customer.

Retention Rate

Two questions are critical when determining the model used for predicting retention rate: first, is the customer–firm relationship 'contractual' or 'non-contractual'? Second, when customers quit the relationship, are they 'lost for good', or is there 'always a share' that can be obtained from them? Contracts dominate B2B transactions, but several non-contractual situations also exist, such as the relationship between a firm and an office supplies vendor. In contractual settings in which customer defection is observed, a binary logit or probit model can be used as a function of covariates to predict retention. Neslin et al. (2006) review several models that academics and practitioners submitted as part of a 'churn tournament' and find that logit and tree analyses outperform discriminant, explanatory and novice approaches. Moreover, the more than 40 entries in the tournament yielded significant differences in terms of incremental profits for the organization. This shows that model quality and predictive accuracy matter.

For the non-contractual context, three of the key models are the Negative Binomial

Distribution (NBD)/Pareto model (Schmittlein et al. 1987), the purchase timing model (Allenby et al. 1999) and the Markov switching models (Pfeifer and Carraway 2000). The NBD/Pareto model assumes that customers buy at a steady, stochastic rate and then become inactive. More specifically, it models time to drop-out using the Pareto (exponential-gamma mixture) timing model and repeat buying behavior but employs the NBD (Poisson-gamma mixture) counting model to represent activity. The data points entered into the model are quite simple and usually exist in many organizations; for example, time since first purchase, time from first purchase until most recent purchase and total number of transactions. Using these inputs, the NBD/Pareto model predicts the likelihood that a customer is still active or retained at some period t. Applications of the NBD/Pareto model include Reinartz and Kumar (2002, 2003) and Fader et al. (2005).

Hazard models assume that changes (increases) in customer's interpurchase times signal a potential threat of leaving the relationship and therefore require managerial intervention. Interpurchase times are also assumed to follow a generalized gamma distribution, and the model allows for both cross-sectional and temporal heterogeneity. In the context of investment decisions, Allenby et al. (1999) find three segments that vary according to their activity status: superactive accounts, active accounts and inactive accounts. In practice, firms would use the model to identify customers who are likely to move from an active to a less active state by recalculating their probability estimates and monitoring them periodically. Recent applications include Lewis (2006), Venkatesan and Kumar (2004) and Venkatesan et al. (2007).

The final alternative uses Markov switching matrices to model customer–firm relationships (Pfeifer and Carraway 2000; Rust et al. 2004). Markov models assume that the customer–firm relationship progresses through different states and models the transition probabilities of a customer in a certain state moving to other states. While early Markov models estimated transition models on observed states that are more applicable for contractual situations, recent frameworks model customer transitions through unobserved states and therefore are even applicable to non-contractual settings (Netzer et al. 2008).

Rust et al. (2004) argue that the lost-for-good approach understates CLV because it does not allow a defected customer to return. Other researchers argue that this is not a serious problem because customers can be treated as a renewable resource (Drèze and Bonfrer 2009). The NBD/Pareto and hazard model frameworks are applicable to either a lost-for-good or an always-a-share assumption; Markov models are more appropriate for the always-a-share assumption. It might be that the choice between these assumptions is context specific. For example, Gupta and Lehmann (2008) propose that business relationships are more suitable for the always-a-share approach because business customers tend to have relationships with multiple service providers. Business relationships that rely on a single salesperson who 'owns' the customer loyalty are at a high risk of customer churn when the salesperson leaves the firm (Bendapudi and Leone 2002; Palmatier et al. 2007). Therefore, relationships between firms are stronger and longer lasting when there are multiple ties between the firms (Palmatier 2008). Multilevel chain of effects models that connect microlevel interactions between the customer and the firm on customer retention would help inform the relationship dynamics in business environments. Such models would also enable managers to effectively connect salesperson incentives to CLV.

Margins

Customer-provided margins represent the final component of the CLV formulation. Researchers have proposed using average past margins, regression models and probability models to predict these margins. But for a few exceptions (Niraj et al. 2001; Venkatesan et al. 2007), most margin models focus on predicting future revenue and then apply a constant gross margin and retention cost to predict customer margin. In business settings retention costs can vary substantially across customers. Furthermore, it may prove challenging to effectively assemble information on customer interactions across multiple divisions of the same firm. Research on calculating and predicting customer margins is scarce partly because of the challenges involved in accurately estimating the costs of serving a customer.

Pursuing Synergies

Firms might make suboptimal marketing investments for at least three reasons. First, they might view customer acquisition rate and customer retention rate as principal metrics of marketing performance. Second, they might focus too much on the current cost of customer acquisition and retention and not enough on customers' long-term value. Third, they might treat acquisition and retention as independent activities and attempt to maximize both rates. The remedy for all these pitfalls rests on the adoption of CLV-based strategies.

By using the concept of CLV described in this section, firms can optimize the acquisition/retention costs of customers and link such efforts to overall profitability. Such an exercise would help firms decide which customers are worth acquiring or retaining and which dormant customers should be pursued to return to the firm. The knowledge firms acquire in implementing these strategies could be used to acquire prospective customers with high profit potential. This approach to link acquisition and retention of customers to firm profitability is a key contribution of the CLV-based approach. We now examine each of these pitfalls to determine how the concept of CLV applies to each.

In the first pitfall, companies often view customer acquisition rate and customer retention rate as the principal metrics of their marketing performance. This is because the two metrics are easy to understand and track and because they easily correspond to ascertaining the increase or decrease in a company's market share. These metrics may be appropriate for B2B companies in contractual settings, such as communications and technology and component manufacturing. However, using these two metrics in non-contractual settings, such as construction and equipment manufacturing, may lead to problems. Realizing this, many firms have begun taking steps to reward account managers who strive to maximize profitability and not just maximize acquisition and retention rates. However, such an approach may lead managers to focus too much on short-term profitability, the second pitfall.

To analyze the second pitfall, Thomas et al. (2004) tested the relationship among acquisition costs, retention costs and customer profitability. Their analysis shows that the 'casual customers' (32 per cent) constituted the largest segment but accounted for only 20 per cent of the profits. This proves that customers who are easy to acquire and retain may not yield the most profits. In contrast, the 'low maintenance customers' (15 per cent) constituted the smallest segment but generated the largest profits (40 per cent of total profits). The 'royal customers' made up 28 per cent of the total customer base and contributed 25 per cent to the profits. Finally, the 'high maintenance customers' proved the least profitable group of customers; they contributed only 15 per cent to the total profits, even though they made up 25 per cent of the total customer base. These trends and findings can be generalized to other firms and industries, with variations in distribution of profits and customers. Thus, targeting customers who are easy to acquire and retain may not ensure profitable customer management. The CLV approach recommends simultaneously optimizing the acquisition/retention costs and directly linking such efforts to overall profitability. In the pursuit to optimize acquisition and retention costs, managers may often end up maximizing acquisition and retention rates independently, the third pitfall.

Treating acquisition and retention independently indicates that the acquisition and retention departments are not complementing each other. In such situations, the acquisition department will try to acquire as many customers as possible, while the retention department will try to retain as many customers as possible. A potential cause for concern here is that these two scenarios may include customers who are not profitable in the long run. Therefore, the key to strike a balance between acquisition and retention lies in efficient resource allocation between customer acquisition and customer retention. In business environments in which decisions about allocating marketing resources increasingly occur at the individual level, marketers must understand that customers who are easy to acquire and retain may not be the most profitable customers. Traditionally a firm has multiple sales teams, each with a primary responsibility of either customer acquisition or retention. The responsibility of balancing acquisition and retention resources remains at the organization level and entails employing someone such as an industry vertical or customer segment manager. Resource allocation decisions should be not only in terms of acquisition and retention but should also be on the level of choices between various communication channels. Such a balance between acquisition and retention will provide managers with a clear set of attainable, profit-linked marketing goals.

CHANNELS

Having acquired and retained customers, companies aim to realize revenue growth from them. Many companies achieve this by foraying into multiple channels. In many instances, these channels are designed to offer customers a chance both to make purchases through multiple channels and to search for product information in one or more channels and purchase in a completely different channel. For example, in a recent study, Art Technology Group (2010) found that: (1) 78 per cent of the respondents used two or more channels to browse, research and make purchases; (2) 30 per cent used three channels or more; and (3) 43 per cent began their research online or through a mobile device but needed to call a customer service or call center representative to complete the transaction because they could not find the necessary product or service information online.

Similarly, mobile technology is significantly influencing shopping patterns. Since September 2009, many national retailers, such as American Eagle Outfitters, A|X Armani Exchange, Sears, Target and Whole Foods Market, have launched m-commerce sites (Retail Traffic 2010). In January 2010, the California-based specialty apparel seller Wet Seal launched its m-commerce site. The company also added features to its corporate site, such as allowing shoppers to reserve products online, and launched a platform that allows customers to shop with friends in real time through social media. Whole Foods' mobile site contains more than 2000 recipes and store information but not a mobile checkout option, while Wet Seal's mobile site provides customers with inventory updates in real time, nearby store locations and a mobile purchase option. In the B2B space, Staples launched an online version of its catalog for its contract customers in 2007 with the aim to reduce costs and increase its reach to mid-sized businesses. Thus, the role of channels is constantly evolving; the instances of shopping across multiple channels is ever increasing; and the emergence of new media, such as mobile phones, plays a crucial part in reaching out to customers.

So who are these multichannel shoppers? How can a firm identify them? Kumar and Venkatesan (2005) identify the drivers of multichannel shoppers as: (1) customer characteristics; (2) supplier-specific characteristics; and (3) customer demographics. Among the various customer characteristics they tested, customer tenure, purchase frequency and the level of customer-initiated contacts had the highest positive effect on multichannel adoption. For supplier-specific characteristics, combining sales calls with either direct mail or telesales had the highest positive effect on multichannel adoption. The mere identification of multichannel shopping drivers may not be sufficient, because managers generally want to know whether multichannel shoppers are more profitable than single-channel customers. In their study, Kumar and Venkatesan compared the value of single-channel and multichannel shoppers across various customer-based metrics, such as how much a customer spends (revenue), share of wallet, past customer value, the likelihood that a customer will buy in the future (likelihood of staying active) and CLV. The results showed that as customers shop across more channels (from one channel to four channels), they spend more revenue with the firm, spend a higher proportion on the firm (rather than on a competitor), have a higher past profitability (which correlates with future profitability) and have a higher likelihood of buying in the future. Therefore, if firms want to identify candidates to encourage shopping in multiple channels, they should first determine which customers show the right signs of being potential multichannel shoppers based on the drivers and then try to leverage those drivers to encourage multichannel shopping behavior.

In addition to considering CLV scores, companies can consider the marginal profitability of customers in determining the right customers to engage in multichannel shopping (Kumar 2010). By segmenting customers according to high and low levels of CLV scores and the marginal profitability (as represented by the marginal effect of marketing communications), companies can develop an effective transaction and communication-based framework that can offer customized messages to the different customer value segments.

Therefore, a company that aims to implement a campaign to encourage customers to adopt new channels should consider the use of field experiments before reaching out to the entire customer base. Field experiments on a sample of customers will provide insights into the communication approach. Such an exercise also helps the company determine which of its customers shop in multiple channels and which customers are most likely to adopt this new channel. In addition, firms can use responses to the field study to assess the return on marketing investment of a potential campaign to all the customers and whether the customer–firm interactions changed after the customer adopted the new channel. Finally, a field study also helps the company identify prospects who are likely to be multichannel shoppers.

LOOKING AHEAD

In this section we provide three parallel examples of the latest trends in CRM research with implications for B2B research. The examples emphasize the need to build stronger and more compelling relationship offerings to customers. This can be brought by better understanding customer needs through the augmentation of traditional secondary data from CRM systems with primary data from customer-initiated interactions with the firm, such as product returns, and from interactions with customer service employees and salespeople. Useful information from customers includes their product and service preferences; attitudes toward the firm, its salespeople and brands; and their inclination to provide business referrals. An example of more compelling relationship offerings is given through the creation of strong service offerings.

Creating Lasting Relationships Through Service Strategies

In most mature product-focused B2B industries, a key challenge is generating true differentiation and, consequently, the ability to charge a premium price. That is, organizations struggle with the objective to create long-lasting customer relationships in the face of product offers that are rather comparable in terms of technical features, attributes and performance. Likewise, for many standard applications, the technology frontier is sufficiently under command even by non-leading competitors. As a result, frequent supplier switching and extensive price competition occur, making it virtually impossible for B2B manufacturers to achieve reasonable and long-term customer profitability.

To combat this challenge, many B2B manufacturers have identified services as a potential weapon (Reinartz and Ulaga 2008). Manufacturers move into services and customer solutions to solidify their positions in increasingly competitive markets and grow revenues and margins beyond their core product businesses. Even beyond global icons, such as General Electric or IBM, this trend has gained widespread acceptance across multinational corporations and small and medium-sized firms. The rationale for a shift from a goods-dominant to a services-led approach in business markets has been well documented (e.g. Antioco et al. 2008; Davies et al. 2006; Wise and Baumgartner 1999).

When deployed successfully, a services-led strategy can be extremely beneficial. As one senior executive put it, 'Successful services is almost like being married to the customer. It represents a huge barrier to entry for competitors'. That is, companies do recognize the potential positive impact of service strategies on their ability to create and maintain solid and long-term customer relationships. Although managers generally agree that they must move into services, economic results are mixed at best. According to a Bain & Company study, only 21 per cent of companies succeed with service strategies (Baveja et al. 2004). Hancock et al. (2005) find that approximately half of all solution providers realize only modest benefits, and 25 per cent actually lose money. Similarly Sawhney et al. (2004) report notable failed service-based initiatives, including Intel's venture into web-based services and Boeing's move into financial services.

Reinartz and Ulaga (2008) investigate the strategic approach of product-focused manufacturers in the service domain. Here, they uncover distinct practices that separate the unsuccessful from the successful companies. Specifically, they find four different levers for building lasting profitable relationships through services. First, by switching current ancillary services from 'free to fee', companies make customers aware of the value they are providing. Second, because services are heterogeneous in nature, manufacturers must streamline back-office operations to produce services efficiently. Third, services need to be sold through an adequately trained sales force. In most cases, services represent a necessary evil for a product-focused sales force. Fourth, before a company can successfully sell complex solutions, it must truly understand customers' problems and design offerings that will solve these problems. This means gathering information on customers' processes and structures.

In general, service strategies have received immense attention in the past few years. Beyond the existing studies, we need to understand better how services can contribute to building lasting relationships in different types of service and product contexts.

Customer Mind-set Measures

The trend toward services and solutions places an even greater emphasis on soft measures of relationship quality, such as satisfaction and overall customer attachment or attitudes toward a firm. However, the ability to build and run extensive behavioral databases about customers has led to a de facto de-emphasis of 'soft' attitudinal information in many organizations. Proponents of the behavioral data approach contend that customer purchase behavior essentially encapsulates underlying attitudes, and because decision-makers are mainly concerned about customer behavior, there is no need to truly worry about underlying attitudes. Reflective of this belief is the massive shift toward analyzing and modeling customer behavior as the core dependent variable instead of attitudinal and intention metrics, which were more prevalent before the availability of customer databases (Gupta and Zeithaml 2006). The entire debate about marketing return on investment (Srinivasan and Hanssens 2009) reflects the underlying sentiment that attitudinal insight is entirely insufficient at the senior decision-making level, whereas behavioral insight is today's benchmark.

Some recent developments indicate a renewed interest in incorporating information on customer attitudes explicitly into marketing strategy. Developing marketing mix and resource allocation strategies that respond to shifts in underlying customer attitudes – in addition to behavioral response – has reappeared as a priority for many firms (Kerin and O'Regan 2008). Several firms, such as Siebel Systems, dunnhumbyUSA, Yankelovich, ZS Associates and IBM, have made large-scale investments in systems that track various customer attitudes, as well as information about customer–firm interactions and customer responses.

Studies linking customer attitudes to marketing actions and sales suggest that information on customer attitudes toward a firm can improve the predictive capability of choice models even when the attitude information is available only at a single period (Horsky et al. 2006). Furthermore, attitudes toward both the firm and the competition need to be included in sales response models (Srinivasan et al. 2008). Venkatesan et al. (2010) assess the value of knowing customer attitudes in predicting CLV and managing customers. They develop a generalized dynamic hierarchical linear model that combines the sales call and sales data that are available at regular time intervals with survey-based customer attitude metrics that are not available at regular intervals. Knowing customer attitudes improves the predictions of customer spending more than customer retention. They find that customer attitudes are more diagnostic for middle-tier customers; that is, customer attitudes help firms identify middle-tier customers with a high potential to transition to top-tier customers. Finally, knowing customer attitudes can improve return on marketing by allowing firms to reduce investments on top-tier customers who are convinced about the firm's products and move resources to middle-tier customers who are still forming their preferences. Business relationships present a good opportunity to incorporate customer mind-set measures into CRM because (1) there are a smaller number of customers to manage; and (2) customers are highly involved in the relationship, which increases the chances of collecting customer attitude measures.

Customer-initiated Activities: Returns and Word of Mouth

Previously we explained how firms can maximize future profits by reaching out to their customers to sell products, services and solutions. However, activities initiated by customers can also contribute toward the firm's future profits, if managed well. Customer-initiated activities in a B2B setting could have both positive and negative implications for the firm. Some of the positive implications of these activities include customers contacting the firm with new needs, customers requiring on-site training programs from the firm (Cannon and Homburg 2001), customers providing feedback to be incorporated into the future purchase orders, and customers providing favorable word of mouth (WOM) to other businesses about the focal firm. Examples of customer-initiated activities having negative implications for the firm include product returns and negative WOM. While it is easy to leverage the positive customer activities to help the financial performance of the firm, the activities with negative implications are not so straightforward. However, a careful analysis of product returns and WOM instances can lead to profitable customer management strategies.

Customers who return products to the firm are not necessarily bad customers. On the contrary, firms should view these returns as opportunities or 'touch points' to interact with the customers and offer a satisfactory return process. Although this might sound counterintuitive, research has shown that too few or too many returns indicate that the customer is a low-CLV customer, and an intermediate number of returns indicate a healthy relationship with the firm. For example, Petersen and Kumar (2010) find that the optimal percentage of product returns that would maximize company profits for a catalog retailer was 13 per cent, or a decrease in product returns of 3 per cent from the actual level. Their reasoning was that as customers begin to return products (up to a threshold), they are becoming more familiar with the firm's different product offerings and distribution channels.

Product returns are more infrequent in the B2B context (owing to longer purchase cycles and a smaller, focused target market), but there are instances when business customers do return products. In such cases, we can expect similar findings to hold for

B2B companies. Other customer-initiated activities that can be considered substitutes for returns in the B2B context include complaints and cancellation requests. To handle complaints, firms should initiate relationship managers to manage key clients. By focusing on resolving the complaint (and not on engaging in any up-selling or cross-selling efforts), firms can handle complaints effectively and possibly prevent them from getting converted into product returns. For cancellation requests, firms should focus on retaining those customers from churning (if they are profitable). In such a scenario, firms can consider setting up a firm credit, which the customer can avail for its future purchases (Kumar 2010). After the customer has been saved, firms can then focus on cross-selling products/services that are more suitable to the customer's needs. Therefore, to determine an optimal product return policy, the firm would need to determine how changes in product return policies affect customer purchase behavior. This can be done using the antecedents of product return behavior as levers for increasing each customer's profitability by maximizing the difference between products purchased and products returned.

With respect to WOM, referral marketing programs are a popular means for B2C firms to acquire new customers. Companies such as AT&T, Sprint PCS, Bank of America and DIRECTV have introduced value-oriented referral incentive programs that reward either the referral or the referring customer, or both. A metric has even been developed to measure a customer's referral value that predicts both the customer's ability and strength to generate profitable referrals (Kumar et al. 2007). However, this is not the case for B2B firms. Instead, they rely on references (or testimonials) from other firms that are already clients of the selling firm to influence purchase decisions.

Many B2B firms, such as Microsoft, SAS and McKinsey, provide their potential clients with testimonials and video references to influence their purchase decisions. Some firms also create a database of customer reference cases for the potential clients to read. In quantifying the value of these business references, Kumar et al. (2010) introduce the concept of business reference value (BRV). The BRV is a metric that measures the ability of a client firm's reference to influence a potential client firm to purchase. They define BRV as the amount of profit the existing client firm can help generate from the potential client firms that purchase products and services as a result of the reference.

To compute the BRV of a customer, the first step is to compute the CLV of the newly acquired customer. Reinartz et al. (2005) demonstrate this approach. The second step is to determine the degree to which all the references obtained affected the new client's purchase decision. This is done by asking the new client to allocate 100 total points between the influence of the reference and all other marketing influences to the purchase decision process. The purpose of this step is to understand the importance of references relative to other marketing activities in influencing a client's purchase decision. The final step, given that the references mattered, is to determine the degree to which each reference obtained influenced the new client's purchase decision. This is done by asking the new client to allocate 100 total points among all the references according to their impact on the purchase decision. For example, if a new client received five different references on a firm, in this step the client allocates 100 points among these five references. While the previous step compared references and other marketing activities, the current step compares the different references obtained by the customer. The product of the values obtained from these steps provides the BRV of a customer.

Using data from a telecommunications and a financial services firm, Kumar et al.

(2010) also identify the following drivers for BRV: (1) the characteristics of the referencing firm (e.g. size, industry); (2) the exchange characteristics of the referencing firm (e.g. how much it purchases, how often it purchases); and (3) the characteristics of the reference (e.g. form of reference, similarity of the referencing firm to the potential client firm). They also tested whether the most profitable customers also had high reference values. Using a decile analysis, they found that high-CLV firms tend to have a high BRV. Specifically, the top six deciles of CLV have the top six deciles of BRV. However, firms with the highest BRVs were in deciles 3, 4 and 5 when ranked on CLV. This finding clearly demonstrates that firms cannot alienate medium-value customers in gaining value from reference programs.

Given that there are no studies in the marketing literature that quantify the value of the references made by client firms, this study has important implications for B2B firms. Furthermore, managers of the selling firm can now identify the best references to influence potential client firms to purchase products and services in the future.

IMPLEMENTING CRM

Customer-centric Organizations

When organizations want to build lasting relationships that create value for both the customers and the focal organization, the type of organizational set-up is likely to have a catalyzing or detracting effect. The ability to create and maintain strong customer relationships should be evaluated, at the minimum, against the background of individual technological (Jayachandran et al. 2005), organizational (Sabherwal et al. 2006) or strategic (Bell et al. 2002) aspects. A key finding that has received prominence in this context is that the building of strong relationships and the management thereof requires a *cross-functional integration* of processes, people, operations and marketing capabilities that is enabled through information, technology and applications (Becker et al. 2009; Reinartz et al. 2004). Although systematically interfacing with a large number of customers over time certainly requires a sound technological basis (e.g. software), technology alone will not suffice. Rather, best-in-class organizations exhibit steadfast senior management commitment, analytical capabilities and alignment of employee incentives with customer management objectives. Therefore, it is important that 'marketing thought' penetrates other functions so that they are included in the mission to attract and retain profitable clients effectively. Table 17.1 provides some future research questions that are relevant for CRM in business settings.

Implementing CLV requires a strategic shift from *product-centric* to *customer-centric* marketing. A product-centric approach is designed to sell products to whoever is willing to buy them, indicating a transactional nature of business. In contrast, a customer-centric approach is designed to serve a portfolio of customers and base the business on relationships with those customers. Such customer centricity is achieved by focusing on interactions between firm and customer, between customers, and between firms, or *interaction orientation*. The interaction orientation results in customers being viewed as both a source of business and a potential business resource for the firm. Such an orientation is achieved by: (1) making more customer-level decisions than aggregate decisions; (2)

Table 17.1   Future research issues for CRM in B2B

Topic	Research Issues
Customer loyalty	1. What is the role of brands in the building of affective loyalty in B2B relationships?
	2. What are optimal levels of investment in customer satisfaction? How should customer satisfaction be balanced with customer profitability?
CLV	1. How should firms model the interaction and synergy among the various steps in a business sales cycle to predict the true cost of acquiring a customer?
	2. What are the value of micro segmentation and of different contacts in the customer firm?
	3. How should firms model the chain of effects that connect interactions in a business relationship and customer retention across multiple levels?
	4. What are the organizational mechanisms to share information effectively on customers' retention costs across silos?
	5. How should firms value business referrals?
Channels	1. How should firms identify customer channel preferences and migrate customers to their preferred and cost-effective channels?
	2. How should firms cross-sell and up-sell in the presence of a channel intermediary?
Customer-centric organizations	1. What are the capabilities needed to best manage customer portfolios of different value tiers?
	2. How can the sales, marketing and services functions interact to build a single face to the customer?
	3. How does customer management technology enable the implementation of a customer-centric organization?

responding to customer needs effectively and efficiently; (3) providing customers with a rich and varied experience; (4) encouraging customer-to-customer interactions; and (5) encouraging customer feedback (Ramani and Kumar 2008). Administering changes to the workforce elements is necessary for a complete implementation. Some of the company-wide human resource changes include: (1) communicating the change in focus through employee-targeted messages; (2) increasing employee interest and participation to support the change; (3) establishing transparency in sharing information and insights about the change process; (4) enabling stakeholders to implement the change on a daily basis; and (5) incorporating monitoring and evaluation procedures to keep the change in place.

Managerial Buy-in of Analytics

Thus far, we have explored the concept of customer loyalty, its implications for business markets and how to measure and manage it to maximize firm profitability. Although the concepts and analyses we present may be the ideal solution, managers still have the task of 'selling' it within their company to implement it. We propose a four-step process to help managers communicate the concepts and strategies and garner the support of the decision-makers within their organizations.

The first step involves presenting the concepts and strategies to the decision-makers.

For example, this chapter shows that customer loyalty does not automatically ensure profitability. Furthermore, the traditional metrics used for measuring the value of the customers are leading to flawed marketing strategies that drain firm resources. Instead, through a forward-looking metric such as CLV, firms can accurately predict the profit brought in by a customer in the future and target similar customers. Concepts such as these must be presented in a way that helps management obtain a deeper understanding of customer loyalty and adopt the proposed concepts as a way forward.

The second step involves presenting best practices of companies that have implemented the proposed concepts and attained success. When managers present best practice applications of firms that implemented these concepts and were able to maximize customer-level revenues and ensure higher profits, it becomes easier and clearer for management to buy into these concepts and understand how they can help the firm when implemented.

The third step involves analyzing a sample data set and comparing it with existing practices. While the first two steps involve communicating the benefits of the proposed concepts and 'selling' them to management, this step involves empirically demonstrating the benefits of adopting the proposed concepts. For example, when the performance of CLV was compared with that of recency, frequency and monetary value and past customer value (backward-looking metrics) for a sample of a B2B high-tech manufacturer, the results showed that the net value generated by the customers scored on CLV was 45 per cent greater than the net revenue generated through customers scored on the backward-looking metrics (Venkatesan and Kumar 2004). This finding helped managers in the B2B firm understand how flawed the backward-looking metrics were in identifying the right customers to target.

The fourth step involves conducting a pilot study on a segment of the firm's customers to demonstrate how the concepts and strategies work. Alternatively, the pilot study could also be done on one business unit of the firm, before extending it to the other units. For example, when IBM wanted to: (1) know which customers to select for targeting; (2) determine the level of resources to be allocated to the selected customers; and (3) select the right customers to be nurtured to increase future profitability, it implemented a pilot study for 35000 of its mid-market customers (firms with between 100 and 999 employees). The results of the study helped IBM identify the right customers to target and led to the reallocation of resources for approximately 14 per cent of the customers, compared with the allocation rules IBM used previously that provided an increase in revenue of $20 million (a tenfold increase) without any changes in the level of marketing investment (Kumar et al. 2008). Such pilot studies provide management with the much-needed confidence to implement new concepts and strategies to the entire organization.

CONCLUSION

Academics and practitioners can benefit tremendously from studies that integrate insights from the CRM and B2B research streams. Because CRM traditionally originated within marketing groups, and business research focuses more on sales force and channels, integration between these streams can also contribute to our understanding of the organization-wide challenge of marketing–sales force collaboration. As Figure

17.1 shows, quantification of the process for developing customer relationships is a good venue for collaboration between CRM and business research. Advances in information technology have tremendously reduced the cost of collecting detailed data on customer transactions and preferences, rendering such integration between CRM and business research more effective and beneficial for firms. Ultimately such integration and collaboration is effective only if an organization is customer focused.

NOTE

1. For the latest findings on CRM strategy, we refer readers to Kumar et al. (2010) and Reinartz and Venkatesan (2008).

REFERENCES

Allenby, Greg M., Robert P. Leone and Lichung Jen (1999), 'A dynamic model of purchase timing with application to direct marketing', *Journal of American Statistical Association*, **94** (June), 365–74.

Anderson, James C. and James A. Narus (1991), 'Partnering as a focused market strategy', *California Management Review*, **33** (3), 95–113.

Anderson, James, James A. Narus and Das Narayandas (2008), *Business Market Management: Understanding, Creating, and Delivering Value*, 3rd edn, Upper Saddle River, NJ: Pearson Prentice Hall.

Antioco, Michael, Rudy K. Moenaert, Adam Lindgreen and Martin G.M. Wetzels (2008), 'Organizational antecedents and consequences of service business orientations in manufacturing companies', *Journal of the Academy of Marketing Science*, **36** (3), 337–58.

Art Technology Group (2010), 'Cross-channel commerce: the consumer view', Research report (March).

Baveja, Sarabjit Singh, Jim Gilbert and Dianne Ledingham (2004), 'From products to services: why it's not so simple', *Harvard Management Update*, **9** (4), 3–5.

Becker, Jan U., Goetz Greve and Sönke Albers (2009), 'The impact of technological and organizational implementation of CRM on customer acquisition, maintenance, and retention', *International Journal of Research in Marketing*, **26** (3), 207–15.

Bell, David, John Deighton, Werner J. Reinartz, Roland T. Rust and Gordon Swartz (2002), 'Seven barriers to customer equity management', *Journal of Service Research*, **5** (1), 77–86.

Bendapudi, Neeli and Robert P. Leone (2002), 'Managing business-to-business customer relationships following key contact employee turnover in a vendor firm', *Journal of Marketing*, **66** (2), 83–101.

Berger, Paul D., Naras Eechambadi, Morris George, Donald R. Lehmann, Ross Rizley and Rajkumar Venkatesan (2006), 'From customer lifetime value to shareholder value: theory, empirical evidence, and issues for future research', *Journal of Service Research*, **9** (2), 156–67.

Bodapati, Anand and Sachin Gupta (2004), 'A direct approach to predicting discretized response in target marketing', *Journal of Marketing Research*, **41** (February), 73–85.

Cannon, Joseph P. and Christian Homburg (2001), 'Buyer–supplier relationships and customer firm costs', *Journal of Marketing*, **65** (1), 29–43.

Davies, Andrew, Tim Brady and Michael Hobday (2006), 'Charting a path toward integrated solutions', *MIT Sloan Management Review*, **47** (3), 39–48.

Day, George S. (2000), 'Managing market relationships', *Journal of the Academy of Marketing Science*, **28** (1), 24–30.

Day, George S. (2006), 'Aligning the organization with the market', *Sloan Management Review*, **48** (1), 41–9.

Dholakia, Ruby R., Jean. L. Johnson, Albert J. Della Bitta and Nikhilesh Dholakia (1993), 'Decision-making time in organizational buying behavior: an investigation of its antecedents', *Journal of the Academy of Marketing Science*, **21** (Fall), 281–92.

Drèze, Xavier and André Bonfrer (2009), 'Moving from customer lifetime value to customer equity', *Quantitative Marketing and Economics*, **7** (3), 289–320.

Fader, Peter S., Bruce G.S. Hardie and Ka Lok Lee (2005), 'Counting your customers the easy way: an alternative to the Pareto/NBD model', *Marketing Science*, **24** (Spring), 275–84.

Farris, Paul W., Neil T. Bendle, Phillip E. Pfeifer and David J. Reibstein (2010), *Marketing Metrics: The Definitive Guide to Measuring Marketing Performance*, 2nd edn, Philadelphia: Wharton School Publishing.

Gulati, Ranjay (2010), *Reorganize for Resilience: Putting Customers at the Center of Your Organization*, Cambridge, MA: Harvard Business Press.

Gupta, Sunil and Donald Lehmann (2008), 'Models of customer value', in Berend Wierenga (eds), *Handbook of Marketing Decision Models*, New York: Springer, pp. 255–90.

Gupta, Sunil and Valarie Zeithaml (2006), 'Customer metrics and their impact on financial performance', *Marketing Science*, **25** (November–December), 718–39.

Gupta, Sunil, Donald Lehmann and Jennifer A. Stuart (2004), 'Valuing customers', *Journal of Marketing Research*, **41** (1), 7–18.

Hancock, Maryanne Q., Roland H. John and Philip J. Wojcik (2005), 'Better B2B selling', *McKinsey Quarterly*, **38** (3), 15–21.

Heskett, James L., Thomas O. Jones, Gary Loveman, W. Earl Sasser Jr and Leonard A. Schlesinger (1994), 'Putting the service-profit chain to work', *Harvard Business Review*, **72** (March–April), 164–74.

Horsky, Dan, Sanjog Misra and Paul Nelson (2006), 'Observed and unobserved preference heterogeneity in brand-choice models', *Marketing Science*, **25** (4), 322–35.

Ittner, Christopher D. and David F. Larcker (1998), 'Are nonfinancial measures leading indicators of financial performance? An analysis of customer satisfaction', *Journal of Accounting Research*, **36** (1), 1–35.

Jaworski, Bernard J. and Ajay K. Kohli (1993), 'Market orientation: antecedents and consequences', *Journal of Marketing*, **57** (July), 53–70.

Jayachandran, Satish, Subhash Sharma, Peter Kaufman and Pushkala Raman (2005), 'The role of relational information processes and technology use in customer relationship management', *Journal of Marketing*, **69** (4), 177–92.

Kerin, Roger A. and Rob O'Regan (2008), *Marketing Mix Decisions: New Perspectives and Practices*, Chicago, IL: American Marketing Association.

Kumar, V. (2010), 'A customer lifetime value-based approach to marketing in the multichannel, multimedia retailing environment', *Journal of Interactive Marketing*, **24** (2), 71–85.

Kumar, V. and Denish Shah (2009), 'Expanding the role of marketing: from customer equity to market capitalization', *Journal of Marketing*, **73** (6), 119–36.

Kumar, V. and Rajkumar Venkatesan (2005), 'Who are the multichannel shoppers and how do they perform? Correlates of multichannel shopping behavior', *Journal of Interactive Marketing*, **19** (2), 44–62.

Kumar, V., J. Andrew Petersen and Robert P. Leone (2007), 'How valuable is word of mouth?', *Harvard Business Review*, **85** (10), 139–48.

Kumar, V., J. Andew Petersen and Robert P. Leone (2010), 'Understanding word of mouth in business markets', working paper, Robinson College of Business, Georgia State University.

Kumar, V., Rajkumar Venkatesan, Tim Bohling and Denise Beckmann (2008), 'Practice prize report – the power of CLV: managing customer lifetime value at IBM', *Marketing Science*, **27** (4), 585–99.

Kumar, V., Lerzan Aksoy, Bas Donkers, Rajkumar Venkatesan, Thorsten Wiesel and Sebastian Tillmanns (2010), 'Undervalued or overvalued customers: capturing total customer engagement value', *Journal of Service Research*, **13** (3), 297–310.

Lambert, Douglas M. and Michael Knemeyer (2004), 'We're in this together', *Harvard Business Review*, **82** (12), 114–22.

Lewis, Michael (2006), 'Customer acquisition programs and customer asset value', *Journal of Marketing Research*, **43** (2), 195–203.

Morgan, Robert M. and Shelby D. Hunt (1994), 'The commitment-trust theory of relationship marketing', *Journal of Marketing*, **58** (3), 20–38.

Narayandas, Das (2005), 'Building loyalty in business markets', *Harvard Business Review*, **83** (9), 131–9, 160.

Neslin, Scott A., Sunil Gupta, Wagner Kamakura, Junxiang Lu and Charlotte H. Mason (2006), 'Defection detection: measuring and understanding the predictive accuracy of customer churn models', *Journal of Marketing Research*, **43** (2), 204–11.

Netzer, Oded, James Lattin and S. Srinivasan (2008), 'A hidden Markov model of relationship dynamics', *Marketing Science*, **27** (2), 185–204.

Niraj, Rakesh, Mahendra Gupta and Chakravarthi Narasimhan (2001), 'Customer profitability in a supply chain', *Journal of Marketing*, **65** (July), 1–16.

Palmatier, Robert (2008), 'Interfirm relational drivers of customer value', *Journal of Marketing*, **72** (4), 76–89.

Palmatier, Robert, Lisa K. Scheer and Jan-Benedict E.M. Steenkamp (2007), 'Customer loyalty to whom? Managing the benefits and risks of salesperson-owned loyalty', *Journal of Marketing Research*, **44** (May), 185–99.

Petersen, J. Andrew and V. Kumar (2010), 'Can product returns make you money?', *Sloan Management Review*, **51** (3), 85–9.

Pfeifer, Phillip E. and Robert L. Carraway (2000), 'Modelling customer relationships as Markov chains', *Journal of Interactive Marketing*, **14** (2), 43–55.

Ramani, Girish and V. Kumar (2008), 'Interaction orientation and firm performance', *Journal of Marketing*, **72** (1), 27–45.

Rangan, V. Kasturi, Rowland T. Moriarty and Gordon S. Swartz (1992), 'Segmenting customers in mature industrial markets', *Journal of Marketing*, **56** (October), 72–82.

Reichheld, Frederick (1996), *The Loyalty Effect*, Boston, MA: Harvard Business Press.

Reinartz, Werner and V. Kumar (2002), 'The mismanagement of customer loyalty', *Harvard Business Review*, **80** (7), 86–94.

Reinartz, Werner and V. Kumar (2003), 'The impact of customer relationship characteristics on profitable lifetime duration', *Journal of Marketing*, **67** (January), 77–99.

Reinartz, Werner and W. Ulaga (2008), 'How to sell services profitably', *Harvard Business Review*, **86** (5), 90–98.

Reinartz, Werner and Rajkumar Venkatesan (2008), 'Decision models for customer relationship management (CRM)', in Berend Wierenga (ed.), *Handbook of Marketing Decision Models*, New York: Springer, pp. 291–326.

Reinartz, Werner, Manfred Krafft and Wayne D. Hoyer (2004), 'The customer relationship management process: its measurement and impact on performance', *Journal of Marketing Research*, **41** (August), 293–305.

Reinartz, Werner, Jacquelyn S. Thomas and V. Kumar (2005), 'Balancing acquisition and retention resources to maximize customer profitability', *Journal of Marketing*, **69** (January), 63–79.

Retail Traffic (2010), 'Becoming mobile', (1 January), available at http://retailtrafficmag.com/retailing/trends/retail_becoming_mobile/, accessed 11 June 2010.

Rust, Roland T., Katherine T. Lemon and Valarie Zeithaml (2004), 'Return on marketing: using customer equity to focus marketing strategy', *Journal of Marketing*, **68** (1), 109–27.

Sabherwal, Rajiv, Anand Jeyaraj and Charles Chowa (2006), 'Information system success: individual and organizational determinants', *Management Science*, **52** (12), 1849–64.

Sawhney, Mohanbir, Sridhar Balasubramanian and Vish V. Krishnan (2004), 'Creating growth with services', *MIT Sloan Management Review*, **45** (2), 34–43.

Schmittlein, David, Donald G. Morrison and Richard Colombo (1987), 'Counting your customers: who are they and what will they do next?', *Management Science*, **33** (January), 1–24.

Shapiro, Benson and Rowland T. Moriarty (1984), 'Organizing the national account force', Marketing Science Institute Working Paper No. 84-101, Cambridge, MA: Marketing Science Institute.

Sheth, Jagdish N. and Atul Parvatiyar (1995), 'Relationship marketing in consumer markets: antecedents and consequences', *Journal of the Academy of Marketing Science*, **23** (4), 255–71.

Srinivasan, Shuba and Dominique Hanssens (2009), 'Marketing and firm value: metrics, methods, findings and future directions', *Journal of Marketing Research*, **46** (3), 293–312.

Srinivasan, Shuba, Koen Pauwels and Vincent Nijs (2008), 'Demand-based pricing versus past–price dependence: a cost–benefit analysis', *Journal of Marketing*, **72** (2), 15–27.

Steenburgh, Thomas, Andrew Ainslie and Peder Hans Engebretson (2003), 'Revealing the information in zipcodes: Bayesian massively categorical variables and aggregated data in direct marketing', *Marketing Science*, **22** (Winter), 40–57.

Thomas, Jacquelyn S. (2001), 'A methodology for linking customer acquisition to customer retention', *Journal of Marketing Research*, **38** (2), 262–8.

Thomas, Jacquelyn S., Werner Reinartz and V. Kumar (2004), 'Getting the most out of all your customers', *Harvard Business Review*, **82** (7–8), 116–23.

Venkatesan, Rajkumar and V. Kumar (2004), 'A customer lifetime value framework for customer selection and resource allocation strategy', *Journal of Marketing*, **68** (4), 106–25.

Venkatesan, Rajkumar, V. Kumar and Timothy Bohling (2007), 'Optimal customer relationship management using Bayesian decision theory: an application to customer selection', *Journal of Marketing Research*, **44** (4), 579–94.

Venkatesan, Rajkumar, Werner Reinartz and Nalini Ravishanker (2010), 'Attitudes toward firm and competition: how do they matter for CRM activities', working paper, Darden School of Business, University of Virginia.

Wise, Richard and Peter Baumgartner (1999), 'Go downstream: the new profit imperative in manufacturing', *Harvard Business Review*, **77** (5), 133–41.

Woodruff, Robert B. (1997), 'Customer value: the next source for competitive advantage', *Journal of the Academy of Marketing Science*, **25** (2), 139–53.

Zeithaml, Valarie (2000), 'Service quality, profitability, and the economic worth of customers: what we know and what we need to learn', *Journal of the Academy of Marketing Science*, **28** (1), 67–85.

18 Trust, distrust and confidence in B2B relationships
*Lisa K. Scheer**

Trust is central in B2B relationships. It increases the 'ability to adapt to unforeseen problems in ways that are difficult to achieve through arm's-length ties' (Uzzi 1996, p. 678) and is the foundation for greater commitment and performance (Palmatier et al. 2007a). Meta-analysis reveals that the 'effect of trust on satisfaction and long-term orientation is even substantially larger than the direct effect of economic outcomes' (Geyskens et al. 1998, p. 242). However, 'while the effects of trust on attitudes and perceptions have been . . . fairly consistent and positive, its effects on behavior and performance' have been weaker (Langfred 2004, p. 385). Although trust has been theorized to improve performance, its actual effect is questionable (Atuahene-Gima and Li 2002; Gundlach and Cannon 2010). Why does trust not consistently generate more favorable performance? Is this due to confusion about what trust is? Critical gaps in our knowledge about trust in B2B relationships remain, including the following:

- What negative effects could result from greater trust, and how can they be mitigated?
- What is distrust? Can it affect B2B relationships differently than the absence of trust?
- How does trust differ from confidence? What are the sources of confidence?

Contemplation of these issues highlights avenues for theory building and empirical investigation as well as managerial insights. Despite extensive prior research, trust is definitely 'worthy of more thorough analysis and a deeper understanding' (Gundlach and Cannon 2010, p. 411).

WHAT IS TRUST?

'Trust is the belief that one's partner can be relied on to fulfill its future obligations and to behave in a manner that will serve the firm's needs and long-term interests' (Scheer and Stern 1992, p. 134). This definition captures the unique character of trust – that the partner is motivated by more than its own immediate, direct self-interest and that this is projected to continue in the future. Trust is evidenced through concurrent attributions about the partner's benevolence; the belief that one's partner is motivated to consider mutual interests and seek joint gain; and the partner's honesty, or the belief that the partner stands by its word and keeps its promises (Ganesan 1994; Kumar et al. 1995a; Larzelere and Huston 1980; Scheer and Stern 1992).[1] I use 'firm' and 'partner' generically to refer to the B2B relationship, but the following discussion can be applied to diverse types of B2B dyads. Inter-organizational trust simultaneously operates at multiple levels: interpersonal trust between boundary spanners, such as purchasing agent and salesperson; personal trust in the counterpart firm, such as that of a traffic manager in a vendor; and inter-firm trust between companies (Fang et al. 2008).

It is widely accepted that the trustee (trusted party) may be a company; more controversial is whether the trustor (trusting party) can be an organization (e.g. Blois 1998; Mouzas et al. 2007). Gulati (1995) argues that inter-firm trust is a viable construct. For Zaheer et al. (1998, p. 143), it is 'the extent to which organization members have a collectively-held trust orientation toward the partner firm'. Currall and Inkpen (2002, p. 484) note that 'persons, groups, and firms . . . are capable of trust decisions and the measurable actions that follow'. Variance in company policies, standard operating procedures and practices across a firm's business partners inherently signal different levels of manifest organizational trust. Managers have shown little difficulty when asked to report their firms' trust in another organization. Whether it is a collectively held orientation, aggregation of employees' beliefs, or manifestation of company policy, inter-firm trust between organizations *can* be measured and has been examined in a variety of disciplines (Ebert 2009). Care must be taken to focus informants on appropriate referents by consistently referring to the firm's (not the manager's) relationship with the partner company. If appropriate focus is achieved, managers do not simply generalize from their personal trust when reporting organization trust (e.g. Fang et al. 2008; Ganesan 1994). However, inter-firm trust has both organizational and interpersonal antecedents. Lyons and Mehta (1997, p. 255) uncover 'numerous examples of firms investing in what can only be interpreted as . . . social relationships between customers and supplier'.

B2B research nearly universally finds positive effects of trust, but this may be an artifact of the search for hypothesized positive effects. Researchers seldom posit that trust will reduce positive outcomes and almost never theorize that trust may lead to negative outcomes. According to Fang et al. (2008, p. 95), researchers 'have focused too narrowly by investigating only the beneficial effects of trust. The implicit limited scope may have missed potential negative effects and limited the understanding of the full range of trust's effects'. Unmeasured dysfunctional consequences could well be the missing mediating mechanism responsible for trust's inconsistent empirical effects on performance. Dysfunctional consequences can arise from misplaced, naive or excessive trust.

POTENTIAL DYSFUNCTIONAL CONSEQUENCES OF TRUST

The most obvious risk is *misplaced trust*, or trust in an untrustworthy partner. To trust is to be vulnerable to exploitation or betrayal (Hardin 2001; McEvily et al. 2003) because of the 'risk or "moral hazard" that untrustworthy agents will act . . . to harm rather than to benefit a trusting counterpart' (Smith 2005, p. 300). Trust can undermine contractual safeguards' effectiveness (Lui and Ngo 2004), creating greater potential for successful opportunism. 'While cozy relationships sound good in theory, such relationships also provide an opportunity for covert activities designed to systematically cheat a partner' (Anderson and Jap 2005, p. 78). Unless the partner is highly dependent on the firm, misplaced trust can be damaging and costly.

Trusting an *untrustworthy* business partner can have devastating effects, but complications of trust in a *trustworthy* partner are less acknowledged or understood. *Naive trust* is the underestimation of risk associated with greater reciprocal trust. Higher trust, though beneficial, also exposes the firm to greater potential loss (Mayer et al. 1995). But, as Blois (1998, p. 204, italics in original) observes, 'while it is a *theoretical possibility* you do not believe it is a *realistic probability* that they will act in a manner that would disadvantage you'. Having trust in a partner encourages the firm to rely less on formal control mechanisms (e.g. Selnes and Sallis 2003). In addition, belief that a partner can be trusted allows a manager to reallocate time and attention to other relationships in which benevolent intentions are not the norm.

As reciprocal trust increases, firm and partner incur greater objective risk from their trusting behaviors, but they *perceive* less risk. Complacency is a natural by-product of reciprocal trust, leading to underestimation of costs and blindness to unintended consequences. It insidiously undermines 'relationships in which the parties are confident and optimistic about their collaboration' (Anderson and Jap 2005, p. 76). 'High levels of trust might have "hidden costs" that limit the effectiveness of working relationships' (Selnes and Sallis 2003, p. 84), such as the following:

- *Groupthink:* As mutual trust builds, value systems converge and common identity may lead to excessive homogeneity (Selnes and Sallis 2003).
- *Inertia:* Trust can inhibit critical information search (Selnes and Sallis 2003) and promote relational inertia, particularly under formalized decision-making (Fang et al. 2008).
- *Lower responsiveness to the external environment:* Greater trust can inhibit relationships with others outside the relationship (Cook et al. 2005) and lead to lower responsiveness to the external environment (Fang et al. 2008).
- *Misallocation of resources:* Strong relational norms can cloud the firm's ability to make sound investment decisions (Brown et al. 2009).
- *Erosion of innovation:* Creative processes and innovation can be undermined (Cook et al. 2005; Selnes and Sallis 2003).
- *Suppression of constructive conflict:* Negative or critical information may not be exchanged freely for fear of undermining the positive relationship atmosphere (Selnes and Sallis 2003).
- *Misdirected discretion:* Trusted B2B partners perform their roles with great autonomy and may be reluctant to seek input when uncertain. Costly initiatives can be pursued that would not have been undertaken had both parties been consulted (Langfred 2004).
- *Obliviousness to crumbling relationship foundations:* Complacency can render the firm oblivious to shifts in the conditions that initially gave rise to trust (Hardin 2001), such as changes in the partner's competitive environment or turnover in management personnel.

'Quite apart from the downside of trust are the *costs* involved in creating, upholding, and maintaining trust' (McEvily et al. 2003, p. 100). Even if no negative effects occur, there is nonetheless an optimal level of trust (Wicks et al. 1999) that maximizes the firm's benefits relative to its costs. At some point, the benefits of investing more to achieve greater trust are outweighed by the costs. *Excessive trust* exceeds the optimum. A full cost–benefit assessment of trust must encompass the costs of building and maintaining trust, the costs of either naive trust or the safeguards employed to deter it, and the costs of misplaced trust. Awareness of potential negative consequences of trust raises the question: can distrust be functional?

DISTRUST

Distrust is the belief that a business partner is likely to undermine or actively work against the firm's interests. 'Distrust is not necessarily bad or destructive; indeed, it can be good and protective when it is well directed' (Cook et al. 2005, p. 60), such as when it prevents misplaced trust. Although distrust minimizes potential loss, it also prevents potential gains from foregone relationships with trustworthy partners (Cook et al. 2005; Gambetta 2000; Hardin 2001). As Table 18.1 summarizes, distrust in B2B relationships has been the focus of a handful of studies, standing in stark contrast to the voluminous research on trust. This may be due to the assumption that distrust is simply the absence of trust. Distrust goes well beyond the passive lack of trust, however, because it involves active *negative expectations* about another's intentions and actions (Cook et al. 2005; Lewicki et al. 1998). Distrust is rooted in 'a dominant conflict of B's interests with A's' (Cook et al. 2005, p. 63). Within any domain, significant trust and distrust cannot coexist. However, a firm can *neither trust nor distrust* its partner.

Table 18.2 summarizes how distrust differs from trust in nature, antecedents and

Table 18.1   Relative research emphasis on selected concepts in B2B relationships

Focal Concept	# of Peer-Reviewed Articles in Marketing Journals		# of Peer-Reviewed Articles in Management Journals	
	B2B	**B2B & Sales**	**B2B**	**B2B & Sales**
Trust	347	409	418	511
Distrust	3	4	16	19
Confidence	50	79	42	83
(Inter)dependence	143	170	147	174
Fairness	45	70	79	112
Opportunism	52	62	77	84
Specific investments	65	75	110	127
Transaction cost	98	120	196	219
Commitment	390	506	285	435

Notes:
Marketing journals include marketing, market, retail, supply or logistics in the title. Management journals include manage, organization, inter-organization, inter-firm or business in the title. The search was conducted on 10 March 2011, using Business Source Premier. The B2B search pertained solely to articles that included terms in the abstract such as B2B, business-to-business, joint venture, strategic alliance, inter-firm, inter-organizational, channel or buyer–seller. The 'B2B & Sales' search also included sales, salesperson, salespeople, sales force, boundary spanner and purchasing. Effort was made to find all articles that mentioned the focal concept and synonyms in the abstract, while excluding other uses of the term. Specifically, searches focused on trust, excluding antitrust, trustee, estate, investment trust and REIT; distrust or mistrust; confidence, excluding confidence interval; dependence or interdependence; fairness or justice; opportunism or opportunistic; specific, idiosyncratic, transaction-specific, TSI, RSI, or relationship-specific assets or investments; transaction cost, TCA or TCE; commitment. Articles referring to 'consumer' in the abstract were omitted.

Table 18.2 Comparison of distrust, trust and alignment of interests

	Sources of Confidence		
	Distrust	Trust	Alignment of Interests
NATURE			
Attribution about partner	Partner motivated to undermine or actively work against the firm.	Partner motivated by collective interests.	Partner motivated by compatible self-interest.
Durability	Resistant to change in response to positive actions of partner.	Easily undermined by negative actions of partner.	Vulnerable to change in the dyad's external environment.
Type of reciprocity	Episodic reciprocity	Complex reciprocity	Episodic reciprocity
Firm's relative dependence	Threatening	Not threatening	Threatening in volatile environments
Interdependence magnitude	Greater interdependence avoided.	Greater interdependence welcomed.	Greater interdependence welcomed.
Perception of risk	Perceived risk > objective risk.	Perceived risk < objective risk.	Perceived risk ≈ objective risk.
ANTECEDENTS			
Prior relationship	No prior interaction required.	Repeated prior interaction required.	No prior interaction required.
Development time	Can develop quickly.	Requires significant time.	Can develop quickly.
Reputation effects	Reputation has greater effect and endures after direct interaction.	Reputation has lesser effect but is irrelevant after direct interaction.	Reputation has minimal effect.
Role of interpersonal relationships	Can be strongly affected by cross-firm interpersonal relationships.	Can be strongly affected by cross-firm interpersonal relationships.	Minimal effect of cross-firm interpersonal relationships.
CONSEQUENCES			
Implications if attribution about partner is incorrect	Opportunity cost of foregone long-term gains is potentially large.	Opportunity cost is limited to the short-term loss.	Opportunity cost is limited to the short-term loss.
Potential long-term gains	Low potential long-term gains.	High potential long-term gains.	Moderate potential long-term gains.
Short-term gain/loss potential	Potential short-term gain ≈ loss.	Potential short-term gain < loss.	Potential short-term gain > loss.
Relationship time horizon	Low continuity intentions	High continuity intentions	Moderate continuity intentions
Information sharing	Low	High	Moderate
Investment in RSIs	Low willingness, even when bilateral.	Greater willingness, uni- or bilateral.	Greater willingness if bilateral.
Interpretation of ambiguity	Presumption of guilt.	Strong presumption of innocence.	Mild presumption of innocence.

consequences. For example, when trust exists, the firm will tend to have a presumption of innocence toward the partner, but distrust leads to a presumption of guilt. Positive acts are suspect and unlikely to be reciprocated (Vlaar et al. 2007), while negative actions reinforce the prevailing distrust and are likely to be reciprocated (Gambetta 2000). Punitive capability (Kumar et al. 1998), even if not exercised, is viewed as threatening. Distinguishing between trust and distrust leads to the realization that eliminating grounds for distrust is more critical than building trust because trust-building initiatives are likely to be viewed with suspicion unless distrust has been allayed. A voluntary B2B relationship cannot survive distrust, but it can thrive despite low trust if the partners have confidence in each other.

CONFIDENCE, TRUST AND ALIGNMENT OF INTERESTS

Confidence is 'perceived certainty about satisfactory partner cooperation' (Das and Teng 1998, p. 492) and the belief that the partner will behave in a desired manner. Knowledge of past behavior patterns, incentives and restraints on behavior can enable reasonably accurate predictions of future partner behavior (Lewicki and Bunker 1996). Confidence thus involves expectations about the partner's predictable behavior but does not address motivations for behavior (Das and Teng 1998).

The two primary sources of a firm's confidence – trust in the partner and alignment of the partner's and firm's self-interests – represent different motives for the partner's behavior (see Figure 18.1). Trust is closely associated with confidence, so much so that the distinction between the concepts has often been blurred, and confidence per se has

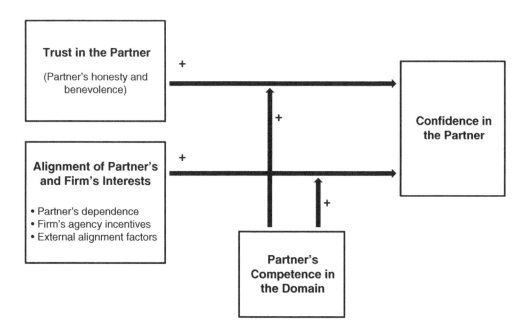

Figure 18.1   Sources of confidence

rarely been investigated. Trust and confidence are not equivalent, however. Although trust 'implies a willingness to rely . . . the opposite is not necessarily the case' (Blois 1998, p. 199). One can have confidence despite the lack of trust (e.g. Das and Teng 1998; Gulati 1995; Lewicki and Bunker 1996; Lyons and Mehta 1997). Confidence can also be generated through alignment of the partner's self-interest with the firm's self-interest. Alignment of interests is driven by 'rational elements of interorganizational relationships' (Mouzas et al. 2007, p. 1018) and is based on consideration of the relative economic merits of alternative courses of action (Doney and Cannon 1997; Lewicki and Bunker 1996; Lyons and Mehta 1997). When the partner's self-interest motivates it to maintain the relationship with and to engage in behavior desired by the firm, the firm has calculative confidence in the partner. For example, Wal-Mart has little need to trust its smaller US suppliers; calculative confidence is generated because it is in those suppliers' self-interests to do business with Wal-Mart. People may trust their primary care physician, but confidence in a surgeon is often more calculative; it is in the surgeon's self-interest for the patient to have a good outcome. Alignment of interests is generated by the partner's dependence on the firm, the firm's agency incentives and external factors that align the firm's and the partner's interests.

Dependence is the partner's need to maintain a relationship with the focal firm to achieve its goals (Beier and Stern 1969; Kumar et al. 1995a). The greater the partner's dependence on the firm, the less motive it has to undermine the firm or the firm–partner relationship. The partner's self-interest assessment encompasses both benefit-based dependence and cost-based dependence (Scheer et al. 2010). *Agency incentives* are the firm's explicit actions to align the partner's short-term behaviors with the firm's interests, such as monitoring (Gundlach and Cannon 2010) or the contingent or non-contingent exercise of power (Scheer and Stern 1992). *External alignment factors* are elements in the competitive environment that promote alignment versus divergence of interests. Firm and partner have different interests based on their unique resource constraints and linkages to their environments (Mukherji et al. 2007). Examples of external alignment factors include short-term economic rationales for alternative courses of action, government mandates that boost primary demand, regulations that disadvantage products, or switching inducements offered by competitors. When external factors align the partner's self-interest with the firm's, they motivate behavior desired by the firm, generating confidence in the partner.

Trust and calculative confidence based on alignment of interests differ in their nature, origin and effects, as Table 18.2 indicates. For example, aligned interests can develop quickly with no history of firm–partner interaction because of shifting external conditions, such as when a potential customer's current supply chain incurs a disastrous, long-term disruption. In contrast, trust requires repeated interaction, often over extended periods, and is inherently grounded in the firm–partner relationship.

Trust and self-interest alignment represent distinct motivations for why the partner's behavior can be reliably predicted, and thus both generate *general confidence* in a business partner. Despite high general confidence, however, a firm's confidence in that partner in a specific context can be low. The partner must also have sufficient *competence in the relevant domain*, that is, 'skills, competencies, and characteristics' (Mayer et al. 1995, p. 712) that enable the partner to meet its obligations and fulfill its role (Doney and Cannon 1997; Lui and Ngo 2004). Although competence is relatively enduring, its mere existence 'does not ensure that knowledge and skills will be applied in beneficial ways' (Smith 2005, p. 306). Whether the partner deploys its abilities is discretionary and thus variable. The firm has confidence that the partner will deploy its abilities on the firm's behalf when the partner is motivated either by collective interests or because it is in the partner's self-interest to do so.

As Figure 18.1 indicates, partner competence in the focal domain is a boundary condition that moderates the impact of trust and alignment of interests on confidence. Insufficient competence renders the partner's motivations irrelevant because it prevents relationship development or results in termination. Below the competence threshold, the firm will have no confidence in the partner in that situation regardless of its general confidence inspired by trust and aligned interests. For this reason, competence is taken as a given in many *ongoing* B2B relationships. The implicit domain of a firm's confidence is the partner's current role in the business relationship, including functions, duties, activities, requirements and responsibilities. Competence in the current role may not extend to new domains, however, and will not lead to cooperation in new spheres of business unless the partner is perceived to be competent in those areas as well. For example, a trusted current retailer may not be well suited to distribute a radically new product requiring unique knowledge and expertise. The firm's trust in that retailer is unchanged, but its confidence in that retailer in the specific context is low. In any specific situation, the firm's trust and its perceptions of the partner's dependence, agency incentives, external alignment factors and domain-relevant competence all affect the firm's confidence in that partner – and many other behaviors, attitudes and outcomes of interest.

TRUST, ALIGNMENT OF INTERESTS AND DISTRUST: IMPLICATIONS FOR RELATIONSHIP DEVELOPMENT

Juxtaposing trust and distrust, as Figure 18.2 depicts, reveals insights into relationship development. Initial interactions between firm and partner occur in a state of *evaluative neutrality*. A small degree of trust is present, possibly coexisting with a low level of distrust. The parties have reputational information about each other, but uncertainty is great, and expectations are modest. They contemplate doing business because they perceive no apparent conflicting interests and believe there may be *compatible interests* such that both can achieve their independent goals (Polzer et al. 1998; Thompson 1990). Each must evaluate the other party as having domain-relevant competence to perform its role.

Pursuit of compatible self-interests will naturally dominate initial interactions, reducing agency problems (Mukherji et al. 2007). It is critical, however, that firms resolve concerns that give rise to distrust promptly. Trust is low, and the shadow of the future (Poppo et al. 2008) is predominant. 'Repeated transactions can be structured such that the parties have a "self-enforcing contract"; . . . understandings will not be violated because violation goes against each party's own self interest' (Bensaou and Anderson 1999, p. 462). If initial dealing reveals opportunism, malevolence or conflicting interests, a state of *suspicion* will result. *Conflicting interests* exist when a firm's pursuit or achievement of its objectives inherently impedes the partner's objectives. When there are conflicting interests and incompatible goals, partner actions and relationship-building initiatives will be scrutinized for hidden motives. Suspicion is a transitional state because, unless concerns are promptly dispelled, the relationship is unlikely to survive. A firm will remain in a *distrusting* B2B relationship only if it has no viable alternatives.

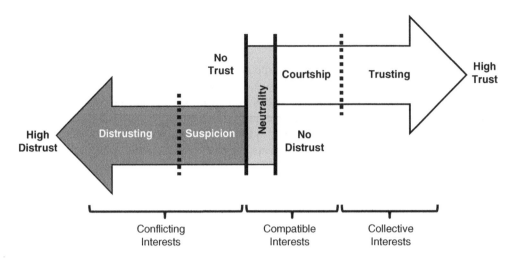

Figure 18.2   Distrust and trust in relationship development

Conversely, if initial interactions verify compatible interests and willingness and ability to work together, the firm and partner transition into *stable neutrality*. The relationship will not necessarily progress beyond this state. If both parties perceive alignment of compatible interests and competence, and neither desires a closer relationship, they can satisfactorily pursue their respective goals through their arm's-length relationship. Many B2B relationships remain in comfortable neutrality with low relational exchange. Firms cannot manage highly enmeshed relationships with all business partners.

Interest compatibility creates the potential for a deeper relationship (Polzer et al. 1998; Thompson 1990), but proactive steps must be taken to determine if the potential can be realized. The firm can strive to deepen the relationship in pursuit of its self-interest and enter the *courtship* stage. Altering external alignment factors is typically beyond a firm's control. Agency incentives can be deployed, but they are of short duration and limited effectiveness. Usually, deepening a relationship requires the firm to accept greater dependence on the partner. The firm signals its interest by taking actions that expose it to loss if exploited by the partner. As Figure 18.3 depicts, significant relationship-specific investments (RSIs) early in a B2B relationship exhibit commitment, demonstrate willingness to be vulnerable and to incur greater dependence, and signal tentative confidence in the partner. If RSIs are strategically selected to generate uniquely favorable outcomes for the partner as well, they enhance interdependence. For these reasons, RSIs can inspire the partner both to perceive greater alignment of interests and to place greater trust in the firm, thus enhancing partner confidence. This multifaceted impact helps explain RSIs' substantial effect on relational outcomes (Palmatier et al. 2007a).

Courtship is a transitory state. If the partner has no interest in a deeper relationship, the firm could settle for stable neutrality. If, however, the firm wants a deeper relationship for strategic reasons, it must find a partner with a similar relationship orientation (Palmatier et al. 2008). A relationship-seeking partner will not exploit the vulnerabilities arising from the firm's initial RSIs, but instead will respond with strategically selected RSIs of its own. 'Trust leads to risk taking, and risk taking, in turn, buttresses a sense

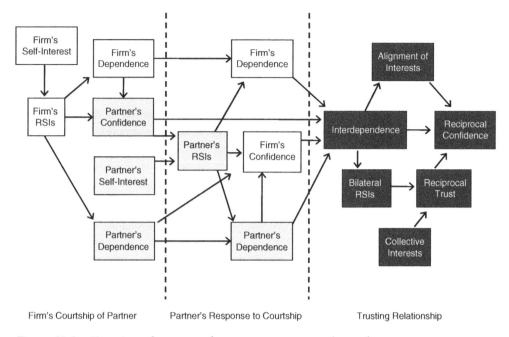

Figure 18.3 Transition from courtship stage to trusting relationship

of trust' (Das and Teng 1998, p. 503). 'Acting on trust when trust is reciprocated can lead to successful cooperation and hence to mutual benefit and potentially to significant gain' (Ullmann-Margalit 2002, p. 533). If the more powerful party deals fairly with the more vulnerable party (Kumar et al. 1995b) and opts for constructive use of its power (Geyskens et al. 1996), the relationship can deepen.

Over time, the history of favorable interactions between firm and partner, or the shadow of the past (Poppo et al. 2008), provides the foundation for greater trust, interdependence and confidence. The parties recognize additional compatible interests (Polzer et al. 1998; Thompson 1990) and develop new congruent goals. The discrete, episodic reciprocity of the arm's-length relationship transitions to the more enmeshed, complex reciprocity of relational exchange (Lund 2010), motivating bilateral RSIs and greater reciprocal trust (O'Donnell et al. 2008). Ultimately, if both parties prioritize *collective interests* over their own short-term self-interests, a *trusting* relationship is achieved. By reducing the costs of monitoring and guarding against opportunism, encouraging better investment decisions, and ensuring rapid and flexible responses to unforeseen events (Lyons and Mehta 1997), reciprocal trust and confidence enable strategies and outcomes that neither party could achieve alone.

RESEARCH IMPLICATIONS

Consideration of the potential dysfunctional consequences of trust, understanding of distrust as more than simply the absence of trust, and the realization that confidence can be based not only on trust but alternatively on the alignment of interests all point to several intriguing issues worthy of research. Great potential for theory development exists because collectively, research has seldom examined the dark side of trust, largely ignored other sources of confidence and neglected distrust. Examples of theoretical propositions include the following:

- In the early stages of a B2B relationship, preventing or eliminating distrust is critical. Trust-building activities are pointless unless concerns giving rise to distrust are resolved first.
- In arm's-length relationships, and in the early stages of a B2B relationship, confidence will be based primarily on the alignment of interests, particularly on external alignment factors.
- In most relationships in a firm's B2B portfolio, confidence will be based primarily on aligned interests. In the firm's most important B2B relationships, however, trust will be critical.
- In arm's-length relationships, some degree of confidence is required to achieve stable neutrality, but there may or may not be trust.
- Confidence based on trust will extend to a wider variety of situations and into the more distant future than calculative confidence. Both types of confidence will have similar effects on short-term attitudes, immediate behaviors and actions that have short-term consequences, but they will have different effects on behaviors and decisions with a longer time horizon.
- As long as the partner's self-interest aligns closely with the firm's, damage from misplaced trust will be low. When interests are not aligned, even moderate trust renders the firm vulnerable to the costs of misplaced trust, such as partner opportunism.
- Turnover in boundary spanners and management personnel can damage confidence by undermining inter-firm trust but will not affect the alignment of interests.
- The domain of confidence in arm's-length relationships will be narrower than in close relationships characterized by complex reciprocity (Lund 2010).
- When conditions in a relationship and within the environment are stable, competence will extend beyond the current domain. As dynamism within an industry increases, concerns about partner competence become more germane.
- Overt self-interest-seeking behavior that does not undermine collective interests will not erode trust or negatively affect the B2B relationship.
- Effective covert opportunism requires the prevention of partner distrust. Covert opportunism will be accompanied by suppression of *overt* negative behavior and maintenance of current cooperation (Wang et al. 2010) to prevent suspicion. This may occur when a firm engages in sabotage before exiting a relationship or when a firm covertly withholds inputs to redress negative inequity (Scheer et al. 2003).

In addition, some general implications regarding research design can be drawn:

- Because suspicion and courtship states are inherently transitory, cross-sectional research methods are unlikely to capture relationships in those states. Longitudinal research, retrospective critical incident studies, case studies, experiments, simulations or other methods may be needed.

- When examining outcomes such as cooperation, it may be sufficient to focus on confidence. However, because little is known about the potential interactions of trust and alignment of interests (or specific sources of interest alignment) on performance and other outcomes, researchers should examine both sources of confidence, if possible.
- The moderating effect of competence is unlikely to exist in ongoing relationships because of survival bias. Competence may have a positive effect, if the firm values greater partner competence, or no effect, if additional competence beyond the threshold is irrelevant.

And, finally, some implications for survey-based research can also be gleaned:

- The firm's perceived alignment of interests and trust in the partner can be conceptualized as causal indicators of the higher-order construct of general confidence in the partner. General confidence may affect outcomes such as commitment or overall loyalty to the partner.
- Informants can provide reports about inter-firm trust if both organizations exhibit entitativity (Hamilton and Sherman 1996; Palmatier et al. 2007b). A similar caveat applies when examining a person's trust in a firm.
- When examining inter-firm trust using survey methodology, researchers should reiterate that questions pertain not to the informant's personal experiences but to the firm's relationship with the partner company. In addition, they should consistently make reference to both 'our firm' and 'the partner company' and avoid ambiguous pronouns ('we' or 'they') that easily could be misinterpreted or cue interpersonal relationships.
- When the firm's strategy or behavior is the focal outcome, it is appropriate to examine trust or confidence from only the firm's perspective. When investigating outcomes that are inherently influenced by both parties, such as performance, it is important to consider both the firm's and the partner's perspectives.
- In a mature relationship, a firm is unlikely to pursue collective interests unless it believes that its partner does so as well. Thus, a firm's self-reported trust in its partner and its perception of the partner's trust in the firm are unlikely to differ significantly. However, the firm's perceptions of its partner's trust may be inaccurate, because the firm and partner can have vastly different perspectives of their relationship (Anderson and Jap 2005).

PRACTICE IMPLICATIONS

Managers must be aware of trust's dark-side potential because the risks firms assume have implications not just for the risk-taker but also for employees, investors, business partners and customers who depend on the goods or services produced. In any B2B relationship, managers should diagnose the configuration of confidence in the partner (see Figure 18.4). Because the partner's motivation for present behavior can lead to different

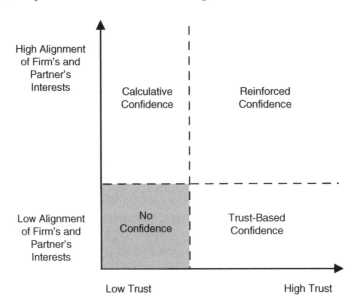

Figure 18.4   Configurations of confidence

future behavior (Larzelere and Huston 1980), understanding the operative sources of confidence becomes more critical as the projected time horizon increases. Calculative confidence extends only to similar situations and is inherently limited in scope, while trust-based confidence and the underlying benevolent motives of the partner are operative in situations with greater variance from current conditions. However, trust-based confidence makes the firm highly vulnerable to misplaced trust because there is little to prevent an untrustworthy partner from exploiting the firm.

Prevention is the first line of defense, but careful vetting of potential partners cannot eliminate misplaced trust. Even if collective interests are initially valued, shifting circumstances or turnover in management can undermine the relationship (Hardin 2001). If self-interests diverge increasingly over time, 'even trustworthy partners can be relied upon to be untrustworthy' (Vlaar et al. 2007, p. 416). Trust reinforced by aligned interests is the best option to mitigate the risk of misplaced trust, but it enhances the risks of naive trust. When a firm and partner each trust the other – and both are aware that their interests align – complacency may result. Efforts to be vigilant may seem redundant, given the parties' implicit motives to cooperate with each other.

Thus, firms should enact policies and procedures to deter or counteract the dysfunctional consequences of naive trust. Negative consequences can be reduced when trust is coupled with control mechanisms (Das and Teng 1998), but some control mechanisms can undermine trust's positive effects (Fang et al. 2008). Unobtrusive, nonconfrontational methods, such as market monitoring, may best preserve the benefits of trust (Gundlach and Cannon 2010) while mitigating negative effects. Firms should establish guidelines to assess specific potential dysfunctions. For example, setting target innovation rates and then gathering data to benchmark against those targets can bring to light declines in the pace of innovation. Procedures should be established to routinely scan the external environment and evaluate elements that may be causing the partner's self-interest to diverge from the firm's, allowing the firm to erect protection against exploitation, if necessary, or work to increase partner dependence or agency incentives. Greater environmental scanning can minimize negative effects on innovation and responsiveness and alert managers to crumbling relationship foundations (e.g. Fang et al. 2008; Gundlach and Cannon 2010).

Internal guidelines and procedures can also help detect excessive trust. In some situations, it may be possible to calculate trusted partner lifetime value, the premium generated by a trusting relationship. In early relationship stages, however, such assessments are speculative. Efforts to build trust seldom bear fruit quickly; returns are reaped only in the future if the relationship deepens. Regardless, RSIs and non-specific investments in building trust should be subjected to retrospective cost–benefit analysis and, when possible, to prospective marginal analysis.

CONCLUSION

Despite the plethora of research examining trust, important issues regarding the dark side of trust, distrust and sources of confidence have not been addressed. Integrating these concepts exposes gaps in our knowledge. Disentangling trust and confidence helps bring clarity and leads to the realization that confidence can be generated by trust or by alignment between the firm's and the partner's self-interests. Contemplation of distrust informs B2B relationship development, particularly the futility of trying to build trust before allaying distrust. Investigations into dysfunctional trust, distrust, aligned self-interests and confidence show promise to advance our knowledge of why some B2B interactions remain satisfactorily arm's-length, why some deepen into relational exchange and why even seemingly strong relationships can be undermined, deteriorate and fail. Many unanswered questions remain. Given the centrality of trust in extant models of B2B relationships, those questions deserve research attention. There is much we do not yet know about trust, distrust and confidence in B2B relationships.

NOTES

*   The author thanks Joseph Cannon, George John, Irina Kozlenkova, Donald Lund and Stephen Hampton for their helpful input on previous versions of this chapter.
1. Benevolence alone could be implemented manipulatively or surreptitiously. Honesty alone does not imply that the partner will go beyond the parameters of the explicitly agreed-upon current role. Benevolence and honesty are often highly correlated, but they are conceptually distinct (Scheer and Stern 1992; Doney and Cannon 1997).

REFERENCES

Anderson, Erin and Sandy D. Jap (2005), 'The dark side of close relationships', *MIT Sloan Management Review*, **46** (3), 75–82.
Atuahene-Gima, Kwaku and Haiyang Li (2002), 'When does trust matter? Antecedents and contingent effects

of supervisor trust on performance in selling new products in China and the United States', *Journal of Marketing*, **66** (July), 61–81.

Beier, Fredrick and Louis W. Stern (1969), 'Power in the channel of distribution', in L.W. Stern (ed.), *Distribution Channels: Behavioral Dimensions*, Boston, MA: Houghton Mifflin, pp. 92–116.

Bensaou, M. and Erin Anderson (1999), 'Buyer–supplier relations in industrial markets: when do buyers risk making idiosyncratic investments?', *Organization Science*, **10** (4), 460–81.

Blois, Keith J. (1998), 'Trust in business relationships: an evaluation of its status', *Journal of Management Studies*, **36** (2), 197–215.

Brown, James R., Jody L. Crosno and Chekitan S. Dev (2009), 'The effects of transaction-specific investment in marketing channels: the moderating role of relational norms', *Journal of Marketing Theory and Practice*, **17** (4), 317–33.

Cook, Karen S., Russell Hardin and Margaret Levi (2005), *Cooperation Without Trust?*, New York: Russell Sage Foundation.

Currall, Steven C. and Andrew C. Inkpen (2002), 'A multilevel approach to trust in joint ventures', *Journal of International Business Studies*, **33** (3), 479–95.

Das, T.K. and Bing-Sheng Teng (1998), 'Between trust and control: developing confidence in partner cooperation in alliances', *Academy of Management Review*, **23** (3), 491–512.

Doney, Patricia M. and Joseph P. Cannon (1997), 'An examination of the nature of trust in buyer–seller relationships', *Journal of Marketing*, **61** (April), 35–51.

Ebert, Tara A.E. (2009), 'Facets of trust in relationships – a literature synthesis of highly ranked trust articles', *Journal of Business Market Management*, **3** (1), 65–84.

Fang, Eric, Robert W. Palmatier, Lisa K. Scheer and Ning Li (2008), 'Trust at different organizational levels', *Journal of Marketing*, **72** (March), 80–98.

Gambetta, Diego (2000), 'Can we trust trust?', in D. Gambetta (ed.), *Trust: Making and Breaking Cooperative Relations*, Oxford: Basil Blackwell, pp. 213–37.

Ganesan, Shankar (1994), 'Determinants of long-term orientation in buyer–seller relationships', *Journal of Marketing*, **58** (April), 1–19.

Geyskens, Inge, Jan-Benedict E.M. Steenkamp and Nirmalya Kumar (1998), 'Generalizations about trust in marketing channel relationship using meta-analysis', *International Journal of Research in Marketing*, **15** (3), 223–48.

Geyskens, Inge, Jan-Benedict E.M. Steenkamp, Lisa K. Scheer and Nirmalya Kumar (1996), 'The effects of trust and interdependence on relationship commitment: a trans-atlantic study', *International Journal of Research in Marketing*, **13** (4), 303–17.

Gulati, Ranjay (1995), 'Does familiarity breed trust? The implications of repeated ties for contractual choice in alliance', *Academy of Management Journal*, **38** (1), 85–112.

Gundlach, Gregory T. and Joseph P. Cannon (2010), '"Trust but verify"? The performance implications of verifications strategies in trusting relationships', *Journal of the Academy of Marketing Science*, **38** (4), 399–417.

Hamilton, David L. and Steven J. Sherman (1996), 'Perceiving persons and groups', *Psychological Review*, **103** (2), 336–55.

Hardin, Russell (2001), 'Distrust', *Boston University Law Review*, **81**, 495–522.

Kumar, Nirmalya, Lisa K. Scheer and Jan-Benedict E.M. Steenkamp (1995a), 'The effects of perceived interdependence on dealer attitudes', *Journal of Marketing Research*, **32** (August), 348–56.

Kumar, Nirmalya, Lisa K. Scheer and Jan-Benedict E.M. Steenkamp (1995b), 'The effects of supplier fairness on vulnerable resellers', *Journal of Marketing Research*, **32** (February), 54–65.

Kumar, Nirmalya, Lisa K. Scheer and Jan-Benedict E.M. Steenkamp (1998), 'Interdependence, punitive capability, and the reciprocation of punitive actions in channel relationships', *Journal of Marketing Research*, **35** (May), 225–35.

Langfred, Claus W. (2004), 'Too much of a good thing? Negative effects of high trust and individual autonomy in self-managing teams', *Academy of Management Journal*, **47** (3), 385–99.

Larzelere, Robert E. and Ted L. Huston (1980), 'The dyadic trust scale: toward understanding interpersonal trust in close relationships', *Journal of Marriage and the Family*, **42** (August), 595–604.

Lewicki, Roy J. and Barbara B. Bunker (1996), 'Developing and maintaining trust in work relationships', in K.M. Moreland and T.R. Tyler (eds), *Trust in Organizations: Frontiers of Theory and Research*, Thousand Oaks, CA: Sage Publications, pp. 114–39.

Lewicki, Roy J., Daniel J. McAllister and Robert J. Bies (1998), 'Trust and distrust: new relationships and realities', *Academy of Management Journal*, **23** (3), 438–58.

Lui, Steven S. and Hang-Yue Ngo (2004), 'The role of trust and contractual safeguards on cooperation in non-equity alliances', *Journal of Management*, **30** (4), 471–85.

Lund, Donald J. (2010), 'Reciprocity in marketing relationships', doctoral dissertation, Trulaske College of Business, University of Missouri, Columbia.

Lyons, Bruce and Judith Mehta (1997), 'Contracts, opportunism, and trust: self-interest and social orientation', *Cambridge Journal of Economics*, **21** (2), 239–57.

Mayer, Roger C., James H. Davis and F. David Schoorman (1995), 'An integrative model of organizational trust', *Academy of Management Review*, **20** (3), 709–34.

McEvily, Bill, Vincenzo Perrone and Akbar Zaheer (2003), 'Trust as an organizing principle', *Organization Science: A Journal of the Institute of Management Sciences*, **14** (1), 91–103.

Mouzas, Stefanos, Stephen Henneberg and Peter Naudé (2007), 'Trust and reliance in business relationships', *European Journal of Marketing*, **41** (9–10), 1016–32.

Mukherji, Ananda, Peter Wright and Jyotsna Mukherji (2007), 'Cohesiveness and goals in agency networks: explaining conflict and cooperation', *Journal of Socio-Economics*, **36** (6), 949–64.

O'Donnell, Edward, Michael L. Mallin and Michael Y. Hu (2008), 'The impact of governance on the development of trust in buyer–seller relationships', *Marketing Management Journal*, **18** (Fall), 76–92.

Palmatier, Robert W., Rajiv P. Dant and Dhruv Grewal (2007a), 'A comparative longitudinal analysis of theoretical perspectives of interorganizational relationship performance', *Journal of Marketing*, **71** (October), 172–94.

Palmatier, Robert W., Lisa K. Scheer and Jan-Benedict E.M. Steenkamp (2007b), 'Customer loyalty to whom? Managing the benefits and risks of salesperson-owned loyalty', *Journal of Marketing Research*, **44** (May), 185–99.

Palmatier, Robert W., Lisa K. Scheer, Kenneth R. Evans and Todd J. Arnold (2008), 'Achieving relationship marketing effectiveness in business-to-business exchanges', *Journal of the Academy of Marketing Science*, **36** (2), 174–90.

Polzer, Jeffrey T., Elizabeth A. Mannix and Margaret A. Neale (1998), 'Interest alignment and coalitions in multiparty negotiation', *Academy of Management Journal*, **41** (1), 42–54.

Poppo, Laura, Kevin Z. Zhou and Sungmin Ryu (2008), 'Alternative origins to interorganizational trust: an interdependence perspective on the shadow of the past and the shadow of the future', *Organization Science*, **19** (1), 39–55.

Scheer, Lisa K. and Louis W. Stern (1992), 'The effect of influence type and performance outcomes on attitude toward the influencer', *Journal of Marketing Research*, **29** (February), 128–42.

Scheer, Lisa K., Nirmalya Kumar and Jan-Benedict E.M. Steenkamp (2003), 'Reactions to perceived inequity in US and Dutch interorganizational relationships', *Academy of Management Journal*, **46** (3), 303–16.

Scheer, Lisa K., C. Fred Miao and Jason Garrett (2010), 'The effects of supplier capabilities on industrial customers' loyalty: the role of dependence', *Journal of the Academy of Marketing Science*, **38** (1), 90–104.

Selnes, Fred and James Sallis (2003), 'Promoting relationship learning', *Journal of Marketing*, **68** (July), 80–95.

Smith, Carole (2005), 'Understanding trust and confidence: two paradigms and their significance for health and social care', *Journal of Applied Psychology*, **22** (3), 299–316.

Thompson, Leigh (1990), 'Negotiation behavior and outcomes: empirical evidence and theoretical issues', *Psychological Bulletin*, **108** (3), 515–32.

Ullmann-Margalit, Edna (2002), 'Trust out of distrust', *Journal of Philosophy*, **99** (10), 532–48.

Uzzi, Brian (1996), 'The sources and consequences of embeddedness for the economic performance of organizations: the network effect', *American Sociological Review*, **61** (4), 674–98.

Vlaar, Pual W.L., Frans A.J. Van den Bosch and Henk W. Volberda (2007), 'On the evolution of trust, distrust, and formal coordination and control in interorganizational relationships: toward an integrative framework', *Group and Organization Management*, **32** (4), 407–29.

Wang, Qiong, Ujwal Kayande and Sandy Jap (2010), 'The seeds of dissolution: discrepancy and incoherence in buyer–supplier exchange', *Marketing Science*, **29** (6), 1109–24.

Wicks, Andrew C., Shawn L. Berman and Thomas M. Jones (1999), 'The structure of optimal trust: moral and strategic implications', *Academy of Management Review*, **24** (1), 99–116.

Zaheer, Akbar, Bill McEvily and Vincenzo Perrone (1998), 'Does trust matter? Exploring the effects of interorganizational and interpersonal trust on performance', *Organization Science*, **9** (2), 141–59.

19 Strategic alliances in a business-to-business environment
Robert E. Spekman

Twenty-five years ago, in my first published paper on collaboration (Spekman and Strauss 1986), we sought to clarify the nature of interdependent buyer–seller relationships from the point of view of resource dependency (Pfeffer and Salancik 1978) and transaction cost economics (Williamson 1985). Building on notions of transaction-specific investments (TSI), uncertainty and product importance, we argued that greater collaboration would be associated with greater TSI, more uncertainty and greater product importance. Our findings suggested that though opportunism can result in abuses, closer ties and non-standard relationships might smooth production and decrease market inefficiencies.

In a *Journal of Marketing* piece two years later (Frazier et al. 1988), we established the notion of *just-in-time* (JIT) *exchanges*, in which suppliers are required to deliver precisely what is needed by the buyer according to quality, quantity and time specifications set by the contract, and the elimination of waste creates a presumption of zero defects.

These two publications identified both why these interdependent organizational forms were worth considering and what might derail them. Most alliance research at the time acknowledged not only the advantages of interdependence but also its darker side: the potential of closer ties to breed opportunism.

In the early 1990s, books by Lewis (1990), Harrigan (1986), Lynch (1989) and others began to espouse the use of *alliances* as a better way to manage relationships among firms. Mostly taking normative views, the books attempted to show how to build an alliance mind-set. Long on anecdotal evidence but short on theory, many of these books, with their lists of dos and don'ts, became important guides for managerial practice. Many of the examples were of buyer–seller relationships, however, and the thought of partnering with one's adversary was a hard pill to swallow at the time; many argued that 'partnering' was merely a new way for a buyer to gain a lower price or some other major concession.

Today it is impossible to open a B2B magazine or trade newspaper and not find a story about strategic alliances. The argument of whether alliances make sense has become a discussion of which type of alliance makes sense, what a successful alliance firm looks like and what core skills and expertise are required. In many industries (e.g. aerospace, pharmaceuticals, biotech), alliances are the rule rather than the exception.

To acquire and utilize a diverse set of capabilities, firms develop alliance strategies that help integrate different disciplines and bodies of knowledge; provide access to technologies, markets and customers that might not be easily reached otherwise; enable the acquisition of R&D; and employ innovations that might otherwise be too costly to implement and might allow one technology or set of standards to dominate another. Strategic alliance thinking represents the integration of economic and social theories and, to firms adept at its practice, can provide a sustainable competitive advantage.

Firms that lack an alliance competence meanwhile tend to be relegated to second-class positions in the markets they serve. Because alliances require a company to change its attitudes and behaviors, old rules no longer apply. To some firms ownership and control are imperative, but in an alliance, one cannot control what one does not own. Other firms are loath to rely on a partner to help them achieve their goals, yet trust is the mortar that binds partners together. To the cautious a contract might provide a degree of protection, but trust is both the key to successful collaboration and, as it happens, a firm's best protection against opportunistic behavior.

What does it mean to be alliance competent? Competence is a multidimensional concept that speaks to the attitudes and behaviors that lead to higher levels of alliance success. Alliance competence suggests that a firm understands the path through which firms that excel at alliances travel as they develop, nurture and manage their own alliances. Firms that are widely recognized as competent are sought out as partners, are selective in their choice of partners and have a well-honed approach to alliance management. They embrace the tenets of collaborative behavior and are better equipped to leverage the full potential of their partners for the benefit of the alliance. My premise is that a sustainable competitive advantage is a function of both partners' resources and skill and their alliance competence. Three elements must work in concert if the firm is to be alliance competent. First, people are essential, and alliances are about relationships, and relationships are about people. Second, knowledge and information is an asset to be shared. Such thinking implies that information becomes the currency of exchange and all parties benefit from its free and open flows. Third, processes, systems and structural factors guide and enable alliance-like behavior. The objective is to improve collaboration and integration across units and across boundaries, with the intent of bringing value to the marketplace.

Fang et al. (2008) imply that alliances are part of a larger class of collaborative entities (co-entity), in which firms work together to achieve outcomes such as developing new products, strengthening supply chains, reaching new markets and reducing operating costs. While I find the term 'collaborative entity' appealing, I do not feel that we need to develop new vocabulary to describe the alliance phenomenon. Fang et al. build their collaborative model on the importance of trust, which is quite consistent with alliance-like thinking. I find it odd, though, that they caution the reader not to generalize to other forms of alliances because they look at only international joint ventures. I would think that by studying a general form of collaborative behavior, some of the core findings would hold across a range of alliances.

For this chapter I begin by discussing the different conceptual frameworks used by scholars to develop the notion of alliances. Next I define *alliances* in the context of these prevailing conceptual frameworks. I identify the stages of alliance development, beginning with strategic intent and partner selection. Then I discuss alliance governance at length. An underexplored topic, governance is the primary source of problems and, for the teams managing each side of the alliance, the essential ingredient. I conclude by noting implications for both managers and academics.

CONCEPTUAL FRAMEWORKS UTILIZED

Much of the work done in the area of alliances grows from a handful of research traditions. These conceptual frameworks provide the foundation on which issues of governance choice are determined. Scholars have relied on transaction cost economics, resource dependency and social exchange theory to derive theoretical explanations for alliance formation, maintenance and termination. Each tradition is described briefly next.

Transaction Cost Economics (TCE)

The major work by Williamson (1975, 1991) states that in conditions of high uncertainty or asymmetry of information, contractual mechanisms break down. When this occurs, there is a probability one partner will act opportunistically to the detriment of the other. Opportunism endangers the performance of the alliance, because each partner will act in its own self-interest. One partner may withhold information and/or resources from the other to protect its own assets or competencies.

This tendency is held in check by trust and other relational norms in which partners acknowledge their interdependence. In addition it is possible that equity alliances, in which partners take an ownership stake in the alliance, reduce the threat of opportunism. Also it is possible to encourage contractual safeguards in which there are penalties assessed to a partner that violates provisions added to the alliance contract. These safeguards could be in the form of poison pills, in which the rules of the game are spelled out clearly and in detail. Such actions often reduce transaction costs, and positive outcomes are more likely.

Resource Dependency (RD)

Resource dependency is based on the notion that because firms compete for resources, success is determined by the resources a firm controls. Given that few are self-sufficient, firms vary in their ability to gather the requisite resources. Dependencies arise when one firm needs the resources controlled by another, placing the less dependent firm in a position of power. Also this lack of self-sufficiency leads to uncertainty in the firms' decision-making capability.

Alliances are one mechanism to deal with these issues. Heide (1994) states that dependence and uncertainty are key antecedents to the formation of any inter-firm relationship. He also posits that TCE parallels RD, in that it views non-market governance as a response to environmental uncertainty and dependence. To the extent that these approaches explain the rise of strategic alliances, they might be considered complementary, not competing, theories.

Social Exchange Theory

If alliances are derived from social networks and based on socially constructed behaviors, it is not surprising to find that social exchange is a condition in which the actions of one party provide the rewards and incentives for the actions of another party over a period of repeated interaction (Homans 1961). The importance of social exchange can be traced to notions of relational contracting (Macneil 1980), social embeddedness (Granovetter 1985) and game theory (Axelrod 1984), as approaches to understanding the nature of alliance partners' interaction. Inter-firm exchange and coordination processes should enhance ties among partners and promote more equitable exchanges. In addition, mutual commitment and trust should result in better alliance outcomes. For example, mutual commitment of resources reduces uncertainty for the alliance partners. Trust can be viewed as confidence in a party's expectations about another's fairness, behavior and goodwill (Ring and Van de Ven 1992). Trust develops over time as partners work together and reflects a positive reputation for non-opportunistic and trustworthy behavior. Trust increases the scope of the relationship, enhances learning, improves communications between partners, enhances collaborative behaviors, facilitates greater joint planning and leads to better outcomes (Muthusamy et al. 2007).

A subfield within a social exchange framework is a network view. At its core a network perspective argues that all firms are embedded in a network in which they collaborate with other firms to create value to serve the marketplace (Granovetter 1985). The network view is a process view in which partners agree to exchange goods over a period of time. Weaker partners are at a disadvantage due to asymmetries caused by size, relative dependency and transaction-specific investments. Chen and Chen (2002) examine alliances between emerging economies (e.g. Taiwan) and developed countries and find that emerging economies tend to partner with larger firms as a vehicle for improving their reputation and credibility. The network paradigm focuses on the contingent nature of the relationship and reinforces the importance of alliances as a means to exchange goods and services. Network thinking has been the hallmark of the IPM Group and the guiding paradigm for many of the studies it has authored. The argument for a network approach stemmed from the belief that firms are inextricably linked and their patterns of interaction are guided by their network connections.

WHAT IS AN ALLIANCE?

In this section, I define an alliance, provide a few examples to clarify the concepts and lead in to a discussion of the different stages through which an alliance progresses. It is hard to find a unitary definition of an alliance because authors tend to tie the definition to what the alliance intends to accomplish. Although the potential outcomes of an alliance are many, it would seem that the definition should focus less on the results and more on the structure and processes that help shape alliance behaviors and attitudes.

A Working Definition

Gulati and Singh (1998) define an alliance as any voluntarily initiated cooperative agreement between firms that involves exchange, sharing or co-development. Such a definition ignores alliances in which a government, another legislative body and/or a more powerful entity mandates that organizations cooperate to achieve a certain goal or outcome. What comes to mind is the international alliance in which the United States and Russia (along with a number of other countries) cooperated to build and deploy the International Space Station. Early in the history of the space station, NASA was told that it would cooperate with the Russians. In this example, the term 'voluntary' does not describe what actually happened. Varadarajan and Cunningham (1995) also talk about pooling resources among cooperating organizations to achieve both common and individual goals. The problem here is that pooling is but one way in which firms can combine their resources; I wonder if alliances in which resources are combined in other ways affect the definition. Other authors tend to focus on the alliance as a way to achieve a competitive advantage (e.g. Culpan 2009). Parkhe (1993) links the goals achieved to the individual strategic intent of the partners.

Despite these differences, there are enough commonalities to generalize that an *alliance* is formed *when two or more independent firms come together to pursue a mutually beneficial goal or shared vision that would be difficult to achieve alone.* Of importance here is that the firms maintain their independence and autonomy and that they pursue mutually beneficial (or compatible) goals that would be difficult to achieve alone. Although this definition implies that the goals are the same, it is quite easy to relax that constraint and argue that the goals can be compatible. That is, even if the goals are not the same, they may be similar, can lead to a common vision or can facilitate the completion of individual goals held by the partners.

Part of the mortar that binds the partners together is trust and commitment. Fang et al. (2008) emphasize the critical nature of trust and operationalize it on three levels. Commitment emerges as key to alliance behavior, whereby partners tend to invest in the relationship to make it more difficult to exit. If two firms are compared to two lengths of rope and the alliance is the knot binding them together, it is in the interest of both firms to ensure the knot is tight and that both contribute to making it tighter. Such a virtuous cycle requires *commitment*, defined as an implicit or explicit pledge of relational continuity between exchange partners (Dwyer et al. 1987).

When US Air's Seth Scofield and British Airways' Sir Colin Marshall met, they shared a vision of seamless global air travel; the United States was the missing link in the network. Although these two firms worked jointly toward a common vision, they maintained their independence and autonomy throughout the process. It was implicitly acknowledged, though not directly stated, that each firm would pursue its self-interest. Yet there are other criteria that surface to help define what a good partner is.

As a first pass, a potential partner must meet the 'three-A' test: it is available, affordable and attractive.[1] In the case of Volvo and Renault, an alliance made sense to the extent that each complemented the other; in addition, they were bound by an equity relationship (defined by the alliance agreement), which was guaranteed by cross-shareholding (i.e. each party held stock in the other's company), a penalty for the party that unilaterally terminated the alliance, and other mechanisms (e.g. poison pills) that made it very hard to break the relationship. Mutually beneficial goals are no guarantee that an alliance will reap equal benefits, but when benefits are evaluated in relation to the amount of risk each partner takes or the proportion of each partner's contribution, a viable alliance will arrive at overall equity that is fair to the partners.

Beyond sharing a strategic direction or vision, a successful alliance requires trust. Trust has been discussed as a complement to contracts, which help enforce the rights and obligations of the partners and serve as a foundation for monitoring and enforcement (Hansen et al. 2008). In this context *trust* is the degree to which, in a risky exchange relationship, one party holds a positive attitude toward the other's goodwill and reliability (Ring and Van de Ven 1992). Trust relates to expectations about the motivations and abilities of another and how those expectations affect partner cooperation (Das and

Teng 1998). If trust exists, the relationship is better able to withstand uncertainty and conflict, because there is greater faith in a positive alliance outcome. Economists define trust in terms of risk and level of calculation, while sociologists tend to emphasize both goodwill and social relations (Das and Teng 1998).

Four trust-related themes can be identified: (1) Trust can be personal or impersonal; (2) trust has three components (promissory, goodwill and competence); (3) the level of trust is likely to vary with factors such as time, previous experience or cultural norms; and (4) the basis of trust can be calculation, knowledge and/or identification (Gill and Butler 2003). Different cultures may conceptualize trust differently, so to understand its dynamics, social relationships must be considered; as a social mechanism for coopera-tion, trust can and may complement or substitute for bureaucratic or contractual mecha-nisms, and when it wanes, a rise in tension and instability in the alliance is likely to result. The threat of opportunism is not as pervasive as one might think, because mechanisms (i.e. control systems) hold it in check. Das and Kumar (2009) contend that where the potential for opportunism exists, alliance partners tend to seek harmony through greater commitment.

Nevertheless alliances are fraught with the potential for conflict. It is generally accepted that 60 per cent of all alliances fail, but the rate of failure is really bimodal: firms that exhibit alliance competence fail at the rate of 20 per cent, and those that lack such competence at 80 per cent. Also mergers and acquisitions fail at a rate approaching 80 per cent (Bruner 2005). An alliance is less costly to initiate than the merger or acquisition and, because the denominator is smaller, has a lower failure rate and a higher return on investment (ROI). In a merger or acquisition, a firm typically buys the entire company, sells the parts it does not want and keeps what is left. In an alliance, a firm seeks to partner only with the most relevant part of another business.

So far we know that alliances are business agreements to combine resources (with or without taking an equity share in the partner) with the intent of leveraging core compe-tencies, penetrating new markets, gaining new technology or learning newer skills and capabilities. Alliances are also used to share risks, because the uncertainty and costs associated with assessing new markets and technology are often prohibitive for a firm to pursue on its own. This perspective is aligned with the less formal definition offered previously, though the language may not be the same. Here I acknowledge that learning is a legitimate outcome of an alliance. I return to the notion of learning and its impact on alliance success later in this chapter.

The aerospace market is replete with alliances intended to share costs and avoid the financial burden of a go-it-alone strategy. One notable example is the joint strike fighter (JSF), touted as a fifth-generation, single-seat, single-engine stealth fighter and the product of an alliance headed by Lockheed Martin, with Northrop Grumman and BAE Systems as major partners. A second example is the 787 Dreamliner, a mid-sized, twin-engine airliner assembled by Boeing in collaboration with multiple international suppliers.

When describing alliances I tend to cast a wide net and include such relationships as consortia, buying groups, co-marketing agreements and joint ventures. Figure 19.1 sum-marizes the range of alliance types, from most vertically integrated to the least formal collaborative relationships.

To determine which kind of alliance applies in a given situation, I rely on the 3Cs: cost,

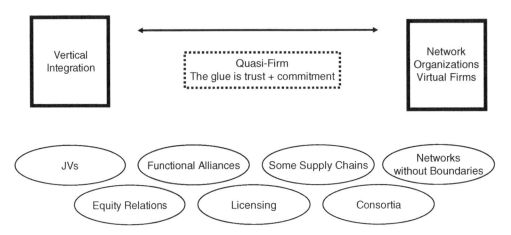

Figure 19.1   Types of organizational structures

control and change. When *cost* is an issue, I advise against a joint venture (JV); of the alliance types, JVs tend to be the most costly, because they often involve combining companies through the formation of subsidiaries, where the alliance partners comprise the board of directors. JVs are also costly to maintain and, if necessary, terminate. In the case of a technology that is *changing* at a fast rate, I tend to suggest the use of licensing, consortia or other alliance types, so that if the technological advantage sought does not materialize, the alliance can be altered more easily. *Control* is meant to capture the ability of one partner to influence the actions of another. Joint ventures and other equity relationships tie the partners more closely and give the more dominant partner a sense of control that would be less likely to exist in other types of alliances. Through partial equity ownership, one partner is better able to influence the behavior of the other. As to how much control a partner needs in an alliance, no consensus exists. Many managers balk at a 50–50 joint venture because they worry about who ultimately has control over the alliance and how they would break a tie, which would slow down any decision-making process. As a result they typically want a 51–49 per cent equity stake, the logic being that the majority holder would eventually rule the day. This logic suffers from the majority fallacy: even a majority holder with a 90 per cent equity position can be held at bay by a minority holder, protracting a stalemate. At the planning or board of director level, the actual percentage of equity held might matter, but at the execution level, it matters little.

Alliance Characteristics

Although there are different forms of alliances that might have advantages in some contexts and not in others, there must exist enough similarities so that the emerging collaborative entity qualifies to be called an alliance. All alliances must share certain common characteristics:

- The sought-after goals may be different but must be compatible.
- To hold opportunism in check, interdependence must be recognized.

- The partners must coordinate and collaborate with a minimum of tension and conflict.
- Trust and commitment, the *sine qua non* of alliances, must exist.
- The alliance must be equitable, though not necessarily equal. Balance in the relationships will occur over time, not at any particular moment in time. That is, if one partner puts 15 per cent into the alliance, it should expect 15 per cent out: no more, no less.
- Alliances are long-term focused, in that they are episodic in nature. What one partner does in one period should affect the other's behavior in a subsequent period, and so on.
- Alliances work best when the partners share similar cultures or have compatible cultural backgrounds. However, while similar cultures ease some of the stresses that affect collaborative relations, if the partners are not aligned on the most basic tenets or fundamental values, there are bound to be problems. Problems can range from issues regarding governance to the formation of the working relationship.

Implied by this list is that the term 'collaboration' suggests a more open and trusting set of relationships than would typically be found in a transactional set of exchanges. Trust is an important element of the relationship, and it can complement the contract or replace it. When firms collaborate, they acknowledge that they are interdependent and that their fates and destinies are linked. Relationships built on compliance and controls do not work. Alliances should be built on strengths and not on weaknesses. When there are duplications in effort or skills, questions of opportunism and disintermediation seem to surface. Complementary assets, skills and capabilities connote that partners recognize the skills brought by their counterparts and attempt to leverage these skills to the advantage of the alliance. Unlike a merger or an acquisition, where one firm absorbs another firm, each firm in an alliance retains its own structure and governance. Performance metrics should be set for the partners and for the alliance. The alliance cannot succeed if one partner achieves its goals and the other does not.

STAGES OF ALLIANCE DEVELOPMENT

As with any process, there are multiple stages through which the development of an alliance must pass, each of which requires different kinds of decisions, has a different outcome and often requires different skills and/or capabilities. Figure 19.2 summarizes one view of the different phases through which a typical alliance might travel as it matures and reaches its end point. Whether the process is three phases or seven is not the point. Of interest here is how problems are addressed and how the skills of the boundary role person (e.g. alliance manager)[2] change over the different phases. During the formulation phase potential partners engage in a search and look for strategic fit, complementarities, shared goals and vision. This stage is often referred to as due diligence, and it gives the potential partners an opportunity to move the alliance from an idea to a concrete reality.

Seven phases of the alliance-building process are highlighted in Figure 19.2, beginning

Anticipation	Engagement	Valuation	Coordination	Investment	Stabilization	Termination
Begin assessment of needs & motivations	Look for complement, congruence, and potential	Making the business case and negotiating the deal	Operational focus, integration, and coordination	Committing resources and people	Managing over time	One of the options as the alliance reaches its endpoint

Source: Modified from Spekman et al. (2000).

Figure 19.2   Stages of alliance development

with 'Anticipation' and ending with 'Termination'. Each phase addresses both business and relationship issues. In the early phases managers begin an assessment of their needs and motivations for the alliance. The focus is on the anticipated outcomes and what the alliance hopes to accomplish. Often a more senior member of the management team envisions a unique solution to a problem facing the firm. The solution often involves forming an alliance. Here the analysis is mostly driven by questions that seek to specify the reason for the alliance and take a first cut at understanding candidates who would qualify as potential partners. As part of its due diligence one firm will state the goals of the proposed alliance and enumerate the skill set needed to fulfill those goals. In the search for a potential partner, the partner selection criteria must align with the skill set that has emerged from the alliance goals. Engagement occurs when the firm meets with prospective partners to share their vision, articulate the business case, determine potential partners' interest and ascertain if there is fit across operational issues, strategic issues and culture.

Valuing is the process by which parties begin their assessment of the exchange rate and the value each party brings to the alliance. Negotiations have for the most part begun, and firms are beginning to calculate the contribution of each partner so that the equity arrangement (if there is one) can be determined. For instance, during the early stages of the Renault–Volvo alliance, it was agreed that though Renault was five times the size of Volvo, Volvo would be given an equal voice in the alliance. Such a gesture signaled that Volvo's contribution to the success of the alliance was important and deemed equal to Renault's. Certainly Volvo's reputation for safety and engineering, as well as its access to the US market, weighed heavily in that decision.

During the process, terms and conditions must be negotiated, sources of known conflict eliminated, performance metrics agreed to, and formal governance established. There are several cautionary points to be made here:

- Avoid 'country club' alliances, where CEOs meet and form the outline for the alliance and then have their people focus on the details. Experience suggests that this approach is a recipe for disaster. Senior management buy-in is critical, but a hand-off from a senior manager to an operational manager rarely goes well. This failure occurs because senior managers tend to work at an abstract level with few details, and such vagueness does not provide adequate direction.
- Because they must live with the outcome of the negotiations, the people who will run the alliance should be directly involved. Often the early work is done by the

business development people, who hand off the alliance to the alliance managers, who must live and die by an alliance they played no part in forming.
- Be careful of attorneys during the formation phase of the alliance. Lawyers tend to write contracts that are untenable, given the business case. While the legal people have an important role to play, they often write contracts that reflect their top priority: protecting the firm. Nevertheless they should be involved in the process, because the contract is the living document that describes what the alliance partners have agreed.
- Once the contract is written, put it away and resist referring to it constantly. If the contract is pulled out and examined, larger problems often surface. I believe that contracts play an essential role, but when they move into the foreground, the spirit of the alliance suffers, and more rigid, contract-like thinking, which is more hierarchical and counter to the alliance process, tends to take over.

An important consideration in the early phases of alliance formation is the manner of negotiations between alliance partners. Issues will arise during the formation of the alliances that will require conflict resolution and are not rooted in opportunism. When ambiguity, uncertainty and tensions brought on by disparate views and goals endanger trust, good conflict resolution techniques can mitigate such negative effects. Problem-solving as an approach leads to more productive outcomes than either contention or yielding to partner demands; its implicit focus on information exchange and a win–win philosophy is likely to result in an integrative solution. Das and Kumar (2009) refer to inter-partner harmony driven by *commitment*, or the desire to sustain the alliance, and *forbearance*, which implies partner interaction based on and conducive to long-term confidence in the alliance. I hope that partners are open, flexible and responsive to each other and avoid rushing to attribute partner behaviors and motivations to anything other than the alliance's success.

Coordinating and investing tend to occur during the normal life of the alliance as parties learn how to align better and work together. Investing is the process by which partners try to tighten the bounds that link them and build a strong and more enduring alliance. Lambe et al. (2002) speak of a virtuous cycle in which partners recommit to the alliance. Each dedicates resources to the alliance, thereby forging a closer, more permanent relationship. We go on to argue that alliance-competent firms are better able to leverage complementary resources and are better at understanding the skills and capabilities of their partners. Only through integrative processes and other means to share knowledge can the alliance achieve its goals.

When problems arise during the management of the alliance, partners often refer to the exit clauses that accompany the formal alliance agreement. I am troubled when termination so quickly becomes the default option. If the alliance is important to both parties, exit as an option is less than satisfactory. I would rather the partners rely on a no-blame review (NBR) (Spekman et al. 2000), which seeks to understand the root cause of the problems, not to place blame. Effort is dedicated to discussing problems and resolving conflicts that have come to affect alliance performance negatively. An NBR may recommend termination, but it is not the default option; partners instead might redefine the alliance, change its course or resume their existing trajectory.

GOVERNANCE OF ALLIANCES

As alliances have grown in importance over the past decade, so have discussions about alliance governance – the process of safeguarding and coordinating alliance activities. At its most basic level, *governance* is a socially constructed set of forces that shape the behavior of the alliance partners, ensuring that the spirit of the alliance will survive its course. Governance provides a structure, reporting system and incentive system for the alliance. It is intended to build on the objectives and goals of the alliance contract or memorandum of understanding by providing for the integration of partners, assigning the right people to the alliance, developing mechanisms for dealing with disagreements and guarding against opportunism and information leakage.

Governance is distinct from leadership; structure and processes alone cannot ensure alliance success. In most alliances joint leadership remains a weakness. Governance typically focuses on making key strategic decisions, providing guidance on strategic vision, resolving disputes and monitoring performance. Alliance leadership focuses on leveraging the skills of partners, empowering other alliance team members to work in support of the alliance goals and objectives and ensuring that the alliance is on track toward the completion of its goals. Yet questions surface regarding roles, responsibility and decision-making authority. Should these issues go unattended, key tasks are not executed; efforts are duplicated, which leads to inefficiency and/or conflict; and because the right people are hard to reach, the alliance underperforms.

Contracts and Trust

To achieve effective alliance governance, mechanisms must help identify key decisions, clearly define processes and roles for making decisions, provide tools and incentives to support the effective implementation of decisions and provide tools to measure results. These formal processes and mechanisms are often supplemented by less formal relational elements, such as trust, that reinforce the objectives of the proposed governance structure. Typically governance has focused on two perspectives: the structural design of a single transaction and relational processes that guide the ongoing relationship of two or more firms. These relational processes emphasize the importance of trust for safeguarding and coordinating the alliance (Faems et al. 2008).

Contracts appear to be devices to safeguard against opportunism by specifying what is and is not permitted. Complex contracts reduce both ability and willingness to behave opportunistically (Parkhe 1993) and serve to coordinate activities by specifying the precise division of labor between partners (Reuer and Arino 2007). Focusing on the single alliance transaction, however, assumes that partners tend to act opportunistically and that as uncertainty increases, so does the likelihood of opportunism (e.g. Williamson 1991). In contrast a relational perspective assumes that partners will behave in a trustworthy manner, especially when past collaborations have been successful.

Trust entails several dimensions that encompass positive expectations about both a partner's ability to perform according to the agreement and own intentions to do the same. In this fashion, trust provides an assurance that information will be used for the greater good and that better communication and information sharing will tend to occur on an informal basis.

Although the research is less than conclusive, there seems to be a reinforcing relationship between these two governance mechanisms. Some studies (Poppo and Zenger 2002) argue that complex contracts facilitate trust-building, whereas others (Malhotra and Murnighan 2002) suggest that these contracts negatively influence the level of trust. Faems et al. (2008) suggest that the initial contract design influences relational dynamics, which in turn affect the application of the contract. A more narrowly defined contract governance structure has a negative impact on trust; a more broadly defined contract governance structure gives rise to goodwill and a more positive trust dynamic. Trust may both supplant the contract and influence the manner in which it is applied, and a more powerful partner is better able to affect the contractual structure than a weaker partner. It follows then that when mutual interdependence and trust exist, the relationship is more likely to continue.

Effects of Task Uncertainty and Asset Specificity on Governance

With uncertainty comes a higher probability of opportunism, which is better controlled by a hierarchical governance form. An equity-based alliance, such as a joint venture, thus is preferred to a market-based alliance, such as licensing. In a review of 63 studies David and Han (2004) show that uncertainty has a positive effect on the use of hierarchical governance in 24 per cent of the cases, a negative effect in 16 per cent, and no effect in 60 per cent. In a TCE framework, governance forms are efficient when they minimize the combined costs of opportunism and administration that arise from uncertainty and asset specificity. Although equity relationships are costly to set up, manage and exit, they specify rights to make future investments and claim returns. Successful alliance experiences lead to positive expectations about future interactions.

Santoro and McGill (2005) demonstrate that alliance partners choose governance structures on the basis of the type of uncertainty they face. For example, firms use more hierarchical governance to control greater uncertainty about partner intentions or capabilities. The higher risks associated with early-stage high-tech alliances become more salient when partners are less familiar with each other. With greater information-sharing, partners can better anticipate contributions and performance, enabling them to use more informal mechanisms to resolve disputes.

An unrelated study (Li et al. 2008) examines partner selection as a mechanism for the control of knowledge leakage. On the basis of prior interactions, it is possible to define a *friend* (prior partner with a higher degree of trust), an *acquaintance* (potential partner with little past interaction) and a *stranger* (potential partner that is unknown). Forming R&D alliances with friends is easy, because there is history, so information should flow more easily. As uncertainty increases, prior experience assumes greater positive significance. Relying on friends can also limit the range of potential partners and lead to path dependencies, though. The knowledge gained through prior contacts can be useful to innovation and competitive success. At the same time some knowledge gained through prior alliance can be harmful if used for one's own gain. Prior knowledge can expose the partner's core knowledge and result in a loss of competitive advantage. Contracts can improve trust by clarifying roles and expectations and generating commitment to the relationships, but if trust lessens the degree of formal governance, it can place the firm at risk. Thus it is the acquaintances that must be treated carefully, because not much is known about them, and knowledge leakage can be a problem.

Equity Versus Non-equity Alliances

Much of the research on governance form in alliances has been based on the distinction between equity and non-equity arrangements. Equity arrangements are typically organized as joint ventures, which most closely relate to a markets–hierarchy continuum, with a separate administrative structure and formal coordination and control mechanisms. Because equity alliances have higher levels of control over partner behavior than non-equity alliances, the latter alliances require higher levels of trust to manage uncertainty over partner behavior. Partners may, through familiarity and past relationships, build enough confidence over time to trade hierarchical control for the flexibility of trust-based non-equity relationships (Gulati 1995). The notion that, absent trust, equity arrangements protect collaborators from opportunistic behavior is subject to debate. What is clear, however, is that equity and non-equity arrangements are subject to different risks.

Casciaro (2003) argues that the exit barriers established in equity arrangements can lead to opportunistic behavior. Conventional wisdom suggests that control is equal to the equity shares held by the partners – that is, more equity equals more control – but this assumption has been challenged on several levels; Mjoen and Tallman (1977) demonstrate that the relative control of parents in a joint venture is more a function of the resources each contributes. These results call into question the relationship between control and equity. Casciaro (2003) takes a different perspective, arguing that the choice of governance structure might be driven by the source of uncertainty facing the alliance. He posits that there are three major sources of uncertainty: task, strategic and partner.

Task uncertainty grows from a contingency perspective (Galbraith 1977) and has been tested by Gulati and Singh (1998), who find a positive relationship between the type of interdependence intrinsic to the task performed in the alliance and the likelihood of adopting equity forms of alliances. The coordination and information processing requirements induced by task uncertainty increase the need for adaption, communication and integrative mechanisms. Even in the presence of full cooperation and coordination, additional uncertainty can arise from the partners' strategic positioning. This strategic uncertainty helps define the role of alliances as risk-sharing entities. The JV permits a firm to explore a new market or technology without fully committing to it. The non-equity alliance, with its lower exit barriers, is less difficult to dissolve than the joint venture. Licensing and supply alliances are associated with lower levels of task and strategic uncertainty because they entail the transfer of resources from one firm to another and often require less coordination. However, depending on the characteristics of the product or service provided during the supply relationship, there could be high task uncertainty. An issue here is that the reliance on partner uncertainty might no longer be as useful as a predictor of equity/non-equity arrangements due to impact of task and strategic uncertainties.

Governance

It has long been assumed that trust is the social lubricant that reduces friction in trading relationships. Over the history of alliance research, we researchers have shown that trust-based governance is contingent on each party's ability to read the other and to learn behaviors. We have noted the perils of misplaced trust due to overestimating the trustworthiness of an acquaintance. We have demonstrated that trust can be used to support an incomplete contract between trading partners. We have shown that the more trust-based governance is used, the more performance improves. But there are limits to the application of trust and its influence on the choice of equity versus non-equity arrangements. There is no question that trust is an important component of any decision to alter the structure of an alliance relationship; however, the decision to pursue an equity or a non-equity alliance is subject to task and strategic uncertainties as well.

I have avoided any discussion of equity relationships in international alliances thus far. These alliances tend to be more complex, due to cultural differences and added performance risks. As noted previously, both the cultural distance and the threat of opportunism can be held in check by an equity alliance. Because historical ties between partners in an international alliance are often limited, learning about a potential partner's credibility is salient. A credible firm often has greater alliance management experience and alliance capability; it also has greater clout and can better leverage its status and reputation. Such skills place these firms in a more powerful position relative to their partner.

Termination

The process of ending an alliance is not well documented, despite the belief that failure is built into the process. That is, alliances are developed to address uncertainty in the marketplace. Given that uncertainty exists, the risk of failure becomes more pronounced. One way of coping is to incorporate preconditions or exit clauses into the contract. These exit clauses are intended to deal with any issues that might affect how the alliance ends and how the resultant products and services, intellectual capital or other proprietary information will be shared or sold after the alliance ends. The argument for incorporating exit clauses flows from the notion that it allows partners to address these concerns without the heat of battle that would arise if the alliance were beginning to falter. When partners are still committed to the alliance, they can make a more objective valuation of the assets or resources dedicated to the alliance and establish a 'fair market value' for the alliance, as well as set the terms for how the proceeds of the alliance will be split among the partners.

I recommend that alliances end amicably, because legal remedies become part of the public record and could leave a black mark on the reputations of firms involved in litigation. If a potential partner firm has a choice, why would it collaborate with another firm that has a reputation for seeking legal remedies to problems? Several telltale signs suggest problems in the alliance, such as when (1) partners talk more about each other than to each other; (2) partners do not assign people of comparable talent to the alliance; or (3) one partner consistently acts opportunistically. Although expectations change over the life of the alliance, if the fundamental reason for the alliance changes for one partner and not the other, there is the potential for a serious rift that must be addressed. If trust is damaged, it should be fixed right away, because it represents the mortar that holds the relationship together.

Reasons against the use of exit clauses are based in the belief that they send the wrong signal and give a way out before that hard work of building strong ties has taken hold. It might sour the relationship at a time when trust is building and partners are fragile. But ask yourself: what do you want your partner to say about you when the alliance terminates? I have recommended a no-blame review as an approach to solving conflict (for a full description, see Spekman et al. 2000). It suffices to say that the premise is taken from the notions articulated in the work 'Getting to Yes', which itself is based on the Harvard Negotiation Project. Simply put, if the alliance is important, it makes little sense to have exit as its default option. If the alliance has merit, partners should work hard to resolve issues and remediate problems. Exit is always an option but perhaps not a good one, even when partners begin to argue. Alliances take hard work, and resorting to exit when problems arise fails to acknowledge the effort required to make an alliance succeed.

IMPLICATIONS FOR B2B MARKETERS

The importance of strategic alliances to B2B marketers cannot be denied, and in recent years their importance has increased for a range of business decisions. The cost of market entry, development of new technology and access to new segments and customers has risen so much that a go-it-alone strategy is no longer viable. More and more we read about alliance competence and the ability of a firm to develop a strategic vision and direction, select the right partner, negotiate a fair contract, establish mutually acceptable performance metrics and manage the formation and eventual dissolution of the alliance.

Yet despite the many articles that provide insight into those factors, the road to failure has been paved by companies with good intentions. Thousands of alliances form yearly, and they fail at a rate of 60 per cent. Given the ebb and flow of alliance relationships, it is reasonable to expect failure as a natural extension of uncertainty. That is, alliances work best under conditions of high uncertainty; if failure were somehow not permitted, at the very least alliance competence would never develop. In any event, uncertainty cannot be avoided.

The key questions that remain are how failure rates might be reduced and the probability of success increased. The dominant theoretical model (transaction cost economics) states that people act opportunistically and with guile, and pursue personal gain to the detriment of their partners, so that the issue becomes one of knowing how to reduce the chance for opportunism and allowing partners to prosper. I have emphasized the importance of trust and other relational variables in mitigating the effects of opportunism, but other strategies exist. For B2B marketers, this chapter offers several suggestions that should serve them well as they venture forth along the alliance path. Portions of the trail are unmarked and hard to navigate, so I provide a map of recommendations in Figure 19.3.

Skills vary as we cycle through the different stages of an alliance. One person alone might not possess all the requisite skills, so an alliance may require a series of managers over the course of its life. Unfortunately alliance formation and management rarely receive the attention they deserve, and many firms do not perceive the importance of developing alliance skills within their own companies, even though the managerial implications are profound. We must work to develop talent that is both alliance aware and alliance competent.

It matters little whether there is an established office of alliance management or if alliance thinking and behaviors are inculcated among all the firm's members. These skills are critical, as suggested by Friedman (2005), who lists collaborative behavior as the

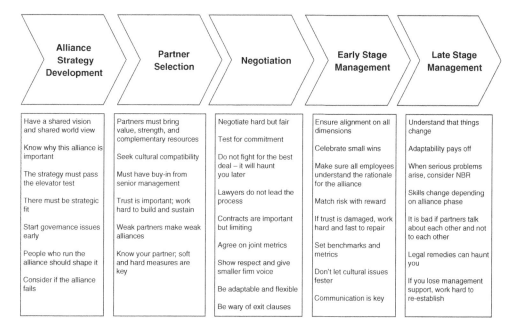

Alliance Strategy Development	Partner Selection	Negotiation	Early Stage Management	Late Stage Management
Have a shared vision and shared world view	Partners must bring value, strength, and complementary resources	Negotiate hard but fair	Ensure alignment on all dimensions	Understand that things change
Know why this alliance is important	Seek cultural compatibility	Test for commitment	Celebrate small wins	Adaptability pays off
The strategy must pass the elevator test	Must have buy-in from senior management	Do not fight for the best deal – it will haunt you later	Make sure all employees understand the rationale for the alliance	When serious problems arise, consider NBR
There must be strategic fit	Trust is important; work hard to build and sustain	Lawyers do not lead the process	Match risk with reward	Skills change depending on alliance phase
Start governance issues early	Weak partners make weak alliances	Contracts are important but limiting	If trust is damaged, work hard and fast to repair	It is bad if partners talk about each other and not to each other
People who run the alliance should shape it	Know your partner; soft and hard measures are key	Agree on joint metrics	Set benchmarks and metrics	Legal remedies can haunt you
Consider if the alliance fails		Show respect and give smaller firm voice	Don't let cultural issues fester	If you lose management support, work hard to re-establish
		Be adaptable and flexible	Communication is key	
		Be wary of exit clauses		

Figure 19.3   Understanding best-in-class behaviors by phase of alliance process

most critical of skills in a 'flat' world marked by increased equity. The list of dos and don'ts in Figure 19.3 presents a challenge to managers who often have difficulty creating internal partnerships, which should be easier.

We often speak of alliances between two firms, but many alliances involve three or more partners. The genome project involved more than two dozen partners from many different countries and institutions. My point is that dyadic relationships are tough enough to manage; when a third partner is added, the complexity increases not arithmetically but geometrically. It would be safe to say that for the practitioner, there is much work to be done to become alliance competent. If trust is a prime example of a key relational variable, it is also necessary to note that trust is fragile, hard to build, and easy to break and that there are a host of constructs that affect the trust-building process.

To complicate issues many of the relationships among the concepts are inconclusive, so it is hard to predict the outcome of a certain action. It can be demonstrated that more alliance experience leads to more alliance competence, which should result in better alliance management. But there is a point at which the capacity to absorb becomes exhausted, and more alliances will only distract from and interfere with alliance management. Cultural differences cannot be ignored either, whether in terms of national or firm-level cultures (e.g. General Motors is very different from Hewlett-Packard) or with regard to functional cultures within disciplines such as marketing, finance and manufacturing. Some of these differences may be subtle, but the impact on management's ability to manage an alliance can be profound.

The skills needed by alliance managers can be divided into two major categories: skills that can be taught and skills that cannot be taught but can be learned over time with the help of a mentor (Spekman et al. 2000). These skills are found more often in alliance-competent firms, where building a cadre of capable alliance managers is an imperative. Skills that can be taught lead to more cross-culturally sensitive managers, known for their alliance capabilities, general business acumen and networks they have established both within and outside the firm. Learned skills lead to a more adaptive and flexible management style, marked by a longer-term view and an enterprise-wide focus. Yet various questions, whose answers would facilitate alliance competence, remain unanswered. What types of learning are most relevant for developing an alliance competence? What skills are most pivotal to alliance success? Experiential learning clearly is key to developing alliance competence, but can the process be shortened?

CONCEPTUAL AND THEORETICAL IMPLICATIONS

The ascendancy of alliances has implications not only for managers but also researchers. Because alliances are a fairly nascent area of academic inquiry, a number of paradigms continue to vie for dominance, with TCE appearing to be the most widely utilized framework.

We thus need to understand better the contributions of resource dependency, social exchange, real options, and network paradigms. My sense is that one approach is not adequate to capture the full effect of those factors on alliance performance, so rather than advocate hegemony, we should be more accepting of competing and complementary conceptual frameworks. For example, research might examine the network effects of international alliances and what occurs when there are power asymmetries between the alliance partners. The goal would be to investigate how the use of complementary paradigms might reveal a fuller picture of partners' interplay, in all its complexity. In an international venue, it would make sense to incorporate cultural constructs as well, to maximize the research's explanatory power.

Although we speak of the importance of trust and its impact on collaboration and performance, researchers may wish to investigate more thoroughly its role in international alliances. It might be useful to examine the extent to which, among partners from different cultures, changes in the partner's strategic direction or management affect the stabilizing effect of trust.

Research is also needed to appreciate the influence of trust on performance. We understand performance metrics, but research has remained mostly silent on issues related to joint goals and maintaining a relationship. That is, alliances are built and sustained by relationship-building activities, and as such, the episodic nature of the relationship becomes important. In a spot market transaction, one cares little about the longevity of the relationship; in the alliance, performance extends from relationship-building to outcome-based metrics. A related topic is the use of learning as a performance measure. Given the lag time between learning and its impact on performance, it might be hard to correlate the two. Adding to the complexity is the notion of absorptive capacity, in that unequal learning rates provide one partner with a stronger bargaining position that introduces tension and instability into an otherwise stable alliance.

Throughout this chapter I have alluded to alliance capabilities, and this topic warrants more extensive research attention. We are aware of the need for strong alliance management skills. Alliance *capability* refers to the mechanisms and routines designed to accumulate, store, integrate and disseminate relevant knowledge about alliance management (Dyer et al. 2001). Which knowledge dissemination methods are most beneficial to alliance management skills and capabilities? What critical skills and competences are required to be adept at effective alliance management? Answers to these questions are necessary to raise the level of alliance success. Few studies emphasize these competencies, but it would be useful to examine what factors encourage and inhibit alliance learning, as well as the development of alliance competencies. Other research might examine whether different types of alliances lead to different learning outcomes. Perhaps joint ventures result in greater learning; a viable rival explanation might also suggest that, considering the level of trust needed in non-equity alliances, these alliances provide better learning opportunities.

In reading many articles comparing alliances to acquisitions, I have started to wonder why more research has not combined resources to examine both approaches. A cross-disciplinary approach would make for better research. For instance, finance studies often use a critical events methodology that compares measures taken before and after a triggering event. Marketing scholars instead tend to rely on factors that appear to enhance results. The two approaches are quite complementary, so I encourage more joint work. Thorny problems are best tackled through multidisciplinary teams that bring complementary skills to bear on them.

CONCLUDING REMARKS

My goal in this chapter has been to explore the topic of alliances and their relevance for the study of B2B markets. Considering the expenses associated with technology development and market access, alliances provide a way for partners to combine and leverage their skills and capabilities to accomplish goals that alone would be difficult to realize. Given the range of alliance options, from consortia to joint ventures, I have chosen not to highlight marketing alliances per se. Instead I have addressed the effect of equity and non-equity alliances on performance and the role of relational variables – trust and commitment – in determining outcomes, both on a goal-and-objectives level and a relationship-formation-and-development level. I have summarized extant literature as it relates to alliance formation and maintenance and recommended fruitful areas of managerial and conceptual inquiry for further study.

We still have a great deal to learn about alliances. For academics and practitioners exploring its unchartered waters, I hope this chapter provides landmarks and directions, and I urge others to take up the call. We have made significant strides, but there is much still to be done.

NOTES

1. Even US Air, despite losing millions of dollars a month, was attractive, in part due to its short-haul expertise. At the time of the alliance (1993), British Airways launched about 200 flights per day from Heathrow to the rest of the world, and US Air launched thousands of short-haul flights from its hub-and-spoke

network. Learning the short-haul business would prepare British Airways for entry into the rest of Europe when deregulation granted foreign carriers the right to carry passengers in country.

2. I prefer the term 'alliance manager' to 'boundary role person' because I consider it more to the point. This person is responsible for managing the alliance for one of the alliance partners, is responsible for all facets of the alliance and is the spokesperson for his or her firm for all issues germane to a particular alliance. Because this person tends to sit at the firm boundary, it is logical to refer to him or her as a 'boundary spanner' too.

REFERENCES

Axelrod, R.M. (1984), *The Evolution of Cooperation*, New York: Basic Books.

Bruner, R. (2005), *Deals from Hell*, New York: John Wiley & Sons.

Casciaro, T. (2003), 'Determinants of governance structure in alliances: the role of strategic, task and partner uncertainties', *Industrial and Corporate Change*, **12** (6), 1223–51.

Chen, H. and T.-Y. Chen (2002), 'Asymmetric strategic alliances: a network view', *Journal of Business Research*, **55** (1), 1007–13.

Culpan, R. (2009), 'A fresh look at strategic alliances: research issues and future directions', *International Journal of Strategic Business Alliances*, **1** (1), 4–23.

Das, T.K. and R. Kumar (2009), 'Interpartner harmony in strategic alliances: managing commitment and forbearance', *International Journal of Strategic Business Alliances*, **1** (1), 24–52.

Das, T.K. and B.S. Teng (1998), 'Resource and risk management in strategic alliance making process', *Journal of Management*, **24** (1), 21–42.

David, R. and S. Han (2004), 'A systemic assessment of the empirical support for transaction cost economics', *Strategic Management Journal*, **25** (1), 39–58.

Dwyer, F.R., P. Schurr and S. Oh (1987), 'Developing buyer–seller relationships', *Journal of Marketing*, **51** (2), 11–27.

Dyer, J., P. Kale and H. Singh (2001), 'How to make strategic alliances work: the role of the alliance function', *MIT Sloan Management Review*, **42** (4), 37–43.

Faems, D., M. Janssens, A. Madhok and B. Van Looy (2008), 'Towards an integrative perspective on alliance governance', *Academy of Management Journal*, **51** (6), 1053–78.

Fang, Eric, Robert Palmatier, Lisa Scheer and N. Li (2008), 'Trust at different organizational levels', *Journal of Marketing*, **72** (2), 80–98.

Frazier, Gary L., Robert E. Spekman and C.R. O'Neal (1988), 'Just-in-time exchange relationships in industrial markets', *Journal of Marketing*, **52** (4), 52–67.

Friedman, Thomas L. (2005), *The World is Flat: A Brief History of the Twenty-First Century*, New York: Farrar, Straus and Giroux.

Galbraith, John R. (1977), *Organizational Design*, Reading, MA: Addison-Wesley.

Gill, J. and R. Butler (2003), 'Managing instability in cross-cultural alliances', *Long Range Planning*, **36** (6), 543–63.

Granovetter, M. (1985), 'Economic action and social structure: the problem of embeddedness', *American Journal of Sociology*, **91** (3), 481–510.

Gulati, R. (1995), 'Does familiarity breed trust? The implications of repeated ties for contractual choice in alliances', *Academy of Management Journal*, **38** (1), 85–112.

Gulati, R. and H. Singh (1998), 'The architecture of cooperation: managing coordination costs and appropriation concerns in strategic alliances', *Administrative Science Quarterly*, **43** (4), 781–814.

Hansen, M.H., R.E. Hoskisson and J.B. Barney (2008), 'Competitive advantage in alliance governance: resolving the opportunism minimization–gain maximization paradox', *Managerial and Decision Economics*, **29** (2–3), 191–208.

Harrigan, K.R. (1986), *Managing for Joint Venture Success*, Lexington, MA: Lexington Books.

Heide, Jan (1994), 'Interorganizational governance in marketing channels', *Journal of Marketing*, **58** (1), 71–85.

Homans, G. (1961), *Social Behavior*, New York: Harcourt, Brace and World.

Lambe, C.J., Robert E. Spekman and Shelby D. Hunt (2002), 'Alliance competence, resources, and alliance success: conceptualization, measurement, and initial test', *Journal of the Academy of Marketing Science*, **30** (2), 141–58.

Lewis, J. (1990), *Partnerships for Profit*, New York: The Free Press.

Li, D., L. Eden, M.A. Hitt and R.D. Ireland (2008), 'Friends, acquaintances, or strangers? Partner selections in R&D alliances', *Academy of Management Journal*, **51** (2), 315–34.

Lynch, R.P. (1989), *Alliance Guide for Business*, New York: John Wiley & Sons.

Macneil, R.I. (1980), *The New Social Contract: an Inquiry into Modern Contractual Relations*, New Haven, CT: Yale University Press.

Malhotra, D. and J. Murnighan (2002), 'The effects of contracts on interpersonal trust', *Administrative Science Quarterly*, **47** (3), 534–59.

Mjoen, H. and S. Tallman (1977), 'Control and performance in international joint ventures', *Organization Science*, **8** (3), 257–74.

Muthusamy, S., M. White and A. Carr (2007), 'An empirical examination of the role of social exchanges in alliance performance', *Journal of Managerial Issues*, **19** (1), 53–75.

Parkhe, A. (1993), 'Strategic alliance structuring: a game theoretic and transaction cost examination of inter-firm cooperation', *Academy of Management Journal*, **36** (4), 794–829.

Pfeffer, J. and G.R. Salancik (1978), *The External Control of Organizations: A Resource Dependence Perspective*, New York: Harper & Row.

Poppo, Laura and T. Zenger (2002), 'Do formal contracts and relational governance function as substitutes or complements?', *Strategic Management Journal*, **23** (8), 707–25.

Reuer, J.J. and A. Arino (2007), 'Strategic alliance contracts: dimensions and determinants of contractual complexity', *Strategic Management Journal*, **28** (3), 313–30.

Ring, P.S. and A.H. Van de Ven (1992), 'Structuring cooperative relationships between organizations', *Strategic Management Journal*, **13** (7), 483–98.

Santoro, M.D. and J.P. McGill (2005), 'The effect of uncertainty and asset co-specialization on governance in biotechnology alliances', *Strategic Management Journal*, **26** (13), 1261–9.

Spekman, Robert E. and D. Strauss (1986), 'An exploratory investigation of a buyer's concern for factors affecting more collaborative buyer–seller relationships', *Industrial Marketing and Purchasing*, **1** (3), 26–43.

Spekman, Robert E., L.A. Isabella and T.C. MacAvoy (2000), *Alliance Competence: Maximizing the Value of your Partners*, New York: John Wiley & Sons.

Varadarajan, P.R. and M.H. Cunningham (1995), 'Strategic alliances: a synthesis of conceptual foundations', *Journal of the Academy of Marketing Science*, **24** (4), 282–96.

Williamson, O.E. (1975), *Markets and Hierarchies, Analysis and Antitrust Implications: A Study in the Economics of Internal Organization*, New York: The Free Press.

Williamson, O.E. (1985), *The Economic Institutions of Capitalism: Firms, Markets, Relational Contracting*, New York: The Free Press.

Williamson, O.E. (1991), 'Comparative economic organization: the analysis of discrete structural alternatives', *Administrative Science Quarterly*, **36** (2), 269–96.

20 Learning in coopetitive relationships
Hillbun (Dixon) Ho and Shankar Ganesan

The current business environment poses increasingly thorny challenges to organizations because of increased globalization, cut-throat competition, fast-paced technological innovations, quick product obsolescence and ever-changing consumer needs. These challenges force organizations to look beyond traditional strategies such as differentiation, cost leadership and niche segmentation if they want to outperform their rivals.

As a result many firms have adopted cooperative strategies with their downstream and upstream partners to create win–win situations and positive outcomes for the entire value chain. This practice is consistent with marketing academics' sentiments about the importance of building and maintaining long-term relationships with suppliers and customers across the entire supply chain. Over the past two decades this relationship-oriented philosophy has permeated marketing literature and the business press (Ganesan 1994; Morgan and Hunt 1994).

Current literature provides a deep understanding of firms' vertical relationships, but knowledge of horizontal relationships among firms that occupy similar positions along a supply chain is rather limited. The result is that cooperation between firms that serve the same customer or market segment has drawn limited attention from marketing academics. The focus of this chapter is on cooperation and competition at the same time among firms, a concept often referred to as 'coopetition'. The paucity of research in this area is unfortunate, because alliances among competitors have become popular in the business community. For example, General Motors and Toyota have collaborated to manufacture automobiles, Siemens and Philips have jointly developed semiconductors, Canon has supplied photocopiers to Kodak, and France's Thomson and Japan's JVC manufactured videocassette recorders (Hamel et al. 1989).

Previous research also suggests that firms can learn from their collaborative experience and acquire new knowledge and skills from their collaborative partners (Hamel 1991). The collaborative ventures that offer learning opportunities are often formed by rivals holding complementary technological expertise and skills. Topics investigated include how knowledge is managed in collaborative partnerships (e.g. Khanna et al. 1998), how knowledge is transferred between partners (e.g. Simonin 1999), how knowledge about collaboration develops over time and influences collaboration outcomes (e.g. Powell et al. 1996) and how the acquired knowledge affects performance (e.g. Lane et al. 2001). Although this literature stream has been growing, marketing scholars have paid limited attention to the learning opportunities available to firms collaborating with competitors.

The main purpose of this chapter therefore is to explicate issues related to cooperation among competitors, or 'coopetition'. First, we discuss the nature and distinctive characteristics of coopetition. Second, we propose external and internal factors that are likely to drive the formation of cooperative relationships among competitors. Third, we suggest theoretical frameworks that are relevant to understanding firm behaviors in a coopetitive context. Fourth, we explain the learning and knowledge transfer aspects of coopetition. Fifth, we discuss the inherent challenges that partnering firms face in a coopetitive context. Sixth and finally, we suggest important directions for further research. These ideas are summarized in the framework in Figure 20.1.

Although coopetition can result in a variety of benefits such as increased shareholder value (Kalaignanam et al. 2007), it also entails the pitfalls and challenges that are common to other collaborative partnerships. Because partner firms are also competitors, the difficulty of managing coopetitive ventures, due to hazards such as information asymmetry and behavioral uncertainty, is exacerbated. Thus effective governance and control are important for the sustainability of alliances, which are inherently unstable (Das and Teng 2000). Several studies of horizontal alliances (a form of coopetition) have examined the implications of partnership hazards for the choice of governance structure and alliance type. For example, when the inherent risks in alliances are high, partner firms tend to use equity alliances as the governance structure and limit the alliance scope (Gulati and Singh 1998; Oxley and Sampson 2004). Because these issues have been addressed extensively in extant literature, we focus in this chapter on governance issues related to knowledge sharing and learning.

In summary, this chapter provides a broad overview of the major facets of coopetition. We seek to increase awareness of this important strategic option among managers who plan to develop inter-firm collaborative relationships and to provoke further discussion and investigation of this phenomenon among marketing scholars.

WHAT IS COOPETITION?

The notion of coopetition was used in game theory to show how rivals could cooperate to increase the size of the outcome 'pie' (Brandenburger and Nalebuff 1998). In general, coopetition refers to circumstances in which firms compete and at the same time cooperate to achieve their strategic goals (Luo 2004). Some well-known examples of coopetition include SEMATECH, a research consortium of leading semiconductor manufacturers; NUMMI, a joint venture of Toyota and GM that built cars under both brands; and Airbus, a joint venture of leading aircraft manufacturers in Europe (Gomes-Casseres 1994). As a strategy, competition and cooperation need not be at the polar ends of a continuum (Lado et al. 1997), because within any inter-firm relationship, competition and cooperation can occur concurrently. Firms capable of managing both activities simultaneously can earn higher returns than firms that focus on either competition or cooperation.

In one form of coopetition multiple types of associations, such as competitive and cooperative relationships, can be superimposed and coexist between partnering firms (Ross and Robertson 2007). Alternatively coopetition can refer to two rivals cooperating to attain a bigger overall 'pie' in the marketplace but also competing to appropriate a greater share from that pie. In this case, cooperation enables both firms to expand the pie of outcomes, while competition enables each one to secure a bigger share of such outcomes.

The practice of coopetition mimics the idea of network competition, in which firms that possess complementary resources or competencies join together to compete with

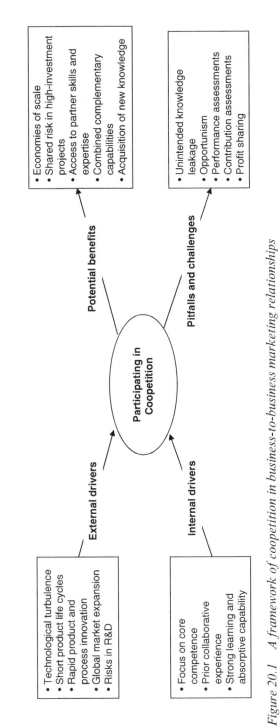

Figure 20.1 A framework of coopetition in business-to-business marketing relationships

other groups of firms (Gomes-Casseres 1994). For example, airline alliances such as Star Alliance, SkyTeam and Oneworld involve groups of airlines competing by increasing the flight network, operational efficiency and services quality of member airlines. Firms participating in coopetition aim to enhance their competitiveness in the marketplace by leveraging synergies among the partners in production, new product development and marketing.

Coopetition is not synonymous with collusion, which violates antitrust legislation. The strategic goals of coopetition usually relate to creating superior value for customers, which in turn generates value for the collaborating firms. In contrast collusion is an agreement between two or more firms to limit open competition by deceiving, misleading or defrauding others of their legal rights or to attain an objective forbidden by law, typically by defrauding or gaining an unfair advantage. Colluding firms agree to divide the market, set prices or limit production, all practices that are illegal. Therefore coopetition is distinct in that it allows partnering firms to gain competitive advantage in the marketplace through improved efficiency and effectiveness, resulting in greater customer value creation.

Competing firms cooperate because participation in activities of common interest enables them to achieve strategic goals and increase individual pay-offs. For instance, competitors form alliances to achieve economies of scale and scope or undertake strategic, high-risk activities (e.g. R&D, new product development). In addition firms have strong incentives to collaborate when the needs of a market segment can be fulfilled more effectively by combining the capabilities and expertise of two rivals (Dhanaraj and Parkhe 2006). Case studies of supply networks show that competing suppliers often work together to serve a common buyer's procurement needs (e.g. Wu and Choi 2005). Furthermore suppliers belonging to a leading buyer's supply network can relate both cooperatively and competitively (Dyer 2000). For example, suppliers may compete in one product market but cooperate in another. In some cases a supplier may purchase product components from another supplier, even though both of them could serve the same customer or buyer. In other cases a supplier could subcontract its manufacturing job to other suppliers that have been designated by the buyer. Sometimes a powerful buyer initiates and guides suppliers' collaboration, creating triadic relationships involving the buyer and its suppliers (Wu and Choi 2005). One type of triadic relationship is referred to as 'coach', in which the buyer coerces two competing suppliers to work together on various production and quality issues to take advantage of the engineering capabilities of both suppliers.

Although collaboration between rivals is motivated by the desire to increase the mutual benefits, coopetition is not free from conflict. Conflict can easily develop because the strategic goals of each party do not always align with the collective goals of the collaboration. In addition because collaboration between rivals is usually confined to a specific market, product domain or corporate function (e.g. R&D), interests may diverge across organizational units or levels within individual firms, owing to the misalignment of goals across the multiple relationships that exist between the rivals. From a learning perspective the cooperative aspect of an alliance arises because each firm needs access to its partner's know-how, and the alliance partners can use their knowledge collectively to produce something beneficial to all parties (Khanna et al. 1998). In contrast the competitive aspect results from each firm's attempt to use its partner's know-how for private gains. This attempt suggests that greater benefits may flow to a firm that is able to learn faster than its partner. Alliance partners need to consider their private benefits (benefits to the individual partner) versus common benefits (benefits to all parties) to optimize their resource allocation under the coopetition paradox.

In summary coopetition is a distinct form of competitive strategy that emphasizes collaborating with a competitor that possesses unique resources, expertise and skills. By pooling resources and competencies, the collaborating parties can attain collective goals that they cannot achieve by working independently. Firms engaging in coopetition aim to become more competitive by accessing and leveraging their competitor's resources and knowledge to develop products, services and solutions of superior value to customers.

EXTERNAL FACTORS AFFECTING COOPETITIVE RELATIONSHIPS

Several environmental factors affect a firm's decision to consider the strategic option of coopetition. First, when multinational companies enter a new market in a foreign country, they often need to partner with firms that are already established players in the domestic market. For example, many US auto manufacturers have formed joint ventures with domestic auto manufacturers in China to gain access to the Chinese automobile market (Luo 2004). The domestic firms know and understand the local business environment, legislation and consumer behavior, and they have strong connections with other local firms that support major supply chain activities. Without local knowledge and expertise, multinational companies are unlikely to succeed in the new markets. However, the most compatible domestic partners usually possess competencies similar to those of the multinational companies, and once these domestic firms acquire the knowledge and expertise of the multinational companies, they could become major competitors in the foreign market.

Second, the modern marketplace is characterized by rapid technological innovation and shorter product life cycles, and frequent changes in consumption trends and fads exacerbate this challenge. Consumers have become so attentive to new trends and accustomed to the launch of new products that they regard firms as un-innovative and non-competitive if they fail to release new models or products on a regular basis. To address this possibility, in many product categories such as consumer electronics and mobile telephones, firms have incorporated features and functions that exceed the actual needs of consumers. The challenge of achieving breakthroughs in technology and converting such breakthroughs into significant consumer value is daunting for many firms, forcing them to invest heavily in R&D to develop products in multiple lines and product categories that are beyond firms' core competencies. Therefore rapid product obsolescence, coupled with the pressure to launch new products, compels firms to consider the option of collaborating with other firms, including competitors. Collaborating with rivals is a desirable strategic choice because competing firms' knowledge base and core competencies are likely to be compatible, and they should have a similar understanding of the market. Furthermore, competing firms usually possess slightly different, yet complementary, capabilities in terms of technological knowledge and skills.

Third, development of new products and technologies in technology-based industries such as semiconductors and pharmaceuticals requires substantial financial resources, rendering it a risky strategic activity. In addition the high failure rate of new products and increasingly strict government regulations further raise the risks firms face. To temper these risks, firms in such industries tend to form alliances with their rivals, pooling their resources and technological expertise to achieve economies of scale and to tackle the complexities involved in developing new products and technologies. Competing firms can also join together to lobby government bodies for policies in support of their industry.

Fourth, coopetitive enterprises are quite important in industries in which establishing technical standards is vital for product success. Coopetition allows competing firms to work together as an influential group to persuade other firms in the industry to adopt technical standards that the group advocates. Collaborating with rivals enables the firm that develops a technical standard to gain a critical mass of adopters rapidly, thus influencing the overall adoption of the standard. Coopetition aimed at establishing industrial technical standards has appeared quite frequently in both the computer industry (e.g. Microsoft OS, Pentium chips) and the electronics industry (e.g. VHS, Blu-ray discs).

ORGANIZATIONAL FACTORS THAT FOSTER COOPETITION

In this section, we identify organizational factors that drive the formation of coopetitive relationships. First, firms with substantial alliance experience, especially in international markets, often seek opportunities for coopetition. Such experience allows firms to develop knowledge and expertise in structuring and managing the collaborative venture, leading to greater operational efficiency and profits. In addition, experience with coopetition enables firms to select a partner with complementary skills, a compatible management style and similar problem-solving approaches (Sivadas and Dwyer 2000). Working with the right partner lowers the risk of opportunism and facilitates the process of conflict resolution through trust, intense communication and commitment (Dyer and Singh 1998). Furthermore a firm's coopetition history creates a reputation of being a reliable and credible partner, and firms with no experience in coopetition tend to solicit partners with established credibility.

Second, firms possessing limited core competencies benefit more from coopetition and are more likely to collaborate with rivals. Given today's increasingly rapid and complex technological innovation, as well as the difficulty of coordinating a global supply chain, firms often do not possess a broad range of capabilities that allows them to excel in a wide spectrum of value chain activities (Gulati and Kletter 2005). Therefore firms must rely on other parties to provide complementary and supplementary value chain functions so they can focus their resources on strengthening their core competencies. For example, aircraft manufacturers outsource the production of component modules to suppliers so they can devote their resources to R&D or the integration of aircraft systems. Not surprisingly suppliers that possess the expertise and skills required to build important components are often competitors in some product markets.

Third, firms adept at learning from the experience of coopetition and acquiring their collaborating partners' knowledge and skills are more likely to participate in coopetition. This receptivity to participation occurs because firms that view coopetition as a learning opportunity benefit more from coopetition (Inkpen 2000). These firms tend to show deeper commitment to the collaborative venture and greater willingness to devote financial and human resources to it. Participating in coopetition allows firms with a strong learning capability to acquire and absorb their rivals' knowledge and skills faster than rivals do. They can capitalize on the collaborative venture to build competencies in areas beyond the scope of the collaboration and systematically incorporate new knowledge throughout their organization, integrating it with existing knowledge. In addition, firms with greater ability to absorb rivals' knowledge and skills can gain more from coopetition, because its rewards are enhanced by developing inter-organizational knowledge transfer routines and skill in governing and managing the collaborative venture.

RELEVANT THEORETICAL PERSPECTIVES

Firms participating in coopetitive relationships seek to enhance their competitiveness in the marketplace. However, organizing and coordinating the collaborative effort is a major challenge, because it entails both common and divergent interests. We define 'collaboration' as the management of the interdependency between two firms to achieve individual and collective goals through joint decision-making and planning. Collaboration requires the partners to interact frequently and depend on each other over a relatively long period. They must also invest relationship-specific resources, share information and establish a proper governance structure for managing and controlling the collaborative venture. In other words collaboration involves tightly coordinated cooperation between partners with significant stakes in the collaborative activities. The type of collaboration can range from a long-term supply agreement to a joint venture with considerable collaboration-specific investments by both partners.

To understand firms' collaborative behaviors in coopetition, scholars have drawn on theories in inter-organizational relationship research, especially transaction cost economics, resource dependence theory, the resource-based view and relational contract theory. Although no single theory can explain the full complexity of firms' collaborative behavior, a few recurrent theoretical perspectives account for the formation and sustainability of collaborative ventures such as strategic alliances and joint ventures. These theories offer insights into the formation, management, maintenance and dissolution of coopetition.

Resource Dependence Theory

According to resource dependence theory, inter-firm collaboration serves as a strategy for firms to cope with the challenges posed by the external environment. As noted previously, external factors likely to drive collaboration include turbulence in world markets, globalization or regionalization of industries, rapid technological change and shortened product life cycles. Through collaboration firms can leverage the resources and capabilities of their strategic partners to compete with other entities in the marketplace. In other words, firms collaborating with a rival aim to exert power, influence or control over the resources or competencies possessed by that rival (Pfeffer and Salancik 1978). Paradoxically when a firm has scarce and valuable resources, it has greater power and control in the collaborative venture. The dependence structure between two partners is crucial for understanding collaborative behaviors because it determines each partner's influence over the other's decisions. More equal bilateral dependence usually has a positive impact on performance as partners work to maintain their relationship and avoid destructive acts, whereas unbalanced, asymmetrical dependence undermines the relationship by lowering the barrier to the use of coercive power (Kumar et al. 1995).

Resource-based View

The resource-based view holds that firms can attain a competitive advantage by possessing rare, difficult to imitate, non-substitutable resources such as assets and organizational competencies (Barney 1991). These assets are valuable because they can generate economic quasi-rents. Resources that are embedded in organizational processes and routines offer a competitive advantage and are more sustainable than physical or human resources. Firms are unable to develop these competencies internally because the value-adding structure is usually uncertain and path-dependent, and thus their generation of rents is causally ambiguous. Firms can use acquisitions to obtain strategic resources, but the cost of acquisitions usually exceeds the profit potential of the acquired resources. Therefore firms must rely on inter-firm relationships such as alliances to gain access to these strategic resources. In addition, studies show that a firm's experience in forming alliances facilitates its further participation in a variety of alliances. A firm's collaborative capability, developed and learned from prior alliance activities, thus becomes a strategic resource (Sivadas and Dwyer 2000).

   The phenomenon of coopetition extends the application of the resource-based view to networked firms' environment. Scarce, hard-to-imitate, non-substitutable resources that provide a sustainable competitive advantage need not be owned directly by firms. By participating in collaborative ventures, firms can mobilize and deploy resources and competencies possessed by their partner. Thus firms can 'acquire' strategic resources from external parties in a cost-effective way instead of developing these resources themselves. Because collaborative ventures allow accessibility to networked partners' resources and competencies, factors that prevent imitation and substitution of strategic resources become less relevant. Consequently the inimitability of resources depends less on the nature of the resources and more on the nature of the relationships between the firm and its partner. Similarly because partners can gain access to the desired resources by participating in coopetition, they have no need to develop substitute resources (Lavie 2006).

Knowledge-based View

The knowledge-based view is an outgrowth of the resource-based view with an emphasis on knowledge – especially about competitors, customers, the marketplace and technology – and organizational processes that act as strategic resources (Teece et al. 1997). Organizational capabilities then result from knowledge integration and application (Grant 1996). According to this view, firms' advantage over markets, as a governance structure, arises from their superior ability to create, transfer and integrate knowledge possessed by individuals and organizational units.

Knowledge resources that contribute to competitive advantage can exist beyond the boundaries of a firm and reside in the firm's network of relationships (Lavie 2006; Uzzi 1997). Firm growth then depends on their ability to access new knowledge from external sources and recombine it with the existing knowledge (Kogut and Zander 1992). A 'relational view' of firms emphasizes that close inter-firm relationships are characterized by specific human assets and knowledge-sharing routines, leading to the strategic importance of generating and acquiring knowledge in inter-firm collaborations (Dyer and Singh 1998). Through human co-specialization, strategic partners 'develop experience working together and accumulate specialized information, language, and know-how' (Dyer and Singh 1998, p. 665). In addition, knowledge-sharing routines enable specialized knowledge to be transferred, recombined and created through direct, intense, frequent face-to-face interactions among employees of the strategic partners.

Case studies demonstrate that firms' knowledge management can extend beyond firm boundaries. Toyota's closely connected supplier network uses routines that facilitate multidirectional knowledge flows among suppliers, motivating them to participate in knowledge creation and to share valuable knowledge openly (Dyer and Nobeoka 2000). In the same vein suppliers producing for both Toyota and the 'Big Three' US auto manufacturers (GM, Ford and Chrysler) find that greater knowledge sharing by Toyota results in more effective learning within their production facilities, specialized for Toyota (Dyer and Hatch 2007). Network resources appear to be relationship-specific and not readily transferable, resulting in significant increases in both supplier and buyer performance.

LEARNING IN COOPETITION

The knowledge-based view and the associated learning perspective suggest that the formation of collaborative relationships or learning alliances is driven by firms' lack of valuable skills and know-how, which their counterparts possess. Thus firms participating in coopetition aim to access, absorb and internalize their partner's knowledge and skills. Researchers have paid increasing attention to collaborative ventures that offer partnering firms opportunities for learning and acquiring partners' knowledge and skills. These collaborative ventures or learning alliances are often formed by rivals that possess complementary capabilities (Rindfleisch and Moorman 2001). We suggest that participating in coopetition offers partners three types of learning opportunities: learning from the collaborative experience, learning from the collaborative partner and learning *with* the collaborative partner.

Learning From the Collaborative Experience

Firms that participate in collaborative ventures such as alliances gain knowledge that can be useful in designing and managing subsequent alliances (Barkema et al. 1997; Gulati 1999). The management of future alliances includes issues such as partner selection, monitoring and control, as well as approaches to extract greater value from the alliance. In addition, prior experience helps firms set realistic expectations, avoid mistakes and respond to new contingencies when establishing and managing future alliances. The notion that learning occurs through collaboration comes from organizational learning theory, which maintains that organizational learning is path dependent and thus that prior learning facilitates the awareness, evaluation and use of new, related knowledge (Cohen and Levinthal 1990). In addition previous experience enables firms to learn about various issues related to the management of alliances, such as assigning dedicated organizational units and employees to oversee daily operations, which allows the firm to capture knowledge about alliance management systematically. Collaborative know-how can mitigate the ambiguousness of knowledge during the partners' knowledge acquisition, because 'collaborative know-how affects the ability of firms to understand and adopt proper procedures for information gathering, interpretation, and diffusion' (Simonin 1999, p. 603).

In general, this type of learning also includes learning about the motives, capabilities, trustworthiness and culture of a specific partner through the collaborative experience, which increases the probability of alliance success, a particularly important factor in collaboration between rivals. Working with an alliance partner can give the firm a better understanding of the overall capability of the partner – information that then is valuable in deciding whether to continue an alliance with the same partner. In addition, accumulated experience with the same partner can have a positive impact on firm performance (Wuyts et al. 2004), because collaborating with repeated partners enhances the transfer of complex, tacit knowledge (Hansen 1999) and generates a deeper understanding of new technologies and innovations. Repeated interactions also allow shared mental models and relationship-specific decision-making heuristics to emerge (Madhavan and Grover 1998; Uzzi 1997).

Learning From the Collaborating Partner

The second kind of learning is that obtained from the collaborating partner. As discussed previously, inter-firm collaborations provide firms with access to their partner's knowledge assets and expertise, such as product and process technology, organizational skills, management practices and customer management skills. Obviously collaboration also opens opportunities for the partnering firms to transfer what they have learned from their counterpart to operations not related to their alliance activities (Khanna et al. 1998) or to develop new competencies by combining the new knowledge with existing knowledge.

Three broad factors determine learning from alliance partners (Hamel 1991): (1) learning intent, or a firm's propensity to view collaboration as an opportunity to learn; (2) transparency or openness of each alliance partner; and (3) receptivity to learning new things, or the partner's capacity to transfer valuable knowledge (Inkpen 2000). These three drivers of learning in turn depend on a broad spectrum of organizational, social and market factors.

Learning intent is 'the self-determination, desire and will of an organization to learn from its partner or collaborative environment' (Simonin 2004, p. 409). Although learning intent is crucial to acquiring knowledge from alliance partners, asymmetrical learning intent may lead to an unstable alliance (Das and Teng 2000). If one firm intends to internalize its partner's knowledge and skills while the partner has no such intentions, the alliance's chances of success are questionable. Once the firm with a strong learning intent internalizes its partner's knowledge and builds competencies comparable to those of its partner, the alliance should tend to dissolve, because the stability of the alliance depends on the relative contributions made by each partner in terms of revealing critical knowledge and skills (Inkpen and Beamish 1997).

Transparency in a learning alliance refers to the accessibility of the partner's knowledge and skills through the interaction between alliance partners. The primary obstacle to openness between partners is fear of unintended, unanticipated knowledge transfer, so that the partner's learning goes beyond what is necessary for the successful execution of joint tasks. This 'knowledge spillover' usually happens at the operational level through interactions between personnel of the alliance partners. To prevent unintended spillover, alliance partners may establish protective systems to control the flow of information and knowledge from one partner to the other (Hamel et al. 1989; Simonin 1999, 2004). However, if both alliance partners protect their critical knowledge and skills by setting up tightly controlled monitoring systems, little collective learning can occur, and the performance of the alliance itself may suffer.

Alliance partners' receptivity to learning new things obviously depends on their capacity to learn, or their 'absorptive capacity'. Absorptive capacity is each firm's ability to value, acquire, assimilate and use external knowledge (Cohen and Levinthal 1990), and it can be crucial to the creation of collaborative value (Dyer and Singh 1998). A firm's capacity to learn reduces the impact of various obstacles that inhibit knowledge acquisition from its alliance partner (Simonin 2004). Yet receptivity also depends on whether the firm believes it can gain relevant and valuable knowledge from its partner (Inkpen 2000, 2005).

Learning With the Collaborating Partner

The last form of learning is learning with an alliance partner to co-create new knowledge to achieve strategic goals of the venture. This co-creation process implies that collective learning occurs through the integration of the partners' different skill sets to create joint learning benefits. Collective learning requires the alliance partners to be highly receptive and transparent and to balance their common and private interests (Larsson et al. 1998). Unfortunately empirical studies examining issues pertinent to collective learning are scarce.

Why is it difficult to create joint value through collective learning? First, alliance partners have appropriation concerns regarding their ability to capture a fair share of the returns from the alliance (Madhok and Tallman 1998). When an alliance involves technology exchange and the limits of the technology are difficult to specify, appropriation concerns increase (Gulati and Singh 1998). The technology or tacit component of the knowledge to be transferred creates the problem of monitoring and the possibility of unobserved violations of contracts. Monitoring problems develop because it is difficult to delimit the precise scope of the technology being transferred and prevent subsequent applications of such technology beyond the confines of the alliance, leading to potential risks of free-riding and misappropriation by the alliance partner. Also the character of knowledge 'makes it difficult for parties to assess accurately the value of the knowledge being exchanged without complete information from the partner, who may not want to reveal such information because it may be proprietary' (Gulati and Singh 1998, p. 788). Thus tacit resources result in a high potential for opportunism when information asymmetry between partners intensifies and the specification and measurement of input, output or contributions are ambiguous. In addition, 'tacitness itself increases the complexity of combining the respective resources of the partners and correspondingly, the relationship-specific expenditures associated with earning those rents' (Madhok and Tallman 1998, p. 332). Because earning quasi-rents by combining tacit resources depends on intensive and ongoing interaction, alliance partners must build compatibility and a strong connection to realize the true value from alliance relationships.

In summary, participation in coopetition affords the partnering firms different types of learning experiences, including learning from the collaborative experience, learning from the partner and learning with the partner. These learning opportunities allow the partnering firms to make their competencies stronger by using the new knowledge to improve current operational processes or to develop new competencies by deploying the new knowledge in untapped business activities. However, significant risks also occur in the inter-firm learning environment, such as unintended knowledge leakage through the interactions of personnel between the partnering firms. We discuss this risk in the next section.

PITFALLS AND CHALLENGES IN COOPETITION

We thus far have discussed the advantages of collaboration with rivals, with an emphasis on learning and knowledge transfer. However, in collaborating with channel members (upstream or downstream) or partners who have little overlap in the markets to be served, firms participating in coopetition face severe challenges. These challenges can come from the external environment, the operation of the collaborative venture or the partnering firms themselves. Although challenges can occur in multiple areas and at different stages of the coopetition, such as when selecting partners, establishing control mechanisms, defining the scope of activities, assigning obligations and responsibilities or dividing returns, our discussion focuses on three important intertwined issues: (1) assessment of venture performance; (2) evaluation of partner contributions and the subsequent distribution of returns; and (3) unintended leakage of knowledge and skills.

Coopetition makes assessing the performance of the venture and individual partners difficult. Because collaborative ventures such as alliances are tools for firms to achieve their strategic goals, the short-term financial gains of the venture may not be the best indicators of performance. What matters most may not be the balance of inputs and outputs but the impact of the venture on the competitive standing of each partner and the strategic options available or foreclosed through the venture. Thus a critically important step is to evaluate the venture's contribution to the strategic goals and standing of individual partners. Unfortunately it is not easy to quantify the extent to which the strategic purposes of collaborative ventures have been achieved. For example, the outcomes of alliances that attempt to gain access to partners' knowledge and skills, to leverage partners' reputation in a product market or geographic area or to gain legitimacy and credibility in foreign markets are not easily measurable. In addition, the performance of certain activities such as R&D cannot be assessed within a short time frame. Even when the performance of these activities can be evaluated, the firm itself may lack a benchmark for comparison. Alliance activities involve external parties' human resources and their contributions, and therefore, the benchmark cannot be the same as the one used to assess each partner's internal activities. Finally, if the interests of individual partners do not align with the goals of the collaborative venture, the firm may attempt to gain unilaterally at the expense of its counterpart by withholding critical resources and valuable information and knowledge. Thus even if such acts compromise the success of the collaborative venture, the opportunistic partner may achieve better performance in the short term.

Coopetition also raises the problem of judging individual partners' contributions accurately and allocating the returns according to their contributions (i.e. value appropriation). Although measuring the contributions of the individual partners in the collaborative venture sounds straightforward, in practice it is quite difficult. In the case of joint ventures the distribution of returns is relatively easy; it can be based on the proportion of equity ownerships belonging to each partner. But collaborative ventures such as alliances might have a different strategic purpose, such as coalition, co-specialization and learning (Child et al. 2005). Each purpose entails a different value creation logic, and thus different metrics should be used to evaluate partner contribution. In coalitions the partners aim to build a network with a critical mass of participants to achieve economies of scale in various strategic activities, such as setting a technical standard. Therefore the main contribution to measure is the partners' ability to strengthen the competitive standing of the coalition as a whole by soliciting new coalition members and creating synergy among them. For co-specialization the partners aim to pool their complementary resources and competencies to perform joint activities.

The measure of a partner's contribution depends on the value of the unique, non-substitutable, hard-to-imitate resources or competencies owned by the partners. Some resources are intangible, such as brand name, company reputation and relationships with enterprises and government in foreign countries; therefore, weighing the value of these assets is extremely difficult. For learning the partners aim to access and acquire knowledge and skills from each other. Thus the expertise and know-how possessed by the partners, as well as the learning opportunities made available to the other, constitute partner contributions. Unless the contributions made by each partner can be estimated and quantified, allocating the returns obtained from the venture to individual partners is quite difficult. Finally the problem of allocating returns becomes even more acute when the partners' competencies complement each other. When partner contributions are highly interdependent, the importance of partner contributions shifts over time, owing to changing environmental factors. The result is an unequal transfer of the benefits to each partner's own business activities, and the allocation of rewards becomes tricky.

Another major challenge in coopetition is the risk of an unintended leakage of knowledge. When firms participate in a collaborative venture, their employees interact frequently across various levels, making the partners' organizational boundaries permeable. To achieve the collective goals of the venture, partners often work together, so shared valuable information and tacit know-how becomes inevitable. Thus the collaborative venture permits the partners to access, acquire, or even internalize their counterpart's knowledge and skills. Much of the knowledge and skill transfer between firms is not specified in the formal terms and conditions of the collaborative ventures. What actually gets traded between the partners is largely determined by the formal and informal interactions of employees, such as engineers and scientists who work in the interface between the partners.

The hazard in alliances is the potential for a learning race, in which partnering firms attempt to 'out-compete' each other in absorbing and internalizing the other's skills and capabilities (Hamel 1991). The party that 'out-learns' its partner can gain greater bargaining power and extract more benefits from the alliance. More important, the firm can use the acquired knowledge for its own private benefits. That is, it gains unilateral benefits by applying the knowledge and skills acquired from its partner to operations unrelated to the collaboration. Therefore and as noted previously firms participating in collaborative partnerships face the risk that their partner opportunistically 'steals' their knowledge for private gains. Although firms can establish control systems to monitor the flow of critical information and knowledge, tightly controlled systems would result in little collective learning and thus compromise the performance of the partnership.

The challenge in coopetition is to share adequate know-how and skills to create competitive advantage for the venture relative to other ventures in the industry while preventing the loss of core competencies to the partner. Firms must monitor the skills and technologies transferred at the interface of the collaborative venture. Although safeguards should be established to prevent the unintended, informal transfer of proprietary information and knowledge, those safeguards cannot signal a lack of trust and commitment (Makhija and Ganesh 1997).

Unfortunately the nature of the knowledge that a firm contributes to the venture largely determines how easily its partner can acquire that knowledge and skills, intentionally or unintentionally. The potential for leakage is greatest when a partner's knowledge contribution is 'explicit', that is, when it can be easily transported (e.g. in engineering drawings, computer storage devices, the heads of a few experts), easily interpreted (documented explicitly or written in a commonly understood language) and easily absorbed (independent of any specific organizational context and history). In joint ventures between US and Japanese firms, American partners often face disadvantages because their knowledge and skills usually entail technological expertise that is generally transparent and susceptible to leakage (Inkpen 2005). In contrast the skills of Japanese partners that are valued by the US partners usually relate to tacit know-how embedded in manufacturing and operational processes. These competencies are highly context specific and deeply embedded in organizational processes and culture, rendering them difficult to transfer.

CONCLUSION

Considering the thorny challenges posed by the global competitive environment, firms face increasing difficulty in maintaining their competitive advantage over time. Rapid changes in market trends and technological advancements accelerate the obsolescence of firms' competencies. In addition, because of time and resource constraints, as well as the significant risks involved in developing new products and entering the global market, firms are compelled to work with strategic partners that possess valuable and inimitable resources. Because resources and skills that give rise to sustainable competitive advantage are path dependent and hard to develop internally, successful firms often hold on to their few core competencies and simultaneously leverage their partners' unique resources and capabilities. Therefore instead of developing competencies across multiple value-chain functions, firms engaged in coopetition join together as dyadic units to use partners' competencies and achieve strategic goals of mutual interest. Because competent partners with a compatible strategic orientation are often competitors, coopetition has become a viable strategic option for firms to compete and sustain their position in the marketplace. However, as this chapter reveals, coopetition entails both advantages and disadvantages. On the one hand, it offers benefits such as accessing and leveraging partner resources and skills, as well as opportunities for bilateral and unilateral learning. On the other hand, the disadvantages include inherent conflicts and challenges such as knowledge leakage, performance assessment and reward sharing.

Research Implications

Although coopetition has significant strategic implications for firms that consider using partnerships or alliances to gain competitiveness in the marketplace, systematic research on different facets of this phenomenon is scarce. It is still unclear what specific circumstances will lead to the formation of coopetition in an industry, the processes by which coopetition creates mutual value and customer value, and whether and how coopetition results in greater profitability and market effectiveness. Research on strategic alliances provides some insights into these issues, but few previous studies have investigated vertical and horizontal alliances separately. Thus understanding of the idiosyncrasies of coopetition remains incomplete. To increase the awareness of both managers and academics regarding the importance of coopetition as a strategic option, this chapter has drawn on different streams of literature to explicate the major facets of coopetition. The issues discussed include the distinctive characteristics of coopetition, environmental and organizational drivers of coopetition, relevant theoretical perspectives, learning in coopetition and challenges faced by firms that consider participating in this type of collaborative venture.

This chapter represents an initial step toward providing a broad overview of coopetition, but some major issues remain underexplored and deserve attention from marketing scholars and managers. Further research should focus on the following noteworthy areas:

- How can partners deal with the inherent conflicts of coopetition and balance its cooperative and competitive sides?
- How should partners tackle various challenges in coopetition, such as assessing performance and sharing rewards equitably among the partners?
- What kind of governance and control mechanisms should be used to structure coopetition to enhance trust and prevent opportunism?
- How do firms evaluate the costs and benefits of collaborating with competitors versus non-competitors?
- Which competitive environments and circumstances motivate firms to consider the strategic option of coopetition?

- What are the managerial implications of simultaneously learning and protecting intellectual assets from misappropriation for firms participating in coopetition?
- Which theoretical perspectives have the most power to explain and predict the development, maintenance and dissolution of coopetition?

Takeaways for Managers

This chapter offers several key insights for managers who are considering coopetition as a strategic alternative. The following list highlights a few important issues that managers should consider:

1. Coopetition is not suitable for every firm. Firms must assess its suitability by considering the economic and technological environments in which they compete. In addition, firms should judge whether they possess the necessary skills, organization structure and organizational culture to support collaborations with their competitors. Firms should evaluate their own absorptive capacity, as well as the intention and transparency of their partners, before pursuing coopetition as a strategic option.
2. Coopetition entails both significant benefits and thorny challenges. Firms must evaluate the pros and cons of coopetition systematically before embarking on this strategic move. Because coopetition can lead to disastrous consequences (e.g. leaking proprietary knowledge assets), firms should not adopt this practice blindly.
3. Prior to the formation of formal coopetitive alliances, firms should examine the purpose of the alliance and the intentions and capabilities of their partners. Understanding these factors will allow firms to deploy the most effective governance and control mechanisms to prevent partner opportunism and avoid conflicts regarding the assessments of individual contributions and shared profits.
4. Coopetition is a collaborative endeavor between firms that happen to be rivals. The collaborating firms should understand the benefits that their partner will accrue and determine mutually agreed, collective goals. Coopetition will not be sustainable if a firm acts opportunistically to obtain unilateral gain at the expense of its partner.
5. Although knowledge-sharing and learning are key outcomes and benefits of coopetition, these results will not happen automatically. Collaborating firms should set up common learning goals and engender learning opportunities for each other. Both firms should have open discussions regarding the specifics of the knowledge to be shared to avoid learning races and misappropriation of partners' knowledge assets.

REFERENCES

Barkema, Harry G., Oden Shenkar, Freek Vermeulen and John H.J. Bell (1997), 'Working abroad, working with others: how firms learn to operate international joint ventures', *Academy of Management Journal*, **40** (2), 426–42.
Barney, Jay B. (1991), 'Firm resources and sustained competitive advantage', *Journal of Management*, **17**, 99–120.
Brandenburger, Adam M. and Barry J. Nalebuff (1998), *Coopetition: A Revolution Mindset that Combines Competition and Cooperation: The Game Theory Strategy That's Changing the Game of Business*, New York: First Currency.
Child, John, David Faulkner and Stephen B. Tallman (2005), *Cooperative Strategy*, New York: Oxford University Press.

Cohen, Wesley M. and Daniel A. Levinthal (1990), 'Absorptive capacity: a new perspective on learning and innovation', *Administrative Science Quarterly*, **35** (March), 128–52.

Das, T.K. and Bing-Sheng Teng (2000), 'Instabilities of strategic alliances: an internal tensions perspective', *Organization Science*, **11** (1), 77–101.

Dhanaraj, Charles and Arvind Parkhe (2006), 'Orchestrating innovation networks', *Academy of Management Review*, **31** (3), 659–69.

Dyer, Jeffrey H. (2000), *Collaborative Advantage – Winning Through Extended Enterprise Supplier Networks*, New York: Oxford University Press.

Dyer, Jeffrey H. and Nile W. Hatch (2007), 'Relation-specific capabilities and barriers to knowledge transfers: creating advantage through network relationships', *Strategic Management Journal*, **27**, 701–19.

Dyer, Jeffrey H. and Kentaro Nobeoka (2000), 'Creating and managing a high-performance knowledge-sharing network: the Toyota case', *Strategic Management Journal*, **21**, 345–67.

Dyer, Jeffrey H. and Harbir Singh (1998), 'The relational view: cooperative strategy and sources of interorganizational competitive advantage', *Academy of Management Review*, **23** (4), 660–79.

Ganesan, Shankar (1994), 'Determinants of long-term orientation in buyer–seller relationships', *Journal of Marketing*, **58** (April), 1–19.

Gomes-Casseres, Benjamin (1994), 'Group versus group: how alliance networks compete', *Harvard Business Review*, **72** (July/August), 62–74.

Grant, Robert M. (1996), 'Toward a knowledge-based theory of the firm', *Strategic Management Journal*, **17** (Winter Special Issue), 109–12.

Gulati, Ranjay (1999), 'Network location and learning: the influence of network resources and firm capabilities on alliance formation', *Strategic Management Journal*, **20**, 397–420.

Gulati, Ranjay and David Kletter (2005), 'Shrinking core, expanding periphery: the relational architecture of high-performing organizations', *California Management Review*, **47** (3), 77–104.

Gulati, Ranjay and Harbir Singh (1998), 'The architecture of cooperation: managing coordination costs and appropriation concerns in strategic alliances', *Administrative Science Quarterly*, **43** (December) 781–834.

Hamel, Gary (1991), 'Competition for competence and inter-partner learning within international strategic alliances', *Strategic Management Journal*, **12**, 83–103.

Hamel, Gary, Yves L. Doz and C.K. Prahalad (1989), 'Collaborating with your competitors and win', *Harvard Business Review*, **66** (January/February), 133–9.

Hansen, Morten T. (1999), 'The search-transfer problem: the role of weak ties in sharing knowledge across organization subunits', *Administrative Science Quarterly*, **44** (March), 82–111.

Inkpen, Andrew C. (2000), 'Learning through joint ventures: a framework of knowledge acquisition', *Journal of Management Studies*, **37** (7), 1019–43.

Inkpen, Andrew C. (2005), 'Learning through alliances: general motors and NUMMI', *California Management Review*, **47** (4), 114–36.

Inkpen, Andrew C. and Paul W. Beamish (1997), 'Knowledge, bargaining power, and the instability of international joint ventures', *Academy of Management Journal*, **22** (1), 177–202.

Kalaignanam, Kartik, Venkatesh Shankar and Rajan Varadarajan (2007), 'Asymmetric new product development alliances: win–win or win–lose partnerships?', *Management Science*, **53** (March), 357–74.

Khanna, Tarun, Ranjay Gulati and Nitin Nohria (1998), 'The dynamics of learning alliances: competition, cooperation, and relative scope', *Strategic Management Journal*, **19**, 193–210.

Kogut, Bruce and Udo Zander (1992), 'Knowledge of the firm, combinative capabilities, and the replication of technology', *Organization Science*, **3** (August), 383–97.

Kumar, Nirmalya, Lisa K. Scheer and Jan-Benedict E.M. Steenkamp (1995), 'The effects of supplier fairness on vulnerable resellers', *Journal of Marketing Research*, **32** (February), 54–65.

Lado, Augustine A., Nancy G. Boyd and Susan C. Hanlon (1997), 'Competition, cooperation, and the search for economic rents: a syncretic model', *Academy of Management Review*, **22** (1), 110–41.

Lane, Peter J., Jane E. Salk and Marjorie A. Lyles (2001), 'Absorptive capacity, learning, and performance in international joint ventures', *Strategic Management Journal*, **22**, 1139–61.

Larsson, Rikard, Lars Bengtsson, Kristina Henriksson and Judith Sparks (1998), 'The interorganizational learning dilemma: collective knowledge development in strategic alliances', *Organization Science*, **9** (3), 285–305.

Lavie, Dovev (2006), 'The competitive advantage of interconnected firms: an extension of the resource-based view', *Academy of Management Review*, **31** (3), 638–58.

Luo, Yadong (2004), *Coopetition in International Business*, Herndon, VA: Copenhagen Business School Press.

Madhavan, Ravindranath and Rajiv Grover (1998), 'From embedded knowledge to embodied knowledge: new product development as knowledge management', *Journal of Marketing*, **62** (October), 1–12.

Madhok, Anoop and Stephen B. Tallman (1998), 'Resources, transactions and rents: managing value through interfirm collaborative relationships', *Organization Science*, **9** (3), 326–39.

Makhija, Mona V. and Usha Ganesh (1997), 'The relationship between control and partner learning in learning-related joint ventures', *Organization Science*, **8** (5), 508–27.

Morgan, Robert M. and Shelby Hunt (1994), 'The commitment–trust theory of relationship marketing', *Journal of Marketing*, **58** (July), 20–38.

Oxley, Joanne E. and Rachelle C. Sampson (2004), 'The scope and governance of international R&D alliances', *Strategic Management Journal*, **25**, 723–49.

Pfeffer, Jeffrey and Gerald R. Salancik (1978), *The External Control of Organizations: A Resource Dependence Perspective*, New York: Harper & Row.

Powell, Walter W., Kenneth W. Koput and Laurel Smith-Doerr (1996), 'Interorganizational collaboration and the locus of innovation: networks of learning in biotechnology', *Administrative Science Quarterly*, **41** (March), 116–45.

Rindfleisch, Aric and Christine Moorman (2001), 'The acquisition and utilization of information in new product alliances: a strength-of-ties perspective', *Journal of Marketing*, **65** (April), 1–18.

Ross, William T. and Diana C. Robertson (2007), 'Compound relationships between firms', *Journal of Marketing*, **71** (July), 108–23.

Simonin, Bernard (1999), 'Ambiguity and the process of knowledge transfer in strategic alliances', *Strategic Management Journal*, **20**, 595–623.

Simonin, Bernard (2004), 'An empirical investigation of the process of knowledge transfer in international strategic alliances', *Journal of International Business Studies*, **35**, 407–27.

Sivadas, Eugene and F. Robert Dwyer (2000), 'An examination of organizational factors influencing new product success in internal and alliance-based processes', *Journal of Marketing*, **64** (January), 31–49.

Teece, David J., Gary Pisano and Amy Shuen (1997), 'Dynamic capabilities and strategic management', *Strategic Management Journal*, **18** (7), 509–33.

Uzzi, Brian (1997), 'Social structure and competition in interfirm networks: the paradox of embeddedness', *Administrative Science Quarterly*, **42**, 35–67.

Wu, Zhaohui and Thomas Y. Choi (2005), 'Supplier–supplier relationships in the buyer–supplier triad: building theories from eight case studies', *Journal of Operations Management*, **24**, 27–52.

Wuyts, Stefan, Stefan Stremersch, Christophe Van Den Bulte and Philip Hans Franses (2004), 'Vertical marketing systems for complex products: a triadic perspective', *Journal of Marketing Research*, **41** (November), 479–87.

21 The organizational buying center: innovation, knowledge management and brand
Wesley J. Johnston and Jennifer D. Chandler

Management of the organizational buying center (OBC) is among the fastest-changing aspects of contemporary business and marketing. Driven largely by rapid technological innovation and the dispersion of global management teams, OBC management has evolved in many ways since its inception more than 40 years ago in the marketing literature. The purpose of this chapter is to review existing OBC knowledge and to identify the most critical practice and research issues facing OBC managers and theorists alike.

According to the Institute for the Study of Business Markets (2010) research priorities, the most pressing OBC management issues include (but are not limited to) the formation of the OBC, prediction of OBC preferences and decision-making criteria and the role of brand and electronic media in OBC processes. These are closely related to the 2010–2012 Marketing Science Institute (2010, p. 5) research priorities that articulate the importance of customer-focused organizations developed 'through the motivation, engagement, management, and appraisal of teams of employees working in collaborative environments'. This includes examining how employees and teams catalyze complex solutions that effectively innovate across product platforms, business models and marketing processes. This chapter sheds some light on these issues.

We begin by reviewing existing OBC knowledge. Then, we identify current B2B marketing trends that relate specifically to OBC management. Finally, we outline future areas of research and practice that might be improved with closer scrutiny of contemporary OBC issues.

EXISTING OBC KNOWLEDGE

What Do We Already Know about the OBC?

The OBC was introduced in marketing more than 40 years ago and refers to the members of an organization who become involved in the buying process for a particular product or service (Johnston and Bonoma 1981; Robinson et al. 1967). Updated in 1996, Johnston and Lewin (1996) advanced the integrated framework for buying center analysis by combining seminal OBC literature from industrial buying behavior and organizational analysis (Robinson et al. 1967; Sheth 1973; Webster and Wind 1972). As we elaborate subsequently, their model includes 11 fundamental constructs that provide a foundation for the further study of the OBC (Chandler and Johnston 2011).

As Figure 21.1 shows, the first and central construct, 'organizational buying process or stages', refers to the tasks of organizational buying, including (1) recognition of need and a general solution, (2) determination of characteristics and quantity, (3) description

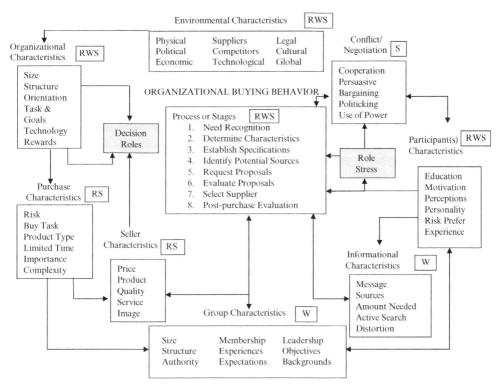

Environmental Characteristics [RWS]

Physical	Suppliers	Legal
Political	Competitors	Cultural
Economic	Technological	Global

Organizational Characteristics [RWS]

Size
Structure
Orientation
Task &
Goals
Technology
Rewards

Decision Roles

ORGANIZATIONAL BUYING BEHAVIOR

Process or Stages [RWS]
1. Need Recognition
2. Determine Characteristics
3. Establish Specifications
4. Identify Potential Sources
5. Request Proposals
6. Evaluate Proposals
7. Select Supplier
8. Post-purchase Evaluation

Conflict/Negotiation [S]

Cooperation
Persuasive
Bargaining
Politicking
Use of Power

Role Stress

Participant(s) Characteristics [RWS]

Education
Motivation
Perceptions
Personality
Risk Prefer
Experience

Purchase Characteristics [RS]

Risk
Buy Task
Product Type
Limited Time
Importance
Complexity

Seller Characteristics [RS]

Price
Product
Quality
Service
Image

Informational Characteristics [W]

Message
Sources
Amount Needed
Active Search
Distortion

Group Characteristics [W]

Size	Membership	Leadership
Structure	Experiences	Objectives
Authority	Expectations	Backgrounds

Notes:
R Indicates constructs contained in the Robinson et al. (1967) model.
W Indicates constructs contained in the Webster and Wind (1972) model.
S Indicates constructs contained in the Sheth (1973) model.
New constructs not contained in any of the original three models.

Source: Johnston and Lewin (1996).

Figure 21.1   An integrated model of organizational buying behavior

of characteristics and quantity, (4) search for potential sources, (5) acquiring and analysis of proposals, (6) proposal evaluation and supplier selection, (7) selection of an order routine and (8) performance feedback and evaluation. The model then outlines different factors that influence OBC processes. The first of these refers to the influence of larger macro-level market forces on the OBC. One such factor includes *environmental* influences, such as political climate, economic pressure, market concentration and cultural environment. Another factor is the *organization* within which the OBC is based, which includes aspects such as organizational size, structure, market orientation, reward programs and goals. There is also the influence of buying *group* or OBC characteristics, such as group size or structure, power, social capital and expectations.

With regard to influences on micro-level OBC processes, the integrated framework also incorporates individual *participants'* (buyers') characteristics, such as education, motivation, perceptions, personality, risk reduction and experience. From the other side of the buying process, the model also recognizes the influence of *seller* characteristics, or the criteria by which potential vendors are evaluated, including price, the ability to meet specifications, product quality, delivery time and after-sales service. It is important to note that this model accounts for some product characteristics as seller characteristics.

With regard to the final purchase decision made by the OBC, the model accounts for *purchase* characteristics, such as product type, perceived risk of the purchase, product complexity and urgency (time pressure) to make a decision. It also accounts for *informational* characteristics, or the source and type of information, such as information garnered from salespeople, trade shows, word of mouth, direct mail and advertising.

Within the OBC, the model describes small group processes as well. For example, the model includes *conflict negotiation* techniques, such as problem-solving or persuasion, and non-rational or inefficient techniques, such as bargaining and politicking. These small group processes in the OBC may also be influenced by organizational-level *decision rules*. These rules can lead to role *stress* (role conflict and ambiguity), role *conflict* (degree of incongruity or incompatibility among purchase expectations), or role *ambiguity* (degree to which clear information is lacking for a satisfactory buying process).

Johnston and Lewin (1996) also find inter-firm and intra-firm influences that affect OBC management. They take a dyadic perspective when referring to *buyer–seller relationships* as the simultaneity of buying and selling activities across firm boundaries; these often focus on, for example, power/dependence between firms, inter-firm behavior monitoring, cooperation/trust, adaptability and commitment. Johnston and Lewin also examine *communication networks*, including communications with employees of other firms through, for example, trade shows or conferences.

EVOLUTION IN THE OBC: PRACTICE AND THEORY

In this section, we discuss three important shifts in OBC practice and theory drawn from Chandler and Johnston's (2011) literature review. These shifts pertain to: (1) the nature of innovation and solutions; (2) knowledge management and electronic media; and (3) the role of the OBC in brand processes. Each of these is discussed next.

The Nature of Innovation and Solutions

The rapid pace of contemporary innovation has intertwined what has come to be known as the OBC with departments within the host firm and often with organizations external to the host firm. In this way, the OBC has expanded beyond traditional procurement departments to include different organizational roles, tasks and positions. Essentially, the tasks and voices of procurement officers, manufacturers, engineers and programmers have become more intertwined with corporate marketing strategy for the firm to respond more quickly to changing market structures. For both sides of the transaction (i.e. both the selling side and the buying side), this is an important shift in thinking with regard to the OBC.

For example, cellular service provider AT&T formed a bridge between its OBC, customer service departments, technical departments and vendors when it incorporated mobile billing into its customer service efforts (Levy 2010). Its vendors, namely Boku, Zong and BilltoMobile, fundamentally assisted AT&T in providing its customers with

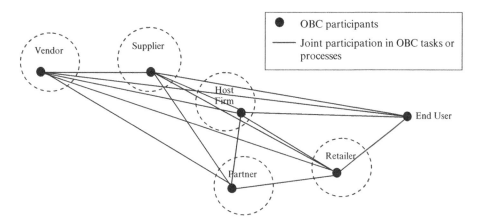

Figure 21.2   The OBC as a bridge and broker across the supply chain

the ability to purchase digital goods through their AT&T mobile phone numbers in lieu of traditional credit cards or PayPal accounts. While highly successful for the smaller vendors, these efforts also pushed AT&T to the forefront of the mobile communications industry. Joint efforts such as these require closer integration among multiple departments and vendors.

Given this, the host firm must often coordinate a holistic cross-channel effort, one that is indiscriminate of traditional firm boundaries. These buying situations are not simple, discrete buy-and-sell transactions, but rather relational exchanges that require ongoing dynamic coordination of varying competences within the firm and also throughout the supply chain. In this scenario, the OBC can be depicted to include OBC participants from various firms in the supply chain (see Figure 21.2). For example, although Boku, Zong and BilltoMobile are AT&T's vendors, they adapted their own corporate strategies to enable mobile billing for AT&T customers. The vendors matched their competences to AT&T's competences, and together, the firms adapted to the buying decision. Needs thus must be continuously evaluated by all the firms involved, a task that is normally ascribed to the OBC with respect to a single firm and a single buying situation. However, these types of buying situations reflect the integration of multiple firms and continuous buying situations. In other words, tasks and processes traditionally associated with a single firm's OBC have been dispersed and layered across departmental and inter-firm boundaries. From either buying or selling firms' perspectives, it has become unclear how these decisions are made. This confusion is further complicated by the simultaneous reciprocal influences that such opportunities exert on multiple firms' competitive strategies.

Successful efforts, such as those of AT&T, do not come easily. Sarin and Mahajan (2001) describe the difficulties associated with managing cross-functional teams charged with the completion of different types of projects. They identify the challenges of harnessing the often-diverse skills, personalities and experiences for productive outcomes, especially given employees trained in highly specialized and technical areas. Figure 21.3 depicts OBC participants within the firm who are assigned to different units or departments. This way of thinking about the people involved in the OBC differs from the

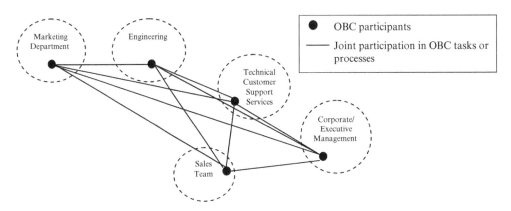

Figure 21.3   The OBC as a bridge and broker inside the firm

traditional OBC conceptualization that focuses on a procurement officer and support staff. Traditionally, OBC processes were largely based on explicit searches for specific goods or services, with the OBC search traditionally 'closing' with the signing of a temporally fixed contract between a seller. Procurement is traditionally considered largely the responsibility of a specific unit of the firm. Given this, the organizational buying process conceptually fitted into stages (as Figure 21.1 outlines) that often proceeded in a linear manner.

However, because contemporary OBC processes have become more intertwined with departments such as product design and engineering and other firms throughout the supply chain, the OBC touches different areas of the firm (see Figure 21.3). As a result, OBC participants are often involved in multiple, ongoing, continuous processes. This has been driven largely by changes in the market, such as, for example, the prominence of reverse marketing. In reverse marketing, the firm receives an order first and then manufactures the product or provides a service plan to fit the order. This differs from traditional marketing in which the first step is to manufacture the product or plan the service, followed by the marketing department performing the traditional tasks of informing, reminding or persuading the customer about finished products or services. In reverse marketing, the marketing department takes on a different role in assisting customers with specifying attributes that create heterogeneity in products or services. Manufacturing is driven more by the ability of customers to make specifications, rather than their ability to buy mass-produced goods or services. In modern OBC management, a key challenge is meeting these specifications in a way that maximizes the success of all those involved throughout the supply chain.

The ability to 'mass-customize' goods and services has prompted the OBC to play an overlooked bridging role between departments and firms. Rather than acting as a supplementary function to the manufacturing process, OBC processes have become more important than ever. OBC processes often involve not only integrating the different functional units within a firm but also integrating the diverse functions sprinkled throughout a supply chain or horizontal partnership network. For example, the manufacturing process, traditionally the strongest driver of corporate strategy, has become one of many functions that are now intertwined with those of the OBC. Rather than existing solely as the 'receiver' of other firms' marketing and sales efforts, the OBC has become fundamental to bridging across departments and organizations to develop customized solutions for the firm's customers. Figures 21.2 and 21.3 show the OBC participants throughout the firm and supply chain.

To begin making sense of the intertwined functions associated with the OBC, we take a process-based view of the firm. A process-based view of the firm regards the tasks and functions of different departments as synchronized elements of an ongoing, dynamic process. Thus the firm is itself an ever-evolving, continuous process that responds to varying market conditions. Dwyer et al. (1987) were among the first to advance the notion of relational exchange by emphasizing the history and future of a relationship between a buyer and a seller. In this way, they followed a single exchange relationship over time and explored how the relationship changed with respect to the buyer and the seller. By doing this, they established relational exchange as a continuous basis through which intertwined processes can evolve across firms. Grönroos (2000) further emphasizes the simultaneity that encompasses all stakeholders within a process, and other researchers (e.g. Morgan and Hunt 1994; Wuyts et al. 2004) underscore the multiplicity inherent in the provision of products and services. Both Prahalad and Ramaswamy (2004) and Vargo and Lusch (2004, 2008) popularized the notion of 'co-creation' in reference to the joint efforts of multiple parties integrated in a single process.

Knowledge Management and Technology in the OBC

Information and knowledge management have also become integral aspects of OBC management (Nonaka 1994). In general, knowledge management refers to the processes of making individual-level knowledge accessible and applicable for firm-level problem-solving. Based in organizational theory, the field of knowledge management has grown rapidly, but little integration of the OBC concept currently exists. The OBC concept is important because it can help explain the diffusion and adoption of knowledge across firm boundaries.

For example, after establishing a clear area of expertise, firms are often unclear which functions they should maintain in-house and which ones they should outsource (Zirpoli and Becker 2010). Zirpoli and Becker (2010) describe an automobile company they call Alpha and its decision to outsource the manufacturing of core functional components in its automobiles. This scenario falls into the traditional realm of OBC management in the B2B marketing literature because there is a specific buying need. Zirpoli and Becker describe how Alpha sent much of its core knowledge-building capacity to vendors by essentially opting to buy functional components rather than manufacturing them in-house. In this case, OBC decision-making had a detrimental effect on knowledge management because outsourcing the core component resulted in knowledge loss that weakened the company's competitive advantage. Zirpoli and Becker further suggest that a more holistic knowledge management approach would have been more beneficial because Alpha would have learned from its suppliers, while buying their parts and components. That is, Alpha could have expanded its own competencies through knowledge gained from suppliers.

However, it is not yet clear how the OBC can serve as a foundation for a comprehensive knowledge management strategy. For example, a unified approach to data collection and management (including data extraction and utilization) would form a strong foundation for a firm-level knowledge management strategy. Buyers and sellers are coming together in non-traditional ways, including distribution channels enabled by, for example, online reverse auctions or mobile devices. Although many firms have access to all kinds of data, they are often unable to use the data because of technological inconsistencies, social policies or norms, corporate rules, or simply inefficient data storage and management issues. Given this, the increasing prevalence of technologically enhanced communication (including the use of wireless devices, email and web-based software) can be foundational for managing knowledge across the firm's functional units, including the OBC. In conjunction with its suppliers, buyers or partner firms, the OBC is often privy to electronic data interchanges and radio frequency identification devices. Such technology can help bridge logistics and inventory discrepancies with the firm's marketing efforts. Customer-generated and end-user-generated content in forums such as Twitter or Facebook, for example, also provide data that can be useful for the management of the OBC.

A way to begin understanding how knowledge and data affect OBC management is to take a resource-based view (RBV) of the firm (Barney 1991, 2001; Penrose 1959; Peteraf 1993). The RBV emphasizes how the firm can draw on resources through its competitive strategy. Traditional RBV emphasizes ownership of resources, but attention is now turning to the management and access of resources that are external to the firm (Srivastava et al. 1998; Wathne and Heide 2004). Along these lines, prior research has shown that shared knowledge among firms can be influenced by how these firms connect with one another (Rindfleisch and Moorman 2001) and build on one another's knowledge (Frazier et al. 2009; Johnson et al. 2004). To this effect, the influence of the marketing department on the activities of the entire firm is well documented (Verhoef and Leeflang 2009).

Role of the OBC in Brand Processes

Relationships with external entities, such as suppliers, vendors, customers and conglomerates, are pivotal for OBC decision-making for many reasons. These processes, or the processes of building and strengthening relationships with other organizations, help manage the risk associated with OBC decision-making. These processes are called 'relational processes' and are important because they help firms mitigate risk by allowing decision-makers to build trust with one another.

One way firms do this is by marking their collaborative relationships as a brand (Keller 1993). A brand refers to 'a name, term, sign, symbol, or design, or combination of them which is intended to identify the goods and services of one seller or group of sellers and to differentiate them from those of competitors' (Kotler 1991, p. 442). Firms typically use brands to differentiate their market offerings from those of other firms. In an OBC context, brands can facilitate faster decision-making and serve as a foundation on which to deepen inter-firm collaborations. For example, consider a manufacturer that supplies a smaller component (e.g. a processing chip) in an end-user device (e.g. a laptop). The smaller component may provide the unique attribute that end users seek, helping solidify how the firm positions the end-user device in the minds of customers. When the smaller component plays the pivotal role of positioning the device in the end-user market, this is called 'ingredient branding' (Kotler and Pfoertsch 2006).

A way to understand how OBC management intersects with brand processes is to take a network perspective of brands. In such cases, the brand is effective because of the work of multiple parties; the brand would not be effective if it were used by one firm on its own. Kotler and Pfoertsch (2006) describe how companies actively create reputations for smaller components hosted in larger devices; one such instance is the popular 'Intel Inside' brand campaign of the early 1990s. Such OBC strategies are based on the ability of smaller procured components to distinguish functional attributes of the host product. Because of this, the relationship between the firms becomes more collaborative and steadfast, which in turn evolves both firms' competitive strategies. Kotler and Pfoertsch acknowledge the complexity inherent in the buying processes of industrial products and underscore the role of a brand in mitigating risk and complexity in these decisions (see also Pfoertsch et al. 2007).

Along the same lines, Ford et al. (2003) elaborate on firms joining together as networks and dynamically affecting one another's strategies in ways other than competition (Achrol and Kotler 1999; Bagozzi 1975). Viewing firms within such networks can help clarify how OBC management and brand processes intersect (Grönroos 2006; Gummesson 2006; Håkansson and Snehota 1995).

ADVANCING THE OBC

Because of changes in the technological, global and economic environments of firms, a framework is needed that links traditional, historical perspectives to the fast-changing contemporary issues outlined previously. Though a seminal and established area of study in the B2B marketing literature, the OBC and its role in emergent topics such as innovation, customized solutions, knowledge management and brand have been largely overlooked. Some OBC aspects are perennial, such as the participation of multiple parties and the dynamic interactions among these parties. However, other aspects have changed, such as the nature of actual participants in the OBC and the intertwining of the OBC process with other processes throughout the firm and supply chain. In addition, firms in today's markets face added pressures of competing across international markets, with fluctuating costs and policies. Thus OBC managers and theorists alike need to develop frameworks that integrate these fundamental changes.

As it was 40 years ago, the fundamental concept of the OBC remains centered on organizational buying decisions. However, these buying decisions have changed dramatically in nature, and as a result, the OBC plays a different role in the firm today. The simplified frameworks originally offered in the marketing literature still apply; however, they must be overlaid onto complex processes. As Figures 21.2 and 21.3 show, the OBC plays a bridging role among departments and firms, often brokering information, resources or knowledge to parties that would otherwise be disconnected without the OBC. Simply put, the OBC itself transcends traditional firm boundaries. To illustrate, the OBC can connect the marketing department with other departments throughout the firm. In this way, the OBC facilitates information and knowledge across traditional firm units. The OBC also connects selling firms with buying firms in ways other than buyer–

seller relationships; many times, the OBC may involve interactions among engineers, developers and programmers from multiple firms who collaborate on product or service specifications. As a fundamental B2B marketing concept, the OBC enables marketing practitioners and theorists to think about the intersections of marketing strategy with these non-marketing units of the firm.

The importance of the OBC is little understood from this perspective. Traditional OBC examinations may focus only on buy–sell scenarios; however, closer examination of buying processes may demonstrate, for example, how buy–sell scenarios are embedded within other important inter-firm processes. Inter-and intra-firm learning, for example, occurs because the OBC facilitates innovation and customized solutions, to name a few. We argue that the seminal OBC framework can provide a formidable foundation in this respect. Two specific notions from the 1996 integrated framework for organizational buying remain especially relevant in today's market environment: (1) the effects of multiple actors' engagement on OBC processes; and (2) identification of the tasks and stages in OBC processes.

Multiple Actor Engagement in the OBC

Traditionally, the practice and theory of OBC management has focused on the purchasing unit of a firm. The multiple parties traditionally involved in the OBC have been limited to this particular unit. As described, however, the OBC has been expanded to include staff and employees across the firm, as well as external organizations such as vendors, suppliers and retailers. Although multiple actors interact dynamically through OBC processes, further research should focus on clarifying who these OBC participants are and how OBC participants interact with one another. As Figure 21.2 shows, the OBC transcends traditional firm boundaries, and OBC participants often interact with others throughout the supply chain. Rather than focusing on dyadic exchange, the focus should be on entire supply chains and how smaller buying processes throughout these supply chains can be more holistically coordinated with the use of technology, particularly electronic data interchanges and radio frequency identification devices. Just-in-time inventory techniques and vendor managed inventory tools are just as important for marketing as they are for operations or logistics management. Because many retailers, for example, now operate in multichannel environments, vendors, suppliers and partners need to understand how to take advantage of web interfaces and inventory management systems. Understanding how these tools can maximize purchase decisions that affect long-term arrangements with vendors, suppliers and customers is an important aspect of OBC management.

To this end, Pankaj Ghemawat (2010) describes in the *Harvard Business Review* how the post-crisis market environment necessitates a stronger management stomach. One of his suggested best practices to combat what he calls 'a new realm of global uncertainty' is to strengthen the fundamental corporate operations inside the firm and begin moving other functions away from the firm's 'home base', all the while maintaining strong coordination of these efforts. Such coordination would imply a proactive technological edge that aids the firm's knowledge management efforts, despite moving certain tasks and functions away from the firm's core. Not only does this require management expertise in facilitating collaboration, but it also requires the ability to identify which tasks, functions and processes should remain within the firm versus those that should be moved outside the firm's home base. This increased dependence on consistent information flows necessitates a stronger understanding of OBC engagement. Implicit within this effort is an exclamation point on the importance of communication tools for OBC participants working across different departments, firms and countries.

Social networks analysis (Wasserman and Faust 1994) is a tool that can offer insight on intra- and inter-firm collaboration across the OBC. For example, Krackhardt and Hanson's (1993) analysis of the 'company behind the chart' reveals how social network analysis clarifies underlying OBC interactions. They identify power and social structures that often affect firm performance. They suggest that most firms have key players who are not in formal positions of power; these key players often interact with individuals from different teams and departments and thereby gain social influence within the firm despite the lack of a corporate title. Given the unprecedented way the OBC has evolved in recent years, such an approach can help pave a smoother road for managers of OBC processes by aiding in the identification of innovative individuals or innovative team structures. With this approach to visualization and the quantification of group processes, it is possible for managers to 'see' how successful multifunctional OBC teams thrive and survive.

Taking this approach further, it is possible to re-examine macro-level environmental characteristics, as Figure 21.1 describes, by focusing instead on the OBC as depicted in Figure 21.2 or Figure 21.3. Figure 21.2 shows that a network approach would involve focusing on the environment of the entire value chain rather than focusing on the political, economic, technological or cultural environment of a single firm. Given this, it is important to quantitatively measure and formalize how the environment of a value chain affects joint efforts among firms. This is possible from a traditional OBC perspective that is expanded to the network/value chain level.

It is important to think holistically about how the buying decision affects processes throughout the firm and the supply chain. Managers and theorists may want to consider the following questions: who is directly affected? Who is indirectly affected? How are the voices of those affected integrated (or not integrated) into the buying decision? Are these voices invited to participate in the buying decision, or are they dissuaded from participation in the buying decision? How does this participation affect the buying decision? Does technological integration assist this buying decision? Why, or why not?

Tasks and Stages in OBC Processes

To examine these questions more closely, we refer back to the traditional tasks of the OBC, as well as the various roles of participants in the OBC. Traditional OBC tasks include the purchase or procurement of a particular product or service, as well as the management of logistics in supply chain deliveries. More specifically, as mentioned previously, the tasks of organizational buying include: (1) recognition of need and a general solution; (2) determination of characteristics and quantity; (3) description of characteristics and quantity; (4) search for potential sources; (5) acquiring and analysis of proposals; (6) proposal evaluation and supplier selection; (7) selection of an order routine; and (8) performance feedback and evaluation (Johnston and Lewin 1996). Typically, these have been studied as stages in a linear process. OBC participants have also been traditionally studied in their completion of these tasks as they enact social roles, such as initiator, user, gatekeeper, influencer, decider and buyer. These OBC roles have typically been studied as responses to the sales efforts of supplier firms.

Although these tasks and stages may remain the same, as we described previously, they also may stretch beyond traditional OBC boundaries. Because these social roles and tasks are now dispersed throughout the firm, they may have moved in responsibility from one person to another or from one unit to another (Akaka and Chandler 2011). In the *Harvard Business Review*, Kanter (2010, p. 42) describes how 'chains of command are being replaced by circles of influence [and how] business fortresses [are being replaced] by collaborative business ecosystems'. It thus is important to identify how teams emerge, collaborate and dissipate, in contrast with previous emphases on the traits and behaviors of powerful stand-alone individuals.

For example, traditional OBC examinations emphasize participant characteristics, such as education, motivation, perceptions and personality. These characteristics are traditionally considered to affect role stress, conflict/negotiation tactics and other small-group processes. However, in contemporary OBC examinations, we call attention to the diversity of participant characteristics and how this diversity can be used as a resource for efficient and effective OBC processes. By following the tasks and stages outlined in foundational OBC research, it is possible to identify where influence and collaboration emerge in the firm and the distribution channel. Rather than focusing solely on buyer response to seller actions, it is possible to examine how OBC participants collaboratively solve problems in the marketplace. Moore (2002) describes the challenges of identifying the true 'owners of the business problem' and indicates how delayering organizations and solutions sales can shed light on the contemporary business models that yield success for multiple firms.

One of the most important directions for OBC research is understanding temporal feedback loops throughout the OBC process, but especially between the final fundamental OBC stage (feedback and evaluation) and the first fundamental OBC stage (need recognition). In traditional OBC research, organizational buying is a discrete process that begins with need recognition and ends with feedback and evaluation. However, it is important to build a stronger mechanism for bridging these stages such that organizational buying can be studied as a real-time, continuous and dynamic process. This is especially important for knowledge management, especially given how firms jointly compete in alliances. Traditionally, the conflict and negotiation processes in OBC management focused on power and consensus building. However, when the traditional tactics of persuasion, bargaining, politicking and use of power are studied from the perspective of knowledge management, it is possible to understand how firms gain access and apply information from OBC processes to their own innovations and solutions.

These feedback loops may also be viewed from different units of analysis. Given the emphasis in this chapter on identifying fundamental OBC decisions and participants, it is important to develop oscillating foci that differentiate among participant-level processes, inter-firm-level processes and supply chain processes (Chandler and Vargo 2011). At the same time, however, these foci must be viewed as different layers of the same OBC system. To study this more deeply, managers and theorists could evaluate how purchase characteristics, such as risk or time constraints, for example, are mitigated at each of these layers and also across each of the layers. Some of the questions that could be asked include the following: when faced with a risky purchase decision, how do OBC participants collaborate? Is collaboration different in risky versus non-risky purchase decisions? Does the OBC behave differently in vertically integrated firms than in alliances? Also, if there is close collaboration among OBC participants across particular firms, how do other firms in the market respond?

CONCLUSION

In examining important B2B marketing topics, managers and theorists alike have relied on supply chain or distribution channel management strategies, which emphasize firm-level management tactics. However, the focus of the OBC provides a different perspective that emphasizes participant-level management; that is, the OBC perspective of B2B marketing examines those who are involved in the buying decision, regardless of department or firm. In response to the fast-changing nature of contemporary management and marketing, this chapter outlines the need to better integrate seminal OBC frameworks: (1) to identify the fundamental buying decision; and (2) to identify the actual OBC participants. Because of the ways that technological innovation and the dispersion of global management teams have changed fundamental business processes, we point practitioners and theorists back to the seminal OBC literature to rethink how innovation, solutions and brand emerge from intra- and inter-firm processes. In short, we argue that it is necessary to look backward in order to move forward. The purpose of this chapter was to review the foundations of OBC knowledge, to identify the most critical OBC practice and research issues and to reintegrate seminal OBC frameworks with contemporary management issues. Given this, the B2B marketing literature provides a strong basis for advancing the practice and theory of the OBC, as well as the practice and theory associated with innovation, solutions, brand and knowledge management.

REFERENCES

Achrol, Ravi S. and Philip Kotler (1999), 'Marketing in the network economy', *Journal of Marketing*, **63** (2), 146–63.
Akaka, Melissa and Jennifer D. Chandler (2011), 'Roles as resources: the dynamic nature of roles in value-creation networks', *Marketing Theory*, forthcoming.
Bagozzi, Richard (1975), 'Marketing as exchange', *Journal of Marketing*, **39** (4), 32–9.
Barney, Jay (1991), 'Firm resources and sustained competitive advantage', *Journal of Management*, **17** (1), 99–120.
Barney, Jay (2001), 'Resource-based theories of competitive advantage: ten-year retrospective on the resource-based view', *Journal of Management*, **27** (6), 643–50.
Chandler, Jennifer and Wesley J. Johnston (2011), 'The organizational buying center as a framework for emergent topics in business-to-business marketing', working paper, University of Hawaii at Manoa.
Chandler, Jennifer and Stephen L. Vargo (2011), 'Contextualization and value-in-context: how context frames exchange', *Marketing Theory*, **11** (1), 35–49.
Dwyer, F. Robert, Paul H. Schurr and Sejo Oh (1987), 'Developing buyer–seller relationships', *Journal of Marketing*, **51** (2), 11–27.
Ford, David, Lars-Erik Gadde, Håkan Håkansson and Ivan Snehota (2003), *Managing Business Relationships*, 2nd edn, Chichester: John Wiley & Sons.
Frazier, Gary, Elliot Maltz, Kersi Antia and Aric Rindfleisch (2009), 'Distributor sharing of strategic information with suppliers', *Journal of Marketing*, **73** (4), 31–43.

Ghemawat, Pankaj (2010), 'Finding your strategy in the new landscape', *Harvard Business Review*, **88** (March), 54–60.

Grönroos, Christian (2000), 'Relationship marketing: the Nordic school perspective', in Jagdish Sheth and Atul Parvatiyar (eds), *Handbook of Relationship Marketing*, Thousand Oaks, CA: Sage Publications, pp. 95–117.

Grönroos, Christian (2006), 'What can service logic offer marketing theory?', in Robert F. Lusch and Stephen L. Vargo (eds), *The Service-Dominant Logic of Marketing: Dialog, Debate, and Directions*, Armonk, NY: M.E. Sharpe, pp. 354–64.

Gummesson, Evert (2006), 'Many-to-many marketing as grand theory: a Nordic school contribution', in Robert F. Lusch and Stephen l. Vargo (eds), *The Service-Dominant Logic of Marketing: Dialog, Debate, and Directions*, Armonk, NY: M.E. Sharpe, pp. 339–53.

Håkansson, Håkan and Ivan Snehota (eds) (1995), *Developing Relationships in Business Networks*, London: Routledge.

Institute for the Study of Business Markets (2010), 'Research priorities', available at http://isbm.smeal.psu.edu/researcher/research-priorities, accessed 12 December 2010.

Johnson, Jean L., Ravipreet S. Sohi and Rajdeep Grewal (2004), 'The role of relational knowledge stores in interfirm partnering', *Journal of Marketing*, **68** (July), 21–36.

Johnston, Wesley J. and Thomas Bonoma (1981), 'The buying center: structure and interaction patterns', *Journal of Marketing*, **45** (3), 143–56.

Johnston, Wesley J. and Jeffrey E. Lewin (1996), 'Organizational buying behavior: toward an integrative framework', *Journal of Business Research*, **35** (1), 1–15.

Kanter, Rosabeth Moss (2010), 'It's time to take full responsibility', *Harvard Business Review*, October, 42–5.

Keller, Kevin (1993), 'Conceptualizing, measuring and managing customer-based brand equity', *Journal of Marketing*, **57** (1), 1–22.

Kotler, Philip (1991), *Marketing Management: Analysis, Planning, Implementation and Control*, Upper Saddle River, NJ: Prentice Hall.

Kotler, Philip and Waldemar Pfoertsch (2006), *B2B Brand Management*, New York: Springer.

Krackhardt, David and Jeffrey Hanson (1993), 'Informal networks: the company behind the chart', *Harvard Business Review*, **71** (4), 104–11.

Levy, Ari (2010), 'AT&T will let customers buy digital music, movies with phones', *BusinessWeek*, 28 October, available at http://www.businessweek.com/technology/content/oct2010/tc20101028_319021.htm.

Marketing Science Institute (2010), *2010–2012 Research Priorities*, Cambridge, MA: Marketing Science Institute.

Moore, Geoffrey (2002), *Crossing the Chasm: Marketing and Selling High-Tech Products to Mainstream Customers*, New York: Harper PaperBacks.

Morgan, Robert M. and Shelby D. Hunt (1994), 'The commitment–trust theory of relationship marketing', *Journal of Marketing*, **58** (3), 20–38.

Nonaka, Ikujiro (1994), 'A dynamic theory of organizational knowledge creation', *Organization Science*, **5** (1), 14–37.

Penrose, Edith (1959), *The Theory of the Growth of the Firm*, New York: John Wiley & Sons.

Peteraf, Margaret A. (1993), 'The cornerstones of competitive advantage: a resource-based view', *Strategic Management Journal*, **14** (3), 179–91.

Pfoertsch, Waldemar, Christian Linder and Jennifer D. Chandler (2007), 'Measuring the value of ingredient brand equity at multiple stages in the supply chain: a component supplier's perspective', in Fredrik Barkovic and Bodo Runzelbacher (eds), *Interdisciplinary Management Research III*, Croatia: Faculty of Economics in Osijek, pp. 571–94.

Prahalad, C.K. and Venkat Ramaswamy (2004), 'Co-creation experiences: the next practice in value creation', *Journal of Interactive Marketing*, **18** (3), 5–14.

Rindfleisch, Aric and Christine Moorman (2001), 'The acquisition and utilization of information in new product alliances: a strength-of-ties perspective', *Journal of Marketing*, **65** (April), 1–18.

Robinson, Patrick J., Charles W. Faris and Yoram Wind (1967), *Industrial Buying and Creative Marketing*, Boston: Allyn & Bacon.

Sarin, Shikhar and Vijay Mahajan (2001), 'The effect of reward structures on the performance of cross-functional product development teams', *Journal of Marketing*, **65** (April), 35–53.

Sheth, Jagdish N. (1973), 'A model of industrial buyer behavior', *Journal of Marketing*, **37** (4), 50–56.

Srivastava, Rajendra K., Tasadduq A. Shervani and Liam Fahey (1998), 'Market-based assets and shareholder value: a framework for analysis', *Journal of Marketing*, **62** (1), 2–18.

Vargo, Stephen L. and Robert F. Lusch (2004), 'Evolving to a new dominant logic for marketing', *Journal of Marketing*, **68** (1), 1–17.

Vargo, Stephen L. and Robert F. Lusch (2008), 'Service-dominant logic: continuing the evolution', *Journal of the Academy of Marketing Science*, **36** (1), 1–10.

Verhoef, Peter and Peter Leeflang (2009), 'Understanding the marketing department's influence within the firm', *Journal of Marketing*, **73** (March), 14–37.

Wasserman, Stanley and Katherine Faust (1994), *Social Network Analysis: Methods and Applications*, Cambridge, UK: Cambridge University Press.

Wathne, Kenneth H. and Jan B. Heide (2004), 'Relationship governance in a supply chain network', *Journal of Marketing*, **68** (1), 73–89.

Webster, Fredrick E., Jr, and Yoram Wind (1972), 'A general model for understanding organizational buying behavior', *Journal of Marketing*, **36** (2), 12–19.

Wuyts, Stefan, Stefan Stremersch, Christophe Van den Bulte and Philip Hans Franses (2004), 'Vertical marketing systems for complex products: a triadic perspective', *Journal of Marketing Research*, **41** (4), 479–87.

Zirpoli, Francesco and Markus Becker (2010), 'What happens when you outsource too much?', *Sloan Management Review*, **52** (2), 59–64.

22 B2B relationship underpinnings of outsourcing[1]
Rajan Varadarajan

- According to news reports, during the latter half of 2009, Delta Air Lines and its alliance partners in the SkyTeam Alliance offered $1 billion in aid to Japan Airlines (JAL) to lure it away from Oneworld Alliance. American Airlines and its alliance partners in the Oneworld Alliance reportedly matched the offer to retain JAL in their alliance network. Despite incurring huge losses in recent years and being saddled with debt, JAL was viewed as an attractive alliance partner by both global airline alliances because of its strong market position in Japan and the rest of Asia and the benefits alliance members envisioned deriving from a code-sharing agreement with JAL (Tabuchi 2009). After weeks of speculation, JAL finally chose to remain in the Oneworld alliance.
- AT&T, a mobile phone service provider, enjoyed an exclusive right to offer Apple smart phones for a limited time. However, during this window, the exclusive agreement was reported to have significantly enhanced AT&T's ability to retain its present customers as well as attract competitors' customers.
- Vizio Inc. is a dominant player in the market for LCD TVs in the United States. By focusing its efforts on design and marketing and contracting production to manufacturers, Vizio has been able to sell its LCD TVs through discount retailers in the United States at substantially lower prices than those of its major competitors, such as Samsung and Sony.

As these examples illustrate, B2B relationships are a critical building block in the *competitive marketing strategies* firms pursue in both B2B and B2C markets. Firms foster B2B relationships with other firms that are *customers, suppliers* and even *competitors,* as well as with firms that fall outside these three groups. For example, firms often enter into strategic alliances (also a B2B relationship) with firms in other industries operating in the same stages of the value chain. These firms, which historically have not been suppliers, customers or competitors of the focal firm, are called 'collaborators'. In accordance with the specific activities or purposes that underpin particular B2B relationships, these relationships have been referred to as: (1) sourcing relationships (between a firm and its suppliers); (2) outsourcing relationships (a firm contracting with another firm to perform an activity that was previously performed in-house); (3) supply chain management relationships (a firm's relationships with its upstream suppliers, downstream channel members, distribution and logistics firms and so on); (4) customer relationship management (CRM) relationships (a firm's relationships with its downstream channel members and other firms to which it outsources specific CRM-related processes and activities); (5) channel management relationships (a firm's relationship with downstream marketing intermediaries); (6) strategic alliance relationships (a firm's relationships with other organizations entailing the pooling of skills and resources to achieve one or more common goals, as well as goals specific to individual alliance partners); and

Table 22.1   An overview of selected B2B relationships

B2B Relationship Type	Relationship with				
	Suppliers	**Customers**	**Competitors**	**Collaborators**	**Others**
Outsourcing[a]					
Production of goods	X		X	X	
Performance of services	X	X	X	X	
Sourcing	X				
Channel		X			
Strategic Alliance					
Marketing alliance		X	X	X	
R&D alliance	X	X	X	X	
Manufacturing alliance			X	X	
...					
Supply Chain					
Management	X	X			
Customer Relationship					
Management	X	X			
Innovation and New					
Product Development	X	X	X	X	

Notes:
a.   Outsourcing refers to a *transitional phase* – a firm transitioning from performing an activity in-house to contracting with an external entity to perform the activity.

The cell entries (X) corresponding to a row (i.e. a particular type of B2B relationship such as outsourcing of performance services) denotes that such B2B relationships can exist between a focal firm and its suppliers, customers, competitors and collaborators. The 'Others' column refers to relationships with entities such as not-for-profit organizations (e.g. cause-related marketing and research partnerships with universities) and non-governmental organizations (NGOs).

(7) co-innovation/collaborative innovation-focused relationships (a firm's relationship with upstream supplier firms, downstream customer firms, competitors and/or strategic alliance partners in the realm of innovation and new product development), to list a few. In addition to these B2B relationships, business relationships that fall under the broader rubric of *inter-organizational* relationships (as opposed to a more narrowly construed domain of B2B relationships) include a firm's relationships with not-for profit institutions (e.g. universities) and not-for-profit organizations (e.g. a firm's relationship in the context of cause-related marketing). Though explored in literature under different labels, some of these relationships overlap with others with regard to their purpose or focal activities. Tables 22.1 and 22.2 provide additional insights into the role of B2B relationships in how firms choose to compete and strive to achieve and maintain competitive positional advantages (i.e. competitive cost advantage and/or differentiation advantage) in the marketplace. Table 22.1 sheds light on the various types of B2B relationships that firms establish with their suppliers, customers, competitors and collaborators. Complementing Table 22.1, Table 22.2 sheds light on the potential strategic role of various types of B2B relationships in reference to competitive strategy at the business-unit level and marketing level. Although both tables are intended to be

Table 22.2   B2B relationship underpinnings of competitive strategy

B2B Relationship Type	Strategic Role of B2B Relationship in Focal Firm					
	Business Strategy		Marketing Strategy			
	Differentiation Advantage[a]	Cost Advantage[a]	Product Strategy[b]	Promotion Strategy[b]	Pricing Strategy[b]	Distribution Strategy[b]
Outsourcing						
Sourcing						
Channel						
Strategic alliance						
Supply chain management						
Customer relationship management						
Innovation and new product development						

Notes:
a.   Individual cells representing relationships in these columns serve to highlight the centrality of B2B relationships to a business's *competitive strategy* (how a business chooses to compete in the marketplace and achieves and sustains a competitive differentiation advantage and/or cost advantage).
b.   Individual cells representing relationships in these columns serve to highlight the centrality of B2B relationships to *marketing strategy* (a business's integrated pattern of decisions that specify its crucial choices regarding marketing behaviors in its interactions with customers to effect specific affective, cognitive and behavioral predispositions in them toward its product in order to facilitate their engaging in revenue-generating transactional and relational exchanges with the organization and thereby enable the organization to achieve specific objectives).

illustrative and representative (e.g. Table 22.2 highlights only certain aspects of business strategy and marketing strategy), they nevertheless highlight the nature and scope of B2B relationships that firms foster with suppliers, customers, competitors and collaborators.

This chapter specifically focuses on B2B relationships in the realm of outsourcing, a long-standing business practice that spans multiple organizational functions, and is organized as follows: First an overview of outsourcing is presented. Second, an overview of selected theoretical perspectives on outsourcing is presented. Third, a conceptual framework delineating outsourcing relationships between a focal firm/ business and its suppliers, customers, competitors and collaborators is presented. Fourth, the role of outsourcing in achieving competitive cost advantage and differentiation advantage (or neutralizing erosion of competitive cost advantage and differentiation advantage) is discussed.[2] The chapter concludes with a brief discussion on related literature streams that address the fundamental issue of a firm's choice between internal organization and market governance from varying orientations. This section also briefly discusses the distinctive aspects of and commonalities between strategic alliances and outsourcing.

OUTSOURCING: AN OVERVIEW

Outsourcing is a pervasive business practice in organizational functions, such as accounting (e.g. bookkeeping and payroll processing), facilities maintenance, human resources management, information systems management, logistics and supply chain management, manufacturing and marketing. Outsourcing refers to the practice of a firm contracting with another firm to perform an activity that was previously performed in-house. The outsourced activity could be either the manufacturing of a *good* or the performance of a *service*. Outsourcing to third-party firms based in other countries is commonly referred to as 'offshore outsourcing', and sourcing from a firm's subsidiaries located in other countries (an intra-organizational and not an inter-organizational cooperative relationship) is commonly referred to as 'offshoring'. Regardless, both offshore outsourcing and offshoring essentially constitute international trade in goods and services (Mankiw and Swagel 2006). Notwithstanding the current high level of interest in offshore outsourcing and offshoring, both constitute only a slice of a much larger business phenomenon. For example, both outsourcing by firms that does not transcend national boundaries and outsourcing to entities other than to a firm's suppliers are pervasive. A firm's decision to outsource is often driven by and drives (i.e. is influenced by and facilitates) the emergence of specialist organizations in various fields and the associated scale-driven cost efficiencies.

Outsourcing refers to a transitional phase – a firm transitioning from performing an activity in-house to contracting with another organization to perform the activity. Beyond the transitional phase, the steady state is *sourcing* from another organization. For example, in the area of marketing, firms routinely entrust the performance of specific services to specialist organizations, such as advertising agencies; sales promotion agencies (e.g. firms that specialize in fulfillment of sales promotion offers, in-store product sampling and processing of money-off coupons); market research agencies; public relations management firms; and firms specializing in selling, distribution and warehousing; supply chain management; and debt collection. In general, the term 'outsourcing' is not used to refer to performance of activities that have been *traditionally* sourced by firms to other organizations, such as to advertising agencies and public relations firms. Moreover in certain industries, sourcing may often be the only viable business model, either for all firms or for a subgroup of firms. A case in point is the practice of newspapers sourcing some of their news-gathering activity (particularly, news gathering in other countries) to external entities, such as Reuters and the Associated Press. In the absence of such an arrangement, it would not be possible for most newspapers to publish news happenings in various parts of the world.

THEORETICAL PERSPECTIVES ON OUTSOURCING: AN OVERVIEW

Transaction cost analysis (TCA) posits that firms choose a mode of transaction (market governance versus internal organization) that minimizes the sum of production and transaction costs. If adaptation costs, performance costs and safeguarding costs are absent or low, firms will favor market governance. If these costs are high enough to exceed the production cost advantages of market governance, firms will favor internal organization (Rindfleisch and Heide 1997). A considerable body of research in various business disciplines (e.g. accounting, information systems, manufacturing, marketing) has examined a firm's choice between performing an activity within its boundaries and outsourcing to an external entity from a TCA perspective. However, authors have voiced concerns about the logic of basing the make versus buy decision solely on cost considerations to the exclusion of other considerations, such as the potential impact of the decision on the overall business strategy (see McIvor 2008). Prior research has also contended that TCA overstates the desirability of either integration or explicit contractual safeguards in certain exchange settings. For example, Poppo and Zenger (2002) note that trust and its underlying normative behaviors operating as self-reinforcing safeguards are more effective and less costly than contracts and vertical integration.

To achieve and sustain a position of *competitive cost advantage*, a firm's resources and capabilities must enable it to produce a product that offers the same set of benefits as its competitors' product offerings at a lower cost. To achieve and sustain a position of *competitive differentiation advantage*, a firm's resources and capabilities must enable it to produce a product that offers more benefits than and/or superior benefits to its competitors' offerings, and customers' preference for these differentiating features enable it to command a higher price in the marketplace. The *competitive advantage/resource-based/ capabilities-based view of the firm* suggests that firms choose to focus their efforts on achieving and sustaining a high level of competence in performing a core set of activities that are critical to their success in an industry and outsourcing activities that are not critical and/or activities that they do not have a distinctive capability to perform. However, firms need to guard against falling into the trap of viewing as core activities those that are performed in-house and as non-core activities those that are outsourced; in other words, viewing activities as core versus non-core as a consequence of a firm's outsourcing decisions rather than its determinant (Mukherji and Ramachandran 2007). Furthermore, as Porter (2001) notes, increased levels of outsourcing by players in an industry can lead to homogenization of skills and resources.

The *comparative advantage explanation* suggests that cross-border outsourcing is a manifestation of the forces of free trade and international specialization in the production of goods and services. If a good or service can be produced at a lower cost in another country, importing rather than producing it domestically allows a country to put its resources to more productive uses. Countries are best off when they focus on sectors in which they have a comparative advantage (Drezner 2004; Mankiw and Swagel 2006).

According to the *ability and motivation explanation*, for firms with a high level of know-how in a particular area, the relative cost of using that know-how is low. With the greater *ability* of firms possessing a high level of know-how resulting in lower costs, such firms will have a greater preference for performing an activity in-house rather than outsourcing. Firms with a low level of know-how are *motivated* to acquire a certain threshold level of know-how to be able to assimilate new know-how. Therefore, firms with a low level of know-how will also have a greater preference for performing an activity in-house. Stremersch et al. (2003) posit that collectively, the ability and motivation considerations lead to a curvilinear relationship. The preference for outsourcing over performing an activity in-house will be greater in firms with moderate levels of know-how than in firms with high or low levels of know-how.

While the TCA and comparative advantage explanations of outsourcing are primarily

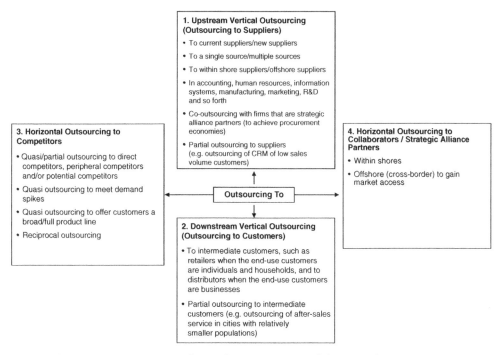

Figure 22.1   B2B outsourcing relationships: a conceptual framework

cost focused, the competitive advantage and ability–motivation perspectives span both cost and non-cost considerations. While the TCA and competitive advantage perspectives are broad in scope, the comparative advantage and ability–motivation perspectives are somewhat limited with regard to the breadth of contexts in which they may be applicable. For example, Stremersch et al. (2003) advance the ability–motivation explanation on outsourcing in specific reference to a technology-intensive decision context (outsourcing of system integration versus in-house system integration).

B2B OUTSOURCING RELATIONSHIPS: A CONCEPTUAL FRAMEWORK

Figure 22.1 presents a conceptual framework that distinguishes between a firm's outsourcing relationships with its suppliers, customers, competitors and collaborators.

- Upstream vertical outsourcing: Outsourcing by a firm to its current and/or new suppliers.
- Downstream vertical outsourcing: Outsourcing by a firm to its customers, specifically intermediate customers.
- Horizontal outsourcing to competitors: Outsourcing by a firm to its direct competitors, peripheral competitors and potential competitors.

- Horizontal outsourcing to collaborators: Outsourcing by a firm to its collabora-
tors/strategic alliance partners.

Upstream Vertical Outsourcing

Upstream vertical outsourcing can include a firm either outsourcing to a third-party firm
with which it currently does not have a supplier relationship (i.e. establishment of a new
buyer–seller relationship) or outsourcing additional activities that are currently being
performed in-house to one of its current suppliers (i.e. broadening of the scope of an existing buyer–seller relationship). Although outsourcing to new suppliers, particularly in the
context of offshore outsourcing, is common, case histories pertaining to the broadening of
the scope of outsourcing to current suppliers provide valuable insights into potential opportunities for firms. Consider, for example, the practice of customers shipping defective products that are under warranty to the after-sales service centers of manufacturers. Much of the
responsibility of shipping the defective products to manufacturers and back to customers
is normally handled by specialist transportation and logistics firms under long-term contracts. A relatively recent development involves these firms investing in developing in-house
after-sales servicing capabilities at their transportation hubs to repair an array of high-end
consumer products, such as laptop computers, DVD players and cell phones manufactured
by different firms (products that are normally shipped through an overnight parcel service
because of their high value relative to volume). Typically, the repair of such products entails
replacing a defective module (e.g. the hard drive in a laptop computer) or component (e.g.
the microprocessor in a laptop computer) or rectifying a software programming glitch in
the product by reinstalling the software. When the nature of the defects is more complex,
offering the customer a replacement product may often be more economical, relative to costs
associated with replacement parts and labor for repairing the product. Although the defective product may be mailed to the same location by customers who had purchased different
brands of the product made by competing firms in an industry, the after-sales service providers customize the shipping address to specific manufacturers of the product. Similarly, the
repaired product is shipped to customers in containers that are customized to specific manufacturers. Here, in addition to the revenue stream associated with providing transportation
and logistics services, by offering customized after-sales service to multiple manufacturers of
a product from a single facility, the supplier firm is able to generate a second revenue stream.
Manufacturers of products such as laptop computers also benefit from this arrangement. By
outsourcing the task of repairing defective products to transportation and logistics firms,
in addition to achieving savings in repair costs (due to scale economies associated with the
logistics firm providing the same repair services to many competing manufacturers) and
shipping costs (the defective product being shipped only to the hub city of the logistics firm),
manufacturers are also able to offer their customers a quicker turnaround.

This example illustrates upstream vertical outsourcing to suppliers in the context of
after-sales customer service, but outsourcing is also commonplace during even earlier
stages, following a sale. For example, when a customer places an order for a desktop
computer online, the CPU is assembled and shipped from the facilities of the PC manufacturer. The PC manufacturer could be either the seller firm or another firm to which the
seller has outsourced manufacturing. The LCD monitor that goes with the desktop computer is shipped directly to the customer from the warehouse of the LCD manufacturer

(with both the LCD and the shipping carton customized to the seller's brand name). A third shipping carton containing ancillary items, such as the keyboard, mouse and connecting wires, is directly shipped from the warehouse of a third firm. All three cartons are delivered to the customer together by a transportation and logistics firm.

While the characteristics of certain products (compact and high-value products, such as laptop computers and digital cameras) may be amenable to a greater degree of *centralized after-sales service outsourcing* (i.e. the defective products being shipped by customers to a central location), the characteristics of other products (bulky products, such as refrigerators, freezers, washers and dryers) necessitate sellers to outsource to a *decentralized network of after-sales service providers.* For example, the outsourcing of on-site repair and after-sales service to different firms in different geographic regions of the country is growing among manufacturers and retailers of large household appliances. That is, in place of an in-house nationwide after-sales service network, firms outsource the provision of on-site after-sales service to a network of regional firms. A variation of this is the seller retaining in-house after-sales service provision in larger population centers and outsourcing after-sales service provision to third parties in smaller population centers.

Downstream Vertical Outsourcing

An alternative to firms outsourcing the provision of after-sales service upstream to providers of logistics and transportations services is downstream vertical outsourcing to the firm's intermediate customers (i.e. the firm's marketing intermediaries, or retailers). Here again, the marketing intermediaries to whom such activities are outsourced achieve cost efficiencies by performing the service to multiple competing firms in a product category.

Technological advances often play an important role in outsourcing to end-use institutional customers. An example is package shipping service providers, such as FedEx and UPS, which outsource to their institutional customers the tasks of scheduling pick-up of parcels over the Internet, printing and affixing shipping labels on packages, tracking the status of packages shipped online, and verifying whether the parcel has been delivered to the addressee. All these activities were previously performed by an employee or agent representing the shipping-service provider, either face-to-face or over the telephone.

Horizontal Outsourcing to Competitors

Quasi outsourcing (partial outsourcing) to competitors is a common business practice. For example, a firm may invest in manufacturing capacity (plant and equipment) and workforce to meet steady state demand and, when feasible, outsource to competitors the production of additional quantities needed to meet seasonal demand and/or unanticipated spikes in demand. In addition, in their quest to offer a broader product line, firms often outsource the manufacturing of some of the product items constituting their full product line to their direct or peripheral competitors. Examples include US auto manufacturers offering lower price, small and fuel-efficient cars manufactured by automobile manufacturers based in Japan and Korea under their brand names. A firm's decision to resort to such partial outsourcing may be driven by the competitive imperative to offer a broad product line but lacking the resources and capabilities needed to do so in-house. In other instances, the manufacturing of key components, such as engine and transmission, is outsourced to competitors. Differences in the minimum efficient scale (higher at the component level than at the assembly level) are often a major consideration in outsourcing to competitors at the component level.

Quasi outsourcing to competitors can take the form of *reciprocal outsourcing*. For example, in the airline industry, an airline that operates several flights in and out of city A but only a few flights in and out of cities B, C and D may outsource the performance of certain ground services in cities B, C and D to other airlines that have a dominant presence in these cities and reciprocally perform these services in city A for these airlines. Similarly, if the fleet of airline A comprises 70 per cent Boeing and 30 per cent Airbus planes and that of airline B comprises 30 per cent Boeing and 70 per cent Airbus planes, reciprocal outsourcing of maintenance and overhaul can be mutually beneficial. That is, both firms may be able to achieve significant cost savings by specializing in maintenance and overhaul of the type of airplanes that account for the larger percentage of their respective fleets and engaging in reciprocal outsourcing.

In addition to quasi outsourcing to competitors, quasi outsourcing to *upstream suppliers* is also a widespread business practice. For example, a common practice in the airline industry is retaining in-house CRM of the firm's high-value customers (platinum customers, or frequent fliers who, on average, fly more than 1 million miles or 500 000 miles annually on the airline) and outsourcing the CRM of customers who travel on the airline less frequently to third-party firms. Another variation of quasi outsourcing of services to suppliers is the practice of outsourcing the *doing* aspects of CRM and performing in-house the *thinking* aspects of CRM (e.g. CRM analytics).

Horizontal Outsourcing to Collaborators

Chief among the issues that are central to competitive strategy are 'how to compete' and 'where to compete'. As a means to gain access to certain country markets, a firm may outsource the manufacturing of certain components or the performance of certain services to firms based in those countries (i.e. market access in exchange for outsourcing). Outsourcing to strategic alliance partners in specific countries may also be driven by considerations such as meeting local content stipulations for products imported into a country. For example, with regard to outsourcing in the aerospace industry, the building of modern-day planes critically depends on a global supply network and the willingness of companies to use state-of-the-art technologies whenever they can find them (Epstein and Crown 2008). In addition, outsourcing to firms in other countries works to the advantage of airplane makers when they try to sell to carriers based in these countries.

Lowering Cost Versus Achieving Greater Differentiation Through Outsourcing

Firms are often faced with the imperative to outsource to lower the costs associated with the production of a product (good or service) and therefore to be *price competitive* in the marketplace. For some firms, outsourcing can be a competitive imperative from the standpoint of lowering operating costs. Consider, for example, the case of legacy passenger airlines based in the United States (relatively older airlines whose workers are largely unionized) that are faced with challenges such as increasing jet fuel prices, limits to lowering labor costs when negotiating with unionized work groups (e.g. pilots,

	At a higher cost	At about the same cost	At a lower cost
Better than we can	7 Knowledge-intensive activities (R&D, new product development, consulting)	8	1
As well as we can	6	9	2
Not as well as we can, but above and beyond the acceptable threshold	5	4	3 • CRM • In-house: High volume (more profitable) customers • Outsource: Low volume (less profitable customers)

Figure 22.2   Cost versus quality underpinnings of outsourcing

mechanics, flight attendants), and price competition from newer airlines with non-unionized workforces. Faced with a competitive imperative to lower costs, some of the legacy airlines have outsourced their CRM-related activities to firms located in countries at a comparative advantage with respect to an important factor cost (i.e. labor costs) to varying degrees. The outsourced CRM activities include both customer-interfacing front office operations (e.g. reservations) and customer-non-interfacing back office operations (e.g. CRM analytics). In other instances, firms are faced with the imperative to outsource to be able to offer specific features in their product offerings and therefore to be *features competitive* in the marketplace. A case in point (discussed previously) is the practice of automobile manufacturers partially outsourcing to their competitors the manufacturing of certain models to be able to offer a full line to their customers.

While cost has been the principal focus on whether firms should perform an activity in-house or outsource it, quality (all factors other than cost) can also be a major consideration in certain outsourcing decisions. Firms can be differentially predisposed (cost driven versus quality driven) toward outsourcing activities that are *low in knowledge intensity* (e.g. data entry) versus *high in knowledge intensity* (e.g. R&D, consulting). Figure 22.2 provides additional insights into this issue. Here, cells 1, 2 and 3 are representative of cost considerations being the principal driver of outsourcing. The activities listed in cell 7 are representative of quality considerations being the principal driver of outsourcing (i.e. activities that are high in knowledge intensity/salient in credence attributes).

Products can be broadly classified as search, experience and credence products, or as products salient in search versus experience versus credence attributes (Darby and Karni 1973; Nelson 1970). Search attributes refer to the attributes of a product whose quality can be inferred before purchase, such as the picture quality of a television set. Experience attributes refer to the attributes whose quality can be inferred only after purchase and consumption of a product, such as the quality of food at a restaurant. Credence attributes refer to the attributes whose quality buyers lack the wherewithal to objectively assess either before or after purchase and consumption. In reference to outsourcing, exemplars of products salient in credence attributes include services such as management consulting and R&D. In the context of two recent additions to the business lexicon, *business process outsourcing* is illustrative of outsourcing of a product that is salient in search attributes, and *knowledge process outsourcing* is illustrative of outsourcing of a product that is salient in credence attributes. Currie et al. (2008) list several distinctive characteristics of knowledge processes outsourced (e.g. processes that are analytical, complex and unstructured; require extensive and complex domain knowledge on the part of the service provider; and result in the creation of intellectual property).

As Figure 22.2 shows, a dynamic perspective of cost versus quality as the principal consideration in a firm's outsourcing decision must take into account the projected trajectory of cost and quality over time. For example, one possible scenario is improvement in quality (due to learning effects) and reduction in cost (due to efficiency effects, learning effects and competitive effects). A second possible scenario is improvement in quality (due to learning effects and upward progression of vendors along the value chain) and increase in cost (due to cost increases associated with upward progression of vendors along the value chain and quality improvements and competition for a limited pool of workers possessing the requisite skills); that is, a net increase in cost notwithstanding reduction in cost due to efficiency effects, learning effects and competitive effects.

ROLE OF TECHNOLOGY IN OUTSOURCING AND CESSATION OF OUTSOURCING

Technology-driven Outsourcing

During the past decade, the confluence of several technological forces at a global level has enabled firms to achieve significant cost savings through offshore outsourcing of a whole new range of business processes and services. Chief among them is the emergence of an Internet-enabled global information and communications infrastructure, coupled with a sharp decline in the cost of global communications (communicating through text and voice) and the cost of computing (information processing). The impact of these forces has been particularly pronounced on the outsourcing of services due to most business processes and services being amenable to being broken down into discrete modules. Specifically, through digitization, *information-centric service modules* have been outsourced offshore. By leveraging the low-cost Internet-enabled global information and communications infrastructure, firms have outsourced their information-centric services to countries at a comparative advantage with respect to labor costs, as opposed to importing workers from these countries to perform the service within the firm's premises. The potential to achieve significant cost reductions through offshore outsourcing spans digitization of information (e.g. image scanning from analog to digital, text scanning from analog to digital, text re-entry from analog to digital, transcription from voice [analog] to text in digital form) and storage and retrieval of digitized information. Furthermore, there are fewer barriers to international trade in services than to international trade in goods. Information-centric services can be transmitted and received in digital form (exported and imported) instantaneously.

Technology-driven Automation and Cessation of Outsourcing

Before and during the 1980s, most of the processing of manufacturers' money-off coupon promotions by US-based firms was outsourced to firms based in either Mexico or the Caribbean region. Though not to the same extent, a sizable portion of the processing of manufacturers' rebate offer promotions (e.g. low denomination rebate offers) was also outsourced to firms based in either Mexico or the Caribbean region. For example, a PO Box or street address in El Paso, Texas (separated by the Rio Grande from Juarez, Mexico), was often the mailing address to which the retailers were required to submit money-off coupons redeemed at their stores and consumers were required to submit the completed rebate forms, proof of purchase and other supporting documentation (e.g. cash register receipts). That is, a critical element of the economics of manufacturers' money-off coupon promotions and low-denomination rebate offers was firms' ability to use low-cost labor in Mexico or the Caribbean region to perform the labor-intensive aspects of the promotions. In recent years, however, the bar codes embedded in money-off coupons enable these coupons to be electronically scanned at the retail cash registers. As a consequence, the labor-intensive task of physically counting the coupons to compute the total amount a manufacturer owes to a retailer toward money-off coupons has been made obsolete; reimbursement to retailers is now largely automated.

Furthermore, in the face of advances and innovations in self-service technology, information technology, communication technology, the Internet and information digitization, cost considerations favor device-enabled micro outsourcing to end-use customers rather than serving the customers by way of a B2B outsourcing relationship with a vendor firm. On the one hand, device-enabled micro outsourcing to end-use customers entails substantial front-end investments by the firm in new equipment and facilities (high fixed costs), but the variable costs associated with serving individual customers can be extremely low, tending toward zero. On the other hand, outsourcing the performance of services to an offshore vendor (to take advantage of lower cost of labor in certain offshore locations) can lead to a substantial reduction in fixed costs (investments in equipment and facilities) and a modest reduction in variable costs. In effect, the fixed and variable cost characteristics of device-enabled outsourcing to end-use customers (self-service) compared with outsourcing of the performance of services by human agents (offshore outsourcing) can be a major consideration in a firm's choice between the two.

DISCUSSION AND CONCLUSION

Although the focus of this chapter is limited to issues related to outsourcing and its potential to contribute to a firm's competitive cost and differentiation advantage, as highlighted in Tables 22.1 and 22.2, they constitute only one aspect of a firm's web of B2B relationships that define its competitive strategy at the business-unit and marketing level. Building on these two tables, a synthesis of extant literature and further research could provide a more comprehensive perspective of the strategic role of a firm's B2B

BOX 22.1   MOTIVES UNDERLYING ENTRY OF FIRMS INTO
STRATEGIC ALLIANCES

1. *Market entry and market position-related motives:* (a) to gain access to new international markets; (b) to circumvent barriers to entering international markets posed by legal, regulatory and/or political factors; (c) to defend market position in present markets; and (d) to enhance market position in present markets.
2. *Product-related motives:* (a) to fill gaps in present product line and (b) to broaden present product line.
3. *Product-market-related motives:* (a) to enter new product-market domains and (b) to enter or maintain the option to enter evolving industries whose product offerings may emerge as either substitutes for or complements to the firm's product offerings.
4. *Market structure modification-related motives:* (a) to reduce potential threat of future competition, (b) to raise entry barriers/erect entry barriers and (c) to alter the technological base of competition.
5. *Market entry timing-related motives:* to accelerate pace of entry into new product-market domains by accelerating pace of R&D, product development and/or market entry.
6. *Resource Utilization Efficiency-related motives:* (a) to lower manufacturing costs and (b) to lower marketing costs.
7. *Resource extension and risk reduction-related motives:* (a) to pool resources in light of large outlays required and (b) to lower risk in the face of large resource outlays required, technological uncertainties, market uncertainties and/or other uncertainties.
8. *Skills enhancement-related motives:* (a) to learn new skills from alliance partners and (b) to enhance present skills by working with alliance partners.

Source: Adapted from Varadarajan and Cunningham (1995).

---

relationships on strategy at the firm, business-unit and marketing levels. For example, in a strategic alliance, the cooperating organizations pool certain resources and skills to achieve common goals and/or goals specific to the alliance partners. Such pooling of skills and resources may involve individual partners in an alliance focusing on either different stages of the value chain to which they have the potential to contribute the most toward the alliance achieving a competitive advantage or the same stage of the value chain. In the context of the former, rather than being viewed as entailing the *pooling* of skills and resources, an alliance can alternatively be viewed as a firm outsourcing the performance of activities related to a particular stage in the value chain to its alliance partner. The potential overlap between outsourcing and strategic alliances notwithstanding, considerable divergence exists in the motives underlying B2B outsourcing relationships and B2B strategic alliance relationships. Box 22.1 provides an overview of the motives underlying firms entering into strategic alliances with other firms.

The question whether to perform specific activities within the boundaries of the firm or outside the boundaries is of ongoing concern to firms. This chapter has primarily focused on B2B relationships in the context of outsourcing, but the broader issue of market governance versus internal organization has also been explored in other related literature streams, such as vertical integration and strategic alliances. In addition to firm actions that are explicitly referred to as outsourcing, a broad array of firm actions also referred to as 'make versus buy', 'vertical integration versus vertical disintegration (contraction)', 'disintermediation versus intermediation', and 'use of an in-house sales force versus sales force affiliated with a third-party firm' also focus on the same underlying phenomenon: namely, the choice between market governance and internal organization. Similarly, to varying degrees, the actions of firms described using phrases such as 'externalization of low-value-added value chain activities in firms', 'the hollowing of corporations', 'the transformation of firms into virtual enterprises', and 'contracting and subcontracting' also pertain to the broader issue of market governance versus internal organization.

NOTES

1. Portions of this chapter are based on Varadarajan (2009).
2. Most large firms in most parts of the world (i.e. the prototypical large firm of the twenty-first century) are multibusiness firms. In this context, the term 'firm' refers to the firm at large (the corporate entity), and 'business' refers to a specific business or strategic business unit in the portfolio of the multibusiness firm. In such firms, customers, competitors, suppliers and potential alliance partners are specific to individual businesses in the firm's portfolio (e.g. customers, competitors and suppliers of General Electric's jet engines business versus home appliances business). In a single-business firm, however, the terms 'firm' and 'business' refer to one and the same entity. While the outsourcing-related issues addressed in this chapter could be either in the context of the firm at large, as in a single-business firm, or in a specific business unit in a multibusiness firm, for ease of exposition, the term 'firm' is used for both.

REFERENCES

Currie, Wendy L., Vaughan Michell and Oluwakemi Abanishe (2008), 'Knowledge process outsourcing in financial services: the vendor perspective', *European Management Journal*, **26** (2), 94–104.
Darby, Michael R. and Edi Karni (1973), 'Free competition and the optimal amount of fraud', *Journal of Law and Economics*, **16** (April), 67–86.
Drezner, Daniel W. (2004), 'The outsourcing bogeyman', *Foreign Affairs*, **83** (3), 22–34.
Epstein, Keith and Judith Crown (2008), 'Globalization bites Boeing', *BusinessWeek*, 13 March, available at http://www.businessweek.com/magazine/content/08_12/b4076032773142.htm.
Mankiw, N. Gregory and Phillip Swagel (2006), 'The politics and economics of offshore outsourcing', *Journal of Monetary Economics*, **53** (5), 1027–56.
McIvor, Ronan (2008), 'What is the right outsourcing strategy for your process?', *European Management Journal*, **26** (1), 24–34.
Mukherji, S. and J. Ramachandran (2007), 'Outsourcing: practice in search of a theory', *IIMB Management Review*, **19** (2), 103–10.
Nelson, Phillip (1970), 'Information and consumer behavior', *Journal of Political Economy*, **78** (2), 311–29.
Poppo, Laura and Todd Zenger (2002), 'Do formal contracts and relational governance function as substitutes or complements?', *Strategic Management Journal*, **23**(8), 707–25.
Porter, Michael E. (2001), 'Strategy and the Internet', *Harvard Business Review*, **79** (3), 62–79.
Rindfleisch, Aric and Jan B. Heide (1997), 'Transaction cost analysis: past, present and future applications', *Journal of Marketing*, **61** (October), 30–54.
Stremersch, Stefan, Allen M. Weiss, Benedict G.C. Dellaert and Ruud T. Frambach (2003), 'Buying modular systems in technology-intensive markets', *Journal of Marketing Research*, **40** (August), 335–50.

Tabuchi, Hiroko (2009), 'Delta and American offer aid to Japan Airlines', *The New York Times*, 18 November, available at http://www.nytimes.com/2009/11/19/business/global/19air.html.

Varadarajan, Rajan (2009), 'Outsourcing: think more expansively', *Journal of Business Research*, **62** (November), 1165–72.

Varadarajan, Rajan and Margaret H. Cunningham (1995), 'Strategic alliances: a synthesis of conceptual foundations', *Journal of the Academy of Marketing Science*, **23** (Fall), 282–96.

PART V

PERSONAL SELLING AND SALES MANAGEMENT

23 Salesperson effectiveness: a behavioral perspective
Kevin Bradford and Barton A. Weitz

Salespeople are the principal vehicle through which B2B firms, particularly firms with a complex and differentiated offering, communicate and exchange information with their customers. Wotruba (1991) identifies the following roles for salespeople within a firm's marketing program: (1) informer; (2) persuader; (3) problem solver; and (4) value creator. In the traditional informer, persuader and problem solver roles, or roles that we collectively refer to as influencer roles, salespeople focus on informing customers about the firm's products and convincing them that these products and services will satisfy their needs and solve their problems. While salespeople engaged in these influencer roles consider the needs of their customers when developing and implementing sales strategies, the alternatives they present to customers are typically limited to their firm's current products and services.

In response to changes in the market environment, such as increasing customer consolidation, product commoditization and globalization, more emphasis is being placed on the value creator role of B2B salespeople. In the value creator role, salespeople draw on the resources of their firms to develop idiosyncratic solutions for their customers' problems. Since these offerings are typically unique to a specific customer relationship, it is difficult for competitors to duplicate the offerings, and thus these offerings have the potential for building a long-term competitive advantage for the buyer–seller dyad over competing dyads. However, developing idiosyncratic solutions is risky because the selling and buying firms need to share sensitive information and make investments that are unique to the relationship. Thus salespeople in a value creator role are responsible for developing and maintaining relational exchanges with their customers – relationships in which their firms and the firms' customers devote their attention to 'increasing the pie' over the long term rather than 'dividing the pie'. This emerging value creator/relationship management role for salespeople supports the growing emphasis that B2B firms, in general, are placing on developing long-term, partnering relationships with their best and most promising customers rather than broadening their customer base with more transactional relationships (Jones et al. 2005; Weitz and Bradford 1999).

Salespeople in the traditional and value creating roles have different goals, engage in different activities and use different sets of knowledge, skills and abilities (KSAs). The measures of effectiveness differ for the two salesperson roles. Short-term sales is a more important performance measure for evaluating influencers, while longer-term measures, such as share of wallet and customer commitment, are more appropriate for assessing the performance of value creators. Finally, the nature of sales management also changes in response to the different skills and support needed by the salespeople.

Table 23.1 summarizes the behaviors of salespeople, their KSAs and the sales management practices used to develop KSAs for salespeople in the more traditional influencer role and the emerging value creation role. We begin by examining research that explores the KSAs needed to be effective in the traditional role (upper-left-hand corner) and the

Table 23.1   Key factors affecting salesperson effectiveness in role

Role Characteristics for Effective Performance	Influencer	Value Creator/Relationship Manager
Salesperson	• Adaptive selling • Complex knowledge structure • Interpersonal mentalizing • Emotional intelligence • Communication skills	• Internal selling • Political skills • Creative thinking • Trust building • Conflict management • Relationship-enhancing activities
Sales Management Programs	• Organizing knowledge • Sharing knowledge • Motivating knowledge development	• Job rotation • Salesperson selection • Training on relationship building

sales management practices for developing these KSAs (lower-left-hand corner). We examine the KSAs salespeople need in the value creation role and associated sales management practices (the left-hand side of Table 23.1) in the second half of the chapter.

EFFECTIVENESS OF SALESPEOPLE IN TRADITIONAL INFLUENCER ROLE

Salespeople in the traditional influencer role use assertive strategies and tactics to convince customers to buy products (Weitz and Bradford 1999). Research examining the effectiveness of salespeople in a traditional influencer role has focused on uncovering salesperson behaviors, behavioral predispositions and capabilities related to performance. For example, experimental studies have explored the effectiveness of 'hard sell', emotional appeals versus 'soft sell', rational appeals; 'canned' versus 'extemporaneous' presentations; and personal versus product messages. Correlational studies have investigated the relationships between personality traits/behavioral predispositions and salesperson performance (see Weitz 1981 for a review).

In general, the results of this research have failed to identify behavioral predispositions or aptitudes that account for a large amount of variance in performance for salespeople. In addition, the results of this research are quite inconsistent and, in some cases, even contradictory.

In light of the lack of success in identifying sales behaviors, behavioral predispositions and KSAs universally related to salesperson performance, researchers have focused on identifying the situational constructs that moderate the salesperson characteristic–performance relationship. Most salespeople encounter a wide variety of customers and sales situations, and research suggests that they need to be flexible and adapt their selling activities to the nature of the sales situation (Weitz et al. 1986). Thus the effective practice of adaptive selling is a key KSA for salespeople in the traditional influencer role (see Franke and Park 2006).

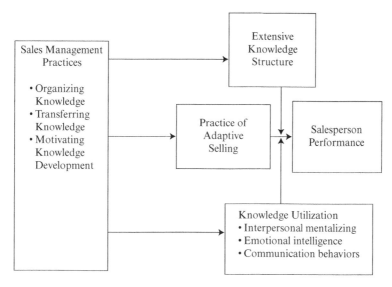

Figure 23.1   Adaptive selling and sales performance

Figure 23.1 provides a framework for describing the relationship between the practice of adaptive selling and salesperson performance. To practice adaptive selling effectively, salespeople need a complex knowledge structure and the ability to utilize that knowledge effectively. Sales management practices can motivate salespeople to practice adaptive selling and to acquire and utilize the knowledge and skills that increase effectiveness.

Adaptive Selling

Adaptive selling is 'the altering of sales behaviors during a customer interaction or across customer interactions based on perceived information about the nature of the selling situation' (Weitz et al. 1986, p. 175). This approach enables salespeople to tailor messages to fit individual customers' needs and preferences. Salespeople engaged in adaptive selling customize their sales strategy to fit the needs of each customer and sales situation and adapt their behaviors across customers, across time and within a customer interaction (see Weitz 1978).

When salespeople are adaptive, they exploit the unique capability of personal selling compared with other marketing communication media. In addition to developing and implementing unique sales presentations tailored to each customer, adaptive salespeople can make rapid adjustments in their sales strategies in response to their customers' reactions. Other marketing communication vehicles (e.g. mass media, sales promotions, point-of-purchase displays, packaging, websites) are restricted to delivering messages targeted toward a 'typical' customer in a market segment, and the opportunity to make timely adjustments is limited.

Research confirms that adaptive selling behavior improves salesperson performance regardless of the circumstances (e.g. Boorom et al. 1998; Franke and Park 2006;

Jaramillo and Grisaffe 2009; Spiro and Weitz 1990; Weitz et al. 1986). Recent studies have concluded that adaptive selling enables salespeople to become more customer oriented (Franke and Park 2006) and mediates the effect of customer orientation on sales performance (Jaramillo and Grisaffe 2009). Giacobbe et al. (2006, p. 121) find support for a positive effect of adaptive selling on sales performance even in 'non-adaptive' selling situations, in which adaptive selling is 'expected to be less effective (perhaps ineffective or even counterproductive)'. When distributor salespeople sold a consumer durable directly to household buyers, adaptive selling explained 27 per cent of the variation in sales performance. Last, a salesperson's adaptive selling behavior is positively related to his or her achievement of both long-term and short-term sales goals (Chakrabarty et al. 2010).

Knowledge Structure for Effective Adaptive Selling

To practice adaptive selling effectively, salespeople need an elaborate knowledge structure of sales situations, sales behaviors and contingencies that link specific sales strategies and behaviors to sales situations (Weitz et al. 1986). Salespeople, like other experts in problem-solving situations, operate in an extremely complex domain. Rather than reacting to each new situation, salespeople accumulate a base of experiences and probably organize these experiences into categories of selling situations so that the past experiences can be readily accessed and applied when they confront new customers and new selling situations.

The categorical model of memory indicates that knowledge is organized into categories with two types of knowledge – procedural and declarative knowledge – associated with each category (Rosch and Lloyd 1978, p. 46). Declarative knowledge is the set of facts associated with the category, such as the nature of the relationship between the salesperson and the customer, the benefits sought by the customer and the stage of the sales process. Procedural knowledge is the sales behaviors that are appropriate when confronting that situation (Leigh and Rethans 1984). Thus, declarative knowledge provides the basis for recognizing different sales situations, and procedural knowledge indicates what should be done when encountering those situations. When confronting a sales situation, salespeople use the declarative knowledge to categorize the present situation according to its similarity to a sales situation category in the salesperson's memory. Then they can access from memory the sales approach, or the procedural knowledge, for dealing with the situation effectively. The degree to which salespeople can effectively adapt depends on the number of sales situation categories they have in memory (Sharma et al. 2007; Sujan et al. 1988).

Knowledge Utilization

Both researchers and practitioners have recognized the relationship between more knowledge and more effective selling performance. For example, Weitz et al. (1986) find that performance was better for salespeople who had more knowledge about their customers and knew more about selling strategies. Three KSAs that enable salespeople to use their knowledge base effectively are interpersonal mentalizing, emotional intelligence and communication skills.

Interpersonal mentalizing

Interpersonal mentalizing is a salesperson's ability to take into account the intentions and mental states of customers. It is an unconscious process that occurs automatically during customer interactions. Salespeople who possess an ability to interpersonally mentalize are able to better alter their interactions with customers according to the perceived wants and needs revealed during customer interactions. Dietvorst et al. (2009) conceptualize this construct and have developed a scale to measure it.

Emotional intelligence

An aspect of intelligence associated with effective adaptive selling is emotional intelligence. Emotional intelligence is the ability to perceive emotions, assimilate emotion-related feelings, understand the information transmitted by those emotions and manage them. Thus salespeople high in emotional intelligence can manage and perceive emotions effectively and use this information to adapt their sales presentations.

Communication behaviors related to building an elaborate knowledge structure

Salespeople develop and use an elaborate knowledge structure by collecting information about customers, by asking questions, listening to customers and interpreting customers' non-verbal cues. Salespeople use this information to accurately categorize the sales situation and draw on past experience for selecting appropriate sales behaviors (Castleberry and Shepherd 1993). Although the research on effective information collection by salespeople is limited (see Ramsey and Sohi 1999; Shepherd et al. 1997 for exceptions), some cognitive skills associated with effective information collection are the ability to evaluate the content of communications, to understand and remember communications and to evaluate the affective state of customers using non-verbal cues. Salespeople who possess these skills engage in behaviors such as taking notes, restating what customers have said, summarizing the major issues raised by customers, employing non-verbal cues to demonstrate interest, asking questions and encouraging conversation by using 'I see' or 'uh huh' responses (Weitz et al. 2007). In the following section, we introduce some activities that sales management can undertake to improve salesperson effectiveness in the influencer role.

BUILDING KNOWLEDGE AND SKILLS IN SALESPEOPLE IN TRADITIONAL INFLUENCER ROLES

Sales management activities that can help develop elaborate knowledge structures in salespeople and encourage and facilitate their use include: (1) training salespeople in how to organize their knowledge more effectively; (2) transferring knowledge residing in the firm to salespeople; and (3) motivating salespeople to develop their knowledge structure (Sujan et al. 1986).

Training on Organizing Knowledge

Organizing knowledge into sales situation categories containing declarative and procedural knowledge helps salespeople adapt effectively to a wide range of sales situations.

However, some bases for categorizing sales situations are more effective than others. In general, organizing categories according to deep characteristics, such as factors related to the customer's decision process (e.g. beliefs about products, importance of product characteristics), instead of surface characteristics (e.g. customer's age, gender) is more functional. These deep characteristics are typically associated with effective sales approaches.

Often sales training programs provide information on the firm's products and the typical customer needs but fail to connect the information about a customer's needs with the sale approaches best used to interact with that customer type. The categories used to organize knowledge need to link declarative and procedural knowledge.

Transferring Company Knowledge to Salespeople

Often B2B firms undertake market research to develop new products and communication programs, but this information rarely trickles down to the sales force. Information on the firm's market segments is particularly useful to the sales force because it can serve as a starting point for developing sales situation categories.

The best and most experienced salespeople have probably developed the most elaborate knowledge. They have the most categories, they organize their categories with deep characteristics, and they have both declarative and procedural knowledge. However, these expert salespeople draw on their knowledge bases automatically; that is, they do not consciously sift through their knowledge base when confronting a sales situation, match the situation with similar situations encountered previously, and then access an effectively employed sales strategy. Thus although it might be difficult for experienced, high performance salespeople to verbally express the knowledge accumulated, it is critical to incorporate this type of experience to develop effective training programs. For example, expert salespeople's experiences can be used to create role play about typical situations encountered and problems solved when selling a product.

Motivating Salespeople to Develop their Knowledge Structure

Sales management can use three approaches to motivate salespeople to develop an elaborate knowledge base: (1) provide process rather than outcome feedback; (2) encourage salespeople to analyze their successes and failures and appropriately attribute their performance; and (3) make work fun.

Provide process feedback
Sales managers often accompany salespeople on customer visits and review the interaction after the sales call. The focus of these feedback sessions is on whether the salespeople achieved a desirable objective. However, this performance feedback is not as effective in developing knowledge as process feedback, that is, diagnostic feedback on salespeople's actions that resulted in desirable or undesirable outcomes (Sujan et al. 1994).

Feedback on what causes outcomes, rather than the outcomes themselves, also helps salespeople focus on the activities associated with their job. This process feedback builds intrinsic interest in the job, makes the job itself more rewarding and promotes the exploration and development of an elaborate knowledge structure.

Encourage strategy attributions for successes and failures

All salespeople fail as well as succeed. Most firms recognize and reward successes, but failures can also be important learning experiences. The ability to learn from mistakes is an important competency for building an elaborate knowledge structure. When analyzing their successes and failures, salespeople should assign reasons for their performance, which in turn facilitates learning. That is, taking credit for successes and blaming failures on factors beyond their control (e.g. poorly designed products, late delivery) does not promote salesperson learning. In contrast, attributing undesirable outcomes to poor strategies leads salespeople to learn from their mistakes. Doing so also promotes learning because the salespeople are motivated to try a different approach the next time they encounter the sales situation (Sujan et al. 1986).

Thus when discussing sales situations with salespeople, sales managers should ask 'why' questions that prompt the salespeople to give reasons for their performance. Sales managers should also encourage the salespeople to attribute successes and failure to factors they can control rather to uncontrollable circumstances, such a tough customer or a lack of inherent sales aptitude.

Make work fun

Salespeople receive two types of rewards for doing their job: extrinsic and intrinsic rewards. Extrinsic rewards are rewards that others give, such as compensation, promotions and recognition. This type of reward typically encourages salespeople to work harder (e.g. to make more sales calls), but it can also distract them from the activities associated with their jobs. Extrinsic rewards focus attention on outcomes rather than processes and suggest that salespeople are working to receive the extrinsic rewards rather than finding the work itself rewarding.

Intrinsic rewards are rewards that salespeople get from doing their job, such as personal rewards from interacting with and solving customer problems. Salespeople motivated by intrinsic rewards try to master their assigned tasks, explore new and better ways to do their job and acquire the knowledge needed to be more effective at their jobs. Sales managers can create intrinsic interest in selling among their salespeople by making the selling itself rewarding and fun. Intrinsic interest motivates salespeople to develop their knowledge base and skills and master tasks for which they are responsible.

Although incentive compensation motivates salespeople to work harder, an overemphasis on incentives can lead them to feel that compensation is the only reason they are working. Incentives can actually diminish intrinsic orientation, and sales management should be wary of these potential negative effects, particularly for new salespeople who need to focus on developing their skills. In the following sections we focus on the behaviors and KSAs salespeople need in the value creator/relationship management role and the sales management practices supporting the development of those KSAs.

EFFECTIVENESS OF SALESPEOPLE IN THE VALUE CREATOR/ RELATIONSHIP MANAGER ROLE

The nature of buyer–seller relationships has evolved from a focus on increasing the number of simple transactional relationships with multiple partners to long-term relationships with a select few customers. While there is considerable research on the characteristics of effective influencer salespeople, research on the characteristics needed to be effective in this emerging value creation/relationship management role is limited.

Critical behaviors and skills that lead salespeople to be effective as value creator/ relationship managers include: (1) engaging in internal selling; (2) using political skills; (3) thinking creatively; (4) building trust; (5) managing conflict; and (6) undertaking relationship-enhancing activities. Next, we discuss these behaviors and skills, as well as the sales management practices that support their development.

Engaging in Internal Selling

In their value creation role, salespeople need to be effective in building relationships with both internal support personnel in their organization and their customers. To offer idiosyncratic value to their customers, many B2B firms are bundling services with their product offerings. Salespeople help identify these customized bundling opportunities and coordinate their delivery (Liu and Leach 2001; Sheth and Sharma 2008). Offerings with a significant service component require greater coordination in the selling firm to meet buyer needs, thus requiring salespeople to work closely with internal support staff. To engage in internal selling, salespeople need to develop and build close working relationships with employees in their firms (Bell et al. 2004). Salespeople also need to develop extensive knowledge of their firm's resources, knowledge of the personnel who control these resources (Homburg et al. 2002) and skills at convincing these employees to support their efforts to provide innovative offerings. Internal support helps salespeople develop more creative and comprehensive solutions for their customers.

Internal selling involves both vertical and lateral relationships in organizations. Vertical relationships include salesperson–sales manager, salesperson–supervisor and salesperson–organization relationships. Lateral relationships include salesperson–team member and salesperson–co-worker relationships. Understanding how to nurture these relationships and to engage in and execute a relationship development process orientation across all relationships (whether internal or external to the organization) benefits the firm and the salesperson (Üstüner and Godes 2006).

Using Political Skills

Organizations are political areas, and some organizational members are more skillful than others in dealing with their firms' politics. To garner internal support, salespeople need to be savvy in working with employees and groups within their firms. Political skills are defined as 'the ability to effectively understand others at work and to use such knowledge to influence others to act in ways that enhance one's personal and/or organizational objectives' (Ahearn et al. 2004, p. 311). Thus politically skilled salespeople understand the needs of internal support people and adapt their approach to influence them accordingly.

The four dimensions of political skills are: (1) social astuteness; (2) interpersonal influence; (3) apparent sincerity; and (4) networking ability (Ferris et al. 2005). Politically skillful salespeople are sensitive to and accurate in perceiving the situation in which they are attempting to gain support; adapt behavior to each situation; are, or appear to be, honest, open, and forthright; and are adept at developing and using networks of people with their firms.

Networking refers to 'behaviors that are aimed at building, maintaining, and using informal relationships that possess the (potential) benefit of facilitating work-related activities of individuals' (Wolff and Moser 2009, p. 196). Through internal networking, salespeople identify and build relationships with company employees who can help them offer special consideration to their customers. The more proactive salespeople's internal networking activities, the more informed they will be of the various resource pools available to facilitate their sales efforts. Plouffe and Barclay (2007) suggest that salespeople who proactively navigate their work environment are more likely to benefit from internal support; for example, by receiving priority in allocations of sales resources and having rules and policies bent to suit their sales needs.

Experienced salespeople are able to identify ways to help satisfy customer needs and achieve superior performance (O'Hara et al. 1991; Pettijohn et al. 1999). To create value, salespeople need experience within the company and with potential support people, in addition to customers. One approach to gain this experience is by rotating salespeople through several internal firm positions. Another approach is to conduct events in which salespeople and support staff interact with each other in both business and social contexts.

Thinking Creatively

Creativity is the production of novel and useful approaches to accomplish a task (Amabile 1983). Novelty implies that creative solutions differ from the conventional practices in a firm, and usefulness indicates that creative solution selling activities and outcomes provide benefits to the parties in the relationship. Creativity plays an important role in the performance of value-creating salespeople (Chonko et al. 2002; Woodman et al. 1993). Creative offerings often involve relationship-specific assets that are difficult for competitors to recognize and duplicate and thus can lead to strategic advantage (Kogut 1988).

Research on personal and organizational creativity identifies three critical characteristics of creative people: (1) resources; (2) creative processes; and (3) intrinsic motivation (Amabile 1988; Amabile and Conti 1999). Resources are the salesperson's knowledge about both firm resources and customers. Depth of knowledge gives the salesperson the ability to explore a wide variety of potential approaches to combine resources and develop creative selling offerings. The creative processes component includes techniques that salespeople use to consider new perspectives, such as using analogies, suspending judgment and making the familiar strange. While knowledge and creative processes facilitate the development of creative solutions, the third component, intrinsic motivation, drives salespeople to engage in the process of developing creative offerings.

Three broad organizational factors stimulate creativity in organizations: (1) organizational encouragement to innovate, or the basic orientation of the organization and its support of creativity and innovation; (2) the resources the firm makes available to employees engaged in creative work; and (3) the provision of challenging and interesting work, specification of overall goals, and formation of work teams by drawing together people with diverse skills and perspectives (Zhang and Bartol 2010).

Aspects of organizational encouragement include upper management valuing creativity, offering supportive responses to new ideas, and collaborating rewards and recognition for the development of creative offerings across the organization. A critical factor affecting creativity involves granting salespeople both autonomy in their day-to-day work and ownership of and control over their own work and ideas. Although extreme pressures can undermine creativity, some pressure can have a positive effect if salespeople believe the pressure is due to the intellectually challenging nature of the task itself. Finally, internal conflict and formal management structures can impede creativity.

Building Trust

Exchanging information with customers is critical, and salespeople bear much of the burden for this formidable role. Because salespeople occupy boundary-spanning positions, they are primarily responsible for acquiring the skills necessary to perform the information exchange function in their task environment and are considered important sources of information about their customers (Lambert et al. 1990; Leifer and Delbecq 1978). Therefore, building trust to encourage information exchange is a critical skill for salespeople.

Trust between the salesperson and the customer occurs when the customer is confident in the salesperson's reliability and integrity (Anderson and Narus 1984; Morgan and Hunt 1994). The relationship between marketing exchanges and trust is well supported (i.e. Doney and Cannon 1997), as are the related benefits of trust and information exchange. When trust occurs in a relationship between the salesperson and the customer, coordinated behavior will likely occur, constructive dialogue will transpire, and cooperative solutions will be developed. Because risk is associated with disclosure of information, an element of trust must exist for disclosure to transpire. As the disclosure of information deepens, the associated risk also increases, as does the ability of the buyer and seller to solve problems predicated on the disclosure of sensitive and confidential information, which is typical for parties engaged in close buyer–seller relationships. Disclosure occurs if the customer trusts that the salesperson will use pertinent, sensitive or confidential information to develop a positive outcome and not misuse the information. If customers do not trust the salesperson, they will be less likely to disclose. Two factors associated with trust are competency and proactive information sharing.

Competency
Competency consists of the groups of skills, abilities and characteristics that enable a party to influence some specific domain (Mayer et al. 1995). The domain of competency affords a person confidence in tasks related to his or her area of responsibility (Mayer et al. 1995). Salesperson competency affects customer confidence; that is, customers must believe that the salesperson has the competence to solve problems before they share the information necessary to solve the problem (Schurr and Ozanne 1985).

Proactive information sharing
Salespeople often make significant idiosyncratic or transaction-specific investments (TSIs) to improve relationships with their customers. Salespeople who are committed to their customers can help them differentiate themselves in the marketplace and develop

competitive advantages by spending the time necessary to develop the best solutions to deliver more effective and efficient solutions (Jap and Ganesan 2000). Some examples of these investments include spending time to understand customers' business problems, providing depth and detail on company products and services not openly available, and offering access to customer-related company resources for problem-specific education. When salespeople make TSIs, their customers perceive the investments as credible pledges of commitment to the relationship (Anderson and Weitz 1992). Social penetration theory posits that as the salesperson offers and shares credible pledges of commitment, the customer feels obligated to reciprocate, thus creating a normative interaction environment of information sharing. In earlier stages of a relationship, these norms have not formed, and communication and information exchange is not deep and resembles professional courtesy. As TSIs deepen, information exchange expands to sensitive and confidential sharing, and the relationship strengthens. This iterative relational process requires a skilled salesperson and hinges on the customer's perception of the salesperson's investment in the relationship.

Managing Conflict

The previously discussed behaviors and skills reflect the salespeople's ability to develop a unique offering for customers – the value creation aspect of this emerging role for salespeople. However, salespeople also need to develop and maintain a long-term relationship with customers. Conflict management is an important skill for salespeople who manage relationships (Biong and Selnes 1996; Bradford and Weitz 2008; Tellefsen and Eyuboglu 2002; Weitz and Bradford 1999).

As the scope of interactions between buyers and sellers broadens and intensifies, conflicts are likely to arise from increased interdependences (Dahrendorf 1959; Thomas 1976). Customers in long-term relationships are also the most challenging to serve satisfactorily because they are sensitive to and significantly affected by inadequacies on the part of the selling companies and salespeople on whom they depend (Jackson 1985). As companies in partnering relationships become closer to each other, relationship norms play a critical role, and transgressions of these rules are treated more seriously (Roloff and Cloven 1990).

However, conflict, when handled effectively, can also function to affect business relationships positively (e.g. Bradford and Weitz 2008). Conflict can serve as a medium through which problems can be aired and solutions derived (Coser 1956; Deutsch 1973). It can serve integrative functions through the voicing of each party's perspectives (Coser 1956) and can enhance the ability to work together in the future (Brown 1983). Stern et al. (1996) posit that conflict motivates parties to adapt to, grow and seize new opportunities. Fundamental to the positive effects of conflict is that 'creative action on the part of some party to the conflict is needed if the conflict is to be successfully resolved' (Rosenbloom 1987, p. 121).

Undertaking Relationship-enhancing Activities

To develop relationships, salespeople engage in relationship-enhancing activities, or actions, resources and efforts focused on strengthening customer relationships (Crosby et al. 1990). Relationship-enhancing activities include social interaction on business and non-business activities, sharing of sensitive information regarding the business and marketplace, adaptive and constructive policies and procedures, and all other initiatives that cultivate a relational character in the seller–customer interaction (Anderson and Weitz 1992; Jap and Ganesan 2000; Palmatier et al. 2007). The goal of relationship-enhancing activities is to convert highly qualified potential customers into committed and trusted business partners (Berry 1995; Crosby et al. 1990; De Wulf et al. 2001).

BUILDING KNOWLEDGE AND SKILLS IN THE VALUE CREATOR/RELATIONSHIP MANAGER ROLE

The skills that salespeople need to perform in the value creator/relationship manager role develop through fundamental knowledge transfer processes, such as those associated with the various methods of training. For high performance in this role, sales managers need to implement and incorporate the following knowledge transfer methods: (1) job rotation; (2) salesperson selection; and (3) targeted training.

Job Rotation

Job rotation is the salesperson's strategic, regular change of jobs within the roles most pertinent to the delivery of value to customers. These include administrative roles, production roles and the roles associated with customer contact, such as frontline sales jobs, frontline sales management, brand management, logistics and sales training. Job rotation helps salespeople learn through experience, and experience enables the salesperson to develop solutions for customers as well as form teams of the appropriate functional experts to assist and support customer interaction efforts. Franke and Park (2006) find that experienced salespeople are more likely to have a customer orientation. That is, experienced salespeople have a greater ability to identify ways to help satisfy customer needs, a long-term orientation and more repeat customers. In addition, experiences gained through job rotation can expedite learning and more fully expose salespeople to the resources needed to be successful as a value creator (O'Hara et al. 1991; Pettijohn et al. 1999). Experience is an antecedent of both job performance and satisfaction.

Salesperson Selection

A key job challenge for sales managers is to recruit and select effective salespeople. Hiring ineffective or non-performing salespeople affects the firm's ability to be successful in customer interaction situations. It is also costly because, beyond sales performance, it often directly affects the bottom line in terms of turnover and additional training. When done effectively though, salesperson selection can be a boon for the firm. Selecting salespeople most appropriate in the value-creating role can positively affect the firm's relationships with its customers through enhanced communication, better expertise, and salespeople similarity which expedites the engagement of relationship development activities (Palmatier et al. 2006).

Targeted Training

Sales training is among the most important factors for developing salespeople who are responsible for creating value for customers. Training salespeople in this particular role affects performance and differs from training salespeople to perform in the traditional influencer role. The most important topics to which these salespeople should be exposed include activities related to value creation and relationship management, such as actions, behaviors and efforts focused on strengthening customer relationships. The activities include social interaction, adaptive policies and procedures, conflict management, project management and all other initiatives that nurture a relational disposition in the salesperson–customer interaction (Anderson and Weitz 1992; Jap and Ganesan 2000). In addition, activities related to improving the efficiency, not just the effectiveness, of salespeople should be included to help salespeople develop knowledge and skills associated with profitable selling, such as understanding processes and acquisition of resources necessary to accomplish the role most effectively (Gwinner et al. 1998).

Beyond these topics for development, sales managers have other challenges associated with training, some of which are not idiosyncratic to the development of salespeople but rather are representative of the challenges all sales managers face, and perhaps more so when responsibilities include managing relationship managers. These topics include justifying training idiosyncratic to the relationship manager role. For example, establishing the amount of money that managers should spend on developing relationship managers, as opposed to the traditional influencer role, and justifying the expenditures are key challenges for sales managers with this responsibility. In addition, sales managers must measure the success of their training efforts, and traditional methods of evaluating the effectiveness of training efforts associated with performance must be updated to reflect relationship development strategies, goals and objectives.

RESEARCH IMPLICATIONS

As B2B firms focus more attention on building long-term, win–win relationships with key customers, the role of the salespeople shifts from influencer to value creator/relationship manager. Salespeople in this emerging role engage in activities that require behaviors and KSAs beyond those needed to be successful in the traditional influencer role. Different sales management practices are needed to support these value creator salespeople.

The nature of buyer–seller relationships is evolving to include both salespeople proficient in the traditional influencer role who focus on shorter-term objectives and strategies and simple transactions with a multitude of partners, and salespeople who are responsible for creating value for their customers and developing longer-term relationships with a select few customers (Kalwani and Narayandas 1995; Weitz and Bradford 1999). Recognizing the need for both roles and understanding the factors that lead to the development of each role and are associated with effectiveness are critical for organizational performance. Salespeople in the traditional role of influencer and salespeople in the role of value creator or relationship manager have similar keys to success. However, the importance of the salesperson effectiveness factors discussed in this chapter differs depending on the roles of the salespeople.

Salespeople have a portfolio of relationships within and across customers, and understanding how to manage across the portfolio is imperative. Factors that affect salesperson effectiveness in the traditional influencer role are associated with the achievement of shorter-term objectives in dealing with customers; that is, they are related to the development of professional relationships with customers and the development of repeat and profitable businesses. Similarly, the factors related to the effectiveness of salespeople in the value creator/relationship manager role are instrumental and necessary, but these salespeople go beyond the traditional influencer role by developing innovative solutions that involve the development of relationship-specific offerings that enhance long-term profits.

REFERENCES

Ahearn, Kathleen K., Gerald R. Ferris, Wayne A. Hochwarter, Ceasar Douglas and Anthony P. Ammeter (2004), 'Leader political skill and team performance', *Journal of Management*, **30** (3), 309–27.

Amabile, Teresa M. (1983), 'The social psychology of creativity: a componential conceptualization', *Journal of Personality & Social Psychology*, **45** (August), 357–76.

Amabile, Teresa M. (1988), 'A model of creativity and innovation in organizations', in B.M. Staw and L.L. Cummings (eds), *Research in Organizational Behavior*, Vol. 10, Greenwich, CT: JAI Press, pp. 123–67.

Amabile, Teresa M. and Regina Conti (1999), 'Changes in the work environment for creativity during downsizing', *Academy of Management Journal*, **42** (December), 630–40.

Anderson, Erin and Barton A. Weitz (1992), 'The use of pledges to build and sustain commitment in distribution channels', *Journal of Marketing Research*, **29** (1), 350–64.

Anderson, James C. and James A. Narus (1984), 'A model of the distributor's perspective of distributor–manufacturer working relationships', *Journal of Marketing*, **48** (Fall), 62–74.

Bell, Simon J. and Bülent Mengüç and Sara L. Stefani (2004), 'When customers disappoint: a model of relational internal marketing and customer complaints', *Journal of the Academy of Marketing Science*, **32** (Spring), 112–26.

Berry, Leonard L. (1995), 'Relationship marketing of services: growing interest, emerging perspectives', *Journal of the Academy of Marketing Science*, **23** (4), 236–45.

Biong, Harald and Fred Selnes (1996), 'The strategic role of the salesperson in established buyer–seller relationships', Marketing Science Institute, Report No. 96-118.

Boorom, Michael L., Jerry R. Goolsby and Rosemary P. Ramsey (1998), 'Relational communication and traits and their effect on adaptiveness and sales performance', *Journal of the Academy of Marketing Science*, **26** (1), 16–30.

Bradford, Kevin D. and Barton A. Weitz (2008), 'Salesperson's management of conflict in buyer–seller relationships', *Journal of the Academy of Marketing Science*, **29** (1), 25–42.

Brown, D.L. (1983), *Managing Conflict at Organizational Interfaces,* Reading, MA: Addison-Wesley.

Castleberry, Stephen B. and David Shepherd (1993), 'Effective interpersonal listening and personal selling', *Journal of Personal Selling & Sales Management*, **13** (Winter), 35–49.

Chakrabarty, Subhra, Gene Brown and Robert E. Widing (2010), 'Closed influence tactics: do smugglers win in the long run?', *Journal of Personal Selling & Sales Management*, **30** (1), 23–32.

Chonko, Lawrence B., Eli Jones, James A. Roberts and Alan J. Dubinsky (2002), 'Role of environmental turbulence, readiness for change, and salesperson learning in the success of sales force change', *Journal of Personal Selling & Sales Management*, **22**, (Fall), 227–45.

Coser, L.A. (1956), *The Functions of Social Conflict*, New York: Free Press.

Crosby, Lawrence A., Kenneth R. Evans and Deborah Cowles (1990), 'Relationship quality in services selling: an interpersonal influence perspective', *Journal of Marketing*, **54** (3), 68–81.

Dahrendorf, R. (1959), *Class and Class Conflict in Industrial Society*, Stanford, CA: Stanford University Press.

De Wulf, Kristoff, Gaby Odekerken-Schröder and Dawn Iacobucci (2001), 'Investments in consumer relationships: a cross-country and cross-industry exploration', *Journal of Marketing*, **65** (October), 35–50.

Deutsch, M. (1973), *The Resolution of Conflict*, New Haven, CT: Yale University Press.

Dietvorst, Roeland, Willem Verbeke, Richard Bagozzi, Carolyn Yoon, Marion Smits and Aad van der Lugt (2009), 'A sales force-specific theory-of-mind scale: tests of its validity by classical methods and functional magnetic resonance imaging', *Journal of Marketing Research*, **46** (5), 653–68.

Doney, Patricia M. and Joseph P. Cannon (1997), 'An examination of the nature of trust in buyer–seller relationships', *Journal of Marketing*, **61** (April), 35–51.

Ferris, Gerald R., Darren C. Treadway, Robert W. Kolodinsky, Wayne A. Hochwarter, Charles Kacmar, Ceasar Douglas and Dwight D. Frink (2005), 'Development and validation of the political skill inventory', *Journal of Management*, **31**, 126–52.

Franke, George R. and Jeong-Eun Park (2006), 'Salesperson adaptive selling behavior and customer orientation: a meta-analysis', *Journal of Marketing Research*, **43** (4), 693–702.

Giacobbe, Ralph, Donald R. Jackson, Lawrence A. Crosby and Claudia M. Bridges (2006), 'A contingency approach to adaptive selling behavior: selling situations and salesperson characteristics', *Journal of Personal Selling & Sales Management*, **26** (2), 115–142.

Gwinner, Kevin P., Dwayne D. Gremler and Mary Jo Bitner (1998), 'Relational benefits in services industries: the customer's perspective', *Journal of the Academy of Marketing Science*, **28** (2), 101–14.

Homburg, Christian, John P. Workman Jr and Ove Jensen (2002), 'A configurational perspective on key account management', *Journal of Marketing*, **66** (April), 38–60.

Jackson, B.B. (1985), *Winning and Keeping Industrial Customers: The Dynamics of Customer Relationship*, Lexington, MA: D.C. Heath.

Jap, Sandy D. and Shankar Ganesan (2000), 'Control mechanisms and the relationship life cycle: implications of safeguarding specific investments and developing commitment', *Journal of Marketing Research*, **37** (2), 227–45.

Jaramillo, Fernando and Douglas B. Grisaffe (2009), 'Does customer orientation impact objective sales performance? Insight from a longitudinal model in direct selling', *Journal of Personal Selling & Sales Management*, **29** (2), 167–78.

Jones, Eli, Steven Brown, Andris A. Zoltners and Barton A. Weitz (2005), 'Changing environment of selling and sales management', *Journal of Personal Selling & Sales Management*, **25**, 104–13.

Kalwani, Manohar U. and Narekasari Narayandas (1995), 'Long-term manufacturer–supplier relationships: do they pay off for supplier firms?', *Journal of Marketing*, **59** (January), 1–16.

Kogut, Bruce (1988), 'Joint ventures: theoretical and empirical perspectives', *Strategic Management Journal*, **9** (4), 319–32.

Lambert, Douglas M., Howard Marmorstein and Arun Sharma (1990), 'The accuracy of salespersons' perceptions of their customers: conceptual examination and empirical study', *Journal of Personal Selling & Sales Management*, **10** (Winter), 1–9.

Leifer, Richard and Andre Delbecq (1978), 'Organizational/environmental interchange: a model of boundary spanning activity', *Academy of Management Review*, **3** (1), 40–50.

Leigh, Thomas W. and Arno J. Rethans (1984), 'A script-theoretic analysis of industrial purchasing behavior', *Journal of Marketing*, **48** (4), 22–32.

Liu, Annie H. and Mark P. Leach (2001), 'Developing loyal customers with a value-adding sales force: examining customer satisfaction and the perceived credibility of consultative salespeople', *Journal of Personal Selling & Sales Management*, **21** (Spring), 147–56.

Mayer, Roger C., James H. Davis and F. David Schoorman (1995), 'An integrative model of organizational trust', *Academy of Management*, **20** (3), 709–34.

Morgan, Robert M. and Shelby D. Hunt (1994), 'The commitment–trust theory of relationship marketing', *Journal of Marketing*, **58** (July), 20–38.

O'Hara, Bradley S., James S. Boles and Mark W. Johnston (1991), 'The influence of personal variables on salesperson selling orientation', *Journal of Personal Selling & Sales Management*, **11** (Winter), 61–7.

Palmatier, Robert W., Rajiv P. Dant, Dhruv Grewal and Kenneth R. Evans (2006), 'Factors influencing the effectiveness of relationship marketing: a meta-analysis', *Journal of Marketing*, **70** (October), 136–55.

Palmatier, Robert W., Lisa K. Scheer, Jan-Benedict E.M. Steenkamp (2007), 'Customer loyalty to whom? Managing the benefits and risks of salesperson-owned loyalty', *Journal of Marketing Research*, **44** (2), 185–99.

Pettijohn, L.S., C.E. Pettijohn and A.J. Taylor (1999), 'An empirical investigation of the relationship between retail sales force performance appraisals, performance and turnover', *Journal of Marketing Theory & Practice*, **7** (Winter), 39–52.

Plouffe, Christopher R. and Donald W. Barclay (2007), 'Salesperson navigation: the intraorganizational dimension of the sales role', *Industrial Marketing Management*, **36** (4), 528–39.

Ramsey, Rosemary P. and Ravipreet S. Sohi (1999), 'Listening to your customers: the impact of perceived salesperson listening behavior on relationship outcomes', *Journal of the Academy of Marketing Science*, **25** (2), 127–37.

Roloff, M.E. and D.H. Cloven (1990), 'When partners transgress: maintaining violated relationships', in

Daniel J. Canary and Laura Stafford (eds), *Communication and Relational Maintenance*, San Diego, CA: Academic Press, pp. 23–43.

Rosch, Eleanor and Barbara B. Lloyd (1978), *Cognition and Categorization*, Oxford: Lawrence Erlbaum Associates.

Rosenbloom, B. (1987), *Marketing Channels: A Management View*, 3rd edn, New York: Dryden Press.

Schurr, Paul H. and Julie L. Ozanne (1985), 'Influences on exchange processes: buyer's preconceptions of a seller's trustworthiness and bargaining toughness', *Journal of Consumer Research*, **11** (March), 939–53.

Sharma, Arun, Michael Levy and Heiner Evanschitzky (2007), 'The variance in sales performance explained by the knowledge structures of salespeople', *Journal of Personal Selling & Sales Management*, **27** (2), 169–81.

Shepherd, C. David, Stephen B. Castleberry and Rick E. Ridnour (1997), 'Linking effective listening with salesperson performance: an exploratory investigation', *Journal of Business and Industrial Marketing*, **12** (5), 315–22.

Sheth, Jagdish N. and Arun Sharma (2008), 'The impact of the product to service shift in industrial markets and the evolution of the sales organization', *Industrial Marketing Management*, **37** (May), 260–69.

Spiro, Rosann and Barton A. Weitz (1990), 'Adaptive selling: conceptualization, measurement, and nomological validity', *Journal of Marketing Research*, **27** (February), 61–9.

Stern, Louis, Adel El-Ansary and Anne Coughlan (1996), *Marketing Channels*, 5th edn, Englewood Cliffs, NJ: Prentice Hall.

Sujan, Harish, Mita Sujan and James R. Bettman (1988), 'Knowledge structure differences between more effective and less effective salespeople', *Journal of Marketing Research*, **25** (1), 81–6.

Sujan, Harish, Baron A.Weitz and Nirmalya Kumar (1994), 'Learning orientation, working smart, and effective selling', *Journal of Marketing*, **58** (July), 39–52.

Sujan, Harish, Barton A. Weitz and Mita Sujan (1986), 'Knowledge, motivation, and adaptive behavior: a framework for improving selling effectiveness', *Journal of Marketing*, **50** (October), 174–91.

Tellefsen, Thomas and Nermin Eyuboglu (2002), 'The impact of a salesperson's in-house conflicts and influence attempts on buyer commitment', *Journal of Personal Selling & Sales Management*, **22** (3), 157–72.

Thomas, Kenneth W. (1976), 'Conflict and conflict management', in Marvin D. Dunnette (ed.), *Handbook of Industrial and Organizational Psychology*, Chicago, IL: Rand McNally, pp. 889–935.

Üstüner, Tuba and David Godes (2006), 'Better sales networks', *Harvard Business Review*, **84** (7–8), 102–12.

Weitz, Barton A. (1978), 'Relationship between salesperson performance and understanding of customer decision making', *Journal of Marketing Research*, **15** (4), 501–16.

Weitz, Barton A. (1981), 'Effectiveness in sales interactions: a contingency framework', *Journal of Marketing*, **45** (Winter), 85–103.

Weitz, Barton A. and Kevin D. Bradford (1999), 'Personal selling and sales management: a relationship marketing perspective', *Journal of the Academy of Marketing Science*, **27** (2), 241–54.

Weitz, Barton A., Stephen B. Castleberry and John F. Tanner (2007), *Selling: Building Partnerships*, 6th edn, New York: McGraw-Hill/Irwin.

Weitz, Barton A., Harish Sujan and Mita Sujan (1986), 'Knowledge, motivation, and adaptive behavior: a framework for improving selling effectiveness', *Journal of Marketing*, **50** (4), 174–91.

Wolff, Hans-Georg and Klaus Moser (2009), 'Effects of networking on career success: a longitudinal study', *Journal of Applied Psychology*, **94** (1), 196–206.

Woodman, Richard W., John E. Sawyer and Ricky W. Griffin (1993), 'Toward a theory of organizational creativity', *Academy of Management Review*, **18** (April), 293–321.

Wotruba, Thomas R. (1991), 'The evolution of personal selling', *Journal of Personal Selling & Sales Management*, **11** (3), 1–12.

Zhang, XiaoMeng and Kathryn M. Bartol (2010), 'Linking empowering leadership and employee creativity: the influence of psychological empowerment, intrinsic motivation, and creative process engagement', *Academy of Management Journal*, **53** (1), 107–28.

24 Boundary work and customer connectivity in B2B front lines

Jagdip Singh, Detelina Marinova and Steven P. Brown

To build long-term customer relationships, salespeople play a critical boundary-spanning role that can be an inimitable source of competitive strength (Cannon and Perreault 1999; Doney and Cannon 1997; Rackham and DeVincentis 1998; Weitz and Bradford 1999). A key characteristic of such roles is the boundary work[1] that salespeople perform to develop strategies and tactics to manage their interfaces with customers (Adams 1976; Brown 1990; McFarland et al. 2006; Soldow and Thomas 1984; Solomon et al. 1985; Spiro and Weitz 1990). Recent studies suggest that new realities are reconfiguring and redefining boundary work in the front lines of B2B interfaces. For example, Hunter and Perreault (2007) focus on salespeople's relationship-forging tasks or tactics that 'blur' boundaries by building strong relationships. Grayson (2007) finds that salespeople must enact divergent boundary roles of 'friends' and 'businesspeople' and manage the inherent conflict between them to build effective relationships. Likewise, in reviewing the evolution of sales roles in B2B contexts, Bradford et al. (2010, p. 241) observe that an embedded sales role emerges in which a salesperson's effectiveness depends on functionally integrating 'organizational subunits' with 'customer's subunits' to create customized solutions.

These recent studies underscore Heide and Wathne's (2006, p. 85) assessment that boundary work raises 'practical barriers' to developing customer relationships and that many 'firms frequently fail in these efforts'. Consistent with this, Evans et al. (1998, p. 32) note that 'considerable development' of a theory of boundary work is needed for 'successful relationship sales strategies'.

The purpose of this chapter is to motivate development of boundary role theory that responds to emerging realities of boundary work and stimulates an organizing framework to germinate new directions for theory and practice. Specifically, the chapter's objectives are twofold. First, we provide a focused review of the boundary role research in B2B contexts. In doing so, we outline its key theoretical principles and critically assess prior empirical work. Our review reveals that boundary role theory has received widespread attention in the literature but also that most studies are guided by a tactical rather than strategic focus. Second, we describe features of boundary work that demand a strategic perspective and rethinking of the premises of contemporary boundary role theory. In particular, we focus on customer-, competitor- and organization-driven forces that are dramatically shifting the nature and scope of boundary work (Bradford et al. 2010; Davie et al. 2010; Jones et al. 2005).

To develop the implications of these forces, we use the rhetorical device of a myth–reality framework to highlight five specific challenges to contemporary boundary role theory. Although contrasting myths of contemporary role theory with evolving realities of boundary work risks exaggeration of differences, it is constructive for provoking theory development and new research directions. We recognize that useful theories, as boundary role theory certainly is, are rarely static and cast in stone; rather, they evolve with the phenomena they represent, and certain principles derived from them may enable a useful rhetorical contrast. In this sense, our myth–reality framework should be viewed as a device for sharpening differences to motivate a discontinuous shift in the evolution of boundary role theory. Specifically, we develop five lines of myth–reality differences and build on them to suggest fresh approaches to boundary role theory in B2B marketing. We begin with a review of relevant literature.

BOUNDARY ROLE THEORY IN B2B FRONT LINES: ORIGINS AND REVIEW

Role theory has emerged as one of the most prominent paradigms for understanding sales performance and other frontline capabilities, in part because it develops coherent role identities from the integration of performative and social role dimensions (that is, it portrays roles as enacted specifically with respect to particular relational partners; e.g. Belasco 1966; Biddle 1986; Burke and Reitzes 1981; Sarbin and Allen 1968; Solomon et al. 1985). Role theory asserts that salespeople, using mastery over a wide range of routines, scripts and associated behaviors (Leigh and McGraw 1989), enact a coherent set of behaviors and activities that are recognizable markers of prototypical, easily categorized role identities (Arnett et al. 2003; Elsbach 2004; Fiske and Taylor 1991). For example, successful enactment of a prototypical identity (e.g. 'friend') validates and confirms a salesperson's standing in the customer's mind as someone who can be trusted to collaborate constructively. In addition, salespeople's enactment of a prototypical identity (e.g. 'friend') invokes socially coded scripts that allow customers to infer the unspoken norms and expectations that guide interactions toward desired outcomes (e.g. mutual cooperation and commitment; Solomon et al. 1985).

Building on microsociological notions of rituals, codes and artifacts in symbolic interactionism (Sarbin and Allen 1968), much research in marketing has conceived of roles as a useful unit of analysis for understanding a wide range of boundary work phenomena in B2B contexts. For example, Dudley and Narayandas (2006) discuss Hewlett-Packard's selling and training approach as being built around the roles of 'value-added supplier' (with focus on specialized services and knowledge) and 'trusted advisor' (with focus on total solutions), which salespeople are trained to enact with customers.

Empirical work on role theory in marketing has roots in Belasco's (1966) early observations of a salesperson's role demands. Rizzo et al.'s (1970) development of validated scales to measure role conflict and ambiguity provided a boost to boundary role work in marketing. By the mid-1990s, Brown and Peterson (1993) were able to quantitatively review 59 studies that focused specifically on salesperson role conflict and ambiguity in relation to performance and job satisfaction. Applications of boundary role theory are now evident in research involving a wide range of boundary-spanning contexts, including customer service employees, buyers, retail managers, product managers and account managers, in addition to salespeople, who remain the most studied group. Thus, although early studies of boundary roles focused on salesperson roles, the underlying theory has been enriched and empirical generalizations achieved by application to a diversity of frontline roles.

Providing a comprehensive review of the vast body of work on boundary roles in marketing is virtually impossible within the confines of a chapter and is beyond the scope of our current effort (for a recent review, see Singh and Saatcioglu 2008). Our purpose is to present the key themes and approaches that typify boundary role theory applications in marketing. Accordingly, we identified a sampling of key articles published between 1990 and 2010 in five major marketing journals (*Journal of Marketing*, *Journal of Marketing Research*, *Journal of Retailing*, *Journal of the Academy of Marketing Science* and *Journal of Business Research*) using the search words 'boundary', 'role' and 'theory'.[2] We reviewed each article identified as a candidate for inclusion to ensure that the reported study: (1) used some aspect of boundary role theory; (2) had empirical content; and (3) did not use the same data as another included study. In addition, consistent with the focus of this handbook, we generally preferred articles for inclusion that involved B2B contexts. We summarized studies that met these criteria by identifying the role theory concepts used, role theory hypotheses, sample type and key findings. Table 24.1 provides an abbreviated version of our review. Space limitations do not permit inclusion of a full version, which is available in a web appendix (see http://handbook.isbm.org).

Although a review of Table 24.1 confirms the widespread application of boundary role theory in diverse marketing contexts, in general empirical research has focused on boundary *roles*, paying little attention to the underlying boundary *strategy* they are designed to support or to the specific role *behaviors* that are required to support different roles. As a result, much of what is known about marketing boundary roles is tactical (e.g. how to enhance salesperson performance) and predominantly rooted in theoretical paradigms of control, coping and constraint (e.g. how to control salesperson behavior and effort, how to facilitate salesperson coping with role stress, how role stress constrains salesperson performance). Largely absent from the literature are studies that focus on strategic issues related to organizational front lines, such as salespeople's role in shaping firm boundaries (e.g. maintain or blur them), sustaining competitive advantages (e.g. innovate organizational systems for customer value creation) and learning from market interactions (e.g. new knowledge is generated at customer interfaces).

Such a view of the nature and limits of roles is problematic because it is based on past realities that in today's markets may be more myth than fact. Three forces combine to reconfigure and redefine boundary work at B2B interfaces. First, dissatisfied with homogeneous products and services for their heterogeneous needs and wants, customers increasingly demand customization in boundary interactions. Customization is essentially a boundary problem, the solution to which lies in the dynamics of boundary interactions. To customize, organizations need to incorporate the specific needs and wants of individual customers, as revealed in past or current boundary interactions. Some customers may desire an arm's-length (acquaintance) relationship characterized by clearly defined boundaries, whereas others may prefer a close (friend) relationship that blurs organizational boundaries. Moreover, customer needs for customization may change dynamically over time. In response, organizations have shifted attention from

Table 24.1   Selected review of the literature on boundary role theory in marketing

Authors	Role Theory Concepts	Role Theory Hypotheses	Sample	Findings
Crosby, Evans and Cowles (1990)	Relational Quality	Relationship quality, defined by similarity, domain expertise and role behaviors, affects salesperson's effectiveness.	469 randomly selected life insurance policy holders; 25 to 44 years age group.	Relational role behaviors are the strongest predictor of relationship quality; however, relationship quality is not associated with effectiveness.
Lusch and Serpkenci (1990)	Role Stress Theory and Individual Differences	Self-esteem, achievement orientation, and inner-direction are negatively associated with job tension and positively with job satisfaction. Job tension diminished performance and satisfaction.	182 retail store managers.	Job tension significantly impairs performance, and substantially reduces satisfaction. Managers with higher achievement orientation and inner directedness experience lower tension.
Singh and Rhoads (1991)	Role Ambiguity	Boundary spanner's role ambiguity has multidimensional facets (e.g. company, boss, customers) that relate differentially with job outcomes (e.g. performance, satisfaction).	472 US-based members of the Sales and Marketing Executives association. 216 boundary spanners (sales and service) from divisions of a US-based Fortune 500 industrial manufacturer.	Job satisfaction is affected more strongly by company and boss role ambiguity, while job performance is influenced more strongly by customer ambiguity. Global measures of role ambiguity under-identify the ambiguity experienced by boundary spanners.
Brown and Peterson (1994)	Role Stress and Effort	Role stressors diminish effort, while competitiveness and instrumentality enhance it. In turn, effort directly and indirectly influences job satisfaction.	380 US-based sales people involved in door-to-door selling of durable products.	Role conflict, but not role ambiguity, reduces effort. Effort has a direct rather than indirect effect on satisfaction and performance.

Author (Year)	Theory	Description	Sample	Findings
Challagalla and Shervani (1996)	Role Stress (e.g. customer role ambiguity) and Control (e.g. information, reward) Theories	Output, activity and capability controls reduce the level of role ambiguity; which subsequently has a negative effect on satisfaction and performance.	270 salespeople from five industrial product divisions of two Fortune 500 companies.	Information-based controls consistently diminish supervisor and customer role ambiguity, while punishments have mixed effects. Reward controls have marginal influence on role ambiguity. Customer role ambiguity is more detrimental for performance, while supervisor role ambiguity is more significant for reducing satisfaction.
Hartline and Ferrell (1996)	Role Stress Theory; Employee-Role Interface	Role ambiguity and conflict negatively influence customers' service quality evaluations; this effect is mediated by self-efficacy, job satisfaction, and adaptability.	561 customer contact employees in the hotel industry.	Role ambiguity has significant negative effects, as proposed; whereas role conflict does not. Role conflict is positively influenced by empowerment and increases self-efficacy.
MacKenzie, Podsakoff and Ahearne (1998)	Role Theory; Distinguishing In-role and Extra-role Performance	Role ambiguity and conflict negatively influence in-role performance. In-role performance positively affects organizational commitment and satisfaction, both of which enhance extra-role performance.	672 commission salespeople from a large insurance company.	As proposed, role ambiguity and conflict diminish in-role performance. In addition, role ambiguity and conflict directly and negatively affect commitment and satisfaction. Weak results obtained for extra-role performance.
Singh (1998)	Role Stress Theory	Role stressors (role ambiguity, conflict and overload) and job characteristics (feedback, autonomy have an inverted U-relationship with job performance). Job characteristics such as feedback, autonomy also have an inverted U-relationship.	Sample 1: 1850 members of Sales and Marketing Executives (SME) association. Sample 2: 520 sales and marketing professionals Fortune 500 MNCs.	Inverted U-effects are generally not supported. Significant linear effects and interaction effects between role stressors and job characteristics are obtained.

Table 24.1 (continued)

Authors	Role Theory Concepts	Role Theory Hypotheses	Sample	Findings
Flaherty, Dahlstrom and Skinner (1999)	Role Stress Theory	Discrepancy in salesperson's perceived and desired organizational customer orientation influences role conflict and ambiguity. Role variables negatively affect customer-oriented selling performance.	402 salespeople from various firms.	Both role ambiguity and conflict are amplified by customer orientation discrepancy. Only role ambiguity substantially constrains customer-oriented selling performance.
Shoemaker (1999)	Salesperson Role and Leadership Practices Model	Evolving salesperson role focuses on five practices: (1) Challenging the Process, (2) Inspiring a Shared Vision, (3) Enabling Others to Act, (4) Modeling the Way and (5) Encouraging the Heart which are positively related to salesperson role clarity and job satisfaction.	158 salespeople from an electrical/electronic control component manufacturer.	Leadership role practices are positively associated with job satisfaction. No significant relationships among leadership practices and self-efficacy were found. With one exception, leadership role practices are positively associated with role clarity.
Atuahene-Gima and Li (2002)	Role Stress (e.g., ambiguity) and Control (e.g., process, outcome) Theories	Role ambiguity diminishes supervisee trust, and this negative effect is stronger in China than in the US.	Chinese sample consisted of 157 onsite interviews from salespersons located in Beijing's High Technology Experimental Zone. US sample frame consisted of 190 salespeople who worked in manufacturing firms.	Role ambiguity interacts with supervisee trust to enhance sales performance in the Chinese sample; in contrast US sample shows a marginally negative interaction effect.

Author	Topic	Description	Data	Findings
De Jong, Ruyter and Lemmink (2004)	Role Diversity, Role Stress, Inter-role Behavior	Tolerance for self-management and flexibility of team members positively affect employees' perceptions of the Self-Managing Teams (SMT) service climate.	Multi-source data comprising: (1) a longitudinal study of 61 SMT members yielding 939 survey responses at time 1 and 730 responses at time 2, and (2) 1884 customer surveys.	Tolerance for self-management, flexibility, and inter- and intrateam support have a direct, positive impact on individual employees' service-climate perceptions. SMT service climate perceptions have a positive impact on customer perceived service quality and share of customer and a negative effect on sales productivity.
Bhuian, Mengüç and Borsboom (2005)	Role Stress Theory	Role ambiguity and conflict have nonlinear effects on job performance, job satisfaction, life satisfaction and turnover intentions. The nonlinear effects include inverted-U and triphasic relationships.	203 salespersons and their sales managers representing 11 industrial companies in New Zealand.	Mixed support for non-linear effects, although the effects are unequivocally dysfunctional (e.g., negative for job satisfaction).
Ferguson, Paulin and Bergeron (2005)	Contractual and Relational Governance of Boundary Spanners	Boundary spanner closeness to the client company is positively related to the use of relational versus contractual governance in the exchange and greater exchange performance.	60 business clients and their account managers at seven commercial banks in three countries.	In regard to exchange performance, relational governance is more predominant governance mechanism than contractual governance. Also closeness between boundary spanner and the client company positively affects exchange performance.

Table 24.1 (continued)

Authors	Role Theory Concepts	Role Theory Hypotheses	Sample	Findings
Harris, Artis, Walters and Licata (2006)	Resourcefulness and Stressors in Customer Service Roles	Role ambiguity and role conflict are negatively associated with resourcefulness. Customer orientation mediates the effect of resourcefulness on job satisfaction.	140 employees of a large bank in Southeastern US.	Role stressors constrain the resourcefulness of service employees, and act as an countervailing force against the: (1) positive effects of resourcefulness on job satisfaction and (2) negative effects of resourcefulness on intentions to turnover.
Karatepe, Yavas, Babakus and Avci (2006)	Role stress, role ambiguity and self efficacy, role conflict and job satisfaction	The negative relationship between: (1) role ambiguity and self-efficacy, (2) role conflict and self efficacy, (3) role ambiguity and job satisfaction, and (4) role conflict and job satisfaction is stronger for frontline female employees than male employees.	362 usable surveys from frontline employees working in 21 banks in the Turkish Republic of Northern Cyprus.	Role conflict has a significantly stronger impact on females' job satisfaction.
Arnold, Flaherty, Voss and Mowen (2009)	Cognitive Appraisal Theory; Role Stress Theory	A highly competitive climate diminishes the negative relationship between a retail employee's perception of role conflict, role ambiguity and family–work conflict and job efficacy. The positive relationship between a retail employee's job satisfaction and performance will be stronger in a more competitive climate.	374 responses (262 for supervisor related performance) collected from a national sample of retail store employees of a large US-based retailer.	Support for the moderating effect of climate on the role ambiguity–job efficacy relationship, such that the harmful effect of role ambiguity is lessened when competitive climate is high. Higher levels of job satisfaction result in improved performance when the competitive climate is perceived as high.

Homburg, Wieseke and Bornemann (2009)	Role Orientation and Playing	The more the frontline employees adopt customer orientation roles, the greater their accuracy of customer needs knowledge. The more the frontline employees participate in role playing training the greater their accuracy of customer needs knowledge.	Two large-scale field studies in German travel agencies. Study 1: 215 employees and 370 customers in 92 travel agencies. Study 2: 105 travel agencies with 237 employees and 489 customers.	Role orientation and role-playing training have an interactive effect on accuracy of customer need knowledge.
Joshi (2010)	Salesperson Role Behaviors	Role behaviors that build salesperson trustworthiness amplify the positive influence of compliance-generating strategies, and mitigate the negative influence of compliance-impeding strategies.	149 product managers in industrial machinery, electronic/electrical equipment and transporation industries.	Enhancing and protective effects of salesperson trustworthiness are supported. Salespeople are encouraged to engage in role behaviors that build trustworthiness.
Bell, Mengüç and Widing (2010)	Social Learning in Individual Salesperson Roles	Organizational learning is bolstered when salespeople include learning in their roles; Organizational climate for learning and efficiency of information dissemination amplify this effect.	422 area sales managers from 113 retail stores.	Salesperson learning mediated by organizational learning significantly enhances store performance. Learning climate amplifies the effect of salesperson learning, but dissemination efficiency does not.

boundary *transactions* to boundary *interactions* that build, grow and sustain customer relationships. Boundary interactions go beyond consummating exchanges to include boundary bridging and blurring (Hunter and Perreault 2007). In boundary bridging, organizations reach out to customers to access knowledge about how their products and services solve idiosyncratic customer problems in situ. Through boundary blurring, organizations make boundaries permeable to facilitate knowledge development and transfer through customer co-production and co-creation processes. Together, boundary bridging and blurring enrich both the breadth and depth of variation in boundary roles.

Second, technological advances and globalization have intensified competitive pressures. For example, in a survey of practitioners in B2B markets, Zoltners et al. (2008) find that managers identified external threats in terms of 'increasing buyer power', 'new competitors entering markets', 'competitors offering lower prices', 'industry deregulation' and 'new forms of distribution threatening existing channels'. Technology has opened markets by demolishing barriers and allowing far-flung competitors to enter new markets with few constraints. It has also enabled those endowed with abundant resources to influence markets dramatically by pressuring prices and setting new price–quality frontiers.

Ironically, the increasing intensity of competition has amplified the importance of boundary work in achieving sustainable competitive advantage. For example, Boaz et al. (2010) surveyed more than 1200 purchasing managers to find that though they insisted that price was a dominant factor, their *actual* vendor performance evaluation was more heavily influenced by overall sales experience. Critical to overall sales experience is boundary work that engages customers effectively with meaningful interactions, demonstrates competence in effective problem-solving based on sound product knowledge and breeds trust by placing customers' interests above self-interest. Although these topics are seeping into empirical research on boundary work in marketing (Hunter and Perreault 2007), theoretical development of boundary role theory has lagged.

Third, to cope with increasingly uncertain and competitive environments, firms have begun to think strategically about boundary work by actively managing the scope and significance of boundary roles (Storbacka et al. 2009). In the area of sales management, this shift is evident in the growing interest in key account and strategic account management (KAM/SAM). These approaches view boundary roles as critical, not just for facilitating exchanges but also for forging and building the lifetime value of long-term relationships with key customers (Homburg et al. 2002). This approach acknowledges that boundary role personnel manage the organization's most important asset: its customers.

From this point of view, boundary work encompasses the task of leading inter-functional coordination efforts to respond to customization needs and management for profitability in customer relationships (Storbacka et al. 2009). Many KAM/SAM programs involve cross-functional teams, including marketing personnel that salespeople coordinate in the interest of connecting closely with customers (Homburg et al. 2002). Using case studies in B2B contexts, Storbacka et al. (2009) identify three themes that characterize the evolving sales role: (1) from sales as a function to customer management as a process; (2) from isolated to integrated sales departments that rely on

Table 24.2 Changing boundary work for customer connectivity: myths and new market realities

Myth	Reality
Boundary roles are a consequence of well-defined job descriptions and the people who fill them.	Boundary roles are a consequence of emergent processes for keeping marketing promises.
Effectiveness of boundary roles involves implementation issues, such as execution of customer-contact scripts and reliable performance.	Effectiveness of boundary roles involves building dynamic customer interface capabilities that create value, are hard to imitate and yield competitive advantages.
Organizational boundaries are exogenous to boundary roles. The purpose of theory is to understand and manage boundary roles for effective maintenance of organizational boundaries.	Organizational boundaries are endogenous to boundary roles. The purpose of theory is to understand the interconnectedness of boundary managing and making for organizational effectiveness.
Theories for understanding boundary roles are rooted in human resource logics, such as control, motivation and empowerment.	Theories for understanding boundary roles are rooted in marketing logics, such as relationships, value and competition.
Boundary roles are central to knowledge exploitation.	Boundary roles are as central to knowledge exploitation as they are to knowledge exploration.

cross-functional teams; and (3) from operational focus on selling to strategic focus on customer problem-solving. Emergent practice in B2B relationships is moving toward *inter*-organizational project teams that either involve two or more suppliers teaming up to provide superior solutions to a buyer or involve members from buyer and seller organizations collaborating to provide customized solutions to buyers (Jones et al. 2005).

Despite this increasing attention to the expanding role of team selling in practice, theoretical and empirical research remains limited. In a rare empirical study, Stock (2006) finds that *inter-organizationality* in buyer–seller teams – the degree to which power and membership is balanced – enhances team effectiveness, especially when market and technological uncertainty are high. Thus, approaches to boundary roles that do not take into account their expanded scope (e.g. blurred internal and external boundaries; management of relationship value) are likely to be out of step with emergent practice.

Collectively, customer-, competitor- and organization-driven forces challenge key principles and concepts of boundary role theory, as we develop next. As noted previously, we present these challenges in a myth–reality rhetorical framework in which we present boundary role principles that are out of step with emergent practice as myths. We purposely build this contrast to stimulate (or perhaps provoke) fresh theoretical ideas, with full recognition that we risk drawing black-and-white comparisons in some gray areas. Table 24.2 summarizes the five key contrasts we develop to challenge conventional thinking about boundary roles and crystallize emergent ideas for new conceptualizations.

CHALLENGES TO CONTEMPORARY BOUNDARY ROLE THEORY: MYTH AND REALITY

Myth 1: Boundary Roles are a Consequence of Well-defined Job Descriptions and the People who Fill Them

Conventional wisdom in role theory construes 'boundary roles' as a means for translating supplier and buyer goals into sets of specific expectations for boundary spanner performances (Adams 1976; Biddle and Thomas 1966). Often, organizational manuals, training programs and cultural norms institutionalize role expectations by specifying desired behaviors of individual salespeople. In turn, role behaviors can be monitored and linked to incentives to align salesperson goals with those of the firm. However, this does not imply that role expectations are free of conflict or ambiguity (Singh and Saatcioglu 2008). Because of their different goals, supervisors and customers may have different, often contrasting role expectations; supervisors expect salespeople to give priority to organizational goals, while customers expect salespeople to give priority to their goals. Likewise, behavior–goal linkages can rarely be fully specified unambiguously. Although role theory does not discuss goal-directed role expectations explicitly, it does theorize concepts such as role conflict and ambiguity as resulting from the differing behavioral expectations of diverse role partners (e.g. suppliers, customers). Moreover, drawing from the literature on role stress, boundary role theory offers a sturdy framework for examining the functional and dysfunctional consequences of conflicted and ambiguous role expectations for salespeople's performance and well-being (Kahn et al. 1964).

This approach, focusing on human capital, encourages firms to strike a balance between role expectations and organizational support to ensure the effectiveness and welfare of boundary spanners (Singh 1998). Findings from this literature suggest that the organization's setting of role expectations and boundary spanners' efforts to meet them are complex processes that can result in dysfunctional outcomes for organizations and their employees.

Emergent conceptions of boundary roles reject the deterministic notions that role expectations are relatively static and prescribed by external role partners with enough specificity to enable consistent and uniform performances by groups of role incumbents. Recent research has noted that individuals do not simply enact socially encoded roles. Instead, as customer-, competition- and organization-driven forces increase market dynamism and uncertainty, salespeople proactively craft their *own* roles to satisfy environmental demands (e.g. What activities should I perform?) and shape their interactions (e.g. How should I interact with role partners? (Griffin et al. 2007; Wrzesniewski and Dutton 2001)). Although many roles involve sets of core activities and interactions that allow little flexibility (e.g. salespeople must meet sales quotas and interact with customers), role boundaries are also usually fuzzy, allowing emergent activities and interactions. These are often improvisational in response to unexpected contingencies and, in turn, result in dynamic change in roles (Ilgen and Hollenbeck 1992). Wrzesniewski and Dutton (2001) observe that when individuals have some flexibility, they attempt to assert control over outcomes and bring meaning to their roles through proactive role crafting. That is, individuals make situational claims about 'who they are and why what they do matters as part of the social identity created at work' without altering their authentic identity (Wrzesniewski and Dutton 2001, p. 180).

Thus, salespeople may claim the social identity of 'friend' to invoke scripts favoring intimacy and affection because they perceive this as conducive to favorable role outcomes. However, this 'strategic' identity may be limited to work, apply only to select customers and be distinct from other identities enacted with other customers. Griffin et al. (2007) note that role crafting is especially relevant when desired outcomes are uncertain and interdependent.

Focus on role crafting extends and transcends work on adaptive selling and influence tactics in sales management (Brown 1990; McFarland et al. 2006; Spiro and Perreault 1979; Spiro and Weitz 1990). Buyer heterogeneity renders a 'one-size-fits-all' approach ineffective and requires salespeople to adapt role crafting to the perceived needs of individual buyers and situations in which they interact (Spiro and Weitz 1990; Szymanski and Churchill 1990). Because both buyer needs and situations evolve and are not easily predictable, salespeople need to be continuously mindful of emergent changes and craft the roles they enact to maintain and build relationships with individual buyers (McFarland et al. 2006). Salespeople may also anticipate changes and engage in role crafting to influence buyer expectations and respond proactively. Role crafting constitutes a flexible, dynamic approach to boundary work that requires ambidexterity in the enactment of disparate roles.

Although few prior studies have advanced theoretical frameworks for adaptive boundary work, recent empirical studies highlight its theoretical relevance. For example, McFarland et al. (2006) find that salespeople are effective only when they match influence tactics to the individual orientations of buyers. No studies to date have examined salespeople's efforts to enact roles that match buyer orientations and create particular types of relationships with them. Practitioner reports suggest that such boundary work is common, and academic research acknowledges its importance (Brown 1990; Saxe and Weitz 1982).

Myth 2: Effectiveness of Boundary Roles Involves Implementation Issues, such as Execution of Customer-contact Scripts and Reliable Performance

The diverse body of boundary role literature in marketing indicates that providing an effective, efficient customer interface is the primary requirement of organizational front lines (Table 24.1). This is evident in the boundary role outcomes that are often examined in the marketing literature. Consistent with *customers'* role expectations that sales and service agents will be effective in fulfilling their needs, providing creative solutions and anticipating future problems, research has examined relationship quality, customer satisfaction and trust as key boundary work outcomes. In addition, consistent with the supplier organization's role expectation that sales and service agents will be efficient in serving customers, studies have focused on sales performance, productivity and profitability outcomes. Pursuing the divergent objectives of providing *effective* solutions and *efficient* operations exposes boundary agents to tensions and stress, as indicated by a substantial volume of research on role stress (Goolsby 1992; Hartline and Ferrell 1996; Singh 1998). A typical organizational response to the efficiency–effectiveness tension in boundary roles is development of exemplary scripts for customer contact and problem-solving that can be used for training and setting role expectations. The work of Solomon et al. (1985) constitutes an early attempt to elaborate on the notion of role scripts in service settings. Subsequent scripting of role performances has become a staple in professional selling (e.g. SPIN 'situation, problem, implication, need pay-off' selling; Friedman 2004). Scripting has been viewed as a quality control device to ensure that boundary agents do not deviate from desired actions and reliably deliver target outcomes.

Emerging practice, driven by customer, competitor and organizational forces, recognizes that a firm's competitive strength lies in consistently delivering superior value to customers who are differentially attracted to the company's products and services. To achieve this, a firm needs to build dynamic capabilities for providing superior value to heterogeneous customers without sacrificing operational efficiency. In conventional thinking, making special accommodations for customers constitutes a 'shock' to an efficiently designed value delivery system. However, in emergent thinking, boundary agents serve a critical role in developing individualized relationships with buying organizations and offer customized solutions with minimal disruption of the efficient operation of the firm's value delivery system. In this sense, a central element in emergent practice is the buffering role of boundary spanners in simultaneously accommodating the variability of customer needs and preserving the operational efficiency of core organizational processes.

Boundary work often involves tasking second-order boundary-spanning agents with handling customer demands that cannot be adequately addressed by the frontline agent. An example is a system that allows for escalating levels of customer service through utilization of technologically mediated frontline systems. Customer service problems that cannot be resolved on the boundary result in either dissatisfied customers and negative word of mouth or costly disturbances to the value delivery system to resolve the problem. Thus, customer selection and prioritization of efforts to serve customers who respond most favorably to the firm's value proposition have important strategic implications. Designing boundary work from a systems perspective remains a neglected theoretical and empirical topic.

More typically, firms are upgrading (i.e. *upskilling*) boundary roles to infuse them with capabilities for sensing and responding to dynamic and unpredictable customer heterogeneity. Boundary agents are viewed as problem-solvers who work closely with customers to co-create value customized for individual customers' needs. Such a view, which is increasingly becoming incorporated into the core principles of relationship marketing, redefines the meaning of scripts and deviations from them. While scripts are guides to behavior based on past experiences, deviations from them are deliberate efforts to collaborate, customize and co-create. Deviating from scripts to respond to changing customer needs and conditions is essential to boundary agent effectiveness. Thus, firm performance is enhanced by allowing boundary agents to deviate from standard scripts to accommodate customer heterogeneity, while buffering internal processes to promote operational efficiency. In this sense, the emergent view of boundary roles redefines the effectiveness–efficiency paradox as a frontline issue and highlights the importance of its resolution for enhancing firms' competitive position.

Myth 3: Organizational Boundaries are Exogenous to Boundary Roles

Conventional studies of contemporary boundary role theory focus on effectiveness in meeting or exceeding expectations set by organizations, including sales quota, complaints handled, customer satisfaction and service quality (Behrman and Perreault 1984; Hunter 2004; Singh 1998; Solomon et al. 1985). Thus, much research has embraced theoretical perspectives that predict the influence of different individual, group, organizational and environmental factors on boundary role effectiveness. The premise underlying these theories is that organizational boundaries are fixed or exogenous and that they remain stable to allow predictions of boundary role effectiveness without accounting for endogeneity or variability in boundaries.

Focusing on boundary roles and performance in them without considering the boundaries themselves ignores the boundary-making function of personnel who occupy boundary roles. Charged with responsibility for forging and growing relationships with external role partners, boundary role occupants do not simply execute scripted routines outlined in given job manuals. Indeed, in many cases, they cannot. Most formal job requirements are incomplete contracts that do not fully specify role expectations or the specific boundaries that define the role (Wrzesniewski and Dutton 2001). Given incomplete contracts, role occupants must craft and construct their roles and negotiate boundaries with relational partners during role enactment. In this sense, role boundaries and expectations are emergent processes that occur during and are not separate from or antecedent to role enactment.

For example, in a B2C context, Price and Arnould (1999) found that role boundaries varied substantially in practice; some customers were averse to forming commercial friendships and preferred an arm's-length relationship, whereas others welcomed strong friendly bonds based on reciprocal self-disclosure. Likewise, in a B2B context, Heide and Wathne (2006) take a more dynamic view of boundary roles by viewing 'friends' (a relational identity that blurs boundaries) and 'businesspeople' (a transactional identity that affirms boundaries) as two extremes on a continuum and role partners engaged in a continuous negotiation of boundaries for mutual benefit. More important, because of the constant tension between the relational and transactional identities (Grayson 2007), role boundaries are neither predictable nor stable. Instead, they depend on how role partners craft and enact their roles.

Thus, boundary making and boundary managing are symbiotically linked processes that are inherent to boundary roles. Viewing boundary roles from this perspective reveals limitations of conventional theoretical approaches that omit the boundary-making function. In practice, outsourcing decisions amount to determinations of where firm boundaries should be located. The nature of boundary roles, in terms of demands imposed by customer, firm and transactional characteristics, is a primary influence on firms' boundary location decisions. Boundaries are not exogenous but are determined in large part by decisions regarding the most efficient and effective ways to fulfill boundary *roles.*

Myth 4: Theories for Understanding Boundary Roles are Rooted in Human Resource Logics

As is evident from the preceding discussion, a great volume of research has relied on theories of role stress, control and motivation to better understand boundary roles. Research drawing on role stress theory examines challenges posed by conflicting or ambiguous roles and individuals' coping mechanisms to maintain effectiveness and avoid burnout (Goolsby 1992). Research based on control theory explores how the focus (e.g. process or outcome), degree (tight or loose) and form (e.g. formal or informal) of organizational control systems direct boundary spanners toward organizational goals (Challagalla and Shervani 1996). Likewise, motivational studies examine how role occupants can be influenced to invest personal resources to achieve normative types and levels of performance using extrinsic incentives, goal setting and identity engagement, among other factors (Brown et al. 1997, 1998).

Although these theoretical approaches differ in perspective, they share a common focus on managing boundary-spanning personnel effectively. Conventional theories of human resources typically focus on practices and procedures for selecting, motivating, training and retaining employees to meet predetermined objectives. Such theoretical approaches are well suited to problems of managing for boundary role effectiveness, but they are not as well adapted to problems that involve dynamic boundary management processes.

Although recent human resource theories are beginning to embrace strategic perspectives, meaningful conceptions of emergent boundary practices require a fundamental departure from current approaches to focus on concepts such as learning, innovation and adaptability in customer interactions. Human resource theories do not provide adequate frameworks for addressing these concepts. Relationship theory begins to address these issues by shifting attention from roles to relationships by focusing on establishing, developing and maintaining sustainable relational exchanges with customers (Morgan and Hunt 1994). This shift does not diminish the significance of boundary roles. In their meta-analysis, Palmatier et al. (2006, p. 151) conclude that relationship marketing strategies are more effective when 'they are focused on building interpersonal relationships between boundary spanners [and customers] than [when they are] focused on building customer–firm relationships'. Weitz and Bradford (1999) characterized this shift as a move from 'making sales' to 'making and keeping relationships' through a partnering role of the salesperson rooted in relational selling (Crosby et al. 1990; Joshi 2010).

Likewise, the framework of the service-dominant (S-D) logic is consistent with boundary making because it emphasizes the centrality of value-creating processes in marketing-oriented organizations. In the S-D logic, the customer is always a co-creator of value, and marketing is an enabler ('facilitator and structurer') of the co-production process. The focus on customer primacy, in co-creation with boundary spanners, emphasizes boundary making, as individual boundary agents craft roles that enable co-creation of value for customers in light of their individual needs and contexts (Joshi 2010). Finally, the literature on sustainable competitive advantage has increasingly coalesced around a knowledge-based view of marketing organizations that coheres with relationship marketing and value co-creation perspectives. According to this view, organizations that are more effective in capturing new knowledge generated at customer interfaces *and* transferring it for use across organizational units are more likely to survive than those that are less adept at knowledge capture and transfer (Homburg et al. 2009). Although the role of knowledge in boundary spanning has received some attention in the marketing literature, the emergent view of knowledge-based organizations redefines and restructures boundary roles in ways that go far beyond conventional thinking.

Myth 5: Boundary Roles are Central to Knowledge Exploitation

Consistent with the conventional view of boundary roles, much contemporary research has been guided by the idea that boundary roles are fulfilled through top-down learning processes that exploit organizational knowledge. That is, rules and responsibilities emanating from the top levels of the organization are woven into boundary roles, which boundary role personnel then learn and enact. For example, Lam et al. (2010) demonstrate that through their actions, top managers function as marketing-oriented role models for middle managers and work group expert peers who, in turn, serve as envoys of market-oriented behavior to frontline employees.

Thus, the marketing strategy literature has traditionally developed frameworks characterizing intelligence dissemination as movement from strategic decision-makers to employees (or from marketing managers to non-marketing managers), who employ this intelligence in performing their job functions (e.g. Maltz and Kohli 2000). In a similar vein, Bharadwaj et al. (1993) argue that a critical factor for achieving competitive advantage in service organizations is corporate culture, characterized as a set of values and beliefs that govern the way employees act. Sharma et al. (2000) discuss how salespeople's knowledge structures with respect to customer needs are developed through proactive training and supervision. They conclude that when knowledge structures are rich and distinctive, they positively influence sales performance. Likewise, Morhart et al. (2009) show that structured training fosters frontline learning of brand-specific transformational leadership skills. In a similar vein, De Ruyter et al. (2009) examine the effectiveness of environmental information dissemination and its use in organizational front lines, and Sundaram et al. (2007) investigate the impact of salespeople's use of technology designed for distribution of market intelligence on individual sales performance. Finally, Wang and Netemeyer (2002) estimate the impact of job structure (e.g. autonomy) and task demands on salespeople's learning, which in turn influences their self-efficacy and service performance.

Emergent practice challenges the earlier focus on knowledge exploitation in boundary roles. The change and uncertainty wrought by customer-, competitor- and organization-driven forces foreshadow an enlarged scope of boundary work that emphasizes knowledge generation, rather than just exploitation. Knowledge generation involves exploration or 'the pursuit of knowledge, of things that might come to be known' (Levinthal and March 1993, p. 105) and involves 'variation, risk taking, experimentation, play, flexibility, discovery, [and] innovation' (March 1991, p. 71). Day (2000) argues that most working knowledge about customer relationships, especially in B2B settings, is tacit, dispersed and held by individual salespeople and account managers. Harnessing this dispersed knowledge is a key adaptive capability and an essential ingredient of competitive advantage. Joshi (2010) notes that B2B selling activity in the past two decades has shifted, such that salespeople must be skilled not only in managing customer relationships but also in communicating market knowledge back to the organization. He develops a process through which salespeople can successfully change the way product management teams develop and modify products. Similarly, Bell et al. (2010) find that salesperson learning has the potential to enhance retail performance of the firm by increasing its capacity for organizational learning. Furthermore, De Jong et al. (2004) recognize facets of bottom-up learning in their framework of service climate in boundary-spanning self-managed teams (SMTs). In operationalizing service climate, they capture the extent to which boundary-spanning SMTs make suggestions for improving service quality. Their findings indicate that the service climate of boundary-spanning SMTs has positive effects on perceived service quality and customer share and a negative effect on sales productivity, particularly for non-routine services.

The preceding is in line with emerging research that reveals the intricate role of frontline autonomy in effective services management. Marinova et al. (2008) demonstrate that frontline autonomy mediates the effects of strategic orientations for quality and productivity on revenue, efficiency and customer satisfaction. They also show that unit cohesion enhances the positive influence of autonomy on revenue and customer satisfaction without increasing its negative effect on productivity. Overall, functional mechanisms that support boundary role execution, such as frontline autonomy and self-management, are conducive to generation of knowledge-in-practice by frontline employees.

A bottom-up learning process is needed to codify such practice-driven knowledge and transform it for use in organizational adaptation and change. Knowledge generation and exploitation processes are closely linked and dynamically embedded in boundary roles. New theoretical approaches that jointly address knowledge exploration and exploitation processes are needed to help organizations maximize performance outcomes and more thoroughly integrate the contribution of front lines to organizational learning in marketing thought. Research has argued that for a firm to experience continual and long-term success, it must establish a balance between exploratory and exploitative activities (March 1991; Raisch et al. 2009). Theoretical approaches that focus narrowly on exploitation, however compelling, are unlikely to offer adequate explanations for the emergent practice.

MANAGERIAL IMPLICATIONS AND CONCLUSIONS

Managerially, this chapter focuses on and develops the implications of emerging market realities that increasingly challenge, and even marginalize, premises and predictions of contemporary boundary role theory in marketing. These new realities include customer-driven focus on co-creation and solution selling, competition-driven pressure on value creation and innovation and organizational emphasis on sales productivity and inter-functional cooperation. Admittedly, to highlight their implications, we have pushed the challenges of new realities to exaggerate contrasts and highlight differences. Nevertheless, the new market realities are significant enough to require that managers shed long-held principles, view boundary roles from new perspectives and construct fresh approaches. Managers as well as researchers motivated to pursue these possibilities should consider at least five clear implications of our work.

First, we recommend that managers consider and adopt new perspectives on boundary roles within their organizations that reflect emergent market realities and then systematically leverage these new perspectives for boundary spanner effectiveness. Managers may find it particularly useful to partner with researchers and consultants to support development of new role constructs (e.g. role crafting) and theorize their influence on boundary spanner performance, satisfaction and commitment. With rare exceptions, most role research in marketing has relied on outdated role constructs developed in the 1960s by management scholars. Original grounded work is needed that begins with in situ studies of role behaviors and practices of boundary spanners in B2B contexts to germinate new constructs that are meaningful instruments for understanding emergent realities. This area of development is ripe for practitioner–scholar partnership.

Second, our research suggests that managers develop a differentiated consideration of organizational boundaries that is rooted in a strategic perspective of boundary roles. With this differentiated perspective, organizational boundaries are neither fixed nor constant for all customers. Rather, managers need to strategically evaluate the following questions: for which customers should they blur boundaries, and conversely, for which customers should they maintain boundaries? What kinds of role behaviors are differentially associated with these choices? The answers are not obvious. Customers that are smaller in size and/or lower in profitability may be strategically more important because they offer unique boundary-learning opportunities not found elsewhere. Thus, managers are well advised to map and examine the relationship between boundary roles and organizational boundaries and the patterns associated with firm effectiveness.

Third, building on the differentiated perspective, we can advise managers that effective boundary management will probably require dynamic shifting among boundary making, blurring and maintaining functions in systematic patterns for the *same* customer. A customer who is in boundary-blurring relationships today may be involved in boundary-maintaining relationships tomorrow. Fresh thinking is needed to understand boundary role behaviors that support such dynamic transitions. From a theoretical perspective, this means that scholars and researchers need new theories for understanding boundary roles and boundary management as a dynamic strategic process with explicit consideration of the rate and direction of change. Such dynamic frameworks for navigating boundary making and blurring and maintaining functions are likely to yield new insights to guide managers' quest for sustainable competitive advantage.

Fourth, our research emphasizes that emergent realities will require that managers understand the knowledge-creating capabilities of boundary roles and the organizational implications of its exploitation. The learning capabilities that reside in organizational boundaries and the distinct competitive advantages they represent are both currently underappreciated and undertheorized. Boundary role behaviors that are crucial to such learning capabilities are unknown. Researchers can play a critical role in opening the black box of boundary role learning processes. Such processes can be understood as bottom-up learning, which has attracted recent attention and development. More grounded and experimental work is needed to develop a pragmatic mapping of boundary role behaviors conducive to learning and to determine whether such behaviors come at the cost of short-term effectiveness. Practitioners and scholars alike are challenged to resist viewing boundary role learning as inherently useful. Little is known about the extent to which knowledge generated through boundary role processes is useful and can be exploited to drive enterprise-wide change in managing organizational boundary roles.

Fifth, and finally, managers will need to rethink hiring, training and motivational approaches for boundary spanners based on new theorizing of boundary roles proposed here. New models are needed to understand how to attract, motivate and retain boundary spanners capable of conceiving and performing boundary role behaviors that respond, not to extant thinking, but to new and emergent realities. Our study is a blueprint for managers and researchers to embark on fresh thinking and develop new models.

NOTES

1. We use the term 'boundary work' to refer broadly to cognitive and behavioral efforts of salespeople to manage their boundaries with customers and develop relationships of appropriate type and intensity with a diversity of customers. We develop this term further herein.
2. While searching the literature, we identified several well-cited articles from the *Journal of Personal Selling & Sales Management* in the review. We included these articles in our review; however, we did not intend to conduct a more thorough search of this journal.

REFERENCES

Adams, J.S. (1976), 'The structure and dynamics of behavior in organizational boundary roles', in Marvin D. Dunnette (ed.), *Handbook of Industrial and Organizational Psychology*, Chicago, IL: Rand McNally, pp. 1175–99.
Arnett, B. Dennis, Steve D. German and Shelby D. Hunt (2003), 'The identity salience model of relationship marketing success: the case of nonprofit marketing', *Journal of Marketing*, **67** (2), 89–105.
Arnold, Todd, Karen E. Flaherty, Kevin E. Voss and John C. Mowen (2009), 'Role stressors and retail performance: the role of perceived competitive climate', *Journal of Retailing*, **85** (2), 194–205.
Atuahene-Gima, Kwaku and Haiyang Li (2002), 'When does trust matter? Antecedents and contingent effects of supervisee trust on performance in selling new products in China and the United States', *Journal of Marketing*, **66** (3), 61–81.
Behrman, Douglas N. and William D. Perreault Jr (1984), 'A role stress model of the performance and satisfaction of industrial salespersons', *Journal of Marketing*, **48** (4), 9–21.
Belasco, James (1966), 'The salesman's role revisited', *Journal of Marketing*, **30** (April), 6–8.
Bell, Simon J., Bülent Mengüc and Robert Widing II (2010), 'Salesperson learning, organizational learning and retail store performance', *Journal of the Academy of Marketing Science*, **38** (2), 187–201.
Bharadwaj, Sundar G., P. Rajan Varadarajan and John Fahy (1993), 'Sustainable competitive advantage in service industries: a conceptual model and research propositions', *Journal of Marketing*, **57** (4), 83–99.
Bhuian, Shahid N., Bulent Mengüc and Rene Borsboom (2005), 'Stressors and job outcomes in sales: a triphasic model versus a linear-quadratic-interactive model', *Journal of Business Research*, **58** (2), 141–50.
Biddle, Bruce J. (1986), 'Recent developments in role theory', *Annual Review of Sociology*, **12** (August), 67–92.
Biddle, Bruce J. and Edwin J. Thomas (1966), *Role Theory: Concepts and Research*, New York: John Wiley & Sons.
Boaz, Nate, John Murnane and Kevin Nuffer (2010), 'The basics of business-to-business sales success', *McKinsey Quarterly*, (May), 11–13.
Bradford, Kevin, Steven Brown, Shankar Ganesan, Gary Hunter, Vincent Onyemah, Robert Palmatier, Dominique Rouzies, Rosann Spiro, Harish Sujan and Barton Weitz (2010), 'The embedded sales force: connecting buying and selling organizations', *Marketing Letters*, **21** (3), 239–53.
Brown, Steven P. (1990), 'Use of closed influence tactics by salespeople: incidence and buyer attributions', *Journal of Personal Selling & Sales Management*, **10** (Fall), 17–29.
Brown, Steven P. and Robert A. Peterson (1993), 'Antecedents and consequences of salesperson job satisfaction: meta-analysis and assessment of causal effects', *Journal of Marketing Research*, **30** (1), 63–77.
Brown, Steven P. and Robert A. Peterson (1994), 'The effect of effort on sales performance and job satisfaction', *Journal of Marketing*, **58** (2), 70–80.
Brown, Steven, William L. Cron and John W. Slocum Jr (1997), 'Effects of goal-directed emotions on salesperson volitions, behavior, and performance: a longitudinal study', *Journal of Marketing*, **61** (1), 39–50.
Brown, Steven P., William L. Cron and John W. Slocum Jr (1998), 'Effects of trait competitiveness and perceived intraorganizational competition on salesperson goal setting and performance', *Journal of Marketing*, **62** (4), 88–98.
Burke, Peter J. and Donald C. Reitzes (1981), 'The link between identity and role performance', *Social Psychology Quarterly*, **44** (June), 83–92.
Cannon, Joseph P. and William D. Perreault Jr (1999), 'Buyer–seller relationships in business markets', *Journal of Marketing Research*, **36** (4), 439–60.
Challagalla, Goutam N. and Tasadduq A. Shervani (1996), 'Dimensions and types of supervisory control: effects on salesperson performance and satisfaction', *Journal of Marketing*, **60** (January), 89–105.
Crosby, Lawrence A., Kenneth R. Evans and Deborah Cowles (1990), 'Relationship quality in services selling: an interpersonal influence perspective', *Journal of Marketing*, **54** (3), 68–81.

Davie, Christopher, Tom Stephenson and Maria V. de Uster (2010), 'Three trends in business-to-business sales', *McKinsey Quarterly*, (May), 1–4.

Day, George S. (2000), 'Managing market relationships', *Journal of the Academy of Marketing Science*, **28** (1), 24–30.

De Jong, Ad, Ko de Ruyter and Jos Lemmink (2004), 'Antecedents and consequences of service climate in boundary-spanning self-managing service teams', *Journal of Marketing*, **68** (2), 18–35.

De Ruyter, Ko, Ad de Jong and Martin Wetzels (2009), 'Antecedents and consequences of environmental stewardship in boundary-spanning B2B teams', *Journal of the Academy of Marketing Science*, **37** (4), 470–87.

Doney, Patricia M. and Joseph P. Cannon (1997), 'An examination of the nature of trust in buyer–seller relationships', *Journal of Marketing*, **61** (April), 35–51.

Dudley, Robert C. and Das Narayandas (2006), 'A portfolio approach to sales', *Harvard Business Review*, **84** (July–August), available at http://hbr.org/2006/07/a-portfolio-approach-to-sales/ar/1.

Elsbach, Kimberly D. (2004), 'Interpreting workplace identities: the role of office décor', *Journal of Organizational Behavior*, **25** (1), 99–128.

Evans, Kenneth, D. Good and T. Hellman (1998), 'Relationship selling: new challenges for today's sales managers', in G. Bauer, M. Baunchalk, T. Ingram and R. LaForge (eds), *Emerging Trends in Sales Thought and Practice*, Westport, CT: Quorum Books, pp. 31–60.

Ferguson, Ronald J., Michèle Paulin and Jasmin Bergeron (2005), 'Contractual governance, relational governance, and the performance of interfirm service exchanges: the influence of boundary-spanner closeness', *Journal of the Academy of Marketing Science*, **33** (2), 217–34.

Fiske, Susan T. and Shelley E. Taylor (1991), *Social Cognition*, 2nd edn, New York: McGraw-Hill.

Flaherty, Theresa, Robert Dahlstrom and Steven J. Skinner (1999), 'Organizational values and role stress as determinants of customer-oriented selling', *Journal of Personal Selling & Sales Management*, **19** (Spring), 1–18.

Friedman, Walter A. (2004), *Birth of a Salesman: The Transformation of Selling in America*, Cambridge, MA: Harvard University Press.

Goolsby, Jerry R. (1992), 'A theory of role stress in boundary spanning positions of marketing organizations', *Journal of the Academy of Marketing Science*, **20** (March), 155–64.

Grayson, Kent (2007), 'Friendship versus business in marketing relationships', *Journal of Marketing*, **71** (4), 121–39.

Griffin, Mark A., Andrew F. Neal and Sharon K. Parker (2007), 'A new model of work role performance: positive behavior in uncertain and interdependent contexts', *Academy of Management Journal*, **50** (2), 327–47.

Harris, Eric G., Andrew B. Artis, Jack H. Walters and Jane W. Licata (2006), 'Role stressors, service worker job resourcefulness, and job outcomes: an empirical analysis', *Journal of Business Research*, **59** (4), 407–15.

Hartline, Michael D. and O.C. Ferrell (1996), 'The management of customer-contact service employees: an empirical investigation', *Journal of Marketing*, **60** (4), 52–70.

Heide, Jan B. and Kenneth H. Wathne (2006), 'Friends, businesspeople, and relationship roles: a conceptual framework and a research agenda', *Journal of Marketing*, **70** (3), 90–103.

Homburg, Christian, Jan Wieseke and Torsten Bornemann (2009), 'Implementing the marketing concept at the employee–customer interface: the role of customer need knowledge', *Journal of Marketing*, **73** (4), 64–81.

Homburg, Christian, John Workman Jr and Ove Jensen (2002), 'A configurational perspective on account management', *Journal of Marketing*, **66** (2), 38–60.

Hunter, Gary (2004), 'Information overload: guidance for identifying when information becomes detrimental to sales force performance', *Journal of Personal Selling & Sales Management*, **24** (2), 91–100.

Hunter, Gary and William D. Perreault Jr (2007), 'Making sales technology effective', *Journal of Marketing*, **71** (1), 16–34.

Ilgen, Daniel R. and John R. Hollenbeck (1992), 'The structure of work: job design and roles', in Marvin D. Dunnette and Leaetta M. Hough (eds), *Handbook of Industrial and Organizational Psychology*, Palo Alto, CA: Consulting Psychologists Press.

Jones, Eli, Steven Brown, Andris Zoltners and Barton Weitz (2005), 'The changing environment of selling and sales management', *Journal of Personal Selling & Sales Management*, **24** (2), 105–11.

Joshi, Ashwin W. (2010), 'Salesperson influence on product development: insights from a study of small manufacturing organizations', *Journal of Marketing*, **74** (1), 94–107.

Kahn, Robert L., Donald M. Wolfe, Robert P. Quinn, J. Diedrick Snoek and Robert A. Rosenthal (1964), *Organizational Stress: Studies in Role Conflict and Ambiguity*, New York: John Wiley & Sons.

Karatepe, Osman M., Ugur Yavas, Emin Babakus and Turgay Avci (2006), 'Does gender moderate the effects of role stress in frontline service jobs?', *Journal of Business Research*, **59** (10–11), 1087–93.

Lam, Son K., Florian Kraus and Michael Ahearne (2010), 'The diffusion of market orientation throughout the organization: a social learning theory perspective', *Journal of Marketing*, **74** (5), 61–79.

Leigh, Thomas W. and Patrick F. McGraw (1989), 'Mapping the procedural knowledge of industrial sales personnel: a script-theoretic investigation', *Journal of Marketing*, **53** (1), 16–34.

Levinthal, Daniel A. and James G. March (1993), 'The myopia of learning', *Strategic Management Journal*, **14** (Winter), 95–112.
Lusch, Robert F. and Ray R. Serpkenci (1990), 'Personal differences, job tension, job outcomes, and store performance: a study of retail store managers', *Journal of Marketing*, **54** (1), 85–101.
MacKenzie, Scott B., Philip M. Podsakoff and Michael Ahearne (1998), 'Some possible antecedents and consequences of in-role and extra-role salesperson performance', *Journal of Marketing*, **62** (3), 87–98.
Maltz, Elliot and Ajay K. Kohli (2000), 'Reducing marketing's conflict with other functions: the differential effects of integrating mechanisms', *Journal of the Academy of Marketing Science*, **28** (Fall), 479–92.
March, James G. (1991), 'Exploration and exploitation in organizational learning', *Organizational Science*, **2** (February), 71–87.
Marinova, Detelina, Jun Ye and Jagdip Singh (2008), 'Do frontline mechanisms matter? Impact of quality and productivity orientations on unit revenue, efficiency, and customer satisfaction', *Journal of Marketing*, **72** (2), 28–45.
McFarland, Richard G., Goutam N. Challagalla and Tasadduq A. Shervani (2006), 'Influence tactics for effective adaptive selling', *Journal of Marketing*, **70** (4), 103–17.
Morgan, Robert M. and Shelby D. Hunt (1994), 'The commitment–trust theory of relationship marketing', *Journal of Marketing*, **58** (3), 20–38.
Morhart, Felicitas M., Walter Herzog and Torsten Tomczak (2009), 'Brand-specific leadership: turning employees into brand champions', *Journal of Marketing*, **73** (6), 122–42.
Palmatier, Robert W., Rajiv P. Dant, Dhruv Grewal and Kenneth R. Evans (2006), 'Factors influencing the effectiveness of relationship marketing: a meta-analysis', *Journal of Marketing*, **70** (4), 136–53.
Price, Linda L. and Eric J. Arnould (1999), 'Commercial friendships: service provider–client relationships in context', *Journal of Marketing*, **63** (4), 38–56.
Rackham, Neil and John DeVincentis (1998), *Rethinking the Sales Force: Redefining Selling to Create and Capture Customer Value*, New York: McGraw-Hill.
Raisch, S., Julian Birkinshaw, Gilbert Probst and Michael L. Tushman (2009), 'Organizational ambidexterity: balancing exploitation and exploration for sustained performance', *Organization Science*, **20** (4), 685–95.
Rizzo, J.R., Robert J. House and S.I. Lirtzman (1970), 'Role conflict and ambiguity in complex organizations', *Administrative Science Quarterly*, **15** (2), 150–63.
Sarbin, Theodore R. and Vernon L. Allen (1968), 'Role Theory', in G. Lindzey and E. Aronson (eds), *Handbook of Social Psychology*, 2nd edn, Reading, MA: Addison-Wesley.
Saxe, Robert and Barton A. Weitz (1982), 'The SOCO scale: a measure of the customer orientation of salespeople', *Journal of Marketing Research*, **19** (3), 343–51.
Sharma, Arun, Michael Levy and Ajith Kumar (2000), 'Knowledge structures and retail sales performance: an empirical examination', *Journal of Retailing*, **76** (1), 53–69.
Shoemaker, Mary E. (1999), 'Leadership practices in sales managers associated with the self-efficacy, role clarity and job satisfaction of individual industrial salespeople', *Journal of Personal Selling & Sales Management*, **19** (4), 1–19.
Singh, Jagdip (1998), 'Striking a balance in boundary-spanning positions: an investigation of some unconventional influences of role stressors and job characteristics on job outcomes of salespeople', *Journal of Marketing*, **62** (3), 69–86.
Singh, Jagdip and Gary K. Rhoads (1991), 'Boundary role ambiguity in marketing-oriented positions: a multi-dimensional, multifaceted operationalization', *Journal of Marketing Research*, **28** (3), 328–38.
Singh, Jagdip and Argun Saatcioglu (2008), 'Role theory approaches for effectiveness of marketing oriented boundary spanners: comparative review, configural extension and potential contributions', in Naresh K. Malhotra (ed.), *Review of Marketing Research*, Vol. 4, New York: M.E. Sharp, pp. 148–82.
Soldow, Gary F. and Gloria Penn Thomas (1984), 'Relational communication: form versus content in the sales interaction', *Journal of Marketing*, **48** (Winter), 84–93.
Solomon, Michael R., Carol Surprenant, John A. Czepiel and Evelyn G. Gutman (1985), 'A role theory perspective on dyadic interactions: the service encounter', *Journal of Marketing*, **49** (Winter), 99–111.
Spiro, Rosann L. and William D. Perreault Jr (1979), 'Influence use by industrial salesmen: influence strategy mixes and situational determinants', *Journal of Business*, **52** (July), 435–55.
Spiro, Rosann L. and Barton A. Weitz (1990), 'Adaptive selling: conceptualization, measurement, and nomological validity', *Journal of Marketing Research*, **27** (1), 61–9.
Stock, R. Maria (2006), 'Interorganizational teams as boundary spanners between supplier and customer companies', *Journal of the Academy of Marketing Science*, **34** (4), 588–99.
Storbacka, Kaj, Lynette Ryals, Iain A. Davies and Suvi Nenonen (2009), 'The changing role of sales: viewing sales as a strategic, cross-functional process', *European Journal of Marketing*, **43** (7–8), 890–906.
Sundaram, Suresh, Andrew Schwarz, Eli Jones and Wynne W. Chin (2007), 'Technology use on the front line: how information technology enhances individual performance', *Journal of the Academy of Marketing Science*, **35** (February), 101–12.

Szymanski, David M. and Gilbert A. Churchill Jr (1990), 'Client evaluation cues: a comparison of successful and unsuccessful salespeople', *Journal of Marketing Research*, **27** (2), 163–74.

Wang, Guangping and Richard G. Netemeyer (2002), 'The effects of job autonomy, customer demandingness, and trait competitiveness on salesperson learning, self-efficacy, and performance', *Journal of the Academy of Marketing Science*, **30** (3), 217–28.

Weitz, Barton A. and Kevin D. Bradford (1999), 'Personal selling and sales management: a relationship marketing perspective', *Journal of the Academy of Marketing Science*, **27** (2), 241–54.

Wrzesniewski, Amy and Jane E. Dutton (2001), 'Crafting a job: revisioning employees as active crafters of their work', *Academy of Management Review*, **26** (2), 179–201.

Zoltners, Andris, Prabhakant Sinha and Sally Lorimer (2008), 'Sales force effectiveness: a framework for researchers and practitioners', *Journal of Personal Selling & Sales Management*, **28** (Spring), 115–31.

25 Key account management
Christian Homburg and Torsten Bornemann

Companies have always paid particular attention to their most important customers. The importance of a customer can arise from strategic factors, such as the customer's potential to enhance the supplier's image, and from financial factors, such as the customer's profitability. With increasing power on the customer side, resulting from account concentration and centralization of procurement activities, a systematization of these 'particular attention' activities has become necessary (Capon 2001). This need for systematization is reflected in the foundation of the Strategic Account Management Association established in 1964, which, according to its mission statement, is 'devoted to developing, promoting and advancing the concept of customer supplier collaboration through communities of practice'. At the beginning of the 1970s, research on the management of the most important accounts, called 'key accounts' or 'national accounts', commenced (Workman et al. 2003).

The objective of key account management (KAM) is to reap the economic benefits of long-term relationships with important customers. The advantages for the customer are obvious: preferential treatment, better service and often lower prices. However, these particular attention activities, which can range from special conditions regarding marketing mix elements to the vertical integration of the supply chain, have additional costs. As a result, relationships with the most important customers sometimes become unprofitable for the supplier (Reinartz and Kumar 2002). Napolitano (1997) even argues that the majority of all KAM programs do not yield any additional value for the supplier. Diligent management of the most important customers thus is required to design KAM effectively (Davies and Ryals 2009).

A recent content analysis comparing academic literature on KAM with practitioners' priorities reveals that in the past 30 years, research on KAM has increased significantly from decade to decade, providing evidence of ongoing academic interest in the topic (Guesalaga and Johnston 2010). At the same time, however, practitioners' needs have diverged from what is covered in academic literature. Whereas researchers have devoted large efforts studying the reasons suppliers adopt KAM, practitioners are especially interested in organizational aspects related to the implementation of KAM. In addition, the complexity of the topic often leads researchers to examine just a single aspect or certain perspectives in more detail. Against this background, this chapter compiles important findings and systemizes them. In the first section of the chapter, we lay the groundwork by defining KAM and connecting the KAM approach to related research areas and relevant theoretical concepts. In the second and main section, we provide an in-depth discussion of the dimensions of KAM, including the determinants of KAM adoption, the design of KAM and its performance implications. The chapter closes with implications for managerial practice and an agenda for future research.

FUNDAMENTALS OF KAM

Definition of KAM

The term KAM became accepted in the literature relatively late. The management of a company's most important customers was first discussed as national account management (NAM), a term that was already common in practice. With increasing internationalization and globalization of both suppliers and customers, this term was extended to global account management (GAM) or strategic account management (SAM; Montgomery et al. 1998). The renaming of the National Account Management Association to the Strategic Account Management Association emphasizes this shift as well. Today, KAM is the most accepted term in research publications (Homburg et al. 2002).

On a very general level, KAM can be defined as the additional activities and/or special personnel dedicated to a company's most important customers (Workman et al. 2003). In contrast with non-recurring transaction-oriented activities, additional activities within the KAM approach constitute relational commitments aimed at creating long-term customer relationships (McDonald et al. 1997). Moreover, this definition entails that KAM identify and select customers that are important to the company in some way. The importance of customers can arise from strategic and financial factors, which we discuss in-depth in the section on the selection of key accounts.

Research Areas related to KAM

The establishment and maintenance of relationships with (important) customers and the customer-oriented organization of marketing and sales activities are not unique to the KAM approach but are also discussed in important research areas that are conceptually related to KAM. From a marketing perspective, these areas encompass the literature on personal selling, relationship marketing and research on market orientation (Workman et al. 2003). Within these research fields, KAM is often treated as a sub-area. Moreover, additional insights can be gained from supply chain management (SCM), which focuses on the buyer's point of view (McDonald 2000). In the following, we provide a brief overview of these research areas and point out their relation to KAM.

Research on *personal selling* has traditionally examined aspects related to the performance of salespeople in their interaction with customers (Churchill et al. 1985) and has generated important findings on the performance implications of relationship-building activities and salesperson characteristics. In this research stream, the provision of additional services to strategically important customers is considered a refinement of personal selling: 'National account management thus is an extension, improvement, and outgrowth of personal selling' (Shapiro and Wyman 1981, p. 104). Although this research enhances knowledge about individual key account managers, it neglects aspects related to organizational adaptation that are highly relevant for the implementation of KAM. In recent years, however, the level of analysis in personal selling research has shifted from the individual salesperson to selling teams that are permanently assigned to customer accounts (Weitz and Bradford 1999). The focus on selling teams reflects the recognition that functional groups other than marketing may be important to establish long-term relationships. Because aspects related to cross-functional coordination are also relevant for the implementation of KAM, researchers have explicitly linked KAM to the team-selling literature (Moon and Armstrong 1994, p. 19): 'Conceptually, national account teams can be viewed as selling teams . . . that service large, complex customers'. An important difference, however, is that team-selling research does not examine inter-organizational activities, which are central aspects of KAM.

Such inter-organizational aspects are the focus of the newer discipline of *relationship marketing*, which focuses on how relationships between suppliers and customers are established and maintained (Berry and Parasuraman 1991). Indeed, Nevin (1995, p. 327) identifies KAM as a facet of relationship marketing: 'Although there are a range of perspectives on relationship marketing, it historically has been associated with attempts by firms to develop long-term relationships with certain customers or key accounts'. In contrast with KAM, however, relationship marketing does not deal with intra-organizational issues.

Research on *market orientation* brings together both intra-organizational and inter-organizational perspectives by focusing on 'a set of tangible actions that a firm initiates as well as the underlying culture that enables a firm to keep track of demand and supply variations in the marketplace and orchestrate appropriate responses to such changes' (Varadarajan and Jayachandran 1999, p. 134). Thus, the concept of market orientation combines a focus on customer needs without neglecting the importance of interfunctional coordination, which is explicitly regarded as one of the core components of market orientation (Narver and Slater 1990). Consequently, KAM research has relied on the concept of market orientation when deriving intra-organizational factors affecting organizational effectiveness, such as top management involvement and organizational culture (Workman et al. 2003). A fundamental difference from KAM is that research on market orientation does not differentiate between important and average customers.

The complementary discipline of SCM examines the buyer's point of view and focuses on cost reduction and quality management (McDonald 2000). However, SCM relationships, just like KAM relationships, are characterized by their long-term nature, a limited number of collaboration partners (suppliers in this case) and the need for mutual trust (Ryals and Humphries 2007). Many KAM relationships also contain arrangements targeted at harmonizing the supply chain (Lambe and Spekman 1997). Juxtaposing important dimensions of KAM and SCM, Ryals and Humphries (2007) find overlap among the need for value creation, trust and reliability, creativity and flexibility, stability, and communication.

This short overview shows that the simultaneous focus on intra- and inter-organizational aspects and on selected customers instead of the market as a whole clearly differentiates KAM from related research areas in marketing.

Theoretical Background

The management of key accounts requires the coordination of inter- and intra-organizational processes as well as the development of trust and commitment to establish long-lasting relationships (Lambe et al. 2001). Therefore, KAM can be examined from both an organizational and a relational perspective.

From an organizational perspective, the contingency approach, resource dependence theory and transaction cost theory constitute relevant theories; they all refer to inter-organizational aspects, such as the allocation of power, and intra-organizational aspects related to coordination. The *contingency approach* proposes that the organizational structure of a company must be adapted individually to the situation and environmental influences to achieve maximum efficiency in a given context (Zeithaml et al. 1988). Empirical research following the contingency approach focuses on the interplay among situational determinants, characteristics of the organizational design and the respective performance implications. These three aspects also constitute the framework for the subsequent discussion of the dimensions of KAM.

Resource dependence theory argues that companies depend on external actors who exert control on limited resources that are important for the companies' survival. A supplier's key accounts control critical resources, such as money (in exchange for the supplier's products), or certain technologies. In their main work on resource dependence theory, Pfeffer and Salancik (1978, p. 54) provide the example of components suppliers in the US automotive industry that strongly depend on General Motors as their key account: 'The small suppliers are quite dependent on General Motors, which, in controlling the market for cars, also controls the market for parts'. As a result, 'organizations will (and should) respond more to the demands of those organizations or groups in the environment that control critical resources' (Pfeffer 1982, p. 193). Only reactively fulfilling requirements, however, is detrimental in the long run, as it leads to a loss of bargaining power and freedom of decision. Therefore, it is necessary to have an active management of existing dependencies by linking resource owners to the company through 'inter-organizational linkage activities' (Pfeffer 1982, p. 200). The introduction of KAM thus can be interpreted as a linkage activity initiated by a supplier with customers who control resources deemed as critical. Empirical research indeed provides evidence that in relationships with key accounts, the supplier's dependence is greater than in relationships with other customers (Ivens and Pardo 2008).

Transaction cost theory focuses on the identification of the most efficient organizational mode to complete transactions: 'Firms seek to align transactions, which differ in their attributes, with governance structures, which differ in their costs and competencies, in a discriminating (mainly transaction cost economizing) way' (Williamson 1991, p. 79). The different approaches for carrying out transactions can be divided into market, firms (hierarchies) and bilateral governance (hybrids). Whereas market refers to exchange between autonomous economic entities, firm transactions describe modes of exchange in which one entity encompasses both sides of the transaction and some form of subordination and consolidated ownership exists. Bilateral governance involves an arrangement between these two extremes. In contrast with market, parties involved in bilateral governance strive to establish a long-term relationship with the respective transaction partner, in which both parties stay legally autonomous (Wengler 2007). The efficacy of any of these organizational arrangements must be evaluated according to the costs resulting from the transaction's asset specificity and the associated uncertainty. Constituting a form of bilateral governance, KAM requires a certain degree of asset specificity; that is, a certain degree of idiosyncratic investments through special activities, resources and actors (McDonald et al. 1997). To constitute an effective organizational arrangement, these relationship-specific investments should reduce the uncertainty the supplier faces in the relationship with the key account. Testing this assumption, Ivens and Pardo (2008) indeed find that in KAM relationships, suppliers' relationship-specific investments are higher and relationship-specific uncertainty is lower than in relationships with other customers. Moreover, by differentiating between varying degrees of asset specificity, transaction cost theory provides a framework for distinguishing between different approaches to KAM, depending on the intensity of additional activities that are performed for important customers (see the section below on design elements of KAM programs).

From a relational perspective, the relevance of 'soft' factors in KAM relationships is emphasized. In line with the assumptions of new institutional economics, exchange relationships are characterized by bounded rationality, uncertainty and opportunism. Because of the complexity of KAM relationships, the use of comprehensive contracts to mitigate these problems is often not feasible. Social exchange theory therefore proposes non-contractual mechanisms, such as trust and commitment, that result from the principle of generalized reciprocity. Over time, these mechanisms lead to mutually agreed-on rules for behavior (Lambe et al. 2001; Narayandas and Rangan 2004). The commitment–trust theory (Morgan and Hunt 1994), for example, considers commitment and trust 'key mediators', which essentially contribute to the success of relationship marketing and enhance cooperative behavior.

DIMENSIONS OF KAM

In line with the contingency approach, KAM can be described by its determinants, the respective organizational design and corresponding performance implications. This section therefore first identifies important determinants of KAM. Subsequently, questions related to the design of KAM programs are answered, including the selection of key accounts and the implementation of KAM. Finally, relational and financial performance implications are discussed.

Determinants of KAM Adoption

Despite its high complexity and the associated costs and coordination efforts, the adoption of KAM programs has steadily increased (Wengler et al. 2006). Against this background, it is not surprising that the question of *why* companies adopt KAM programs has sparked enormous research interest, whereas this question is regarded as less relevant from practitioners' point of view (Guesalaga and Johnston 2010). A first and quite obvious determinant of KAM adoption that has been identified in the literature very early and directly emanates from the contingency approach is the size of the selling company and the associated complexity (Stevenson and Page 1979). Most determinants of KAM adoption, however, lie beyond the control of the supplier. These external determinants include characteristics of the revenue structure in business and industrial markets, market maturity and the resulting competitive intensity, account concentration and procurement concentration (Gosselin and Bauwen 2006; Millman and Wilson 1999; Stevenson and Page 1979).

A common observation in industrial markets is a Pareto-distributed revenue structure: 20 per cent of customers account for 80 per cent of revenues. The existence of a small number of important customers directly implies the need for a special treatment of these accounts. In addition, maturation and consolidation of industries, accompanied by waves of mergers and acquisitions, has led to increasing competitive intensity and further account concentration (Capon 2001). Suppliers may introduce KAM programs to escape the resulting competitive pressure through close business relationships with their customers. These may demand special conditions regarding pricing, logistics and interfaces with the supplier (Montgomery and Yip 2000). Moreover, multinational customers tend to rationalize their supply base to reduce procurement complexity and to increase operational efficiency, which can be achieved by aligning the supply chain with a preferably small number of suppliers (McDonald 2000; Millman and Wilson 1999). These customers also have begun to systemize their most important supplier relationships in an analogous manner, using concepts such as key supplier management (KSM) and SCM (Ryals and Humphries 2007).

Design of KAM

The design of KAM is arguably the most important issue from a practitioner's point of view (Guesalaga and Johnston 2010). However, because knowledge on important design elements alone does not necessarily make up a good KAM program, the following section also considers issues related to the selection of key accounts and the implementation of the program. Figure 25.1 depicts the aspects considered in the following sections.

The selection of key accounts

The selection of customers for a KAM program is an essential step that determines the relational and economic success of the program. Research on criteria for the selection of key accounts has identified both strategic and financial factors on which the selection of key accounts can be based. Strategic factors include the customer's potential to enhance the supplier's image and reputation as well as possibilities for the common development of new markets and products (Millman and Wilson 1999). To get the most out of such an intense strategic relationship, a certain degree of 'fit' between supplier and customer is essential (Toulan et al. 2006). This fit can arise from a matching of customer needs and core competencies of the supplier (Napolitano 1997) or can be related to the companies' strategy, operational business or employees (Richards and Jones 2009). Williams Companies, the US-based energy and communications firm and winner of the Strategic Account Management Association's Performance Award 2001, describes the selection process for its Alliance Development Group (ADG) program as follows: 'ADG starts evaluating the strength of the current relationships and then determines how Williams fits with the potential alliance target culturally, financially, geographically, and strategically. In initial meetings, ADG meets with no less than a vice president' (Sperry 2001, p. 31).

Financial selection criteria include potential and present sales volume, current profitability and potential for profit (Boles et al. 1999; Napolitano 1997). In most companies, sales volume-related aspects prevail because they are easy to measure (McDonald et al. 1997; Wengler et al. 2006). However, the calculation of a customer's

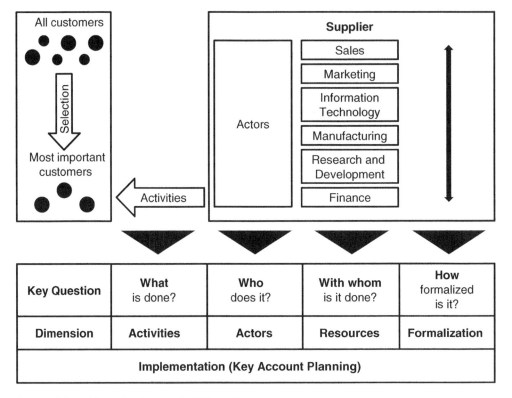

Notes: Adapted from Homburg et al. (2002, p. 44).

Figure 25.1   Design of KAM

profitability based on his or her lifetime value provides a much more reliable means to assess the customer's 'keyness' for the supplier. The calculation of customer lifetime value (CLV) requires an assessment of KAM-specific cost and revenue drivers (for an example, see Ryals and Holt 2007). Having identified these drivers, the value of a customer can be defined as the future stream of revenues from that customer (CR) minus the future stream of costs (CC) for the expected relationship length from $t = 1$ to n:

$$CLV = \sum_{t=1}^{n} \frac{(CR_t - CC_t)}{(1 + i)^t},$$

where i is a discount rate (Ryals 2005).

When selecting key accounts, existing relationships should not be considered in isolation. Instead, the whole portfolio of customers with varying importance for the supplier should be taken into account because their importance based on the defined criteria can vary tremendously over time (Piercy and Lane 2006; Ryals and Rogers 2007). Thus, a once derived evaluation and selection should be reviewed on a regular basis (Homburg et al. 2009).

Design elements of KAM programs

To systemize design elements of KAM programs, the A-R-A model (activities–resources–actors) is used and extended by the aspect of formalization, which is regarded as an own decision variable (Homburg et al. 2002). The *activities* of KAM contain aspects related to marketing mix elements, such as internationally harmonized prices, mutual product development, exchange of information, or the joint coordination of working processes in the context of vertical integration in the value chain (Lambe and Spekman 1997; Napolitano 1997). Customer requirements can serve as a starting point when determining the different activities that determine a particular KAM relationship. The factors that have generally been found to be of great importance to key accounts are internationally uniform conditions, consistency in quality and performance, and reduction of complexity by coordination and harmonization of processes (Cespedes 1992; Montgomery et al. 1998).

In general, the intensity and proactiveness of the pursued activities differentiate them from activities for average customers. Whereas *intensity* refers to the degree to which additional activities are performed for key accounts, *proactiveness* describes the extent to which the supplier initiates these activities (Workman et al. 2003). If KAM is demanded by the customer, and thus introduced reactively, the customer's willingness to coordinate the purchasing division internally is greater, which in turn facilitates adaptation at the supplier side. The reactive introduction of KAM can often be observed under conditions of high process complexity. If the supplier initializes KAM proactively, more effort must be put into the adaptation of the customer's organizational structure. However, such a proactive design is more effective than a reactive design because the supplier can design activities that correspond to his or her own interests (Workman et al. 2003). Proactive designs are more often observed when product complexity is high (Brehmer and Rehme 2009).

The *actors* of KAM appear in entirely different tasks and hierarchy levels. In some KAM programs, sales and/or marketing managers also take on the role of a key account manager (part-time KAM), whereas in others, a full-time KAM position exists (Pegram 1972). In the following, the term 'key account manager' refers to the main contact to the key account, regardless of who holds this position. A key account manager's role is twofold: he or she must coordinate internal processes and, at the same time, create additional value for customers (Georges and Eggert 2003). These functions may have special requirements with regard to the key account manager, such as long-term orientation, honesty, creative problem-solving and understanding of customer requirements (Boles et al. 1996).

To create value for the customer, exact knowledge of the respective customer's needs is necessary (Homburg et al. 2009). Thus, a central task of key account managers is regular communication with the customer. Communication enhances mutual trust, improves coordination and enables synergetic solutions through the exchange of strategic information (Morgan and Hunt 1994; Schultz and Evans 2002). In contrast with a sales manager, a key account manager's primary task is to perform an advisory function for the customer (Sharma 2007). Communication and strategic skills are also related to the effectiveness of a key account relationship. The ability to think strategically mainly affects the quality of communication and the customer's trust in the salesperson, which have a decisive positive influence on the effectiveness of the program. Intrapreneurial skills, which are defined as 'entrepreneurship inside the corporation' and are associated with informal influence within the supplying company, do not have an effect on the quality of communication but rather on trust and subsequently the effectiveness of the program (Sengupta et al. 2000). These two strongly correlating skills should be taken into account when selecting key account managers and designing training programs and incentive systems.

Key account relationships do not necessarily need to be managed by a single key account manager. The assignment of a *team* can be an alternative option, especially for large and complex customers (Arnett et al. 2005). Selling teams should preferably have functionally different backgrounds to enhance mutual activities with the key account at different functional interfaces (Moore 1994). Effective teams have a direct impact on the strategic value of a relationship and the degree of collaboration and commitment (Arnett et al. 2005). Moreover, organizational learning and knowledge transfer are accelerated, which in turn facilitates adaptation to the customer's requirements (Nätti et al. 2006). Coordination within the team can be achieved by a formalization of different roles, analogous to purchasing teams on the customer side (Georges and Eggert 2003).

An additional aspect that must be considered is the degree to which *senior management* is involved in a KAM program. For the customer, senior management participation serves as a strong signal of commitment to the relationship, enabling 'board to board' contact (Millman and Wilson 1999). Moreover, a central characteristic of KAM is that strategic aspects are considered that go beyond regular sales activities. Participation of senior management members, in advisory or even operational functions, helps align the program's strategic objectives with functional requirements (Homburg et al. 2002; Napolitano 1997).

Having decided on the actors involved in the program, adequate incentive systems must be implemented, as remuneration schemes for key accounts should entail different aspects than those for regular salespeople (Arnett et al. 2005; Sengupta et al. 2000). Key account managers are often remunerated with a higher fixed portion and a lower bonus portion. The important aspect, however, is not that the performance-related portion is relatively lower but that it refers to indicators based on long-term considerations of performance measurement. One possibility to measure team performance, for example, is to incorporate the degree of collaboration with the customer and the strategic value of the relationship as perceived by the customer (Arnett et al. 2005).

The adaptation of structures to customer needs associated with the introduction of KAM requires the availability and adequate allocation of internal *resources* (Georges and Eggert 2003). To implement the aforementioned activities, internal collaboration of diverse functional areas such as marketing and sales, logistics, manufacturing, information technology and finance and accounting is necessary (Yip and Madsen 1996). Key account managers, who traditionally belong to the sales function, may not always have the authority to command these resources (Homburg et al. 2002). The resulting departmental 'jockeying' constitutes one of the major hurdles in the implementation of effective KAM programs (Millman and Wilson 1999). One way to ensure interdepartmental cooperation is to grant the key account manager special organizational power (i.e. access to *non-marketing* and *non-sales* resources in addition to marketing and sales resources; Homburg et al. 2002) or to involve senior management in the program. Another way is to establish a relationship-oriented culture in the company (Jaworski and Kohli 1993). The degree to which people involved in the management of key accounts pursue a

Table 25.1   Taxonomy of approaches to KAM

Variable / KAM approach	Top management KAM	Middle management KAM	Operating-level KAM	Cross-functional, dominant KAM	Unstructured KAM	Isolated KAM	Country club KAM	No KAM
Activity intensity	**Medium-high**	Medium	**Medium-high**	**High**	Medium	Medium	*Low*	*Low*
Activity proactiveness	Medium	Medium	*Low-medium*	**High**	*Low-medium*	Medium	*Low*	*Low-medium*
Approach formalization	**Very high**	High	Rather high	**Very high**	Low	Rather low	*Very low*	Low
Top management involvement	**Very high**	Medium	Low	High	*Very low*	Medium-high	High	Low
Use of teams	Much	Little	**Much-very much**	**Very much**	Little	Medium	*Very little*	*Very little*
Selling center *esprit de corps*	Rather strong	Rather weak	Rather strong	**Strong**	**Strong**	*Weak*	Rather weak	*Weak*
Access to marketing and sales resources	Rather low	High	Low	**Very high**	Rather high	Medium	**Very high**	*Very low*
Access to non-marketing and non-sales resources	*Low*	Medium	*Low*	**High**	Medium	*Low*	Medium	*Low*

Notes: Means in the highest band are in bold; means in the lowest band are in italics. Adapted from Homburg et al. (2002, p. 50).

common goal, called 'esprit de corps', could be identified as one of the major drivers of KAM effectiveness (Workman et al. 2003).

Formalization refers to the degree to which policies and procedures for the handling of key accounts are defined and established. An explicit definition of roles and responsibilities facilitates coordination among the involved functional areas in a complex organization (Georges and Eggert 2003), which is why KAM programs tend to be less formalized in smaller companies, in which processes are less complex and thus easier to coordinate in an informal way (Wengler et al. 2006). However, a high degree of formalization may negatively affect KAM effectiveness because it implies a certain rigidness of and lack of flexibility in the adaptation of structures to individual customer needs (Workman et al. 2003). Another way to formalize KAM programs is the use of contracts. The degree to which contracts are desired depends on the distribution of power between the involved parties. Empirical research shows that the stronger party favors informal agreements because it can exert its power more easily when it is not bound to contractual conditions (Narayandas and Rangan 2004).

Using the corresponding values of the discussed design elements of KAM programs, Homburg et al. (2002) empirically developed a taxonomy of approaches to KAM, which Table 25.1 depicts. With regard to KAM effectiveness and performance at the organizational level, the no KAM and the isolated KAM approach perform worst. The best performance at the organizational level arises from top management KAM (with regard to profitability) and from cross-functional KAM (with regard to performance in the market and adaptiveness). Cross-functional KAM also exhibits the highest values for KAM effectiveness (Homburg et al. 2002), providing evidence for the criticality of inter-departmental cooperation.

Implementation of KAM
The implementation of KAM includes the previously discussed selection of key accounts and the design of the different elements of the KAM program. To ensure the achievement of efficiency- and effectiveness-related objectives, careful planning and monitoring during all phases of the implementation is necessary (Ryals and Rogers 2007). Several studies have identified prototypical phases of KAM relationships. McDonald et al.'s (1997) relational development model, for example, describes five phases based on the nature of the relationship (transactional to collaborative) and the level of the supplier's involvement with the customer.

Davies and Ryals's (2009) transitioning model differentiates four prototypical phases of KAM programs based on an examination of the extent to which different elements are implemented over time: introducing KAM, embedding KAM, optimizing KAM and continuous improvement. They also consider performance-related aspects in these different phases. During the *introduction phase*, the supplier decides to implement a KAM program and identifies specific key accounts. In this phase, the focus is on the actual set-up of the program and the definition of activities, though the impact of this dedication of resources on long-term profits is often neglected. In the *embedding phase*, planning procedures are introduced and roles within the program are defined. The introduction of planning and monitoring procedures now shows the costs associated with the program, often leading to disillusion. Critical in this phase is ongoing support by senior management. The *optimizing phase* entails much higher investments to align organizational structures and increase service levels. Astonishingly, a reduction of performance monitoring can be observed, oftentimes replaced by benchmarking against competitors. Finally, companies that have reached the *continuous improvement phase* become more selective regarding the granting of additional activities to key accounts and may even reduce the number of key accounts. Moreover, senior management, which is more important to establish KAM, is less involved in this phase to reduce costs. Davies and Ryals (2009, p. 1041) conclude that 'KAM is a long-term organization-wide change management process, taking in excess of 6 years to impact and that impacts upon the whole organization infrastructure, from top management through to product development and service providers'.

The observation that, oftentimes, no detailed *ex ante* analysis of the benefits and costs associated with the implementation of KAM is made is also shared by Wengler et al. (2006). In their study, only 3 of 35 interviewed managers conducted a formal cost–benefit calculation before the actual implementation of KAM. As a consequence, the costs associated with the set-up of the program, the required changes of the organizational structure, and the maintenance costs of keeping the program active are often underestimated. By introducing planning and control systems at an early stage, these costs can be quantified and contrasted with the value created for the supplier and the customer. Moreover, a detailed key account planning in advance can speed up the whole implementation process. Ryals and Rogers (2007, p. 217) recommend the inclusion of the following aspects in a key account plan:

- *Relationship overview/executive summary*: current performance analysis, current initiatives, financial targets and planning assumptions.
- *Key account overview*: key account's business environment (e.g. competitive situation, challenges).
- *Objectives and strategy*: identification and prioritization of key opportunities with the key account.
- *Customer alignment*: customer's critical success factors, relative performance of the supplier and strategies for managing the relationship.
- *Relationship management*: contact mapping of the customer's decision-making unit (analysis of the buying center).
- *Implementation plan*: detailed tactics, budget, risks and contingencies.

Performance Implications of KAM

The ultimate question for a company considering the adoption of KAM is whether such an approach actually increases performance. In the following, performance implications of KAM are divided into relational and financial performance (Richards and Jones 2009). Moreover, the question whether KAM relationships are more successful than other types of relationships is considered.

Relational performance implications

Because a main goal of KAM programs is to intensify and stabilize the supplier's relationships with its most important customers, relationship-related aspects constitute important performance outcomes. These aspects, subsumed under labels such as KAM effectiveness (Workman et al. 2003) and relationship effectiveness (Richards and Jones 2009), include trust, information sharing, reduction of conflicts and commitment to the relationship. Trust and commitment, when transferred from the individual level of sales and procurement managers to the organizational level, can also help attenuate detrimental effects arising from an imbalance of power in the relationship (Narayandas and Rangan 2004).

However, KAM status alone does not guarantee high levels of relational performance. Ivens and Pardo (2007), for example, found that though KAM relationships are characterized by a greater commitment on the customer side, trust and satisfaction are not necessarily greater than in regular customer relationships. One explanation for this finding is that key accounts, aware of their high status, may exhibit higher expectations regarding the KAM relationship than would be the case in a regular relationship. Other than the granting of KAM status per se, the discussed design elements of KAM influence relational performance. Whereas activities and resources are important drivers of relational performance, actors are less important and formalization even exerts a negative impact (Workman et al. 2003).

Financial performance implications

Empirical research on financial performance implications shows that KAM effectiveness positively affects market success and profitability (Workman et al. 2003). However, the most effective designs of KAM (in this case top management KAM and cross-functional KAM; see Table 25.1) are not necessarily the most profitable ones. For these designs, overall costs are higher, for example, because of the use of teams or a higher intensity of key account-directed activities (Homburg et al. 2002). This finding reflects the often unconditional provision of added value in KAM programs stemming from the hope of increasing the key account's commitment (Ivens and Pardo 2007). In addition, the dependence on only a few important customers may negatively affect the achievable price level (Piercy and Lane 2006). Therefore, control mechanisms for performance measurement, which we presented when discussing the implementation of KAM, should be set up at an early stage (Davies and Ryals 2009). An adaptation of activities for the key account according to CLV, for example, can be implemented very easily and helps avoid such pitfalls (see Ryals 2005 for an example).

DISCUSSION

Implications for Managerial Practice

This chapter provides an overview of important elements of KAM and their inter-dependencies. KAM can have positive relational and financial implications for both partners by reducing complexity and adding value. We have discussed that the selection of key accounts, one of the most critical decisions for a firm, should be based on economic and strategic criteria. Marriott's Alliance Account Program, for example, focuses on accounts with $25 million in actual or potential lodging per year, but the selection also considers whether the account has a centralized purchasing process and is present in various parts of the world. The program's stated goal is not just to sell rooms but to maintain a partnership to realize mutual long-term objectives (Sperry 2002).

With regard to the activities that constitute the core of a KAM program, a thorough understanding of the key account's business challenges is important. One of the customers in Marriott's Alliance Account Program is Siemens, the Munich-based electrical engineering and electronics firm. Marriott supported Siemens's travel management centralization process by acting as a link between the Siemens headquarters and various country travel groups, which enabled the introduction of a centralized pricing scheme for Siemens.

We have also shown that a key aspect enhancing the effectiveness of KAM is the involvement of senior management. In the Marriott–Siemens relationship, both companies soon discovered that their complementary skills could provide a basis for much more than a simple buyer–seller relationship. With the involvement of top executives from both companies, Marriott and Siemens founded a joint venture that installed high-speed Internet access in Marriott's US properties, a competence brought into the relationship by Siemens. Both companies then began developing state-of-the-art wireless applications for hotels, with a special focus on business travelers. Marriott's long-term benefits of having a world-class communication infrastructure are obvious, and extend far beyond the Marriott–Siemens relationship. As Sperry (2002, p. 3) noted, 'Two corporate giants . . . saw an operational and strategic fit and more than made the best of it'.

Future Research

Although a substantial body of KAM research exists, several aspects warrant further examination. A content analysis of KAM research identified 64 articles published on KAM from 1979 to 2009 (Guesalaga and Johnston 2010). Although qualitative and descriptive studies prevail over this period, in the last decade an increase in more advanced methods, such as structural equation modeling, could be observed. Of note, the focus of research articles does not necessarily mirror practitioners' interests. A large number of research articles focus on aspects such as determinants of KAM and elements of KAM, which are regarded as less important from practitioners' point of view, whereas managerially relevant aspects such as organizing for KAM and adaptation of KAM approaches received relatively little research interest. Within these categories, the role of senior management and approaches for internal alignment and coordination could be identified as highly relevant for practitioners (Guesalaga and Johnston 2010).

Although empirical research has shown that top management involvement positively influences the performance of KAM programs (Workman et al. 2003), the question of *how* senior management should be integrated still remains to be answered. The continuum here reaches from a purely advisory role to concrete functional tasks. In the Marriott example, top management involvement turned out to be particularly effective when the focus was on long-term strategic objectives of mutual interest for both companies. Moreover, the question arises whether the main benefits from top management involvement originate from the facilitation of interdepartmental coordination or from the signaling of commitment in relation to the customer. Also worth examining are conditions that lead to detrimental effects of top management involvement.

We have also discussed the aspect of internal alignment in the context of design elements of KAM programs. Possibilities to ensure internal alignment are the use of formal (by the involvement of senior management) or informal power, the use of teams that represent the different functions involved, and the creation of a customer-focused culture that leads to a sense of belonging and a common goal. Although the effects of these factors on KAM effectiveness have already been studied empirically (Workman et al. 2003), the question regarding whether they affect internal alignment and subsequently performance outcomes remains to be answered.

Another KAM-related issue that deserves further research attention is an examination that encompasses the whole portfolio of a supplier's customer relationships. A simple differentiation between key accounts and regular accounts is too simplistic for several reasons. First, the decision to adopt KAM requires an allocation of resources that may also affect other relationships. Although research has shown that the introduction of KAM enhances overall profitability (Workman et al. 2003), an explicit examination of interdependencies between different kinds of relationships may be fruitful. What are the implications of KAM for the management of small accounts, which constitute the vast majority of customers for most suppliers? Second, an adequate selection of key accounts should consider the respective key account's lifetime value (Ryals 2005). This lifetime value, however, is dynamic and subject to change (Homburg et al. 2009). Therefore, a worthwhile research issue is a longitudinal examination of KAM performance and the identification of determinants that affect the 'keyness' of the relationship based on CLV.

This brief and by no means exhaustive overview of research issues shows that there are still plenty of possibilities to make a research contribution that practitioners and academics alike will highly value.

REFERENCES

Arnett, D.B., B.A. Macy and J.B. Wilcox (2005), 'The role of core selling teams in supplier–buyer relationships', *Journal of Personal Selling & Sales Management*, **25** (1), 27–42.

Berry, L.L. and A. Parasuraman (1991), *Marketing Services*, New York: Free Press.

Boles, J.S., H.C. Barksdale and J.T. Johnson (1996), 'What national account decision makers would tell salespeople about building relationships', *Journal of Business and Industrial Marketing*, **11** (2), 6–17.

Boles, J., W. Johnston and A. Gardner (1999), 'The selection and organization of national accounts: a North American perspective', *Journal of Business and Industrial Marketing*, **14** (4), 264–75.

Brehmer, P.O. and J. Rehme (2009), 'Proactive and reactive: drivers for key account management programmes', *European Journal of Marketing*, **43** (7), 961–84.

Capon, N. (2001), *Key Account Management and Planning*, New York: Free Press.

Cespedes, F.V. (1992), 'Sales cooperation: an exploratory study', *Journal of Personal Selling & Sales Management*, **12** (3), 13–29.

Churchill, G.A., N.M. Ford, S.W. Hartley and O.C. Walker (1985), 'The determinants of salesperson performance: a meta-analysis', *Journal of Marketing Research*, **22** (2), 103–18.

Davies, I.A. and L.J. Ryals (2009), 'A stage model for transitioning to KAM', *Journal of Marketing Management*, **25** (9–10), 1027–48.

Georges, L. and A. Eggert (2003), 'Key account managers' role within the value creation process of collaborative relationships', *Journal of Business-to-Business Marketing*, **10** (4), 1–22.

Gosselin, D.P. and G.A. Bauwen (2006), 'Strategic account management: customer value creation through customer alignment', *Journal of Business and Industrial Marketing*, **21** (6), 376–85.

Guesalaga, R. and W. Johnston (2010), 'What's next in key account management research? Building the bridge between the academic literature and the practitioners' priorities', *Industrial Marketing Management*, **39** (7), 1063–8.

Homburg, C., V. Steiner and D. Totzek (2009), 'Managing dynamics in a customer portfolio', *Journal of Marketing*, **73** (5), 70–89.

Homburg, C., J. Wieseke and T. Bornemann (2009), 'Implementing the marketing concept at the employee–customer interface: the role of customer need knowledge', *Journal of Marketing*, **73** (4), 64–81.

Homburg, C., J.P. Workman and O. Jensen (2002), 'A configurational perspective on key account management', *Journal of Marketing*, **66** (2), 38–60.

Ivens, B.S. and C. Pardo (2007), 'Are key account relationships different? Empirical results on supplier strategies and customer reactions', *Industrial Marketing Management*, **36** (4), 470–82.

Ivens, B.S. and C. Pardo (2008), 'Key-account-management in business markets: an empirical test of common assumptions', *Journal of Business & Industrial Marketing*, **23** (5), 301–10.

Jaworski, B.J. and A.K. Kohli (1993), 'Market orientation: antecedents and consequences', *Journal of Marketing*, **57** (3), 53–70.

Lambe, J.C. and R.E. Spekman (1997), 'National account management: large account selling or buyer–supplier alliance?', *Journal of Personal Selling & Sales Management*, **17** (4), 61–74.

Lambe, J.C., M.C. Wittmann and R.E. Spekman (2001), 'Social exchange theory and research on business-to-business relational exchange', *Journal of Business-to-Business Marketing*, **8** (3), 1–36.

McDonald, M. (2000), 'Key account management: a domain review', *Marketing Review*, **1** (1), 15–34.

McDonald, M., T. Millman and B. Rogers (1997), 'Key account management: theory, practice and challenges', *Journal of Marketing Management*, **13** (8), 737–57.

Millman, T. and K. Wilson (1999), 'Processual issues in key account management: underpinning the customer-facing organisation', *Journal of Business and Industrial Marketing*, **14** (4), 328–37.

Montgomery, D.B. and G.S. Yip (2000), 'The challenge of global customer management', *Marketing Management*, **9** (4), 22–9.

Montgomery, D.B., G.S. Yip and B. Villalonga (1998), 'The use and performance effect of global account management: an empirical analysis using structural equations modeling', working paper, Graduate School of Business, Stanford University.

Moon, M.A. and G.M. Armstrong (1994), 'Selling teams: a conceptual framework and research agenda', *Journal of Personal Selling & Sales Management*, **14** (1), 17–41.

Moore, C.M. (1994), *Group Techniques for Idea Generating*, Thousand Oaks, CA: Sage Publications.

Morgan, R.M. and S.D. Hunt (1994), 'The commitment–trust theory of relationship marketing', *Journal of Marketing*, **58** (3), 20–38.

Napolitano, L. (1997), 'Customer–supplier partnering: a strategy whose time has come', *Journal of Personal Selling & Sales Management*, **17** (4), 1–8.

Narayandas, D. and K.V. Rangan (2004), 'Building and sustaining buyer–seller relationships in mature industrial markets', *Journal of Marketing*, **68** (3), 63–77.

Narver, J.C. and S.F. Slater (1990), 'The effect of a market orientation on business profitability', *Journal of Marketing*, **54** (4), 20–35.

Nätti, S., A. Halinen and N. Hanttu (2006), 'Customer knowledge transfer and key account management in professional service organizations', *International Journal of Service Industry Management*, **17** (4), 304–19.

Nevin, J.R. (1995), 'Relationship marketing and distribution channels: exploring fundamental issues', *Journal of the Academy of Marketing Science*, **23** (4), 327–34.

Pegram, R.M. (1972), *Selling and Servicing the National Account*, New York: The Conference Board.

Pfeffer, J.S. (1982), *Organizations and Organization Theory*, London: Pitman.

Pfeffer, J.S. and G.R. Salancik (1978), *The External Control of Organizations: A Resource Dependence Perspective*, New York: Harper and Row.

Piercy, N. and N. Lane (2006), 'The underlying vulnerabilities in key account management strategies', *European Management Journal*, **24** (2), 151–62.

Reinartz, W.J. and V. Kumar (2002), 'The mismanagement of customer loyalty', *Harvard Business Review*, **80** (7), 86–94.

Richards, K.A. and E. Jones (2009), 'Key account management: adding elements of account fit to an integrative theoretical framework', *Journal of Personal Selling & Sales Management*, **29** (4), 305–20.

Ryals, L.J. (2005), 'Making customer relationship management work: the measurement and profitable management of customer relationships', *Journal of Marketing*, **69** (4), 252–61.

Ryals, L.J. and S. Holt (2007), 'Creating and capturing value in KAM relationships', *Journal of Strategic Marketing*, **15** (5), 403–20.

Ryals, L.J. and A.S. Humphries (2007), 'Managing key business-to-business relationships: what marketing can learn from supply chain management', *Journal of Service Research*, **9** (4), 312–26.

Ryals, L.J. and B. Rogers (2007), 'Key account planning: benefits, barriers and best practice', *Journal of Strategic Marketing*, **15** (2–3), 209–22.

Schultz, R.J. and K.R. Evans (2002), 'Strategic collaborative communication by key account representatives', *Journal of Personal Selling & Sales Management*, **22** (1), 23–31.

Sengupta, S., R.E. Krapfel and M.A. Pusateri (2000), 'An empirical investigation of key account salesperson effectiveness', *Journal of Personal Selling & Sales Management*, **20** (4), 253–61.

Shapiro, B.P. and J. Wyman (1981), 'New ways to reach your customers', *Harvard Business Review*, **59** (4), 103–10.

Sharma, A. (2007), 'The shift in sales organizations in business-to-business services markets', *Journal of Services Marketing*, **21** (5), 326–33.

Sperry, J.P. (2001), '2001 SAMA Performance Award winner: Williams Company Alliance Development Group', *Velocity*, **3** (3), 30–32.

Sperry, J.P. (2002), '2002 SAMA Performance Award winner: Marriott International and Siemens', *Focus Europe* (a supplement to *Velocity*), **2** (3), 1–4.

Stevenson, T.H. and A.L. Page (1979), 'The adoption of national account marketing by industrial firms', *Industrial Marketing Management*, **8** (1), 94–100.

Toulan, O., J. Birkinshaw and D. Arnold (2006), 'The role of interorganizational fit in global account management', *International Studies of Management and Organization*, **36** (4), 61–81.

Varadarajan, P.R. and S. Jayachandran (1999), 'Marketing strategy: an assessment of the state of the field and outlook', *Journal of the Academy of Marketing Science*, **27** (2), 120–43.

Weitz, B.A. and K.D. Bradford (1999), 'Personal selling and sales management: a relationship marketing perspective', *Journal of the Academy of Marketing Science*, **27** (2), 241–54.

Wengler, S. (2007), 'The appropriateness of the key account management organization', *Journal of Business Market Management*, **1** (4), 253–72.

Wengler, S., M. Ehret and S. Saab (2006), 'Implementation of key account management: who, why, and how? An exploratory study on the current implementation of key account management programs', *Industrial Marketing Management*, **35** (1), 103–12.

Williamson, O.E. (1991), 'Strategizing, economizing, and economic organization', *Strategic Management Journal*, **12** (2), 75–94.

Workman, J.P., C. Homburg and O. Jensen (2003), 'Intraorganizational determinants of key account management effectiveness', *Journal of the Academy of Marketing Science*, **31** (1), 3–21.

Yip, G.S. and T.L. Madsen (1996), 'Global account management: the new frontier in relationship marketing', *International Marketing Review*, **13** (3), 24–42.

Zeithaml, V.A., P.R. Varadarajan and C.P. Zeithaml (1988), 'The contingency approach: its foundations and relevance to theory building and research in marketing', *European Journal of Marketing*, **22** (7), 37–64.

26 Sales force compensation: research insights and research potential

Anne T. Coughlan and Kissan Joseph

Today's B2B selling environment is characterized by much complexity. Key drivers of this complexity include group sales efforts, multipart sales offerings and multibusiness unit participation on single deals (CFO Research Services 2010). Furthermore, the selling process is evolving from a transactional focus to consultative and enterprise-level selling with a corresponding shift in competencies from price and problem solving to value creation (Rackham and De Vincentis 1999). However, despite this increase in complexity, practitioners still demand compensation plans that are relatively simple, error free and cost effective (CFO Research Services 2010).

Against this backdrop, it is timely to review the role of sales force compensation in B2B organizations. Indeed, sales force compensation is one of the most powerful tools in a B2B firm's arsenal for influencing sales and profitability. The purpose of a sales compensation plan is to *motivate* members of the sales force and/or sales management, so that the firm can *coordinate* the salesperson's (or sales team's or sales hierarchy's) activities with the firm's own profit-maximizing goals. This would not be a difficult management problem were salespeople's goals and objectives aligned with the firm's profit maximization goal. But practitioners and researchers alike have long recognized the fundamental divergence between the objectives of firms and their salespeople; the academic literature's extensive work on *agency theory* seeks to find compensation and motivation solutions to precisely this problem, in sales force and other principal–agent contexts.

Ours is not the first article to survey and summarize the literature on sales force compensation and motivation (see also Albers 2002; Coughlan 1993; Coughlan and Sen 1989; Mantrala et al. 2010). We do not replicate the summaries included in these articles; rather, we focus on issues that merit heightened attention. Given the application focus, our review is organized by substantive problem areas. This allows us both to report on what *is* known in the academic literature and to comment on areas that are *under-researched* and, thus, ripe for future investigation.

The B2B firm has a multidimensional sales compensation problem to solve. Decisions to be made include:

- deciding on the elements of compensation to offer, including not just the standard salary and commission, which have been extensively studied in the literature, but also quota–bonus schemes, the use of monitoring in place of incentives, spiffs (special performance incentives for field force; see Zoltners et al. 2006, p. 378), sales contests, team selling compensation and compensation based on group sales performance even without team selling;
- determining actual reward levels, and setting the appropriate balance between and among them (when multiple compensation tools are used);

- deciding whether to delegate price setting to the sales force, and if so, what degree of price dispersion to allow, and whether to link compensation to the chosen level of prices;
- setting pay differentials for sales professionals at different levels in the sales organization;
- setting the time horizon over which to offer rewards;
- setting jointly optimal sales compensation levels and sales training investments;
- managing total compensation costs in light of sales force turnover; and
- establishing metrics on which incentives are based (e.g. whether a bonus is awarded for group or individual performance, and what the minimum quota amount is above which bonus is earned; linking incentive pay to salespeople's ability to forecast sales).

We first discuss research insights on compensation elements to offer to salespeople, followed by a summary of results on how much to pay and how to balance salary versus incentive pay. We next survey results on the choice to delegate pricing authority to the sales force and its impact on compensation. Finally, we discuss the remaining challenges, in which academic research results are sparser and therefore in which the opportunity for future research is bright.

COMPENSATION ELEMENTS OVERVIEW

The array of possible elements of sales force compensation is limited only by the imagination of managers setting sales compensation plans. However, most compensation plans include salary (a fixed payment) and one or more elements of incentive pay, such as commission or bonus. Salary is a fixed payment to the salesperson, independent of his or her productivity (though *adjustments* in salary from year to year are very likely to be related to the salesperson's previous year's productivity). Commission is typically awarded as a *percentage* of some outcome measure; commonly, as a percentage of sales revenue or of profit or gross margin generated by the salesperson. Bonus pay is typically awarded as a lump sum and is contingent on reaching a goal set by management over some time horizon (e.g. monthly, quarterly, yearly), such as selling more than a prespecified quota amount or reaching sales goals for a particular product.

Beyond these core compensation elements, other elements of sales compensation include spiffs, sales contest awards, team sales compensation and cross-territory compensation. Compensation may be awarded on the basis of performance across varying *time horizons* or varying *metrics*; compensation (both total payouts and degree of reliance on incentive pay) also typically varies across different levels of the sales hierarchy within a firm. Table 26.1 defines each of these compensation components and their incentive effects and horizons.

We next discuss research insights on the first two elements in Table 26.1 (salary and commission on sales) in light of the connected questions of *how much compensation to offer in total* and *what the optimal mix is between salary and incentive pay*. We then turn to discussions of the research insights on quota–bonus plans, sales contests, spiffs and group selling compensation, and whether and when direct sales force monitoring

Table 26.1   Compensation components: definitions, incentives, horizons

Compensation Component	Definition	Incentive Effect?	Horizon?
Salary	Fixed payment independent of current performance	Risk avoidance in short run; future salary adjustments depend on current performance	Adjusted yearly
Commission: Paid on Sales	Payment of X per cent of sales revenue (can be product specific or paid on total sales)	Work to sell highest-commission product and/or sell to easiest-to-close sales	Monthly (typically)
Commission: Paid on Gross Margin	Payment of X per cent of gross margin (can be product specific or paid on total gross margin)	Work to sell highest-margin product; requires divulging gross margins to sales force	Monthly (typically)
Bonus: Paid Individually for Performance over Quota	Lump-sum payment for sales over minimum quota amount	Hit quota volume this period; may cause salesperson to 'sandbag' sales to meet quota next period	Monthly, quarterly, yearly
Bonus: Paid from Fixed Pool	Lump sums awarded from a pool of fixed total size, when a salesperson hits quota target	Achieve quota sales volume; capped incentive due to fixed size of total bonus pool (especially if likelihood of making quota is high for other salespeople)	Monthly, quarterly, yearly
Spiff	Commission on sales paid by manufacturer directly to *salespeople* of the independent distributor or rep firm, *not* to the distributor or rep firm itself	Allocate increased effort to spiffed product	Short-term (1–3 months) (e.g., offered on new products, products to be discontinued)
Sales Contest	Lump-sum monetary or in-kind payments for performance relative to other individuals	Increased short-term effort; competitive in nature	Short-term (1–3 months)
Team Selling Award	Commission or bonus based on sales by a team of multiple salespeople	Increased team effort; may lead to free-riding by some team members	Monthly, quarterly, or on closing the sale, however long it takes
Cross-Territory Commission	Per cent commission paid on the basis of group sales achievement, without team selling, to all salespeople in the group	Increased effort due to diversification of risk	Monthly, quarterly

(facilitated by the ever-increasing sophistication of monitoring and information technologies) is preferable to the use of indirect incentives for sales performance. We close with a discussion of underresearched problems in the sales compensation area, which provide fruitful avenues for future research.

HOW HIGH SHOULD TOTAL COMPENSATION BE, AND WHAT IS THE OPTIMAL SALARY/INCENTIVE SPLIT?

Total compensation offered to a salesperson is the sum of the amounts earned through any and all of the compensation components used by the firm (see Table 26.1). However, among the components, *salary* plays a special role: although it is typically adjusted on an annual basis, in response to some aggregate measures of market pay norms and salesperson achievement, it is the one compensation component that is offered to the salesperson without immediate dependence on any sales or profitability outcome.

It therefore is natural to consider not only how much should be paid in total to the salesperson but also how that amount should be split between salary and incentive pay in general. The literature has shown that these two questions are closely interlinked: the optimal amount of total pay depends on the split between certainty and at-risk compensation, mediated by the salesperson's degree of risk aversion.

Agency theory provides a useful lens through which to analyze this fundamental sales compensation problem.[1] Agency theory posits a *principal* (the firm or the sales manager acting on behalf of the firm) whose objective is to maximize the firm's expected profit (thus, the firm is assumed to be risk neutral). Profit is a positive function of sales and a negative function of compensation to an *agent* (the salesperson). Sales themselves are assumed to be a positive but stochastic function of the amount of sales effort.[2] The salesperson is assumed to maximize expected utility, which is a positive function of his or her compensation and a negative function of the selling effort exerted. The salesperson is also assumed to be risk averse. Risk aversion blunts the motivating impact of incentives; all else being equal, increases in risk aversion decrease the effort put forth by the salesperson.

The difference in risk attitudes of the principal (firm) and agent (salesperson) would not prevent the firm from being able to set compensation to elicit a profit-maximizing effort level, if it were possible to observe sales effort perfectly. Knowing the salesperson's utility function and, thus, his or her trade-off between income and the disutility for work, the firm would be able to calculate the optimal number of hours for the salesperson to work – the number that just balances the value of generating another hour's worth of expected sales and the cost of compensating the salesperson for an incremental hour of work (i.e. lost leisure). In this case, the firm would offer a contract to the salesperson specifying an all-salary compensation plan, with the amount of salary contingent on the salesperson working the profit-maximizing number of hours, in which this salary payment is just large enough to make the salesperson willing to take the job.[3] This outcome is known as the 'first-best' case.

However, consistent with the realities of sales management, agency theory also assumes that the firm cannot observe sales effort, it can only observe actual sales achieved. The handy contractual solution outlined previously is then not possible, because its success hinges on payment for *effort exerted*. When only sales *outcomes* can be observed, and the salesperson's utility function values both leisure and income, an apparently low sales outcome could be due simply to poor luck or to effort shirking on the part of the salesperson; similarly, an apparently high sales outcome could be due to very hard work on the salesperson's part or simply to good luck (even with some shirking on effort).

Under these circumstances, the agency-theoretic model shows that when salary and/or commission are the allowable compensation elements, the best possible sales compensation contract offers *expected utility* equal to the salesperson's next best available opportunity; this is logical because, otherwise, the salesperson would leave this firm and take a better job. The optimal compensation plan also includes a *mixture* of salary and commission on sales; the incentive pay induces the salesperson to work harder than would a pure-salary plan, but unfortunately it also inflicts risk on the salesperson. Salary helps mitigate, but does not fully obviate, the risk the salesperson faces. This compensation plan therefore does not induce the effort level of the first-best case, because the salesperson's risk aversion causes him or her to favor leisure (which generates utility *for sure*) over incremental selling effort (which generates income only *in expectation*) on the margin. The higher the optimal amount of *leverage* in the plan (the ratio of incentive pay to total pay), the less risk averse the salesperson is and the higher is his or her hourly sales productivity. Table 26.2 lists other comparative-static effects of parameters on optimal compensation amount and structure, profitability and sales effort.

Table 26.2 shows that sales compensation tilts toward the surety of salary pay when the salesperson is more risk averse or when there is simply more risk in the environment; either way, it is unproductive to thrust more risk on the salesperson's shoulders through a more highly leveraged pay plan, when the risk-neutral firm is better suited to handle it. The results also show, though, that when the pay plan is less leveraged (i.e. when the ratio of salary to expected income rises), sales effort falls and firm profitability concomitantly falls. When the outside market promises better alternative compensation, the agency-theoretic framework predicts both higher total pay and less leverage in the pay plan, resulting in lower firm profitability and sales effort. Higher-cost firms are predicted to offer lower and less leveraged total compensation, again resulting in lower profitability and lower sales effort. More productive salespeople are offered higher total compensation, exert more effort and accrue more profit for the firm. And, finally, salespeople selling products with greater inherent popularity (i.e. greater sales even with minimal or no sales effort exertion) are offered lower salaries, and their firms make more profit, though other predictions vary depending on specific model assumptions.

These agency-theoretic predictions have been empirically tested in multiple research studies. In general, the empirical tests fail to reject the overall theory, though specific studies test only a subset of the available hypotheses (and may include other variables as controls). As Table 26.3 highlights, hypotheses regarding *expected total income* and the *salary/total pay ratio* are tested, rather than those predicting salary, commission rate, profit or sales effort. The effects of sales effort effectiveness, outside earnings opportunities and risk aversion are consistent with the predictions of the theory. The effect of uncertainty in the sales response function on leverage in the pay plan is consistent with the theory, but there is no support for the expected negative relationship between sales response function uncertainty and total pay. Overall, however, the empirical evidence

Table 26.2   Predictions from agency-theoretic sales compensation models[1]

Effect of Increased:	Effect on Optimal:					
	Salary	Commission Rate	Expected Total Income	Salary/ Expected Income Ratio	Firm Profit	Sales Effort
Uncertainty in Sales Response Function	(+)	(–)	(–)	(+)	(–)	(–)
Salesperson Risk Aversion	(+)	(–)	(–)	(+)	(–)	(–)
Marginal Cost of Production	(+)	(–)	(–)	(+)	(–)	(–)
Salesperson Outside Earning Opportunity	(+)	(–)	(+)	(+)	(–)	(–)
Effectiveness of Sales Effort*	(–)	(+)	(+)	(–)	(+)	(+)
Base Sales Level (with zero sales effort)	(–)	Ambiguous	Ambiguous	Ambiguous	(+)	Ambiguous

Notes:
1. Adapted from Basu et al. (1985) and Lal and Srinivasan (1993). Basu et al. analyze both gamma and binomial error distributions for the sales response function. Lal and Srinivasan assume an exponential salesperson utility function and sales response function with a normal error distribution. In a few cases, the Lal and Srinivasan's predictions differ from those of Basu et al. For example, Lal and Srinivasan predict no effect of Salesperson Outside Earning Opportunity on effort or the commission rate. In addition, higher sales effort effectiveness leads to a lower salary, higher commission rate, higher total income, lower salary–total pay ratio, higher profit, and higher effort. Basu et al. do not publish comparative-static effects of risk aversion on optimal outcomes. The effect of a higher Base Sales Level varies depending on the underlying error distribution in the sales response function; only the unambiguous effects are listed in this table.
(+) means a positive effect on the optimal variable level; (–) means a negative effect on the optimal variable level; 'Ambiguous' means the effect cannot be signed or differs across different sales response functional forms.
*   Effectiveness of 'Sales Effort' predictions are as in Lal and Srinivasan (1993).

is consistent with agency-theoretic rationales for pay. Clearly, future research could do more to investigate the effects of these factors on sales effort and firm profitability as well.

Beyond these basic agency-theoretic predictions, the empirical articles include other factors as controls or predictors of sales force pay amounts and/or leverage. Using data aggregated to the company level from Dartnell Corporation, Coughlan and Narasimhan (1992) find that the presence of a career path for salespeople is associated with less leverage in the pay plan; this is hypothesized to hold because offering the promise of a job promotion (future pay-off for today's effort) is a substitute for incentive pay (current pay-off for today's effort), so when it is available, incentive pay is not as important an effort motivator on the margin in the optimal sales compensation plan. Coughlan and Narasimhan also find that firms set a longer horizon for incentive pay (e.g. commissions paid out every quarter rather than every month) the longer is the sales performance

Table 26.3   Empirical evidence on predictions from agency-theoretic sales compensation models

Predicted Effect on Optimal Expected Total Income of:	Coughlan and Narasimhan (1992)	Joseph and Kalwani (1995)	Misra, Coughlan and Narasimhan (2005)	Rouzies et al. (2009)
Uncertainty in Sales Response Function (−)	Not significant	Not supported	Negative, but not significant	NA
Salesperson Risk Aversion (−)	NA	Negative, but not significant	NA	NA
Salesperson Outside Earning Opportunity (+)	Positive	NA	Positive	Positive
Effectiveness of Selling Effort (+)	Positive	NA	Positive	NA
Predicted Effect on Optimal Ratio of Salary/Expected Total Income of:				
Uncertainty in Sales Response Function (+)	Positive	Positive (but only when risk aversion is high)	Positive	NA
Salesperson Risk Aversion (+)	NA	Positive	NA	NA
Salesperson Outside Earning Opportunity (+)	Positive	NA	Positive	Positive
Effectiveness of Selling Effort (−)	Negative	NA	Negative	NA

Notes:
NA denotes not applicable because this hypothesis was not tested in the research in question.
Rouzies et al. (2009) summarize their hypotheses for the field sales force, though they also present hypotheses and tests thereof for compensation of sales managers.

horizon (as measured by the time a salesperson has to make quota); thus, firms seek to match incentive awards to sales performance timing.

Misra et al. (2005) extend the classic agency-theoretic sales compensation model to include firm size, which they predict is positively associated with the pay plan's leverage (ratio of incentive to total pay) and with total pay itself. Both predictions are supported in the data analysis, which re-estimates Coughlan and Narasimhan's (1992) data (from 1986) and compares them with analogous data from 1996.

Joseph and Kalwani (1995) use survey data and find that the size of the sales force is associated with higher leverage in the pay plan, consistent with Misra et al. (2005); Joseph and Kalwani (1995) also show that pay plan leverage is positively associated with the proportion of salesperson time spent on direct selling activities, consistent with the need to provide strong incentives for well-allocated selling time.

Rouzies et al. (2009) investigate the influence of the taxation system on the split between salary and incentive pay, using a multicountry European data set measured at the disaggregated level of the salesperson (not the sales force, as other studies are forced to do). These data use the 'Hay point'[4] as a measure of job challenge, a correlate of the opportunity cost of the salesperson's time. This research hypothesizes that the compensation plan will be more highly leveraged (i.e. rely more heavily on incentive pay) the more burdensome are either: (1) employee taxes; or (2) employer taxes. Indeed, companies motivate their sales forces in response not only to the standard agency-theoretic factors but also to the tax burden. The reasoning behind this result is that when tax burdens are high, achieving the desired differential in *net* (take-home) pay between excellent and average performers requires a disproportionately greater differential in *gross* (pre-tax) pay. Offering compensation that is more heavily incentive weighted allows the firm to economize on total compensation costs (it does not have to pay high *employer* taxes on highly salaried salespeople) and allows salespeople to pay higher taxes only when they achieve excellent sales performance.

Rouzies et al. (2009) also examine the interrelationship between total (take-home) pay and the leverage in the pay plan and find that they are positively related. This is consistent with the agency-theoretic logic that when the compensation plan makes the salesperson bear more risk (because of its heavier reliance on incentive pay), the firm must commensurately offer a risk premium through a *total* pay level that is higher.

These results show solid support for the agency-theoretic approach to predicting sales compensation levels and leverage. However, the focus in this literature on two compensation elements, salary and generic incentive pay, masks the subtleties of using various types of incentives for particular motivational purposes in the sales force. Therefore, we now turn to a survey of the results on the use of quota–bonus plans, sales contests, and spiffs and group commission compensation awards.

QUOTA–BONUS PLANS

The agency-theoretic approach has been very useful in delineating the essential trade-offs inherent in employing salary versus incentive compensation. In this analysis, the resulting optimal compensation offered to the salesperson is mathematically represented as a non-linear and continuous function of sales. However, empirical surveys reported in the literature suggest that real-world sales organizations frequently differ from this idealized representation on account of discontinuities introduced through a quota–bonus plan (Joseph and Kalwani 1998). That is, firms often employ bonus payments pegged to some predetermined level of performance, which is typically called the quota. Moreover, the slope of the compensation function usually exhibits a sharp upward kink at the point of the quota. Typically, the quota is based on sales volume, but many other dimensions of performance, such as division profitability, new accounts, sales of new products, account retention and customer satisfaction, are also frequently employed (Joseph and Kalwani 1998).

This departure from the agency-theoretic representation of a smooth, non-linear compensation function does not diminish the essential logic of the approach. However, it does provide opportunities for bringing the theory closer to the operational realities of designing compensation plans for the sales force. The works reviewed next illustrate this premise.

Raju and Srinivasan (1996) formally observe that a quota–bonus scheme is essentially a piecewise linear compensation plan with a discontinuity at the quota. They compare the performance of this piecewise linear compensation plan with the optimal, non-linear plan derived in Basu et al. (1985). For reasonable values of the parameter space, they demonstrate that the non-optimality emerging from this approximation is less than 1 per cent. They thus make a strong case for employing piecewise linear plans in practice. The piecewise linear quota–bonus plan also provides the real benefit of communicating a single plan to the entire sales force but altering the quota (point of discontinuity) to account for salesperson or territory heterogeneity.

Mantrala et al. (1994) recognize another important aspect of heterogeneity, namely, that salespeople may differ in their preferences with regard to various quota–bonus combinations. They propose a conjoint-based task to elicit this preference structure and use these preferences as constraints in the firm's optimization problem that involves designing a common quota–bonus plan across the entire sales force. In essence, they design compensation plans while explicitly recognizing heterogeneity in salesperson preferences for different quota–bonus pairs.

Ross (1991) and Gaba and Kalra (1999) highlight yet another important behavioral feature that is likely to arise when salespeople face the discontinuity inherent in a quota–bonus plan: specifically, that salespeople may modify their account selection strategies (high pay-off, high risk vs. low pay-off, low risk) as a function of their current standing relative to quota. Ross argues that this behavior calls for additional managerial monitoring of salesperson performance relative to quota with attendant interventions to ensure that salespeople's account selection choices are consistent with company policy. In a similar vein, Gaba and Kalra suggest that the stringency of quotas or contests should take into account the type of clients the firm desires to acquire.

Quota–bonus schemes can also enable firms to learn about market demand. Mantrala et al. (1997) demonstrate how quotas can be employed not only to motivate salespeople but also to generate valuable information back to the firm about unknown territory characteristics. They explicitly derive the period-by-period quota-setting rule by employing Bayesian adaptive control methodology.

More recently, Steenburgh (2008) and Chung et al. (2009) examine the use of both quarterly and annual bonuses and their impact on sales productivity. They find that bonuses help stimulate enhanced productivity. Notably, an annual bonus rewards high performance, while quarterly bonuses serve as pacers to keep the sales force on track to achieve annual sales quotas. These results imply that concern in the prior theoretical literature that salespeople may strategically 'time' their sales to earn bonuses, without increasing the firm's sales, may be overstated. Misra and Nair (2009) observe a similar phenomenon; they model dynamics of quota–bonus plan incentives and find that the distance to the quota horizon (e.g. with a three-month quota horizon, the maximum distance is three months and the minimum is zero) significantly influences sales performance. Early in the quota period, sales per week are low; they rise as the salesperson nears the quota level (implying accelerating effort exertion) but then fall when the salesperson reaches approximately 40 per cent of quota (which typically happens in the first two months of the three-month quota period); this suggests that the salesperson knows he or she will make quota by the end of the period and therefore does not need to overexert on sales effort.

In summary, various researchers have fruitfully examined several operational aspects of quota–bonus schemes. Nevertheless, there remain many avenues for future research. These include:

- How can territory and salesperson characteristics be employed to determine the level of quota?
- Given performance relative to quota for a given period, how are quotas set for the next period?
- How are quota–bonus plans set when there are multiple measures of performance?
- How are multiple performance measures best combined?

SALES CONTESTS

Sales contests reward salespeople for their performance *relative to* another salesperson or other salespeople. Contests are defined along many dimensions, including (Murphy et al. 2004; Zoltners et al. 2006):

- contest goal (outcome-based, process-based, or a combination of the two);
- competitive format (individual or team, single or multiple prizes);
- award type (cash merchandise, travel);
- contest duration;
- award value; and
- contest theme.

Although contests are often designed so that it is possible for everyone to win, through the establishment of individual performance goals rather than a winner-takes-all format, it is also common to limit the total number of possible contest winners to some intermediate range.[5] Presumably, a contest is more effective the more attractive its attributes are to the salespeople competing in it. With this underlying maintained hypothesis, Murphy et al. (2004) use expectancy theory to investigate salespeople's contest design preferences. Using a conjoint task, they find that, on average, field salespeople prefer the following:

- outcome-based goals to either process-based goals or a combination of outcome-based and process-based goals;
- a mid-range of number of winners to either a winner-takes-all or an all-can-win contest design;
- cash awards, followed by travel awards; merchandise is least preferred;
- sales contests with a moderate duration of about one sales cycle to either longer or shorter contest lengths; and
- contests with greater award values.

Murphy et al. (2004) attribute the first finding to the idea that field salespeople are used to being out on their own rather than being monitored and supervised closely by a manager, so outcome-based rewards are most consistent with their work styles. The finding that cash is most motivational was contrary to the theoretical predictions but is consistent with a more economics-focused predictive framework, as is the result on greater award values. These findings, though particular to the sales forces surveyed, still provide guidelines about how the details of contest implementation might work best.

In the analytic literature, contests are also known as 'tournaments'.[6] In its simplest form, consider a two-person sales contest. The salesperson with the highest sales achieved over the contest horizon is the *winner*, and the other salesperson is the *loser*. The winner and loser earn contest compensation, with the winner's prize (obviously) higher than the loser's prize. (In the academic literature, often the loser's prize is set equal to zero as an anchoring point, without loss of generality to the predictive results.) One reason sales contests can be extremely effective motivators is that the pay-out scheme naturally nets out systematic risk (i.e. the risk that pervades the sales response functions of all territories).

Some key properties of contests affect how hard salespeople work to win and, thus, how profitable it is to run a contest. One is the *degree of similarity or difference in sales potential across territories*. Consider the classic contest compensation: the top sales producer wins the prize. Then, if territories have sufficiently similar potential, a contest offers a 'good horse race', that is, one in which the outcome is not a foregone conclusion. Without a 'good horse race', neither top nor mediocre salespeople will be motivated to work hard, and the contest will fail. This is obvious in the case of a salesperson who knows he or she has no chance of winning the contest prize (why work hard when there is no compensation for it at the end of the contest period?). Even the obvious winner also has little incentive to work hard, because he or she already knows he or she will win in the end. It is only necessary to exert a minimal amount of effort to prevent the next best (or next most likely to win) salesperson from beating him or her.

When territories have significantly different sales potentials, the firm can still run a highly motivational sales contest, but not with a standard 'top producer wins the prize' compensation rule. Instead, if the firm employs some sort of handicap, or if it segments the territories to create subgroups of territories whose potentials are similar enough within-group, the 'good (adjusted by handicaps) horse race' is restored. For example, the handicap might measure performance above quota (e.g. those discussed in the section above on quota–bonus plans); the salesperson with the highest performance above quota would then be the winner, not the salesperson with the highest performance in absolute terms.

Another important factor in running a successful sales contest is the *variance in the effort-to-sales relationship*. One might casually think that high variance lessens the profitability of running a contest, but this intuition is incorrect. For a given amount of difference in potentials across territories, there must be some uncertainty in the effort-to-sales relationship for a contest to motivate high sales effort. If there were no uncertainty, the outcome would be obvious even before the contest started: the salesperson with the highest territory potential could exert a high enough amount of effort to win *for sure*. Such a contest would fail to motivate the whole sales force to work hard. In contrast, some uncertainty in the sales response function makes it possible for hard work to pay off even when a salesperson's territory has a slightly lower average potential than another territory, thus giving the entire sales force a reason to try to win.

That being said, the optimal amount of variance in the sales response function is not infinite; one important mediating factor is salespeople's *attitude toward risk*. The more risk averse salespeople are, the larger the expected pay premium must be to induce them to bear the risk of competing in a sales contest. Even supposing equal average territory productivity levels, it is true that for any level of variance in the sales response function, there must be a maximum degree of risk aversion beyond which there is no contest that covers the compensation cost (including risk premiums) of running it; thus, there is a natural limit on the feasibility of contests in general.

Yet another contributing factor to the success and optimal design of contests is the degree of correlation in outcomes across sales territories. Most of the academic research on contests implicitly or explicitly assumes that there is a *positive* correlation in outcomes, and when this is so, a contest is more likely to be feasible the stronger is the positive correlation between territory outcomes. Even for negatively correlated territory outcomes, it can be feasible to design a sales contest that motivates high effort and covers its compensation costs. The issue in such cases is whether an alternative incentive compensation option would work better. Caldieraro and Coughlan (2009) compare the profitability of offering a sales contest versus a compensation plan with a salary plus commission, in which the commission structure can be on own sales only or on own sales and cross-territory sales (a 'group commission'). When these three compensation options are possible, a contest is more likely to be optimal:

- the lower is risk aversion in the sales force;
- the less disutility there is for sales effort exertion;
- the more similar sales potentials are across territories;
- the more similar salespeople's sales effort productivities are; and
- the more positively correlated outcomes are across territories.

Too strong a departure from these tendencies not only makes a sales contest a less profitable compensation mechanism for the firm but also eventually makes it infeasible (i.e. it does not lead to high effort exertion in the sales force).

The firm contemplating offering a sales contest usually faces budgetary constraints in allocating the overall marketing budget. Murthy and Mantrala (2005) consider this problem, in which the budget must be allocated between advertising expenditures and contest prizes. Both marketing mix expenditures positively affect sales, with advertising increasing the productivity of sales effort and contest prizes increasing effort incentives as well. Murthy and Mantrala find that the proportion of the promotional budget to allocate to the contest is greater: (1) the less sales uncertainty there is; (2) the lower is the salesperson's disutility for sales effort; (3) the lower is risk aversion in the sales force; and (4) the more effective sales effort is in generating sales. A balanced allocation between advertising and contest funding is optimal, with the proportionate funding of the contest depending interactively on sales force size and the planned number of contest winners. Specifically, the optimal contest funding proportion *drops* as sales force size increases if a low enough percentage of the sales force is planned to win a prize in the contest. This is because fewer absolute salespeople stand to win, and thus the motivational power of the contest decreases.

Gaba and Kalra (1999) extend the basic contest literature by considering the possibility that the salesperson can choose not only overall sales effort but also the *variance* of the sales response function he or she faces. For example, a salesperson could choose to target one big customer with strong sales effort; although this customer has a relatively low conversion-to-sales probability, the expected order size if the customer does convert is huge. Alternatively, the salesperson could follow a less risky strategy and target many 'smaller fish', each of which has a higher conversion probability but a lower expected order size. Gaba and Kalra show that when risk (i.e. variance in the sales response function) is a choice variable of the salesperson along with sales effort, a contest with only a few prizes (for the topmost performers) induces salespeople to undertake riskier prospecting strategies than a contest offering prizes to more contestants. They find support for their analytic predictions in experimental tests.[7]

The questions of the number of salespeople who should be winners and how to allocate the rewards in a contest are the focus of Kalra and Shi's (2001) study. They find that optimal contest design depends on the number of salespeople vying for rewards, their risk aversion and the degree of uncertainty in the sales response function. Salespeople are predicted to exert less effort the more salespeople they are competing with and the greater the sales response function uncertainty. The optimal number of contest winners is predicted to increase with salesperson risk aversion and the number of salespeople and to fall with increases in sales response function uncertainty; the optimal monetary spread between adjacent awards is predicted to decrease, the more risk averse salespeople are.

Lim et al. (2009) test some of Kalra and Shi's (2001) predictions. Using experimentation both in the laboratory and in the field, they examine the prediction that the optimal contest involves multiple prizes (rather than one) and that these prizes are both rank ordered to match the ordinal performance of the winners and are also unique in value (no duplicate prizes). Their research question then is whether the greatest effect of a contest occurs when the firm complicates the contest by offering multiple prizes, uniquely rank ordered, or, alternatively, whether a contest with multiple prizes of the same value works just as well. They find that moving from a single winner-takes-all contest prize structure to a multiple-prize structure *does* boost sales performance. But there is no performance enhancement when the multiple prizes are rank ordered and unique, versus the same in value. They conclude that the prize structure need not be as complicated as Kalra and Shi suggest; it can simply determine the number of winners and the equal prize value for all winners, rather than also needing to calculate the optimal spread between awards.

Finally, a set of primarily empirical studies uncovers some insights into the dynamic nature of incentives in tournaments. Sales contest administrators are often concerned about the problem of 'gaming the system', for example, by saving up precontest sales until the start of the contest period and/or pushing postcontest sales into the contest period to artificially inflate contest performance, to the detriment of orders around the contest period and possibly also to the long-term relationship with the customer. Gopalakrishna et al. (2006) show that this concern may be overstated. In an empirical study of an insurance company, they find some evidence of a precontest trough; however, the incremental sales during and even following the contest period led to net new sales. Furthermore, the increased effort spent on selling the contest-award product did not lessen sales of other products in the agents' portfolios. Finally, the contests were profitable to the firm.

Other empirical contest research findings support the theoretical predictions about contest design and outcomes and thus suggest the theory's applicability in both B2B and other general sales contexts:[8]

- When the contest has a longer time horizon, larger contest winning amounts increase performance, but only with a time lag, suggesting that the *dynamics of competition in the contest* affect effort exertion throughout the contest period.
- The higher the *marginal return to effort late in the contest period*, the harder a contestant works to win the tournament in later periods of a dynamic contest horizon.
- If one contestant has a strong lead in the tournament at any given point in time, this lessens the effort level of other contestants.
- Contestants who are behind in the contest in early periods increase their effort, in an attempt to catch up to the leader; they lose motivation only when the gap with the leader is too great. A winner who is very far ahead also loses motivation to exert high effort in later periods of the contest. Thus, a 'poor horse race' really does decrease motivation for both the eventual losers and the eventual winner.
- Effort levels are lower in tournaments with a higher number of contestants, even for a fixed percentage of winners.

In summary, sales contests have proved to be effective short-term effort motivators for salespeople. It is rather obvious that higher prize payments elicit higher effort levels, but many other findings, both theoretical and empirical, are much more subtle in nature. Managers wanting to implement good contests can focus on contests that: (1) provide multiple prizes (not winner-takes-all); (2) provide some incremental incentive to do better but do not necessarily have elaborate multi-tier winning levels; and (3) run for one to two sales cycles. Managers should be aware that effort is likely to intensify later in a long-term contest, even if effort does not seem to be aggressive early on, and that effort is higher when the contest offers a 'good horse race' but that there are conditions when contests are not feasible to implement (e.g. when cross-territory outcomes are insufficiently positively correlated, when salespeople are too risk averse, when variance in sales response functions is too small or extremely high, and when territory potentials are too disparate).

With these caveats, we now turn to some other sales incentives. These include spiffs and compensation awards based on the performance of multiple salespeople.

SPIFFS AND COMPENSATION BASED ON MULTIPLE SALESPEOPLE'S PERFORMANCE

In this section, we examine other sales force incentive pay components not previously reviewed: spiffs and group commission compensation awards. Spiffs are payments salespeople receive for short-term and well-defined sales performance activities. Firms may use spiffs to promote a new-to-the-market product or to intensify sales effort during a slow post-holiday season, for example. Firms can offer spiffs to their own employee sales force; however, in this context they are quite similar to quota–bonus plans. Thus, in the discussion here we focus on a more interesting application of spiffs: their use as direct compensation awards to the salespeople of a *channel intermediary's sales force*.[9]

Consider the situation in which a firm sells through the manufacturer's rep firms, which act as the firm's 'feet on the street' (i.e. they perform the same functions as an employee sales force but are employees of the intermediary, not of the manufacturer). As in any intermediary channel, the manufacturer loses important elements of control when selling through a rep firm, including the right to directly monitor or offer compensation for the sales force's activities on behalf of the manufacturer. An agency problem arises that is more complicated than that described in the previous section, because it requires the manufacturer to seek a compensation plan that aligns the incentives of both the *salespeople of the rep firm* and the *rep firm itself* with the firm's incentives. The usual compensation structure among a manufacturer, its rep firm and the rep firm's salespeople involves a commission on sales offered by the manufacturer to the rep firm and a salary plus incentive compensation contract offered by the rep firm to its employee sales reps. The rep firm typically carries an array of complementary products that together create a synergistic product line; thus, the compensation plan is designed to give the reps incentives to help the rep firm maximize *its* profits (a goal that is not coincident with that of maximizing the *manufacturer's* profits). Other products in the reps' line may carry a higher marginal commission or bonus rate than this manufacturer's product, so the effort exerted on behalf of this manufacturer's product may be lower than the manufacturer would prefer.

Against this backdrop, Caldieraro and Coughlan (2007) show that spiffs can move the rep firm channel closer to the coordinated outcome in situations in which compensation plans are not quickly adjustable. When multiple products (each with its own, different productivity of sales effort) are sold by a single manufacturer through the rep firm, when common commission rates are offered by the manufacturer to the rep firm for both products, and when common commission rates are offered by the rep firm to its salespeople for both products, the authors show that it is optimal to spiff the *lower-sales-productivity* product to the rep firm's sales force. In this case, the spiff allows the manufacturer to raise the effective incentive on the harder-to-sell product to equal that on the easier-to-sell product, thus restoring the incentives of the rep firm's sales force to work hard on *both* products. Note that this result is reversed in the case of competing manufacturers offering the same two products to the rep firm; then, it is optimal for the manufacturer of the *higher-sales-productivity* product to offer a spiff to the rep firm. This reversal results from the ability of the manufacturer of the higher-sales-productivity product to 'outbid' the other manufacturer for the time and effort of the rep's sales force. If the higher-sales-productivity manufacturer does not engage in optimal spiffing behavior, the manufacturer of the lower-sales-productivity product might be able to offer a spiff high enough to claim the favored position in the rep's product line-up. The higher-sales-productivity manufacturer thus is forced to spiff the rep firm's sales force just enough to make it uneconomical for the other manufacturer to bother to offer spiffs.

In short, spiffs are an optimal way to increase the flexibility of incentive payments to the intermediary's sales force. (If all compensation plans were infinitely flexible, spiffs would not work because they would simply cause the rep firm and the competing manufacturer to instantaneously adjust their own compensation plans to restore the original incentives.) Whether the stronger or weaker product is optimally spiffed depends on whether the external effects of spiffing are internalized by the same manufacturer or are inflicted on a competing manufacturer. When externalities are internalized, the weaker product should be spiffed; when attempting to deter a weaker competitor from appropriating sales effort 'share', a spiff on the stronger product has the appropriate deterrence effect.

The spiffing results rely on an assumption that the same sales force sells both products, and therefore there is a need to try to rationalize salespeople's time allocation across the products. What if, instead, the firm manages salespeople who each have their own territories and sell the same product, but the territories themselves have some degree of non-zero covariance? Can the firm take advantage of this covariance and improve its profitability by preserving the incentive to exert effort, while lessening total compensation costs? Caldieraro and Coughlan (2009) show that such a benefit is indeed possible when territory outcomes exhibit a negative covariance, through the addition of a *group commission* rate to the standard salary-plus-own-territory-commission compensation structure. The more negatively correlated the outcomes across the territories in question, the more important the group commission payment becomes as a percentage of total pay. The reason for this is that the group commission effectively 'pools the risk' that any one salesperson who operates in one territory faces. When a poor outcome occurs in one territory, the negatively correlated other territory is likely to have a good outcome. The group commission thus provides co-insurance for the two salespeople, lessening the compensation swings that would otherwise occur with the standard salary-plus-commission plan. This smoothing of compensation is valuable to a risk-averse sales force, and therefore the firm incurs a lower total compensation cost when using the group commission plan with negatively correlated sales territories.

These co-insurance benefits can be so powerful that they make it more profitable for the firm to allocate salespeople to territories with negative outcome correlations (a 'diversification' strategy) than to higher-productivity territories with positive correlations. Specifically, suppose the firm has three sales territories it could fill and must decide which territories to assign to two salespeople. Two of the three territories' outcomes are positively correlated (indeed, they may be of the identical type, with perfectly positively correlated outcomes and identical marginal sales productivities), and a third has slightly lower sales productivity but exhibits negative correlation with the first territory type. Then, the diversification strategy becomes relatively more profitable: (1) the stronger is the available negative cross-territory correlation; (2) the less are the differences in cross-territory sales productivity; (3) the lower is the variance of sales in the new territory type; (4) the more risk averse the salespeople are; and (5) the more costly it is to exert high sales effort. Furthermore, offering a group commission plan can dominate offering a sales contest when these conditions are strong enough.

These analyses show the value of thinking beyond the standard compensation components when designing the sales compensation plan. Selling through the efforts of an intermediary may require extra compensation components (e.g. spiffs) to offer effective incentives directly to those generating sales for the firm. Alternatively, the firm can take advantage of assets already available in its own sales force, such as the pre-existing outcome correlations across territories, to design a compensation plan that preserves the incentives to sell hard, while saving compensation dollars overall. The general principle in all these instances is that the firm should implement the least expensive compensation plan structure, which nevertheless does the best job in aligning the sales force's incentives with its own.

MONITORING OR INCENTIVES?

Although incentives are a powerful lever for controlling the sales force and have been the focus of much prior research, casual empiricism suggests that many elements of salesperson behavior are controlled through managerial monitoring. Joseph and Thevaranjan (1998) explicitly analyze the firm's joint decisions both about which costly incentive levels to offer and what investments to make in salesperson monitoring. A balance between the two sales management strategies is derived, recognizing that even though it is costly, monitoring beneficially allows the firm to lower its compensation costs both by reducing the amount of incentive compensation offered and by allowing the hiring of more risk-averse (and, thus, relatively more inexpensive) salespeople.

The choice between managing the sales force through incentives and managing through monitoring has been discussed in depth in the marketing literature examining what are called 'outcome-based control' (incentive plan design) and 'behavior-based control' (facilitated by monitoring).[10] In outcome-based control, little managerial direction is provided (i.e. there is little monitoring); instead, the emphasis is on the achievement of results (i.e. reliance on an incentive-heavy compensation plan). In contrast, behavior-based control is characterized by high levels of managerial intervention and the utilization of subjective measures of inputs (i.e. monitoring); when such intervention is both possible and cost effective, it leaves little reason for incentive pay and suggests a compensation plan more heavily weighted toward salary.

The essential ideas behind behavior-based control and output-based control merit renewed attention because of the continued development and advancement of new information technologies to help monitor and manage the salesperson's activities. These technologies improve sales management's information on field sales activities, suggesting the value of a renewed appraisal of the most appropriate balance between outcome-based (incentive) and behavior-based (monitoring) control elements in the sales compensation process. Sales force automation technologies, for example, provide a window into each salesperson's prospect funnel and account-specific calling patterns. Similarly, the availability of monitoring technologies has altered the use of performance metrics and the nature of risk sharing in the trucking industry (Hubbard 2000). It is possible that a similar evolution will occur in sales force settings as firms obtain greater visibility of and feedback on the salesperson's activities.

Future research avenues in the domain of sales force control include:

- How is technology affecting the performance metrics employed in sales force compensation contracts?
- How is technology affecting the extent of risk sharing in compensation contracts?
- How is technology affecting job design for salespeople?
- What factors inhibit the embrace of sales force automation technologies? For example, these technologies typically reduce the importance of previously unique value-added assets owned by the salesperson; consequently, new agency problems are likely to emerge.

PRICE DELEGATION

By virtue of their proximity to customers and to the market in general, salespeople are often better informed about customers' willingness to pay (WTP) and price sensitivity than their sales managers or higher executives at their firms. This suggests the potential value of delegating the pricing decision to the sales force, because it could result in appropriate pricing that maximizes sales success for a given level of sales force effort.

However, salespeople may not always have the firm's best interests at heart. The literature on sales force price delegation emphasizes that salespeople value both leisure and income and thus may exert less effort than the firm would like. Salespeople are also likely to be more risk averse than their employers, which leads them to seek the 'safe sale' rather than to reach for possibly higher WTP prospects but with a higher probability of failure. Although firms and sales managers may engage in monitoring effort to check on salespeople's work ethics and choices of sales targets, monitoring is costly and imperfect. These countervailing factors have been considered in both analytic and empirical articles on the price delegation question.

The main analytical findings with regard to the use of price delegation are as follows:

- The way incentive compensation is awarded affects the viability of price delegation. If commission is awarded on the basis of sales volume rather than profit margin, price delegation is not advisable, because the salesperson will maximize his or her income by setting a low price and thus achieving high sales (Bhardwaj 2001).
- Delegating pricing to the sales force can be a strategic competitive tool to soften price competition (Bhardwaj 2001). When commissions are awarded on the basis of profit margin, then the lower the commission rate, the higher the price the salesperson will set. Thus, the stronger the price competition, the greater is the value of delegating pricing to the sales force.
- Limiting price delegation can be profitable, even when salespeople's *ability* to find high-WTP customers exceeds that of the firm, because it can increase the effort salespeople exert to find customers willing to pay at least the minimum permitted price (Joseph 2001). This finding is of interest because it distinguishes between the salesperson's *inherent* superior knowledge of customers' WTP (Lal 1986) and his or her *potential* to discover WTP. If discovering WTP takes effort, delegating pricing decisions creates a pernicious incentive for the salesperson to underinvest in the WTP discovery process.
- This finding is mitigated by the proportion of high-WTP customers naturally occurring in the population of sales prospects. Joseph (2001) finds that only if the cost of WTP discovery is either very low or very high is price delegation optimal. If it is very low, the salesperson's effort to discover high-WTP customers is not very costly to him or her and the agency problem in price delegation is minimal. If it is very high, limiting price delegation by dictating a minimum threshold for pricing is not appropriate because it causes the salesperson to lose too many sales.
- When salespeople actually do possess valuable private information about WTP that is unknown to the firm, sales force compensation based on the *accuracy of a salesperson's forecast* can substitute for the need to delegate pricing authority to the sales force (Mishra and Prasad 2004, 2005). If the firm can contract with its

salesperson after the salesperson's revelation of information about market conditions (e.g. through forecasted sales), the firm's profits are the same whether it centralizes pricing or delegates it. This finding emphasizes that price delegation's value is in its ability to allow the firm to use the salesperson's superior (but private) knowledge about market conditions.

Empirical research generates findings generally consistent with these predictions. In one study of 222 German sales organizations across multiple industries, Hansen et al. (2008) find that price delegation is *less likely* when the firm is concerned about agency problems, specifically the salesperson shirking on effort and thus needing to charge a lower price. They also find a lower likelihood of using price delegation when the compensation plan awards commission on the basis of sales rather than profit margin and that price delegation is more likely the more the firm engages in monitoring (holding constant the efficacy of monitoring). In a subsequent survey of 181 industrial machinery and electrical engineering companies in Germany, Frenzen et al. (2010) find that price delegation is more likely the greater is the information asymmetry between the firm and the salesperson about market conditions, the more difficult it is to engage in high-quality monitoring, and the less risk averse are salespeople. They find that price delegation is positively linked to higher firm performance, especially with high market uncertainty and well-informed salespeople.

Overall, sales compensation managers can view price delegation as an important and useful tool for maximizing firm profits. This is particularly the case when salespeople's market information is clearly superior to that of the firm and when the agency problems associated with delegating pricing are either *de minimus* or can be controlled through mechanisms such as monitoring or the judicious choice of compensation contracts to offer.

CONCLUSION: UNDERRESEARCHED AREAS IN SALES COMPENSATION

This review presents a summary of research findings in some key areas of sales compensation: how high total pay should be, the appropriate degree of leverage (ratio of incentive to total pay), quota–bonus plans, sales contests, spiffs, multi-salesperson compensation, the choice of monitoring or incentives, and the decision whether to delegate pricing to the sales force.

Although much has been done in the past two decades, myriad questions remain to be attacked in the sales compensation arena. We close with a brief list of some of these:

● What should relative pay differences be, and what structural differences should there be, for B2B sales professionals at different levels of the sales organization: field salespeople, sales managers and key account managers? The results for field salespeople versus sales managers are presented in an empirical study of five European countries (Rouzies et al. 2009) and show that sales managers receive take-home pay from 25 to 50 per cent higher than field salespeople (depending on industry and country); their pay leverage is not much different (the largest difference being between field salespeople, 12 per cent, and sales managers, 8 per cent, in Germany); field salespeople's take-home pay increases at a *decreasing* rate with job challenge, while sales managers' take-home pay increases at an *increasing* rate with job challenge (consistent with the multiplier effect of a good sales manager on his or her many subordinates); and more aggressive taxation systems lead to more highly leveraged pay for both field salespeople and sales managers. Despite these insights, more can be done to compare optimal and actual pay structures and levels for different sales professional job levels.

- What are the right metrics on which to base sales compensation awards, and what metrics are commonly used today? For example, current research does not elucidate what a reasonable minimum quota amount is above which bonus should be earned; whether a bonus should be awarded for individual or group performance, and under what conditions; or whether and when to base commission pay on profit, gross margin, market share gains or sales. Answers to such questions will not be the same in all industries, sales force sizes, or countries, but some commonalities may emerge from further research.

- What is the right time horizon for sales force compensation? Misra and Nair (2009) comment that 'there exists no straightforward algorithm that would implement an exhaustive search over the multidimensional compensation space and uncover the optimal second best compensation policy' – including the right horizon over which to pay salespeople. Their study suggested that shortening the quota horizon from three months to one month improved profitability. Coughlan and Narasimhan (1992) find a positive relationship between the sales performance horizon and the incentive pay horizon. These insights form a tantalizing start but invite future inquiry.

- What is the proper interrelationship between compensation structures/amounts and sales force training? How does the combination of training and compensation affect sales force turnover, and what is the optimal tripartite combination of compensation structure, training levels and turnover? This is a key question because, as in Murthy and Mantrala's (2005) research, the firm must make a decision on the relative allocation of marketing and sales funds across training and compensation. Through training, the firm in effect can create a higher-productivity salesperson; while such a person brings in more revenue, they also cost more in terms of compensation. If in addition the firm's training program is so excellent as to spur competitors to 'pick off' already-trained salespeople, the firm's turnover costs may swamp the benefits of better-trained salespeople. Additional theoretical and empirical research on this question thus is warranted.

- What is the overall optimal compensation plan, and why should the firm prefer one type of extra incentive component to another? We indicate in this review a few examples of comparative analyses of one compensation investment versus another, but more such comparisons across multiple alternative incentive plans could uncover general rules for preferring one to another incentive type.

- More generally, how do compensation decisions interact with other important decisions, such as sales force structure, territory design, sales force selection, marketing–sales coordination and so forth? Most likely, dependencies are important in practice. For example, there may be interesting trade-offs between productivity and compensation costs as B2B firms move from specialized to generalized sales forces. Similarly, territory design can moderate salesperson productivity and, thereby, the incentive effects of compensation. Even more comprehensive research foci could consider joint sales force/organizational decisions, such as how to design compensation schemes to better coordinate the sales function with the marketing or new product development functions in the firm.

These research ideas are only a subset of all the possible ways we expect research insights to continue to be created in the area of sales compensation. We encourage our colleagues to attack these and other directions in the future.

NOTES

1. See, for example, Basu and colleagues (1985) and Lal and Srinivasan (1993). Summary articles that comment on the agency-theoretic approach include Coughlan (1993), Coughlan and Sen (1989), Bergen et al. (1992) and Albers (1996).
2. The classic agency-theoretic problem assumes that prices are set outside the sales management sphere and thus are a parameter of the sales response function. Later work examines the advisability of granting the salesperson the right to set price and to choose the amount of selling effort; see the 'Price delegation' section for details on results in the literature with this extension.
3. Because the firm is lifting all risk bearing from the salesperson's shoulders, any combination of salary and incentive pay that also produces the same total pay for the same number of hours worked is an equivalently profitable compensation solution.
4. The Hay Group is the world's largest compensation consulting firm and the innovator of the Hay point metric for measuring job challenge. The construct has been exhaustively calibrated across many companies, industries and job classifications to create a reliable and comparable measure of the sophistication of the tasks and duties of various job types.
5. Murphy et al. (2004) refer to a 20 to 40 per cent winner rate as common, citing Churchill et al. (2000) and Colletti et al. (1988). Zoltners et al. (2006) note that with a fixed contest budget, the firm faces a trade-off between offering a high winning likelihood with low prize values and offering one or a few large prize values. Both options have some 'traction' value, implying that a balance in the middle is likely to be best in many sales situations.
6. See Lazear and Rosen (1981), Green and Stokey (1983), Nalebuff and Stiglitz (1983), O'Keefe et al. (1984) and Prendergast (1999) for the basics of tournament compensation models in the economics literature.
7. In a different context, an empirical study of NASCAR and International Motor Sports Association auto racing (Becker and Huselid 1992) generates similar findings to those of Gaba and Kalra (1999), but only in terms of the 'spread' between adjacent prize amounts rather than in terms of the number of prizes. This suggests the robustness of these findings and their applicability in many B2B contexts.
8. See Ehrenberg and Bognanno (1990), who study the behavior of men's Professional Golf Association tour, for the results on dynamic effects in contests. See Casas-Arce and Martinez-Jerez (2009) for the results on contestant positions (relative and actual) on motivation to exert effort.
9. This discussion is based on Caldieraro and Coughlan (2007).
10. Key references in this area include (but are not limited to) Anderson and Oliver (1987), Bergen et al. (1992), Eisenhardt (1985, 1989), Cravens et al. (1993), Celly and Frazier (1996), Oliver and Anderson (1994) and Grant and Cravens (1996).

REFERENCES

Albers, Sonke (1996), 'Optimization models for salesforce compensation', *European Journal of Operational Research*, **89** (1), 1–17.
Albers, Sonke (2002), 'Salesforce management: compensation, motivation, selection, and training', in Barton

A. Weitz and Robin Wensley (eds), *Handbook on Marketing*, Thousand Oaks, CA: Sage Publications, pp. 249–66.

Anderson, Erin and Richard L. Oliver (1987), 'Perspectives on behavior-based versus outcome-based control systems', *Journal of Marketing*, **51** (4), 76–88.

Basu, Amiya K., Rajiv Lal, V. Srinivasan and Richard Staelin (1985), 'Salesforce compensation plans: an agency theoretic perspective', *Marketing Science*, **4** (4), 267–91.

Becker, Brian E. and Mark A. Huselid (1992), 'The incentive effects of tournament compensation systems', *Administrative Science Quarterly*, **37** (2), 336–50.

Bergen, Mark, Shantanu Dutta and Orville C. Walker Jr (1992), 'Agency relationships in marketing: a review of the implications and applications of agency and related theories', *Journal of Marketing*, **56** (2), 1–24.

Bhardwaj, Pradeep (2001), 'Delegating pricing decisions', *Marketing Science*, **20** (2), 143–69.

Caldieraro, Fabio and Anne T. Coughlan (2007), 'Spiffed-up channels: the role of spiffs in hierarchical selling organizations', *Marketing Science*, **26** (1), 31–51.

Caldieraro, Fabio and Anne T. Coughlan (2009), 'Optimal sales force diversification and group incentive payments', *Marketing Science*, **28** (6), 1009–26.

Casas-Arce, Pablo and F. Asis Martinez-Jerez (2009), 'Relative performance compensation, contests, and dynamic incentives', *Management Science*, **55** (8), 1306–20.

Celly, Kirti Sawhney and Gary L. Frazier (1996), 'Outcome-based and behavior-based coordination efforts in channel relationships', *Journal of Marketing Research*, **33** (2), 200–210.

CFO Research Services (2010), *Managing Sales Incentive Compensation Amid Uncertainty*, New York: CFO Publishing.

Chung, Doug, Thomas Steenburgh and K. Sudhir (2009), 'Do bonuses enhance sales productivity? A dynamic structural analysis of bonus-based compensation plans', working paper, Yale School of Management.

Churchill, Gilbert A., Neil M. Ford, Orville C. Walker, Mark W. Jonston and John F. Tanner Jr (2000), *Sales Force Management: Planning, Implementation, and Control*, 6th edn, Homewood, IL: Irwin.

Colletti, Jerome A., David J. Cichelli, S.D. Linser, J.F. Martin, D.S. Schattinger and Gary S. Tubridy (1988), *Current Practices in Sales Incentives*, New York: The Alexander Group.

Coughlan, Anne T. (1993), 'Salesforce compensation: a review of MS/OR advances', in J. Eliashberg and G.L. Lilien (eds), *Handbooks in Operations Research and Management Science*, Vol. 5, Amsterdam: Elsevier Science Publishers BV, pp. 611–51.

Coughlan, Anne T. and Chakravarthi Narasimhan (1992), 'An empirical analysis of sales-force compensation plans', *Journal of Business*, **65** (1), 93–121.

Coughlan, Anne T. and Subrata K. Sen (1989), 'Salesforce compensation: theory and managerial implications', *Marketing Science*, **8** (4), 324–42.

Cravens, David W., Thomas N. Ingram and Raymond W. LaForge (1993), 'Behavior-based and outcome-based salesforce control systems', *Journal of Marketing*, **57** (4), 47–59.

Ehrenberg, Ronald G. and Michael L. Bognanno (1990), 'Do tournaments have incentive effects?', *Journal of Political Economy*, **98** (6), 1307–24.

Eisenhardt, Kathleen M. (1985), 'Control: organizational and economic approaches', *Management Science*, **31** (2), 134–49.

Eisenhardt, Kathleen M. (1989), 'Agency theory: an assessment and review', *Academy of Management Review*, **14** (January), 57–74.

Frenzen, Heiko, Ann-Kristin Hansen, Manfred Krafft, Murali K. Mantrala and Simone Schmidt (2010), 'Delegation of pricing authority to the sales force: an agency-theoretic perspective of its determinants and impact on performance', *International Journal of Research in Marketing*, **27**, 58–68.

Gaba, Anil and Ajay Kalra (1999), 'Risk behavior in response to quotas and contests', *Marketing Science*, **18** (3), 417–34.

Gopalakrishna, Srinath, Jason Garrett, Murali K. Mantrala and J. David Moore (2006), 'Determining the effectiveness of sales contests', working paper, College of Business, University of Missouri–Columbia.

Grant, Ken and David W. Cravens (1996), 'Examining sales force performance in organizations that use behavior-based sales management processes', *Industrial Marketing Management*, **25** (5), 361–71.

Green, Jerry R. and Nancy L. Stokey (1983), 'A comparison of tournaments and contracts', *Journal of Political Economy*, **91** (3), 349–64.

Hansen, Ann-Kristin, Kissan Joseph and Manfred Krafft (2008), 'Price delegation in sales organizations: an empirical investigation', *Business Research*, **1** (1), 94–104.

Hubbard, Thomas N. (2000), 'The demand for monitoring technologies: the case of trucking', *Quarterly Journal of Economics*, **115** (2), 533–60.

Joseph, Kissan (2001), 'On the optimality of delegating pricing authority to the sales force', *Journal of Marketing*, **65** (1), 62–70.

Joseph, Kissan and Manohar U. Kalwani (1995), 'The impact of environmental uncertainty on the design of salesforce compensation plans', *Marketing Letters*, **6** (3), 183–97.

Joseph, Kissan and Manohar U. Kalwani (1998), 'The role of bonus pay in salesforce compensation plans', *Industrial Marketing Management*, **27**, 147–59.

Joseph, Kissan and Alex Thevaranjan (1998), 'Monitoring and incentives in sales organizations: an agency-theoretic perspective', *Marketing Science*, **17** (2), 107–23.

Kalra, Ajay and Mengze Shi (2001), 'Designing optimal sales contests: a theoretical perspective', *Marketing Science*, **20** (2), 170–93.

Lal, Rajiv (1986), 'Delegating pricing responsibility to the sales force', *Marketing Science*, 5 (2), 159–68.

Lal, Rajiv and V. Srinivasan (1993), 'Compensation plans for single- and multi-product salesforces: an application of the Holmstrom–Milgrom Model', *Management Science*, **39** (7), 777–93.

Lazear, Edward P. and Sherwin Rosen (1981), 'Rank-order tournaments as optimum labor contracts', *Journal of Political Economy*, **89** (5), 841–64.

Lim, Noah, Michael J. Ahearne and Sung H. Ham (2009), 'Designing sales contests: does the prize structure matter?', *Journal of Marketing Research*, **46** (3), 356–71.

Mantrala, Murali K., Kalyan Raman and Ramarao Desiraju (1997), 'Sales quota plans: mechanisms for adaptive learning', *Marketing Letters*, **8** (4), 393–405.

Mantrala, Murali K., Prabhakant Sinha and Andris A. Zoltners (1994), 'Structuring a multiproduct sales quota-bonus plan for a heterogeneous sales force: a practical model-based approach', *Marketing Science*, **13** (2), 121–44.

Mantrala, Murali K., Sonke Albers, Fabio Caldieraro, Ove Jensen, Kissan Joseph, Manfred Krafft, Chakravarthi Narasimhan, Srinath Gopalakrishna, Andris Zoltners, Rajiv Lal and Leonard Lodish (2010), 'Sales force modeling: state of the field and research agenda', *Marketing Letters*, **21** (3), 255–72.

Mishra, Birendra K. and Ashutosh Prasad (2004), 'Centralized pricing versus delegating pricing to the sales-force under information asymmetry', *Marketing Science*, **23** (1), 21–7.

Mishra, Birendra K. and Ashutosh Prasad (2005), 'Delegating pricing decisions in competitive markets with symmetric and asymmetric information', *Marketing Science*, **24** (3), 490–97.

Misra, Sanjog and Harikesh Nair (2009), 'A structural model of sales-force compensation dynamics: estimation and field implementation', working paper, Simon School of Business, University of Rochester.

Misra, Sanjog, Anne T. Coughlan and Chakravarthi Narasimhan (2005), 'Salesforce compensation: an analytical and empirical examination of the agency theoretic approach', *Quantitative Marketing and Economics*, **3**, 5–39.

Murphy, William H., Peter A. Dacin and Neil M. Ford (2004), 'Sales contest effectiveness: an examination of sales contest design preferences of field sales forces', *Journal of the Academy of Marketing Science*, **32** (2), 127–43.

Murthy, Pushkar and Murali K. Mantrala (2005), 'Allocating a promotion budget between advertising and sales contest prizes: an integrated marketing communications perspective', *Marketing Letters*, **16** (1), 19–35.

Nalebuff, Barry J. and Joseph E. Stiglitz (1983), 'Prizes and incentives: toward a general theory of compensation and competition', *Bell Journal of Economics*, **14** (1), 21–43.

O'Keefe, Mary, W. Kip Viscusi and Richard J. Zeckhauser (1984), 'Economic contests: comparative reward schemes', *Journal of Labor Economics*, **2** (1), 27–56.

Oliver, Richard L. and Erin Anderson (1994), 'An empirical test of the consequences of behavior- and outcome-based sales control systems', *Journal of Marketing*, **58** (4), 53–67.

Prendergast, Canice (1999), 'The provision of incentives in firms', *Journal of Economic Literature*, **37** (1), 7–63.

Rackham, Neil and John De Vincentis (1999), *Rethinking the Sale Force*, New York: McGraw-Hill.

Raju, Jagmohan S. and V. Srinivasan (1996), 'Quota-based compensation plans for multiterritory heterogeneous salesforces', *Management Science*, **42** (10), 1454–62.

Ross, William T., Jr. (1991), 'Performance against quota and the call selection decision', *Journal of Marketing Research*, **28** (3), 296–306.

Rouzies, Dominique, Anne T. Coughlan, Erin Anderson and Dawn Iacobucci (2009), 'Determinants of pay levels and structures in sales organizations', *Journal of Marketing*, **73** (6), 92–104.

Steenburgh, Thomas J. (2008), 'Effort or timing: the effect of lump-sum bonuses', *Quantitative Marketing & Economics*, **6**, 235–56.

Zoltners, Andris A., Prabhakant Sinha and Sally E. Lorimer (2006), *The Complete Guide to Sales Force Incentive Compensation*, New York: AMACOM.

27 Sales force performance: a typology and future research priorities
Michael Ahearne and Son K. Lam

In marketing research and practice in a selling context, performance implications are often demonstrated at the individual, business unit, or company level. Since Ford et al.'s (1985) book on sales force performance, the literature on sales force performance has become entrenched. Therefore, we take this opportunity to reflect on this voluminous body of research to chart future research avenues.

The purposes of this chapter are threefold. First, we survey the literature on sales force performance to evaluate how this important criterion variable has been defined, operationalized and measured. Using this survey, we develop a typology of sales force performance measures. To this end, we categorize sales force performance into topical areas along two dimensions – positive versus negative performance and behavioral versus outcome performance – and show how in-role and extra-role behavioral performance fit into the typology. Second, we identify future research topics in each of those areas. Third, we provide brief methodological notes for exploring these new topics. The organization of the chapter also follows this order.

We contribute to the ongoing conversation about sales force evaluation in two ways. The chapter provides not only a comprehensive review of the current state of the literature but also a useful typology for academic researchers and practitioners to appreciate and make sense of the complexity of sales force evaluation. In addition, in each topical area of sales force evaluation, we identify opportunities for further research that will inform managers of effective ways to evaluate performance. Given the focus of the chapter, we confine our discussion only to sales force performance and do not examine its antecedents. Interested readers can refer to the work of Churchill et al. (1985) for a meta-analytical review of these antecedents and Bagozzi (1978) for a social psychological treatment of the topic.

DEFINITIONS

Previous research has defined performance as a salesperson's contribution to the goals of the organization (Churchill et al. 1985). This contribution can take the form of sales productivity and behaviors that are the precursors to sales productivity. MacKenzie et al. (1998; see also Netemeyer et al. 1997) suggest that in evaluating salesperson performance, managers should also take into account organizational citizenship behaviors (OCBs), or discretionary behaviors on the part of the salesperson that directly promote the effective functioning of an organization, without necessarily influencing the salesperson's objective sales productivity. As we allude to subsequently, OCBs are a special type of extra-role behavior. From these perspectives, our working definition of sales force performance is the sales force's contribution to the organization's goals and to the effective functioning of the organization and work groups. Note that this contribution can be either positive or negative.

In evaluating performance, it is important to distinguish between inputs and outputs and between productivity and efficiency. The input versus output distinction is based on prior research on behavioral and outcome control (Anderson and Oliver 1987; Jackson et al. 1983; Jackson et al. 1995; Krafft 1999), which we describe in more detail in the next section. More broadly, input measures can go beyond salespeople's effort to include territory workload and market potential (Boles et al. 1995). Productivity refers to the contribution of salespeople to organizational performance, which can be behavioral (e.g. number of sales calls) or outcome (e.g. sales revenue). Therefore, productivity is synonymous with performance, or effectiveness. Finally, efficiency refers to the ratio of output to input. Efficiency is central to sales force performance evaluation that relies on data envelopment analysis (DEA) (Boles et al. 1995).

A TYPOLOGY OF SALES FORCE PERFORMANCE MEASURES

Before developing a typology of sales force performance measures and research streams, we conducted an extensive survey of how previous marketing research has operationalized and measured sales force performance. We limited our literature search to premiere journals. These include *Journal of Marketing Research*, *Journal of Marketing* and *Marketing Science*. We paid particular attention to studies on selling and sales management that appeared in these publications in the past 21 years (1990–2010). In our survey of the literature, we included studies that examine performance at the individual and group level (e.g. sales teams, self-managed teams, business units).[1] Because the focus of this handbook is on B2B marketing, we did not include studies that examine selling and services in a B2C context. Table 27.1 provides details of the measures used.

Measuring Sales Force Performance

Several noteworthy trends emerge from Table 27.1. First, the majority of studies use subjective (self-rated, other-rated) rather than objective performance. The most-often-used scale for measuring subjective performance is Behrman and Perreault's (1982) scale. Sujan et al. (1994) added two items to this scale on identifying attractive prospects and assisting sales supervisors to meet their goals. Dubinsky and Mattson (1979) developed another often-adapted scale in a retail context. Second, the most popular form of performance measured is in-role and positive behavior. Third, research on sales force extra-role behavior seems to be limited to OCBs. Fourth, few studies have examined negative performance, such as opportunistic behavior (Jaworski and MacInnis 1989; Ramaswami and Singh 2003). Finally, although many studies have examined the role of sales managers and sales supervisors, the majority of studies have focused on leadership, feedback and control systems. However, sales managers and supervisors fulfill many other important roles as well.

Sales force performance measures can serve a variety of purposes, such as benchmarking, compensation, control, selection or promotion consideration. Not only are these the logical next steps in performance evaluation, but they also determine which measures are appropriate in performance evaluation. To maintain the focus of the chapter on

Table 27.1   Existing performance measures and their use in premiere academic research

Article	Journal	Rating		Discretion		Control		Focus of analysis				
		Subjective	Objective	In-Role	Extra-Role	Outcome	Behavior	Sales Rep	Manager Role	Co-worker Role	Group Climate	Customer Role
MacKenzie, Podsakoff and Fetter 1993	JM	X	X	X	X	X	X	X	X			
Singh 1993	JM	X		X				X	X	X	X	X
Johnston and Kim 1994	JM	X		X			X	X				
Oliver and Anderson 1994	JM	X		X		X	X	X	X			
Challagalla and Shervani 1996	JM	X		X		X		X	X			
Singh, Verbeke and Rhoads 1996	JM	X		X		X	X	X			X	
Brown, Cron and Slocum 1997	JM	X		X		X	X	X				
Netemeyer et al. 1997	JM	X			X	X	X	X	X		X	
Brown, Cron and Slocum 1998	JM		X	X		X		X			X	
Singh 1998	JM	X		X		X	X	X				
Singh 2000	JM	X		X		X	X	X	X			
Ramaswami and Singh 2003	JM	X		X		X	X	X	X			
Verbeke et al. 2008	JM	X	X	X		X		X				
Ahearne et al. 2010a	JM		X	X		X		X				
Lam, Kraus and Ahearne 2010	JM		X	X		X	X	X	X	X	X	
Spiro and Weitz 1990	JMR	X		X		X	X	X	X			
Johnston et al. 1990	JMR	X		X			X	X		X		
Singh and Rhoads 1991	JMR	X		X		X	X	X				
Sujan, Weitz and Kumar 1994	JMR	X		X		X	X	X	X			
Chandrashekaran et al. 2000	JMR	X		X			X	X				
Palmatier, Scheer and Steenkamp 2007	JMR	X		X		X	X	X	X			X
Ahearne et al. 2010b	JMR		X	X	X	X	X	X	X		X	

Notes: JM = *Journal of Marketing*, and JMR = *Journal of Marketing Research*.

498

sales force performance measures and typology, we refer interested readers to Albers (2006) for more details. It is worth mentioning, however, that the purpose of measuring performance also determines the type of measures used and the data analytical strategy. As we allude to subsequently, individual evaluation (e.g. control, a focus on effectiveness) and relative evaluation (e.g. benchmarking, a focus on efficiency) call for different analytical techniques. Besides, because sales force evaluation for compensation purposes may require both individual and relative evaluation (e.g. comparing a focal salesperson with the best salesperson), managers may need to rely on a combination of primarily objective measures to be fair and analytical techniques to account for differences across sales territories and customer requirements.

Dimensions of Sales Force Performance Typology

Many studies beyond those we examine have tapped into other aspects of sales force performance or services behavior that are relevant to sales management. Thus, a typology of sales force performance will be incomplete if we do not include these studies. With that in mind, from our intensive review of the literature, we suggest that two important dimensions of sales force performance are positive versus negative performance and behavioral versus outcome performance. In the positive performance category, previous research has distinguished in-role from extra-role behavior. Extra-role behaviors are 'positive social acts which are not formally specified role requirements; they are not specifically assigned to individuals as activities to be performed as part of the job' (Brief and Motowidlo 1986, p. 712). Therefore, in-role versus extra-role performance captures what salespeople actually do relative to their role descriptions. In the negative performance category, previous research has shown that salespeople may engage in behavior that is not beneficial to the firm or the customers, such as unethical behavior or opportunistic behavior (Jaworski and MacInnis 1989).

The literature also informs that the distinction between behavioral versus outcome performance is critical (Anderson and Oliver 1987). According to Anderson and Oliver (1987, p. 51), under an outcome-based control system, 'salespeople are left alone to achieve results in their own way using their own strategies', and they 'are held accountable for their results (outcomes) but not for how they achieve the results (inputs or behavior).' Conversely, a behavior-based control system is 'typified by high levels of supervisor monitoring, direction and intervention in activities, and subjective and more complex methods of evaluating performance, typically centered on the salesperson's job inputs' (Oliver and Anderson 1994, p. 53). Much research has been developed to refine this distinction (e.g. Challagalla and Shervani 1996). Outcome control criteria can be sales, market shares, accounts, profit and orders taken, while behavior control tools can be product knowledge, presentation quality, closing ability and services performed (Anderson and Oliver 1987; Cravens et al. 1993; Jackson et al. 1995; Oliver and Anderson 1994). The behavioral–outcome performance dimension in our typology reflects what firms do to motivate, measure and reward sales force performance. Note that for the breadth of the measures, behavioral/outcome and positive/negative performance dimensions incorporate almost all performance measures in the literature. Figure 27.1 categorizes various types of performance measures along the two dimensions.

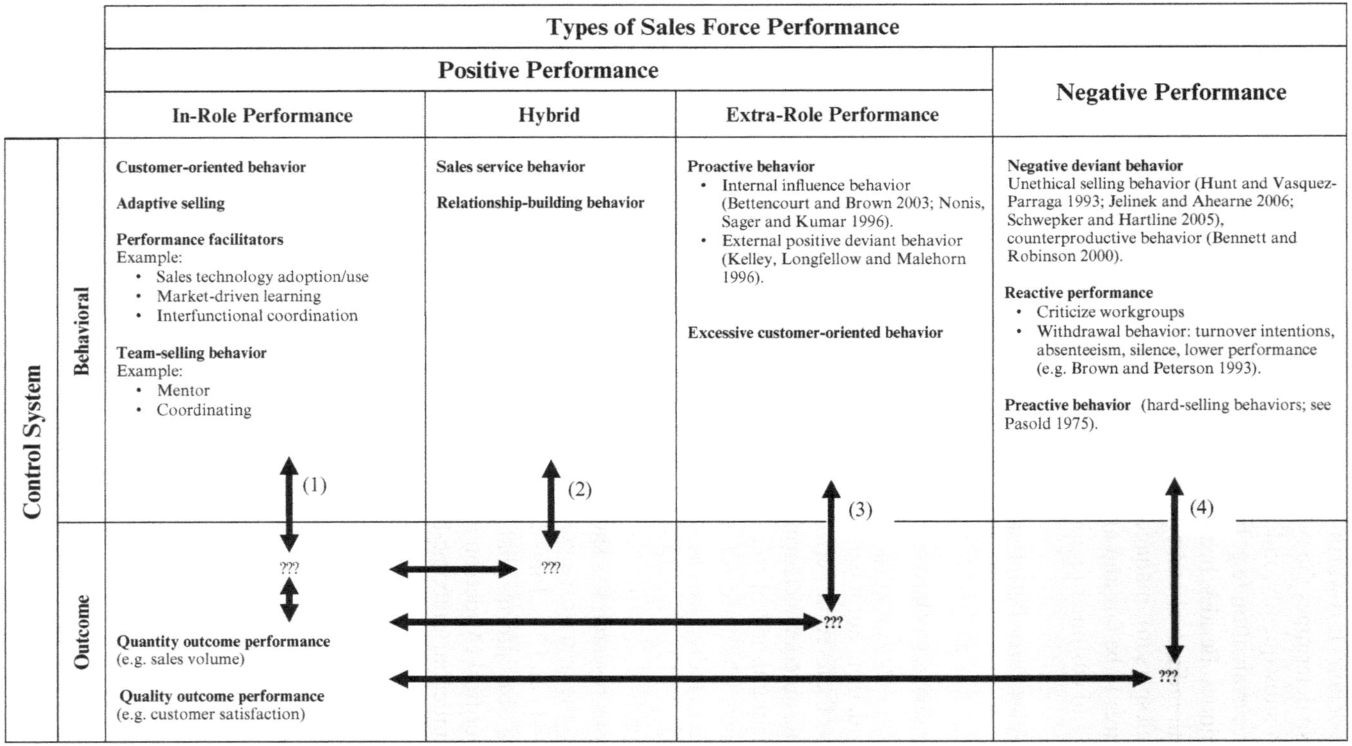

Types of Sales Force Performance

	Positive Performance			Negative Performance
Control System	**In-Role Performance**	**Hybrid**	**Extra-Role Performance**	
Behavioral	**Customer-oriented behavior** **Adaptive selling** **Performance facilitators** Example: • Sales technology adoption/use • Market-driven learning • Interfunctional coordination **Team-selling behavior** Example: • Mentor • Coordinating	**Sales service behavior** **Relationship-building behavior**	**Proactive behavior** • Internal influence behavior (Bettencourt and Brown 2003; Nonis, Sager and Kumar 1996). • External positive deviant behavior (Kelley, Longfellow and Malehorn 1996). **Excessive customer-oriented behavior**	**Negative deviant behavior** Unethical selling behavior (Hunt and Vasquez-Parraga 1993; Jelinek and Ahearne 2006; Schwepker and Hartline 2005); counterproductive behavior (Bennett and Robinson 2000). **Reactive performance** • Criticize workgroups • Withdrawal behavior: turnover intentions, absenteeism, silence, lower performance (e.g. Brown and Peterson 1993). **Proactive behavior** (hard-selling behaviors; see Pasold 1975).
Outcome	**Quantity outcome performance** (e.g. sales volume) **Quality outcome performance** (e.g. customer satisfaction) (1) ???	(2) ???	(3) ???	(4) ???

Notes: To avoid clusters, this figure does not reflect the respective levels of analysis (e.g. company, work group, individual).

Figure 27.1   A typology of performance measures

In developing this typology, we do not posit that these types of performance are independent of one another. Rather, our intent is quite the opposite.[2] In the next section, we delve deeper into each type of sales force performance.

Positive In-role Performance

Previous research has examined in-role performance from both outcome and behavioral performance perspectives. Although there are many types of behavioral and outcome in-role performance, they tend to fall into six major groups: customer-oriented behavior, adaptive selling behavior, performance-facilitating behavior, team-selling behavior, and quantity and quality outcome performance.

Customer-oriented behavior
Early work on salesperson behavior conceptualizes selling activities as following either a self-serving sales orientation to maximize short-term sales performance or a customer orientation. Customer-oriented selling is 'the practice of the marketing concept at the level of the individual salesperson and customer' (Saxe and Weitz 1982, p. 343). Research that uses the SOCO (selling orientation–customer orientation) scale is voluminous (Saxe and Weitz 1982). However, Franke and Park's (2006) meta-analysis shows that the relationship between customer orientation and performance outcomes is mixed and weak.

Adaptive selling behavior
Adaptive selling is defined as 'the altering of sales behaviors during a customer interaction or across customer interactions based on perceived information about the nature of the selling situation' (Weitz et al. 1986, p. 175). Similar to customer orientation, the relationship between adaptive selling and performance outcomes is significant when performance outcome is self-rated, but not manager rated (Spiro and Weitz 1990). Franke and Park (2006) found that adaptive selling behavior significantly increases customer-oriented selling, but the reverse is not true. Furthermore, adaptive selling behavior is more strongly related to performance than customer-oriented selling, regardless of the source of measures being used.

Performance-facilitating behavior
The literature has discussed multiple quantitative behavioral performance measures, such as sales calls, selling expense, ancillary activities, time utilization and qualitative behavioral/attitudinal measures (Jackson et al. 1995). Examples of these ancillary activities include sales technology adoption and use (Ahearne et al. 2008), market-driven learning such as competitive intelligence activities (Le Bon and Merunka 2006), and interfunctional coordination such as interacting with the marketing function (Homburg and Jensen 2007; Smith et al. 2006). Marshall et al. (1999) provide a comprehensive list of sales force activities in B2B sales. Performance-facilitating behavior can be qualitative and/or quantitative in nature.

Team-selling behavior
With increased use of team-based selling, researchers have begun to examine sales force behavior at the work-group level rather than at the individual level (e.g. Ahearne

et al. 2010b; De Jong et al. 2004). While this stream of research is still nascent in the marketing field, the literature on work groups and teams is voluminous in other fields (Guzzo and Dickson 1996). Of note is the widely used input–process–output (Hackman 1987; Steiner 1972) model, which posits that team *inputs* (e.g. team, supervisor, organizational and contextual characteristics) influence team *processes* (e.g. planning, strategy formulation, conflict management) and *emergent states* (e.g. cohesiveness, group potency), which ultimately lead to team *outputs* (e.g. effort, performance, efficiency). That being said, there is still room for further research, as we allude to subsequently.

Quantity and quality outcome performance

Some performance criteria can be expressed in comparable units (e.g. sales volume in dollars, number of new customers), but outcome performance, such as customer satisfaction and service quality, is considered quality in nature. Quality outcome performance refers to how quantity outcome performance is achieved (e.g. Singh 2000). This distinction is particularly important for both research and practice because quantity outcome performance can be readily compared across salespeople, sales teams and companies, while comparison of quality outcome performance is subject to various measurement issues. Recent research has also emphasized the importance of providing a competitive analysis of a customer's performance ratings about multiple companies (Ahearne et al. 2007). This approach is particularly important if managers want to use performance measures as a benchmarking tool (e.g. Albers 2006).

Positive Extra-role Performance

By definition, extra-role performance is not formally rewarded. Most extra-role performance activities are behavioral performance rather than outcome performance. We revisit the link between extra-role behavioral performance and outcome performance shortly.

OCBs

OCBs have been broadly studied in both management and marketing literature streams. Because of the many high-quality reviews (e.g. Organ et al. 2006), we do not discuss this behavior in detail in this chapter. However, a few points warrant mentioning here. First, extra-role behavior can be beneficial to the person being helped and the work-group climate but may hurt business unit performance (Podsakoff and MacKenzie 1994). Second, Podsakoff and MacKenzie (1997) distinguish between organization-directed and customer-directed extra-role behavior. This distinction is important, but empirical research examining customer-directed extra-role behavior is sparse (e.g. Wuyts 2007). Wuyts (2007) argues that while organization-directed extra-role behavior can be one-sided, customer-directed extra-role behavior is embedded in a dyadic relationship, and therefore the relationship between customer-directed extra-role behavior and relationship profitability is contingent on partner characteristics and environmental conditions.

Proactive performance: internal and external

We refer to positive deviant behavior as proactive behavioral performance.[3] There has been surprisingly little research in this area, given the relationship nature in the B2B selling context. Proactive behavior consists of constructive behavior or behavior with honorable intentions, aimed at correcting the situation without sacrificing the interests of the company while keeping the customer satisfied. Proactive behavior falls into the category of positive deviance, defined as intentional behavior that departs from the norms of a referent group in *honorable* ways (Spreitzer and Sonenshein 2004). These norms can be unit or organizational norms, industry norms, practice norms or general principles of business norms. In the context of selling, these referent groups include not only the company but also the customers. Other researchers have also referred to this type of positive deviant behavior as prosocial rule-breaking behavior (Morrison 2006) and constructive deviance (Warren 2003). Examples of proactive coping behavior include salesperson deviant discretion behavior (Kelley et al. 1996) and internal influence tactics (Bettencourt and Brown 2003; Nonis et al. 1996).

Similar to extra-role behavior, proactive behavioral performance can be internally conducted, such as internal influence to change the situation (Bettencourt and Brown 2003), or externally directed at customers (Kelley et al. 1996). For example, deviant discretion behaviors arise in a service delivery context 'when employees exercise discretion but have not been empowered to do so, or when employees have utilized inappropriate decision criteria (as judged by the organization) during the exercise of routine or creative discretion' (Kelley et al. 1996, p. 138).

Certain sales force behavioral performance cannot always be classified as in-role or extra-role. We refer to these as hybrid behavioral performance. For example, Ahearne et al. (2007) propose the concept of sales service behaviors as behaviors after the initial sales that aim to nurture and develop the exchange relationship. They conceptualize sales service behaviors as consisting of five dimensions: diligence; information communication; inducements; empathy; and sportsmanship. The first three dimensions are in-role, and the last three dimensions are extra-role. Another type of behavior that has recently emerged is salesperson creative performance, defined as the number of new ideas generated and novel behaviors exhibited by the salesperson in performing his or her job activities (Wang and Netemeyer 2004).

Negative Performance

In Hirschman's (1970) theory of loyalty, dissatisfied people often decide to exit an organization in silence; if they cared and did not want to exit the organization, they would voice their concern. However, the absence of voice within the organization or overt voice does not mean these customers do not engage in negative behavior inside and outside the organization. Analogously, these types of negative behaviors are like cancer, spreading silently throughout the work group and destroying the life source of the organization and its members. Next we identify three negative behaviors that have received academic attention.

Negative deviant behavior

Deviant behavior can be negative, and negative deviant behavior can fall into two types: *internal* and *external*. This stream of research follows the tradition in industrial organizational psychology. Robinson and Bennett (1995, p. 556) define employee negative deviance as 'voluntary behavior that violates significant organizational norms and in so doing threatens the well-being of an organization, its members, or both.' However, this type of behavior is not necessarily unethical behavior.

Podsakoff and MacKenzie's (1997) typology includes anticitizenship behaviors. We use the term 'internal' rather than Podsakoff and MacKenzie's 'company-directed' term because these deviant behaviors can occur at the team or work-group levels. Negative deviant behavior can also be external. We use the term 'external' to Podsakoff and MacKenzie's 'customer-directed' term because these negative deviant behaviors do not necessarily involve customers, but rather the external stakeholders in general. For example, an unsatisfied salesperson can criticize the company on forums outside working hours, and this information is accessible to all external stakeholders, including potential job candidates. These websites are now quite popular (e.g. www.cafepharma.com, www. glassdoor.com).

Several studies in applied psychology have examined internal negative deviant behavior (Bennett and Robinson 2000; Robinson and Bennett 1995). Research on external negative deviant behavior focuses on unethical selling practice (Hunt and Vasquez-Parraga 1993; Schwepker and Hartline 2005). Recent sales research has examined this behavior from the organizational, interpersonal and external perspective (Jelinek and Ahearne 2006).

Reactive behavior
This type of behavior reflects a 'take the situation as is' mentality in the form of withdrawal and passive behavior. These reactive behaviors can include a heightened intention to leave a job or quitting the job altogether. Prior research on selling and sales management has examined this phenomenon (e.g. Brown and Peterson 1993; Lucas et al. 1987; MacKenzie et al. 1998).

Preactive behavior
In this type of behavior, the salesperson forces the customer to conform to the seller's requirements (Pasold 1975). In competitive markets, however, a salesperson can rarely pursue such hard-selling tactics.

Toward a Cybernetic and Dynamic Viewpoint of Sales Force Performance

Thus far we have identified two key dimensions of sales force performance to propose a typology. In this typology, we never assume that behavioral performance leads to outcome performance because of various contingencies (e.g. salesperson experience, salesperson informal power) and intervening factors. These missing links, represented as question marks in Figure 27.1, warrant further research. Here we emphasize two elements that have not received much academic attention and pose a daunting challenge to practice: namely cybernetics and dynamics of sales force performance.

A cybernetic viewpoint
Central to cybernetics, a general theoretical framework that pertains to the functioning of self-regulating systems, is the feedback loop. For example, in developing a cybernetic theory of stress, Edwards (1992, p. 245) categorizes two classes of outcomes

of stress: (1) psychological and physical health, or the employee's well-being; and (2) coping, or efforts to prevent or reduce the negative effects of stress on well-being. According to this theory, stress damages well-being and activates coping, which in turn influences employee well-being both directly and indirectly through the determinants of stress.

In line with this cybernetic perspective, salespeople may engage in behavioral performance to cope with role stress (e.g. role conflict, role ambiguity) or a negative work event rather than pursuing outcome goals (Brown et al. 2005). Certainly, certain types of behavioral performance are instrumental in achieving outcome performance. If behavioral performance is instrumental in resolving role stress, it may not be successful. In such a case, behavioral performance can actually impair outcome performance. For example, a salesperson who engages in upward influence may not always be successful. Such failure may be disheartening and thus impair his or her performance.

Feedback relationships between extra-role performance and in-role performance may also exist. For example, Podsakoff and MacKenzie (1994) find a negative relationship between OCBs and the quantity of performance. They speculate that because of the high turnover rate in the insurance industry, the short-term increase in inexperienced agents' productivity resulting from experienced agents' help may not offset the corresponding decrease in sales productivity that experienced agents must incur. They also speculate that members in teams that perform well are more likely to engage in extra-role behaviors.

A dynamic viewpoint

It takes time for different types of behavioral performance to turn into quantifiable outcome performance. For example, a long sales cycle may be needed to transform an initial sales call into actual sales. Although the time gap between prospecting and farming is widely accepted, our extensive review of the literature on sales force performance revealed only a few studies that explicitly examine this substantive research question (e.g. Chonko et al. 2000; Smith et al. 2006).

Objective Versus Subjective Ratings

The issues of predictive validity difference between subjective and objective performance measures are not new in the marketing literature (Ailawadi et al. 2004; Churchill et al. 1985; Rich et al. 1999) or in the management literature (for a recent review, see Jaramillo et al. 2005). The strength of the relationship between a predictor and an objective performance typically varies widely depending on the source of performance rating. For example, in Franke and Park's (2006) meta-analysis on salesperson adaptive selling behavior, the relationship between adaptive selling behavior and self-rated performance is .261, that between adaptive selling behavior and manager-rated performance is merely .089 and that between adaptive selling behavior and objective performance is only .149. In the same meta-analysis, Franke and Park report that the correlation among self-rated, manager-rated and objective performance is between .25 to .35.

CHALLENGES IN SALES FORCE PERFORMANCE EVALUATION: MANAGERIAL PERSPECTIVE

In addition to the literature review, we also conducted a brief qualitative survey about the challenges sales executives experience when they evaluate sales force performance. This step complements the literature review to ensure that our proposed further research priorities are both substantively and theoretically applicable. We sent a Web link of a brief survey to senior sales managers of companies that sponsor two nationally known sales centers in the United States. We received 13 responses from sales executives in various industries, from insurance sales to industrial distribution. We tabulate the challenges these sales executives encountered in Table 27.2. We coded each of the challenges into two major groups: (1) locus of challenge, in which we follow the exact categorization we used in Table 27.1 in reviewing prior academic research on sales force performance evaluation (i.e. subjective versus objective ratings, in-role versus extra-role, outcome versus behavior and focus of performance evaluation); and (2) specific areas of challenges, which include three subcategories: the information that managers rely on or need to acquire to perform the evaluation, evaluation flexibility and adjustments, and other challenges (e.g. goal incompatibility, goal setting, priorities).

Three important issues that have not received much academic research emerged. First, managers report that sales force performance evaluation is challenging partly because of external factors beyond their and even salespeople's control. For example, managers must evaluate salespeople using fixed criteria while the market keeps changing. Although marketing research has examined this phenomenon (e.g. Albers 2000; Homburg et al. 2009a), more research remains to be done. Second, in franchising contexts such as insurance and travel agencies, firms may not have complete control over the sales force because agents are independent contractors. An understanding of how to motivate salespeople who do not formally belong to the firm is another notable research area. For example, what motivates the owner of a franchised insurance agent to pass along the incentives received from the franchisor to the sales representatives or their customers? Third, leader–follower congruence of goals and strategic priorities is also not easily evaluated by sales managers. We return to these themes in the next section.

FURTHER RESEARCH AVENUES

In this section, we identify several research questions that can be explored conceptually or empirically. We do not attempt to create an exhaustive list of possible research questions, but rather focus on research areas that are substantively and theoretically important to the field.

Under-researched Sales Force (Behavioral and Outcome) Performance

Although the literature on sales force performance has recognized that salespeople at different career stages may behave very differently (Cron and Slocum 1986) and that customer–company relationships evolve through various phases that call for different selling emphasis, most empirical research has been cross-sectional. In addition, our

Table 27.2   Sales executives' major challenges in sales force performance evaluation

| Challenges | Locus of Challenge | | | | | | | | | Specific Areas of Challenge | | |
| | Subjective vs. Objective | | In-Role vs. Extra-Role | | Outcome vs. Behavior | | Focus of Evaluation | | | Info. for Eval. | Evaluation Flexibility and Adjustment | Others (goals, priorities) |
	Sub.	Ob.	In	Ex.	Out.	Beh.	Sales Rep.	Cust.	Others (Managers and Peers)			
Accurate information; Reports (many places to obtain data on performance, all different).	X	X			X	X	X	X	X	X	X	
Keeping accountability for daily activities; Tracking production; Understanding and managing the number of qualified prospects sales reps deal with in a given week; Evaluating their daily sales skills.			X		X	X	X	X		X		
Productivity and time management: Are they being the most productive with their time; Commitment to investing time necessary to attain results; Priority: Are they spending their time with the right accounts.	X	X	X		X	X	X	X		X		
Inability to see how they interact with their customers every day; Distance: reps are spread out across the country; 'Since they are mostly working out of their homes, how can we know they are really seeing customers.'	X		X			X	X	X		X		
If they are working up to their potential.	X		X		X	X	X			X		
Pipeline management.	X	X	X		X	X	X	X		X		
Consistency of performance.		X	X		X	X	X			X	X	

Table 27.2 (continued)

Challenges	Subjective vs. Objective		In-Role vs. Extra-Role		Outcome vs. Behavior		Focus of Evaluation			Specific Areas of Challenge		
										Info. for Eval.	Evaluation Flexibility and Adjustment	Others (goals, priorities)
	Sub.	Ob.	In	Ex.	Out.	Beh.	Sales Rep.	Cust.	Others (Managers and Peers)			
Heterogeneity/Internal: Judging performance of tenured vs. newly hired employees; 'Most of our sales force is younger so they are just learning the "ropes" and need time to develop before truly evaluating.'	X	X	X		X	X	X			X	X	
Heterogeneity/External: Different markets/territories encounter different opportunities and challenges that may be harder to overcome; Different markets don't always have different objectives.	X	X	X		X	X	X				X	
'Since we represent over 5000 vendors, how can they be credible to the customers with so many vendors (industrial distribution).'			X			X		X				X
Change issues: The changing value of the dominant product and service offering; Changing initiatives and priorities during the year.	X	X	X		X	X		X			X	

508

Challenge / Issue					
Inconsistency between personal sales objectives and outside business objective; If they are inefficient because of outside influences (e.g. family issues); Is their motivation in line with corporate goals?	X	X	X	X	X
Disconnection between top management and direct reports on the nature and priorities of their function.			X	X	X
Agents are independent contractors: It can be difficult to change their behaviors (insurance sales).				X	X
'If I am giving them correct support': Helping reps develop and nurture referral networks; Helping reps develop the habits that lead to a higher number of sales from qualified prospects; Investment of the new associates to take the time to invest in themselves outside company training (off-time investment).			X	X	X
Difficulty of driving results without direct authority.			X	X	X

typology reveals underresearched sales force performance that warrants more academic attention. Next are specific research questions:

1. *Long-term versus short-term impact of salesperson behavior*: What is the long-term impact of sales force behavior? How do firms measure and quantify this long-term impact? What are some of the implications for a reward system for individual-selling and team-selling structures?
2. *Dynamics of the buyer–seller relationship*: Little empirical research exists on how the role of salespeople changes over the various phases of the buyer–seller relationship (e.g. Dwyer et al. 1987). Most research has focused on selling, but not on after sales (for a rare conceptual treatment, see Challagalla et al. 2009). Some research questions include the following: what is the role of the salesperson in relationship dissolution? What social networks do salespeople rely on when they sell at different relationship stages (e.g. Üstüner and Godes 2006)?
3. *Salesperson as a competitive intelligence agent*: How do firms motivate salespeople to engage in competitive intelligence agent activities? Is competitive intelligence an in-role or extra-role performance?
4. *Salesperson covert behavior*: What are some salesperson covert behaviors? What are the implications for the firm and its customers? In addition, if the concept of customer loyalty to the salesperson rather than the company exists (Palmatier et al. 2007), how do firms manage these relationships? Although some studies have examined the impact on the firm when the key salesperson leaves (Bendapudi and Leone 2002), additional research is needed. On the flip side, salespeople may strongly identify with the customers they serve and may engage in excessive customer-oriented behaviors (Lam 2007). This type of behavior refers to situations in which a salesperson who grows too close to a customer might sacrifice company resources to satisfy the customer's needs. Further research is needed to examine this phenomenon.
5. *Behavior-based control system and extra-role behavior*: Does a behavioral-based control system capture extra-role behavior? Should firms formally reward salespeople for engaging in extra-role behavior? What are some implications for control system research if it is normatively appropriate to recognize and reward certain extra-role behavior?
6. *Managing the external sales force*: How do firms motivate outsourced salespeople or salespeople who do not formally belong to the firm, such as in franchised contexts? Should the franchisor leave everything to the franchisee when it comes to performance evaluation? Should the franchisor also monitor the behaviors of franchisees' sales force?
7. *New and dynamic input–output conceptual models*: What are the underlying processes linking the behavioral performance to outcome performance (we denote these as question marks in Figure 27.1)? How do these processes unfold over time?

Level of Analysis: Team Selling

Over the past 15 years, many companies have shifted from a traditional sales model featuring individual sales representatives to a team-based selling approach (Moon and Armstrong 1994). As many as 75 per cent of today's companies sell in teams (Cummings

2007). Ahearne et al. (2010b) posit that studying sales teams is difficult for at least two reasons: (1) Team performance (output) is a complex function of many different inputs, processes, and emerging cognitive and emotional states; and (2) team members may not perceive/experience the inputs, processes and emergent states in the same way.

Sales teams are unique in the sense that apart from individual behavior, the interaction between team members may give rise to work-group climates that also determine how each team member is perceived and behaves. Furthermore, findings in the team and work-group literature may not necessarily apply to the context of selling teams because of the boundary-spanning nature of the selling task. More specifically, most research on teams focuses on teams that are isolated from the world outside the firm, while members of sales teams interact both within the team and in selling activities to external customers. Some useful research questions include the following:

1. How should sales team performance be evaluated while balancing between individual inputs and collective outputs?
2. What are some of the antecedents and consequences of perceptual differences between supervisors and salespeople? Although this relationship may not always apply in a team context, it becomes even more complicated in a team-selling context.
3. Are perceptual differences always bad? What are some desirable perceptual differences (e.g. to avoid groupthink) and in what context?
4. A related topic is the role of work-group peers and co-workers. Although this research question also applies to contexts other than selling in teams (e.g. Kohli and Jaworski 1994), it becomes even more important in a team-selling context because of more social interactions and shared rewards. Recent marketing research has addressed this issue from an internal marketing perspective (e.g. Lam et al. 2010; Wieseke et al. 2009), but much remains to be learned about how salespeople can learn from one another.

Salespeople as Brand Ambassadors: The Role of Internal Marketing

Previous research has suggested that internal marketing helps with external marketing over time. For example, the service–profit chain posits that employee satisfaction leads to customer satisfaction. Empirical evidence, however, is mixed. In a meta-analysis using dyadic data, Brown and Lam (2008) find that this correlation is quite low, only .20. Recent theorization has suggested an alternative to the traditional service–profit chain. This research suggests that leadership style and dyadic tenure moderate the organizational identification transfer from top managers to middle managers and middle managers to sales reps. Sales reps' identification with the organization transfers to customers' identification with the firm, and this transfer process generates higher sales revenues (Homburg et al. 2009b; Maxham et al. 2008; Wieseke et al. 2009).

A related topic is how social media can influence salesperson performance. Prior research has shown that salespeople can be an important internal audience to advertising (Gilly and Wolfinbarger 1998). However, marketing communications have evolved from the one-way model to the co-creation, interactive model, and thus much remains to be learned about the role of salespeople as generators and recipients of these messages. Some important research questions include the following:

1. What types of firms should be doing internal marketing? Can internal marketing be harmful?
2. What is the difference between internal marketing, internal branding and internal market orientation?
3. How do salespeople process firm-related information that is generated by external stakeholders?

Performance During Times of Change

Much research has ruled out seasonality, especially the work on quota setting (e.g. Zoltners et al. 2006). However, sales force performance can fluctuate because of reasons other than seasonality. We focus our discussion here on sales force performance during times of change. 'Change is fundamental to a modern business organization as a means to keep up with evolving market demands and to stay competitive' (Ye et al. 2007, p. 156). Indeed, practitioners and scholars alike agree that change is ubiquitous and can be unexpectedly instigated by external forces, such as competitors or regulators, or strategically initiated by firms to stay competitive. However, little research has examined how change may affect sales force performance. Many relationships found in existing literature may not hold during times of change. For example, Ahearne et al. (2010b) show that during a switch to a new customer relationship management system, the relationship between salesperson traits and performance is non-linear and more complex than a simple positive or negative relationship.

Change can take several forms: intended changes initiated by the focal firm (e.g. territory realignment, new product introduction, downsizing, new market entry) and unintended changes brought on by external influences (e.g. market downturns, competitor actions, a misconduct scandal, loss of a key account, mergers and acquisitions). Change can be preannounced or unexpected. Furthermore, regardless of whether the change is planned or unplanned, not all changes are disruptive. A different adaptation model would be expected for a change that is enhancing (as opposed to disruptive), such as when a primary competitor goes out of business and drives customers to the focal firm, or when the company hires additional salespeople. These areas deserve additional research (Ahearne et al. 2010a).

Middle Managers

Much of previous research in sales has focused on salespeople. Although the literature on supervisors in a sales setting is also prolific, much of this research has focused on leadership styles (charismatic, transformational, transactional), feedback (Sujan et al. 1994), supervisors' orientation (Kohli et al. 1998), control styles (Challagalla and Shervani 1996) and, more recently, brand-specific leadership (Morhart et al. 2009). Recent research has revisited the notion of middle managers as linking pins (Lam et al. 2010; Wieseke et al. 2009). Some research questions are as follows:

1. How do firms measure sales managers' performance? What is unique about evaluating sales managers' performance in comparison with salesperson performance?
2. What are the specific traits and roles of middle-level sales managers?

3. What are the antecedents and consequences of top manager–sales manager and sales manager–salesperson congruence on performance? Such congruence can be in terms of their goals, strategic orientations or strategic priorities.
4. Insofar as the leader can influence sales reps' performance, sales reps' behavior can also influence sales managers' performance. What are some of the mechanisms through which this upward influence can occur? Which manager characteristics facilitate upward influence? Such upward influence also represents a challenge in empirical multilevel research.

DEA

The performance measures we have discussed so far focus on individual performance and ignore efficiency. Boles et al. (1995) propose the use of DEA to evaluate salespeople. Horsky and Nelson (1996) suggest the use of DEA to evaluate the size of the sales force and productivity. This approach to sales force performance evaluation focuses on relative evaluation rather than individual evaluation. In other words, DEA provides a benchmark, either internally within a unit or externally across units. For a review of the evolution of this method, see Seiford (1996).

Briefly, DEA is a method for measuring the efficiency of any process or unit that is characterized by multiple inputs and outputs. Researchers first compute the maximum attainable output (i.e. the optimal level of output) by examining the inputs and outputs of the peer group of salespeople. This step produces an efficient frontier that represents the optimal output levels that correspond to given levels of inputs. Researchers then compare the actual outputs of a focal salesperson to this maximum attainable output or the efficient frontier. Salespeople who are at the frontier are considered efficient, and those who are less efficient reside within the frontier. Unfortunately, surprisingly few applications of this idea exist in marketing research. DEA is particularly useful for examining several important sales performance phenomena. For example, in situations when change happens, it is important to understand how managers adjust the weights of inputs and what inputs should be included (or excluded) in estimating the efficiency frontier. However, DEA is a mathematical technique that is sensitive to the selection of inputs and outputs to be included, and the data required to perform the method can be daunting.

METHODOLOGICAL NOTES

Previous marketing research has examined the ramifications of performance rating source (e.g. self-rating, peer rating, manager rating) and objective versus subjective performance measures. We refer interested readers to the literature we previously reviewed for further detail. Here we focus on the following issues: (1) level of analysis; (2) performance during times of change; and (3) measurement issues.

Level of Analysis

Table 27.1 reveals that previous research has mostly focused on the individual level. More recently, team selling has become more popular in practice (Moon and

Armstrong 1994). Unfortunately, the marketing literature has lagged behind practice. Little research has incorporated work groups (e.g. team level) and cross-level analyses in which work-group variables moderate a lower-level relationship or lower-level constructs mediate the influence of work-group variables on an individual outcome (e.g. Ahearne et al. 2010b; De Jong et al. 2004). Conceptually, the composition models that specify the functional relationships between phenomena at the individual and group level are critical in conducting group-level research (Chan 1998). These composition models and the functional relationships they embody provide a systematic framework for mapping the transformation of the phenomena across levels, and therefore they permit more precise conceptualization. Two of the most important composition models are the additive model, in which the group mean translates the individual-level phenomena to the team level, and the dispersion model, in which the standard deviation translates the individual-level phenomena to the team level. Dispersion models treat variability within a team as a theoretically significant phenomenon in its own right. This is in contrast with traditional multilevel research, which treats within-group variability as an error (Chan 1998). Research in the management literature has shown that within-group differences play an important role in team performance. However, there are various differences (see Harrison and Klein 2007), and thus empirical research is needed.

In the sales team literature, the additive model has been widely used while the dispersion model has rarely been used (cf. Venkatesh et al. 2001). This is unfortunate because a lack of consensus or disagreement can arise from quantitative differences on a single attribute or dimension (e.g. opinions, belief, values, attitudes) or qualitative differences in kind (e.g. race, gender, functional background, information) across team members (Harrison and Klein 2007).

An important concept in work-group level research is work-group diversity. There are multiple measures of diversity (Harrison and Klein 2007; Roberson et al. 2007). Therefore, researchers who study sales teams should pay particular attention to the type of dispersion of interest to select the most appropriate form of measure. Another important concept in work-group research is homology, which is based on the assumption that the relationships between a set of constructs maintain some level of similarity across levels of analysis (Chen et al. 2005). Some empirical research shows that this is not always the case. For example, MacKenzie et al. (1999) find that OCBs matter more for managers than for salespeople. Additional research is needed to examine what relationships between which construct exhibit this homologous nature.

Performance During Times of Change

A methodological question is: during times of change, how do researchers measure performance? Singer and Willett (2003) posit that to study change, researchers need: (1) multiple waves of data; (2) a continuous outcome that changes systematically over time; and (3) a sensible metric for time. In the context of B2B selling, tracking longitudinal performance can be challenging (Rindfleisch et al. 2008). Guidelines for studying individual change and empirical model building are also available in other literature streams outside marketing (Bliese and Ployhart 2002; Bryk and Raudenbush 1987; Hofmann et al. 1993).

Measurement Issues

When performance ratings are solicited from different sources, disagreement among raters is almost inevitable. Two perspectives exist regarding this disagreement. The first stream treats disagreement as methodological artifacts and creates a method to adjust for such measurement error. The second stream views inter-rater disagreement as meaningful differences to be explained and acted on. For example, the Johari windows (Luft and Ingham 1955) provide the people being rated with a 2×2 matrix (self-awareness versus other-awareness). Much research is needed to identify the antecedents and consequences of these disagreements and even perceptual biases. Another measurement challenge is how to measure deviant behavior, even for positive deviant behavior. In this respect, sales researchers can refer to the applied psychology literature on deviant behavior (e.g. Bennett and Robinson 2000).

MANAGERIAL IMPLICATIONS

This chapter provides several managerial implications. First, through a comprehensive review of the literature and a survey with sales executives, we demonstrate the complexity of sales force performance evaluation. There are multiple dimensions along which managers can evaluate sales force performance, many of which are subjective and some of which are not always aligned. Second, we have identified important missing links across various types of underresearched performance measures, which we depict as question marks in Figure 27.1. Thus, it is extremely important for managers to understand the big picture of performance evaluation. Third, it is important for managers to realize that behavioral outcome can be measured and observed in terms of the type of behavior and frequencies with which salespeople engage in the behavior. As we mentioned, positive behavioral performance, such as helping team members, can become detrimental if it takes away valuable productive time from those who offer to help. Finally, although we identify several important challenges in performance evaluation, we also offer managers useful methodological notes for gathering and analyzing performance information. In this regard, depending on the purpose of performance measuring (e.g. evaluation, benchmarking, promotion consideration), managers may want to place more emphasis on a particular performance measure and analytical approach than others.

CONCLUSION

In this chapter we have discussed how sales force performance has been studied and how marketing researchers can further the understanding of this topic. We open the chapter with a survey of previous research and then create a typology of performance measures and identify future research avenues. We also lay out some methodological challenges and opportunities for future researchers. A caveat is worth mentioning: sales force performance is a function of a multitude of variables, some of which are under the salesperson's control and some of which are not. Previous research has examined possible interactions and synergy between sales force efforts and other marketing mix variables (e.g. Boulding et al. 1994; Gatignon and Hanssens 1987). In examining sales force performance, researchers should not lose sight of the fundamental marketing principle.

NOTES

1. We treat studies that measure turnover intention as measuring behavioral performance.
2. Although the relationship between effort and outcome performance is significantly positive, outcome performance does not always mediate the relationship between effort (i.e. a type of behavioral performance) and job satisfaction (Brown and Peterson 1994).
3. Spreitzer and Sonenshein (2004, p. 836) propose that OCBs are not the same as positive deviance.

REFERENCES

Ahearne, Michael, Ronald Jelinek and Eli Jones (2007), 'Examining the effect of salesperson service behavior in a competitive context', *Journal of the Academy of Marketing Science*, **35** (4), 603–16.

Ahearne, Michael, Eli Jones, Adam Rapp and John Mathieu (2008), 'High tough through high tech: the impact of salesperson technology usage on sales performance via mediating mechanisms', *Management Science*, **54** (April), 671–85.

Ahearne, Michael, Son K. Lam, John Mathieu and Willy Bolander (2010a), 'Why are some salespeople better at adapting to organizational change?', *Journal of Marketing*, **74** (May), 65–79.

Ahearne, Michael, Scott B. MacKenzie, Philip M. Podsakoff, John E. Mathieu and Son K. Lam (2010b), 'The role of consensus in sales team performance', *Journal of Marketing Research*, **47** (June), 458–69.

Ailawadi, Kusum L., Rajiv P. Dant and Dhruv Grewal (2004), 'The difference between perceptual and objective performance measures: an empirical analysis', Working Paper No. 04-103, Marketing Science Institute.

Albers, Sonke (2000), 'Sales-force management', in Keith Blois (ed.), *The Oxford Textbook of Marketing*, Oxford: Oxford University Press, pp. 292–317.

Albers, Sonke (2006), 'Salesforce management: compensation, motivation, selection and training', in Barton Weitz and Robin Wensley (eds), *Handbook of Marketing*, Thousand Oaks, CA: Sage, pp. 248–66.

Anderson, Erin and Richard L. Oliver (1987), 'Perspectives on behavior-based versus outcome-based sales-force control systems', *Journal of Marketing*, **51** (October), 76–88.

Bagozzi, Richard P. (1978), 'Salesforce performance and satisfaction as a function of individual difference, interpersonal, and situational factors', *Journal of Marketing Research*, **15** (November), 517–31.

Behrman, Douglas N. and William D. Perreault Jr (1982), 'Measuring the performance of industrial salespersons', *Journal of Business Research*, **10** (3), 355–70.

Bendapudi, Neeli and Robert P. Leone (2002), 'Managing business-to-business customer relationships following key contact employee turnover in a vendor firm', *Journal of Marketing*, **66** (2), 83–101.

Bennett, Rebecca J. and Sandra L. Robinson (2000), 'Development of a measure of workplace deviance', *Journal of Applied Psychology*, **85** (3), 349–60.

Bettencourt, Lance A. and Stephen W. Brown (2003), 'Role stressors and customer-oriented boundary-spanning behaviors in service organizations', *Journal of the Academy of Marketing Science*, **31** (4), 394–408.

Bliese, Paul D. and Robert E. Ployhart (2002), 'Growth modeling using random coefficient models: model building, testing, and illustrations', *Organizational Research Methods*, **5** (4), 362–87.

Boles, James S., Naveen Donthu and Ritu Lohtia (1995), 'Salesperson evaluation using relative performance efficiency: the application of data envelopment analysis', *Journal of Personal Selling & Sales Management*, **15** (3), 31–49.

Boulding, William, Eunkyu Lee and Richard Staelin (1994), 'Mastering the mix: do advertising, promotion, and sales force activities lead to differentiation?', *Journal of Marketing Research*, **31** (May), 159–72.

Brief, Arthur P. and Stephan J. Motowidlo (1986), 'Prosocial organizational behaviors', *Academy of Management Review*, **11** (4), 710–25.

Brown, Steven P. and Son K. Lam (2008), 'A meta-analysis of relationships linking employee satisfaction to customer responses', *Journal of Retailing*, **84** (3), 243–55.

Brown, Steven P. and Robert A. Peterson (1993), 'Antecedents and consequences of salesperson job satisfaction: meta-analysis and assessment of causal effects', *Journal of Marketing Research*, **30** (1), 63–77.

Brown, Steven P. and Robert A. Peterson (1994), 'The effect of effort on sales performance and job satisfaction', *Journal of Marketing*, **58** (April), 70–80.

Brown, Steven P., William L. Cron and John W. Slocum Jr (1997), 'Effects of goal-directed emotions on salesperson volitions, behavior, and performance: a longitudinal study', *Journal of Marketing*, **61** (1), 39–50.

Brown, Steven P., William L. Cron and John W. Slocum Jr (1998), 'Effects of trait competitiveness and perceived intraorganizational competition on salesperson goal setting and performance', *Journal of Marketing*, **62** (4), 88–98.

Brown, Steven P., Robert A. Westbrook and Goutam Challagalla (2005), 'Good cope, bad cope: adaptive and maladaptive coping strategies following a critical negative work event', *Journal of Applied Psychology*, **90** (4), 792–8.

Bryk, Anthony S. and Stephen W. Raudenbush (1987), 'Application of hierarchical linear models to assessing change', *Psychological Bulletin*, **101** (1), 147–58.

Challagalla, Goutam N. and Tasadduq A. Shervani (1996), 'Dimensions and types of supervisory control: effects on salesperson performance and satisfaction', *Journal of Marketing*, **60** (January), 89–105.

Challagalla, Goutam, R. Venkatesh and Ajay K. Kohli (2009), 'Proactive postsales services: when and why does it pay off?', *Journal of Marketing*, **73** (March), 70–87.

Chan, David (1998), 'Functional relations among constructs in the same content domain at different levels of analysis: a typology of composition models', *Journal of Applied Psychology*, **83** (2), 234–46.

Chandrashekaran, Murali, Kevin McNeilly, Frederick A. Russ and Detelina Marinova (2000), 'From uncertain intentions to actual behavior: a threshold model of whether and when salespeople quit', *Journal of Marketing Research*, **37** (November), 463–79.

Chen, Gilad, Paul D. Bliese and John E. Mathieu (2005), 'Conceptual framework and statistical procedures for delineating and testing multilevel theories of homology', *Organizational Research Methods*, **8** (4), 375–409.

Chonko, Lawrence B., Terry N. Loe, James A. Roberts and John F. Tanner (2000), 'Sales performance: timing of measurement and type of measurement make a difference', *Journal of Personal Selling & Sales Management*, **20** (1), 23–36.

Churchill, Gilbert A., Jr, Neil M. Ford, Steven W. Hartley and Orville C. Walker (1985), 'The determinants of salesperson performance: a meta-analysis', *Journal of Marketing Research*, **22** (May), 103–18.

Cravens, David W., Thomas N. Ingram, Raymond W. LaForge and Clifford E. Young (1993), 'Behavior-based and outcome-based salesforce control systems', *Journal of Marketing*, **57** (October), 47–59.

Cron, William L. and John W. Slocum Jr (1986), 'The influence of career stages on salespeople's job attitudes, work perceptions, and performance', *Journal of Marketing Research*, **23** (May), 119–29.

Cummings, Betsy (2007), 'Group dynamics', *Sales & Marketing Management*, **159** (1), 8.

De Jong, Ad, Ko de Ruyter and Jos Lemmink (2004), 'Antecedents and consequences of the service climate in boundary-spanning self-managing service teams', *Journal of Marketing*, **68** (April), 18–35.

Dubinsky, A.J. and B. Mattson (1979), 'Consequences of role conflict and ambiguity experienced by retail salespeople', *Journal of Retailing*, **55** (Winter), 70–86.

Dwyer, F. Robert, Paul H. Schurr and Sejo Oh (1987), 'Developing buyer-seller relationships', *Journal of Marketing*, **51** (April), 11–27.

Edwards, Jeffrey R. (1992), 'A cybernetic theory of stress, coping, and well-being in organizations', *Academy of Management Review*, **17** (2), 238–74.

Ford, Neil M., Gilbert A. Churchill Jr and Orville C. Walker Jr (1985), *Sales Force Performance*, Lexington, MA: Lexington Books.

Franke, George R. and Jeong-Eun Park (2006), 'Salesperson adaptive selling behavior and customer orientation: a meta-analysis', *Journal of Marketing Research*, **43** (November), 693–702.

Gatignon, Hubert and Dominique M. Hanssens (1987), 'Modeling marketing interactions with application to salesforce effectiveness', *Journal of Marketing Research*, **24** (August), 247–57.

Gilly, Mary C. and Mary Wolfinbarger (1998), 'Advertising's internal audience', *Journal of Marketing*, **62** (January), 69–88.

Guzzo, Richard A. and Marcus W. Dickson (1996), 'Teams in organizations: recent research on performance and effectiveness', *Annual Review of Psychology*, **47** (1), 307–38.

Hackman, R. (1987), 'The design of work teams', in J. Lorsch (ed.), *Handbook of Organizational Behavior*, Englewood Cliffs, NJ: Prentice Hall, pp. 315–42.

Harrison, David A. and Katherine J. Klein (2007), 'What's the difference? Diversity constructs as separation, variety, or disparity in organizations', *Academy of Management Review*, **32** (4), 1199–228.

Hirschman, Albert O. (1970), *Exit, Voice, and Loyalty: Responses to Decline in Firms, Organizations, and States*, Cambridge, MA: Harvard University Press.

Hofmann, David A., Rick Jacobs and Joseph E. Baratta (1993), 'Dynamic criteria and the measurement of change', *Journal of Applied Psychology*, **78** (2), 194–204.

Homburg, Christian and Ove Jensen (2007), 'The thought worlds of marketing and sales: which differences make a difference?', *Journal of Marketing*, **71** (July), 124–42.

Homburg, Christian, Viviana V. Steiner and Dirk Totzek (2009a), 'Managing dynamics in a customer portfolio', *Journal of Marketing*, **73** (September), 70–89.

Homburg, Christian, Jan Wieseke and Wayne D. Hoyer (2009b), 'Social identity and the service–profit chain', *Journal of Marketing*, **73** (March), 38–54.

Horsky, Dan and Paul Nelson (1996), 'Evaluation of salesforce size and productivity through efficient frontier benchmarking', *Marketing Science*, **15** (4), 301–20.

Hunt, Shelby and Arturo Z. Vasquez-Parraga (1993), 'Organizational consequences, marketing ethics, and salesforce supervision', *Journal of Marketing Research*, **30** (February), 78–90.

Jackson, Donald W., Jr, Janet E. Keith and John L. Schlacter (1983), 'Evaluation of selling performance: a study of current practices', *Journal of Personal Selling & Sales Management*, **3** (2), 42–51.

Jackson, Donald W., Jr, John L. Schlacter and William G. Wolfe (1995), 'Examining the bases utilized for evaluating salespeople's performance', *Journal of Personal Selling & Sales Management*, **15** (4), 57–65.

Jaramillo, Fernando, Francois A. Carrillat and William B. Locander (2005), 'A meta-analytic comparison of managerial ratings and self-evaluations', *Journal of Personal Selling & Sales Management*, **25** (4), 315–28.

Jaworski, Bernard J. and Deborah J. MacInnis (1989), 'Marketing jobs and management controls: toward a framework', *Journal of Marketing Research*, **26** (November), 406–19.

Jelinek, Ronald and Michael Ahearne (2006), 'The enemy within: examining salesperson deviance and its determinants', *Journal of Personal Selling & Sales Management*, **26** (4), 327–44.

Johnston, Mark W., A. Parasuraman, Charles M. Furell and William C. Black (1990), 'A longitudinal assessment of the impact of selected organizational influences', *Journal of Marketing Research*, **27** (August), 333–44.

Johnston, Wesley J. and Keysuk Kim (1994), 'Performance, attribution, and expectancy linkages in personal selling', *Journal of Marketing*, **58** (4), 68–81.

Kelley, Scott W., Timothy Longfellow and Jack Malehorn (1996), 'Organizational determinants of service employee's exercise of routine, creative, and deviant discretion', *Journal of Retailing*, **72** (2), 135–57.

Kohli, Ajay K. and Bernard J. Jaworski (1994), 'The influence of coworker feedback on salespeople', *Journal of Marketing*, **58** (October), 82–94.

Kohli, Ajay K., Tasadduq A. Shervani and Goutam N. Challagalla (1998), 'Learning and performance orientation of salespeople: the role of supervisors', *Journal of Marketing Research*, **35** (2), 263–74.

Krafft, Manfred (1999), 'An empirical investigation of the antecedents of sales force control systems', *Journal of Marketing*, **63** (July), 120–34.

Lam, Son K. (2007), 'Excessive customer-oriented behaviors in sales', in Andrea L. Dixon and Karen A. Machleit (eds), *2007 AMA Winter Educators' Conference Proceedings*, Chicago: American Marketing Association, p. 79.

Lam, Son K., Florian Kraus and Michael Ahearne (2010), 'The diffusion of market orientation throughout the organization: a social learning theory perspective', *Journal of Marketing*, **74** (September), 61–79.

Le Bon, Joel and Dwight Merunka (2006), 'The impact of individual and managerial factors on salespeople's contribution to marketing intelligence activities', *International Journal of Research in Marketing*, **23** (4), 395–408.

Lucas, George H., Jr, A. Parasuraman, Robert A. Davis and Ben M. Enis (1987), 'An empirical study of salesforce turnover', *Journal of Marketing*, **51** (3), 34–59.

Luft, Joseph and Harry Ingham (1955), 'The Johari window: a graphic model of interpersonal awareness', *Proceedings of the Western Training Laboratory in Group Development*, Los Angeles: University of California, Los Angeles.

MacKenzie, Scott B., Philip Podsakoff and Michael Ahearne (1998), 'Some possible antecedents and consequences of in-role and extra-role salesperson performance', *Journal of Marketing*, **62** (July), 87–98.

MacKenzie, Scott B., Philip M. Podsakoff and Richard Fetter (1993), 'The impact of organizational citizenship behavior on evaluations of salesperson performance', *Journal of Marketing*, **57** (1), 70–80.

MacKenzie, Scott B., Philip Podsakoff and Julie Beth Paine (1999), 'Do citizenship behaviors matter more for managers than for salespeople', *Journal of the Academy of Marketing Science*, **27** (4), 396–410.

Marshall, Greg W., William C. Moncrief and Felicia G. Lassk (1999), 'The current state of sales force activities', *Industrial Marketing Management*, **28** (1), 87–98.

Maxham, James G., III, Richard G. Netemeyer and Donald R. Lichtenstein (2008), 'The retail value chain: linking employee perceptions to employee performance, customer evaluations, and store performance', *Marketing Science*, **27** (2), 147–67.

Moon, Mark A. and Gary M. Armstrong (1994), 'Selling teams: a conceptual framework and research agenda', *Journal of Personal Selling & Sales Management*, **14** (1), 17–30.

Morhart, Felicitas M., Walter Herzog and Torsten Tomczak (2009), 'Brand-specific leadership: turning employees into brand champions', *Journal of Marketing*, **73** (September), 122–42.

Morrison, Elizabeth W. (2006), 'Doing the job well: an investigation of pro-social rule breaking', *Journal of Management*, **32** (1), 5–28.

Netemeyer, Richard G., James S. Boles, Daryl O. McKee and Robert McMurrian (1997), 'An investigation into the antecedents of organizational citizenship behaviors in a personal selling context', *Journal of Marketing*, **61** (July), 85–98.

Nonis, Sarath A., Jeffrey K. Sager and Kamalesh Kumar (1996), 'Salespeople's use of upward influence tactics (UITs) in coping with role stress', *Journal of the Academy of Marketing Science*, **24** (1), 44–56.

Oliver, Richard L. and Erin Anderson (1994), 'An empirical test of the consequences of behavior- and outcome-based sales control systems', *Journal of Marketing*, **58** (October), 53–67.

Organ, Dennis W., Phillip M. Podsakoff and Scott B. MacKenzie (2006), *Organizational Citizenship Behavior: Its Nature, Antecedents, and Consequences*, Thousand Oaks, CA: Sage Publications.

Palmatier, Robert W., Lisa K. Scheer and Jan-Benedict E.M. Steenkamp (2007), 'Customer loyalty to whom? Managing the benefits and risks of salesperson-owned loyalty', *Journal of Marketing Research*, **44** (May), 185–99.

Pasold, Peter W. (1975), 'The effectiveness of various modes of sales behavior in different markets', *Journal of Marketing Research*, **12** (May), 171–6.

Podsakoff, Philip M. and Scott B. MacKenzie (1994), 'Organizational citizenship behaviors and sales unit effectiveness', *Journal of Marketing Research*, **31** (August), 702–13.

Podsakoff, Philip M. and Scott B. MacKenzie (1997), 'Impact of organizational citizenship behavior on organizational performance: a review and suggestion for future research', *Human Performance*, **10** (2), 133–51.

Ramaswami, Sridhar N. and Jagdip Singh (2003), 'Antecedents and consequences of merit pay fairness for industrial salespeople', *Journal of Marketing*, **67** (October), 46–66.

Rich, Gregory A., William H. Bommer, Scott B. MacKenzie, Philip M. Podsakoff and Jonathan L. Johnson (1999), 'Apples and apples or apples and oranges? A meta-analysis of objective and subjective measures of salesperson performance', *Journal of Personal Selling & Sales Management*, **19** (4), 41–52.

Rindfleisch, Aric, Alan J. Malter, Shankar Ganesan and Christine Moorman (2008), 'Cross-sectional versus longitudinal survey research: concepts, findings, and guidelines', *Journal of Marketing Research*, **45** (June), 261–79.

Roberson, Quinetta M., Michael C. Sturman and Tony L. Simons (2007), 'Does the measure of dispersion matter in multilevel research?', *Organizational Research Methods*, **10** (4), 564–88.

Robinson, Sandra I. and Rebecca J. Bennett (1995), 'A typology of deviant workplace behaviors: a multidimensional scaling study', *Academy of Management Journal*, **38** (2), 555–72.

Saxe, Robert and Barton A. Weitz (1982), 'The SOCO scale: a measure of the customer orientation of salespeople', *Journal of Marketing Research*, **19** (August), 343–51.

Schwepker, Charles H., Jr and Michael D. Hartline (2005), 'Managing the ethical climate of customer-contact service employees', *Journal of Service Research*, **7** (4), 377–97.

Seiford, Lawrence M. (1996), 'Data envelopment analysis: the evolution of the state of the art', *Journal of Productivity Analysis*, **7** (2–3), 99–137.

Singer, Judith D. and John B. Willett (2003), *Applied Longitudinal Data Analysis*, New York: Oxford University Press.

Singh, Jagdip (1993), 'Boundary role ambiguity: facets, determinants, and impacts', *Journal of Marketing*, **57** (2), 11–31.

Singh, Jagdip (1998), 'Striking a balance in boundary-spanning positions: an investigation of some unconventional influences of roles stressors and job characteristics on job outcomes of salespeople', *Journal of Marketing*, **62** (3), 69–86.

Singh, Jagdip (2000), 'Performance productivity and quality of frontline employees in service organizations', *Journal of Marketing*, **64** (April), 15–34.

Singh, Jagdip and Gary K. Rhoads (1991), 'Boundary role ambiguity in marketing-oriented positions: a multidimensional, multifaceted operationalization', *Journal of Marketing Research*, **28** (3), 328–38.

Singh, Jagdip, Willem Verbeke and Gary K. Rhoads (1996), 'Do organizational practices matter in role stress processes? A study of direct and moderating effects for marketing-oriented boundary spanners', *Journal of Marketing*, **60** (3), 69–86.

Smith, Timothy M., Srinath Gopalakrishna and Rabikar Chatterjee (2006), 'A three-stage model of integrated marketing communications at the marketing–sales interface', *Journal of Marketing Research*, **43** (November), 564–79.

Spiro, Rosann L. and Barton A. Weitz (1990), 'Adaptive selling: conceptualization, measurement, and nomological validity', *Journal of Marketing Research*, **27** (February), 61–9.

Spreitzer, Gretchen M. and Scott Sonenshein (2004), 'Toward the construct definition of positive deviance', *American Behavioral Scientist*, **47** (6), 828–47.

Steiner, L.D. (1972), *Group Process and Productivity*, New York: Academic Press.

Sujan, Harish, Barton A. Weitz and Nirmalya Kumar (1994), 'Learning orientation, working smart, and effective selling', *Journal of Marketing*, **58** (July), 39–52.

Üstüner, Tuba and David Godes (2006), 'Better sales networks', *Harvard Business Review*, **84** (July–August), 102–12.

Venkatesh, R., Goutam Challagalla and Ajay K. Kohli (2001), 'Heterogeneity in sales districts: beyond individual-level predictors of satisfaction and performance', *Journal of the Academy of Marketing Science*, **29** (3), 238–54.

Verbeke, Willem J., Frank D. Belschak, Arnold B. Bakker and Bart Dietz (2008), 'When intelligence is (dys)functional for achieving sales performance', *Journal of Marketing*, **72** (4), 44–57.

Wang, Guangping and Richard Netemeyer (2004), 'Salesperson creative performance: conceptualization, measurement, and nomological validity', *Journal of Business Research*, **57** (8), 805–12.

Warren, Danielle E. (2003), 'Constructive and destructive deviance in organizations', *Academy of Management Review*, **28** (4), 622–32.

Weitz, Barton A., Harish Sujan and Mita Sujan (1986), 'Knowledge, motivation, and adaptive behavior: a framework for improving selling effectiveness', *Journal of Marketing*, **50** (October), 174–91.

Wieseke, Jan, Michael Ahearne, Son K. Lam and Rolf van Dick (2009), 'The role of leaders in internal marketing', *Journal of Marketing*, **73** (March), 123–45.

Wuyts, Stefan (2007), 'Extra-role behavior in buyer–seller relationships', *International Journal of Research in Marketing*, **24** (4), 301–11.

Ye, Jun, Datelina Marinova and Jagdip Singh (2007), 'Strategic change implementation and performance loss in the front lines', *Journal of Marketing*, **71** (4), 156–71.

Zoltners, Andris A., Prabhakant Sinha and Sally E. Lorimer (2006), *The Complete Guide to Sales Force Incentive Compensation: How to Design and Implement Plans that Work*, New York: American Management Association.

28 Building a winning sales force in B2B markets: a managerial perspective
Andris A. Zoltners, Prabhakant Sinha and Sally E. Lorimer

THE POWER OF PERSONAL SELLING IN B2B ENVIRONMENTS

The ability to create and sustain strong relationships with customers is a key success factor in B2B markets. Sales forces can be highly effective at communicating and delivering value to business customers and consequently help a company achieve its financial goals. According to a 2009 *Selling Power* magazine survey, companies such as Microsoft, Xerox, Cisco, IBM and General Electric (GE), all of which generate a large majority of their revenues though B2B sales, each have more than 14000 salespeople in the United States alone. By our estimates (Zoltners et al. 2009), the amount invested in US sales forces exceeds $800 billion a year, more than three times the $241 billion spent on all media advertising (Barclay's Capital 2009) and 35 times the $22.7 billion spent on online advertising in 2009 (IAB 2010). On average, companies invest about 10 per cent of their annual revenues in their sales forces to pay for salaries, benefits, taxes, bonuses, travel expenses, computers and other administrative and field support for salespeople and their managers.

The significance of the sales force goes beyond its cost. The sales force is perhaps the most highly empowered organization within many companies. Usually working alone and unsupervised, salespeople are entrusted with a company's most important asset: its relationship with its customers. Often salespeople have considerable control over this relationship; to some customers, the salesperson *is* the company. Because of the sales force's critical impact on customer relationships, its effect on company revenues and market share is significant. We have observed through our interactions with corporate sales leaders and executives in a wide range of businesses around the world that in any given situation, a *very good* sales force – one that has talented salespeople who engage in the right selling activities – produces at least 10 per cent more revenues in the short term than an average sales force of the same size. In the long term the revenue impact can be much greater: 50 per cent or more.

Although a good sales force is a powerful asset for a company, the source of its very power also makes it difficult to control, direct and manage. The sales force consists of people, each with their own capabilities, motivators and values. People bring flexibility, creativity and initiative to the sales process; they can adapt sales strategies and messages as needed to meet individual customer needs and build customer loyalty. But at the same time, they bring egos and the need for security and meaning. Unlike advertising, salespeople cannot be turned on and off. Unlike a website, they cannot be expanded and upgraded overnight.

Sales forces enable B2B companies to build strong personal relationships with customers through face-to-face interaction and hands-on problem solving. This personal attention has high sales impact. Yet at the same time, personal selling is expensive. It costs a company much more to make a face-to-face sales call than it does to contact customers through a call center or the web. Consequently a sales force is most appropriately deployed to select customers, products and selling activities; specifically, those for which the benefit is worth the cost. When deployed to the right opportunities, an effective sales force is an invaluable asset for a B2B company: a powerful customer-facing force that can be a source of considerable competitive advantage.

A FRAMEWORK FOR UNDERSTANDING AND IMPROVING THE SALES FORCE

Managing a sales force successfully starts with understanding the various components and linkages that explain how a sales force influences company results.

What Defines Sales Force Success?

Since 1987 we have been teaching an executive-level course entitled *Accelerating Sales Force Performance* at Northwestern University's Kellogg School of Management as well as in other global venues. Each time we teach the course, we ask the sales leaders in attendance, 'How do you know when you have a successful sales force?' Their answers, both spontaneous and reflective, span a wide range of topics. Figure 28.1 provides some typical responses, organized around several dimensions of sales force effectiveness that link logically to one another. Sales leaders tell us that in a successful sales force, *salespeople* with strong skills, capabilities, values and motivations engage in the right kinds of *activity* to drive *customer results*, and customer results ultimately determine *company results*.

Companies often focus on financial results as a sign of sales force success; a sales force that achieves its goals consistently is considered 'excellent'. Yet the responses in Figure 28.1 also show that there are many dimensions to sales force success. Company financial results are only a partial indication of how good a sales force really is. Making the numbers is a sign of success, but it can also be a sign of luck. An assessment of a sales force requires looking at multiple dimensions of success, including:

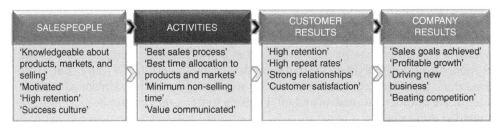

SALESPEOPLE	ACTIVITIES	CUSTOMER RESULTS	COMPANY RESULTS
'Knowledgeable about products, markets, and selling' 'Motivated' 'High retention' 'Success culture'	'Best sales process' 'Best time allocation to products and markets' 'Minimum non-selling time' 'Value communicated'	'High retention' 'High repeat rates' 'Strong relationships' 'Customer satisfaction'	'Sales goals achieved' 'Profitable growth' 'Driving new business' 'Beating competition'

Figure 28.1   How sales leaders describe a successful sales force: four dimensions of sales force success

Figure 28.2   Sales force system framework: SFE drivers and their impact

- Are goals being achieved across product lines? (Company results)
- Are customers' needs being met? (Customer results)
- Are salespeople engaged in the right activities? (Activities)
- Does the sales force have strong skills, knowledge and capabilities? (Salespeople)

The Sales Force System Framework and Sales Force Effectiveness (SFE) Drivers

Sales leaders influence sales force success through their decisions and through the various processes, systems and programs for which they are responsible. We call them the *sales force effectiveness (SFE) drivers* (see Figure 28.2). The SFE drivers form the root of the sales force system. By impacting salespeople and their activities, the SFE drivers affect customer and ultimately company results. Sales leaders can build excellence in all dimensions of the sales force system by doing an excellent job managing the SFE drivers.

The SFE drivers are organized into five categories. Figure 28.2 provides several examples of drivers for each category. The five categories were derived based on our observations of how different SFE drivers influence the sales force system.

- *Definer* SFE drivers, such as sales force size and structure, define the sales organization by specifying sales force investment levels, organizational structure and roles for salespeople.
- *Shaper* SFE drivers, such as sales force hiring and training programs, shape the members of the sales force by influencing sales force skills, capabilities and values.
- *Enlightener* SFE drivers, such as sales data and tools, enlighten the sales force by providing the information salespeople and managers need to understand customers and to be successful.
- *Exciter* SFE drivers, such as sales incentive compensation and other motivation programs, generate excitement within the sales force by inspiring salespeople to work hard and succeed.
- *Controller* SFE drivers, such as sales force performance management systems and goal setting, control and direct sales force activities to keep the sales force on course to achieve company goals.

Individual SFE drivers can have influences in multiple ways, yet for simplicity, the framework lists them in the SFE driver category where they generally have the most significant impact. For example, the driver 'incentives' is categorized as an exciter because the right incentive plan motivates salespeople to work hard to achieve challenging goals. However, an incentive can also have an impact as a shaper if it helps attract the right type of person to the sales job, or as a controller, because by aligning incentives with the right products or customers, the company communicates to salespeople what it wants them to do.

The roots of a successful sales force system are these SFE drivers. Sales leaders can seek solutions to sales force issues, challenges and concerns by looking to the SFE drivers, as well as by ensuring that all drivers are well-managed and in alignment with company business strategies. An excellent sales force implements best practices with each and every SFE driver, thereby creating a sales force of talented salespeople, encouraging quality sales activity and generating superior results.

A Sales Leader's Perspective on Adapting and Improving the Sales Force

To gain perspective on the challenges and opportunities that sales leaders face in driving sales force effectiveness, we draw on an inventory of sales force issues specified by the sales leaders who attended our *Accelerating Sales Force Performance* course. These leaders come from B2B companies in a broad range of industries and countries. Prior to attending the course, we asked the sales leaders, 'What sales force productivity issues are you currently faced with?' Our initial purpose for asking the question was to learn about sales leader needs so we could tailor course content appropriately. In 1995 we began building a database of course attendee responses to our question; by 2010 we had captured and categorized more than 2400 responses from 868 sales leaders. In addition to helping us with course content the database has enabled us to learn much about how sales leaders view sales force success and about the challenges that sales organizations face.

Sales leaders face many opportunities and challenges that bring about a need to adapt and improve their sales forces. Our inventory reveals that most of the issues that sales leaders face fall into four categories (see Table 28.1). The discussion here shows how the sales force system framework (Figure 28.2) guides sales leaders who face each of these four situations through a logical and comprehensive decision-making process for determining what action to take to improve their sales forces.

Situation 1: When External Events Bring About a Need for Sales Force Change

Sales forces need to change when external events require an appropriate reaction. How effectively a sales force responds to events can have a huge profit impact. The sales force system framework helps sales leaders assess how events affect the sales force so they can determine what SFE driver adjustments are required to keep the company on a success track. Figure 28.3 shows a decision-making process for helping a sales force adapt successfully to external events.

Example 1.1: Adapting to environmental change at United Airlines
United Airlines (UA) had a sales organization that built and managed contractual partnerships between UA and corporate travel departments and travel agencies. The sales

Table 28.1   Four situations that create a need for sales for adaptation and improvement

Situation (% of Responses)	Examples of Responses from our Inventory of Sales Force Issues
Events occur externally to the sales force (13%)	• 'We must adapt to changing customer needs and new technologies.' • 'New competitors are entering our markets.' • 'The economy is moving into a recession.' • 'The company product line is shifting.' • The company has acquired another firm with salespeople who have relationships with our customers.'
Issues emerge within the sales force (43%)	• 'We are losing too many top performers.' • 'Salespeople lack closing skills.' • 'Salespeople don't spend enough time prospecting.' • 'Customers are confused by the lack of coordination among product sales specialists.' • 'We are not achieving quota consistently.'
The company wants to improve sales force effectiveness (3%)	• 'Management has taken a keen interest in improving global sales effectiveness.' • 'We just launched a new "Sales Effectiveness and Growth Initiative" aimed at improving sales force performance.'
Issues emerge within an SFE driver (41%)	• 'Territory alignment needs to change: large differences in territory potential are creating unfairness in the sales force.' • 'Recruiting processes need improvement so we can attract better sales talent.' • 'Sales information is lacking: Accuracy and timeliness of sales dashboards are inadequate due to IT problems.' • 'Sales compensation plans need to change to reflect our business priorities.' • 'Goal setting processes result in unfair sales targets.'

organization's mission was to capture a disproportionate share of high-profit travel (largely business travel) for UA. For many years, UA's sales success was driven primarily by price and by personal relationships between salespeople and their customers. In the early 2000s, a number of events – including the declines in air travel following September 11, 2001, high fuel prices, and inflexible labor agreements – created significant financial challenges for UA and the entire airline industry.

What the company did   UA's leadership team transformed the company's sales approach. It replaced the traditional 'price and relationship' sales model with a new value-based, consultative sales model that required salespeople to work closely with corporate and travel agent customers to understand their needs and tailor a customer-specific mix of airline routes and seats, consultative services, travel management and support programs and comfort and productivity offerings for business travelers – offerings that created business value well beyond best price alternatives.

To implement the new selling model, UA used a structured decision process (see Figure 28.3) to identify high impact SFE drivers that were no longer aligned well with the new sales approach. SFE driver changes that the company implemented included:

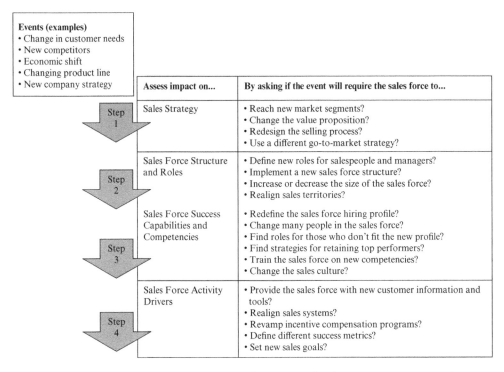

Events (examples)
• Change in customer needs
• New competitors
• Economic shift
• Changing product line
• New company strategy

	Assess impact on...	By asking if the event will require the sales force to...
Step 1	Sales Strategy	• Reach new market segments? • Change the value proposition? • Redesign the selling process? • Use a different go-to-market strategy?
Step 2	Sales Force Structure and Roles	• Define new roles for salespeople and managers? • Implement a new sales force structure? • Increase or decrease the size of the sales force? • Realign sales territories?
Step 3	Sales Force Success Capabilities and Competencies	• Redefine the sales force hiring profile? • Change many people in the sales force? • Find roles for those who don't fit the new profile? • Find strategies for retaining top performers? • Train the sales force on new competencies? • Change the sales culture?
Step 4	Sales Force Activity Drivers	• Provide the sales force with new customer information and tools? • Realign sales systems? • Revamp incentive compensation programs? • Define different success metrics? • Set new sales goals?

Figure 28.3   Decision-making process for adapting a sales force to major external events

● *Sales strategy changes*: With extensive input from customers and from the sales and marketing teams, UA developed a new value proposition and a new sales process for delivering that value to customers.

● *Sales force structure and role changes*: UA changed the size and structure of its sales force and redesigned field sales territories to support implementation of the new sales process. It also added a telesales team to support selected smaller accounts more efficiently.

● *Sales force skill and capability changes*: UA developed a new sales force competency model and revised its hiring profile accordingly. It re-interviewed sales people for jobs, retaining only those who had the capabilities and desire to adapt to the new selling model. Approximately 30 per cent of salespeople had to be replaced.

● *Sales force activity changes*: To help the sales force carry out the activities required for the new sales process, UA revised its sales force training and established mechanisms for best practice sharing. It developed a suite of technology products to assist salespeople in classifying customers, creating customized product offerings and reinforcing value to customers. It also revamped goal setting and performance management systems to reinforce the new selling model.

● *Alignment across the SFE drivers*: UA aligned its entire portfolio of SFE drivers around its new sales strategy, thus ensuring consistency of all sales force decisions, processes, systems and programs with company goals and strategies.

The new sales model had positive results for UA's sales force, its customers and the company. Salespeople found the new sales approach more strategic and professional. Customers said the new approach was more tailored to their needs and priorities. Sales results were good following implementation, as UA established contractual partnerships with many high priority new accounts and renewed contracts with many high priority existing accounts. Company leaders felt that the new sales model made substantial performance contributions worldwide in an industry environment fraught with continued challenges. They hired Jeff Foland, the consulting principal who had managed the sales force transformation project, as their new vice president of worldwide sales. According to Foland (Zoltners et al. 2009):

> the success of the sales force transformation came from anchoring everything around deep customer insights, institutionalizing a structured sales process that we supported with training and tools, introducing call planning discipline, explicitly defining what success means and how sales managers should coach salespeople to succeed, and recognizing good performance by creating heroes and holding them up for the organization to see.

Situation 2: When Specific Issues or Concerns Emerge Within the Sales Force

The best companies do not limit their focus on sales force effectiveness to times when major marketplace or company events compel change. Instead sales leaders at these companies engage in ongoing *effectiveness hunts*, seeking to discover specific issues or concerns that reside within the sales force system, including deficiencies in the skills and capabilities of *salespeople*, inappropriate or insufficient sales *activity* or early signs of trouble with *customer* or *company results*. Issue-driven diagnoses allow sales leaders to identify which SFE drivers should be modified to remedy specific issues and concerns. Two examples show how such diagnoses lead to enhanced sales effectiveness.

Example 2.1: Addressing sales force effectiveness concerns at an insurance company

Sales leaders at an insurance company were concerned about excessive staff turnover. The sales force sold insurance policies to corporations to include in employee benefits packages. Salespeople earned all of their pay in the form of commissions on sales. More than 60 per cent of the new salespeople hired left the company before completing their first year of employment. For years while the market was growing, this high level of sales force turnover was an expected part of the company's successful business model. The company recruited thousands of new salespeople every year, knowing that those who discovered that they were unsuited for the job would leave quickly. Yet as the market became saturated, the model stopped working well. With less favorable market opportunities, too many people with good long-term potential were leaving too quickly, and the company's investment in recruiting and training was no longer paying off because not enough people stayed long enough to produce significant results.

What the company did   When the company discovered that salespeople who made their first sale quickly were much more likely to stay than those who struggled for months to make a sale, it launched a three-pronged effort to improve the early success of new recruits. First, it began giving new salespeople a few existing customer accounts that had good growth potential. Second, it invested in improved training and coaching programs

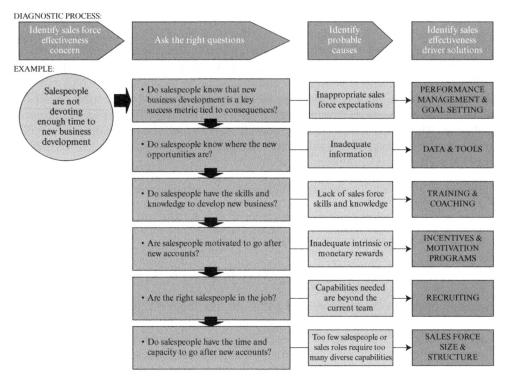

Figure 28.4   Process for diagnosing sales force concerns at a B2B company

for new salespeople. Third, by developing a more targeted profile for screening candidates during the recruiting process, the company improved the quality of its new recruits. These initiatives helped new salespeople with good long-term potential get off to a faster start, thereby increasing retention. The company also began paying salespeople a small salary for their first year only, in addition to paying them commissions. This change gave new salespeople money to survive on while they built the skills and customer relationships that would enable their long-term success.

Example 2.2: Using a diagnostic process to address new business development concerns at a B2B company

Sales leaders at a B2B company were concerned that salespeople spent almost all of their time with loyal, comfortable customers and were not devoting enough time to new business development. Bringing new customers on board would be critical for achieving new revenue growth goals in a competitive market.

What the company did   Sales leaders used the sales force system framework to guide a diagnosis that could trace the causes of their concern back to the root SFE drivers that might provide solutions (see Figure 28.4).

Leaders structured the diagnosis around a series of questions aimed at identifying probable causes and ultimately solutions. The questions were sequenced so that those asked first linked to SFE drivers that were easier to change. For example, adjustments to performance management processes, goals, data and tools could be made fairly quickly and without significant disruption to the sales force. The questions near the bottom of Figure 28.4 led to SFE drivers that were more challenging to change, such as the recruiting program and the size and structure of the sales force. Because these drivers determined the people in the sales force and the assignment of customer responsibility, changing them would be more disruptive and harder to implement, and it would take longer to have an impact. Through the diagnosis, sales leaders identified remedies in two of the easier-to-change SFE drivers: training and performance management. First, because many salespeople lacked confidence in approaching new accounts, the company implemented a new training program aimed at improving the prospecting and new business development skills of salespeople. Second, leaders elevated the importance of new account development in the performance management process by tracking new business development metrics by territory and giving salespeople specific goals for these metrics. These changes prompted an increase in new business development activity and ultimately results.

The questions that sales leaders at the B2B company used to diagnose their particular concern can be adapted to address a variety of challenges faced by sales forces. Some companies will have considerable success effecting change by leveraging the easier-to-change SFE drivers. Others will have to rely on the harder-to-change SFE drivers to create an effective solution. Solutions to the most difficult sales force challenges typically involve adjustments to multiple SFE drivers.

Situation 3: When the Company Wants to Improve Sales Force Effectiveness

Because sales force effectiveness is strongly linked to top- and bottom-line performance, corporate initiatives aimed at increasing overall sales force effectiveness are quite common at B2B companies. GE has a leadership team responsible for improving the competence and productivity of salespeople. The team includes sales effectiveness directors for every major GE business unit and a corporate 'Global Manager of Sales Programs & Sales Force Effectiveness' who is charged with developing consistent frame works and best practices for GE sales forces and propagating them across the company's numerous businesses around the world.

The best sales force effectiveness initiatives rely on diagnostic tools and structured approaches to identify and implement sales force changes with high impact. For example, by analyzing cross-sectional territory-level data, it is possible to gain insights into how well various SFE drivers are performing (examples appear later in this chapter, in Figures 28.6 and 28.7). Benchmarking against competitors and keeping up with industry best practices can also help companies discover opportunities to increase their sales force effectiveness.

Many companies have revealed powerful ways to improve their sales forces by observing the traits and activities of the best performers within their own companies. Top performers – those who have achieved the best results relative to the potential in their territory – demonstrate what level of performance is possible in a sales force. Substantial improvements in sales force effectiveness can be made by investing in sales force programs, systems and processes that enable the company to learn from the best salespeople.

Then by sharing what it learns with average-performing salespeople, the company increases the average sales force performance level. B2B companies have implemented numerous effectiveness-enhancing changes as a result of what they have learned by studying the behaviors of top performers.

Example 3.1: Novartis learns from its top-performing salespeople
With operations in 140 countries around the world, the healthcare products company Novartis seeks to constantly improve the effectiveness of its many sales organizations.

What the company did   Beginning in 2001, Novartis sales leaders conducted annual sales force effectiveness reviews. Using structured processes and analytic tools, they identified high-priority opportunities to improve sales force performance by implementing effectiveness-enhancing sales force changes throughout the world. In one initiative, sales leaders identified a set of success behaviors that differentiated the company's top performing salespeople from average performers. Sales leaders then incorporated the set of success behaviors into a training program for the entire sales organization. They also implemented new coaching tools and realigned the performance management process to emphasize these success behaviors. Salespeople who had been trained and coached to emulate the behaviors of top performers earned more favorable perceptions among their customers. An industry survey asked customers to select the best industry salesperson that they interacted with, and the Novartis salespeople who had completed the training were selected 46 per cent of the time, compared with only 22 per cent of the time for salespeople who did not complete the training. Customers' preferences were also linked to better sales results.

Example 3.2: Prioritizing based on performance and impact at a healthcare company
Leaders of the Swiss division of a global healthcare company sought to improve sales force effectiveness. Their preliminary diagnosis had revealed a large list of SFE drivers that were candidates for improvement, yet they felt that the company would get the best results by prioritizing the drivers and focusing improvement efforts on a small number of the most important ones first.

What the company did   Leaders created a performance scorecard (see Figure 28.5) to assess sales force effectiveness and prioritize initiatives according to their likely impact. The scorecard profiled each SFE driver in terms of two measures: performance and strategic impact. The performance score reflected how competent or capable the selling organization was at maximizing each SFE driver. These scores were derived using data analysis, benchmarking and the input of company leaders and other experts. The strategic impact scores measured the importance of each SFE driver for the organization's ability to succeed in the current economy. The company used management judgment and input from outside experts to derive the strategic impact scores.

The performance scorecard provided a snapshot of the organization's performance and the strategic impact of the SFE drivers. The position of each driver on the scorecard suggested an action:

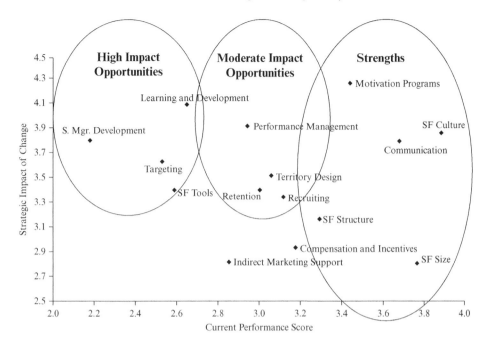

Figure 28.5   Example sales force performance scorecard for the Swiss division of a healthcare company

- Low strategic impact and high performance (e.g. sales force size): maintain at current levels.
- High strategic impact and high performance (e.g. motivation programs): monitor closely to ensure that performance does not slip.
- Low strategic impact and low performance (e.g. indirect marketing support): monitor to see whether impact increases over time.
- Low performance and high strategic impact (e.g. training, sales manager develop-ment, targeting, sales force tools): these SFE drivers presented the greatest oppor-tunity for effectiveness gains and as such were considered top priorities for sales leaders.

When selecting SFE driver priorities from a performance scorecard, another con-sideration is the ease of implementation for enhancing the SFE drivers. Some SFE drivers are easier to change and will have quick impact; others require change that is more disruptive and difficult for the sales force, and it will take longer to have an impact.

A performance scorecard is very specific to a company and its condition at the time the assessment is conducted. SFE drivers move to the right as the sales force's performance improves and to the left as performance slips when changes in the environment render current practices less effective or when sales leaders and individual salespeople fail to maintain high performance standards. Drivers move up or down as their strategic impact changes due to modifications in environmental conditions and company strategy. Sales

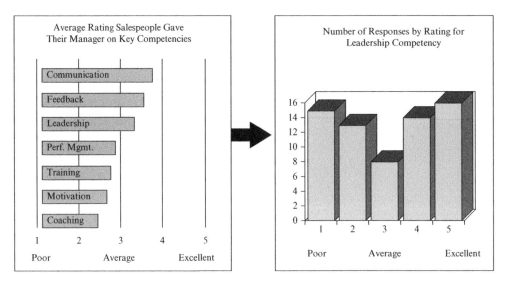

Figure 28.6   *How salespeople rated managers on seven key competencies*

leaders gain particular insights when they conduct such assessments on a regular basis and track changes over time.

Situation 4: When Issues or Concerns Emerge Within a Specific SFE Driver

Quite often, sales leaders focus on single SFE driver solutions for their effectiveness enhancement initiatives. Consider two examples.

Example 4.1: Addressing sales manager weakness at a hospital supply company

A company that sold hospital supplies assessed its sales management team by asking sales-people to complete anonymous evaluations of their managers on important competencies (see Figure 28.6). The average rating that salespeople gave their managers was nowhere near 'excellent' for any of the seven competencies that leaders felt were critical to sales manager success; managers were rated 'below average' on four of these competencies. The distribution of scores on every competency followed a disturbing bimodal pattern (Figure 28.6 shows the pattern for leadership). Although many salespeople gave their manager an excellent rating on leadership, almost equally as many rated their manager poor, and rela-tively few gave their manager an average rating. This bimodal trend occurred for the other managerial competencies as well. The survey results confirmed sales leaders' hypothesis that the sales force was carrying a number of weak managers.

What the company did   Realizing that, in time, an ineffective sales manager brings down the performance of all of the territories that he or she manages, the company initiated a serious effort to upgrade the quality of its sales management team. Managers for whom the upgrade did not produce the desired results were reassigned to individual contributor roles.

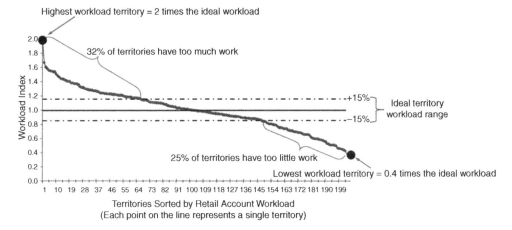

Figure 28.7   Analysis of territory workloads for retail merchandising

Example 4.2: Addressing sales territory design concerns at a cosmetics company
A cosmetics company employs retail merchandisers who regularly stock shelves, set up displays and take inventories in retail stores that sell the company's products. An analysis of the annual account workload in each merchandiser's territory revealed that the majority of territories had workloads that were outside the acceptable range of what a merchandiser can accomplish in a year (see Figure 28.7): 32 per cent of territories had too much work for the merchandiser to handle effectively, and 25 per cent had too little work to keep a merchandiser fully busy.

What the company did   The company increased its sales force effectiveness and retailer coverage significantly by reassigning under-covered profitable accounts from high-workload territories to merchandisers who had time to cover those accounts more effectively.

A Need for Multidriver Solutions

Often sales leaders turn to drivers that are highly visible (e.g. compensation), non-threatening (e.g. training), or offer new hope (e.g. customer relationship management) while overlooking SFE drivers that are less obvious and more difficult to change, such as culture, leadership and recruiting. Most difficult sales force challenges require multiple SFE driver solutions, including solutions in both the visible and the less obvious categories. By linking sales force issues and concerns with a comprehensive list of potential SFE driver solutions, the sales force system framework helps sales leaders develop complete solutions to the issues they face while keeping all the SFE drivers well aligned with company goals and strategies.

A PERSPECTIVE FOR RESEARCHERS ON ADAPTING AND IMPROVING THE SALES FORCE

By providing a holistic view of how all the components and linkages within sales forces work together and interact, the sales force system framework helps researchers understand the impact of their work within the context of the broader sales force system. There is a good deal of descriptive and normative research to help sales leaders understand each of the SFE drivers individually. Our inventory of sales academic research (updated from the original, Zoltners et al. 2008) includes 220 recent sales-related articles from the *Journal of Marketing, Journal of Marketing Research, Journal of Personal Selling and Sales Management* and *Marketing Science.* These articles were discovered through searches of electronic research databases for articles published between 2001 and 2009 that used subject keywords such as 'salespeople', 'sales management' and 'personal selling'. The articles are categorized according to the SFE drivers that have salience in the article abstracts.

Statistics derived from the inventory show that the majority of sales research has a narrow focus. In particular, 168 of the articles focus on at least one SFE driver; 129 articles (77 per cent) focus on a single SFE driver. Only 11 articles consider three or more SFE drivers. Although there is some indication that the breadth of research has increased recently (7 of the 11 articles focusing on multiple SFE drivers were published between 2007 and 2009), most research continues to explore the impact of just one SFE driver at a time. We have suggested some best practices for each SFE driver individually (Zoltners et al. 2009), and we also propose some processes for looking comprehensively across multiple drivers to address important sales force issues, challenges and dilemmas (as in Figure 28.4).

Research that expands beyond a single SFE driver focus by looking at the impact of individual SFE drivers in the context of the entire sales force system can be of great value to sales leaders. SFE driver decisions affect *salespeople* and *activities* and ultimately drive *customer* and *company results*. Research that focuses on understanding each of these linkages and the interactions that exist among the SFE driver decisions can help sales leaders make better decisions that increase sales effectiveness. The causal model in Figure 28.8 lays out important hypotheses at an aggregate level regarding how key linkages in the sales force system work.

The *SFE drivers* affect customer and company *results* through *salespeople* and *activities*. Salespeople and activities have several dimensions. Salespeople need *capabilities* (knowledge, skills, abilities) and *motivation* if they are to execute sales activities effectively. At the same time, the effective execution of sales activities requires a sufficient *quantity* and *quality* of activity, as well as the proper *allocation* of activity to the right customers, products and sales tasks. With the right quantity, quality and allocation of activity, a sales force can produce the desired customer and company *results*.

The components and dimensions in Figure 28.8 are linked together by hypothesized causal relationships. The arrows indicate our hypotheses regarding the linkages that exist and the strength of their impact. Strength of impact is an ordinal classification: the thickest arrows signify linkages with the strongest impact, and the thinnest, dashed arrows represent linkages with the weakest impact. The lack of an arrow suggests

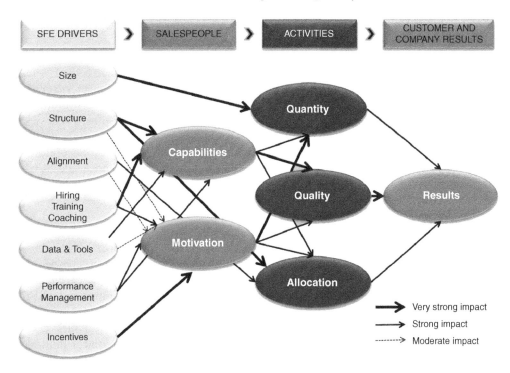

Figure 28.8   Hypotheses: how key linkages in the sales force system work together to drive results

no meaningful linkage exists between the components. For example, incentives have very strong impacts on salespeople's motivation but no meaningful impact on their capabilities. Motivation has a very strong impact on the quantity of activity and a strong impact on the quality and allocation of activity. Data and tools have strong impacts on salespeople's capabilities and moderate impacts on their motivation. Most SFE drivers affect sales activities through one or both of the salespeople dimensions. We hypothesize that three SFE drivers influence activities directly: size has a very strong impact on the quantity of an activity that a sales force can deliver, and alignment and structure affect the allocation of activity across products, markets and sales territories.

Figure 28.8 thus suggests a possible research agenda for understanding how SFE driver decisions affect salespeople, activities and ultimately results. Researchers can help sales leaders measure each component, measure the strength of the relationships between the components and gain insight about how the components and linkages differ by industry and with varied business conditions and levels of sales process complexity.

By helping sales leaders understand how SFE driver decisions affect all of the linkages and components of the sales force system within the context of the business environment, researchers can help sales leaders determine the most appropriate role for each of the SFE drivers. This will enable sales leaders to create and maintain more effective sales organizations.

CONCLUSION

Sales forces have high impact on both revenues and costs for B2B companies, yet managing a sales force successfully is a significant challenge. An excellent sales force has talented *salespeople* who engage in the right *activities* to meet *customer* needs and drive *company results*. The best way to create, maintain and continuously improve an excellent sales force is to ensure that the company decisions, processes, programs and systems that affect salespeople – the *sales force effectiveness drivers* – are well-managed and in alignment with company business strategies. Several key insights are relevant for sales leaders and researchers who seek to enhance sales force effectiveness.

Key Insights for Sales Leaders

- Improve sales force effectiveness by improving the sales force effectiveness drivers: the decisions, processes, systems and programs that affect salespeople and their activities and thus determine results. A sales force is only excellent if the SFE drivers are excellent. The way to improve results is to improve the SFE drivers.
- Look to SFE drivers when seeking solutions to specific sales force issues, challenges and concerns. Bringing about effective change usually requires multiple SFE driver adjustments and looking beyond frequent go-to drivers such as training and incentives.
- SFE drivers have impacts on the sales force system over varied time horizons. Some drivers (e.g. training, incentives) have immediate impact. The impacts of other drivers (e.g. sales force structure and culture) take longer to show up in the results. When adjusting the SFE drivers, think about sales force needs over time and work to enable success not only today but also tomorrow and the day after.
- There are synergistic effects within the portfolio of SFE drivers. Your sales force decisions, processes, systems and programs are most powerful when they are aligned with one another in support of business goals and strategies. For example a complex sales process requires *hiring* salespeople with the right capabilities, *training* them on critical skills and providing them with *data and tools* to enable their success. An *incentive plan* that pays salespeople a commission on all sales requires a *sales territory alignment* that ensures adequate opportunity for every salesperson to succeed.
- Assess the SFE drivers regularly but especially when your selling environment is changing. Seek constant sales force effectiveness improvement by selecting a few high-impact SFE drivers to improve every year.

Key Insights for Researchers

- The sales force system comprises many complex components and linkages. Running a sales force is like running a business. The issues range from strategy development to managing human resources, logistics, operations and finances to establishing an organizational culture. Researchers need to broaden their research paradigms to help with these important marketing mix decisions.

- The impact of various linkages within the sales force system differs by industry and with the level of sales process complexity. Research is valuable when it provides insight on how impactful the SFE drivers are within the context of the specific selling environment. The dynamics in a simple sales environment (e.g. store merchandising of consumer packaged goods) are quite different from those in a complex sales environment (e.g. selling customized high-tech products to global corporations).

- In addition to building research around SFE drivers, focus on specific, frequent sales force *issues* or *concerns* (e.g. how to motivate a complacent sales force, increase retention of salespeople, change a sales process as customer needs evolve). Such research can aid understanding of which SFE drivers are most useful for addressing different challenges.

- Mathematical models are powerful aids to practitioners' decision-making about some SFE drivers (e.g. sales force size, territory alignment, incentive compensation). For SFE driver decisions that are currently incompatible with mathematical models (e.g. finding the right sales force structure, establishing a success culture, discovering the most effective coaching approaches), researchers can enhance understanding by creating thinking frameworks that support structured and comprehensive decision-making processes.

- The sales force system is highly complex, making it difficult to study comprehensively. Researchers face many challenges, including a lack of data in the public domain, companies reluctant to share their own data and considerable heterogeneity across sales environments, which creates complexity beyond what simple approaches can capture. By studying one or a subset of the components and linkages of the sales force system, while acknowledging the role of those components and linkages within the holistic system, researchers can continue to build insights useful to practitioners. In time a meta-analysis that summarizes and synthesizes insights across studies can significantly enhance understanding of sales force system dynamics.

There is opportunity for sales leaders to learn much from the research performed to date in the area of sales force effectiveness. At the same time, researchers can discover many new research opportunities by learning more about the issues and challenges that practitioners face. As the sales environment continues to change and increase in complexity, it is important that researchers and practitioners work together to enhance understanding of the best ways to manage all of the SFE drivers for optimal business impact.

REFERENCES

Barclay's Capital (2009), 'US advertising revenue by medium', available at http://www.businessinsider.com/us-advertising-spending-by-medium-2009-10.

IAB (2010), 'IAB internet advertising revenue report – 2009 full year results', April, p. 3, available at http://www.iab.net/media/file/IAB-Ad-Revenue-Full-Year-2009.pdf.

Selling Power (2009) '500 largest sales forces in America', October, pp. 43–60.

Zoltners, Andris A., Prabhakant Sinha and Sally E. Lorimer (2008), 'Sales force effectiveness: a framework for researchers and practitioners', *Journal of Personal Selling and Sales Management*, Spring, pp. 115–31.
Zoltners, Andris A., Prabhakant Sinha and Sally E. Lorimer (2009), *Building a Winning Sales Force: Powerful Strategies for Driving High Performance*, New York: Amacom.

29 The impact of the Internet on B2B sales force size and structure

Murali K. Mantrala and Sönke Albers

Since its commercialization in the mid-1990s, the Internet has become one of the most revolutionary forces in history to hit business in general and B2B (including 'industrial' and 'services') markets in particular – an economic sector expected to grow to $15 trillion in 2010 (Sheth and Sharma 2008).[1] The Internet represents the single most important technology of this generation for firms to cut costs, improve service, expand markets and deal more effectively with customers (Litan and Rivlin 2001). In their pioneering study, Varian et al. (2002) reported that the earliest and most pervasive Internet-based technologies that businesses adopted were customer-facing solutions (e.g. e-marketing, customer service and support, e-commerce solutions). In addition, Giga Information Group (now part of Gartner Group) estimated that the cost savings from business use of e-commerce would reach $1.25 trillion by 2002 (Masterson 1999). A significant proportion of these projected savings stem from the reduction in SG&A (sales, general and administrative) costs. Organizations in the United States expected that their Internet business solutions would help them save more than $150 billion in such costs by 2005. The most frequently mentioned savings were from reduction in customer support costs, followed by reduced costs of human resources, sales and marketing (Varian et al. 2002).

Since Varian et al.'s (2002) study, the invention and diffusion of new Internet-based technologies, applications and services useful for business and e-commerce have proceeded rapidly. For example, within the past decade Web 1.0 evolved into Web 2.0, and innovative technologies have emerged, such as 'software as a service' (Saas) and cloud computing (Internet-based computing on demand), which make it easier for firms of all sizes to harness the power of the Internet in a flexible way. Applying these technologies, vendors such as Salesforce.com have made powerful sales force automation (SFA) and customer relationship management (CRM) web-based tools and applications more accessible to many businesses. Research on the adoption of such SFA and CRM technologies and their effects on sales force performance and management is rapidly growing (e.g. Ahearne et al. 2007; Ahearne et al. 2008; Buttle et al. 2006). Our objectives in this chapter, however, are broader and twofold: (1) to review and document how the Internet is used in B2B buying and selling today; and (2) to conceptualize the Internet's evolving impact on sales force size and structure with propositions for further investigation.

MOTIVATION FOR CHAPTER'S OBJECTIVES

The sales force is a potent instrument of marketing communication and is easily the most significant demand-generating budget item for many industrial firms (e.g. Albers et al. 2010; Mantrala et al. 2010). Even so, with the advent of the Internet, the future of sales forces was much debated among strategic thinkers at the beginning of the new millennium (e.g. Porter 2001; Rackham and De Vincentis 1999; Sharma 2002; Sharma and Tzokas 2002; Sheth and Sisodia 1999). Some predicted that the Internet would lead to significant downsizing, if not disintermediation, of firms' traditional business sales organizations ('selling without the sales force'; Sheth and Sisodia 1999). These authors reasoned that the Internet adds value to firms by lowering specific transaction costs associated with many of the activities traditionally performed by sales personnel, such as providing product information, negotiating and contracting, collecting payments, and supervising delivery (e.g. Marshall et al. 1999). According to Rackham and De Vincentis (1999, p. 3), by some estimates 'at least half of today's selling positions will be gone within five years'. However, an opposing school of thought argued that Internet-based technologies would never replace salespeople (because buyers value the human touch; Bendapudi and Leone 2002; Lewin et al. 2010) but could enhance their efficiency and effectiveness (e.g. Ahearne and Rapp 2010; Piercy and Lane 2003; Porter 2001). In this vein, Long et al. (2007) document how firms integrated various Internet-based tools existing at the time to improve salesperson efficiency and effectiveness at every stage of the classic selling process.

Over time, it has become evident that the Internet has not disintermediated B2B sales forces in general, even though some industries have downsized during the past decade (e.g. real estate brokerages, travel agencies, financial services) (Lane and Piercy 2004; Lewin et al. 2010).[2] Conversely, sales forces have even expanded in other industries (e.g. high-technology). Dell Computers successfully integrated both Internet-based and direct sales force channels in its business models and has recently announced plans to expand its sales force by 4000 (Ladendorf 2010). Thus, though largely anecdotal, the empirical evidence so far provides little support for the disintermediation hypothesis.

Still, most observers agree that the Internet has severely buffeted traditional B2B sales strategies and organizations and has increased uncertainty about the futures of sales jobs in many industries (e.g. Sharma et al. 2010). Legat and Woehr (2004) call it a cataclysmic shock that 'makes classical sales management obsolete'. Reflecting this view, many sales consultants today refer to 'Sales 2.0' as the new Internet-enabled sales paradigm (which aligns the selling process more closely and collaboratively with the buying process, e.g. Trailer 2009) that has replaced Sales 1.0 (i.e. the classical sales paradigm). From an academic viewpoint, it is debatable how much of the Sales 2.0 thinking is really new; many of its core ideas (e.g. adaptive selling, relationship selling) have been available for some time (see Bradford et al. 2010; Spiro and Weitz 1990; Weitz and Bradford 1999). However, the essentially universal access to the Internet for both buyers and sellers is certainly quite new, and Sales 2.0 thinking clearly accounts for these contemporary technological developments.

Despite the importance and gravity of the early predictions, systematic study of the Internet's impact on B2B sales force size and structure is sparse. Now, however, as the first decade of the new millennium has drawn to a close, the timing is right to offer a fresh conceptual framework and agenda for systematic study of the Internet's effects to better guide evolving B2B sales force strategy. The need is urgent considering the many billions of dollars in sales force investments, and the hundreds of thousands of B2B sales jobs, perceived to be at stake around the world (e.g. Jones et al. 2005; Sharma et al. 2010; Zoltners et al. 2008). This chapter attempts to meet this need.

Notably, this chapter's focus on the impact of the prevailing Internet-enabled information environment on B2B sales organization, as distinct from B2B companies'

Internet marketing strategies and investments, differs from that of extant work in several information technology (Internet-) related business marketing management research streams, as listed below:

- the evolution and impact of Internet strategies, investments and integration in B2B marketing and sales strategies and tactics in general (e.g. Avlonitis and Karayanni 2000; Jap and Mohr 2002; Lichtenthal and Eliaz 2003);
- the adoption, use and efficacy of SFA in B2B markets (e.g. Ahearne et al. 2008; Speier and Venkatesh 2002);
- B2B multichannel selling strategy, cannibalization and conflict (e.g. Jap and Mohr 2002; Rosenbloom 2007; Webb and Lambe 2007);
- the functioning and performance of online B2B exchanges (e.g. Day et al. 2003) and electronic marketplaces (e.g. Bakos 1997); and
- the impact of Web 2.0 technologies (e.g. blogging, search engine optimization, social media) on B2B marketing practices in general (e.g. Steenburgh and Narayandas 2010).

In contrast, our work focuses on how the Internet-based information environment affects B2B buying and selling processes and, consequently, sales force size and structure. It also offers a conceptual model and propositional inventory for further investigation.

The remainder of this chapter is organized as follows: first, we detail our organizing conceptual framework. This framework considers the Internet as a bundle of technologies for computer-mediated communication, which in some of its facets (e.g. Mohr and Nevin 1990) and interactive properties emulates those of an industrial salesperson (see Weitz's 1978 model). Second, we describe the classic formulations of the B2B buying process and personal selling process and summarize how firms employ various Internet communication technologies at different 'stages' of these processes. Third, we outline how advances in the nature of information derived from these Internet-based technologies are transforming key aspects of B2B buying, namely, *buying center complexity* and *buying process* dependence on Internet-based versus sales force-based information. We also discuss the degree to which the Internet is transforming the classic selling process from a *seller-driven* to a *buyer-driven* process and how buyer–seller interactions are being transformed. Fourth, we present the implications of these Internet-based changes in B2B buying and selling for sales force size and structure in the form of propositions. We conclude with a summary of the managerial and research implications.

ORGANIZING CONCEPTUAL FRAMEWORK

An Overview

From the B2B sales force perspective, the Internet is a revolutionary platform, characterized as intelligent, ubiquitous and flexible, and by instant and constant connectivity (Sharma 2002), *for getting and providing information*. The Internet's fundamental benefits include information acquisition and provision through *one-way* communication (e.g. users searching over sites and reading pages), *two-way* communication (e.g. email

Table 29.1   Ways of communication offered by the Internet

Nature of Communication Involved

'One-way'	'Two-way'	'Multiway'
World Wide Web (WWW), e.g. vendor websites, third-party websites, web feeds, podcasts	Email	Webcasts
Web search engines, e.g., Google, Yahoo	Instant messaging	Web conferencing (w/wo VOIP), e.g. webinars
	Online chat	Virtual events, e.g. virtual tradeshows
	VOIP	Social media, e.g. blogs; microblogs such as Twitter; collaborative projects such as Wikipedia; social/professional networking sites such as Facebook, LinkedIn; content communication such as YouTube, Slideshare; virtual social worlds such as Second Life

exchanges between two people) and *multiway* – that is, one-to-many or many-to-many – communication (e.g. usage of social networking media such as LinkedIn). Further, the Internet today allows users to communicate with one another through a variety of methods: synchronous, asynchronous, text, audio and video. Our schema includes Internet-based communications involved in both B2B e-commerce and offline sales. Table 29.1 summarizes this classification of Internet information communication technologies.

Contemporary Internet communication technologies have radically transformed the attributes of marketing information available to actors in B2B markets. In particular, the Internet has greatly enhanced the quantity, quality (richness), currency and verifiability of information available to buyers and sellers, as well as the speed and scope of the information collected, while lowering the costs of collection (though not necessarily the costs of *processing* the information, which would limit the amount of Internet information gathered and used; e.g. Coiera 2000). (Note that this is not an exhaustive list of Internet information attributes but rather specifies seven that we see as distinctive and highly relevant in B2B buying and selling. The Appendix provides a description of these selected attributes of Internet information.)

In our conceptualization, Internet-based changes in attributes of information available to B2B buyers and sellers affect: (1) buying center complexity; (2) the nature (Internet- vs. salesperson-dependence) of the buying process; (3) the nature (buyer-driven vs. seller-driven) of the selling process; and (4) the nature (goods-dominant vs. services-dominant) of buyer–seller interpersonal interactions. The nature of the product, the nature of the purchase and the nature of the buyer–seller exchange all moderate these effects. Subsequently, the Internet information-induced changes on the buying and selling sides and their interaction have significant implications for sales force size and structure. Two key moderating factors at this stage are the nature of competition and environmental uncertainty. Figure 29.1 depicts this conceptual framework. The inspiration for the framework stems from findings of recent market research studies of Internet usage by business buyers and sellers, which we summarize next.

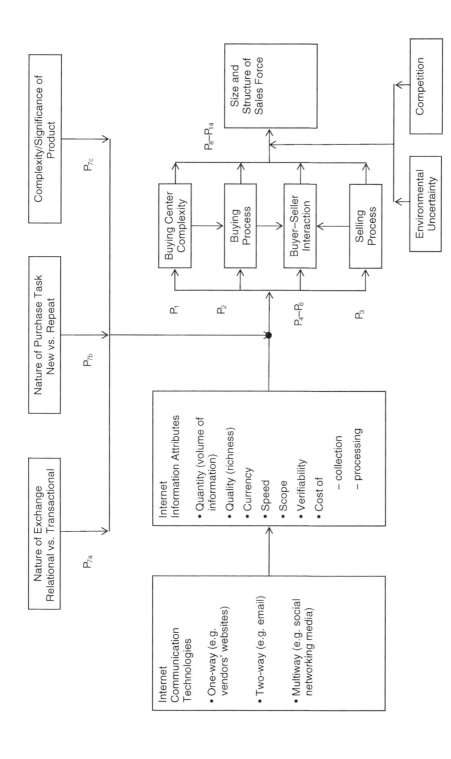

Figure 29.1 Organizing conceptual framework

Table 29.2   Buying and selling processes and Internet use

Buying Process	Internet Technology Usage	Selling Process	Internet Technology Usage
Need recognition	Internet searches (vendor websites, Google), chat rooms, blogs, video blogs (YouTube), social media (Twitter, Facebook, LinkedIn)	Prospect finding and obtaining leads	Buyers' website
Definition of requirements	B2B exchanges/ marketplaces/portal websites; Tailored online communities	Qualifying leads	Inbound: Search engine advertising; contextual ads; business databases; email (outbound); B2B portals; exchanges; virtual trade shows; social media; webinars; podcast; webcasts
Determination of specifications	Third-party websites	Pre-approach: Finding possible contacts within company	Buyer's employees blogs; intranet/extranets
Search for and qualification of suppliers	Mainstream search engine (Google, Yahoo, Microsoft); vendor site; B2B vertical search engine; enterprise information site; extranets	Approach: Classify buyers	Own websites; webcasts
Requests for proposals	Email; reverse auctions; user-generated content	Presentation: Communications and demonstrations	Own websites; Skype; Webex; web conferencing; online demos
Supplier proposal evaluation	Forums, panels, blogs	Handling objections	Own websites; online reviews; weblinks to independent sites
Supplier selection/ order routine	Electronic data interchange	Closing	Online marketing; online payment systems
Negotiations and purchase		Follow-up	Online tracking system
Qualifying the purchase afterward	Email	Customer engagement and retention	Internet-based CRM

Industrial Buyers' and Sellers' Usage of Internet-based Communication Media

Table 29.2 displays the traditional textbook descriptions of the steps or stages in industrial (B2B) buying and selling processes side by side. The realism of these classic 'linear' conceptualizations of how industrial buyers (sellers) make (influence) buying decisions has been questioned for some time (e.g. Moncrief and Marshall 2005; Spiro and Weitz

1990; Weitz and Bradford 1999). However, these conceptualizations serve a useful purpose of accounting for all the activities that must occur in any logical buying and selling process. What is of interest is how the Internet is transforming the way these activities are being conducted. Table 29.2 also displays several Internet technologies reportedly used today at various stages of these processes.

Use of Internet information technologies in the buying process
Several recent market research reports suggest that the Internet is profoundly affecting the classic depiction of the B2B buying process. First, B2B buyers are increasingly turning to online sources earlier in their process, to research purchases before calling a 'live' sales rep. Specifically, MarketingSherpa's (Balegno 2009) 2009–2010 B2B Marketing Benchmark Report, based on a survey of technology buyers who make purchases greater than $25 000 (i.e. large, consultative purchases), found that more than 24 per cent of the respondents reported increasing usage of search engines, virtual trade shows, business news/information websites, vendors' websites, technology B2B websites and social media (blogs and social networks). In contrast, 37 per cent of the respondents in this survey indicated *decreasing usage* of face-to-face events and trade shows. (Interestingly, a nearly ten-year-old investigation of industrial buyers' perceptions of the Internet as a communication tool found that personal experience, travel to meeting sites and attendance at tradeshows were perceived as more useful than the Internet; see Deeter-Schmelz and Kennedy (2002).) The upshot of these trends is that B2B buyers' face-to-face conversations with vendors tend to occur more in the later stages of the buying cycle.

Second, helped both by their intranets and extranets linking collaborators such as suppliers and distributors, B2B buyers are more than ever manifesting themselves as a buying unit comprised of multiple decision-makers: a big-ticket purchase will be evaluated by a team of people, including, for example, the initial recommender, someone making the business case, a purchasing agent, and someone from legal and finance departments. Moreover, the vertical involvement of higher-level executives in the buying process is increasing (BUYERsphere 2010).

Third, B2B buyers are pursuing a more 'massively multichannel' buying process than ever before; however, channel weightings and their sequence vary according to the phase of the buying process. In general, supplier websites and Web searches figure prominently in the early stages (identifying needs, identifying suppliers) of B2B buying processes but much less so in the later supplier selection phase. The BUYERsphere report findings indicate that despite being hyped considerably, the role and influence of social media in the B2B buying process are still minimal. Specifically, 10 per cent or less of respondents in the BUYERsphere study indicated that communication through social media (e.g. blogs, Twitter, Facebook, LinkedIn) played a role in the buying process stages of identifying needs, identifying potential suppliers and selecting a supplier. Indeed, more traditional communications, such as industry press reports, word of mouth and events/ seminars, continue to be used more than social media in B2B markets. However, blogs, Twitter and Facebook do have high influence *when* they are used (BUYERsphere 2010). Further, Ramos and Young (2009) report that 91 per cent of technology decision-makers were 'spectators'; that is, those who are reading blogs, watching user-generated videos and participating (if not contributing much to conversations) in other social media, and 69 per cent said they were using this technology for business purposes. Moreover, these trends may accelerate with the arrival of the next generation of industrial buyers who grew up using social media in their formative years.

Use of Internet information technologies in the B2B selling process

Table 29.2 lists the variety of Internet tactics/technologies reportedly used by marketing/sales management at various stages of the B2B selling process (a review of the many opportunities for integration of Internet tools in the selling process is provided by Long et al. 2007). Recent surveys indicate that marketers are relying more on company websites and email, followed by public relations, trade shows (in person) and search marketing (MarketingProfs LLC 2009). However, they use virtual trade shows (the least-frequently-used tactic) and traditional tactics, including outdoor media, radio and television advertising, on a relatively infrequent basis. Again, the actual selling process in the Internet age is far from being a smooth linear process from one stage to the next, whose timing and flow is controlled by the seller. Rather, it involves many touch points, two-way interactions and backtracking that are a consequence of increasingly well-informed and networked prospects and buyers (e.g. Court et al. 2009).

IMPACT OF THE INTERNET ON B2B BUYING AND SELLING: SOME PROPOSITIONS

Effects of Internet Information on Buying Center Complexity

Originally, the concept of a 'buying center' in industrial selling referred to the people within an organization who become involved in the buying process for a product or service (Johnston and Bonoma 1981; Johnston and Chandler 2011; Robinson et al. 1967). However, some influential people or parties with stakes in the purchase can also be located in external organizations. Taking an 'open-systems' perspective, Dawes et al. (1998) argue that these parties should be treated as an external buying center group. We adopt this perspective in the following discussion.

As Figure 29.2 shows, we treat buying center complexity as a formative construct whose facets include the buying center's *size* (number of actively involved decision participants), *diversity* (number of functional areas of the firm represented in the buying center or *lateral involvement*) (e.g. Lewin and Donthu 2005), *executive or vertical involvement* (the frequency with which senior officers of the company intervene in the purchase decision), *dispersion* (the geographic distances of participants from the purchasing department) and *external involvement* (the frequency of inputs from parties outside the buying organization).

Prior research suggests that people who control the flow of information into and around the buying center gain power and have more influence on the decision (effectively equivalent to a reduction in the buying center's size from a seller's viewpoint) (e.g. Dawes et al. 1998; Pettigrew 1972). However, the Internet (including the company's intranet, extranet and social media networks) enables more dispersed stakeholders not only to stay connected but also to be better informed and participate more efficiently and effectively, thus reducing power concentration at the center. In effect, the average size of the buying center increases. Internet information attributes also facilitate greater diversity,

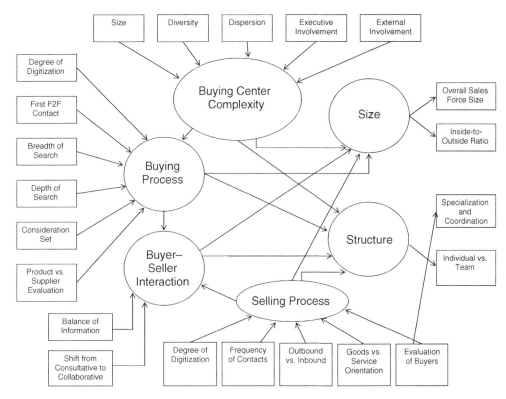

Figure 29.2 How Internet-induced changes in selling and buying processes influence sales force size and structure

vertical involvement and external involvement in the buying process. Together, these effects make the seller's task more difficult because it must coordinate and convince multiple decentralized but connected and well-informed decision-makers (e.g. Malone 1999) rather than one (centralized) person. In light of all these effects on the buying and selling sides, we propose the following:

P_1: *As Internet-based information improves (in terms of one or more of the noted characteristics), buying center complexity faced by sellers increases.*

Effects of Internet Information on Buying Process (Internet-dependence vs. Seller-dependence)

We view the buying process as a formative construct whose facets include the buying center's *degree of digitization* (e.g. investments in electronic data interchange with vendors, recourse to reverse auctions; e.g. Haruvy and Jap 2011), *breadth of search* (e.g. the geographic scope of search) over suppliers/products, *depth of search* (the bits of information gathered per alternative before meeting any vendor) over selected suppliers'/products' attributes, *size of the consideration set of suppliers* (who may be personally contacted), *product- versus supplier-focused direct evaluation*, and *postponement* (late timing) *of first direct (face-to-face) personal contact* (see Figure 29.2).

As Internet technologies' costs decrease, and knowledge of and familiarity with them and the attributes of information they provide increase (new generations of buyers are more tech-savvy than their senior counterparts), we expect a greater degree of digitization of purchasing management among B2B companies. This is already evident in the growing trend of reverse auctions in the B2B marketplace (Jap 2002). For the same reasons, we expect the breadth and depth of searches with respect to alternatives through the Internet to increase. Moreover, buyers are likely to keep their consideration sets open and to add to them with a more intense information collection in settings of greater uncertainty (e.g. those experiencing a faster pace of technological change; Heide and Weiss 1995). Internet information attributes enable buyers not only to assemble larger consideration sets but also to be more informed about the alternatives, without direct personal contacts with any vendor's salespeople. It is only at the choice stage of the purchase process, rather than at the earlier consideration stage, that direct contacts with sellers' salespeople might be necessary. That is, buyers can resolve much of their uncertainty with Internet information and postpone the time of first direct contact with the vendor's sales force.

Furthermore, because of the greater quantity of objective information buyers possess about each alternative remaining in consideration, it is likely that the focus of the first and subsequent direct contacts that buyers have with salespeople is more on assessing the fit of the supplier's organization (than just the 'product') and its total 'solution' (as defined by Tuli et al. 2007). That is, we expect the evaluation of alternatives remaining in the buyer's consideration set to be more focused on *relational processes* and not just product suitability to the buyer. This expectation is consistent with Heide and Weiss's (1995) findings that greater buyer uncertainty *lowers* the probability of switching from an existing vendor to a new one, despite creating a larger consideration set earlier in the buying process. Any new vendor under consideration who wants to displace an existing vendor will need to establish why his or her *firm*, beyond the product, would be a better option for the buyer than the latter's current supplier. Because the buyer has more knowledge of the existing supplier's solution, the buyer is likely to drive such a supplier evaluation discussion. Thus, we propose the following:

P_2: *As Internet-based information improves (in terms of one or more of the noted characteristics), the buying process as a whole becomes more (less) Internet-dependent (seller-dependent).*

Effects of Internet Information on Selling Process (Buyer-driven vs. Seller-driven)

As Figure 29.2 indicates, we view the selling process as a formative construct whose facets include the supplier's *degree of digitization of selling activity* (Johnson and Bharadwaj 2005), *emphasis on inbound (vs. outbound) marketing* (i.e. marketing and selling strategies and practices that *pull* prospective customers to a business or product through the use of Web 2.0 tools and applications, such as blogging and search engine optimization; e.g. Halligan and Shah 2010; Steenburgh et al. 2009), *frequency of direct (salesperson) contacts with existing versus new customers, goods- versus service-dominant orientation* (e.g. Bradford et al. 2010; Sheth and Sharma 2008) and *sellers' precontact search for and evaluation of buyers* (e.g. sales lead generation and qualification). From the prior literature and industry trends review, we expect the Internet's technological advances and familiarity (to younger workers) to increase: (1) the digitization of selling activity; (2) the emphasis on inbound marketing; (3) a service-dominant orientation; (4) salespeople's evaluations of potential buyers before first contact; and (5) the frequency of salespeople's contacts with existing customers. Taken together, these effects represent a selling process transforming into one that is led much more by the buyer than by the seller.

P_3: As Internet-based information improves (in terms of one or more of the noted characteristics), the B2B selling process becomes increasingly buyer-driven.

Impact of Internet Information on Buyer–Seller Interpersonal Interaction

In parallel with the Internet's transformative effects on the buying center, buying process and selling process, we expect that Internet information directly affects individual buyer–seller interpersonal interactions whenever and however they occur. As Figure 29.2 depicts, the facets of such interactions of particular relevance here are: (1) the *balance of information* or symmetry of information possessed by both sides when they interact; and (2) *the nature of the interaction: transactional, consultative,* or *collaborative* (which entails a degree of 'co-creation' of solutions for the customer; e.g. Sheth et al. 2000).

The Internet enables buyers to be more informed about a seller's product and competing alternatives' attributes and performance than in the past. Through blogs and social networking media, a buyer can also gather more information about the service and reputation of a supplier remaining in its consideration set. In turn, the seller has access to much of the same information about alternatives and also can perform a more detailed search to qualify whether a particular buyer is worth pursuing further. As a result, we expect both buyers and sellers to be more symmetrically informed about the products, users, alternative suppliers and each other because of the information available on the Internet. While previously the seller tended to have informational advantages going into an interaction with a buyer, this is no longer the case today. That is, the Internet has become the great equalizer. Thus, we propose the following:

P_4: As Internet-based information improves, buyer–seller interactions commence with more balanced (symmetric) information.

However, information not available on the Internet before a first engagement is precise knowledge of whether, in what form and how well the two sides may do business together. That is, we expect issues of the potential form, fit or 'match' between the organizations to dominate product-related conversation. Therefore, we propose the following:

P_5: As Internet-based information improves (in terms of one or more of the noted characteristics), the first (or early) direct interactions between the buyer and the seller will become increasingly 'organizational-match'-focused rather than product-focused.

In the 1980s and 1990s, at the urging of sales specialists, many B2B sales organizations moved toward consultative selling to win and keep customers (e.g. Rackham and

De Vincentis 1999). Today, however, Internet information available to buyers enables them to be better informed of what they need and the available options to meet these needs before any direct interactions with sellers. Correspondingly, the need for sellers to 'educate' buyers about their offerings has diminished, especially in situations in which the buyer's needs are fairly standard and the options are well known and documented on the Internet, even if untried by the buyer. In such circumstances, the Internet enables sellers to shift back from effective but costly consultative selling to more efficient transactional selling. At the same time, Internet connections enable a shift from consultative selling to collaborative interaction in co-creating solutions to meet novel needs of buying organizations. Therefore, we propose the following:

P_6:   As Internet-based information improves (in terms of one or more of the noted characteristics), the first (or early) B2B buyer–seller interactions will shift (a) from consultative to transactional selling in the case of well-known offerings to meet standard needs and (b) from consultative to collaborative selling (co-created offerings) to meet new and more customized needs.

Moderator Effects

We expect three factors to moderate the effect of the Internet on buyer–seller relationships (see Figure 29.1): (1) the *nature of the purchase task*, or 'buyclass' (Anderson et al. 1987; Robinson et al. 1967); (2) the *nature of the exchange* (e.g. one-time (transactional) event or part of an ongoing relationship (relational)); and (3) *the nature of the product* (technical complexity and product's significance in terms of purchase expenditures, e.g. Lilien and Wong 1984). In general, we expect the following:

P_7:   The positive effect of advances in Internet information on buying center complexity, the buying process, the selling process and the buyer–seller interaction enhances as (a) product complexity increases, (b) buyclass shifts from a 'routinized' buy to a 'new' task, and (c) the nature of exchange changes from transactional to relational.

Rationale: there is greater uncertainty about the purchase and the satisfaction it will provide when the product is complex or significant, the nature of the purchase is new and the deal can make or break a relationship. To reduce this uncertainty, the parties will search for and gather more information through both formal and informal (e.g. social media) Internet-based sources. More vertical, lateral and external stakeholders can be expected to be involved and provide their inputs in such situations. Conversely, when products are less complex or significant, the buyclass nature is more routinized and the nature of the exchange is more transactional, we expect the effects of Internet information to attenuate.

IMPACT OF INTERNET-INDUCED CHANGES IN B2B BUYING AND SELLING ON SALES FORCE SIZE AND STRUCTURE

In this section we offer several implications of Internet-induced changes on the buying and selling sides, and in buyer–seller interaction, for sales force size and structure. We distinguish first between 'inside' and 'outside' (field) sales forces (e.g. Boyle 1996; Narus and Anderson 1986). Traditionally, inside sales representatives typically do not leave the office and are responsible for taking orders over the telephone and handling customer complaints. These reps are frequently responsible for generating sales leads, acquiring new clients by 'cold calling' various organizations and arranging contacts or meetings for outside sales representatives. Conversely, outside sales reps spend much of their time traveling to and visiting current clients and prospective buyers. A hallmark of the outside sales rep is face-to-face (F2F) contact with the customer. During a sales call, outside reps discuss the client's needs and suggest how their product can meet those needs. They may show samples or catalogs that describe the items and discuss prices, availability and ways their products can save money and boost productivity. One recent survey reports that the average inside (lead generation) to outside rep ratio in the United States is 1 to 3.5 (The Bridge Group 2009). However, this ratio could be increasing. Another survey by James Oldroyd, a professor at Sungkyunkwan University in Seoul, Korea, reports that inside sales jobs in North America will grow by 800000 during the 2009–2012 period while growth in outside sales positions will stagnate (see http://www.insidesales.com/news). This trend is consistent with Narus and Anderson's (1986) observations that firms focus on inside sales reps as the primary promotional contact, gatherer of competitive intelligence and provider of minor technical and problem-solving assistance to customers. Subsequently, following a study of one firm that found that inside sales performance affected customer satisfaction more than the company's field force, Boyle (1996) observed that changing communication technologies as well as ever-increasing costs of F2F selling had much to do with the growing profile of inside sales reps in selling organizations. However, this phenomenon has not been subjected to much systematic research since the Internet's tremendous advances during the past decade.

We now propose several selected implications of Internet-induced effects for inside and outside sales force size and structure. In doing so, we appeal to several communication and organization theories.

Implications for Sales Force Size

According to media richness theory, organizations process information to reduce uncertainty and equivocality (Daft and Lengel 1986). Uncertainty is defined as the difference between the amount of information required to perform the task and the amount of information already possessed. Equivocality is defined as the ambiguity of the task, caused by conflicting interpretations about a group situation or environment, as would exist in a complex buying center with participants from different levels, functions and locations. Therefore, as information increases, uncertainty and equivocality decrease. In addition, media richness theory posits that commonly used media work better for certain tasks than others. Specifically, Daft and Lengel (1986) conclude that written media are preferred for unequivocal messages while F2F media are preferred for equivocal messages. Daft et al. (1987) present a media richness hierarchy based on four criteria: feedback, multiple cues, language variety and personal focus. The richest communication medium is F2F meetings, followed by telephone, email, and memos and letters (Rice and Shook 1990).

Early studies of computer-mediated communications (e.g. the Internet) found that

F2F media were richer media because they use verbal communication enriched by facial cues to convey information and relay quick feedback to other parties. Media richness theory proposes that F2F media are preferred for equivocal messages (ambiguity) while written or computer-mediated media are preferred for unequivocal messages (e.g. Barkhi et al. 1999).

On the basis of media richness theory, we expect the effectiveness of F2F selling (i.e. outside sales reps) to increase as buying center complexity increases. Therefore, we propose the following:

P_8:   *As Internet-induced buying center complexity increases, the outside-to-inside sales force size ratio increases.*

However, P_2 and P_3 predict that with advances in Internet information, the B2B buying process is becoming more Internet-dependent and the corresponding selling process is becoming more buyer-driven, in which timely responses to potential buyers are key to remaining in consideration as well as qualifying these leads coming in through inbound marketing methods. This implies more inside selling capability, leading us to propose the following:

P_9:   *As B2B buying processes become more Internet-dependent, the size of the inside sales force increases.*

P_{10}:   *As B2B selling processes become more buyer-driven, the size of the inside sales force increases.*

The evolving nature of buyer–seller interactions due to the Internet's influence has mixed implications for the ratios of outside to inside sales force sizes. Specifically, in a complex and significant new purchase setting, if the buyer and seller are symmetrically informed but still pursuing an interaction, we expect the conversation to be supplier fit and total solution-focused and thus suitable for F2F interaction. In such circumstances, we propose the following:

P_{11}:   *In complicated and significant purchase settings, as information symmetry in buyer–seller interactions increases and the interactions become more collaborative, the outside-to-inside sales force size ratio increases.*

P_{12}:   *In more standard and/or less significant purchase settings, as information symmetry in buyer–seller interactions increases and the interactions become more transactional, the outside-to-inside sales force size ratio decreases.*

Implications for Sales Force Structure

As buying center complexity increases, we expect the demands of buying center coordination to exceed one salesperson's 'bandwidth' (e.g. Zoltners et al. 2008). Specialization by some activity is the natural solution when organizational activity becomes too complicated for one person. Specialists have greater knowledge and expertise and thus are more adaptive to and can more effectively handle non-routine tasks in settings in which performance is difficult to assess and the environment is complex and uncertain (Ruekert et al. 1985).

Internet-induced changes in the B2B buying and selling processes also make the selling task for a new seller selected for F2F discussions by a buyer more complex because the buyer's focus at this stage is on evaluating supplier fit more than product fit. In addition, in new task, complex product and relational exchange settings, the actual F2F interaction is more intense and tends to involve multiple representatives from the selling side (e.g. sales, marketing, logistics, finance) as the two sides attempt to determine fit. Therefore we propose the following:

P_{13a}:   *In new task, complex product and relational exchange situations, B2B sellers' use of sales teams will increase as*:

- Internet-induced buying center complexity increases;
- the buying process becomes more Internet-dependent;
- the selling process becomes more buyer-driven; and
- the buyer–seller interaction becomes more collaborative.

More specifically, various types of sales teams exist, and the appropriateness of any depends on the nature of the buying center complexity. Thus:

P_{13b}:   *The increase in buying center complexity (i) due to more Internet-induced vertical involvement increases multilevel team selling; (ii) due to more Internet-induced lateral involvement increases cross-functional team selling; and (iii) due to more Internet-induced external involvement increases inside (e.g. marketing-sales) team selling.*

P_{13c}:   *The increase in buying center complexity due to more geographic dispersion increases key-account management by account teams.*

P_{13} deals with team selling to a specific complex account. In the various versions of this scenario, specialized reps coordinate activities to provide solutions for the customer. That is, the coordination must take place at the account level. Thus, we propose the following:

P_{14}:   *As an account's Internet-induced buying center complexity increases, an account manager responsible for all sales to that account is likely to coordinate team selling.*

Moderator Effects

We expect two key factors – environmental uncertainty and intensity of competition – to moderate the proposed effects of Internet-induced changes in B2B buying and selling on sales force size and structure (see Figure 29.1). An increase in either factor makes any buying situation more challenging and more complex. Consequently, we expect that an increase in either or both of these factors increases the demand for more inside sales support and more team selling.

IMPLICATIONS FOR MANAGERS AND RESEARCHERS

Key Managerial Implications

This chapter discusses how contemporary Internet-induced changes in B2B buying center complexity, buying and selling processes, and buyer–seller interactions have profound implications for firms' B2B sales force strategy (i.e. sizing and structure). However, the notion of selling 'without the sales force' is applicable only in a few transactional and routinized product buying situations. In general, the need for a sales force remains, even though the Internet enables buyers to be more information-empowered, the buying process has become more Internet-dependent, and the selling process has become more buyer-driven. Nor do these changes necessarily imply that firms will have smaller sales forces. Rather, selling organization size and design must become much more guided by and finely attuned and responsive to how Internet-empowered customers want to do business. This implies a radical shift in traditional sales force strategy from seller- and product-focused to an *outside-in* (Day and Moorman 2010) sales organization design. As a result, the sales force size of many firms may actually grow in the Internet era, but much of that increase will probably occur in the number of inside rather than outside salespeople. Moreover, as proposed in this chapter, more contemporary B2B sales forces are likely to be organized as teams of outside and inside specialists led by account executives. Such Internet-induced changes in sales force design have numerous other implications for sales managers that are beyond the scope of this chapter but will undoubtedly imply much more sophisticated and complex sales forces in the future.

Key Directions for Future Research

This chapter takes a first step toward more systematic study of the effects of the new Internet information-enriched world of B2B buying and selling on sales force size and structure. We provide a conceptual framework that connects the Internet's attributes to changes in the business buying and selling processes, buyer–seller interaction and their implications for sales organizations. The framework offers several propositions to drive future empirical research. Currently, empirical data on the effects of Internet-based technologies on B2B sales force size and structure are sparse and largely confined to business consultants' reports. More rigorous empirical research that tests hypotheses derived from a theoretical framework is needed, and our proposed framework could serve as a starting point. In addition, this framework and our propositions could be extended to consider other aspects of sales organization and management, such as sales force compensation, recruiting and training. Future qualitative and survey-based research combined with growing secondary data-based empirical studies would help improve this framework.

CONCLUSIONS

In this chapter we focused on the Internet's effects on sales force size and structure. We acknowledge that we have barely scratched the surface of inquiry into the Internet's effects on B2B sales forces. Additional research is needed to guide fresh thinking about the best way to redesign, deploy and manage B2B sales organizations that is in tune with the realities and fast-paced developments of the new Internet Age. Classical sales management thinking seems increasingly obsolete, and much of the material in current sales management textbooks is outdated at best and irrelevant at worst. The need for new research on optimal B2B sales force organization and management in today's world is urgent. We hope this chapter serves to trigger such research in the immediate future.

NOTES

1. Following Litan and Rivlin (2001), for the purposes of this research, we define 'Internet business solutions' or simply 'Internet' as any initiative that combines the Internet with networking, software and computing hardware technologies to enhance or improve existing business processes or create new business opportunities.
2. The US Bureau of Labor Statistics (BLS) continues to project growth in 'sales and related occupations', but the rate of growth has declined during the past decade, from a projected 12 per cent increase in employment from 2000 (15.5 million jobs) to 2010 (17.4 million jobs) to a projected 6.2 per cent increase from 2008 (15.9 million jobs) to 2018 (16.9 million jobs) (see BLS Employment Projections 2000–2010 (http://www.bls.gov/opub/ted/2001/dec/wk1/art02.htm) and 2008–2018 (http://www.bls.gov/news.release/ecopro.nr0.htm)).

REFERENCES

Ahearne, Michael and Adam Rapp (2010), 'The role of technology at the interface between salespeople and consumers', *Journal of Personal Selling & Sales Management*, **30** (2), 111–20.

Ahearne, Michael, Douglas E. Hughes and Niels Schillewaert (2007), 'Why sales reps should welcome information technology: measuring the impact of CRM-based IT on sales effectiveness', *International Journal of Research in Marketing*, **24**, 336–49.

Ahearne, Michael, Eli Jones, Adam Rapp and John Mathieu (2008), 'High touch through high tech: the impact of salesperson technology usage on sales performance via mediating mechanisms', *Management Science*, **54** (4), 671–85.

Albers, Sönke, Murali K. Mantrala and Shrihari Sridhar (2010), 'Personal selling elasticities: a meta-analysis', *Journal of Marketing Research*, **47** (October), 840–53.

Anderson, Erin, Wujin Chu and Barton Weitz (1987), 'Industrial purchasing: an empirical exploration of the buyclass framework', *Journal of Marketing*, **51** (July), 71–86.

Avlonitis, George J. and Despina A. Karayanni (2000), 'The impact of internet use on business-to-business marketing examples from American and European companies', *Industrial Marketing Management*, **29**, 441–59.

Bakos, J. Yannis (1997), 'Reducing buyer search costs: implications for electronic marketplaces', *Management Science*, **43** (12), 1676–92.

Balegno, Sergio (2009), 'MarketingSherpa's 2009–10 B2B Marketing Benchmark Report', available at http://www.sherpastore.com, accessed 26 May 2010.

Barkhi, Reza, Varghese S. Jacob and Hasan Pirkul (1999), 'An experimental analysis of face to face versus computer mediated communication channels', *Group Decision and Negotiation*, **8**, 325–47.

Bendapudi, Neeli and Robert P. Leone (2002), 'Managing business-to-business customer relationships following key contact employee turnover in a vendor firm', *Journal of Marketing*, **66** (April), 83–101.

Boyle, Brett A. (1996), 'The importance of the industrial inside sales force: a case study', *Industrial Marketing Management*, **25** (5), 339–48.

Bradford, Kevin, Steven Brown, Shankar Ganesan, Gary Hunter, Vincent Onyemah, Robert Palmatier, Dominique Rouziès, Rosann Spiro, Harish Sujan and Barton Weitz (2010), 'The embedded sales force: connecting buying and selling organizations', *Marketing Letters*, **21**, 239–53.

The Bridge Group (2009), 'Lead generation metrics and compensation report', available at www.bridge-groupinc.com, accessed 8 February 2011.

Buttle, Francis, Lawrence Ang and Reiny Iriana (2006), 'Sales force automation: review, critique, research agenda', *International Journal of Management Reviews*, **8** (4), 213–31.

BUYERsphere (2010), 'Survey of B2B buyers' use of social media. Report on the survey findings', available at http://www.baseone.co.uk/beyond/Buyersphere_report.pdf, accessed 8 February 2011.

Coiera, Enrico (2000), 'Information economics and the internet', *Journal of the American Medical Informatics Association*, **7** (3), 215–21.

Court, David, Dave Elzinga, Susan Mulder and Ole Jørgen Vetvik (2009), 'The consumer decision journey', *McKinsey Quarterly*, (June), 1–11.

Daft, Richard L. and Robert H. Lengel (1986), 'Organizational information requirements, media richness and structural design', *Management Science*, **32** (5), 554–71.

Daft, Richard L., Robert H. Lengel and Linda Kiebe Trevino (1987), 'Message equivocality, media selection, and manager performance: implications for information systems', *MIS Quarterly*, **11** (3), 354–66.

Dawes, Philip L., Don Y. Lee and Grahame R. Dowling (1998), 'Information control and influence in emergent buying centers', *Journal of Marketing*, **62** (July), 55–68.

Day, George and Christine Moorman (2010), *Strategy from the Outside In: Profiting from Customer Value*, New York: McGraw-Hill.

Day, George S., Adam J. Fein and Greg Ruppersberger (2003), 'Shakeouts in digital markets: lessons from B2B marketplaces', *California Management Review*, **45** (2), 131–50.

Deeter-Schmelz, Dawn R. and Karen Norman Kennedy (2002), 'An exploratory study of the internet as an industrial communication tool examining buyers' perceptions', *Industrial Marketing Management*, **31**, 145–54.

Halligan, Brian and Dharmesh Shah (2010), *Inbound Marketing: Get Found Using Google, Social Media, and Blogs*, Hoboken, NJ: John Wiley & Sons.

Haruvy, Ernan and Sandy D. Jap (2011), 'Designing B2B Markets', in Gary L. Lilien and Rajdeep Grewal (eds), *Handbook of Business-to-Business Marketing*, Cheltenham, UK and Northampton, MA, USA: Edward Elgar Publishing.

Heide, Jan and Allen Weiss (1995), 'Vendor consideration and switching behavior for buyers in high-technology markets', *Journal of Marketing*, **59** (July), 30–43.

InsideSales.com (2009), 'New research shows growth of 800,000 jobs over next three years in inside sales', available at http://www.insidesales.com/news, accessed 8 February 2011.

Jap, Sandy D. (2002), 'Online reverse auctions: issues, themes, and prospects for the future', *Journal of the Academy of Marketing Science*, **30** (4), 506–25.

Jap, Sandy D. and Jakki J. Mohr (2002), 'Leveraging Internet technologies in B2B relationships', *California Management Review*, **44** (4), 24–38.

Johnson, Devon S. and Sundar Bharadwaj (2005), 'Digitization of selling activity and sales force performance: an empirical investigation', *Journal of the Academy of Marketing Science*, **33** (1), 3–18.

Johnston, Wesley J. and Thomas V. Bonoma (1981), 'The buying center: structure and interaction', *Journal of Marketing*, **45** (Summer), 143–56.

Johnston, Wesley and Jennifer Chandler (2011), 'The organizational buying center: innovation, knowledge management and brand', in Gary L. Lilien and Rajdeep Grewal (eds), *Handbook of Business-to-Business Marketing*, Cheltenham, UK and Northampton, MA, USA: Edward Elgar Publishing.

Jones, Eli, Steven P. Brown, Andris A. Zoltners and Barton A. Weitz (2005), 'The changing environment of selling and sales management', *Journal of Personal Selling & Sales Management*, **25** (2), 105–11.

Ladendorf, Kirk (2010), 'Dell plans to hire 4000 for sales jobs', AllBusiness.com, 29 June, available at http://www.allbusiness.com/company-activities-management/sales-selling-sales/14722612-1.html, accessed 19 February 2011.

Lane, Nikala and Nigel F. Piercy (2004), 'Strategic customer management: designing a profitable future for your sales organization', *European Management Journal*, **22** (6), 659–68.

Legat, Dieter and William Woehr (2004), 'Revolution in sales management', Delta Institute, 17 February, available at http://www.sales-system-management.ch/Downloads/Sales-Management-Revolution.pdf, accessed 19 February 2011.

Lewin, Jeffrey E. and Naveen Donthu (2005), 'The influence of purchase situation on buying center structure and involvement: a select meta-analysis of organizational buying behavior research', *Journal of Business Research*, **58**, 1381–90.

Lewin, Jeffrey E., Wim Biemans and Wolfgang Ulaga (2010), 'Firm downsizing and satisfaction among United States and European customers', *Journal of Business Research*, **63**, 697–706.

Lichtenthal, J. David and Shay Eliaz (2003), 'Internet integration in business marketing tactics', *Industrial Marketing Management*, **32**, 3–13.

Lilien, Gary L. and M.A. Wong (1984), 'An exploratory investigation of the structure of the buying center in the metalworking industry', *Journal of Marketing Research*, **21** (February), 1–11.

Litan, Robert E. and Alice M. Rivlin (2001), 'Projecting the economic impact of the Internet', *American Economic Review*, **91** (2), 313–17.

Long, Mary M., Thomas Tellefsen and J. David Lichtenthal (2007), 'Internet integration into the industrial selling process', *Industrial Marketing Management*, **36** (5), 676–89.

Malone, T.W. (1999), 'Is "Empowerment" just a fad? Control, decision-making, and information technology', *BT Technology Journal*, **17** (4), 141–4.

Mantrala, Murali K., Sönke Albers, Kissan Joseph, Manfred Krafft, Chakravarthi Narasimhan, Fabio Caldieraro, Ove Jensen, Srinath Gopalakrishna, Rajiv Lal, Andris Zoltners and Leonard Lodish (2010), 'Sales force modeling', *Marketing Letters*, **21** (3), 255–72.

MarketingProfs LLC (2009), 'B2B marketing in 2009: trends in strategies and spending', *MarketingProfs Research Insights*, available at http://www.slideshare.net/piglet1/b2b-marketing-in-2009-trends-in-strategies-and-spending, accessed 21 July 2010.

Marshall, Greg W., William C. Moncrief and Felicia G. Lassk (1999), 'The current state of sales force activities', *Industrial Marketing Management*, **28**, 87–98.

Masterson, Michele (1999), 'E-commerce to generate $1.25 trillion in savings by 2002', *E-Commerce Guide*, 5 August, available at http://www.internetnews.com/ec-news/article.php/175961/E-Commerce-To-Generate-125-Trillion-in-Savings-By-2002.htm.

Mohr, Jakki and John R. Nevin (1990), 'Communication strategies in marketing channels: a theoretical perspective', *Journal of Marketing*, **54** (October), 36–51.

Moncrief, William C. and Greg W. Marshall (2005), 'The evolution of the seven steps of selling', *Industrial Marketing Management*, **34**, 13–22.

Narus, James A. and James C. Anderson (1986), 'Industrial distributor selling: the role of outside and inside sales', *Industrial Marketing Management*, **15**, 55–62.

Pettigrew, Andrew M. (1972), 'Information control as a power resource', *Sociology*, **6** (2), 187–204.

Piercy, Nigel F. and Nikala Lane (2003), 'Transformation of the traditional salesforce: imperatives for intelligence, interface and integration', *Journal of Marketing Management*, **19**, 563–82.

Porter, Michael E. (2001), 'Strategy and the Internet', *Harvard Business Review*, (March), 2–19.

Rackham, Neil and John De Vincentis (1999), *Rethinking the Salesforce: Redefining Selling to Create and Capture Value*, New York: McGraw-Hill.

Ramos, Laura and G. Oliver Young (2009), 'The social technographics of business buyers: how technology buyers engage with social media', Forrester Research Report.

Rice, Ronald E. and Douglas E. Shook (1990), 'Relationships of job categories and organizational levels to use of communication channels, including electronic mail: a meta-analysis and extension', *Journal of Management Studies*, **27** (2), 195–229.

Robinson, Patrick J., Charles W. Faris and Yoram Wind (1967), *Industrial Buying and Creative Marketing*, Boston, MA: Allyn & Bacon.

Rosenbloom, Bert (2007), 'Multi-channel strategy in business-to-business markets: prospects and problems', *Industrial Marketing Management*, **36** (1), 4–9.

Ruekert, Robert W., Orville C. Walker Jr and Kenneth J. Roering (1985), 'The organization of marketing activities: a contingency theory of structure and performance', *Journal of Marketing*, **49** (Winter), 13–25.

Sharma, Arun (2002), 'Trends in Internet-based business-to-business marketing', *Industrial Marketing Management*, **31**, 77–84.

Sharma, Arun and Nikolaos Tzokas (2002), 'Personal selling and sales management in the Internet environment: lessons learned', *Journal of Marketing Management*, **18** (3), 249–58.

Sharma, Dheeraj, Jule B. Gassenheimer and Bruce L. Alford (2010), 'Internet channel and cannibalization: an empirical assessment of sales agents' perspective', *Journal of Personal Selling & Sales Management*, **30** (3), 209–22.

Sheth, Jagdish N. and Arun Sharma (2008), 'The impact of the product to service shift in industrial markets and the evolution of the sales organization', *Industrial Marketing Management*, **37** (3), 260–69.

Sheth, Jagdish N. and Rajendra Sisodia (1999), 'Revisiting marketing's lawlike generalizations', *Journal of the Academy of Marketing Science*, **27** (1), 71–87.

Sheth, Jagdish N., Rajendra Sisodia and Arun Sharma (2000), 'The antecedents and consequences of customer-centric marketing', *Journal of the Academy of Marketing Science*, **28** (1), 55–66.

Speier, Cheri and Viswanath Venkatesh (2002), 'The hidden minefields in the adoption of sales force automation technologies', *Journal of Marketing*, **66** (July), 98–111.

Spiro, Rosann and Barton A. Weitz (1990), 'Adaptive selling: conceptualization, measurement, and nomological validity', *Journal of Marketing Research*, **27** (February), 61–9.

Steenburgh, Thomas and Das Narayandas (2010), 'The impact of Web 2.0 on business-to-business marketing', Working paper, Harvard Business School, Harvard University.

Steenburgh, Thomas, Jill Avery and Naseem Dahod (2009), 'HubSpot: inbound marketing and Web 2.0', HBS Case Study 9-509-049.

Trailer, Barry (2009), 'What is sales 2.0?', *CustomerThink: CRM, CEM & Social Media*, 5 June, available at http://www.customerthink.com, accessed 23 January 2011.

Tuli, Kapil R., Ajay K. Kohli and Sundar G. Bharadwaj (2007), 'Rethinking customer solutions: from product bundles to relational processes', *Journal of Marketing*, **71** (July), 1–17.

Varian, Hal, Robert E. Litan, Andrew Elder and Jay Shutter (2002), 'The net impact study: the projected economic benefits of the Internet in the United States, United Kingdom, France and Germany, V2.0', available at http://www.netimpactstudy.com/NetImpact_Study_Report.pdf, accessed 23 January 2011.

Webb, Kevin L. and C. Jay Lambe (2007), 'Internal multi-channel conflict: an exploratory investigation and conceptual framework', *Industrial Marketing Management*, **36** (1), 29–43.

Weitz, Barton (1978), 'Relationship between salesperson performance and understanding of customer decision making', *Journal of Marketing Research*, **25** (November), 501–16.

Weitz, Barton A. and Kevin Bradford (1999), 'Personal selling and sales management: a relationship marketing perspective', *Journal of the Academy of Marketing Science*, **27** (2), 241–54.

Zoltners, Andris A., Prabhakant Sinha and Sally E. Lorimer (2008), 'Sales force effectiveness: a framework for researchers and practitioners', *Journal of Personal Selling & Sales Management*, **28** (2), 115–31.

APPENDIX

Detail on Selected Information Attributes

Quantity: This refers to the volume of pertinent information available. Aided by today's powerful search engines, the Internet allows users to find, access and compile a much greater *quantity* of information, on any business or product, and from a much wider array of sources, than in pre-Internet days.

Quality: This refers to the richness of information available. For example, information on the Internet is multimedia-capable of having colored images, sound and video. These can be expensive to produce, but increasingly there are open sources of these types of content that are free of charge. When produced, the price of distribution of the information is nominal compared with that of producing hard-copy brochures, CDs and films.

Currency: This refers to the timeliness of information available. The Internet is 'open for business' always ('24/7') and allows users to access the very latest information entered by sources, such as business news sites, blogs and Twitter, whenever they want.

Verifiability: This refers to the validity of information available. The Internet allows rapid verification of one source's information by cross-checks with multiple other trusted sources (e.g. friends on Facebook, or respected professional peers on LinkedIn).

Speed of information collection: This refers to the time taken to acquire relevant information on a subject from the time the need for it arises. Today's advanced search engines and broadband technologies on the Internet enable relevant digitized information on a particular topic to be found, retrieved and downloaded very rapidly (one-gigabit-per-second Internet upload and download speeds are now available). What may have taken many hours or days to acquire in the past now may take only a few minutes or even seconds.

Scope of information collection: This refers to the diversity and locations of sources of relevant information being sought. (By and large) the Internet knows no geographic boundaries; a user can get information about any issue from sources anywhere in the world that are connected to the Internet. Furthermore, smartphones and other mobile devices enable users to obtain wireless Internet-delivered information from anywhere and wherever they are stationed or on the move.

Cost of information collection: The Internet has dramatically reduced search and other (e.g. transportation and delivery) costs associated with the acquisition and communication of information compared with pre-Internet days.

PART VI

TECHNOLOGY AND B2B MARKETING

30 Toward a theory of technology marketing: review and suggestions for future research[1]
Jakki J. Mohr, Sanjit Sengupta and Stanley Slater

Marketing of high-technology products appeared as a unique topical domain in the literature in the early to mid-1980s with the arrival of books and articles dedicated to the topic (Davidow 1986; Shanklin and Ryans 1984a). During these early stages, experts in the field of technology marketing debated whether marketing of high-technology products required different marketing practices than traditional goods and services (Moriarty and Kosnik 1987, 1989; Shanklin and Ryans 1984b). Although these experts agreed that marketing for technology-based products and innovations required adroit use of standard marketing strategies (including segmentation, targeting and positioning; customer relationship management; pricing; sales and distribution, to name just a few), they also acknowledged that because technology-based products are introduced into an environment characterized by rapid obsolescence, customer uncertainty, technological turbulence and competitive volatility, marketing was particularly important to the success of such products. Because of these differences in marketing strategy and because technology fields continue to expand in scope and importance to customers, the firms marketing them and society in general (Davidson and Leavy 2007; McKenna 2002), it is vital that marketing scholarship acknowledge and capture this domain in its theories and research.

Research in the area of technology marketing tends to take one of three approaches. The first approach simply uses technology industries and/or high-tech companies as a context or setting to test standard marketing theories and hypotheses (e.g. Mohr et al. 1996). Some of these studies find that the context itself presents unique and interesting characteristics. So, the second approach focuses specifically on the unique characteristics of high-tech markets and their implications for marketing theory and practice (e.g. Chandy and Tellis 1998; Stremersch et al. 2007). Because of the unique characteristics that technology markets pose – to the companies marketing them, to the customers adopting them and to the partners allied in the process (channel members, third-party software developers and other 'complementors') – studies in this stream suggest that high-tech marketing requires adaptations and modifications to standard marketing theories and strategies. A third approach to technology marketing research offers a direct assessment of whether marketing for high-tech products requires different theories and strategies than other products/markets. This contingency-based approach explicitly addresses differences in marketing strategies for high-technology innovations compared with more incremental/standard innovations.

Although the debate continues about whether marketing for high-tech products requires different theories and strategies than other products/markets, the research we overview in this chapter suggests that, similar to other areas in the marketing discipline – for example services marketing or B2B marketing – technology marketing is evolving into a unique sub-specialty (see Gronhaug and Moller 2005).[2] As Stremersch and Van Dyck (2009, p. 16, italics added) conclude in their framework of research issues for the life sciences (one high-tech industry):

> As with the advent of any new field, there are as many cynics who claim that nothing is fundamentally different about life sciences marketing and that conventional insights can easily be extended to such markets without adaptation as there are enthusiasts who embrace these markets as being as different as the moon is from the earth. The former group often finds a dominant argument in the data-driven nature of the original contributions to life sciences marketing. However, in itself, *this is not a reason an industry cannot be guided by different principles, thus leading to unique challenges.* The same applies to the argument that some challenges are also present in other industries.

Indeed, our review indicates that research in the discipline of technology marketing continues to develop in volume, rigor and contributions to marketing theory. The attention devoted to this sub-specialty in the following ways further suggests that this area is an increasingly unique domain in the marketing area:

- Special issues of journals focused on the marketing of technology-based products and services (see Kim and Huarng 2011; Mohr and Shooshtari 2003; Sarin and Mohr 2008; Sengupta and Puumalainen 2011),
- Specialty journals devoted to technology marketing (e.g. *International Journal of Technology Marketing*),
- The American Marketing Association's Technology & Marketing Special Interest Group.

The purpose of this chapter is to provide an overview of the state-of-the-art in both research and practice in the field of technology marketing.[3] First, we discuss the domain of technology marketing and why the unique characteristics of this domain create unique marketing-related problems for theory and practice. Second, we provide a brief summary of the state-of-the-art in managerial practice in this field. Third, we present an overview of the basic approaches to research in the area of technology marketing, addressing strengths and weaknesses of each approach. A key insight arising from our overview is that the time is ripe to coalesce the body of knowledge into a cogent theory of technology marketing. Toward this end, we offer suggestions for research to refine marketing theory in this complicated and fast-moving arena.

THE DOMAIN OF TECHNOLOGY MARKETING: CHARACTERISTICS AND IMPLICATIONS FOR A UNIQUE APPROACH TO MARKETING

High-technology markets are characterized by the development of breakthrough innovations based on significant amounts of scientific and technical know-how (John et al. 1999). Technological innovations often introduce radically new performance attributes relative to existing technologies that can result in obsolescence of the prior platform (Govindarajan and Kopalle 2006). Often referred to as 'technology-push' or 'supply-side' markets (Shanklin and Ryans 1984b), some of the defining characteristics of such markets are as follows (Mohr et al. 2010):[4]

- lack of clearly defined competitors, because either the technology is so new it has no direct competitors or its competitors arise from different technological alternatives;
- new technologies that are developed in the absence of a well-defined market opportunity; indeed, the various applications of a new technology can be so diverse that the market opportunity that ultimately drives the success of the technology is completely unimagined at the outset;
- high levels of fear, uncertainty and doubt in customers' purchase and adoption decisions, resulting in a 'balkiness' or hesitancy in purchase behavior (Dhebar 1996);
- lack of reliability of the new technology's performance and of the vendor's ability to deliver and provide service; uncertainty about technological obsolescence;
- unit-one costs in development (i.e. the cost of producing the very first unit is very high relative to the variable costs of reproducing subsequent units); such a situation typically arises when know-how (or knowledge embedded in the design of the new technology) represents a substantial portion of the value of the product; and
- the presence of network effects, which means that the value of a product increases as more users adopt that product (e.g. Tellis et al. 2009).

These characteristics of the technology marketing context have specific implications for how high-tech companies are managed (e.g. Chandy and Tellis 1998), which marketing strategies are used (e.g. Aaker and Jacobson 2001), how customers make purchasing decisions (e.g. Thompson et al. 2005) and how the industry evolves (in terms of dominant designs, platform-based competition and technology trajectories; e.g. Srinivasan et al. 2006). Indeed, because high-tech markets are riskier than traditional markets, they tend to have a smaller tolerance/margin for error (Moriarty and Kosnik 1989), and paradoxically, high-tech companies may be ill-prepared to address the greater marketing complications because they are less likely to have a well-respected, well-trained staff of marketing professionals (Mohr et al. 2006, 2010).

As a result of these defining characteristics of technology innovations, companies and markets, the field of technology marketing has evolved and developed, much like B2B marketing and services marketing have evolved as subdisciplines within marketing over time. As Gronhaug and Moller (2005, p. 92) note with respect to the evolution of technology marketing as a subdiscipline in its own right: '[S]uch narrowing of focus allows for concentrating on specific problems . . . allowing for the development of more elaborated concepts, theories, and methodological approaches to deal with these specific problems more adequately, not covered in depth in the "mother" discipline.'

In terms of specific technologies (per the output-based approach to defining technology; Mohr et al. 2010), many technological developments are in industrial or B2B technologies, such as robotics, nanotechnology, and web-based and information and communications technologies used to enhance business productivity or effectiveness, to name a few. High-tech markets also include many customer-facing technologies (B2C), such as consumer electronics, information communications technologies (e.g. hardware, software), the use of online technologies (e.g. e-tailing, social networking, online search) and telecommunications technologies. Given the focus of this handbook, we pay particular attention to research on B2B technologies,[5] while acknowledging that much of the research is generalizable to both B2C and B2B firms.

STATE-OF-THE-ART IN MANAGERIAL PRACTICE IN TECHNOLOGY MARKETING

The current state-of-the art with respect to managerial practice in technology marketing is probably best captured in the popular books of Geoffrey Moore on *Crossing the Chasm* (Moore 1991, and updated editions in 1995, 1999, 2002 and 2006; see also his follow-on books: Moore 1995, 1999). Essentially, Moore modifies Rogers' (1962) original theory of adoption and diffusion of innovations for technology adoption decisions, by acknowledging that the word-of-mouth process breaks down between early adopters and early majority customers of technology. This breakdown results in the presence of a 'chasm' in high-tech markets, a period in which, despite some initial sales success, sales growth slows or falls off (empirically validated by Goldenberg et al. 2002), often never to be regained. The selection of a 'beachhead', or a single target market from which to launch the company's marketing efforts; the development of a 'whole product' so that pragmatist customers will be able to purchase a complete end-to-end solution; and the evolution of the distribution channel are key aspects of managerial practice based on the popularity of Moore's ideas.

In addition, practicing managers in the field of technology marketing have access to a variety of books (see Bibliography at end of chapter). Though useful and grounded in practice, these resources tend to lack empirical testing. Thus scholarly research on the marketing of technology and innovation can validate these popular approaches and offer distinct insights for the field of technology marketing.

APPROACHES TO RESEARCH ON TECHNOLOGY MARKETING

The research on the marketing of technology and innovation can be categorized in three major ways:[6]

1. Research that uses high-technology industry contexts (products, managers, customers) to test theoretical and/or substantive marketing issues: no specific hypotheses are offered about how or why high-tech contexts require any differences in theories or managerial implications (see Web Exhibit 30.A);
2. Research that specifically identifies unique characteristics of high-technology industries and/or products that necessitate adaptations to existing theory or a unique theoretical lens: this research typically explores only high-technology contexts/radical innovations (see Web Exhibits 30.B and 30.C); and
3. Research based explicitly on the notion that different types of products (innovations) require different types of marketing strategies to be successful in the market-

place: this contingency-type research includes a direct comparison between types of products (e.g. breakthrough vs. incremental innovations) to draw conclusions for the marketing of radical or breakthrough innovations and/or high-velocity, turbulent environments specifically (see Web Exhibit 30.D).

In addition to categorizing research in technology marketing according to the relative degree of inclusion/focus on unique characteristics of high-tech products (and the corresponding ability to derive a theory of technology marketing specifically), categorization can be based on the unit of analysis of the study. These levels of analysis include the following:[7]

- *Industry-level studies*, which provide, for example, an analysis of the evolution of technology in the industry over time (e.g. Anderson and Tushman 1990; Bayus 1998; Sood and Tellis 2005).
- *Firm-level studies* (both at the intra- and inter-organizational levels), which examine issues related to the company itself; for example, company survival rates (pioneering advantage) (e.g. Srinivasan et al. 2004), managerial decision-making within the firm (e.g. Chandy and Tellis 1998), cross-functional interactions and the effects of firm-level characteristics (e.g. Gupta et al. 1986), and alliances and networks as part of the firm's strategy (e.g. Sivadas and Dwyer 2000; Swaminathan and Moorman 2009).
- *Customer-level studies*, which examine the unique characteristics of customer technology adoption decisions (e.g. Srinivasan et al. 2002; Wu et al. 2003);[8] this area includes not only the adoption and diffusion of innovations process (Gatignon and Robertson 1989; Parasuraman and Colby 2001) but also the impact of specific feature sets and attributes (either emotional or objective) on customer choice behavior (Jayachandran et al. 2005; Zhu et al. 2006). Customer-level studies also include the development of forecasting models and tools to model the take-off of technology-based products (Agarwal and Bayus 2002; Golder and Tellis 1997; Norton and Bass 1987).
- *Public policy-level studies*, which offer specific guidance to policy officials about regulating technology markets (Hoskisson et al. 2004; Teece 1986). Policy-related issues arise for topics such as privacy policies (e.g. with respect to Internet and health care-related technologies), company antitrust considerations (a rather large concern in technology markets in which de facto monopolies can arise from the success of dominant designs and platforms; Ford and Ryan 1981) and the balance between government and industry/company responsibility for development of and access to critical technologies (e.g. rural broadband for small businesses for economic development and/or development of space technologies, aerospace, or other technologies deemed in the public interest).

The following subsections, organized according to the initial three research categories – whether the research considered the high-tech context, whether it identified and incorporated unique characteristics of technology markets and whether it explicitly compared high-tech/radical innovations and other types of innovations – include research from all the levels of analysis. The intent of this illustrative overview is to provide insights into each approach's strengths and weaknesses with respect to theoretical development in the field of technology marketing. Our position is that research that explicitly provides a theoretical distinction and empirically documents the differences in marketing strategies and customer buying behavior between radical and incremental innovation is necessary to develop a coherent theory of technology marketing.

High-technology as the Research Context

Empirical marketing research requires data to conduct hypothesis testing; certainly, high-technology industries, companies or customers can serve as a possible context for such testing. Using high-technology as a research context means that data are collected from a sample of technology companies or customers to test standard marketing theories and hypotheses (for illustrative studies, see Web Exhibit 30.A). This stream of research, set in a high-tech context to test general substantive and/or theoretical marketing issues, covers a wide range of marketing topics, including new product development in high-tech companies, communication strategies in high-tech distribution channels, alliances in high-tech industries and marketing performance measurement in high-tech companies, to name a few. These topics collectively offer insights into a wide range of marketing practices and theories.

However, with respect to technology marketing in particular, the intent of the studies in this stream of research was *not* to build a theory for technology marketing per se, nor was it to determine how the unique aspects of the high-tech context require different marketing strategy considerations. Rather, the intent was to test standard marketing issues/phenomena. If anything, the unique aspects of the high-tech context were either ignored or used as a 'strong case' test of a particular theory; that is, if the hypotheses were supported in a technology-based context, because the context is characterized by the extreme conditions in technology markets, the context provides a rigorous test of the particular relationship being tested. Indeed, sometimes the context itself was used to explain the findings:

> This signal [the stock market's use of information regarding alliances in the software industry] may be particularly valuable in network markets, such as the software industry studied here. In these markets, a strong network can be integral to the success of new products and allow a firm to erect barriers to entry. Further research should examine this winner versus loser finding of alliance capability in other network industries. (Swaminathan and Moorman 2009, p. 63)

Two caveats should be considered in drawing conclusions for the scholarship and practice of technology marketing when using high-technology samples as the context for research: first, given the increasing evidence (summarized in the next two sections) that the marketing of technology-intensive, radical innovations requires adaptations and modifications to standard marketing theories, issues of generalizability warrant increased scrutiny. Indeed, research set in high-technology contexts often ends up explaining unexpected findings based on the context, lending credibility to the view that the unique characteristics of these environments require adaptations to marketing theory. Second, putting the label 'high-tech' (or technologically intensive, or a similar modifier) in a title or in the positioning of a piece of research does not build unique insights about the field of high-technology marketing. As Sarin and Mohr (2008, p. 628) note: 'Researchers must utilize the unique characteristics of high-tech industries to extend existing marketing theories and concepts, find limitations and boundary conditions of existing theories, and propose new paradigms for research in this area.'

Simply calling a piece of research 'high-tech' and relatedly offering the suggestion that high-tech is a unique field when the research has not explicitly modeled any unique high-tech factors does not contribute to theory building in this area. Indeed, research labeled as 'high-tech' must be critically evaluated to identify explicitly what adaptations and modifications to standard marketing theory and practice the research hypothesizes and tests. If no explicit points of difference are acknowledged, high-tech becomes the context for the contribution rather than the substance of the contribution. When the unique characteristics of high-technology contexts are addressed explicitly in the conceptual/ hypothesis development, the research is working toward developing a theory of technology marketing. This is the thrust of the second stream of research in high-technology marketing.

Unique Characteristics of High-tech Markets Requiring Unique Theoretical Approaches

Research that specifically identifies unique characteristics of high-technology industries and products develops adaptations to existing theory and/or a unique theoretical lens to understand these markets. Studies in this stream explicitly include variables designed to capture unique aspects of the high-tech environment that affect marketing strategies of high-tech companies and/or purchase decisions of high-tech customers.

The pioneering work of Capon and Glazer (1987) represents some of the earliest theoretical developments that explicitly acknowledge the unique characteristics of technology (based on embedded know-how) and how knowledge embodied in the firm's strategy is a major asset. Because the economics of information (or know-how) operate differently from the economics of traditional goods, unique approaches to marketing strategy are required. Capon and Glazer developed a technology portfolio framework to guide marketing strategy decisions in companies that are increasingly driven by technological considerations. John et al.'s (1999) conceptual framework was another notable step in the development of a theory of high-technology marketing. They also use the unique characteristics of knowledge (know-how creation, dissemination and use) to identify eight features of technology-intensive markets and how those features subsequently affect marketing strategy decisions explicitly.

Web Exhibits 30.B and 30.C provide overviews of illustrative empirical research following this tradition.[9] This category of research has done much to advance a theory of technology marketing. By first explicitly identifying the unique aspects of the technology marketing context (e.g. network externalities (Srinivasan et al. 2006), the innovator's dilemma (Chandy and Tellis 2000)) and then empirically testing the impact of those factors on firm- and customer-level decisions, managers and scholars have come to realize that, indeed, technology markets require adaptations to firm- and customer-level decision-making to cope with the unique characteristics of technology markets.

A possible limitation of studies in this second stream is that most do not use a 'control' sample; thus whether the phenomena under study would occur similarly in less technology-intensive environments or non-high-tech companies is unknown/untested. (In some cases, the phenomena under study may not be relevant in a non-high-tech setting.) The third category of research on technology marketing provides this explicit test.

Differential Marketing for Different Types of Innovations

This third approach explicitly recognizes that breakthrough (radical) innovations require different marketing strategies than the strategies used for other types of products/ innovations: 'Market planning that explicitly recognizes and accounts for the strategic distinction between market-driven [incremental] and innovation-driven [technology-push] research goes a long way toward yielding better corporate performance.' (Shanklin and Ryans 1984b, p. 167)

Shanklin and Ryans' (1984b) development of the continuum of incremental versus breakthrough innovations created the impetus for this initial development (see also Rangan and Bartus 1995). Other typologies of innovation also exist (e.g. disruptive vs. sustaining, modular vs. architectural; see Mohr et al. 2010, p. 25), but the incremental versus radical/breakthrough distinction tends to be the most commonly used in this stream of research.

More explicitly, a key premise underlying the research in this category is that marketing strategy is contingent on the type of innovation. By appropriately matching marketing strategies and tools to the different types of innovation (e.g. incremental vs. breakthrough), companies enhance their odds of success. Known as the contingency theory of high-technology marketing (Gardner 1990; Gardner et al. 2000; Mohr 2001), research following this approach includes a direct comparison of different types of innovations, highlighting how and under what conditions high-tech marketing for breakthrough technologies differs from that for more standard products/incremental innovation (see also Gronhaug and Moller 2005). Web Exhibit 30.D provides an overview of some of the findings from the empirical research in this stream.

The logic of contingent effects for different types of innovations occurs across a wide range of marketing topics, such as strategy (first-mover advantage/pioneers), market orientation and corporate social responsibility, to name a few. Research following the contingency-type logic of technology marketing sometimes uses proxies for types of innovations or high-tech environments, such as environmental turbulence, technology uncertainty and product risk/complexity. In addition, some research, without explicitly developing the idea of different strategies for different types of industries/products, uses industry and/or product as a control variable, further establishing the notion of different types of marketing strategies for different types of products/innovations.

To be sure, much conceptual development based on contingency theory for high-technology marketing could be tested empirically. For example, Lee (2002) acknowledges that the characteristics of high-tech products, including high per-unit costs, rapid obsolescence and competitive volatility, make standard supply-chain management practices ill-equipped to deal with the risks and uncertainties in these markets. His tailored supply-chain model for four types of uncertain environments warrants empirical testing. Similarly, Barton et al. (1995) argue in their conceptual work that market research methods must be aligned with the type of innovation being developed. For incremental innovations, new product developments align with the current market; customer needs are generally known, and traditional marketing research, such as focus groups, surveys, concept tests, conjoint studies and test markets, can be useful to match new product characteristics with customer needs. In contrast, standard marketing research tools typically do not address new uses or new benefits and are less effective when customers are unfamiliar with the product being researched. Moreover, standard research tools cannot help firms develop truly breakthrough (radical) innovations. Therefore, for breakthrough products or for rapidly changing markets, useful market research techniques include, for example, customer visits, empathic design, lead-user process, quality function deployment and prototype testing. This match between market research methodologies and types of innovations also warrants empirical testing.

To empirically establish that a particular type of innovation (e.g. disruptive, technology-driven, radical) requires a particular type of marketing, an explicit comparison is made with incremental innovations or a 'control' sample of traditional products/ contexts. Research in this third category adds another level of sophistication to the field of technology marketing, establishing a foundation for a theory of technology marketing explicitly based on the differences between types of innovation. In this spirit we emphasize a few of these contributions.

Consistent with the contingency theory of high-tech marketing, matching a firm's strategy (pioneer) to the type of innovation (incremental) will enhance its odds of success (Min et al. 2006). Conversely, mismatching a pioneering strategy to a breakthrough innovation will lower the odds of success – unless the market is characterized by network effects (Srinivasan et al. 2004). These studies highlight the very complicated intersection of product factors (type of innovation) and market conditions that affect firm strategy and performance in high-tech markets.

Moreover, a firm that is extremely competent in exploiting its current competencies will be successful with radical innovation only with a dose of exploration as well (Atuahene-Gima 2005); existing competencies seemingly provide the necessary absorptive capacity for the firm to fully leverage the new knowledge gained in competence exploration. Importantly, scoring high on both orientations (exploitation and exploration) has a negative effect on innovation performance.

Another area in which the idea of a contingent approach to marketing strategy for breakthrough versus incremental products is established is that of R&D–marketing interactions (Gupta et al. 1986; Song and Thieme 2009). Scientists and engineers (R&D) drive the process of technology-push innovation. An important question for marketing practice and theory is what role marketing should play for emerging technologies – those that have long gestation periods for development (e.g. nanotechnology, hydrogen fuel cells that have not yet crossed the chasm). In addition to providing market feedback to developers, marketing personnel potentially have a very important role to play in educating stakeholders (financiers, government, complementors, the general public) and in employing communication media (e.g. press relations, social media) to influence these stakeholders. Although R&D tends to have a stronger, more influential role in breakthrough products, marketing tends to have a greater role in more incremental products. Because the possibilities for the application of new, breakthrough technologies tend to be either non-obvious or very numerous, engineering should not proceed in isolation from market-related feedback. Thus, for breakthrough products, the early interface efforts between R&D and marketing should address what industry the company should compete in, what the conceivable market opportunities are and what the market development priorities are. The cross-functional interaction helps determine desired product features and assess engineering feasibility.

TOWARD A THEORY OF TECHNOLOGY MARKETING: DISCUSSION AND IMPLICATIONS FOR FUTURE RESEARCH

The technology marketing research stream includes studies set in a high-tech context, albeit without much explicit theorizing or testing about the unique characteristics or specific adaptations to marketing strategy (Web Exhibit 30.A). Moving from context to identification of the unique characteristics of high-tech markets (Capon and Glazer 1987; John et al. 1999) provides the necessary foundation to begin building a theory of technology marketing (e.g. Christensen 2006). Web Exhibits 30.B and 30.C summarize some of the illustrative research on the unique characteristics of, for example, the shape of technology life cycles, emergence of dominant designs in the presence of network effects, the effects of indirect network effects (e.g. impact of software development on hardware sales), firms' development of their own disruptive innovations, and the impact of firm strategy (pioneer vs. fast follower) in markets characterized by, for example, network effects. Research that explicitly addresses these unique characteristics of technology markets is necessary to continue to evolve and develop a theory of technology marketing, with unique scholarly contributions promising new insights into theory and practice.

In addition to research on how the unique characteristics of high-tech markets affect strategic marketing, research that explicitly contrasts marketing strategies of technology-based products with more traditional products provides a rigorous approach to creating a theory of technology marketing. Web Exhibit 30.D summarizes research that explicitly contrasts types of innovations (e.g. radical vs. incremental innovations). The findings from this body of research indicate that matching marketing strategies appropriately to the type of innovation enhances firm performance (compared with using one marketing tool kit for all types of innovations). Indeed, contingent-effects logic greatly enhances both managers' decision-making and scholars' understanding of the adaptations and modifications required in technology markets (compared with more standard, traditional product marketing). Much remains to be done in this regard to further coalesce a dedicated theory of technology marketing.

In line with these approaches to developing a theory of technology marketing, and in the spirit of articulating important managerial and theoretical questions, we encourage and advocate additional research along the following lines:[10]

1. Because they can be widely distributed over the Internet, digital goods (e.g. software or on-demand services, such as cloud computing or video teleconferencing) pose unique challenges and opportunities. Distinguishing between high-tech products in general and those that are primarily digital offers another, finer-grained lens on technology marketing; strategies for digital high-tech goods may require their own adaptations. The complications and opportunities for these digital goods are probably unique enough that they may warrant their own contingency-type theory: physical high-tech products versus digital high-tech products. For example, issues related to the long tail (Anderson 2008) and distribution of digital goods are topics

that researchers have begun exploring (e.g. Elberse 2008; Shapiro and Varian 1998a, 1998b). In addition, despite the presence of Moore's Law[11] and its impact on pricing/ costs for physical products (the law was originally formulated in the semiconductor industry), pricing complexities for digital goods are of high interest; at the extreme, the zero-marginal cost structure of these goods suggests a pricing structure of 'free' (e.g. Anderson 2009).

2. Pricing of high-tech products in general seems to be an underresearched area (for an exception, see Grenadier and Weiss 1997), including the valuation of technologies in their early stages.

3. Issues related to transforming intellectual property into products that offer economic and social value are at the heart of high-tech companies. Yet, because of the complicating factors in technology markets, these decisions are very difficult to make. Indeed, how technology start-ups decide what product form to offer in the market is a vital but under-researched topic. Frias et al. (2010) take a step in this direction, examining factors that affect whether a firm licenses its know-how to other companies, offers a component (or intermediate product) to other companies in the industry, or markets a product in its final form (as a system). This decision has implications for a firm's vertical positioning decision – where in the industry's supply chain it will compete, which in turn has implications for who its customers and competitors will be. Yet, to our knowledge, this is the first research to examine this important managerial decision.

Frias et al. (2010) draw some of the background literature for their study from the field of the 'commercialization of technology' (see also Jolly 1997; Nevens et al. 1990). This stream of research has emerged fairly independently from the technology marketing research. Integrating these two streams of literature holds potential theoretical and managerial insights. For example, research on the issues related to licensing strategies (e.g. Lichtenthaler 2007), technology transfer and valuation methodologies would be important additions to the field of technology marketing.

4. The issue of ecosystems[12] as a primary source of value and success for high-tech products is increasingly obvious (Adner 2006). For example, competition between platforms (Moore 1997), 'the app economy' (MacMillan et al. 2009), and the difficulties in some industries in getting the requisite infrastructure in place to deliver the value of new technology (think charging infrastructure for electric cars and high-speed networks for smart phones) all highlight the importance of the ecosystem. Certainly, the literature on alliances can inform the issue of technology ecosystems, but the theoretical questions and managerial implications of this broadened notion of competition remain under-researched.

Relatedly, the pros and cons of *open platforms*, in which a technology company offers its underlying technology to multiple players in the industry (e.g. Google's approach to developing the Android operating system and the ecosystem built on that platform), versus *walled gardens* (e.g. Apple's more proprietary, controlled approach to development of its ecosystem) are also under-researched (Knowledge@ Wharton 2007). On the one hand, because the technology can be deployed across multiple products inexpensively, open platforms have the potential to generate network effects more quickly; on the other hand, Apple's walled-garden approach (potentially much more expensive) relies extensively on its clout with content providers (e.g. music, movies). Evaluating the underlying issues of these two approaches will help firms to manage their ecosystem strategies better.

Other important topics based on the trend toward competition between platforms/ ecosystems include: (1) predicting where the tipping point occurs between a dominant (legacy) platform and a new ecosystem; and (2) incentives and governance structures for complementary developers.

5. With respect to the differences between radical and incremental innovations, a large stream of research explores how companies come to develop radical innovations (Berchicci and Tucci 2010; Kelley 2009; O'Connor 2008). Although not all radical innovations are technological in nature, the theories and managerial insights offered from the research on radical innovations are certainly useful for generating a theory of technology marketing.

We strongly urge research to examine further the differences in marketing strategy between high-technology products/firms and more traditional products/firms, as follows:

- Experts exhort technology managers to delineate a precise beachhead from which to launch their marketing initiatives. To our knowledge, this basic premise has never been empirically validated. Do technology firms benefit disproportionately from a narrow selection of target market (as advocated by Geoffrey Moore's model of selecting a beachhead to 'cross the chasm')? Or, conversely, might a wider net allow the best market opportunities to present themselves in a more organic fashion? For a similar logic on how firms might approach market opportunities in base-of-the-pyramid (BOP) markets, see Simanis (2010).

- Technology companies are often enamored with the feature set (technical specifications) and functional form of their invention. However, customers of technology are often befuddled by the engineer's description of what the technology is and how it works. In extreme cases, the engineer's explanations never get to the specific value proposition: what problem will the technology solve for the customer? Because it articulates the notion of the exchange of one party's specialized knowledge and competencies for the benefit of another, service-dominant logic (Vargo and Lusch 2004, 2008) might be particularly beneficial in the technology arena. For example, many technology marketing experts advocate a greater reliance on value (solutions to customers' problems) than on the underlying technology. Therefore, utilization of the service-dominant logic paradigm may be particularly relevant and promising to technology marketing. Relatedly, how technology companies come to craft their value propositions is unexplored in the field; yet it is critically important for practicing managers.

- Anecdotal evidence suggests wide variance in the organizational culture of high-tech firms – from Apple's highly secretive, closed approach, to Microsoft's very hierarchical and competitive culture, to Google's reputed open and innovative culture. Do these various types of organizational culture (e.g. Deshpandé et al. 1993) offer differential value to high-technology firms under different conditions? Related research could explore the relative impact of organizational culture, organizational structure and planning processes on a firm's radical innovation capability (compared with incremental innovation capabilities).

- Leaders exert a strong influence on their organizations. In technology companies, do these leaders require different skills than leaders in more traditional companies? Again, anecdotal evidence from the visionary leadership of Apple's Steve Jobs might indicate that the visibility and style of leaders in technology companies possibly exert more influence (e.g. on a firm's radical innovation capability) and potentially have greater risks/exposure of poor decisions because of the highly dynamic technology environments.

6. Even while a cogent theory of technology marketing develops, addressing the unique characteristics of technology markets and the differences in marketing strategies between radical and incremental innovations, technology marketing researchers and managers also must stay abreast of general marketing issues. Important, timely and relevant topics that affect marketing in general, and technology marketing in particular, include the following:

- *BOP markets* (e.g. Mahajan and Banga 2005; Prahalad 2004). Technological innovations have great potential to offer solutions to problems arising in BOP markets, such as those related to health care, education, information and so forth (e.g. Mohr et al. 2010; Simanis 2010). Research on the opportunities and challenges technology companies face in BOP markets would offer insights to complement this important stream of research and value to the populations living in these markets.

- *Development of appropriate marketing metrics* (Srivastava et al. 1998). The development of marketing metrics in technology markets poses unique challenges. For example, the application of traditional financial metrics has been described as an 'innovation killer' (Christensen et al. 2008). Consistent with the notion that technology marketing requires a unique theoretical and managerial lens, metrics related to innovation performance, ecosystem development and firm value (particularly in markets characterized by network effects) must be crafted for the unique conditions that exist in technology markets. For example, is market share a more important metric than profits in markets in which platform-based competition is the primary driver of success?

- *Sustainability in business strategies.* Considerations about a firm's carbon footprint continue to increase in importance. Mohr et al. (2010) argue that technology companies are leading the way in reducing environmental impacts and that high-tech customers are particularly sensitive to the environmental friendliness of technology (e.g. energy efficiency, use of chemicals and toxins in production). For example, reducing energy-related operating expenses is the main reason companies pursue sustainable IT operations, beyond 'doing the right thing' for the environment (Jana 2008); the Green Electronics Council introduced the Electronic Product Environmental Assessment Tool (EPEAT) to allow customers to reliably gauge the sustainability (environmental impact) of high-tech products. Research exploring the effect of environmental considerations on customer adoption decisions relative to other considerations would be timely, as would understanding how technology firms leverage sustainability in their marketing strategies.

7. Finally, because the technology field generally is considered leading edge – if not 'bleeding edge' – scholars of technology marketing should lead in forging new theories and methodologies. For example, scholars such as Von Hippel (1986) and Leonard and Rayport (1997) have pioneered new methodologies to generate novel insights in markets in which customers find it difficult to articulate their needs or to understand the promise that new technologies offer. In this vein, a promising development to generate new insights for breakthrough technologies is the emerging field of biomimicry (Benyus 1997). Biomimicry refers to 'the conscious seeking of inspiration, the search for finding new and better ways to do things, through understanding nature and the principles of biology' (Mohr et al. 2010, p. 211). It has led to disruptive, breakthrough innovations in fields as diverse as industrial technologies (fans and turbines in engines), energy (power from ocean waves), architecture and building, and consumer products (automotive, apparel). Yet research on how firms leverage biomimicry in their technology development is lacking. For example, what types of firms are most likely to benefit from using biomimicry in their innovation processes? This is but one example of an area in which technology marketers (both managers and scholars) have the leading-edge knowledge and skills to offer new contributions to theory and practices, contributions currently unknown and waiting to be discovered.

This section is an initial enumeration of the many important topics in technology marketing that warrant additional research. As noted previously, managers in technology marketing face something of a double-jeopardy situation (Mohr et al. 2006): the context requires a highly sophisticated understanding of how marketing works, but high-technology firms tend not only to lack marketing competencies but also to underinvest in marketing-related activities relative to technology development. Thus, although marketing needs are particularly acute in technology markets, technology managers tend to be undertrained in marketing. Moreover, scholars have tended not to view technology marketing as a subdiscipline in its own right. We hope our review and ideas in this chapter inspire others to pursue this interesting, dynamic and important field; to investigate these questions further to provide managers with the guidance they need; and ultimately to create a theory of technology marketing.

NOTES

1. This chapter makes extensive reference to additional material that can be found on the ISBM Handbook website (see http://handbook.isbm.org).
2. As in other areas of marketing, much valuable research is conducted in companion fields; indeed, the management of technology as a sub-specialty in the management area has long been recognized not only with specialized journals but also with specialized degree programs.
3. Admittedly, the goal of summarizing the state-of-the-art regarding theory and practice in the arena of technology marketing is beyond the scope of any one chapter when entire books are devoted to this expansive topic (e.g. Mohr et al. 2010).
4. The US government defines high-technology industries on the basis of either input criteria (e.g. R&D expenditures or the number of technical employees) or output measures (product classifications determined by a panel of experts based on whether industry output embodies new or leading-edge technologies) (e.g. Mohr et al. 2010, pp. 9–10).
5. Although participation and adoption of electronic marketplaces in a B2B firm's operations (Grewal et

al. 2010; Grewal et al. 2001) are part of the domain of technology marketing, because there is a separate chapter in this handbook devoted to B2B electronic commerce, we do not provide a full review of this aspect of B2B technology marketing.

6. Though lacking clear 'bright lines' between each category, this categorization serves a useful purpose in examining the strengths and weaknesses of each approach and in identifying avenues for further research.

7. Methodological approaches to data gathering can include both qualitative (case study histories) and quantitative (either survey/perceptual data collected from managers or secondary data collected from the firm or from other secondary data sources) techniques.

8. In addition, customer adoption of technology comprises a rather large area in the management information systems research stream, focused on the technology acceptance model (TAM) (e.g. Venkatesh and Davis 2000).

9. Many studies fall somewhere in the gray area between 'high-tech as context' (category 1) and 'unique high-tech characteristics that generate unique insights for marketing theory' (category 2). For example, some of the studies in Web Exhibit 30.B (e.g. at the managerial/firm level) use high-technology settings primarily as context while also offering specific insights for the high-tech domain because the research questions addressed are applicable primarily to high-tech companies.

10. Independent of the notion of explicitly developing a theory of technology marketing, experts have previously established research agendas in this area (Hauser et al. 2006; Mohr and Sarin 2009; Srinivasan 2008; Tellis 2008); scholars in the area of technology marketing are strongly encouraged to dissect this excellent work.

11. Moore's Law states that the performance of a technology doubles roughly every 18 months while the cost to produce that level of performance remains constant. Alternatively, the price of technology is cut in half every 18 months to deliver the same level of performance.

12. An ecosystem is sometimes referred to as 'the network', or a firm's network of partners. Note that this use of the word 'network' differs greatly from the specific characteristic of 'network effects' in technology markets. These two meanings of 'network' could lead to potential confusion and misunderstanding. Note also that the word 'ecosystem' in business has a very different connotation than the notion of environmentally friendly, ecological business strategies, or 'green business'.

REFERENCES

Aaker, David and Robert Jacobson (2001), 'The value relevance of brand attitude in high-technology markets', *Journal of Marketing Research*, **38** (4), 485–93.

Adner, Ron (2006), 'Match your innovation strategy to your innovation ecosystem', *Harvard Business Review*, **84** (April–May), 98–107.

Agarwal, Rajshree and Barry L. Bayus (2002), 'The market evolution and sales takeoff of product innovations', *Management Science*, **48** (August), 1024–41.

Anderson, Chris (2008), *The Long Tail, Revised and Updated Edition: Why the Future of Business is Selling Less of More*, New York: Hyperion.

Anderson, Chris (2009), *Free: The Future of a Radical Price*, New York: Hyperion.

Anderson, Philip and Michael Tushman (1990), 'Technological discontinuities and dominant designs: a cyclical model of technological change', *Administrative Science Quarterly*, **35**, 604–34.

Atuahene-Gima, Kwaku (2005), 'Resolving the capability–rigidity paradox in new product innovation', *Journal of Marketing*, **69** (4), 61–83.

Barton, Dorothy, Edith Wilson and John Doyle (1995), 'Commercializing technology: understanding user needs', in V.K. Rangan et al. (eds), *Business Marketing Strategy*, Chicago: Irwin, pp. 281–305.

Bayus, Barry (1998), 'An analysis of product lifetimes in a technologically dynamic industry', *Management Science*, **44** (June), 763–75.

Benyus, Janine (1997), *Biomimicry: Innovation Inspired by Nature*, New York: McGraw-Hill.

Berchicci, Luca and Christopher L. Tucci (2010), 'There is more to market learning than gathering good information: the role of shared team values in radical product definition', *Journal of Product Innovation Management*, **27** (7), 972–90.

Capon, Noel and Rashi Glazer (1987), 'Marketing and technology: a strategic coalignment', *Journal of Marketing*, **51** (3), 1–14.

Chandy, Rajesh and Gerard Tellis (1998), 'Organizing for radical product innovation: the overlooked role of willingness to cannibalize', *Journal of Marketing Research*, **35** (4), 474–87.

Chandy, Rajesh and Gerard Tellis (2000), 'The incumbent's curse? Incumbency, size, and radical product innovation', *Journal of Marketing*, **64** (3), 1–17.

Christensen, Clayton (2006), 'The ongoing process of building a theory of disruption', *Journal of Product Innovation Management*, **23** (January), 39–55.

Christensen, Clayton M., Stephen P. Kaufman and Willy Shih (2008), 'Innovation killers: how financial tools destroy your capacity to do new things', *Harvard Business Review*, **86** (January–February), 98–105.

Davidow, William (1986), *Marketing High Technology*, New York: The Free Press.

Davidson, Alistair and Brian Leavy (2007), 'Interview with innovation guru Geoffrey Moore: seeking solutions to intractable problems', *Strategy & Leadership*, **35** (5), 4–8.

Deshpandé, Rohit, John Farley and Frederick Webster (1993), 'Corporate culture, customer orientation, and innovativeness in Japanese firms: a quadrad analysis', *Journal of Marketing*, **57** (1), 23–37.

Dhebar, Anirudh (1996), 'Speeding high-tech producer, meet the balking consumer', *Sloan Management Review*, **37** (2), 37–49.

Elberse, Anita (2008), 'Should you invest in the long tail?', *Harvard Business Review*, **86** (July–August), 88–96.

Ford, David and Chris Ryan (1981), 'Taking technology to market', *Harvard Business Review*, **59** (March–April), 117–26.

Frias, Kellilynn, Mrinal Ghosh and Robert Lusch (2010), 'Product form choice: a multi-method approach for understanding the "commercialized form" of innovations in entrepreneurial and business markets', working paper, University of Arizona.

Gardner, David (1990), 'Are high-technology products really different?', Working Paper #90-1706, University of Illinois at Urbana-Champaign.

Gardner, David, Frank Johnson, Moonkyu Lee and Ian Wilkinson (2000), 'A contingency approach to marketing high technology products', *European Journal of Marketing*, **34** (9/10), 1053–77.

Gatignon, Hubert and Thomas S. Robertson (1989), 'Technology diffusion: an empirical test of competitive effects', *Journal of Marketing*, **53** (1), 35–49.

Goldenberg, Jacob, Barak Libai and Eitan Muller (2002), 'Riding the saddle: how cross-market communications can create a major slump in sales', *Journal of Marketing*, **66** (2), 1–16.

Golder, Peter and Gerard Tellis (1997), 'Will it ever fly? Modeling the takeoff of really new consumer durables', *Marketing Science*, **16** (3), 256–70.

Govindarajan, Vijay and Praveen Kopalle (2006), 'The usefulness of measuring disruptiveness of innovations ex post in making ex ante predications', *Journal of Product Innovation Management*, **23** (January), 12–18.

Grenadier, Steven and Allen M. Weiss (1997), 'Investments in technological innovations: an options pricing approach', *Journal of Financial Economics*, **44** (3), 397–416.

Grewal, Rajdeep, Anindita Chakravarty and Amit Saini (2010), 'Governance mechanisms in business-to-business electronic markets', *Journal of Marketing*, **74** (4), 45–62.

Grewal, Rajdeep, James Comer and Raj Mehta (2001), 'An investigation into the antecedents of organizational participation in business-to-business electronic markets', *Journal of Marketing*, **65** (3) 17–33.

Gronhaug, Kjell and Kristian Moller (2005), 'High-tech marketing: fact or fiction?', *Finnish Journal of Business Economics*, **1**, 91–104.

Gupta, Ashok K., S.P. Raj and David Wilemon (1986), 'A model for studying R&D–marketing interface in the product innovation process', *Journal of Marketing*, **50** (2), 7–17.

Hauser, John, Gerard J. Tellis and Abbie Griffin (2006), 'Research on innovation: a review and agenda for marketing science', *Marketing Science*, **25** (6), 687–720.

Hoskisson, Robert, Daphne Yiu and Hicheo Kim (2004), 'Corporate governance systems: effects of capital and labor market congruency on corporate innovation and global competitiveness', *Journal of High Technology Knowledge Management Research*, **15** (2), 293–315.

Jana, Reena (2008), 'Green IT: corporate strategies', *BusinessWeek*, 11 February, available at http://www.businessweek.com/innovate/content/feb2008id/20080211_204672.htm.

Jayachandran, Satish, Subhash Sharma, Peter Kaufman and Pushkala Raman (2005), 'The role of relational information processes and technology use in customer relationship management', *Journal of Marketing*, **69** (4), 177–92.

John, George, Allen Weiss and Shantanu Dutta (1999), 'Marketing in technology-intensive markets: toward a conceptual framework', *Journal of Marketing*, **63** (Special Issue), 78–91.

Jolly, Vijay (1997), *Commercializing New Technologies: Getting from Mind to Market*, Boston, MA: Harvard Business School Press.

Kelley, Donna (2009), 'Adaptation and organizational connectedness in corporate radical innovation programs', *The Journal of Product Innovation Management*, **26** (5), 487–501.

Kim, Sang-Hoon and K.H. Huarng (2011), 'Winning strategies for innovation and high-technology product management', *Journal of Business Research*, **64** (11), 1147–50.

Knowledge@Wharton (2007), 'Who's the winner in the tug-of-war between "walled garden" and "open plain" strategies?', 5 September, available at http://knowledge.wharton.upenn.edu/article.cfm?articleid=1804, accessed 28 March 2011.

Lee, Hau (2002), 'Aligning supply chain strategies with product uncertainties', *California Management Review*, **44** (Spring), 105–19.

Leonard, Dorothy and Jeffrey F. Rayport (1997), 'Spark innovation through empathic design', *Harvard Business Review*, **75** (November–December), 102–13.

Lichtenthaler, Ulrich (2007), 'The drivers of technology licensing: an industry comparison', *California Management Review*, **49** (Summer), 67–89.

MacMillan, Douglas, Peter Burrows and Spencer E. Ante (2009), 'Inside the app economy', *BusinessWeek*, 22 October, available at http://www.businessweek.com/magazine/content/09_44/b4153044881892. htm?chan=magazine+channel_top+stories.

Mahajan, Vijay and Kamini Banga (2005), *The 86 Percent Solution: How to Succeed in the Biggest Market Opportunity of the 21st Century*, Upper Saddle River, NJ: Wharton School Publishing.

McKenna, Regis (2002), *Total Access, Giving Customers What They Want in an Anytime, Anywhere World*, Cambridge, MA: Harvard Business School Press.

Min, Sungwook, Manohar U. Kalwani and William T. Robinson (2006), 'Market pioneer and early follower survival risks: a contingency analysis of really new versus incrementally new product-markets', *Journal of Marketing*, **70** (1), 15–33.

Mohr, Jakki (2001), *Marketing of High-Technology Products and Innovations*, 1st edn, Upper Saddle River, NJ: Prentice Hall.

Mohr, Jakki and Shikhar Sarin (2009), 'Drucker's insights on market orientation and innovation: implications for emerging areas in high-technology marketing', *Journal of the Academy of Marketing Science*, **37** (Spring), 85–96.

Mohr, Jakki and Nader Shooshtari (2003), 'Introduction to the special issue: marketing of high-technology products and innovations', *Journal of Marketing Theory and Practice*, **11** (Summer), 1–11.

Mohr, Jakki, Robert Fisher and John R. Nevin (1996), 'Integration and control in interfirm relationships: the moderating role of collaborative communication', *Journal of Marketing*, **60** (3), 103–15.

Mohr, Jakki, Sanjit Sengupta and Stanley Slater (2010), *Marketing of High-Technology Products and Innovations*, 3rd edn, Upper Saddle River, NJ: Prentice Hall.

Mohr, Jakki, Stanley Slater and Sanjit Sengupta (2006), 'Foundations for successful high-technology marketing', in R. Verburg, R.J. Ortt and W.M. Dicke (eds), *Managing Technology and Innovation: An Introduction*, London: Routledge Publishing, pp. 84–105.

Mohr, Jakki, Stanley Slater and Sanjit Sengupta (2010), 'Technology marketing', in Hossein Bidgoli (ed.), *The Handbook of Technology Management*, Vol. 2, Hoboken, NJ: John Wiley & Sons, pp. 421–34.

Moore, Geoffrey (1991), *Crossing the Chasm*, New York: HarperCollins.

Moore, Geoffrey (1995), *Inside the Tornado*, New York: HarperBusiness.

Moore, Geoffrey A. (1999), *The Gorilla Game: Picking Winners in High Technology*, New York: HarperBusiness.

Moore, James (1997), *The Death of Competition: Leadership and Strategy in the Age of Business Ecosystems*, New York: Harper Paperbacks.

Moriarty, Rowland and Thomas Kosnik (1987), 'High-tech vs. low-tech marketing: where's the beef?', Harvard Business School Case #9-588-012.

Moriarty, Rowland and Thomas Kosnik (1989), 'High-tech marketing: concepts, continuity, and change', *Sloan Management Review*, **30** (Summer), 7–17.

Nevens, T. Michael, Gregory L. Summe and Bro Uttal (1990), 'Commercializing technology: what the best companies do', *Harvard Business Review*, **68** (May/June), 154–62.

Norton, John and Frank Bass (1987), 'Diffusion theory model of adoption and substitution for successive generations of technology intensive products', *Management Science*, **33** (September), 1069–86.

O'Connor, Gina Colarelli (2008), 'Major innovation as a dynamic capability: a systems approach', *Journal of Product Innovation Management*, **25**, 313–30.

Parasuraman, A. and Charles L. Colby (2001), *Techno-Ready Marketing: How and Why Your Customers Adopt Technology*, New York: The Free Press.

Prahalad, C.K. (2004), *The Fortune at the Bottom of the Pyramid: Eradicating Poverty Through Profits*, Upper Saddle River, NJ: Wharton School Publishing.

Rangan, V. Kasturi and Kevin Bartus (1995), 'New product commercialization: common mistakes', in V.K. Rangan et al. (eds), *Business Marketing Strategy*, Chicago, IL: Irwin, pp. 63–75.

Rogers, Everett (1962), *Diffusion of Innovations*, New York: The Free Press.

Sarin, Shikhar and Jakki Mohr (2008), 'An introduction to the special issue on marketing of high-technology products, services, and innovations', *Industrial Marketing Management*, **37** (August), 626–8.

Sengupta, Sanjit and Kaisu Puumalainen (2011), 'Guest editors: marketing of emerging technologies', *International Journal of Technology Marketing*, forthcoming.

Shanklin, William and John Ryans (1984a), *Essentials of Marketing High Technology*, Lexington, MA: DC Heath.

Shanklin, William and John Ryans (1984b), 'Organizing for high-tech marketing', *Harvard Business Review*, **62** (November–December), 164–71.

Shapiro, Carl and Hal R. Varian (1998a), *Information Rules: A Strategic Guide to the Network Economy*, Cambridge, MA: Harvard Business School Press.

Shapiro, Carl and Hal R. Varian (1998b), 'Versioning: the smart way to sell information', *Harvard Business Review*, (November–December), 106–14.

Simanis, Erik (2010), 'Needs, needs everywhere but not a base of the pyramid market to tap', in T. London and S. Hart (eds), *Next Generation Business Strategies for the Base of the Pyramid: New Approaches for Building Mutual Value*, Upper Saddle River, NJ: Pearson, pp. 103–28.

Sivadas, Eugene and Robert Dwyer (2000), 'An examination of organizational factors influencing new product success in internal and alliance-based processes', *Journal of Marketing*, **64** (1), 31–49.

Song, Michael and Jeff Thieme (2009), 'The role of suppliers in market intelligence gathering for radical and incremental innovation', *Journal of Product Innovation Management*, **26**, 43–57.

Sood, Ashish and Gerard Tellis (2005), 'Technological evolution and radical innovation', *Journal of Marketing*, **69** (3), 152–68.

Srinivasan, Raji (2008), 'Sources, characteristics, and effects of emerging technologies: research opportunities in innovation', *Industrial Marketing Management*, **37** (August), 633–40.

Srinivasan, Raji, Gary Lilien and Arvind Rangaswamy (2002), 'Technological opportunism and radical technology adoption: an application to e-business', *Journal of Marketing*, **66** (3), 47–60.

Srinivasan, Raji, Gary Lilien and Arvind Rangaswamy (2004), 'First in, first out? The effects of network externalities on pioneer survival', *Journal of Marketing*, **68** (1), 41–58.

Srinivasan, Raji, Gary Lilien and Arvind Rangaswamy (2006), 'The emergence of dominant designs', *Journal of Marketing*, **70** (2), 1–17.

Srivastava, Rajendra, Tasadduq Shervani and Liam Fahey (1998), 'Market-based assets and shareholder value: a framework for analysis', *Journal of Marketing*, **62** (1), 2–18.

Stremersch, Stefan and Walter Van Dyck (2009), 'Marketing of the life sciences: a new framework and research agenda for a nascent field', *Journal of Marketing*, **73** (4), 4–30.

Stremersch, Stefan, Gerard Tellis, Philip Hans Franses and Jeroen L.G. Binken (2007), 'Indirect network effects in new product growth', *Journal of Marketing*, **71** (3), 52–74.

Swaminathan, Vanitha and Christine Moorman (2009), 'Marketing alliances, firm networks and firm value creation', *Journal of Marketing*, **73** (5), 52–69.

Teece, David (1986), 'Profiting from technological innovation: implications for integration, collaboration, licensing, and public policy', *Research Policy*, **15**, 285–305.

Tellis, Gerard (2008), 'Important research questions in technology and innovation', *Industrial Marketing Management*, **37** (August), 629–32.

Tellis, Gerard, Eden Yin and Rakesh Niraj (2009), 'Does quality win? Network effects versus quality in high-tech markets', *Journal of Marketing Research*, **46** (2), 135–49.

Thompson, Debora Viana, Rebecca Hamilton and Roland Rust (2005), 'Feature fatigue: when product capabilities become too much of a good thing', *Journal of Marketing Research*, **42** (4), 431–42.

Vargo, Stephen and Robert Lusch (2004), 'Evolving to a new dominant logic for marketing', *Journal of Marketing*, **68** (1), 1–17.

Vargo, Stephen and Robert Lusch (2008), 'Service dominant logic: continuing the evolution', *Journal of the Academy of Marketing Science*, **36** (1), 1–10.

Venkatesh, Viswanath and Fred D. Davis (2000), 'A theoretical extension of the technology acceptance model: four longitudinal field studies', *Management Science*, **46** (February), 186–204.

Von Hippel, Eric (1986), 'Lead users: a source of novel product concepts', *Management Science*, **32** (July), 791–805.

Wu, Fang, Vijay Mahajan and Sridhar Balasubramanian (2003), 'An analysis of e-business adoption and its impact on business performance', *Journal of the Academy of Marketing Science*, **31** (September), 425–47.

Zhu, Kevin, Kenneth L. Kraemer and Sean Xu (2006), 'The process of innovation assimilation by firms in different countries: a technology diffusion perspective on e-business', *Management Science*, **52** (10), 1557–76.

BIBLIOGRAPHY OF POPULAR PRESS BOOKS ON TECHNOLOGY MARKETING

Bowen, James E. (2004), *Building High-Tech Product Companies: The Maelstrom Effect*, Mason, OH: Thomson South-Western.

Davidow, William (1986), *Marketing High Technology*, New York: Free Press.

McGrath, Michael (2000), *Product Strategy for High Technology Companies*, New York: McGraw-Hill.

Moore, Geoffrey (1991), *Crossing the Chasm*, 1st edn, New York: HarperCollins.

Moore, Geoffrey (1995), *Inside the Tornado*, New York: HarperBusiness.

Moore, Geoffrey A. (1999), *The Gorilla Game: Picking Winners in High Technology*, New York: HarperBusiness.

Nesheim, John L. (2000), *High Tech Start Up*, New York: Free Press.

Reddy, Allan C. (1997), *The Emerging High-Tech Consumer*, Westport, CT and London: Quorum Books.

Ryan, Rob (2001), *Entrepreneur America*, New York: HarperBusiness.

Ryans, Adrian, Roger More, Donald Barclay and Terry Deutscher (2000), *Winning Market Leadership in Technology Intensive Industries*, Toronto: John Wiley & Sons.

Shanklin, William and John K. Ryans Jr (1984), *Essentials of Marketing High Technology*, Lexington, MA: DC Heath.

Sowter, Colin (2000), *Marketing High-Tech Services*, Aldershot, UK: Gower Publishing.

Viardot, Eric (1998), *Successful Marketing Strategy for High-Tech Firms*, Boston and London: Artech House.

Weinstein, Art (2004), *Handbook of Market Segmentation: Strategic Targeting for Business and Technology Firms*, Binghamton, NY: Haworth Press.

31 Key questions on innovation in the B2B context
Gerard J. Tellis, Rajesh K. Chandy and Jaideep C. Prabhu

Innovation is a critical driver of the improvement in performance of customers, the growth and success of firms and the wealth of nations. Firms need to innovate constantly to offer superior value to their customers or face rivals that do so. Innovation can be in products or processes; in platform, design or component technologies; or in business models. Innovation is as vital in B2B markets as it is in consumer markets. Firms that produce and market to other firms often do so in response to specifications set by end customers. However, in the new intensely competitive marketplace, meeting specifications is no longer adequate. Suppliers need to innovate increasingly to exceed the specifications demanded by their customers or satisfy these specifications at much lower cost. Furthermore, as markets change rapidly, firms must predict the future needs of their customers to meet them in a timely way. Finally, in today's highly global marketplace, new suppliers arise from numerous developed and emerging economies. Being at the cutting edge of innovation helps ensure that firms can successfully serve their customers and are not made obsolete by competitors with a superior product or better processes.

In such a competitive and global environment, although much is known because of extensive research on innovation, several important questions still remain unanswered. This chapter identifies ten major topics in innovation, summarizes the major contributions of and issues in those topics and outlines the following key research questions for the future:

- Developing innovations
  1. Why do great firms fail?
  2. What is the role of top managers in innovation?
  3. Should firms make or buy innovations?
  4. What is business model innovation? What is its role in the B2B context?
- Commercializing innovations
  5. How do technologies evolve?
  6. Is network or quality more important for success?
  7. Should hardware or software come first?
- Fruits of innovation
  8. What is the pay-off to innovation?
  9. What is the role of innovation in emerging markets?
  10. What drives the wealth of nations?

These research questions are organized within the three major stages of innovation: developing innovations, commercializing innovations and the fruits of innovation. Although these stages frequently overlap, and the boundaries between them can be fuzzy, they provide a useful framework to organize the innovation journey (Yadav et al. 2007).

DEVELOPING INNOVATIONS

1. Why do Great Firms Fail?[1]

Given the importance of innovation for the survival and success of firms, we would expect that they would invest massive amounts of time, equipment and personnel into research for innovation. The largest firms in each market would have the most resources for this task. Therefore, they would be the most successful at innovation and would grow to dominate the next technological platform. As such, wealth would lead to greater wealth. However, history reveals that large, wealthy firms frequently fail. Indeed, great market leaders in one generation sometimes do not even survive the next generation. For example, leadership in the PC market moved from Altair, to Tandy, to Apple, to IBM, to Compaq, to Dell, to Hewlett-Packard (Tellis and Golder 1996, 2001). Why does prior strength not lead to continued strength?

Researchers have put forth several theories to explain why great firms fail. Schumpeter (1942) at least initially attributed failure to the disadvantages of large size. Foster (1986) attributed the failure of firms to the emergence of a new technology and the commitment of old dominant firms to the old technology. Failure occurred when the new technology crossed the old technology in performance. Continuing with the technological explanation, Utterback (1994) attributed failure to the type of technology. Failure occurred not merely if a new technology merged, but if the new technology was competence destroying rather than competence enhancing (Tushman and Anderson 1986). Christensen (1997) went a step further and attributed failure to the single-minded focus of established firms on meeting needs of the mass market of customers served by the old technology. That focus blinded them to the emergence of a new technology that was inferior to the old technology on the primary dimension of performance but superior on some secondary dimension that satisfied only a niche market. Failure occurred when the new technology surpassed the performance of the old technology even on the primary dimension. Chandy and Tellis (1998) attributed failure to the internal culture of the firm. A firm whose culture focuses on the future, instills internal competition and is willing to cannibalize past successful products is more likely to embrace innovations and stay ahead of the game (see Tellis et al. 2009a).

Which of these theories best explains the failure of firms, especially in a B2B context? They have not been tested strictly against each other in a rigorous field experiment or empirical study. Therefore, the jury is still out.

2. What is the Role of Top Managers in Innovation?

In general, B2B markets involve a limited set of customers, relative to B2C markets. Moreover, transaction values tend to be large and purchase cycles long in B2B markets (Brennan et al. 2007). For these reasons, and given the critical role of innovation in B2B markets, managers in the upper echelons of firms often play an active role in innovation activities in B2B firms.

Existing research suggests that top managers can have powerful effects in promoting or discouraging innovation in their firms. In a recent study, when asked 'Who is the biggest force driving innovation at your company?' 45 per cent of managers indicated that it was their firm's CEO (Boston Consulting Group 2006). CEOs such as Steve Jobs at Apple, Andy Grove and Gordon Moore at Intel and Bill Hewlett at Hewlett-Packard are celebrated for their apparent success in driving innovation in their firms.

Top managers play a crucial role in driving innovation in their firms for at least four reasons (Boyd et al. 2010; Tellis et al. 2009a). First, top managers can play an *informational* role by helping identify new market opportunities and orienting the attention of others in the firm toward these opportunities. Second, they play a *decisional* role by helping determine the level and type of innovation-related investments made in the firm. Third, they play a *relational* role by managing the firm's relationships with top stakeholders (e.g. major customer accounts, investors, alliance partners, employees) who are relevant to the innovation task. Fourth, and perhaps most important, they play a *cultural* role by shaping the values, attitudes and practices that are promoted or discouraged within the firm. Each of these effects could affect innovation outcomes.

Given the importance of CEOs and other top managers in innovation, scholars have sought to formally examine their role in innovation. Some have highlighted the importance of delving into managers' backgrounds and experiences to predict their emphasis on innovation. For example, some scholars have suggested that top executives with backgrounds in 'output'-oriented functions, such as marketing, R&D and sales, put greater emphasis on product innovation than those with backgrounds in 'throughput'-oriented functions, such as accounting/finance, production, administration and legal (Finkelstein and Hambrick 1996; Hambrick and Mason 1984). Others have noted that top managers' attention patterns have a strong impact on innovation, in that firms with CEOs who tend to focus on the future and on entities external to the firm are more innovative than others (Yadav et al. 2007). Executive compensation schemes may also affect innovation outcomes, in that long-term compensation packages may be associated with a greater focus on innovation activities that pay off over a long time horizon (see Makri et al. 2006).

Despite recent progress in understanding the role of top managers in innovation, much remains unknown. Are top managers in B2B firms more engaged in innovation activities than those in B2C firms? What are the roles of different members of top management teams (e.g. CEOs, CFOs, CMOs) in the innovation journey? How do corporate boards affect innovation? Are top managers in privately held firms more long-term oriented (and thus more encouraging of innovation) than top managers in equivalent publicly held firms, who face quarterly earnings pressures? Should top managers get directly involved in picking ideas and opportunities for innovation? These are all topics that could benefit from additional research.

3.   Should Firms Make or Buy Innovations?

Large corporations often depend on the innovation of their suppliers. In this sense, their suppliers provide not only the materials, parts and services for the current mix of products but also the innovations to improve them or develop new ones. For example, in developing the Boeing 787 Dreamliner, Boeing decided to outsource the manufacture and even research of approximately 70 per cent of the plane to firms all over the world (Kotha and Nolan 2005). This included outsourcing the wings, the part of the aircraft that Boeing considered its 'crown jewels'. In the past Boeing reserved manufacture of the wings to internal divisions only. Moreover, Boeing outsourced such manufacture even though it was well known that some of the firms building these parts had aspirations to grow into manufacturing entire planes themselves. Was Boeing nurturing the competitors of tomorrow? Would these suppliers one day threaten, if not displace, its dominance of the airplane manufacturing business?

Increasingly, firms actively work with outside entities – not only suppliers but also customers, academic institutions and even competitors – to develop new products and services. This process of working with outside entities to create and market innovations is called 'open innovation' (Chesbrough 2004). The open innovation efforts of Procter & Gamble (P&G) have received a good deal of attention in recent years. For decades P&G developed its new products entirely within its laboratories and tended to ignore or reject new ideas that were 'not invented here'. A few years ago P&G decided to abandon its policy of developing most new products internally to developing at least 50 per cent of its products from the outside (Huston and Sakkab 2006). This policy involves the sourcing of new ideas and innovation from outside the firm or outsourcing even R&D to outside firms. Although most P&G products are targeted to end consumers, the successful implementation of the firm's open innovation strategy relies on collaborating actively with *business* partners and suppliers. For example, the development of P&G's Mr. Clean brand of water-activated microscrubbers, which 'magically' erase tough household messes, involved collaboration with BASF, the large German chemicals company. P&G's open innovation efforts were partly inspired by the B2B innovation story of Goldcorp, a Canadian mining company. Goldcorp made the dramatic decision to open geological data about its mine (data that was zealously guarded from outsiders before) to the world at large (Tapscott and Williams 2008; Taylor and LaBarre 2007). The firm organized a competition for innovative ideas from outsiders and offered a monetary prize for the best ideas on where it should dig for gold within the mine. Within two weeks, the firm received over 1100 ideas from more than 50 countries. Of the ideas from the 110 semi-finalists in the competition, more than 50 per cent were new to the company, and 80 per cent of these ideas yielded gold. Goldcorp went from mining 53 000 ounces of gold per year at a cost of $360 per ounce in 1995, before the open innovation effort, to mining 500 000 ounces of gold at $60 per ounce after incorporating external sources of ideas. Of note, the inspiration for Goldcorp's competition came when its CEO learned about the remarkable success of the Linux operating system community in building a computer operating system with voluntary contributions of ideas and effort.

The Linux case (and, more generally, the open source software context) alludes to another rich source of externally developed innovation: lead users (Von Hippel 1986). Lead users are people who face needs that are not yet, but eventually will be, available in the marketplace, and therefore they are well positioned to solve these needs themselves (Von Hippel 1986). By seeking out such users, firms can obtain promising ideas often at little or no cost that can serve customer needs more effectively than internally generated ideas. Many firms have used lead users' efforts to develop successful innovations.

However, recent research indicates that lead users are not the only types of customers who can provide valuable contributions to innovation activities (Bendapudi and Leone 2003; Grewal et al. 2006). Many leading-edge firms are engaging with customers more generally in their innovation efforts, in a process called 'co-creation' (Prahalad and Ramaswamy 2000). O'Hern and Rindfleisch (2009, p. 4) define co-creation as a 'collaborative new product development activity in which customers actively contribute and select various elements of a new product offering'. Recent research has identified customer segments that might serve as especially productive sources of co-created innovation (Hoffman et al. 2010). Despite this progress, much remains unknown about the co-creation process (see Hoyer et al. 2010; O'Hern and Rindfleisch 2009). Why are some firms more successful at co-creation than others? What motivates some customers to co-create with companies, and why are some better sources of innovations than others? What incentives should be offered to customers for their co-creation efforts? Do monetary incentives help or hurt the likelihood of engaging in co-creation and the outcomes of co-creation efforts?

The question regarding whether a firm should manufacture or buy its supplies (whether innovation related or otherwise) has been a perennial strategy issue. One theory enlightening the solution has been that of transaction costs. That is, a firm should manufacture when the transaction costs of buying from the outside exceed the costs of acquiring the expertise to manufacture on the inside (Walker and Weber 1984). However, this example illustrates a far more complex set of problems and opportunities that firms face in the global economy today. Products are now so complex and centers of excellence so highly distributed around the world that a firm would be unwise to completely ignore good innovations and expertise that lie outside the firm (Rigby and Zook 2002). What is the core technology, if any, that a firm should reserve for internal development? When should a firm go outside for ideas, and when should it stay inside? In which country should a firm locate its R&D, and how should it recruit and organize its talent for this task?

Other important issues arise when a firm chooses to manufacture its innovation. For example, how should a firm organize to be innovative? Should it use a functional or divisional structure? If the latter, should it resort to cooperating divisions, competing divisions, spin-outs, or spin-offs? These are important issues that merit research.

4.   What is Business Model Innovation? What is its Role in the B2B Context?

A recent influential survey found that 'business model' innovation is the most important form of innovation for CEOs across the globe (IBM Global CEO Study 2006). The survey also found that firms that emphasize business model innovation grow far faster than firms that undertake product or process innovation alone. However, despite considerable recent interest in the phenomenon of business model innovation, there is still little consensus about what such innovation involves. Velu et al. (2010) combine a review of existing studies (Brandenburger and Stuart 1996; Gambardella and McGahan 2010; Johnson et al. 2008; Zott and Amit 2008) with their own interviews with managers to propose that business model innovations involve systemic changes to a firm's customer value proposition along with changes to its accompanying operating structure. Such changes involve changing multiple elements of the customer value proposition along with the accompanying cost structure of the business (Susarla et al. 2009). For example, Amazon.com was an innovation that involved changes not only to the customer value proposition but also to the product (a far greater assortment than any bricks-and-mortar book retailer, made possible in part by a B2B marketplace), distribution (books available everywhere and all the time through the Internet), price (lower prices in general) and promotion (access to online customer reviews about products and retailers). Changes also occurred in the cost structure of Amazon.com's offering through reduced overheads and greater economies of scale. Amazon.com's B2B customers as well as end customers seem to have benefited from its innovation in business models.

Given its systemic nature, business model innovation poses both opportunities and challenges for new venture and incumbent firms alike. New ventures such as Amazon.com can exploit new technologies, such as the Internet, to create significantly new value propositions for consumers that can also be delivered at radically lower cost levels. In this way, firms can come to create and dominate new sectors or even industries. But because business model innovation is more than just product or process innovation, and is often both at the same time, major questions remain about: (1) how new ventures should go about doing business model innovation; (2) the resources and capabilities they require to succeed at such innovation; and (3) the organizational and strategic challenges they face in doing so.

For incumbent firms with existing business models, their superior resources can help them innovate and remain dominant. However, as considerable research shows, radical product innovation is hard enough for most incumbents to undertake because of their commitment to existing technologies and customer segments. Given the systemic nature of business model innovation, this form of innovation is likely to be even harder for incumbent firms than product innovation. Thus, bricks-and-mortar book distributors, such as Barnes & Noble and Borders, have faced particular difficulties in trying to develop an Internet business model in addition to their existing business model. How do incumbents reinvent their business models? What challenges do they face in doing so? How can they leverage their existing resources and capabilities to do so? How are the challenges incumbents face different from those new entrants face? These are questions around which little empirical research currently exists.

Business model innovation raises issues about how firms manage their relationships with other businesses in both B2C and B2B contexts. Even in B2C contexts, because of the systemic nature of business model innovation, such innovation involves working not only with end consumers (because of the role of the value proposition) but also with suppliers and distributors (because of the role of the firm's operating structure). Compared with incumbent firms, how do new ventures manage the inter-firm relationships needed for business model innovation? Further research is needed to shed light on this question.

In purely B2B contexts, the way firms manage their relationships with other firms becomes even more crucial to the successful development and delivery of new business models. Given that the business buying process is different from that of consumers, a key question is: does business model innovation differ significantly in the B2B than the B2C context? Relatedly, are business model innovations more or less frequent in the B2B than the B2C context? Are they easier or harder to develop in the B2B than the B2C context? Does this development vary depending on whether the innovating firm is a new venture or an incumbent? Given the paucity of research on these topics, finding answers to these questions holds the promise of a rich stream of research, with significant implications for academics and managers alike.

COMMERCIALIZING INNOVATIONS

5. How do Technologies Evolve?

A commonly observed phenomenon in innovation is the replacement of one technology by another. For example, digital photography has largely replaced film photography, online air reservation is rapidly replacing travel agencies, and open source software is threatening commercial software. In printing, ink-jet and laser technologies replaced dot matrix printing, and both are steadily improving in performance. Which one will win, or will thermal printing replace both? A change in technology involves huge costs in equipment, training and management for firms. More important, transitions in technologies often cause the demise of or at least the tripping up of giant incumbents. For example, although IBM's mainframe business did not seem immediately threatened by the emergence of microcomputers, the lower cost and increasing power of the latter ultimately encroached on IBM's lucrative B2B business in mainframe computers. Thus, predicting the path of technological evolution can be a great advantage for an incumbent or entrant. How do technologies evolve?

Foster (1986) proposed a simple theory to explain technological evolution. He suggested that technological performance on some key dimension, as a function of research effort, evolved along an S-shaped curve. Curves for rival technologies crossed once. So, a good strategy was to switch from an old technology on the mature or upper flat of its S curve to a new technology on the upward or growth trajectory of its S curve. However, Sood and Tellis (2005a, 2005b, 2011) show that this simple model is rarely, if ever, true. Technologies evolve along step functions, with multiple crossings and huge spikes in performance after periods of long dormancy. How can a firm predict the path of this evolution given this messy real world? What theory or model can throw light on the phenomenon? Is the pace of technological evolution increasing? If so, where is it heading? These are unanswered questions with billion-dollar implications for the firms locked in combat on rival technologies.

Technological innovations are particularly salient because most new consumer products based on new technologies are initially developed in B2B contexts. Mobile phones, room air conditioners, microwave ovens and videotape recorders are commonly viewed as consumer products today, but they got their start as innovations for businesses. Indeed, the B2B market may be the launch pad for many, if not most, major consumer innovations (Golder and Tellis 1993; Tellis and Golder 2001). Conversely, some products introduced for consumer markets may become so successful that they encroach on B2B markets. This phenomenon raises the following questions: how do technologies diffuse from B2B to B2C markets, or vice versa? Which is a preferred launching pad for new products? How do these two markets cross-subsidize the evolution of technologies?

6. Is Network or Quality More Important for Success?

A not uncommon phenomenon in the age of high-technology or Internet products, whether B2B or B2C, is that a single product has an overwhelming market share. For example, Intel, Microsoft Windows, Microsoft Office, eBay, Facebook and Amazon. com all dominate their respective markets. And in some cases, dominance occurs quite fast and reaches 70 to 85 per cent market share. Why does this phenomenon occur? Analysts attribute it to direct or indirect network effects. Direct or user-based network effects occur when the benefit from a product increases with the number of other users of the product. Alibaba.com maintains its dominant position as the world's largest B2B portal in part because millions of businesses buy and sell on it. Microsoft Excel's usefulness to users increases as more users use the same program. Indirect network effects occur when the benefit of a product increases with the number of accessories or add-ons that run with or on it. For example, smartphones that run iPhone and Android operating systems become more useful as the number of mobile applications ('apps') that run on them grows.

Some economists have argued that in the presence of network effects, a brand that takes an early lead, either because of entering the market early or through some accident, may end up with the highest market share (Church and Gandal 1993; Farrell and Saloner 1985; Katz and Shapiro 1985). This phenomenon is sometimes called 'path dependence' because the market share path of the brand depends on some early accident (Besen and Farrell 1994). The argument goes that network effects or path dependence could be so strong that an inferior brand could dominate its market and even lock out superior quality or lower-priced alternatives.

Some researchers have argued that the case for network effects and path dependence is overstated (Liebowitz and Margolis 1999; Tellis et al. 2009b, 2009c); yet the dominance of brands that are known to have many flaws persists (e.g. Windows). What are the real causes of market success and dominance of innovations for high-tech and Internet products? Are network effects more important than quality for such products? How do such networks develop, and what control do managers have over them? Do inferior brands really win out through accidents of history? Answers to these questions have important implications for managers and public policy-makers.

7. Should Hardware or Software Come First?

When two products are related by indirect network effects they pose another problem for managers and policy-makers: which product should come first? Such linked products often have a hardware component and a software component. For example, the PC (hardware) is more useful as the number of programs (software) run off it increases. More generally, the hardware may be considered a heavy investment category, while the software may be considered a light investment category.

The presence of indirect network effects raises the proverbial chicken-and-egg problem (Caillaud and Jullien 2003; Gandal 1994; Gupta et al. 1999). Should firms invest in the hardware or the software first? Hardware manufactures argue that without programs, consumers will not buy the hardware. Software manufacturers argue that without hardware, the software is meaningless. This dilemma is what has delayed and continues to delay the easy spread of ethanol or electric cars in the United States. In the latter case, the link is between cars and the network of refueling stations. Some analysts argue that the issue has no solution, similar to the chicken-and-egg problem. However, a solution could come from many sources, including commitment, level of investment, or regulation (Stremersch et al. 2007). How prevalent is the problem of first investment for such linked products? Should hardware or software come first? Under which conditions? When, if ever, and how should government intervene to break the impasse between hardware and software suppliers for the benefit of consumers? Research to answer these questions can serve multiple publics.

FRUITS OF INNOVATION

8.   What is the Pay-off to Innovation?

Managers typically invest in innovation by comparing the investment costs with the future market revenues of an innovation. However, the pay-off from innovations is often in the distant and uncertain future. Not only must managers discount the profits from future time periods, but they must also factor in the uncertainties from ever earning those revenues. Some analysts suggest turning to the stock market to assess how the market values investments in innovations. The logic from doing so is that the market is efficient, so the stock price reflects current and discounted future cash flows that would accrue to the firm given all the information available at the time. Any abnormal return in the stock price (beyond the normal for the whole market) on some announcement of innovation would reflect the value of that innovation at the time of the announcement.

A few studies have shown that the market does indeed show 'abnormal returns' to certain events in the life cycle of developing and commercializing an innovation (Chaney et al. 1991; Rao et al. 2008; Sorescu et al. 2003). Nevertheless, these findings raise a host of important issues (Sood and Tellis 2008). What is the right metric and approach for evaluating the returns to an innovation? If abnormal returns are the focus, what are the abnormal returns to various stages of an innovation, such as initiation, development and commercialization? What are the total returns to all stages and events in the life of an innovation? Do investments in innovation ultimately pay off in terms of total returns? Answers to these questions are of critical importance in determining the value of investments in innovation and advising managers and investors about strategies on which they should focus.

9.   What is the Role of Innovation in Emerging Markets?

For much of the twentieth century, innovation was the preserve of the developed economies of North America, Western Europe and Japan. The world's largest spenders on innovation were mostly Western or Japanese multinational corporations (MNCs) that, even while outsourcing manufacturing to China in the 1980s and back-office processes to India in the 1990s, located their R&D activities at home, close to headquarters. If they chose to locate R&D away from their home country, they typically did so in other developed or triad economies. In the late 1990s and the 2000s, however, this trend was reversed, so much so that China and India in particular, but also Brazil and, to a certain extent, Russia, are now major destinations for large MNC R&D centers (Tellis et al. 2010). For example, General Electric and IBM currently locate their largest R&D centers in India.

The phenomenon of the offshoring of R&D is accompanied by the related phenomenon of the outsourcing of innovation to other companies, both MNCs and domestic companies, in emerging economies. Specifically, the R&D centers of many large MNCs in emerging markets form relationships with other local companies as a means to tap into ideas and expertise that others have. These ideas may be technical or market related and can be local or global in nature.

The twin phenomena of offshoring and outsourcing of innovation to emerging markets raise several questions for researchers and managers alike. What is driving these phenomena? Given that R&D and innovation are strategic assets imperiled by offshoring and outsourcing, how do firms manage the potential loss of intellectual property to competitors, especially those they also partner with in the R&D/innovation process? What kinds of activities – technological versus market development, local versus global application – do MNCs in emerging markets pursue? How do they combine their activities in emerging markets with their activities in their R&D centers in other parts of the world, especially in developed economies?

Increasingly, it is not only foreign, developed country MNCs that innovate in emerging markets. More and more Chinese, Indian and Brazilian firms are investing in R&D and exploiting their home cost and market advantage to innovate for global markets. These firms are also acquiring foreign, developed country firms to acquire advanced technology they can leverage to compete globally. For example, not only has India's Tata Motors domestically developed the Nano, the world's cheapest car, but it has also acquired the UK's Jaguar and Land Rover to give it access to technology and brands at the high end of the price spectrum. The rise of firms from emerging markets and their increasing focus on innovation raise several questions of interest. Is the type of innovation of emerging market firms different from that of developed country firms? Specifically, do emerging market firms excel at low-cost product and process innovation rather than high-end, technological innovation? Do they undertake more business model innovation than product innovation? Can they successfully take their domestic innovations to global markets? How will they compete with Western MNCs through innovation in the long run? These types of questions hold the promise of a rich stream of research with significant implications for academics and managers alike.

10.   What Drives the Wealth of Nations?

Researchers have long been intrigued with the questions: what drives the wealth of nations, and what is the role of innovation in it? Many disciplines have addressed these questions and have come up with quite varied answers. One obvious candidate includes raw materials, which many people assume are the most important cause of wealth. Along these lines, recent research has argued that geography plays a critical role in enabling the harnessing of crops and animals for the development of prosperity (Diamond 1999; Morris 2010). However, could the lack of raw mineral, agricultural or animal resources lead people to be innovative, while abundance of these resources leads people to be lazy? Some authors have argued that a key driver of wealth is a particular religion, which makes believers more materialistic, industrious and innovative than believers in other religions (Weber 1930). Other authors have argued that climate is a critical factor that fosters a work ethic of innovation and industriousness (Parker 2000). Still other authors have argued for the importance of social and political systems (e.g. patent law), which have given people the incentives to be innovative (Landes 1999). Economists have argued for the role of regulation, investment in R&D and education of the work force (Furman et al. 2002). In contrast with these perspectives, a recent study argues that firm culture is the most important determinant of a country's innovativeness (Tellis et al. 2009a).

Innovations have enabled even countries with minimal raw materials (e.g. Japan) to develop and become wealthy. Furthermore, the innovations of these countries arise from entrepreneurs and firms within the country rather than from governments. In this context, B2B markets may play two roles. First, as explained previously, these markets could serve as the launch pad for innovations, including those that ultimately become consumer products. Second, highly innovative firms may serve as the hub of a highly innovative cluster of B2B suppliers. For example, Apple, Boeing, Microsoft and Intel serve as the nexus of an innovative cluster of B2B firms. The innovations of the hub stimulate and are enhanced by innovations of its B2B suppliers.

An overview of history shows that no country or civilization has been permanently dominant or wealthy. Wealth has not led to greater wealth and success, as some of the aforementioned explanations would lead one to conclude. Rather, history has been witness to the perennial rise and fall of civilizations. Thus any explanation of this complex but important problem needs to take into account the failure of any one nation to remain innovative and wealthy permanently. Moreover, even within a nation, clusters of innovativeness (e.g. Silicon Valley) rise and fall with time. The answer to this problem is not merely of historical importance. It informs public and government policy and firm strategy today.

Key research questions are the following: what causes nations to be innovative? Is it climate, geography, culture, religion, economics or politics? Does the innovativeness of a country affect the innovativeness of firms within it? Or does the innovativeness of a country rest on the innovation of its firms? Are there innovative clusters within countries? If so, what drives that phenomenon, and how can it be replicated? Is the location of a firm's R&D department merely one of operational efficiency, or does it affect the innovativeness of the department and the firm? What is the role of B2B firms in the innovativeness of major organizations? To what extent are consumer innovations driven by innovations of the manufacturers versus innovations of their suppliers?

CONCLUSION

Innovation is an important force in markets today, and it is just as vital in B2B as it is in B2C markets. Despite extensive research over the years and across many disciplines, much still remains to be known about innovation, especially in a B2B context. As we argue in this chapter, the B2B context is in some ways similar to the B2C context and in some ways different. Moreover, we could argue that the B2B context is more widespread. Even firms that eventually serve end consumers need to work with other firms to innovate and serve these consumers better. Although much existing knowledge about innovation in a B2C context can be extended to the B2B context, research remains to be conducted to better understand when and how innovation in the two contexts differs. The goal of this chapter has been to outline what is already known and what remains to be done and to trigger interest in finding answers to the questions that remain.

NOTE

1. Parts of this chapter borrow from Tellis (2008).

REFERENCES

Bendapudi, Neeli and Robert P. Leone (2003), 'Psychological implications of customer participation in co-production', *Journal of Marketing*, **67** (January), 14–28.

Besen, Stanley M. and Joseph Farrell (1994), 'Choosing how to compete: strategies and tactics in standardization', *Journal of Economic Perspectives*, **8** (2), 117–31.

Boston Consulting Group (2006), *Innovation 2006*, Boston, MA: Boston Consulting Group.

Boyd, J. Eric, Rajesh K. Chandy and Marcus Cunha Jr (2010), 'When do chief marketing officers affect firm value? A customer power explanation', *Journal of Marketing Research*, **47** (December), 1162–76.

Brandenburger, A. and S.H. Stuart (1996), 'Value-based business strategy', *Journal of Economics and Management Strategy*, **5** (1), 5–25.

Brennan, Ross, Louise Canning and Ray McDowell (2007), *Business-to-Business Marketing*, London: Sage Publications.

Caillaud, Bernard and Bruno Jullien (2003), 'Chicken & egg: competition among intermediation service providers', *RAND Journal of Economics*, **34** (2), 309–28.

Chandy, Rajesh K. and Gerard J. Tellis (1998), 'Organizing for radical product innovation: the overlooked role of willingness to cannibalize', *Journal of Marketing Research*, **35** (4), 474–87.

Chaney, Paul K., Timothy M. Devinney and Russell S. Winer (1991), 'The impact of new product introductions on the market value of firms', *Journal of Business*, **64** (4), 573–610.

Chesbrough, Henry (2004), *Open Innovation*, Cambridge, MA: Harvard Business School Press.

Christensen, Clayton M. (1997), *The Innovator's Dilemma: When New Technologies Cause Great Firms to Fail*, Boston, MA: Harvard Business School Press.

Church, Jeffrey and Neil Gandal (1993), 'Complementary network externalities and technological adoption', *International Journal of Industrial Organization*, **11**, 239–60.

Diamond, Jared (1999), *Guns, Germs, and Steel: The Fates of Human Societies*, New York: Norton and Company.

Farrell, Joseph and Garth Saloner (1985), 'Standardization, compatibility and innovation', *RAND Journal of Economics*, **16** (1), 70–83.

Finkelstein, S. and D. Hambrick (1996), *Strategic Leadership: Top Executives and Their Effects on Organizations*, St Paul, MN: West Publishing Co.

Foster, R. (1986), *Innovation: The Attacker's Advantage*, New York: Summit Books.

Furman, J.L., M.E. Porter and S. Stern (2002), 'The determinants of national innovative capacity', *Research Policy*, **31**, 899–933.

Gambardella, A. and A. McGahan (2010), 'Business-model innovation: general purpose technologies and their implications for industry structure', *Long Range Planning*, **43** (2–3), 262–71.

Gandal, Neil (1994), 'Hedonic price indexes for spreadsheets and an empirical test for network externalities', *RAND Journal of Economics*, **25** (1), 160–70.

Golder, Peter and Gerard J. Tellis (1993), 'Pioneering advantage: marketing fact or marketing legend', *Journal of Marketing Research*, **30** (May), 158–70.

Grewal, Rajdeep, Gary Lilien and Girish Mallapragada (2006), 'Location, location, location: how network embeddedness affects project success in open source systems', *Management Science*, **52** (7), 1043–56.

Gupta, Sachin, Dipak C. Jain and Mohanbir S. Sawhney (1999), 'Modeling the evolution of markets with indirect network externalities: an application to digital television', *Marketing Science*, **18** (3), 396–416.

Hambrick, Donald and Phyllis A. Mason (1984), 'Upper echelons: the organization as a reflection of its top managers', *Academy of Management Review*, **9** (2), 193–206.

Hoffman, Donna L., Praveen K. Kopalle and Thomas P. Novak (2010), 'The "right" consumers for better concepts: identifying consumers high in emergent nature to develop new product concepts', *Journal of Marketing Research*, **47** (October), 854–65.

Hoyer, Wayne, Rajesh Chandy, Matilda Dorotic, Manfred Krafft and Siddharth Singh (2010), 'Customer participation in value creation', *Journal of Service Research*, **13** (3), 283–96.

Huston, Larry and Nabil Sakkab (2006), 'Connect and develop: inside Procter & Gamble's new model for innovation', *Harvard Business Review*, **84** (3), 58–66.

IBM Global CEO Study (2006), *Expanding the Innovation Horizon*, IBM Global Business Services, available at http://www-07.ibm.com/sg/pdf/global_ceo_study.pdf, accessed 7 February 2011.

Johnson, W., C. Christensen and H. Kagermann (2008), 'Reinventing your business model', *Harvard Business Review*, **86** (12), 50–59.

Katz, Michael L. and Carl Shapiro (1985), 'Network effects, competition, and compatibility', *American Economic Review*, **75** (3), 425–40.

Kotha, Suresh and Richard Nolan (2005), *Boeing 787: The Dreamliner*, Boston, MA: Harvard Business Publishing.

Landes, David (1999), *The Wealth and Poverty of Nations: Why Some are so Rich and Some so Poor*, New York: W.W. Norton.

Liebowitz, Stan J. and Stephen Margolis (1999), *Winners, Losers & Microsoft*, Oakland, CA: The Independent Institute.

Makri, M., P.J. Lane and L. Gomez-Mejia (2006), 'CEO incentives, innovation, and performance in technology-intensive firms', *Strategic Management Journal*, **27** (11), 1057–80.

Morris, Ian (2010), *Why the West Rules for Now*, New York: Farrar, Straus and Groux.

O'Hern, Matthew S. and Aric Rindfleisch (2009), 'Customer co-creation: a typology and research agenda', in Naresh K. Malholtra (ed.), *Review of Marketing Research*, Vol. 6, Armonk, NY: M.E. Sharpe, pp. 84–106.

Parker, Philip (2000), *Physioeconomics*, Cambridge, MA: MIT Press.

Prahalad, C.K. and Venkat Ramaswamy (2000), 'Co-opting customer competence', *Harvard Business Review*, **78** (January–February), 79–87.

Rao, Raghunath, Rajesh Chandy and Jaideep Prabhu (2008), 'The fruits of legitimacy: why some new ventures gain more from innovation than others', *Journal of Marketing*, **72** (4), 58–75.

Rigby, Darrell and Chris Zook (2002), 'Open-market innovation', *Harvard Business Review*, **80** (10), 5–12.

Schumpeter, Joseph (1942), *Capitalism, Socialism, and Democracy*, New York: Harper.

Sood, Ashish and Gerard J. Tellis (2005a), 'Technological evolution and radical innovation?', *Journal of Marketing*, **69** (July), 152–68.

Sood, Ashish and Gerard J. Tellis (2005b), 'The S-curve of technological change: strategic law or self-fulfilling prophecy?', Marketing Science Institute Working Paper.

Sood, Ashish and Gerard J. Tellis (2008), 'Do innovations pay off? Total stock market returns to innovation', *Marketing Science*, **28** (3), 442–56.

Sood, Ashish and Gerard J. Tellis (2011), 'Demystifying disruptions: a new model for understanding and predicting disruptive technologies', *Marketing Science*, forthcoming.

Sorescu, Alina, Rajesh Chandy and Jaideep Prabhu (2003), 'Sources and financial consequences of radical innovation: insights from pharmaceuticals', *Journal of Marketing*, **67** (October), 82–102.

Stremersch, Stefan, Gerard J. Tellis, Philip Hans Franses and Jeroen L.G. Binken (2007), 'Indirect network effects in new product growth', *Journal of Marketing*, **71** (July), 52–74.

Susarla, A., A. Barua and A. Whinston (2009), 'A transaction cost perspective of the "software as a service" business model', *Journal of Management Information Systems*, **26** (2), 205–40.

Tapscott, Don and Anthony Williams (2008), *Wikinomics*, London: Atlantic Books.

Taylor, William and Polly LaBarre (2007), *Mavericks at Work: Why the Most Original Minds in Business Win*, New York: HarperCollins.

Tellis, Gerard J. (2008), 'Important research questions in technology and innovation', *Industrial Marketing Management*, **37** (6), 629–32.

Tellis, Gerard J. and Peter N. Golder (1996), 'First to market, first to fail? The real causes of enduring market leadership', *Sloan Management Review*, **37** (2), 65–75.

Tellis, Gerard J. and Peter N. Golder (2001), *Will and Vision: How Latecomers Grow To Dominate Markets*, Burr Ridge, IL: McGraw-Hill.

Tellis, Gerard J., Jaideep C. Prabhu and Rajesh K. Chandy (2009a), 'Radical innovation across nations: the preeminence of corporate culture', *Journal of Marketing*, **73** (January), 3–23.

Tellis, Gerard J., Yiding Yin and Rakesh Niraj (2009b), 'Does quality win? Network effects versus quality in high-tech markets', *Journal of Marketing Research*, **46** (April), 135–49.

Tellis, Gerard J., Yiding Yin and Rakesh Niraj (2009c), 'Why and how quality wins over network effects and what it means', in 'Commentaries and Rejoinder to "Does quality win? Network effects versus quality in high-tech markets"', *Journal of Marketing Research*, **46** (April), 160–62.

Tellis, Gerard J., A. Eisingerich, R. Chandy and J. Prabhu (2010), 'Competing for the future: patterns in the global location of R&D centers by the world's largest firms', working paper, Marshall School of Business, University of Southern California.

Tushman, Michael L. and P. Anderson (1986), 'Technological discontinuities and organizational environments', *Administrative Science Quarterly*, **31** (3), 439–65.

Utterback, James M. (1994), *Mastering the Dynamics of Innovation*, Boston, MA: Harvard Business School Press.

Velu, Chander, Jaideep C. Prabhu and Rajesh K. Chandy (2010), 'Evolution or revolution: business model innovation in network markets', working paper, Judge Business School, University of Cambridge.

Von Hippel, Eric (1986), 'Lead users: a source of novel product concepts', *Management Science*, **32** (7), 791–805.

Walker, Gordon and David Weber (1984), 'A transaction cost approach to make-or-buy decisions', *Administrative Science Quarterly*, **29**, 373–91.

Weber, Max (1930), *The Protestant Ethic and the Spirit of Capitalism*, Talcott Parsons, trans., New York: Charles Scribner's Sons.

Yadav, Manjit S., Jaideep C. Prabhu and Rajesh K. Chandy (2007), 'Managing the future: CEO attention and innovation outcomes', *Journal of Marketing*, **71** (October), 84–101.

Zott, C. and R. Amit (2008), 'Exploring the fit between business strategy and business model: implications for firm performance', *Strategic Management Journal*, **29** (1), 1–26.

32 The Stage-Gate® system for product innovation in B2B firms
Robert G. Cooper

The Stage-Gate® system has become the most widely used methodology for conceiving, developing and launching new products among B2B firms. Indeed, an estimated 70 to 75 per cent of companies that develop new products have implemented a robust idea-to-launch system, such as Stage-Gate (APQC 2002; Cooper et al. 2005; Griffin 1997).[1] The benefits of such a process have been well documented, and many well-managed B2B companies, such as Emerson Electric, ITT, Siemens, Corning Glass, BASF and 3M, have prospered and profited from using Stage-Gate. (Stage-Gate is trademarked, and thus it is known by different names: Emerson Electric and BASF call it Phase-Gate; General Electric uses the term Tollgate system; at Procter & Gamble, it's called SIMPL; the US Army calls it TARGET; and the UK government uses the name Gateways).

Benchmarking studies reveal that many firms still struggle with their new product systems and methodologies, though. For example, new products continue to have an alarming failure rate: of every nine new product concepts, only one becomes a commercial success, according to Product Development and Management Association (PDMA) studies (Adams and Boike 2004a, 2004b; APQC 2002; Griffin 1997). A review of many investigations suggests that about 40 per cent of new products fail at launch, even after all the voice of the customer (VoC) efforts, product tests and customer trials. And in only 21.3 per cent of companies do new product efforts meet annual profit objectives (Cooper et al. 2004a).

Thus it's time to get back to the basics, to look at why new products win; that is, to define the critical success drivers and determine how to build them into an idea-to-launch methodology. The first part of this chapter does this: it provides an overview of factors that correlate most strongly with successful product innovation, when success is measured at the project level,[2] including the key variables that differentiate successful new products from unsuccessful ones. Next it provides a brief introduction to the Stage-Gate system, an idea-to-launch methodology that incorporates these and other success drivers. In addition this chapter shows what leading B2B firms have done to streamline, adapt and improve their stage-and-gate method: how they have moved beyond the traditional gating process and evolved to the next-generation idea-to-launch Stage-Gate system. Finally this chapter identifies important research questions that provide useful directions for research into the practical side of product innovation.

SEVEN CRITICAL SUCCESS DRIVERS

Research into new product success and failure has revealed critical success drivers that distinguish successful projects or businesses from unsuccessful ones (APQC 2002;

Cooper 2001, 2004, 2011; Cooper et al. 2004a, 2004b, 2005; Cooper and Kleinschmidt 1987, 1990, 1994, 1995). The key is to understand the drivers first, then build them into an operational model for driving new products to market. This section provides a brief overview of some of the more important success drivers, which can and have been built into the Stage-Gate system.

A Unique Superior Product (Differentiated Product that Delivers Unique Benefits and Compelling Value Propositions to Customers or Users) Drives New Product Profitability

Delivering products with unique benefits and real value to users separates winners from losers more often than any other single factor (APQC 2002; Cooper 2001, 2004, 2011; Cooper et al. 2004a, 2004b, 2005; Cooper and Kleinschmidt 1987, 1990, 1994, 1995). Such superior products have five times the success rate, over four times the market share and four times the profitability compared with products lacking this ingredient. Product advantage, superiority or differentiation as the key determinant of success is a recurring theme in many new product studies. The fact that differentiated, superior products are key to success should come as no surprise to product innovators. Apparently though, it isn't obvious to everyone: study after study shows that 'reactive products' and 'me-too' offerings are the rule rather than the exception in many businesses' new product efforts, and the majority fail to produce large profits!

A closer look at exceptional businesses, as in Figure 32.1, shows that the 'best innovators'[3] emphasize certain factors in their new-product efforts (Cooper et al. 2004a, 2004b, 2005):

- they launch products whose *main benefits* are really important to the customer or user, at a 4:1 ratio compared with poor performers;
- their products offer the customer *new and unique benefits* not available in competitive products, by a huge 8:1 ratio compared with poor performers;
- they deliver new products that offer *better value for money* to the customer or user, compared with competitors (three times more so);
- their new products are superior to competing products in terms of *meeting customers' and users' needs* (by a 4:1 ratio versus poor performers);
- they launch *better quality products* – however the customer or user measures quality – than poor performers, by a 2:1 ratio.

A point of distinction for Figure 32.1: benefits are what customers or users value and pay money for; product attributes, features, functionality and performance are the things that engineers, scientists and designers build into products. Often benefits and features are connected, but sometimes the designers get it wrong, so that added product features and performance do not yield additional benefits for customers or users.

Building in the Voice of the Customer (Market-driven and Customer-focused New Product Process) is Critical to Success

A thorough understanding of customers' or users' needs and wants, the competitive situation and the nature of the market is an essential component of new product success.

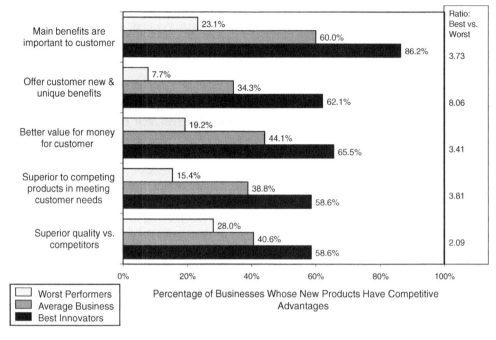

Sources: APQC 2002; Cooper 2001, 2004, 2011; Cooper et al. 2004a, 2004b, 2005; Cooper and Kleinschmidt 1987, 1990, 1994, 1995.

Figure 32.1   A unique, superior product is the top driver of performance results

This finding is supported in virtually every study of product success factors (Cooper 2004). Recurring themes include:

- needs recognition;
- understanding user needs;
- market need satisfaction;
- constant customer contact;
- strong market knowledge and market research;
- quality of execution of marketing activities;
- more spending on the front-end market-related activities.

Conversely, a failure to adopt a strong market focus in product innovation, an unwillingness to undertake the needed market assessments or to build in the voice of the customer (VoC) and leaving the customer out of product development spells disaster. Poor market research, inadequate market analysis, weak market studies, test markets, market launch and inadequate resources devoted to marketing activities are common weaknesses found in virtually every study of why new products fail (Griffin and Page 1993; Cooper 2001, 2004).

The best innovators are leaders when it comes to a strong market focus, as Figure 32.2 reveals (APQC 2002; Cooper 2001, 2004, 2011; Cooper et al. 2004a, 2004b, 2005; Cooper and Kleinschmidt 1987, 1990, 1994, 1995). They:

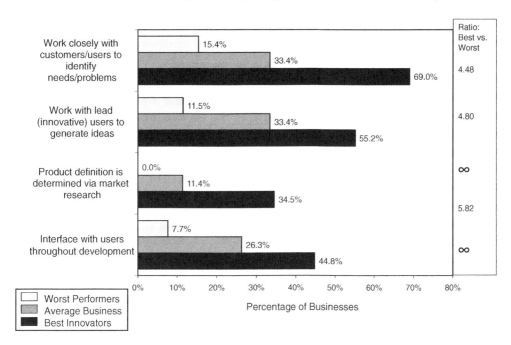

Sources: APQC 2002; Cooper 2001, 2004, 2011; Cooper et al. 2004a, 2004b, 2005; Cooper and Kleinschmidt 1987, 1990, 1994, 1995.

Figure 32.2   Voice of the customer & market insight strongly affects innovation performance results

- work closely with customers and users to identify needs, problems and 'points of pain', 4.5 times more so than poor performers;
- work with lead or innovative users who are 'ahead of the wave' to generate new product ideas (by a 5:1 ratio versus poor performers);
- determine their product definitions through market research; that is, VoC insights are major inputs to product definition (remarkably, *none* of the poor performing businesses do this, and such input is a practice of only 11 per cent of average businesses);
- interface with customers throughout the entire development process, not just at the beginning and end, by a 6:1 ratio compared with poor performers.

Doing the Homework and Front-end Loading the Project is Key to Success: Due Diligence Before Development Pays Off!

Homework or due diligence is critical to winning. Countless studies reveal that the steps that precede the actual design and development of the product make the difference between winning and losing. For example, one of Toyota's seven principles of innovation stipulates that projects be 'front-end loaded', that a higher proportion of work be shifted to the earlier stages of the development project (Morgan 2005). The best innovators are much more proficient when it comes to these activities in the fuzzy front end of projects; they do their homework (see Figure 32.3), including:

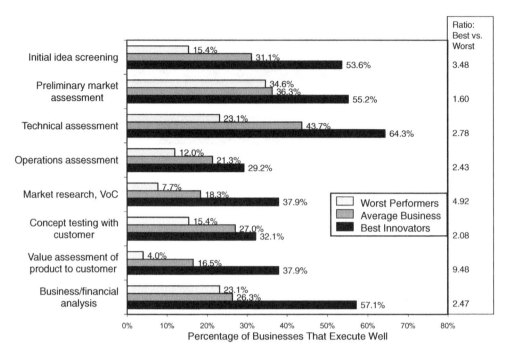

Sources: APQC 2002; Cooper 2001, 2004, 2011; Cooper et al. 2004a, 2004b, 2005; Cooper and Kleinschmidt 1987, 1990, 1994, 1995.

Figure 32.3 *Quality of execution in the fuzzy front end strongly affects innovation*
  success

- idea screening: the first decision to initiate the project;
- preliminary market assessment: a market overview of market size, potential, competitive situation and possible product acceptance;
- technical assessment: determining the technical risks and identifying probable technical solutions and routes;
- operations assessment: looking at sources of supply, manufacturing and operations issues;
- market research: VoC work to determine customers' or users' needs and requirements;
- concept testing: testing the product concept with the customer or user;
- value assessment: determining the value or economic worth of the product to the customer;
- business and financial analysis just before the decision to 'Go to Development' (i.e. building the business case).

Another issue is the balance within the homework stage. The best innovators strike an appropriate balance between market/business-oriented tasks and technological activities, whereas poor performers tend to push ahead on the technical side and just pay lip service to marketing and business issues in the early stages of the project. Figure 32.3 shows how much better the best innovators execute the homework activities, especially the early-stage marketing/business tasks. Surprisingly, most firms confess to serious weaknesses in the front-end or pre-development steps of their new product process. 'More homework means longer time to market' is a frequently voiced complaint. It is a valid concern, but experience has shown that homework pays for itself in reduced development times, as well as improved success rates:

1. Evidence points to a much higher likelihood of product failure if the homework is omitted. So the choice is between more work early on or much increased odds of failure.
2. Better project definition, the result of solid homework, speeds up the development process. One of the major causes of time slippage is poorly defined projects as they enter the development stage, leading to vague targets and moving goalposts.
3. Given the inevitable product design evolution that occurs during the life of a project, the time to make the majority of design changes is early: more homework upfront anticipates these changes and enables them to occur earlier in the process rather than later, when they are more problematic.

Sharp and Early Product and Project Definition and Avoiding Scope Creep and Unstable Specs mean Higher Success Rates and Faster Time to Market

How well the project and product are defined prior to entering development is a major success factor, with positive impacts on profitability and reduced time to market. Looking at the data in Figure 32.4, including how much better the best innovators get the product defined before embarking on the development stage (APQC 2002; Cooper 2001, 2004, 2011; Cooper et al. 2004a, 2004b, 2005; Cooper and Kleinschmidt 1987, 1990, 1994, 1995):

- the best innovators clearly *define the benefits* to be delivered to the customer (by a 4:1 ratio compared with poor performers);
- the *target market* (who will buy the product) is clear, and so is the positioning strategy, or how the product will be positioned in the customer's mind and versus competitors;
- the product *concept* is also well defined for what the product will be and do;
- the product definition is *stable* and does not keep changing as development proceeds;
- the product *features, attributes and specifications* are well defined.

In contrast, a failure to define the product and project scope before development begins is a major cause of both new product failure and serious delays in time to market. Although early and stable product definition is consistently cited as a key to success, businesses continue to perform poorly here, as Figure 32.4 shows. Terms such as 'unstable product specs' and 'project scope creep' describe far too many new product projects in success versus failure studies.

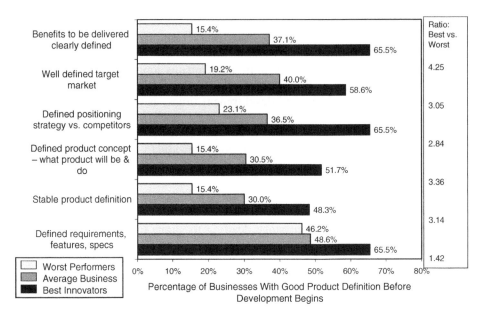

Sources: APQC 2002; Cooper 2001, 2004, 2011; Cooper et al. 2004a, 2004b, 2005; Cooper and Kleinschmidt 1987, 1990, 1994, 1995.

Figure 32.4   Sharp, stable and fact-based product definition before development begins is key to successful new products

Unless these five bulleted items are clearly defined, written down and agreed to by all parties prior to entering the development stage, the odds of failure increase by a factor of three:

1.   building a product definition step into the new product system forces more attention on front-end or pre-development activities;
2.   this definition serves as a communication tool and guide – an all-party agreement or 'buy in', so that each functional area has a clear and consistent definition of what the product and project are;
3.   this definition provides a clear set of objectives for the development stage of the project and for the technical team members: no moving goalposts and no fuzzy targets!

Achieving the ideal of a stable product definition is a challenge, though; even the best innovators struggle, as Figure 32.4 shows. Many markets are quite fluid and dynamic, and 'things change'. Thus the notion of the traditional '100 per cent design freeze' prior to development may not apply in some dynamic markets, such as IT products and software. Instead, the concept of agile or spiral development may be more appropriate (as discussed subsequently in this chapter) to deal with fluid markets, where some elements of the product's design remain 'variable' and 'to be decided' as the project proceeds through Development. However, the fluid nature of markets is not an excuse for omitting the front-end homework and at least striving for stability in product definition.

Successful Businesses Focus: Fewer Development Projects, Better Projects and the Right Mix of Projects by Adopting a Systematic Portfolio Management Method and Building Tough Go/Kill Decision Points into Idea-to-launch Systems

Most companies suffer from too many projects and not enough resources to mount an effective or timely effort for each. This scenario is the result of a lack of adequate project evaluation and prioritization (i.e. poor portfolio management), with negative results: first, scarce and valuable resources are wasted on mediocre or low-value projects. Second, truly deserving projects do not receive the resources they should. The result is that good projects are starved of resources and move at a crawl.

The desire to weed out bad projects, coupled with the need to focus limited resources on the best projects, means that tough Go/Kill and prioritization decisions are necessary. That is, *effective portfolio management* in the form of making the right development investment decisions must be an integral part of the idea-to-launch system. It results in a sharper focus, higher success rates and shorter times to market.

Yet project evaluations are consistently cited as weakly handled or non-existent: decisions involve the wrong people from the wrong functions (no functional alignment); no consistent criteria are used to screen or rank projects; or there is simply no will to kill projects at all as projects take on lives of their own. For example, only 31.1 per cent of businesses screen new product ideas properly, and only 26.3 per cent of firms undertake a proficient business and financial analysis as part of their business cases (Figure 32.3). Looking at the portfolio management practice results in Figure 32.5 (APQC 2002; Cooper 2001, 2004, 2011; Cooper et al. 2004a, 2004b, 2005; Cooper and Kleinschmidt 1987, 1990, 1994, 1995):

- only 21 per cent of firms have a *formal and systematic portfolio management system* in place to help decide which development investments to make;
- only 24 per cent have the right number of projects for the available resource, whereas 76 per cent have *too many projects* for their limited resources;
- only a quarter of businesses do a good job of *prioritizing* and ranking projects;
- only 21 per cent of firms' portfolios contain *high-value projects* to the corporation;
- only 19 per cent boast a *good balance* of projects; most firms have far too many small, insignificant developments.

By comparison, the best innovators do a much better job in project selection and portfolio management, though they too are far from perfect.

A critical problem is too many projects for the limited resources available, as in Figure 32.5. This gap stems from the reluctance to kill projects, resulting in no project priorities. Typically resources are removed from projects a little at a time (rather than making a tough kill decision), such that they end up being spread so thinly that all projects are set up for failure (Cooper and Edgett 2003).

Some companies thus redesign their idea-to-launch system to create a *funneling*

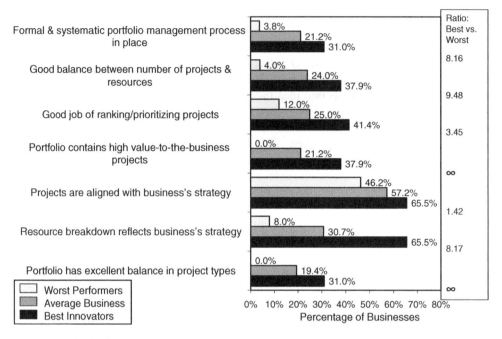

Sources: APQC 2002; Cooper 2001, 2004, 2011; Cooper et al. 2004a, 2004b, 2005; Cooper and Kleinschmidt 1987, 1990, 1994, 1995.

Figure 32.5 *To achieve optimum portfolios of the best projects and the right mix, an effective portfolio management system is essential*

process, which successively weeds out the poor projects; they have built in decision points in the form of *tough gates.* At gate reviews, senior management rigorously scrutinizes projects and makes Go or Kill and prioritization decisions. The use of visible Go/Kill criteria at gates improves decision effectiveness. Fortunately certain project characteristics have been identified that consistently separate winners from losers, which should be used as criteria in a scorecard format for project selection and prioritization (discussed subsequently in this chapter).

Project selection and picking winning new product projects is only part of the task, though. Another goal is selecting the right *mix and balance* of projects in the development portfolio, seeking strategic alignment in the portfolio and ensuring that the business's spending on development projects mirrors its strategic priorities. Figure 32.6 dramatically reveals that portfolio management and project mix really matter: the most successful innovating companies have a decidedly different development portfolio mix from the rest (Cooper 2005). Note that among the poor performers, 40 per cent of their portfolios consist of 'incremental product improvements and changes'. But for the best innovators, 65 per cent of their portfolios are dedicated to more innovative products: new-to-the-world, genuinely new and major revision products. Many businesses have thus moved to more formal portfolio management systems to help them allocate resources effectively and achieve the right mix and balance of development projects.

	Worst Performers	Average Business	Best Performers
Promotional Developments & Package Changes	12%	10%	6%
Incremental Product Improvements & Changes	40%	33%	28%
Major Product Revisions	19%	22%	25%
New-to-the-Business Products	20%	24%	24%
New-to-the-World Products	7%	10%	16%
	~45%	~55%	~65%

|——— 10-Point Steps ———|

Best performers focus more on innovative and game-changing projects

Source: Cooper 2005.

Figure 32.6   Breakdown of projects by project type: different portfolios for best versus worst performers in product innovation

A Well-conceived, Properly Executed Launch is Central to New Product Success, and a Solid Marketing Plan is at the Heart of Such a Launch

Not only must the product be superior, but its benefits must be communicated aggressively. A quality launch is strongly linked to new product profitability. Consider how the best innovators fare in Figure 32.7:

- they do the necessary market research to understand buyer or customer behavior and better craft the launch plan;
- they conduct a test market or a trial sale to validate the marketability of the new product and test elements of the market launch plan;
- they undertake a solid pre-launch business analysis;
- most important, they execute the launch proficiently, by a ratio of 3:1 compared with poor innovators.

A well-integrated, properly targeted launch does not occur by accident, however; it is the result of a fine-tuned marketing plan, properly backed and resourced, and proficiently executed. Marketing planning, or moving from marketing objectives to strategy and marketing programs, is a complex process and must be woven into the idea-to-launch system. For example, defining the target market and the development of a positioning strategy, one of the core steps in developing a marketing plan, is part of the

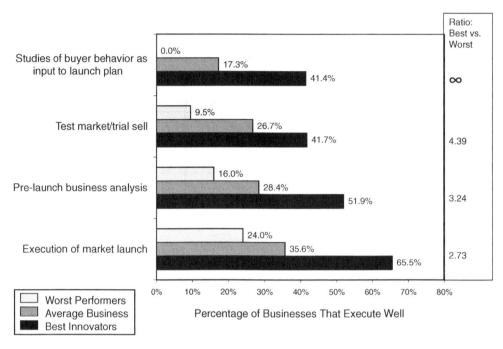

Sources: APQC 2002; Cooper 2001, 2004, 2011; Cooper et al. 2004a, 2004b, 2005; Cooper and Kleinschmidt 1987, 1990, 1994, 1995.

Figure 32.7   Market launch and related actions are important facets of the idea-to-launch process

product definition step, just before Development begins (Success Driver 4). Furthermore answers to many key questions, such as how customers buy, must come from market research investigations built into the idea-to-launch methodology (Figure 32.7). Finally each element of the launch plan, such as the sales force plan, has been crafted with the help of the pertinent functional area, ensuring a credible plan in which the resources are all in place. Indeed project teams in best practice companies develop a preliminary launch plan very early, even before Development begins, as part of their business case.

The Right Organizational Structure, Design and Teams Drive Product Innovation Success

Product innovation is very much a team effort. Do a post-mortem on any bungled new product project and invariably you will find each functional area doing its own piece of the project, with very little communication between players and functions (i.e. a fiefdom mentality) and no real commitment of individual players to the project. Many studies concur that the way the project team is organized and functions strongly influences project outcomes (APQC 2002; Cooper 2001, 2004, 2011; Cooper et al. 2004a, 2004b, 2005; Cooper and Kleinschmidt 1987, 1990, 1994, 1995).

The best innovators organize their new product project teams as shown in Figure 32.8.

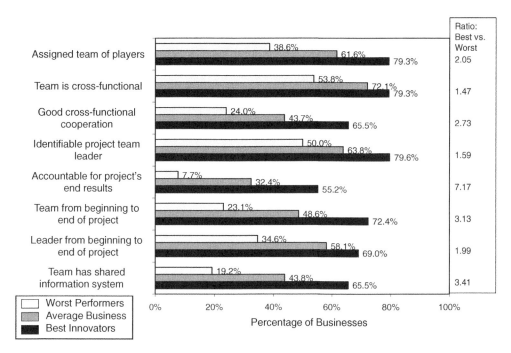

Source: APQC 2002; Cooper 2001, 2004, 2011; Cooper et al. 2004a, 2004b, 2005; Cooper and Kleinschmidt 1987, 1990, 1994, 1995.

Figure 32.8   The way development project teams are organized strongly affects innovation performance

First, there is a *clearly assigned team* of players for each significant development project, including the people who are part of the project and their time commitments specified. What is surprising is that this practice is not evident in almost any businesses today: only 61.6 per cent of businesses have clearly assigned project teams for innovation, and the best innovators outperform the worst by 2:1. Most important, this defined project team should be a *cross-functional team*, with members from technical, sales, marketing, operations and other departments – a practice now embraced by a majority of businesses. Cross-functional cooperation on the team is also critical, avoiding time and effort wasted on politics, conflicts or interdepartmental prejudices. Ensuring harmony and cooperation among team members is normally the role of the project leader, but in some firms, training in how to be a good team player is provided. Surprisingly this tactic is a moderately weak aspect of most businesses' new product efforts, with only 43.7 per cent of businesses reporting good cross-functional cooperation within project teams.

Second, there is a clearly *identified team leader* in the best innovator firms, a person in charge and responsible for driving the project. The team leader's role is similar to that of the leader of a business start-up and entrepreneurial enterprise, such that the leader not only leads the team but also promotes the project, seeks resources and handles external interfaces, especially with senior management.

Third, *project team accountability* is key to innovation success, as Figure 32.8 shows.

That is, when a project leader and team present a business case to senior management – such as sales projections, profit estimates or the expected launch date – and the project is approved, these 'projections' become commitments (Cooper and Mills 2005). The concept of accountability makes sense, yet only a third of businesses actually apply this principle, even as the best innovators embrace team accountability by a 7:1 ratio. The lack of accountability and team continuity leads to many negative results: over-estimated initial projections and a significant failure to follow through to achieve the promised results. Another best practice is that the project team and the project leader *remain on the project* from beginning to end, not just for a single phase.

Fourth, the final best practice in Figure 32.8 is a *centrally shared information system* for project team members. This centralized communication and IT system permits sharing of project information and allows several team members to work concurrently on the same document, even across functions, locations or countries.

INTEGRATING SUCCESS DRIVERS INTO AN OPERATIONAL MODEL

The next step is to take these and other best practices and success drivers and incorporate them into a model, methodology or 'playbook' for driving new products to market. That's how Stage-Gate® was born. It was originally developed from academic research on B2B firms that modeled what the winners, both companies and project teams, do to excel (Cooper 1990). Yet too many projects and businesses miss the mark: key steps and activities missing, poor organizational design and leadership, inadequate quality of execution, lack of data integrity and timelines missed. So project teams need help in the form of a playbook based on what winning teams do. Stage-Gate is simply that playbook. Thus a Stage-Gate system is a conceptual and operational map for moving new product projects from idea to launch and beyond, and a blueprint for managing the new product development process to improve effectiveness and efficiency.

In its simplest form Stage-Gate consists of a series of stages, where the project team undertakes the work, obtains the needed information and does the subsequent data integration and analysis, followed by gates at which Go/Kill decisions are made to continue to invest in the development project or cut the losses and get out of a bad project. A typical Stage-Gate system designed for major product developments is shown in Figure 32.9 (Cooper 2001). The process begins with an ideation stage, called Discovery, and ends with the Post-Launch review. Note that there are three front-end stages (Discovery plus two homework stages) before serious financial commitments are made at the Go-to-Development gate.

Stages

The idea-to-launch process can be visualized as a series of stages, with each stage comprising a set of required or recommended activities needed to progress the project to the next gate. The stages are prescriptive and based on the success drivers and best practices observed in winning teams and projects. Each stage is designed to gather information

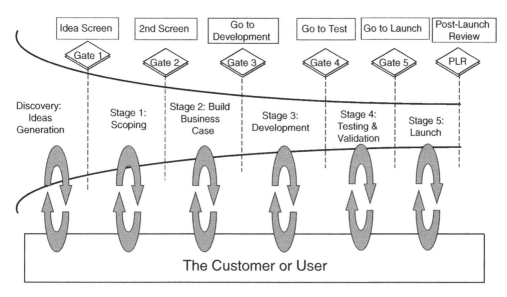

Sources: Cooper 2001, 2011.

Figure 32.9 *Overview of a typical Stage-Gate® system for major new product developments*

to reduce key project uncertainties and risks; the information requirements thus define the purpose of each of the stages. The activities within stages are undertaken in parallel and by a team of people from different functional areas within the firm; tasks within each stage are done concurrently. Each stage is cross-functional, so there is no 'R&D stage' or 'Marketing stage' but rather, every stage includes marketing, R&D, operations, sales and engineering. No department 'owns' any one stage. Each subsequent stage typically costs more than the preceding one. The process thus is an incremental commitment and a series of increasing bets. But with each step and increase in project cost, the uncertainties are driven down, so risk is well managed. The stages, as shown in Figure 32.9, are:

0. *Discovery*: Pre-work designed to discover opportunities and generate new product ideas.
1. *Scoping*: A quick, preliminary investigation and scoping of the project. This stage provides inexpensive information based largely on desk research to narrow the field of projects before Stage 2.
2. *Build the Business Case*: A much more detailed investigation involving primary research, both market and technical, that produces a business case. This stage is when the bulk of the vital homework is done and most market studies are conducted. It results in a business case that includes the product definition, the project justification and a project 'go-forward' plan.
3. *Development*: The actual detailed design and development of the new product, along with some product testing work. The deliverable at the end of Stage 3 is an alpha- or

lab-tested product. Full operations (production) and market launch plans are also developed in this potentially lengthy stage.

4. *Testing and Validation*: Tests or trials in the marketplace, lab and plant verify and validate the proposed new product, its marketing and operations through field trials or beta tests, test markets or trial selling and operations trials.

5. *Launch*: Commercialization is the beginning of full operations, marketing and selling. The market launch, operations and post-launch monitoring plans thus are executed.

At first glance, this overview seems to portray the stages as relatively simple steps in a logical process. Yet this model is only a high-level view of a generic process: a *conceptual* model. In a real organization's process, the *operational* model provides the details of each stage, including a detailed list of activities within a stage, the how-to aspects of each activity, best practices and even required deliverables from each stage. In short the drill-down provides a detailed and operational playbook for the project team – everything it needs to know and do to complete that stage of the process and project.

The high-level conceptual model in Figure 32.9 is also fairly domain-neutral. Although originally based on B2B firms, Stage-Gate has been adopted by both B2B and B2C firms, by service and physical product companies and even by governments and public organizations, including the US Department of Energy and Department of Defense (Molitoris 2010). But the operational model gets customized and adapted for each organization. Thus the details of the model vary by type of business (B2B versus B2C), by industry (process versus non-process industries) and even by organization within a particular industry.

For example, in the B2B version of Stage-Gate, Stage 3, Development, where detailed product design and physical development takes place, is industry specific (e.g. the chemical industry employs lab work, lab experiments and lab-based pilot plants in Stage 3; for engineered products and equipment firms, Stage 3 is largely computer-based design work and rapid prototyping). Similarly Stage 4, Testing and Validation, employs different testing methodologies (again largely depending on the industry, such as beta tests for IT products versus field trials for engineered equipment). Even in Stage 2, Build the Business Case, though the components of a business case may seem fairly domain neutral – product definition, financial justification and a 'go forward' plan – what constitutes these components (e.g. product definition) is industry specific.

Gates

Following each stage is a gate, or a Go/Kill decision point, as in Figure 32.9. Gates serve as quality control check points, Go/Kill and prioritization decision points and points for agreeing on the path forward and resources for the next stage of the project. The structure of each gate is similar; they consist of the following:

- *Deliverables*, or what the project leader and team bring to the gate (e.g. results of a set of completed activities), which are visible and based on a standard menu for each gate.

- *Criteria* by which the project will be judged by gatekeepers (senior management). *Must meet criteria* or knock-out questions (checklist) weed out misfit projects quickly. *Should meet criteria* get scored and added (often with a point-count system) to prioritize projects.
- *Outputs*, which include the decision (Go, Kill, Hold, Recycle), an approved action plan for the next stage, resources committed and a set of deliverables and date for the next gate.

NEXGEN STAGE-GATE: AN ADAPTIVE, FLEXIBLE, SCALABLE SYSTEM

Stage-Gate has evolved significantly since it was first introduced in the late 1980s. Indeed, some companies are working on their third-generation versions of their idea-to-launch methodologies. This section of the chapter describes some approaches that leading B2B firms have built in to improve new product productivity and to deal with the quickening pace of change as they move to their next generation Stage-Gate systems.

Not Linear but Spiral Development

Project teams are often guilty of charging into development with a product definition based on information that was right at the time, or thought to be right. But it wasn't, or customer requirements changed, or a new competitive product has been introduced. And when the product is finally developed and then market-tested or moved into full market launch (Stages 4 or 5 in Figure 32.9), the team discovers that the product is not quite right for the market.

A traditional linear approach means that the project team must then recycle back to the Development stage and make the necessary changes to the product and its design. In contrast smart project teams practice spiral or agile development and adapt and adjust their project in real time (Cooper 2006a, 2008a, 2008b). Similar to linear teams, they do their front-end homework (VoC, competitive analysis, concept testing) and define the product using the currently best available information. But here's the difference: very quickly, an adaptive-spiral team creates a first version of the product (often virtual) and tests it with the customer, seeking immediate feedback, as in Figure 32.10. Customers do not know what they are looking for until they see it, so the project team puts something in front of the customer as early as possible to confirm the design. The team uses this feedback to produce the next, more complete version of the product, in the form of a working model or *protocept*. These fast-paced teams remove unnecessary rework and quickly move to the finalized product by undertaking a series of iterative steps or loops: build, test, obtain feedback, revise. By the time the product is ready for customer trials or tests in Stage 4 (Figure 32.9), the customer has already confirmed the product at least several times. The loops are deliberately built into the entire idea-to-launch process, from Scoping through Development and into Testing (they are not reactive, knee-jerk actions), and when sketched on a flow diagram, they appear as spirals, as in Figure 32.10.

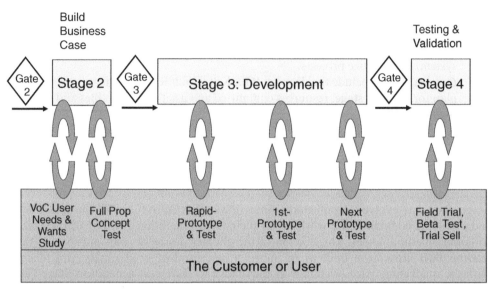

Source: Cooper and Edgett 2005.

Figure 32.10   *Spiral development: a series of 'build-test-feedback-revise' iterations gets*
the product right without wasted time

A Flexible Process, not a Rigid one

Flexibility is built into the gates. For example decision options at each gate include 'go forward' or 'cycle back' to the previous stage. Thus there are many routes through the model, including multiple iterations between stages. Some firms have added a 'conditional Go' option at gates to accelerate projects, whereby the project is approved, conditional on certain future events or information occurring or being true.

Another facet of flexibility is simultaneous or concurrent execution, such that key activities and even entire stages overlap, rather than waiting for perfect information before moving forward. It is acceptable to move activities from one stage to an earlier one and, in effect, overlap stages. At Toyota, for example, the rule is to synchronize processes for simultaneous execution (Morgan 2005). Effective concurrent execution requires that each subsequent activity maximizes the utility of the stable information available from the previous activity as it becomes available. Development teams do not wait for perfect information; they do the most they can with the portion of the data they have that is not likely to change.

Simultaneous execution usually adds risk to a project. For example the decision to purchase production equipment before field trials are completed in order to reduce long order lead times may be a good application of simultaneous execution. But it is risky, because the project may be cancelled after dedicated production equipment has been purchased. Thus the cost of delay must be weighed against the cost and probability of being wrong.

Stage-Gate is also a prescriptive but flexible guide, in that the model only suggests best practices, recommended activities and deliverables. Few activities and deliverables are mandatory. The project team has much discretion over which activities to execute and which not to do. For example in most firms, the project team presents its proposed go-forward plan at each gate, including what needs to be done to make the project a success. The gatekeepers commit the necessary resources and, in so doing, approve the plan. But it is the project team's plan that gets approved, not simply a mechanistic implementation of a standardized process.

Scaled to Suit Different Risk Levels

Stage-Gate has become a scalable process, to suit very different types and risk levels of projects: from very risky and complex platforms or technology developments to low-risk product extensions and modifications, and even to rather simple sales force requests (Cooper 2006a; Cooper and Edgett 2005).

When first implemented, there was only one version of Stage-Gate, typically a five-stage, five-gate model to handle larger, more complex development projects, as in Figure 32.9. But some projects seemed too small to put through the full five-stage model, and thus project teams circumvented it. The problem was that these smaller projects – such as line extensions, modifications or sales force requests – though individually small, collectively consumed the bulk of development resources. Thus a contradictory situation emerged, whereby projects that represented the majority of development resources fell outside the system.

Each project, large and small, has risk, consumes resources and must be managed; however, not all need to go through the full five-stage process. The process has thus morphed into multiple versions to fit business needs and accelerate projects. Figure 32.11 shows some examples: Stage-Gate® XPress for projects of moderate risk, such as improvements, modifications and extensions, or Stage-Gate® Lite for very small projects, such as simple sales force requests.

Multiple Versions to Handle Platform and Technology Development Projects

In addition Stage-Gate is no longer limited to new product projects (Ajamian and Koen 2002; Koen 2003). Other types of projects, including platform developments, process developments or exploratory research projects, compete for similar resources, need to be managed and thus merit their own version of a stage-and-gate process. For example, ExxonMobil Chemical has designed a three-stage, three-gate version of its Stage-Gate process to handle upstream research projects (Cohen et al. 1998); numerous other organizations (Timex, Lennox, Sandia Labs, Bosche, Donaldson) have adopted unique gating systems to handle fundamental research, technology development or platform projects (Cooper 2006b).

A Leaner System with No Waste

Over time, most companies' product development processes have become too bulky, cumbersome or bureaucratic. Thus smart companies have borrowed the

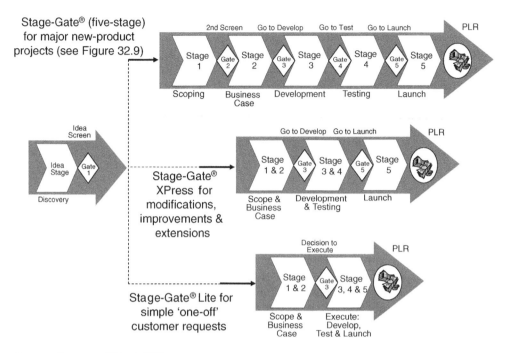

Source: Cooper and Edgett 2005.

Figure 32.11   Stage-Gate® is scalable to suit different risk levels of projects

concept of *value stream analysis* from lean manufacturing and applied it to their new product process to remove waste and inefficiency in their next-generation Stage-Gate system.

A value stream is simply the connection of all the process steps with the goal of maximizing customer value (Fiore 2005). In product development, a value stream represents the linkage of all value-added and non-value-added activities associated with the creation of a new product. The value stream map portrays the value stream or product development process, critical for identifying both value-added and non-value-added activities, which makes it an essential tool for improving the innovation process.

In employing value stream analysis, a taskforce creates a map of the value stream (i.e. the firm's current idea-to-launch process) for typical development projects. All the stages, decision points and key activities are mapped, with typical time ranges for each activity and decision. Often it becomes clear that there is a huge difference between the way the process is supposed to work and the way it works in reality.

Once the value stream is mapped, the taskforce dissects the innovation process, examining all procedures, required deliverables, documents and templates, committees and decision processes, looking for time wasters. Once time wasters and non-value-added activities are spotted, the taskforce works to remove them. The result invariably is a much more streamlined, less bulky idea-to-launch system.

Effective Governance

Gates with teeth

Perhaps the greatest challenge that users of stage-and-gate processes face is making the gates work well: as go the gates, so goes the process! In a robust gating system, poor projects are spotted early and killed, and projects in trouble are detected and sent back for rework or redirection on course. But as quality control checkpoints, the gates are not effective in too many companies. Gates are rated one of the weakest areas in product development, with only 33 per cent of firms claiming they have tough, rigorous gates throughout the idea-to-launch process (Cooper et al. 2004b).

A recurring problem is that gates are either non-existent or lack teeth (Jenner 2007): once underway, projects are rarely killed. In poorly managed firms, after the initial Go decision, the gates amount to little more than a project update meeting or a milestone checkpoint. Thus instead of the well-defined funnel, firms end up with a tunnel, where everything that enters comes out the other end, good and bad. Yet management is deluded into believing that it has a functioning gating process.

Gates are not merely project review meetings or milestone checks. They must have teeth and involve Go/Kill, resource allocation and investment decisions. Gates are where senior management meet to decide whether the company should continue to invest in the project, based on the latest information, or to cut losses and get out of a bad project (Cooper 2009a). A significant percentage of projects should be killed – in a typical company, well more than half – as they move through the first three gates in Figure 32.9.

Resource commitment meetings

Approval decisions are meaningless unless resources are committed. Too often, the gate review meeting produces a Go decision, without any resources committed. That is, projects get approved, but resources are not, which means a hollow Go decision that leads to too many projects in the development pipeline. There is no limit to the number of projects that can be approved as long as no resources are ever committed!

In an effective gating system, the project leader and team must leave the gate meeting with the resources they need to advance their project. Gates must be a resource commitment meeting, where a Go decision means the project leader and team receive a commitment of resources for their project. In addition to enabling the team to move its project ahead in a timely fashion, specified resource commitments at gates place a limit on the number of projects that can be approved, so the pipeline does not get overloaded.

Leaner and simpler gates

Some of the information that gating systems demand may be interesting. Yet often much of what is delivered to gates is not essential to the gate decision. Detailed explanations of how the market research was done or sketches of what a new molecule looks like add no value to the decision. The emphasis in lean gates is making expectations clear to project teams and leaders. They are not required to provide an 'information dump' to gatekeepers (Belair 2007). The key principles state:

- information only has a value to the extent it improves a decision;
- deliverables to a gate should provide decision-makers with only that information they need to make an effective and same-day decision.

Page restrictions, templates with text and field limits and solid guides are tactics favored by many progressive firms.

Built-in Portfolio Management

Effective portfolio management for making the right investment decisions is an integral part of a Stage-Gate system. Gates are designed for Go/Kill and resource allocation decisions; portfolio management provides a broader view of the totality of active projects. Thus gates provide an evaluation of individual projects in depth and one at a time, and gatekeepers make investment decisions from the beginning to the end of the project (Gates 1–5 in Figure 32.9). In contrast, portfolio reviews are holistic and consider the entire set of projects, obviously with less depth per project than gates. Portfolio reviews take place periodically; two to four times per year is the norm (Edgett 2007). They deal with issues such as achieving the right mix and balance of projects in the portfolio, project prioritization and aligning the portfolio with the business's strategy.

Most firms rely on traditional financial criteria, such as net present value (NPV), internal rate of return (IRR) or the payback period to rate and rank order projects. But there are other methods to improve portfolio management within Stage-Gate that also prove effective (Cooper and Edgett 2006; Cooper et al. 1999, 2002, 2004b).

Strategic buckets to achieve the right balance and mix of projects

Strategic buckets require senior management to make a priori strategic choices about how they wish to spend their development resources. The method is based on the premise that the strategy becomes real when the firm starts spending money. In using strategic buckets, strategic resource split decisions are made by senior management across project types (e.g. new products, improvements, cost reductions, technology developments), by market or business areas, by technologies (base, pacing, embryonic) or by geographies. After these splits are strategically decided at the beginning of each year, projects and resources are tracked. Pie charts reveal the actual split in resources (year to date) versus the target split, according to the strategic choices. These pie charts, reviewed during portfolio reviews, ensure that resource allocation mirrors the strategic priorities of the business. This method has proven an effective way to ensure that the right balance and mix of projects is achieved in the development pipeline; for example, to ensure that the pipeline is not overloaded with small, short-term and low-risk projects.

Scorecards to make better Go/Kill and prioritization decisions

Scorecards are based on the premise that qualitative criteria or factors are often better predictors of success than financial projections. (It is not that the financial models are wrong; rather, the data input are notoriously inaccurate, especially early in the development project when the difficult Go/Kill decisions must be made.) In using a scorecard approach, the business develops a list of approximately six to eight key criteria that are known predictors of success (an example for Gate 3 is in Box 32.1). Projects are scored

BOX 32.1   A BEST PRACTICES GATE 3 SCORECARD FOR NEW PRODUCT PROJECT SELECTION

Factor 1: Strategic Fit & Importance

- Alignment of project with our business's strategy
- Importance of project to the strategy
- Impact on the business

Factor 2: Product & Competitive Advantage

- Differentiated product in eyes of customer/user
- Product delivers unique customer (or user) benefits
- Product offers customer (or user) excellent value for money (compelling value proposition)
- Positive customer/user feedback on product concept (concept test results in Stage 2)

Factor 3: Market Attractiveness

- Market size
- Market growth & future potential
- Margins earned by competitors in this market
- Competitiveness – how intense & tough the competition is (negative item)

Factor 4: Core Competencies Leverage

- Project leverages our core competencies & strengths in:
    - Technology (design, development, IP)
    - Production or operations
    - Marketing (reputation, brand, communications)
    - Distribution & sales force

Factor 5: Technical Feasibility

- Size of technical gap (straightforward to do)
- Technical complexity (few barriers, solution envisioned)
- Familiar technology to our business
- Our technical track record on these types of projects
- Technical results to date (proof of concept in Stage 2)

Factor 6: Financial Reward versus Risk

- Size of financial opportunity
- Financial return (NPV, IRR, payback period)
- Productivity Index
- Certainty of financial estimates
- Level of risk & ability to address risks

Notes
- New-product projects are scored by the gatekeepers at the gate meeting, using all *six factors*, listed on a scorecard (0–10 scales).
- The scores are tallied and displayed electronically for discussion.
- The Project Attractiveness Score is the weighted or unweighted sum of the six factor scores, subtracted from 100.
- A score of 60–65 out of 100 is usually required for a Go decision.

Source: Adapted from Cooper and Edgett 2006.

---

on these criteria by senior management at the gate meetings. The total score becomes a key input into the Go/Kill gate decision and, along with other factors, helps prioritize projects at portfolio review meetings. Different scorecards and criteria can be used for different types of projects.

Productivity Index to help prioritize projects
This useful extension of the NPV is employed in portfolio reviews to prioritize projects when resources are constrained. The Productivity Index is a financial approach based on the theory of constraints: to maximize the value of a development portfolio subject to a constraining resource, take the variable to be maximized (e.g. NPV) and divide it by the constraining resource (e.g. person-days or costs) that is required to complete the project:

Productivity Index (PI) = Forecasted NPV/Person-Days to Complete Project.

OR

PI = Forecasted NPV/Cost to Complete Project.

The PI is used to rank projects until out of resources in that particular bucket. Projects at the top of the list are Go projects, receive resources and are accelerated to market. Projects beyond the resource limit are placed on hold or killed. The method maximizes the value of the development portfolio yet stays within existing resource limits.

Built-in Continuous Improvement

Many next-generation Stage-Gate systems build in a tough Post-Launch Review to instill accountability for results and foster a culture of continuous improvement. Continuous improvement is one of the main tenets of lean manufacturing and lends itself readily to applications to product innovation. Continuous improvement in product development has three major elements (Cooper 2006a; Cooper and Edgett 2008):

1. *Performance metrics in place* to measure how well a specific new product project performs. Were the new product's profits on target? Was it launched on time?
2. *Establishing team accountability for results*, with all members of the project team fully responsible for performance results when measured against these metrics.
3. *Building in learning and improvement*, such that when the project team misses the targets, management focuses on fixing the cause rather than putting a bandage on the symptom or, even worse, punishing the team.

There are three benefits of this approach. First, estimates of sales, profits and time to market are much more realistic when project teams are held accountable for them. (Note that the estimates come from the project team, typically delivered at Gate 2 or 3 in Figure 32.9.) Second, with clear objectives, the project team can focus and work diligently to achieve them. Expectations are clear (Cooper and Mills 2005). Third, if the team misses the target, causes are sought and improvements to the process made to prevent a recurrence of the cause, which ensures closed loop feedback and learning (Ledford 2006).

An 'Open System'

Stage-Gate now accommodates *open innovation* and handles the flow of ideas, intellectual property, technology and even totally developed products into the company from external sources, as well as the flow outward (Chesbrough 2003). Companies such as Kimberly Clark, General Electric and Air Products & Chemicals have modified their Stage-Gate processes to build in the necessary flexibility, capability and systems and support to enable this network of partners, alliances and outsourced vendors from idea generation through launch.

Innovation achieved by partnering with external firms and people has been around for decades in the form of joint ventures, venture groups, licensing arrangements and even venture nurturing. Open innovation is a broader version that includes not only these traditional partnering models but all types of collaborative or partnering activities, and with a wider range of partners than in the past.

In the traditional or closed innovation model, inputs at project initiation come from internal and some external sources, such as customer inputs, marketplace ideas, market information or strategic planning inputs. Then the process becomes very internal and closed: the R&D group proceeds with the task of inventing, evolving and perfecting technologies and products, often for immediate deployment, though sometimes for use at a later date (Docherty 2006). In contrast, with open innovation, companies look inside-out and outside-in, across all aspects of the innovation process, including ideation, development and commercialization. Some companies have thus adapted their Stage-Gate models to include open innovation, as in Figure 32.12 (Grönlund et al. 2010). Adaptations include the following (Cooper and Edgett 2005, 2007):

- *Ideation or discovery stage*: Not only do companies look externally for customer problems to be solved or unmet needs to be satisfied, but they solicit inventors, start-ups, small entrepreneurial firms, partners and other sources of available technologies that can be used in internal or joint developments.

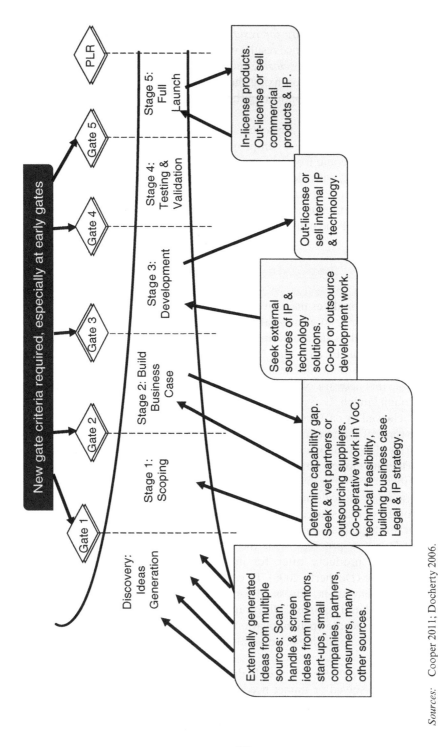

New gate criteria required, especially at early gates

Gate 1 — Gate 2 — Gate 3 — Gate 4 — Gate 5 — PLR

Discovery: Ideas Generation

Stage 1: Scoping

Stage 2: Build Business Case

Stage 3: Development

Stage 4: Testing & Validation

Stage 5: Full Launch

Externally generated ideas from multiple sources: Scan, handle & screen ideas from inventors, start-ups, small companies, partners, consumers, many other sources.

Determine capability gap. Seek & vet partners or outsourcing suppliers. Co-operative work in VoC, technical feasibility, building business case. Legal & IP strategy.

Seek external sources of IP & technology solutions. Co-op or outsource development work.

Out-license or sell internal IP & technology.

In-license products. Out-license or sell commercial products & IP.

Sources: Cooper 2011; Docherty 2006.

Figure 32.12 Open innovation Stage-Gate features external interfaces (inbound and outbound) at multiple points in the process

620

- *Development stage*: Established companies seek help in solving technology problems or undertaking parts of the physical development work from scientists and engineers external to the corporation, or they acquire external innovations that already have been productized. They also out-license internally developed intellectual property that is not being utilized.
- *Launch or commercialization stage*: Companies sell or out-license already-developed products if more value can be realized elsewhere; they in-license and acquire already-commercialized products that provide immediate sources of new growth.

Automating Stage-Gate

Progressive companies recognize that automation greatly increases the effectiveness of their new product systems. The new software designed to support stage-and-gate methodologies makes it easier for everyone, from project leaders to executives, to use the process, which enhances its adoption. Another benefit is information management: the key participants have access to effective displays of relevant information. Project teams see what they need to do to advance their project and cooperate globally with other team members on vital tasks. Executives have the information to make Go/Kill decisions and stay on top of the portfolio of projects.[4]

NEW RESEARCH NEEDED

Stage-Gate was conceived from academic research, which began shortly after I completed my doctoral degree. Research in and about Stage-Gate has become my career's work, resulting in well over 150 articles in academic journals, by me and my colleagues. Despite its academic roots, though, Stage-Gate has become the most widely used system for driving new products to market by industry.

Over the years, our approach for designing research studies has been to begin with a practitioner problem or question, then to craft a methodologically sound study that served both academic and practitioner communities. In this vein, here are some potential research questions relevant to both audiences regarding how to get new products to market:

1. What are the main drivers of new product success (or, in more academic terms, what discriminates successful new product developments from unsuccessful developments)? The unit of analysis could be either the new product project or the entire business unit, division or company.
2. What are the different types of idea-to-launch methodologies that firms employ, beyond those depicted in Figures 32.9, 32.11 and 32.12? What are their impacts, both negative and positive? And what have businesses done to overcome deficiencies?
3. Does a formal idea-to-launch process stifle creativity and innovation? How have progressive companies overcome this potential problem? Have new versions of stage-and-gate systems enhanced fundamental research, technology developments,

creative innovations and higher risk projects (e.g. Ajamian and Koen 2002; Koen 2003)?

4. What new best practices are businesses adopting to accelerate development projects and/or improve productivity in product development? What are their respective impacts?

5. How do companies select new product projects (or undertake portfolio management)? Which selection methods give the best results, when 'results' are measured multidimensionally?

6. Does 'open innovation' really work, or is it all hype? What have been the impacts of open innovation? The costs? How has the idea-to-launch system been tailored to accommodate open innovation (e.g. Grönlund et al. 2010)?

7. Can 'lean methodology', so popular in a manufacturing context, be applied to streamline the product innovation process to remove waste and non-value-added work? How can firms achieve continuous improvement in product innovation?

NOTES

1. Stage-Gate is a registered trademark of the Product Development Institute Inc. This chapter draws from several articles by the author. See Cooper (2008a, 2008b, 2009a, 2009b).
2. Another body of research looks at success factors at the business level and identifies a somewhat different set of success drivers (e.g. Cooper 2004).
3. 'Best innovators' are the top 20 per cent of firms in terms of new product results, when measured on ten performance metrics: new product profitability, meeting sales and profit objectives, percentage of sales from new products, on-time performance and so on (Cooper et al. 2004a).
4. Multiple software products have been certified for use with Stage-Gate. See http://www.stage-gate.com.

REFERENCES

Adams, Marjorie and Doug Boike (2004a), 'PDMA Foundation CPAS Study Reveals New Trends', *Visions*, **28** (July), 26–9.

Adams, Marjorie and Doug Boike (2004b), *The PDMA Foundation's 2004 Comparative Performance Assessment Study (CPAS)*, Chicago, IL: Product Development and Management Association.

Ajamian, Greg and Peter A. Koen (2002), 'Technology Stage Gate: a structured process for managing high risk, new technology projects', in Paul Beliveau, Abbie Griffin, and Stephen Somermeyer (eds), *The PDMA Toolbox for New Product Development*, New York: John Wiley & Sons, pp. 267–95.

American Productivity and Quality Center (APQC) (2002), *New Product Development Best Practices Study: What Distinguishes the Top Performers*, Houston, TX: American Productivity and Quality Center.

Belair, Georgette (2007), 'Beyond gates: building the right NPD organization', *Proceedings, First International Stage-Gate Conference*, St Petersburg Beach, FL, available at http://www.stage-gate.com.

Chesbrough, Henry (2003), *Open Innovation: The New Imperative for Creating and Profiting from Technology*, Cambridge, MA: Harvard Business School Press.

Cohen, Lorraine Y., Paul W. Kamienski and Ramon L. Espino (1998), 'Gate system focuses industrial basic research', *Research-Technology Management*, **41** (July–August), 34–7.

Cooper, Robert G. (1990), 'Stage-Gate systems: a new tool for managing new products', *Business Horizons*, **33** (May–June), 44–54.

Cooper, Robert G. (2001), *Winning at New Products: Accelerating the Process from Idea to Launch*, 3rd edn, Reading, MA: Perseus Books.

Cooper, Robert G. (2004), 'New products: what separates the winners from the losers', in *The PDMA Handbook of New Product Development*, 2nd edn, New York: John Wiley & Sons, pp. 3–18.

Cooper, Robert G. (2005), 'Your NPD portfolio may be harmful to your business's health', *Visions*, **29** (April), 22–6.

Cooper, Robert G. (2006a), 'Formula for success', *Marketing Management Magazine*, (March–April), 21–4.

Cooper, Robert G. (2006b), 'Managing technology development projects – different than traditional development projects', *Research-Technology Management*, **49** (November–December), 23–31.

Cooper, Robert G. (2008a), 'The Stage-Gate idea-to-launch process – update, what's new and NexGen systems', *Journal of Product Innovation Management*, **25** (May), 213–32.

Cooper, Robert G. (2008b), 'NexGen Stage-Gate® – what leading companies are doing to re-invent their NPD processes', *Visions*, **32** (September), 6–10.

Cooper, Robert G. (2009a), 'Effective gating: make product innovation more productive by using gates with teeth', *Marketing Management Magazine*, (March–April), 12–17.

Cooper, Robert G. (2009b), 'How companies are re-inventing their idea-to-launch methodologies', *Research-Technology Management*, **52** (March–April), 47–57.

Cooper, Robert G. (2011), *Winning at New Products: Creating Value through Innovation*, 4th edn, New York: Basic Books.

Cooper, Robert G. and Scott J. Edgett (2003), 'Overcoming the crunch in resources for new product development', *Research-Technology Management*, **46** (May–June), 48–58.

Cooper, Robert G. and Scott J. Edgett (2005), *Lean, Rapid and Profitable New Product Development*, Ancaster, ON: Product Development Institute, available at http://www.stage-gate.com.

Cooper, Robert G. and Scott J. Edgett (2006), 'Ten ways to make better portfolio and project selection decisions', *Visions*, **30** (June), 11–15.

Cooper, Robert G. and Scott J. Edgett (2007), *Generating Breakthrough New Product Ideas: Feeding the Innovation Funnel*, Ancaster, ON: Product Development Institute, available at http://www.stage-gate.com.

Cooper, Robert G. and Scott J. Edgett (2008), 'Maximizing productivity in product innovation', *Research Technology Management*, **51** (March–April), 47–58.

Cooper, Robert G. and Elko J. Kleinschmidt (1987), 'What makes a new product a winner: success factors at the project level', *R&D Management*, **17** (July), 175–89.

Cooper, Robert G. and Elko J. Kleinschmidt (1990), *New Products: The Key Factors in Success*, Chicago, IL: American Marketing Association.

Cooper, Robert G. and Elko J. Kleinschmidt (1994), 'Determinants of timeliness in new product development', *Journal of Product Innovation Management*, **11** (November), 381–96.

Cooper, Robert G. and Elko J. Kleinschmidt (1995), 'New product performance: keys to success, profitability and cycle time reduction', *Journal of Marketing Management*, **11**, 315–37.

Cooper, Robert G. and M. Mills (2005), 'Succeeding at new products the P&G way: a key element is using the "innovation diamond"', *Visions*, **29** (October), 9–13.

Cooper, Robert G., Scott J. Edgett and Elko J. Kleinschmidt (1999), 'New product portfolio management: practices and performance', *Journal of Product Innovation Management*, **16** (July), 333–51.

Cooper, Robert G., Scott J. Edgett and Elko J. Kleinschmidt (2002), *Portfolio Management for New Products*, 2nd edn, New York: Perseus Publishing.

Cooper, Robert G., Scott J. Edgett and Elko J. Kleinschmidt (2004a), 'Benchmarking best NPD practices – Part 1: culture, climate, teams and senior management's role', *Research-Technology Management*, **47** (January–February), 31–43.

Cooper, Robert G., Scott J. Edgett and Elko J. Kleinschmidt (2004b), 'Benchmarking best NPD practices – part 2: strategy, resources and portfolio management practices', *Research-Technology Management*, **47** (May–June), 50–60.

Cooper, Robert G., Scott J. Edgett and Elko J. Kleinschmidt (2005), 'Benchmarking best NPD practices – part 3: the NPD process & decisive idea-to-launch activities', *Research-Technology Management*, **47** (January–February), 43–55.

Docherty, Michael (2006), 'Primer on "open innovation": principles and practice', *Visions*, **30** (April), 13–15.

Edgett, Scott J. (2007), *Portfolio Management: Optimizing for Success*, Houston, TX: American Productivity and Quality Center.

Fiore, Clifford (2005), *Accelerated Product Development*, New York: Productivity Production Press.

Griffin, Abbie (1997), *Drivers of NPD Success: The 1997 PDMA Report*, Chicago, IL: Product Development and Management Association.

Griffin, Abbie and Albert L. Page (1993), 'An interim report on measuring product development success and failure', *Journal of Product Innovation Management*, **9** (1), 291–308.

Grönlund, Johan, David. R. Sjödin and Johan Frishammar (2010), 'Open innovation and the Stage-Gate process: a revised model for new product development', *California Management Review*, **52** (Spring), 105–31.

Jenner, Stephen (2007), 'Gates with teeth: implementing a centre of excellence for investment decisions', *Proceedings, First International Stage-Gate Conference*, St Petersburg Beach, FL, available at http://www.stage-gate.com.

Koen, Peter (2003), 'Tools and techniques for managing the front end of innovation: highlights from the May 2003 Cambridge conference', *Visions*, **27** (October).

Ledford, Randall D. (2006), 'NPD 2.0: raising Emerson's NPD process to the next level', in *Innovations*, St Louis, MO: Emerson Electric Company, pp. 4–7.
Molitoris, Heather (2010), 'TARDEC is right on TARGET', *US Army TARDEC Accelerate Magazine*, Summer, 24–9.
Morgan, James (2005), 'Applying lean principles to product development', Report from SAE International Society of Mechanical Engineers, available at http://www.shop.sae.org.

33 B2B e-commerce
Venkatesh Shankar

There is growing interest among academics and managers in B2B electronic commerce (e-commerce). Broadly speaking B2B e-commerce is commerce between companies over an electronic medium or network, which could be based on proprietary information technology or the ubiquitous Internet. Thus B2B commerce includes transactions and relationships between business entities.

The US Census Bureau estimates that approximately 94 per cent of all e-commerce is B2B e-commerce and that B2B e-commerce is worth $3.4 trillion (http://www.census. gov/econ/estats/faqs.html). Many US B2B markets or industries are big. For example the chemical industry is worth $1.6 trillion, the telecom industry $900 billion and the construction industry $800 billion. The sizes of these industries and markets offer tremendous opportunities for electronic commerce.

These opportunities coexist, however, with challenges inherent to B2B e-commerce, due to its differences with B2C e-commerce. B2B e-commerce differs from B2C e-commerce in three important ways. First, it is bigger in value and more complex than is B2C. Second, it is more relationship-oriented than is B2C. Although e-commerce is not done through a face-to-face human interface, it can be facilitated, enhanced and supplemented by human interactions. Moreover frequent electronic interchanges create a long-term orientation in interchanges between business entities. Thus, B2B e-commerce is more relationship-oriented than is B2C e-commerce. Third, unlike B2C e-commerce, B2B e-commerce involves industry or domain expertise and entails fundamental buyer behavior shifts (Mantrala and Albers 2011).

Given these differences, researchers and practitioners are interested in a better understanding of several important topics relating to B2B e-commerce. These issues include B2B electronic data interchange (EDI), extranet, B2B exchanges or e-marketplaces and international B2B e-commerce. In this chapter, I discuss these issues in the B2B environment by providing an overview of e-commerce in the B2B environment according to an organizing framework. I review the essentials of e-commerce in B2B markets. I also summarize what is known about EDI, extranet, B2B exchange and international B2B e-commerce. To conclude, I outline implications for researchers and practitioners.[1]

AN ORGANIZING FRAMEWORK FOR B2B E-COMMERCE

Broadly speaking B2B e-commerce involves interactions between buyers and sellers over the electronic medium. An organizing framework for B2B e-commerce appears in Figure 33.1. Electronic commerce connects business sellers and buyers through different forms or platforms such as EDI, extranet and exchange. B2B e-commerce includes several activities such as product information provision, order taking, order tracking, pricing

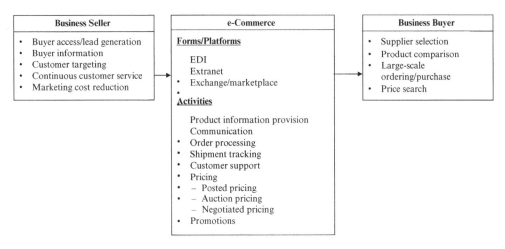

Figure 33.1   An organizing framework for B2B e-commerce

and promotions. Sellers in B2B industries use B2B e-commerce to access a wide range of buyers, to generate a high number of sales leads, to continuously support customers and to reduce overall marketing costs. Buyers seek to gain from a wide selection of suppliers, economies of scale and the ability to search for better prices. By engaging efficiently and effectively in several business activities over the electronic medium, buyers and sellers improve their business performance.

Among the different activities, pricing is a critical activity that thrives in the B2B e-commerce environment. Pricing takes place primarily in three ways over the electronic medium: posted/fixed pricing, auction pricing and negotiated pricing. The electronic medium is ideally suited for posted pricing and auctions. Different types of auctions such as regular auctions and reverse auctions are now increasingly common on the Internet. Online auctions have important effects on buyer–supplier relationships (Jap 2007). Buyers obtain concessions from sellers through dynamic bidding processes and reverse auctions. Because bidders are often anonymous with respect to one another, they tend to undercut others in the hope of winning the bid. Consequently online trust, critical to purchases on the Internet (Bart et al. 2005), is severely tested between the buyer and the seller. Online trust can be enhanced by improving the website's navigation and presentation and building the value of the brand (Bart et al. 2005).

B2B firms make other strategic decisions in the Internet-enabled business environment. These decisions are based on a good understanding of the effects of B2B e-commerce on key elements of business. For instance B2B e-commerce has important effects on reducing transaction costs (Garicano and Kaplan 2001), so cost reduction is an important objective for B2B firms in e-commerce. Furthermore online trust relates positively to the intent to purchase and is thus key to success in B2B e-commerce (Bart et al. 2005; Shankar et al. 2002).

B2B EDI AND EXTRANET

EDI and extranets are inter-organizational systems that were the forerunners of today's B2B e-commerce. EDI has been the topic of research primarily in information management (Holland et al. 1992; Srinivasan et al. 1994; Wang and Seidmann 1995). It helps rationalize physical resources such as inventories across the supply chain while also consolidating the competitive positions of the adopters (Kekre and Mukhopadhyay 1992). Srinivasan et al. (1994) find that electronic sharing of data between suppliers and buyers can provide substantial support for the achievement of high unit fill rates.

Extranets have also been studied, albeit more sparsely than EDI (e.g. Kale et al. 2001). Extranets are shared inter-organizational information systems based on the Internet that use a web browser (Kale et al. 2001). Conceptually extranets offer additional benefits, such as lower need for capital, reduced transaction costs, flexible communication and multilevel integration (Kale et al. 2001).

Theoretically the benefits of extranet over EDI include improved relations with supply chain partners, better dissemination of product information to customers, faster response times and increased customer and/or supplier satisfaction. Kale et al. (2001) show, however, that the benefits of extranets are primarily soft, customer service-oriented improvements that may not offer short-term revenue or profit growth. Extranets typically require less investment than EDI. Kale et al. (2001) also find that extranets differ fundamentally from EDI with regard to supply chain management. For instance there is no need for large transaction volumes or a large number of supply chain partners to begin realizing the benefits of extranet implementation, as is typically the case with EDI because of its large capital outlay. In addition firms believe that extranets improve the performance of the supply chain (Kale et al. 2001).

However, extranet adoption is associated with concerns as well (Kale et al. 2001). These concerns relate to data security and processing speed. The simplicity of access to extranets makes them vulnerable to the same security threat as that for any information system open to public access. Protection measures such as firewalls, proxy servers, passwords, encryption, digital certificates and public key infrastructure are therefore critical issues for companies that implement extranets. In addition, Internet data transfer rates are typically not as fast as the EDI rates, so most high volume traffic continues to be carried over private value-added networks and direct leased lines. The advantages of EDI, such as network reliability, scalability, processing power and around-the-clock support, outweigh the low cost advantages of extranets for high-volume users. Thus firms must make trade-offs related to the benefits and drawbacks of extranets.

B2B E-MARKETPLACES OR EXCHANGES

Aimed at overcoming some of the limitations of EDI and extranets, e-marketplaces or exchanges have emerged as a major development in the B2B arena. B2B e-marketplaces or exchanges have also attracted the attention of many researchers (e.g. Grewal et al. 2010; Grewal et al. 2001; Kaplan and Sawhney 2000).

At the height of the dot.com boom, hundreds of exchanges existed. Only a handful remain today. A few large exchanges, such as Covisint, Verticalnet and Ventro, ramped up fast, only to crash in a few years. There are major reasons for their failures. First, these exchanges did not gain traction with buyers or sellers because they did not provide compelling benefits. Second, they underestimated the behavioral change needed on the part of buyers and sellers to migrate to a new e-commerce platform. Third, they were not perceived as adequately neutral or authentic in domain knowledge. Fourth, they could not extract adequate value from participants (buyers and sellers) to maintain a sustainable business model. As a result, surviving B2B exchanges had to reinvent themselves as more focused, leaner, more value-adding (for buyers and sellers) and more practical e-commerce platforms than before.

In this section, I discuss the benefits and types of exchanges, the factors driving the formation of exchanges and its speed, success drivers of exchanges, key decision issues for industry incumbents, impediments to success for incumbent-formed exchanges and ways industry incumbents can participate in exchanges.

B2B exchanges provide both buyers and sellers with benefits along six dimensions: namely, exchange efficiency, information utility, place utility, assortment utility, time utility and supply chain efficiency.

- *Exchange efficiency*: an e-marketplace offers a substantial reduction of costs. If costs are linear with the number of links between buyers and sellers, an e-marketplace can reduce exchange costs substantially, by as much as one third. If there are four suppliers and four buyers, then an e-marketplace can lower the number of links from sixteen to eight.
- *Information utility*: a B2B exchange provides a seamless, searchable and interactive platform for buyers and sellers to gather, transmit and share information. This information utility enables participants to make effective decisions, resulting in improved results.
- *Place utility*: an e-marketplace offers high levels of convenience for buyers and sellers. It is a one-stop source for information and transactions. It is both a medium and a channel connecting all the participants involved.
- *Assortment utility*: B2B exchanges offer buyers a wide selection of products from multiple suppliers. The electronic exchange also offers the ability to choose quickly and conveniently from this wide selection.
- *Time utility*: the ability to share information and transact around the clock (24/7) is an important benefit for both buyers and sellers in an electronic exchange. This ability decreases the downtime for decision-making and implementations for participants.
- *Supply chain efficiency*: a well-designed B2B exchange with multiple suppliers and buyers offers the potential to integrate supply chains in an industry, leading to more efficient transaction, transportation, logistics and financial systems.

From a seller's perspective, B2B exchanges offer some benefits as well. They allow sellers to reach more customers, gather more information about potential buyers, provide more effective targeting and help serve customers better. From a buyer's standpoint, exchanges also offer a wider selection of suppliers, the ability to compare different choices, the ability to price search among several suppliers and a price advantage for small buyers. By offering advantages to both buyers and sellers, exchanges provide substantial savings to the end-users in any industry.

There are two broad types of exchanges: vertical and horizontal. Vertical exchanges are those for vertical markets/industries, ranging from plastics to energy to flowers. Horizontal exchanges are organized around activities such as capital equipment recovery, reverse logistics and employee benefits.

Vertical Exchanges

The vertical is the more common type of exchange. For example in the energy vertical market, houstonstreet and pantellos are two e-marketplaces. In the telecom industry, arbinet and globalcapacity are examples of vertical e-marketplaces. Examples of exchanges in other industries include partminer (computers and electronics), vipar (truck parts), and omnexus (plastics). A partial list of vertical exchanges appears in Box 33.1.

B2B vertical exchanges can be classified into four types (see Figure 33.2):

- Independent exchanges (e.g. fast parts, digital marketplace). These are known as butterfly-type exchanges, which are highly fragmented on both (buy and sell) sides of the exchange.
- Buyer-driven exchanges (e.g. auto exchange, energy exchange, aerospace exchange). This type of exchange works well in buyer-dominated industries.
- Supplier-driven exchanges (e.g. metals, airlines). This type of exchange works well in supplier-dominated industries.
- Supplier and buyer-driven exchanges. These exchanges are rare because it is very difficult for many buyers and sellers in a single vertical exchange to get together and form an exchange. However, when done right, they offer both buyers and sellers the most benefits from an e-marketplace.

There are also four broad types of business models or mechanisms used in e-marketplaces (see Figure 33.2): catalog, auction, market exchange and barter.

- *Catalog mechanism*: this mechanism involves demand and supply matching for small ticket items through prespecified, published prices. Popular examples of e-marketplace business models are SciQuest.com and MROdirect.com.
- *Auction mechanism*: in this mechanism, there is spatial matching of perishable or used products through bidding over the exchange prices for specific items. A popular example of such an e-marketplace model is Ariba.com.
- *Market exchange mechanism*: here, demand and supply are temporally matched for commodity items, with market makers facilitating liquidity. A popular example of such an e-marketplace model is Arbinet.com.
- *Barter mechanism*: in this mechanism, goods are exchanged without much transfer of cash. Typically this mechanism is used for exchanges of manufacturing capacity and assets with high transportation costs. A good example is Barterexchange.com.

From a marketing perspective, an e-marketplace can be viewed as an extension of a distribution channel. Channel design is typically based on channel service outputs, such

BOX 33.1   EXAMPLES OF B2B EXCHANGES OR E-MARKETPLACES

General

www.exostar.com: Exchange connecting supply chain members in a variety of industries

www.elemica.com: Supply chain network for 25 industries, including tires, rubber, chemical and energy

www.covisint.com: Healthcare and manufacturing supply chain information solutions

Automotive

www.hdamerica.com: Demand aggregation exchange for heavy vehicles parts

www.vipar.com: Demand aggregation for truck parts

Business services

www.purchasepro.com (Perfect Commerce): On-demand procurement and sourcing solutions

www.works.com: Secure electronic payment solutions over global credit card network

www.onvia.com: Government business analysis solutions

www.freightquote.com: Aggregator of shipping services

www.sword-ctspace.com: Document management and collaboration workflow applications in construction and engineering industries

Chemicals

www.airproducts.com/markets/paints_and_Coatings_InfoCenter/www.paint. org/index.htm: Paints exchange

www.omnexus.com: E-marketplace for plastics and elastomer injection materials

Computers and electronics

www.partminer.com: Electronics parts distribution network

Energy

www.houstonstreet.com: Trading exchange for crude oil and refined products

www.pantellos.com: E-marketplace for electric, natural gas distribution, natural gas pipeline and other energy sectors

Jewelry

www.polygon.net: Exchange for jewelry

Telecommunications

www.arbinet.com: Global voice and IP communication services exchange

www.globalcapacity.com: Integrated supply chain management of telecommunication networks

www.InterXion.com: Datacentre exchange

www.itquotes.com: Procurement of IT and telecommunication services

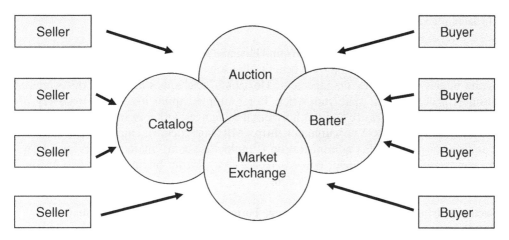

Figure 33.2   e-marketplace business mechanisms/models

Table 33.1   Typology of e-marketplaces

Exchange Interrelationship	Orientation	
	Cost reduction	Value addition
Low	Procurement exchange	Supply chain exchange
High	Procurement web	Networked web

as information utility, place utility, assortment utility and time utility. Prior research in marketing channels has examined channel coordination issues according to single manufacturer–single buyer and single manufacturer–multiple buyer frameworks (e.g. McGuire and Staelin 1983). A typical e-marketplace involves multiple manufacturers (sellers) and multiple buyers. Not much is known about coordinating designs in such a framework.

Vertical electronic marketplaces can be classified along two dimensions: the business orientation of firms and exchanges and the degree of interconnectedness among the different vertical or horizontal exchanges. The business orientation of firms can be either cost reduction or value addition. Exchange interrelationship can be low or high. Depending on the combination of these factors, four possible types of e-marketplace systems are possible, as Table 33.1 shows. A procurement exchange is characterized by a cost-reduction orientation and low interconnectedness between the buyers and sellers. A supply chain exchange is associated with weak relationships among buyers and sellers but a value addition orientation by the supplier. When buyers look to reduce costs but have strong relationships with sellers, a procurement web results. Finally, when sellers are oriented toward value addition and are highly connected with the buyers, a networked web type of exchange emerges. As an exchange becomes more effective over time, it is likely to evolve from a procurement exchange to a networked web.

Horizontal Exchanges

Horizontal exchanges are organized around business activities, such as capital equipment recovery, reverse logistics, employee benefits, logistics monitoring, project management, media buying and energy management. Horizontal exchanges are based on common business processes that span industries. For example capital investment recovery or surplus equipment sales are popular horizontal exchanges. Other examples of horizontal exchanges include MRO procurement (http://MROdirect.com), employee information management and benefits administration (Employease.com), managed services (www. gxs.com), project management (sword-ctspace.com), media buying (www.google.com/ doubleclick) and procurement (ariba.com).

Factors Driving Independent B2B Exchange Formation and the Speed of Formation

Four major factors drive the formation of independent B2B exchanges: economies of scale in transaction processing, value of information acquired in buying and selling, anonymity of buyers' and sellers' information and marketplace expertise. Two major factors then drive the speed at which B2B exchanges are formed: transaction efficiency and buyer/seller sophistication.

- *Transaction inefficiency*: transactions between buyers and sellers are significantly suboptimal in many industries, such as automobiles. Typically in such industries, information flows are poor, there are complex or multilayered distribution channels, and the fragmented supplier or customer bases leave money on the table for both buyers and sellers in their transactions. Such industries are ideal for successful B2B exchanges.
- *Buyer/seller sophistication*: sophisticated buyers or sellers facilitate B2B exchanges. If some buyers or sellers are sophisticated, in that they have business processes in place and are technologically savvy, they accelerate the formation and adoption of e-marketplaces.

Success Drivers of Exchanges

Firms creating e-marketplaces should carefully weigh the advantages and disadvantages of pioneering the market (Varadarajan et al. 2008). Several factors determine the success of e-marketplaces, including:

- the degree of fragmentation in the buyers' and suppliers' markets;
- the level of inefficiency in existing supply chain;
- network strength (critical mass-generating ability);
- domain expertise and relationships;
- master cataloging and metadata scheme capabilities to aggregate catalogs;
- expanding the exchange model to allow for simultaneous, automated multiparty transactions;
- the degree of process standardization and extendibility;
- core capability of process knowledge and workflow automation;

- complementarity of industry-specific knowledge and process capability;
- customizability of process capability.

An exchange will be likely to succeed if inefficiency is high in the existing supply chain, fragmentation is high, firms have strong domain expertise, the exchange allows more business processes, the exchange automates and standardizes the processes and work-flows and the exchange customizes process capability to buyers and sellers.

Key Decision Issues for Industry Incumbents

In making decisions about creating or participating in exchanges, industry incumbents face several difficult questions, such as:

- Do we spin out a new company to form an exchange?
- Do we take a stake in the new exchange?
- Do we partner with competitors? If so, how?
- Who will control the exchange?
- How will we integrate our current systems with the exchange?
- In which exchange should we participate?

The answers to these important questions depend on the following factors:

- centrality of items transacted in the exchange to the company;
- criticality of the exchange to business performance;
- switching costs;
- the ability of the exchange to disrupt the business model.

If the items transacted in the exchange are critical to the firm and the exchange is vital for an incumbent firm, then the incumbent should participate in the exchange. In contrast, if the switching costs are low, incumbents can afford to play in other exchanges. Furthermore, if the exchange threatens to upset the existing business model of the incumbent firm, the firm may want to consider participating in other exchanges.

Grewal et al. (2001) examine the antecedents and consequences of firms' decisions to participate in B2B electronic markets. According to them, a firm's information technology (IT) capabilities influence its participation and performance in electronic markets.

In addition, some critical issues relate to e-marketplaces, including market entry (timing and scale), channel conflict, expansion of offering scope, sources of long-term advantage, growth and diversification and buyer versus seller bargaining power.

Impediments to Success for Incumbent-formed Exchanges

Incumbent-formed exchanges face many hurdles in becoming successful. In particular, industry incumbents often:

- do not have a good horizontal collaborative record;
- may not have sufficient technology skills;

- may not be up to speed with Internet speed of design and implementation;
- confront antitrust issues;
- face minority supplier issues.

Incumbents should undertake major initiatives to surmount these hurdles. They could spend to acquire the necessary skills and recruit appropriate talented individuals who can work at Internet speed. They should avoid the traps of becoming a monopoly or ignoring minority suppliers.

How Industry Incumbents can Participate in the Exchange

To be successful, incumbents might consider the following ways to play in the exchange game: plan for future rather than current e-marketplaces; think B2B2C; treat the e-marketplace as a disruptive innovation; work toward evolving exchanges; participate in business mechanisms that offer competitive advantage; and have a technology strategy before investing.

Grewal et al. (2010) study the effect of governance of B2B electronic markets on their performance. Specifically they examine three governance mechanisms that market makers use to manage markets: monitoring, community building and self-participating mechanisms. Their analysis of survey data from B2B electronic markets suggests that monitoring is effective for reputed market makers when demand is highly uncertain; community building works best if prices rarely change; and self-participating is powerful for reputed market makers when prices continually change.

INTERNATIONAL B2B E-COMMERCE

The explosive growth in the use of the digital medium continues to alter the global marketplace and global marketing in important ways. In the B2B environment, the digital medium and global Internet marketing strategy have both direct and moderating effects on the impact of marketing mix decisions (e.g. product development, communication, pricing, distribution) on firm performance (Shankar and Meyer 2009).

With regard to global product development, the Internet significantly influences the effectiveness and speed of new product development and its impact on firm performance (Costlow 2006). In technological B2B markets in particular, speed to market is critical to the success of new products. For example in the auto industry, by virtually connecting product development team members across the globe, firms have shrunk product development cycles from a high of 60 months to a low of 18.

The Internet also has an important role for the effects of both company- and user-generated communication efforts on firm performance. User groups and technical communities now expedite problem-solving in the global e-marketplace. However, due to differences in culture, the stage of market development and technological sophistication across countries, B2B firms must adapt their digital communication strategies for different countries (Shankar and Donato 2003).

With regard to global pricing, the web allows more pricing transparency but also offers opportunities for differentiation across countries. Typically pricing is done in local currencies, so transparency does not always adversely affect a firm's pricing across countries. Because many B2B markets depend on local suppliers in different countries, customers expect and understand differences in prices across countries.

With regard to global distribution, the web may serve as either a substitute or a complementary channel in different global markets. By coordinating the Internet with the other channels in each country, firms can improve their performance in global markets.

In the future continued Internet penetration and the surge in mobile media may further alter B2B e-commerce (Shankar and Balasubramanian 2009). For example businesses use mobile devices to track products using radio frequency identification (RFID) technology, order taking, fulfillment and customer service. Research on the digital medium and global B2B marketing is still growing, and many important questions remain largely underexplored. More research is needed to understand the relationships among the Internet, mobile media, marketing mix decisions and firm performance in a global B2B context.

The explosive growth in mobile media and communication suggests that mobile marketing and commerce in the B2B environment is a ripe area for future research (Shankar and Balasubramanian 2009). Internet-enabled B2B innovations such as electronic account reconciliation services are also gaining research attention (e.g. Dotzel and Shankar 2010) and represent a fruitful avenue for additional research.

IMPLICATIONS FOR RESEARCHERS

Future B2B exchanges will include increased use of social media. Already some exchanges are using social media, such as tradekey, alibaba, vertmarkets, fyIndOut, choiceVendor and resourceNation. Tradekey connects traders to wholesalers, buyers, manufacturers and distributors across more than 200 countries in 27 categories, from agricultural to transportation products. FyIndOut.com, a B2B social media hub, promotes itself as 'the central place to find and promote business information, applications, and services'. It allows B2B vendors to list their products and services, such as accounting and web conference applications, for free and interact with both prospects and buyers to research sellers and post reviews of them. Vendors pay for interested leads. The ChoiceVendor B2B vendor review platform is similar to FyIndOut.com but makes money by offering features for subscribers who seek vendors. SalesForce.com's AppXchange and Google App Marketplace are exchanges for web-based applications. The Resource Nation business resource marketplace links sellers and buyers of several B2B products and services, such as payroll outsourcing, laser printers and buildings. In this marketplace vendors are prescreened by a credit reporting agency and can receive qualified leads for a fee.

Much previous research in marketing, information systems and economics focuses on a single good or product. A promise of e-marketplaces is that they can enable the selection and bundling of multiple products. This capability has significant implications for marketplace design. Therefore an important research question is: how should the design of an e-marketplace be different if it uses multiple products and their combinations?

Despite the growing popularity of e-marketplaces, not much is known about the effectiveness of alternative design mechanisms in IT-mediated environments. As advocates of specific e-marketplaces choose combinations of the mechanisms or specialize in certain mechanisms, we need greater knowledge about the following issues:

1. What are the relative merits of alternative design mechanisms for e-marketplaces? Some traditional criteria for evaluating effectiveness include exchange efficiency, information utility, place utility, assortment utility, time utility and supply chain efficiency. Research is needed to evaluate critically how design mechanisms perform on these effectiveness criteria and uncover the trade-offs among them.
2. What factors should govern the choice of marketplace design mechanisms in specific contingency conditions? Information systems and marketing literature have extensively examined inter-organizational systems and channel coordination issues in the context of a single seller and multiple buyers (Choudhury 1997). How might this literature extend to the case of multiple buyers and suppliers? How do the issues of incentive compatibility affect the trade-offs among the different marketplace design mechanisms? Do specific information systems design principles influence the trade-offs among marketplace design mechanisms? Other topics that need more investigation include the effectiveness of marketplace design mechanisms, the effects of IT mediation, criteria for evaluating the effectiveness of e-marketplace design mechanisms and contingency factors that influence the effectiveness of e-marketplace design mechanisms.
3. With regard to global B2B e-commerce, several questions merit further research. How can firms seamlessly integrate their e-commerce platforms across different exchanges in different countries? What e-commerce mechanism can best tap into the diversity of new product ideas across the world? How can firms maintain price consistency across different countries in an increasingly transparent environment? How can B2B firms maintain a central image, yet adapt their value propositions across countries by participating in different B2B exchanges and communicating across multiple electronic platforms around the world?

The answers to these questions can provide a strong foundation for global B2B e-commerce strategies.

IMPLICATIONS FOR PRACTITIONERS

The findings from research into B2B e-commerce have important implications for practitioners. Because B2B e-commerce lowers transaction costs, it can enable managers to improve their operational efficiency. The finding that online trust is critical and driven by navigation, presentation and brand suggests that B2B managers should carefully plan and design their e-commerce platforms and improve their brand's value proposition.

Insights into EDI and extranets suggest that managers should design better information-sharing and collaborative e-commerce platforms. Because research shows that the benefits of extranets are primarily soft, and because they do not require a large initial investment, managers could use them primarily to enhance supply chain performance. In choosing between EDI and extranets, managers should compare the benefits of extranets with those of EDI – such as network reliability, scalability and around-the clock support – for their firms.

Buyer and seller organizations could analyze the benefits of B2B exchanges along the six dimensions and focus on the best dimensions to improve value for the other party. With a deep understanding of the types of vertical and horizontal exchanges and the associated business models, as well as their pros and cons, executives of both incumbent and new firms can determine the most effective exchange and business model in which to participate. Similarly a thorough understanding of the factors that drive exchange formation and the success drivers of exchanges can lead to the design of better exchanges and enable buyers and sellers to choose the best exchange in which to participate. An exchange is most likely to succeed if there is high existing supply chain inefficiency, if fragmentation is high, if firms have strong domain expertise, if the processes are stand-ardized and if the process capability is customized to fit buyers and sellers. Buyers and sellers can identify the exchanges most likely to succeed for them and participate accord-ingly.

Incumbent industry players should invest to acquire the necessary skills and recruit the right talented people who can work at the pace of the web, without becoming a monopoly or ignoring minority suppliers. They should also anticipate B2B e-commerce in the future and prepare for the right B2B platform and business model. Market makers should choose a governance mechanism from monitoring, community building and self-participating mechanisms, depending on their reputation, uncertainty of demand and changes in their prices.

Firms can benefit from exchanges by using more self-service technologies. B2B firms can also learn from B2C firms such as eBay and Amazon to design the best B2B e-commerce platforms and exchanges. Managers of firms can work toward making B2B e-commerce more customer-centric. They may want to look for new business models and communities that will enrich participants' experience in B2B exchanges.

Knowledge about global B2B e-commerce is critical for important decisions. Managers of firms can use a global e-commerce platform to reduce their product development lead times significantly. They could use adapted company- and user-generated communica-tion messages across countries to improve awareness and preference among their cus-tomers worldwide. Managers also might use differences in the local prices of supplies to formulate tight global pricing strategies using the web and coordinate e-commerce channels by country.

By using mobile media applications in areas such as inventory tracking, order fulfillment and customer service, managers can improve their firms' B2B value propo-sitions for clients and enhance B2B e-commerce, both on the web and through mobile devices.

NOTE

1. I do not discuss the effects of the Internet on B2B sales forces. For greater detail on this topic, see Mantrala and Albers (2011).

REFERENCES

Bart, Yakov, Venkatesh Shankar, Fareena Sultan and Glen L. Urban (2005), 'Are the drivers and role of online trust the same for all web sites and consumers? A large scale exploratory empirical study', *Journal of Marketing*, **69** (4), 133–52.

Choudhury, V. (1997), 'Strategic choices in the development of interorganizational information systems', *Information Systems Research*, **8** (1), 1–24.

Costlow, Terry (2006), 'Design goes global: web fuels collaborative product development', *Design News*, 20 March, p. 61.

Dotzel, Thomas and Venkatesh Shankar (2010), 'Asymmetries between Internet-enabled and people-enabled B2B service innovations', Working Paper, McGill University, CA.

Garicano, Luis and Stephen N. Kaplan (2001), 'The effects of business-to-business e-commerce on transaction costs', *Journal of Industrial Economics*, **49** (December), 463–85.

Grewal, Rajdeep, Anindita Chakravarty and Amit Saini (2010), 'Governance mechanisms in business-to-business electronic markets', *Journal of Marketing*, **74** (4), 48–62.

Grewal, Rajdeep, James M. Comer and Raj Mehta (2001), 'An investigation into the antecedents of organizational participation in business-to-business electronic markets', *Journal of Marketing*, **65** (3), 17–33.

Holland, Chris, Geoff Lockett and Ian Blackman (1992), 'Planning for electronic data interchange', *Strategic Management Journal*, **13** (7), 539–50.

Jap, Sandy D. (2007), 'The impact of online reverse auction design on buyer–supplier relationships', *Journal of Marketing*, **71** (1), 146–59.

Kale, Rahul, Venkatesh Shankar, Elliott Rabinovich and Martin Dresner (2001), 'Extranet and supply chain management', Working Paper.

Kaplan, Stephen N. and Mohanbir S. Sawhney (2000), 'E-hubs: the new B2B marketplace', *Harvard Business Review*, **78** (3), 97–103.

Kekre, Sunder and Tridas Mukhopadhyay (1992), 'Impacts of electronic data interchange technology on quality improvement and inventory reduction programs: a field study', *International Journal of Production Economics*, **28**, 265–82.

Mantrala, Murali K. and Sonke Albers (2011), 'The impact of the Internet on B2B sales force size and structure', in Gary L. Lilien and Rajdeep Grewal (eds), *Handbook of Business-to-Business Marketing*, Cheltenham, UK and Northampton, MA, USA: Edward Elgar.

McGuire, Timothy and Richard Staelin (1983), 'An industry equilibrium analysis of downstream vertical integration', *Marketing Science*, **2** (2), 161–92.

Shankar, Venkatesh and Sridhar Balasubramanian (2009), 'Mobile marketing: a synthesis and prognosis', Tenth Anniversary Special Issue, *Journal of Interactive Marketing*, **23** (2), 118–29.

Shankar, Venkatesh and Mary P. Donato (2003), 'Personalization of global sales and marketing activities in the digital economy', in Nirmal Pal and Arvind Rangaswamy (eds), *Power of One*, University Park, PA: eBRC Press, pp. 103–21.

Shankar, Venkatesh and Jeff Meyer (2009), 'Internet and international marketing', in Masaaki Kotabe and Christiaan Helsen (eds), *Handbook of International Marketing*, Thousand Oaks, CA: Sage, pp. 451–67.

Shankar, Venkatesh, Glen L. Urban and Fareena Sultan (2002), 'Online trust: a stakeholder perspective, concepts, implications, and future directions', *Journal of Strategic Information Systems*, **11** (December), 325–44.

Srinivasan, Kannan, Sunder Kekre and Tridas Mukhopadhyay (1994), 'Impact of electronic data interchange technology on JIT shipments', *Management Science*, **40** (10), 1291–304.

Varadarajan, Rajan, Manjit S. Yadav and Venkatesh Shankar (2008), 'First-mover advantages in an Internet-enabled market environment: conceptual framework and propositions', *Journal of Academy of Marketing Science*, **36** (3), 293–408.

Wang, E. and Abraham Seidmann (1995), 'Electronic data interchange: competitive externalities and strategic application policies', *Management Science*, **41** (3), 401–18.

34 Designing B2B markets
Ernan Haruvy and Sandy Jap

In 2009, the Global 2000 firms earned revenues of more than $32 trillion and spent $11.8 trillion with 134 500 trading partners on average (Forbes.com 2010). A central goal in the research on business markets is to improve the efficiency and effectiveness of these transactions. Substantial literature in marketing considers organizational exchange issues from a variety of perspectives. A special issue of *Marketing Letters* summarizes the knowledge to date and highlights opportunities for research on various issues ranging from analytical and empirical models of manufacturer–retailer interactions and promotional strategies (Ailawadi et al. 2010, Coughlan et al. 2010), to sales force incentives (Mantrala et al. 2010) and design (Bradford et al. 2010), to B2B marketing and new product management (Lilien et al. 2010), to channel design issues (Sa Vinhas et al. 2010) and governance (Rindfleisch et al. 2010). Another important area of inter-organizational exchange includes negotiation strategies and their outcomes (Ganesan 1993; Srivastava and Chakravarti 2009).

These research streams implicitly approach the dyad (buyer–seller or manufacturer–retailer or reseller) as the relevant unit of analysis. However, there is also growing recognition that organizational exchange performance is at least in part determined by factors external to the dyad; much of this work is rooted in social network theory and the impact of network properties on exchange (Houston et al. 2004; Van den Bulte and Wuyts 2007; Wuyts and Geyskens 2005; Wuyts et al. 2004). In this chapter we broaden the unit of analysis even further to consider the *market* the relevant unit of analysis, involving multiple buyers or sellers who bid on products and services using a market clearing mechanism (i.e. competitive pricing), such as an auction. These markets have become increasingly common over the past decade as a result of the Internet and are widely used across a variety of industries because of their demonstrated ability to drive exchange performance. For example, savings generated in online B2B auctions is in the range of 10–40 per cent, which is substantial (Victor 2008).

Researchers and practitioners face unique challenges in understanding B2B online pricing mechanisms, as well as their design and execution, compared with B2C or consumer-to-consumer (C2C) markets. In this chapter our goal is to highlight these challenges (i.e. the non-binding nature and role of non-price considerations and inter-organizational relationships) and the implications for product assortment managements and the general design of B2B markets. We compare the emerging themes and issues in these areas with the historical perspective in traditional auction literature, which has its genesis in microeconomics, industrial organization, game theory and behavioral economics. Much of the research reviewed here relies on proprietary data that were painstakingly gathered in primary data collection efforts across multiple firms, industries and product categories. Thus, this work provides an understanding of auction design, bidding behavior and auction-based market phenomena, which is complementary to the growing research stream in marketing on B2C or C2C auctions based on eBay and other widely available online market data.

Specifically, we examine three areas in depth. The first issue regards the product to be auctioned and the various options for which these products would be offered within an auction, whether in regard to sequential product offerings or online and offline offerings. We then turn to the second issue of bidder behavior and strategies in B2B auctions. Third, we close with a section on the mechanism design, including issues of price visibility, and consider the roles of guarantees and price premiums. Within each of these broad themes we discuss the significance of differentiated bidders and inter-organizational relationships in B2B markets and the implications for the firm. We conclude with a consideration of additional issues germane to future research.

UNIQUE CHALLENGES OF B2B MARKET RESEARCH AND DESIGN

In general, consumer auctions are forward auctions, meaning that buyers compete against one another for the right to *buy* the auctioned item. For most efficient consumer auction formats, the buyer with the highest or second-highest bid wins. B2B auctions can certainly take place as forward auctions. Examples include livestock auctions (Buccola 1982), flower auctions (Heezen and Baets 1996), land auctions (Colwell and Yavaş 1994) and acquisition of companies or strategic business units (DePamphilis 2007). Also common are markets for businesses that are interested in small quantities of relatively homogeneous goods (e.g. uBid auctions). However, most B2B auctions are *reverse*; that is, the sellers bid against one another for the right to *sell* to a buyer. In standard *binding* reverse auctions, which we refer to as *price-based* mechanisms, the buyer begins by preparing a set of detailed specifications, such as a request for quotes or information. Suppliers respond through a live bidding event. All the bidding is conducted on the basis of price, and the buyer commits to award the contract to the *lowest* bidder (or second-lowest bidder), provided the bidder can meet the contract specifications.

Buyer-determined End Rules

An alternative, commonly used reverse auction mechanism is a *non-binding*, or *buyer-determined*, mechanism. Suppliers respond through a live auction event and bid on price; yet, rather than commit to awarding the contract to the lowest bidder, the buyer instead reserves the right to factor other non-price criteria, such as product quality and delivery reliability, into the selection of the ultimate winner. Thus, our traditional view of price-based 'auctions' needs to be expanded in B2B contexts. In essence, buyers may assign a weight to non-price attributes to rank the bids (assuming the winner is not chosen randomly). The weight can vary from zero (meaning that the auction reduces to a pure price-based auction) to infinity (meaning that winner selection is not at all based on price). Any finite set of weights can imply monetizing the non-price attributes; thus, each bidder j can be scored as follows:

Score(bidder j) = Monetary nonprice measure for bidder j – bid by bidder j, where the bidder with the highest score wins, rather than the bidder with the lowest price. This constitutes a quasi-linear utility in which the bid enters linearly, and it is a common form in marketing (Rao 2009).

Non-binding auctions are surprisingly common. Anderson and Frohlich (2001, p. 60) report that 'clients do not normally make award decisions on bid day. In the days and weeks that follow the bidding event, buyers examine bid results, review supplier information (such as supplier capability, quality certifications, and manufacturing processes), and sometimes conduct a buyer audit before making a final decision. The client does not have to select the lowest bidder'. Jap (2002, p. 510) reports that 'the vast majority of [FreeMarkets procurement] auctions used in the marketplace today do not determine a winner . . . and the buyer may reserve the right to select a winner on any basis'.

Differentiated Bidders

Thus, in many B2B markets, bidders are *differentiated* on the basis of their non-price value to the bid-taker,[1] which is an underexamined feature in the historical auction literature. And although the auction literature has acknowledged the existence of such actions (Branco 1997; Che 1993) and documented such asymmetries in public works (Bajari 1998) or school milk auctions (Pesendorfer 2000; Porter and Zona 1999), the vast majority of research on auctions does not account for such differences. This is because an important assumption of the theoretical work on auctions to date (and the reality of most consumer auctions) is that bidders are non-differentiated on non-price attributes, so the bid-taker is indifferent to whether the bids originate from one bidder or another. The auction mechanism clears the market only on the basis of price, and the bid-taker will accept the lowest price offer from any bidder and will value the bids equally. Of course, bidders can be heterogeneous in their valuations, but they are only discriminated on the basis of their bid prices. With this approach, simplifying assumptions about bidder symmetry (Milgrom and Weber 1982) make the equilibrium estimation mathematically tractable.

In one approach to accounting for bidder differentials, the use of a *multidimensional* auction format, the bid-taker explicitly specifies to suppliers its *ex ante* weighing of non-price aspects of the exchange. Research into such auctions originated with government auctions, particularly the department of defense contracts (Anton and Yao 1987; Boger and Liao 1988; Mayer 1987), though auctioning monopoly franchises (Riordan and Sappington 1987) was also considered around the same time. For example, Che (1993) and Branco (1997) analytically characterize auctions of two dimensions: price and quality. Che demonstrates the revenue equivalence between first-price and second-price multi-attribute reverse auctions with endogenous non-monetary attributes, and Chen-Ritzo and colleagues (2005) consider three dimensions: price, quality and delivery time. Subsequent empirical work delineates the potential limit of this approach. Engelbrecht-Wiggans et al. (2007) find that two-dimensional auctions may not improve buyer profits if the number of bidders is small and cost and quality are either largely independent or negatively correlated because, under these conditions, the buyer can get a high-quality seller at bargain prices. This effect dissipates as the number of sellers increases.

In the marketplace, the use of multidimensional auctions is not a widespread practice, as it requires a well-defined and commonly known scoring rule *ex ante*, which may be cumbersome or difficult to construct in advance. An alternative to dealing with complex prespecification algorithms may be to couple a price-based mechanism with some form of non-competitive contract, as these are more profitable and cost effective than price-based auctions and less complex than a full-blown combinatorial auction (Engelbrecht-Wiggans et al. 2007). Tunca and Wu (2009) use an analytical model to demonstrate when a single stage (i.e. a reverse English auction) is efficient for price discovery and the conditions under which such an approach would be inefficient. They find that when the number of bidding suppliers is high, a single-stage approach is efficient, especially when capacity is rigid. In contrast, a two-stage process that reveals supplier information in the second stage (i.e. a subset of suppliers from the first-stage process undergoes additional negotiations or an alternative market mechanism) is more effective if production is highly scalable and may be more preferable when production is of intermediate scalability.

Inter-organizational Relationships

An important differentiator of B2B and B2C exchanges is the potential for the development of a long-term relational exchange. Because B2B exchange can involve repeated purchases of significant stakes and complexity (i.e. in terms of inventory, equipment and logistical costs), there is a large body of literature in marketing on the development of cooperative relational exchange: relationships that are marked by trust and commitment (Anderson and Weitz 1992; Morgan and Hunt 1994; Wuyts and Geyskens 2005), cooperation and information exchange (Macneil 1980; Mohr and Nevin 1990) and the development of mutual benefits and strategic advantage (Anderson and Narus 1990; Jap 1999). Such relationships are different from non-price attributes because their presence (and even their potential presence) can systematically affect bidding strategies before the auction and can be subsequently affected post-auction by the bidding strategies that occurred during the auction event. As the interactions between the parties become computer mediated, relationship states can deteriorate. For example, Gattiker et al. (2007) use an experimental approach to demonstrate that sellers who participate in online reverse auctions report significantly lower trust in their buyer counterparts than those who negotiated face-to-face.

Using pre- and post-surveys of bidder relationship states (e.g. propensity for a relationship with the buyer, willingness to make investments, relationship satisfaction) in online reverse auctions, Jap and Haruvy (2008) find that bidders with higher relationship propensity (both past and future) and a greater willingness to make specific investments with the buyer before the auction bid less aggressively during the course of the auction, while bidders who bid aggressively during the auction reduce their propensity for a relationship and sour incumbent satisfaction with the buyer post-auction (see also Carter and Stevens 2006). This research was the first to use field data to examine bidding behavior during the auction with factors *outside* the auction mechanism (both before and after), but more important, it suggests that bidders systematically intertwine and trade off bid prices and non-price attributes against each other as part of their strategic bidding behavior.

The need to manage and account for inter-organizational relationships can also result in the creation of hybrid pricing mechanisms that combine price-competitive aspects and non-competitive contracts. For example, Engelbrecht-Wiggans and Katok (2006) investigate a mechanism that combines auctions with non-competitive contracts; an auction among a set of bidders sets the price, and the buyer contracts 'non-competitively' with other suppliers to provide goods at whatever price the auction sets. This mechanism assumes that buyers want to continue their relationships with preferred suppliers and at the same time allow the market to set prices. Engelbrecht-Wiggans and Katok find that this hybrid mechanism outperforms the pure auction mechanism, underscoring a firm's need to account for and protect valuable inter-organizational relationships in the design and usage of auction mechanisms.

Tunca and Zenios (2006) develop a formal model that compares price-based auctions and long-term relational contracts and find that price-based auctions enhance the enforceability of relational contracting mechanisms and the provision of high-quality goods when the market size is large. However, if the premium that consumers are willing to pay for quality over the marginal production cost is sufficiently high and the provider of high-quality intermediate parts is sufficiently patient, a relational contracting mechanism will dominate a price-based auction. In contrast, if the quality premium is only moderate, both mechanisms – relational contracting and price auctions – can coexist in equilibrium. The previously mentioned studies represent important first steps for better understanding how and when price-based versus relational-based mechanisms are useful. Still needed, though, is research that identifies the industry characteristics (e.g. fast or slow clock speed industries) under which these mechanisms are more effective, and the sustainability of their outcomes over time.

Finally, Emiliani and Stec (2001) caution that B2B auctions can inflict long-term damage on buyer–supplier relationships and hamper cooperation and collaboration. In a series of studies on the impact of buyer-determined online reverse auctions, Jap (2003, 2007) demonstrates how the level of price visibility – that is, the extent to which every bidder can observe every bid during auction event – undermines relationship outcomes (i.e. increases supplier opportunism suspicions and decreases willingness to make specific investments or work with the buyer in the future). These studies are described in more detail in the section on price visibility. However, one limitation of this stream of research is that the demonstrated impact on performance outcomes has only been observed immediately after the auction. To this end Carter and Kaufmann's (2007) survey of more than 300 industrial buyers suggests that the opportunism associated with these auctions significantly reduces relationship trust and increases dysfunctional conflict and that these effects ultimately undermine suppliers' non-price performance in the exchange. Although these results confirm the potential long-term consequences of online reverse auctions on supply relationships, additional demonstrations of relationship damage and a better understanding of the conditions under which they are more or less likely to occur should continue to be a key priority for future research.

IMPLICATIONS FOR PRODUCT ASSORTMENTS AND OFFERINGS

As a second major task, any market designer must choose the products to be offered, the manner in which the products will be bundled (or unbundled) with complements (or substitutes), how it will be offered (e.g. online or offline), and the location of the products or market. In this section, we examine several significant decisions for product assortments and offerings in B2B markets: complements and package bidding, substitutes and forward-looking behavior, and online versus offline options.

Complements and Package Bidding

A critical issue in B2B auctions is that each auctioned product or contract is generally not considered as a stand-alone event, but rather as part of a larger strategic objective. When a seller is bidding for the right to supply a particular buyer, the seller may aim to supply more than that particular contract in the specific auction. That is, it may not be cost effective for the seller to win a single contract if it loses all complementary auctions. Auctions are considered *complements* when the value of winning both auctions is greater than the sum of winning them individually. This creates a common problem, the 'exposure problem', in which bidders may be hesitant to compete aggressively on items if there is a risk of obtaining only part of the desired set of items. The literature on complementarities in auctions is large (see Milgrom 2000) due in large part to government (Federal Communications Commission) spectrum auctions, and many solutions have been proposed to address complementarities.

One of the best-known solutions is the 'simultaneous ascending auction' (Milgrom 2000), which reduces, but does not eliminate the exposure problem. This auction was first introduced in 1994 to sell licenses to use bands of radio spectrum in the United States. A simultaneous ascending auction calls for bidding on multiple items in rounds. In each round, bidders simultaneously make sealed bids for any item. After the round, results are posted. For each item, these results show the new bids and bidders, the 'standing high bid' and the corresponding bidder. A bidder may withdraw bids, but there is a penalty for doing so: if the selling price of the item is less than the bid, the bidder pays the difference. Package bidding, in which bidders can place bids on combinations of items, eliminates the exposure problem, and auctions with package bidding are called 'combinatorial auctions'. Package bidding addresses the exposure problem, but it also creates a threshold problem. A 'threshold problem' exists if efficient combinations of small bidders are unable to coordinate a response to an aggressive package bid by a large bidder. A related feature that government auctions share with business auctions is the possibility of split awards, which have received attention with government auctions as a motivation (Anton and Yao 1989, 1992).

Although the field has made great progress, it is largely theoretical. We would like to see statistical methods for capturing potential complementarities according to the preferences of competitors, based on their observed bids and inferred bid strategies in overlapping or simultaneous auctions by the same seller. This would require some restrictive assumptions about bidder strategies but would be of tremendous assistance to the auctioneer in deciding on an optimal auction format that accounts for complementarities. It would also assist bidders in mounting an effective competitive response to aggressive competitors who attempt to exploit complementarities to their advantage.

Substitutes and Forward-looking Behavior

Two auctions are considered substitutes if the value of winning both is lower than the sum of winning them individually; this causes the opposite of the complementarities issue. Sequential auctions for the same or similar items or contracts are not uncommon in B2B exchanges. The bidder should anticipate the value of winning a present auction as well as the value of winning a future one. There is some empirical work on sequential auctions. For example, Donald et al. (2006) tackle the problem of estimating the parameters of the distributions of values and of participation costs in sequential auctions. Regarding auction design, Carare (2007) uses a search model to deduce the effect on bids of imposing a stationary reserve price in sequential auctions of identical objects. Using data collected from online auctions, he finds substantial gains in revenue from the imposition of a reserve price.

A stream of work also examines bidding behavior and market design in sequential auctions. For example, Jofre-Bonet and Pesendorfer (2003) analyze bidding in repeated highway B2B auctions using the first-order conditions for optimality. Zeithammer's (2006) research on sequential consumer auctions in eBay provides a plethora of insights. He shows that when rational forward-looking bidders participate in sequential auctions for imperfect substitutes, they can shade their bids when there are sufficiently many future auctions and these auctions are sufficiently near in the future. This result raises the question: how should a bidder bid against other strategic forward-looking bidders? Milgrom and Weber (1982) answer this question for the case of a sequential auction for exactly identical perfect substitutes: all bidders who participate in each auction shade their bids just enough to arbitrage away any potential price decline. When the auctioned objects are not identical but still substitutes because of buyer capacity constraints (e.g. two pairs of tickets to different but concurrent shows), Zeithammer (2009) shows that equilibrium bidding can be non-intuitive. For example, even bidders who prefer the object auctioned second will still bid on the object auctioned first because it allows them to gauge the strength of the competition.

The impact of bidder forward-looking behavior on seller profits is almost always negative because of bid shading. Thus, the question arises: how should the seller sell in a sequential auction marketplace with forward-looking bidders? Although it may seem that the seller could eliminate bid shading by selling infrequently, a long-lived seller facing overlapping generations of consumers cannot eliminate bid shading entirely (Zeithammer 2007a). However, Zeithammer (2007a) finds that bid shading is self-regulating because it turns itself off whenever the existence of the market is threatened by low seller profits. Zeithammer calls this effect the market's 'self-preservation instinct' and suggests that auctioneers and regulators need not worry about forward-looking bid shading. Rather, such bid shading helps markets clear at the correct prices when sellers merely offer units for sale and the market determines prices through auctions.

Alternatively, bid shading can be eliminated through commitment and adaptation (Zeithammer 2007b). When announcing a future auction for a second unit of the same good reduces today's bids, the seller may want to credibly limit the number of units he or she sells. Conversely, the seller could use the outcome of the first auction to inform the sale of the second unit. These two selling regimes, commitment and adaptation, are mutually exclusive (Zeithammer 2007b). Adaptation involves learning about remaining demand from early prices, and commitment requires a seller forgo such learning and make all selling decisions at the beginning of the game. The analysis implies that neither regime dominates the other. Commitment may reduce bid shading by bidders, but adaptation may resolve the demand uncertainty inherent in auction markets and can be more efficient. Thus, an adaptive seller can capture sufficient efficiency gains to prefer adaptation to commitment. The seller's choice of regime should depend on the gains from trade: when the expected gains from trade are low, commitment dominates adaptation, and vice versa.

The finding that adaptation can dominate precommitment is important because it seems to contradict Schelling's (1960) principle of commitment in which the seller should never prefer adaptation: in a dynamic game, the player able to precommit to arbitrary future actions should be better off than the player restricted to play subgame perfect strategies. Zeithammer (2008) resolves this inconsistency, showing that a seller who can condition the second auction on the first price exceeding a publicly announced threshold is always better off than an adaptive seller. Of note, the commitment to a threshold may unravel informative bidding strategies in the first auction since a unique invertible bidding equilibrium exists only for the Dutch auction format, and only when the second auction is sufficiently discounted by the bidders. Therefore when the bidders are sufficiently strategic, the seller may not learn much about remaining demand from early auctions.

More theoretical research into sequential B2B auctions is needed. Unlike consumer auctions in which the buyer and seller are likely to be anonymous (or nearly anonymous) strangers, B2B auctions involve a repeated and complex dynamic interplay between the same set of buyers and sellers. Losing at a particular price in one auction not only reveals something about the competition (Zeithammer 2009) but also affects the relationship (mutual investment and trust) between bidder and buyer (Jap and Haruvy 2008). Thus, the transfer between one auction and the next is not purely informational in nature but may involve real value changes. Unlike B2B auctions, consumer sequential auctions are also likely to be either substitutes or unrelated. Complement auctions are possible (as in collector sets), thus creating an exposure problem (see previous section on complements), but the problem is not as common or as pressing as in B2B auctions and therefore has not garnered any attention in the consumer sequential auction literature. Future B2B auctions may be either complements or substitutes. A complex mix can generally be anticipated, and approaches to handling a mix of future substitutes and complements have not been developed. Future research should also examine whether and how the auction *sequence* of complement and substitute auctions might affect performance.

Online Versus Offline Assortments

Investigations into B2B auctions in B2B markets split from the public auction literature with the advent of the Internet; the impact of the Internet has received considerable attention in both the consumer (see Haruvy and Popkowski-Leszczyc 2009; Park and Wang, 2009) and the B2B (see Emiliani 2000; Emiliani and Stec 2001) auction literature. Internet-based auctions have drastically lowered transaction costs and expanded the choice set of firms on both sides of the market (Jap 2002; Sashi and O'Leary 2002).

Favorable prices and other terms are obtained by increasing competition among suppliers. Additional advantages include the reduction of time and overhead associated with the sourcing decision (Emiliani 2000; Emiliani and Stec 2001; Judge 2001; Richards 2000; Sheridan 2001; Tully 2000). Third-party providers of auction services also claim that they can broaden the pool of potential suppliers competing for the buying company's business.

However, research on dynamic product assortments and offerings in B2B settings is still in a nascent stage. A common fundamental question pertains to the impact on auction revenue of conducting auctions online or face-to-face. A related issue is how bidding behavior is affected when bidders participate online (through a web browser) or face-to-face (i.e. physical presence at the auction). Although the issue may have no bearing on markets for products of standard or unvarying quality, such as consumer packaged goods, books, or any new product, it can complicate the bidding task for used products or products that contain variance in specific attributes, such as used cars, homes, memorabilia and markets for dating. Online bidders, unable to easily and more richly inspect product quality variation, have an informational disadvantage. This might suggest that online bidders will gravitate toward products with less unique variation in specific attributes, since they cannot visually inspect and handle the product. Alternatively, it might be that online bidders accept (or concede) that they are at an information disadvantage and do not need to physically touch or inspect the auction item.

In their examination of more than 85 000 wholesale auction sales over a two and a half year period, Overby and Jap (2009) found evidence for both theories, with the former emerging before the latter. Specifically, they find that initially online buyers are more likely to gravitate toward vehicles with little variation, but over time, as they adapt to the online bidding interface, they are more likely to purchase products with *both* minimal and maximal variation in their attributes. However, online buyers are less likely to purchase cars with conditions in between these two extremes. They also find that, consistent with a long-tail story, online buyers are more likely to bid for products with low availability (i.e. rare) in the market.

IMPLICATIONS FOR BIDDING BEHAVIOR AND STRATEGIES

In this section, we consider the implications of B2B markets on strategic bidding behavior. We begin with an examination of how bidder valuations might be distributed and then consider how bidding behavior is typically operationalized and examined. The findings in this area are primarily based on research in which consumers bid for individual products or pieces, but they are nevertheless generalizable to B2B auction contexts.

Bidder Valuations

The most commonly examined distinction among bidders is their valuation of the auction item or contract (i.e. whether these valuations are private, affiliated or common). Affiliated valuations exist when bidder valuations for the item are correlated among bidders. In common value auctions, all bidders have the same value for the item but different signals regarding what that price might be: no single bidder knows the true value of the item. Both common values and affiliated values imply that bidders in B2B auctions can gain a strategic advantage by observing competitive bidding activity and may compromise their strategic position by revealing information about themselves through their own bids. In contrast, independent private values are bidders' values that are uncorrelated with each other. The most common examples of common value auctions include categories with clear secondary markets or resale values, such as commodities, real estate and cars. Affiliated values are generally accepted in art auctions or other collectors' items.

These distinctions are particularly relevant in B2B auctions because of the differentiating non-price attributes. Quality attributes in particular critically affect bidder scores, as explained previously. The score is the reverse auction equivalent of valuation; thus, each bidder may have private information about his or her own relative advantage and learns more about his or her quality standing by observing others' bids, which in turn reflect their own information. Because the quality differential is the key to winning the auction, this has a parallel in affiliated valuation models.

Bidder Behavior

In B2B markets, theory on bidding behavior is still emerging, though exceptions include the winner's curse and some consideration of intimidation and collusion in auctions (Cramton and Schwartz 2000, 2002). The behavioral literature on bidding in auctions has focused primarily on measures of bidder aggressiveness, including the rate at which bids are submitted, the price concessions the bids offer, and the number of bids offered over the course of the auction. The bidding rate, or the total number of bids during the auction divided by the auction duration, pertains to the bidders' speed of response to other bids (Häubl and Popkowski-Leszczyc 2006; Katok and Kwasnica 2002; and Tuunainen et al. 2001). Essentially, it represents a rescaling, or normalization, of the total bids offered over the course of the auction. The total number of bids, including multiple bids, reflects the bidder's commitment to winning (Ariely and Simonson 2003; Wilcox 2000). Finally, the total price concession, or the difference between a bidder's first and last bids, gives insight into the bidder's commitment to win and his or her defensiveness against competition. Together, these three measures reflect a bidder's commitment to winning and aggressiveness. In an alternative approach, Park and Bradlow (2005) model bidder commitment as a latent, time-varying construct. Using a database of notebook auctions, they develop a general parametric framework that gives insight into whether bidders bid, who bids, when they bid and how much they bid.

Assessment Tools

Along with the evolution in conceptualizing bidder behavior (i.e. in light of bidder differentiation, measurement and the bidding interface), there is growing attention on how best to leverage and represent the plethora of point-by-point bid data made so easily available by the Internet. New statistical estimation techniques are needed for effective data mining to drive decision-making, prediction and operational decisions (Pinker et al. 2003).

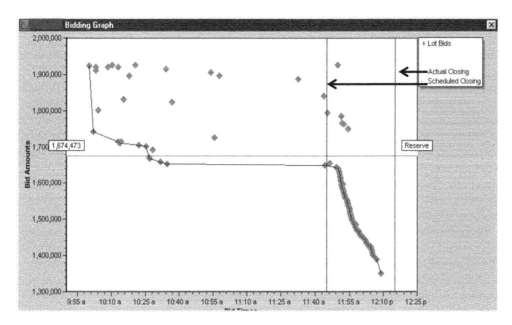

Notes: The horizontal axis denotes time over the course of the auction. Diamonds represent bids received over the course of the auction. The solid line traces the lowest bid at any point in time.

Source: Jap (2002).

Figure 34.1   Bidding activity in online reverse auctions

Another promising direction is the development of decision support systems for price discovery in B2B markets. For example, as a consequence of differentiated bidders and the emergence of buyer-determined reverse auction markets, bidders may self-adjust their price bids to account for their non-price advantages (and disadvantages). Thus, in many buyer-determined reverse auctions we observe many bids above the lowest bid over the course of the auction (see Figure 34.1). Thus, buyers need a way to assess whether a supplier has bid aggressively or cautiously held back. To this end, Jap and Naik (2008) developed BidAnalyzer, an optimization algorithm using state-space models and a Kalman filtering technique, not only to predict the ending bids of an auction (based on initial bid activity) but also to give insight into whether the supplier has held back in its bidding (implying that there is still money to be gained from post-auction negotiations) or has bid too aggressively (and perhaps is in danger of a winner's curse). However, further research is needed on both the development of decision support models and the general process of price discovery in B2B markets.

IMPLICATIONS FOR MECHANISM DESIGN

Finally, in this section we consider buyers' mechanism choice, which principally consists of the degree of price visibility and the use of guarantees or price premiums.

Price Visibility

The price visibility in an auction captures the extent to which bidders can observe every price bid made over the course of the event and can vary along a continuum of visibility. In a full price visibility auction format, all bidders can see every competitive bid (though they typically do not know the bidder's identity). In a partial price visibility auction, bidders cannot see every bid but receive some feedback on their bid's placement relative to others. For example, bidders may receive rank-ordering feedback on their bid price (i.e. they are told that their bid is in first, second or third place) or they may be told only what the first price bid is at any point in time (i.e. no insight into the placement or ordering of any other bids). At the other extreme, a sealed bid auction format is one in which the bidders do not see any information on competitive bids; there is only one round of bidding, which obviates the need for a responsive bid.

In buyer-determined reverse auctions, does the price visibility in the mechanism format lead to similar or differential performance (e.g. savings in reverse auctions)? Jap (2003) compares the savings from sealed bid and full price visible auctions and observes no difference. Instead, she finds that savings are specific to product category type and not to price visibility alone. At one level, this suggests that performance, particularly in this type of auction, is probably driven by additional factors other than the price visibility dimension alone. With this in mind and given the pervasiveness of buyer-determined auction formats in the marketplace, a stream of research examines how price visibility design choices, sometimes in conjunction with other mechanism formats, affect the buyer's or seller's welfare. For example, Engelbrecht-Wiggans et al. (2007) demonstrate that full price visibility in buyer-determined auctions increases the buyer's welfare given a sufficient number of bidders (~four) and product quality is positively related to the bidder's costs. Under these conditions, rational experienced bidders will incorporate their non-price attributes into their bids, and though this will result in higher prices and lower cost reductions relative to a price-based auction, the additional value for buyers who may choose a supplier other than the lowest bidder more than compensates for the loss in price savings.

The intermediate forms of price visibility are a unique characteristic of procurement mechanisms and deserve more research attention and systematic investigation. The theoretical auction literature has primarily focused on either full price visibility or sealed bid mechanisms, but it is the marketplace that is developing and experimenting with intermediate forms of visibility.

Another possible mechanism is to couple the full price visibility mechanism with a non-competitive contract before the auction in a hybrid format. Engelbrecht-Wiggans and Katok (2006) test such an approach, in which the non-competitive contract enables bidders to commit to providing specific volumes at a price determined by the auction. The coupling with a non-competitive contract format outperforms price-based auctions because the non-competitive contracts have a positive expected profit, and the costs of conducting an auction with both mechanisms are as low as or lower than a price-only reverse auction under a variety of conditions. By decoupling volume commitments from price bid competition, this format gives suppliers the opportunity to highlight desirable non-price attributes, thus creating a more effective mechanism than the price-based format alone.

A final stream of research considers how price visibility in buyer-determined B2B auctions affects the inter-organizational relationships (both prospective and existing) between the buyer and bidders (Jap 2003, 2007). Jap (2003) contrasts the impact of sealed bid auctions with full price visibility auctions and finds that bidders feel extremely threatened in full price visible reverse auctions. Specifically, she finds that suspicions of opportunism – that is, the belief that the buyer will actively seek their self-interest (i.e. cheat and extort) at the bidder's expense – are significantly greater and that these suspicions persist, even though the buyer is actually *not* engaging in or attempting to engage in such behavior. This implies that negative suspicions, whether rightly or wrongly, may color bidder perceptions of the event; to the extent that bidders rely on these perceptions in the future, this could imply negative long-term consequences for buyers from suppliers. On the positive side, Jap also finds that full price visible auctions can serve as an effective wake-up call for incumbent suppliers because current suppliers are more willing to make dedicated investments to the buyer than new suppliers in these auctions.

In a subsequent study involving 25 auctions across four industries, Jap (2007) further illuminates how the auction mechanism affects inter-organizational relationship outcomes. She finds that in buyer-determined B2B auctions, the larger the number of bidders, the larger the economic stakes, and the less visible the price in the auction, the better the impact on the relationship (i.e. suspicions of opportunism, overall satisfaction and future expectations). Unsurprisingly, large price drops over the course of the event have the opposite effect on the relationship. In price-determined auctions opportunism suspicions are exacerbated with full price visibility mechanisms and tempered as the economic stakes increase.

Guarantees, Premiums and Penalties

Market makers can also use price guarantees to attract sellers and buyers (Greenleaf et al. 1993; Greenleaf et al. 2002). Though a common approach in art auctions, it has yet to be investigated in B2B auctions. Auction houses might offer sellers a price guarantee for a minimum amount regardless of the auction outcome (taking ownership of the art if it does not sell) and then charge the seller a commission for prices that exceed the guarantee. In general, these approaches profit sellers at the expense of the auction houses, primarily because of the seller's ability to negotiate these circumstances (Greenleaf et al. 2002). Conversely, auction houses may use buy-in penalties with sellers, or the amount they must pay if the property does not sell. This motivates sellers to set a lower reserve price, which increases expected total revenue. This approach typically Pareto-dominates auctions that only use seller commissions (Greenleaf and Sinha 1996).

For art buyers, auction houses might use a premium, or a percentage (typically ~25 per cent) of the first proportion of revenue gained. Premiums typically raise prices because most bidders fail to fully weight the premium during the bidding process and perceive the total cost as lower than it is. This phenomenon is similar to what consumers do with shipping costs, as illustrated in applications of partitioned pricing (Morwitz et al. 1998).

In this section, we have reviewed various individual aspects of format or mechanism design that are commonly considered. Auction mechanisms can be created using some or all aspects of the design. These possibilities represent a wide-open area for future research. There is a need to understand the potential interactive effects of these format characteristics on performance, particularly with respect to buyer-determined auctions. In industrial contexts, repeat purchases are often the norm. Price premiums that vary dynamically is one topic in this vein that remains for future research.

We close this section on a broader note by considering the possibility of *competition* between auction formats or elements of the auction mechanism. In its simplest form, the issue of competition would raise questions regarding the omission/inclusion of one element (e.g. the ending rule) and its impact on bidding strategy. Roth and Ockenfels (2002) attribute the greater sniping behavior (i.e. last-minute bidding) that is greater on eBay than on Amazon.com to eBay's fixed end time compared with the soft close time on Amazon.com. Analytical and simulation-based research on auctions suggests that competitive market formats can coexist in equilibrium (Chen et al. 2005), and even for markets of varying sizes (Ellison et al. 2004). Critical next steps for research on this topic require new data sets and problems, statistical techniques, and more attention to the role of heterogeneity and differentiated bidders on mechanism performance (Haruvy et al. 2008).

CONCLUSIONS

The purpose of this chapter has been to serve as a primer for researchers, academics and practitioners interested in the design of auction-based markets for B2B exchange. Clearly, the high complexity and unique context characteristics related to these markets need to be explored. These complexities and idiosyncrasies also represent opportunities to examine significant departures from classical auction theory based on price and bidder valuation characterizations. Another goal has been to illuminate some of the trade-offs that buyers, sellers and market-makers should consider as they design and structure these pricing and exchange mechanisms.

An obvious next step to this type of work would address how to successfully embed these auction mechanisms in a larger online context and how to generate value for all members involved. This is the challenge that Ariba faces with its online commerce cloud. Its online network is home to more than 4.8 million buyers and sellers from over 16 000 organizations who source and sell over $450 million in goods and services and conduct over 100 000 purchase, sales and financial transactions daily. Empowering these participants to interact, collaborate and exchange with each other more efficiently is the firm's ultimate goal. These outcomes and challenges are the same in most marketing verticals as well. In this vein, future research might examine the role and use of auctions in purchase and supply *networks*. For example, it could be that the use of auctions by network members with high centrality may be more or less effective at staving off the negative relationship effects of online reverse auctions. Or it could be that they differentially *benefit* from their usage relative to non-central network members.

Finally, we hope that this chapter will infect some readers with the same enthusiasm that we have for this area. We have found it to be an exciting place 'to hang our hat' with significant economic impact and managerial implications, as well as a long-term future.

NOTE

1. These non-price attributes are exogenous.

REFERENCES

Ailawadi, Kusum, Eric T. Bradlow, Michaela Draganska, Vincent Nijs, Robert P. Rooderkerk, K. Sudhir, Kenneth C. Wilbur and Jie Zhang (2010), 'Empirical models of manufacturer–retailer interaction: a review and agenda for future research', *Marketing Letters*, **21** (3), 273–86.

Anderson, Erin and Barton Weitz (1992), 'The use of pledges to build and sustain commitment in distribution channels', *Journal of Marketing Research*, **29** (1), 18–34.

Anderson, James C. and James A. Narus (1990), 'A model of distributor firm and manufacturer firm working partnerships', *Journal of Marketing*, **54** (1), 42–58.

Anderson, Jamie and Mark Frohlich (2001), 'Free markets and online auctions', *Business Strategy Review*, **12** (2), 59–68.

Anton, James J. and Dennis A. Yao (1987), 'Second sourcing and the experience curve: price competition in defense procurement', *RAND Journal of Economics*, **18** (1), 57–76.

Anton, James J. and Dennis A. Yao (1989), 'Split awards, procurement, and innovation', *RAND Journal of Economics*, **20** (4), 538–52.

Anton, James J. and Dennis A. Yao (1992), 'Coordination in split award auctions', *Quarterly Journal of Economics*, **107** (2), 681–707.

Ariely, Dan and Itamar Simonson (2003), 'Buying, bidding, playing or competing? Value assessment and decision dynamics in online auctions', *Journal of Consumer Psychology*, **13** (1–2), 113–23.

Bajari, Patrick (1998), 'A structural econometric model of the first price sealed bid auction with asymmetric bidders', working paper, Department of Economics, Stanford University.

Boger, Dan C. and Shu S. Liao (1988), 'Quantity-split strategy under two-contractor competitive procurement environment', Naval Postgraduate School, NPS-54-88-008.

Bradford, Kevin, Stephen Brown, Shankar Ganesan, Gary Hunter, Vini Onyemah, Robert Palmatier, Dominique Rouziès, Roseann Spiro, Harish Sujan and Barton Weitz (2010), 'The embedded sales force: connecting buying and selling organizations', *Marketing Letters*, **21** (3), 239–54.

Branco, Fernando (1997), 'The design of multidimensional auctions', *RAND Journal of Economics*, **28** (1), 63–81.

Buccola, Steven T. (1982), 'Price trends at livestock auctions', *American Journal of Agricultural Economics*, **64** (1), 63–9.

Carare, Octavian (2007), 'Reserve prices in repeated auctions', working paper, Department of Economics, University of Texas at Dallas.

Carter, Craig R. and Lutz Kaufmann (2007), 'The impact of electronic reverse auctions on supplier performance: the mediating role of relationship variables', *Journal of Supply Chain Management*, **43** (1), 16–26.

Carter, Craig R. and Cynthia Kay Stevens (2006), 'Electronic reverse auction configuration and its impact on buyer price and supplier perceptions of opportunism: a laboratory experiment', *Journal of Operations Management*, **25**, 1035–54.

Che, Yeon-Koo (1993), 'Design competition through multidimensional auctions', *RAND Journal of Economics*, **24** (4), 668–80.

Chen, Rachel R., Robin O. Roundy, Rachel Q. Zhang and Ganesh Janakiraman (2005), 'Efficient auction mechanisms for supply chain procurement', *Management Science*, **51** (3), 467–82.

Chen-Ritzo, Ching-Hua, Terry P. Harrison, Anthony M. Kwasnica and Douglas J. Thomas (2005), 'Better, faster, cheaper: an experimental analysis of a multiattribute reverse auction mechanism with restricted information feedback', *Management Science*, **51** (12), 1753–62.

Colwell, Peter F. and Abdullah Yavaş (1994), 'The demand for agricultural land and strategic bidding in auctions', *Journal of Real Estate Finance and Economics*, **8** (2), 137–49.

Coughlan, Anne T., S. Chan Choi, Wujin Chu, Charles A. Ingene, Sridhar Moorthy, V. Padmanabhan, Jagmohan S. Raju, David A. Soberman, Richard Staelin and Z. John Zjang (2010), 'Marketing modeling reality and the realities of marketing modeling', *Marketing Letters*, **21** (3), 317–34.

Cramton, Peter and Jesse A. Schwartz (2000), 'Collusive bidding: lessons from the FCC spectrum auctions', *Journal of Regulatory Economics*, **17** (3), 229–52.

Cramton, Peter and Jesse A. Schwartz (2002), 'Collusive bidding in the FCC spectrum auctions', *Contributions to Economic Analysis & Policy*, **1** (1), 1–19.

DePamphilis, Donald (2007), *Mergers, Acquisitions, and Other Restructuring Activities: An Integrated Approach to Process, Tools, Cases, and Solutions*, 4th edn, San Diego, CA: Elsevier/Academic Press.

Donald, Stephen G., Harry J. Paarsch and Jacques Robert (2006), 'An empirical model of the multi-unit, sequential, clock auction', *Journal of Applied Econometrics*, **21** (8), 1221–47.

Ellison, Glenn, Drew Fudenberg and Markus Möbius (2004), 'Competing auctions', *Journal of the European Economic Association*, **2** (1), 30–66.

Emiliani, Mario L. (2000) 'Business-to-business online auctions: key issues for purchasing process improvement', *Supply Chain Management*, **5** (4), 176–86.

Emiliani, Mario L. and David J. Stec (2001), 'Online reverse auction purchasing contracts', *Supply Chain Management*, **6** (3–4), 101–5.

Engelbrecht-Wiggans, Richard and Elena Katok (2006), 'e-sourcing in procurement: theory and behavior in reverse auctions with non-competitive contracts', *Management Science*, **52** (4), 581–96.

Engelbrecht-Wiggans, Richard, Ernan Haruvy and Elena Katok (2007), 'A comparison of buyer-determined and price-based multi-attribute mechanisms', *Marketing Science*, **26** (5), 629–41.

Forbes.com (2010), 'The global 2000', (21 April), available at http://www.forbes.com/lists/2010/18/global-2000-10_The-Global-2000_Rank.html, accessed 28 February 2011.

Ganesan, Shankar (1993), 'Negotiation strategies and the nature of channel relationships', *Journal of Marketing Research*, **30** (2), 183–203.

Gattiker, Thomas F., Xiaowen Huang and Joshua L. Schwarz (2007), 'Negotiation, email and internet reverse auctions: how sourcing mechanisms deployed by buyers affect suppliers' trust', *Journal of Operations Management*, **25**, 184–202.

Greenleaf, Eric A. and Atanu R. Sinha (1996), 'Combining buy-in penalties with commissions at auction houses', *Management Science*, **42** (4), 529–40.

Greenleaf, Eric A., Ambar G. Rao and Atanu R. Sinha (1993), 'Guarantees in auctions: the auction house as negotiator and managerial decision maker', *Management Science*, **39** (9), 1130–45.

Greenleaf, Eric A., Ma Jun, Qiu Wanhua, Ambar G. Rao and Atanu R. Sinha (2002), 'Note on "Guarantees in auctions: the auction house as negotiator and managerial decision maker"', *Management Science*, **48** (12), 1640–44.

Haruvy, Ernan and Peter Popkowski-Leszczyc (2009), 'Bidder motives in cause-related auctions', *International Journal of Research in Marketing*, **26** (4), 324–31.

Haruvy, Ernan, Peter Popkowski-Leszczyc, Octavian Carare, James Cox, Eric Greenleaf, Wolfgang Jank, Sandy Jap, Young-Hoon Park and Michael Rothkopf (2008), 'Competition between auctions', *Marketing Letters*, **19** (3–4), 431–48.

Häubl, Gerald and Peter T.L. Popkowski-Leszczyc (2006), 'Bidding frenzy: how the speed of competitor reaction influences product valuations in auctions', working paper, School of Business, University of Alberta.

Heezen, Judith and Walter Baets (1996), 'The impact of electronic markets: the case of the Dutch flower auctions', *The Journal of Strategic Information Systems*, **5** (4), 317–33.

Houston, Mark B., Michael Hutt, Christine Moorman, Peter H. Reingen, Aric Rindfleisch, Vanitha Swaminathan and Beth Walker (2004), 'A network perspective on marketing strategy performance', in Donald Lehmann and Christine Moorman (eds), *Assessing Marketing Strategy Performance*, Cambridge, MA: Marketing Science Institute, pp. 249–70.

Jap, Sandy D. (1999), 'Pie-expansion efforts: collaboration processes in buyer–supplier relationships', *Journal of Marketing Research*, **36** (4), 461–75.

Jap, Sandy D. (2002), 'Online, reverse auctions: issues, themes, and prospects for the future', *Journal of the Academy of Marketing Science*, **30** (4), 506–25.

Jap, Sandy D. (2003), 'An exploratory study of the introduction of online reverse auctions', *Journal of Marketing*, **67** (3), 96–107.

Jap, Sandy D. (2007), 'The impact of online reverse auction design on buyer–supplier relationships', *Journal of Marketing*, **71** (1), 146–59.

Jap, Sandy D. and Ernan Haruvy (2008), 'Interorganizational relationships and bidding behavior in industrial online reverse auctions', *Journal of Marketing Research*, **45** (5), 550–61.

Jap, Sandy D. and Prasad Naik (2008), '*BidAnalyzer*: a method for estimation and selection of dynamic bidding models', *Marketing Science*, **27** (6), 949–60.

Jofre-Bonet, Mireia and Martin Pesendorfer (2003), 'Estimation of a dynamic auction game', *Econometrica*, **71** (5), 1443–89.

Judge, Paul C. (2001), 'How I saved $100 million on the web', *Fast Company*, **43**, 174–81.

Katok, Elena and Anthony M. Kwasnica (2002), 'Time is money: the effect of clock speed on seller's revenue in Dutch auctions', Pennsylvania State University, ISBM Report 11-2002.

Lilien, Gary L., Rajdeep Grewal, Douglas Bowman, Min Ding, Abbie Griffin, V. Kumar, Das Narayandas, Renana Peres, Raji Srinivasan and Qiong Wang (2010), 'Calculating, creating and claiming value in business markets: status and research agenda', *Marketing Letters*, **21** (3), 287–300.

Macneil, Ian R. (1980), *The New Social Contract: An Inquiry into Modern Contractual Relations*, New Haven, CT: Yale University Press.

Mantrala, Murali K., Sönke Albers, Fabio Caldieraro, Ove Jensen, Kissan Joseph, Manfred Krafft, Chakravarthi Narasimhan, Srinath Gopalakrishna, Andris Zoltners, Rajiv Lal and Leonard Lodish (2010), 'Sales force modeling: state of the field and research agenda', *Marketing Letters*, **21** (3), 255–72.

Mayer, Andrew (1987), 'Military procurements: basic principles and recent developments', *George Washington Journal of International Law and Economics*, **21**, 165–87.

Milgrom, Paul (2000), 'Putting auction theory to work: the simultaneous ascending auction', *Journal of Political Economy*, **108** (2), 245–72.

Milgrom, Paul and Robert J. Weber (1982), 'A theory of auctions and competitive bidding', *Econometrica*, **50** (5), 1089–122.

Mohr, Jakki and John R. Nevin (1990), 'Communication strategies in marketing channels: a theoretical perspective', *Journal of Marketing*, **54** (4), 36–51.

Morgan, Robert M. and Shelby D. Hunt (1994), 'The commitment-trust theory of relationship marketing', *Journal of Marketing*, **58** (3), 20–38.

Morwitz, Vicki G., Eric A. Greenleaf and Eric J. Johnson (1998), 'Divide and prosper: consumers' reactions to partitioned prices', *Journal of Marketing Research*, **35** (4), 453–63.

Overby, Eric and Sandy Jap (2009), 'Electronic and physical market channels: a multiyear investigation in a market for products of uncertain quality', *Management Science*, **55** (6), 940–57.

Park, Young-Hoon and Eric T. Bradlow (2005), 'An integrated model for bidding behavior in internet auctions: whether, who, when, and how much', *Journal of Marketing Research*, **42** (4), 470–82.

Park, Young-Hoon and Xin Wang (2009), 'Online and name-your-own-price auctions: a literature review', in Vithala R. Rao (ed.), *Handbook of Pricing Research in Marketing*, Cheltenham, UK and Northampton, MA, USA: Edward Elgar Publishing, pp. 419–34.

Pesendorfer, Martin (2000), 'A study of collusion in first-price auctions', *Review of Economic Studies*, **67** (232), 381–411.

Pinker, Edieal J., Abraham Seidmann and Yaniv Vakrat (2003), 'Managing online auctions: current business and research issues', *Management Science*, **49** (11), 1457–84.

Porter, Robert H. and J. Douglas Zona (1999), 'Ohio school milk markets: an analysis of bidding', *RAND Journal of Economics*, **30** (2), 263–88.

Rao, Vithala (2009), *Handbook of Pricing Research in Marketing*, Cheltenham, UK and Northampton, MA, USA: Edward Elgar Publishing.

Richards, B. (2000), 'Dear supplier: this is going to hurt you more than it hurts me . . .', *Ecompany Now*, **1** (1), 136–42.

Rindfleisch, Aric, Kersi Antia, Janet Bercovitz, James R. Brown, Joseph Cannon, Stephen J. Carson, Mrinal Ghosh, Susan Helper, Diana C. Robertson and Kenneth H. Wathne (2010), 'Transaction costs, opportunism, and governance: contextual considerations and future research opportunities', *Marketing Letters*, **21** (3), 211–22.

Riordan, Michael H. and David E.M. Sappington (1987), 'Awarding monopoly franchises', *American Economic Review*, **77** (3), 375–87.

Roth, Alvin E. and Axel Ockenfels (2002), 'Last-minute bidding and the rules for ending second-price auctions: evidence from eBay and Amazon auctions on the Internet', *American Economic Review*, **92** (4), 1093–103.

Sa Vinhas, Alberto, S. Chatterjee, Shantanu Dutta, Adam Fein, Joseph Lajos, Scott Neslin, Lisa Scheer, William Ross and Qiong Wang (2010), 'Channel design, coordination, and performance: future research directions', *Marketing Letters*, **21** (3), 223–38.

Sashi, C.M. and Bay O'Leary (2002), 'The role of Internet auctions in the expansion of B2B markets', *Industrial Marketing Management*, **31** (2), 103–10.

Schelling, Thomas (1960), *The Strategy of Conflict*, Boston, MA: Harvard University Press.

Sheridan, John H. (2001), 'Proceed with caution', *Industry Week*, **250** (2), 38–44.

Srivastava, Joydeep and Dipankar Chakravarti (2009), 'Channel negotiations with information asymmetries: contingent influences of communication and trustworthiness reputations', *Journal of Marketing Research*, **46** (4), 557–72.

Tully, Shawn (2000), 'The B2B tool that really is changing the world', *Fortune*, **141** (6), 132–7.

Tunca, Tunay I. and Qiong Wu (2009), 'Multiple sourcing and procurement process selection with bidding events', *Management Science*, **55** (5), 763–80.

Tunca, Tunay I. and Stefanos A. Zenios (2006), 'Supply auctions and relational contracts for procurement', *Manufacturing and Service Operations Management*, **8** (1), 43–67.

Tuunainen, Virpi Kristiina, Eric van Heck and Otto Koppius (2001), 'Auction speed as a design variable for internet auctions', working paper, Rotterdam School of Management, Erasmus University.

Van den Bulte, Christophe and Stefan Wuyts (2007), 'Social networks and marketing', *MSI Relevant Knowledge Series*, Cambridge, MA: Marketing Science Institute.

Victor, Ron (2008), 'What is online reverse auction?', available at http://ezinearticles.com/?What-is-Online-Reverse-Auction?&id=1775310, accessed 10 December 2008.

Wilcox, Ronald T. (2000), 'Experts and amateurs: the role of experience in internet auctions', *Marketing Letters*, **11** (4), 363–74.

Wuyts, Stefan and Inge Geyskens (2005), 'The formation of buyer–supplier relationships: detailed contract drafting and close partner selection', *Journal of Marketing*, **69** (4), 103–17.

Wuyts, Stefan, Stefan Stremersch, Christophe Van den Bulte and Philip Hans Franses (2004), 'Vertical marketing systems for complex products: a triadic perspective', *Journal of Marketing Research*, **41** (4), 479–87.

Zeithammer, Robert (2006), 'Forward-looking bidding in Internet auctions', *Journal of Marketing Research*, **43** (3), 462–76.

Zeithammer, Robert (2007a), 'Strategic bid-shading and sequential auctioning with learning from past prices', *Management Science*, **53** (9), 1510–19.

Zeithammer, Robert (2007b), 'Optimal selling in dynamic auctions: adaptation versus commitment', *Marketing Science*, **26** (6), 859–67.

Zeithammer, Robert (2008), 'Commitment in sequential auctioning: advance listings and threshold prices', *Economic Theory*, **38** (1), 187–216.

Zeithammer, Robert (2009), 'Sequential auctions with information about future goods', working paper, Anderson School of Management, University of California, Los Angeles.

PART VII

METHODOLOGICAL ISSUES

35 Qualitative research methods for investigating business-to-business marketing questions
Abbie Griffin

Qualitative research methods started to be used for research in the management field in the mid-1980s, with the major texts explicating these techniques first published in the middle of that decade (e.g. Miles and Huberman 1994; Yin 1984). Shortly thereafter these research methods started to move into use in our field of B2B marketing. One of the first articles to be published in an A-level marketing journal using these methods was Kohli and Jaworski's (1990) article developing the market orientation construct, published in the *Journal of Marketing* (*JM*). Shortly thereafter Workman (1993) published his ethnographic study of marketing's role in new product development (NPD) in the *Journal of Marketing Research* (*JMR*). Both he and several other young academics had success publishing in *JM* and *JMR* in the 1990s, introducing these research methods to the field of marketing. This chapter uses several of these articles as examples and illustrations throughout.

In the 10 years from 1997 to 2006 inclusive, 170 articles based on qualitative methods were published (about 16 per cent of the total published) in the three journals that focus exclusively on the B2B realm: *Industrial Marketing Management* (*IMM*), *Journal of Business-to-Business Marketing* (*JBBM*) and *Journal of Business and Industrial Marketing* (*JBIM*). Of those articles, 145 (85 per cent) used single or multiple case studies as the research method (Piekkari et al. 2010). Currently approximately 20 per cent of the articles published in *IMM* and *JBIM*, totaling about 30 articles per year, use qualitative research methods; again, predominantly case studies. *IMM* considers the case study research method important enough to the field that the first issue of Volume 39 (January 2010) was a special issue with 13 articles devoted to understanding how to 'use case studies to advance B2B marketing theory and practice' (LaPlaca 2010, p. 1).

This chapter defines what qualitative research is, outlines when and why qualitative methods are most appropriate, briefly describes the different types of qualitative research methods, presents the general research process for qualitative research, reviews advice on what constitutes rigor in qualitative research and then closes with a review of the state of the field for published qualitative research.

WHAT IS QUALITATIVE RESEARCH ANYWAY?

This chapter adopts the following definition:

> Qualitative research is a situated activity that locates the observer in the world. It consists of a set of interpretive, material practices that make the world visible. These practices . . . turn the world into a series of representations, including field notes, interviews, conversations,

photographs, recordings, and memos to the self. At this level, qualitative research involves an interpretive, naturalistic approach to the world (Denzin and Lincoln 2005, p. 3).

Qualitative research questions 'how' and 'why' something happened in the natural world and focuses on context. These questions allow researchers to investigate issues of process and explain how outcomes are achieved. Qualitative researchers view social phenomena holistically, and qualitative research typically produces a rich, thick description of that world. In our field, qualitative research takes place in and between organizations and investigates the complex processes taking place in and across those organizations in their entirety. It produces thick descriptions and complex models of organizational processes and relationships, as well as how individuals participate in them.

For example, Workman's (1993) *JMR* article investigated the processes by which the marketing function in one firm was involved in NPD. This investigation required understanding the entire complex, multifunctional process of product development: what needs to be done at what point in the process, who is responsible for what aspects of development, how decisions get made and so on, as well as how the marketing function fits into all of these steps, both formally and informally.

Grewal et al. (2007) investigated relationships occurring across firm boundaries. They researched how inter-firm linkages were affected by catastrophic disruptions, or crises, that alter patterns of demand, including both natural phenomena (hurricanes) and human-made crises (terrorism). They explored how these crises affected relationships with both customers and suppliers, as well as the role that inter-firm linkages play in crisis management, resulting in a process model of crisis management.

Qualitative methodologies thus give researchers the ability to investigate complex organizational processes and relationships from a holistic perspective. They allow researchers to approach settings or phenomena of interest without assuming a priori that they know what will be important, focusing instead on discovering what is important. They produce rich descriptions that can be used to describe, explore or explain phenomena and either generate or refine theory.

WHEN TO USE QUALITATIVE METHODS

Because of the output they generate, qualitative methods can be used for multiple purposes:

- to find interesting problems;
- as a precursor to a survey-based empirical study;
- as an end in itself in understanding a phenomenon or generating theory.

Qualitative Research as a Preliminary Research Phase

One difficulty many academics have is coming up with interesting (doable and publishable) research questions. Qualitative methods can be used to help identify potentially interesting research questions. As John Hauser (1998, p. 73) wrote: 'I was never able to set forth a theory without spending time in the field. It's amazing how much insight one can obtain from a manager who is facing a difficult (and scientifically interesting) problem'. The qualitative data Hauser obtained from managers helped him develop theories for how to model their problem(s).

Initial information about potentially interesting problems can be obtained just by informally chatting with managers. However, using a more formal interview process that moves from casual observations and conversations to a more systematic inquiry may increase the probability that a researcher will come to understand all the different aspects of a phenomenon. Formally creating an interview guide about the research question of interest, reviewing it with colleagues in the domain for completeness and understand-ability and then consistently using it in conversations with managers (interviews with informants) increases the likelihood of uncovering unexpected insights into the details of a problem that could affect the approach taken to try and model it, empirically under-stand it or solve it through some other means.

Many academics use qualitative research as a precursor to fielding a piece of large-scale survey research. Qualitative research can help a researcher identify the relevant theories that might be used to develop a testable empirical model, fill in contextual details to fully specify a model and rigorously develop new scales. Churchill (1979) explicitly recommended the use of qualitative research in the item generation phase of scale devel-opment. Many academics never publish an article based just on the qualitative findings. However, they use the outputs of their qualitative research to justify the structure of the model tested in the empirical manuscript or to develop the scales. A quantitative study with a higher likelihood of publication is likely to result from a more systematic and rigorously conducted qualitative inquiry.

Qualitative Research as the End Result of the Project

Qualitative research as an end result is done for one of three purposes:

- describe a phenomenon;
- explore a phenomenon;
- explain a phenomenon.

A descriptive study documents and describes a phenomenon. In general the research questions ask about the salient actions, events, beliefs, attitudes and social structures and processes in the phenomenon. Because theory is neither developed nor tested, descriptive qualitative research is the most difficult type to get published. Workman's (1993) article on marketing's role in NPD and Drumwright's (1994) article on socially responsible organizational buying are examples of descriptive qualitative research. The results of Workman's research included a listing and description of the types of formal and infor-mal actions marketing takes in influencing NPD. Drumwright's research resulted in rich description of a four-category typology of firm actions with regard to socially respon-sible buying. It is important to note that both of these articles were groundbreaking in their domain: no research had investigated either topic previously. Only because they were groundbreaking did a description of the phenomenon make a sufficient contribu-tion to new knowledge to warrant publication in an A-level marketing journal.

An exploratory study is undertaken to investigate a little-understood phenomenon, for the purpose of identifying or discovering important categories of meaning and generating hypotheses for further research. The general research questions are:

- what is happening in this organization?
- what are the salient themes, patterns or categories of meaning?
- how are these themes linked?

Since 1994, qualitative B2B research articles published in A-level marketing journals have all been exploratory in nature: Drumwright (1998), Gilly and Wolfinbarger (1998), Workman et al. (1998) and Narayandas and Rangan (2004). Drumwright's (1998) article took the next step in her investigation into organizational social responsibility, this time looking at advertising with a social dimension. In this article she went beyond just description to create a simple, direct-effect conceptual model of the antecedents to the perceived success of a social advertising campaign. Gilly and Wolfinbarger (1998) investigated how a firm's advertising affects its employees' attitudes toward the company, creating a conceptual model and hypotheses for testing by later researchers.

Workman et al.'s (1998) research investigated how marketing is organized in firms. In addition to creating a typology of and descriptions for the organizational structures found, they developed a general conceptual framework and propositions addressing how firm- and strategic business unit (SBU)-specific factors are associated with the different organizational structures and antecedent relationships for two specific, non-structural marketing organization-dependent variables: dispersion of marketing research and cross-functional power of marketing. Finally, Narayandas and Rangan (2004) investigated how firms in mature industries build and sustain relationships with important suppliers, using data collected from both sides of the customer–supplier dyad. This research resulted in several complex propositions about how these relationships form, build and remain in place over time.

The most difficult form of qualitative research to execute is an explanatory study. Its purpose is to explain the patterns related to the phenomenon in question and to identify plausible relationships shaping the phenomena. Although an exploratory study may produce a model of simple direct-effect relationships, explanatory studies produce much more complex models of a topic and all of its themes, including complex interactions between those themes. Kohli and Jaworski's (1990) *JM* article explicating the market orientation construct, antecedents, consequences and numerous antecedent and moderator propositions is an excellent example.

The difference between an exploratory and explanatory study lies in the completeness and complexity of the model and propositions proposed. An exploratory study uncovers *some* themes and direct effect relationships, which generally can be tested empirically using regression modeling because they are relatively simple. An explanatory study instead develops a more completely specified model, frequently with multiple mediators and moderators. Figure 35.1 exemplifies the types of output generated from an explanatory study (Mish 2009). As proposed, this model is not empirically testable because of its complexity, and it requires a significant amount of text to convey all of the meanings contained within this figure. The same is true for the initially proposed market orientation model in Kohli and Jaworski (1990). Typically, to test these types of models, subsequent researchers carve out a subset of the overall structure to test at any one time.

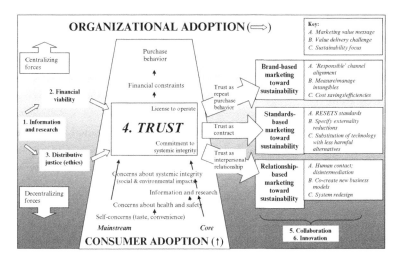

Source: Mish (2009), reprinted with permission.

Figure 35.1   Trust fulcrum model of marketing for sustainability

In summary, understanding how to execute a rigorously performed qualitative research project can result in a publishable piece of research, either directly or indirectly. To publish directly in A-level journals, the research will need to be at least exploratory if not explanatory in nature. Recently it seems to have become more difficult to publish qualitative research in business marketing topics in the field's A-level journals. It may be helpful to publish the initial qualitative model in a domain-specific journal (e.g. *IMM*, *Journal of Product Innovation Management, Journal of Service Research*), then target empirical research that tests the model to an A-level journal. Good qualitative research can indirectly improve the likelihood of publication of an empirical project by refining a theoretical model to be tested empirically or aiding in scale development. Thus the ability to execute a qualitative research project rigorously should be one methodology in researchers' arsenal of capabilities.

QUALITATIVE RESEARCH METHODOLOGIES

This section briefly describes the most frequently used qualitative methodologies and provides primary resources that offer more detail about how to execute each method rigorously.

Interviews

The simplest qualitative method is in-depth interviews. Interviews can be sufficient when the phenomenon under investigation is less complex and the research is more tightly designed, as when Hebda et al. (2007) interviewed triads about their different perspectives on the same rather narrow issue: how to motivate serial innovators. Showing how the human resource managers' perspectives on this point differed from those of the innovator and the innovator's manager helped create sufficient new knowledge to warrant publication. Sources that describe how to execute interviews include Kvale (1996), Merton et al. (1990) and Rubin and Rubin (2005).

Case Study Research

One of the dominant research methods encouraged by and published in *IMM* in the past 10 years is case studies (see Chapter 36 for additional detail). A case study is a relatively intensive study and analysis of a single instance of a phenomenon, process or firm, gathering data very broadly. Case research is most appropriate when researchers are interested in complex questions that require an understanding of the context to understand the phenomenon. It is best for more broadly defined research topics. The Radical Innovation Project, for example, defined its mission as performing research that would produce new theories, insights and data to test ways for improving the practice of managing radical innovation in large, established companies (Leifer et al. 2000). Therefore they longitudinally studied one radical innovation project in each of 10 companies, investigating how projects were executed in the context of both the research organization and the larger business unit. Yin (1984, 2003a, 2003b) has written extensively on case study research methods.

Participant Observation and Ethnography

Participant observation directly observes people's daily behavior. When it is carried out over a long time period, it is referred to as ethnography. Ethnography produces a close and intimate familiarity with a given group of individuals, their language and their practices, through intensive involvement with that group in its natural environment. Ethnographers come to understand and describe a socio-cultural scene from the emic, or insider's, perspective. In business marketing research, it can be helpful in understanding how people actually participate in processes within the firm, whether they be manufacturing, NPD or decision-making processes. Ethnography can help a researcher link what people say they do to what they actually do and uncover discrepancies. Workman (1993) studied marketing's role in NPD processes using a nine-month ethnographic approach. Three key sources of information are Fetterman (1998), Jorgensen (1989) and van Maanen (1988).

Action Research

In action research, an organization wishing to make a particular change and a researcher with an idea about how to intervene to help it make that change work collaboratively to develop and implement the intervention. They then jointly analyze the results, determine the intervention's level of success, and either apply another intervention to improve on its success or develop and implement a mechanism to disseminate the intervention across the organization. Although action research has not typically been viewed as equally 'scientific' as some other qualitative methodologies in the United States, it is still frequently employed in Europe, especially in the United Kingdom. For a detailed description of the method, see McIntyre (2007).

Grounded Theory

Theory is the set of concepts used to define and/or explain some phenomenon. Grounded theory is the discovery of theory from data systematically gathered and analyzed through the research process. Grounded theorists begin with an area of study and allow theory to emerge from the data. The literature review typically is completed after developing an independent analysis of the data. Theorizing from data is a complex activity that entails not only conceiving or intuiting ideas or concepts but also formulating them into logical, systematic and explanatory schema. Grounded theory can be produced from interviews (Griffin et al. 2009) or case studies (Eisenhardt 1989; Kester et al. 2011). Rather than a pure research 'method', it is an approach to knowledge creation. The original source on this method is Glaser and Strauss (1967). Eisenhardt (1989) also advanced knowledge of developing grounded theory from case studies as it applies to managerial research questions. Additional useful references include Strauss and Corbin (1998), Charmaz (2006) and Bryant and Charmaz (2010).

Multiple Methods Simultaneously

Because of the complexity of the phenomena under investigation, many business marketing qualitative researchers use multiple methods in their investigations. Kester et al. (2011), for example, used a combination of in-depth interviewing, archival analysis of firm documents and participant observations of meetings in a grounded theory, four-case study of how business units make NPD portfolio decisions. Documents provided data about the process as it should be done, according to corporate policy; interviews provided data about what managers said they did; and observations showed how decisions actually were made. Multiple methods frequently help researchers triangulate their data to secure an in-depth understanding of the phenomena in question. Thus successful qualitative researchers should have an understanding of many of the different methodologies that constitute the field.

QUALITATIVE RESEARCH PROCESS

The process for executing qualitative research (Figure 35.2) differs in several ways from experimental or survey research. In experimental and survey research, collected data cannot be changed or added to without running another experiment or fielding another survey. Nor can a data collection instrument be changed once the first data are collected, without abandoning the data already collected and starting over again. The sample also cannot be changed mid-process. In qualitative research, though, the data are collected iteratively, the instrument can be changed or added to as needed and even the sample composition can be modified throughout the data collection and analysis phases. Finally data analysis – or the steps in the shaded box in Figure 35.2 – is much more complex and difficult and demands significant cognitive effort and time. The next sections overview each of the research process steps with examples. Sources for designing qualitative research include Marshall and Rossman (2006) and Maxwell (1996).

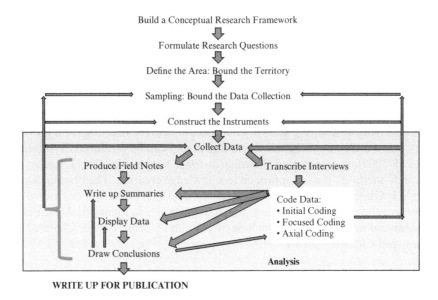

Figure 35.2   General research process

Build a Conceptual Research Framework

All researchers come to a project with some orienting ideas. The question in building a conceptual framework is how much should come from the extant theory before entering the field and how much should emerge from the data collected in the field. On one end of the spectrum are tightly designed studies with well-delineated constructs. For example, Hebda et al.'s (2007) tightly designed research on motivating and demotivating highly successful technologists employed well-defined, motivation-related constructs from the human resources literature as a basis for inquiry. On the other hand, researchers doing truly grounded theory enter the field with a very loosely designed study (emergent design) and allow virtually the entire conceptual framework to emerge from the data. Emergent designs are more appropriate for exploring more complex phenomena. The sample and data collection instruments may change significantly during data collection and analysis. Because very little was known about marketing's role in NPD in high-tech companies, Workman's (1993) research was a loosely designed study.

Most qualitative projects fall between the ends of this spectrum. Several of my publications (e.g. Griffin et al. 2007, 2009) on serial innovators provide good examples: we started with Amabile's (1983) componential creativity model as the underlying framework to investigate how serial innovators innovate. During the investigation, other constructs (e.g. perspective, political ability) arose, which changed the overall framework materially.

Formulate Initial Research Questions

Formulating initial research questions helps researchers organize how they will execute the rest of the project, as each question represents a facet of an empirical domain to explore. The way these questions are organized may also help researchers understand what they want to know first or most importantly about a phenomenon. These questions thus help make the theoretical assumptions more explicit. They also may shape sampling decisions and point directly toward specific data-gathering devices or even specific initial interview questions.

Good research questions are answerable (doable), substantively relevant (should-doable), and 'want-to-doable' (Silverman 2005). An answerable research question is one for which the data required to answer the question are, if not obvious, then at least imaginable and obtainable. Substantively relevant questions are scientifically and/or theoretically interesting and worthwhile, justifying the investment to be spent on the research effort. They need to contribute materially to theory, practice, social issues and/or policy, ultimately making them publishable. A 'want-to-doable' question is one that will keep a researcher's interest piqued for the long period of time and significant effort it will take to execute and write up the research. This is no small point in selecting a research project to pursue.

Research questions can be theoretical in nature, site-specific or focused on specific populations. Kohli and Jaworski's (1990, p. 1) research question, for example, was theoretical: their goal was to provide 'a foundation for the systematic development of a theory of market orientation'. Workman's (1993) research on marketing's role in NPD was a site-specific question. My research question about innovators focused on a specific population: how do serial innovators repeatedly develop breakthrough innovations in large, mature US firms?

Define the Area: Bound the Territory

This step in the research process says as much about what will be *excluded* from the research as it says about what will be *included*. Bounds that may need to be defined include topics, geographies and populations. The goal is to make the research 'doable'. Bounding the territory is important for matching the project scope to the time, money and manpower available.

Notice that the serial innovators research question, in addition to naming the focal population of interest, delimits the kind of companies in which these innovators would be sought. It specifically eliminates people working in start-ups and those from outside the United States, because we thought a priori that the resource and cultural differences in these types of businesses and geographies might change the findings materially. We also bounded this work to innovators residing in US firms in part because we had no budget for overseas travel.

Sampling: Bound the Data Collection

On the one hand, enough data must be collected to demonstrate that a comprehensive data set has been obtained that allows researchers to derive the relationships and conclusions they have drawn. On the other hand, more data collection means more time and money.

In research for business markets, sampling occurs at several different levels: industry, firm and people within firms. The number and types of industries and firms dictates the research generalizability. The number of documents reviewed, people interviewed and meetings attended indicates the depth of the data gathered, which relates to the ability to move from description through exploration and into explanation, as well as to issues of validity and reliability. Qualitative research sampling is more likely to be purposive, theoretical or convenient in nature than random, as is frequently desired in survey and experimental research. Snowball techniques frequently have to be used to find the right kinds of organizations for the research, then to network into the organization and find the right people to whom to talk.

In purposive sampling, industries, firms and individuals are chosen as research sites or informants because they have a specific feature that relates to the phenomenon being investigated in some important way. Researchers must think critically about the parameters of the phenomenon and choose the organizations carefully to reflect those parameters. For example when studying NPD portfolio decision-making, Kester et al. (2011) chose four specific cases: two firms from industries with sophisticated portfolio decision-making processes and two from industries that were the least sophisticated. Data were thus gathered about both 'good' decision-making processes and those that were likely to be associated with less-than-stellar outcomes.

Theoretical sampling is similar to purposive sampling, except that the cases are chosen strictly in terms of their relevance to the theoretical underpinnings of the research. Researchers add cases representing different aspects of the theoretical position until theoretical saturation is reached, which is the point at which incremental learning is minimal (Glaser and Strauss 1967). In theoretical sampling it is critical to include 'deviant' cases. For example Kester et al.'s (2011) purposive sampling plan did not quite reach the level of theoretical sampling because they did not include a firm that was not just 'less sophisticated' in terms of making portfolio decisions but one that made *no* portfolio decisions whatsoever.

Many times for business marketing research, a topic is so difficult to find relevant informants for that a convenience sample must be used. For example, serial innovators are only 1 in 50 to 200 of the employees in a firm's research division (Vojak et al. 2006). To find them, we started by querying various contacts about whether they knew of any such people in their organization. Then we contacted any individuals they named to determine whether they really were serial innovators, using a series of screening questions.

Questions always arise about how many cases to undertake and people to interview. Eisenhardt (1989, p. 545) suggests that:

> while there is no ideal number of cases, a number between 4 and 10 usually works well. With fewer than 4 cases, it is often difficult to generate theory with much complexity, and its empirical grounding is likely to be unconvincing . . . With more than 10 cases, it quickly becomes difficult to cope with the complexity and volume of the data.

Griffin and Hauser (1993) found that 20 interviews produced about 90 per cent of the data theoretically available.

These recommendations vary of course with the complexity of the phenomenon under investigation. Hebda et al. (2007), looking specifically at motivation, collected data from 22 innovator–manager–human resource manager triads. However, across the total serial innovator project, more than 60 serial innovators and about the same number of managers and co-workers were interviewed. Because this overall project was very complex, with the aim of understanding how serial innovators repeatedly innovated, what kind of people they were and how they developed into innovators, many in-depth interviews were needed.

Construct the Instruments

The objective of data collection instruments is to enable the researcher to gather *all* of the information needed from *each* of the research sites or interviewees. There are two major kinds of instruments: those that help the researcher collect artifacts and those for interviewing.

Artifact collection instruments can be as simple as checklists of material to be collected. For research on organizations, it may include items such as organizational charts, mission statements, strategy statements, procedures and policies, and descriptions of processes. For example Kester et al. (2011) collected organizational charts, NPD strategy statements and the portfolio decision-making procedure policy and process statements.

Qualitative research interview instruments generally ask open-ended questions. The objective is to get informants to tell the story of their knowledge of and involvement with the particular phenomena or person of interest. Interviews are most frequently semi-structured. It is best to think of the instruments as guides rather than protocols to be strictly followed. The guide contains the major topics about which the researcher wants to gather data and any sub-topics or specific issues within those major topics that might act as prompts or reminders for special aspects of the phenomenon to cover in more depth. The looser the research design, the more the research guide will change as insights are gleaned from initial interviewees and new topics are added.

Our initial serial innovator research guide contained questions about how informants innovated, with prompts for additional details about the process, who was involved when, how decisions were made, the market research used and how they managed politics. It also had questions about creativity, motivation and expertise acquisition, following the initial conceptual framework of Amabile (1983). The first few interviews, however, unexpectedly revealed information that innovators may have unusual perspectives on the world. We thus expanded the set of topics to include issues about their worldview, or perspective, and found in the end that this part of context was an important differentiator between innovators and other technologists in the firm.

Collect the Data

Collecting data is about logistics (never run out of batteries for the digital recorder, get to the right place at the right time for the interview), organization (collect all the artifacts the first time, have all the instruments, get the full story in the proscribed time period), personality (smile and relax during the interview, even if you crashed the car on the way to it) and energy (no more than three to four one-hour interviews per day). Good sources on how to interview include Kvale (1996), Merton et al. (1990) and Rubin and Rubin (2005).

Data collection can take from two to three months for a tightly bounded and closely designed study (e.g. Hebda et al. 2007) to nine to twelve months for an ethnography (e.g.

Workman 1993) or a multiple case study (e.g. Kester et al. 2011) to four to ten years for studies of highly complex phenomena such as serial innovators or radical innovation. Longer projects such as the latter are likely to result in multiple papers and possibly a book (Griffin et al. 2012; Leifer et al. 2000).

Data Analysis: Coding and Displaying

Data analysis takes roughly two to five times the amount of time data collection takes. Data analysis proceeds first within informant, then within case and finally across cases. Miles and Huberman (1994) provide what is considered the bible for how qualitative data analysis should be done. Additional general resources on data analysis include Bryant and Charmaz (2010), Charmaz (2006), Coffey and Atkinson (1996) and Srinivasan, Chapter 38 of this book.

After an interview is transcribed, coding begins. Coding is hard, obsessive work, the insights from which often can lead to further data collecting. Coding can start from a list of previously identified categories (Griffin et al. 2009; Hebda et al. 2007) or emerge strictly from the transcripts in a grounded theory fashion (Kester et al. 2011). Most typically codes emerge using a bit of both. Coding takes place in three stages: initial, focused and axial.

Initial coding is done informant by informant to obtain detailed information related to the phenomena from the transcripts (Miles and Huberman 1994). The set of codes should be evaluated systematically after every three to five interviews, to group them into collections of higher-level (more abstract) codes and emerging theoretical categories.

These higher-level codes and emerging categories form the basis of second-level, focused coding, which is more conceptual in nature, synthesizing and explaining larger segments of data (Charmaz 2006). The 'constant comparative method' (Bryant and Charmaz 2010) compares information from different informants across interviews and observations within each case, adding new codes as needed or adding details to previously identified codes and themes.

The third analysis step is axial coding, which specifies the properties and dimensions of a category and relates categories to subcategories (Charmaz 2006). Axial coding focuses on discovering relationships between theoretical categories. Many different kinds of data displays can be used to help uncover relationships and interactions among different themes within the data. Axial coding is required to move from descriptive research that identifies themes and typologies to exploratory and explanatory studies that produce frameworks and theory.

Writing Up Qualitative Research; Or, 'It Ain't Research Until It's Published'

Before writing up a research project, researchers should present it orally in as many venues as possible. It frequently can take four to six presentations of qualitative research and receiving feedback to nail down the positioning of the research within extant literature, identify the gap the research addresses, determine whether the amassed evidence is sufficient to support the conclusions, refine the story line and identify all of the rich nuances that make the findings not just interesting but compelling. It is easier and faster to do it in PowerPoint than in prose.

Before starting to write up qualitative research for publication, pick a target journal and review other recent qualitative research articles from that journal. Position the article within the literature, and use the language of that journal. To ensure that the exposition meets current publication standards, review Beverland and Lindgreen (2010), Easterby-Smith et al. (2008), Gibbert et al. (2008), Piekkari et al. (2010) and Pratt (2008, 2009). An excellent resource on composing qualitative research is Golden-Biddle and Locke (2007).

One of the most difficult aspects of writing up qualitative research is figuring out how to parse the research most effectively. A qualitative project frequently produces far too many findings for just one article. Determining what to leave out can be heart-wrenching; however, going into more depth about the findings of one aspect may be easier than trying to cover everything. In our serial innovator research, for example, one article just covered what motivates and demotivates innovators (Hebda et al. 2007), another published the overall conceptual framework (Griffin et al. 2009), a third contrasted innovators with those who take on other roles in the NPD process such as champions (Griffin et al. 2007) and yet another focused on how innovators manage politics in the organization (Price et al. 2009).

The key in writing up qualitative research, and the real difference between writing up other empirical research and qualitative research, is persuading readers that the findings presented are credible and believable. The next section of this chapter addresses best practices that should help researchers achieve these goals.

ON BEING PUBLISHABLE: EXECUTING AND DEMONSTRATING QUALITY AND RIGOR IN QUALITATIVE RESEARCH

One reason that publishing qualitative research can be difficult is because to date there has been no 'boilerplate' for how to craft a great qualitative article (Pratt 2008, 2009). To remedy this situation, Pratt (2008, 2009) developed suggestions to help authors through the execution, exposition and publication processes.

Management academics who have published articles based on qualitative research frequently believe that their articles were accepted because the article contributed to theory (Table 35.1). A further 14 per cent indicated that their article's links to existing theory contributed to its acceptance. These two answers strongly suggest that articles that merely describe are far less likely to get accepted for publication than those that extend theory or build new theory. Sampling then should be purposive or theoretical, with the number of cases investigated and the depth of data collection within cases matched to the complexity of the phenomenon under investigation, such that theory can be developed.

The second and fourth most important acceptance criteria were novelty and good writing. These points are major differentiators between getting quantitative versus qualitative research published. A paper testing a model with survey data can be boring or pedantically written and still get published, as long as it contributes sufficient new knowledge to warrant publication. This possibility is just not the case with qualitative papers, which must be both novel and well written.

First, qualitative research must be novel in some fashion. Qualitative research

Table 35.1   *Top criteria mentioned for qualitative article acceptance by respondents as authors*

Criteria	Frequency (n = 87)
Contribution to theory	52%
Novelty (theory, context or methods)	41%
Transparent, exhaustive, well-articulated methods	31%
Good writing (interesting or compelling)	31%
Editor and reviewer qualities	17%
Links to existing theory	14%

Source: Pratt (2008).

produces the theory and models that survey researchers test later. Qualitatively investigating a domain in which a significant amount of quantitative research already has been done is unlikely therefore to lead to a publishable piece of research. When queried as to why they thought their 1990 paper on market orientation was published in *JM*, Kohli and Jaworski responded: 'It was on a topic that was central to the field of marketing and yet ill-understood. The qualitative field-work helped define the market orientation construct in a simple, memorable way that allowed for its richness to be captured'. In other words, their topic was both novel and important.

Second, successful qualitative researchers must be far better writers than is required for quantitative researchers. We need to think in terms of making our data tell a story – a *compelling* story – to readers. Not only does the writing need to be grammatically correct, clear and succinct, but the argumentation and reasoning must be crystal clear and logical. Through his research, Pratt (2008) identified three tensions surrounding qualitative research that are associated with how it is written and that specifically contribute to the difficulty of getting it published.

The first is the tension of having to break from existing theory (create a new theory) while still being firmly embedded in extant theory. On the one hand, grounded theory research projects specifically start with no theory. On the other hand, the research ultimately must be positioned within extant literature, so that the contribution to new theory development is clear. For example for our recent grounded theory article (Kester et al. 2011), no one had previously investigated the processes by which portfolio decisions are made, and no extant theories guided our research. However, in the end, aspects of the theory developed linked to previously developed theories in the innovation, marketing and management domains. This linkage had to be made explicit before the article was accepted for publication.

The second tension has to do with providing sufficient detail about the methods used to conduct the research and analyze the data, such that the research quality is transparent to the reader, but still adhering to the page limits and format required by the journal. Just citing Yin (1984, 1994, 2003a) regarding how the research was executed or Miles and Huberman (1994) for how the data were analyzed is not sufficient. Yet a methods section usually should be less than five pages long. A researcher cannot provide the codebook developed or the memos that uncovered the relationships between the themes. Pratt

(2008, 2009) suggested that a good qualitative research methods section should answer the questions proposed in the list below:

1. Why this study?
   a. Why are qualitative methods appropriate?
   b. Am I building, elaborating or testing theory?
2. Why study here?
   a. What is the nature of the context I am examining?
   b. What was my rationale for choosing this context?
3. What am I studying and why?
   a. Am I sampling events, cases, people etc.?
   b. What is my sampling strategy?
4. How did I study these things?
   a. How did I analyze the data?
   b. How did I link data with theory?

The third tension a qualitative researcher must balance is between showing too much data (showing) versus interpreting data too much for the readers (telling). Good writing is integrally tied to how evidence is brought to bear to convince the audience of the validity of the theory developed in the research. Pratt (2009) offered two important suggestions to help researchers balance this tension. The first is to use organizing figures to clarify the researcher's own thinking about a project, even if some or all of them do not make it into the final manuscript. Pratt's (2009) second suggestion was to 'Show data – in a smart fashion'. Showing is a data depth issue. Data must be presented to provide sufficient evidence to the audience that the theory being developed holds across cases, which is frequently best done in tables that can present more data compactly. However, additional data (other than those in the tables) are needed in the text to help tell the story. These data should be carefully chosen to be relevant to the argument being made. They put the 'compelling' in the writing and keep the reader involved in the argument.

The next section closes this chapter by covering actual published quality and rigor, based on three analyses: two from the January 2010 special issue of *IMM* on case-based research in B2B marketing (Beverland and Lindgreen 2010; Piekkari et al. 2010) and one from the management field (Gibbert et al. 2008), which frequently publishes qualitative research in A-level journals. Both the *IMM* articles find that 'there seem to be no single set of "best practice" recommendations in the disciplinary context of industrial marketing' (Piekkari et al. 2010, p. 110).

THE STATE OF THE FIELD FOR EXECUTING AND DEMONSTRATING QUALITY AND RIGOR IN QUALITATIVE RESEARCH

Beverland and Lindgreen (2010), considering how quality should be evaluated, took the positivist perspective in Table 35.2. They analyzed 105 qualitative case studies published in *IMM* between 1971 and 2006 across four eras, constructed on the basis of the methodological advancements in the field: 1971–79, 1980–89, 1990–99 and 2000–06. In

Table 35.2   Positivist quality criteria for case research

Design Test	Theoretical Explanation of the Concept (Yin 1994)	Operationalized Through
Construct Validity	To ensure that correct operational measures have been established for the concepts being studied.	1. Triangulation though multiple sources of data or interviews. 2. Providing readers with a chain of evidence using cross-case tables or quotes from informants. 3. Allowing interviewees to review the draft case and feedback.
Internal Validity	To make sure that a causal relationship – certain relationships lead to other conditions – have been established (only for explanatory or causal case studies).	1. Pattern matching through cross-case analysis. 2. Searching for negative cases, ruling out or accounting for alternative explanations. 3. Time-series analyses.
External Validity (Generalizability)	To prove that the domain to which a case study's findings belong can be generalized.	1. Specification of the population of interest. 2. Replication logic in multiple case studies.
Reliability	Demonstrating that the findings from a case study can be replicated if the case study procedures are followed.	1. A standardized interview protocol. 2. Constructs well defined and grounded in extant literature. 3. Providing an audit trail by providing access to data.

Sources: Beverland and Lindgreen (2010), as adapted from Beverland and Lockshin (2003) and Flint et al. (2002).

general, Beverland and Lindgreen regarded the methodological information contained in *IMM's* articles as less than encouraging. Only 22.8 per cent of these articles addressed issues of validity (both internal and construct; they found too few cases of either to assess them separately), 16.2 per cent addressed reliability, and 23.8 per cent addressed generalizability. However, they also found that methodological rigor has been improving over time. Prior to 1990, *IMM* published about one case-based article a year. Information provided in the articles that would allow readers to assess their research rigor and quality was incomplete and inconsistent. The authors believed this situation was due in part to the 'fragmented nature of accepted practices in business and marketing research during this time' (Beverland and Lindgreen 2010, p. 59).

The 1980s was also a seminal period for publications providing guidance on conducting qualitative case research, including Sage's *Qualitative Research* series. By the 1990s, there was thus more information about, as well as more concurrence in, what constituted quality and rigor in qualitative research methods. Therefore 1990–99 was a transitional period for case research published in *IMM*. The journal published approximately three times as many case-based articles a year than it had previously, and more authors specifically addressed issues of research quality. However, much of what was provided still was incomplete, and that which was provided was inconsistent across articles. Some authors

Table 35.3 Theoretical best practice guidelines for the linear model of case-based research

Phases of Case Study Process	Key Decisions	Best Practice Recommendations
Relating theory to empirical data	Research purpose	• Clarity of purpose: descriptive, exploratory, explanatory • Theory development prior to data collection
Choosing and justifying empirical cases	Number of case studies Sampling strategy	• Decision made prior to data collection • Purposeful sampling • Use of literal or theoretical replication
Establishing case boundaries	Defining the unit of analysis Defining the temporal scope	• Specified as holistic or embedded • Longitudinal or cross-sectional design
Selecting appropriate data sources	Multiple sources of evidence	• Use multiple sources • Explicit triangulation
Analyzing findings and data reduction	Method/process of data analysis	• Explicit application of analytical techniques such as pattern matching • Use initial theoretical propositions to steer appropriate analytical strategy
Ensuring quality of data	Method of verification	• Construct validity • External validity • Internal validity • Reliability
Writing up and presenting case data	Presentation and discussion of findings	• Choice of report structure should be aligned with research purpose and case audience • Case report may not need to include rich narrative

Source: Piekkari et al. (2010), based on Halinen and Törnroos (2005) and Yin (2003a).

provided substantial detail about how they conducted the study but no specific data; others provided significant amounts of data in the text and tables but very little information about the methods or analysis, apart from a description of the context.

The 2000–06 period saw more case-based research published, about 10 articles per year, and further improvements in methodological quality. Nearly 90 per cent of the articles provided sufficient information to allow judgments on the findings' boundary conditions (external validity, generalizability). More than 30 per cent addressed construct validity. Finally, information that supported assessments of the reliability of the research was presented in about 30 per cent of the articles. However, little or no information appeared in relation to internal validity. While progress clearly has been made, Beverland and Lindgreen (2010) suggested that further improvement still is needed in the amount of first-hand access readers have to raw data, demonstrations of triangulation (both aspects of construct validity), the use of cross-case pattern matching and the inclusion of negative validity (both aspects of internal validity).

Piekkari et al. (2010) started with the theoretical framework of Halinen and Törnroos (2005), who interpreted Yin's (2003a) key guidelines for how to execute the case research process rigorously in the specific context of B2B marketing (Table 35.3). In their best practice recommendations, they listed validity and reliability issues (those issues focused on by Beverland and Lindgreen) as key decisions to be taken under the heading 'Ensuring quality of data'. Then Piekkari et al. analyzed 145 case study articles published in the past 10 years in *IMM*, *JBBM* and *JBIM*, three top business marketing journals, for evidence of best practices. Unfortunately they concluded that in general business marketing case research was commonly unsophisticated. The vast majority of studies had not moved past descriptive themes to causal ordering and theory. However, some of the best practices from Table 35.3 appeared in a subset of the articles:

- Relating theory to empirical data: Theory-building case studies.
- A purposive sampling strategy based on phenomenon parameters (45.5 per cent).
- Appropriate data sources sought:
  - Multiple data sources, including in-depth interviews, observation and archival records.
  - Multiple informant perspectives, including employees, managers and external actors.
- Analyses of findings and data reduction performed rigorously (29.0 per cent), with:
  - Data coding aided by specialist software.
  - Data analysis by pattern matching and constant comparative method.
- Ensuring data quality through
  - Triangulation techniques (33.1 per cent).
  - Respondent validation of case study findings and reports (17.2 per cent).

These findings indicate that authors are beginning to pay attention to some issues of validity and reliability, especially construct validity. Whereas Beverland and Lindgreen (2010) found little evidence of internal validity being addressed in their study of *IMM* articles, Piekkari et al. (2010) found that at least some investigators were starting to address it through their use of more sophisticated analysis techniques, such as pattern matching and cross-case constant comparative methods. However, both studies suggest that B2B marketing researchers have a long way to go in learning how to execute valid and reliable exploratory and explanatory qualitative research and then write it up, such that the article clearly demonstrates its validity and reliability.

Gibbert et al. (2008) investigated case study rigor in the management literature. Of the 2643 articles published in the top 10 management journals between 1995 and 2000, 159 (6.0 per cent) were based on case research methods. The authors identified 15 specific methodological practices demonstrating internal validity (3), construct validity (6), external validity (3) and reliability (3), according to Yin (1994) and Cook and Campbell (1979). To demonstrate rigor in a methodological sense, two-thirds of the category's practices had to be demonstrated in the article. Articles published in three top-tier journals (*Academy of Management Journal*, *Administrative Science Quarterly* and *Strategic Management Journal*) demonstrated construct, internal and external validity more frequently than those published in seven other management journals (Table 35.4). However, even in the top-tier journals, only external validity (bounding the phenomenon, providing sufficient contextual details to demonstrate

Table 35.4   Composite quality of case research in management journals

Journal	Total Case Articles	Internal Validity (%)	Construct Validity (%)	External Validity (%)	Reliability (%)
Three top-tier journals[1]	22	40.9[2]	36.4[2]	72.7[2]	27.3
Seven other journals	137	8.8	10.9	48.2	15.3
All management journals	159	13.2	14.5	51.6	17.0

Notes:
1. These top-tier journals are *Academy of Management, Administrative Science Quarterly* and *Strategic Management Journal.*
2. Top-tier percentages are greater than those for the seven other journals and statistically significant at $p < .10$.

Source: Adapted from Gibbert et al. (2008).

generalizability) was adequately dealt with by more than half of the published studies. Reliability (demonstrating that the case findings can be replicated if the research procedures are followed) was the least frequently demonstrated quality in top-tier journals.

Comparing the low numbers that Piekkari et al. (2010) reported against those offered by Gibbert et al. (2008), it would appear that the rate at which business marketing researchers publishing in *IMM, JBBM* and *JBIM* demonstrate construct validity (30 per cent) is approximately the same as management researchers publishing in the top-tier journals (36.4 per cent); external validity (50 per cent) is the same as found in the seven other management journals (48.0 per cent); and internal validity (30 per cent) rates come closer to the level found in top-tier journals (40.9 per cent) rather than the other management journals (8.8 per cent).

Publishing qualitative research in top-tier marketing and management journals is difficult. These three analyses suggest that this situation has arisen, at least in part, because of researchers' inability to demonstrate the validity and reliability of their research convincingly to reviewers and editors.

CONCLUSION

IMM in particular has encouraged qualitative research in B2B marketing and become a prime outlet for this type of research. As Beverland and Lindgreen (2010) and Piekkari et al. (2010) clearly have pointed out, the quality of the published research to date in B2B marketing could be improved significantly. They, along with Pratt (2008, 2009), provide clear paths that researchers can use to improve their research questions, execution of the qualitative project, analysis of the data and exposition of the research in publishable articles. We need to keep striving to improve the rigor and quality of the qualitative research we execute, write up and submit for publication.

Even as we improve this rigor, quality and exposition, a B2B marketing scholar who uses qualitative research methods as his or her *sole* investigative technique may find it difficult to publish consistently in A-level journals, as is commonly required to obtain tenure. Yet qualitative research methods must be one of the methodologies in a researcher's methodological toolbox, because they allow for the investigation of complex, evolving processes, relationships and interactions, such as are found in organizations marketing to other firms. These methods can also provide rich insights to practitioners in firms trying to understand how these complex processes operate in their firms.

REFERENCES

Amabile, Teresa M. (1983), 'Social psychology of creativity: a componential conceptualization', *Journal of Personality and Social Psychology*, **45**, 357–77.

Beverland, Michael and Adam Lindgreen (2010), 'What makes a good case study? A positivist review of qualitative case research published in *Industrial Marketing Management*', *Industrial Marketing Management*, **39** (1), 56–63.

Beverland, Michael and L. Lockshin (2003), 'A longitudinal study of customers' desired value change in business-to-business markets', *Industrial Marketing Management*, **32**, 8653–66.

Bryant, A. and Katherine Charmaz (2010), *The SAGE Handbook of Grounded Theory*, London: Sage Publications.

Charmaz, Katherine (2006), *Constructing Grounded Theory: A Practical Guide Through Qualitative Analysis*, London: Sage Publications.

Churchill, Gilbert A., Jr (1979), 'A paradigm for developing better measures of marketing constructs', *Journal of Marketing Research*, **16** (February), 64–73.

Coffey, A. and P. Atkinson (1996), *Making Sense of Qualitative Data: Complementary Research Strategies*, Thousand Oaks, CA: Sage Publications.

Cook, T.D. and D.T. Campbell (1979), *Quasi-Experimental Design: Design and Analysis Issues for Field Settings*, Skokie, IL: Rand McNally.

Denzin, N.K. and Y.S. Lincoln (eds) (2005), *The Sage Handbook of Qualitative Research*, 3rd edn, Thousand Oaks, CA: Sage Publications.

Drumwright, M.E. (1994), 'Socially responsible organizational buying: environmental concern as a noneconomic buying criterion', *Journal of Marketing*, **58** (July), 1–19.

Drumwright, M.E. (1998), 'Company advertising with a social dimension: the role of noneconomic criteria', *Journal of Marketing*, **60** (October), 71–87.

Easterby-Smith, M., K. Golden-Biddle and K. Locke (2008), 'Working with pluralism: determining quality in qualitative research', *Organizational Research Methods*, **11** (3), 419–29.

Eisenhardt, Kathleen M. (1989), 'Building theories from case study research', *Academy of Management Review*, **14** (4), 532–50.

Fetterman, D.M. (1998), *Ethnography: Step by Step*, 2nd edn, Thousand Oaks, CA: Sage Publications.

Flint, D.J., R.B. Woodruff and S.F. Gardial (2002), 'Exploring the phenomenon of customers' desired value change in a business-to-business context', *Journal of Marketing*, **66** (October), 102–17.

Gibbert, M., W. Ruigrok and B. Wicki (2008), 'What passes as a rigorous case study?', *Strategic Management Journal*, **29**, 1465–74.

Gilly, Mary C. and Mary Wolfinbarger (1998), 'Advertising's internal audience', *Journal of Marketing*, **62** (January), 69–88.

Glaser, Brian G. and Anselm L. Strauss (1967), *The Discovery of Grounded Theory: Strategies of Qualitative Research*, London: Wiedenfeld and Nicholson.

Golden-Biddle, K. and K. Locke (2007), *Composing Qualitative Research*, Thousand Oaks, CA: Sage Publications.

Grewal, Raj, Jean L. Johnson and S. Sarker (2007), 'Crises in business markets: implications for interfirm linkage', *Journal of the Academy of Marketing Science*, **35**, 398–416.

Griffin, Abbie and John R. Hauser (1993), 'The voice of the customer', *Marketing Science*, **12** (1), 1–27.

Griffin, Abbie, Raymond L. Price and Bruce A. Vojak (2012), *Serial Innovators: How Individuals Create and Deliver Breakthrough Innovations in Existing Organizations*, Palo Alto, CA: Stanford University Press.

Griffin, Abbie, Edward W. Sim, Raymond L. Price and Bruce A. Vojak (2007), 'Exploring differences between inventors, champions, implementers and serial innovators in developing new products in large, mature firms', *Creativity and Innovation Management*, **16** (December), 422–36.

Griffin, Abbie, Raymond L. Price, Matthew M. Maloney, Bruce Vojak and Edward W. Sim (2009), 'Voices from the field: how exceptional electronic industrial innovators innovate', *Journal of Product Innovation Management*, **26** (March), 222–40.

Halinen, A. and J.-A. Törnroos (2005), 'Using case methods in the study of contemporary business networks', *Journal of Business Research*, **58**, 1285–97.

Hauser, John R. (1998), 'The role of mathematical models in the study of product development', *14th Paul D. Converse Symposium*, Chicago, IL: American Marketing Association.

Hebda, John M., Abbie Griffin, Bruce A. Vojak and Raymond L. Price (2007), 'The motivation of technical visionaries in large American companies', *IEEE Transactions on Engineering Management*, **54** (August), 433–44.

Jorgensen, D.L. (1989), *Participant Observation: A Methodology for Human Studies*, Thousand Oaks, CA: Sage Publications.

Kester, Linda, Abbie Griffin, Erik Jan Hultink and Kristina Lauche (2011), 'Modeling portfolio decision-making processes', *Journal of Product Innovation Management* (forthcoming).

Kohli, Ajay K. and Bernard J. Jaworski (1990), 'Market orientation: the construct, research propositions, and managerial implications', *Journal of Marketing*, **54** (July), 1–18.

Kvale, S. (1996), *Interviews: An Introduction to Qualitative Research*, London: Sage Publications.

LaPlaca, Peter J. (2010), 'Letter from the editor', *Industrial Marketing Management*, **39** (1), 1–4.

Leifer, Richard, Christopher M. McDermott, Gina Colarelli O'Connor and Lois S. Peters (2000), *Radical Innovation: How Mature Companies Can Outsmart Upstarts*, Cambridge, MA: Harvard Business Press.

Marshall, C. and G.B. Rossman (2006), *Designing Qualitative Research*, Thousand Oaks, CA: Sage Publications.

Maxwell, J.A. (1996), *Qualitative Research Design: An Interactive Approach*, Thousand Oaks, CA: Sage Publications.

McIntyre, A. (2007), *Participatory Action Research*, Thousand Oaks, CA: Sage Publications.

Merton, R.K., Marjorie Fiske and Patricia L. Kendall (1990), *The Focused Interview*, New York: The Free Press.

Miles, R. and A.M. Huberman (1994), *Qualitative Data Analysis: A Sourcebook of New Methods*, 2nd edn. Thousand Oaks, CA: Sage Publications.

Mish, Jenny (2009), 'Centralizing and decentralizing forces in the development of sustainable markets: a study of food product standards', doctoral dissertation, University of Utah.

Narayandas, Das and R.K. Rangan (2004), 'Building and sustaining buyer–seller relationships in mature industrial markets', *Journal of Marketing*, **68** (July), 63–77.

Piekkari, R., E. Plakoyiannaki and C. Welch (2010), '"Good" case research in industrial marketing: insights from research practice', *Industrial Marketing Management*, **39** (1), 109–17.

Pratt, Michael G. (2008), 'Fitting oval pegs into round holes: tensions in evaluating and publishing qualitative research in top-tier North American journals', *Organizational Research Methods*, **11** (3), 481–509.

Pratt, Michael G. (2009), 'From the editors: for the lack of a boilerplate: tips on writing up (and reviewing) qualitative research', *Academy of Management Journal*, **52** (5), 856–62.

Price, Raymond L., Abbie Griffin, Bruce A. Vojak, Nathan Hoffman and Holli Burgon (2009), 'Innovation politics: how serial innovators gain organizational acceptance for breakthrough new products', *International Journal of Technology Marketing*, **4** (2–3), 165–84.

Rubin, H.J. and I.S. Rubin (2005), *Qualitative Interviewing: The Art of Hearing Data*, 2nd edn, Thousand Oaks, CA: Sage Publications.

Silverman, D. (2005), *Doing Qualitative Research*, 2nd edn, London: Sage Publications.

Strauss, Anselm and Julie Corbin (1998), *Basics of Qualitative Research: Techniques and Procedures for Developing Grounded Theory*, Thousand Oaks, CA: Sage Publications.

Van Maanan, John (1988), *Tales of the Field on Writing Ethnography*, Chicago, IL: University of Chicago Press.

Vojak, Bruce, Abbie Griffin, Raymond L. Price and Konstantin Perlov (2006), 'Characteristics of technical visionaries as perceived by American and British industrial physicists', *R&D Management*, **36** (1), 17–24.

Workman, John P., Jr. (1993), 'Marketing's limited role in new product development in one computer systems firm', *Journal of Marketing Research*, **30** (November), 405–21.

Workman, John P., Jr, Christian Homburg and Kjell Gruner (1998), 'Marketing organization: an integrative framework of dimensions and determinants', *Journal of Marketing*, **62** (July), 21–41.

Yin, R.K. (1984), *Case Study Research: Design and Methods*, Thousand Oaks, CA: Sage Publications.

Yin, R.K. (1994), *Case Study Research: Design and Methods*, 2nd edn, Thousand Oaks, CA: Sage Publications.

Yin, R.K. (2003a), *Case Study Research: Design and Methods*, 3rd edn, Thousand Oaks, CA: Sage Publications.

Yin, R.K. (2003b), *Applications of Case Study Research*, Thousand Oaks, CA: Sage Publications.

36 Case study research in business-to-business contexts: theory and methods
Arch G. Woodside and Roger Baxter

Case study research (CSR) focuses on describing, understanding, predicting and/or controlling for the individual process, animal, person, household, organization, group, industry, culture or nationality (Woodside 2010). This definition is intentionally broader than the definition that Yin (1994, p. 13) proposes: 'A *case study* is an empirical inquiry that investigates a contemporary phenomenon within its real life context, especially when the boundaries between phenomenon and context are not clearly evident'. Yet for any given study, focusing the research issues, theory and/or empirical inquiry on the individual constitutes the central feature of CSR. As Skinner notes (1966, p. 21), 'instead of studying a thousand rats for one hour each, or a hundred rats for ten hours each, the investigator is likely to study one rat for a thousand hours'. This view is not intended to imply that CSR is limited to a sample of n = 1. Reports of multiple case studies are widely available in organization science, especially in B2B contexts (e.g. Nutt 1984, 1993). In marketing literature, Howard and Morgenroth (1968) illustrate how to transform the research context in one supply chain from n = 1 to n > 30 by examining alternative thought/action routes taken in separate, but seemingly similar, decisions.

Without using the term, Howard and Morgenroth (1968) create an 'ethnographic decision tree model' (Gladwin 1989) that includes five principal parties in a corporate context: a senior decision-maker, a regional manager, a local distributor and two sets of competitors. They test the predictive validity of their model by comparing actual price decisions by the focal firm with price decision forecasts by the model using a holdout sample of pricing decisions. Analogous to Skinner's observation about studying one rat for a thousand hours, Howard and Morgenroth (1968) study multiple price decisions in one firm.

Along with their inclusion of predictive validation, Howard and Morgenroth (1968) provide a seminal study that shows that multiple paths lead to price increases, decreases and no price change; they describe the rationales used by executives for specific decision paths; and their model expresses directly the assumptions (thinking and emotions) of executives making the decisions. Howard and Morgenroth's (1968) case study describes, explains and predicts behavior (i.e. thinking, deciding and outcomes) of a decision-making unit across multiple decisions.

Howard and Morgenroth (1968) illustrate two core principles of decision-making by organizations.

Principle 1.   Antecedent conditions form both simple and complex paths leading to one or more alternative outcomes, and complex paths almost always precede change outcomes.

Principle 2.   Conjoining antecedent conditions (i.e. antecedent paths or 'causal recipes') is a sufficient but not necessary path for change outcomes; more simply multiple routes are available for a price increase or decrease, creating or adopting of an innovation, hiring a new executive and all other decisions relating to instances when the firm changes direction (Huff et al. 2001).

This chapter's objectives include four outcomes. First, the chapter serves to inform readers about core assumptions concerning B2B relationships that serve as rationales for conducting CSR in B2B contexts. Second, the chapter provides brief summaries of exemplar methods in previous B2B CSR studies. Third, the review of these studies provides principles for advancing a contextual-focus view in how firms make sense of their environments and make and implement decisions. Fourth, the chapter provides examples of useful strategy implications that result from CSR reports.

CORE WORKING PROPOSITIONS SERVING AS RATIONALES FOR CSR

Five core working propositions about B2B relationships appear in the following paragraphs. First, B2B relationships include direct or sequential interactions among two or more persons. Thus a salesperson seemingly interacting alone with a customer receives prior direction and reports back to a sales manager and frequently other salespersons in her firm; a buyer in the customer firm also receives prior direction and reports to a purchasing manager and members of formal and informal buying centers.

Second, because participants differ in their perspectives and prior experiences to some important extent in B2B contexts, important differences occur in their descriptions of B2B processes and the causes and outcomes of these processes. To clarify and deepen knowledge of what is happening and how participants interpret thinking, actions and outcomes, case study researchers prefer to observe meetings and interview two or more persons who interact in B2B contexts. For example case study researchers prefer to interview a B2B buyer and a B2B vendor separately as well as observe their face-to-face meetings rather than relying on responses to a survey from one or the other participant.

Figure 36.1 illustrates these ideas and emphasizes the point that B2B contexts and processes involve several time periods (days, weeks, months and years). Case study researchers have a strong preference to apply a triangulation of methods in collecting data: interviews of participants, analyses of documents and direct observation of events such as meetings that are relevant for the same B2B process. Case study researchers tend to interview the same persons on more than one occasion because they recognize that B2B processes are dynamic and occur over several time periods.

Third, most thinking occurs unconsciously; humans have limited access to their unconscious thoughts (Bargh and Morsella 2008; Wegner 2002; Wilson 2002; Woodside 2006). Respondents are frequently unaware and may not admit to the idea that unconscious thinking affects their behavior. People, including executives, also may believe their answers to questions accurately portray reality, but answers from different executives in the same firm on the same topic are likely to vary considerably depending on their job function, preferences, abilities and limited vantage of the process under study (Nisbett and Wilson 1977; Pettigrew 1975; Woodside and Samuel 1981).

Consequently some researchers apply methods that are attempts to bring unconscious

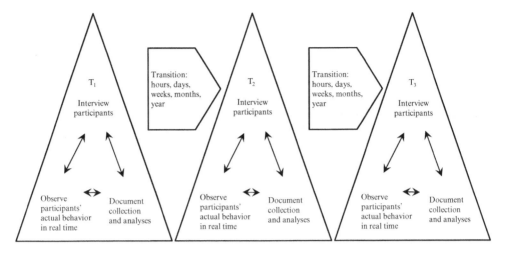

Notes: The use of three time periods is arbitrary; the key point is that the case study researcher often prepares written narratives of interviews, direct observations and document analyses, then presents these narratives to selected participants in the following time period to verify that they include the details reported, observed and found in the previous time period. For examples, see Nutt (1993) and Howard and Morgenroth (1968).

Figure 36.1   Triangulation in CSR

thinking to the surface. For example cognitive mapping in organizational research contexts encourages organizational members to share their idiosyncratic sensemaking of organizational reality and give insights into the actual values and beliefs guiding their behaviors in their immediate social context. Cognitive maps are 'visual representations that establish a landscape, or domain, name the most important entities that exist within that domain, and simultaneously place them within two or more relationships' (Huff and Jenkins 2002, p. 2). Von Wallpach and Woodside (2009) study the implicit thinking of B2B executives by asking respondents to create cognitive maps and metaphorical representations of persons in their firm as animals using a forced metaphor elicitation technique (FMET) (for details on using FMET, see Woodside 2004, 2008). The following excerpt is illustrative of their findings:

> When asked to assign animals to single persons in his cognitive map, depicting these persons' characteristics and roles, Eric's [product innovation team manager] first comment is 'Wow, the idea to use animal symbols is really not bad'. Eric begins with his team: P27 is a rooster. He is proud, an alpha animal and Eric's official representative who would like to have more of a leading role in the team. P52 is a sheep, at times too generous with herself and others. P51 is a fox, not an insidious fox but a cunning, smart fox (Von Wallpach and Woodside 2009, p. 410).

Fourth, humans edit their thoughts before responding to questions to defend their egos, appear rational and hide information that they believe is best kept confidential to themselves and/or their firm, especially when talking with an interviewer for the first time or completing a written survey. Figure 36.2 illustrates the third and fourth principles in the context of a buyer and seller in a B2B context—along with the researcher observing their interaction. Figure 36.2 shows the complexities of the processes that occur and the

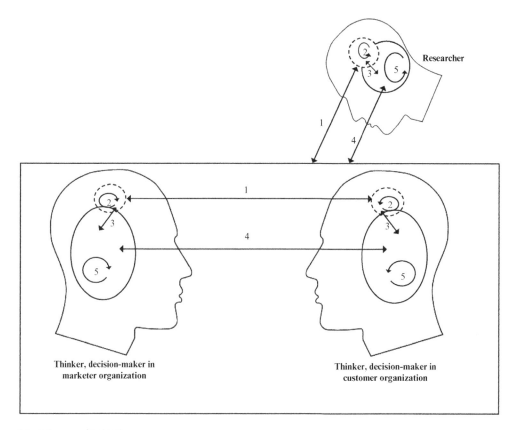

Mental processing levels:
1. Verbalized thoughts.
2. Conscious editing of thoughts surfacing from subconscious and mixing/spreading with thoughts verbalized and heard.
3. Thoughts surfacing and being stored in subconscious.
4. Unconscious processing between parties.
5. Unconscious processing within the individual.

Figure 36.2   Multiple mental processes in research on industrial marketing-buying thinking

opportunities for distortion. Consequently case study researchers employ methods that include but go beyond asking questions; these additional methods include document analysis (Pettigrew 1973, 1975, 1995), direct observation (Mintzberg 1979) and FMET (von Wallpach and Woodside 2009).

Fifth, thinking and making decisions in B2B relationships include creating satisficing (Simon 1956) rules; decision-makers do not attempt to identify and select optimal solutions even when they report doing so. Rather they create and apply simple heuristics, or rules that represent paths to accepting and rejecting options. These satisficing rules involve yes/no mental paths that include two or more attributes; not a compensatory evaluation involving sums of scores on the –3 to +3 scales that reflect five or so attributes. That is, B2B decision-makers do not use compensatory heuristics even

Concept variables:

I = individual
G = group
⟷ = conversation
→ = path of events
E = event
B = behavior
T = time
SB = sentiments
and beliefs

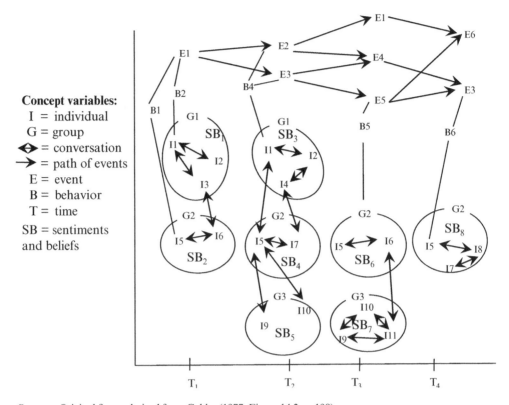

Source: Original figure, derived from Calder (1977, Figure 14.2, p. 198).

Figure 36.3 Concepts and propositions in CSR

when they report doing so (Woodside and Wilson 2000). Consequently research on key success factors (Cooper 1998) is insufficient for forecasting B2B behavior accurately; no one key success factor is sufficient or necessary for accepting or rejecting an option in a B2B context. Identifying key success paths and key failure paths instead is necessary to forecast B2B outcomes accurately. This chapter includes examples of both.

Figure 36.3 illustrates the core assumptions from this section. Note that time and observability represent the *x*- and *y*-axes, respectively. In contrast with most respondent self-reported surveys, time and observability are the principal explicit dimensions in most case studies. CSR recognizes that B2B relationship enactments include specific events (milestones) that connect through time and that group meetings occur before, during and after these enactments. A key conclusion from Figure 36.3 and the assumptions about B2B contexts is that most CSR requires substantial time to collect data in real-life settings. Participants' self-reports in one-shot surveys are a poor meal and cannot document the dynamics and nitty-gritty details of B2B processes, including implicit sentiments and beliefs. To clarify and deepen understanding, this chapter includes CSR summaries that display these assumptions and how they operate in specific B2B contexts. The examples come from studies that employ CSR methods.

EXAMPLE CSR METHODS IN B2B CONTEXTS

This section includes brief descriptions of six CSR methods that researchers apply in B2B literature: direct research and observing B2B processes; decision systems analysis (DSA); ethnographic decision tree modeling (EDTM); content analysis; degrees-of-freedom analysis (DFA); and fuzzy-set qualitative comparative analysis (see www.fsqca.com).

Direct Research and Observing B2B Processes

Direct research includes entering B2B contexts and observing the activities and interviewing the participants in B2B processes. Direct research applies Mintzberg's (1979, p. 582) definition of a strategy, 'a pattern in a stream of decisions', such that the 'central theme has been the contrast between "deliberate" strategies, that is, patterns intended before being realized, and "emergent" strategies, patterns realized despite or in the absence of intentions'. Direct research includes observing B2B contexts, with the researcher in situ for a week, month, several months or even a year or longer. Direct research includes data triangulation; the heart of the method is onsite interviews and face-to-face observations of B2B processes.

Mintzberg (1979) describes seven themes in his CSR studies that relate to B2B contexts. The discussion here covers the first two themes: (1) The research is purely descriptive (not prescriptive) as far as possible; and (2) it relies on simple – in a sense, inelegant – methodologies (e.g. sitting in a manager's office and observing what she does).

Eichenwald (2000) and Woodside and Samuel (1981) include participant observation in B2B contexts. In *The Informant* (Eichenwald 2000), an executive in an international manufacturing firm becomes an undercover researcher (with hidden cameras and listening devices) to collect data showing his colleagues planning and conducting illegal price-fixing deals with executives in other firms.

In most studies, participant observation data collection is overt and obtrusive, with the organizations' members' knowledge that a researcher is present for the purposes of observing, describing and explaining what is occurring in the organization. Woodside and Samuel (1981) apply an overt ethnographic approach to develop flow diagrams of the information processes and decision-making stages of corporate and plant executives in developing corporate purchasing agreements with suppliers.

The two-year, direct observation case study by Cyert et al. (1956) is essential reading for honing skills in CSR methods in B2B contexts. They propose four elements (i.e. behavioral principles) in their study of a firm's decision process focusing on the 'feasibility of using electronic data-processing equipment [a mainframe computer] in a medium size corporation that engages both in manufacturing and in selling through its own widely scattered outlets' (Cyert et al. 1956, p. 238).

Decision Systems Analysis (DSA)

DSA includes building ethnographic and generalized visualizations (maps) and text explanations of the sensemaking steps, interactions of people, decision processes and outcomes in real-life B2B contexts. DSA is an operational method for Mintzberg's seventh theme: building theoretical configurations of what happens in organizations.

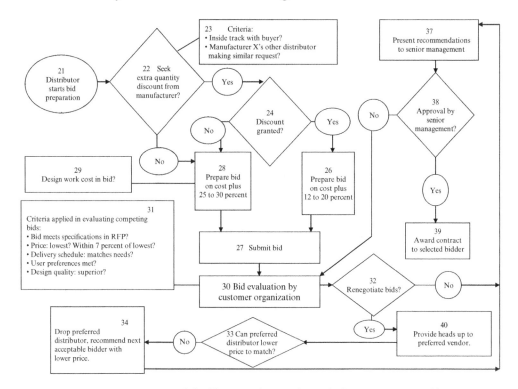

Figure 36.4   Contingency model of large order marketer bid preparation and buyer award process

Hulbert et al. (1972) were the first to describe the theory and empirical steps of conducting DSA in B2B contexts. Examples with elaborations in B2B contexts include Capon and Hulbert (1975), Howard et al. (1975), Hulbert (1981, 2003), Johnston and Bonoma (1981), Na et al. (2009) and Vyas and Woodside (1984). Figure 36.4 is an example map from a DSA of the thoughts, decisions and outcomes involving manufacturers, distributors and customers in the United States office furniture industry. Woodside (2003) provides additional maps and explanations of the configural processes in this B2B context.

Figure 36.4 offers a specific example of the visual generalization of the B2B processes in Figure 36.3. Several individuals and firms appear in Figure 36.4 during what appears at first blush to be a muddling-through process (Lindblom 1959). DSA helps clarify and deepen understanding of real-life B2B processes and removes the mud in the context and the cataracts from the eyes of the viewer.

Ethnographic Decision Tree Modeling (EDTM)

EDTM features the following characteristics: data on search for information, sensemaking, creating heuristics and choice in non-programmed or semi-programmed decisions collected in real-life field settings, whereby the researcher asks or observes an individual or group of decision-makers to think aloud or role play as they perform the process, once per several individuals or groups (usually n < 20) or several times (usually n > 20) by the same individual or group. EDTM creates binary flow models leading to specific decision outcomes (e.g. accept versus reject a new product; increase, decrease or keep price the same) and tests the efficacy of the models to predict outcomes in a holdout sample of cases.

Gladwin (1989; Gladwin et al. 2002) provides several insightful ethnographic studies set in B2B contexts. Her studies create composite EDTM representations of real-life B2B decisions. For example, in Eastern Zambia, this methodology provided insight into the decisions of small-scale farmers (121 case studies), including female-headed households, to adopt agroforestry innovations in the form of improved fallows (Gladwin et al. 2002). Using data from Phillips (1968), Montgomery (1975) provides a gatekeeper analysis of the multiple decision processes of the same supermarket buying committee, which deliberated on accepting or rejecting 124 manufacturers' product proposals, which constitute 124 case studies. The resulting analysis has several characteristics of EDTM. Figure 36.5 is a decision tree model of the thinking and deciding process of the supermarket buying committee (executives, not consumers shopping in supermarkets), created from Montgomery's (1975) gatekeeper analysis.

In Figure 36.5 no one simple antecedent condition is sufficient or necessary to cause 'accept' or 'reject' outcomes. The committee first considers whether or not the manufacturer's (M) reputation is strong. If the reputation is strong, a second issue arises: is the product in the proposal significantly new? The configuration (causal recipe) of a strong reputation and a significantly new product is sufficient for the committee to accept the manufacturer's proposal. This configuration is not necessary for gaining acceptance; other routes (paths) can lead to acceptance. A manufacturer with a weak reputation can propose a new product that gains acceptance ('yes' responses in path 1 → 4 → 9). Several paths also lead to rejection. Even a proposal from a manufacturer with a strong reputation faces rejection if it does not offer a significantly new product or fails to provide substantial promotional support.

Howard and Morgenroth (1968) and Morgenroth (1964) provide EDTMs of decision-makers in the same petroleum company making pricing decisions. Their analysis includes the use of a holdout sample to test the predictive validity of the final version of the study's EDTM. These two papers are essential reading for CSR in B2B contexts.

Woodside and Wilson (2000) provide EDTMs of individual and group decisions of both manufacturer and customer firms for industrial solvents. The study describes substantial variance in price settings for different decision paths by the manufacturer. It confirms the view that multiple, complex, antecedent conditions (causal recipes or configurations) rather than simple antecedent conditions are sufficient (but no recipe is necessary) for causing a high price, with other causal paths leading to a low price.

Content Analysis

Examining written communications such as minutes of meetings is one example of content analysis. Asking participants to read and help revise drafts of EDTMs and a researcher's written case report on the participants' decision processes is another example. Pettigrew's (1975, 1995) longitudinal analysis of written communications

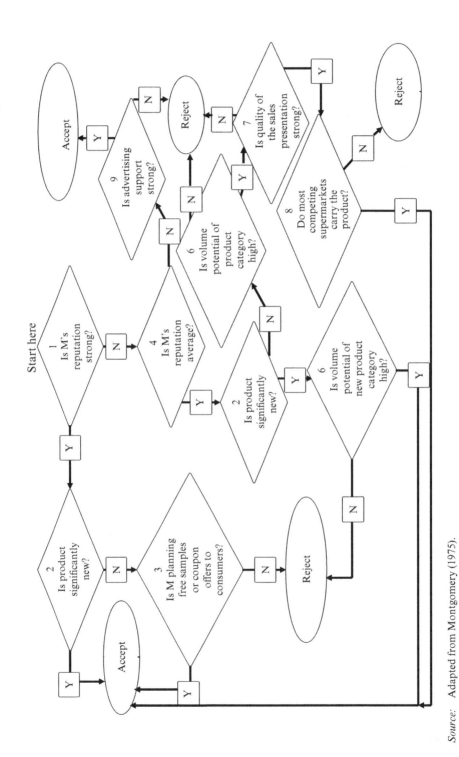

Source: Adapted from Montgomery (1975).

*Figure 36.5   An ethnographic decision process model of supermarket committee buying decisions about a manufacturer's (M's) new
product offering*

among senior, middle and first-line managers is an example of a content analysis of multiple communications, written and read by participants (with Pettigrew as a researcher) in a B2B context. Pettigrew's findings support his conclusion that the middle manager in his study revised and controlled both the content and the flow of communications in ways unrecognized by senior and first-line managers. Pettigrew concludes that the middle manager's gatekeeping actions enabled him to direct both the senior managers and first-line managers to accept his views about selecting and rejecting competing vendors: hence the title of Pettigrew's seminal article, 'The industrial purchasing decision as a political process'.

Morgenroth's (1964) study includes several revisions of EDTMs, each based on content analyses by participants of the decision processes in earlier versions of Morgenroth's maps. Thus the researcher asked participants to reflect further on and help revise the researcher's interpretations and mapping of the decision process. Morgenroth kept returning to the participants for follow-up interviews and new versions of his maps until both he and the participants were satisfied with the accuracy and completeness of the final EDTM.

Woodside et al. (2005) and Pattinson and Woodside (2009) propose a five-level hermeneutic analysis framework. Figure 36.6 summarizes the initial levels of understanding and research on B2B decision making, up to four levels of hermeneutic analysis. Level I depicts the specific interpretations of the B2B executives' descriptions and explanations of what happened and why for a focal decision. In Figure 36.1 the Level I analysis shows that mental models are crafted and revised during the decision and action under study at time *t*.

Degrees-of-Freedom Analysis (DFA)

DFA is an attempt to deepen understanding and accuracy in a case study by identifying how well the features in the case match competing explanations (normative theories and theories-in-use by participants) about what has happened, as well as the explanations of the causes and outcomes relevant to what has happened. Campbell (1975) introduces and advocates DFA in case study research. He maintains that this pattern-matching activity is analogous to having degrees of freedom in a statistical test:

> In a case study done by an alert social scientist who has thorough local acquaintance, the theory he uses to explain the focal difference also generates predictions or expectations on dozens of other aspects of the culture, and he does not retain the theory unless most of these are also confirmed. In some sense, he has tested the theory with *degrees of freedom* [emphasis added] coming from the multiple implications of one theory (Campbell 1975, pp. 181–2).

Woodside (2010) provides for details and statistical testing of DFA in B2B contexts.

Fuzzy-Set Qualitative Comparative Analysis (FS/QCA)

The FS/QCA method bridges quantitative and qualitative approaches because the methods in this tool kit are simultaneously qualitative and quantitative (Ragin 2008). FS/QCA focuses on analyzing alternative combinations of antecedent conditions that represent causal complexity rather than the analysis of net effects; it identifies causal

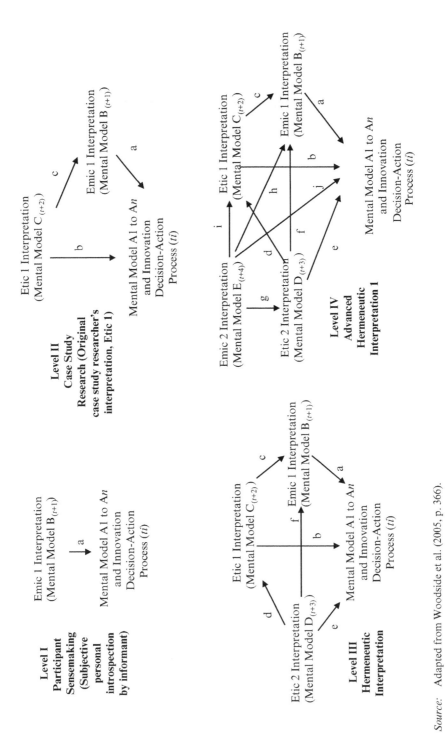

Source: Adapted from Woodside et al. (2005, p. 366).

Figure 36.6 Hermeneutic interpretation of sensemaking in B2B innovation decisions: action processes

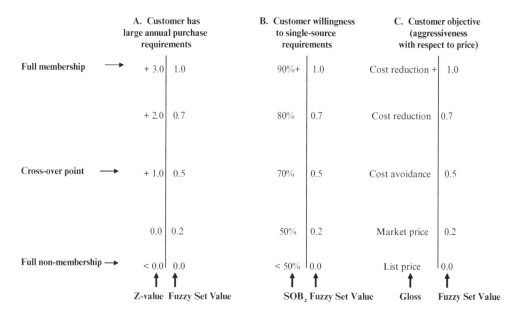

Notes:
SOBx = share of business awarded to Firm X (focal firm).
Code = Buyer statement indicating aggressive stance in price negotiation with Firm X (focal firm):
cost reduction + indicates the buyer wants a lower price for next year in real terms and extras (e.g. free
construction); cost avoidance indicates buyer wants price increase to be less than rate of inflation.

Figure 36.7   Fuzzy set scaling examples

recipes (specific combinations of causally relevant ingredients relating to an outcome)
and thereby unravels causal complexity.

FS/QCA builds on set theory and fuzzy set analysis (Zadeh 1965), using Boolean
rather than matrix algebra. Examining all logically possible combinations of causal conditions makes it possible to construct experimental design-like contrasts (i.e. only one
causal condition at a time may vary) and thus offers a thorough analysis of the effects of
relevant causal conditions. In effect the impact of each cause is examined in all logically
possible contexts (2^k configurations of conditions, where k = number of causal conditions) (Ragin 2008).

The following discussion is a brief introductory example. A fuzzy set scale allows for
fine gradations of the degree of membership in a causal conditional recipe. A fuzzy set
can be viewed as a purposively calibrated scale transformation of a continuous variable.
Such calibration is possible only through the use of theoretical and substantive knowledge that is essential in the specification of the three qualitative breakpoints (full membership = 1.0, full non-membership = .0, maximum ambiguity, or the crossover point
= .5; Ragin 2008).

Figure 36.7 illustrates the creation of three fuzzy-set, purposively calibrated scales
from case data in a B2B process study of marketing and purchasing industrial chemicals
(Woodside and Wilson 2000). Less than 1 per cent of all customers of a large manufacturer of industrial chemicals were fully in the group of customers with large purchase

Table 36.1   Fuzzy set scores for customer SOB awarded to supplier firm X

Customer Firm Case Number	A. Large Customer	B. Willingness Single Source	C. Price Objective	A·B·C	Y. Customer SOBx Annual Agreement
1	.9	.7	.9	.7	1.0
2	.6	.7	.8	.6	.9
3	.9	.2	1.0	.2	.8
4	.5	.9	.3	.3	.5
5	.2	.9	.6	.2	.9
6	.2	.2	.2	.2	.5
7	.9	.2	.3	.2	.3
8	.7	.9	.1	.1	.6
9	.1	.3	.9	.1	.4
10	.1	.4	.1	.1	.3
11	.6	.9	1.0	.6	.2

requirements. Rather the customers of the manufacturing firm with purchase requirements for chemicals could be classified as more out than in the group defined by large customer requirements. The manufacturer classified customers willing to single-source at least 90 per cent of their purchase requirements for the category as fully in the membership of customers willing to single-source. Customers buying 50 per cent of their chemical requirements from this manufacturer were more out than in this form of membership. Finally customers aggressively demanding price reductions and additional benefits (e.g. the manufacturer must build storage facilities on the customers' site at no charge) are fully in the membership of aggressive with respect to price setting. Those that demand cost avoidance objectives (i.e. price increases less than inflation rates for the category) represent the crossover point. Customers that express a willingness to pay market prices are classifiable as more out than in the group of aggressive with respect to price setting.

Three common operations on fuzzy sets are set negation, set intersection (logical 'and') and set union (logical 'or'). In the logical 'and' condition, compound sets form from the combination of two or more sets, an operation commonly known as set intersection. Mid-level dots indicate such set intersection for the three causal conditions (e.g. A·B·C). With fuzzy sets, taking the minimal membership score of each case in the sets that are combined accomplishes a logical 'and'.

Table 36.1 includes the fuzzy set scores and set intersection of their three-way combination (causal recipe) for 11 customers in the industrial chemicals study. The intersection scores are equal to the lowest score from the three prior columns in Table 36.1. The numeric intersection value indicates the degree to which each case is more in or out of the intersection membership. A fuzzy set can be negated to indicate the degree that the case is not a member. To calculate membership in the negation of fuzzy set A (denoted ~A), simply subtract membership in set A from 1.0: (Membership in set ~A) = 1.0 − (Membership in set A), or ~ A = 1.0 − A, where ~ indicates negation. Thus for customer case number 1, its membership in (not a member of the large customer group) has score equal to 1.0 − .9 = .1.

Negation membership in the 'not a large customer' group is asymmetric with membership in the target concept of small customer membership; that is, a customer can be more

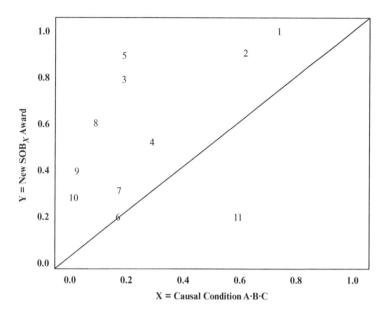

Notes:
Consistency $(Y_i \le X_i) = \sum [\min (X_i, Y_i)] / \sum (X_i) = 27/27 = 1.00$ without customer case number 11.
$= 29/33 = .88$ with customer case number 11.
Coverage $(X_i \le Y_i) = \sum [\min X_i, Y_i)] / \sum (Y_i) = 27/62 = .44$ without customer case number 11.
$= 29/64 = .45$ with customer case number 11.

Figure 36.8   *Plot of Y (new SOBx award) by causal condition A·B·C (n = customer case number)*

out than in the large customer membership (not a member of large customers) but still not be a full member of the small customer membership. This point holds for the other two causal conditions (B and C) in Table 36.1 as well. Dual coding of key causal conditions has important theoretical benefits.

Two or more sets can also be joined through the logical 'or', which is the union of sets. The logical 'or' directs the researcher's attention to the maximum of each case's memberships in the component sets. Membership in the set formed from the union of two or more fuzzy sets is the maximum value of its memberships in the component sets. An addition sign indicates the logical 'or', such that the logical 'or' membership for case 1 for the combination of the three causal conditions in Table 36.1 equals A + B + C = .9.

With fuzzy sets, membership scores in one set (causal condition or combination of causal conditions) that are less than or equal to their corresponding membership scores in another set (e.g. the outcome) indicates a subset relationship. In Table 36.1 the causal recipe membership score for A·B·C is consistently less than or equal to the corresponding membership scores in the customer share of business awarded to firm X (i.e. chemical manufacturer) – with the exception of customer case 11.

Figure 36.8 shows the plot of the causal recipe of the intersection representing the conjunction of the causal conditions (A·B·C) and the outcome membership of customer share of business awarded to firm X. The pattern of results is consistent with an argument of sufficient causation. An upper-left triangular plot, with the degree of membership in the causal combination on the horizontal axis and the degree of membership in the outcome on the vertical axis, signals the fuzzy set relation. The plot also shows the sufficiency but not necessity for the conjunction of A·B·C on the outcome membership. Other paths to high membership scores on the outcome condition exist (e.g. firm 5 has a low score for the complex condition A·B·C but nevertheless has a high score on the outcome condition), but this observation does not take away from the finding of sufficiency of high membership scores in the causal recipe resulting in high membership scores in the outcome condition. The argument of sufficiency but not necessity informs the occurrence of multiple (different) paths to high scores for the outcome condition.

Measures of Associations

Consistency, similar to significance, signals whether or not an empirical connection merits the close attention of the investigator. If findings from the membership analysis are inconsistent with the hypothesized relation, the hypothesis or conjecture is not supported (Ragin 2008). Coverage, like strength of association in statistical analysis, indicates the empirical relevance or importance of a set–theoretic connection. Coverage estimates assess the proportion of cases following a path to high outcome scores; coverage is a straightforward indicator of the empirical importance of a causal combination (Ragin 2008) and indicates the share of cases with high values on the outcome condition that the specified antecedent condition represents. The formulas and specific estimates for consistency and coverage for the causal combination (conjunction A·B·C) appear below the graph in Figure 36.8. The evaluation of the set relationships between the causal recipe and the outcome condition indicates high consistency and a moderate amount of coverage.

The uniqueness of case 11 in the findings in Table 36.1 and Figure 36.8 merits further attention, and its discussion extends Gibbert's (2006) observations about generalizing about uniqueness. Further discussion about customer 11 with the manufacturer confirmed its unique relationship. The manufacturer's sales manager reported its monthly complaints and continuing attempts to renegotiate prices during the annual contract. Although the sales manager did not use the expression, customer 11 reflects the industrial customer equivalent to van Maanen's (1978) 'asshole' in his study of a distinct type of person who is familiar to police officers. Thus the unique findings indicate a paradox worthy of further investigation, because '[g]eneralizability demands the research findings are not idiosyncratic to the firm or the sample of firms studied' (Gibbert 2006, p. 124). The researcher should look for the presence of further 'assholes' or other seemingly unique cases before concluding that adding condition D is relevant for model building and testing.

Creating a fourth causal condition, ~D = 'not an asshole', would place all customers in Table 36.1 above the crossover point (.5) except for customer 11. Customer 11's low score on this causal condition (~D = .00) shifts its conjunction score (A·B·C·~D = .00) to the left and results in high consistency for this more complex (causal recipe) explanation of the outcome condition.

Table 36.1 and Figure 36.8 examine only one causal condition's relation to the outcome condition. Additional causal conditions warrant examination, such as A, B,

C; A·B; A·C; B·C; ~A·~B·~C; and ~A·B·C among others. Ragin et al. (2007) provide a software program to ease the calculations involved in creating complex conditions and estimating their consistency and coverage (www.fsqca.com).

USEFUL STRATEGY AND THEORY IMPLICATIONS RESULTING FROM CASE REPORTS

This section offers a few insights into how CSR reports may influence planning, implementing and evaluating strategies in B2B contexts. Because B2B CSR often contain nitty-gritty details of processes relating to thinking, deciding and doing among interacting participants, paths that lead to successful versus unsuccessful outcomes are identifiable. Several CSR methods inherently recognize that the B2B researcher needs to explicitly include time to collect data and model B2B relationships (Woodside 2006), which is a valuable insight for both researchers and managers.

What does a manufacturer with an average reputation need to do to gain new product acceptance by executives in a supermarket buying committee? Figure 36.5 indicates two strategy paths that lead to acceptance for such a manufacturer. The point here is that creating accurate EDTMs is helpful for identifying specific actions necessary to implement in specific, real contexts.

CSR methods include the use of empirical positivistic (statistical) tests. For example using DFA to test the efficacies of competing theories compares hits and misses to the features present in a case. However, case study researchers have a natural bias against seven-point scales. Mintzberg (1979) provides a telling explanation for this bias.

With direct research, content analysis, FS/QCA and additional CSR methods, the researcher stays close to the data and can use alternative metrics to test the accuracy of complex antecedent conditions and paths leading to success and failure – rigorously and in terms that relate to real-life contexts. Such testing achieves the objective of generalizing the findings to multiple decisions (e.g. EDTM by Howard and Morgenroth 1968; Gladwin et al. 2002) and across multiple cases (e.g. FS/QCA by Ragin 2008; Woodside 2010).

SUMMARY

CSR is an inquiry focusing on describing, understanding, predicting and/or controlling the individual process, animal, person, household, organization, group, industry, culture or nationality. Any combination of the following purposes may serve as the major objective of CSR: description, understanding, prediction or control. However, deep understanding of the actors, interactions, sentiments and behaviors occurring for a specific process through time is the principal objective of the case study researcher. The researcher should consider using explicit auto-driving tools to bring up unconscious mental processes among informants (e.g. hermeneutic spiral, Pattinson and Woodside 2009; Woodside et al. 2005).

Core criticisms made by case study researchers of large-sample surveys consisting of interviews of one person, informal group or organization include: (1) the failure to confirm reported conversations, behaviors and events; (2) the failure to collect the necessary detail to gain a deep understanding of the mechanics and reasons embedded in the processes examined; and (3) the use of response scales too far removed from the reality of what they intend to measure.

Core variables in CSR include individual and group behaviors through time, resulting in a sequence of paths of events (decisions, performance outcomes and revelatory incidents). Beliefs and sentiments held by individuals and groups are additional core variables that CSR reports. No one CSR method is appropriate for all studies. Explanations with examples of additional CSR methods are available elsewhere (e.g. Woodside 2010). The coverage in this chapter serves to introduce theory and methods useful for doing CSR in B2B contexts.

ACKNOWLEDGMENTS

The authors acknowledge the helpful comments of their colleagues on previous drafts of this chapter: Abbie Griffin, University of Utah; Gary Lilien, Pennsylvania State University; and Carol M. Megehee, Coastal Carolina University.

REFERENCES

Bargh, John A. and Ezequiel Morsella (2008), 'The unconscious mind', *Perspectives on Psychological Science*, **3** (1), 73–9.
Calder, Bobby J. (1977), 'Structural role analysis of organizational buying: a preliminary investigation', in Arch G. Woodside, Jagdesh N. Sheth and P.D. Bennett (eds), *Consumer and Industrial Buying Behavior*, New York: Elsevier, pp. 193–200.
Campbell, Donald T. (1975), 'Degrees of freedom and the case study', *Comparative Political Studies*, **8** (2), 178–93.
Capon, Noel and James Hulbert (1975), 'Decision systems analysis in industrial marketing', *Industrial Marketing Management*, **4**, 143–60.
Cooper, Robert G. (1998), 'Benchmarking new product performance: results of the best practices study', *European Management Journal*, **16**, 1–17.
Cyert, Richard M. and James G. March (1963), *A Behavioral Theory of the Firm*, Englewood Cliffs, NJ: Prentice-Hall.
Cyert, Richard M., H.A. Simon and D.B. Trow (1956), 'Observation of a business decision', *Journal of Business*, **29** (October), 237–48.
Eichenwald, Kurt (2000), *The Informant: A True Story*, New York: Broadway Books.
Gibbert, Michael (2006), 'Generalizing about uniqueness', *Journal of Management Inquiry*, **15** (2), 145–51.
Gladwin, Christina H. (1989), *Ethnographic Decision Tree Modeling*, Newbury Park, CA: Sage.
Gladwin, Christina H., J.S. Peterson and A.C. Mwale (2002), 'The quality of science in participatory research: a case study from Eastern Zambia', *World Development*, **30** (4), 523–43.
Howard, John A. and William M. Morgenroth (1968), 'Information processing model of executive decision', *Management Science*, **14** (3), 416–28.
Howard, John A., James M. Hulbert and John U. Farley (1975), 'Organizational analysis and information system design: a decision process perspective', *Journal of Business Research*, **3** (April), 133–48.
Huff, Anne and Mark Jenkins (2002), *Mapping Strategic Knowledge*, London: Sage.
Huff, Anne S., James O. Huff and Pamela Barr (2001), *When Firms Change Direction*, New York: Oxford University Press.
Hulbert, James M. (1981), 'Descriptive models of marketing decisions', in Randall L. Schultz and Andris A. Zoltners (eds), *Marketing Decisions Models*, New York: North-Holland, pp. 19–53.
Hulbert, James M. (2003), 'Organizational analysis and information system design: a road revisited', *Journal of Business and Industrial Marketing*, **18** (6/7), 509–13.

Hulbert, James M., John U. Farley and John A. Howard (1972), 'Information processing and decision making in marketing organizations', *Journal of Marketing Research*, **9** (February), 75–7.

Johnston, Wesley J. and Thomas V. Bonoma (1981), 'The buying center: structure and interaction patterns', *Journal of Marketing*, **45** (Summer), 143–56.

Lindblom, Charles E. (1959), 'The science of muddling through', *Public Administration Review*, **19** (February), 79–99.

Mintzberg, Henry (1979), 'An emerging strategy of "direct" research', *Administrative Science Quarterly*, **24** (December), 582–9.

Montgomery, D.F. (1975), 'New product distribution: an analysis of supermarket buyer decisions', *Journal of Marketing Research*, **12** (3), 255–64.

Morgenroth, William M. (1964), 'Method for understanding price determinants', *Journal of Marketing Research*, **1** (3), 17–26.

Na, Woon Bong, Roger Marshall and Arch G. Woodside (2009), 'Decision system analysis of advertising agency decisions', *Qualitative Market Research: An International Journal*, **12** (2), 153–70.

Nisbett, Richard E. and Timothy D. Wilson (1977), 'Telling more than we can know: verbal reports on mental processes', *Psychological Review*, **84**, 231–59.

Nutt, Paul C. (1984), 'Types of organizational decision processes', *Administrative Science Quarterly*, **29** (3), 414–50.

Nutt, Paul C. (1993), 'The formulation processes and tactics used in organizational decision making', *Organization Science*, **4** (2), 226–51.

Pattinson, Hugh M. and Arch G. Woodside (2009), 'Capturing and (re)interpreting complexity in multi-firm disruptive product innovations', *Journal of Business and Industrial Marketing*, **24** (1), 61–76.

Pettigrew, Andrew M. (1973), *The Politics of Organizational Decision Making*, London: Tavistock.

Pettigrew, Andrew M. (1975), 'The industrial purchasing decision as a political process', *European Journal of Marketing*, **9** (March), 4–19.

Pettigrew, Andrew M. (1995), 'Longitudinal field research on change: theory and practice', in George P. Huber and Andrew H. Van De Ven (eds), *Longitudinal Field Research Methods*, Thousand Oaks, CA: Sage, pp. 91–125.

Phillips, Louis A. (1968), 'An exploratory study of factors which determine the initial distribution of selected categories of products on supermarket shelves', unpublished Master's thesis, Sloan School of Management, Massachusetts Institute of Technology.

Ragin, Charles C. (2008), *Redesigning Social Inquiry: Fuzzy Sets and Beyond*, Chicago, IL: Chicago University Press.

Ragin, Charles, K. Drass and S. Davey (2007), 'Fuzzy-Set/Qualitative Comparative Analysis 2.0', available at http://www.u.arizona.edu/Bcragin/fsQCA/software.shtml.

Simon, Herbert A. (1956), 'Rational choice and the structure of the environment', *Psychological Review*, **63**, 129–38.

Skinner, Burrhus F. (1966), 'Operant behavior', in W.K. Honig (ed.), *Operant Behavior: Areas for Research and Application*, New York: Appleton-Century-Crofts, pp. 12–32.

Van Maanen, John (1978), 'The asshole', in P.K. Manning and J. Van Maanen (eds), *Policing: A View from the Street*, Santa Monica, CA: Goodyear Publishing, available at http://petermoskos.com/readings/Van_Maanen_1978.pdf.

Von Wallpach, Sylvia and Arch Woodside (2009), 'Theory and practice of enacted internal branding: theory, practice, and an experiential learning case study of an Austrian B2B company', in M. Glynn and Arch G. Woodside (eds), *Business-to-Business Brand Management, Advances in Business Marketing and Purchasing*, Vol. 15, London: Emerald Publishing, pp. 389–425.

Vyas, Niren and Arch G. Woodside (1984), 'An inductive model of industrial supplier choice processes', *Journal of Marketing*, **47**, 30–44.

Wegner, Daniel M. (2002), *The Illusion of Conscious Will*, Cambridge, MA: Bradford Books and MIT Press.

Wilson, Timothy D. (2002), *Strangers to Ourselves: Discovering the Adaptive Unconscious*, Cambridge, MA: Belknap.

Woodside, Arch G. (2003), 'Middle-range theory construction of the dynamics of organizational marketing–buying behavior', *Journal of Business & Industrial Marketing*, **18** (4/5), 309–35.

Woodside, Arch (2004), 'Advancing from subjective to confirmatory personal introspection in consumer research', *Psychology & Marketing*, **21** (12), 987–1010.

Woodside, Arch (2006), 'Overcoming the illusion of will and self-fabrication: going beyond naïve subjective personal introspection to an unconscious/conscious theory of behavior explanation', *Psychology & Marketing*, **23** (3), 257–72.

Woodside, Arch G. (2008), 'Using the forced metaphor-elicitation technique (FMET) to meet animal companions within self', *Journal of Business Research*, **61** (5), 480–87.

Woodside, Arch G. (2010), *Case Study Research: Theory, Methods and Practice*, Bingley, UK: Emerald.
Woodside, Arch G. and David M. Samuel (1981), 'Observation of centralized corporate procurement', *Industrial Marketing Management*, **10**, 191–205.
Woodside, Arch G. and Elizabeth J. Wilson (2000), 'Constructing thick descriptions of marketers' and buyers' decision processes in business-to-business relationships', *Journal of Business and Industrial Marketing*, **15**, 354–69.
Woodside, Arch G., Hugh H. Pattinson and Kenneth E. Miller (2005), 'Advancing hermeneutic research for interpreting interfirm new product development', *Journal of Business and Industrial Marketing*, **20**, 364–79.
Yin, Robert K. (1994), *Case Study Research: Design and Methods*, Thousand Oaks, CA: Sage Publications.
Zadeh, L.A. (1965), 'Fuzzy sets', *Information and Control*, **8**, 338–53.

37 Survey research in B2B marketing: current challenges and emerging opportunities
Aric Rindfleisch and Kersi D. Antia

> Surveys are extensions of our natural tendencies to seek information by means of questioning and learning about wholes by selecting parts. (Schuman 1982, p. 21)

Survey research often provides answers to the questions B2B scholars commonly ask. For example, knowledge of the topics covered in this handbook, including sales force performance (Ahearne and Lam 2012), agency theory (Banerjee et al. 2012), buyer–seller relationships (Bowman 2012) and interorganizational trust (Scheer 2012), has largely been obtained through managerial surveys. As a further testament, survey research has been the primary means of inquiry for every empirical article that has won the American Marketing Association's prestigious Louis W. Stern Award, including Anderson and Weitz (1992), Cannon and Homburg (2001), Jap and Ganesan (2000), Lusch and Brown (1996) and Mohr et al. (1996). Survey research also provides essential inputs to several leading economic indicators of the business environment, including unemployment estimates, new business formation projections and gross domestic product statistics (Landefeld et al. 2008). Thus, in addition to being commonly employed, surveys are capable of providing exceptional insights into B2B activity.

Despite its ubiquity and utility, many academics seem skeptical of survey research, and editors and reviews tend to scrutinize this technique heavily. This skepticism and scrutiny is not undeserved, as the limitations of survey research are well documented. For example, responses to survey items can be tainted by a variety of biases, including non-response bias, social desirability bias, acquiescence bias, extreme response bias and common method variance (CMV) bias, among others (Armstrong and Overton 1977; Baumgartner and Steenkamp 2001; Podsakoff et al. 2003; Steenkamp et al. 2010; Van Rosmalen et al. 2010). As survey researchers, we acknowledge these limitations and readily admit that a poorly executed survey can easily lead to faulty conclusions. Thus, rather than dismissing these limitations, our objective is to identify three major challenges facing B2B survey research – namely: response rate, CMV and causal inference – and offer a set of solutions for managing these concerns. We focus on these three particular challenges because they correspond to three key steps in the survey research process (see Table 37.1). Specifically, when conducting a survey study, researchers must first identify who will be surveyed and how to persuade them to respond (i.e. interrogation). Typically, the majority of the people identified will elect not to respond, which may lead to potential CMV bias. Next, researchers must determine which questions to ask and how to ask them (i.e. inquiry). However, if these questions are not designed properly, CMV bias may confound the results. Finally, researchers must interpret the data they collect and develop a set of conclusions (i.e. interpretation). Unfortunately, because these conclusions are based on correlational data, forming strong causal insights from survey data is often difficult.

Table 37.1   Survey research framework

Steps	Key Issues	Challenges	Opportunities
Interrogation	Who will be asked and how will we get them to respond?	Non-response bias	Multiple respondents Multiple organizations
Inquiry	What questions will be asked and how will we ask them?	CMV bias	Online surveys Split-sample designs
Interpretation	What interpretations will we conclude from their answers?	Causal inference	Using surveys to affect behavior

In addition to providing a set of actionable guidelines for addressing survey research challenges, we strive to advance the cause of survey research by identifying five emerging opportunities: multiple informants; multiple organizations; online survey administration; split sample designs; and use of surveys to affect behavior. As Table 37.1 shows, these opportunities map onto the three steps of the survey process and provide survey researchers with a set of tools for enhancing interrogation, inquiry and interpretation. Because these three key survey research steps are common to both B2B academics and practitioners, the challenges and guidelines we address in this chapter are generally applicable to both audiences.[1]

CURRENT CHALLENGES

B2B scholars have employed survey research for more than seven decades (e.g., Faville 1936; Frederick 1937; Lanyon 1939). This longevity is a testament to survey research's unique value as a means of obtaining answers to the questions that B2B scholars ask. In contrast with consumer research, B2B activity is considerably less amenable to experimental investigation (for exceptions, see Armstrong and Collopy 1996; Blyalogosky et al. 2006; Dahl and Moreau 2002). Thus, the topics of interest to B2B researchers are more easily measured than manipulated. This substitution of measurement for manipulation lies at the heart of survey research's benefits as well as its limitations. For example, while survey research provides the ability to obtain precise measurement control (Jap and Anderson 2004), the act of measurement may produce unwanted biases and limit causal inferences (Rindfleisch et al. 2008). In this section, we identify three key survey limitations that B2B scholars commonly face, and offer a set of solutions for minimizing their impact. Table 37.2 provides a summary of these limitations and their solutions.[2]

Response Rate

We define response rate as the percentage of eligible participants who return at least a partially completed survey. A survey's response rate is usually calculated by dividing the number of actual respondents by the number of eligible respondents (Wiseman and Billington 1984). Eligible respondents are those individuals or organizations that actually receive the survey instrument. Thus, surveys that are returned as non-deliverable are typically not considered eligible. In recent years, survey studies in the B2B domain have

Table 37.2   Survey research challenges and solutions

Challenge	Solution	Key Works
1. Response rate	*Design*: Monetary incentive; pre- and post-contact *Analysis*: Comparison of early vs. late respondents; comparison of respondents vs. non-respondents	Armstrong and Overton (1977) Childers and Ferrell (1979) Yu and Cooper (1983)
2. CMV	*Design*: Mix-scaled formats; collecting data from multiple respondents; marker variable inclusion *Analysis*: Nested confirmatory factor analysis models; marker variable analysis	Doty and Glick (1998) Lindell and Whitney (2001) Podsakoff et al. (2003)
3. Causal inference	*Design*: Longitudinal data collection; well-developed conceptualization *Analysis*: Non-recursive SEM models; Granger causality	Einhorn and Hogarth (1986) Marini and Singer (1988) Rindfleisch et al. (2008)

typically displayed response rates between 20 and 45 per cent (e.g., Ganesan et al. 2005; Jap and Haruvy 2008; Palmatier 2008; Wuyts and Geyskens 2005).

A low response rate is potentially problematic for at least two reasons. First, a low response rate may limit a researcher's ability to draw valid inferences. This limitation is commonly known as non-response bias (Schaeffer et al. 1991). Non-response bias has been demonstrated across several contexts (Schaeffer et al. 1991; Yu and Cooper 1983) and is a common concern of both reviewers and editors (Kamakura 2001). Second, B2B surveys are often sent to a relatively small sample of individuals or organizations. In these cases, a low response rate may severely constrain the number of respondents, which challenges a researcher's ability to examine potential moderators or boundary conditions and limits the use of analytical procedures, such as structural equation modeling (SEM; Gerbing and Anderson 1988) and moderated regression analysis (Cohen et al. 2003). Thus, B2B scholars should design surveys that minimize the risk of non-response bias and assess the degree of possible bias after collecting survey data.

Design solutions

During the past five decades, survey researchers have examined a variety of techniques and tactics for improving a survey's response rate (e.g. Childers and Ferrell 1979; Frazier and Bird 1958; Yammarino et al. 1991; Yu and Cooper 1983). The evidence collected thus far suggests that the two best means of increasing response rate are to contact potential respondents multiple times (i.e. pre- and post-survey) and provide them with a (prepaid) monetary incentive (Armstrong 1975; Childers and Ferrell 1979; Yu and Cooper 1983). As Yu and Cooper (1983, p. 36) note, 'there is no strong empirical evidence demonstrating the effectiveness of any techniques other than the use of monetary incentives and follow-up contacts'. Thus, we recommend that B2B scholars: (1) establish contact with their potential respondents before sending a survey; (2) include a prepaid monetary incentive with the survey instrument; and (3) follow up after the survey has been sent. Adherence to these three simple steps should significantly increase a survey's response rate.

Analysis solutions

In addition to these design recommendations, B2B scholars should try to assess the degree of potential non-response bias. The most commonly employed means of non-response bias assessment is to compare early (i.e. initial mailing) and late (i.e. follow-up mailing) respondents (Armstrong and Overton 1977; Sax et al. 2003). This comparison should test for differences in both the means and variances for the key measures across both groups of respondents (e.g. Ganesan et al. 2005). A lack of significant differences suggests that non-response bias is unlikely. This technique is largely based on the assumption that late respondents are similar to non-respondents (Armstrong and Overton 1977). Although this assumption may be of questionable validity, it is seldom challenged by reviewers or editors.

Nonetheless, we recommend that B2B scholars supplement this early versus late assessment with a comparison of the characteristics of respondents versus non-respondents (Armstrong and Overton 1977). This comparison is typically conducted through a simple t-test; a lack of significant differences between the two groups suggests that non-response bias is unlikely (e.g. Rindfleisch and Moorman 2003). Researchers seeking a more sophisticated approach can apply a two-stage Heckman analysis to both assess and possibly correct for non-response bias (see Sales et al. 2004). This comparative approach provides the added benefit of actually assessing (rather than inferring from late respondents) the characteristics of non-respondents. However, it is often difficult to implement because of respondent anonymity or a lack of readily available information about non-respondent characteristics. Thus, comparisons of respondents and non-respondents may not be feasible in every B2B study. In these cases, a comparison of early and late respondents should be sufficient as an analytical assessment of non-response bias.

CMV

CMV is systematic error variance due to the use of a single measurement approach (e.g. a cross-sectional survey) (Podsakoff et al. 2003). Prior research suggests that CMV can be quite substantial and, in some cases, may even exceed the amount of trait variance for a particular measure (Cote and Buckley 1987). Across various academic disciplines, CMV accounts for approximately 30 per cent of the total variance in a given survey. This variance may bias results (i.e. CMV bias) by leading researchers to mistakenly believe that the observed covariance between two or more measures is due to an association between their traits. The danger of CMV bias is a current concern of many reviewers and editors and often poses a stiff challenge for B2B survey studies (Jap and Anderson 2004; Kamakura 2001). However, despite the relatively high presence of CMV found in many surveys, a growing chorus suggests that, in general, this variance is unlikely to bias survey results (e.g. Doty and Glick 1998; Malhotra et al. 2005; Rindfleisch et al. 2008). Thus, CMV risk may be lower than commonly believed. Nonetheless, B2B scholars need to be attuned to this limitation and should try to minimize CMV during survey design and assess the degree of potential CMV bias after collecting their survey data.

Design solutions

CMV has been attributed to contextual, respondent and measurement influences (Podsakoff et al. 2003; Rindfleisch et al. 2008). Most B2B scholars have limited control over context or respondents, and so our recommendations focus on reducing CMV through careful measurement procedures. Because CMV is more likely to occur in surveys that employ a common format across multiple measures, the use of a variety of scale formats (e.g. Likert, semantic differential, constant sum) or anchors (e.g. five-point, seven-point) should reduce this unwanted variance (Lindell and Whitney 2001). Varying scale formats is especially important for outcome measures, which should be assessed at least slightly differently from a survey's predictors. In addition to varying scale formats, B2B scholars can minimize CMV bias by collecting their outcome measures from a different set of respondents or from the same respondents at a later time (Rindfleisch et al. 2008). This type of physical or temporal separation is typically the most effective way to reduce CMV but is not always feasible to implement. Thus, these techniques are often recommended but seldom followed (for exceptions, see Atuahene-Gima 2005; Bolton and Lemon 1999; Im and Workman 2004; Jap 1999).

Analysis solutions
In addition to preventing CMV bias through careful survey design, B2B scholars should attempt to assess and control for this potential bias. Thus, we provide a brief overview of various CMV analysis approaches.[3] The most widely used CMV assessment technique is Harman's one-factor test (Podsakoff and Organ 1986). Essentially, this test entails forming a confirmatory factor analysis model in which all the items across a study's various measures are specified as predictors of a single underlying latent construct. Usually, this model displays rather poor fit indexes, which is viewed as evidence that CMV is unlikely to taint the measures reflected by these items (e.g. Frazier et al. 2009). Although this approach is appealing in terms of its simplicity, it is increasingly viewed as an inferior and insufficient means to assess CMV bias.

B2B researchers interested in employing a more rigorous assessment of CMV bias can find several options in Podsakoff et al.'s (2003) comprehensive review of CMV research. In particular, we recommend their nested modeling approach. Basically, this technique entails specifying two confirmatory factor analysis models: one in which a survey's items are specified to load on their hypothesized traits (i.e. trait model) and one in which these items are specified to load on both their hypothesized traits and a common method factor (i.e. trait and method model). A comparative assessment of the relative fit indexes for each model provides insight into the degree to which CMV may be biasing a survey's results. This approach has the added benefit of allowing researchers to separate observed variance into trait, method and error components.

Another useful approach for assessing and controlling for potential CMV bias is Lindell and Whitney's (2001) marker variable approach.[4] This technique harnesses the power of both design and analysis solutions and can be used in combination with other approaches, such as the nested modeling approach. Essentially, this technique entails designing a survey to include at least one theoretically unrelated (i.e. 'marker') variable. After data collection is completed, researchers can assess the degree of correlation between this marker and their key constructs. Because this marker variable is theoretically unrelated, the largest correlation coefficient between it and their key constructs is considered an indicant of CMV and can be partialled out. Regardless of the approach taken, we recommend that survey researchers employ a comparative analysis that contrasts results that account for CMV with those that do not. According to Doty and Glick

(1998), this comparative assessment often reveals substantive findings that are broadly similar, which suggests that though some degree of CMV is likely to be present in all survey studies, this variance may not always bias a survey's results.

Causal Inference

Causal inference is the ability to infer causality from observed empirical relations (Marini and Singer 1988). Because most B2B studies attempt to explain or predict organizational activity, causal inferences are often drawn (either explicitly or implicitly) from survey data. Typically, these causal inferences are based on cross-sectional surveys, which are usually collected from a single organizational respondent at a single point in time (Rindfleisch et al. 2008). Therefore, these studies lack temporal separation between their predictors and outcomes. This lack of separation makes it difficult to decipher which variable is the cause and which is the effect. As a result, reviewers and editors often view survey data as correlational in nature and unable to provide much, if any, causal insights (Rindfleisch et al. 2008).

Design solutions
Because temporal separation is a widely acknowledged means of inferring causality, the most common solution for enhancing a survey's causal insights is the collection of longitudinal data (Jap and Anderson 2004). Although this solution is appealing in concept, longitudinal data collection can be quite costly in terms of both time and money. In addition, the collection of data at a later point in time can introduce a new set of biases both among respondents and non-respondents, and may lead to only a modest gain in causal inference ability (Rindfleisch et al. 2008). Thus, this solution is often invoked but seldom implemented.[5]

As an alternative to longitudinal data collection, survey researchers can enhance causal inference by developing a strong and convincing conceptual foundation (Wittink 2004). According to the principle of *coherence*, results that display strong nomological validity and closely align with theoretical expectations provide an important marker of causality (Einhorn and Hogarth 1986; Hill 1965; Marini and Singer 1988). In particular, B2B researchers can significantly enhance causal inference through the strategic use of conceptually driven moderators and boundary conditions. Moderators can help tease out causes from effects by shedding light on underlying processes and mechanisms. Likewise, finding that an effect occurs under theoretically plausible conditions but not theoretically implausible ones provides considerable causal attributions.

Analysis solutions
Beyond designing a study that is longitudinal in nature and/or based on well-developed theory, survey researchers can gain added causal insights using a variety of analytical approaches. We discuss two methods in particular. The first approach employs a non-recursive SEM that incorporates cyclical paths (i.e. from $X \rightarrow Y \rightarrow Z$ and back again from $Z \rightarrow Y \rightarrow X$) (Jöreskog and Sörbom 1993). This technique enables survey researchers to model potential feedback loops by estimating a path from an outcome variable back to its theorized predictors, thus allowing for richer causal insights (Martens and Haase 2006). Rather than assume a unidirectional flow from X to Y, non-recursive SEM

allows for the specification and testing of reciprocal relations (from X to Y and Y to X). Perhaps most appealing of this class of models is that they can be estimated using cross-sectional data (Wong and Law 1999). Specification of such feedback loops is not a trivial task, however, and requires careful attention to order and rank identification conditions in order to properly estimate these rather complex models. Fortunately, recent advances in contemporary SEM software (AMOS, LISREL and M*plus*) have eased this task by including full information-based maximum likelihood estimators as part of their stand-ard packages.

The second approach, which is commonly known as Granger causality, involves an attempt to 'establish causality' between an outcome (*Y*) and its predictor (*X*) by using lagged instruments that assess changes in *X* over time (Granger 1969). Though elegant in its approach, Granger causality does not actually prove causality, is difficult to interpret in practice and requires the collection of longitudinal data. Nevertheless, this approach seems to be gaining usage among contemporary marketing scholars (e.g. Luo and Homburg 2007, Trusov et al. 2009) as a means to validate causal relations.

EMERGING OPPORTUNITIES

By addressing concerns about response rate, CMV and causal inference, survey research-ers can provide added confidence in the validity of their data collection approach and increase their study's prospects of a favorable reception by reviewers and editors. However, we recommend that B2B scholars set a more ambitious goal and strive not only to address current concerns but also to leverage emerging opportunities to provide added value to their research. Specifically, we discuss five important survey-related trends that B2B scholars should consider when embarking on a new research project.

Multiple Respondents

B2B researchers are typically interested in studying organizational-level phenom-ena. However, their surveys usually elicit the perspective of only a single respondent from each organization (e.g. Antia and Frazier 2001; Ganesan et al. 2005; Wuyts and Geyskens 2005). This incongruity is usually justified by arguing that these respondents are 'key informants' that have unique and valuable knowledge of their organization's activities (Campbell 1955).

Although the logic of key informants is widely accepted, many B2B scholars also recognize that data provided by a single organizational respondent (even a key inform-ant) is generally less reliable than data provided by multiple respondents (John and Reve 1982; Phillips 1981). This recognition seems to be growing because of increasing concerns about the risks of CMV bias. As a result, an increasing number of B2B studies are employing multiple respondents (e.g. Atuahene-Gima 2005; Im and Workman 2004; Ramani and Kumar 2008).

Unfortunately, organizational respondents often provide divergent, and sometimes contradictory, responses to survey measures. This divergence, combined with the added cost and effort of collecting data from multiple respondents, makes the use of this approach somewhat problematic. Kumar et al. (1993) offer three approaches for dealing with divergent responses: (1) latent trait; (2) aggregation; and (3) consensus. We briefly review each of these three approaches.

The latent trait approach, based on the well-known multiple trait–multiple method (Campbell and Fiske 1959), partitions the variance of divergent organizational responses into three separate components: trait (the latent construct of interest), method (the particular informant) and random error. Though appealing in its precision, this approach is often plagued by a lack of statistical convergence due to the widely disparate starting values that characterize multiple respondents.

The aggregation approach attempts to synthesize divergent organizational responses by aggregating responses across multiple informants. The most common aggregation approach is a simple computation of the (unweighted) mean response across an organization's respondents. Though appealing in its simplicity, this approach often results in biased measures because the arithmetic mean tends to be skewed by outliers. In essence, the mean gets 'stretched' by the responses that are the most divergent.

The consensus approach strives to minimize divergence across organizational respondents by asking these respondents to resolve their differences through discussion. This approach, however, requires a great deal of effort from both the researchers and the respondents, and may introduce unwanted biases, such as social desirability and group-think. Considering the limitation of all three approaches, Kumar et al. (1993) recommend a hybrid technique that combines the elements of each approach. Although this recommendation is intuitively appealing, it is nevertheless costly and difficult to implement.

As an alternative means to manage divergence across organizational respondents, Van Bruggen et al. (2002) recommend a simple variant of the aggregation approach. Specifically, they suggest that survey researchers should manage divergent responses by first assessing (i.e. scoring) the competence of each respondent.[6] Researchers can then use these competence scores to compute a weighted arithmetic mean across all an organization's respondents. This method significantly outperforms the simple arithmetic mean-based aggregation approach and strikes a balance between validity and ease of implementation. Alternatively, B2B scholars might avoid this problem by asking different individuals within an organization to complete different portions of the survey instrument according to their expertise and knowledge. For example, a survey about the impact of co-marketing alliances on firm performance could ask brand managers to answer questions about the degree of communication and trust among alliance members and ask chief financial officers to report information about firm performance.

Integrating Multi-organizational and Intra-organizational Perspectives

Whether as a response to CMV-related concerns or as a natural evolution of the field, B2B scholars are increasing the scope of their data collection and analysis efforts beyond a single firm or a dyadic relationship. Recent examples of this broadened scope include Wathne and Heide's (2004) investigation of relationship governance in a supply chain network, Palmatier et al.'s (2007) study of boundary-spanning sales personnel and McFarland et al.'s (2008) examination of supply chain contagion. A common underlying premise across all these studies is the notion that a focal organization's activities and outcomes affect, and are affected by, external entities (e.g. suppliers, customers, downstream channel partners).

Although surveys of multiple organizations have significantly broadened the scope of B2B research, this approach presents several challenges. First, many of these studies collect survey data from hundreds or even thousands of organizations (e.g. Dahlstrom and Nygaard 1999; Homburg et al. 2009). These types of large-scale surveys require significant investments in terms of both time and money.[7] Second, the coding of data from multiple organizations usually requires the matching of responses across organizational respondents (e.g. Wathne and Heide 2004). This matching process hinges on a researcher's ability to persuade respondents to provide the names and contact details of their counterparts in one or more external entities, which often results in substantial sample attrition (usually 60–75 per cent). Third, the appropriate analysis of matching data across multiple organizations requires more than a passing familiarity with new modeling techniques, such as multilevel regression. Fortunately, these multilevel methods are relatively straightforward extensions of traditional regression techniques and are well detailed by both Raudenbush and Bryk (2002) and Hox (2010).

The use of multilevel regression provides B2B scholars with the ability to obtain a more nuanced understanding of organizational phenomena. Specifically, this technique allows B2B scholars to assess relationships within a firm (e.g. Wiesecke et al. 2009), between a firm and its key constituents (e.g. Homburg et al. 2009) or even across multiple firms in a value chain (e.g. McFarland et al. 2008). Multilevel techniques are not only a natural conceptual fit with B2B inquiry but also reasonably accessible to most B2B scholars through standard software packages, such as SAS, STATA and HLM.

A researcher might hypothesize, for example, that the level of trust between two firms engaged in an alliance is a function of specific investments made by each partner. The impact of both sets of investments is typically reflected in a pair of fixed (beta) coefficients. Extending this analytical approach to a multilevel setting, a researcher might instead allow each beta coefficient to vary as a function of the expectations of continuity held by employees within each firm. Employees thus are considered level-1 units nested within level-2 firms (Raudenbush and Bryk 2002), and it is possible to 'unpack' variation in trust to causes attributable to the participating firms, as well as to their respective employees. Conceptually, multilevel techniques facilitate the much called for 'opening up of the organizational black box'. Thus, we encourage B2B scholars to consider expanding the scope of their surveys to examine research issues spanning both across and within organizations.

Online Surveys

Traditionally, B2B surveys have been mainly administered by mail. Thus, much of the knowledge not only of organizational activity but also of survey research methodology has been informed by this approach. For example, the bulk of research on response rates focuses on techniques for enhancing responses to surveys delivered by mail (e.g. Childers and Ferrell 1979; Yammarino et al. 1991; Yu and Cooper 1983). However, an increasing number of B2B surveys are now being administered online (e.g. Jap 2007; Ramani and Kumar 2008; Srinivasan and Moorman 2005). We briefly explore this emerging trend and examine its benefits and limitations.

Compared with mail surveys, an online approach confers several benefits to researchers. First and foremost, because they eliminate printing and mailing costs, online surveys are considerably more cost effective than mail surveys (Couper 2008; Kaplowitz et al. 2004). Second, online surveys typically provide real-time data capture and greatly reduce coding errors (Jap and Anderson 2004). Third, online surveys can be easily customized to each respondent, thereby allowing for more sophisticated survey designs, such as split-sample approaches (which we discuss next).

Despite these benefits, the modality (i.e. computer-based) of online surveys presents important limitations that B2B researchers need to consider carefully. Because of this modality, online surveys are perceived as less confidential than mail surveys (Couper 2008; Sax et al. 2003). In addition, online surveys are considerably less portable than the paper surveys respondents receive by mail (Jap and Anderson 2004).[8] Online surveys may also appear to be much longer than their paper equivalents. For example, a four-page paper version of a survey conducted by Sax et al. (2003) required 32 pages (an 8-to-1 ratio) on a computer to present the same amount of information.

Considering these limitations, it is perhaps not surprising that online surveys generally obtain lower response rates than their offline counterparts (Lozar Manfreda et al. 2008; Sax et al. 2003).[9] Moreover, because response rate research has largely been conducted on mail surveys, the findings from this body of work may be of limited applicability to online surveys (Couper 2008).[10] For example, although monetary incentives are a key means to increase response rates for mail surveys, they seem to be considerably less effective for online surveys (Sax et al. 2003). As an alternative approach, B2B researchers should consider employing a mixed-modality strategy, such as preceding an online survey with a notification letter by regular mail (Kaplowitz et al. 2004) or conducting a mail survey with an online option (Sax et al. 2003). These types of mixed-modality strategies can bring an online survey's response rate up to the level found for surveys conducted by regular mail (Kaplowitz et al. 2004; Sax et al. 2003).

In the aggregate, we believe that the benefits of online surveys greatly exceed their limitations. Thus, we have personally switched from paper to online survey administration and enthusiastically recommend this approach to our B2B colleagues. Researchers can choose from several freely available online survey design packages, such as Survey Monkey (www.surveymonkey.com) and Zoomerang (www.zoomerang.com). However, we are particularly fond of Qualtrics (www.qualtrics.com) and appreciate its high degree of functionality and flexibility. Although Qualtrics is a fee-based service, many universities subscribe to this service and offer complimentary access to their faculty and doctoral students.[11]

Split Samples

Most, if not all, survey researchers have faced the unenviable problem of having too many questions and too little space. A typical B2B survey includes multiple latent constructs, each reflected in or formed by multiple items (Churchill 1979). Thus, it is not uncommon for a B2B survey instrument to contain more than 150 items.

Inordinately long surveys impose a burden on potential respondents and can result in low response rates, item non-response and undesirable response styles (Bradburn et al. 2004). Thus, survey researchers face a trade-off 'between more data per variable, but lesser quality data [and] lesser data per variable, but higher quality data' (Vriens et al. 2001, p. 16). As a means to balance this trade-off, survey scholars advocate managing survey length (Dillman et al. 2009). For example, Childers and Ferrell (1979) suggest that to enhance response rates, mail surveys should not exceed four pages. Although these types of survey-length guidelines provide helpful rules of thumb, they are often difficult to put into practice.

As an alternative solution to this dilemma, marketing scholars have recently advocated the use of split questionnaire design (SQD) (Adiguzel and Wedel 2008; Vriens et al. 2001).[12] This technique provides a tractable means of conducting comprehensive surveys while minimizing respondent fatigue. In essence, a SQD breaks up a massive survey instrument into several smaller blocks of questions and then systematically administers sets of these blocks across potential respondents so that, across the total sample, responses to all questions are obtained. This technique is analogous to conjoint choice experiments or factorial experiment design, both of which focus on obtaining an aggregate perspective through a disaggregated approach.

Survey scholars interested in employing the SQD technique can choose from two variants. The first variant, proposed by Vriens et al. (2001), recommends the employment of a core block of questions administered to all respondents combined with multiple blocks of questions randomly administered to various subsets of respondents. Although this SQD approach is easy to administer, it offers limited statistical properties. More important, the random assignment of question blocks to sample subsets can lead to information loss. This limitation is addressed by another variant SQD technique that Adiguzel and Wedel (2008) propose. Their approach splits a broader survey into smaller blocks by presenting respondents with a partial set of the items constituting a given construct and then recovers missing data through various imputation techniques. Although both SQD variants require more effort in terms of design and analysis than a conventional survey approach, they offer a means to maximize the benefits and minimize the costs of fielding a large-scale survey.

Using Surveys to Affect Behavior

B2B scholars share an unwritten assumption that surveys provide a means to assess what respondents think and do. As survey researchers, we share this assumption and have made considerable use of surveys to assess various types of B2B activity (e.g. Frazier et al. 2009; Ganesan et al. 2005; Rindfleisch and Moorman 2003). However, we also acknowledge that surveys may affect the behavior they try to assess.

The idea that measurement affects (rather than just assesses) outcomes has been raised in many disciplines, ranging from psychology (Fiske and Campbell 1992) to physics (Robertson 1929). Within the marketing domain, Simmons et al. (1993, p. 327) suggest that 'the measurement process may create, rather than capture, market-place opinion and produce a spurious consistency among these created opinions'. This spurious consistency has been labeled 'self-generated validity' and occurs because answers to earlier questions provide diagnostic and accessible inputs for responses to later questions (Feldman and Lynch 1988). For example, Simmons et al. (1993) demonstrate that earlier questions about political attitudes strongly affect later questions about voting intentions.

To combat this validity threat, survey researchers should pay close attention to the order in which survey questions are presented (Schwarz 1999).

More recently, a growing body of research in the field of consumer behavior has demonstrated that survey questions affect not only intentions but also actual behavior (e.g. Fitzsimons and Morwitz 1996; Morwitz and Fitzsimons 2004; Sprott et al. 2006). Fitzsimons and Morwitz (1996, p. 1) suggest that 'the process of survey measurement actually changes respondents' attitudes, intentions, and behaviors'. This change is known as the 'question–behavior effect' and has been documented across a range of contexts in both laboratory and field settings (see Sprott et al. 2006 for a review). For example, Morwitz and Fitzsimons (2004) find that surveying consumer purchase intentions exerts a positive impact on actual purchase behavior at both the brand and the category level. The question–behavior effect is akin to the principle of self-generated validity and is believed to occur because the act of responding to questions about intentions provides accessible inputs for subsequent purchase decisions (Morwitz and Fitzsimons 2004). These inputs are not fleeting effects but rather persist for several months following survey measurement (Sprott et al. 2006).

Although the study of how survey questions affect respondent behavior has largely been the province of consumer researchers, we believe that the question–behavior effect is also likely to occur among managerial respondents. Thus, we strongly encourage B2B scholars to investigate this important but underacknowledged effect. In addition to exploring the impact of this effect on survey validity, B2B researchers should examine the degree to which question accessibility can actually influence (and possibly improve) managerial behavior. For example, do managers who respond to questions about their firms' degree of market orientation exhibit more of this orientation following survey administration? The possibility that surveys can affect (rather than just assess) managerial behavior is an exciting prospect and, if validated, has the potential to breathe new life into the realm of B2B survey scholarship.

CONCLUDING REMARKS

Survey research is an important means of inquiry for B2B scholars. This method is well established and provides unique benefits by allowing researchers to measure phenomena in a naturalistic setting rather than manipulating it in a laboratory. However, as Schuman (1982, p. 25) notes, 'No method offers a panacea.' Thus, as with all inquiry techniques, survey research also entails several limitations. Our chapter identifies three of these limitations and offers solutions for reducing their potential adverse impact (see Table 37.2 for a guidepost). We recommend that B2B scholars follow this guidepost when conducting and reporting survey research. In addition to addressing survey research's limitations, we recommend that B2B scholars seek opportunities for extending the scope of survey research and enriching its influence. Our chapter identifies five opportunities in particular, but there are likely to be several more that will emerge in the years ahead. Through this dual effort of minimizing limitations and maximizing opportunities, B2B scholars can help ensure that survey research remains an important and vital means of obtaining answers to their research questions.

NOTES

1. Because B2B academics are mainly concerned with deriving valid explanations, they may wish to pay particular attention to our discussion of causality, multiple respondents and multiple organizations. In contrast, because B2B practitioners are mainly concerned with developing accurate predictions, they may wish to pay particular attention to our discussion of non-response bias, online surveys and split sample designs.
2. Because our goal is concision rather than comprehensiveness, our coverage of survey limitations and solutions captures a limited slice of a rich and complex domain. B2B scholars wanting a deeper exploration of the nuances of survey research should consult more comprehensive treatises (e.g. Bradburn et al. 2004; Dillman et al. 2009; Wright and Marsden 2010).
3. For a more thorough examination of various CMV assessment techniques, see Podsakoff et al. (2003).
4. See Malhotra et al. (2005) for a variant of this approach.
5. See Bolton and Lemon (1999) and Jap (1999) for notable exceptions.
6. Respondent qualification questions (i.e. degree of organizational knowledge or number of years of employment) can double as competence scores.
7. These investments are usually somewhat offset by the cooperation of one or more sponsoring organizations.
8. This portability limitation may be eliminated in the near future because tablet-based computing devices, such as the iPad, are rapidly diffusing.
9. Extant research suggests that, on average, response rates for online surveys are 10 per cent lower than their mail counterparts (Lozar Manfreda et al. 2008; Sax et al. 2003). However, this difference may vary considerably depending on a wide number of topical, contextual and respondent characteristics.
10. Some online surveys may not have a predefined sampling frame, which makes it extremely difficult to estimate non-response (Couper 2008).
11. For a listing of universities with Qualtrics subscriptions, see www.qualtrics.com/clients/.
12. For more information about this technique, see Raghunathan and Grizzle (1995).

REFERENCES

Adiguzel, Feray and Michel Wedel (2008), 'Split questionnaire design for massive surveys', *Journal of Marketing Research*, **45** (October), 608–17.
Ahearne, Michael and Son Lam (2012), 'Sales force performance: a typology and future research priorities', in Gary Lilien and Rajdeep Grewal (eds), *Handbook of Business-to-Business Marketing*, Cheltenham, UK and Northampton, MA, USA: Edward Elgar Publishing.
Anderson, Erin and Barton Weitz (1992), 'The use of pledges to build and sustain commitment in distribution channels', *Journal of Marketing Research*, **29** (February), 18–34.
Antia, Kersi D. and Gary L. Frazier (2001), 'The severity of contract enforcement in interfirm channel relationships', *Journal of Marketing*, **67** (October), 67–81.
Armstrong, J. Scott (1975), 'Monetary incentives in mail surveys', *Public Opinion Quarterly*, **39** (Spring), 111–16.
Armstrong, J. Scott and Fred Collopy (1996), 'Competitor orientation: effects of objectives and information on managerial decisions and profits', *Journal of Marketing Research*, **33** (May), 188–99.
Armstrong, J. Scott and Terry S. Overton (1977), 'Estimating nonresponse bias in mail surveys', *Journal of Marketing Research*, **14** (August), 396–402.
Atuahene-Gima, Kwaku (2005), 'Resolving the capability-rigidity paradox in new product innovation', *Journal of Marketing*, **69** (October), 61–83.
Banerjee, Ranjan, Mark Bergen, Shantanu Dutta and Sourav Ray (2012), 'Applications of agency theory in B2B marketing: review and future directions', in Gary Lilien and Rajdeep Grewal (eds), *Handbook of Business-to-Business Marketing*, Cheltenham, UK and Northampton, MA, USA: Edward Elgar Publishing.
Baumgartner, Hans and Jan-Benedict E.M. Steenkamp (2001), 'Response styles in marketing research: a cross-national investigation', *Journal of Marketing Research*, **38** (May), 143–56.
Blyalogosky, Eyal, William Boulding and Richard Staelin (2006), 'Stuck in the past: why managers persist with new product failures', *Journal of Marketing*, **70** (April), 108–21.
Bolton, Ruth N. and Katherine N. Lemon (1999), 'A dynamic model of customers' usage of services: usage as an antecedent and consequence of satisfaction', *Journal of Marketing Research*, **36** (May), 171–86.
Bowman, Douglas (2012), 'Evolution of buyer-seller relationships', in Gary Lilien and Rajdeep Grewal (eds),

Handbook of Business-to-Business Marketing, Cheltenham, UK and Northampton, MA, USA: Edward Elgar Publishing.

Bradburn, Norman, Seymour Sudman and Brian Wansink (2004), *Asking Questions: The Definitive Guide to Questionnaire Design: For Market Research, Political Polls, and Social and Health Questionnaires*, New York: John Wiley & Sons.

Campbell, Donald T. (1955), 'The informant in quantitative research', *American Journal of Sociology*, **60** (January), 339–42.

Campbell, Donald T. and Donald W. Fiske (1959), 'Convergent and discriminant validation by the multitrait-multimethod matrix', *Psychological Bulletin*, **56** (2), 81–105.

Cannon, Joseph P. and Christian Homburg (2001), 'Buyer–supplier relationships and customer firm costs', *Journal of Marketing*, **65** (January), 29–43.

Childers, Terry L. and O.C. Ferrell (1979), 'Response rates and perceived questionnaire length in mail surveys', *Journal of Marketing Research*, **16** (February), 64–73.

Churchill, Gilbert A. (1979), 'A paradigm for developing better measures of marketing constructs', *Journal of Marketing Research*, **16** (August), 429–31.

Cohen, Joel, Patricia Cohen, Stephen G. West and Leona S. Aiken (2003), *Applied Multiple Regression/Correlation Analysis for the Behavior Sciences*, Mahwah, NJ: Lawrence Erlbaum Associates.

Cote, Joseph A. and M. Ronald Buckley (1987), 'Estimating trait, method, and error variance: generalizing across 70 construct validation studies', *Journal of Marketing Research*, **24** (August), 315–18.

Couper, Mick P. (2008), *Designing Effective Web Surveys*, Cambridge, UK: Cambridge University Press.

Dahl, Darren W. and Page Moreau (2002), 'The influence and value of analogical thinking during new product ideation', *Journal of Marketing Research*, **39** (February), 47–60.

Dahlstrom, Robert and Arne Nygaard (1999), 'An empirical investigation of ex post transaction costs in franchised distribution channels', *Journal of Marketing Research*, **36** (May), 160–70.

Dillman, Donald A., Jolene D. Smyth and Leah Melani Christian (2009), *Internet, Mail, and Mixed-Mode Surveys: The Tailored Design Method*, 3rd edn, New York: John Wiley & Sons.

Doty, D. Harold and William H. Glick (1998), 'Common methods bias: does common methods variance really bias results?', *Organizational Research Methods*, **1** (October), 374–406.

Einhorn, Hillel J. and Robin M. Hogarth (1986), 'Judging probable cause', *Psychological Bulletin*, **99** (January), 3–19.

Faville, David E. (1936), 'Comparison of chain and independent grocery stores in the San Francisco area', *Journal of Marketing*, **1** (October), 87–90.

Feldman, Jack A. and John G. Lynch Jr (1988), 'Self-generated validity: effects of measurement on belief, attitude, intention and behavior', *Journal of Applied Psychology*, **73** (August), 421–35.

Fiske, Donald T. and Donald W. Campbell (1992), 'Citations do not solve problems', *Psychological Bulletin*, **112** (3), 393–5.

Fitzsimons, Gavan and Vicki G. Morwitz (1996), 'The effect of measuring intent on brand-level purchase behavior', *Journal of Consumer Research*, **23** (June), 1–11.

Frazier, Gary L., Elliot Maltz, Kersi D. Antia and Aric Rindfleisch (2009), 'Distributor sharing of strategic information with suppliers', *Journal of Marketing*, **73** (July), 31–43.

Frazier, George and Kermit Bird (1958), 'Increasing the response of a mailed questionnaire', *Journal of Marketing*, **22** (October), 186–7.

Frederick, J. George (1937), 'New uses for marketing research', *Journal of Marketing*, **2** (October), 132–3.

Ganesan, Shankar, Alan J. Malter and Aric Rindfleisch (2005), 'Does distance still matter? The role of geographic proximity in new product development', *Journal of Marketing*, **69** (October), 44–60.

Gerbing, David W. and James C. Anderson (1988), 'An updated paradigm for scale development incorporating unidimensionality and its assessment', *Journal of Marketing Research*, **25** (May), 186–92.

Granger, Clive (1969), 'Investigating causal relations by econometric models and cross-spectral methods', *Econometrica*, **37** (3), 424–38.

Hill, Austin Bradford (1965), 'The environment and disease: association or causation?', *Proceedings of the Royal Society of Medicine*, **58** (5), 295–300.

Homburg, Christian, Jan Wiesecke and Wayne Hoyer (2009), 'Social identity and the service-profit chain', *Journal of Marketing*, **73** (March), 38–54.

Hox, Joop (2010), *Multilevel Analysis: Techniques and Applications*, 2nd edn, New York: Routledge.

Im, Subin and John P. Workman Jr (2004), 'Market orientation, creativity, and new product performance in high-technology firms', *Journal of Marketing*, **68** (April), 114–32.

Jap, Sandy D. (1999), 'Pie-expansion efforts: collaboration processes in buyer–supplier relationships', *Journal of Marketing Research*, **36** (November), 461–75.

Jap, Sandy D. (2007), 'The impact of online reverse auction design on buyer–supplier relationships', *Journal of Marketing*, **71** (January), 146–59.

Jap, Sandy D. and Erin M. Anderson (2004), 'Challenges and advances in marketing strategy field research', in

Christine Moorman and Donald R. Lehmann (eds), *Assessing Marketing Strategy Performance*, Cambridge, MA: Marketing Science Institute, pp. 269–92.

Jap, Sandy D. and Shankar Ganesan (2000), 'Control mechanisms and the relationship life cycle: implications for safeguarding specific investments and developing commitment', *Journal of Marketing Research*, **37** (May), 227–45.

Jap, Sandy D. and Ernan Haruvy (2008), 'Interorganizational relationships and bidding behavior in industrial online reverse auctions', *Journal of Marketing Research*, **45** (October), 550–61.

John, George and Torger Reve (1982), 'The reliability and validity of key informant data from dyadic relationships', *Journal of Marketing Research*, **22** (November), 517–24.

Jöreskog, Karl and Dag Sörbom (1993), *LISREL 8: User's Reference Guide*, Chicago, IL: Scientific Software International.

Kamakura, Wagner A. (2001), 'From the editor', *Journal of Marketing Research*, **38** (February), 1–2.

Kaplowitz, Michael D., Timothy D. Hadlock and Ralph Levine (2004), 'A comparison of web and mail survey response rates', *Public Opinion Quarterly*, **68** (1), 94–101.

Kumar, Nirmalya, Louis W. Stern and James C. Anderson (1993), 'Conducting interorganizational research using key informants', *Academy of Management Review*, **36** (6), 1633–51.

Landefeld, J. Steven, Eugene P. Seskin and Barbara M. Fraumeni (2008), 'Taking the pulse of the economy: measuring GDP', *Journal of Economic Perspectives*, **22** (Spring), 193–216.

Lanyon, Alan C. (1939), 'The mortality of Baltimore fuel dealers', *Journal of Marketing*, **4** (July), 68–72.

Lindell, Michael K. and David J. Whitney (2001), 'Accounting for common method variance in cross-sectional research design', *Journal of Applied Psychology*, **86** (1), 114–21.

Lozar Manfreda, K., M. Bosnjak, J. Berzelak, I. Haas and V. Vehovar (2008), 'Web surveys versus other survey modes: a meta-analysis comparing response rates', *International Journal of Market Research*, **50** (1), 79–114.

Luo, Xueming and Christian Homburg (2007), 'Neglected outcomes of customer satisfaction', *Journal of Marketing*, **71** (April), 133–49.

Lusch, Robert F. and James R. Brown (1996), 'Interdependency, contracting, and relational behavior in marketing channels', *Journal of Marketing*, **60** (October), 19–38.

Malhotra, Naresh K., Sung S. Kim and Ashutosh Patil (2005), 'Common method variance in IS research: a comparison of alternative approaches and a reanalysis of past research', *Management Science*, **52** (December), 1865–83.

Marini, Margaret Mooney and Burton Singer (1988), 'Causality in the social sciences', *Sociological Methodology*, **18**, 347–409.

Martens, Matthew P. and Richard F. Haase (2006), 'Advanced applications of structural equations modeling in counseling psychology research', *The Counseling Psychologist*, **34** (November), 878–911.

McFarland, Richard G., James M. Bloodgood and Janice M. Payan (2008), 'Supply chain contagion', *Journal of Marketing*, **72** (March), 63–79.

Mohr, Jakki J., Robert J. Fisher and John R. Nevin (1996), 'Collaborative communication in interfirm relationships: moderating effects of integration and control', *Journal of Marketing*, **60** (July), 103–15.

Morwitz, Vicki G. and Gavan J. Fitzsimons (2004), 'The mere-measurement effect: why does measuring intentions change actual behavior?', *Journal of Consumer Psychology*, **14** (1–2), 64–74.

Palmatier, Robert W. (2008), 'Interfirm relational drivers of customer value', *Journal of Marketing*, **72** (July), 76–89.

Palmatier, Robert W., Lisa K. Scheer and Jan-Benedict E.M. Steenkamp (2007), 'Customer loyalty to whom? Managing the benefits and risks of salesperson-owned loyalty', *Journal of Marketing Research*, **44** (May), 185–99.

Phillips, Lynn W. (1981), 'Assessing measurement error in key informant reports: a methodological note on organizational analysis in marketing', *Journal of Marketing Research*, **18** (November), 395–415.

Podsakoff, Philip M. and Dennis W. Organ (1986), 'Self-reports in organizational research: problems and prospects', *Journal of Management*, **12** (4), 531–44.

Podsakoff, Philip M., Scott B. MacKenzie, Jeong-Yeon Lee and Nathan P. Podsakoff (2003), 'Common method biases in behavioral research: a critical review of the literature and recommended remedies', *Journal of Applied Psychology*, **88** (5), 879–903.

Raghunathan, Trivellore E. and James Grizzle (1995), 'A split questionnaire survey design', *Journal of the American Statistical Association*, **90**, 54–63.

Ramani, Girish and V. Kumar (2008), 'Interaction orientation and firm performance', *Journal of Marketing*, **72** (January), 27–45.

Raudenbush, Stephen W. and Anthony S. Bryk (2002), *Hierarchical Linear Models: Applications and Data Analysis Methods*, 2nd edn, Thousand Oaks, CA: Sage Publications.

Rindfleisch, Aric and Christine Moorman (2003), 'Interfirm cooperation and customer orientation', *Journal of Marketing Research*, **40** (November), 421–36.

Rindfleisch, Aric, Alan J. Malter, Shankar Ganesan and Christine Moorman (2008), 'Cross-sectional versus longitudinal survey research: concepts, findings, and guidelines', *Journal of Marketing Research*, **45** (June), 261–79.

Robertson, Howard Percy (1929), 'The uncertainty principle', *Physical Review*, **34** (1), 163–4.

Sales, Anne E., Mary E. Plomondon, David J. Magid, John A. Spertus and John S. Rumsfeld (2004), 'Assessing response bias from missing quality of life data: the Heckman method', *Health and Quality of Life Outcomes*, **2**, 623–32.

Sax, Linda J., Shannon K. Gilmartin and Alyssa N. Bryant (2003), 'Assessing response rates and nonresponse rates in web and paper surveys', *Research in Higher Education*, **44** (August), 409–32.

Schaeffer, Nora Cate, Judith A. Seltzer and Marieka Klawitter (1991), 'Estimating nonresponse and response bias: resident and nonresident parents' report about child support', *Sociological Methods & Research*, **20** (1), 30–59.

Scheer, Lisa K. (2012), 'Trust, distrust and confidence in B2B relationships', in Gary Lilien and Rajdeep Grewal (eds), *Handbook of Business-to-Business Marketing*, Cheltenham, UK and Northampton, MA, USA: Edward Elgar Publishing.

Schuman, Howard (1982), 'Artifacts are in the mind of the beholder', *American Sociologist*, **17** (February), 21–8.

Schwarz, Norbert (1999), 'Self-reports: how the questions shape the answers', *American Psychologist*, **54** (February), 93–105.

Simmons, Carolyn J., Barbara A. Bickart and John G. Lynch Jr (1993), 'Capturing and creating public opinion in survey research', *Journal of Consumer Research*, **20** (September), 316–29.

Sprott, David E., Eric R. Spangenberg, Lauren G. Block, Gavan J. Fitzsimons, Vicki G. Morwitz and Patti Williams (2006), 'The question–behavior effect: what we know and where we go from here', *Social Influence*, **1** (2), 128–37.

Srinivasan, Raji and Christine Moorman (2005), 'Strategic firm commitments and rewards for customer relationship management in online retailing', *Journal of Marketing*, **69** (October), 193–200.

Steenkamp, Jan-Benedict E.M., Martijn de Jong and Hans Baumgartner (2010), 'Socially desirable response tendencies in survey research', *Journal of Marketing Research*, **47** (April), 199–214.

Trusov, Michael, Randolph E. Bucklin and Koen Pauwels (2009), 'Effects of word-of-mouth versus traditional marketing: findings from an internet social networking site', *Journal of Marketing*, **73** (September), 90–102.

Van Bruggen, Gerrit, Gary Lilien and Manish Kacker (2002), 'Informants in organizational marketing research: why use multiple informants and how to aggregate responses', *Journal of Marketing Research*, **39** (November), 469–78.

Van Rosmalen, Joost, Hester van Herk and Patrick J.F. Groenen (2010), 'Identifying response styles: a latent-class multinomial logit model', *Journal of Marketing Research*, **47** (February), 157–72.

Vriens, Marco, Michel Wedel and Zsolt Sandor (2001), 'Split questionnaire designs: a new tool in survey design and panel management', *Marketing Research*, **13** (Summer), 14–19.

Wathne, Kenneth H. and Jan B. Heide (2004), 'Relationship governance in a supply chain network', *Journal of Marketing*, **68** (January), 73–89.

Wiesecke, Jan, Michael Ahearne, Son K. Lam and Rolf van Dick (2009), 'The role of leaders in internal marketing', *Journal of Marketing*, **73** (March), 123–45.

Wiseman, Frederick and Maryann Billington (1984), 'Comment on a standard definition of response rates', *Journal of Marketing Research*, **21** (August), 336–8.

Wittink, Dick R. (2004), '*Journal of Marketing Research*: 2Ps', *Journal of Marketing Research*, **41** (February), 1–6.

Wong, Chi-Sum and Kenneth S. Law (1999), 'Testing reciprocal relations by nonrecursive structural equation models using cross-sectional data', *Organizational Research Methods*, **2** (January), 69–87.

Wright, J. and Peter Marsden (2010), *Handbook of Survey Research*, 2nd edn, Bingley, UK: Emerald.

Wuyts, Stefan and Inge Geyskens (2005), 'The formation of buyer–seller relationships: detailed contract drafting and close partner selection', *Journal of Marketing*, **69** (October), 103–17.

Yammarino, Francis J., Steven J. Skinner and Terry L. Childers (1991), 'Understanding mail survey response behavior: a meta-analysis', *Public Opinion Quarterly*, **55** (4), 613–39.

Yu, Julie and Harris Cooper (1983), 'A quantitative review of research design effects on response rates to questionnaires', *Journal of Marketing Research*, **20** (February), 36–44.

38 Marketing metrics for B2B firms
Raji Srinivasan

Marketers are increasingly pressured to demonstrate the return on their firms' marketing investments. As John Quelch (2005) noted in the *Wall Street Journal*:

> Today's boards want chief marketing officers who can speak the language of productivity and return on investment and are willing to be accountable. In recent years, manufacturing, procurement, and logistics have all tightened their belts in the cause of improved productivity. As a result, marketing expenditures account for a larger percentage of many corporate cost structures than ever before. Today's boards don't need chief marketing officers who have creative flair but no financial discipline. They need ambidextrous marketers who offer both.

Against this backdrop in business practice, marketing scholars have emphasized the importance of marketing metrics (Srivastava et al. 1998, 1999), especially as it relates to firm performance, including accounting performance (e.g. Erickson and Jacobson 1992) and shareholder value metrics (e.g. McAlister et al. 2007; Mizik and Jacobson 2003). Over the past few decades, marketers in business practice have developed myriad metrics for evaluating marketing performance (see Farris et al. 2009). Some of these include awareness, preference, purchase intent, share of wallet, customer satisfaction, loyalty and repeat purchase rate, to name a few.

A large body of empirical work has examined the effects of various marketing actions, including branding (e.g. Rao et al. 2004), advertising (e.g. McAlister et al. 2007; Singh et al. 2005) and customer relationships (e.g. Gupta et al. 2004). Prior work in marketing has also studied metrics on profits (e.g. Erickson and Jacobson 1992), stock returns (e.g. Mizik and Jacobson 2003), intangible value (e.g. Rao et al. 2004; Srinivasan 2006) and systematic risk (McAlister et al. 2007).

My review of the marketing metrics literature as it pertains to B2B firms indicates two broad streams of research. The first stream of research focuses on the development of marketing metrics (e.g. customer satisfaction, market share, profits, stock returns) primarily using the B2C context (e.g. mass media advertising, discrete goods and services, end consumers). However, B2B firms have distinctive characteristics in terms of customers (other firms), products (total solutions) and marketing communications (integrated multimedia communications), so many of the marketing metrics developed in the context of B2C firms have limited applicability to B2B firms.[1]

The second stream of research focuses on issues relevant to B2B firms. Much of the research examines the performance implications of marketing actions of B2B firms, generating useful insights into marketing metrics. For example, drawing on the notions of relational capabilities and absorptive capacity, Johnson et al. (2004) examine the effects of interactional, functional and environmental knowledge stores on relationship quality and relationship portfolio effectiveness. Narayandas and Rangan (2004) study the evolution of three industrial buyer–seller relationships in mature industrial markets and find that weaker firms can thrive in long-term relationships with powerful partners through the development of high levels of interpersonal trust across the dyad. Narayandas (2005) identifies the drivers of customer loyalty in B2B markets, which are very different from those in B2C markets.

Other studies have generated insights into the drivers to leverage profitability in B2B relationships (e.g. Bowman and Narayandas 2004; Kalwani and Narayandas 1995), and still others have focused on customer lifetime value (Kumar et al. 2008; Palmatier 2008) and the various factors that affect customer profitability and customer equity in B2B relationships, such as customer referrals (Kumar et al. 2010) and interaction orientation (Ramani and Kumar 2008). Palmatier and colleagues focus on the factors influencing inter-organizational relationships, including trust (Fang et al. 2008) and salesperson-owned loyalty (Palmatier et al. 2007).

My review indicates that though these studies in the B2B area provide rich insights into the effectiveness of marketing programs, many focus on the inter-organizational relationships between suppliers and buyers that characterize B2B markets. However, B2B firms have many distinctive characteristics other than inter-organizational relationships that remain unexplored in general, but specifically with respect to marketing metrics.

In the remainder of this chapter, I discuss the many distinctive characteristics of B2B firms and the challenges they face. I also identify research questions for marketing scholars and practitioners interested in the area of marketing metrics for B2B firms.

DISTINCTIVE CHARACTERISTICS OF B2B FIRMS: WHY THAT MATTERS FOR MARKETING METRICS

Webster and Wind (1972, p. 2) define organizational buying as the decision-making process by which formal organizations establish the need to purchase products and services and identify, evaluate and choose among alternative brands and services. B2B goods and services are, by definition, purchased by executives on behalf of their organizations. Transaction values in B2B transactions can be very high, sometimes running into several millions of dollars; sellers tend to customize products for their customers; and tools of conventional mass marketing are not appropriate in B2B markets. Sales executives and key account managers are deployed to develop, nurture and maintain customer relationships with the buyer firms. In this section, I discuss the distinctive characteristics of B2B markets and the resultant research questions in the area of marketing metrics for B2B firms.

B2B Goods and Services are Relatively Complex

Unlike in the B2C context, firms purchase B2B goods and services either for their consumption (e.g. office supplies) or as input for their production process to produce goods and services for their end consumers (e.g. chemicals to manufacture detergents). B2B goods and services are typically more complex and sophisticated than B2C goods and services. Often the benefits and costs of the products to either the seller or the buyer may not be known before (or even after) the buyer uses the products. In addition, in many cases the products and services sold to business customers are inputs to the buyer's production process, which may entail the consideration of technical specifications, total cost of ownership and compatibility with the buyer's products and end customers. Physical products are often only a small part of the overall customer solution in the B2B context. Thus the selling proposition in this context must present value-based differentiated solutions that can support the rational buying decisions of the seller firms (Tuli et al. 2007). Firms customize these customer solutions, which typically involve a combination of goods and services, to address a customer's particular requirement. Business processes essential to the development of customer solutions in B2B markets include defining requirements, customizing and integrating goods and/or services, deploying the solutions and then providing post-deployment support.

Given this paradigm shift in conceptualization of products across B2C (discrete products) and B2B (customized solution selling with emphasis on relationship processes) markets, a pertinent question is whether insights into new product development metrics and product management (e.g. Griffin and Page 1996) on discrete off-the-shelf products and services prevalent in B2C firms can be extended to a customer solutions paradigm in B2B firms. Additional research questions that emerge include the following:

- What are the appropriate metrics for the development of customer solutions for B2B firms? Are the various metrics developed in the B2C context (e.g. time to market, time to commercialization) valid and relevant for B2B firms?
- What key (e.g. chain of command, culture) and relational processes should be managed for the effective development and marketing of customer solutions in B2B firms? Which functional areas (i.e. marketing, research and development, operations, sales) and routines of interaction and coordination among departments should be set up for fast and effective solution delivery? What metrics should be created to monitor the degree and quality of information transmission and utilization among departments? Given the high importance of the direct sales force, what metrics should be developed that enable the sales department to participate in the solution creation process and also solution delivery?
- Given the large component of services involved in customer solutions, what are appropriate measures for customer value (from a customer's perspective)?
- Given the intrinsic opportunities to mix and match goods and services across the B2B firm's various customers, what, if any, are the opportunities to develop decision-making tools that allow efficient matching of customers' needs to the B2B firm's solution offerings?

B2B Selling Process is Long and Complex and Involves Many Actors

The purchase cycle for most B2B products is very long, frequently extending over several months, and several stages in the selling process are critical, starting with prospect identification and ending with the receipt of payment for the purchase. Each of these different stages makes unique demands on the seller firm, has different processes and therefore calls for distinctive measures of performance.

In addition, multiple parties in the purchasing organization influence the decision-making process in B2B markets. (I discuss the buying center in detail in a later section.) Therefore, the seller firm must identify and reach multiple parties in multiple tiers within the prospect's organization with different offerings and related messaging that resonate with each person's interests and concerns.

The B2B selling relationship is often not exclusive or direct. Frequently, the complex network of partners involved in the B2B buying process includes not only executives from different functions from the seller and buyer organizations but also consultants, specification experts and external agencies from outside the seller and buyer firms who significantly influence the selling process.

Thus insights on market outcome measures, such as customer satisfaction (Anderson and Sullivan 1993), focused on the satisfaction of a set of homogeneous end consumers more applicable to B2C firms may not apply to the complex network of various actors, each of whom have very different roles, motivations and needs in the B2B buying process. Some research questions that emerge here include the following:

- What are the appropriate metrics to measure the market performance of the various actors in a B2B firm's sales network? What is the influence of the different actors (e.g. buying agent, consultant, key account managers, sales manager) in the network on the firm's sales, profit and shareholder performance?
- What are the different types of direct and indirect ties among actors in both the selling and the buying process? Which embedded structures and relationships among these actors influence each actor's social capital and, thus, influence the selling or buying process?
- Given the long life cycle of the selling process, how can firms develop metrics to ensure that they build a diversified portfolio of sales leads, prospects and customers that are in different stages of the selling process? Specifically, how does a diversified portfolio of business prospects affect the firm's performance, including systematic and idiosyncratic risk? Finally, which metrics that track the movement of sales leads into prospects and prospects into customers, time to move, and rate of movement of potential buyers across the stages, should be developed to predict firm performance and risk?

B2B Customers are Few and Very Large

Unlike B2C firms, which have thousands, if not millions, of consumers for many of their products, B2B firms often have hundreds, dozens, or, in some cases, only a handful of customers. In most cases, B2B firms know their potential customers and vice versa, and so awareness generation may not be as important in B2B markets as they are in B2C markets. The more important aspect of the B2B customer management process is to understand customers' needs, requirements and constraints, which vary not only across various organizations but also across the various people involved in the buying process.

As a result, unlike marketing to consumers in B2C markets, marketing to B2B customers does not occur through highly controlled, homogeneous, mass media-based promotion programs. Rather, crucial to the success of B2B marketing programs are one-to-one marketing programs built through ongoing personal interactions between the executives of the buyer firms and the teams of trained, multifunctional experts of the seller firms.

Thus, marketing metrics developed in the B2C context of many different customers (e.g. market share), with more or less homogeneous needs and preferences, may not apply to B2B firms with a few, very large customers with substantially heterogeneous needs and preferences. Some research questions that emerge include the following:

- What appropriate metrics should be developed to manage large key accounts? What is the periodicity of measuring these metrics?
- Given the intrinsic risk of exposure of B2B firms to these large accounts, what is the effect of this risk on the variability of firms' profits and cash flows? Which specific marketing actions should B2B firms take to reduce the risk associated with these few and large customers?

Supplier–Customer Relationships are Close and Evolve Over Time in B2B Firms

Critical to the B2B firm's competitive advantage and performance is the development and maintenance of customer relationships. Thus B2B relationships cannot be viewed as multiple independent transactions; rather, the interdependency of the transactions creates its own dynamic over time. The process of relationship evolution can be subject to termination at any point through customer causes (ceasing of category consumption), competitive causes, or internally unintended (attrition through service problems) or internally intended (customer firing) causes. The effect of transaction-specific investments on relationship commitment in manufacturer–retailer relationships differs across the different stages of the relationship life cycle (Jap and Ganesan 2000). Specific marketing metrics research questions that emerge include the following:

- How should B2B firms manage the customer relationship management process as the customers transition through the various stages of the relationship life cycle?
- Does the profitability of the B2B firm's customers vary across the different stages of the relationship life cycle? Are there some marketing mix interventions that are more (or less) effective for the B2B firm's customers in the different stages of the relationship life cycle?
- Can a B2B firm's customers be too close to the relationship life cycle, resulting in negative performance consequences for the B2B firm?
- What, if any, are investors' responses to the B2B firm's termination of customer relationships? Do they differ across customer relationships in different stages of the life cycle?

B2B Buying Situations Vary Considerably

Business buyers face many different types of decisions when buying goods and services for their organizations (Robinson et al. 1967). The complexity of the decisions buyers face depends on the buying situation, including the nature of the organization's problem that the considered product is designed to address, newness of the buying requirement, number of executives involved in the decision-making, amount of investment required, and the time frame for the decision-making. Robinson et al. (1967) identify three types of buying situations: the straight rebuy, the modified rebuy and a new task:

1. *Straight rebuy*: The purchasing department reorders the product on a routine basis (e.g. office supplies, cleaning services) and chooses suppliers from an approved list of vendors. In-suppliers make an effort to ensure that price and product-quality specifications are complied with and the ordering system is automated. Out-suppliers try to break through with a small order and then enlarge share of wallet of the customer firm.
2. *Modified rebuy*: The buyer modifies product specifications, prices, delivery requirements or other terms (e.g. new business consulting project), which typically involves additional sets of actors from the supplier and customer firms. The in-suppliers consider a modified rebuy situation a threat to their account, while out-suppliers perceive it as an opportunity to break through into the account.
3. *New task*: The customer firm buys a product for the first time (e.g. turnkey services to build a new fabrication facility). The greater the cost and/or risk, the larger the number of participants involved, and the greater their information gathering, the longer the buyer takes to make a purchase decision.

There are no clear analogs to these three B2B buying situations in the B2C context. The following marketing metrics research questions emerge here:

●   What marketing mix interventions can the firm undertake to transition a customer along the different buying situations?
●   What metrics can be developed in situations when the B2B firm fails to close the deal to sell the product to the customer? Can these 'failed' situations be recovered through post-failure marketing communication efforts?

There are Many Stages in the Buying Process

Robinson et al. (1967) identify eight stages in the B2B buying process, called 'buy phases', within an overall buy-grid framework. Table 38.1 describes the buying stages involved in a new-task buying situation. In a straight-rebuy or modified-rebuy situation, some of these stages may be eliminated.

The buying process begins when an executive in the buyer firm recognizes a problem or need that can be met by purchasing a good or service. Next, the buyer determines the needed item's general characteristics and required quantity. This process varies across different types of products. For simple items, this process tends to be simple; for complex items, the process may involve many engineers, users and external consultants. The buyer next identifies the most appropriate suppliers through trade directories, Internet search engines, contacts with other firms, trade advertisements and trade shows. The buyer then invites qualified suppliers to submit proposals. Again the proposal solicitation process will vary across different products. For expensive, complex products, the proposal is often a detailed document with extensive supporting information. After evaluating the proposals, the buyer invites a few suppliers to make formal presentations of their products and offers. Before selecting suppliers, the buying center specifies desired supplier attributes and indicates the relative importance of these attributes. The different suppliers are then rated on various evaluation

Table 38.1 Buy phases in the buy-grid framework

Buy Phases	Buy Phase Description	Buy Classes		
		New Task	Modified Rebuy	Straight Rebuy
1. Problem recognition	Starts the buying process by recognition of problem, which triggers need for product.	Yes	Maybe	No
2. General need description	The buyer determines the needed item's general characteristics and quantity.	Yes	Maybe	No
3. Product specification	This may involve multiple managers in the buyer's firm, including technical, production, marketing and sales.	Yes	Yes	Yes
4. Supplier search	Established through trade directories and B2B electronic exchanges.	Yes	Maybe	No
5. Proposal solicitation	The buyer invites qualified suppliers to submit quotations and chooses a subset of suppliers to make a formal presentation.	Yes	Maybe	No
6. Supplier selection	The buying center specifies desired supplier attributes, rates their importance and rates suppliers. The buyer then selects suppliers according to evaluation criteria.	Yes	Maybe	No
7. Order-routine specification	After selecting supplier, the buyer negotiates the final order, quantity, delivery schedule, return policies and so forth.	Yes	Maybe	No
8. Performance review	The buyer periodically reviews the performance of the chosen suppliers.	Yes	Yes	Yes

criteria, which vary depending on the type of product and buying situation. The buying center may also attempt to negotiate with preferred suppliers for better prices and terms before making the final decision. After selecting the suppliers, the buyer negotiates the final order and lists the technical specifications, the quantity needed, the expected time of delivery, return policies and so forth. Finally, after the order is placed and the products delivered, the buyer periodically reviews the performance of the chosen suppliers, which then leads the buyer to continue, modify or terminate a supplier relationship.

Marketing programs in the B2C context do not need to deal with the multiple elements of the buy-grid framework involved in the B2B context. Marketing metrics research questions that emerge for B2B firms with respect to the buy-grid framework include the following:

- What proactive marketing program initiatives can the B2B firm undertake to move the firm's proposal for products through the buying phases of the buy-grid framework? How can the firm measure its performance in the different stages?
- What performance review metrics can the buyer firm initiate to manage its supplier relationships more effectively?

There are Many Participants in the B2B Buying Process

Webster and Wind (1972) call the decision-making unit of a buying organization the 'buying center'. The buying center comprises all the individuals and groups that participate in the purchase decision-making process and share common goals and risks arising from the decisions. In addition, all members of the organization play any one of the following seven roles in the purchase decision process:

1. *Initiators*: Executives in the buyer firms who request that something be purchased. Sometimes these executives may be users of the product. In many cases, they are designated to place requests for goods and services.
2. *Users*: Executives in the buyer firms who use the product. In many cases, the users initiate the buying process and define the product requirements.
3. *Influencers*: People in the buyer firms who influence the buying decision. They often define specifications for the product and approve the product specifications and pricing. Typically, technical and research and development managers are important influencers in the B2B buying process.
4. *Deciders*: Executives in the buyer firms who decide on the product requirements, pricing and suppliers. The higher the value of the B2B product in question, the higher is the level of the decider executive in the buyer firm.
5. *Approvers*: Executives in the buyer firms who authorize the proposed purchase decisions. Again, the higher the value of the B2B product in question, the higher is the level of the approver executive in the buyer firm.
6. *Buyers*: Executives in the buyer firms who have formal authority to select the supplier and arrange the purchase terms.
7. *Gatekeepers*: Executives in the buyer firms who have the power to prevent sellers or information from reaching the buying center.

Again, there are no clear analogs of the buying center-based decision-making in the B2C context. Research questions that emerge here include the following:

- Which product performance metrics do the different members of the buying center desire for the B2B firm's products? What, if any, are the trade-offs in product performance metrics across the different members of the buying center?
- What is the nature of the influence of the cross-buying center nodes on each other? Does the nature of these influences change depending on the buying situation (straight rebuy, modified rebuy and new order)?
- How do the buying center's different members (e.g. initiators, users, influencers) influence word of mouth, including customer referrals, about the seller firm?

Purchasing Orientations Vary Across Buyer Firms

An organization's approach to acquiring resources and capabilities from external supply markets – that is, its purchasing orientation – is guided by the expected contribution of purchasing to the organization's performance. Purchasing orientations (i.e. buying orientation, procurement orientation and supply chain management orientation) can differ across industries and firms, and even within an organization, depending on the product to be sourced (Dobler and Burt 1996).

Historically, purchasing departments were situated at the lower end of the firm's hierarchy, and their approach mostly depicted a buying orientation. A buying orientation pertains to purchasing practices whose principal purpose is to achieve reductions in the money spent on goods and services. However, the recognition that the purchasing department not only saved costs and improved profitability but also dramatically influenced the firm's strategic advantage led many firms to change these departments' focus from short-term, tactical to long-term strategic. That is, the emphasis in these departments shifted from a focus on 'the best deal' to optimizing purchase resources to increase both the strategic advantage of the firm's products and the productivity of the firm's manufacturing processes, in what is known as procurement orientation. Increasingly, the procurement orientation is more evident when the purchasing managers simultaneously seek cost reductions and quality improvements. Such buyers develop collaborative relationships with major suppliers and seek savings through superior cost management at various stages of the procurement process. Finally, some firms have broadened the scope of their purchasing department beyond the immediate suppliers to include customers, premised on the notion that the firm's performance is related to the integrated supply chain performance within the firm, resulting in a supply chain management orientation of the purchasing department.

Of the three orientations, the supply chain management orientation is the most progressive because the purchasing department's focus is further broadened to a strategic, value-adding role in the development of the buyer firm's products, including the purchase of raw materials, production of products, and selling and delivery of products to the buyer firm's end consumers. The different purchasing orientations of buyer firms are a key input to B2B firms' marketing strategies, including the development of product offerings and associated marketing programs. Research questions that emerge for B2B firms here include the following:

- What are the effects of the different types of orientation of a B2B firm's business customers (buying orientation, procurement orientation and supply chain management orientation) on the firm's sales, profits and shareholder performance?
- Do investors pay attention to the buyer firms' buying orientations? How does each purchasing department orientation in a B2B firm's portfolio of customers affect the firm's shareholder value?

B2B Buying Processes Often Involve Professional Purchasing

Business goods and services are often purchased by trained purchasing agents, whose job function is to buy products for their organizations. Purchasing agents must comply with their organizations' purchasing policies, constraints and requirements. These professional buyers may belong to professional buying organizations, such as the National Association of Purchasing Managers, whose goal is to improve professional buyers' effectiveness. Thus, business marketers usually deal with experts who want to perform better in their jobs and therefore must provide technical information

Table 38.2   Integrated marketing communication mix of B2B firms

Communication Objectives	Potential Customers	Communication Tools
Awareness	Leads	Advertising, direct mail, publicity, industry conferences
Interest	Inquiries	Brochures, videos, recorded demonstrations, websites, trade shows
Evaluation	Prospects	Telemarketing, field sales visits
Trial	New customers	Field sales visits, inside sales calls
Purchase	Established customers	Transactional and relationship teams, key account management, thought leadership

Notes: Adapted from Anderson and Narus (2004).

and support to the professional purchase managers. No parallel situation exists in the B2C context. Specific marketing metrics research questions that emerge here include the following:

- What are the metrics relevant to measuring the B2B firm's performance (e.g. information provision) with respect to professional purchase managers?
- What kinds of referral systems exist to document the experience of purchasing managers in an industry, and what types of firms operate such referral systems? What are and should be the attributes of the referral system so as to improve the buying process for all firms in the industry? What metrics should be developed that track and penalize opportunistic firm behavior in referral systems, and what industry standards should govern such a system?
- What is the role of Internet-based user-generated content generated by professional purchasing managers? How does this content affect customer referrals and customer acquisition efforts?

Complex, Integrated Marketing Communications

Given the complexity of the buying process, the large number of actors in the buying unit, the different types of products, and the different kinds of buying situations that extend over long periods, B2B firms face an onerous task with respect to communicating their products to customers. Added to this mix is the emphasis that individual organizational buyers place on the purchase decision. That is, different actors in the buying unit may be interested in different aspects of the product's characteristics, including the technical specifications, reliability and prices. For example, users of the product are typically interested in the product's performance, while approvers are interested in the product's price and delivery terms. Thus, an integrated marketing communications program that uses multiple messages, across different media, at different stages of the buying process, aimed at different actors in the buying unit is an integral part of the B2B firm's marketing program (Anderson and Narus 2004).

Table 38.2 describes the stages through which a buyer progresses when engaging in communications from the B2B firm. The stages in the model are linked to the processes

New Customer/Prospect/Buying Phase	Key Seller: Communications Objective and Tasks		Relative Communication Effectiveness	
	Communications Objectives	Task	Low	High
Need recognition	Generate awareness	Prospecting		
Developing product specifications	Feature comprehension	Opening relationship/qualifying prospect		
Search and qualification of suppliers	Lead generation	Qualifying prospect		
Evaluation	Performance comprehension	Presenting sales message		
Supplier selection	Negotiation of terms/offer customization	Closing sales		
Purchase feedback	Reassurance	Account service	Advertising	trade shows	personal selling

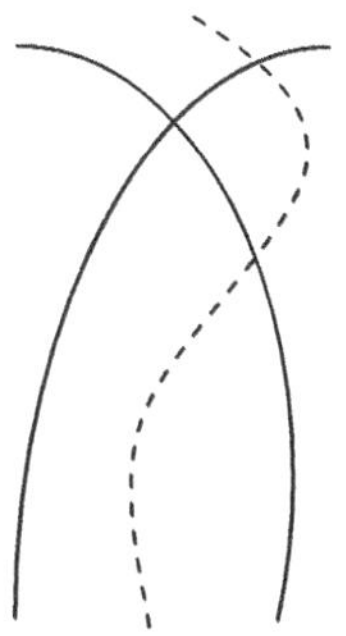

Notes: Adapted from Gopalakrishna and Lilien (1995).

Figure 38.1 Relative effectiveness of business communication tools

a company enacts to acquire and retain customers and to the communications tools that may be used in different stages of the process. Figure 38.1 describes the various stages in the buying phase, the seller's communications objectives and tasks for each stage, and the relative effectiveness of business communication tools: namely advertising, trade shows and personal selling (Gopalakrishna and Lilien 1995). As Table 38.2 and Figure 38.1 show, integrated marketing communications in the B2B context is a complex, multifaceted task that involves the coordination of multiple messages, multiple media and multiple audiences over time.

Integrated marketing communications are prevalent in B2B markets, and the challenges that complex B2B buying processes pose are unique given the complexity of the products and the heterogeneous preferences of the different buy phases in the buy-grid framework. Marketing metrics research questions that emerge in this area include the following:

- What are the optimal investments in the different elements of the integrated marketing communications programs? Should investments vary across different types of products, various stages of the B2B buying process and various buying situations?
- What is the role of face-to-face communications for B2B firms, given the growing role of electronic communications? This is especially worthy of investigation in the context of trade shows, which have been studied extensively in the B2B context.
- How can B2B firms effectively leverage Internet-based new media communication tools, such as search engines and social networking websites (e.g. LinkedIn), for marketing communications?

Table 38.3   Summary comparison of performance metrics across B2B and B2C firms

Defining Characteristics	Performance Metrics: B2B Firms	Performance Metrics: B2C Firms
B2B goods and services are relatively complex	Complex metrics involving hybrids of goods and services.	Simpler metrics based on singular units of goods and services.
B2B selling process is long and complex and involves many actors	Performance metrics over time and across many actors in customer firms.	Shorter time frames involving fewer, frequently single customers.
B2B customers are few and very large	Granular metrics over fewer customers, making comparisons challenging.	Large-scale metrics over a large number of customers.
Supplier–customer relationships are close and evolve over time in B2B firms	Qualitative metrics derived from personal interactions are important.	Greater reliance on quantitative market-based performance metrics.
B2B buying situations vary considerably	Challenges in comparing performance metrics across buying situations.	Easier to compare performance metrics across customers.
There are many stages in the buying process	Integration of performance metrics varies across the many stages in the buying process.	Fewer performance metrics across few stages in the buying process.
There are many participants in the buying process	Integration of performance metrics varies across the many participants in the buying process.	Fewer performance metrics across more similar customers.
Purchasing orientations vary across buyer firms[a]	Need for customized performance metrics based on purchasing orientations of customer firms.	—
B2B buying processes often involve professional purchasing	Professional purchasing in customer firms with different systems poses challenges to supplier firms in development of standardized performance metrics.	—
Complex, integrated marketing communications	Use of different performance metrics, some qualitative and others quantitative, poses challenges.	—

Note: a   In some cases, the B2C performance metric comparison is not relevant.

Summary

As this chapter shows, the B2B marketplace contains distinctive characteristics that differ from those in the B2C marketplace. Table 38.3 provides a summary of these differences and their implications on the different performance metrics for B2B firms and B2C firms. These substantial differences have implications for both marketing scholars and practitioners. For scholars, these differences suggest an immense research opportunity. For B2B marketers, these differences highlight both the need to be cognizant of the challenges when measuring the performance of their marketing actions and the need to customize performance metrics pertinent to the B2B marketplace.

CHALLENGES FACING B2B FIRMS: IMPLICATIONS FOR MARKETING METRICS

In addition to the distinctive characteristics of B2B firms, B2B firms face unique challenges. However, these challenges provide an opportunity for developing marketing metrics specific to B2B firms, which I discuss next.

Increased Offshoring and Outsourcing of Products

The growing competition from firms outside the United States for both goods and services is increasingly challenging B2B firms today. During the past decade, manufacturing of goods for both end consumers and organizations has shifted to China, Vietnam and other Far East countries, in which labor costs are much lower than those in the United States. Although outsourced manufacturing is not entirely new to firms, the scope of outsourcing is unprecedented and is expected to increase in the future. However, the offshoring of services is new, and for the first time in their history, many firms are obtaining various services, including high-value-added services (e.g. product design, technical support), from overseas firms. Marketing metrics research questions in this area include the following:

- What are the effects of offshoring and offshore outsourcing of goods and services in B2B firms? Do they vary across goods and services? Across industries and firms within industries?
- What are the most effective governance mechanisms (e.g. organizational and financial structure) for ensuring the best outcomes for B2B firms with regard to offshoring and offshore outsourcing?
- Can US B2B firms serve as outsourcing destinations for firms in countries outside the United States that are shopping around for goods and services? What characteristics of B2B firms will increase their desirability to foreign buyer firms?
- What types of outsourced portfolios are firms creating, and is there a diversity of products and services in such portfolios? What are the appropriate metrics to measure the attributes of an outsourced portfolio? How do such portfolio attribute metrics influence firm returns and risk?

Increasing Role of B2B E-Commerce

The growth of B2B e-commerce is frenetic and is expected to continue in the coming decade. This growth is expected to occur through various Web-based vehicles, including the following:

1. *catalog sites*, where firms can order thousands of products using electronic catalogs;
2. *vertical markets*, where firms both up and down the supply chain in a given industry can congregate electronically to buy and sell products and services;

3. *auction sites*, where buyers can typically purchase across diverse markets;
4. *exchange markets*, where products and services are traded and prices change rapidly;
5. *private exchanges*, where large firms with extensive requirements of products and services operate private exchanges to link with specially invited groups of suppliers and partners over the Web.

Online B2B selling offers many advantages, including reducing costs for both buyers and sellers, reducing the time between order and delivery, consolidating purchasing systems, and forging more efficient relationships between partners and buyers. However, the disadvantages of online B2B selling include the erosion of supplier–buyer loyalty because of a lack of face-to-face communication, increase of price competition and potential security threats. Marketing metrics research questions that emerge in this area include the following:

●   What are the most effective marketing program interventions that B2B firms can undertake to ensure customer loyalty and price realizations in B2B online formats?
●   What is the relative value to the firm of alternative B2B online formats (e.g. auction sites, private and public exchanges)? In terms of profits and shareholder value?
●   Do the performance parameters of organizational buying (e.g. product quality, prices, timely delivery) vary across the different B2B online formats?

New Pricing Models

Information-based products and services are increasingly being given away for free. This 'free-pricing' trend has been enabled by the marginal cost of the Internet's underlying technologies, including storage, bandwidth, information processing and processing power. Consequently, the cost of adding an additional customer has become negligible, allowing firms to price their offerings at zero. For example, in the advertising-supported model, a product or service is given away for free in exchange for advertising to be displayed. The media model is a traditional example of an advertising-based free-pricing model. A magazine's main source of income comes from the space it sells to advertisers based on the profile of its readers. Thus, advertisers are the magazine's real customers because readers pay a heavily subsidized price for a subscription. A well-known advertising-supported model in online media and information technology is that practiced by Google, which gives away services (e.g. storage, computing software, search, email) for free to its customers because advertisers pay for their ads to appear on search pages.

Although the threats from free products and services are real and pertinent, given the recency of the phenomenon, marketing scholars have not examined research questions in this area. Marketing metrics research questions that emerge in this area include the following:

●   How are the emerging new free-pricing business models threatening traditional models, and under what conditions will such threats increase or decrease for B2B firms?

- How can B2B firms develop customer solution offerings to address the threats from the free-pricing products and services being offered by non-traditional Internet-based firms (e.g. Google, Yahoo)?
- Are some B2B market segments (e.g. geographic segments) more vulnerable than others to the threats from free-pricing models? What differentiated and customized marketing programs can B2B firms develop to address different market segments?
- What types of partnerships and alliances can B2B firms develop with non-traditional Internet-based firms to integrate their product offerings with the free products and services from Internet-based firms? These may include leveraging the B2B firm's customer relationships and product offerings.
- Should some products and services in the B2B firm's offerings be given away freely to increase the firm's ability to compete with non-traditional Internet-based firms?

CONCLUSION

Most of the marketing metrics in the marketing literature have been developed using the context of B2C firms, reducing their applicability to B2B firms, which have distinctive characteristics in terms of customers, products and marketing systems. In this chapter, I have identified several key distinctive features of B2B firms and proposed related research questions in the area of marketing metrics for B2B firms, to stimulate further work in this area. Empirical research in the area would extend marketing theory and contribute useful insights for managers in B2B firms.

NOTE

1. In this chapter, I use the term B2C to denote exemplar B2C product markets (e.g. fast-moving consumer goods, retailing) and acknowledge that some B2C product markets (e.g. computer systems, telecommunications) have characteristics (e.g. rational decision-making, multiple decision-makers, solution selling) similar to those of B2B product markets, while some B2B product markets (e.g. office supplies) have characteristics (e.g. important role for brands, individual decision-making) similar to those of B2C product markets.

REFERENCES

Anderson, Eugene W. and Mary W. Sullivan (1993), 'The antecedents and consequences of customer satisfaction for firms', *Marketing Science*, **12** (2), 125–43.
Anderson, James C. and James A. Narus (2004), *Business Market Management: Understanding, Creating, and Delivering Value*, 2nd edn, New York: Pearson Education.
Bowman, Douglas and Das Narayandas (2004), 'Linking customer management effort to customer profitability in industrial markets', *Journal of Marketing Research*, **41** (4), 433–47.
Dobler, D.W. and D.N. Burt (1996), *Purchasing and Supply Management*, 6th edn, New York: McGraw-Hill.
Erickson, Gary and Robert Jacobson (1992), 'Gaining comparative advantage through discretionary expenditures: the returns to R&D and advertising', *Management Science*, **38** (9), 1264–79.
Fang, Eric, Robert W. Palmatier and Jan-Benedict E.M. Steenkamp (2008), 'Effect of service transition strategies on firm value', *Journal of Marketing*, **72** (September), 1–15.
Farris, Paul W., Neil T. Bendle, Phillip E. Pfeifer and David J. Reibstein (2009), *Marketing Metrics: Fifty+ Metrics Every Executive Should Master*, Philadelphia: Wharton School Publishing.

Gopalakrishna, Srinath and Gary L. Lilien (1995), 'A three-stage model of industrial trade show performance', *Marketing Science*, **14** (1), 22–42.

Griffin, Abbie and Albert Page (1996), 'PDMA success measurement project: recommended measures for product development success and failure', *Journal of Product Innovation Management*, **13** (6), 478–96.

Gupta, Sunil, Donald R. Lehmann and Jennifer Stuart (2004), 'Valuing customers', *Journal of Marketing Research*, **41** (February), 7–18.

Jap, Sandy D. and Shankar Ganesan (2000), 'Control mechanisms and the relationship life cycle: implications for safeguarding specific investments and developing commitment', *Journal of Marketing Research*, **37** (May), 227–45.

Johnson, Jean L., Ravi Sohi and Rajdeep Grewal (2004), 'The role of relational knowledge stores in interfirm partnerships', *Journal of Marketing*, **68** (July), 21–36.

Kalwani, Manohar U. and Narakesari Narayandas (1995), 'Long-term manufacturer–supplier relationships: do they pay off for supplier firms?', *Journal of Marketing*, **59** (January), 1–16.

Kumar, V., J. Andrew Petersen and Robert P. Leone (2010), 'Driving profitability by encouraging customer referrals: who, when and how', *Journal of Marketing*, **74** (September), 1–17.

Kumar, V., Rajkumar Venkatesan, Timothy Bohling and Denise Beckmann (2008), 'The power of CLV: managing customer lifetime value at IBM', *Marketing Science*, **27** (4), 585–99.

McAlister, Leigh, Raji Srinivasan and MinChung Kim (2007), 'Advertising, research and development, and systematic risk of the firm', *Journal of Marketing*, **71** (January), 35–48.

Mizik, Natalie and Robert Jacobson (2003), 'Trading off between value creation and value appropriation: the financial implications of shifts in strategic emphasis', *Journal of Marketing*, **67** (January), 63–76.

Narayandas, Das (2005), 'Building loyalty in business markets: tool kit', *Harvard Business Review*, **83** (9), 131–9.

Narayandas, Das and V. Kasturi Rangan (2004), 'Building and sustaining buyer–seller relationships in mature industrial markets', *Journal of Marketing*, **68** (July), 63–77.

Palmatier, Robert W. (2008), 'Interfirm relational drivers of customer value', *Journal of Marketing*, **72** (July), 76–89.

Palmatier, Robert W., Lisa K. Scheer and Jan-Benedict E.M. Steenkamp (2007), 'Customer loyalty to whom? Managing the benefits and risks of salesperson-owned loyalty', *Journal of Marketing Research*, **44** (May), 185–99.

Quelch, John A. (2005), 'Ambidextrous marketing', *Wall Street Journal Eastern Edition*, **246** (October 11), B2.

Ramani, Girish and V. Kumar (2008), 'Interaction orientation and firm performance', *Journal of Marketing*, **72** (January), 27–45.

Rao, Vithala R., Manoj K. Agarwal and Denise Dahlhoff (2004), 'How is manifest branding strategy related to the intangible value of a corporation?', *Journal of Marketing*, **68** (October), 126–41.

Robinson, P.J., C.W. Farris and Y. Wind (1967), *Industrial Buying and Creative Marketing*, Boston, MA: Allyn & Bacon.

Singh, Manohar, Sheri Faircloth and Ali Nejadmalayeri (2005), 'Capital market impact of product marketing strategy: evidence from the relationship between advertising expenses and cost of capital', *Journal of the Academy of Marketing Science*, **33** (4), 432–44.

Srinivasan, Raji (2006), 'Dual distribution and intangible firm value: franchising in restaurant chains', *Journal of Marketing*, **70** (July), 120–35.

Srivastava, Rajendra K., Tasadduq A. Shervani and Liam Fahey (1998), 'Market-based assets and shareholder value: a framework for analysis', *Journal of Marketing*, **62** (January), 2–18.

Srivastava, Rajendra K., Tasadduq A. Shervani and Liam Fahey (1999), 'Marketing, business processes, and shareholder value: an organizationally embedded view of marketing activities and the discipline of marketing', *Journal of Marketing*, **63** (Special Issue), 168–79.

Tuli, Kapil R., Ajay K. Kohli and Sundar G. Bharadwaj (2007), 'Rethinking customer solutions: from product bundles to relational processes', *Journal of Marketing*, **71** (July), 1–17.

Webster, Frederick E., Jr, and Yoram Wind (1972), *Organizational Buying Behavior*, Upper Saddle River, NJ: Prentice Hall.

Name index

Aaker, D. 215, 565
Abratt, R. 184, 208 (in Bendixen et al.)
Achrol, R. 74, 114, 393
Adams, J. 131, 302, 433, 444
Adams, M. 596
Adiguzel, F. 709
Adner, R. 573
Adler, P. 97
Agarwal. M. (in Rao et al.) 715
Agarwal, R. 567
Agrawal, J. (in Kamakura et al.) 199
Ahearne, Michael 437, 449 (in Lam et al.),
    496–520, 539, 540, 541, 699, 707
  in Lim et al. 47–8, 51, 485
  in Wieseke et al. 301, 707
Aiken, L. (in Cohen et al.) 701
Ailawadi, K. 505, 639
Ainslie, A. (in Steenburgh et al.) 317
Ajamian, G. 613
Akdeniz, M. 97
Albaum, G. 138
Albers, Sönke 49, 293, 326 (in Becker et al.),
    473, 493, 499, 502, 506, 539–59, 625, 638
  in Mantrala et al. 7, 639
Alderson, W. 117
Alford, B. (in Sharma et al.) 540
Algesheimer, R. 80
Allen, V. 434
Allenby, G. 318
Amabile, T. 425, 666, 669
Ambler, T. 277, 280, 282, 284
Amit, R. 586
Andaleeb, S. 140
Anderson, C. 572, 573
Anderson, E. 44, 45, 74, 255, 277, 280, 283,
    285, 299, 301–2, 305, 333–4, 339, 343,
    427–9, 493, 497–9, 550, 642, 699–700
  in Rouzies et al. 127, 137, 142, 479–80, 491
Anderson, J. 16, 19, 28, 31, 35, 99, 101, 140,
    220, 250–52, 282, 286, 297–9, 303, 305,
    313, 426, 551, 641–2, 701–2, 704, 705–6
    (in Kumar et al.), 708, 718, 724
Anderson, P. 567, 583
Ang, L. (in Buttle et al.) 539
Ante, S. (in MacMillan et al.) 573
Antia, Kersi D. 74, 639 (in Rindfleisch et al.),
    699–714
  in Frazier et al. 93, 392

Antioco, M. 322
Arabie, P. 197
Argyres, N. 104
Ariely, D. 648
Arino, A. 358
Armstrong, G. 458, 510, 514
Armstrong, J. 699, 700, 701, 702
Arnett, D. 434, 464
Arnold, D. (in Toulan et al.) 461
Arnold, T. 440
Arnould, E. 447
Arrfelt, M. (in Hult et al.) 101
Artis, A. 440
Ashforth, B. 127
Atkinson, P. 670
Atuahene-Gima, K. 332, 438, 571, 703, 705
Auh, S. 94
Autry, C. 96
Aversa, N. (in Gensch et al.) 183
Avery, J. (in Steenburgh et al.) 548
Avici, T. 440
Avlonitis, G. 541
Avlontia, G. 256
Axelrod, R. 350
Azzaro, M. (in Schultz et al.) 167, 172, 177

Babakus, E. 440
Bacon, L. (in Naik et al.) 195
Bagozzi, R. 393, 421 (in Dietvorst et al.)
Bailey, S. 175
Baker, G. 45, 46
Baker, S. 217
Baker, W. 83, 254, 280, 281, 284
Bakker, A. (in Verbeke et al.) 498
Bakos, J. 541
Balasubramanian, S. 322–3 (in Sawhney et al.),
    567 (in Wu et al.), 635
Balegno, S. 545
Balogh, P. 240
Banerjee, Ranjan 41–53, 699
Banga, K. 575
Banting, P. 230
Baratta, J. (in Hofmann et al.) 514
Barclay, D. 425
Barczyk, C. 231
Bargh, J. 681
Barich, H. 182, 184–5
Barkema, H. 376

Zadeh, L. 691
Zaheer, A. 333, 334 (in McEvily et al.)
Zahorik, A. (in Kordupleski et al.) 98
Zajac, E. 54, 55
Zaltman, G. 21
    in Moorman et al. 140, 282, 283, 296,
        297
Zander, U. 376
Zane, L. 161
Zawada, C. (in Marn et al.) 251, 253
Zbaracki, M. (in Dutta et al.) 263
Zeckhauser, R. (in O'Keefe et al.) 493
Zeithaml, C. (in V. Zeithaml et al.) 459
Zeithaml, V. 277, 293, 305, 314, 323, 459
    in Rust et al. 311, 315, 318
Zeithammer, R. 645, 646
Zenger, T. 359, 404
Zenios, S. 643
Zenor, M. (in Dillon et al.) 197

Zhang, C. 45, 257 (in Cavusgil et al.)
Zhang, J. (in Ailawadi et al.) 639
Zhang, R. (in Chen et al.) 652
Zhang, X. 425
Zhiang, L. (in Yang et al.) 79
Zhou, K. (in Poppo et al.) 339, 341
Zhu, K. 567
Zirger, B. 119
Zirpoli, F. 391
Zjang, Z. (in Coughlan et al.) 639
Zoltners, Andris A. 30, 32, 442, 473, 482, 493,
        512, 521–38, 540, 553
    in Jones et al. 417, 433, 443
    in Mantrala et al. 7, 481, 539, 639
    in Rouzies et al. 127, 137, 142
Zook, C. 586
Zott, C. 586
Zou, S. 257
    in Morgan et al. 90, 98

Subject index